Introduction to Psychology: Gateways to Mind and Behavior

16e

Dennis Coon

John Mitterer
Brock University

Tanya Martini
Brock University

CENGAGE

Australia • Brazil • Canada • Mexico • Singapore • United Kingdom • United States

CENGAGE

***Introduction to Psychology: Gateways to Mind and Behavior*, Sixteenth Edition**
Dennis Coon, John Mitterer, Tanya Martini

SVP, Higher Education & Skills Product: Erin Joyner

VP, Higher Education & Skills Product: Thais Alencar

Product Director: Laura Ross

Product Manager: Colin Grover

Product Assistant: Jessica Witczak

Learning Designer: Natasha Allen

Senior Content Manager: Christy Frame

Digital Delivery Lead: Allison Marion

Director, Marketing: Neena Bali

Marketing Manager: Trisha Salata

IP Analyst: Deanna Ettinger

IP Project Manager: Kelli Besse

Production Service: Lori Hazzard, MPS Limited

Designer: Bethany Bourgeois

Cover Image Source: *Poco Libre*, Stephen Harlan

Library of Congress Control Number: 2020922577

Student Edition:
ISBN: 978-0-357-37139-8

Loose-leaf Edition:
ISBN: 978-0-357-37146-6

Cengage
200 Pier 4 Boulevard
Boston, MA 02210
USA

Printed at CLDPC, USA, 07-21

Dedication

To Sevren

—DC

To Rue Elizabeth Pante

—JM

To David, Callum, and Ronan

—TM

About the Authors

Courtesy of Dennis Coon

Dennis Coon is a publishing phenomenon and one of the best-selling authors in the field of psychology. His innovative instructional methods and student-focused style make his works perennial favorites among instructors and students alike. To date, more than two million students have learned psychology with a Coon text as their guide. Dr. Coon graduated with a B.A. in psychology from the University of California, Riverside, and earned his PhD in social psychology from the University of Arizona. He is also coauthor, with John Mitterer and Tanya Martini, of *Psychology: Modules for Active Learning, 15th Edition.*

Courtesy of John Mitterer

John Mitterer was awarded his PhD in cognitive psychology from McMaster University. He has taught psychology at Brock University to more than 30,000 introductory psychology students. He is an award-winning teacher whose several teaching awards include a National 3M Teaching Fellowship, the Canadian Psychological Association Award for Distinguished Contributions to Education and Training in Psychology, and the Brock University Don Ursino Award for Excellence in the Teaching of Large Classes. He has created textbooks and support materials for both students and instructors, and he has published and lectured on undergraduate instruction throughout Canada and the United States.

Courtesy of Callum Williams

Tanya Martini obtained her PhD in developmental psychology from the University of Toronto. In addition to introductory psychology, she also teaches research methods, human learning, and courses aimed at facilitating students' understanding of career-related skills. She has received both the Brock University Distinguished Teaching Award, and the Chancellor's Chair for Teaching Excellence. Dr. Martini's research examines how undergraduates think about the skills that are being fostered during university experiences, both inside and outside the classroom. She's also interested in how we can improve students' understanding of career-related skills so that they are in a better position to leverage them when they apply for jobs or post-graduate programs. In addition to her position at the university, Dr. Martini currently sits on the advisory board for the Socio-Emotional Skills Initiative that has been undertaken by the Conference Board of Canada.

Brief Contents

Contents

2 Brain and Behavior 52

3 Human Development 82

4 Sensation, Attention, and Perception 116

5 States of Consciousness 158

6 Conditioning and Learning 190

7 Memory 224

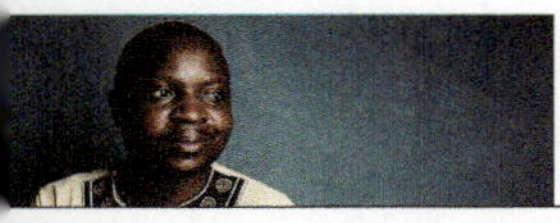

8 Cognition, Language, and Creativity 258

9 Intelligence 286

10 Motivation and Emotion 314

11 Sex, Gender, and Sexuality 348

12 Personality and Individual Differences 380

13 Health Psychology 410

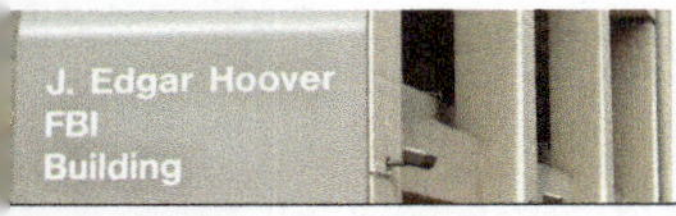

14 Psychological Disorders 440

15 Therapies 472

16 Social Thinking and Social Influence 502

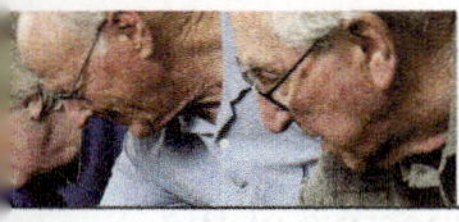

[[ ]] Preface

To You, the Student—An Invitation to Learn Psychology with Us

Greetings from your authors! We look forward to being your guides as you explore the exciting field of psychology and our ever-evolving understanding of human behavior. In a very real sense, we wrote this book about you, for you, and to you. We sincerely hope you will find, as we do, that what you learn is at once familiar, surprising, and challenging.

Reading *Introduction to Psychology: Gateways to Mind and Behavior*

We have done all we could to make *Gateways to Mind and Behavior* enjoyable to read and relevant to your everyday life. Each chapter takes you on a journey into a different realm of psychology, where you will explore areas such as personality, abnormal behavior, memory, consciousness, and human development. Each one is complex and fascinating in its own right, with many pathways, landmarks, and interesting detours for you to discover. Like any journey of discovery, your exploration of psychology will help you better understand yourself, others, and the world around you. It's definitely a trip worth taking.

Studying Effectively with *Introduction to Psychology: Gateways to Mind and Behavior*

As would be the case on any interesting trip, studying psychology will be most rewarding if you adopt a reflective attitude. Psychologists believe that answers to important questions come through engaged and careful thought, observation, and inquiry. Put another way, they often ask "How can we step outside ourselves to look objectively at how we live, think, feel, and act?" As simple as that approach may seem, this type of careful consideration takes practice to develop. *Gateways to Mind and Behavior*, then, is your gateway, or passport, to an adventure in active, reflective learning, not just passive reading.

We offer at least two different ways to help you develop this type of reflective approach to your studies. First, to help you get off to a good start, we strongly encourage you to read our short "manual," *Psychology and Your Skill Set: Reflective Studying*, which precedes Chapter 1. In it, we describe what you can learn by taking this course, including the skills you'll develop that can be helpful in both your personal and professional life. In *Reflective Studying*, you'll also read about a variety of well-established study skills that you can use to get the most out of your psychology course, and your other courses as well.

Second, a set of *guided notes* is available for each chapter. Developed using the well-established Cornell method of note-taking, we have created them to help you distill the most important aspects of each chapter and develop good study aids to assist you in preparing for tests. Available as MS Word files, you can use the guided notes to help organize your thinking about the material, focus on key ideas and concepts, and practice summarizing important points in your own words.

To You, the Instructor—An Invitation to Teach Psychology with Us

Thank you for choosing *Introduction to Psychology: Gateways to Mind and Behavior* for your students and for your course. Marcel Proust wrote, "The real voyage of discovery consists not in seeing new landscapes but in having new eyes." It is in this spirit that we have written this book—our goal is to promote not just an interest in human behavior but an appreciation for the perspective of the psychological scientist as well.

As the authors of this textbook, we have together accumulated over 80 years of classroom experience, teaching tens of thousands of college and university students. Although we have found most students to be generally well intentioned, our modern world certainly does immerse them in their work, careers, families, intimate relationships, and popular culture. As we compete for ever-more-limited student attention, we need to motivate our students to read and educate them about how to learn effectively—learning, after all, is a life-long endeavor (Matthew & Sternberg, 2009; Paternoster & Pogarsky, 2009).

We have explicitly designed and written the sixteenth edition of *Gateways to Mind and Behavior* to foster this type of deeper student engagement with the field of psychology. We believe that this will result in better memory for what has been read and

studied, and a deeper understanding of how to become more reflective learners and thinkers. To help you and your students reach these goals, we have designed this edition around two key goals:
integrating support to address instructor learning objectives and ***integrating support for active student learning***. In the sections below, we discuss each of these in more detail.

Integrating Support to Address Instructor Learning Objectives

This edition of *Gateways* has a new structure; one that we believe will make it easier for instructors to customize their use of the book to address their specific learning outcomes, regardless of whether they are driven by department/state standards or by personal preference. Specifically, each chapter is now organized around approximately five sections that represent the "big ideas and issues" in that particular area of psychology. Each of these self-contained sections begins with a set of learning outcomes that are compatible with Bloom's Taxonomy and ends with a short *Reflective Practice* box that allows students to receive some immediate formative feedback regarding their understanding of the key concepts and ideas from that section. We believe that structuring the book around a smaller number of key topics like this will allow instructors the flexibility to customize their course by having students read only those sections that are central to their unique learning objectives.

In addition, we have worked hard to bring the sixteenth edition of *Gateways* in line with the new recommendations put forth by the APA's Introductory Psychology Initiative (APA-IPI), while still maintaining the past edition's compatibility with the broader APA Guidelines for the Undergraduate Major. There are three main themes that appear throughout the textbook that are relevant to the APA-IPI. The first is related to *Human Diversity*, and these sections include material that ranges from the way that culture shapes moral reasoning to the way that poverty shaped the impact felt by families during COVID-19. Our discussions of human diversity include race, ethnicity, culture, SES, gender, sexual orientation, and age. Too often, such differences needlessly divide people into opposing groups. Our aim throughout this book is to discourage stereotyping, prejudice, discrimination, and intolerance. To that end, all pronouns and examples involving females and males are equally divided by gender. In artwork, photographs, and examples, we have also set out to portray the rich diversity of humanity.

The second APA-IPI theme that appears throughout the book is called *Studying the Science*. These sections model good critical thinking on topics such as adolescent mental health and the replication crisis, but they're also intended to emphasize how thinking in psychology has evolved with new research, and to highlight areas in which we're still searching for answers (e.g., How should we best conceptualize intelligence? How can we best manage implicit bias in the workplace?).

Finally, you'll see APA-IPI sections throughout the book related to *Psychology in Everyday Life*, which emphasize how psychological science can be applied to the world around us, including topics such as using laptops to take notes in class, intersex athletes competing at the Olympics, and celebrity endorsements to promote marketing campaigns. Table P.1 underscores the text's compatibility with the APA-IPI and Table P.2 shows how it can help you and your students meet the American Psychological Association's (2013) Guidelines for the Undergraduate Major.

In addition to our new format and compliance with APA initiatives, this edition of *Gateways* has a newly revised and expanded Instructor Companion Site that includes an *Instructor's Resource Manual,* which provides a wealth of teaching tips and classroom resources; *Cengage Learning Testing Powered by Cognero* featuring questions correlated to learning objectives, Bloom's taxonomy level, and difficulty; and *PowerPoint slides* providing concept coverage with dynamic animations, photographs, and video. Each of these resources has been designed with your needs in mind and will support you in successfully addressing the learning objectives you've created for your course.

Integrating Support for Active Student Learning

We have built in a number of features into the new edition of *Gateways* that we believe will assist students in honing their active learning skills. We'd like to draw your attention to four of them: *assisting with active reading*, *scaffolding student note-taking*, *promoting empirically-supported learning strategies*, and *emphasizing practical applications*.

Assisting with Active Reading

We have incorporated a number of features into the text itself that are intended to help students to learn actively as they are reading. These features include:

New Bloom's-oriented learning outcomes act as advance organizers to help guide student reading

Research suggests that, when included at the beginning of each chapter, learning outcomes help students build cognitive maps of upcoming topics and guide reading in productive ways (Ausubel, 1978; Gurlitt et al., 2012). The sections in each chapter of *Gateways* begin with a number of clearly-defined learning outcomes to prime student interest and focus their attention on the key ideas that they will encounter.

▲ TABLE P.1 APA-IPI Objectives Addressed by Reading *Introduction to Psychology: Gateways to Mind and Behavior,* 16e

Psychology Content: Identify basic concepts and research findings	
1.1. Define and explain basic psychological concepts.	All chapters, with support provided by *Glossary* and *Guided Notes*
1.2. Interpret research findings related to psychological concepts.	Sections 1.5–1.7 (*Research Methods*) Section 1.8 (*Psychology and Your Skill Set: Information Literacy*) *Studying the Science* sections
1.3. Apply psychological principles to personal growth and other aspects of everyday life.	*Psychology and Your Skill Set* sections *Psychology and Everyday Life* sections
Scientific Thinking: Solve problems using psychology methods	
2.1. Draw logical and objective conclusions about behavior and mental processes from empirical evidence.	Sections 1.5–1.7 (*Research Methods*) Section 1.8 (*Psychology and Your Skill Set: Information Literacy*) *Studying the Science* sections
2.2. Describe the advantages and limitations of various research strategies.	Sections 1.5–1.7 (*Research Methods*) *Studying the Science* sections
2.3. Design, conduct, or evaluate psychological research.	Sections 1.5–1.7 (*Research Methods*) *Studying the Science* sections
2.4. Evaluate how psychological science can be used to counter unsubstantiated statements, opinions, or beliefs.	Sections 1.5–1.7 (*Research Methods*) Section 1.8 (*Psychology and Your Skill Set: Information Literacy*)
Key Themes: Provide examples of psychology's integrative themes	
3.A. Psychological science relies on empirical evidence and adapts as new data develop.	All chapters, with a specific emphasis in *Studying the Science* sections
3.B. Psychology explains general principles that govern behavior while recognizing individual differences.	All chapters, with specific emphasis in *Human Diversity* sections
3.C. Psychological, biological, social, and cultural factors influence mental processes and behavior.	All chapters, with specific emphasis on Section 1.4 (*Biopsychosocial Model*) Section 17.4 (*Psychology and Your Skill Set: Diversity and Inclusion*) *Human Diversity* sections
3.D. Our perceptions filter our experiences of the world through an imperfect personal lens.	Sections 4.5–4.6 (*Attention and Perception*) Section 5.5 (*Psychology and Your Skill Set: Metacognition*) *Human Diversity* sections
3.E. Applying psychological principles can change our lives and communities in positive ways.	Section 18.3 (*Community Psychology*) Section 11.5 (*Civic Engagement*) *Psychology and Your Skill Set* sections *Psychology and Everyday Life* sections
3.F. Ethical principles guide psychology research and practice.	Sections 1.5–1.7 (*Research Methods*) Section 3.5 (*Ethical Behavior*)
3.G. Psychologists strive to promote respect for human diversity in its many forms.	All chapters, with specific emphasis in Section 17.4 (*Psychology and Your Skill Set: Diversity and Inclusion*) and *Human Diversity* sections

Active questioning is emphasized and modeled

How can questioning be built into a textbook? This new edition of *Gateways* continues its long tradition of using italicized *Dialogue Questions*, such as the previous sentence. They are typically the sorts of questions that students might find themselves thinking as they begin reading a section of text. As such, they model a dialogue in which the questions and the reactions of students are anticipated. They also clarify difficult points in a lively give-and-take between questions and responses.

Formative feedback is provided to students as they read

Within chapters, each main section concludes with a *Reflective Practice* box that allows students to test their recall and further develop their understanding of the topics presented. Each *Reflective Practice* box begins with a series of short, noncomprehensive quiz questions to help students actively process information and assess their progress. These questions, which are not as difficult as in-class tests, are meant to offer a sample of what students could be asked about various topics. Students who miss any items are encouraged to backtrack and clarify their understanding before reading further.

Reflective Practice boxes also include *Think Critically* questions. These stimulating questions challenge students to think critically and analytically about psychology. Each is followed by a brief answer with which students can compare their own thoughts. Many of these answers are based on research and are informative in their own right. Finally, *Reflective Practice* boxes conclude with *Self-Reflect* questions that encourage students to connect new concepts with personal experiences and prior knowledge.

▲ TABLE P.2 APA Skills Guidelines 2.0 Addressed by Reading *Introduction to Psychology: Gateways to Mind and Behavior*, 16e

Chapter	Topic of Chapter	Skills in Action Topic	Chapter Addresses Material from APA Guidelines 2.0
Introduction	How to Study	Reflective Studying	4.1, 5.2, 5.3, 5.5
1	The Foundations of Psychological Science	Information Literacy	1.1, 1.2, 1.3, 2.1, 2.2, 2.3, 2.4, 2.5, 3.1
2	Brain and Behavior	Self-Regulation	1.1, 1.2, 5.2
3	Human Development	Ethical Behavior	1.1, 1.2, 2.5, 3.2, 5.1
4	Sensation, Attention, and Perception	Communication	1.1, 1.2, 4.1, 4.2, 4.3, 5.4
5	States of Consciousness	Metacognition	1.1, 1.2, 5.2, 5.3
6	Conditioning and Learning	Behavioral Self-Management	1.1, 1.2, 5.2
7	Memory	Giving Memorable Presentations	1.1, 1.2, 4.2, 5.3
8	Cognition, Language, and Creativity	Creativity and Innovation	1.1, 1.2, 1.3, 2.3, 2.5
9	Intelligence	Emotional Intelligence	1.1, 1.2, 3.2, 3.3, 4.3, 5.1, 5.4
10	Motivation and Emotion	Positivity and Optimism	1.1, 1.2, 1.3, 2.5, 4.3, 5.4
11	Sex, Gender, and Sexuality	Civic Engagement	1.3, 3.2, 3.3, 4.3, 5.2, 5.3, 5.4
12	Personality and Individual Differences	Leadership	1.1, 1.2, 2.1, 3.3, 5.1, 5.2, 5.4
13	Health Psychology	Stress Management	1.1, 1.2, 1.3, 3.3, 5.1
14	Psychological Disorders	Perseverance	5.2, 5.3, 5.5
15	Therapies	Managing Mental Health Issues	1.1, 1.2, 1.3, 3.3
16	Social Thinking and Social Influence	Teamwork	1.1, 1.2, 3.2, 3.3, 4.3, 5.1, 5.4
17	Prosocial and Antisocial Behavior	Diversity and Inclusion	1.1, 1.2, 1.3, 2.5, 3.2, 3.3, 4.3, 5.1, 5.4
18	Applied Psychology	Career Preparation	1.1, 1.2, 1.3, 2.3, 5.1, 5.5
Appendix	Statistics	Statistical Literacy	1.1, 2.1, 2.2, 2.4, 4.1

Built-in reading aids assist students in mastering key concepts and ideas

These reading aids include:

- Boldface terms, robust illustrations, and summaries of information relevant to the learning outcomes at the end of each chapter.
- *Bridges*, which are clearly marked in-text links to other material relevant to the reading at hand. For example, a student reading about the Freudian theory of dreams will encounter a bridge to a relevant discussion of psychoanalysis in a later chapter.
- *Placeholders*—different colored text and small geometric shapes—are used to draw attention to figure and table references in the text and make it easier for students to return to the section that they were reading after they have paused to view a table or figure.
- The *glossary function* has been made as powerful as possible. The *Main Glossary*, at the end of the book, is integrated with the *Subject Index*, making it easy to link important definitions to where they are discussed in the text. All glossary items are bold and defined in-text when the term is first encountered. In addition, the parallel *Running Glossary* defines key terms in the margins of the relevant pages, making it easy for students to find, study, and review important terms.

Scaffolding Student Note-Taking

We've noticed that many students struggle to take a good set of notes based on their reading of college texts. To address this issue, this new edition of *Gateways* comes with guided notes that are designed to scaffold students' ability to address the learning outcomes by extracting the most important information from each chapter. The notes, which are available as MS Word files, were developed using the well-established Cornell method of note-taking.

Each set of notes begins with a single-page multi-level summary of the chapter called *The Big Picture*, which gives students a bird's eye view of the chapter as a whole and emphasizes the structure that's created with headers and subheaders. The guided notes themselves focus students' attention on information relevant to the learning outcomes and press them to generate their own examples and summarize important ideas in their own words. Concept maps that are included with the notes are designed to assist students in recognizing the relationships between ideas presented in each section so that they can make important connections.

Promoting Empirically-Supported Learning Strategies

One of our goals with *Gateways* was to ensure that students begin thinking about skills during your course. Given its far-reaching implications, one that we spend considerable time on relates to effective learning. In the text itself, effective learning is promoted in a few places. First, the introduction (*Psychology and Your Skill Set: Reflective Studying*, which precedes Chapter 1) outlines some of the key features of reflective cognition and underscores its links to deeper understanding and memory. It also introduces students to specific empirically-supported strategies for a variety of different assessments, including multiple choice and short/long answer question formats.

Emphasizing Practical Applications

To further encourage students' reading, we have emphasized the many ways that psychology relates to practical problems in daily life. As mentioned earlier, this edition of the texts includes new *Psychology in Everyday Life* sections that tackle the role of psychology in addressing issues relevant to the world around us. Another major feature of this book is the *Psychology and Your Skill Set* sections that are found at the end of each chapter. These high-interest discussions bridge the gap between theory and practical applications by exploring how psychology has contributed to our understanding of the skills that are valuable at work and in our relationships.

We believe that it is fair for students to ask, "Does this mean anything to me? Can I use it? Why should I learn it if I can't?" These two unique sections found throughout the text allow them to see the benefits of adopting new ideas from this text, and they breathe life into psychology's concepts.

Introduction to Psychology: Gateways to Mind and Behavior—What's New in the 16th Edition?

On the content side, the 16th edition of *Introduction to Psychology: Gateways to Mind and Behavior* has been extensively updated and features some of the most recent, reliable, and interesting findings from psychological science, plus fully updated statistics. The following sections provide some highlights regarding the new topics and features that appear in this edition.

Chapter 1: The Foundations of Psychological Science

- The new organization of this chapter includes the following major sections:

1.1 Commonsense Psychology	1.5 Core Features of Psychological Science
1.2 What Psychologists Do	1.6 Experimental Research
1.3 The History of Psychological Science	1.7 Nonexperimental Research
1.4 Contemporary Psychological Science and the Biopsychosocial Model	1.8 Psychology and Your Skill Set: Information Literacy

- The structure of Section 1.2 (*What Psychologists Do*) has been simplified to address two major themes: conducting psychological research and "helping people," or clinical work.
- Section 1.3 (*History of Psychological Science*) has been reorganized such that contemporary approaches are more clearly contrasted against historical ones.
- Section 1.5 (*Core Features of Psychological Science*) now includes a designated section on the types of data collected by psychological scientists (i.e., self-report/surveys, observational data, physiological data). New material in this section also introduces qualitative methods of inquiry. In addition, a new *Studying the Science* segment explains the importance of replicating scientific findings and the various reasons that can account for replication failures.
- Section 1.7 (*Nonexperimental Research*) now brings together all of the material related to nonexperimental methods (i.e., quasi-experiments, correlational research, cases studies).
- Section 1.8 (*Information Literacy*) includes new material related to the pressing need to check sources at a time when it is so easy to create misleading or biased web-based content, as well as quick and practical suggestions related to lateral reading, which is the primary method employed by professional fact checkers.

Chapter 2: Brain and Behavior

- The new organization of this chapter includes the following major sections:

2.1 The Nervous System	2.4 The Subcortex and Endocrine System
2.2 Brain Research	2.5 Psychology and Your Skill Set: Self-regulation
2.3 The Cerebral Cortex	

- Section 2.3 (*The Cerebral Cortex*) contains more recent research concerning mirror neurons that questions their role in autism.
- Section 2.5 (*Self-Regulation*) includes a new *Studying the Science* segment that addresses recent efforts to replicate Mischel's famous "marshmallow test," and how poverty can impact the results of such self-regulation tasks.

Chapter 3: Human Development

- The new organization of this chapter includes the following major sections:

3.1 The Forces That Shape Development: Nature and Nurture	3.4 Language, Cognitive, and Moral Development
3.2 Physical and Perceptual Development	3.5 Psychology and Your Skill Set: Ethical Behavior
3.3 Emotional and Social Development	

- Section 3.1 (*Nature and Nurture*) now contains a new segment about epigenetics that describes, in very simplified terms, how epigenetic factors work to alter gene expression and their impact on development across the lifespan.
- Sections 3.2, 3.3, and 3.4 have been reorganized to adopt a chronological approach within each of these "topical areas" of development. Specifically, each topical area begins with a discussion of development in infancy and childhood, followed by a discussion of development in adolescence and adulthood.
- Section 3.2 (*Physical and Perceptual Development*) has new material detailing perceptual development beyond the visual system to include lifespan changes in hearing, taste, and smell.
- Section 3.3 (*Emotional and Social Development*) now includes recent research related to adolescent mental health concerns, as well as information about the positivity effect that has been repeatedly observed in research related to adults' emotional lives. This section also includes new material related to emerging adulthood, and introduces readers to established literature demonstrating that shrinking social networks in older adulthood is less about disengagement and more about purposefully prioritizing relationships that are the most rewarding.
- Section 3.4 (*Language, Cognitive, and Moral Development*) has been streamlined and reorganized to make way for an expanded discussion of theory of mind research, as well as more recent cognitive developmental research related to executive functions, academic learning, and children's memory.
- Section 3.5 (*Ethical Behavior*) includes a new *Human Diversity* section that outlines alternative bases for making moral decisions that go beyond the traditional focus on justice and care, outlining how they are important, in particular, in cultures outside of the West.

Chapter 4: Sensation, Attention, and Perception

- The new organization of this chapter includes the following major sections:

4.1 Sensation	4.5 Attention
4.2 Vision	4.6 Perception
4.3 Hearing	4.7 Psychology and Your Skill Set: Communication
4.4 Chemical and Somesthetic Senses	

- Section 4.1 (*Sensation*) has been rewritten to further clarify the process of transduction, and the section on sensory selection has been reorganized to make clear the four specific ways in which selection can take place.
- Sections 4.2 to 4.4, which relate to the basic sensory modalities, have all been reorganized to focus on how transduction occurs in that particular modality. A new *Psychology in Everyday Life* segment describes the phenomenon of motion sickness in terms of new material on multimodal integration.
- Section 4.5 (*Attention*) provides expanded coverage on processes related to attention, including new material related to multitasking. The importance of goals in guiding attention is also highlighted with new research that has been connected to inattentional blindness. This section concludes with a newly-written *Psychology in Everyday Life* section that addresses recent research on mind-wandering.
- Section 4.6 (*Perception*) has been reorganized to emphasize how transduction and experience contribute to both similarities and differences in human perception. In doing so, we draw in new references to popular culture (#thedress; Yanni vs. Laurel). A new *Human Diversity* segment discusses the other-race effect observed in face perception studies, and a new *Psychology in Everyday Life* segment discusses research related to the use of virtual reality in clinical contexts.

Chapter 5: States of Consciousness

- The new organization of this chapter includes the following sections:

5.1 States of Consciousness	5.4 Drug-Altered Consciousness
5.2 Hypnosis and Meditation	5.5 Psychology and Your Skill Set: Metacognition
5.3 Sleep	

- Section 5.3 (*Sleep*) includes new research on sleep disorders.
- Section 5.4 (*Drug-Altered Consciousness*) has updated information on state laws related to cannabis, new research on caffeine, and new statistics related to fentanyl overdoses.

Chapter 6: Conditioning and Learning

- The new organization of this chapter includes the following major sections:

6.1 The Basics of Learning	6.4 Observational Learning
6.2 Classical Conditioning	6.5 Cognitive Learning
6.3 Operant Conditioning	6.6 Psychology and Your Skill Set: Behavioral Self-Management

- Material related to conditioning has been streamlined to allow for a significantly expanded discussion of observational and cognitive learning.
- Section 6.4 (*Observational Learning*) includes new material that connects observational learning to workplace behavior (e.g., how people learn the type of inappropriate behavior that was the focus of the #metoo movement) and media coverage of real-life tragedies such as mass shootings (i.e., copycat crimes). Material related to observational learning and mediabased violence has been updated, and a new *Studying the Science* segment unpacks why researchers sometimes come up with conflicting findings regarding the connection between media violence and aggression.

- Section 6.5 (*Cognitive Learning*) is now more clearly aimed at students interested in pursuing careers in education, as well helping students to better understand their own learning. Newly-written material covers the distinction between school and educational psychologists, Bloom's Taxonomy, and factors that influence cognitive learning (e.g., learner characteristics and learning strategies). Two *Studying the Science* sections look carefully at mindset and learning styles, areas in which newer findings have not always aligned with original research. This section concludes with a new segment on educational technology, including research that specifically examines the costs and benefits of using laptops in the classroom for note-taking.

Chapter 7: Memory

- The new organization of this chapter includes the following major sections:

7.1 A General Model of Memory	7.5 Accuracy of Long-Term Memory
7.2 Sensory & Short-Term (Working) Memory	7.6 Improving Your Memory
7.3 Long-Term Memory	7.7 Psychology and Your Skill Set: Giving Memorable Presentations
7.4 Remembering and Forgetting	

- This chapter now more clearly delineates memory systems (that is, types of memory) from memory processes, and emphasizes the general process of encoding as the means of moving information from working memory into long-term memory.
- Section 7.3 (*Long-Term Memory*) has been substantially reworked, elaborating on the idea that LTM is organized primarily based on meaning. This section also addresses the importance of LTM (i.e., the problem with adopting a view that people don't need to remember because they can just "Google it"), drawing on findings demonstrating that extensive prior knowledge in LTM helps with both quickly understanding new information and with remembering it later.
- Section 7.4 (*Remembering and Forgetting*) has been reorganized to focus on factors that do promote encoding and those that (surprisingly) do not, backed up by newer research that builds on the classic "penny" study. Updated views on forgetting (including its benefits for learning and the distinction between active and passive forgetting) and the reconstructive nature of remembering have also been added to this section.

Chapter 8: Cognition, Language, and Creativity

- The new organization of this chapter includes the following major sections:

8.1 The Basic Units of Cognition	8.4 Creative Thinking
8.2 Problem Solving	8.5 Psychology and Your Skill Set: Creativity and Innovation
8.3 Intuition, Decision-Making, and Cognitive Biases	

- Section 8.1 (*The Basic Units of Cognition*) includes updated information about bilingualism.
- Section 8.2 (*Problem Solving*) includes an expanded discussion of the different problem-solving strategies employed by experts and novices, drawing students' attention to the link between problem solving and memory.
- Section 8.3 (*Intuition, Decision Making, and Cognitive Biases*) now introduces readers to the role of psychology in the emerging field of behavioral economics. It also has a new section that describes the availability heuristic, as well as updated information on choice overload (including the conditions under which it does *not* occur).

Chapter 9: Intelligence

- The new organization of this chapter includes the following major sections:

9.1 Defining Human Intelligence	9.4 Genetic and Environmental Contributions to Intelligence
9.2 Measuring Intelligence	9.5 Thinking Ethically About Intelligence
9.3 Intellectual Giftedness and Disability	9.6 Psychology and Your Skill Set: Emotional Intelligence

- Section 9.1 (*Defining Human Intelligence*) has been reorganized to include more general material from other sections, and discusses the strengths and weaknesses associated with multiple conceptualizations of intelligence.
- Section 9.2 (*Measuring Intelligence*) includes newer research concerning developmental change in traditional IQ measures.
- Section 9.4 (*Genetic and Environmental Contributions to Intelligence*) describes newer research related to genetic contributions to intelligence, including the findings of large-scale studies suggesting that intelligence is the product of a large number of genes. Also included in this section is updated information about the role of the environment, including an attempt to clarify conflicting research findings related to the role of programs such as Head Start.
- Chapter 9.5 (*Thinking Ethically About Intelligence*) includes new information from large-scale genetic studies emphasizing the need to avoid over-simplifying the concept of race, and its relation to IQ test scores. A new *Psychology in Everyday Life* section expands on prior coverage of artificial intelligence (AI), and includes a new discussion about AI privacy concerns, particularly those associated with the facial recognition programs now in use in many parts of the United States.

Chapter 10: Motivation and Emotion

- The new organization of this chapter includes the following major sections:

10.1 The Basics of Motivation	10.4 The Four Basic Aspects of Emotion
10.2 Biological Motives	10.5 Connecting the Four Basic Aspects of Emotion
10.3 Stimulus and Learned Motives	10.6 Psychology and Your Skill Set: Positivity and Optimism

- Section 10.1 (*The Basics of Motivation*) outlines newer findings related to the history of Maslow's hierarchy of needs, including some misconceptions about his ideas.
- Section 10.3 (*Stimulus and Learned Motives*) contains a more nuanced account of the Yerkes-Dodson law with a new figure that helps to explain how the relationship between arousal and performance depends on the ease of the task.
- Section 10.4 (*The Four Basic Aspects of Emotion*) now situates our discussion of emotion in the context of emotion-related experience, physiology, expression (i.e , behavior), and cognitions. In terms of behavior, newer research related to the importance of posture, eye gaze, and tone of voice has been included, and a new *Psychology in Everyday Life* section discusses new findings related to emotion contagion. Another new section describes emotion regulation, including the effectiveness of a variety of well-studied regulatory strategies.
- Section 10.5 (*Connecting the Four Basic Aspects of Emotion*) includes an updated treatment of Schachter and Singer's two-factor theory. A new *Studying the Science* section takes a closer look at Paul Ekman's basic emotion theory, including elements that have and have not been supported in more recent research.

Chapter 11: Sex, Gender, and Sexuality

- The new organization of this chapter includes the following major sections:

11.1 Sexual Development and Orientation	11.4 Sexual Relationships
11.2 Gender Identities and Roles	11.5 Psychology and Your Skill Set: Civic Engagement
11.3 Sexual Responses, Attitudes, and Behaviors	

- This chapter has been updated to reflect recent recommendations about the language that should be used to describe members of the LGBTQ community.
- Section 11.1 (*Sexual Development and Orientation*) contains a new *Psychology in Everyday Life* section related to the participation of intersex athletes in international competitions such as the Olympics.
- Section 11.3 (*Sexual Responses, Attitudes, and Behaviors*) includes newer research related to current sexual attitudes and behavior, as well as updated statistics on STDs.
- Section 11.4 (*Sexual Relationships*) has a brand-new section related to sexual harassment, including information designed to help students identify instances of harassment and potential responses.
- Section 11.5 (*Civic Engagement*) has updated information about young people's leadership and participation in major initiatives such as the Global Climate Strike.

Chapter 12: Personality and Individual Differences

- The new organization of this chapter includes the following major sections:

12.1 Theories of Personality	12.4 Factors Influencing Personality
12.2 Traits	12.5 Psychology and Your Skill Set: Leadership
12.3 Personality Assessment	

- Section 12.1 (*Theories of Personality*) has been reorganized to directly contrast key terms (e.g., personality, individual differences, temperament). Subsections related to theoretical perspectives have been rewritten in a parallel format (including each one's conceptions about the structure, dynamics, and development of personality) to make it easier for students to draw direct comparisons between them.
- Section 12.2 (*Traits*) includes a new *Human Diversity* section that highlights the HEXACO model of personality, and directly contrasts it with the Big Five. Two other new sections outline how a wide array of personalities can be explained with just a small number of trait-related factors, and the distinction between trait and type (e.g., Myers-Briggs) approaches to personality.

Chapter 13: Health Psychology

- The new organization of this chapter includes the following major sections:

13.1 Biopsychosocial and Behavioral Contributions to Health	13.4 Improving Health Through Coping
13.2 Stress and Health	13.5 Psychology and Your Skill Set: Stress Management
13.3 Improving Health with Treatment	

- Section 13.1 (*Biopsychosocial and Behavioral Contributions to Health*) has been substantially reworked to include greater emphasis on cultural differences in the extent to which practitioners adhere to the medical vs. biopsychosocial models of health. It also more clearly explains how the three components of the biopsychosocial model are relevant to health psychologists' work. A new *Human Diversity* section addresses the role of poverty in contributing to the health-related consequences of COVID-19.
- Section 13.2 (*Stress and Health*) has been reorganized and streamlined to make way for new content in other sections.
- Section 13.3 (*Improving Health with Treatment*) is brand new and focuses broadly on the role of the biopsychosocial model in understanding the likelihood of seeking and complying with treatment from a health-care provider. Specific topics include: factors related to recognizing illness and seeking treatment (including complementary and alternative medicine), reasons for treatment noncompliance, and how health care practitioners can minimize the likelihood that noncompliance will occur. A *Studying the Science* section explores people's use of the Internet to find information during the COVID-19 pandemic.
- Section 13.4 (*Improving Health Through Coping*) has been streamlined to make way for content in other sections, but includes new material on relationship-focused coping.

Chapter 14: Psychological Disorders

- The new organization of this chapter includes the following major sections:

14.1 Psychopathology: Classification and Causes	14.4 Anxiety and Anxiety-Related Disorders
14.2 Psychotic Disorders	14.5 Psychology and Your Skill Set: Perseverance
14.3 Mood and Personality Disorders	

- Section 14.1 (*Classification and Causes*) has been reorganized to focus on four ways to define abnormality and the advantages and disadvantages of using the DSM-5 as a means of classifying mental health concerns.
- Section 14.3 (*Mood and Personality Disorders*) includes changes to language related to suicide that are in keeping with suggestions made by the American Foundation for Suicide Prevention.
- In all sections of this chapter, there is a greater emphasis on the biopsychosocial model as a means of understanding psychopathology.

Chapter 15: Therapies

- The new organization of this chapter includes the following major sections:

15.1 The Origins and Effectiveness of Psychotherapy	15.4 Medical Therapies
15.2 Behavior Therapies	15.5 Psychology and Your Skill Set: Managing Mental Health Issues
15.3 Cognitive and Humanistic Therapies	

- Section 15.1 (*The Origins and Effectiveness of Psychotherapy*) brings together general information about psychotherapies (e.g., history, classification, methods of establishing effectiveness) that had previously been distributed throughout the chapter.
- Section 15.2 (*Behavior Therapies*) now more clearly delineates two therapeutic techniques based on classical conditioning (aversion and exposure therapies) and two based on operant conditioning (token economies and a new section on intensive behavioral intervention, which is often used in the treatment of autism). The different types of exposure therapy (flooding, systematic desensitization, modeling) are also more clearly delineated.
- Section 15.3 (*Cognitive and Humanistic Therapies*) provides a clearer explanation of rational-emotive behavior therapy as one of the first examples of a cognitive behavior therapy.
- Section 15.4 (*Medical Therapies*) includes updated information related to brain stimulation therapies.

Chapter 16: Social Thinking and Social Influence

- The new organization of this chapter includes the following major sections:

16.1 The Fundamentals of Social Groups	16.3 Social Influence
16.2 Attitudes	16.4 Psychology and Your Skill Set: Teamwork

- Section 16.1 (*The Fundamentals of Social Groups*) brings together general information about groups (ingroups vs. outgroups, characteristics of groups, characteristics of individuals within groups) that was previously distributed throughout the chapter. This section also includes a more nuanced discussion of attribution theory, with a new table that shows how consistency, distinctiveness, and consensus impact the likelihood that an internal vs. external attribution will be made.
- Section 16.3 (*Social Influence*) includes a streamlined section on mere presence that allows for a more in-depth discussion of conformity (including new material on Sherif's famous autokinetic study) and compliance (including new research from behavioral economists related to "nudges"). A new *Studying the Science* section explores Milgram's obedience studies in greater depth, examining a broader range of his experimental conditions and what they tell us about the likelihood that people will (or will not) obey orders.
- Section 16.4 (*Teamwork*) now makes reference to COVID-19 and its impact on our understanding of the effectiveness of virtual teams.

Chapter 17: Prosocial and Antisocial Behavior

- The new organization of this chapter includes the following major sections:

17.1 Affiliation and Attraction	17.3 Antisocial Behavior: Aggression, Conflict, and Prejudice
17.2 Prosocial Behavior: Helping Others	17.4 Psychology and Your Skill Set: Diversity and Inclusion

- Section 17.2 (*Prosocial Behavior*) now clarifies the relationship between altruism and prosocial behavior, and distinguishes between self-oriented and other-oriented motives for prosocial behavior. An expanded section on the factors that influence prosocial behavior is also included. Finally, a new *Studying the Science* section explores the construct of empathy.
- Section 17.3 (*Antisocial Behavior*) now distinguishes between direct and indirect aggression, providing examples from everyday life. Two new *Studying the Science* sections examine emerging work related to microaggressions (and some of the challenges associated with studying them) and the utility of the implicit association task (IAT). Finally, new material addresses the health consequences that stem from experiencing chronic prejudice and the utility of diversity training initiatives in the workplace.

Chapter 18: Applied Psychology

- The new organization of this chapter includes the following major sections:

18.1 Industrial/Organizational Psychology	18.3 Legal, Community, and Sports Psychology
18.2 Environmental Psychology	18.4 Psychology and Your Skill Set: Career Preparation

- Section 18.1 (*Industrial/Organizational Psychology*) has been reorganized and the discussion of flexible working has been expanded to include a discussion of this topic in relation to COVID-19.
- In Section 18.2 (*Environmental Psychology*), previous material on space habitats has been eliminated to allow for expanded coverage of human impacts on the environment.
- Section 18.3 (*Legal, Community, and Sports Psychology*) now distinguishes the related fields of legal and forensic psychology. Material about educational psychology has been moved to Chapter 6 (Conditioning and Learning); in its place is a brand-new section introducing students to community psychology.
- Section 18.4 (*Career Preparation*) contains some new suggestions for students to consider as they think about a possible career.

Appendix: A Psychologist's Skill Set: Statistical Literacy

- We have clarified the relationship between measures of central tendency and measures of variability to help readers understand their distinct contribution to descriptive statistics. The utility of correlations in making predictions has been further emphasized.

A Complete Course—Teaching and Learning Supplements

A rich array of supplements accompanies *Introduction to Psychology: Gateways to Mind and Behavior*, including several that make use of the latest technologies. These supplements are designed to make teaching and learning more effective. Many are available free to professors or students. Others can be packaged with this textbook at a discount. Contact your local sales representative for more information on any of the listed resources.

Instructor Resources

Teaching an introductory psychology course is a tremendous amount of work, and the supplements listed here should help make it possible for you to concentrate on the more creative and rewarding facets of teaching. Go to login.cengage.com to create an account and log in.

The Instructor Companion Site

The Instructor Companion Site for this title includes an *Instructor's Resource Manual*, which provides a wealth of teaching tips and classroom resources; *Cengage Learning Testing Powered by Cognero* featuring questions correlated to learning objectives, Bloom's taxonomy level, and difficulty; *Guided Notes for students* to assist with their note-taking; and *PowerPoint slides* providing concept coverage with dynamic animations, photographs, and video.

Summary

We sincerely hope that both teachers and students will consider this book and its supporting materials a refreshing change from the ordinary. Creating it has been quite an adventurous journey for us; one that we look forward to sharing with you in the chapters that follow. We hope that you enjoy the ride.

Acknowledgments

Psychology is a cooperative effort requiring the talents and energies of a large community of scholars, teachers, researchers, and students. Like most endeavors in psychology, this book reflects the efforts of many people. We deeply appreciate the contributions of the following professors, whose sage advice has contributed to the ongoing updates reflected in new editions of *Introduction to Psychology: Gateways to Mind and Behavior:*

Dr. Robin Akawi
Sierra Community College
Faren R. Akins
University of Arizona
Avis Donna Alexander
John Tyler Community College
Clark E. Alexander
Arapahoe Community College
Tricia Alexander
Long Beach City College
Dennis Anderson
Butler Community College
Lynn Anderson
Wayne State University
Nancy L. Ashton
R. Stockton College of New Jersey
Scott A. Bailey
Texas Lutheran University
Carol Baldwin
Salish Kootenai College
Frank Barbehenn
Bucks County Community College
Michael Bardo
University of Kentucky
Larry W. Barron
Grand Canyon University
Linda M. Bastone
Purchase College, SUNY
Brian R. Bate
Cuyahoga Community College
Hugh E. Bateman
Jones Junior College
Evelyn Blanch-Payne
Oakwood College
Cheryl Bluestone
Queensborough Community College–CUNY
Galen V. Bodenhausen
Michigan State University
Aaron U. Bolin
Arkansas State University
Tom Bond
Thomas Nelson Community College
John Boswell
University of Missouri, St. Louis
Anne Bright

Jackson State Community College
Soheila T. Brouk
Gateway Technical College
Derek Cadman
El Camino Community College
James F. Calhoun
University of Georgia
Dennis Cogan
Texas Tech University
Lorry Cology
Owens College
William N. Colson
Norfolk State College
Chris Cozby
California State University, Fullerton
Corinne Crandell
Broome County Community College
Thomas L. Crandell
Broome County Community College
Charles Croll
Broome Community College
Daniel B. Cruse
University of Miami
Keith E. Davis
University of South Carolina–Columbia
Diane DeArmond
University of Missouri, Kansas City
Patrick T. DeBoll
St. John's University
Dawn Delaney
University of Wisconsin–Whitewater
Jack Demick
Suffolk University
Lorraine P. Dieudonne
Foothill College
H. Mitzi Doane
University of Minnesota–Duluth
Wendy Domjan
University of Texas at Austin
Roger A. Drake
Western State College of Colorado
John Dworetzky
Glendale Community College
Bill Dwyer
Memphis State University
Thomas Eckle
Modesto Community College
David Edwards
Iowa State University
Raymond Elish
Cuyahoga Community College
Diane Feibel
University of Cincinnati–Raymond Walters College
Paul W. Fenton
University of Wisconsin, Stout
Christopher Ferguson
Stetson University
Dave Filak
Joliet Junior College
Oney D. Fitzpatrick, Jr.
Lamar University
Linda E. Flickinger
Saint Clair County Community College
William F. Ford
Bucks County Community College
Marie Fox
Metropolitan State College of Denver
Chris Fraser
Gippsland Institute of Advanced Education
Christopher Frost
Southwest Texas State University
Eugenio J. Galindro
El Paso Community College
Irby J. Gaudet
University of Southwestern Louisiana
David Gersh
Houston Community College
David A. Gershaw
Arizona Western College
Andrew R. Getzfeld
New Jersey City University
Carolyn A. Gingrich
South Dakota State University
Perilou Goddard
Northern Kentucky University
Michael E. Gorman
Michigan Technological University
Peter Gram
Pensacola Junior College
David A. Gries
State University of New York, Farmingdale
R. J. Grisham
Indian River Community College
John Grivas
Monash University
Anne Groves
Montgomery College
Michael B. Guyer
John Carroll University
Janice Hartgrove-Freile
North Harris College
Raquel Henry
Kingwood College
Callina Henson
Oakland Community College–Auburn Hills
Anne Hester
Pennsylvania State University–Hazleton Campus
Gregory P. Hickman
The Pennsylvania State University–Fayette
Don Hockenbury
Tulsa Junior College
Sidney Hockman
Nassau Community College
Gordon Hodson
Brock University
Barbara Honhart
Lansing Community College
John C. Johanson
Winona State University
James A. Johnson
Sam Houston State University
Myles E. Johnson
Normandale Community College
Pat Jones
Brevard Community College
Richard Kandus
Menifee Valley Campus
Bruno M. Kappes
University of Alaska–Anchorage
Charles Karis
Northeastern University
John P. Keating
University of Washington
Patricia Kemerer
Ivy Tech Community College
Cindy Kennedy
Sinclair Community College
Shaila Khan
Tougaloo College
Richard R. Klene
University of Cincinnati
Ronald J. Kopcho
Mercer Community College
Darla Korol
Nebraska Indian Community College
Mary Kulish
Thomas Nelson Community College
Billie Laney
Central Texas College
Phil Lau
DeAnza College
Robert Lawyer
Delgado Community College
Walter Leach
College of San Mateo
Christopher Legrow
Marshall University
Lindette I. Lent
Arizona Western College
Elizabeth Levin
Laurentian University
Julie Lewis
Georgian College
Elise B. Lindenmuth
York College of Pennsylvania
Linda Lockwood
Metropolitan State College of Denver
Philip Lom
West Connecticut State University
Cheryl S. Lynch
University of Louisiana–Lafayette
Salvador Macias, III
University of South Carolina, Sumter
Abe Marrero

Rogers State University
Al Mayer
Portland Community College
Michael Jason McCoy
Cape Fear Community College
Edward R. McCrary III
El Camino College
Yancy B. McDougal
University of South Carolina, Spartanburg
Mark McGee
Texas A&M University
Angela McGlynn
Mercer County Community College
Mark McKinley
Lorain County Community College
Chelley Merrill
Tidewater Community College
Beth Moore
Madisonville Community College
Feleccia R. Moore-Davis
Houston Community College System
Edward J. Morris
Owensboro Community College
Wynema Morris
Nebraska Indian Community College
Edward Mosley
Pasiac County Community College
James Murray
San Jacinto University
Gary Nallan
University of North Carolina–Ashville
Andrew Neher
Cabrillo College
Don Nelson
Indiana State University
Steve Nida
Franklin University
Peggy Norwood
Tidewater Community College
James P. B. O'Brien
Tidewater Community College
Frances O'Keefe
Tidewater Community College
Steve G. Ornelas
Central Arizona College
Laura Overstreet
Tarrant County College
Darlene Pacheco
Moorpark College
Lisa K. Paler
College of New Rochelle
Debra Parish
Tomball College
Cora F. Patterson
University of Southwestern Louisiana
Leon Peek
North Texas State University
John Pennachio
Adirondack Community College
Peter Phipps
Sullivan County Community College
Steven J. Pollock
Moorpark College
Jack Powell
University of Hartford
Ravi Prasad
Texas Tech University
Derrick L. Proctor
Andrews University
Douglas Pruitt
West Kentucky Community College
Robin Raygor
Anoka-Ramsey Community College
Richard Rees
Glendale Community College
Paul A. Rhoads
Williams College
Harvey Richman
Columbus State University
Marcia Rossi
Tuskegee University
Jeffrey Rudski
Mulhenberg College
James J. Ryan
University of Wisconsin, La Crosse
John D. Sanders
Butler County Community College
Nancy Sauerman
Kirkwood Community College
Michael Schuller
Fresno City College
Pamela E. Scott-Johnson
Spelman College
Carol F. Shoptaugh
Southwest Missouri State University
Harold I. Siegel
Rutgers University
Richard Siegel
University of Massachusetts, Lowell
Nancy Simpson
Trident Technical College
Madhu Singh
Tougaloo College
Glenda Smith
North Harris Community College
Steven M. Smith
Texas A&M University
Francine Smolucha
Moraine Valley Community College
Michael C. Sosulski
College of DuPage
Lynn M. Sprott
Jefferson Community College
Donald M. Stanley
North Harris County College
Julie E. Stokes
California State University–Fullerton
Catherine Grady Strathern
University of Cincinnati
Harvey Taub
Staten Island Community College
Christopher Taylor
University of Arizona
Carol Terry
University of Oklahoma
Laura Thompson
New Mexico State University
Richard Townsend
Miami-Dade Community College–Kendall Campus
Bruce Trotter
Santa Barbara City College
Susan Troy
Northeast Iowa Community College
Pat Tuntland
Pima College
Paul E. Turner
David Lipscomb University
A. D. VanDeventer
Thomas Nelson Community College
Mark Vernoy
Palomar College
Charles Verschoor
Miami-Dade Community College–Kendall Campus
Frank Vitro
Texas Women's University
John Vojtisek
Castleton State College
Francis Volking
Saint Leo University
David W. Ward
Arkansas Tech University
Paul J. Wellman
Texas A&M University
Sharon Whelan
University of Kentucky
Robert Wiley
Montgomery College
Thomas Wilke
University of Wisconsin, Parkside
Carl D. Williams
University of Miami
Don Windham
Roane State Community College
Kaye D. Young
North Iowa Area Community College
Michael Zeller
Mankato State University
Margaret C. Zimmerman
Virginia Wesleyan College
Otto Zinser
East Tennessee State College

Producing *Introduction to Psychology: Gateways to Mind and Behavior* and its supplements was a formidable task. We are especially indebted to each of the following individuals for supporting this book, beginning with Stephen Harlan, the brilliant digital artist who created "Poco Libre," which graces the cover of this textbook (you can see more of Stephen's art at his website, http://harlanart.com).

We also wish to thank the gifted group of professionals at Cengage and elsewhere who have so generously shared their knowledge and talents over the past two years. These are the people who made it happen:

At Cengage, we are especially grateful to our Product Manager, Colin Grover, for his savvy and unconditional support.

We also want to single out Christy Frame. As our Senior Content Manager, Christy patiently kept us on track and offered many deeply appreciated suggestions.

Tricia Salata, Natasha Allen, Kim Buettler, Kelli Besse, and Deanna Ettinger, along with so many others, played key roles.

Thank you also Lori Hazzard from MPS Limited, and Nishabhanu Beegum and Sri Ranjani from Lumina Datamatics.

Up in St. Catharines, Barbara Kushmier, Kayleigh Hagerman, Heather Mitterer, and David and Callum Williams pitched in to lend a hand.

Last of all and, of course, not least, we would like to thank our spouses, Sevren, Heather, and David, for making the journey worthwhile.

Introduction to

Psychology:

Gateways to Mind and Behavior

16e

Introduction
Psychology and Your Skill Set: Reflective Studying

fizkes/Shutterstock.com

Gateway Theme It is possible to learn more efficiently and effectively by being reflective about reading, note-taking, and studying.

Chapter Outline

Well Hello There!

As your authors, we are delighted to welcome you to the "manual" for this textbook. No! Don't skip this, please. We understand that few people want to start a new adventure by reading a manual—they would prefer to just step off the airplane and begin their vacation, get right into that new computer game, or start using their new camera or smartphone. But please be patient and take some time to read this short chapter—we think it will almost certainly increase your odds of success in this course.

Successfully learning psychology depends on how *reflective* you are as you read your textbook, listen during your classes, and study for exams. Students who get good grades tend to work more reflectively, not just longer or harder. They also tend to understand and remember more of what they've learned long after their exams are over. In this introduction, we share our thoughts on why psychology provides a good foundation for being successful in your personal and professional life, before going on to outline a variety of ways to become a more reflective learner.

I.1 Why Study Psychology?

GATEWAYS LEARNING OUTCOME:
After reading this section you should be able to:

I.1.1 Explain how studying psychology will help you in your personal and professional life

As you begin exploring the field of psychology, you may well be asking yourself what you'll get out of it. In general, most of your courses will offer you opportunities to learn in two important ways. The first has to do with course *content*—in this introductory psychology course, the content is what you'll learn about the field of psychology. This includes what psychological research tells us about memory, social relationships, brain functioning, children's development, and psychopathology (to name just a few topics). But taking a psychology course will also promote your learning in a second way—specifically, it will teach you about *skills* that you'll need to be successful in your personal and professional life.

What do you mean by "skills"? When we talk about skills, we're often talking about things that you can do, such as communicate clearly or work well with others. But in some cases, the term *skills* can also refer to personal characteristics; for example, independence, tolerance, and adaptability are often considered to be important skills.

These two broad categories of learning—content and skills—are outlined in the American Psychological Association's (APA) *Guidelines for the Undergraduate Psychology Major* (*version 2.0*) (American Psychological Association, 2013). It is well worth having a look at the full document (which is available online), but you can start by having a look at ▲ Table I.1.

Do you assume that your only goal is to memorize "the facts," or knowledge base, of psychology? If so, as you can see in Table I.1, you are thinking in terms of Goal 1. But what about the other goals listed there? Suppose you are given an assignment that involves working in small groups to evaluate some published research articles. Would you wonder why you have to work with other students? Or wish your professor would just get to the point and tell you what the articles are about? Understanding that your education is also about acquiring skills—like being able to think critically (Goal 2), consider diverse points of view (Goal 3), communicate clearly (Goal 4), and work as part of a team (Goal 5)—makes it easier for you to appreciate that professors set up assignments to build skills, as well as furthering what you know about psychology.

One of the things that you might notice as you look through Table I.1 is that many of the skills listed aren't really specific to psychology—they're likely to be just as relevant to someone majoring in history or business or biology. After all, people in all disciplines need to understand how to communicate well, work well with others, and behave ethically.

Some of the most important advice we can give you, then, is to remember to focus on the skills that you are learning throughout your studies at university, whether in psychology or other subjects. They may not always seem obvious when you're reading a textbook or when you're completing your assignments, but when it comes time for you to hit the job market, you'll be happy that you did.

▲ Table I.1 APA Guidelines for the Undergraduate Psychology Major

Goal 1: Knowledge Base of Psychology
Goal 2: Scientific Inquiry and Critical Thinking
Goal 3: Ethical and Social Responsibility in a Diverse World
Goal 4: Communication
Goal 5: Professional Development

Adapted from American Psychological Association, 2013. For complete details, go to: www.apa.org/ed/precollege/about/learning-goals.pdf.

A StockStudio/Shutterstock.com

Working on developing your skills may seem like a waste of your time compared with putting that time into learning course content. But don't sell it short; your skill set will be just as important as your content expertise whether you go on to post-graduate education or a career.

Psychology and Your Skill Set

To understand why your skill set is important, have a look at ▲ Table I.2, which lists a few of the career opportunities open to psychology majors.

Travel agent? Think about it for a moment. A travel agent may not need psychology content expertise, such as being able to list Freud's stages of psychosexual development or explain what psychological functions are controlled by the different parts of the brain. But it *would* help to be able to work independently, do your own research, be able to make presentations to individuals or groups, have some sensitivity to cross-cultural issues, write well, and, in general, work well with people. While these sorts of skills can be learned in other ways, studying psychology provides a "golden opportunity" for you to develop an impressive set of skills that are valued by many employers.

▲ Table I.2 A Skills-Based List of Some Potential Careers for Psychology Majors

Addictions counselor	Manager
Administration	Market research analyst
Advertising	Marketing
Career/employment counselor	Mental health worker
Case worker	Motivational researcher
Child care worker	Personnel
Child welfare worker	Population studies researcher
Community worker	Probation or parole officer
Correctional officer	Professional consultant
Counselor	Program coordinator
Cultural diversity consultant	Psychiatric assistant or aide
Customs or immigration agent	Public health statistician
Daycare worker, supervisor	Public opinion interviewer
Educational counselor	Public relations
Entrepreneur	Psychology professor
Fundraiser or development officer	Recreation specialist
Gerontology	Research assistant
Government researcher	Sales representative
Health services	Social services/social worker
Hospice coordinator	Teaching
Human resources	Technical writer
Immigration officer	Travel agent
Labor relations specialist	Youth worker

Adapted from Canadian Psychological Association (2017).

How This Book Will Help You with Skill Development

You probably won't be surprised to learn that *Introduction to Psychology: Gateways to Mind and Behavior* has been written with the APA *Guidelines* in mind, in an effort to help you further develop your career-related skill set. Here are some skills highlights:

- **Application Skills:** One skill that employers value is the ability to see connections and apply learning from one situation to another. In this book, we have a number of sections about *Psychology in Everyday Life* which are intended to make clear how the findings from psychological science can be seen all around us.
- **Research and Critical Thinking Skills:** We will introduce you to science and psychology research, from the research methods in Chapter 1 to the Statistical Literacy Appendix (and everywhere in between!). An important element of research is critical thinking, which encompasses a wide array of related skills including defining problems, searching for and evaluating information to address those problems, and synthesizing information that you gather. But critical thinking skills matter in many careers beyond research, so in this book we've tried to model it whenever we can. In particular, scattered throughout the book you'll find sections called *Studying the Science*, in which we specifically focus on thinking critically about complex topics such as the link between media violence and aggression.
- **Cultural Awareness Skills:** OK, so we can't take you on a field trip to Japan, but throughout this book, we invite you to reflect on the differences among people of different ethnicities, sexual orientations, ages, and genders. Developing these skills will be particularly important when you find yourself having to work with others whose background or belief system is not the same as your own. Throughout this text, you'll find sections titled *Human Diversity*, which will draw your attention to the wide variation in human characteristics and behaviors.
- **Psychology and Your Skill Set:** In the remainder of this Introduction we discuss a full set of study skills, from how to read and listen for understanding to how to take tests and overcome procrastination. In addition, at the end of each chapter you'll also encounter a *Psychology and Your Skill Set* section. Each of these sections connects the field of psychology to a skill that is likely to be useful across a broad range of career paths. These sections, combined with the digital resources for this book, will allow you to measure your skill level and give you practical ideas you can use to improve your skill set.

Of course, we understand that the classroom isn't the only place to learn skills that can help you in your personal life and career. Many college and university students will also have part-time jobs, or they will participate in other learning experiences such as community-based volunteering, student government or clubs, or study abroad. Often, the skills that you develop through these extracurricular experiences will support or complement the skills that you can learn through the assignments that you'll complete for your courses.

For example, common part-time student jobs involving interaction with the public (e.g., waiting tables, customer service, or retail jobs) often help to build *verbal* communication skills such as the ability to speak to others, and to listen effectively to what others are saying. In contrast, class assignments often build *writing* skills and the ability to *read and understand* complex material. When you are attempting to persuade an employer that you have a broad range of communication skills, then, you should make sure that you discuss what you have learned from a variety of experiences both inside and outside of the classroom to demonstrate the full range of your abilities.

Reflective Learning: The Most Important Ingredient

Simply deciding that you want to learn some content or skills isn't going to actually make it happen. To understand why, think about the last time you spent the evening relaxing in front of the

William Haefeli/Conde Nast/Cartoon bank

"I'm too busy going to college to study."

television. It probably was fun, but you may have noticed that you didn't think too much about what you were watching and that your subsequent memories are not detailed. You were engaging in **experiential processing**, more or less passively soaking up the experience (Kahneman, 2011; Norman, 1994).

Now contrast that with your experience in a recent job interview. It is highly unlikely that you got through the interview by relying on experiential processing alone (and even less likely that you landed the job if you did). Instead, you probably actively and carefully listened to the questions and put some serious effort into thinking through the implications of answering in different ways before responding. No drifting off here; you were focused and controlled until you left the interview, when you likely breathed a much-deserved sigh of relief. By reacting mindfully (Siegel, 2010), you engaged in **reflective processing** (Kahneman, 2011; Norman, 1994). Rather than just having the experience, you *actively thought* about it. Similarly, **reflective learning** occurs when you engage in deliberately reflective and active self-regulated study (Anthony, Clayton, & Zusho, 2013; Mega, Ronconi, & De Beni, 2014). Here, in general, is how you can promote reflective learning of both content and skills:

1. **Set specific, objective learning goals.** Begin each learning session with specific goals in mind. What knowledge or skills are you trying to master? What do you hope to accomplish (Pychyl, 2013)? The learning outcomes that precede each section will help you with this task.
2. **Plan a learning strategy.** How will you accomplish your goals? Make daily, weekly, and monthly plans for learning. Then put them into action.
3. **Be your own teacher.** Effective learners silently give themselves guidance and ask themselves questions. For example, as you are learning, you might ask yourself, "What are the important ideas here? What do I remember? What don't I understand? What do I need to review? What should I do next?"
4. **Monitor your progress and correct your strategy when necessary.** Reflective learning depends on self-monitoring. Exceptional learners keep records of their progress toward learning goals (pages read, hours of studying, assignments completed, and so forth). They quiz themselves, use study guides, and find other ways to check their understanding while learning. Consider asking yourself these questions regularly as you work toward mastering both course content and skills: Do any specific areas of your work need improvement? If you are not making good progress toward long-range goals, do you need to revise your short-term targets? If you fall short of your goals, you may need to adjust how you budget your time. You may also need to change your learning environment to deal with distractions such as browsing the web, daydreaming, talking to friends, or testing the limits of your hearing with your new ear buds.
5. **Reward yourself.** When you meet your daily, weekly, or monthly goals, reward your efforts in some way, such as going to a movie or downloading some new music. Be aware that self-praise also rewards learning. Being able to say "Hey, I did it!" can be rewarding. In the long run, success, self-improvement, and personal satisfaction are the real payoffs for learning.

If you discover that you lack certain knowledge or skills, ask for help, take advantage of tutoring programs, or look for information beyond your courses and textbooks. Knowing how to reflectively enhance learning can be a key to lifelong enrichment and personal empowerment (Van Blerkom, 2012).

I.2 Reflective Reading: How to Tame a Textbook

GATEWAYS LEARNING OUTCOME:
After reading this section you should be able to:

I.2.1 Describe how you can get the most out of this textbook

One powerful way to get the most out of this textbook is to be more reflective through **self-reference**. As you read, relate new facts, terms, and concepts to your own experiences and information that you already know well. Doing this will make new ideas more personally meaningful and easier to remember. **Critical thinking** is another powerful way to be more reflective. Remember, critical thinkers pause to evaluate, compare, analyze, critique, and synthesize what they are reading (Chaffee, 2015). You should, too. In Chapter 1, we will learn how to think critically about psychological science.

Does this really work? You bet! Using a reflective reading strategy improves learning and course grades (Taraban, Rynearson, & Kerr, 2000). It also results in enhanced long-term understanding. Simply reading straight through a textbook chapter can give you intellectual indigestion. That's why it's better to stop often to reflect, review, and digest information as you read.

Going Digital

Digital media can also offer several ways to learn more reflectively from this textbook. You can get a good start by exploring MindTap.

MindTap

MindTap is a highly personalized, fully online learning platform that integrates in one site all of the authoritative content, assignments, and services that accompany your textbook, *Introduction to Psychology: Gateways to Mind and Behavior*.

What can I expect to get out of MindTap? Many of the more active elements of reflective learning are better presented digitally. There is room, for example, to include only a few practice quizzes in a print textbook (and you, the reader, have to self-score them). In contrast, digital media make it feasible to present more extensive practice materials, as well as to provide immediate feedback.

MindTap has been designed to make it easier for you to engage in reflective learning by presenting the entire course (yup, the textbook, too) through a reflective learning path that includes video and other interactive activities. You will be able to complete reading assignments, annotate your readings, complete homework, get detailed instant feedback on Guided Practice Activities, and interact with quizzes and assessments. MindTap includes a variety of apps known as "MindApps," allowing functionality such as having the text read aloud to you, as well as synchronizing your notes with your personal Evernote account. MindApps are woven into the MindTap platform and enhance your learning experience with this textbook.

Psychology Websites

As you read (reflectively, of course) through this textbook, you may, from time to time, find yourself wanting to read more about a particular topic. Consider following up by looking up some of the references included in this text. For example, suppose that you were just reading about procrastination and wanted to learn more about the reference *Pychyl* (2013). You can look up all in-chapter references in the "References" section at the back of this text. There, you will find that *Pychyl* (2013) is a book about overcoming procrastination.

Sometimes, though, the reference that you are interested in will be a psychology journal article. To locate journal articles, you can use PsycINFO, a specialized online database offered by the American Psychological Association (APA). **PsycINFO** provides summaries of the scientific and scholarly literature in psychology. Each record in PsycINFO consists of an abstract (short summary), plus notes about the author, title, source, and other details. Entering the author's or authors' name(s) and article title will bring you to the article in question. Also, all PsycINFO entries are indexed using key terms. Thus, you can search for various topics by entering words such as *procrastination*, *postpartum depression*, or *creativity* and find research papers on any topic in psychology that might interest you.

Most colleges and universities subscribe to PsycINFO. You can usually search PsycINFO from a terminal in your college library or computer center—for free. PsycINFO can also be directly accessed (for a fee) through the Internet via APA's PsycINFO Direct service. For more information on how to gain access to PsycINFO, check out www.apa.org/pubs/databases/psycinfo/index.aspx. Beware, though: Many of the primary research papers available through PsycINFO are highly technical. Don't be put off by this; read and digest what you can. You'll pick up some interesting information and become a better psychology student in the process.

Aside from PsycINFO, there are a number of good websites that you can consult for reliable information about psychology. For example, the American Psychological Association (APA) and the Association for Psychological Science (APS) maintain online libraries of general-interest articles on many topics. They are well worth consulting when you have questions about psychological issues. You'll find them at www.apa.org and www.psychologicalscience.org. For links to recent articles in newspapers and magazines, check the APA's PsycPORT page at www.apa.org/news/psycport/index.aspx. Other high-quality websites include those maintained by other professional organizations, such as the National Institute of Mental Health (www.nimh.nih.gov). (■ See Section 1.8 for more on the important skill of information literacy.)

I.3 Reflective Note-Taking: LISAN Up!

GATEWAYS LEARNING OUTCOME:
After reading this section you should be able to:

I.3.1 Describe how you can get the most out of class time

Just as studying a textbook is best done reflectively, so, too, is learning in class (Norman, 1994). Like effective reading, good notes come from actively seeking information. A **reflective listener** avoids distractions and skillfully gathers ideas. Here's a listening/note-taking plan that works for many students. The letters LISAN, pronounced like the word *listen*, will help you remember the steps:

- L = *Lead. Don't follow.* Read assigned materials before coming to class. Try to anticipate what your teacher will say by asking yourself questions. If your teacher provides course notes or

Experiential processing Thought that is passive, effortless, and automatic.

Reflective processing Thought that is active, effortful, and controlled.

Reflective learning Deliberately reflective and active self-guided study.

Self-reference The practice of relating new information to prior life experience.

Critical thinking An ability to evaluate, compare, analyze, critique, and synthesize information.

PsycINFO A searchable online database that provides brief summaries of the scientific and scholarly literature in psychology.

Reflective listener A person who knows how to maintain attention, avoid distractions, and actively gather information from lectures.

Microsoft PowerPoint® overheads before lectures, survey them before coming to class. Reflective questions can come from those materials or from study guides, reading assignments, or your own curiosity.

- I = *Ideas*. Every lecture is based on a core of ideas. Usually, an idea is followed by examples or explanations. Ask yourself often, "What is the main idea now? What ideas support it?"
- S = *Signal words*. Listen for words that tell you what direction the instructor is taking. For instance, here are some signal words:

There are three reasons . . .	Here come ideas
Most important is . . .	Main idea
On the contrary . . .	Opposite idea
As an example . . .	Support for main idea
Therefore . . .	Conclusion

- A = *Actively listen*. Sit where you can get involved and ask questions. Bring questions that you want answered from the last lecture or from your text. Raise your hand at the beginning of class or approach your professor before the lecture. Do anything that helps you stay active, alert, and engaged.
- N = *Note taking*. Students who take accurate lecture notes tend to do well on tests (Williams & Eggert, 2002). However, don't try to be a tape recorder. Listen to everything, but be selective and write down only key points. If you are too busy writing, you may not grasp what your professor is saying. When you're taking notes, it might help to think of yourself as a reporter who is trying to get a good story (Ryan, 2001; Wong, 2015).

Most students take reasonably good notes—and then don't use them! Instead, they wait until just before exams to review. By then, their notes have lost much of their meaning. If you don't want your notes to seem like chicken scratches, it pays to review them periodically (Ellis, 2016).

Using and Reviewing Your Notes

When you review, you will learn more if you take these extra steps (Ellis, 2016; Pychyl, 2013; Santrock & Halonen, 2013):

- As soon as you can, reflect on your notes to fill in gaps, complete thoughts, and look for connections among ideas.
- Remember to link new ideas to what you already know.
- Summarize your notes. Boil them down and organize them.
- After each class session, write down several major ideas, definitions, or details that are likely to become test questions. Then, make up questions from your notes and be sure that you can answer them.

The letters *LISAN* are a guide to active listening, but listening and good note-taking are not enough. You must also review, organize, reflect, extend, and think about new ideas. Use active listening to get involved in your classes, and you will undoubtedly learn more (Van Blerkom, 2012).

I.4 Reflective Study Strategies: Making a Habit of Success

GATEWAYS LEARNING OUTCOME:
After reading this section you should be able to:

I.4.1 Describe how you can best prepare for tests

Grades depend as much on effort as they do on intelligence. But good students work more efficiently, not just harder, and that's true when they study as well as when they write exams. In this section we provide some tips for improving your studying and test-taking skills.

Strategies for Studying

In an interesting paper, researchers reviewed more than 700 research articles on 10 of the most commonly used learning strategies to determine which ones were the most effective (Dunlosky et al., 2013). One of the study strategies most commonly used by students—highlighting or underlining material in the text or lecture notes—was found to be a particularly *ineffective* way to master the material, largely because it doesn't usually promote active or reflective learning. If you cannot imagine your textbook without the pretty neon colors, make sure that you combine your highlighting with one (or more!) of the effective strategies that we discuss below.

Test Yourself

A great way to improve grades is to take practice tests before the real one (Karpicke & Blunt, 2011; Sutterer & Awh, 2016), and this strategy came out as a clear winner in the review of learning strategies. In other words, reflective studying should include **self-testing**, in which you pose questions to yourself. You can use flashcards, online quizzes in MindTap, a study guide, or any other means that you find helpful. You'll also find *Reflective Practice* self-tests at the end of each major section of this textbook. As you study, try to anticipate potential test questions and be sure you can answer them. Studying without self-testing is like practicing for a basketball game without shooting any baskets.

Use Spaced Study Sessions

Another clear winner in the review of learning strategies was the use of spaced study sessions. It is reasonable to review intensely before an exam. However, you're taking a big risk if you are only cramming (learning new information at the last minute). Spaced practice is much more efficient (Dunlosky et al., 2013; Sternberg, 2017). **Spaced practice** consists of a large number of relatively short study sessions. Long, uninterrupted study sessions are called **massed practice**. (If you "massed up" your studying, you probably messed it up, too.) Cramming places a big burden on memory. Generally, you shouldn't try to learn anything new about a subject during the last day before a test. It is far better to learn small amounts every day and review frequently.

Other Suggestions for Studying

Ideally, you should study in a quiet, well-lit area free of distractions. If possible, you should also have one place only for studying. Do nothing else there: keep magazines, social media sites, friends, cell phones, pets, video games, televisions, and other distractions out of the area (Przepiorka, Błachnio, & Díaz-Morales, 2016). In this way, the habit of studying will become strongly linked with one specific place.

Also, many students *underprepare* for exams, and most *overestimate* how well they will do. A solution to both problems is **overlearning**, in which you continue studying beyond your initial mastery of a topic. In other words, plan to do extra study and review *after* you think you are prepared for a test. One way to overlearn is to approach all tests as if they will be essays. That way, you will learn more completely, so you really "know your stuff."

Strategies for Taking Tests

OK, but what about actually taking the tests? Are there any strategies for that? You bet! You'll do better on all types of tests if you observe the following guidelines (Van Blerkom, 2012; Wong, 2015):

1. Read all directions and questions carefully. They may give you good advice or clues about what to include in your answer and how to format it.
2. Survey the test quickly before you begin.
3. Answer easy questions before spending time on more difficult ones.
4. Be sure to answer all questions.
5. Use your time wisely.
6. Ask for clarification when necessary.

Objective Tests

Several additional strategies can help you do better on objective tests. Such tests (multiple-choice and true–false items) require you to recognize a correct answer among wrong ones or a true statement versus a false one. Here are some strategies for taking objective tests:

1. Relate the question to what you know about the topic. Then read the alternatives. Does one match the answer that you expected to find? If none match, reexamine the choices and look for a partial match.
2. Read all the choices for each question before you make a decision. Here's why: if you immediately think that *a* is correct and stop reading, you might miss seeing a better answer like both *a* and *d*.
3. Read rapidly and skip items that you are unsure about. You may find free information in later questions that will help you answer difficult items.
4. Eliminate certain alternatives. With a four-choice multiple-choice test, you have one chance in four of guessing right. If you can eliminate two alternatives, your guessing odds improve to 50–50.
5. Be sure to answer any skipped items, unless there is a penalty for guessing. Even if you are not sure of the answer, you may be right. If you leave a question blank, it is automatically wrong. When you are forced to guess, don't choose the longest answer or the letter that you've used the least. Both strategies lower scores more than random guessing does.
6. Some people might say: "Don't change your answers on a multiple-choice test. Your first choice is usually correct." Those people would be wrong. If you change answers, you are more likely to *gain* points than to lose them. This is especially true if you are uncertain of your first choice, or it was a hunch and your second choice is more reflective (Higham & Gerrard, 2005).
7. Search for the one best answer to each question. Some answers may be partly true, yet flawed in some way. If you are uncertain, try rating each multiple-choice alternative on a 1 to 10 scale. The answer with the highest rating is the one you are looking for.
8. Remember that few circumstances fall at the extremes. Answers that include superlatives such as *always* or *never* are often false.

Essay Tests

Essay questions are a weak spot for students who lack organization, don't support their ideas, or don't directly answer the question (Van Blerkom, 2012). When you take an essay exam, try the following:

1. Read the question carefully. Be sure to note key words, such as *compare*, *contrast*, *discuss*, *evaluate*, *analyze*, and *describe*. These words all demand a certain emphasis in your answer.
2. Answer the question. If the question asks for a definition and an example, make sure that you provide both. Providing just a definition or just an example will get you half marks.
3. Reflect on your answer for a few minutes and list the main points that you want to make. Just write them as they come to mind. Then rearrange the ideas in a logical order and begin writing. Elaborate plans or outlines are not necessary.
4. Don't beat around the bush or pad your answer. Be direct. Make a point and support it. Get your list of ideas into words.
5. Look over your essay for errors in spelling and grammar. Save this for last. Your ideas are more important. You can work on spelling and grammar separately if they affect your grade.

Short-Answer Tests

Tests that ask you to fill in a blank, define a term, or list specific items can be difficult. Usually, the questions themselves contain little information. If you don't know the answer, you won't get much help from the questions. The best way to prepare for short-answer tests is to overlearn the details of the course. As you study, pay special attention to lists of related terms.

Again, it is best to start with the questions whose answers you're sure you know. Follow that by completing the questions

Self-testing Evaluating learning by posing questions to yourself.

Spaced practice Practice spread over many relatively short study sessions.

Massed practice Practice done in a long, uninterrupted study session.

Overlearning Continuing to study and learn after you think that you've mastered a topic.

whose answers you think you probably know. Questions whose answers you have no idea about can be left blank.

See Figure I.1 for a summary of study skills.

Study Skills Checklist

Time Management
- Make formal schedule
- Set specific goals

Study Habits
- Study in specific area
- Pace study and review
- Create memory aids
- Test yourself
- Overlearn

Reading
- Use reflective SQ4R method
- Study while reading
- Review frequently

Note Taking
- Listen actively
- Use LISAN method
- Review notes frequently

Figure I.1 Study skills checklist.

Managing Procrastination

All these techniques are fine. But what can I do about procrastination? **Procrastination**, the tendency to put off working on unpleasant tasks, is almost universal. (When campus workshops on procrastination are offered, many students never get around to signing up!) Even when procrastination doesn't lead to failure, it can cause much suffering (Hensley, 2016; Sirois & Tosti, 2012; Wohl, Pychyl, & Bennett, 2010). Procrastinators work only under pressure, skip classes, give false reasons for late work, and feel ashamed of their last-minute efforts. They also tend to feel frustrated, bored, and guilty (Pychyl, 2013).

Why do so many students procrastinate? Many students equate grades with their personal worth—that is, they act as if grades tell whether they are good, smart people who will succeed in life. By procrastinating, they can blame their poor work on a late start rather than a lack of ability (Haghbin, McCaffrey, & Pychyl, 2012). After all, it wasn't their best effort, was it? Perfectionism is a related problem. If you expect the impossible, it's hard to start an assignment. Students with high standards often end up with all-or-nothing work habits (Rice, Richardson, & Clark, 2012).

While procrastination can be a real problem for students, most can improve by learning to manage time effectively, setting realistic goals, and considering their attitude toward learning. We have already discussed general study skills, so let's consider these other strategies in a little more detail.

Time Management

A **weekly time schedule** is a written plan that allocates time for study, work, and leisure activities. To prepare your schedule, make a chart showing all the hours in each day of the week. Then fill in times that are already committed: sleep, meals, classes, work, team practices, lessons, appointments, and so forth. Next, fill in times when you will study for various classes. Finally, label the remaining hours as open or free times. Each day, you can use your schedule as a checklist. That way, you'll know at a glance which tasks are done and which still need attention (Pychyl, 2013).

You may also find it valuable to make a **term schedule** that lists the dates of all quizzes, tests, reports, papers, and other major assignments for each class. The beauty of sticking to a schedule is that you know you are making an honest effort. It will also help you avoid feeling bored while you are working or guilty when you play.

Be sure to treat your study times as serious commitments, but respect your free time, too. And remember, students who study hard and practice time management *do* get better grades (Nandagopal & Ericsson, 2011).

Goal Setting

As mentioned earlier, students who are reflective, active learners set **specific goals** for studying. Such goals should be clear-cut and measurable (Pychyl, 2013). If you find it hard to stay motivated, try setting goals for the semester, the week, the day, and even for single study sessions. Also, be aware that more effort early in a course can greatly reduce the stress that you might experience later. If your professors don't give frequent assignments, set your own day-by-day goals. That way, you can turn big assignments into a series of smaller tasks that you can complete. An example would be reading, studying, and reviewing eight pages a day to complete a 40-page chapter in five days. For this textbook, reading one section every day or two might be a good pace. Remember, many small steps can add up to an impressive journey.

Developing a Positive Attitude

A final point to remember is that you are most likely to procrastinate if you think that a task will be unpleasant. Students often think that something must be wrong if learning doesn't come easily, but in fact the opposite is true—real learning is effortful. That doesn't mean it has to be unpleasant, though—in fact, reflective students can almost always find ways to make schoolwork interesting and enjoyable (Mega, Ronconi, & De Beni, 2014). Try to approach your schoolwork as if it were a game, a sport, an adventure, or simply a way to become a better person. The best educational experiences are challenging, yet fun (Santrock & Halonen, 2013).

Virtually every topic is interesting to someone, somewhere. For example, you may not be particularly interested in the sex life of South American tree frogs, but a biologist might be fascinated. (Another tree frog might be, too.) If you wait for teachers to make everything in their courses interesting, you are missing the point. Interest is a matter of *your attitude* (Sirois & Tosti, 2012).

Getting Out What You Put In

There is a distinction in Zen between *live* words and *dead* words. Live words come from personal experience; dead words are about a subject. This book will be only a collection of dead words unless you accept the challenge of taking an intellectual journey. You will find many helpful, useful, and exciting ideas in the pages that follow. To make them yours, you must set out to actively and reflectively learn as much as you can. The ideas presented here should get you off to a good start. Good luck!

For more information, consult any of the following books:

Chaffee, J. (2015). *Thinking critically* (11th ed.). Belmont, CA: Cengage Learning/Wadsworth.

Ellis, D. (2016). *The essential guide to becoming a master student* (4th ed.). Boston, MA: Cengage Learning.

Pychyl, T. A. (2013). *Solving the procrastination puzzle: A concise guide to strategies for change.* New York: Tarcher/Penguin.

Santrock, J. W., & Halonen, J. S. (2013). *Your guide to college success: Strategies for achieving your goals* (7th ed.). Belmont, CA: Cengage Learning/Wadsworth.

Van Blerkom, D. L. (2012). *College study skills: Becoming a strategic learner* (7th ed.). Belmont, CA: Cengage Learning/Wadsworth.

Wong, W. (2015). *Essential study skills* (8th ed.). Belmont, CA: Cengage Learning/Wadsworth.

Reflective Practice

Psychology and Your Skill Set: Reflective Studying

1. The facts you pick up during your academic studies are the most important aspect of your education. T or F?
2. Setting learning goals and monitoring your progress are important parts of ________________ learning.
3. When using the LISAN method, students try to write down as much of a lecture as possible so that their notes are complete. T or F?
4. Spaced study sessions are usually superior to massed practice. T or F?
5. According to research, you should almost always stick with your first answer on multiple-choice tests. T or F?
6. To use the technique known as *overlearning*, you should continue to study after you feel you have mastered a topic. T or F?
7. Procrastination is related to seeking perfection and equating self-worth with grades. T or F?

THINK CRITICALLY

8. How is the LISAN method reflective?

SELF-REFLECT

- What career paths are you considering? What skills do you think would be valuable in a job like that? Do you already possess these skills? If so, how might you strengthen them? If not, what kinds of experiences can you undertake during your degree to develop these skills? One of the best ways to begin answering these questions is to sit down and undertake an inventory of the skills you have learned from your psychology studies and elsewhere.

Answers: 1. F. 2. reflective 3. F 4. T 5. F 6. T 7. T 8. Both encourage people to be reflective and to actively seek information as a way of learning more effectively.

Procrastination The tendency to put off working on unpleasant tasks.

Weekly time schedule A written plan that allocates time for study, work, and leisure activities during a one-week period.

Term schedule A written plan that lists the dates of all major assignments for each of your classes for an entire term.

Specific goals Goals with clearly defined and measurable outcomes.

CHAPTER IN REVIEW

Gateways to Reflective Studying

Summary: Gateways Learning Outcomes

I.1 Why Study Psychology?

I.1.1 Explain how studying psychology will help you in your personal and professional life

Two broad categories of learning relate to *content* (that is, the subject matter) and *skills*. Psychology students learn a variety of skills during their studies, including research skills, critical thinking skills, cultural awareness skills, communication skills, and personal skills. All of these can be useful at work or in your personal life. The study of psychology will also prepare you for many potentially rewarding careers. Some of those exist within the field of psychology, but the skills learned in a psychology degree can also be applied to a wide range of other career paths.

I.2 Reflective Reading: How to Tame a Textbook

I.2.1 Describe how you can get the most out of this textbook

Reflective reading, which involves actively thinking about what is being read, is better than passive reading. Using digital media offers another way to be more reflective about your reading.

I.3 Reflective Note-taking: LISAN Up!

I.3.1 Describe how you can get the most out of class time

Reflective learning in class involves active listening. One way to be a more active listener in class is to follow the five steps of the LISAN method: lead, don't follow; identify the main ideas; pay attention to signal words; actively listen; engage in good note taking.

I.4 Reflective Study Strategies: Making a Habit of Success

I.4.1 Describe how you can best prepare for tests

More reflective studying involves studying in a specific place, using spaced study sessions, trying mnemonics, testing yourself, and overlearning. Remember that more specialized strategies may be needed for objective tests, essay tests, and short-answer tests. Avoid procrastination through time management, setting goals, and making learning an adventure.

1 The Foundations of Psychological Science

Gateway Theme Psychology is a profession and a science. Psychologists rely on scientific methods to critically answer questions about behavior.

Chapter Outline

- **1.1** Commonsense Psychology: Not Necessarily "Common" or "Sense"
- **1.2** What Psychologists Do
- **1.3** The History of Psychological Science: A Trip Through Time
- **1.4** Contemporary Psychological Science and the Biopsychosocial Model
- **1.5** The Core Features of Psychological Science
- **1.6** Experimental Research: Where Cause Meets Effect
- **1.7** Nonexperimental Research: Losing (a Bit of) Control
- **1.8** Psychology and Your Skill Set: Information Literacy

Living in a Tree House

When Nate Madsen was 25 years old, he learned that loggers were cutting down giant redwoods in a grove that had become his refuge—a restful spot where he could leave behind the stressors of student life. Determined not to simply watch as the trees were destroyed, Nate climbed 160 feet into the branches of a giant redwood and stayed there for more than two years. During that time, he endured heavy rain and winds from above and harassment from people below. Friends climbed up ropes to visit and then abseiled back down to the ground. From his perch with the spectacular view, Nate watched the birds and the bears and, with the help of a donated laptop computer and some very understanding professors, he completed his college degree. And though he didn't climb down for his graduation ceremony, at least 70 people turned up at the base of the tree to help him celebrate his academic success.

"What could Nate possibly have been *thinking*?," you might wonder. But you might equally wonder why people get married, grow roses, become suicide bombers, go to college, or live out their lives in monasteries. You might even wonder, at least sometimes, why *you* do some of the things you do. In other words, the odds are that you are curious about human behavior (just like your authors, we should point out). That may even be a part of the reason that you are taking a course in psychology and reading this book.

We humans have always been curious about humankind. Even the word *psychology* is thousands of years old, coming from the ancient Greek roots *psyche*, meaning mind, and *logos*, meaning knowledge or study. Psychology, then, started out as the study of mind and the contemporary field of psychology is an ever-changing vista of people and ideas that can help you better understand yourself and others. Psychology is about love, stress, therapy, persuasion, hypnosis, perception, memory, death, conformity, creativity, learning, personality, aging, intelligence, sexuality, emotion, happiness, wisdom, and much more. This book is a guided tour of human behavior. We hope you enjoy the voyage.

1.1 Commonsense Psychology: Not Necessarily "Common" or "Sense"

GATEWAYS LEARNING OUTCOMES:
After reading this section you should be able to:

1.1.1 Explain why people fail to recognize that "commonsense" beliefs are often false

1.1.2 Distinguish between superstition, pseudoscience, and science

If psychology has been around for centuries isn't it by now mostly common sense? Because we deal with ourselves and others every day, it is tempting to think that we already know what is true in psychology. But you may be surprised to learn how many "commonsense" beliefs about human behavior are false. For example, have you ever heard that some people are left-brained and some are right-brained? Or that subliminal advertising really works? Or that playing Mozart's music to infants will boost their intelligence? It turns out that these widely held beliefs, and many others, are simply wrong (Lilienfeld et al., 2010).

How could that be? From the perspective of contemporary psychology, common sense is frequently wrong because we humans are vulnerable to **uncritical acceptance**—a failure to evaluate claims with sufficient logical rigor. Instead, we have a tendency to accept beliefs as true for illogical reasons, such as:

- having someone we respect or trust assure us that the claims are true
- believing the claims despite having weak or nonexistent evidence
- frequently encountering repetitions of claims, especially from multiple sources or the media
- wanting the claims to be true

As a consequence, we all too often are tempted to accept commonsense beliefs, false news, urban legends, and even outrageous claims about the powers of healing crystals, miraculous herbal remedies, psychics predicting their future, and so forth. Consider astrology horoscopes, which generally contain mostly flattering traits. Naturally, when your personality and your future are described in *desirable* terms, it is hard to deny that the description has the ring of truth (Rogers & Soule, 2009). On the other hand, how much acceptance would astrology receive if all horoscopes read like this:

> **Virgo:** Your nitpicking is unbearable to your friends. You are cold, unemotional, and usually fall asleep while making love. You have no chance of ever finding a person who will love you. Virgos make good doorstops.

But even when a horoscope contains a mixture of good and bad traits, it may seem accurate because we humans are also vulnerable to **confirmation bias**, the tendency to remember or notice things that confirm our expectations and ignore the rest (Lilienfeld, Ammirati, & Landfield, 2009). For example, how well does the following astrological description describe your personality?

> You have many personality strengths, with some weaknesses to which you can usually adjust. You tend to be accepting of yourself. You are comfortable with some structure in your life but do enjoy diverse experiences from time to time. Although on the inside you might be a bit unsure of yourself, you appear under control to others. You are sexually well adjusted, although you do have some questions. Your life goals are more or less realistic. Occasionally, you question your decisions and actions because you're unsure that they are correct. You want to be liked and admired by other people. You are not using your potential to its full extent. You like to think for yourself and don't always take other people's word without thinking it through. You are not generally willing to disclose to others because it might lead to problems. You are a natural introvert, cautious, and careful around others, although there are times when you can be an extrovert who is the life of the party.

A psychologist read a similar summary to college students who thought they were taking a personality test. Though their astrological signs spanned the range from Aquarius to Capricorn, only a few students in the sample felt that the description was *in*accurate. But if you reread the description, you will see that it contains both sides of several personality dimensions ("You are a natural introvert … although there are times when you can be an extrovert …"). Its apparent accuracy is an illusion based on confirmation bias.

Confirmation bias, which can occur unconsciously, is similar to *cherry picking*, the deliberate selection of evidence and arguments to support one's own beliefs while ignoring contradictory evidence or arguments (Boudry, Blancke, & Pigliucci, 2015). Conscious or not, this is a surefire way to protect yourself from confronting your mistaken beliefs. It is also a surefire way to remain mistaken (Schick & Vaughn, 2014).

Science, Pseudoscience, and Superstition

The entire belief system of astrology is based on the types of flawed observations and flawed reasoning characteristic of uncritical acceptance. As such, it can be considered a type of **superstition**, an unfounded belief held without objective evidence or in the face of falsifying evidence. If the unfounded belief system seems scientific, it is sometimes called a **pseudoscience** or "false science." Many other beliefs are also pseudoscientific. For example, *phrenology* was popularized in the early 1800s by Franz Gall, a German anatomy teacher. Phrenology claimed that the shape of the skull reveals personality traits. However, psychological research has clearly demonstrated that bumps on the head have nothing to do with talent or ability. The phrenologists were so far off that they listed the part of the brain that controls hearing as a center for combativeness!

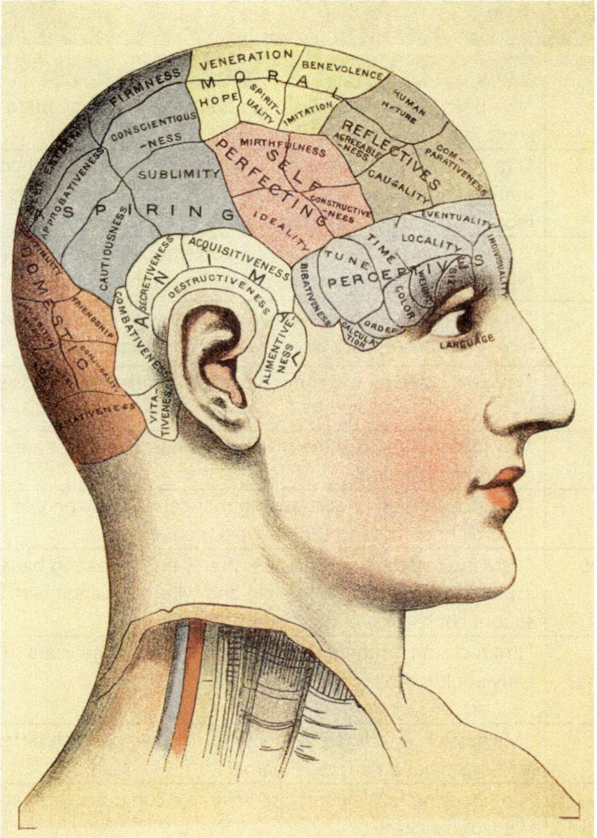

Universal History Archive/Universal Images Group/Getty Images

Phrenology was an attempt to assess personality characteristics by examining various areas of the skull. Phrenologists used charts such as the one shown here as guides. Like other pseudopsychologists, phrenologists resisted attempts to empirically verify their concepts.

Graphology, the study of handwriting as a predictor of personality, is a more recent example of pseudoscience. Though examining handwriting can be useful for detecting forgeries, graphologists score no better than average on tests of accuracy in rating personality (Dazzi & Pedrabissi, 2009; Furnham, Chamorro-Premuzic, & Callahan, 2003).

In contrast to superstition and pseudoscience, practicing **science** requires that we take an objective approach to answering questions using careful observations and experiments. The data that we gather need to be evaluated impartially, avoiding the temptation to engage in confirmation bias, or cherry picking only the results we want to see. As scientists, some psychologists do research to establish the validity of claims such as those put forward about astrology and graphology. Psychological researchers also work to discover new knowledge, or to apply psychology to solve problems in fields such as mental health, business, education, sports, law, medicine, and the design of machines (Bayne & Jinks, 2013). Other people who work in the area of psychological science include teachers who share their knowledge with students and clinicians who work to assist people with their problems. Let's take a closer look at the wide range of career paths that are possible in psychology.

1.2 What Psychologists Do

GATEWAYS LEARNING OUTCOMES:
After reading this section you should be able to:

1.2.1 Name some areas in which psychological scientists do research

1.2.2 Describe the work carried out by clinical and counseling psychologists

Every **psychologist** is highly trained in the methods, knowledge, and theories of psychological research. Psychologists have usually earned a master's degree or a doctorate, typically requiring several years of postgraduate training. About 31 percent are employed full time at colleges or universities (including medical schools), where they teach and do research, consulting, or therapy. The remainder give psychological tests, do research in other settings, or serve as consultants to business, industry, government, or the military. In fact, at present, the American Psychological Association (APA) consists of more than 50 divisions, each reflecting special skills or areas of interest.

Psychological Research

No matter where they are employed, or what their area of specialization is, many psychologists do research. Some do *basic research,* in which they seek knowledge for its own sake. For example, a psychologist might study memory simply to understand how it works. Others do *applied research* to solve immediate practical problems, such as finding ways to improve athletic performance (Davey, 2011). Some do both types of research. Some of the major areas of research are listed in ▲ Table 1.1.

Research involving animals was mentioned in some of the psychology specialties listed in Table 1.1. Why is that? You may be surprised to learn that psychologists are interested in the behavior of *any* living creature—from flatworms to humans. Indeed, some comparative psychologists spend their entire careers studying rats, cats, dogs, parrots, or chimpanzees.

Uncritical acceptance The tendency to believe claims because they seem true or because it would be nice if they were true.

Confirmation bias The tendency to remember or notice information that fits one's expectations, while forgetting or ignoring discrepancies.

Superstition Unfounded belief held without evidence or in spite of falsifying evidence.

Pseudoscience Unfounded belief system that seems to be based on science.

Science An objective approach to answering questions that relies on careful observations and experiments.

Psychologist A person highly trained in the methods, factual knowledge, and theories of psychology.

▲ Table 1.1 Types of Psychologists and What They Do

Specialty		Typical Activities	Sample Research Topic
Biopsychology	B*	Researches the brain, nervous system, and other physical origins of behavior	"I've been doing some exciting research on how the brain controls hunger."
Clinical	A	Does psychotherapy; investigates clinical problems; develops methods of treatment	"I'm curious about the relationship between early childhood trauma and adult relationships and how it can help adults be more successful in their marriages."
Cognitive	B	Studies human thinking and information-processing abilities	"I want to know how reasoning, problem solving, memory, and other mental processes relate to playing computer games."
Community	A	Promotes community-wide mental health through research, prevention, education, and consultation	"How can we prevent the spread of sexually transmitted diseases more effectively? That's what I want to understand better."
Comparative	B	Studies and compares the behavior of different species, especially animals	"I'm fascinated by the communication abilities of porpoises."
Consumer	A	Researches packaging, advertising, marketing methods, and characteristics of consumers	"My job is to improve the marketing of products that are environment-friendly."
Counseling	A	Does psychotherapy and personal counseling; researches emotional disturbances and counseling methods	"I am focused on understanding more about why people become hoarders and how to help them stop."
Cultural	B	Studies the ways in which culture, subculture, and ethnic group membership affect behavior	"I am interested in how culture affects human eating behavior, especially the foods that we eat and whether we eat with a spoon, chopsticks, or our fingers."
Developmental	A, B	Conducts research on infant, child, adolescent, and adult development; does clinical work with disturbed children; acts as a consultant to parents and schools	"I'm focusing on the transitions from the teenage years to early adulthood."
Educational	A	Investigates classroom dynamics, teaching styles, and learning; develops educational tests, evaluates educational programs	"My passion is to figure out how to help people with different learning styles be effective learners."
Engineering	A	Does applied research on the design of machinery, computers, airlines, automobiles, and so on for business, industry, and the military	"I'm studying how people use wearable computer interfaces, like Google Glass."
Environmental	A, B	Studies the effects of urban noise, crowding, attitudes toward the environment, and human use of space; acts as a consultant on environmental issues	"I am concerned about global warming and want to understand what impact rising temperatures have on human culture."
Evolutionary	B	Studies how behavior is guided by patterns that evolved during the long history of humankind	"I am studying some interesting trends in male and female mating choices."
Forensic	A	Studies problems of crime and crime prevention, rehabilitation programs, prisons, and courtroom dynamics; selects candidates for police work	"I am interested in improving the reliability of eyewitness testimony during trials."
Gender	B	Researches differences between males and females, the acquisition of gender identity, and the role of gender throughout life	"I want to understand how young boys and girls are influenced by gender stereotypes."
Health	A, B	Studies the relationship between behavior and health; uses psychological principles to promote health and prevent illness	"How to help people overcome drug addictions is my field of study."
Industrial-organizational	A	Selects job applicants; does skills analysis; evaluates on-the-job training; improves work environments and human relations in organizations and work settings	"Which plays a greater role in successful management styles, intelligence or emotion? That is my question."
Learning	B	Studies how and why learning occurs; develops theories of learning	"Right now, I'm investigating how patterns of reinforcement affect learning. I am especially interested in superstitious conditioning."
Medical	A	Applies psychology to manage medical problems, such as the emotional impact of illness, self-screening for cancer, and compliance in taking medicine	"I want to know how to help people take charge of their own health."
Personality	B	Studies personality traits and dynamics; develops theories of personality and tests for assessing personality traits	"I am especially interested in the personality profiles of people who are willing to take extreme risks."
School	A	Does psychological testing, referrals, and emotional and vocational counseling of students; detects and treats learning disabilities; improves classroom learning	"My focus is finding out how to keep students in school instead of having them drop out."
Sensation and perception	B	Studies the sense organs and the process of perception; investigates the mechanisms of sensation; develops theories about how perception occurs	"I am using a perceptual theory to study how we are able to recognize faces in a crowd."
Social	B	Investigates human social behavior, including attitudes, conformity, persuasion, prejudice, friendship, aggression, helping, and so forth	"My interest is interpersonal attraction. I place two strangers in a room and analyze how strongly they are attracted to each other."

*Research in this area is typically applied (A), basic (B), or both (A, B).

This timber wolf is wearing a tracking collar. Through tracking studies and other tests, psychologists are better able to understand how wild wolves think and communicate (Range, Möslinger, & Virányi, 2012). Since wolves are endangered across much of their historical range, this understanding may prove crucial in enhancing efforts to conserve these intriguing creatures.

Although only a small percentage of psychological studies involve animals, this work has the potential to answer many important questions (Baker & Serdikoff, 2013). Some psychologists use an **animal model** to discover principles that apply to humans. For instance, animal studies have helped us understand stress, learning, obesity, aging, sleep, and many other topics. Psychology can also benefit animals. Behavioral studies can help us better care for domestic animals and those in zoos, as well as conserve endangered species in the wild.

Helping People

I thought that all psychologists did therapy and treated abnormal behavior! Actually, only about 45 percent of psychologists are directly involved in providing mental health services. Although most psychologists help people in one way or another, those who are specifically interested in emotional problems usually specialize in clinical or counseling psychology (see Table 1.1). A **clinical psychologist** treats psychological problems or does research on therapies and mental disorders. In contrast, a **counseling psychologist** generally treats milder problems, such as troubles at work or school.

To become a clinical psychologist, you need to have a doctorate (PhD, PsyD, or EdD). Most clinical psychologists have a PhD and follow a *scientist-as-practitioner* model—that is, they are trained to do either research or therapy. Many do both. Other clinicians earn the PsyD (Doctor of Psychology) degree, which emphasizes therapy skills rather than research (Stricker, 2011).

Does a psychologist need a license to offer therapy? Yes. Psychologists must also meet stringent legal requirements. To work as a clinical or counseling psychologist, you must have a license issued by a state examining board. However, the law does not prevent people from calling themselves almost anything else they choose—therapist, rebirther, primal feeling facilitator, cosmic aura balancer, or life skills coach—or from selling "psychological" services to anyone willing to pay. Beware of people with self-proclaimed titles. Even if their intentions are honorable, they may have little actual training.

Licensed clinical and counseling psychologists must also follow an ethical code that stresses (1) high levels of competence, integrity, and responsibility; (2) respect for people's rights to privacy, dignity, confidentiality, and personal freedom; and, above all, (3) protection of the client's welfare (American Psychological Association, 2017a; Barnett et al., 2007). (■ See Section 3.5 for more information about ethics.)

Beyond Psychologists: Other Mental Health Professionals

Clinical and counseling psychologists often coordinate their efforts with psychiatrists, psychoanalysts, counselors, and other mental health professionals. Each has a specific blend of training and skills. For example, a **psychiatrist** (sometimes called a *shrink*, a slang term derived from the term *head shrinkers*) is a medical doctor who treats serious mental disorders, often by prescribing drugs. Today, clinical psychology and psychiatry are somewhat more similar than in years gone by—many psychiatrists use psychotherapy, for example, and psychologists in Iowa, Idaho, New Mexico, Louisiana, and Illinois can also legally prescribe drugs (as can psychologists in the U.S. military). It will be interesting to see whether other states grant similar privileges in the years to come (McGrath & Moore, 2010).

A **psychoanalyst** is a psychiatrist or psychologist who has a very specific approach to psychotherapy. According to an old stereotype, to be a psychoanalyst, you must have a moustache and goatee, spectacles, a German accent, and a well-padded couch. In reality, though, psychoanalysts have an MD or PhD degree, plus further training in Freudian psychoanalysis.

In many states, counselors also do mental health work. A **counselor** is an adviser who helps solve problems with marriage, career, school, work, or the like. To be a licensed counselor (such as a marriage and family counselor, a child counselor, or a school counselor) typically requires a master's degree (though it doesn't have to be in psychology), plus one or two years of full-time supervised counseling experience. Counselors learn practical helping skills and do not treat serious mental disorders.

Animal model In research, an animal whose behavior is studied to derive principles that may apply to human behavior.

Clinical psychologist A psychologist who specializes in the treatment of psychological and behavioral disturbances or who does research on such disturbances.

Counseling psychologist A psychologist who specializes in the treatment of milder emotional and behavioral disturbances.

Psychiatrist A medical doctor with additional training in the diagnosis and treatment of mental and emotional disorders.

Psychoanalyst A mental health professional (usually a medical doctor) trained to practice psychoanalysis.

Counselor A mental health professional who specializes in helping people with problems that do not involve serious mental disorders.

One of the key things that characterizes all psychologists is their belief in the importance of psychological science. Even those who focus on doing therapy are invested in making sure that the techniques they use with clients are *evidence-based*, that is, supported by research. Research in psychology has a long and interesting history that dates back more than 100 years, and many of its guiding ideas have changed over time. Let's take a closer look at some of the key people and ideas that have helped to shape psychology.

Reflective Practice

What Psychologists Do

1. Horoscopes provided by astrology are stated in positive terms, which have a "ring of truth." This fact is the basis of
   a. falsification
   b. uncritical acceptance
   c. confirmation bias
   d. critical thinking

Match the following research areas with the topics that they cover.

2. Developmental — **A.** Attitudes, groups, psychology leadership
3. Learning — **B.** Behavior as related to the legal system
4. Personality — **C.** Brain and nervous system
5. Sensation and perception — **D.** Child psychology
6. Biopsychology — **E.** Individual differences, motivation
7. Social psychology — **F.** Processing sensory information
8. Forensic psychology — **G.** Conditioning, memory
9. A psychologist who specializes in treating human emotional difficulties is called a(n) ____________ psychologist

THINK CRITICALLY

10. Based on what you've read in this chapter, evaluate the following statement: *Superstitions like astrology and graphology are harmless.*

SELF-REFLECT

- How stringently do you evaluate your own beliefs and the claims made by others? For which topics are you most likely to fall victim to confirmation bias?
- At first, many students think that psychology is primarily about abnormal behavior and psychotherapy. Did you? How would you evaluate the field now?

Answers: 1. b 2. D 3. G 4. E 5. F 6. C 7. A 8. B 9. clinical or counseling 10. False. Although superstitions may seem like no more than a quaint nuisance, they can do real harm. For example, people seeking treatment for psychological disorders may become the victims of self-appointed "experts" who offer ineffective, pseudoscientific therapies (Kida, 2006; Lilienfeld, Ruscio, & Lynn, 2008). Or imagine being turned down for a job by a graphologist who was hired by the company to evaluate your suitability by analyzing your handwriting. Even a graphological society recommends that handwriting analysis should not be used to select people for jobs (Simner & Goffin, 2003).

1.3 The History of Psychological Science: A Trip Through Time

GATEWAYS LEARNING OUTCOMES:
After reading this section you should be able to:

1.3.1 Explain the method that Wundt and Titchener used to study conscious experience and the limitations of this method

1.3.2 Contrast Titchener's structuralist approach to psychology with

(a) the Gestalt approach developed by Wertheimer
(b) the functionalist approach developed by James
(c) the behaviorist approach developed by Watson and Skinner
(d) the psychoanalytic approach developed by Freud
(e) the cognitive approach
(f) the humanists' approach developed by Maslow and Rogers

Most historians now agree that scientific psychology truly took hold in the late 1800s in Leipzig, Germany (Kardas, 2014). There, in 1879, Wilhelm Wundt (VILL-helm Voont), the father of psychology, set up a laboratory to study the mind. How, Wundt wondered, do we experience sensations, images, and feelings?

Wundt (and psychologists ever since) relied on **scientific observation**. Although casual observation also relies on gathering *empirical evidence* (information gained from direct observation), scientific observation is *systematic* (that is, carefully planned) and *intersubjective* (that is, many observers can confirm what's been seen). For example, has anyone ever told you that people in New York City (or Paris, or wherever) are rude? While this statement may be based on observation, it would not be considered scientific if it's based on just one person's experience. It's possible that this person simply had a bad encounter on a single visit and may well have nothing to say about New Yorkers or Parisians in general. Basically, then, taking a scientific approach says, "Let's take a more objective look" (Stangor, 2015; Stanovich, 2013).

Introspection and Structuralism

In his efforts to be scientific, Wundt systematically observed and measured objective stimuli of various kinds (e.g., lights, sounds, and weights). A **stimulus** is any physical energy that affects a person and evokes a response [stimulus: singular; stimuli (STIM-you-lie): plural]. He then presented various stimuli to observers, who were asked to "look within" via **introspection**, which is defined as the personal observation of mental events such as thoughts, feelings, and sensations. If you were to focus on a nearby object and carefully describe aloud your inner thoughts, feelings, and sensations about it you would be *introspecting*. In this way, introspection can be seen as the precursor to *self-report methods* of gathering data that psychologists use today (■ see Section 1.5).

Aware that casual introspection may be unreliable, Wundt sought to train his *introspectionists* to be systematic and scientific as they looked inward to report their reactions to various stimuli (Asthana, 2015). Over the years, Wundt studied vision, hearing, taste, touch, memory, time perception, and many other topics. By insisting on systematic observation and measurement, he asked some interesting questions and got contemporary psychology off to a good start as the scientific study of mental events (Schultz & Schultz, 2016).

Wilhelm Wundt (1832–1920). Wundt is credited with making psychology an independent science, separate from philosophy. Wundt's original training was in medicine, but he became deeply interested in psychology. In his laboratory, Wundt investigated how sensations, images, and feelings combine to make up personal experience.

Edward Titchener (TICH-in-er) brought Wundt's ideas about introspection to the United States, naming them **structuralism**—the study of sensations and personal experience analyzed as basic elements.

But you can't analyze conscious experience in the same way as a chemical compound, can you? Although even Wundt didn't think that you could do that, the structuralists tried to explore "mental chemistry," mostly through introspection. For instance, an observer might hold an apple and decide that she or he had experienced the item's hue (color), roundness, and weight. Another question that a structuralist might have asked is, "What basic tastes mix together to create complex flavors as different as broccoli, lime, bacon, and strawberry cheesecake?"

The Shortcomings of Introspection

The early psychologists all relied mainly on introspection, casual or otherwise, for observations of the mind in action. But right from the beginning, introspection proved to be a poor way to answer psychological questions (Benjafield, 2015). No matter how insightful the individual, systematic the observations, or well-trained the introspectionists, results from one introspection to the next frequently disagreed. Even worse, there was no way to settle intersubjective differences. Think about it: If you and a friend both introspect on your perceptions of an apple and end up listing different basic elements, who would be right?

As if this were not problem enough, in 1901 one of Wundt's students, Karl Marbe, reported a dramatic example of what has come to be called **imageless thought** (Hergenhahn & Henley, 2014). He asked trained introspectionists to introspect while they compared two objects of different weights, holding one weight in each hand. They could clearly describe their experiences of each weight and which one was heavier, but they could not describe the mental process of judging which one was heavier. As Marbe put it, the thought process of comparing the weights did not form a conscious "image." Thus, not only did introspection fail to yield reliable, consistent observations of the mind at work, but it also appeared that some of the mind's work was not even open to introspection.

To appreciate the full implications of the discovery of imageless thought, let's have a close look at a more recent study. Imagine that you are one of the shoppers that psychologists Timothy Wilson and Richard Nesbitt invited to examine four pairs of silk stockings hanging on a rack. The shoppers were asked a deceptively simple question: "Which pair is the highest quality, and why?" (Wilson & Nisbett, 1978). The results can be found in ● Figure 1.1. As you can see, the order in which the stockings were displayed strongly influenced which pair was chosen.

What's important here is that all the stockings were objectively identical. Also, each pair appeared equally often in each of the four serial positions. This was achieved by changing the order of the four pairs before each shopper made a choice. This made it impossible that the pair in position D was actually consistently of better quality.

If the shoppers were introspectively aware of the underlying psychological processes that resulted in their choices, they surely would have identified serial position as a relevant factor. Amazingly, while serial position *objectively* influenced the shoppers' choice, no shopper gave serial position as a *subjective* reason for his or her choice. Apparently, you are not always the best judge of why you behave the way you do (Wilson, 2004). That is, even when introspection does yield information, there is no guarantee that the information is accurate.

What reasons did the shoppers give? If you think about it, it *would* be odd to hear someone say, "The pair in position D are the best because they are on the far right." Apparently, not knowing exactly why they made their choice, the shoppers gave the sorts of reasons that you (and they) might expect a thoughtful shopper to give: smoothness, visual appearance, color, weave, and so on. They gave plausible but incorrect answers such as, "I chose the pair in position D because they were the sheerest and most elastic."

Scientific observation An empirical investigation structured to answer questions about the world in a systematic and intersubjective fashion (i.e., observations can be reliably confirmed by multiple observers).

Stimulus Any physical energy that an organism senses.

Introspection Personal observation of your own thoughts, feelings, and behavior.

Structuralism Study of sensations and personal experience analyzed as basic elements.

Imageless thought An old term describing the inability of introspectionists to become subjectively aware of some mental processes; an early term describing the cognitive unconscious.

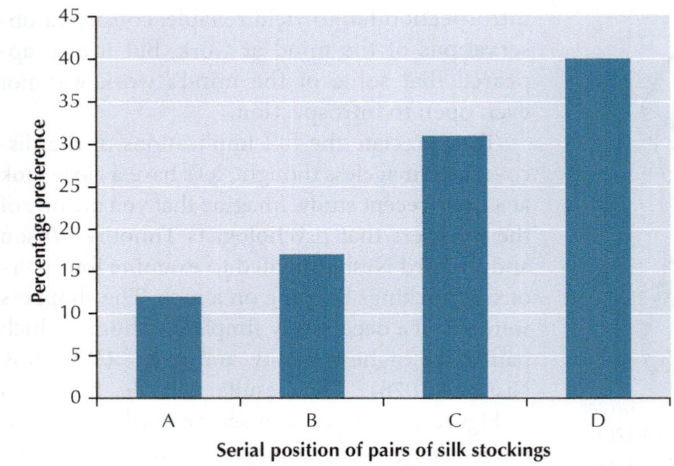

Figure 1.1 The effects of serial position on preference. The four pairs of silk stockings in this experiment were labeled A, B, C, and D, from left-to-right. The results clearly show that the serial position of the individual pairs of stockings, that is, where each pair appeared in the "lineup," influenced shopper's preferences. (Data adapted from Wilson & Nisbett, 1978.)

Wilson and Nisbett's finding is only one of hundreds of similar reports, dating back to Marbe. Taken together, they confirm that much of our thinking actually takes place in the **cognitive unconscious**, a part of the mind of which we are subjectively unaware and which is therefore not open to introspection (see, e.g., Bar-Anan, Wilson, & Hassin, 2010; Nisbett & Wilson, 1977). We will encounter the cognitive unconscious many times during our exploration of psychology. (■ For example, in Chapter 7 we explore the accuracy of police lineups. Given what you now know, just imagine being arrested on suspicion of committing a murder … and being assigned to position D in a four-person lineup.)

So does imageless thought take place in the cognitive unconscious? Precisely! Try it for yourself. Close your eyes and extend both hands palms up while a friend gives you two objects of different weights, one in each outstretched palm. You will certainly become aware of the sensations associated with each object and should notice that you *immediately* know which is heavier. It will just "pop into your mind." But *how* did you decide this? Marbe couldn't know it in 1901, but by documenting an example of the *cognitive unconscious* in action, he set in motion a debate that would eventually result in the rejection of introspectionism.

Gestalt Psychology

Imagine playing "Happy Birthday" on a flute and then on a guitar. The guitar duplicates none of the flute's sounds. Yet the melody is still recognizable—so long as the *relationship* between the notes remains the same.

Now imagine what would happen if you played the notes of "Happy Birthday" in the correct order, but at a rate of one per hour. What would you have? Nothing! The separate notes would no longer be a melody. Perceptually, the melody is more than the individual notes that define it.

Observations like these launched the Gestalt school of thought. German psychologist Max Wertheimer (VERT-hi-mer) was the first to advance the Gestalt viewpoint. It is inaccurate, he said, to introspectively analyze psychological events into pieces, or elements, as the structuralists tried to do. Accordingly, **Gestalt psychology** studied experiences of thinking, learning, personality, and perception as whole units, not by analyzing them into parts as structuralists did. Gestalt psychology also inspired a type of psychotherapy (■ see Section 15.3). Their slogan was, "The whole is greater than the sum of its parts." In fact, the German word *Gestalt* means form, pattern, or whole.

Max Wertheimer (1880–1941). Wertheimer first proposed the Gestalt viewpoint to help explain perceptual illusions. He later promoted Gestalt psychology as a way to understand not only perception, problem solving, thinking, and social behavior, but also art, logic, philosophy, and politics.

Functionalism

American scholar William James further broadened psychology to include animal behavior, religious experience, abnormal behavior, and other interesting topics. James's brilliant first book,

This design is entirely made up of broken circles. However, as the Gestalt psychologists discovered, our perceptions have a powerful tendency to form meaningful patterns. Because of this tendency, you will probably see a cube in this design, even though it is only an illusion. Your whole perceptual experience exceeds the sum of its parts.

William James (1842–1910). William James was the son of philosopher Henry James, Sr., and the brother of novelist Henry James. During his long academic career, James taught anatomy, physiology, psychology, and philosophy at Harvard University. James believed strongly that ideas should be judged in terms of their practical consequences for human conduct.

Principles of Psychology (1890), helped establish the field as a separate discipline (Kardas, 2014).

James's interest in how the mind functions to help us adapt to the environment grew into **functionalism**, a school of psychology that considers behaviors in terms of active adaptations. James regarded consciousness as an ever-changing *stream* or *flow* of images and sensations, not a set of lifeless building blocks, as the structuralists claimed.

The functionalists admired Charles Darwin, who deduced that creatures evolve in ways that favor survival. According to Darwin's principle of **natural selection**, physical features that help plants and animals adapt to their environments are retained in evolution. Similarly, the functionalists wanted to find out how the mind, perception, habits, and emotions help us adapt and survive.

What effect did functionalism have on contemporary psychology? Functionalism brought the study of animals into psychology. It also promoted educational psychology (the study of learning, teaching, classroom dynamics, and related topics). Learning makes us more adaptable, so the functionalists tried to find ways to improve education. For similar reasons, functionalism spurred the rise of *industrial/organizational* psychology, the study of people at work. (■ Today, educational psychology and industrial/organizational psychology remain two major applied specialties; ■ see Sections 6.5 and 18.1 for more information about these topics.)

Behaviorism

John B. Watson objected strongly to the study of the "mind" or conscious experience and launched a school of thought referred to as **behaviorism**. He believed that introspection was unscientific precisely because there is no objective way to settle disagreements between observers. Watson realized that he could study the behavior of animals even though he couldn't ask animals questions or know what they were thinking (Hergenhahn & Henley, 2014). He simply observed the relationship between any *stimuli* (i.e., events in the environment) and an animal's **response** (any muscular action, glandular activity, or other identifiable aspect of behavior). These observations were objective because they did not involve introspecting based on subjective experience. Why not, he asked, apply the same objectivity to study human behavior? For Watson and many other behaviorists, psychology was *not* the study of mind; it was the study of *behavior*. In this way, the behaviorists championed the use of *observational methods* of gathering data, which are still widely used by psychologists today (■ see Section 1.5).

John B. Watson (1878–1958). Watson's intense interest in observable behavior began with his doctoral studies in biology and neurology. Watson became a psychology professor at Johns Hopkins University in 1908 and advanced his theory of behaviorism. He remained at Johns Hopkins until 1920, when he left for a career in the advertising industry!

Psychologists ever since have agreed with Watson and systematically study behavior directly in order to draw more valid conclusions. Would you say it's true, for instance, that "the clothes make the man"? Or do you believe that "you can't judge a book by its cover"? Why introspect about it? As psychologists, we simply look at some people who are well dressed and some who are not and, through scientific observation, find out who makes out better in a variety of situations.

Watson also adopted Russian physiologist Ivan Pavlov's (ee-VAHN PAV-lahv) concept of *conditioning* to explain most behavior (a *conditioned response* is a learned reaction to a particular stimulus; ■ see Section 6.1). He believed conditioning could be used to change people's actions, and what happened to them as a result. You may not be surprised to learn, then, that Watson famously claimed, "Give me a dozen healthy infants, well-formed, and my own special world to bring them up in, and I'll guarantee to take any one at random and train him to become any type of specialist I might select—doctor, lawyer, artist, merchant-chief, and yes, beggarman and thief" (Watson, 1913/1994).

Would most psychologists today agree with Watson's claim? No. The early behaviorists believed that all responses are *determined* by stimuli. Today, this is regarded as an overstatement. Just the same, by stressing the study of observable behavior, behaviorism helped make psychology a natural science rather than a branch of philosophy.

Cognitive unconscious The part of the mind of which we are subjectively unaware and that is not open to introspection.

Gestalt psychology Study of thinking, learning, and perception in whole units, not by analysis into parts.

Functionalism School of psychology that considers behaviors in terms of active adaptations.

Natural selection Darwin's theory that evolution favors those plants and animals best suited to their living conditions.

Behaviorism School of thought in psychology that emphasizes study of observable actions over study of the mind.

Response Any muscular action, glandular activity, or other identifiable aspect of behavior.

B. F. Skinner (1904–1990). Skinner studied simple behaviors under carefully controlled conditions. In addition to advancing psychology, Skinner hoped that his radical brand of behaviorism would improve human lives.

Radical Behaviorism

The best-known behaviorist, B. F. Skinner (1904–1990), believed that our actions are controlled by rewards and punishments in a process called operant conditioning. Many of Skinner's ideas about learning grew out of his work with rats and pigeons. Nevertheless, he believed that the same laws of behavior apply to humans. (■ See Section 6.2 for more information about operant conditioning.) As a **radical behaviorist**, Skinner not only rejected introspection, he also rejected the concept of *mind* as an inappropriate subject matter for scientific psychology. Skinner believed that behavior can be explained without any reference to mental events such as *thinking* (Schultz & Schultz, 2016).

Behaviorists deserve the credit for much of what we know about learning, conditioning, and the proper use of rewards and punishments. Skinner was convinced that a culture based on positive reinforcement could encourage desirable behavior. He also opposed the use of punishment because it doesn't teach correct responses. Too often, he believed, misguided rewards and punishments lead to destructive actions that create problems such as overpopulation, pollution, and war.

Behaviorism is also the source of behavior therapy, which uses learning principles to change problem behaviors such as overeating, unrealistic fears, or temper tantrums. (■ See Section 15.2 for more information about behavior therapy.)

Psychoanalytic Psychology

As behaviorism's distrust of introspection pushed American psychology to grow more scientific, an Austrian doctor named Sigmund Freud, who also distrusted introspection, was developing radically different ideas that opened new horizons in art, literature, and history, as well as psychology (Barratt, 2013). Freud believed that mental life is like an iceberg: Only a small part is exposed. He called the area of the mind that lies outside personal awareness the *unconscious*. Today, Freud's notion is often referred to as the **dynamic unconscious**, to differentiate it from the concept of the *cognitive unconscious* (Zellner, 2011). According to Freud, our behavior is deeply influenced by unconscious thoughts, impulses, and desires—especially those concerning sex and aggression.

Freud theorized that many unconscious thoughts are *repressed*, or held out of awareness, because they are threatening. But sometimes, he said, they are revealed by dreams, emotions, or slips of the tongue. (Freudian slips are often humorous, as when a student who is late for class says, "I'm sorry I couldn't get here any later.") Because of this, Freud held that you cannot take people's self-reports literally, since much is left out and much of the rest is disguised. To more accurately interpret self-reports, he created **psychoanalysis**, the first fully developed psychotherapy, or "talking cure" to explore unconscious conflicts and emotional problems. (■ See Section 15.1 for more details.)

Sigmund Freud (1856–1939). For over 50 years, Freud probed the unconscious mind. In doing so, he altered contemporary views of human nature. His early experimentation with a "talking cure" for hysteria is regarded as the beginning of psychoanalysis. Through psychoanalysis, Freud added psychological treatment methods to psychiatry.

Like the behaviorists, Freud believed that all thoughts, emotions, and actions are *determined*. In other words, nothing is an accident. If we probe deeply enough, we will find the causes of every thought or action. Unlike the behaviorists, he believed that unconscious processes (not external stimuli) were responsible for what people do. Freud was also among the first to appreciate that childhood affects adult personality (perhaps best expressed in the quote by poet William Wordsworth, "the child is father to the man").

It wasn't long before some of Freud's students modified his ideas. Known as **neo-Freudians** (*neo* means "new" or "recent"), they accepted some of Freud's theory but revised parts of it. Many, for instance, placed less emphasis on sex and aggression and more on social motives and relationships. Some well-known neo-Freudians are Alfred Adler, Anna Freud (Freud's daughter), Karen Horney (HORN-eye), Carl Jung (yoong), Otto Rank (rahnk), and Erik Erikson. Today, Freud's ideas have been altered so much that few strictly psychoanalytic psychologists are left. However, his legacy is still evident in **psychodynamic theory**, which continues to emphasize internal motives, conflicts, and unconscious forces (Moran, 2010).

Cognitive Psychology

When the radical behaviorists rejected introspection as a legitimate scientific method, they also deliberately ignored the role that thinking plays in our lives. This approach was eventually criticized as "throwing the baby out with the bath water." Eventually, behaviorism became less radical, as references to mental processes (thinking, or *cognition*) began to be used to explain even the behavior of animals (Zentall, 2002, 2011). As an example, let's say that a rat frequently visits a particular location in a maze because it offers access to food. A behaviorist would say that the rat visits this location because it is rewarded by the pleasure of eating each time that it goes there. A *cognitive behaviorist* would add that, in addition, the rat *expects* to find food at the location. This is the cognitive part of the rat's behavior.

By the late 1950s, **cognitive psychology** took form as the study of information processing, thinking, reasoning, and problem solving (Goldstein & Brockmole, 2017; Neisser, 1967). Unlike radical behaviorism, cognitive psychology is open to studying the mind and mental events. Like behaviorism (and unlike introspectionism), cognitive psychology relies primarily upon objective observation rather than subjective introspection.

But how can cognitive psychology objectively study subjective mental events without introspection? The answer lies in the concept of *operational definitions*. An **operational definition** defines a scientific concept by stating the specific actions or procedures used to measure it. Suppose, for example, we want to objectively study hunger, a mental event that we all experience subjectively. We might operationally define the intensity of hunger by counting the number of hours of food deprivation. After all, it stands to reason that someone who has not eaten for 12 hours is most likely hungrier than she was after not having eaten for 3 hours.

Here's another example: Suppose we give a list of words to be studied and then, sometime later, ask for the words to be recalled from memory. We could operationally define memory accuracy as the number of words written down correctly divided by the total number of words originally presented. Again, it stands to reason that someone who correctly wrote down only 30 percent of the words has a less accurate memory for those words than someone who correctly wrote down 85 percent of the words.

Abraham Maslow (1908–1970). As a founder of humanistic psychology, Maslow was interested in studying people of exceptional mental health. Such self-actualized people, he believed, make full use of their talents and abilities. Maslow offered his positive view of human potential as an alternative to the schools of behaviorism and psychoanalysis.

Humanistic Psychology

For a time, radical behaviorism and psychoanalysis combined to offer the unsettling view that we humans don't consciously know much about ourselves. Eventually, *humanists* like Abraham Maslow and Carl Rogers questioned the Freudian idea that we are ruled solely by unconscious forces. They also were uncomfortable with the radical behaviorist emphasis on conditioning and the rejection of mental events, such as thinking, as appropriate topics for scientific psychology (Schultz & Schultz, 2016).

Each of these two views has a strong undercurrent of **determinism**—the idea that behavior is determined by forces beyond our control. Instead, humanists stress **free will**, our ability to make conscious, voluntary choices. Of course, past experiences and the unconscious do affect us. Nevertheless, humanists believe that people can freely *choose* to live more creative, meaningful, and satisfying lives.

Humanistic psychology, then, is the study of people as inherently good and consciously motivated to learn and improve. Humanists believe that everyone has this potential, and they seek ways to help it emerge. Humanists are interested in psychological needs for love, self-esteem, belonging, self-expression, creativity, and spirituality. Such needs, they believe, are as important as our biological urges for food and water. For example, newborn infants deprived of human love may die just as surely as they would if deprived of food. Maslow's concept of self-actualization is a key feature of humanism. **Self-actualization** refers to the process of fully developing personal potential.

How scientific is the humanistic approach? Initially, humanists were less interested in treating psychology as a science. They stressed subjective factors, such as one's self-image, self-evaluation, and frame of reference. (*Self-image* is your perception of your own body, personality, and capabilities. *Self-evaluation* refers to appraising yourself as good or bad. A *frame of reference* is a mental perspective used to interpret events.) Today, humanists still try to understand how we perceive ourselves and experience the world. However, most now do research to test their ideas, just as other psychologists do (Schneider, Bugental, & Pierson, 2001). Like the very early psychologists, they believe that mental events are important; however, unlike the structuralists, they do not believe that our mental lives can be easily divided into distinct building blocks.

▲ Table 1.2 presents a summary of psychology's early development.

Radical behaviorism A behaviorist approach that rejects both introspection and any study of mental events, such as thinking, as inappropriate topics for scientific psychology.

Dynamic unconscious In Freudian theory, the parts of the mind that are beyond awareness, especially conflicts, impulses, and desires not directly known to a person.

Psychoanalysis Freudian approach to psychotherapy emphasizing the exploration of the unconscious using free association, dream interpretation, resistances, and transference to uncover unconscious conflicts.

Neo-Freudians Psychologists who accept the broad features of Freud's theory but have revised the theory to include the role of cultural and social factors while still accepting some of its basic concepts.

Psychodynamic theory Any theory of behavior that emphasizes internal conflicts, motives, and unconscious forces.

Cognitive psychology The study of information processing, thinking, reasoning, and problem solving.

Operational definition Defining a scientific concept by stating the specific actions or procedures used to measure it. For example, hunger might be defined as the number of hours of food deprivation.

Determinism The idea that all behavior has prior causes that would completely explain one's choices and actions if all such causes were known.

Free will The ability to freely make choices that are not controlled by genetics, learning, or unconscious forces; the idea that human beings are capable of making choices or decisions themselves.

Humanistic psychology Study of people as inherently good and motivated to learn and improve.

Self-actualization The process of fully developing personal potentials.

▲ **Table 1.2 The Early Development of Psychology**

Perspective	Date	Notable Events
Experimental psychology	1879	• Wilhelm Wundt opens the first psychology laboratory in Germany
	1883	• The first psychology lab in the United States is founded at Johns Hopkins University, in Baltimore, Maryland
	1886	• The first psychology textbook published in the United States; written by John Dewey
Structuralism	1898	• Edward Titchener advances psychology based on introspection
Functionalism	1890	• William James publishes *Principles of Psychology*
	1892	• The American Psychological Association is founded
Psychodynamic psychology	1895	• Sigmund Freud publishes his first studies
	1900	• Freud publishes *The Interpretation of Dreams*
Behaviorism	1906	• Ivan Pavlov reports his research on conditioned reflexes
	1913	• John Watson presents the behaviorist viewpoint
Gestalt psychology	1912	• Max Wertheimer and other researchers advance the Gestalt viewpoint
Humanistic psychology	1942	• Carl Rogers publishes *Counseling and Psychotherapy*
	1943	• Abraham Maslow publishes *A Theory of Human Motivation*
Biopsychology	1949	• Donald Hebb publishes *The Organization of Behavior*
Cognitive psychology	1956	• George Miller publishes *The Magic Number Seven, Plus or Minus Two*

Reflective Practice

The History of Psychological Science: A Trip Through Time

1. The cognitive unconscious is
a. better studied objectively
b. inaccessible through introspection
c. outside subjective awareness
d. all of the above

Match the following psychological approaches with the appropriate historical figure.

2. Structuralism — **A.** Maslow
3. Humanistic — **B.** Freud
4. Functionalism — **C.** Titchener
5. Psychoanalytic — **D.** Wertheimer
6. Radical behaviorism — **E.** James
7. Gestalt — **F.** Watson
8. Behaviorism — **G.** Skinner

THINK CRITICALLY

9. Modern sciences like psychology are built on intersubjective observations, which can be verified by two or more independent observers. Based on your reading, evaluate whether structuralism met this standard, giving reasons for your answer.

SELF-REFLECT

- Which of the historical approaches to psychology best matches your own thinking about human thinking and behavior? Why?

Answers: 1. b 2. C 3. A 4. E 5. B 6. G 7. D 8. F 9. No, it did not. Structuralism's downfall was that each observer examined the contents of his or her own mind—which is something that no other person can observe.

1.4 Contemporary Psychological Science and the Biopsychosocial Model

GATEWAYS LEARNING OUTCOMES:
After reading this section you should be able to:

1.4.1 Explain the three perspectives that comprise the biopsychosocial model

1.4.2 Explain the advantages of the biopsychosocial model for describing complex behavior

1.4.3 Explain why early psychological research was prone to gender and culture bias

Today, most psychologists accept that **psychology** is the scientific study of behavior and mental processes (appropriately operationally defined). It is this reliance on objective scientific observation to systematically answer questions about all sorts of behaviors and mental processes that distinguishes psychology from many other fields, such as history, law, art, and business (Stanovich, 2013).

What does "behavior" refer to in that definition of psychology? Any directly observable action or response—eating, hanging out, sleeping, talking, or sneezing—is a *behavior*. So are studying, gambling, watching television, tying your shoes, giving someone a gift, and reading this book. But psychologists haven't left out the mind; they also objectively study mental events, such as dreaming, thinking, remembering, understanding what you read, and making decisions about stockings (or murder suspects), as well as other mental processes (Jackson, 2016).

Key insights from the early schools of thought continue to influence contemporary psychology. Some early systems, such as structuralism, have disappeared entirely, while new ones have gained prominence. Also, viewpoints such as functionalism and Gestalt psychology have been absorbed into newer, broader perspectives. Freudian psychoanalysis continues to evolve into the broader *psychodynamic view.* Although many of Freud's ideas have been challenged or refuted, psychodynamic psychologists continue to trace our behavior to unconscious mental activity. They also seek to develop therapies to help people lead happier, fuller lives. The same is true of humanistic psychologists, although they stress subjective, conscious experience and the positive side of human nature.

Today, though, one overarching perspective has gained prominence. The **biopsychosocial model** accepts that human behavior, mental processes, and overall well-being are strongly influenced by a combination of *biological, psychological,* and *social* factors (Woods, 2019).

Let's take a closer look at the three components of the biopsychosocial model.

The Biological Perspective

The **biological perspective** seeks to explain behavior in terms of biological principles such as genetics, brain processes, and evolution. **Evolutionary psychology** is an approach that emphasizes inherited, adaptive aspects of behavior and mental processes. *Biopsychologists* and others who study the brain and nervous system, such as biologists and biochemists, comprise the broader field of **neuroscience**. Using new techniques, *neuroscientists* are producing exciting insights about how the brain relates to thinking, feelings, perception, abnormal behavior, and other topics.

The Psychological Perspective

The **psychological perspective** views behavior as the result of psychological processes within each person. This view continues to emphasize scientific observation, just as the early psychologists did. However, cognitive psychology has gained prominence in recent years as researchers have devised suitable operational definitions and research methods to objectively study mental processes, such as thinking, memory, language, perception, problem solving, consciousness, and creativity (Reed, 2013). With a renewed interest in thinking, it can be said that psychology has finally "regained consciousness" (Robins, Gosling, & Craik, 1998).

The Social Perspective

The **social perspective** stresses the impact that social contexts, such as crowds, groups, and cultures, have on human behavior. Many characteristics of our social world, such as access to education, ethnicity, religion, and poverty, affect the social norms that guide behavior. **Social norms** are rules that define acceptable and expected behavior for members of various groups.

Putting the Three Perspectives Together

As all-encompassing as this may at first seem, in practice the biopsychosocial model cannot by itself tell us *which* particular biological, psychological, and social factors influence any particular behavior—only more detailed research can yield specific answers. Instead, this model serves as a constant reminder of the value of taking into account multiple perspectives, because doing so allows us to better understand complex human behaviors (▲ Table 1.3). For example, *anorexia nervosa* is an eating disorder involving unrealistic thoughts about body image and behaviors such as excessive exercise and restrictive eating (■ see Section 10.2). To properly understand this disorder using a biopsychosocial model, it's important to fully consider the biological (anomalies on chromosome 12), psychological (high need for control), and social (exposure to idealized body images presented in the media) factors that play a role in triggering this potentially fatal disorder (Hausenblas et al., 2013). Table 1.3 gives an overview of the perspectives associated with the biopsychosocial perspective.

Human Diversity and the Biopsychosocial Model

One of the real benefits of a model that considers biological, psychological, and social factors is that it is better able to capture the full range of diversity that we see in human thinking and behavior. Though the study of human diversity is well established in contemporary psychology, it took some time for psychology to realize its importance, and to incorporate it into everyday psychological theory and practice. This delay stemmed mainly from the fact that the founders of psychology were not a very diverse group (you may have noticed that all of the early psychologists mentioned in our look at the history of psychology were Caucasian men). This

Psychology The scientific study of behavior and mental processes.

Biopsychosocial model An approach acknowledging that biological, psychological, and social factors interact to influence human behavior and mental processes.

Biological perspective The attempt to explain behavior in terms of underlying biological principles.

Evolutionary psychology Approach that emphasizes inherited, adaptive aspects of behavior and mental processes.

Neuroscience The broader field of biopsychologists and others who study the brain and nervous system, such as biologists and biochemists.

Psychological perspective The traditional view that behavior is shaped by psychological processes occurring at the level of the individual.

Social perspective The focus on the importance of social contexts in influencing the behavior of individuals.

Social norms Rules that define acceptable and expected behavior for members of a group.

▲ Table 1.3 Perspectives of the Biopsychosocial Model

Biological Perspective

Biopsychological View

Key idea: *Human and animal behavior is the result of internal physical, chemical, and biological processes.*

Seeks to explain behavior through activity of the brain and nervous system, physiology, genetics, the endocrine system, and biochemistry; a neutral, reductionistic, and mechanistic view of human nature.

Evolutionary View

Key idea: *Human and animal behavior is the result of the process of evolution.*

Seeks to explain behavior through principles based on natural selection; a neutral, reductionistic, and mechanistic view of human nature.

Psychological Perspective

Behaviorist View

Key idea: *Behavior is shaped and controlled by one's environment.*

Emphasizes the study of observable behavior and the effects of learning; stresses the influence of external rewards and punishments; a neutral, scientific, and somewhat mechanistic view of human nature.

Cognitive View

Key idea: *Much human behavior can be understood in terms of the mental processing of information.*

Concerned with thinking, knowing, perception, understanding, memory, decision making, and judgment; explains behavior in terms of information processing; a neutral, somewhat computerlike view of human nature.

Psychodynamic View

Key idea: *Behavior is directed by forces within one's personality that are often hidden or unconscious.*

Emphasizes internal impulses, desires, and conflicts—especially those that are unconscious; views behavior as the result of clashing forces within personality; a somewhat negative, pessimistic view of human nature.

Humanistic View

Key idea: *Behavior is guided by one's self-image, by subjective perceptions of the world, and by the need for personal growth.*

Focuses on subjective, conscious experience, human problems, potentials, and ideals; emphasizes self-image and self-actualization to explain behavior; a positive, philosophical view of human nature.

Social Perspective

Social View

Key idea: *Behavior is influenced by one's social and cultural context.*

Emphasizes that behavior is related to the social and cultural environment within which a person is born, grows up, and lives from day to day; a neutral, interactionist view of human nature.

inadvertently introduced narrowness into early psychological theory and research.

For example, Lawrence Kohlberg (1969) proposed an influential theory about how we develop moral values. His studies suggested that women were morally "immature" because, compared to men, they were not as concerned with justice when making moral decisions. Many years later, Carol Gilligan (1982) provided evidence that women were more likely to make moral choices based on caring, rather than justice. When moral decision making is examined from this point of view, it was men who were morally immature. (■ Today, we recognize that both justice and caring perspectives may be essential to adult wisdom. ■ See Section 3.4 for more details.)

There are two main reasons why early psychological theories were prone to this type of **gender bias in research**. The first is that because the majority of early researchers and clinicians were men, women rarely had an opportunity to contribute their perspectives to the research being carried out, or the theories being developed. Without women's input into the research agenda, topics of significant interest to women were also more likely to be ignored by many investigators.

The second issue that contributed to gender bias was the tendency for research to focus on male participants, and to assume that results observed with men would also hold true for women. Without directly studying women, though, it's impossible to know the extent to which this assumption is true. A related problem occurs when researchers combine results from men and women. Doing so can hide important male–female differences. A final problem related to research participants is that unequal numbers of men and women may volunteer for some kinds of research. For example, in studies of sexuality, more male college students volunteer to participate than females (Wiederman, 1999). Conversely, more females than males participate in studies of nursing (Polit & Beck, 2013).

As important as they are, male–female differences are but one type of human diversity. Similar types of bias also arise when it comes to people of different ages, sexual orientations, and ethnic groups (Denmark, Rabinowitz, & Sechzer, 2005; Guthrie, 2004). Perhaps the most general research bias of all becomes clear when you consider that many of psychology's conclusions are based on people who are WEIRD (that is, from **W**estern, **E**ducated, **I**ndustrialized, **R**ich, and **D**emocratic societies). For example, to this day, the vast majority of human participants in psychology experiments are recruited from introductory psychology courses. (This fact led psychologist Edward Tolman to note that much of psychology is based on two sets of subjects—rats and college freshmen!)

While the reliance on WEIRD research participants does not automatically invalidate the results of psychology experiments, it may place limitations on their implications. According to Henrich, Heine, and Norenzayan (2010), we have a strongly ingrained tendency to assume that what Western researchers discover while studying Western research participants is the norm in human behavior and that the behavior of those in other societies is unusual. However, after a careful review of studies comparing Westerners to people from other societies, these researchers concluded that exactly the opposite is the case. *We* in North America and Western Europe are WEIRD, and so we should be careful about making assumptions that what we learn from studying behavior in our society illuminates the behavior of people in non-Western societies. Too often in the past, the unstated standard for determining what is average, normal, or correct has been the behavior of middle-aged, white, heterosexual, middle-class Western men (Henrich, Heine, & Norenzayan, 2010).

Margaret Washburn (1871–1939). In 1908, Washburn published *The Animal Mind*, an influential textbook on animal behavior. In 1921 she became the second female to serve as President of the American Psychological Association (Mary Whiton Calkins was the first).

Francis Cecil Sumner (1895–1954). Sumner served as chair of the Psychology Department at Howard University and wrote articles critical of the underrepresentation of African Americans in American colleges and universities.

Inez Beverly Prosser (c. 1895–1934). Prosser was one of the early leaders in the debate about how to best educate African-American children.

More recently, though, psychologists have started asking important questions such as: Do the principles of Western psychology apply to people in all cultures? Are some psychological concepts invalid in other cultures? Are any universal? As psychologists have probed such questions, one thing has become clear: **cultural relativity**—the idea that behavior must be judged relative to the values of the culture in which it occurs—can greatly affect our understanding of "other people." Most of what we think, feel, and do is influenced, in one way or another, by the social and cultural worlds in which we live (Baumeister & Bushman, 2017; Henrich, Heine, & Norenzayan, 2010). This includes not just everyday thinking and behavior, but also the diagnosis and treatment of mental disorders (Lum, 2011). To be effective, psychologists must be sensitive to people who are ethnically and culturally different from themselves (Lowman, 2013). (■ See Section 15.1 for a discussion of the impact of culture on therapy.)

It's worth noting that although women and ethnic minorities were long underrepresented among psychologists, there *were* a few pioneers (Minton, 2000). In 1894, Margaret Washburn became the first woman to be awarded a PhD in psychology. By 1906 in the United States, about 1 psychologist in 10 was a woman. In 1920, Francis Cecil Sumner became the first African American man to earn a doctoral degree in psychology. Inez Beverly Prosser, the first African American female psychologist, was awarded her PhD in 1933.

Fortunately, psychology is coming to better reflect human diversity as the proportion of women and racial/ethnic minorities in the psychology workforce continues to increase (American Psychological Association, 2015b). For example, according to a 2014 survey of members of the American Psychological Association (American Psychological Association, 2015a):

- 57 percent of members are women, and 9 percent are racial/ethnic minorities
- 49 percent of members working full time in universities, colleges, and other academic settings are women, and 14 percent are racial/ethnic minorities
- 57 percent of members holding PhD degrees (or equivalent) are women, and 9 percent are racial/ethnic minorities

The American Psychological Association (APA) has also recently recognized the importance of educating the public about diversity in the field of psychology. In conjunction with the Smithsonian Institute, the APA Women's Programs Office has developed the *I Am Psyched!* program to celebrate the role of women of color in psychology. To maximize exposure, *I Am Psyched!* is now a traveling exhibit that has traveled from coast to coast, visiting more than 50 colleges in the United States.

In closing, we should note that the issue of diversity is not solely of academic concern. We are rapidly becoming a multicultural society. By 2044, more than half of all Americans will be members of minority groups such as African American, Hispanic, Asian American, Native American, or Pacific Islander (Colby & Ortman, 2016). In some large cities such as Detroit and Baltimore, minority groups

Gender bias in research A tendency for females and female-related issues to be underrepresented in research, whether psychological or otherwise.

Cultural relativity The idea that behavior must be judged relative to the values of the culture in which it occurs.

Rawpixel.com/Shutterstock.com

As illustrated by this photo of office co-workers, America is becoming more diverse. To fully understand human behavior, personal differences based on age, race, culture, ethnicity, gender, and sexual orientation must be taken into account.

have already become the majority. An appreciation of the fuller spectrum of human diversity can enrich your life as well as your understanding of psychology (Helgeson, 2012).

Reflective Practice

Contemporary Psychological Science and the Biopsychosocial Model

1. Which of the following is ***not*** a perspective included in the biopsychosocial model?
   a. Social perspective
   b. Clinical perspective
   c. Psychological perspective
   d. Biological perspective
2. A psychotherapist is working with a person from an ethnic group other than her own. She should be aware of how cultural relativity and ______________ affect behavior.
   a. information literacy errors
   b. operational definitions
   c. biased sampling
   d. social norms
3. Gender bias in research was a problem that stemmed in part from the fact that there were very few female researchers in psychology. T or F?
4. WEIRD science refers to the fact that many ideas in psychology are based on participants from societies that are Western, ______________, Industrialized, Rich, and ______________.

THINK CRITICALLY

5. Evaluate the following statement: *All sciences are interested in controlling the phenomena that they study.*

SELF-REFLECT

- In what ways are your own judgments of other people guided by factors such as your gender and culture?

Answers: 1. b 2. d 3. T 4. Educated, Democratic 5. False. Astronomy and archeology are examples of sciences that do not share psychology's fourth goal. Think about it for a moment: No one can control the stars or the past.

1.5 The Core Features of Psychological Science

GATEWAYS LEARNING OUTCOMES:
After reading this section you should be able to:

1.5.1 Explain the goals of contemporary psychology

1.5.2 Define critical thinking, and identify the five principles of critical thinking

1.5.3 Outline the six steps of the scientific method

1.5.4 Describe three types of data gathered by psychological scientists, including the challenges faced by psychologists who use them

It's clear from reading about psychology's history and more recent ideas such as the biopsychosocial model that both critical thinking and the scientific method are at the heart of contemporary psychology. But what are the larger goals of psychologists?

Psychology's Goals

As scientists, our ultimate goal is to benefit humanity (O'Neill, 2005). More specifically, the goals of psychology are to *describe, understand, predict,* and *control* behavior. What do those goals mean in practice? Let's see.

Description

Answering psychological questions often begins with a careful description of behavior. **Description**, or naming and classifying, is typically based on making a detailed record of scientific observations. Descriptions of behavior might include the observation that women attempt suicide more often than men, or that men are more likely than women to succeed in their efforts to end their lives. Another example of description is the finding that when many bystanders are present during an emergency, we often find that few—if any—people will step up to provide help.

But a description doesn't explain anything, does it? No. While useful knowledge begins with accurate descriptions, descriptions fail to answer the important "why" questions. *Why* do more women attempt suicide, and *why* do more men succeed at it? *Why* are bystanders often unwilling to help in an emergency?

Understanding

We have met psychology's second goal when we can explain an event. That is, **understanding** usually means that we can state the causes of a behavior. For example, research on bystander apathy reveals that people often fail to help when *other* possible helpers are nearby. Why? Psychologists' efforts to understand this phenomenon suggest that a diffusion of responsibility occurs. Basically, when lots of people are present, no single individual feels personally obligated to pitch in. As a result, the more potential helpers there are, the less likely it is that anyone will help (Aronson, Wilson, & Akert, 2013). (■ Bystander apathy and conditions that influence whether people will help in an emergency are of great interest to social psychologists. ■ See Section 17.2 for details.)

Prediction

Psychology's third goal, **prediction**, is the ability to forecast behavior accurately. Notice that our explanation of bystander apathy makes a prediction about the chances of getting help; specifically we might predict that the more people that are present during an emergency, the less likely it is that any one of them will provide help. If you've ever been stranded on a busy freeway with car trouble, you'll recognize the accuracy of this prediction: Having many potential helpers nearby is no guarantee that anyone will stop to help.

Control

Description, explanation, and prediction seem reasonable, but is control *a valid goal?* Control may seem like a threat to personal freedom. However, to a psychologist, **control** simply refers to the ability to alter the conditions that affect behavior. If social psychologists are able to suggest conditions that would minimize bystander apathy and those suggestions are implemented, then control has been exerted. Similarly, if a clinical psychologist helps a person overcome a terrible fear of heights, control is involved. If you suggest changes in a classroom that help students learn better, you have exerted control. Control is also involved in designing cars to keep drivers from making fatal errors. Clearly, though, psychological control must be used wisely and humanely.

In summary, psychology's goals are a natural outgrowth of our desire to understand behavior. Basically, they boil down to asking the following questions:

- What is the nature of this behavior? What does it look like? (description)
- Why does this behavior occur? (understanding and explanation)
- Can we forecast when the behavior will occur? (prediction)
- What conditions affect the behavior? Should we use our knowledge of those conditions to change it? (control)

Sinseeho/Shutterstock.com

Some psychologists specialize in administering, scoring, and interpreting psychological self-report tests, such as tests of intelligence, creativity, personality, or aptitude. This specialty, which is called *psychometrics*, is often used to address psychology's third goal: predicting future behavior.

To achieve their goals of describing, understanding, predicting, and controlling behavior, psychologists rely on critical thinking and the scientific method. Critical thinking in psychology most often takes the form of collecting empirical evidence to evaluate theories, as guided by the scientific method. It would be impossible to accurately answer most questions about human behavior without the aid of scientific research methods.

Thinking Critically to Meet Psychology's Goals

Critical thinking in psychology is a type of reflection (you *did* read *Psychology and Your Skill Set—Reflective Studying*, right?) that involves asking whether a particular belief can be supported by both scientific theory and observation (Vaughn, 2016; Yanchar, Slife, & Warne, 2008).

Critical thinkers are willing to challenge both conventional and unconventional wisdom by asking hard questions (Ruggiero, 2015). For this and many other reasons, learning to think critically is one of the lasting benefits of a college education.

For example, when it comes to achieving our goals, is it better to focus on how far we still have to go before we reach a goal, or should we focus on what we have already accomplished? Critical thinkers might immediately ask: "Is there any theory to support stressing either a goal focus or an accomplishment focus? Is there any empirical evidence either way? What could we do to find out for ourselves?" (Be on the lookout later in this chapter for some evidence concerning this question.)

Critical Thinking Principles

The heart of critical thinking is a willingness to actively *reflect* on ideas. Critical thinkers evaluate ideas by deliberately probing for weaknesses in their reasoning and analyzing the evidence supporting their beliefs. They question assumptions and look for alternative conclusions. True knowledge, they recognize, comes from constantly revising our understanding of the world. Critical thinking relies on the following basic principles (Jackson & Newberry, 2016; Ruggiero, 2015; Vaughn, 2016):

1. *Few truths transcend the need for logical analysis and empirical testing.* Whereas religious beliefs and personal values are often held as matters of faith, most other ideas can and should be evaluated by applying the rules of logic, evidence, and the scientific method.
2. *Authority or claimed expertise does not automatically make an idea true or false.* Just because a teacher, guru, celebrity,

Description In scientific research, the process of naming and classifying.

Understanding In psychology, being able to state the causes of a behavior.

Prediction In psychology, an ability to accurately forecast behavior.

Control In psychology, altering conditions that influence behavior.

Critical thinking In psychology, a type of reflection involving the support of beliefs through scientific explanation and observation.

or authority is convincing or sincere doesn't mean that you should automatically believe (or disbelieve) that person. Naively accepting (or denying) the word of an expert is unscientific and self-demeaning unless you ask, "Is this a well-supported explanation, or is there a better one? What evidence convinced her or him?"

3. *Judging the quality of the evidence is crucial.* Imagine that you are a juror in a courtroom, judging claims made by two battling lawyers. To decide correctly, you can't just weigh the *amount* of evidence. You must also critically evaluate the *quality* of the evidence. Then you can give greater weight to the most credible facts.
4. *Critical thinking requires an open mind.* Be prepared to consider daring departures and go wherever the evidence leads. However, don't become so open-minded that you are simply gullible. Astronomer Carl Sagan once noted, "It seems to me that what is called for is an exquisite balance between two conflicting needs: the most skeptical scrutiny of all hypotheses that are served up to us and at the same time a great openness to new ideas" (Kida, 2006, p. 51).
5. *Critical thinkers often wonder what it would take to show that a "truth" is false.* **Falsification** is the deliberate attempt to uncover how a commonsense belief or scientific theory might be false. Critical thinkers adopt an attitude of actively seeking to *falsify* beliefs, including their own. They want to find out when they are wrong, even if it is difficult to accept. As Susan Blackmore (2000, p. 55) said when her studies caused her to abandon some long-held beliefs, "Admitting you are wrong is always hard—even though it's a skill that every psychologist has to learn." On the plus side, finding out what is wrong with a belief often points the way to improving it. Similarly, critical thinkers can be more confident in beliefs that have survived their attempts at falsification.

To put these principles into action, here are some questions to ask as you evaluate new information (Jackson & Newberry, 2016; Ruggiero, 2015; Vaughn, 2016):

1. What is the claim being made? Is it understandable? Does it make logical sense? Does it fit into an existing theory? What are the implications of the claim? Is there another possible explanation? Is it a simpler explanation?
2. What empirical tests of this claim have been made (if any)? How good is the evidence? (In general, scientific observations provide the highest quality evidence.) Can the claim be falsified?
3. Who did the tests? How reliable and trustworthy were the investigators? Do they have conflicts of interest (for example, are they being paid or rewarded in some other way for making these claims)? Do their findings appear to be objective? Has any other independent researcher duplicated the findings?

Using the Scientific Method to Meet Psychology's Goals

Psychology generally follows the **scientific method**, a form of critical thinking based on the systematic collection of evidence, accurate description and measurements, precise definitions, controlled observations, and repeatable results (Jackson, 2016; Yanchar, Slife, & Warne, 2008). As we noted previously, the first step in the scientific method is the careful recording of observations, the foundation of all science (Stanovich, 2013). To be *scientific*, our observations must be *systematic*, so they reveal something reliable about behavior.

The Six Steps of the Scientific Method

In its ideal form, the scientific method has six steps (Figure 1.2). All six steps are found in the following example, from Florida State University psychologist Kyle Conlon and his colleagues (2011). Conlon wondered whether goals are more attainable if people maintain a goal focus (stressing how much remains to be done to achieve the goal) or an achievement focus (stressing how much has already been accomplished). These researchers decided to find out.

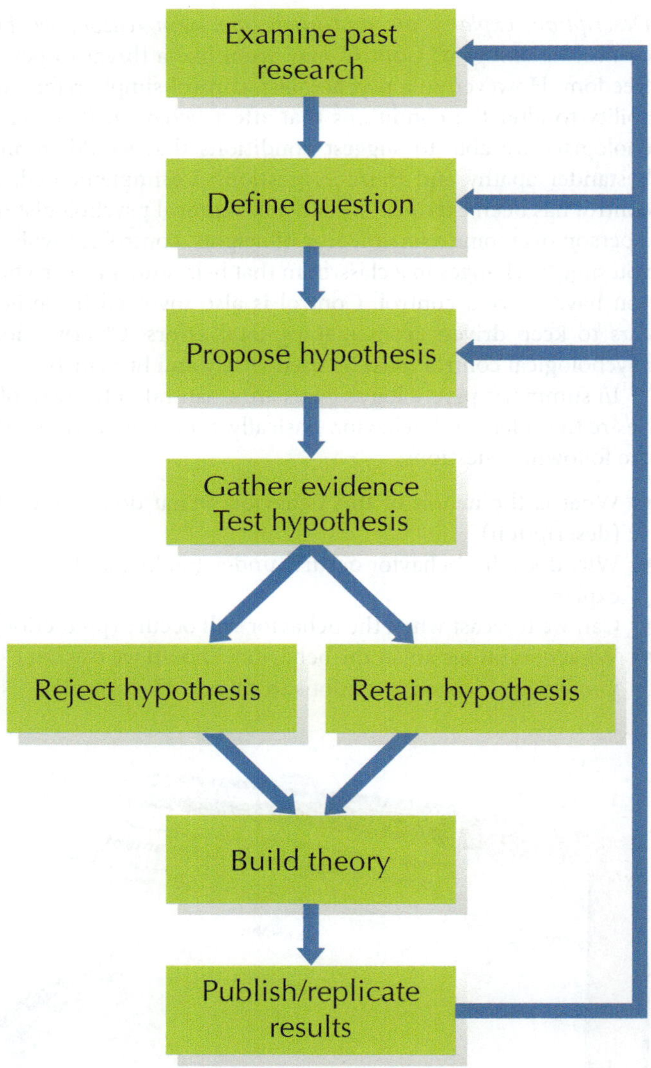

Figure 1.2 The scientific method. Psychologists use the logic of science to answer questions about behavior. Specific hypotheses can be tested in a variety of ways, including naturalistic observation, correlational studies, controlled experiments, case studies, and surveys. Psychologists revise their theories to reflect the evidence they gather. New or revised theories then lead to new observations, problems, and hypotheses.

1. Examine Past Research

The researchers reviewed previously published studies, noting that both goal-focused and achievement-focused approaches are popular. If the goal is weight loss, for example, one goal-focused approach is to count down the pounds (only 10 pounds to go!), while one achievement-focused approach is to celebrate milestones. (Congratulations on losing the first 10 pounds!)

2. Define the Question

The researchers also noted that maintaining a goal focus seems to inspire more goal-oriented behaviors. Thus, they defined their main question as "Will people lose more weight if they maintain a goal focus compared to an achievement focus?"

3. Propose a Hypothesis

What exactly is a hypothesis? A theoretical question or statement (like "Will people lose more weight if they maintain a goal focus or if they maintain an achievement focus?") is usually too vague to be assessed directly. In contrast, a **hypothesis** (hi-POTH-eh-sis) is the predicted outcome of an experiment or an educated guess about the relationship between variables. In other words, a hypothesis is a *testable* hunch about behavior, or a statement about the outcome you believe you'll see. In this study, the hypothesis was that *people who adopted a goal focus would lose more weight than those who had an achievement focus.*

Theoretical questions are transformed into testable hypotheses through operational definitions (as we saw earlier in this chapter, an *operational definition* states the exact procedures used to measure a concept). Conlon and his colleagues began by creating a 12-week exercise program involving weekly group meetings and a companion website. Operationally defining weight loss was straightforward; participants were weighed on a standard digital scale at the beginning of the weight-loss period and once every week until the program ended.

Measuring someone's goal focus or achievement focus was a bit harder since these terms refer to mental processes. Fortunately, operational definitions also allow mental processes that are not directly observable to be tested in real-world terms (see Figure 1.3). Conlon and his colleagues modified their weight-loss program so that the weekly surveys, feedback, and group

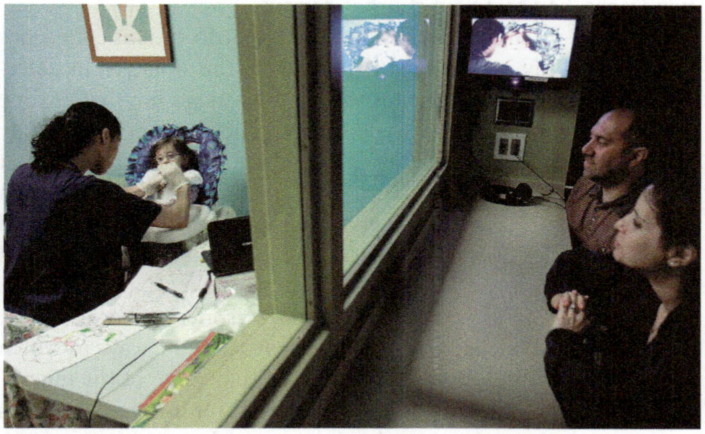

The Star-Ledger/Robert Sciarrino/The Image Works

Applying the scientific method to the study of behavior requires careful observation. Here, two psychologists observe and record a session in which a child's eating behavior is being studied.

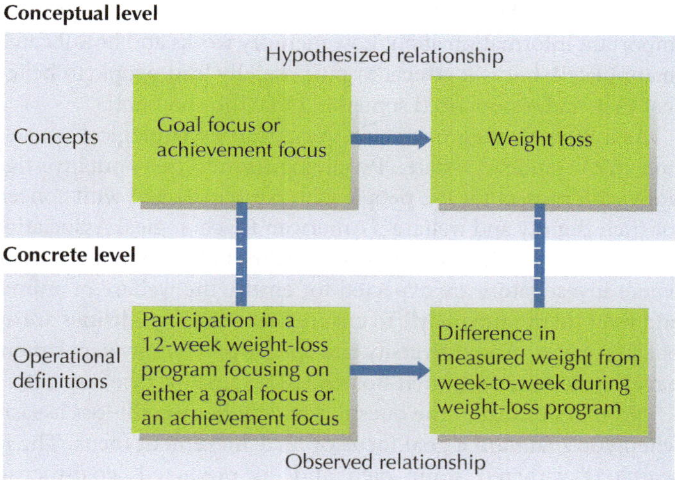

Figure 1.3 Operational definitions. Operational definitions are used to link concepts with concrete observations. Conlon and his colleagues (2011) define their weight-loss programs in enough detail that other researchers can confirm both the validity of their operational definitions and the accuracy of their results. Operational definitions vary in how well they represent concepts. For this reason, many different experiments may be necessary to draw clear conclusions about hypothesized relationships in psychology.

discussions revolved around either a goal focus or an achievement focus. They then assigned a third of their participants to one program or the other (the final third was assigned to a "control" group without either focus). For example, every week, goal-focused participants were asked to describe how much more weight they needed to lose to reach their goal, while achievement-focused participants were asked to describe how much weight they had already lost.

4. Gather Evidence/Test Hypothesis

In the next step, scientists will gather data (from animals or humans) to test their hypothesis. An examination of psychological research will reveal that researchers can collect many different types of data and different procedures, or methods, to test hypotheses. The types of data and research methods that psychologists use are described later in this chapter.

Aren't there rules about how scientists must treat people and animals when they gather evidence? Absolutely! It probably won't come as a surprise to you that psychological research sometimes raises *ethical* questions. For example, is it ethical to carry out research with small children or adults with dementia, given that they are unable to give their consent to participate in the research? Or what about some classic research in which psychologists demonstrated that it was possible to "plant" false memories in the minds of their participants,

Falsification The deliberate attempt to uncover how a commonsense belief or scientific theory might be false.

Scientific method A form of critical thinking based on careful measurement, controlled observation, and repeatable results.

Hypothesis Predicted outcome of an experiment, or an educated guess about the relationship between variables.

who genuinely believed them to be true? This research provided important information about how memory works and how it can be manipulated, but is it ethical to purposefully lead people to believe that they had experienced something that they had not?

As a reply to such questions, American Psychological Association (APA) guidelines state: "Psychologists must carry out investigations with respect for the people who participate and with concern for their dignity and welfare" (American Psychological Association, 2017a; see ▲ Table 1.4). Ethical guidelines also apply to animals, where investigators are expected to "ensure the welfare of animals and treat them humanely." To ensure that ethical guidelines are applied properly, most university and college psychology departments have Institutional Research Boards (IRBs) that oversee research.

Now let's return to the question of whether weight loss is easier when you maintain a goal focus or an achievement focus. The researchers gathered some data and, as predicted, goal-focused individuals lost more weight than did either achievement-focused or control group individuals. They also reported being more committed to reaching their goal weights. Accordingly, the evidence gathered provided support for the researchers' hypothesis.

5. Build Theory

How do theories fit in? A **theory** is a system of ideas designed to interrelate concepts and facts in a way that summarizes existing data and predicts future observations. Good theories summarize observations, explain them, allow prediction, and guide further research. Without theories of forgetting, personality, stress, mental illness, and the like, psychologists would drown in a sea of disconnected facts (Stanovich, 2013). (■ One of the major limitations of Freudian personality theory is that many of its concepts are not testable or falsifiable. ■ See Section 12.1.)

Conlon and his colleagues interpreted their results as consistent with theories of motivation that stress the importance of being aware of how much work remains to be done to achieve a goal. The results were also portrayed as extending these theories into the field of health psychology and as being relevant to the design of health-intervention programs.

6. Publication and Replication of Results

Because scientific information must always be *publicly available*, the results of psychological studies are usually published in professional journals (see ▲ Table 1.5). That way, other researchers can read about the results and make their own observations if they doubt the study's findings (Gravetter & Forzano, 2016). In a scholarly article published in the *Journal of Experimental Social Psychology*, Conlon and his colleagues (2011) describe the question they investigated, the methods they used, and the results of their study comparing goal-focused and achievement-focused dieters.

▲ Table 1.4 Basic Ethical Guidelines for Psychological Researchers

Do no harm.
Describe risks accurately to potential participants.
Ensure that participation is voluntary.
Minimize any discomfort to participants.
Maintain confidentiality.
Do not invade privacy unnecessarily.
Use deception only when absolutely necessary.
Remove any misconceptions caused by deception (i.e., debriefing).
Provide results and interpretations to participants.
Treat participants with dignity and respect.

▲ Table 1.5 Outline of a Research Report

- **Abstract** Research reports begin with a brief summary of the study and its findings. The abstract lets you get an overview of the contents without reading the entire article.
- **Introduction** The introduction describes the question to be investigated. It also provides background information by reviewing prior studies on the same or related topics.
- **Method** This section tells how and why observations were made. It also describes the specific procedures used to gather data. That way, other researchers can repeat the study to see if they get the same results.
- **Results** The outcome of the investigation is presented. Data may be graphed, summarized in tables, or statistically analyzed.
- **Discussion** The results of the study are discussed in relation to the original question. Implications of the study are explored and further studies may be proposed.

Studying the Science: The Importance of Replicating Scientific Results

Just as researchers are obliged to treat participants ethically, they are also obliged to report on their data in an ethical manner. This means that the methods must be reported accurately, and that researchers cannot "cherry pick" only the results that they want people to see when the findings are published.

The importance of treating data ethically was highlighted recently when it became clear that publications based on a famous psychological study—the Stanford Prison Experiment—had misreported the conditions under which information was gathered, and the findings that were obtained (Le Texier, 2019). In this compelling study, the researchers assigned 12 young men to be either "guards" or "prisoners" in a simulated prison. Early articles based on the research suggested that the men quickly became immersed in the roles they were assigned. Those assigned to be guards allegedly became cruel and abusive, while those assigned to be prisoners became passive and despondent, with some demonstrating high levels of desperation. The situation at the "prison" became so dire that the study, which was initially supposed to last two weeks, had to be cut short at day six.

Publications and presentations by Zimbardo and his colleagues about this study emphasized the power of the situation in determining our behavior; in other words, they suggested that anyone can be overcome by social roles and the norms that accompany them (Zimbardo et al., 1971). It has come to light, though, that some of the study's methods and results were misrepresented in a way that allowed the researchers to tell the story that they wanted to report, rather than one that accurately depicted what happened in the study (Le Texier, 2019). For example, rather than the guards spontaneously acting cruelly toward the prisoners, it became clear that they were coached by the researchers as to the ways in which they should behave. It has also emerged that some of the guards' and prisoners' behaviors were not genuine, but instead were acts put on by the participants to lend drama to the scenario.

Misrepresentations of a study's methods and results create challenges when it comes to *replicating* (repeating) its findings.

Psychologists care about replication because if others are able to reproduce the results of a study, those results become more credible. Unfortunately, efforts to replicate some famous studies in psychology—including the Stanford Prison Experiment—have sometimes been unsuccessful. This has resulted in what some people refer to as a *replication crisis* in psychology, and it received widespread attention in the media (Shrout & Rodgers, 2018).

It's important to note that failures to replicate published work often have nothing to do with distorting or falsifying a study's methods or results. Indeed, this sort of misrepresentation is rare in psychology. Sometimes a failed replication is related to the fact that the exact methods of the initial study were not observed in the replication attempt. Another reason has to do with historical choices about which studies got published. In the past, there was a preference to publish only research studies that were novel and reported interesting relationships. If a researcher found, for example, that there was *no* relationship between early trauma and depression in adulthood, she would likely have had much more difficulty getting that study published in a journal than a researcher who did find such a relationship. We refer to this problem as a *publication bias*, and it leads to a general sense that these relationships are more prevalent than they really are because in the past we never saw the studies that found no evidence for them (Wichert, 2019).

Perhaps one of the most important factors in replication failures, though, is the samples from which psychologists gather data. It's possible, for example, that the participants in the original study were somewhat restricted, and consequently findings observed with that sample might not generalize to other groups. This problem occurs when researchers recruit very few participants for their study (that is, the study has a small sample size), but you may remember that we also discussed this problem in relation to studies in which all of the participants were men, or people from WEIRD societies. If the originally published research was based on a restricted sample, then it's probably not too surprising that efforts to replicate it with another group of people might be unsuccessful.

Another reason that might contribute to replication failures relates to the passage of time. It's possible, for example, that while the initial findings were true, they no longer hold. For example, imagine that you carried out a study in the 1950s that examined attitudes toward parenting and found that people generally saw parenting as "women's work." If you were to carry out the same study today, do you think you would find the same thing? In all likelihood, we would find a failure to replicate the results of that original study, but that's primarily because attitudes about parenting have shifted considerably since the original work was done and not because there was anything flawed about the study itself.

It's worth noting that psychology is not the only field that is experiencing a replication crisis. Fields such as medicine, business, and economics are also experiencing challenges with replicating their findings. To their credit, though, psychologists have moved quickly to address the problem. Journals are now much more committed to publishing work that finds no evidence of relationships, for example, and researchers have redoubled their efforts to gather evidence from much larger samples that better represent diverse experiences. Perhaps most important, there is a general move toward making psychology an open and transparent science in which researchers agree to make their data, materials, and computer code available to other scientists who want to use them for the purposes of replication.

Evidence to Address Psychology's Goals: From Tests to Testosterone

Step 4 in the scientific method is all about gathering evidence. One of the things that's striking about psychologists is the wide variety of ways in which they gather evidence, or data. The data that psychologists gather is often classified as being either *quantitative* or *qualitative*. Quantitative data are represented as numbers, while qualitative data are usually represented as words or pictures (including videotaped behavior). For example, a psychologist interested in test anxiety might ask a research participant to use a 7-point scale to rate how anxious they feel when asked to take an exam, with a 1 representing "very little or no anxiety" and a rating of 7 indicating "extremely high levels of anxiety." These numeric data are a quantitative assessment of test anxiety.

However, researchers can also elect to study test anxiety by gathering qualitative data. For example, the researcher might ask the participants to describe, in their own words, what their experience is like when they go into an exam, including how they felt physically (sweaty palms or racing heart, perhaps), their emotional responses and their thoughts while taking the test. Each person's report will likely be different, but the researcher will look for common themes in these descriptions.

Let's take a closer look at the types of data you're likely to see in psychological research.

Self-report Data

Sometimes psychologists would like to ask everyone in the world a few well-chosen questions: "What form of discipline did your parents use when you were a child?" "What is the most dishonest thing you've done?" When we ask people to answer them, we are gathering **self-report data**, which is probably the most common form of data that psychologists use. In some cases, we ask participants to self-report their answers in their own words, either by writing things down or giving an answer verbally in an interview (qualitative responses). Other times, we'll ask them to complete a test, questionnaire, or survey and provide answers on a scale (quantitative responses).

Surveys and Sampling

A **survey** is a form of self-report data in which participants are asked the same questions (Babbie, 2016; Thrift, 2010). Usually, we are interested in surveying entire populations. A **population**—the group of people from which a sample is drawn—might be all the people in a particular category (for example, all college students or all single women). Because surveying entire populations

Theory Comprehensive explanation of observable events.

Self-report data Information that is provided by participants about their own thoughts, emotions, or behaviors, typically on a questionnaire or during an interview.

Survey Descriptive research method in which participants are asked the same questions.

Population The entire group of people from which a sample is drawn.

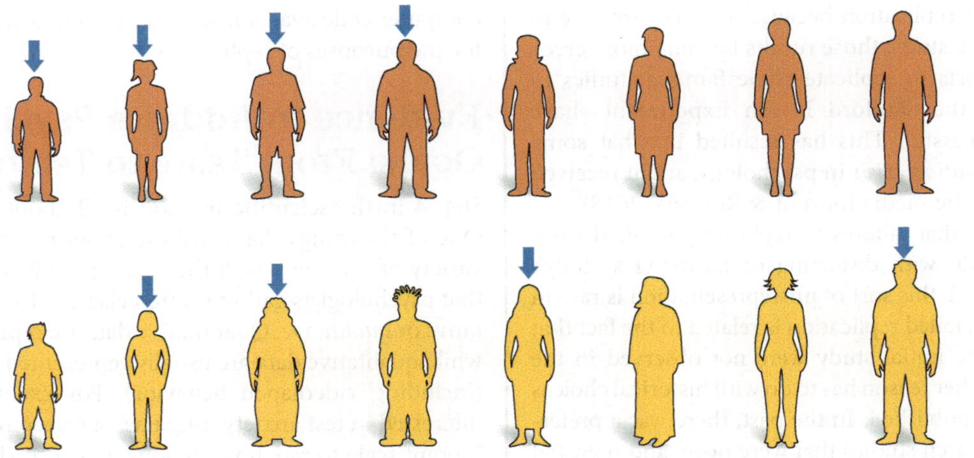

● **Figure 1.4 Random sampling** If you were conducting a survey in which a person's height might be an important variable, the nonrandom sample of shorter people would be very unrepresentative. The random sample, selected using a table of random numbers, better represents the group as a whole.

is often not feasible, typically a **sample**—a subset of a population being studied—is asked a series of carefully worded questions.

In some research studies surveys are carried out in person or via telephone; in others, they might be carried out via the Internet. Web-based research can be a cost-effective way to reach large groups of people, especially those who are not easy to survey any other way (Gosling & Mason, 2015). Internet studies have provided interesting information about topics such as anger, decision making, racial prejudice, what disgusts people, religion, sexual attitudes, and much more. Biased samples can limit web-based research (it isn't easy to control who answers your online questionnaire), but psychologists are getting better at gathering valid information online (Weigold, Weigold, & Russell, 2013).

Are there any problems with data gathered from surveys? If a survey is administered to a **representative sample**—a sample that accurately reflects a larger population—we can draw conclusions about the larger population without polling every person. For a sample to be representative, it must include the same proportion of men, women, young people, old people, professionals, blue-collar workers, Republicans, Democrats, Caucasians, African Americans, Native Americans, Latinos, Asians (and other groups!) as one would find in the population as a whole. Representative samples are often obtained by *randomly* selecting who will be included (● Figure 1.4).

Contemporary surveys like the Gallup and Harris polls use random samples and can therefore be quite accurate. However, if a survey is based on a biased sample, it could paint a false picture. A **biased sample** does not accurately reflect the population from which it was drawn. Surveys done by magazines, websites, and online information services can be quite biased. For example, surveys on gun-control laws done by *O: The Oprah Magazine* and *Guns and Ammo* magazine would probably produce different results—neither of which would likely represent the general population. For many years, the vast majority of human participants in psychology experiments have been recruited from North American and Western Europe, and a large proportion come from introductory psychology courses. In our earlier discussion about diversity, we described this as WEIRD science (that is, Western, Educated, Industrial, Rich, and Democratic). While sampling from such groups does not automatically invalidate the results of psychological studies, it may place important limitations on the extent to which we can generalize the findings to other groups (Henrich, Heine, & Norenzayan, 2010). For this reason, psychologists using the survey method go to great lengths to ensure that their samples are representative.

Even well-designed surveys may be limited by a second problem: **social desirability**. If a psychologist were to ask you detailed questions about your sexual history and current sexual behavior, how accurate would your replies be? Would you exaggerate? Would you be embarrassed? Replies to survey questions are not always accurate or truthful. Many people show a distinct, deliberate tendency to give polite or socially desirable answers. For example, answers to questions concerning sex, drinking or drug use, income, and church attendance tend to be less than truthful. Likewise, the week after an election, more people will say they voted than actually did—and the ones who did vote may not be honest about who they voted for (Babbie, 2016).

Observational Data

Sometimes psychologists' data come from observing participants' behavior. **Observational data** can be either *naturalistic* or *structured*. **Naturalistic observations** take place in a *natural setting* (the typical environment in which a person or animal lives), without any interference from the researcher. For example, in 1960, Jane Goodall first observed a wild chimpanzee in Tanzania use a grass stem as a tool to remove termites from a termite mound (Van Lawick-Goodall, 1971). Psychologists doing naturalistic studies make a special effort to minimize bias by keeping a detailed record of their data and observations, sometimes with the help of video recordings.

In contrast, **structured observations** are those in which psychologists put each participant in the same position and then watch their

© Jolyon Troscianko 2006

Some psychological scientists observe animal behavior, either in person or using video. Here, a new Caledonian crow is wearing a tiny "crow cam" barely half the weight of a silver dollar, allowing researchers to record its use of twigs to forage for food (Rutz & St. Clair, 2012).

behavior. For example, if we were interested in studying empathy, we might have children come to a research lab and have a researcher pretend to trap their finger in a door and express pain. The researcher would express their pain in exactly the same way for each child and would then watch to see how the children responded. Notice that observations provide only *descriptions* of behavior. To *explain* observations, we may need information from other research methods.

Are there any problems with data gathered from observations? The **observer effect**—changes in a subject's behavior caused by an awareness of being observed—is a major problem with observational data. Naturalists should be careful to keep their distance and avoid making friends with the animals that they are watching. Likewise, if you are interested in why automobile drivers have traffic accidents, you can't simply get in people's cars and start taking notes. As a stranger, your presence would likely change the drivers' behaviors. When possible, the observer effect can be minimized by concealing the observer. Another solution is to use hidden recorders. One naturalistic study of traffic accidents was done with video cameras installed in 100 cars (Dingus et al., 2006). It turns out that most accidents are caused by failing to look at the traffic in front of the car (keep your eyes forward!).

Observer bias is a related problem in which observers see what they expect to see or record only selected details (Gravetter & Forzano, 2016). Observer bias is a special case of confirmation bias, which was discussed earlier in this chapter. A good example of observer bias comes from a classic study in which teachers were told to watch a videotape of a boy. In this experiment, the teachers were randomly assigned to one of four groups and each group was given different information about the boy (he was labeled as either learning disabled, mentally challenged, emotionally disturbed, or "normal"). Though every teacher watched a video of the same boy, and in spite of the fact that the boy was completely "normal," the teachers in each group still gave widely different ratings of his

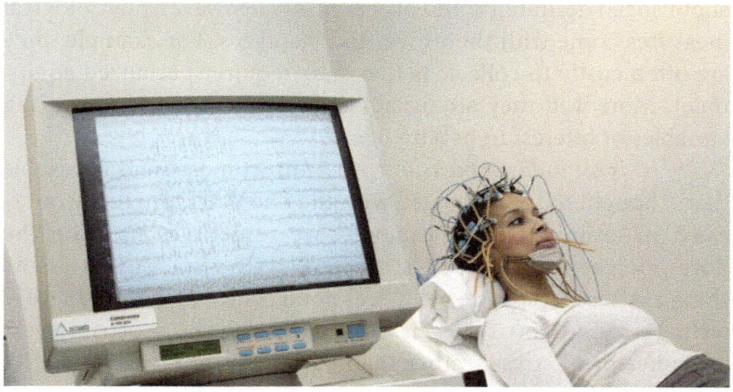

AJPhoto/Science Source

The scientific study of dreaming was made possible by use of the EEG, a device that records the tiny electrical signals generated by the brain as a person sleeps. The EEG converts these electrical signals to a written record of brain activity. Certain shifts in brain activity, coupled with the presence of rapid eye movements, are strongly related to dreaming.

behavior that reflected the label they had associated with him (Foster & Ysseldyke, 1976).

Physiological Data

More recently, psychological researchers have also begun to use physiological measures of psychological states. **Physiological data** are typically quantitative and can be gathered using tools that map brain activity (such as EEG or fMRI; ■ see Section 2.2), the functioning of the heart, the tension in our muscles, and the dilation of our pupils. Some studies also gather information about the levels of hormones such as *cortisol* (to assess stress), *testosterone* (as a measure of aggression), and *oxytocin* (an indicator of affiliation). One of the reasons that physiological data have become so popular in psychological research is that they reduce concerns

Sample Subset of a population being studied.

Representative sample A small, randomly selected part of a larger population that accurately reflects characteristics of the whole population.

Biased sample A subpart of a larger population that does not accurately reflect characteristics of the whole population.

Social desirability Deliberate tendency to provide polite, socially acceptable responses.

Observational data Data that come from watching participants and recording their behavior.

Naturalistic observation Observing behavior as it unfolds in natural settings.

Structured observation Observing behavior in situations that have been set up by the researcher.

Observer effect Changes in an organism's behavior brought about by an awareness of being observed.

Observer bias The tendency of an observer to distort observations or perceptions to match his or her expectations.

Physiological data Data that come from participants' physiological processes (including measures of the brain and heart, muscles, and the production of hormones).

about social desirability and observer bias. However, physiological measures come with their own disadvantages. For example, they are often costly to collect, as they may require specialized equipment. Moreover, they are usually *indirect* methods of measuring variables of interest to psychologists.

What is an indirect measure? An indirect measure is a variable that's thought to be associated with the one that we're really interested in examining. For example, we sometimes measure the hormone cortisol to assess stress levels. Cortisol isn't the same thing as stress, of course, but there's good evidence that when we're feeling stressed, cortisol levels will also rise. Because cortisol is just an indicator of stress (rather than equivalent to stress itself), it's considered an indirect measure.

In closing, valid psychological theories are built upon critical thinking and data gathered using the scientific method, not superstitions, pseudoscience, fads, opinions, or wishful thinking. But just because psychological scientists agree on the scientific method doesn't mean that they all do research in exactly the same way. In fact, there are a few different methods that researchers can use to address their hypotheses. For the most part, these methods can be broadly classified as being either *experimental* or *nonexperimental.* In the next two sections, we'll take a closer look at each one.

Reflective Practice

The Core Features of Psychological Science

1. A psychologist does a study to see whether exercising increases a sense of well-being. In the study, she will be testing a(n)
   a. theoretical statement
   b. hypothesis
   c. empirical definition
   d. unfalsifiable theory
2. For the survey method to be valid, a representative sample of people must be polled. T or F?
3. Critical thinking involves asking whether a belief can be supported by scientific theory and observation. T or F?

THINK CRITICALLY

4. A psychologist conducting a survey at a shopping mall (The Gallery of Wretched Excess) flips a coin before stopping passersby. If the coin shows heads, he interviews the person; if it shows tails, he skips that person. Evaluate whether the psychologist has obtained a random sample, providing evidence for your answer.

SELF-REFLECT

- Follow the steps of the scientific method to propose a testable hypothesis and decide how you would gather evidence. (But don't worry—you don't have to publish your results.)
- Google "Critter cam" and find one that you can watch. What species did you watch? What behaviors might you observe and record?

Answers: 1. B 2. T 3. T 4. The psychologist's coin flips *might* produce a reasonably good sample of people *at the mall*. The problem is that people who go to the mall may be mostly from one part of town, from upper-income groups, or from some other nonrepresentative group. The psychologist's sample is likely to be seriously flawed.

1.6 Experimental Research: Where Cause Meets Effect

GATEWAYS LEARNING OUTCOMES:
After reading this section you should be able to:

1.6.1 Differentiate between independent, dependent, and extraneous variables in an experiment

1.6.2 Explain how experiments allow psychological scientists to make statements about cause and effect

1.6.3 Outline how psychological scientists evaluate the results of an experiment

1.6.4 Describe two problems associated with experiments, and how they can be controlled

While different research strategies may be used to investigate human behavior, most of them are aimed at investigating relationships between two or more variables. A **variable** is any factor or characteristic that can change (or vary) across people, situations, and/or time. Examples of variables include human characteristics such as biological sex, age, ethnicity, or marital status, as well as more "psychological" variables such as motivation, extraversion, psychopathy, intelligence, and memory. Still other variables are linked to our behavior; for example, drug use, eating behavior, and exercise. Researchers will do one of two things with the variables they study: They will either *manipulate* them, or they will *measure* them—we'll come back to this idea a number of times as we introduce you to experimental research, and again in Section 1.7 when we discuss nonexperimental research.

One method of doing research is particularly useful in terms of allowing us to make claims about whether one variable can *cause* change in another. If our goal is to clarify whether there is a cause-and-effect relationship between variables, then we must usually conduct an **experiment** (Stangor, 2015). Because of their ability to allow for causal claims, experiments are generally accepted as the most powerful scientific research tool. As an example, let's say that we're interested in discovering whether smartphone use while driving *causes* people to engage in more unsafe driving behaviors. The two variables that we're studying in this experiment are smartphone use and unsafe driving behaviors.

Experimental Variables

When we carry out an experiment, the variables we're interested in studying are classified as being one of three types:

1. An **independent variable** is the suspected *cause* for differences in behavior. In the case of our study, the independent variable is smartphone use. The independent variable is *manipulated* by the researcher, which means that the researcher chooses the values that this variable takes (more on this in a moment!).

2. A **dependent variable** is a variable that measures any effect of manipulating the independent variable. In our study, the dependent variable is unsafe driving behaviors. The term "dependent" is appropriate, because this variable is thought to *depend* on the independent variable—that is, dependent variables reveal the *effects* that independent variables have on behavior. As such, researchers *measure* the dependent variable to examine whether it has been affected by manipulations to the independent variable.
3. An **extraneous variable** is a condition or factor that a researcher wants to prevent from affecting the outcome of the experiment. They are variables that, like the independent variable (smartphone use), are believed to influence the dependent variable (unsafe driving behavior). In our study, extraneous variables might include the weather on the days that the drivers are tested, the time of day, lighting conditions, and so forth. How can we make sure they don't affect the outcome of our study? Usually, it is done by making all conditions (except the independent variable) *exactly* alike for everyone who takes part in our study. Put another way, we try to *control* extraneous variables, and we *measure* them to ensure that they have not affected the dependent variable.

Experimental Groups and Random Assignment

Psychology experiments are fundamentally about comparing groups of people. The simplest psychological experiment is based on two groups of **experimental subjects**—animals or people whose behavior is investigated (human subjects are typically called **participants**). The **experimental group** is the group that receives the treatment that the study is designed to test (in the preceding example, this would be the group that used a smartphone). The **control group** includes the subjects who do not receive the treatment being investigated (in the preceding example, this would be the group that didn't use a smartphone).

Remember how we said that the independent variable is manipulated by the researcher, who chooses the values that this variable takes? You can see that each of the groups in this study is exposed to a different "level" or "condition" of the independent variable (smartphone use in the preceding example). In this example, then, the independent variable has just two levels, or conditions: one is "using a smartphone" and the other is "not using a smartphone." The researcher manipulates which participants are exposed to the condition "using a smartphone" and which are exposed to the condition "not using a smartphone." Other than the independent variable whose levels that are intentionally manipulated by the researcher, the experimental group and the control group are treated exactly alike. The researcher does not manipulate the dependent measure—it's simply measured for each person in the control and experimental groups, and then a mean (or average) score is calculated for each group. Ultimately, then, we want to compare the average scores on the dependent variable for the experimental and control groups to see whether they differ as a result of having been exposed to the two levels of the independent variable.

Kritsada Namborisut/Shutterstock.com

Do you talk or text on your smartphone while driving?

To perform an experiment, then, you would do the following:

1. Create two or more groups of participants. These groups should be alike in all ways *except* for the independent variable. In our study, that would mean that one group would be assigned to use a smartphone during the driving task (the experimental group) and the other group would be told to not use a smartphone during the driving test (the control group).
2. Ensure that all other variables that could affect the dependent variable (extraneous variables) are controlled. Examples of extraneous variables are the number of hours slept the night before the test, driving experience, and familiarity with the vehicle used in the experiment.
3. Measure the dependent variable (unsafe driving behaviors) for everyone in the study. In our study, unsafe driving will be operationally defined by the number of unsafe behaviors displayed on a test of driving ability.
4. Compare the two groups on the dependent variable that you have measured to see if there is a difference between them.

Variable Factor or characteristic manipulated or measured in research.

Experiment A study in which the investigator manipulates at least one variable while measuring at least one other variable.

Independent variable Variable manipulated by the researcher in an experiment.

Dependent variable The element of an experiment that measures any effect of the manipulation.

Extraneous variable A condition or factor that may change and is excluded from influencing the outcome of an experiment.

Experimental subjects Humans (also referred to as *participants*) or animals whose behavior is investigated in an experiment.

Participants Humans whose behavior is investigated in an experiment.

Experimental group Group that receives the treatment the study is designed to test.

Control group Subjects in an experimental study who do not receive the treatment being investigated.

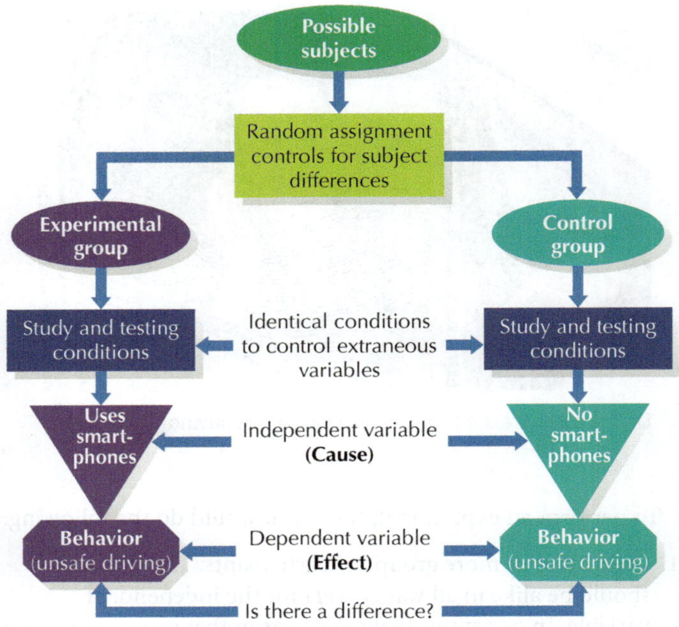

Figure 1.5 A simple experiment. Elements of a simple psychological experiment to assess the effects of using smartphones while driving on unsafe driving behaviors.

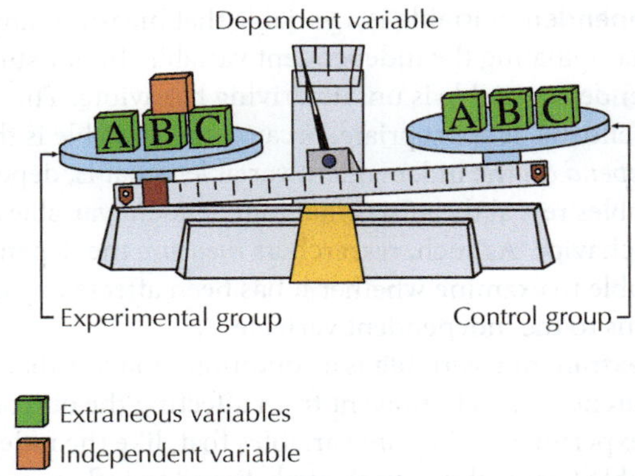

Figure 1.6 Controlling extraneous variables. Experimental control is achieved by balancing extraneous variables for the experimental group and the control group. For example, both groups could be formed so that the average age (A), education (B), and intelligence (C) of group members are the same. Then the independent variable can be applied to the experimental group. If their behavior (the dependent variable) changes (in comparison with the control group), the independent variable must be causing the change.

The experiment that we describe here has actually been carried out by a team of researchers. Psychologist David Strayer and his colleagues have confirmed that almost all drivers talking on cellphones drive no better than people who are legally drunk, and texters perform even worse (Drews et al., 2009; Strayer, Drews, & Crouch, 2006; Watson & Strayer, 2010).

Is a control group really needed? Can't people just drive a car while navigating using a smartphone to see if they are less safe? Less safe than what? The control group provides a *point of reference* for comparison with the scores in the experimental group. Without a control group, it would be impossible to tell whether using smartphones had any effect on driving safety. If the number of unsafe behaviors shown by the experimental group is greater than that of the control group, we can conclude that using smartphones (the independent variable) causes people to drive less safely (dependent variable). If there is no difference, it's clear that the independent variable had no effect on driving safety.

Ok, but how do we know that the people in one group aren't just worse drivers than those in the other group before the experiment started? It's true that personal differences in driving ability might affect the experiment. However, an extraneous variable like this one can be controlled by *randomly* assigning people to groups. In our driving experiment, this could be done by simply flipping a coin for each participant: heads, and the participant is in the experimental group; tails, it's the control group.

Random assignment is the use of chance to place subjects in experimental and control groups. In practice, this means that a participant has an equal chance of being in either the experimental group or the control group. *Random assignment is the defining feature of a true experiment, and it's essential to our ability to make cause-and-effect claims about the variables we're studying.* Why? Because random assignment balances out personal differences in the two groups, helping us to control the extraneous variables. In our study, for example, random assignment would help to ensure that there are few (if any) differences in the number of people in each group who are better (or worse) drivers, women or men, comfortable navigating with a global positioning system (GPS) or not, hungry, or any other extraneous variable that might influence the dependent variable. When all of the extraneous variables are controlled and the only difference between the groups is the independent variable (using a smartphone or not), then any decline in driving safety *must* be caused by using the smartphone, and it becomes possible to make a causal claim about the relationship between those two variables (Figures 1.5 and 1.6).

Evaluating Experimental Results

If the experimental group using the smartphones performed more unsafe driving behaviors than the control group, then we can conclude that the independent variable really made a difference, right? Almost—but one last issue remains. Suppose the smartphone users demonstrated 30 unsafe driving behaviors on the test and the control group that was not using the smartphones demonstrated only 15. Such a big difference almost certainly means that the smartphone users were driving in a less safe manner. But suppose that the difference was 30 unsafe behaviors versus 29? In other words, how big a difference do we have to find before we can conclude that the driving test scores are meaningfully different?

Fortunately, this question can be handled statistically. Reports in psychology journals almost always include a statement like this one: "Results were **statistically significant**." This means that the obtained results would occur rarely by chance alone. To be statistically significant, a difference must be large enough that it would occur by chance in fewer than 5 out of 100 experiments. Of course, you may remember from the last step of the scientific method that findings also become more convincing when they can be *replicated* (repeated) by other researchers. (See the Statistical Literacy Appendix for more information on inferential statistics.)

As you might guess, numerous studies are done on important topics in psychology. Although each study adds to our understanding, the results of various studies don't always agree. Let's say that we are interested in whether males or females tend to be greater risk takers. A computer search would reveal that many studies have investigated various types of risk taking (for example, smoking, fast driving, or unprotected sex).

Is there a way to combine the results of the studies? Yes! A statistical technique called **meta-analysis** can be used to combine the results of many studies as if they were all part of one big study (Cooper, 2010). In other words, a meta-analysis is a study of the results of other studies. In recent years, meta-analyses have been used to summarize and synthesize mountains of psychological research. This allows us to see the big picture and draw conclusions that might be missed in a single, small-scale study.

Potential Problems with Experiments

Suppose that a researcher hypothesizes that the drug amphetamine (a stimulant) improves learning. She explains her hypothesis to all of her participants and gives the experimental group participants an amphetamine pill before they begin studying. People in the control group get nothing. Later, she assesses how much each participant learned. Does this experiment seem valid? Well, it isn't.

Why not? The experimental group took the drug and the control group didn't. Differences in the amount they learned must have been caused by the drug, right? Actually, this study has two significant problems that would compromise our ability to make any kind of claim about the relationship between amphetamines (the independent variable) and learning (the dependent variable). One is research participant bias, the other is researcher bias.

Research Participant Bias

If you look carefully at the description of the study, you'll see that the amphetamine might not be the only difference between the groups. First, because of what they were told about the hypothesis, participants in the experimental group likely *expected* to learn more (as compared to the control group). Any observed differences between groups, then, might reflect *differences in expectations between the groups* and not the actual effect of the drug. In a well-designed experiment, you must be careful what you tell participants. Small bits of information might create **research participant bias**—changes in participants' behavior caused by the influence of their expectations.

Second, notice also that experimental group participants swallowed a pill, and control participants did not. Even if the participants were not told about the hypothesis, it could be that those who swallowed a pill unconsciously *expected* to do better. After all, pills are medicine, aren't they? This alone might have created a **placebo effect**—a change in experience or behavior due to a participant's expectation that a drug or treatment will do something.

Placebo effects create a significant challenge for researchers. We know that if a **placebo** (plah-SEE-bo; an inactive substance or treatment that looks the same as the real, active substance or treatment) has any effect, it must be based on suggestion, not chemistry (White & McBurney, 2013). Even so, placebo effects can be quite powerful and usually account for at least one-third of the apparent effectiveness of the official treatment. For instance, a placebo saline injection is 70 percent as effective as morphine in reducing pain. That's why doctors sometimes prescribe placebos—especially for complaints that seem to have no physical basis. Placebos have been shown to affect pain, anxiety, depression, alertness, tension, sexual arousal, cravings for alcohol, and many other processes (Justman, 2011; Wampold et al., 2005).

How could an inert substance have any effect? Placebos alter our expectations, both conscious and unconscious, about our own emotional and physical reactions (Vance, 2016). Because we associate taking medicine with feeling better, we expect placebos to make us feel better, too (Benedetti, 2009; Czerniak & Davidson, 2012). After a person takes a placebo, brain activity linked with pain is reduced, so the effect is not imaginary (Wager et al., 2004).

Controlling Research Participant Bias

To manage research participant bias, you need to begin by ensuring that participants do not know whether they are in the experimental or the control group, and they are unaware of the hypothesis that's being tested in the study. Addressing the placebo effect is more challenging. To control for a placebo effect, the researcher would do better to give the experimental group an amphetamine pill and the control group a placebo.

Using these two strategies together yields a **single-blind study**, in which everyone gets a treatment that looks the same; that is, all participants are given the same instructions, and everyone gets a pill or injection. The only difference is the independent variable—people in the experimental group get the real drug, and those in the control group get a placebo. Participants will be "blind" to the condition they're in (that is, whether they are receiving a real drug or a placebo). If all participants are blind as to the hypothesis under investigation and whether or not they received the drug, their expectations (conscious *and* unconscious) tend to be similar. Any difference in their behavior is likely to be caused by the drug itself.

It's worth noting that even a single blind arrangement is not enough to protect the validity of experimental results, because researchers themselves sometimes unwittingly affect experiments by influencing participants. Let's see how this occurs.

Researcher Bias

Even if a researcher uses a single-blind procedure to avoid deliberately biasing participants, **researcher bias**—changes in behavior caused by the unintended influence of a researcher—remains a

Random assignment Use of chance to place subjects in experimental and control groups.

Statistically significant Experimental results that would rarely occur by chance alone.

Meta-analysis A statistical technique for combining the results of many studies on the same subject.

Research participant bias Changes in the behavior of study participants caused by the unintended influence of their own expectations.

Placebo effect Changes in behavior due to participants' expectations that a drug (or other treatment) will have some effect.

Placebo Inactive substance or treatment that is distinguishable from a real, active substance or treatment.

Single-blind study Research in which the subjects do not know which treatment they receive.

sebra/Shutterstock.com

The placebo effect is a major factor in medical treatments. Would you also expect the placebo effect to occur in psychotherapy as well? It does, which complicates studies on the effectiveness of new psychotherapies, but likely also enhances the effectiveness of psychotherapy (Justman, 2011).

problem. Experimenters run the risk of finding what they expect to find; this is a form of confirmation bias.

Researcher bias even applies outside the laboratory. Psychologist Robert Rosenthal (1973) reported a classic example of how expectations influence people: At the U.S. Air Force Academy Preparatory School, 100 student pilots were randomly assigned to five different math classes. Their teachers did not know about this random placement. Instead, each teacher was told that his or her students either had unusually high or low ability. Students in the classes labeled as "high ability" improved much more in math scores than those in "low-ability" classes. Yet, the initial randomization made it likely that the average ability of all the classes was roughly equal. Why, then, would we see differences in how much the students in those classes improved?

Although the teachers were not conscious of any bias, apparently they subtly communicated their expectations to students. Most likely, they did this through their tone of voice, body language, and encouragement or criticism. Their hints, in turn, created a self-fulfilling prophecy that affected the students. A **self-fulfilling prophecy** is a prediction that prompts people to act in ways that make the prediction come true. For instance, many teachers underestimate the abilities of ethnic minority children, which hurts the students' chances for success (Jussim & Harber, 2005). In short, people sometimes become what we predict for them. It is wise to remember that others tend to live *up* or *down* to our expectations of them (Madon et al., 2011).

Controlling Researcher Bias

Because of research participant bias and researcher bias, it is common to keep both participants *and* researchers blind to the treatment conditions. In a **double-blind study**, research is conducted so that neither the researcher nor the subjects know which subjects received which treatment. This not only controls for research participant bias, but it also keeps researchers from unconsciously influencing participants.

How can the researchers be blind—it's their experiment, isn't it? The researchers who designed the experiment, including preparing the pills or injections, typically hire research assistants to collect data from the participants. The research assistants are blind in that they do not know which pill or injection is a drug or placebo, or whether any particular participant is in the experimental or control group.

Double-blind testing has shown that at least 50 percent of the effectiveness of antidepressant drugs, such as the antidepressant drug Prozac, is due to the placebo effect (Kirsch & Sapirstein, 1998; Rihmer et al., 2012). Much of the popularity of herbal health remedies is also based on the placebo effect (Seidman, 2001).

Reflective Practice

Experimental Research: Where Cause Meets Effect

1. To understand cause and effect, a simple psychological experiment is based on creating two groups: the ________ group and the ________ group.
2. Three types of variables must be considered in an experiment: ________ variables (which are manipulated by the experimenter); ________ variables (which measure the outcome of the experiment); and ________ variables (factors to be excluded in a particular experiment).
3. A researcher performs an experiment to learn whether room temperature affects the amount of aggression displayed by college students under crowded conditions in a simulated prison environment. In this experiment, the independent variable is which of the following?
   a. room temperature
   b. the amount of aggression
   c. crowding
   d. the simulated prison environment
4. A procedure used to control both research participant bias and researcher bias in psychological experiments is the
   a. single-blind study
   b. controlled experiment
   c. double-blind study
   d. random assignment of participants

THINK CRITICALLY

5. Evaluate the loophole in the following statement: "I've been taking vitamin C tablets, and I haven't had a cold all year. Vitamin C is great!"

SELF-REFLECT

- We all conduct little experiments to detect cause-and-effect connections. If you enjoy music, for example, you might try listening with different types of headphones. One question might be, "Does the use of earbuds versus sound-cancelling headphones [the independent variable] affect the enjoyment of music [the dependent variable]?"

Answers: 1. experimental, control 2. independent, dependent, extraneous 3. a 4. c 5. The statement implies that vitamin C prevented colds. However, not getting a cold could be a coincidence. A controlled experiment with a group given vitamin C and a control group not taking vitamin C is needed to learn whether vitamin C has any effect on susceptibility to colds.

1.7 Nonexperimental Research: Losing (a Bit of) Control

GATEWAYS LEARNING OUTCOMES:
After reading this section you should be able to:

1.7.1 Differentiate between quasi-experiments and true experiments

1.7.2 Explain what is meant by correlational research, and how the degree of association between two variables is assessed in correlational research

1.7.3 Describe the conditions under which case studies are useful

At the beginning of Section 1.6, we noted that many psychological studies are aimed at investigating relationships between two or more variables, and that those variables will either be manipulated or simply measured by researchers. In an experimental study, we study the relationship between the independent and dependent variables. We do this by randomly assigning people to experience different levels of the independent variable in the control and experimental groups (that is, the independent variable is *manipulated*), and we *measure* the effect of manipulating the independent variable on the dependent variable. If the dependent variable differs for the two groups, then we know that the independent variable affects the dependent variable (that is, there is a relationship between them).

Sometimes, though, psychologists want to look at differences between groups even though they aren't able to randomly assign people to those groups (that is, they cannot manipulate the independent variable). At other times they may not be interested in differences between groups but instead want to simply measure variables as they naturally occur and then look at the general relationship between those variables (for example, the relationship between the size of a person's social network and depression). In these instances, psychologists gather evidence and test hypotheses using nonexperimental methods (Jackson, 2016). Here, we'll talk about three types of nonexperimental research: quasi-experiments, correlational research, and case studies.

Quasi-Experiments

We saw earlier that when we conduct an experiment, we need to expose the experimental and control groups to different "levels," or conditions, of the independent variable. We also found out that in a true experiment the participants are *randomly assigned* to a group, and that this random assignment is really important because it helps to ensure that there are unlikely to be differences between the groups at the outset (that is, it controls for extraneous variables). In fact, *random assignment is the defining feature of a true experiment.*

Sometimes, though, it is not possible to randomly assign people to the control and experimental groups. Imagine, for example, that we're interested in finding out whether exposure to a natural disaster is related to symptoms of post-traumatic stress disorder (PTSD). In this case, the independent variable would be whether or not someone is exposed to a natural disaster, and the dependent variable would be the presence of PTSD symptoms. You can probably see where this example is going: You would never, ever convince an Ethics Review Board to allow you to run a study in which you randomly assigned people to a group that was going to experience an earthquake or a tsunami, just so that you could determine whether it caused them to show signs of PTSD (even if you did happen to know how to bring such a natural disaster about).

Here's another example: If you were interested in finding out whether getting older causes people to become more conservative in their political beliefs, the independent variable would be age (older or younger), and the dependent variable would be a measure of political beliefs. Try randomly assigning people to be either "old" or "young" in your experiment—there's simply no messing around with people's age (much as some people try!). The same is true for any study in which the independent variable is sex, ethnicity, religion, or any other characteristic that is inherently part of who we are—you can't randomly assign people to different levels of these variables.

When random assignment to the experimental and control groups is not possible—either because it would be unethical or because it's impossible—then we aren't carrying out a true experiment, and consequently *we cannot make cause-and-effect statements about the relationship between the independent and dependent variables.* We can still compare the groups on the dependent variable, but we can't be totally sure that they were equivalent at the outset. As a result, these studies are called **quasi-experimental studies**.

Correlational Research

The term **correlational research** refers to any study that quantifies the degree to which two (or more) variables are associated. In these studies, we are not manipulating any variables or comparing groups of participants; instead, we are simply measuring variables as they naturally occur and then looking at whether those variables seem to be associated, or correlated, with one another.

Researcher bias Changes in participants' behavior caused by the unintended influence of a researcher's actions.

Self-fulfilling prophecy A prediction that prompts people to act in ways that make the prediction come true.

Double-blind study Research in which neither the observer nor the subjects know which subjects received which treatment.

Quasi-experimental study A descriptive study in which researchers wish to compare groups of people, but cannot randomly assign them to groups.

Correlational research Descriptive study that quantifies the degree to which events, measures, or variables are associated.

Let's say that a psychologist notes an association between the IQs of parents and their children, between beauty and social popularity, or between anxiety and test performance. A **correlation** exists when two variables are linked together in an orderly way (■ see the Statistics Appendix). While an experimental study allows us to test cause-and-effect relationships between variables, a correlational study is focused more on making *predictions* about one variable using what we know about another variable.

For example, John Simister and Cary Cooper (2005) decided to find out if there is a correlation between the weather and crime. They obtained data on temperatures and criminal activity in Los Angeles over a four-year period. When they graphed air temperature and the frequency of aggravated assaults, a clear relationship emerged. Assaults and temperatures rise and fall more or less in parallel. Knowing the temperature in Los Angeles now allows us to predict whether the number of aggravated assaults will increase.

Correlational research is at the heart of most "big data" that are gathered by companies, especially on the web, because it allows us to make predictions about people's thinking and behavior. For example, when Netflix and Amazon make recommendations about movies you might want to watch or books that you might want to buy, those predictions are based on correlations that they have observed in their customer base in the past. If their correlational data suggest that buying Agatha Christie novels is correlated with buying books by Stephen King, for example, then you may find yourself faced with automatic "You Might Like . . ." suggestions that include Christie's *Murder on the Orient Express* after purchasing *It* by Stephen King.

Understanding Associations Using Correlation Coefficients

When we examine the correlation between two variables, we're generally interested in two things: its *strength* and its *direction*. The strength and direction of a relationship can be seen in a scatterplot, but they can be expressed more simply as a **correlation coefficient**. The correlation coefficient can be calculated as a number falling somewhere between +1.00 and −1.00.

Strength of the Association

We learn about the strength of a relationship (that is, how well we can predict one variable if we know something about the other) by looking at the number in the correlation coefficient (ignoring the positive or negative sign). The bigger the number, the stronger the relationship and the better your ability to make predictions. What this means, then, is that a correlation of −.85 is actually stronger than a correlation of +.36—if you ignore the sign, you'll see that .85 is a bigger number than .36. Similarly, correlations of −.52 and +.52 are equally strong: Your ability to predict one variable from the other is the same in both cases.

Drawing graphs of relationships helps us to see the strength of the relationship (see ● Figure 1.7). If the number in the correlation coefficient is zero or close to zero, the association between two measures is weak or nonexistent (see ● Figure 1.7*c*). For example, the correlation between shoe size and intelligence is zero. (Sorry, size 12 readers.) With a zero correlation, points are scattered randomly on the graph and look like a circle; predicting one variable from the other is impossible.

As the number increases the relationship becomes stronger, and it becomes easier to predict one variable if you know the value of the other. Correlations of +1.00 or −1.00 are considered "perfect" in the sense that if you know the value of one variable, you will be able to predict the other with perfect accuracy. Perfect relationships are represented by a straight line on the graph (see ● Figures 1.7*a* and 1.7*e*). (■ For more detail about calculating and graphing correlations, see the Statistical Literacy Appendix.)

In reality, perfect relationships between variables are very, very rare. For example, the correlation between the IQs of parents and children is just .35; between identical twins it's .86. This means that if you have a pair of identical twin boys and you know the IQ of only one of them, you'll be much more accurate in predicting

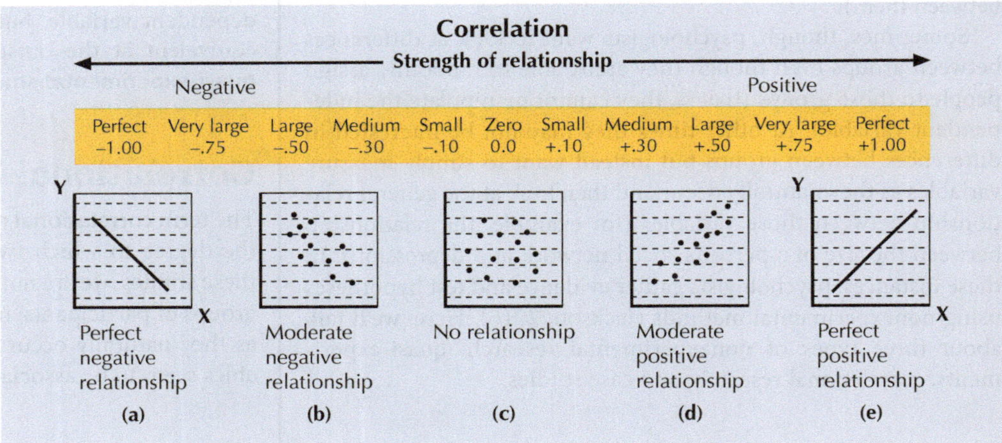

● **Figure 1.7 Correlation coefficients.** The correlation coefficient tells how strongly two measures are related. These graphs show a range of relationships between two measures, X and Y. If a correlation is negative (a), increases in one measure are associated with decreases in the other. (As Y gets larger, X gets smaller.) In a positive correlation (e), increases in one measure are associated with increases in the other. (As Y gets larger, X gets larger.) The center-left graph (b; a moderate negative relationship) might result from comparing time spent playing computer games (Y) with grades (X): More time spent playing computer games is associated with lower grades. The center graph (c; no relationship) would result from plotting a person's shoe size (Y) and his or her IQ (X). The center-right graph (d; a moderate positive relationship) could be a plot of grades in high school (Y) and grades in college (X) for a group of students: Higher grades in high school are associated with higher grades in college.

his twin brother's IQ than you will his mother's or father's IQ. (Correlations between the IQs of family members are used to estimate the degree to which intelligence is affected by heredity and environment; see Section 9.4).

Direction of the Association

The direction of a correlation is represented by its sign (+ or −). In a *positive correlation*, higher scores on one measure are matched by higher scores on the other. For example, a positive correlation exists between high school grades and college grades; students who do well in high school tend to do well in college (and vice versa; see Figure 1.7*d*). In a *negative correlation*, higher scores on one measure are associated with lower scores on the other. We might observe, for instance, a negative correlation between the number of hours that students play computer games and their grades—that is, more play is associated with lower grades. (This is the well-known "computer game–zombie" effect; see Figure 1.7*b*.)

Wouldn't that show that playing computer games too much causes lower grades? It might seem so, but as we noted previously, the best way to be confident that a cause-and-effect relationship exists is to perform a controlled experiment. It's entirely possible that the reverse interpretation is true here: people who do poorly at school are drawn to other activities besides schoolwork, causing them to seek out computer games. That's an important point, so let's explore it further.

Correlation and Causation

Correlational studies help us discover relationships and make predictions. However, correlation *does not* demonstrate **causation** (a cause–effect relationship) (Ruggiero, 2015). For instance, it could be that students who aren't interested in their classes have more time for computer games. If so, then their lack of study and lower grades is the result of lack of interest rather than excessive game playing (which would be another result of lack of interest in classes). Just because one thing *appears* to be related directly to another does not mean that a cause-and-effect connection exists.

Here is another example of mistaking correlation for causation: What if a psychologist discovers a correlation between parents who smoke cigarettes and juvenile delinquency in their children? Does this show that parental smoking *causes* juvenile delinquency? Perhaps, but maybe it's that juvenile delinquents drive their parents to take up smoking in an effort to handle the stress of dealing with them! Alternatively, maybe both parental smoking and juvenile delinquency are related to some *third variable*, such as socioeconomic status (SES). Poorer parents are more likely to be smokers, and poorer juveniles are more likely to become delinquents (see Figure 1.8).

To reiterate, just because one thing *appears* to cause another does not *confirm* that it does. It's always possible that the causal relationship is the reverse of what you suspect, or that a third variable is responsible for the relationship. The best way to be confident that a cause-and-effect relationship exists is to perform a controlled experiment.

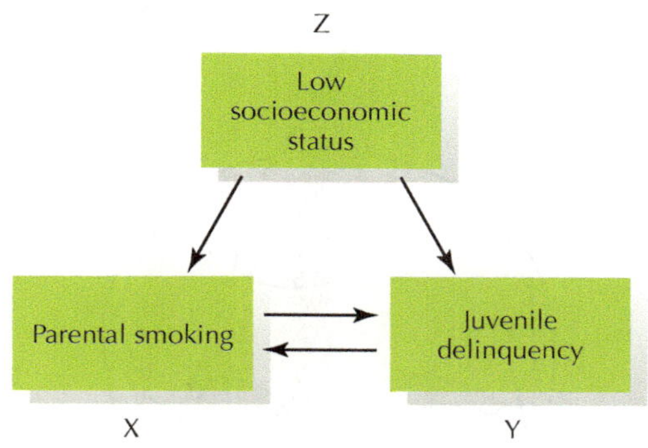

Figure 1.8 Correlation and causality. A correlation between two variables might mean that X causes Y, that Y causes X or that some other, third, variable, Z causes *both* X and Y.

Case Studies

It may be impractical, unethical, or impossible to use the experimental method to study rare events, such as unusual mental disorders, childhood geniuses, or rampage school shootings (Harding, Fox, & Mehta, 2002). In such instances, a **case study (clinical method)**—an in-depth analysis of the behavior of one person or a small number of people—may be the best source of information. (Because clinical psychologists rely heavily on case studies, this is also referred to as the *clinical method*.) Since case studies lack formal control groups, the conclusions that can be drawn are limited. Nevertheless, case studies can provide special opportunities to answer interesting questions about rare events.

Case studies have been especially useful for investigating mental disorders, such as depression or psychosis (Wedding & Corsini, 2014). For instance, a classic case study in psychology concerns the Genain sisters, identical quadruplets. In addition to having identical genes, all four women developed schizophrenia before age 24 (Duncan, 2013). The chances of identical quadruplets all *accidentally* developing schizophrenia are about 1 in 1.5 billion. The Genains, who have been studied for more than 55 years, were in and out of psychiatric hospitals most of their lives. The fact that they share identical genes suggests that heredity influences disorders such as schizophrenia. The fact that some of the sisters are

Correlation The existence of a consistent, systematic relationship between two events, measures, or variables.

Correlation coefficient A statistical index ranging from −1.00 to +1.00 that indicates the direction and degree of correlation.

Causation The act of causing some effect.

Case study (clinical method) In-depth analysis of the behavior of one person or a small number of people.

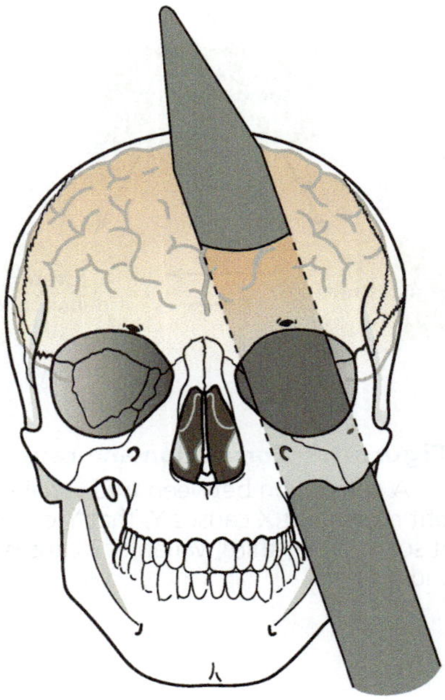

● **Figure 1.9 The case of Phineas Gage.** Some of the earliest information on the effects of damage to frontal areas of the brain came from a case study of the accidental injury of Phineas Gage (illustrated here).

more disturbed than others suggests that environmental conditions also affect mental illness. Myra, the least ill of the four, was the only sister who was able to avoid her father, an alcoholic who terrorized, spied on, and sexually molested the girls. Thus, cases like theirs provide insights that can't be obtained by any other means (Mirsky et al., 2000). (■ See Section 14.2 for more information about the causes of schizophrenia.)

Case studies may also be used to study unusual accidents or other natural events. Gunshot wounds, brain tumors, accidental poisonings, and similar disasters have provided much information about the human brain. One remarkable case was reported by Dr. J. M. Harlow (1868). Phineas Gage, a young foreman on a work crew, had a 13-pound steel rod driven into the front of his brain by a dynamite explosion (● Figure 1.9). Amazingly, he survived the accident. Within two months, Gage could walk, talk, and move normally, but the injury forever changed his personality. Instead of the honest and dependable worker he had been before, Gage became a surly, foul-mouthed liar. Dr. Harlow carefully recorded the details of what was, perhaps, the first in-depth case study of an accidental frontal lobotomy (the destruction of front brain matter).

▲ Table 1.6 summarizes the key research methods that we have covered in this chapter.

A Look Ahead

In this chapter, we've learned that science is a powerful way of asking questions about the world and getting unbiased, trustworthy answers. But in this book, we're not just interested in having you master information about psychology—we also want to help you start to think about developing your skill set. For that reason, each chapter includes a *Psychology and Your Skill Set* at the end of each chapter that connects the material you will read with information about related skills that can be helpful in your personal life, as well as in the world of work. Many of the skills that employers are interested in—teamwork, critical thinking, and communication, for example—are topics of great interest to people who do psychological research. To complete this chapter, then, let's take a look at how we can think more critically about information reported in the popular press and on social media. You should find this an interesting way to conclude our opening tour of psychology and its methods.

▲ Table 1.6 Comparison of Psychological Research Methods

	Advantages	Disadvantages
Experimental methods	Clear cause-and-effect relationships can be identified; powerful controlled observations can be staged; no need to wait for a natural event	May be somewhat artificial; some natural behavior not easily studied in the laboratory (field experiments may address these objections)
Quasi-experimental methods	Allows for comparison of groups based on naturally occurring variables that are of interest to psychologists but that cannot be manipulated (e.g., sex, exposure to trauma, adoption)	Little or no control is possible; cause-and-effect relationships cannot be confirmed
Correlational methods	Demonstrates the existence of relationships; allows prediction; can be used in a lab, clinic, or natural setting	Little or no control is possible; cause-and-effect relationships cannot be confirmed; relationships may be coincidental
Clinical methods	Allows investigation of rare or unusual problems or events	Little or no control is possible; does not provide a control group for comparison; subjective interpretation is often necessary; a single case may be misleading or unrepresentative

Reflective Practice

Nonexperimental Research: Losing (a Bit of) Control

1. Correlation typically demonstrates causation. T or F?
2. Which correlation coefficient represents the strongest relationship?
   a. −0.86 b. +0.66 c. +0.10 d. +0.09
3. A method that allows psychologists to look closely at rare events is called ______________________.
4. In a quasi-experiment we cannot make cause-and-effect statements because
   a. the dependent variable isn't known
   b. the independent variable isn't known
   c. there are too many extraneous variables
   d. we cannot randomly assign people to groups, and so we cannot be sure that the groups were equivalent at the outset.

THINK CRITICALLY

5. On a podcast, a guest discussed an "experiment" in which they demonstrated that Democrats and Republicans differ in terms of their comfort with feelings of threat. Evaluate whether this is really an experiment, explaining why or why not.

SELF-REFLECT

- See if you can identify at least one positive correlation and one negative correlation that involve human behavior.

Answers: 1. F 2. –.86 3. case study 4. d 5. It's not an experiment. It's a quasi-experiment because although they were interested in studying the differences between groups, the independent variable of interest (political party) isn't one that allows for random assignment.

1.8 Psychology and Your Skill Set: Information Literacy

GATEWAYS LEARNING OUTCOMES:
After reading this section you should be able to:

1.8.1 Name six ways that people can critically evaluate information found in the popular press and on social media

1.8.2 Create a plan to analyze and evaluate information that you are exposed to in the popular press and on social media

In this section we explore *information literacy*, or how to think critically about the information that we are exposed to every day. Some of that information may come from people that you talk to regularly (for example, your friends, or parents, or even your college professors). Much of it may also come from the popular media. But contemporary media—especially the Internet—functions as a giant echo chamber, awash with rumors, hoaxes, half-truths, false news, and urban legends like the one about giant alligators living in New York sewers (Hughes, 2008).

Unfortunately, a great deal of what you will encounter is based on entertainment value rather than critical thinking or science (Ruggiero, 2015). Let's face it: In this era of Internet bots and trolls, and when many people have easy access to software that can realistically alter images and video, you simply can't believe everything you read. Or hear. Or even see! What, for example, should you make of reports that people can learn to use the power of their minds to protect their feet while they walk on hot coals? Should you be impressed or skeptical? Here are some suggestions for thinking about the information that's presented in the media (Lawson, Jordan-Fleming, & Bodle, 2015).

Separating Fact from Fiction in the Media

Suggestion 1: Consider the source of information. The popular media provides an endless stream of information. The Internet, in particular, has transformed our ability to access information in very positive ways: Suddenly, you can find vast amounts of material simply by doing a Google search on your smartphone (but not while driving, right?). But it's becoming clear that there's also a downside to having such easy access. Good information is readily available, but so is unreliable information and provocative content that stirs people up. Nowhere is this more evident than on the various social media platforms (e.g., Facebook, Instagram, Twitter, Snapchat, YouTube) that people gravitate toward on a daily basis.

Lots of people are concerned about "fake news"—online content that is blatantly untrue. So-called "zombie stories" (stories that are repeatedly debunked but refuse to die) abound, and they seem to increase in number every year (as you'd expect from … well … zombies). And of course, people lie outright on the web all the time.

Truthfully, though, obviously fake news is not really the biggest problem we have when it comes to online information. One of the things that's much more challenging now is the ability to critically evaluate material that's biased or poorly informed, but not obviously so. To be very clear, it's not that people are dumb, or easily duped. Rather, website development has evolved to a point where it's sometimes really hard to figure out who or what the source of the website's information is—some websites that are definitely biased or ill-informed (and occasionally genuine purveyors of "fake news") look really slick, and totally trustworthy.

Determining the credibility of a web-based source can be tricky, but there are a few strategies that you can use (Caulfield, 2017). Your go-to strategy should be similar to that of professional fact checkers who work for organizations such as Snopes or Politifact. When these experts want to establish the credibility of an Internet source, their first move—ironically—is to *leave* the webpage they're checking out and search the web to see what other people are saying about the person or group that's behind that site. This strategy is referred to as *reading laterally* and is often helpful in establishing whether the site you're investigating is likely to be providing information that's biased in some particular way (McGrew, Ortega, Breakstone, & Wineburg, 2017).

Here's an example: In many states, politicians have periodically put forward the idea of raising the minimum wage. Such increases are usually pretty controversial. Credible sounding arguments against it (e.g., people will be laid off or fewer people will be hired because employers won't be able to afford the cost; the cost of everything will rise substantially) are often pitted against those in favor of it (it will give lower income people and students more money to spend, thus stimulating the economy).

In the United States, one website that has weighed in on the question of whether it's a good idea to raise the minimum wage is www.minimumwage.com. If you go to the website, you'll see that it's very professional looking and seems like a credible source of information. But try doing a little lateral reading: Type minimumwage.com into a search engine and then move past results that are from the page itself. Looking at other sources on the web, you'll find that the minimumwage.com website is maintained by an organization called the Employment Policies Institute (EPI). You'll also find that this organization is headed by someone who lobbies for the restaurant and hotel industry (and therefore likely has an interest in seeing the minimum wage stay low). Perhaps most important, lateral reading will reveal that a *New York Times* investigative reporter found no evidence that there *was* an EPI office.

Of course, this investigation doesn't mean that everything on the minimumwage.com website is false. Instead, what it reveals is that the information is likely to be biased in favor of a particular position. Knowing this should encourage you to think more critically about what you read on that site and search out information that speaks to the other side of the debate.

Suggestion 2: Beware of claims based on poor—or carefully selected—evidence, and don't overgeneralize. For conclusions to be trustworthy, they need to come from research that has been carefully designed. For example, researchers need to ask their questions in such a way that they will not get misleading or biased information from their participants. This means avoiding questions that are vague and unclear, as well as those that are likely to "lead" participants to one particular answer. Statements in the media that are supported by poor data are unlikely to stand the test of time, so it's important to look closely at the quality of the information on which any claim is based.

Of course, even good research can still be used to support claims that are totally misleading. Imagine a website reporting that a new form of therapy has been associated with reduced symptoms of autism in three high-quality research studies. That's quite exciting, right? Maybe not. What the website may have failed to report is that the beneficial effects of the therapy are short term, or that five other studies found that this new form of therapy doesn't seem to work at all. This type of "cherry-picking" is common in the popular media. People are quick to report findings that are in line with the story that they want others to believe but fail to note findings that are contradictory. You should always be looking for *disconfirming* evidence—even if it means seeking out information that conflicts with something you want to believe. Beware of confirmation bias!

Finally, it's important to distinguish between comments in the media that are based on evidence from a large number of people and those that come from one or two examples, anecdotes, or testimonials. The media is often keen to overgeneralize a finding that is based on one or two cases, suggesting that it should apply to everyone. Unfortunately, such *individual cases* (or even several) tell us nothing about what is true *in general* (Stanovich, 2013). For example, good research studies based on large groups of people show that smoking increases the likelihood of lung cancer. It is less relevant if you know a lifelong heavy smoker who is 95 years old. The general finding is the one to remember.

Suggestion 3: Always consider alternative explanations and remember that some things just happen by chance. If you see a person crying, is it correct to assume that she or he is sad? It seems reasonable to make this assumption, but it could easily be wrong. Maybe he or she just peeled some onions or is trying contact lenses for the first time.

Or consider how the Boston Red Sox won the World Series in 2004 after many members of the team began wearing a particular metal-impregnated twisted rope necklace designed to "stabilize the electricity flow through the body." Do you think that the necklaces provided the players with some sort of mystical batting and throwing abilities? While it might be tempting to think that those necklaces brought about something extraordinary, it's always important to stop and consider what else may have caused the events you've observed. The 2004 Red Sox team was a group of dedicated athletes. It's more likely that their success at the World Series was a function of their hard work and talent, and not their choice of jewelry.

But what about your good friend Beth, who tells you that she had a dream about someone that she hadn't seen for months, and then met that very same person at the mall the next day. Do you think that Beth has special powers? What alternative explanation could there possibly be? The truth is not likely to be nearly as exciting as finding out that your friend is psychic: Although such occurrences make for a good story, the reality is that events like meeting a friend at the mall after a long time happen by chance all the time.

Suggestion 4: Ask yourself if there was a control group. The key importance of a control group in any experiment is frequently overlooked by the unsophisticated—an error to which you are no longer susceptible! The popular media are full of reports of experiments performed without control groups: "Talking to Plants Speeds Growth"; "Special Diet Controls Hyperactivity in Children"; "Graduates of Firewalking Seminar Risk Their Soles."

Consider the last example. Expensive commercial courses have long been promoted to teach people to walk barefoot on hot coals. Firewalkers supposedly protect their feet with a technique called "neurolinguistic programming." Many people have paid good money to learn the technique, and most do manage a quick walk on the coals. But is the technique necessary? And is anything remarkable happening?

To really answer these questions, we need a comparison group that has not learned the technique to see if they, too, can walk on the coals. Fortunately, physicist Bernard Leikind has provided one. Leikind showed with volunteers that anyone (with reasonably callused feet) can walk over a bed of coals without being burned. This is because the coals, which are made of light, fluffy carbon, transmit little heat when touched. The principle involved is similar to briefly putting your hand in a hot oven without touching

Toru Yamanaka/AFP/Getty Images

Firewalking certainly looks dramatic, but looks can be deceiving.

any of its surfaces. If you touch a pan, you will be burned because metal transfers heat efficiently. But if your hand stays in the heated air, you'll be fine because air transmits little heat (Kida, 2006; Mitchell, 1987). Mystery solved!

Suggestion 5: Look for errors in distinguishing between correlation and causation. As you now know, it is dangerous to presume that one thing *caused* another just because they are correlated. In spite of this, you will see many claims based on questionable correlations. Here's an example of mistaking correlation for causation: Jeane Dixon, a well-known astrologer, once answered a group of prominent scientists—who had declared that there is no scientific foundation for astrology—by saying, "They would do well to check the records at their local police stations, where they will learn that the rate of violent crime rises and falls with lunar cycles." Dixon, of course, believed that the moon affects human behavior.

If it is true that violent crime is more frequent at certain times of the month, doesn't that prove her point? Far from it. Increased crime could be due to darker nights, the fact that we expect others to act crazier during a full moon, or any number of similar factors. Besides, direct studies of the alleged lunar effect have shown that it doesn't occur (Dowling, 2005). Moonstruck criminals, influenced by a bad moon rising, are the stuff of fiction (Iosif & Ballon, 2005).

Suggestion 6: Beware of oversimplifications, especially those motivated by monetary gain. You'll find as you read this textbook that most psychological behaviors and phenomena like emotional well-being, healthy relationships, and a good memory typically have multiple causes and often develop over many years. For this reason, you should immediately question any claims that suggest, for example, that the cause of aggression has been established. Clearly, people's aggressive behaviors occur for many reasons, including how their parents treated them, the coping strategies that they have learned, and possibly even how their brains are wired.

Likewise, websites that promise to reveal "the secret to unlimited joy, health, money, relationships, love, youth: everything you have ever wanted" should be immediately suspect. According to these sites, all you need to do is send your desires out to the universe and the universe must respond by granting your wishes. And all it will cost you is the price of ordering a video. (It's no secret that the promoters are the real winners in this game.)

Summary

We are all bombarded daily with such a mass of new information that it is difficult to absorb it all. The available knowledge in an area like psychology, biology, or medicine is so vast that no single person can completely know or comprehend it. With this reality in mind, it becomes increasingly important that you become a critical, selective, and informed consumer of information (Lilienfeld et al., 2010).

Reflective Practice

Psychology and Your Skill Set: Information Literacy

1. Popular media reports usually stress objective accuracy. T or F?
2. The finding that people can walk on hot coals after taking a "firewalking" course demonstrates that the course is necessary for people who want to learn this skill. T or F?
3. Blaming the lunar cycle for variations in the rate of violent crime is an example of mistaking correlation for causation. T or F?
4. If a psychology student uses a sleep-learning device to pass a midterm exam, it proves that the device works. T or F?

THINK CRITICALLY

5. Imagine that you have come across a claim on Twitter reporting on a new study indicating that immunizing children has been conclusively linked to autism in children. How could you evaluate the truth of this claim?

SELF-REFLECT

- How actively do you evaluate and question claims made by an authority or found in the media? Could you be a more critical consumer of information? *Should* you be a more critical consumer of information?

Answers: 1. F 2. F 3. T 4. F 5. You could begin by doing a lateral search on the person or organization behind the study, and then do the same for the person or organization responsible for the tweet—you would be looking for any evidence of bias. You should also go directly to the source (that is, the original article) to ensure that the claims are not misrepresenting (or oversimplifying) what was reported in the paper itself.

CHAPTER IN REVIEW

Gateways to the Foundations of Psychological Science

Summary: Gateways Learning Outcomes

1.1 Commonsense Psychology: Not Necessarily "Common" or "Sense"

1.1.1 Explain why people fail to recognize that "commonsense" beliefs are often false

Commonsense beliefs are often false, but people fail to recognize this because they do not tend to evaluate them critically (uncritical acceptance) and because we seek evidence that confirms, and avoid evidence that contradicts, our beliefs (confirmation bias), regardless of the quality of that evidence.

1.1.2 Distinguish between superstition, pseudoscience, and science

Superstitions are unfounded beliefs that change little over time because they are held without objective evidence or in the face of falsifying evidence. Scientific-sounding superstitions are referred to as pseudoscience. Science requires that we take an objective approach to answering questions using careful observations and experiments.

1.2 What Psychologists Do

1.2.1 Name some of the areas in which psychological scientists do research

Some psychologists work primarily as researchers, and psychological research can be basic or applied. Researchers may study animals either because they are interested in animal behavior or because animals provide a model of human behavior. The field of psychology now has dozens of specialties, including developmental, forensic, community, environmental, and industrial/organizational (see Table 1.1).

1.2.2 Describe the work carried out by clinical and counseling psychologists

Some psychologists work primarily as clinicians, helping other people with mental health issues. They often work alongside other mental health workers (e.g., psychiatrists, psychoanalysts, and counselors) whose training and methods differ considerably. Clinical psychologists treat mental disorders and emotional problems; counseling psychologists treat milder problems including difficulties at work or school.

1.3 The History of Psychological Science: A Trip Through Time

1.3.1 Explain the method that Wundt and Titchener used to study conscious experience and the limitations of this method

Wilhelm Wundt used introspection (personal observation of mental events) to study conscious experience. His student, Titchener, took these methods to the United States and referred to his approach as structuralism, a kind of "mental chemistry" based on introspection.

However, introspection is of limited use as a research method since there is little consistency between the introspective reports of different people and because of the discovery of imageless thought, the finding that people may be subjectively unaware of their own mental processes and the cognitive unconscious.

1.3.2 Contrast Titchener's structuralist approach to psychology with:

a. the Gestalt approach developed by Wertheimer

Gestalt psychologists such as Wertheimer believed in the value of introspection, but disagreed with structuralists like Titchener about the experience. While structuralists valued the idea of analyzing psychological events in terms of their individual components, Gestalt theorists felt that these events could only be studied as whole units.

b. the functionalist approach developed by James

William James saw mental events as a continuous stream of events rather than the static building blocks proposed by Titchener's structuralist approach. He developed functionalism in an effort to better understand how behavior helped us to adapt to the environment. His interest in adaptation created a natural bridge with Darwin's views of natural selection and evolution.

c. the behaviorist approach developed by Watson and Skinner

Behaviorists rejected introspection and structuralism, choosing instead to study objective behavior. Radical behaviorists rejected the study of mind altogether.

d. the psychoanalytic approach developed by Freud

Sigmund Freud distrusted introspection and developed psychoanalysis to emphasize the unconscious origins of behavior and the importance of properly interpreting the hidden meaning of conscious thoughts.

e. the cognitive approach

The cognitive approach involves studying mental processes, just as Wundt and Titchener did. However, cognitive psychologists approach the study of mental processes more objectively than Wundt and Titchener by operationally defining them in terms of objective measures.

f. the humanists' approach developed by Maslow and Rogers

Humanistic psychology embraced conscious experience, human potential, and personal growth. Though they believed in the importance of mental events, they did not believe they could be subdivided into individual building blocks, as Titchener's structuralist approach suggested

1.4 Contemporary Psychological Science and the Biopsychosocial Model

1.4.1 Explain the three perspectives that comprise the biopsychosocial model

The three perspectives include: biological (behavior is the result of biological and evolutionary processes, such as genetics and the nervous system), psychological (behavior is the result of psychological processes, such as thinking and memory), and social (behavior is the result of social contexts, such as culture).

1.4.2 Explain the advantages of the biopsychosocial model for explaining complex behavior

The biopsychosocial model holds that human behavior and mental processes are best understood by combining insights from biology (including biopsychology and evolutionary psychology), psychology (including motivation thinking, personality, perception, and language), and the social world (including culture, access to education, and poverty). Because it considers the three perspectives simultaneously, it is better able to explain complex human behavior (such as eating disorders) and the full range of human diversity.

1.4.3 Explain why early psychological research was prone to gender and culture bias

Gender bias was inadvertently introduced into psychological research because most early psychologists were Caucasian men, and because the participants in much of the early research were men. Similarly, culture bias stems from an overreliance on research participants who are from WEIRD (Western, Educated, Industrialized, Rich, and Democratic) societies.

1.5 The Core Features of Psychological Science

1.5.1 Explain the goals of contemporary psychology

Psychologists' goals are description (name and classify behavior through detailed records), understanding (state causes of behavior), prediction (forecast behavior), and control (alter conditions that influence behavior).

1.5.2 Define critical thinking, and identify the five principles of critical thinking

Critical thinking in psychology is a type of open-minded reflection involving the support of beliefs with scientific explanation and observation.

Critical thinking requires:

1. performing logical analysis/empirical testing
2. refusing to believe information based on claimed expertise
3. evaluating the *quality* of the evidence
4. evaluating evidence *for* and *against* the claim with an open mind
5. seeking to falsify claims

1.5.3 Outline the six steps of the scientific method

1. Make observations
2. Define the problem
3. Propose a hypothesis
4. Gather evidence/test hypothesis
5. Build theory
6. Publish results

1.5.4 Describe three types of data gathered by psychological scientists, including the challenges faced by psychologists who use them

1. *Self-report, including interviews, tests, questionnaires, and surveys*

   Self-report data may be compromised if the sample of respondents is not representative (that is, it does not accurately reflect the larger population), or if participants provide answers that are socially desirable rather than truthful.

2. *Observational data, including natural and structured observations*

   Observational data can be compromised by the observer effect (changes in a subject's behavior as a result of being watched) and observer bias (observers seeing what they want or expect to see).

3. *Physiological data, including measures of heart rate, brain activity, and hormones.*

   Physiological data are often more expensive to collect because they require specialized equipment. In addition, these measures are often indirect assessments of the variables that they attempt to assess.

1.6 Experimental Methods: Where Cause Meets Effect

1.6.1 Differentiate between independent, dependent, and extraneous variables in an experiment

Independent variables are assumed to be the "cause" in a cause-and-effect relationship between variables, and are controlled by the researcher (in the sense that the researcher randomly assigns participants to experience one version, or level, of the independent variable).

Dependent variables are assumed to be the "effect" in a cause-and-effect relationship between variables, and are measured by the researcher.

Extraneous variables are variables (other than the independent variable) that are believed to influence the dependent variable. They are controlled by the researcher, who attempts to keep them the same for all participants in the study.

1.6.2 Explain how experiments allow psychological scientists to make statements about cause and effect

Experiments involve comparing two or more groups of subjects that differ only regarding the independent variable. Random assignment helps to ensure that the groups are equivalent in all ways except for their experience of the independent variable. Effects on the dependent variable are then measured. All other conditions (extraneous variables) are held constant. Because the independent variable is the only difference between the experimental group and the control group, it is the only possible cause of a change in the dependent variable.

1.6.3 Outline how psychological scientists evaluate the results of an experiment

To be taken seriously, the results of an experiment must be statistically significant (they would occur very rarely by chance alone). Put another way, the control group and the experimental group must demonstrate a difference on the dependent variable that is large enough that it is unlikely to have occurred by chance. It also strengthens an experimental result if the research can be replicated.

1.6.4 Describe two problems associated with experiments, and how they can be controlled

1. *Research participant bias (changes in participant behavior based on their expectations), including the placebo effect.* To control for this problem, researchers can ensure that they give a placebo to the control group, and they can make use of single-blind procedures, which means that participants do not know whether they are in the experimental or control group.
2. *Researcher bias (changes in participant behavior brought about by researcher influence).* To control for this problem, researchers can make use of double-blind procedures, which means that neither the research participants nor the researchers collecting data know who was in the experimental group or the control group.

1.7 Nonexperimental Methods: Losing (a Bit of) Control

1.7.1 Differentiate between quasi-experiments and true experiments

As is the case with a true experiment, quasi-experiments involve comparing two or more groups to establish whether they differ on the dependent variable. Unlike true experiments, it is either unethical or impossible to randomly assign participants to groups. As a result, it is not possible to establish cause-and-effect relationships using quasi-experiments.

1.7.2 Explain what is meant by correlational research, and how the degree of association between two variables is assessed in correlational research

In correlational research, psychologists try to assess the degree of association between two variables. A correlation coefficient is computed to gauge the strength of the relationship between these variables. Correlation coefficients range from −1.00 to +1.00. The magnitude of the number (ignoring the sign) describes how strong the association between the variables is (that is, how well you can predict one variable from the other). The sign (− or +) tells you whether the relationship is positive (as the value of one variable increases, the other also increases) or negative (as the value of one variable increases, the other decreases).

1.7.3 Describe the conditions under which case studies are useful

Case studies—an in-depth analysis of one person or a small number of people—are most often employed when psychologists are interested in studying rare events.

1.8 Psychology and Your Skill Set: Information Literacy

1.8.1 Name six ways that people can critically evaluate information found in the popular press and on social media

1. Consider the source of information, reading laterally
2. Beware of poor or carefully selected information
3. Consider alternative explanations and remember things happen by chance
4. Check to ensure that reported studies had a control group
5. Distinguish between correlation and causation
6. Beware of oversimplifications

1.8.2 Create a plan to analyze and evaluate information that you are exposed to in the popular press and on social media

We hope that after reading this section, you'll be able to use the suggestion provided to feel confident evaluating the information that you see and read in a variety of sources!

2 Brain and Behavior

FOTOKITA/Shutterstock.com

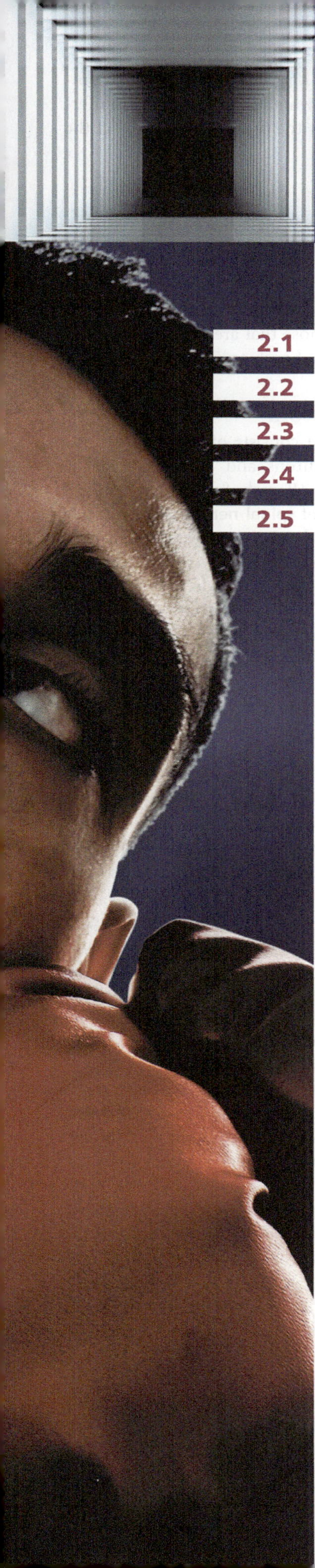

Gateway Theme **Brain activity is the source of human consciousness, intelligence, and behavior.**

Chapter Outline

Punch-Drunk

He died of a self-inflicted gunshot wound. Not to his head, mind you, but to his chest, because he wanted to leave his brain to science. Two-time Super Bowl winner Dave Duerson blamed his post-football troubles, including memory loss, difficulty spelling words, depression, and moodiness, on the repeated concussions that he suffered on the playing field. Sure enough, an autopsy revealed signs of a unique type of brain injury—*chronic traumatic encephalopathy*—that has been found in dozens of other NFL players, as well as athletes from other violent sports such as hockey and boxing. The boxers even have a name for it: *punch-drunk*. Sports leagues like the NFL and NHL are now taking notice as former players continue to file lawsuits and demand compensation. In 2018, it was estimated that claims filed over concussion-related brain injuries by retired NFL players alone will eventually reach 1.4 billion dollars.

We don't normally notice the key role the nervous system—and especially the brain—plays in all that makes us human. But those who suffer from injuries to the nervous system quickly realize that it's critical for everyday tasks like brushing your teeth and reading this book, as well as more complex things like making music of exquisite beauty, seeking a cure for cancer, or falling in love with someone wonderful. Let's take a closer look at how this amazing system works.

2.1 The Nervous System

GATEWAYS LEARNING OUTCOMES:
After reading this section you should be able to:

2.1.1 Outline the major divisions of the nervous system

2.1.2 Identify the important parts of a neuron

2.1.3 Describe how neurons operate and communicate with each other

2.1.4 Distinguish between neuroplasticity and neurogenesis

The human nervous system is undeniably amazing—it may even be the most complex structure in existence (Sporns, 2013). Let's begin with an overview of the nervous system by following Mike and Molly, who are out in the park with their football. As they run, jump, and throw the ball, a blaze of activity lights up many of the 100 billion or so nerve cells—or *neurons*—that make up their nervous systems.

It probably won't surprise you to know that something so complicated has different parts, each of which is responsible for different tasks. Let's take a closer look at the different branches of the nervous system.

Branches of the Nervous System

The nervous system can be broken down into two main branches: the central and peripheral nervous systems (see Figure 2.1). Together, they allow you to carry out tasks that are very simple, like raising your hand, as well as those that are much more complicated, like surfing the waves off a beach on Oahu.

The Central Nervous System

The **central nervous system (CNS)** consists of the brain, which contains the majority of your neurons and does most of the "computing," and the spinal cord (Banich & Compton, 2011). The **spinal cord** is a large column of **spinal nerves** that transmits information between the brain and the **peripheral nervous system (PNS)**, which includes all parts of the nervous system beyond the brain and spinal cord. Suppose that Mike decides to throw the football to Molly. The decision is made in the brain and is then transmitted to the spinal cord. His spinal cord then relays the message to the PNS which then directs Mike's body, right hand, and arm to throw the ball.

Are nerves the same as neurons? No. A **neuron** (NOOR-on) is a single cell in the nervous system that transmits information. Neurons, as we will soon see, are tiny. You usually need a microscope to see one. **Nerves** are large bundles of many neuron fibers (called *axons*). You can easily see nerves without magnification.

Oops. The football is sailing much higher than Mike anticipated. To catch it, a huge amount of information must quickly be collected by Molly's muscles (I need to run faster if I want to catch it), as well as her eyes (The ball is moving over toward the picnic area!) and other senses (What's that barking behind me? Will I lose my balance if I try to jump and catch the ball?). That information is sent to her brain to be interpreted through a variety of pathways. For example, information from her muscles flows back to her brain via the spinal nerves, while input from her eyes, ears, and sense of balance arrives via the **cranial nerves**, which connect the PNS to the brain directly, and do not pass through the spinal cord. Decisions based on this input must be made in the brain, and messages are then sent back out to direct countless muscle fibers (move my body and hands to catch that ball while avoiding that couple and their dog sitting on the lawn behind me).

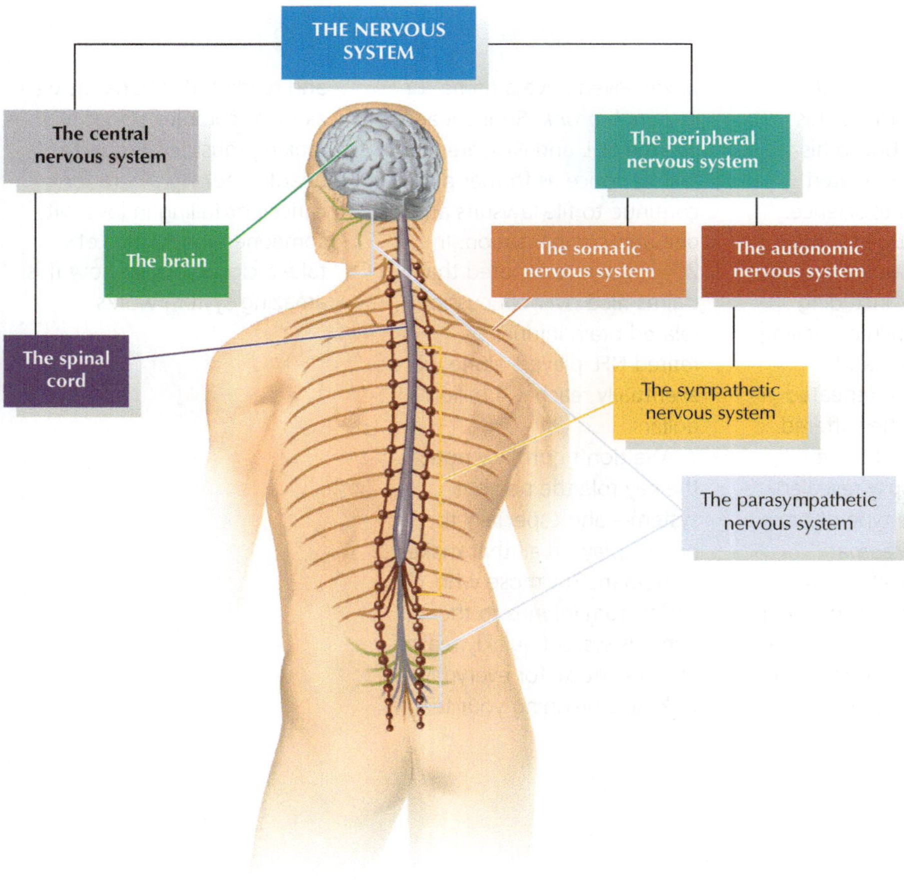

Figure 2.1 Divisions of the nervous system. The nervous system can be divided into the central nervous system, made up of the brain and spinal cord, and the peripheral nervous system, composed of the nerves connecting the body to the central nervous system.

The Peripheral Nervous System

As we mentioned earlier, the peripheral nervous system (PNS) comprises all elements of the nervous system that lie outside of the central nervous system (brain and spinal cord). The peripheral nervous system can be divided into two major parts. The **somatic nervous system (SNS)** is the network linking the spinal cord with the body and sense organs. In general, it controls voluntary behavior, such as when Molly lurches backwards to catch the football. In contrast, the **autonomic nervous system (ANS)** is the collection of neurons that carry information to and from internal organs and glands. The word *autonomic* means self-governing. Activities governed by the ANS, such as heart rate, digestion, and perspiration, are mostly vegetative or automatic.

The SNS and ANS work together to coordinate the body's internal reactions to events in the world outside the body. For example, messages carried by the SNS can make Molly's hand move to catch the ball, and when the dog lunges at her the SNS controls her leg muscles so that she can jump out of the way. At the same time, her ANS activates her internal organs, raising her blood pressure and quickening her rate of breathing. If Molly feels a burst of fear when she almost steps on the dog, or a surge of love for Mike when he shows concern, that activity will also be carried by her ANS. (The ANS plays a central role in our emotional lives. In fact, without the ANS, a person would feel little emotion; see Section 10.4.)

The ANS can be further divided into the *sympathetic* and *parasympathetic* branches. In essence, the **sympathetic nervous system** is the division of the autonomic nervous system that coordinates arousal, while the **parasympathetic nervous system** is the part of the autonomic nervous system that quiets the body and conserves energy (Figure 2.2). The sympathetic branch energizes Molly's heightened reaction to the lunging dog. It is responsible for initiating the "fight or flight" reaction during times of danger or high emotion. Right after she escapes the dog, she has to stop and catch her breath for a moment while her parasympathetic branch returns her internal organs to a lower level of arousal. Of course, both branches of the ANS are always active. At any given moment, their combined activity determines the degree to which your body is relaxed or aroused.

It's clear from this discussion that the nervous system is remarkable in terms of its ability to allow for all kinds of complex behaviors. Oddly enough, though, any single neuron is not very smart—it takes many of them just to make Molly blink. Yet individual neurons are the building blocks of the nervous system. Understanding how they work is a good first step in better understanding how the nervous system functions.

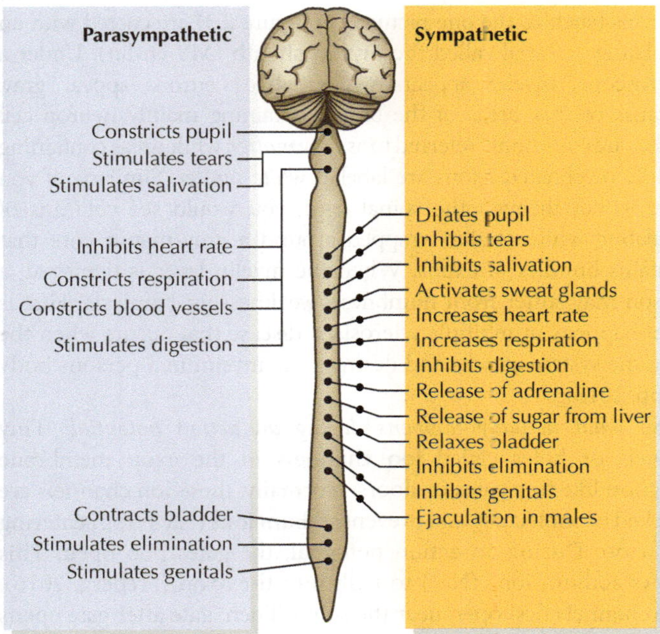

Figure 2.2 Branches of the ANS. Both branches control involuntary actions. The sympathetic system generally activates the body. The parasympathetic system generally quiets it. The sympathetic branch relays its messages through clusters of neurons outside the spinal cord.

Neurons: The Building Blocks of the Nervous System

While neurons come in very different shapes and sizes, most have four basic parts (Figure 2.3). The **dendrites** (DEN-drytes), which look like tree roots, are neuron fibers that receive incoming messages. The **cell body**, or *soma* (SOH-mah), receives information from the dendrites. The **axon** (AK-sahn) is the fiber that carries information away from the cell body of a neuron. Axons branch out into even thinner fibers ending in bulb-shaped **axon terminals**.

Like miniature cables, millions of miles of axons carry messages through the brain and nervous system (Breedlove, Watson, &

Central nervous system (CNS) The brain and spinal cord.

Spinal cord A column of nerves that transmits information between the brain and the peripheral nervous system.

Spinal nerves Major nerves that carry sensory and motor messages in and out of the spinal cord.

Peripheral nervous system (PNS) The parts of the nervous system outside the brain and spinal cord.

Neuron A cell in the nervous system that transmits information.

Nerve A bundle of neuron axons.

Cranial nerves Major nerves that leave the brain without passing through the spinal cord.

Somatic nervous system (SNS) A network linking the spinal cord with the body and sense organs.

Autonomic nervous system (ANS) The collection of axons that carry information to and from internal organs and glands.

Sympathetic nervous system (sympathetic branch) The division of the autonomic nervous system that coordinates arousal.

Parasympathetic nervous system (parasympathetic branch) The division of the autonomic nervous system that quiets the body and conserves energy.

Dendrites Neuron fibers that receive incoming messages.

Cell body The part of the neuron or other cell that contains the nucleus of the cell.

Axon A fiber that carries information away from the cell body of a neuron.

Axon terminals Bulb-shaped structures at the ends of axons that form synapses with the dendrites and cell bodies of other neurons.

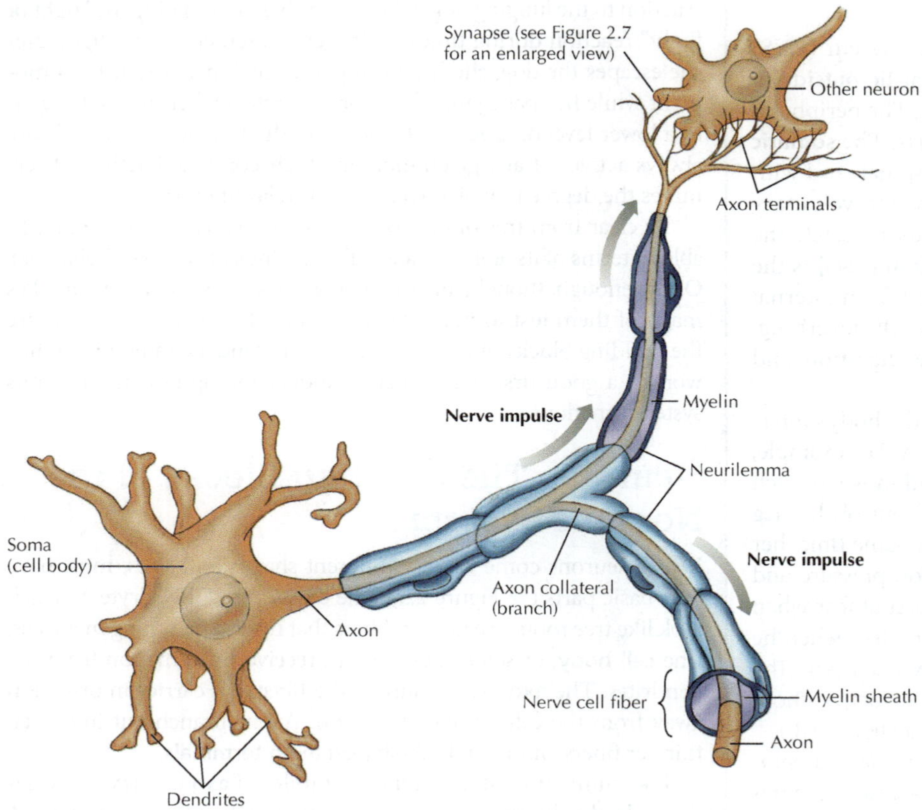

Figure 2.3 A stylized neuron. Action potentials usually travel from the dendrites and cell body to the branching ends of the axon.

Rosenzweig, 2013). Although some axons are only 0.1 millimeter long (about the width of a human hair or a pencil line), others stretch for several feet through the nervous system (from the base of your spine to your big toe, for instance). Large bundles of axons comprise most of the spinal cord and the nerves of the peripheral nervous system (PNS). By forming connections with the dendrites of other neurons, axon terminals allow information to pass from neuron to neuron.

As impressive as neurons are, they don't act alone. They are sustained by the *glial cells* that surround them, which are charged with providing physical support and insulation, removing waste, and providing nutrients. Once thought of as silent servants to neurons, recent research suggests that glia are far more important and sophisticated than scientists had initially believed. For one thing, there are too many of them to ignore: they outnumber neurons by a ratio of 9 to 1. For another, they aren't silent—they do indeed communicate with one another, often after "listening in" on the activity of the neurons they surround. Most recently, neuroscientists have suggested that glia should be viewed as partners to neurons, with each making a unique contribution to the smooth functioning of the nervous system (Fields, 2013).

How Neurons Work: Action Potentials

So how does a neuron actually send messages from the dendrites to the axon terminals? Neural function is primarily electrical. Electrically charged molecules called *ions* (EYE-ons) are found both inside and outside of each neuron. Some of these ions have a positive electrical charge, whereas others have a negative charge. When a neuron is inactive (or resting), more of the plus, or positive, charges exist outside the neuron and more minus, or negative, charges exist inside. As a result, the inside of each resting neuron has a slight negative electrical charge.

The electrical charge of an inactive neuron is called its **resting potential**. But neurons seldom get much rest. Messages constantly arrive from other neurons, causing the resting potential to fluctuate. Some inputs excite the neuron, slightly raising the resting potential, while others inhibit the neuron, slightly lowering the resting potential. If enough excitatory inputs arrive within a short span of time, the overall electrical charge will rise quite a bit. When the charge is high enough, the neuron will reach its **threshold**, or trigger point for firing (Figure 2.4). When a neuron reaches its threshold, an **action potential**, a brief change in a neuron's electrical charge, sweeps down the axon at up to 200 miles per hour (Figure 2.5). That may seem fast, but it still takes at least a split second to react to this electrical message that's being carried by a neuron. That's one of the reasons it's so difficult to return a 130-mile-per-hour professional tennis serve!

How does an action potential move so fast? The axons of some neurons (such as the one pictured in Figure 2.3) are coated with an insulating material called the **myelin sheath** (MY-eh-lin). Under a microscope, myelin appears white, while neurons appear gray. Because of this, areas of the brain containing mainly neuron cell bodies are commonly referred to as *gray matter*, while areas containing mainly myelinated axons are labeled *white matter*. Similarly, if you were to cut through the spinal cord, you would see columns of insulating white matter wrapped around a gray-matter core that contains bundles of axons. When the myelin layer is damaged, a person may suffer from numbness, weakness, or paralysis. That is what happens in multiple sclerosis, a disease that occurs when the immune system attacks and destroys the myelin in a person's body (Kipp, 2016).

So what actually happens during an action potential? Tiny tunnels or holes called **ion channels** in the axon membrane function like tiny gates or doors. Normally, these ion channels are blocked by molecules that prevent sodium ions (Na^+) from entering the axon. During an action potential, the gates pop open. This allows sodium ions (Na^+) to rush into the axon (Freberg, 2016). The channels first open near the soma. Then, gate after gate opens down the length of the axon as the action potential zips along (Figure 2.6).

Each action potential is an *all-or-nothing event* (it occurs completely or not at all). You might find it helpful to picture the axon as a row of dominoes set on end. Tipping over the dominoes is an

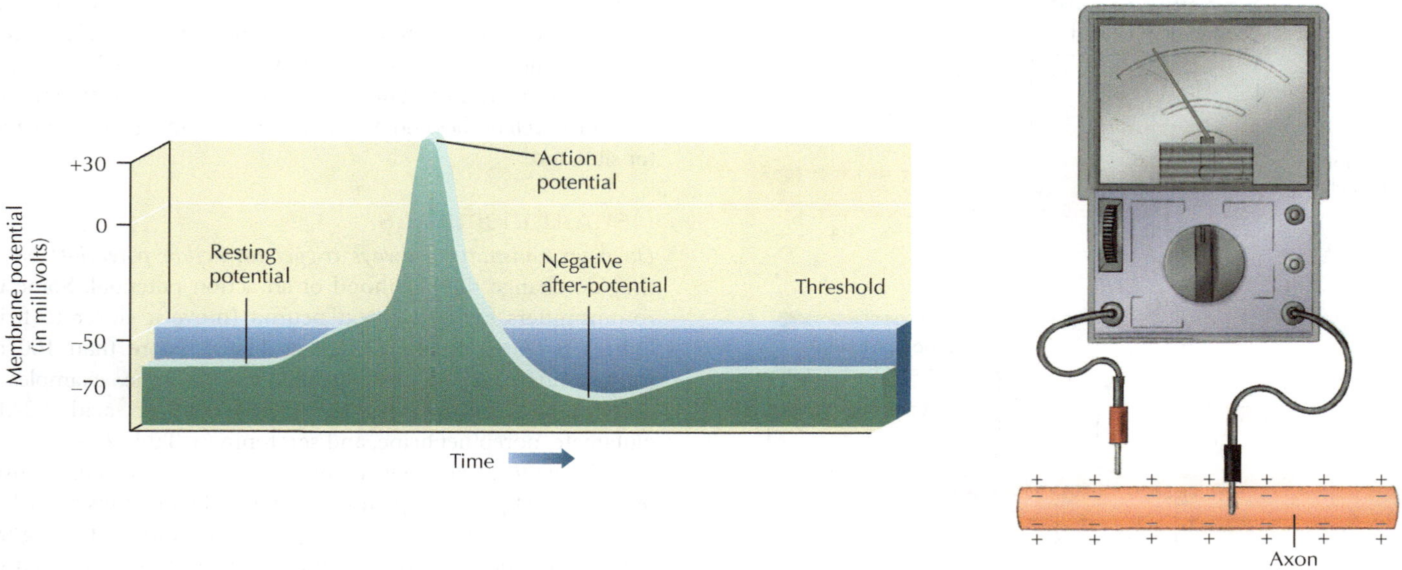

Figure 2.4 Measuring electrical activity in the neuron. Tiny electrical probes called *microelectrodes*, placed inside and outside an axon, measure its activity. The inside of an axon at rest is about –60 to –70 millivolts, compared with the outside. Electrochemical changes in a neuron generate an *action potential*. When sodium ions (Na^+) that have a positive charge rush into the cell, its interior briefly becomes positive. After the action potential, positive potassium ions (K^+) flow out of the axon and restore its negative charge. (See Figure 2.5 for further explanation.)

all-or-nothing act. Once the first domino drops, a wave of falling blocks zips rapidly to the end of the line. Similarly, when an action potential is triggered near the soma, a wave of activity travels down the length of the axon.

After an action potential, the cell briefly dips below its resting level and becomes less able to fire. This **negative after-potential** occurs because potassium ions (K^+) flow out of the neuron while the membrane gates are open (Figure 2.6). After a nerve impulse, ions flow both into and out of the axon, recharging it for more action. In our model, this is the equivalent of taking a moment to set up the row of dominoes again. Soon, however, the axon is ready for another wave of activity.

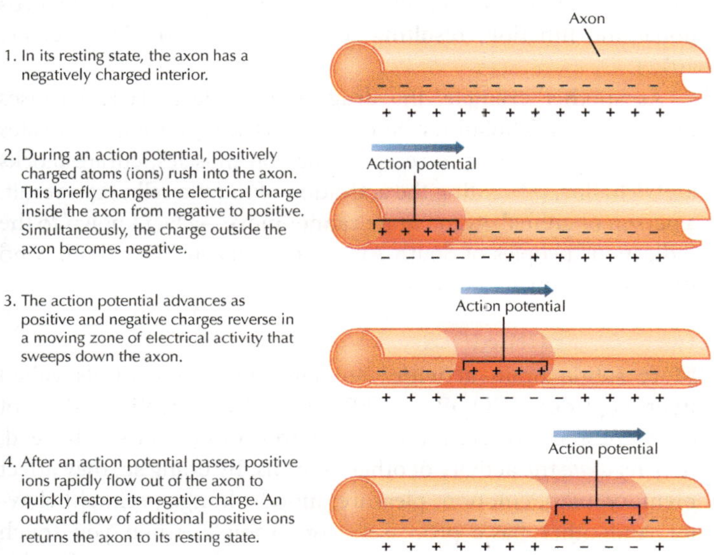

Figure 2.5 The action potential. The inside of an axon normally has a negative electrical charge, and the fluid surrounding an axon is normally positive. As an action potential passes along the axon, these charges reverse, so that the interior of the axon briefly becomes positive. This process is described in more detail in Figure 2.6.

Synaptic Transmission

So what happens when the action potential gets to the end of the axon terminals? Remarkably, individual neurons do not physically touch each other; they are separated by a microscopic gap called the **synapse** (SIN-aps). **Synaptic transmission** occurs when an action potential reaches the tips of the axon terminals and releases a **neurotransmitter** (NOOR-oh-TRANS-mit-ers)—a chemical that

Resting potential The electrical charge of an inactive neuron.

Threshold In neurons, the point at which a nerve impulse is triggered.

Action potential A brief change in a neuron's electrical charge.

Myelin sheath Insulating material that covers some axons.

Ion channels Tiny openings through the axon membrane.

Negative after-potential A drop in electrical charge below the resting potential.

Synapse A microscopic space over which messages pass between two neurons.

Synaptic transmission The chemical process that carries information from one neuron to another.

Neurotransmitter A chemical that moves information from one nervous-system cell to another.

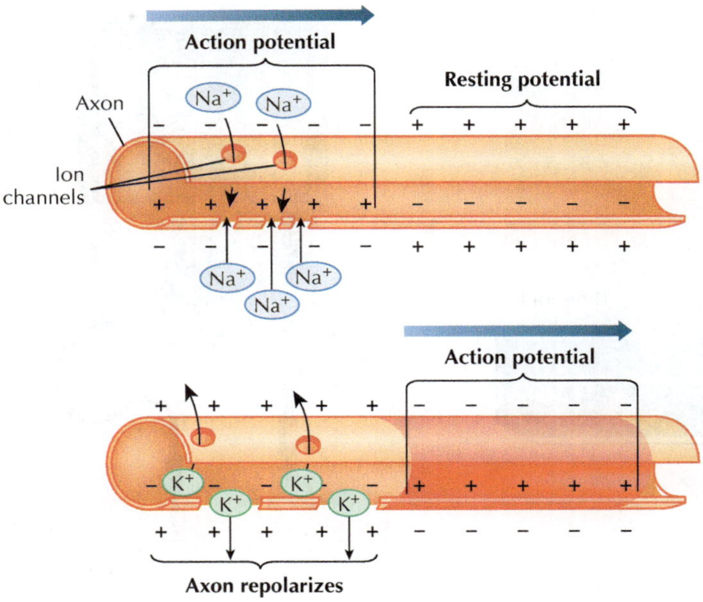

Figure 2.6 The interior of an axon. The right end of the top axon is at rest. Thus, it has a negative charge inside. An action potential begins when ion channels open and sodium ions (Na^+) rush into the axon. In this drawing, the action potential travels from left to right along the axon. In the lower axon, the action potential has moved to the right. After it passes, potassium ions (K^+) flow out of the axon. This quickly renews the negative charge inside the axon, so that it can fire again. Sodium ions that enter the axon during an action potential are pumped out more slowly. Removing them restores the original resting potential.

moves information from one neuron to another—into the synaptic gap (Figure 2.7).

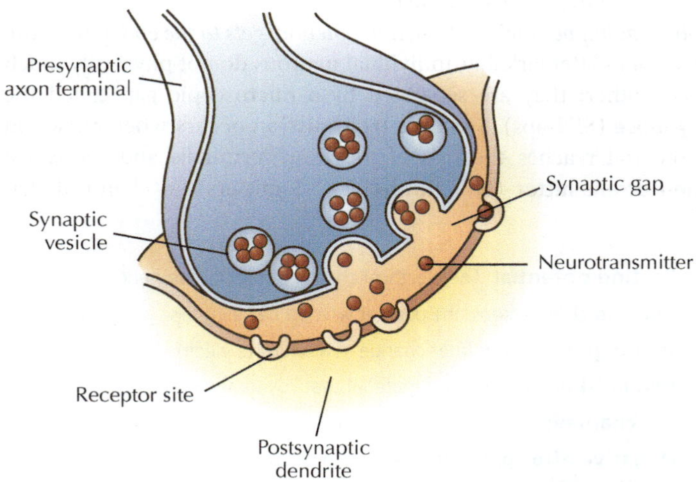

Figure 2.7 The synapse. Neurotransmitters are stored in tiny sacs called *synaptic vesicles* (VES-ih-kels). When an action potential reaches the end of an axon, the vesicles move to the surface and release neurotransmitters. These molecules cross the synaptic gap to affect the next neuron. The size of the gap is exaggerated here; it is actually only about one-millionth of an inch. Some transmitter molecules excite the next neuron and some inhibit its activity.

When neurotransmitters cross over a synapse, they temporarily bond to special receiving areas on the next neuron called receptor sites (see Figure 2.7). Each tiny **receptor site** on the cell membrane is sensitive to neurotransmitters. The sites are found in large numbers on neuron cell bodies and dendrites. Muscles and glands have receptor sites, too.

Neurotransmitters

Do neurotransmitters always trigger an action potential? No, but they do change the likelihood of an action potential. Some neurotransmitters *excite* the next neuron (move it closer to firing). Others *inhibit* it (make firing less likely). More than 100 neurotransmitters are found in the brain. Some examples are acetylcholine, dopamine, gamma-aminobutyric acid (GABA), glutamate, norepinephrine, and serotonin (▲ Table 2.1).

Why are there so many neurotransmitters? Some neurotransmitters are used by specific pathways that interlink regions of the brain. It is as if different pathways speak different languages. Perhaps this helps prevent confusing crosstalk or intermixing of messages. For example, the brain has a reward or pleasure system that communicates mainly via dopamine (DOPE-ah-meen) (Mark et al., 2011; Syed et al., 2016).

Slight variations in neurotransmitter function may be related to temperament differences in infancy and personality differences in adulthood (Ashton, 2013). Outright disturbances of any neurotransmitter can have serious consequences. For example, too much dopamine may cause schizophrenia (Howes, McCutcheon, & Stone, 2015), whereas too little serotonin may underlie depression (Torrente, Gelenberg, & Vrana, 2012).

Many drugs mimic, duplicate, or block neurotransmitters. For example, the chemical structure of *cocaine* is similar to that of dopamine. In the short run, cocaine can trigger an increase in dopamine in the reward system, resulting in a drug high (España et al., 2010). In the long run, the overuse of recreational drugs such as cocaine overstimulates the reward system and disturbs dopamine function, resulting in drug addiction (Taber et al., 2012).

As another example, the drug *curare* (cue-RAH-ree) causes paralysis. Acetylcholine (ah-SEET-ul-KOH-leen) normally activates muscles. By attaching to receptor sites on muscles, curare blocks acetylcholine, preventing the activation of muscle cells. As a result, a person or animal given curare cannot move—a fact known to the indigenous peoples of South America's Amazon River basin, who use curare as an arrow poison for hunting.

Neural Regulators

More subtle brain activities are affected by chemicals called **neuropeptides** (NOOR-oh-PEP-tides). Neuropeptides do not carry messages directly the way neurotransmitters do. Instead, they *regulate* the activity of other neurons. By doing so, they affect memory, pain, emotion, pleasure, moods, hunger, sexual behavior, and other basic processes. For example, when you touch something hot, you jerk your hand away. The messages for this action are carried by neurotransmitters. At the same time, pain may cause the brain to release neuropeptides called *enkephalins* (en-KEF-ah-lins). These opiate-like neural regulators relieve pain and stress. Yet other neuropeptides called *endorphins*

▲ **Table 2.1 Major Neurotransmitters**

Neurotransmitter	Main Mode of Action	Function in the Brain	Effects of Imbalance
Acetylcholine	Excitatory neurotransmitter	Participates in movement, autonomic function, learning and memory	Deficiency may play a role in Alzheimer's disease
Dopamine	Excitatory neurotransmitter	Participates in motivation, reward, planning of behavior	Deficiency may lead to Parkinson's disease, reduced feelings of pleasure; excess may lead to schizophrenia
GABA	Inhibitory neurotransmitter	Major inhibitory effect in the CNS; participates in moods	Deficiency may lead to anxiety
Glutamate	Excitatory neurotransmitter	Major excitatory effect in the CNS; participates in learning and memory	Excess may lead to neuron death and autism; deficiency may lead to tiredness
Norepinephrine	Excitatory neurotransmitter	Participates in arousal, vigilance, and mood	Excess may lead to anxiety
Serotonin	Inhibitory neurotransmitter	Participates in mood, appetite, and sleep	Deficiency may lead to depression and/or anxiety

Adapted from Freberg, 2016; Kalat, 2016; Prus, 2014.

(en-DORF-ins) are released by the pituitary gland. Together, these chemicals reduce the pain from your burn so that it is not too disabling (Bruehl et al., 2012).

Knowing about neural regulators, we now have at least one way to explain the painkilling effect of the placebos (fake pills or injections) that we discussed in Chapter 1—they raise endorphin levels (Price, Finniss, & Benedetti, 2008). A release of endorphins also seems to underlie runner's high, masochism, acupuncture, the euphoria sometimes associated with childbirth, painful initiation rites, and even sport parachuting (Janssen & Arntz, 2001). In each case, pain and stress cause the release of endorphins. In turn, these endorphins induce feelings of pleasure or euphoria similar to being high on morphine. People who say they are "addicted" to running may be closer to the truth than they realize. Ultimately, neural regulators may help explain addiction, depression, schizophrenia, and other puzzling topics.

Neuroplasticity and Neurogenesis

Although it is appropriate to describe the brain as a *biocomputer*, it is not programmed in the usual sense of the word. Instead, it (and you) learns (Kolb & Whishaw, 2013). This capacity of our nervous systems to change in response to experience is known as **neuroplasticity**.

Consider, for example, taxi drivers from London, England, who must learn the names and locations of tens of thousands of streets in order to earn their licenses. Not only do experienced cabbies have superior memory for street information, but the parts of their brains responsible for this learning are also enlarged (Woollett & Maguire, 2011). Similarly, after undergoing cognitive behavior therapy, not only do people with depression become more able to control their negative moods, but images of their brains reveal more normal activity in brain areas related to emotional processing (Ritchey et al., 2011). Finally, consider the more extreme example of Nico and Brooke, teenagers who had large portions of their brains removed as infants. Both are functioning well today; over the years, their brains have literally "rewired" themselves (Immordino-Yang, 2008; Kolb et al., 2011). These studies and many others suggest that every new experience is reflected in synaptic changes in the brain.

If human brains are neuroplastic then could Dave Duerson's brain have healed itself? Although adult brains are much less neuroplastic than those of children, they can be changed with patience and persistence (Livingston-Thomas et al., 2016; Xerri, 2012). Unfortunately for Dave Duerson, who was diagnosed with *chronic traumatic encephalopathy*, the prospects for recovery were not good: The brain damage suffered from repeated head trauma can be extensive and often triggers a subsequent disease process that continues to damage the brain long after the original injuries (Baugh et al., 2012).

It's worth noting that, in addition to changing as a result of experience, the nervous system is "plastic" in another way. Specifically, it has long been known that nerves in the peripheral nervous system (PNS) can *regrow* if they are damaged—this is why patients can expect to regain some control over the nerves in severed limbs once they have been reattached.

In contrast, though, serious injuries, disabilities, or aging processes that affect the CNS were long thought to be permanent because it was widely believed that we are born with all the brain cells we will ever have (Ben Abdallah et al., 2010). However, we now know that the brain is also capable of **neurogenesis** (noor-oh-JEN-uh-sis), the production of new brain cells (Lee, Clemenson, & Gage, 2011). Each day, thousands of new cells originate deep within the brain, move to the surface, and link up with other neurons to become part of the brain's circuitry. This was stunning news to neuroscientists, who must now figure out what the new cells do. Most likely, they are involved in learning, memory, and our ability to adapt to changing circumstances

Receptor site An area on the surface of neurons and other cells that is sensitive to neurotransmitters or hormones.

Neuropeptides Brain chemicals, such as enkephalins and endorphins, that regulate the activity of neurons.'

Neuroplasticity The capacity of the brain to change in response to experience.

Neurogenesis The production of new brain cells.

Reflective Practice

The Nervous System

1. The somatic and autonomic systems are part of the __________ nervous system.
2. The parasympathetic nervous system is most active during times of high emotion. T or F?
3. The __________ and __________ are the receiving areas of a neuron where information from other neurons is accepted.
4. Action potentials are carried down the __________ to the __________.
5. The __________ potential becomes a(n) __________ potential when a neuron passes the threshold for firing.
6. The simplest neural network is a(n) __________.
7. *Neuroplasticity* refers to the capacity of the nervous system to
   a. grow new neurons
   b. cover some axons with a thin layer of cells
   c. quickly recover from action potentials
   d. form new synaptic connections

THINK CRITICALLY

8. Evaluate the effect of a drug that is known to block the passage of neurotransmitters across the synapse.
9. Where in all the brain's "hardware" do you think the mind is found? What is the relationship between mind and brain?

SELF-REFLECT

- How much of the functioning of your brain can you become aware of through introspection?
- How does a neural network differ from the central processing unit of a computer?

Answers: 1. peripheral 2. F 3. dendrites, soma (cell body) 4. axon, axon terminals 5. resting, action 6. reflex arc 7. d 8. Such a drug could have wide-ranging effects, depending on which neurotransmitter(s) it blocked. If the drug blocked excitatory synapses, it would depress brain activity. If it blocked inhibitory messages, it would act as a powerful stimulant. 9. These questions, known as the mind–body problem, have challenged thinkers for centuries. We still don't have any definitive answers. One recent view is that mental states are emergent properties of brain activity—that is, brain activity forms complex patterns that are, in a sense, more than the sum of their parts. Or, to use a rough analogy, if the brain were a musical instrument, then mental life would be like music played on that instrument.

(Cameron & Glover, 2015). The discovery of neurogenesis in adult brains is leading to treatment possibilities that offer new hope for people suffering from a variety of other disabilities, such as depression, addiction, and schizophrenia (Chambers, 2012; Fournier & Duman, 2012).

2.2 Brain Research

GATEWAYS LEARNING OUTCOMES:
After reading this section you should be able to:

2.2.1 Identify three methods that scientists use to understand the structures of the brain

2.2.2 Identify four methods that scientists use to understand the function of brain structures

Your 3-pound brain is wrinkled like a walnut, the size of a grapefruit, and the texture of tofu. How could such a squishy little blob of tissue enable us to run at near-Olympic speeds to catch a train? Or design an electric car? Or read a book to a small child? *Biopsychology* is the study of how biological processes, especially those occurring in the nervous system, relate to the behaviors that we engage in every day.

Along with other neuroscientists, biopsychologists have developed some sophisticated research methods to learn about the various *structures* that make up the brain, as well as which parts control particular mental or behavioral *functions*.

Exploring Brain Structure

Anatomists have learned much about the structure of the brain by cutting apart (*dissecting*) autopsied brains. Dissection reveals that the brain is made up of many anatomically distinct areas comprised of *gray matter* (clusters of neuron cell bodies) interspersed with regions of *white matter* (bundles of myelinated axons), or pathways between those clusters. Fortunately, newer, less invasive technologies, such as *CT scans* and *MRI*, can be used to map brain structures in living brains (Kalat, 2016).

CT Scans

Computed tomography (CT) scans revolutionized the study of the brain by providing clearer images than those provided by conventional X-ray machines. In a CT scan, a computer collects X-rays of a single location taken from a number of different angles and forms them into an image. This procedure can reveal brain structure, as well as the location of strokes, injuries, tumors, and other brain disorders.

MRI Scans

Since they are X-rays, repeated CT scans may expose patients to unhealthy doses of radioactivity. Fortunately, a newer technology with no known side effects, **magnetic resonance imaging (MRI)**, provides even more detailed images than are possible with CT scans. In an MRI scan, a person's body is placed inside a strong magnetic field. Processing by a computer then creates a three-dimensional model of the brain or body. Any two-dimensional plane, or slice, of the body can be selected and displayed as an image on a computer screen. MRI scans allow us to peer into the living brain, almost as if it were transparent. Recent developments in MRI technology have even made it possible to explore pathways in the brain in great detail (Sporns, 2013).

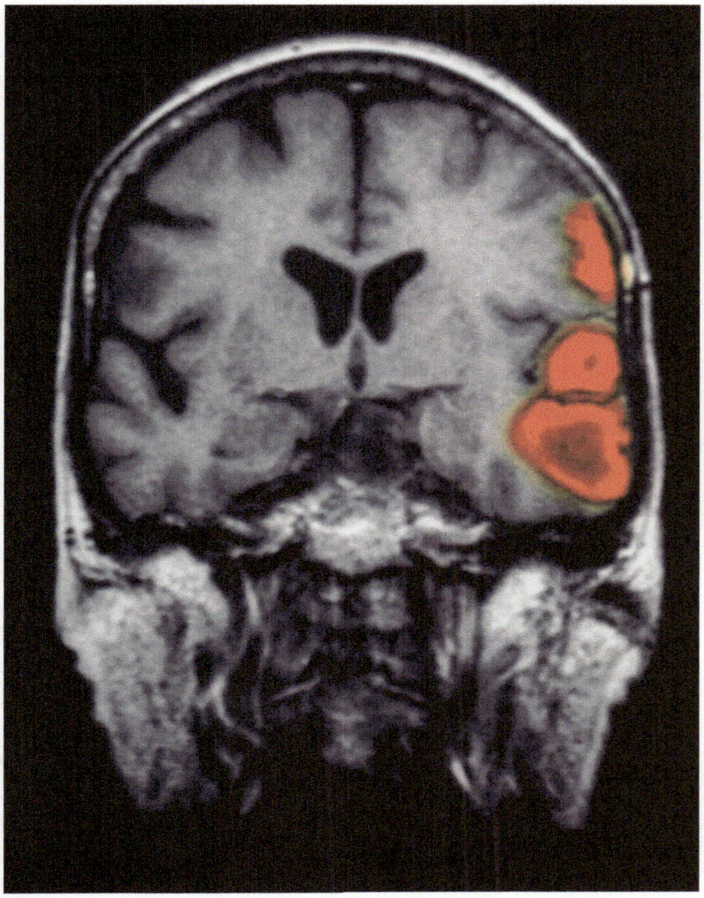

Scott Camazine/Science Source

This brain in this CT scan was damaged by a stroke (shown in red). The location of the stroke determines what mental or behavioral functions have been compromised.

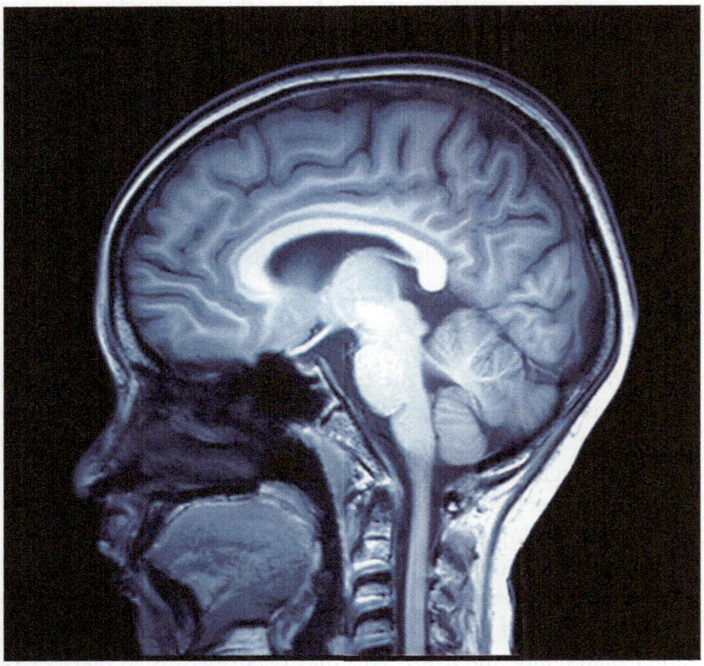

MriMan/Shutterstock.com

An MRI scan of the brain reveals many details. Can you identify any brain regions?

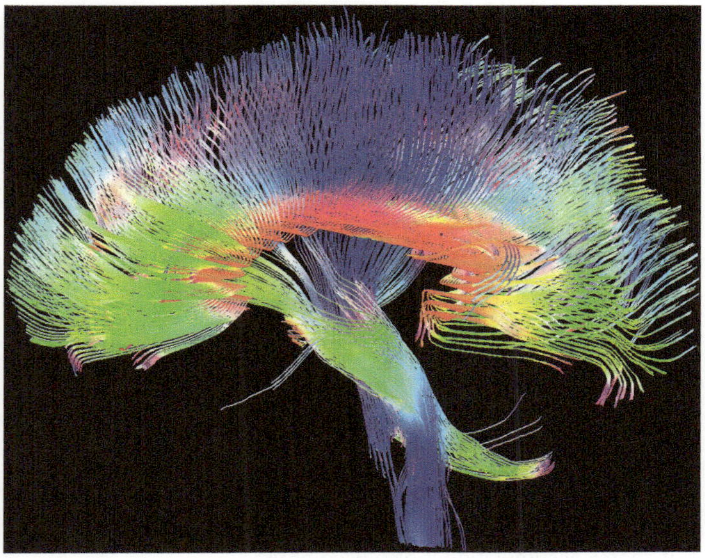

Tom Barrick, Chris Clark, SGHMS/Science Source

This colored MRI image reveals pathways in the brain of a healthy adult. Each pictured thread is a bundle of hundreds of thousands of axons (Human Connectome Project, 2013).

Exploring Brain Function

Imagine a mechanic handing you a car part. Even though you can clearly see the *structure* of the thing (it's about an inch long, with a round knob on one end, and a little prong . . .), you probably won't be able to figure out its *function* (. . . but is it part of the steering system, the brakes, or what?). Similarly, while it is valuable to be able to examine images of different brain structures, such as those made possible by CT scans and MRIs, it is another matter entirely to understand what role those structures play in normal brain function.

So how can we figure out those functions? This is a question psychological scientists have worked many years to answer. To answer questions about the function of various brain functions, we must **localize function** by linking psychological or behavioral capacities with particular brain structures. In many instances, particularly during the early history of psychology, psychological scientists did this through research that involved *case studies.*

Is that like the case study of Phineas Gage that we talked about in Chapter 1? Exactly! You may remember that such case studies examine changes in personality, behavior, or sensory capacity caused by brain diseases or injuries. If damage to a particular part of the brain consistently leads to a particular loss of function, then we say that the function is localized in that structure. Presumably, that part of the brain controls the same function in all of us.

Computed tomographic (CT) scan A computer-enhanced X-ray image of the brain or body.

Magnetic resonance imaging (MRI) An imaging technique that results in a three-dimensional image of the brain or body, based on its response to a magnetic field.

Localization of function The research strategy of linking specific structures in the brain to specific psychological or behavioral functions.

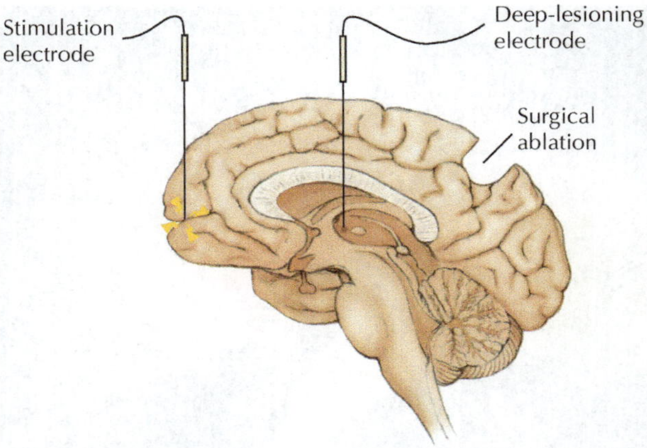

Figure 2.8 Stimulating or removing brain structures. The functions of brain structures are explored by selectively stimulating or removing them. Brain research is often based on electrical stimulation, but chemical stimulation is also used at times.

More recently, psychologists have developed a number of other research methods for localizing brain function and these methods have provided a wealth of information about how the brain works. Let's take a look at a few of them.

Surgical Techniques

In addition to case studies, researchers have learned much from **electrical stimulation of the brain (ESB)** (Figure 2.8). For example, the surface of the brain can be "turned on" by stimulating it with a mild electrical current delivered through a thin insulated wire called an **electrode**. When this is done during brain surgery, the patient can describe the effect of the stimulation. (The brain has no pain receptors, so surgery can be done while a patient is awake. Only local painkillers are needed for the scalp and skull. Any volunteers?) Even structures below the surface of the brain can be activated by lowering a stimulating electrode, insulated except at the tip, into a target area inside the brain. ESB can call forth behavior with astonishing power. Instantly, it can bring about behavioral indicators such as aggression, alertness, eating, drinking, sleeping, movement, euphoria, memories, speech, tears, and more.

An alternative approach is **ablation** (ab-LAY-shun)—the surgical removal of parts of the surface of the brain (see Figure 2.8). When ablation causes changes in behavior or sensory capacity, we also gain insight into the purpose of the missing "part." By using a technique called **deep lesioning** (LEE-zhun-ing), structures below the surface of the brain can also be removed. In this case, an electrode is lowered into a target area inside the brain, and a strong electric current is used to destroy a small amount of brain tissue (see Figure 2.8). Again, any resulting changes in behavior give clues to the function of the affected area.

Are any less invasive techniques available for studying brain function? Absolutely! Evolving technology means that we now have several other techniques that allow us to observe the activity of parts of the brain without doing any damage at all. These include the EEG, PET scan, and fMRI (Freberg, 2016), described next.

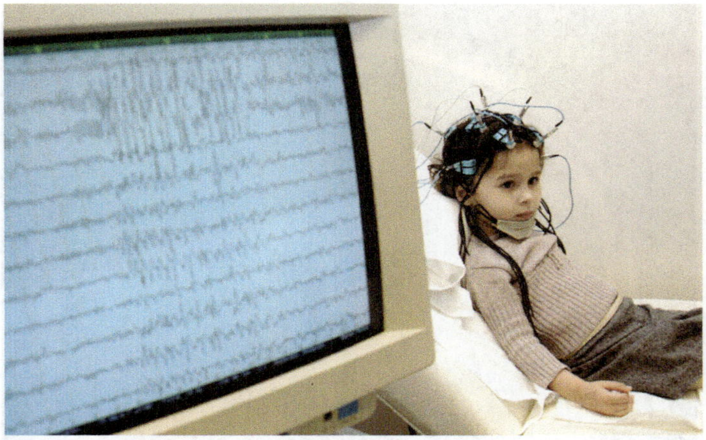

An EEG recording.

EEG

Electroencephalography (ee-LEK-tro-in-SEF-ah-LOG-ruh-fee) measures the waves of electrical activity produced near the surface of the brain. Small electrodes (disk-shaped metal plates) are placed on a person's scalp. Electrical impulses from the brain are detected and sent to an **electroencephalograph (EEG)**, which amplifies these weak signals (i.e., brain waves) and records them on a moving sheet of paper or a computer screen. Various brain-wave patterns can identify the presence of tumors, epilepsy, and other diseases. The EEG also reveals changes in brain activity during sleep, daydreaming, hypnosis, and other mental states. (Section 5.4 explains how changes in brain waves help define various stages of sleep.)

PET Scans

Positron emission tomography (PET) is a high-resolution imaging technique that captures brain activity by attaching radioactive particles to glucose molecules. A PET scan detects positrons (i.e., subatomic particles) emitted by weakly radioactive glucose (sugar) as it is consumed by the brain. Because the brain runs on glucose, a PET scan shows which areas are using more energy. Higher energy use corresponds with higher activity. Thus, by placing positron detectors around the head and sending data to a computer, it is possible to create a moving, color video of changes in brain activity (Figure 2.9). (PET scans suggest that different patterns of brain activity accompany major psychological disorders, such as schizophrenia or depression. See Sections 14.2 and 14.3.)

fMRI Scans

A **functional MRI (fMRI)** uses MRI technology to record activity levels in various areas of the brain. For example, if we scanned your brain while you are reading this textbook, areas of your brain involved in understanding what you read would be highlighted in an fMRI image. (In contrast, if we used MRI, rather than fMRI, we would get a beautiful image of your brain structure without any clues as to which parts of your brain were more or less active.)

Psychiatrist Daniel Langleben and his colleagues have even used fMRI images to examine if a person is lying. As Figure 2.10 shows, the front of the brain is more active when a person is lying rather than telling the truth. This may occur because it takes extra effort to lie, and that extra brain activity is detected with fMRI (Langleben, 2008). Eventually, such findings may validate the use of

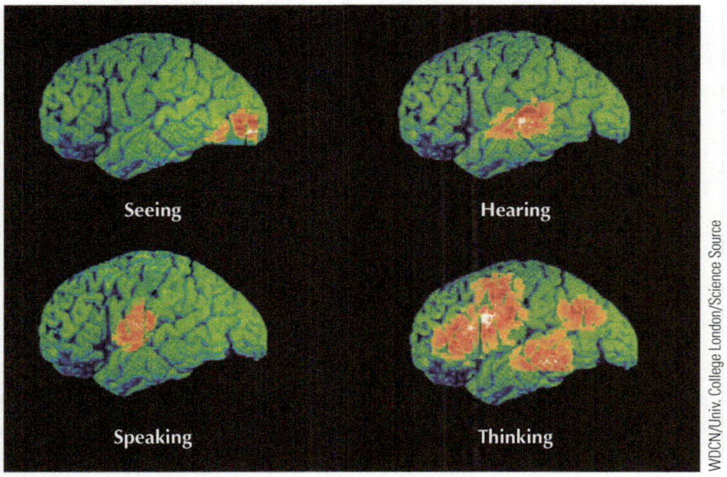

Figure 2.9 PET SCANS. PET scans reveal different patterns of brain activation when we engage in different tasks.

fMRI evidence in courts of law (Langleben & Moriarty, 2013; Rusconi & Mitchener-Nissen, 2013).

Fact or fiction? Do most people really use only 10 percent of their brain capacity? This is one of the lasting myths about the brain—but it is indeed a myth. Brain scans such as the ones we've described here show that *all* parts of the brain are active during waking hours. Obviously, some people make better use of their innate brainpower than others. Nevertheless, a normally functioning brain has no great hidden or untapped reserves of mental capacity.

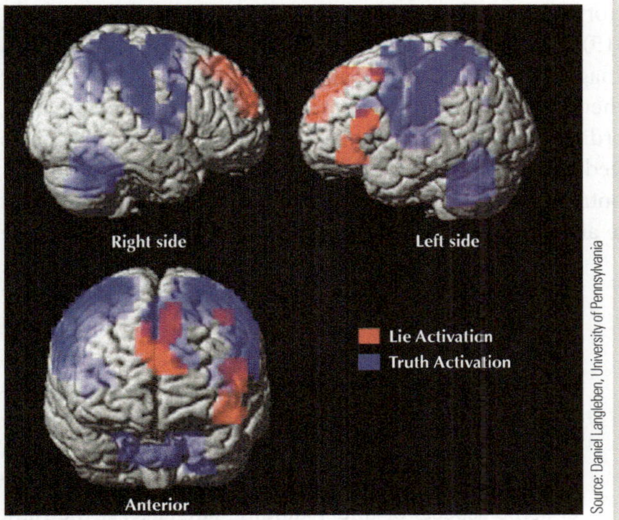

Figure 2.10 fMRI. Participants were asked to tell the truth or to lie while fMRI images of their brains were taken. When compared with telling the truth (shown in blue), areas toward the front of the brain were active during lying (shown in red). (Adapted from Langleben et al., 2005.)

Reflective Practice

Brain Research

1. Which of the following research techniques has the most in common with case studies of the effects of brain injuries?
   a. EEG recording
   b. deep lesioning
   c. microelectrode recording
   d. PET scan
2. CT scans cannot determine which part of your brain plays a role in speech because they
   a. use X-rays
   b. reveal brain structure, not brain activity
   c. reveal brain activity, not brain structure
   d. use magnetic fields
3. ______________ links brain structures to brain functions.
4. People use only 10 percent of their brain capacity. T or F?

THINK CRITICALLY

5. Deep lesioning is used to destroy an area in the hypothalamus of a rat. After the operation, the rat loses interest in food and eating. How would you evaluate the argument made by another scientist who tells you that it would be a mistake to automatically conclude that the destroyed area is a hunger center.

SELF-REFLECT

- You suspect that the function of a certain part of the brain is related to risk taking. How could you use case studies, ablation, deep lesioning, and ESB to determine its structure?
- You want to know which areas of the brain's surface are most active when a person sees a face. Evaluate what methods will you use.

Answers: 1. b 2. b 3. Localization of function 4. F 5. Other factors might explain the apparent loss of appetite. For example, the taste or smell of food might be affected, or the rat might have difficulty swallowing. It also is possible that hunger originates elsewhere in the brain, and the ablated area merely relays the messages that cause the rat to eat.

Electrical stimulation of the brain (ESB) Direct electrical stimulation and activation of brain tissue.

Electrode Any device (such as a wire, needle, or metal plate) used to stimulate or destroy nerve tissue electrically or to record its activity.

Ablation In biopsychology, the surgical removal of tissue from the surface of the brain.

Deep lesioning Removal of tissue within the brain by the use of an electrode.

Electroencephalograph (EEG) A device that records electrical activity in the brain.

Positron emission tomography (PET) A high-resolution imaging technique that captures brain activity by attaching radioactive particles to glucose molecules.

Functional MRI (fMRI) An MRI technique that records activity levels in various areas of the brain.

2.3 The Cerebral Cortex

GATEWAYS LEARNING OUTCOMES:
After reading this section you should be able to:

2.3.1 Explain how the left and right hemispheres of the cerebral cortex differ as a result of lateralization

2.3.2 Name the four lobes of the cerebral cortex and describe their functions

In many ways, we humans are pretty unimpressive creatures. Other animals surpass us in almost every category of strength, speed, and sensory sensitivity. However, we are the stars when it comes to intelligence.

Does that mean humans have the largest brains? No, that honor goes to whales, whose brains can weigh as much as six times more than ours. However, when we compare brain weight to body weight, we find that a whale's brain makes up as little as 1/10,000th of its total weight. The ratio for humans is 1/60. And yet the ratio for tree shrews (small, squirrel-like, insect-eating mammals) is about 1/30. So our human brains are not noteworthy in terms of either absolute or relative weight (Coolidge & Wynn, 2009; Herculano-Houzel, 2012).

So having a larger brain doesn't necessarily make a person smarter? Although a small positive correlation exists between intelligence and brain size, overall size alone does not determine human intelligence (Kievit et al., 2012; Royle et al., 2013). In fact, many parts of your brain are surprisingly similar to corresponding brain areas in other animals, such as lizards. What is different is your **cerebral cortex** (seh-REE-brel), the thin, outer covering of the brain in which high-level processes take place.

The cerebral cortex, which looks a little like a giant, wrinkled walnut, consists of two large hemispheres that cover the upper part of the brain. The two hemispheres are divided into smaller areas known as *lobes.* The cerebral cortex covers most of the brain with a mantle of *gray matter* (spongy tissue made up mostly of cell bodies). Although the cortex is only 3 millimeters thick (one-tenth of an inch), it contains 70 percent of the neurons in the central nervous system. In humans, the cortex is twisted and folded, and it is the largest brain structure (Striedter, Srinivasan, & Monuki, 2015). In lower animals, it is smooth and small (see ● Figure 2.11). The fact that humans are more intelligent than other animals is related to this **corticalization** (KORE-tih-kal-ih-ZAY-shun), or increase in the size and wrinkling of the cortex. Indeed, the human cortex is largely responsible for our ability to see, hear, move, think, as well as the fact that we can use language, make tools, acquire complex skills, and live in complex social groups (Coolidge & Wynn, 2009). Without the cortex, we humans wouldn't be much smarter than toads.

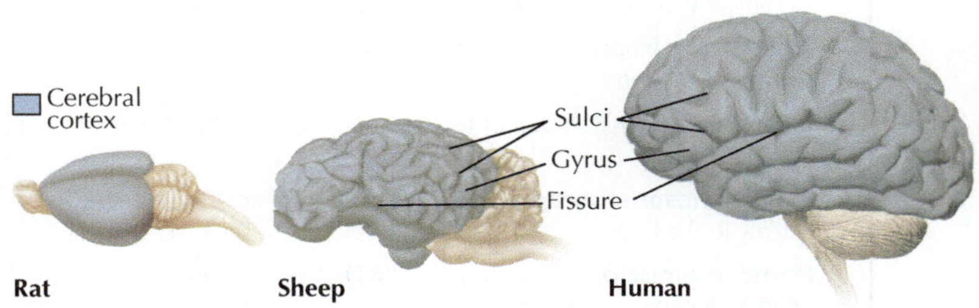

● **Figure 2.11 Corticalization of the human brain.** A more wrinkled cortex has greater cognitive capacity. Extensive corticalization is the key to human intelligence.

The Cerebral Hemispheres

The cortex is composed of two sides, or **cerebral hemispheres** (half-globes), that are connected by a thick band of axon fibers called the *corpus callosum* (KORE-pus kah-LOH-sum) (● Figure 2.12). It has long been known that the cerebral cortex displays **lateralization**, a specialization in the abilities of the left and right hemispheres.

Hemispheric Lateralization

In a very basic way, lateralization results in the left hemisphere controlling physical movement on the right side of the body. Likewise, the right hemisphere controls the left side of the body. If a stroke were to cause you to lose the ability to move your *left* arm, the stroke would have happened in your *right* hemisphere.

Damage to one hemisphere from a stroke may also cause a curious problem called *spatial neglect* (Llorens & Noé, 2016), which is related to attention rather than movement. A spatial neglect patient may pay no attention to one side of their visual field (● Figure 2.13). For example, patients with right hemisphere damage may not eat food on the left side of a plate. Some even refuse to acknowledge a paralyzed left arm as their own (Hirstein, 2005). If you point to the "alien" arm, the patient may well say, "Oh, that's not my arm. It must belong to someone else."

But the effects of lateralization aren't confined to movement and attention. In 1981, Roger Sperry (1914–1994) won a Nobel Prize for his remarkable discovery that the right and left brain hemispheres also perform differently on complex psychological abilities (Gazzaniga, 2015). For example, roughly 95 percent of us use our left brain for language (speaking, writing, and understanding). In addition, the left hemisphere is superior at math, judging time and rhythm, and coordinating the order of small complex movements, such as those needed for speech (Kell et al., 2011; Pinel & Dehaene, 2010).

In contrast, the right hemisphere can produce only the simplest language and numbers. To answer questions, the right hemisphere must use nonverbal responses, such as pointing at objects. But although it is poor at producing language, the right brain is especially good at providing an overall view of the world. It helps us with perceptual skills, such as recognizing patterns and faces. It also helps you express emotions and detect the emotions that other people are feeling (Castro-Schilo & Kee, 2010). And even though the right hemisphere is nearly "speechless," it is superior at some aspects of understanding language. If the right side of the brain is damaged, for example, people lose their ability to understand jokes, irony, sarcasm, implications, and other nuances of language. Basically, the right hemisphere helps us see the overall context in which something is said (Dyukova et al., 2010).

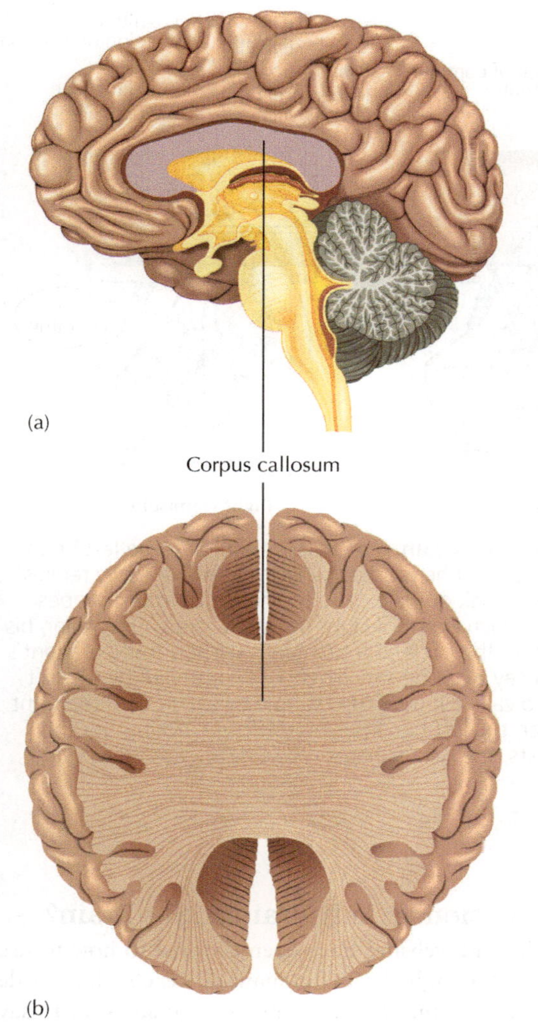

Figure 2.12 The corpus callosum. **(a)** The corpus callosum seems unremarkable when seen in crosssection. **(b)** Seen from above, with the neurons of the cerebral cortex that normally cover it removed, it is easier to appreciate the full extent of this thick band of axon fibers that richly interconnects the two cerebral hemispheres.

In general, then, the left hemisphere is involved mainly with *analysis* (breaking information into smaller parts). It also processes information *sequentially* (in order, one item after the next). In contrast, the right hemisphere appears to be involved in providing us with an overall view of the world, and it processes information *holistically* (all at once) and *simultaneously*. You could say that the right hemisphere is better at assembling pieces of the world into a "big picture"; it sees overall patterns and general connections while the left brain focuses on small details (Figure 2.14). Put another way, the right brain sees the wide-angle view; the left zooms in on specifics (Hübner & Volberg, 2005).

How did Sperry figure this out? Sperry and his student, Michael Gazzaniga, spent lots of time with people who had had a **split-brain operation**. In this rare surgery, the corpus callosum is

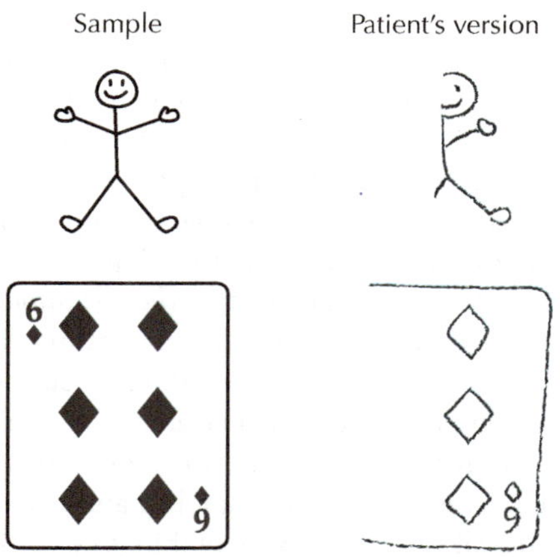

Figure 2.13 Spatial neglect. A patient with right-hemisphere damage asked to copy images will likely neglect the left-hand side when drawing them. Shown images of a human-like stick figure or a playing card, such a patient might produce versions like those shown here. Similar instances of neglect occur in many patients with right-hemisphere damage (Silveri, Ciccarelli, & Cappa, 2011). Of course, a patient with left-hemisphere damage would neglect the right side of these images.

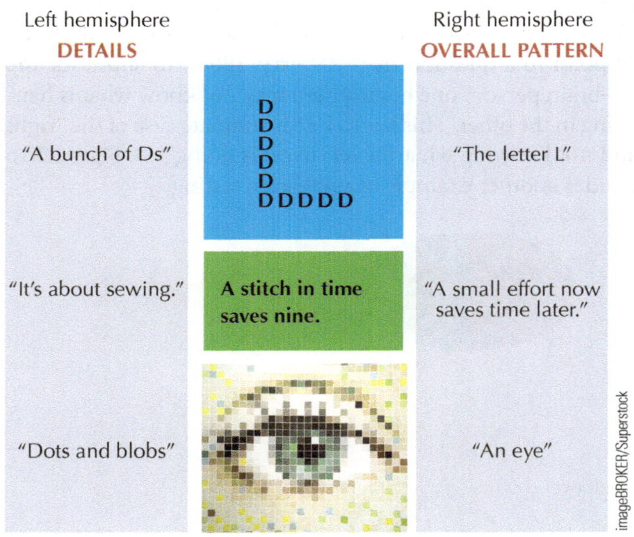

Figure 2.14 Local and global processing. The left and right brains have different information processing styles. The right brain gets the big pattern; the left focuses on small details.

Cerebral cortex The thin, wrinkled outer covering of the brain in which high-level processes take place.

Corticalization An increase in the relative size of the cerebral cortex.

Cerebral hemispheres The left and right sides of the cerebral cortex; interconnected by the corpus callosum.

Lateralization Differences between the two sides of the body, especially differences in the abilities of the brain hemispheres.

cut, typically to control severe epilepsy. Because the corpus callosum joins the two hemispheres, the result is essentially a person with two separate brains in one body (Schechter, 2012). After the right and left brain are separated, each hemisphere has its own separate perceptions, concepts, and impulses to act. It also becomes possible to send information solely to one hemisphere or the other (● Figure 2.15).

How does a split-brain person act after the operation? Having two "brains" in one body can create some interesting dilemmas. One split-brain patient, Karen, had to endure an out-of-control left hand. As Karen put it, "I'd light a cigarette, balance it on an ashtray, and then my left hand would reach forward and stub it out. It would take things out of my handbag and I wouldn't realize, so I would walk away. I lost a lot of things before I realized what was going on" (Mosley, 2011). However, such conflicts are actually rare. That's because both halves of the brain normally have about the same experience at the same time. Also, if a conflict arises, one hemisphere usually overrides the other.

Split-brain effects are easiest to see in specialized testing. For example, we could flash a dollar sign to the right brain and a question mark to the left brain of a patient named Tom (● Figure 2.15 shows how this is possible). Next, Tom is asked to draw what he saw, using his left hand, out of sight. Tom's left hand draws a dollar sign. If Tom is then asked to point with his right hand to a picture of what his hidden left hand drew, he will point to a question mark (Sperry, 1968). In short, for the split-brain person, one hemisphere may not know what is happening in the other. This has to be the ultimate case of the "right hand not knowing what the left hand is doing"! ● Figure 2.16 provides another example of split-brain testing.

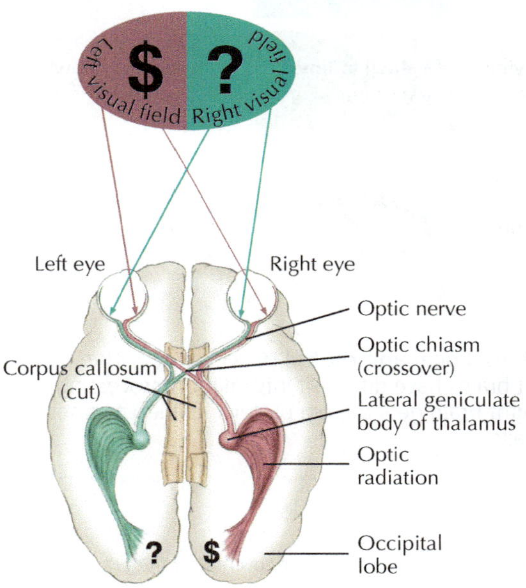

● **Figure 2.15 Basic pathways of vision.** Notice that the left portion of each eye connects to the left half of the brain; likewise, the right portion of each eye connects to the right brain. When the corpus callosum is cut, a split brain results. Then visual information can be sent to just one hemisphere by flashing it in the right or left visual field as the person stares straight ahead.

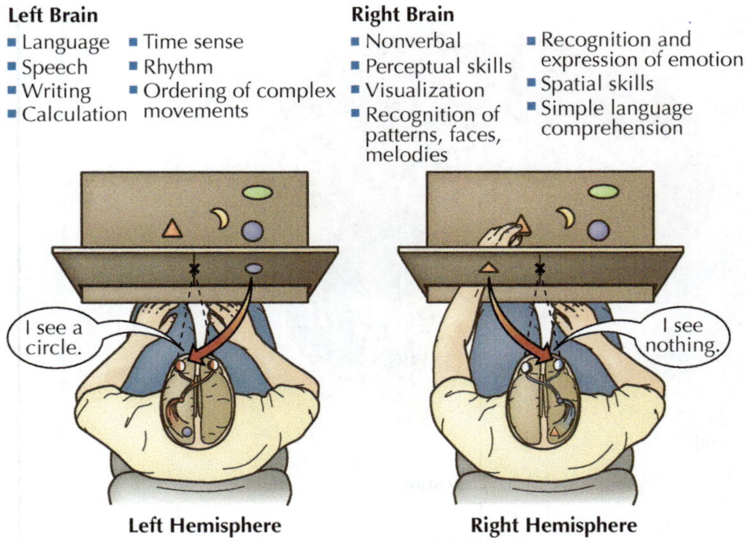

● **Figure 2.16 The split brain.** A circle is flashed to the left brain of a split-brain patient, and he is asked what he saw. He easily replies, "A circle." He can also pick out the circle by merely touching shapes with his right hand, which is out of sight behind a screen. However, his left hand can't identify the circle. If a triangle is flashed to the patient's right brain, he can't say what he saw (speech is controlled by the left hemisphere). He also can't identify the triangle by touch with the right hand. Now, however, the left hand has no difficulty picking out the triangle. In other tests, the hemispheres reveal distinct skills, as listed above the drawing.

Studying the Science: Left Brain/Right Brain?

Numerous books and websites have been devoted to how to use the left brain or the right brain to manage, teach, draw, ride horses, learn, and even make love. Some even go so far as to say that there are people who are "left-brained" and "right-brained." But this is a good example of a "neuromyth," because people normally use both sides of their brain at all times (Nielsen et al., 2013). It's true that some tasks may make *more* use of one hemisphere or the other. But in most real-world activities, the hemispheres share the work. Each does the parts that it does best and shares information with the other side.

A smart brain is one that grasps both the details (left hemisphere) and the overall picture (right hemisphere) at the same time. For instance, during a concert, a guitarist will use her left brain to judge time and rhythm and coordinate the order of her hand movements. At the same time, she will use her right brain to recognize and organize melodies, and monitor the overall sound of the music.

Human Diversity: Lateralization and Sex Differences

How about men's and women's brains? Are they specialized in different ways? Yes, they are. Many physical differences between male and female brains have been found, although their implications are not fully understood (McCarthy et al., 2012). One generalization that may stand the test of time is that the two hemispheres appear to be more interconnected in women than in men (Ingalhalikar et al., 2013; Tomasi & Volkow, 2012). (See ● Figure 2.17.)

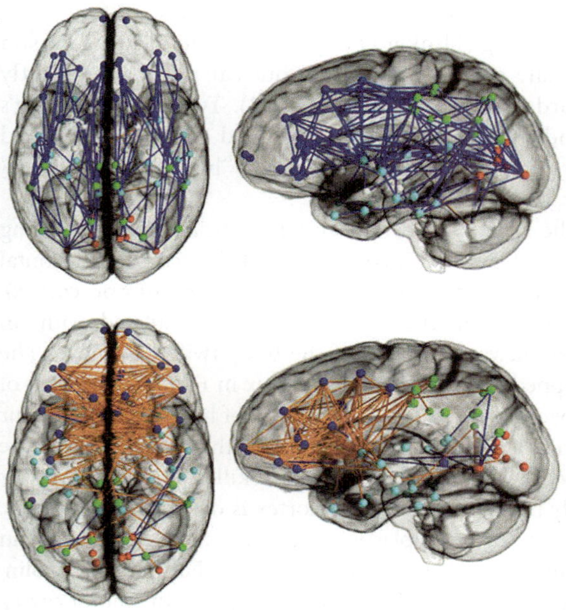

Figure 2.17 Male and female brains. (*top*) Male brains have more front-to-back connections in each hemisphere. (*bottom*) Female brains have more left-to-right connections between hemispheres (Ingalhalikar et al., 2013).

This structural difference may underlie some of the observed functional differences between men's and women's brains. For example, in one classic series of studies, researchers observed brain activity as people did language tasks. Both men and women showed increased activity in a region called Broca's area, on the left side of the brain, exactly as expected (we will further discuss Broca's area later in this chapter). Surprisingly, the *right* side of the brain was also activated in more than half the women tested. Despite this difference, the two sexes performed equally well on a task that involved sounding out words (Shaywitz et al., 1995). Another study, this time focused on intelligence, also found that women were more likely than men to use both sides of their brains (Tang et al., 2010).

It is tempting to conclude that the front-to-back connection pattern of the male hemispheres explains men's readiness to quickly go from perception to action. Similarly, the left-to-right connection pattern in females seems to explain women's greater willingness to combine rational and intuitive judgments. For now, these are just hypotheses that await further research.

Hemispheric Dominance

In addition to lateralization, the cerebral hemispheres may sometimes display *dominance*. For example, what is your **handedness**—do you prefer to use your right hand or your left hand? If you are right-handed, your **dominant hemisphere** is most likely the left hemisphere (and vice versa for left-handedness) (Meguerditchian, Vauclair, & Hopkins, 2013).

Overall hemispheric dominance is difficult to assess based on handedness alone, however. For example, about 95 percent of right-handers process speech in the left hemisphere and are left-brain dominant. But a good 70 percent of left-handers also process speech from the left hemisphere, just as right-handed people do. A smaller proportion of people—19 percent of lefties and 3 percent of righties—use their right brain for language, and are right-brain dominant. Some left-handers (approximately 12 percent) even use both sides of the brain for language processing (Szaflarski et al., 2011).

Mixed dominance is also quite common. While most people (about 75 percent) are strongly right- or left-handed (McManus et al., 2010), the rest show some inconsistency in hand preference. For example, one of your authors plays sports right-handed but writes left-handed. Other people may be *ambidextrous*, preferring either hand (or side) equally. For example, retired professional baseball player Pete Rose, who holds the record for the most hits in a career, was a "switch hitter," batting almost equally well from either the left side or the right side of the plate.

Hemispheric dominance is not restricted to handedness. You may have mixed preferences for using your left or right feet, eyes, and ears. You even have preferences for which nostril you usually breathe through and which direction you lean your head when kissing (Greenwood et al., 2006; van der Kamp & Cañal-Bruland, 2011). (Do you kiss "right"?)

Lobes of the Cerebral Cortex

Each of the two hemispheres of the cerebral cortex can be divided into several smaller *lobes*. Some of the **lobes of the cerebral cortex** are defined by larger fissures on the surface of the cortex. Others are regarded as separate areas because their functions are quite different (Figure 2.18).

The Frontal Lobes

The **frontal lobes** are areas of the cortex associated with movement, sense of self, and higher mental functions. If the frontal lobes are damaged, a patient's personality and emotional life may change dramatically. Remember Phineas Gage, the railroad foreman described in Section 1.7? He's the person who accidentally destroyed much of his frontal cortex. It's likely that Gage's personality changed after he suffered brain damage because the frontal cortex generates our sense of self, including an awareness of our current emotional state (Jenkins & Mitchell, 2011).

Split-brain operation A surgical procedure that involves cutting the corpus callosum.

Handedness A preference for the right or left hand in most activities.

Dominant hemisphere A term usually applied to the side of a person's brain that produces language.

Lobes of the cerebral cortex Areas on the left and right cortex bordered by major fissures or defined by their functions.

Frontal lobes Areas of the cortex associated with movement, the sense of self, and higher mental functions.

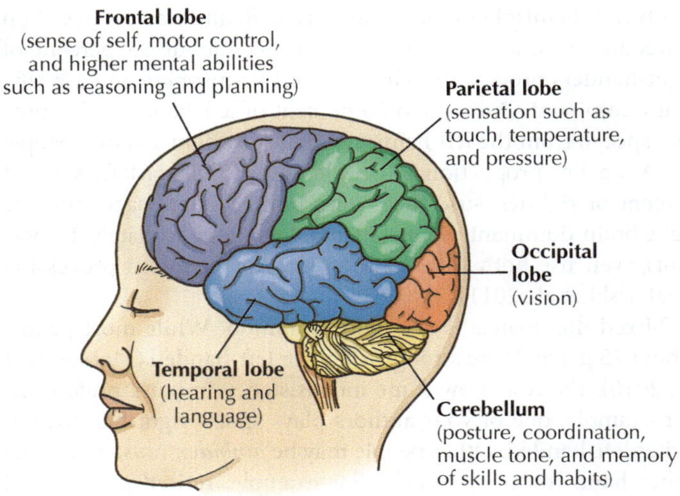

Figure 2.18 Functions of the lobes of the cerebral cortex.

The very front of the frontal lobes is known as the **prefrontal area (cortex)** (Figure 2.19). This part of the brain is responsible for the **executive functions**, the higher-level mental processes that allow us to regulate and coordinate our own thought processes (Gruberger et al., 2015). (Also see the section at the end of this chapter on *self-regulation*, and Section 5.5 on *metacognition*.) Damage to the prefrontal cortex, then, affects reasoning or planning (Roca et al., 2010). This is likely why patients with damage to the prefrontal areas often get stuck on mental tasks and repeat the same wrong answers over and over (Stuss & Knight, 2002).

Outside of the prefrontal cortex, most of the rest of the frontal lobes are usually referred to as *frontal association areas*. Only a small portion of the cerebral cortex (the primary areas) directly controls the body or receives information from the senses. All the surrounding areas, which are called **association areas (association cortex)**, combine and process information. For example, if you see a rose, association areas help you connect your primary sensory impressions with memories, so that you can recognize the rose and name it.

So what psychological functions are generally associated with the frontal lobes? Great question! First, PET and fMRI scans also suggest that much of what we call *intelligence* is related to increased activity in the frontal areas of the cortex (Cole et al., 2012; Nestor et al., 2015). Second, reduced frontal lobe function also leads to greater *impulsivity*, including increased risk for drug addiction (Crews & Boettiger, 2009). In turn, drug abuse can further damage this important area of the brain (Perry et al., 2011).

A third function that has been connected to some frontal association areas is *language*. For example, a person with damage to association areas in the left hemisphere may suffer **aphasia** (ah-FAZE-yah), an impaired ability to use language.

One type of aphasia is related to **Broca's area** (BRO-cahs), a speech center that is part of the left frontal association area (for 5 percent of all people, the area is part of the right frontal association area). (See Figure 2.19.) Damage to Broca's area causes *motor* (or *expressive*) *aphasia*, a great difficulty in speaking or writing (Flinker et al., 2015). Generally, the person knows what she or he wants to say but can't seem to fluently utter the words (Fridriksson et al., 2012). Typically, a patient's grammar and pronunciation are poor and speech is slow and labored. For example, the person may say "bife" for bike, "seep" for sleep, or "zokaid" for zodiac.

Fourth, the frontal lobes are also responsible for controlling *movement*. Specifically, an arch of tissue at the rear of the frontal lobes, called the **primary motor area (primary motor cortex)**, directs the body's muscles. If this area is stimulated with an electrical current, various parts of the body twitch or move. The drawing wrapped around the motor cortex in Figure 2.19 is out of proportion because it reflects the *dexterity* of body areas, not their size. The hands, for example, get more area than the feet. If you've ever wondered why your hands are more skilled or agile than your feet, it's partly because more motor cortex is devoted to the hands. Incidentally, due to neuroplasticity, learning and experience can alter these "motor maps" (Hoenig et al., 2011). For instance, violin, viola, and cello players have larger "hand maps" in the motor cortex (Hashimoto et al., 2004).

Mirror Neurons

The motor cortex is one brain area that contains **mirror neurons**. These neurons become active when we perform an action *and* when we merely observe someone else carrying out the same action. Their story of their discovery, though, was a neuroscience accident. Italian researchers had been reliably recording an increase in the activity of a single neuron in the motor cortex of a monkey as it reached for food. They quite logically concluded that the neuron was a **motor neuron**, and necessary for the monkey's ability to move. But one day when the monkey observed one of the researchers reaching for a snack of his own, that same neuron fired. It was responding as if the monkey had

Does this chimpanzee imitate researcher Jane Goodall by relying on mirror neurons?

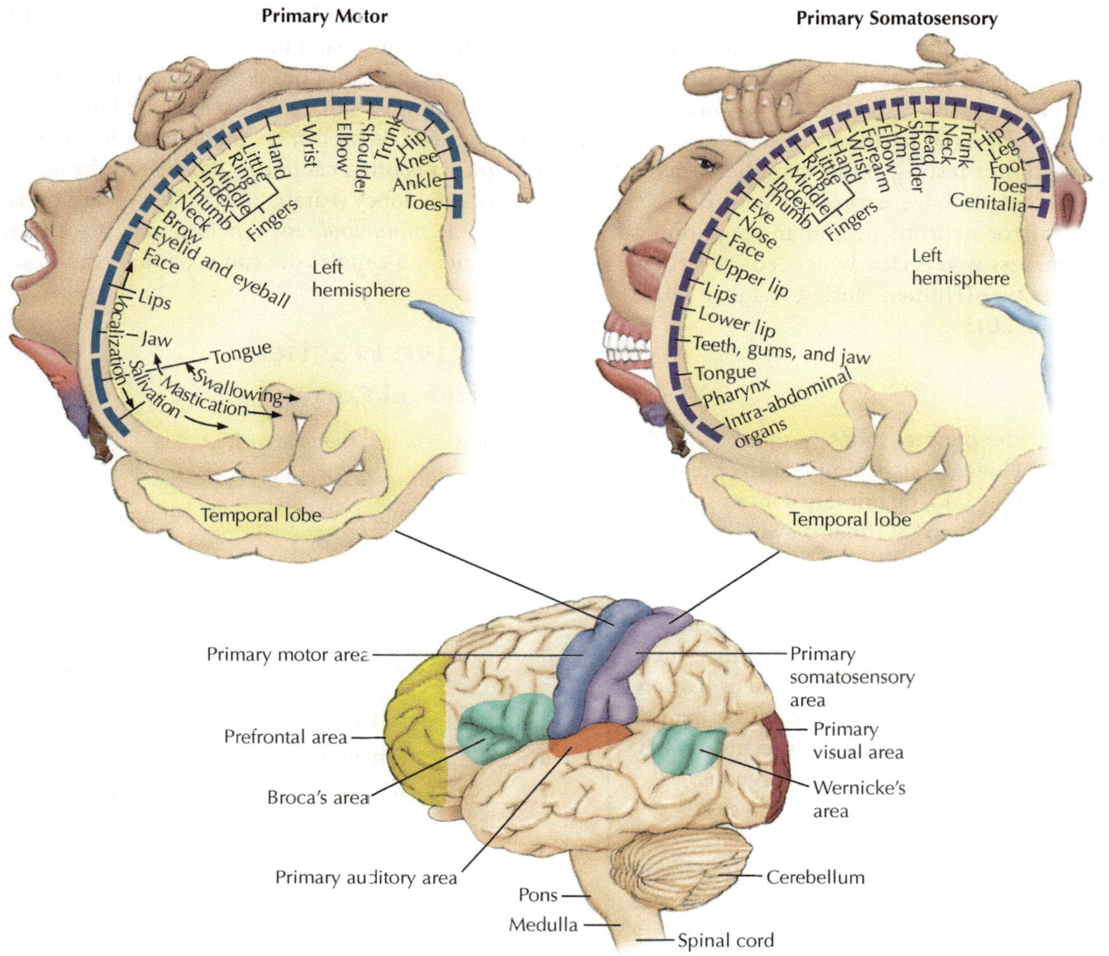

Figure 2.19 Functions of some cortical areas. The lobes of the cerebral cortex and the primary sensory, motor, visual, and auditory areas on each. The top diagrams show (in cross section) the relative amounts of cortex assigned to the sensory and motor control of various parts of the body. (Each cross section, or slice, of the cortex has been turned 90 degrees, so that you see it as it would appear from the back of the brain.)

reached for the food itself *even though the monkey hadn't moved*! Unexpectedly, a neuron involved in controlling a particular motor movement also was activated when the monkey merely observed that same motor movement in someone else. Just like that, the Italians discovered *mirror neurons* (Rizzolatti, Fogassi, & Gallese, 2006).

Their discovery triggered a flood of interest. Researchers were quick to confirm that mirror neurons are found in various areas of the monkey brain and appear to exist in the human brain as well (Molenberghs, Cunnington, & Mattingley, 2012). Psychologists had long assumed that learning new skills by imitating others involved a complicated process. But now it seemed possible that newborn humans (and monkeys) easily imitate others because networks of mirror neurons are activated when an infant watches someone perform an action. Then the same mirror network can be used to perform that action (Cook et al., 2014; Meini & Paternoster, 2012). Psychologists and neuroscientists have also speculated that human empathy (the ability to identify with another person's experiences and feelings) may arise from the activation of mirror neurons

Prefrontal area (prefrontal cortex) The very front of the frontal lobes; involved in the sense of self, executive functions, and planning.

Executive functions The higher-level mental processes that allow us to regulate and coordinate our own thought processes.

Association areas (association cortex) All areas of the cerebral cortex that are not primarily sensory or motor in function.

Aphasia A speech disturbance resulting from brain damage.

Broca's area A language area related to grammar and pronunciation.

Primary motor area (primary motor cortex) A brain area associated with the control of movement.

Mirror neurons Neurons that become active when a motor action is carried out *and* when another organism is observed performing the same action.

Motor neuron A cell in the nervous system that transmits commands from the brain to the muscles.

Autism spectrum disorder A lifetime disorder whose primary features are impaired communication and social interaction.

Parietal lobes Areas of the cortex in which body sensations register.

Primary somatosensory area (primary somatosensory cortex) A receiving area for body sensations.

(Corradini & Antonietti, 2013). (■ See Section 6.4 to read more about imitation.) Because imitation and empathy are connected to **autism spectrum disorder** (a condition whose features are impaired communication and social interaction), researchers have wondered whether mirror neurons may play a role in this disorder as well.

To date, results from studies testing these hypotheses have been mixed and some scientists have expressed considerable doubt about the role of mirror neurons in human functioning (Hickok, 2014). Additional research is clearly needed; nevertheless, the possibilities are exciting (Hunter, Hurley, & Taber, 2013; Oberman & Ramachandran, 2015).

The Parietal Lobes

Bodily sensations register in the **parietal lobes** (puh-RYE-ih-tal), located just behind the frontal lobes. Touch, temperature, pressure, and other somatic sensations flow into the **primary somatosensory area (primary somatosensory cortex)** (SO-mat-oh-SEN-soree) of the parietal lobes. Again, we find that the map of bodily sensations is distorted. In the case of somatosensory cortex, the drawing in ● Figure 2.19 reflects the *sensitivity* of body areas, not their size. For example, the lips are large in the drawing because of their great sensitivity, whereas the back and trunk, which are less sensitive, are much smaller. Notice that the hands are also large in the map of body sensitivity—which is obviously an aid to musicians, typists, watchmakers, massage therapists, lovers, and brain surgeons.

The Temporal Lobes

The **temporal lobes** are located on each side of the brain and are important to hearing. Auditory information is sent via the auditory nerve directly to the **primary auditory area (primary auditory cortex)**. If we did a PET scan of your brain while you listened to your favorite song, your primary auditory area would be the first to "light up," followed by association areas in your temporal lobes. Likewise, if we could electrically stimulate the primary auditory area of your temporal lobe, you would "hear" a series of sound sensations.

A left temporal lobe association area called **Wernicke's area** (VER-nick-ees) also functions as a language site (see ● Figure 2.19; again, for 5 percent of all people, the area is on the right temporal lobe). If it is damaged, the result is a *receptive* (or *fluent*) *aphasia*. Although the person can hear and speak speech normally, he or she has difficulty understanding the meaning of words (Ardila, Bernal, & Rosselli, 2016). Thus, when shown a picture of a chair, someone with Broca's aphasia might say "tssair." In contrast, a Wernicke's patient might *fluently*, but incorrectly, identify the photo as "truck."

The Occipital Lobes

At the back of the brain, we find the **occipital lobes** (awk-SIP-ih-tal), cortical areas that play a role in visual processing. Patients with tumors (cell growths that interfere with brain activity) in the **primary visual area (primary visual cortex)**, the part of the cortex to first receive input from the eyes, experience blind spots in their vision.

Do the primary visual areas of the cortex correspond directly to what is seen? Images are mapped onto the brain, but the map is greatly stretched and distorted (Freberg, 2016). That's why it's important to avoid thinking of the visual area as a little television screen in the brain. Visual information creates complex patterns of activity in neurons; it does *not* make a television-like image.

One of the most fascinating results of brain injury is **visual agnosia** (ag-KNOW-zyah), an inability to identify seen objects. Visual agnosia is often caused by damage to the association areas on the occipital lobes (Farah, 2004). This condition is sometimes referred to as *mindblindness*. For example, if we show Alice, an agnosia patient, a candle, she can see it and can describe it as "a

Reflective Practice

The Cerebral Cortex

See if you can match the following.

1. ______ Corpus callosum	**A.** Visual area
2. ______ Occipital lobes	**B.** Language, speech, writing
3. ______ Parietal lobes	**C.** Motor cortex and abstract thinking
4. ______ Temporal lobes	**D.** Spatial skills, visualization, pattern recognition
5. ______ Frontal lobes	**E.** Speech disturbances
6. ______ Association cortex	**F.** Hearing
7. ______ Aphasias	**G.** Increased ratio of cortex in brain
8. ______ Corticalization	**H.** Bodily sensations
9. ______ Left hemisphere	**I.** Treatment for severe epilepsy
10. ______ Right hemisphere	**J.** Inability to identify seen objects
11. ______ Split brain	**K.** Fibers connecting the cerebral hemispheres
12. ______ Agnosia	**L.** Cortex that is not sensory or motor in function

THINK CRITICALLY

13. If your brain were removed, replaced by another, and moved to a new body, how would you evaluate the "new you"?—your old body with the new brain, or your new body with the old brain?

SELF-REFLECT

- Think of learning the functions of the brain lobes as being like learning countries on a map. Try drawing a map of the cortex. Can you label all the different lobes and name their functions? Where is the primary motor area? The primary somatosensory area? Broca's area? Keep redrawing the map until it becomes more detailed and you can do it easily.

Answers: 1. K 2. A 3. H 4. F 5. C 6. L 7. E 8. G 9. B 10. D 11. I 12. J 13. Although there is no "correct" answer to this question, your personality, knowledge, personal memories, and self-concept all derive from brain activity—a fact which makes a strong case for your old brain in a new body being more nearly the "real you."

long narrow object that tapers at the top." Alice can even draw the candle accurately, but she cannot name it. However, if she is allowed to feel the candle, she will name it immediately. In short, Alice can still see color, size, and shape. She just can't form the associations necessary to perceive the meanings of objects.

An especially fascinating form of mindblindness is **facial agnosia**, an inability to perceive familiar faces (Sacks, 2010; Susilo et al., 2015). One patient with facial agnosia couldn't recognize her husband or mother when they visited her in the hospital, and she was unable to identify pictures of her children. However, as soon as visitors spoke, she knew them immediately by their voices.

Areas devoted to recognizing faces and the emotions they convey lie in association areas in the occipital and frontal lobes (Prochnow et al., 2013). These areas appear to be highly specialized. Why would parts of the brain be set aside solely for processing faces? From an evolutionary standpoint, it is not really so surprising—after all, we are social animals for whom facial recognition is very important.

2.4 The Subcortex and Endocrine System

GATEWAYS LEARNING OUTCOMES:
After reading this section you should be able to:

2.4.1 Name the three major regions of the subcortex, and the parts that make up each one

2.4.2 Explain how the endocrine system works, and describe the action of four endocrine glands

Although our cerebral cortex makes us uniquely human, it is important to recognize the critical role played by our more primitive subcortex and its links to the endocrine system. For example, the cerebral cortex is surprisingly unnecessary for physical survival. You, or at least your body, would continue to live even if you lost large portions of your cerebral cortex. Not so with the subcortex (the brain structures underneath the cerebral cortex) and your endocrine system. Hunger, thirst, sleep, attention, sex, breathing, and many other vital functions are controlled by parts of these areas. Let's take a quick tour (Figure 2.20).

The Subcortex

Like a multilevel parking garage beneath an apartment building, the **subcortex** lies beneath the cerebral hemispheres, and can be divided into three layers: the hindbrain, midbrain, and forebrain.

The Hindbrain

The **hindbrain** is the most primitive part of the brain. It comprises the medulla, pons, reticular formation, and cerebellum.

Medulla and Pons

The **medulla** connects the brain with the spinal cord and controls vital life functions. As a result, various drugs, diseases, and injuries that can disrupt the medulla may end or endanger life. The **pons** acts as a bridge between the medulla and other brain areas, including the cerebellum, and influences sleep and arousal.

The Reticular Formation

A collection of cells and fibers called the **reticular formation (RF)** (reh-TICK-you-ler) lies inside the medulla and pons. As messages flow into the brain, the RF gives priority to some while turning others aside (Freberg, 2016). In doing so, the RF influences *attention*. The RF doesn't fully mature until adolescence, which may be why children have such short attention spans. The RF also modifies outgoing commands to the body. In this way, the RF affects muscle tone, posture, and movements of the eyes, face, head, body, and limbs. At the same time, the RF controls the reflexes involved in breathing, sneezing, coughing, and vomiting.

The RF also keeps us vigilant, alert, and awake. Incoming messages from the sense organs branch into the RF, which bombards the cortex with stimulation, keeping it active and alert. For instance, let's say that a sleepy driver rounds a bend and encounters a deer standing in the road. The driver snaps to attention and applies the brakes. She can thank her RF for arousing the rest of her brain and averting an accident. If you're getting sleepy while reading this section, try pinching your ear—a little pain will cause the RF to momentarily arouse your cortex.

The Cerebellum

The **cerebellum** is also part of the hindbrain. Looking like a miniature cerebral cortex, the cerebellum lies near the base of the brain. Although there is growing evidence that it plays a role in cognition and emotion (Adamaszek et al., 2016; Schmahmann, 2010), the cerebellum primarily regulates posture, muscle tone, and muscular coordination. Without the cerebellum, tasks such as walking, running, or playing catch become impossible.

Temporal lobes Areas of the cortex that include the sites where hearing registers.

Primary auditory area (primary auditory cortex) The part of the temporal lobe that first receives input from the ears.

Wernicke's area A temporal lobe brain area related to language comprehension.

Occipital lobes Cortical areas at the back of the brain that play a role in visual processing.

Primary visual area (primary visual cortex) The part of the occipital lobe that first receives input from the eyes.

Visual agnosia An inability to identify seen objects.

Facial agnosia An inability to perceive familiar faces.

Subcortex A term referring to all brain structures below the cerebral cortex.

Hindbrain A primitive part of the brain that comprises the medulla, pons, and cerebellum.

Medulla The structure that connects the brain with the spinal cord and controls vital life functions.

Pons An area of the hindbrain that acts as a bridge between the medulla and other structures.

Reticular formation (RF) A collection of cells and fibers in the medulla and pons involved in arousal and attention.

Cerebellum The structure in the hindbrain involved in controlling coordination and balance.

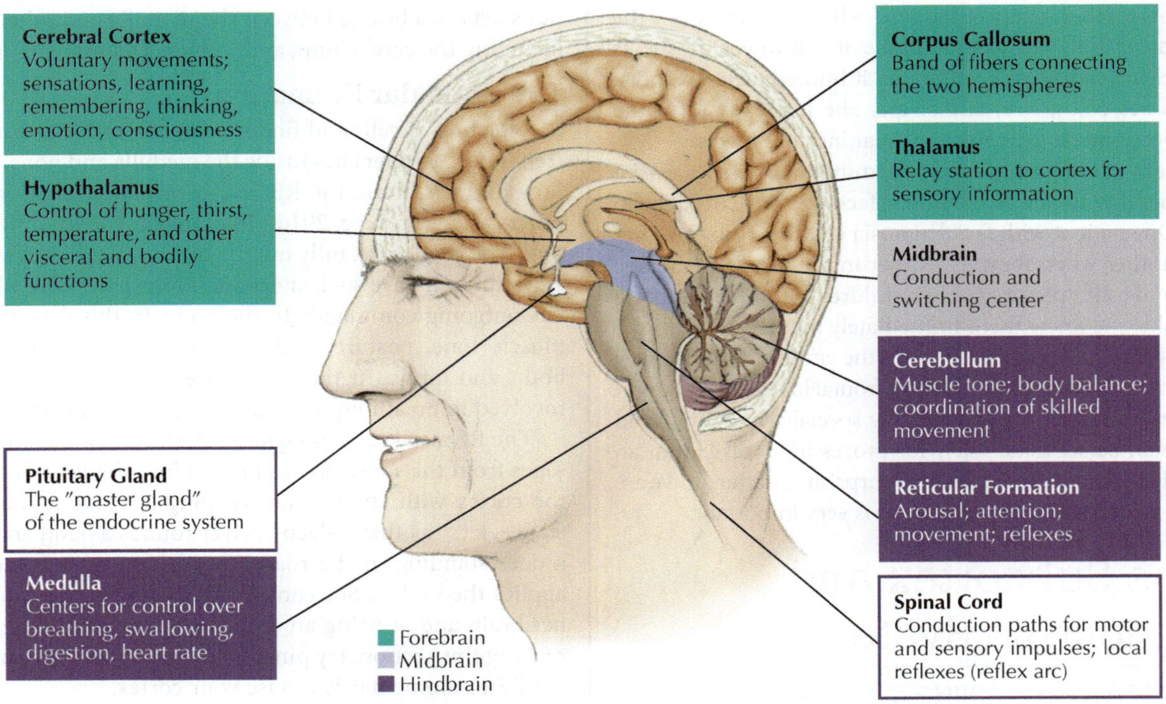

Figure 2.20 Main structures of the human brain. This simplified drawing shows the main structures of the human brain and describes some of their most important features. (You can use the color code in the foreground to identify which areas are part of the forebrain, midbrain, and hindbrain.)

The cerebellum also stores memories related to "know-how," or our skills (Alstermark & Ekerot, 2013). Once again, we see that experience shapes the brain: Musicians and athletes, who practice special motor skills throughout their lives, have larger than average cerebellums (Hutchinson et al., 2003; Park et al., 2012). (Note that "know-what" memories, such as remembering a person's name or knowing what the cerebellum does, are stored elsewhere in the brain; see Section 7.3.)

The Midbrain

The **midbrain** is the brain structure that connects the hindbrain with the forebrain. The midbrain and two hindbrain structures (pons and medulla) make up the *brainstem*, which is the thickening of the spinal cord where it joins the brain. Virtually all communication between the cerebral cortex and the rest of the body passes through the brainstem.

Damage to the brainstem can be devastating, as Kate Adamson will tell you. At the age of 33, a stroke caused catastrophic damage to her brainstem. This event cut off communication between Kate's body and her cortex, leaving her with *locked-in syndrome*. Just before the stroke, she was fine, and the next moment, she was totally paralyzed, trapped in her own body and barely able to breathe (Cruse et al., 2011). Unable to move a muscle, but still fully awake and aware, she was unable to communicate her simplest thoughts and feelings to others.

Kate thought that she was going to die. Her doctors, who thought she was *brain dead*, or at best only minimally conscious, did not administer painkillers as they inserted breathing and feeding tubes down her throat. In time, Kate discovered that she could communicate by blinking her eyes. After a recovery that was miraculous by any measure, she went on to appear before the U.S. Congress and even wrote about her experiences (Adamson, 2004).

Not everyone is so lucky. Just think what might have befallen Kate had she not even been able to blink her eyes (Schnakers et al., 2009). In one chilling study, coma researchers used fMRI to reexamine 54 patients previously diagnosed as being practically brain dead. Patients were repeatedly asked to imagine swinging a tennis racket or walking down a familiar street. Five of the patients showed clearly different brain activity for the two tasks, despite being unable to communicate with doctors in any other way (Monti et al., 2010).

What if they could "will" a computer to speak for them? Right! These results suggest that not all totally locked-in patients are brain dead or minimally conscious. The results also hold out hope that we may eventually be able to develop brain–computer interfaces to help free these patients from their bodily prisons (Laureys & Boly, 2007; Shih & Krusienski, 2012).

The Forebrain

The **forebrain** comprises several brain structures that govern higher-order mental processes, including the cerebral cortex that was discussed earlier in this chapter. Along with the cerebral cortex and corpus callosum, the forebrain also includes the thalamus (THAL-uh-mus), hypothalamus (HI-po-THAL-uh-mus), and limbic system.

Thalamus

The **thalamus** acts as a final "relay" for sensory information on its way to the cerebral cortex. Vision, hearing, taste, and touch all pass through this small, football-shaped structure. Thus, injury to even small areas of the thalamus can cause deafness, blindness, or loss of any other sense, except smell.

Hypothalamus

About the size of a grape, the human **hypothalamus** is a small area of the brain that regulates emotional behaviors and basic biological needs (Kalat, 2016). The hypothalamus affects behaviors as diverse as sex, rage, temperature control, hormone release, eating and drinking, sleep, waking, and emotion. (■ See Section 10.2.)

The hypothalamus is basically a "crossroads" that connects many areas of the brain. It is also the final pathway for many kinds of behavior. That is, the hypothalamus is the last place where many behaviors are organized or "decided on" before messages leave the brain, causing the body to react.

The Limbic System

As a group, the hypothalamus, parts of the thalamus, the amygdala, the hippocampus, and other mainly subcortical structures make up the **limbic system** (● Figure 2.21). The limbic system plays an important role in controlling emotion and memory (LeDoux, 2012). Rage, fear, sexual response, and intense arousal can be localized to various points in the limbic system. Laughter, a delightful part of human social life, also has its origins in here (Wild et al., 2003).

During evolution, the limbic system was the earliest layer of the forebrain to develop. In lower animals, the limbic system helps organize basic survival responses: feeding, fleeing, fighting, and reproduction. In humans, a clear link to emotion remains. The **amygdala** (ah-MIG-dah-luh), in particular, is associated with emotional processing and is strongly related to fear and the memory of fearful experiences (Bergstrom et al., 2013).

The amygdala provides a primitive, quick pathway to the cortex. Like lower animals, we can be startled and, as such, are able to react to dangerous stimuli before we fully know what is going on (Méndez-Bértolo et al., 2016). In situations in which true danger exists, such as in military combat, the amygdala's rapid response may aid survival. However, disorders of the brain's fear system can be very disruptive. An example is the war veteran who involuntarily dives into the bushes when he hears a car backfire.

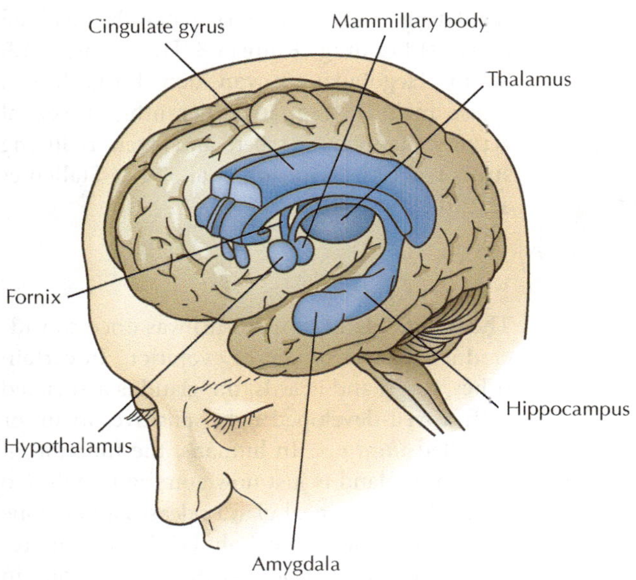

● **Figure 2.21 Parts of the limbic system.** Although only one side is shown here, the hippocampus and the amygdala extend into the temporal lobes at each side of the brain. The limbic system is a sort of primitive core of the brain strongly associated with emotion.

The role of the amygdala in emotion may also explain why people who suffer from phobias and disabling anxiety often feel afraid without knowing why (Lamprecht et al., 2009; Schlund & Cataldo, 2010). For example, people who survive horrible experiences, such as a plane crash, can have debilitating fears years later due to unconscious fear produced by the amygdala. (■ See the discussion of stress-related disorders in Section 14.4.)

Some parts of the limbic system have taken on additional, higher-level functions. A part called the **hippocampus** (HIP-oh-CAMP-us) is important for storing memories (Jurd, 2011; Moscovitch et al., 2016). The hippocampus lies inside the temporal lobes, which is why stimulating the temporal lobes can produce memory-like or dreamlike experiences. The hippocampus also helps us navigate the space around us. The right side of your hippocampus becomes more active, for instance, if you mentally plan a drive across town (Maguire, Intraub, & Mullally, 2016).

Psychologists have also discovered that animals will learn to press a lever to deliver a dose of electrical stimulation to the limbic system (■ see Section 6.2). The animals act like the stimulation is satisfying or pleasurable. Indeed, several areas of the limbic system act as reward, or "pleasure," pathways. Many are found in the hypothalamus, where they overlap with areas that control thirst, sex, and hunger. As we mentioned earlier in this chapter, commonly abused drugs, such as cocaine, amphetamine, heroin, nicotine, cannabis, and alcohol, activate many of the same pleasure pathways. This appears to be part of the reason that these drugs feel so rewarding (Niehaus, Cruz-Bermúdez, & Kauer, 2009; Prus, 2014). You might also be interested to know that music you would describe as "thrilling" activates pleasure systems in your brain. This may explain some of the appeal of music that can send shivers down your spine (Salimpoor et al., 2011). (It also may explain why people pay so much for concert tickets!)

Incidentally, aversive, or "punishment," areas also have been found in the limbic system. When these locations are activated, animals show discomfort and work hard to turn off the stimulation. Because much of our behavior is based on seeking pleasure and avoiding pain, these discoveries continue to fascinate psychologists.

Midbrain A structure that connects the hindbrain with the forebrain.

Forebrain A brain structure, including the limbic system, thalamus, hypothalamus, and cortex, that governs higher-order mental processes.

Thalamus A brain structure that relays sensory information to the cerebral cortex.

Hypothalamus A small area of the brain that regulates emotional behaviors and basic biological needs.

Limbic system A set of brain structures that play important roles in regulating emotion and memory.

Amygdala A part of the limbic system associated with the rapid processing of emotions; especially fear.

Hippocampus Part of the limbic system associated with storing memories.

The Endocrine System

Our behavior is not solely a product of the nervous system. The endocrine (EN-duh-krin) glands form an equally important parallel communication system in the body (Kalat, 2016). The **endocrine system** is made up of glands that secrete *hormones* directly into the bloodstream or lymphatic system (see Figure 2.22). Chemically similar to neurotransmitters, **hormones** are carried throughout the body, where they affect both internal activities and visible behaviors such as puberty, personality, dwarfism, jet lag, and many more.

How do hormones affect behavior? Although we are seldom directly aware of them, hormones affect us in many ways (Kalat, 2016). For example, hormone output from the adrenal glands rises during stressful situations, and androgens (meaning "male" hormones) are related to the sex drive in both males and females. We also know that hormones secreted during times of high emotion intensify memory formation and that at least some of the emotional turmoil of adolescence is due to elevated hormone levels. Not surprisingly, pregnancy and motherhood cause the release of hormones that lead to the changes involved in maternal behavior (Henry & Sherwin, 2012). Even disturbing personality patterns may be linked to hormonal irregularities (Evardone, Alexander, & Morey, 2007). These examples should begin to give you some sense of just how important the glands of the endocrine system are, so let's take a closer look at how they work.

Pituitary Gland

The **pituitary gland** is a pea-sized globe hanging from the base of the brain (see Figure 2.22). The pituitary is often called the "master gland" because it influences the other endocrine glands (especially the thyroid, adrenal glands, and ovaries or testes). These glands in turn regulate such body processes as metabolism, responses to stress, and reproduction. But the master has a master: the pituitary is directed by the hypothalamus, which lies directly above it. In this way, the hypothalamus can affect glands throughout the body. This, then, is the major link between the brain and hormones (Kalat, 2016; Prus, 2014).

One of the pituitary's more important roles is to regulate growth (Beans, 2009). If too little **growth hormone** is released by the pituitary during childhood, a person may remain far smaller than average. If this condition is not treated, a child may be 6 to 12 inches shorter than age-mates. As adults, some will have *hypopituitary* (HI-po-pih-TU-ih-ter-ee) *dwarfism*. Such individuals are perfectly proportioned, but tiny. Regular injections of growth hormone can raise a hypopituitary child's height by several inches, usually to the short side of average.

Too much growth hormone produces *gigantism* (excessive bodily growth). Secretion of too much growth hormone late in the growth period causes *acromegaly* (AK-row-MEG-uh-lee), a condition in which the arms, hands, feet, and facial bones become enlarged. Acromegaly produces prominent facial features, which some people have used as a basis for careers as character actors, wrestlers, and the like.

Oxytocin is another important hormone released by the pituitary. It plays a broad role in regulating many behaviors generally involved in social bonding (Kumsta & Heinrichs, 2013; Stoop, Hegoburu, & van den Burg, 2015). These include pregnancy, parenthood, sexual activity, happiness, trust, and even reducing stress reactions (Gordon et al., 2010; Stallen et al., 2012).

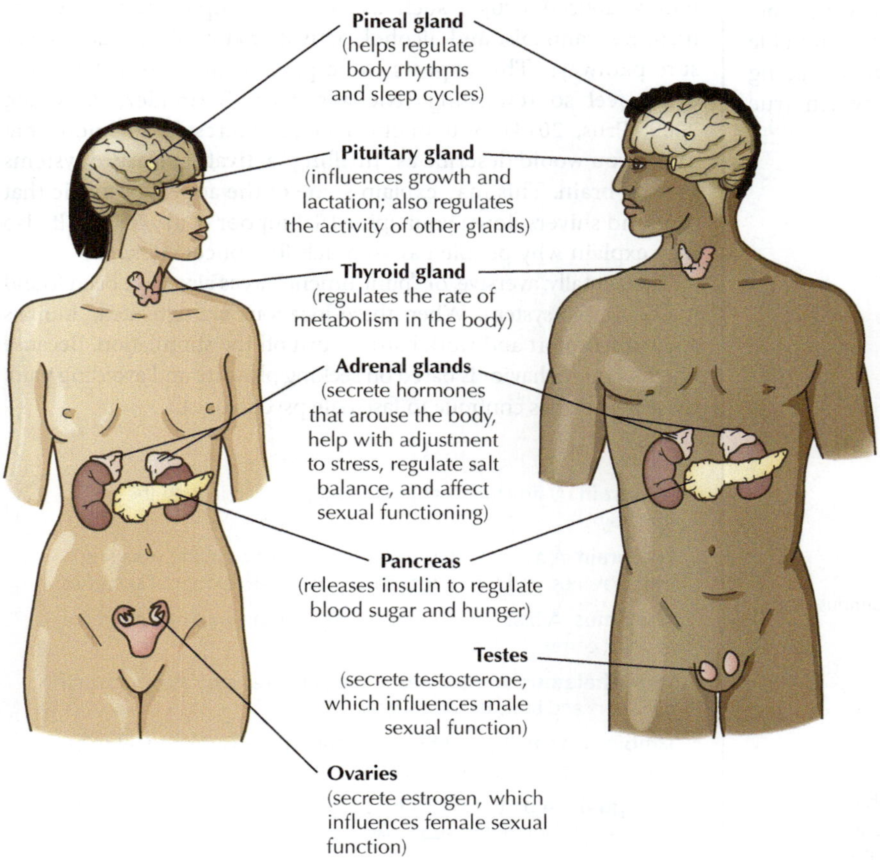

Figure 2.22 The endocrine system.

Pineal Gland

The **pineal gland** (pin-EE-ul) was once considered a useless remnant of evolution. In certain fishes, frogs, and lizards, the gland is associated with a well-developed light-sensitive organ, or so-called *third eye*. In humans, the function of the pineal gland is just now coming to light (so to speak). The pineal gland releases a hormone called **melatonin** (mel-ah-TONE-in) in response to daily variations in light. Melatonin levels in the bloodstream rise at dusk, peak around midnight, and fall again as morning approaches. As far as the brain is concerned, it's bedtime when melatonin levels rise (Norman,

Known as the "cuddle" hormone, oxytocin is released by the pituitary gland in a wide variety of intimate situations. For example, a mother's oxytocin levels play an important role in deepening the mother/child bond during the all-important early years (Feldman et al., 2013).

2009). (■ Melatonin can be used to reset the body's "clock" and minimize jet lag for long-distance pilots, aircrews, and travelers. See Section 10.2.)

Thyroid Gland

The **thyroid gland**, located in the neck, regulates *metabolism*, the rate at which energy is produced and expended in the body. By altering metabolism, the thyroid can have a sizable effect on personality. A person suffering from *hyperthyroidism* (an overactive thyroid) tends to be thin, tense, excitable, and nervous. An underactive thyroid (*hypothyroidism*) in an adult can cause inactivity, sleepiness, slowness, obesity, and depression (Joffe, 2006).

Adrenal Glands

The **adrenal glands** are located just under the back of the rib cage, atop the kidneys. The *adrenal medulla,* or inner core of the adrenal glands, is the source of epinephrine and norepinephrine. (Epinephrine is also known as adrenaline, a word that may be more familiar to you.) **Epinephrine** (ep-eh-NEF-rin), which is associated with fear, tends to arouse the body. **Norepinephrine** (or noradrenaline), which also functions as a neurotransmitter in the brain, also tends to arouse the body, but it is linked with anger.

Fear and anger prepare your body for "fight or flight" action: your heart rate and blood pressure rise; stored sugar is released into the bloodstream for quick energy; your muscles tense and receive more blood; and your blood is prepared to clot more quickly in case of injury. As we discussed earlier in this chapter, these changes are controlled by the autonomic nervous system (ANS). Specifically, the sympathetic branch of the ANS causes the adrenal glands to release epinephrine and norepinephrine.

The *adrenal cortex,* or outer "bark" of the adrenal glands, produces a set of hormones called corticoids (KOR-tih-coids). One of their jobs is to regulate salt balance in the body. A deficiency of certain corticoids can evoke a powerful craving for the taste of salt in humans. The corticoids also help the body adjust to stress, and they are a secondary source of sex hormones. An oversecretion of the adrenal sex hormones can cause *virilism* (exaggerated male characteristics). For instance, a woman may grow a beard, or a man's voice may become so low that it is difficult to understand. Oversecretion early in life can cause *premature puberty* (full sexual development during childhood).

Anabolic Steroids

Testosterone, one of the principal androgens, or "male" hormones, is supplied in small amounts by the adrenal glands. (The testes are the main source of testosterone in males.) Perhaps you have heard about the use of anabolic steroids by athletes who want to "bulk up" or promote muscle growth. Most of these drugs are synthetic versions of testosterone.

Although there is some disagreement about whether steroids actually improve athletic performance, it is widely accepted that they may cause serious side effects (Grönbladh, Nylander, & Hall-berg, 2016; Kanayama et al., 2012). Problems include voice deepening or baldness in women and shrinkage of the testicles, sexual impotence, or breast enlargement in men (Millman & Ross, 2003). Dangerous increases in hostility and aggression ("roid rage") have also been linked to steroid use (Cunningham, Lumia, & McGinnis, 2013; Hartgens & Kuipers, 2004). Increased risk of heart attack and stroke, liver damage, and stunted growth also are common when younger adolescents use steroids. Understandably, almost all major sports organizations ban the use of anabolic steroids.

Endocrine system A network of glands that release hormones into the bloodstream.

Hormones A chemical released by the endocrine glands.

Pituitary gland The master gland of the endocrine system that controls the action of all other glands.

Growth hormone A hormone, secreted by the pituitary gland, that promotes body growth.

Oxytocin A hormone, released by the pituitary gland, that plays a broad role in regulating pregnancy, parenthood, sexual activity, social bonding, trust, and even reducing stress reactions.

Pineal gland A gland in the brain that helps regulate body rhythms and sleep cycles.

Melatonin A hormone released by the pineal gland in response to daily cycles of light and dark.

Thyroid gland An endocrine gland that helps regulate the rate of metabolism.

Adrenal glands Endocrine glands that arouse the body, regulate salt balance, adjust the body to stress, and affect sexual functioning.

Epinephrine An adrenal hormone that tends to arouse the body; epinephrine is associated with fear. (Also known as *adrenaline.*)

Norepinephrine Both a brain neurotransmitter and an adrenal hormone that tends to arouse the body; norepinephrine is associated with anger. (Also known as *noradrenaline.*)

Reflective Practice

The Subcortex and Endocrine System

1. Three major divisions of the brain are the ________________, the ________________, and the ________________.
2. Reflex centers for heartbeat and respiration are found in the
   a. cerebellum
   b. thalamus
   c. medulla
   d. RF
3. A portion of the reticular formation serves as an ________________ system in the brain.
   a. activating
   b. alternate
   c. adjustment
   d. aversive
4. The ________________ is a final relay, or switching station, for sensory information on its way to the cortex.
5. Reward and punishment areas are found throughout the ________________ system, which also is related to emotion.
6. The body's ability to resist stress is related to the action of the ________________ glands.

THINK CRITICALLY

7. Subcortical structures in humans are quite similar to corresponding brain areas in most animals with spinal cords. Why would knowing this allow you to predict, in general terms, what functions the subcortex controls?

SELF-REFLECT

- What are the major subcortical structures, and what functions do they control?
- Why is it especially important to understand the limbic system and the role that it plays in your emotional life?

Answers: 1. hindbrain, midbrain, forebrain 2. c 3. a 4. thalamus 5. limbic 6. adrenal 7. Because the subcortex must be related to basic functions common to all higher animals: motives, emotions, sleep, attention, and vegetative functions such as heartbeat, breathing, and temperature regulation. The subcortex also routes and processes incoming information from the senses and outgoing commands to the muscles.

doble.d/Moment/Getty Images

How about you? As a four-year-old, would you have hung in there for two marshmallows, or would you have settled for one? How about you as an adult?

2.5 Psychology and Your Skill Set: Self-Regulation

GATEWAYS LEARNING OUTCOMES:
After reading this section you should be able to:

2.5.1 Define self-regulation and explain how it can help you in your personal and professional life

2.5.2 Create a plan to improve your self-regulation skills in an area that is important to you

Designed by Stanford psychologist Walter Mischel, the "Marshmallow Test" is often used to examine children's ability to resist temptation. Psychologists refer to this as **self-regulation**—the ability to consciously exert control over our thoughts, feelings, and behaviors. In the "Marshmallow Test," children are asked to forego eating one marshmallow immediately in favor of receiving two later. Amazingly, kids' behavior on this simple task seems to predict important consequences for them many years later. In adulthood, for example, children who were good self-regulators were likely to enjoy better health ("I should probably skip that extra helping of dessert."), more professional success ("I can't party tonight; I have a report to prepare."), and greater financial stability ("Do I really need to buy a bigger TV? I should probably save the money.") (Berman et al., 2013). Given how important self-regulation seems to be at work and in our personal lives, it's helpful to know that self-regulation is a skill that anyone can develop with practice (Mischel, 2014).

The Executive Living in Your Frontal Lobes

For the most part, the roots of self-regulation lie in the brain's frontal lobes (the prefrontal cortex), though some other regions of the brain are also involved. In particular, as mentioned earlier in this chapter, the prefrontal cortex is home to an important set of abilities referred to as *executive functions*, which provide the foundation for higher-level thinking including our ability to demonstrate self-control.

Like an air traffic control system that permits the coordination of incoming and outgoing flights on multiple runways, executive functions coordinate our thinking and behavior so that we can accomplish the things that we need to do. For example, they allow us to pay attention to important things and filter out distractions, prioritize information, make plans, and suppress behaviors that would prevent us from carrying those plans out (Center on the Developing Child at Harvard University, 2011).

Executive functions are at the heart of self-regulation because they allow us to set goals ("I'm going to try to wait and get the two marshmallows instead of eating one now."), make plans that will help us to achieve those goals ("I'm not going to touch the marshmallow."), control our attention and emotions in ways that will be helpful as we work toward our goals ("I'm going to close my eyes so that I don't have to look at the marshmallow while I'm waiting."), and monitor our progress on the goal so that we know if we need to change our strategy ("Only five more minutes before she comes back and I can have two marshmallows. I'm doing great!").

So if self-regulation is based in the brain, is it determined by genetics? Because the ability to control our behavior is so closely connected with the prefrontal cortex, you might imagine that there's little you can do to change how it develops over time. And while it is true that brain development is, in part, controlled by genetics, it's also influenced by our environment and our actions. This is why Walter Mischel believes that self-regulation is a skill that we can all develop.

From Marshmallows to Retirement Funds

If you think about it, there are many times during our adult lives when it becomes important to control the impulse to give in to immediate temptation. Sometime during this semester, for example, you'll probably put aside some time to study for exams rather than going out with friends because you understand that your performance at school can have important implications for your ability to find a job later, after graduation. If you marry and find yourself in a bar with a stranger who is flirting with you, you'll likely want to resist the temptation to cheat on your spouse because you'll recognize that it could one day spell the end of a relationship that is important to you. And when you find yourself with some extra money, you may have to stop yourself from spending it on a new car and instead put it into your retirement savings so that you'll be comfortable many years down the road when you stop working.

There are many more day-to-day examples of how self-regulation can have consequences for later, such as sticking to your diet or your plan to give up cigarettes. Viewed like this, it becomes a bit easier to see how self-regulation has important connections to the quality of our adult lives. Things such as good health and adequate retirement savings often require us to give up immediate rewards for something better later on, even though doing so is really hard work (Baumeister, 2015; Inzlicht & Schmeichel, 2012).

But does the ability to control behavior in childhood really predict what happens so many years later? It may not initially be easy to see how children's behavior in the Marshmallow Test would be connected to something like academic achievement in high school, but Mischel's work clearly suggested that it was. Other work from New Zealand has confirmed and extended these findings (Moffitt et al., 2011). Researchers there followed *every child* born in the small town of Dunedin between 1972 and 1973—more than 1,000 of them!—until they were in their thirties. They assessed the children's self-regulation in a variety of ways, including the children's own comments about their ability to control themselves, reports from parents and teachers, and observations made by the researchers. Later in life, children who had displayed greater levels of self-regulation were doing better on a variety of measures, including ones that assessed health, substance abuse, finances (saving habits, credit card problems), and antisocial behavior, such as criminal activity.

You may be wondering how a child's behavior could be so important to his or her circumstances as an adult decades later. Though the story behind these relationships is complex and involves brain development, it's also likely that when children grow up having had some success with self-regulation—say, their experiences lead them to realize that waiting generally leads to better results than giving in to immediate impulses—they learn that it pays to control themselves and wait for a larger payoff later. As a result, self-regulation starts to become more natural for them, and they will do it more often. When you think about it this way, it's not too hard to see how a simple task like the Marshmallow Test, done during childhood, might be connected to some of the important outcomes that we see later in life. Kids who are learning that it pays to wait will find themselves in better circumstances as they grow up.

Studying the Science: Self-Regulation and Poverty

More recently, researchers have attempted to replicate Mischel's work with larger and more diverse samples of children. In one particular example, psychologists found that, in keeping with Mischel's studies, children's performance on the Marshmallow Test (that is, early self-regulation) was correlated with their academic performance in high school many years later (recall from ■ Section 1.7 that correlations tell us about the relationship between two variables; in this case, the relationship between self-regulation and high school grades). The correlation was smaller than in the original study, a finding that likely reflected the larger and more representative sample (Watts, Duncan, & Quan, 2018).

The key difference, however, was that the more recent study also suggested that the correlation between self-regulation and high school achievement may actually be due to a third factor: affluence. Children from wealthier families, on average, did better on the Marshmallow Test *and* had better grades in high school. So perhaps self-regulation isn't important for high school grades at all—maybe it's just whether you come from a wealthy family that matters. So should we consider the Marshmallow Test to be unimportant in predicting what happens later in life? Did Mischel's early studies get it all wrong?

It's worth noting that Mischel had long realized that children from poorer families did not fare as well as more affluent children on the Marshmallow Test. Decades ago, he noted that whether children opt to eat the marshmallow early isn't only a function of their self-regulation abilities—it's also influenced by their life circumstances (Mischel, 1974). Many studies since have demonstrated the same thing: Living in poverty is an experience that prompts people to take a sure thing now rather than waiting for something more later (Evans et al., 2013). If you're a child from a poor family, then, it probably makes a lot of sense to take the marshmallow that's in front of you instead of hoping that someone really will give you a second one later.

Self-regulation The ability to consciously exert self-control.

This newer research doesn't really contradict Mischel's early work; it simply helps us to better understand the complexity of the relationship between self-regulation and later outcomes like high school grades (Payne & Sheeran, 2018). In effect, a focus on the here-and-now—which makes good sense for people living in poverty—likely compromises their ability to self-regulate in ways that might be beneficial later on. Put another way, it's not *either* affluence *or* self-regulation that influences high school grades; instead, those two factors likely work together to impact future outcomes such as grades, financial stability, and health.

Improving Your Self-Regulation Skills

I can see that self-regulation is important. But if it's really a skill, then how can I get better at it? That's a great question. Imagine, for example, that you are a university student trying to save up for a car so that you don't have to take the bus everywhere. It's hard, though, because there are lots of other ways to spend your money that would give you more immediate pleasure. Maybe you'd like to go out to the pub with your friends or buy some new clothes. Or perhaps you'd like to take a trip during spring break. The tendency to focus on what we want now and ignore the consequences that will come later has been referred to as the *hot emotional system*, and it tends to be associated with the limbic system of the brain. It's the system that will dominate your thinking when you're faced with temptation right now, and it will issue a powerful push to do what you want in that moment. In contrast, the *cool cognitive system* is one that allows you to reflectively consider the potential long-term consequences of your actions (Mischel, 2014). As you might guess, the cool system is associated with the prefrontal cortex, and it's essential for self-regulation.

While it may be difficult to control the hot system when working toward long-term goals like buying a car, researchers such as Walter Mischel have suggested that this is one of the most important ways that people can work toward improving their self-control (Mischel, 2014). There are a number of ways to cool your immediate impulses. For example, work on changing what you pay attention to, a strategy that's called *selective attention* (■ see Section 4.5). Employing selective attention means that you focus on things that are removed from the temptation—in other words, you take your attention away from the things that the hot system is focused on. Rather than looking longingly at a friend's brochures for a sun-filled trip during spring break, you might focus your attention on the cars outside and tell yourself that it won't be long before you can have one yourself.

You might also engage in *cognitive reappraisal*, which essentially means that you try to reframe situations in ways that are more likely to help you stay in control (Duckworth, Gendler, & Gross, 2014). For example, your efforts to save money for a car might lead you to think differently about an invitation to go to the pub with your friends. Instead of feeling as though you're missing out if you limit yourself to one drink while you're out, you might think that you won't need an extra trip to the gym to work off the calories that would come with the extra beer!

Mischel also suggests that it's important to find ways to bring the long-term rewards and consequences to the front of your mind, to ensure that the cool system is in control. One way to do this is by stepping outside of the here and now and clearly imagining your future self suffering the consequences of your impulsive actions. If you're saving for a car, then, imagine yourself still standing at the bus stop in two years because you couldn't stop spending your extra money. If you're trying to quit smoking, clearly picture the doctor showing your future self an X-ray and telling you that you have lung cancer.

While strategies aimed at cooling the hot system are very effective, a second way to improve your self-regulation skills is to simply avoid putting yourself in an environment where the temptation will be too great to resist (Duckworth et al., 2014). We can do this by actively *choosing* or *changing the environments* we find ourselves in, so that we are more likely to do what we know is right in the long term. If you were trying to save money for a car, then, you might decide you aren't going to go out for a pricey dinner and drinks with friends (choosing the environment). Alternatively, if you did go out for dinner, you might make sure that you only take a specified amount of money to spend (changing the environment by restricting what you can buy).

Of course, there may be times when you are faced with temptation and find it difficult to change the environment or your thinking. In such cases, you can still rely on the old-fashioned way of showing self-control: Just say no!

Reflective Practice

Psychology and Your Skill Set: Self-Regulation

1. Executive functions are important to self-regulation because they help us to set goals and work toward them successfully. T or F?
2. The ability to self-regulate in childhood is not related to the ability to self-regulate in adulthood. T or F?
3. Selective attention and cognitive reappraisal are two strategies that can be used to improve self-regulation skills. T or F?

THINK CRITICALLY

4. If you were setting the goal of losing 10 pounds, how could you create a plan that would improve your chances of resisting the temptation of your favorite foods and stick to your diet?

SELF-REFLECT

- What types of goals have you currently set for yourself? What kinds of things are likely to get in the way of you achieving those goals?
- Can you use some of the strategies from this section to help you stay on track with your goals?

Answers: 1. T 2. F 3. T 4. You can use strategies like selective attention (when in the kitchen or a restaurant, focus your attention on something other than the foods you are trying to avoid) or cognitive reappraisal (think about those potato chips in terms of how bad they are for your health). You can also try avoiding environments (e.g., fast food restaurants) where you're likely to give in to temptation.

Gateways to Brain and Behavior

Summary: Gateways Learning Outcomes

2.1 The Nervous System

2.1.1 Outline the major divisions of the nervous system

The nervous system can be divided into the central nervous system (CNS) and the peripheral nervous system (PNS). The CNS is made up of the brain, which carries out most of the "computing" in the nervous system, and the spinal cord, which connects the brain to the PNS. The PNS includes the somatic nervous system (SNS), which carries sensory information to the brain and motor commands to the body, and the autonomic nervous system (ANS), which controls vegetative and automatic bodily processes. The ANS has a sympathetic branch and a parasympathetic branch.

2.1.2 Identify the important parts of a neuron

Key parts of a neuron include the *dendrites* (which receive incoming messages), the *cell body* (which receives information from dendrites), the *axon* (which carries information away from the cell body), and the *axon terminals* (where information is passed along to adjacent neurons).

2.1.3 Describe how neurons operate and communicate with each other

The dendrites and soma of a neuron combine neural input and send it down the axon as an action potential. The action potential travels to the axon terminals. Neural function, including fluctuations of the neuron's resting potential and the firing of the action potential, is basically electrical in nature.

Communication between neurons is chemical. When an action potential reaches the end of the axon terminals, neurotransmitters are released into the synapse and attach to receptor sites on the adjacent neurons, exciting or inhibiting them. Chemicals called *neuropeptides* can also regulate synaptic activity in the brain.

2.1.4 Distinguish between neuroplasticity and neurogenesis

Neuroplasticity refers to the brain's ability to change in response to experiences. While neurons and nerves in the PNS often can regenerate, the term neurogenesis refers to the production of new neurons in the brain.

2.2 Brain Research

2.2.1 Identify three methods that scientists use to understand the structures of the brain

Brain structure is investigated through dissection, as well as less-intrusive CT scans and MRI scans.

2.2.2 Identify four methods that scientists use to understand the function of brain structures

Brain function is investigated through surgical procedures (electrical stimulation, ablation, deep lesioning), as well as less-intrusive EEG recording, PET scans, and fMRI scans.

2.3 The Cerebral Cortex

2.3.1 Explain how the left and right hemispheres of the cerebral cortex differ as a result of lateralization

The cerebral cortex is lateralized, with left and right hemispheres specializing in different abilities. Much of what we have learned about lateralization comes from split-brain patients whose corpus callosum has been surgically cut. Such an operation allows information to be sent to only one hemisphere or another, thus allowing scientists to see how each hemisphere processes the information in the absence of any input from the other hemisphere.

Psychologists have learned that the left hemisphere is good at analysis, and it processes small details sequentially. It contains speech or language centers in most people. It also specializes in writing, calculating, judging time and rhythm, and ordering complex movements. The right hemisphere detects overall patterns; it processes information simultaneously and holistically. It is largely nonverbal and excels at spatial and perceptual skills, visualization, and recognition of patterns, faces, and melodies. It is important to note, however, that while the hemispheres appear to specialize in their functions, there is no merit to the idea that people are "left-brained" or "right-brained."

2.3.2 Name the four lobes of the cerebral cortex and describe their function

1. The *frontal lobes* contain the primary motor area (which includes many mirror neurons) and many association areas that combine and process information. The prefrontal cortex is related to abstract thought and one's sense of self.
2. The *parietal lobes* contain the primary sensory area, which processes bodily sensations.
3. The *temporal lobes* contain the primary auditory area and are responsible for hearing and language.
4. The *occipital lobes* contain the primary visual area, which first receives input from the eyes.

2.4 The Subcortex and Endocrine System

2.4.1 Name the three major regions of the subcortex, and the parts that make up each one

The three regions are the hindbrain, midbrain, and forebrain. The *hindbrain* is made up of the medulla (which contains centers essential for reflex control of heart rate, breathing, and other vegetative functions), the reticular formation (which directs sensory and motor messages and acts as an activating system for the cerebral cortex), and the cerebellum (which maintains coordination, posture, and muscle tone). The pons links the medulla with other brain areas.

The *midbrain* connects the hindbrain to the forebrain. The midbrain and two hindbrain structures (pons and medulla) make up the *brainstem,* which is the thickening of the spinal cord where it joins the brain.

The *forebrain* consists of the thalamus (which carries sensory information to the cortex), the hypothalamus (which exerts control over eating, drinking, sleep cycles, body temperature, and other basic motives and behaviors), and the limbic system (which is related to emotion, reward and punishment, and contains the hippocampus, which is important for forming memories).

2.4.2 Explain how the endocrine system works, and describe the action of four endocrine glands

Endocrine glands serve as a chemical communication system within the body. Hormones from the endocrine glands enter the bloodstream, affecting behavior, moods, and personality. Many of the endocrine glands are influenced by the pituitary (the master gland), which is in turn influenced by the hypothalamus. Thus, the brain controls the body through both the fast nervous system and the slower endocrine system. Four important endocrine glands are:

1. The pituitary gland, which influences many other glands, including the thyroid and adrenal glands. It is also responsible for growth (through the release of growth hormone) and social bonding (through the release of oxytocin).
2. The pineal gland, which regulates the body's internal clock (through the release of melatonin).
3. The thyroid gland, which regulates metabolism.
4. The adrenal glands, which regulate the body's response to stress (through the release of epinephrine and norepinephrine) and sexual development.

2.5 Psychology and Your Skill Set: Self-Regulation

2.5.1 Define self-regulation, and explain how it can help you in your personal and professional life

Self-regulation refers to our ability to control our thoughts, emotions, and behavior. It is associated with the frontal lobes of the brain, which manage our executive functions. Executive functions allow us to set goals, make plans to achieve those goals, control attention and emotions as we work toward our goals, and monitor our progress on the goal so that we know if we need to change our strategy.

Because of its close link to goals, self-regulation in childhood predicts many things connected to personal and professional success, including health, antisocial and criminal behavior, and financial security.

2.5.2 Create a plan to improve your self-regulation skills in an area that is important to you

Self-regulation skills can be improved by changing what we pay attention to, how we think about situations we're in, or the environments we find ourselves in. We hope that after reading this section, you'll be better able to think about how you can use these strategies to help when you need to focus and resist temptation in order to meet your goals!

3 Human Development

Dr. Nancy L. Segal

Gateway Theme The principles of development extend across the life span, helping us better understand not only children, but our own behavior at any age.

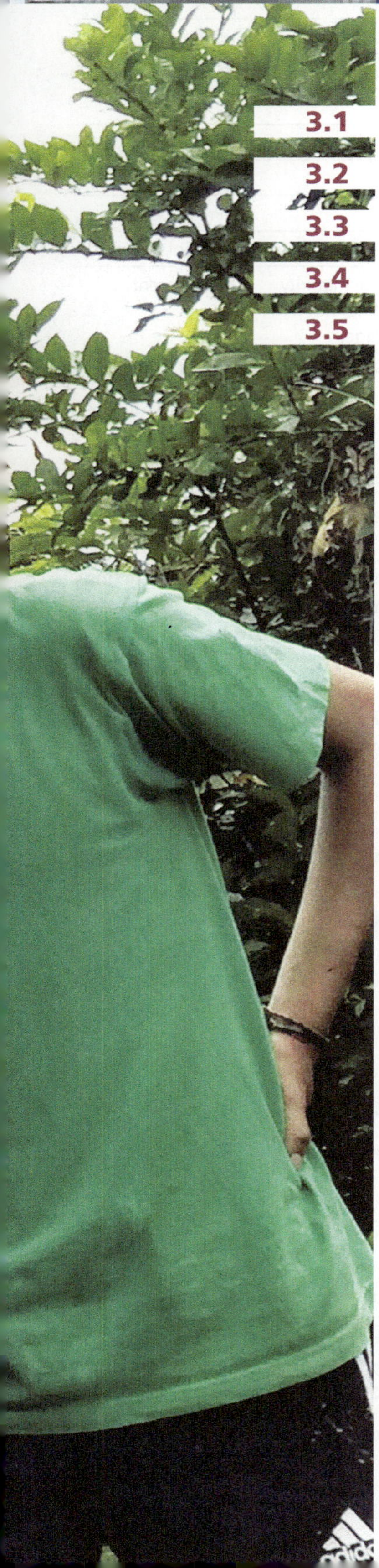

Chapter Outline

Seeing Double

The photo he'd received from his friend Laura was a bit of a shock, and Jorge just couldn't stop staring at it. Before sending it, Laura had told Jorge that on her last trip to Bogotà she'd met someone who could have been his identical twin. The man was a butcher named William, and Laura had convinced him to provide the photo now on the screen in front of Jorge. It was, Jorge thought, like staring at a stranger who seemed to have his face. But William's likeness to Jorge wasn't the only surprise that had been captured by the camera. Looking more closely, it became clear that there was another unknown man sitting next to William in the photo—and that man was the spitting image of Jorge's own fraternal twin, Carlos.

The story of the twins from Bogotá, Columbia, who were switched as babies and met by chance at the age of 25, reads like something that could only happen in a Hollywood movie. Two pairs of identical twin babies happened to be in the same hospital at the same time. But in an accident of fate, one boy from each pair was sent home with the wrong family and both pairs of twins were believed to be fraternal. Jorge and Carlos lived their lives in Bogotá and were encouraged to work hard at school. In contrast, William and his brother Wilber were raised on a very rural farm in Santander. Because the nearest high school was a five-hour walk, the boys finished school at the age of 12 and began working on the farm.

Research tells a fascinating story about human growth and development that centers on the genes we inherit and the environment we inhabit. In this chapter, we'll learn what psychology can tell us about how our genes and environment shape not just our appearance, but our thoughts and emotions, as well as our values and relationships.

3.1 The Forces That Shape Development: Nature and Nurture

GATEWAYS LEARNING OUTCOMES:
After reading this section you should be able to:

3.1.1 Explain how genes impact human development

3.1.2 Explain how the environment impacts human development

3.1.3 Explain how epigenetic factors impact human development

When we think of human development, we tend to think of children "growing up." That's entirely understandable since the developmental changes we experience during infancy, childhood, and adolescence can seem pretty dramatic compared to the relatively gradual developmental changes that characterize adulthood. Regardless, even as adults we never really stop growing. **Developmental psychology**—the study of normal changes in behavior that occur across the life span—involves every stage of life from conception to death, or womb to tomb (Kail & Cavanaugh, 2016; Newman & Newman, 2015). (See ▲ Table 3.1.) Let's spend some time exploring the forces that shape us as we move through the lifespan.

▲ **Table 3.1 Developmental Stages***

Developmental Stage	Approximate Duration	Descriptive Name
Prenatal period	Conception to birth	
Germinal stage	Conception to 2 weeks after conception	Zygote
Embryonic stage	2–8 weeks after conception	Embryo
Fetal stage	8 weeks after conception to birth	Fetus
Infancy	From birth to 1 year	Infant, baby
Childhood	From infancy to adolescence	Child
Early childhood	1–3 years	Toddler
Preschool period	3–6 years	Preschooler
Middle childhood	6–12 years	School-age child
Adolescence	Puberty to full social maturity (it's difficult to define the duration of this stage)	Adolescent
Adulthood	From adolescence to death	Adult
Young adulthood	20–34 years	Emerging adult
Middle adulthood	35–64 years	Mature adult
Late adulthood	65 years and older	Old age

*Note: Various developmental stages have no exact beginning or ending point. The ages are approximate, and each stage may be thought of as blending into the next.

Nature: The Effects of Genetics

The dance of development begins at conception, when a father's sperm cell fertilizes a mother's egg cell (ovum). At that instant, a rapidly developing new organism will begin a long journey, shaped at every stage by an interplay between heredity (our "nature") and environment (our "nurture"). The term **heredity ("nature")** refers mainly to the transmission of genes from parents to offspring at conception. The genetic heritage that will determine so many of our physical and psychological characteristics is referred to as the *genome*.

The Genome

What, exactly, is the genome? A major scientific milestone was reached when the Human Genome Project completed sequencing all 3 billion chemical base pairs in human DNA (U.S. Department of Energy Office of Science, 2015). The nucleus of every human cell contains **deoxyribonucleic acid (DNA)** (dee-OX-see-RYE-bo-new-KLEE-ik), a long, ladderlike chain of pairs of chemical molecules (● Figure 3.1). The order of these molecules, or organic bases, acts as a code for genetic information. The DNA in each cell is the same and contains a record of all the instructions needed to make a human—with room left over!

Human DNA is organized into 46 **chromosomes**. (The word *chromosome* means "colored body.") These rodlike structures in the cell nucleus house the genes. Notable exceptions are sperm cells and ova, which contain only 23 chromosomes. Thus, each of the Bogotá twins received 23 chromosomes from his mother and

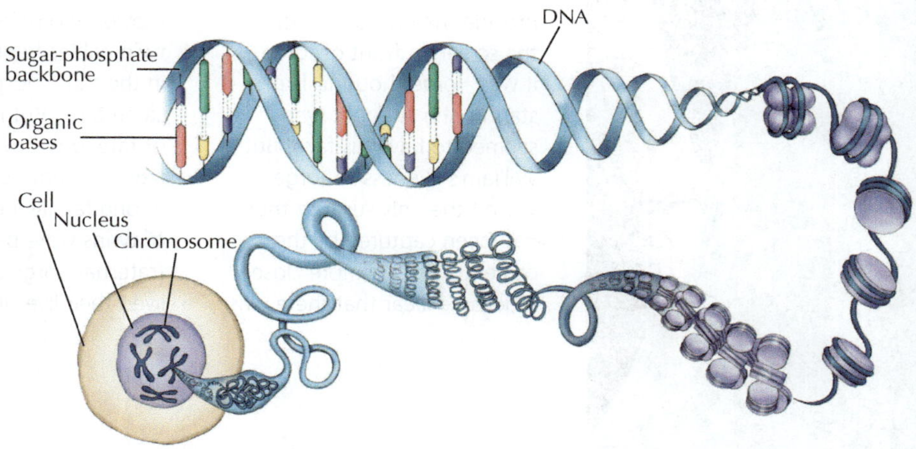

● **Figure 3.1 DNA.** *(Top left)* Linked molecules (organic bases) make up the rungs on DNA's twisted molecular ladder. The order of these molecules serves as a code for genetic information. The code provides a genetic blueprint that is unique for each individual (except identical twins). The drawing shows only a small section of a DNA strand. An entire strand of DNA is composed of billions of smaller molecules. *(Bottom left)* The nucleus of each cell in the body contains chromosomes made up of tightly wound coils of DNA.

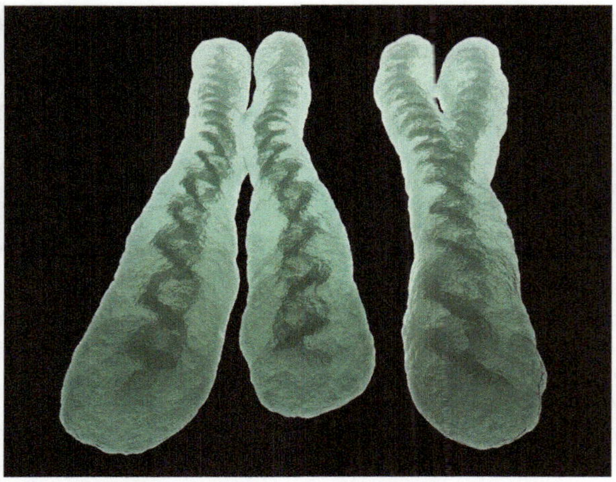

Andrzej Wojcicki/Science Photo Library/Getty Images

A digital illustration of X and Y human chromosomes. (Colors are artificial.)

23 from his father. This is their *genome*. And because the twins were identical, each pair of twins had identical DNA at birth.

Genes are the coded instructions of heredity located on the DNA of each chromosome. Because your chromosomes come in pairs, you have two "versions" (geneticists call them "alleles") of every gene: one version of the gene resides on the chromosome from your mother and the other on the chromosome from your father. If some of the transmitted genes from either parent are defective, the result may be a **genetic disorder** such as sickle-cell anemia, hemophilia, cystic fibrosis, muscular dystrophy, albinism, and some types of intellectual disability.

In rare situations, a single gene is responsible for an inherited feature, such as eye color. Genes may be dominant or recessive. When a **dominant gene** controls a feature like eye color, that feature will appear every time the gene is present. A **recessive gene** must be paired with a second, identical recessive gene before its effect will be expressed. For example, if Jorge got a blue-eye gene from his father and a brown-eye gene from his mother, Jorge would have brown eyes, because brown-eye genes are dominant over blue-eye genes.

Cultura Creative (RF)/Alamy Stock Photo

Twins who share identical genes (identical twins) demonstrate the powerful influence of heredity. Even when they are reared apart, identical twins are strikingly alike in motor skills, physical development, and appearance. At the same time, identical twins are never completely identical and are less alike as adults than they were as children, showing that environmental influences are at work (Freberg, 2016; Larsson, Larsson, & Lichtenstein, 2004).

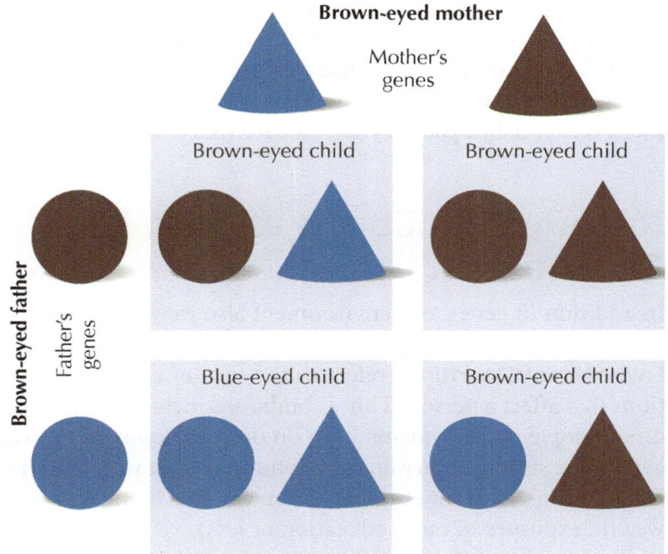

Figure 3.2 Expression of single gene characteristics. Gene patterns for children of brown-eyed parents, where each parent has one brown-eye gene and one blue-eye gene. Because the brown-eye gene is dominant, one child in four will be blue-eyed. Thus, there is a significant chance that two brown-eyed parents will have a blue-eyed child.

If brown-eye genes are dominant, why do two brown-eyed parents sometimes have a blue-eyed child? If one or both parents have two brown-eye genes, the couple's children can only have brown eyes. But what if each parent has one brown-eye gene and one blue-eye gene? In that case, both parents would have brown eyes. Yet, there is one chance in four that their children will get two blue-eye genes and have blue eyes (Figure 3.2).

In actuality, few of our characteristics are controlled by single genes. Instead, most are **polygenic characteristics** (pol-ih-JEN-ik), controlled by many genes, located on different chromosomes, working in combination. So, for example, there is no one gene for height; in fact,

Developmental psychology The study of the normal changes in behavior that occur across the lifespan.

Heredity ("nature") The transmission of physical and psychological characteristics from parents to offspring through genes.

Deoxyribonucleic acid (DNA) A molecular structure that contains coded genetic information.

Chromosomes Rodlike structures in the cell nucleus that house an individual's genes.

Genes Areas on a strand of DNA that carry hereditary information.

Genetic disorders Problems caused by defects in the genes or by inherited characteristics.

Dominant gene A gene whose influence will be expressed each time that the gene is present.

Recessive gene A gene whose influence will be expressed only when it is paired with a second recessive gene of the same type.

Polygenic characteristics Personal traits or physical properties that are influenced by many genes working in combination.

about 200 genetic variations have already been shown to play a role in determining whether children will be short or tall in adulthood (Allen, Estrada, et al., 2010). These observable characteristics that are determined at least in part by genes—blue eyes vs. brown, tall vs. short, very social vs. painfully shy—are referred to as the *phenome*.

Some of the typical features of children with FASD include a small, nonsymmetrical head, a short nose, a flattened area between the eyes, oddly shaped eyes, and a thin upper lip. Many of these features become less noticeable by adolescence. However, intellectual disabilities and other problems commonly follow the FASD child into adulthood.

Nurture: The Effects of the Environment

In addition to genes, our environment also exerts a profound influence on our development right from conception onward. **Environment ("nurture")** refers to the sum of all *external* conditions that affect a person. Those conditions include the effects that other people and the media have on our development, as well as events like serious injury and the conditions that we live in (in the Bogotá twins' case, for example, urban vs. rural homes, poverty vs. wealth, exposure to more education or less).

Prenatal Environment

It's worth noting that the important role of the environment can begin before birth even though the *intrauterine* (interior of the womb) environment is highly protected. For example, during the last few months of a pregnancy, a baby's fetal heart rate will change whenever it perceives the mother's voice (Kisilevsky & Hains, 2011). When mothers experience excess stress, poor health, or poor nutrition during pregnancy, the result can be a smaller, weaker baby at birth (Schetter, 2011).

More ominously, environmental effects can include exposure to **teratogens** during pregnancy (teh-RAT-uh-jen)—harmful substances that can cause birth defects. Although no direct intermixing of blood takes place between a mother and her unborn child, some substances can reach the fetus, including viruses (such as German measles, syphilis, or Zika), environmental hazards (such as lead, radiation, or mercury), and drugs (such as alcohol, cocaine, or nicotine). These environmental conditions affect the developing fetus and become apparent at birth (Lanphear, 2015). In such cases, babies are born with **congenital problems**, or birth defects. Though women are sometimes unknowingly exposed to powerful teratogens, pregnant women often have direct control over them. For example, a woman who takes cocaine or drinks to excess runs a serious risk of injuring her fetus (Minnes et al., 2016). In short, when a pregnant woman takes drugs, her unborn child does, too.

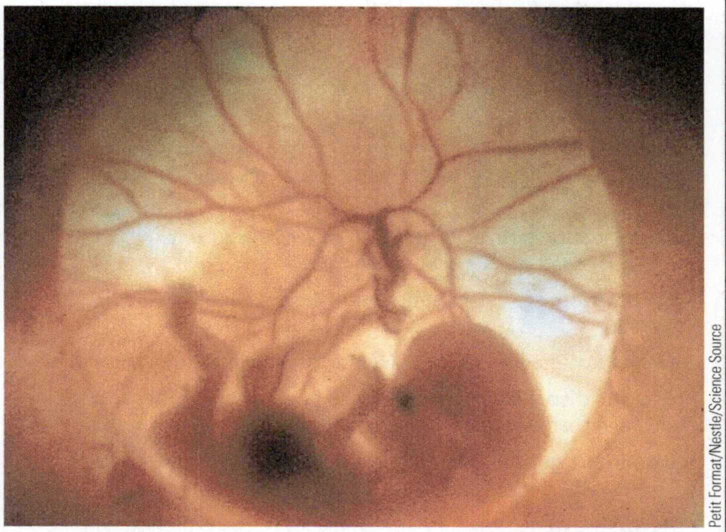

An 11-week-old fetus. Because of the rapid growth of basic structures, the developing fetus is sensitive to a variety of diseases, drugs, and sources of radiation. This is especially true during the first trimester (three months) of gestation (pregnancy).

Unfortunately, in the United States, alcohol and drugs are among the greatest risk factors facing unborn children (Keegan et al., 2010). In fact, repeated heavy drinking during pregnancy is the most common cause of birth defects in the United States (Liles & Packman, 2009). Affected infants have **fetal alcohol spectrum disorder (FASD)**, a collection of conditions occurring in children whose mothers consumed alcohol during pregnancy. The most extreme form of FASD is commonly referred to as *fetal alcohol syndrome (FAS)*. Children born with FASD often have low birth weight, a small head, bodily defects, and facial malformations. Many also suffer from emotional, behavioral, and mental disabilities (Hepper, Dornan, & Lynch, 2012; Jones & Streissguth, 2010).

If a mother is addicted to morphine, heroin, or methadone, her baby may be born with an addiction. Even tobacco use is harmful. Smoking during pregnancy greatly reduces oxygen to the fetus. Heavy smokers risk miscarrying or having premature, underweight babies who are more likely to die soon after birth. Furthermore, children of smoking mothers score lower on tests of language and mental ability (Clifford, Lang, & Chen, 2012).

Postnatal Environment

Once a baby is born, the environment becomes more important because it provides learning experiences. For example, the brain of a newborn baby has fewer *dendrites* (nerve cell branches) and *synapses* (connections between nerve cells) than an adult brain (● Figure 3.3). However, the newborn brain is highly *plastic* (■ capable of being altered by experience; see Section 2.1). During the first three years of life, millions of new neural connections form in the brain every day. At the same time, unused connections disappear. As a result, early learning environments literally shape the developing brain, through the "blooming and pruning" of synapses (Nelson, 1999; Walker et al., 2011).

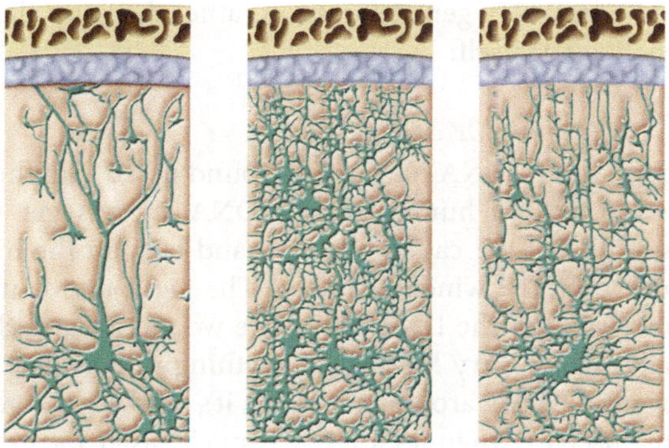

Figure 3.3 Brain development after birth. On the left is an illustration of the neural networks in the brain of a nine-month-old infant. By age two, pictured in the center, the number of synapses and neurons in those networks has dramatically increased. By age four, pictured on the right, the number of synapses and neurons has declined slightly. Nevertheless, at that point, children actually have more brain synapses than adults do. Then, after age ten, the number continues to slowly decline, reaching adult levels at about age sixteen. (BSIP/Science Source)

Sensitive Periods

Early experiences can have particularly lasting effects. For example, children who are abused may suffer lifelong emotional problems (Cicchetti, 2016; Shin, Miller, & Teicher, 2012). At the same time, extra care can sometimes reverse the effects of a poor start in life (Walker et al., 2011). In short, environmental forces guide human development—for better or worse—throughout life.

Why do some experiences have more lasting effects than others? Part of the answer lies in the idea of a **sensitive period**, a time when children are more susceptible to particular types of environmental influences. Events that occur during a sensitive period can permanently alter the course of development (Bedny et al., 2012). For example, forming a loving bond with a caregiver early in life seems to be crucial for optimal development. Likewise, language abilities may become impaired when babies don't hear normal speech during their first year (Gheitury, Sahraee, & Hoseini, 2012).

Deprivation and Enrichment

Some environments can be described as *deprived* or *enriched.* **Deprivation** refers to a lack of normal nutrition, stimulation, comfort, or love. **Enrichment** exists when an environment is deliberately made more stimulating, loving, and so forth.

What happens when children suffer severe deprivation? Tragically, a few mistreated children have spent their first years in closets, attics, and other restricted environments. When discovered, these children may be mute, intellectually disabled, emotionally damaged, and sometimes suffer lifelong consequences (Kennedy et al., 2016; Wilson, 2003). Though such extreme deprivation is unusual, milder perceptual, intellectual, or emotional deprivation occurs in many families, especially those that must cope with poverty (Cicchetti, 2016; Matthews & Gallo, 2011).

Poverty can affect the development of children in at least two ways (Huston & Bentley, 2010; Sobolewski & Amato, 2005). First, poor parents may not be able to give their children necessities and resources such as nutritious meals, health care, or learning

Oleksiy Rezin/Shutterstock.com

Children who grow up in poverty run a high risk of experiencing many forms of deprivation. There is evidence that lasting damage to social, emotional, and cognitive development occurs when children must cope with severe early deprivation.

materials. As a result, impoverished children tend to be sick more often, their cognitive development lags, and they may do more poorly at school. Second, the stresses of poverty also can be hard on parents, leading to marriage problems, less positive parenting, and poorer parent–child relationships. The resulting emotional turmoil can damage a child's socioemotional development. In the extreme, it may increase the risk of delinquent behavior and mental illness.

Can an improved environment enhance development? To answer this question, psychologists have studied *enriched environments* that are especially novel, complex, and stimulating. To illustrate, let's consider the effects of raising rats in a sort of "rat wonderland." In one study, the walls of their cages were decorated with colorful patterns, and each cage was filled with platforms, ladders, and cubbyholes. As adults, these rats were superior at learning mazes. In addition, they had larger, heavier brains, with a thicker cortex (Benloucif, Bennett, & Rosenzweig, 1995). Of course, it's a long leap from rats to people, but if extra stimulation can enhance the intelligence of a lowly rat, it's likely that human

Environment ("nurture") The sum of all external conditions affecting development, including especially the effects of learning.

Teratogen A harmful substance that can cause birth defects.

Congenital problems Defects that originate during prenatal development in the womb.

Fetal alcohol spectrum disorder (FASD) A collection of conditions occurring in children whose mothers consumed alcohol during pregnancy.

Sensitive period During development, a period of increased sensitivity to environmental influences. It also is a time during which certain events must take place for normal development to occur.

Deprivation In development, the loss or withholding of normal stimulation, nutrition, comfort, love, and so forth; a condition of absence.

Enrichment In development, deliberately making an environment more stimulating, nutritional, comforting, loving, and so forth.

infants also benefit from enrichment. Indeed, many studies have shown that enriched environments improve abilities or enhance human development (Phillips & Lowenstein, 2011).

What can parents do to enrich a child's environment? They can encourage exploration and stimulating play by paying attention to what holds the baby's interest. It is better to childproof a house than to put strict limits on what a child can touch. Actively enriching sensory experiences also are valuable. It makes perfect sense to take infants outside, to hang mobiles over their cribs, to place mirrors nearby, to play music for them, or to rearrange their rooms now and then. Children progress most rapidly when they have responsive parents and stimulating play materials at home (Beeber et al., 2007).

Epigenetics: Where Genes and Environment Meet

You might wonder how it can be that every cell in your body has the same coded instructions in the DNA and still look and function differently. A neuron, for example, looks nothing like a skin cell. And neither one of them looks or operates anything like a cell in your liver or your heart. How can the same genetic instructions produce such different cells?

The answer lies in the field of **epigenetics** (literally meaning, *above genetics*), which is the study of changes in organisms that are caused by modifications to gene *expression* rather than alteration of the genetic code itself. That probably sounds a bit complicated, so let's take some time to unpack it a bit.

In humans, epigenetics seems to work in two main ways. The first has to do with the way DNA gets read in each cell, and the second has to do with how DNA is packaged up in each cell. Let's look at each one of these separately.

How DNA Is Read

We know that every cell in the body has the same "blueprint" from the genetic code in your DNA. But before the cells in your body can actually do anything with that genetic code from your genome they need some instructions about how to read it. Armed with those instructions, the cells will then know how to proceed with their development.

Those instructions come from special tags called *methyl groups* that bind to certain genes on the DNA. If what's needed is a skin cell, for example, methyl groups will tag certain genes and those tags will instruct the cell to "Turn on these genes which are essential for a skin cell" and "Turn off these genes which are not necessary for a skin cell."

But if what's needed is a cell for your toenail, the methyl groups will tag different genes, thus providing a different set of instructions. Those tags will indicate to the cell which genes are essential for a toenail (and so should be expressed) and which ones are irrelevant for a toenail (and do not need to be expressed). In this sense, methyl groups are like a switch that can turn particular genes on or off to create the kind of cell that's needed.

What's important to remember is that in both cells—the one that will become a skin cell and the one that will become a toenail cell—the genetic code is identical. However, that code is being *expressed* differently depending on the instructions provided by those methyl tags bound to the cell's DNA. That's why we define epigenetics in terms of gene expression rather than any alteration to the genetic code itself.

How DNA Is Packaged

The long strands of DNA have to be wound up so that they'll fit inside a tiny cell. In humans, those DNA strands get wound around spools that are called histones, and tags on the histones dictate how tight the winding will be. The tags provide instructions about whether the DNA should be wound around the histones really tightly, very loosely, or anything in between. When DNA is wound tightly around a histone, it's hard for the genes to express themselves; when it's loose, it's much easier for the genes to express themselves. Again, then, the actual genetic code isn't changing in this example—the "tightness" of the winding just governs how easy it is for those genes to be expressed.

Epigenetics and Development

To summarize, then, the genome is like the hardware of a computer that does the work and the *epigenome* is like the software, telling the hardware what to do. Put another way, every cell in your body has a unique pattern of tags on the DNA and the histones (the epigenome) and those tags govern exactly what that cell will look like by dictating which genes on your DNA (the genome) will be expressed or ignored.

For developmental psychologists, epigenetics is an important area of study because the epigenome changes over the course of the lifespan. It changes during puberty, pregnancy, and in old age, for example, when the body undergoes significant changes that result from the natural processes of maturation. But the epigenome is also sensitive to environmental conditions. For example, those tags that make up the epigenome will change when we face prolonged periods of stress or poverty. They can also change when we engage in particular behaviors over a long period of time, such as doing drugs, eating poorly, or training for an Ironman competition. Poor conditions or behaviors over the long term may result in epigenetic tags that bind to the wrong genes, for example, and they consequently provide incorrect instructions that lead the cells to become diseased.

The epigenome helps to explain why even identical twins like Jorge and William (and Carlos and Wilber) will not grow up to be exactly the same, even though their genetic code is identical. It's inevitable that identical twins—even the ones who are raised in the same home—will experience some differences in their environments as they grow up. It's those differences in their experiences that can change the epigenome, causing the twins' development to diverge in some ways.

Understanding something about epigenetics makes it clear why the old question "Is nature or nurture more important to development?" doesn't really make sense. Clearly, both are important. Ultimately, the person you are today reflects a continuous *interaction* between heredity and environment (Kalat, 2016). Although heredity gives each of us a variety of potentials and limitations, these are, in turn, affected by environmental influences, such as learning, nutrition, culture, and disease. This ongoing process is called **maturation** (Cummings, 2016). As maturation proceeds over time, genetic instructions and environmental conditions continue to influence body size and shape, height, intelligence, athletic potential, personality traits, sexual orientation, and a host of other human characteristics.

Reflective Practice

The Forces That Shape Development: Nature and Nurture

1. Most inherited characteristics can be described as polygenic. T or F?
2. Environmental factors begin to influence a child's development beginning at
   a. infancy
   b. birth
   c. conception
   d. maturity
3. The orderly sequence observed in the unfolding of many basic responses can be attributed to ______________.
4. As a child develops, a continuous ______________ takes place between the forces of heredity and environment.
5. Epigenetics is strictly related to genetics and has no connection to the environment. T or F?

THINK CRITICALLY

6. Aside from the genes that he passes on, evaluate how fathers contribute to the health of their unborn baby.

SELF-REFLECT

- Can you think of clear examples of some ways in which heredity and environmental forces have combined to affect your development?

Answers: 1. T 2. c 3. maturation 4. interaction (or interplay) 5. F 6. Fathers can play an important role before birth by providing support for the mother, working to minimize her stress when possible and encouraging healthy choices (e.g., a good diet).

3.2 Physical and Perceptual Development

GATEWAYS LEARNING OUTCOMES:
After reading this section you should be able to:

3.2.1 Describe key aspects of physical development across the lifespan

3.2.2 Describe key aspects of perceptual development across the lifespan

Now that we have some basic knowledge about the factors that shape development, let's take a closer look at how our bodies—including our ability to see and hear—change with time.

Physical Development

Physical development is concerned with how our bodies grow and change. If you consider the whole lifespan, it's not hard to see that physical changes are dramatic. Each of us goes from being a tiny infant to an adolescent whose body becomes that of an adult. But even in adulthood our bodies continue to change, often showing frustrating declines. In this section, we'll take a look at these changes in more detail.

Physical Development in Infancy and Childhood

In their mother's womb, the twins Jorge and William rapidly grew from a single fertilized egg cell into an individual collection of more than a trillion differentiated cells, including those that made up their bones, muscles, organs, nerves, and blood. Although at birth the twins would have been unable to survive themselves, they were far from helpless. For example, each would have possessed several adaptive reflexes (Siegler, DeLoache, & Eisenberg, 2014). Let's take a look at some of them.

To elicit the *grasping reflex*, press an object in a newborn's palm, and he will grasp it with surprising strength. Many infants, in fact, can hang from a raised bar, like little trapeze artists. The grasping reflex aids survival by helping infants avoid falling. You can observe the *rooting reflex* (reflexive head turning and nursing) by touching a baby's cheek. Immediately, he will turn toward your finger, as if searching for something. The rooting reflex helps infants find a bottle or a breast. Then, when a nipple touches the infant's mouth, the *sucking reflex* (rhythmic nursing) helps him obtain needed food. Like other reflexes, this is a genetically programmed action.

The *Moro reflex* also is interesting. If an infant's position is changed abruptly, or if he is startled by a loud noise, he will make a hugging motion. This reaction has been compared to the movements that baby monkeys use to cling to their mothers. (We leave it to the reader's imagination to decide whether there is any connection.)

The twins would have rapidly matured past grasping, rooting, sucking, and hugging as they developed more and more motor skills, such as sitting, crawling, standing, and walking. Of course, the *rate* of maturation varies from child to child. Nevertheless, the *order* of maturation is almost universal. For instance, it's likely that the twins were able to sit without support from an adult before they matured enough to stand. Indeed, infants around the world typically sit before they crawl, crawl before they stand, and stand before they walk (● Figure 3.4). More generally, muscular control spreads in a pattern that is *cephalocaudal* (SEF-eh-lo-KOD-ul), meaning from head to toe, and *proximodistal* (PROK-seh-moe-DIS-tul), meaning from the center of the body to the extremities.

Although maturation has a big impact, motor skills don't simply emerge—they need to be practiced so that they can be controlled. When babies are beginning to crawl or walk, they actively try new movements and select those that work. Often, their efforts are aided by parents, siblings, and other caregivers. With practice and assistance, babies fine-tune their movements to be smoother and more effective. Such learning is evident from the very first months of life and continues to improve throughout childhood (Adolph & Berger, 2011).

Epigenetics The study of changes in organisms that are caused by modifications to gene *expression* rather than alteration of the genetic code itself.

Maturation The physical growth and development of the body, brain, and nervous system.

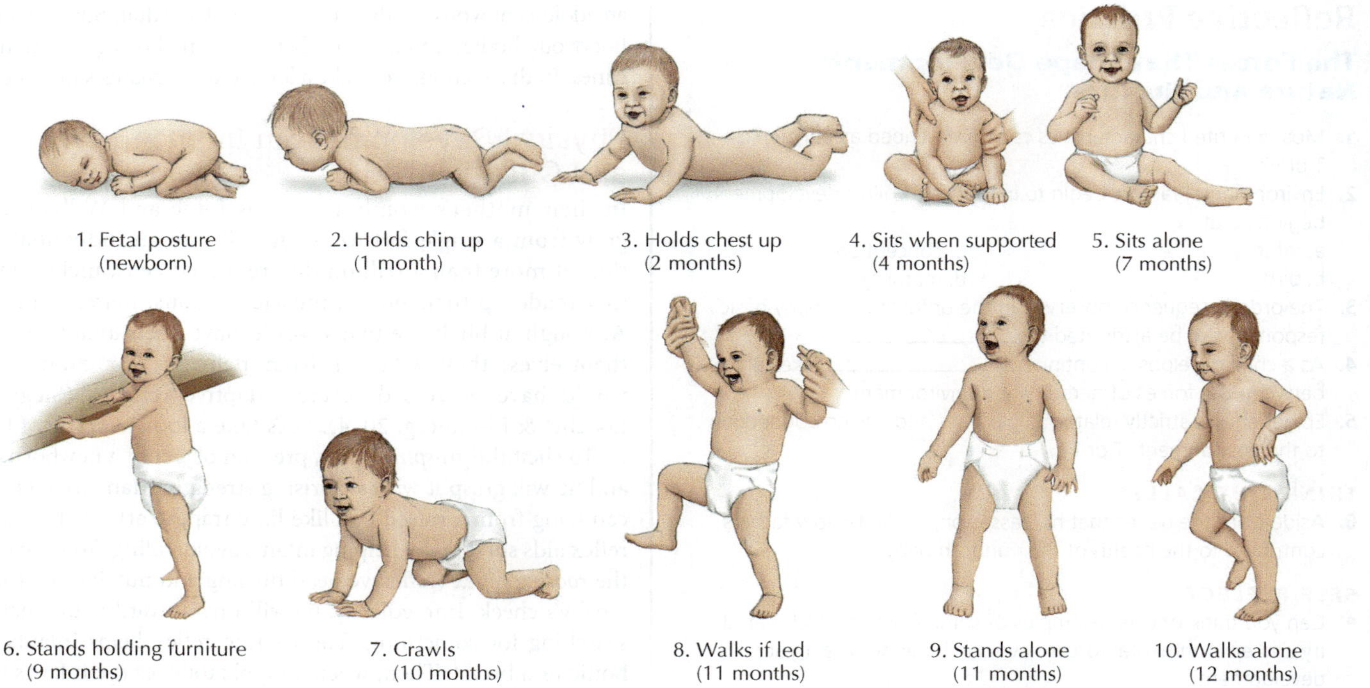

Figure 3.4 Motor development in infancy. Most infants follow an orderly pattern of motor development. Although the order in which children progress is similar, there are large individual differences in the ages at which each ability appears. The ages listed are averages for American children. It is not unusual for many of the skills to appear one or two months earlier than average, or several months later (Adolph & Berger, 2011). Parents should not be alarmed if a child's behavior differs some from the average.

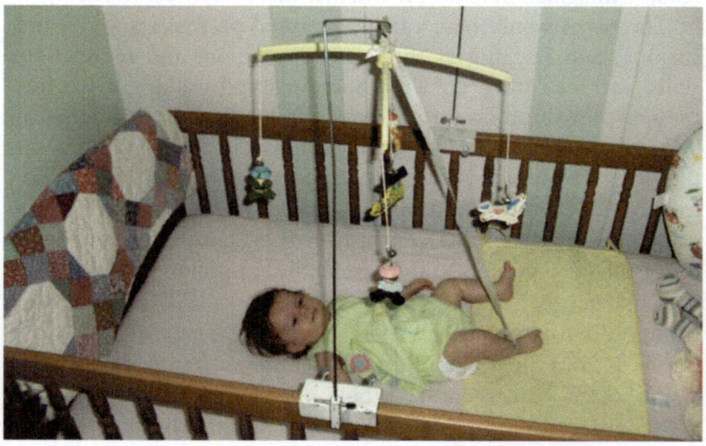

Dr. Carolyn Rovee-Collier

Psychologist Carolyn Rovee-Collier has shown that babies as young as three months old can learn to control their movements. In her experiments, babies lie on their backs under a colorful crib mobile. A ribbon is tied around the baby's ankle and connected to the mobile. Whenever babies spontaneously kick their legs, the mobile jiggles and rattles. Within a few minutes, infants learn to kick faster. Their reward for kicking is a chance to see the mobile move (Hayne & Rovee-Collier, 1995).

Physical Development in Adolescence and Adulthood

The early teenage years usher in a major transition in physical development. During **puberty**, hormonal changes promote both a physical growth spurt and reproductive maturity (Kail & Cavanaugh, 2016). Many people confuse adolescence with puberty. However, puberty is a *biological* event, not a social status—social and intellectual maturity may lie years down the road. In contrast, **adolescence** is the culturally defined period between childhood and adulthood (Bjorklund & Hernández Blasi, 2012).

Almost all cultures recognize this period of transition. However, the length of adolescence varies greatly from culture to culture. For example, most 14-year-old girls in North America live at home and go to school. In contrast, many 14-year-old girls in the rural villages of some less-developed countries have married and may have children. In our culture, 14-year-olds are adolescents. In others, they may be adults.

How much difference does the timing of puberty make? For boys, maturing early is generally beneficial. It typically enhances their self-image and gives them an advantage socially and athletically. Early-maturing boys tend to be more relaxed, dominant, self-assured, and popular. However, early puberty carries some risks because early-maturing boys also are more likely to get into trouble with drugs, sex, alcohol, and antisocial behavior (Steinberg, 2001).

For girls, the advantages of early maturation are less clear-cut. In elementary school, fast-maturing girls are *less* popular and have poorer self-images, perhaps because they are larger and heavier than their classmates (Deardorff et al., 2007). By junior high, however, early development also includes sexual features. This leads to a more positive body image, greater peer prestige, and adult approval. Early-maturing girls tend to date sooner and are more independent and more active in school. However, like their male counterparts, they also are more often in trouble at school and more likely to engage in early sex (Negriff & Trickett, 2010).

Early in adulthood, most of us reach our physical peaks and face a decline thereafter, even if we maintain healthy lifestyles (Aldwin & Gilmer, 2013). Although some adults face far more serious health issues, from heart attacks to cancer, all of us face the inevitable routine wear and tear of aging. How we deal with the decline during later adulthood will strongly influence our degree of life satisfaction and can complicate our personal development, especially after the late fifties. Fortunately, most of the time, declines happen slowly enough that they can be offset by increased life experience (Sigelman & Rider, 2015).

Perceptual Development

Perceptual development focuses on how our senses develop, which in turn shapes the way that we interpret the world around us. Let's take a look at how our senses change over time.

Perceptual Development in Infancy and Childhood

Contrary to common belief, newborn babies are not oblivious to their surroundings. Newborns come into the world equipped to see, hear, smell, taste, and respond to pain and touch. Although their senses are less acute than children and adults, babies are very responsive. For example, from birth, babies are able to follow a moving object with their eyes and will turn in the direction of sounds.

Tests show that newborn vision is not as sharp as that of adults; newborns can most clearly see objects that are about a foot away from them. It is as if they are genetically predisposed to see the people who love and care for them (Leppänen, 2011). Perhaps that's why babies have a special fascination with human faces. Just *hours* after they are born, babies prefer seeing their mother's face rather than a stranger's. When babies are only two to five days old, they will pay more attention to a person who is gazing directly at them rather than one who is looking away (Farroni et al., 2004). Three-day-old babies also prefer complex patterns, such as checkerboards and bull's-eyes, to simpler colored rectangles.

But the role of the environment quickly becomes apparent: When infants reach six months old, they are able to recognize categories of objects that differ in shape or color. By nine months of age, they can tell the difference between dogs and birds or other groups of animals. By one year of age, they will be able to see as well as their parents (Sigelman & Rider, 2015). (■ See Chapter 4 for more information about the processes of sensation and perception.)

In contrast to vision, other senses such as hearing, taste, and smell are quite well developed at birth. Sudden loud sounds, for example, will provoke a startled response from newborns, while soothing, rhythmic sounds will put them to sleep. Research also suggests that babies can distinguish between sweet, salty, sour, and bitter, and show a distinct early preference for things that are sweet. Finally, studies have found that infants respond positively to pleasant smells such as vanilla and strawberries, but will grimace, frown, or turn away from the smell of rotten eggs or ammonia (who wouldn't?).

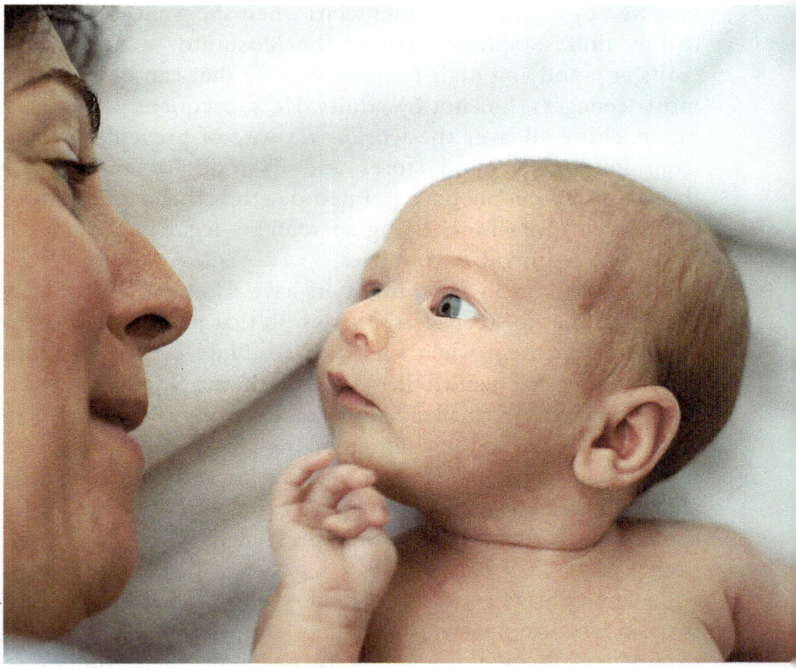
cwa/Alamy Stock Photo

Newborn babies display a special interest in the human face. Infants just days old pay more attention to the faces of people who are gazing directly at them than to people gazing away. A preference for seeing their mother's face develops rapidly and encourages social interactions between mother and baby.

Perceptual Development in Adolescence and Adulthood

Changes in perceptual abilities can continue into adolescence, when some teenagers discover—often to their dismay!—that environmental factors such as reading and watching screens result in a need for glasses or contact lenses. Though less common, hearing problems can also occur in adolescence and young adulthood, often the result of repeated exposure to loud music or other sounds through ear buds and headphones.

But declines in perceptual abilities are most noteworthy in later adulthood. For example, nearly two-thirds of adults over the age of 40 contend with vision problems, many of which can be corrected through glasses, contact lenses, or laser surgery. But more serious vision problems, including macular degeneration, glaucoma, and cataracts, become much more common over the age of 65 (Teutsch et al., 2016).

Hearing loss also becomes more prevalent with age. The ability to hear high-frequency sounds, in particular, begins to decline later in adolescence—a fact that inventor Harold Stapleton was able to exploit. Annoyed that his daughter had been

Puberty Biologically defined period during which a person matures sexually and becomes capable of reproduction.

Adolescence The culturally defined period between childhood and adulthood.

harassed by a group of young teens when she went to the store to buy milk, Stapleton created the Mosquito—a device that emits an annoying high-frequency noise that can be heard by most teenagers, but not by adults. He subsequently marketed his machine all over the world as a way of preventing teens from loitering around stores and in shopping malls. And though many people have pointed out the ethical concerns of using such a machine, doing so remains legal in the United States and many other countries.

Of course, equally savvy inventors have also created Mosquito-type ringtones for teenagers' phones, so that parents and teachers can't hear them when someone is calling. Even the famous magician duo Penn and Teller got in on the act (literally!), developing a magic trick that capitalizes on developmental changes in hearing—parents of the children taking part should be forgiven for their confusion when their young sons and daughters were able to consistently outsmart them on stage (with a little help from some high-frequency sound prompts that the adults could not hear)!

Later in life, of course, hearing loss can become more problematic. For example, nearly half of adults over the age of 75 experience hearing loss at a level that prevents them from properly understanding conversations (National Institute on Aging, 2019). Unfortunately, US data suggest that the majority of people who could benefit from newer technologies, including hearing aids or cochlear implants, do not seek treatment.

Reflective Practice

Physical and Perceptual Development

1. Physical maturation proceeds in a manner that is ____________ (that is, from inside toward the extremities) and ____________ (that is, from head to toe).
2. For boys, early puberty is an advantage. T or F?
3. Newborn babies' vision is just as good as an adult. T or F?
4. Which of the following senses is very well developed in newborns?
   a. hearing
   b. taste
   c. smell
   d. all of the above

THINK CRITICALLY

5. Evaluate why might there be an advantage to babies being born with a preference for human faces, and the ability to recognize their caregivers within a very short time of being born.

SELF-REFLECT

- Did puberty arrive early or late for you? Did this impact your social standing with your classmates at school? In what way?

Answers: 1. Proximodistal; cephalocaudal 2. T 3. F 4. d 5. Babies' chances of survival depend heavily on others protecting them until they are able to fend for themselves. Given that this is the case, it makes sense for babies to show a preference for looking at people, and for their caregivers (who are most likely to protect them) more specifically.

3.3 Emotional and Social Development

GATEWAYS LEARNING OUTCOMES:
After reading this section you should be able to:

3.3.1 Describe key aspects of emotional development across the lifespan

3.3.2 Describe key aspects of social development across the lifespan, including:

(a) the eight psychosocial dilemmas described by Erikson
(b) the importance of temperament and attachment in childhood
(c) what is known about parenting styles, and how they differ across cultures
(d) the characteristics of emerging adults' and older adults' social networks

Socioemotional development is a broad term that takes in all of the psychological research related to the development of social relationships and emotions (including our ability to feel, recognize, and control them). Though social and emotional development are fields that are closely intertwined with one another, we'll consider them separately so that we can highlight the unique findings in each area.

Emotional Development

Researchers interested in emotional development study several aspects of emotion, including emotional experience ("feelings"), emotional expression and control (emotion regulation), and the ability to recognize emotions in others. Let's take a closer look at how these can change over time.

Emotional Development in Infancy and Childhood

A baby's emotional life blossoms rapidly and appears to follow a pattern tied to maturation (Music, 2011; Panksepp & Pasqualini, 2005; see Figure 3.5). Experts have determined this by looking carefully at infants' emotional expressions. Beginning with a general expression of excitement, the newborn's emotional life soon differentiates into cries of distress and coos of delight (Bridges, 1932). Although there is still disagreement on the details (see, e.g., Izard, Woodburn, & Finlon, 2010; Shutter & Camras, 2010), by around six months of age further differentiation allows infants to facially express at least six *basic emotions*: happiness, sadness, fear, anger, surprise, and disgust (Kail & Cavanaugh, 2016). Interestingly, it takes further development before infants can read the expression of emotions on other faces; this ability does not appear before 36 to 48 months (Widen & Russell, 2008). Emotional expression and interpretation, though, appears to be sensitive to cultural norms that govern which emotions are acceptable to display, and which should be controlled (Raval & Walker, 2019).

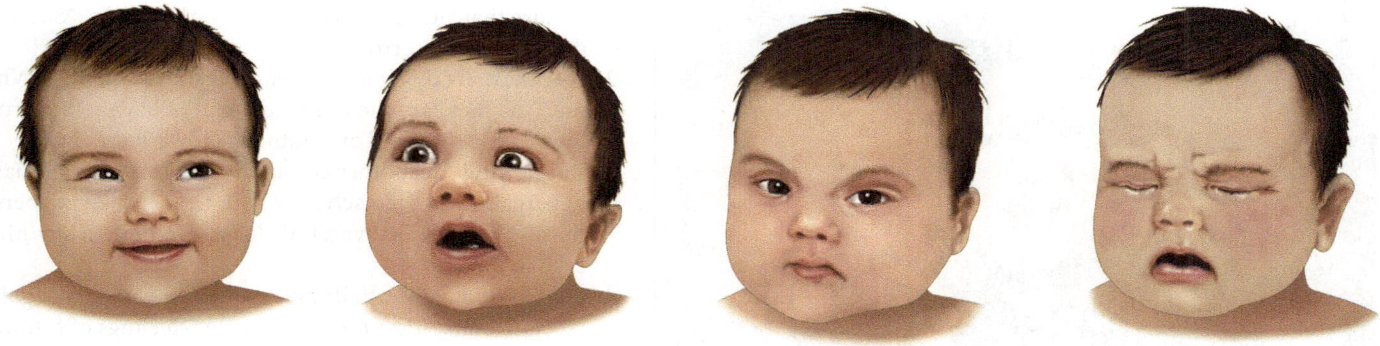

Figure 3.5 Emotional expressions in infants. Infants display many of the same emotional expressions as adults do. Carroll Izard believes that such expressions show that many distinct emotions appear within the first months of life. Parents can expect to see a full range of basic emotions by the end of a baby's first year.

The rapid development of the basic emotions in infants suggests that these emotions are governed by heredity and related to evolution (Izard, 2011; Matsumoto & Hwang, 2019). Perhaps that's why smiling is one of a baby's most common reactions. Smiling may help babies survive by inviting parents to care for them. At first, a baby's smiling is haphazard. By the age of 8 to 12 months, however, infants smile more frequently when another person is nearby (Mcquaid, Bibok, & Carpendale, 2009). This **social smile** is especially rewarding to parents. Infants can even use their social smile to communicate interest in an object, like the time Jorge gazed at his favorite toy and then smiled at his mother (Parlade et al., 2009).

What is an example of a nonbasic emotion? Embarrassment, shame, guilt, and pride are examples of nonbasic and *complex emotions*. To feel these emotions requires a sense of self-awareness, and the ability to self-evaluate. Sometime after about 18 months, infants become able to recognize themselves in a mirror. It is not until this age that infants first become able to experience complex emotions that are closely tied to this sense of self (Shaffer & Kipp, 2014). The range of emotional experience, including the ability to experience emotion blends (e.g., feeling sad and relieved at the same time), continues to expand throughout childhood.

Emotional Development in Adolescence and Adulthood

Research strongly suggests that emotions play an important role in adolescence (Coe-Odess, Narr, & Allen, 2019). Sometimes labeled a time of "storm and stress," emotional experiences and expressions can become more intense than they were during childhood. In particular, there is evidence from surveys to suggest that emotions related to anxiety and depression are becoming more common among adolescents than they were in previous generations (Twenge, 2019). For example, among 16- and 17-year-olds, reports of depression were up almost 70 percent between 2009 and 2017; feelings of anxiety and hopelessness rose by almost the same amount among 18- to 25-year-olds.

Studying the Science: Adolescents' Mental Health

If those data are from a survey, then was the sample representative? Great question! You may remember in ■ Section 1.7 we talked about the importance of having a representative sample when we want to draw accurate conclusions from surveys. These data come from a nationally representative sample of 600,000 Americans, so we can feel reasonably confident about the trends that are being reported.

As a good scientist and critical thinker, you might also be wondering about alternative explanations for these troubling statistics—maybe, for example, those numbers are getting higher because people are just more comfortable talking about depression and anxiety. One way to address this possibility is to look at behaviors—like suicide—that often accompany significant mental health concerns. If numbers are increasing only because people feel more comfortable talking about feeling anxious or depressed (rather than because more people actually *are* anxious or depressed) then we shouldn't necessarily see suicide rates going up—but we do. In fact, suicides increased by 56 percent among 18- and 19-year-olds in the decade between 2008 and 2017; hospital visits related to self-harm (like cutting) were also up during that period.

But we don't want to leave you with the impression that it's all emotional doom-and-gloom during adolescence and young adulthood. In fact, this period provides lots of opportunities for positive emotional experiences and growth (Coe-Odess et al., 2019). Just as importantly, positive emotion during this time period is associated with higher levels of well-being in adulthood (Kansky, Allen, & Deiner, 2016).

But don't people face a "midlife crisis" at some point in their forties or fifties? Although adulthood brings its fair share of challenges, only about a quarter of men and women believe that they have experienced a midlife crisis characterized by strong negative feelings and dissatisfaction (Wethington, Kessler, & Pixley, 2004). It is more common to make a "midcourse correction" at midlife than it is to survive a "crisis" (Freund & Ritter, 2009; McFadden & Rawson Swan, 2012). Ideally, the midlife transition involves reworking old identities, achieving valued goals, finding one's own truths, and preparing for old age. Taking stock may be especially

Socioemotional development Area of psychology concerned with changes in emotions and social relationships.

Social smile Smiling elicited by a social stimulus, such as seeing a parent's face.

D Dipasupil/FilmMagic/Getty Images

Shown here at the Saturday Night Live 40th Anniversary Celebration in 2015, Betty White celebrated her 95th birthday in 2017. Still active after over 80 years as a popular entertainer, Betty is proof that aging does not inevitably bring an end to engaging in challenging activities.

valuable at midlife but reviewing past choices to prepare for the future is helpful at any age. For some people, difficult turning points in life can serve as "wake-up calls" that create opportunities for personal growth (Weaver, 2009).

You might be tempted to think that older adulthood would be associated with the highest levels of negative emotion. After all, older adults are managing declines in physical functioning as well as the loss of friends and family members who are close to them in age. It's somewhat surprising, then, to find that this isn't really the case at all. In fact, despite the emphasis on youth in our culture, middle age and beyond can be a rich period of life in which people feel secure, happy, and self-confident (Lilgendahl, Helson, & John, 2013).

For many adults, age-related physical declines are offset by positive relationships and greater mastery of life's demands (Ryff & Singer, 2009; Wilhelm et al., 2010). What are older adults doing to help them experience these positive outcomes? One of the most stable findings in the research on aging is the *positivity effect*, or the tendency for older adults to pay attention to, and remember, more positive information than negative information (Carstensen & DeLiema, 2018). In addition, compared to adolescents and young adults, older adults also appear to be more skilled at regulating, or controlling, their emotional responses (Scheibe, Sheppes, & Staudinger, 2015). Some research suggests that they do this through a process of situation selection, or choosing to spend most of their time doing things with people that they care about (Sims, Hogan, & Carstensen, 2015) (■ see Section 2.5 for more on the importance of self-regulation and situation selection).

Of course, in the end, death is the biologically inevitable conclusion of every life. A highly influential account of emotional responses to death comes from the work of Elisabeth Kübler-Ross (1926–2004). Over the years, she spent hundreds of hours at the bedsides of the terminally ill, where she observed five basic emotional reactions to impending death (Kübler-Ross, 1975):

1. **Denial and isolation.** A typical first reaction is to deny death's reality and isolate oneself from information confirming that death is really going to occur. Initially, the person may be sure that "it's all a mistake." She or he thinks, "Surely the doctor made an error."
2. **Anger.** Many dying individuals feel anger and ask, "Why me?" As they face the ultimate threat of having life torn away, their anger may spill over into rage toward the living.
3. **Bargaining.** In another common reaction, the terminally ill bargain with themselves or with God. The dying person thinks, "Just let me live a little longer and I'll do anything to earn it."
4. **Depression.** As death draws near and the person begins to recognize that it cannot be prevented, feelings of futility, exhaustion, and deep depression may set in.
5. **Acceptance.** If death is not sudden, many people manage to come to terms with dying and accept it calmly. The person who accepts death is neither happy nor sad, but at peace with the inevitable.

Kübler-Ross's list is best understood as describing typical reactions to impending death. But not all terminally ill persons display each of these reactions, nor do they always occur in this order. In general, one's approach to dying will mirror his or her style of living (Yedidia & MacGregor, 2001). Note, as well, that many of the same reactions accompany any major loss, be it divorce, loss of a home due to fire, death of a pet, or loss of a job.

How can I use this information? First, it can help both the dying and the survivors to recognize and cope with periods of depression, anger, denial, and bargaining. Second, it helps to realize that close friends or relatives may feel many of the same emotions before or after a person's death because they, too, are facing a loss (Leming & Dickinson, 2016). Perhaps the most important thing to recognize is that dying persons need to share their feelings and to discuss death openly (Corr, Nabe, & Corr, 2013). Too often, dying persons feel isolated and separated from others. If someone in your life is dying, be genuine, be ready to listen, be respectful, be aware of feelings and nonverbal cues, be comfortable with silence, and most of all, be there, no matter what (Dyer, 2001).

John Mitterer

Death may be inevitable, but it can be faced with dignity and sometimes even lightheartedly. While she was alive, nobody took Pearl Roberts's health complaints seriously because she always had such a sense of humor.

▲ Table 3.2 Erikson's Psychosocial Dilemmas

Age	Characteristic Dilemma	Successful navigation of this dilemma depends on ...
Birth to 1 year	Trust versus mistrust	Whether parents respond to their dependent babies with warmth, love, and caring for their needs
1–3 years	Autonomy (independence) versus shame and doubt	Responses to children as they express their growing self-control by climbing, touching, exploring, and trying to do things for themselves
3–5 years	Initiative versus guilt	Positive, supportive responses to children as they seek the freedom to play, ask questions, use imagination, and choose activities
6–12 years	Industry versus inferiority	Positive, supportive responses to children as they work on new challenges such as building, painting, cooking, reading, and studying
Adolescence (12–19 years)	Identity versus role confusion	Effective efforts to create an identity that fits well with adolescents' talents, values, life history, relationships, and the demands of the culture. Effective efforts to integrate the experiences of different roles (student, friend, athlete, worker, son, lover) into a unified sense of self
Young adulthood (20–34 years)	Intimacy versus isolation	The ability to care about others and share meaningful experiences with them
Middle adulthood (35–64 years)	Generativity versus stagnation	Striking a balance between caring for oneself, one's family, and providing support for future generations. Engaging in productive or meaningful work
Late adulthood (65 years and older)	Integrity versus despair	The ability to look back on one's life with acceptance and satisfaction

Ted Streshinsky Photographic Archive/Getty Images

Personality theorist Erik Erikson (1903–1994) is best known for his life-stage theory of human development.

Social Development

Social developmentalists examine our interactions with a wide range of others, including family, friends, teachers, romantic partners, co-workers, and clergy. In particular, they're interested in how those relationships can change over time, both in face-to-face interactions and, more recently, online.

In a highly influential book entitled *Childhood and Society*, Erik Erikson (1963) suggested that we face a specific *psychosocial dilemma*, or "crisis," at each stage of life. A **psychosocial dilemma** is a conflict between personal impulses and the social world. Resolving each dilemma creates a new balance between a person and society. A string of "successes" produces healthy development and a satisfying life. Unfavorable outcomes throw us off balance, making it harder to deal with later crises. Life becomes a "rocky road," and personal growth is stunted. ▲ Table 3.2 outlines Erikson's dilemmas.

More recent work in the area of social relationships has expanded on Erikson's ideas. Let's take a look at some of the findings that have emerged from this interesting field of research.

bikeriderlondon/Shutterstock.com

According to Erikson, an interest in future generations characterizes optimal adult development.

Social Development in Infancy and Childhood

Affectional Needs

A baby's **affectional needs**—emotional needs for care, love, and positive relationships with others—are every bit as important as more obvious needs for food, water, and physical care. In part to meet their affectional needs, infants rapidly begin to form close emotional bonds with their primary caregivers (Music, 2011). As infants form their first emotional bond with an adult, usually a parent, they also begin to develop self-awareness and an awareness of others (Easterbrooks et al., 2013). These early social developmental milestones lay a foundation for subsequent relationships with parents, siblings, friends, and relatives (Shaffer & Kipp, 2014).

Psychosocial dilemma A conflict between personal impulses and the social world.

Affectional needs Emotional needs for care, love, and positive relationships with others.

In a classic study of mother–infant relationships, Harry Harlow separated baby rhesus monkeys from their mothers at birth. The real mothers were replaced with **surrogate mothers** (substitutes). Some were made of cold, unyielding wire. Others were covered with soft terry cloth.

When the infants were given a choice between the two mothers, they spent most of their time clinging to the cuddly terry-cloth mother. This was true even when the wire mother held a bottle, making it the source of food. The "love" and attachment displayed toward the cloth replicas was identical to that shown toward natural mothers. For example, when frightened by rubber snakes, wind-up toys, and other "fear stimuli," the infant monkeys ran to their cloth mothers and clung to them for security. These classic studies suggest that attachment begins with **contact comfort**, the pleasant, reassuring feeling that infants get from touching something soft and warm, especially their mother.

Nina Leen/The LIFE Picture Collection/Getty Images

An infant monkey clings to a cloth-covered surrogate mother. Baby monkeys become attached to the cloth "contact-comfort" mother but not to a similar wire mother. This is true even when the wire mother provides food and the cloth mother doesn't. Contact comfort may also underlie the tendency of children to become attached to inanimate objects, such as blankets or stuffed toys.

sergei telegin/Shutterstock.com

Most parents are familiar with the storm of crying that sometimes occurs when babies are left alone at bedtime. Bedtime distress can be a mild form of separation anxiety. As many parents know, it is often eased by the carefully monitored presence of "security objects," such as a stuffed animal or favorite blanket (Donate-Bartfield & Passman, 2004).

Although mothers usually begin to feel bonded to their babies before birth, babies respond more or less equally to everyone for the first few months. By two or three months, though, most babies prefer their mothers to strangers. By about seven months, babies generally become truly attached to their mothers, crawling after them if they can. Shortly thereafter, they begin to form attachments to other people as well, such as their father, grandparents, or siblings (Sigelman & Rider, 2015).

A direct sign that an emotional bond has formed appears around eight to twelve months of age. At that time, babies display **separation anxiety**—crying and signs of fear—when left alone or with a stranger. Mild separation anxiety is normal. When it is more intense, it may reveal a problem. At some point in their lives, about 1 in 20 children suffer from *separation anxiety disorder* (Herren, In-Albon, & Schneider, 2013). These children are miserable when they are separated from their parents, who they cling to or constantly follow. Some fear that they will get lost and never see their parents again. Many refuse to go to school. Children tend to outgrow the disorder (Dick-Niederhauser & Silverman, 2006), but if separation anxiety is intense or lasts for more than a month, parents should seek professional help for their child (Allen, Lavallee et al., 2010).

All things considered, creating a bond of trust and affection between the infant and at least one other person is a key event during the first year of life. It's important to note, however, that the parent–child relationship goes both ways—growing infants influence their parents' behavior at the same time that they are changed by it.

How can babies influence parents? They can't even talk! Newborn babies differ noticeably in **temperament**, the general pattern of attention, arousal, and mood that is evident from birth. This is the hereditary, physical core of personality, and it includes sensitivity, irritability, distractibility, and typical mood (Slagt et al., 2016). According to one influential theory, about 40 percent of all newborns are *easy children,* who are relaxed and agreeable. Another 10 percent are *difficult children,* who are moody, intense, and easily angered. *Slow-to-warm-up children* (about 15 percent) are restrained, unexpressive, or shy. The remaining children do not fit neatly into a single category (Chess & Thomas, 1986).

Because of differences in temperament, some babies are more likely than others to smile, cry, vocalize, reach out, or pay attention. As a result, babies rapidly become active participants in their own development. For example, Jorge was an easy baby who smiled frequently and was easily fed. This encouraged his mother to touch, feed, and sing to him. His mother's affection rewarded Jorge, in turn causing him to smile more.

In this way, a dynamic relationship blossoms between mother and child. For example, good parenting can reciprocally influence a shy child who, in turn, might become progressively less shy. The reverse also occurs: Difficult children may make parents unhappy and elicit more negative parenting. Alternatively, negative parenting can turn a moderately shy child into a very shy one. This suggests that inherited temperaments are dynamically modified by a child's experiences (Bridgett et al., 2009; Kiff, Lengua, & Bush, 2011).

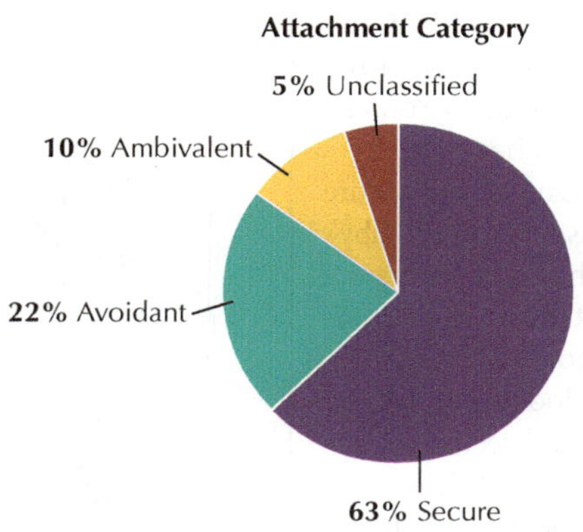

Figure 3.6 Distribution of child attachment. In the United States, about two-thirds of all children from middle-class families are securely attached. About one child in three is insecurely attached. (Percentages are approximate. From Kaplan, 1998)

Attachment

Though the term **attachment** is used often in conversations about parent–child relationships, psychologists think about it in a very narrow way. Specifically, developmental researchers use the term attachment to refer to an infant's feelings of security when they're with their caregiver in unfamiliar (and sometimes stressful) circumstances (Bowlby, 1978). According to psychologist Mary Ainsworth (1913–1999), the quality of attachment is revealed by how babies act when their mothers return after a brief separation in an unfamiliar laboratory environment (Ainsworth, 1989). This method of evaluating infants' responses to separations in the lab is referred to as the *Strange Situation.* Using this procedure, infants who develop a **secure attachment** have a stable and positive emotional bond. They are upset by the mother's (or caregiver's) absence and seek to be near her when she returns. Infants with an **insecure-avoidant attachment** have an anxious emotional bond. They tend to turn away from the mother (or caregiver) when she returns. **Insecure-ambivalent attachment** also is an anxious emotional bond. In this case, babies have mixed feelings: They both seek to be near the returning mother and angrily resist contact with her (Figure 3.6).

What about attachment to fathers? While much of the early research on attachment was done with mothers, we now know that babies also develop attachments with their fathers and other caregivers. Fathers of securely attached infants tend to be outgoing, agreeable, and happy in their marriage. In general, a warm family atmosphere—one that includes sensitive mothering *and* fathering—produces secure children (Gaumon et al., 2016; Mattanah, Lopez, & Govern, 2011).

Different attachment styles are associated with lasting effects (Morley & Moran, 2011; Moutsiana et al., 2014). Infants who are securely attached during infancy later show resilience, curiosity, problem-solving ability, and social skills in preschool. In contrast, attachment failures can be quite damaging (Santelices et al., 2011). Consider, for example, the plight of children raised in severely overcrowded orphanages (Rutter et al., 2009). These children get almost no attention from adults for the first year or two of their lives. Once adopted, many are poorly attached to their new parents. Some, for instance, will wander off with strangers, are anxious and remote, and don't like to be touched

Stephanie Rausser/Stone/Getty Images

A baby's temperament can have an important impact on parent–child interactions. Babies with an easy temperament are likely to be treated differently by their parents than those who have a difficult temperament.

Surrogate mother A substitute mother (in animal research, often an inanimate object or a dummy).

Contact comfort A pleasant and reassuring feeling that human and animal infants get from touching or clinging to something soft and warm, usually their mothers.

Separation anxiety Distress displayed by infants when they are separated from their parents or principal caregivers.

Temperament General pattern of attention, arousal, and mood that is evident from birth.

Attachment Emotional bonding between an infant and its caregivers that results from infants' feelings of security with the caregiver in times of stress or uncertainty.

Secure attachment A stable and positive emotional bond.

Insecure-avoidant attachment An anxious emotional bond marked by a tendency to avoid reunion with a parent or caregiver.

Insecure-ambivalent attachment An anxious emotional bond marked by both a desire to be with a parent or caregiver and some resistance to being reunited.

or to make eye contact with others (O'Conner et al., 2003). In short, for some children, a lack of affectionate care early in life leaves a lasting emotional impact well into adulthood. (■ You can learn more about your adult attachment pattern in Chapter 17.)

How can parents promote secure attachment? One key to secure attachment is a mother who is accepting and sensitive to her baby's signals and rhythms. Poor attachment occurs when a mother's actions are constantly inappropriate, inadequate, intrusive, overstimulating, or rejecting. Examples include a mother who tries to play with a drowsy infant, or one who ignores a baby who is looking at her and vocalizing. The link between sensitive caregiving and secure attachment appears to apply to all cultures (Santelices et al., 2011).

Does commercial day care interfere with the quality of attachment? That depends on the quality of day care. Overall, *high-quality* day care does not adversely affect attachment to parents. In fact, high-quality day care can improve children's social and cognitive skills (National Institute of Child Health and Human Development, 2010). Children in high-quality day care tend to have better relationships with their mothers (or caregivers) and fewer behavior problems. They also have better language abilities (Li et al., 2012). However, all the positive effects just noted are *reversed* for low-quality day care. Low-quality day care *is* risky and *may* weaken attachment (Phillips & Lowenstein, 2011). Poor-quality day care can even create behavior problems that didn't exist beforehand.

Parents seeking quality day care should look for responsive and sensitive care providers who offer plenty of attention and verbal and cognitive stimulation. This is more likely to occur in day-care centers with *at least* the following: (1) a small number of children per caregiver, (2) small overall group size, (3) trained care providers, (4) minimal staff turnover, and (5) stable, consistent care.

Parenting

From the first few years of life, when caregivers are the center of a child's world, through adulthood, the style and quality of parenting can profoundly influence our psychosocial outcomes (Gopnik, 2016). Psychologist Diana Baumrind (1991, 2005) has studied the effects of three major **parental styles**, which are identifiable patterns of parental caretaking and interaction with children. See if you recognize the styles that she describes.

Authoritarian parents enforce rules and require obedience from their children. The child is expected to stay out of trouble and to accept, without question, what parents regard as right or wrong ("Do it because I said so and I'm your mother"). Authoritarian parents tend to discipline their children through **power assertion**—physical punishment or a show of force, such as taking away toys or privileges. As an alternative, they may use **withdrawal of love**, refusing to speak to a child, threatening to leave, or otherwise acting as if the child is temporarily unlovable.

In North American Caucasian families, the children of authoritarian parents are usually obedient and self-controlled; but may also be emotionally stiff, withdrawn, apprehensive, lacking in curiosity, and dependent on adults for approval. In addition, they can develop low **self-esteem** (sense of worth). However, the outcomes for children of authoritarian parents in other cultures can look quite different.

"Your father and I have come to believe that incarceration is sometimes the only appropriate punishment."

Peter Steiner/Cartoon Collection

Overly **permissive parents** give little guidance to their children, allow them a great deal of freedom, and often don't hold them accountable for their actions. Typically, the child has few responsibilities. Rules are not enforced, and the child usually gets his or her way ("Do whatever you want"). Some overly permissive parents genuinely wish to empower their children by imposing few limits on their behavior, making them feel special, and giving them everything they want. But such good intentions can backfire, leaving parents with children who have developed unrealistically high levels of self-esteem and a sense of entitlement (Mamen, 2004). These children may also be dependent, immature, aimless and lacking in self-control (Byrne & O'Brien, 2014).

Finally, Baumrind describes **authoritative parents** as those who supply firm and consistent guidance, combined with love and

ZouZou/Shutterstock.com

Across ethnic communities, norms for effective parenting often differ in subtle ways. In the final analysis, parenting can be judged only if we know what culture or ethnic community a child is being prepared to enter (Sorkhabi, 2012).

affection. Such parents balance their own rights with those of their children. They control their children's behavior through praise, recognition, approval, rules, and reasoning. In North American Caucasian families, this style of parenting produces children who are *resilient* (good at bouncing back after bad experiences) and who develop the strengths that they need to thrive even in difficult circumstances (Azadyecta, 2011; Masten, 2014). The children of authoritative parents are competent, self-controlled, independent, assertive, and inquiring. They know how to manage their emotions and use positive coping skills (Kudo, Longhofer, & Floersch, 2012).

But what about mothers and fathers—don't they parent differently? Yes. Although *maternal influences* (all the effects that a mother has on her child) typically have a greater impact than *paternal influences* (the sum of all effects that a father has on his child). Although fathers are spending more time with their children, mothers still do most of the nurturing and caretaking, especially of young children (Craig, 2006).

Having said that, fathers also make a unique contribution to parenting (Bjorklund & Hernández Blasi, 2012). For example, fathers are more likely to play with their children and tell them stories. In contrast, mothers are typically responsible for the physical and emotional care of their children (Figure 3.7).

It might seem that the father's role as a playmate makes him less important. Not so. From birth onward, fathers pay more visual attention to children than mothers. Fathers are much more tactile (lifting, tickling, and handling the baby), more physically arousing (engaging in rough-and-tumble play), and more likely to engage in unusual play (imitating the baby, for example) (Fletcher, St. George, & Freeman, 2013). In comparison, mothers speak to infants more, play more conventional games (such as peekaboo), and, as noted, spend much more time in caregiving. Young children who spend a lot of time playing with their fathers tend to be more competent in many ways (Fletcher, St. George, & Freeman, 2013; Tamis-LeMonda et al., 2004).

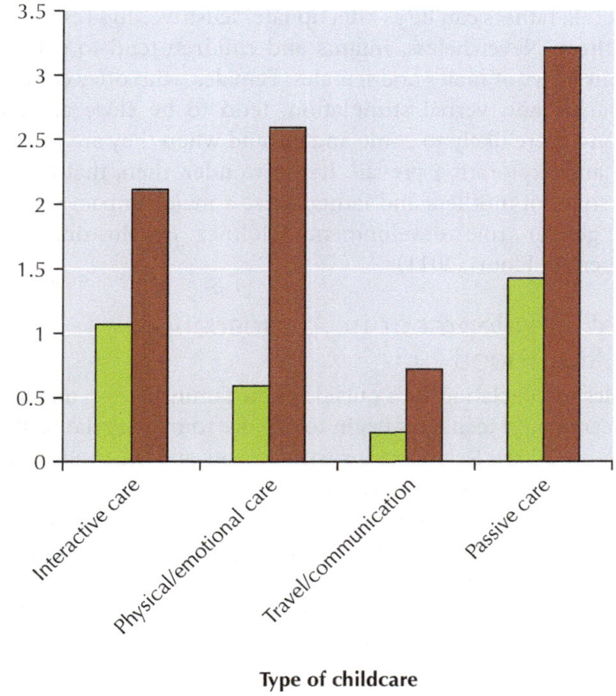

Figure 3.7 Mother–child and father–child interactions. This graph shows what occurred on routine days in a sample of over 1,400 Australian homes. Mothers spend about twice as long each day on childcare than fathers do. Furthermore, mothers spend more time on physical and emotional care (e.g., feeding, bathing, soothing) than on interactive care (e.g., playing, reading, activities); fathers show the reverse pattern. Finally, mothers spend more time on travel (e.g., driving children to sports or music lessons), communication (e.g., talking to teachers about their children), and passive care (e.g., supervising children while they play). (Adapted from Craig, 2006.)

Fathering typically makes a contribution to early development that differs in emphasis from mothering.

Parental styles Identifiable patterns of parental caretaking and interaction with children.

Authoritarian parents Parents who enforce rigid rules and demand strict obedience to authority.

Power assertion The use of physical punishment or coercion to enforce child discipline.

Withdrawal of love Withholding affection to enforce child discipline.

Self-esteem Regarding oneself as a worthwhile person; a positive evaluation of oneself.

Permissive parents Parents who give little guidance, allow too much freedom, or do not require the child to take responsibility.

Authoritative parents Parents who supply firm and consistent guidance combined with love and affection.

Overall, fathers can be as affectionate, sensitive, and responsive as mothers. Nevertheless, infants and children tend to get very different views of males and females. Females, who offer comfort, nurturance, and verbal stimulation, tend to be close at hand. Males are more likely to come and go, and when they are present, action and exploration prevail. It's no wonder, then, that the parental styles of mothers and fathers have a major impact on children's gender role development (Holmes & Huston, 2010; Malmberg & Flouri, 2011).

Social Development in Adolescence and Adulthood

In adolescence relationships outside of the family take on increased significance, and teenagers begin to explore romantic relationships (Giordano, 2003). Relationships with parents and other adults can become strained as adolescents work toward negotiating new norms related to their own independence and decision making. Adolescence is also a time for many adolescents to engage in self-exploration, consider the values that are important to them, and "try on" different roles to establish whether they are comfortable; parents may (or may not!) be happy with those values and roles.

Nowadays, many young people are deferring the transition to adulthood, prolonging identity explorations well into their twenties before they commit to life choices in work and love. Parents and other adults have become increasingly tolerant of **emerging adulthood**, a socially accepted period of extended adolescence, an unstable, in-between, self-focused period of time to develop skills and explore identities and life possibilities (Arnett, 2011, 2016).

It's worth noting, though, that emerging adulthood is not universal across cultures—instead, it seems to be most prevalent in economically wealthy countries such as the United States, Canada, Western Europe, and Australia. To some extent, features of emerging adulthood are also seen in wealthy Asian countries such as Japan and South Korea. For young adults in these countries, emerging adulthood seems to arise as a function of the fact that more years are being spent in school, with fewer prospects for stable employment immediately after graduation.

Antonio Guillem/Shutterstock.com

What identity will this teenager develop as he asks himself, "Who am I?"

The social networks of adults are often large and complex, having expanded beyond one's own family to include relationships with work colleagues, new friendships, and the families of romantic partners. Though some of these relationships are maintained out of necessity rather than preference, in general adults' social relationships are a valuable source of social support for managing the stressors that inevitably accompany the demands of working and raising a family (Walen & Lachman, 2000).

As people move into old adulthood, it's common for the size of the social network to decrease. Previously, it was assumed that this happened as a function of naturally occurring events (the death of siblings and friends; retirement from work) and a general wish to disengage from the social world (Achenbaum & Bengston, 1994). Psychological scientists, however, have suggested that smaller social networks in later adulthood may also be the result of purposeful choice. In particular, there is some evidence to suggest that people actively prune their social network so that they include only those individuals with whom the person enjoys spending time (Carstensen, Isaacowitz, & Charles, 1999).

Reflective Practice

Social and Emotional Development

1. Which of the following is not one of the six basic emotions infants express by six months of age?
   a. disgust
   b. fear
   c. sadness
   d. embarrassment
2. Fathers are more likely to act as playmates for their children, rather than as caregivers. T or F?
3. The development of separation anxiety in an infant corresponds to the formation of an emotional attachment to parents. T or F?
4. Contact comfort refers to the young infant's preference for access to food. T or F?

THINK CRITICALLY

5. Evaluate the following statement: Emotional bonding begins before birth.
6. Assess which parenting style would be most likely to lead to eating disorders in children.

SELF-REFLECT

- Do you think that early attachment affects your life as an adult? Can you think of any examples from your own life? Was your attachment to your mother different from your attachment to your father?

Answers: 1. d 2. T 3. T 4. F 5. It certainly can for parents. When a pregnant woman begins to feel fetal movements, she becomes aware that a baby is coming to life inside her. Likewise, prospective parents who hear a fetal heartbeat at the doctor's office or see an ultrasound image of the fetus often begin to become emotionally attached to the unborn child (Sigelman & Rider, 2015). 6. Authoritarian parents who are too controlling about what their children eat, as well as permissive parents who are too willing to withdraw from conflicts over eating, can create dietary issues in their children (Haycraft & Blissett, 2010).

3.4 Language, Cognitive, and Moral Development

GATEWAYS LEARNING OUTCOMES:
After reading this section you should be able to:

3.4.1 Describe key aspects of language development across the lifespan

3.4.2 Describe key aspects of cognitive development across the lifespan, including:

(a) the central ideas that underlie Piaget's theory of cognitive development

(b) the central ideas that underlie Vygotsky's theory of cognitive development

(c) the focus of more recent research concerning cognitive development

3.4.3 Describe key aspects of moral development across the lifespan, including Kohlberg's three stages of moral development and Carol Gilligan's criticism of this theory

Social developmental research has demonstrated that our relationships with others clearly show important changes over time. However, it's worth noting that those relationships—and our genes—also have important consequences for growth in at least three other areas: our ability to use language, to think and reason about the world (cognitive development), and the development of our values (moral development). We'll take a look at each one of these in the sections that follow.

Language Development

There's something almost miraculous about the rapidity of early language development, which is closely tied to maturation (Gleason & Ratner, 2013). As every parent knows, babies can cry from birth on. By one month of age, they use crying to gain attention. Typically, parents can tell whether an infant is hungry, angry, or in pain simply from the tone of the crying (Nakayama, 2010). Around 6 to 8 weeks of age, babies begin *cooing* (the repetition of vowel sounds such as "oo" and "ah").

By seven months of age, a baby's nervous system is mature enough to allow *babbling*. In the babbling stage, the consonants *b*, *d*, *m*, and *g* are combined with the vowel sounds to produce meaningless language sounds: *dadadadada* or *bababa*. At first, babbling is the same around the world. But soon, the language spoken by parents begins to have an influence (Goldstein et al., 2010)—that is, Japanese babies start to babble in a way that sounds like Japanese, Mexican babies babble in Spanish-like sounds, and so on (Garcia-Sierra et al., 2011).

At about one year of age, children respond to real words such as *no* or *hi*. Soon afterward, the first connection between words and objects forms, and children may address their parents as "Mama" or "Dada." By age 18 months to two years, a child's vocabulary may include 100 words or more. First comes the *single-word stage*, during which children use one word at a time, such as "go," "juice," or "up." Soon after, words are arranged in simple two-word sentences called *telegraphic speech*: "Want-Teddy"; "Mama-gone."

At about the same time that children begin to put two or three words together, they become much more independent. They may assert their independence by saying, "No drink," "Me do it," "My cup, my cup," and the like. After age two, the child's comprehension and use of words takes a dramatic leap forward. From this point on, vocabulary and language skills grow at a phenomenal rate (Fernald, Perfors, & Marchman, 2006). By first grade, the average child will understand around 8,000 words and use about 4,000.

Nature and Nurture in Language Development

What accounts for this amazing language development in childhood? Linguist Noam Chomsky (1986) has long claimed that humans have a **biological predisposition**, or hereditary readiness, to develop language. In other words, he puts significant emphasis on "nature" in his account of language development. According to Chomsky, language patterns are inborn, much like a child's ability to coordinate walking. If such inborn language capacity does exist, it may explain why children around the world use a limited number of patterns in their first sentences. Typical patterns include the following (Mussen et al., 1979): identification ("See kitty."), nonexistence ("Allgone milk."), possession ("My doll."), agent-action ("Mama give."), negation ("Not ball."), and question ("Where doggie?").

While maturation stemming from genetics is certainly an important part of language development (Saxton, 2010), many psychologists feel that Chomsky underestimates the importance of learning, or "nurture" in this domain (Behne et al., 2012; Hoff, 2014). *Psycholinguists* (specialists in the psychology of language) have shown that imitation of adults and rewards for correctly using words (for example, when a child asks for a cookie and is rewarded by receiving one) are an important part of language learning.

Indeed, it seems that parents and children begin to communicate long *before* the child can actually speak. This readiness to interact *socially* with parents may be just as important as the innate language processing emphasized by Chomsky. For

Emerging adulthood A socially accepted period of extended adolescence that is now quite common in Western and Westernized societies.

Biological predisposition The presumed hereditary readiness of humans to learn certain skills, such as how to use language or a readiness to behave in particular ways.

example, parents go to a great deal of trouble to get babies to smile and vocalize. In doing so, they quickly learn to change their actions to keep the infant's attention, arousal, and activity at optimal levels. A familiar example is the "I'm-Going-to-Get-You" game. In it, the adult says, "I'm gonna getcha . . . . I'm gonna getcha . . . . I'm gonna getcha . . . . Gotcha!"

Through such games, adults and babies come to share similar rhythms and expectations (Carroll, 2008). Soon a system of shared **signals** is created, including touching, vocalizing, gazing, and smiling. These signals help lay a foundation for later language use (De Schuymer et al., 2011; Kraus & Slater, 2016). Specifically, signals establish a pattern of "conversational" *turn-taking* (alternate sending and receiving of messages):

Jorge's mom	*Jorge*
	(smiles)
"Oh what a nice little smile!"	
"Yes, isn't that nice?"	(burps)
"Well, excuse you!"	
"Yes, that's better, yes."	(vocalizes)
"Yes."	(smiles)
"What's so funny?"	

From the outside, such exchanges may look meaningless. In reality, they represent real communication (Behne et al., 2012). One study found that six-week-old babies change their gaze at an adult's face when the adult's speech changes (Crown et al., 2002). Infants as young as four months engage in vocal turn-taking with adults (Jaffe et al., 2001). The more children interact with parents, the faster they learn to talk and the faster they develop thinking abilities (Hoff & Tian, 2005). Unmistakably, social relationships contribute to early language learning (Hoff, 2014; Vernon-Feagans et al., 2011).

As they get older, input from their conversation partners becomes even more valuable. For example, when a child makes a language error, parents typically repeat the child's sentence, with needed corrections, or ask a clarifying question to draw the child's attention to the error (Hoff, 2014). In addition, babies actively participate in language learning by asking questions, such as "What dis?" (Domingo & Goldstein-Alpern, 1999).

When they talk to infants, parents use an exaggerated pattern of speaking called **motherese (parentese)**. Typically, they raise their tone of voice, use short, simple sentences, repeat themselves, and use frequent gestures (Gogate, Bahrick, & Watson, 2000). They also slow their rate of speaking and use exaggerated voice inflections: "Did you eat it A-L-L UP?"

What is the purpose of such exchanges? Parents are apparently trying to help their children learn language (Soderstrom, 2007). When a baby is still babbling, parents tend to use long, adult-style sentences. But as soon as the baby says its first word, they switch to parentese. By the time that babies are four months old, they prefer parentese over normal speech (Cooper et al., 1997).

In addition to being simpler, parentese has a distinct "musical" quality (Trainor & Desjardins, 2002). No matter what language mothers speak, the melodies, pauses, and inflections they use to comfort, praise, or give warning are universal. Psychologist Anne Fernald has found that mothers of all nations talk to their babies with similar changes in pitch. For instance, we praise babies with a rising, then falling pitch ("BRA-vo!" "GOOD girl!"). Warnings are delivered in a short, sharp rhythm ("Nein! Nein!" "Basta! Basta!" "No! Dude!"). To give comfort, parents use low, smooth, drawn-out tones ("Oooh poor baaa-by." "Oooh pobrecito."). A high-pitched, rising melody is used to call attention to objects ("See the pretty BIRDIE?") (Fernald, 1989).

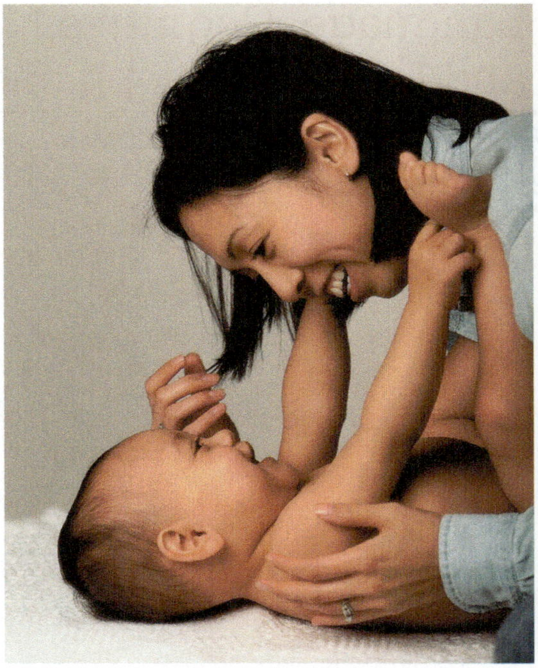
Gary Conner/Photolibrary/Getty Images

As with motherese, parents use a distinctive style when singing to an infant. Even people who speak another language can tell if a tape-recorded song was sung to an infant or an adult (Trehub, Unyk, & Trainor, 1993).

Parentese helps parents get babies' attention, communicate with them, and teach them language (Newman, Rowe, & Bernstein, 2016). Later, as a child's speaking improves, parents tend to adjust their speech to the child's language ability. Especially from 18 months to four years of age, parents seek to clarify what a child says and prompt the child to say more.

In summary, some elements of language are clearly innate, just as Chomsky suggested. Nevertheless, environmental forces also influence which languages we learn, and whether a person will develop simple or sophisticated language skills. The first seven years of life are a sensitive period in language learning (Hoff, 2014). Clearly, a full flowering of speech requires careful cultivation.

Cognitive Development

The term cognition refers to all of the processes that contribute to our thinking. As a consequence, cognitive development is a vast area of research covering everything from thinking and learning to memory and problem solving. What we know from years of study is that babies are smarter than many people think. From an evolutionary perspective, a baby's mind is designed to soak up information, which it does at an amazing pace (Bjorklund, 2012).

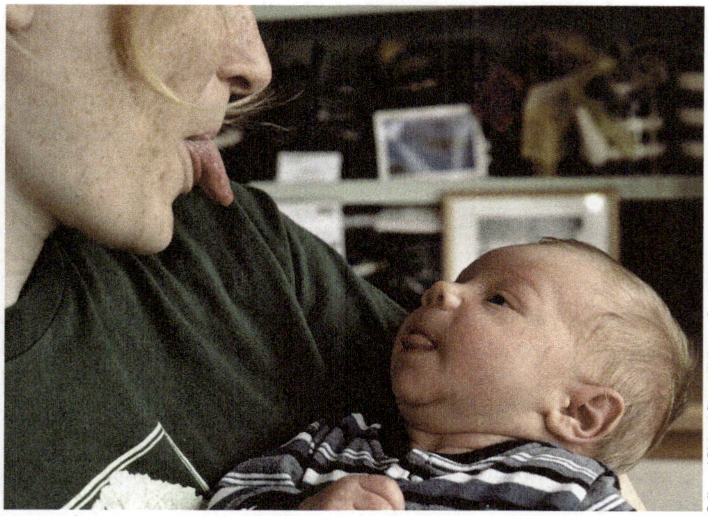

When this mother sticks out her tongue, her infant son imitates her. Is this common? To find out, Andrew Meltzoff videotaped mothers and researchers as they made facial gestures at infants and recorded the infant's responses. The resulting videotapes of both adults and of tested infants helped ensure objectivity.

Jean Piaget (1896–1980). Philosopher, psychologist, and keen observer of children. Many of his ideas came from observing his own children as they solved various thought problems. (It is tempting to imagine that Piaget's illustrious career was launched one day when his wife said to him, "Watch the children for a while, will you, Jean?")

In the first months of life, babies are increasingly able to think, to learn from what they see, to make predictions, and to search for explanations. For example, Jerome Bruner (1983) observed that three- to eight-week-old babies seem to understand that a person's voice and body should be connected. If a baby hears his mother's voice coming from where she is standing, the baby will remain calm. If her voice comes from a loudspeaker several feet away, though, the baby will become agitated and begin to cry.

As another example, psychologist Andrew Meltzoff has found that babies are born mimics. Videos of babies confirm that they imitate adult facial gestures while they can see them. (■ Observational learning, anyone? See Section 6.3.) As early as nine months of age, infants can remember and imitate actions a day after seeing them (Heimann & Meltzoff, 1996; Meltzoff, 2005). Such mimicry obviously aids rapid learning in infancy.

Cognitive Development in Childhood and Adolescence: Piaget's Theory

Swiss psychologist and philosopher Jean Piaget (Jahn pea-ah-ZHAY) (1896–1980) provided some of the first great insights into how children develop thinking abilities when he proposed that children's cognitive skills progress through a series of maturational stages (Barrouillet, 2015). According to Piaget (1951, 1952), children's thinking is, generally speaking, less abstract than that of adults. Put another way, they tend to base their understanding on particular examples and objects that they can see or touch. Also, children use fewer abstract generalizations, categories, and principles.

Over time, though, Piaget demonstrated that children's thinking about a variety of subjects grows more abstract and complex. For example, we know that one of the twins, William, knew nothing about horses when he was born; he had, of course, never seen one. But living on a farm in a rural area he eventually did see horses, and his aunt from La Paz even gave him a stuffed toy horse when she came to visit. He knew the word "horse," and he eventually learned to distinguish them from other similar-looking animals like donkeys. According to Piaget, after many encounters with things related to horses, William had formed a **schema**—an organized learned body of knowledge or skills about a particular topic—in this case, for his understanding of the concept of "horse."

How does this type of learning take place, you might wonder. Piaget proposed that children's thinking—including schema development—improves through mental processes that he called *assimilation* and *accommodation*.

Assimilation refers to the application of an established schema to new objects or problems. Let's say that little William sees a picture of a horse in a book at the school library. He has already seen a live horse in a field, and he has the little stuffed horse that his aunt gave him. He naturally points to the picture and calls out, "Horse!" and his teacher says "Yes! It's a horse." In this case, William adds this new experience with a picture of a horse to his existing concept of *horse*. Because this new experience fits neatly within William's existing schema for horses, Piaget would say that it has been *assimilated* into that schema.

Signals In early language development, behaviors, such as touching, vocalizing, gazing, or smiling, that allow nonverbal interaction and turn-taking between parent and child.

Motherese (parentese) A pattern of speech used when talking to infants, marked by a higher-pitched voice; short, simple sentences; repetition; slower speech; and exaggerated voice inflections.

Schema A mental structure composed of an organized learned body of knowledge or skills about a particular topic, according to Piaget.

Assimilation The application of an established schema to new objects or problems, according to Piaget.

In **accommodation (learning)**, existing schemas are modified to fit new objects or problems. For instance, suppose that while looking at that same book in his school library, William sees a picture of a zebra. Proudly, he again exclaims, "Horse!" This time, his teacher replies, "No, that's a zebra." Little William has *failed to assimilate* the zebra to his horse schema, so now he must *accommodate* by creating a new schema for *zebra*, and modifying his schema of horse (so that it does *not* include black and white stripes!).

Over the course of a lifetime, we develop a very large number of schemas that are stored in memory. In addition to having schemas for animals like horses and zebras, for example, we also develop schemas for each of the people that we know (your eccentric Uncle George), groups of people (university professors), and the places where we spend our time (your home, the place where you work). We also develop behavioral schemas called *scripts*, which contain information about the appropriate ways to act in particular situations. You very likely have a script that tells you what to do when you arrive at a restaurant, for example, as well as one that contains information about the proper way to behave at a funeral.

Piaget's Stages of Cognitive Development

Piaget believed that children's thinking moved through an orderly set of stages that were the same for all children, and that adult-like thinking was not achieved until early adolescence. Let's take a closer look at those stages:

1. Sensorimotor Stage (0–2 Years)

As adults, one of our most useful cognitive strategies is the ability to call something up in your "mind's eye." If we asked you to think about anything familiar, from Albert Einstein to a bag of popcorn, you could likely call up an image that represents those concepts, or ideas. But according to Piaget, newborns, who are in the **sensorimotor stage**, cannot create *internal representations* such as mental images in their minds. As a result, they lack **object permanence**, a recognition that physical things continue to exist even when they are no longer visible. When babies do achieve object permanence, they finally understand that people and things are still "out there in the world" even though they cannot be seen. In fact, the development of object permanence is one of the primary reasons that babies eventually begin to display separation anxiety when their caregivers move out of sight: They finally understand that even though mom or dad has disappeared from view, they continue to exist (and can perhaps be brought back if sufficient noise is made!). (■ Note that language also requires internal representation; see Section 8.1 for more information.)

Because of these limitations in their thinking, babies' cognitive development in the first two years of life is largely concerned with learning to coordinate information from sensory perceptions (what they see and hear, for example) with their motor skills (grabbing what they see, crawling toward what they hear). But sometime during the first year, babies do begin to actively pursue disappearing objects and they can even anticipate the movement of an object that has disappeared behind a screen (Baillargeon & DeVos, 1991). For example, when watching a toy train move along a track, infants would be more likely to look ahead to the end of a tunnel than stare at the spot where the train disappeared. They do this because they understand that the train is still there even though it can't be seen, and that it will continue to move in a straight line, just as it was before it left their sight. In general, then, the child begins to see the world as more *stable* as they move past this stage. Objects cease to appear and disappear magically, and a more orderly and predictable world replaces the confusing and disconnected sensations of infancy.

2. Preoperational Stage (2–7 Years)

Close your eyes. Imagine the room you sleep in. What would it look like if you were perched on the ceiling and your bed was missing? Now you have operated mentally on your image by *transforming* it. According to Piaget, even though children in the **preoperational stage** can form mental images or ideas, they are *pre*operational because they cannot easily use mental *operations*, or **transformations**, to manipulate those images or ideas in their minds.

According to Piaget, during the preoperational stage children display **egocentrism**, believing that everyone sees what they see, and thinks as they do. In a famous study, Piaget had children walk around a three-dimensional model of three adjacent mountains (Piaget and Inhelder, 1956). Various small objects were placed around the three mountains so that they could be seen from some sides but not from others. After the child had had an opportunity to see the model from all sides, a doll was placed at various points around the model and the child was asked to indicate what the doll could see from its position.

Four-year-olds consistently responded with answers that reflected what they themselves could see, regardless of where the doll was positioned. However, by the age of six, there was clear evidence that children understood that someone standing in another location would have a different view and might see things that they could not.

Such egocentrism about the physical world may also explain why children sometimes block your view by standing in front of the television—they assume that if they can see the screen then you must be able to as well! Egocentrism is also at the heart of why young children find the game of peekaboo so entertaining. For a 2-year-old, it's truly amazing to think that if you cover your eyes to block your view of mom, she will no longer be able to see you either!

Pavel L Photo and Video/Shutterstock.com

Crossing a busy street can be dangerous for the preoperational child. Because their thinking is still egocentric, younger children cannot understand why the driver of a car can't see them if they can see the car. Children under the age of seven also cannot judge the speeds and distances of oncoming cars consistently. Likewise, adults can overestimate the "street smarts" of younger children easily. It is advisable to teach children to cross with the light, in a crosswalk, with assistance, or all three.

Figure 3.8 The Sally-Anne task. Developmental psychologists often act out the Sally-Anne task using dolls as a way of establishing whether a child has developed a theory of mind

But egocentrism isn't limited to taking others' perspective on the physical world—we also see it in preschoolers' understanding of other people's mental perspectives. **Theory of mind** research explores children's understanding that people have mental states, such as thoughts, beliefs, and intentions, and that other people's mental states can be different from one's own. One way to assess whether a child understands that other people have their own mental states is the false-belief (or Sally-Anne) task (see Figure 3.8). In this test, a child is shown two dolls, Sally and Anne. Sally has a basket and Anne has a box. Sally puts a marble in her basket and goes out to play. In the meantime, Anne takes the marble from Sally's basket and puts it into her box. Sally comes back and looks for the marble. To assess theory of mind, the child is asked where Sally will look for her marble. Although the child knows that the marble is in Anne's box, the doll Sally does not; thus, the correct answer is that Sally will look in her basket. To answer correctly, then, children must understand that Sally does not have information that they themselves have (Sally has a false belief), and that she will behave based on what she *thinks* is true (and not what the child knows is actually true).

Children younger than four will invariably tell you that Sally will look for the marble in the box—they simply don't understand that Sally's thoughts differ from their own. By the time they reach age four or five, though, typically developing children can reliably demonstrate an understanding that other people's mental states differ from their own (Apperly, 2012; Baillargeon, Scott, & Bian, 2016). Some children diagnosed as being on the autism spectrum, however, struggle with developing a theory of mind (Kimhi, 2014).

Theory of mind is an important developmental milestone. Children need it in order to empathize with other people, for example, since empathy requires an understanding of how others' circumstances are likely to impact their thinking and emotions (see Chapter 17 for more information about empathy). Perhaps less obvious is the fact that theory of mind is also important to children's lie-telling and their ability to keep secrets. Both lies and secrets require a child to provide other people with misleading, false, or no information, and it's critical that the child understand that others will respond in keeping with the information that they have (even if it is false or incomplete), rather than what the child knows to be true.

3. Concrete Operational Stage (7–11 Years)

Remember that one important feature of preoperational thought is that children cannot operate on their mental representations. The hallmark of a child in the **concrete operational stage** is the emerging ability to carry out such mental operations, including tasks that require *reversals.*

Reversibility of thought allows children in the concrete operational stage to "undo" events in their minds, using their mental representations to move backward in time. The development of mental operations such as reversibility allows for the mastery of

Accommodation (learning) Modification of an established schema to fit a new object or problem, according to Piaget.

Sensorimotor stage Piaget's initial stage of development, when the infant's mental activity is only sensory perception and motor skills.

Object permanence Recognizing that physical things continue to exist, even when they are no longer visible.

Preoperational stage Piaget's second stage of cognitive development, characterized by the use of symbols and illogical thought.

Transformation (Piagetian) The mental ability to change the shape or form of a substance (such as clay or water) and to perceive that its volume remains the same.

Egocentrism The belief that everyone sees exactly what you see in the physical world, or that they think about the world in the same way that you do.

Theory of mind The understanding that people have mental states, such as thoughts, beliefs, and intentions and that other people's mental states can be different from one's own.

Concrete operational stage Piaget's third stage of cognitive development, characterized by logical thought.

Tony Freeman/PhotoEdit

Children under age seven intuitively assume that a volume of liquid increases when it is poured from a short, wide container into a taller, thinner one. This boy thinks the tall container holds more than the short one. In reality, each holds the same amount of liquid. Children make such judgments based on the height of the liquid, not its volume.

"Young man, go to your room and stay there until your cerebral cortex matures."

Barbara Smaller/Conde Nast/Cartoon bank

conservation during the concrete operations stage—Piaget's term for the awareness that physical quantities stay constant despite changes in their shape or appearance.

Let's think about a typical child at the age five: If you show her a short, wide glass full of milk and a taller, narrow glass full of milk, most likely she will tell you that the taller glass contains more milk (even if it doesn't). What's even more remarkable, though, is that she will tell you this *even if she watches you pour milk from the short glass into an empty taller glass*. You may wonder how on earth the child could say such a thing—after all, she saw you do the pouring and she knows that you didn't add anything to that taller glass. Why on earth would she think there was more in the second glass just because it's taller?

Children struggle with conservation tasks like this until they are about six to eight years of age. As they get older, though, children can mentally transform the pouring of the milk by mentally *reversing* it, to see that the shape of the container is irrelevant to the volume of milk that it contains. If nothing has been added or taken away, then what they are looking at must be the same even if it looks different. Children have learned conservation when they understand that rolling a ball of clay into a "snake" does not increase the amount of clay (just because it looks longer). Likewise, taking a row of coins and spreading them out does not mean that you have more money (if only!). In each case, the amount of material remains the same, no matter what shape it takes, or how it appears. The original amount of matter is *conserved*.

4. Formal Operational Stage (11 Years and Up)

According to Piaget's theory, after about the age of eleven, children begin to rely less on the concrete objects and specific examples that characterize the concrete operations stage. Thinking is based more on abstract principles, such as democracy, honor, or correlation. Children who reach the **formal operational stage** become self-reflective about their thoughts, and they become less egocentric. Older children and young adolescents also gradually become able to consider hypothetical possibilities (suppositions, guesses, or projections). For example, if you ask a younger child in the concrete operational period, "What do you think would happen if it suddenly became possible for people to fly?" the child might respond, "People can't fly." Older children are better able to consider such possibilities.

Studying the Science: Evaluating Piaget's Ideas

Today, Piaget's theory remains a valuable road map for understanding how children think. On a broad scale, many of Piaget's ideas have held up well. However, there has been disagreement about specific details. Three criticisms are particularly important.

First, according to learning theorists, children continuously gain specific knowledge; they do not undergo stage-like leaps in general mental ability (Miller, 2011; Siegler, 2005). On the other hand, the growth in connections between brain cells occurs in waves that parallel some of Piaget's stages (Lefmann & Combs-Orme, 2013). (See Figure 3.9.) Thus, the truth may lie somewhere between Piaget's stage theory and modern learning theory.

Second, it is now widely accepted that children develop cognitive skills somewhat earlier than Piaget originally thought (Bjorklund, 2012). For example, Piaget believed that infants under the age of one year cannot think (i.e., use internal representations). Such abilities, he

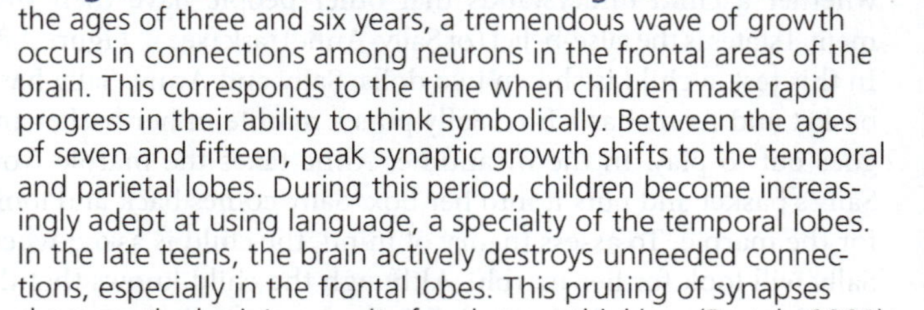

Figure 3.9 Brain maturation and cognition. Between the ages of three and six years, a tremendous wave of growth occurs in connections among neurons in the frontal areas of the brain. This corresponds to the time when children make rapid progress in their ability to think symbolically. Between the ages of seven and fifteen, peak synaptic growth shifts to the temporal and parietal lobes. During this period, children become increasingly adept at using language, a specialty of the temporal lobes. In the late teens, the brain actively destroys unneeded connections, especially in the frontal lobes. This pruning of synapses sharpens the brain's capacity for abstract thinking (Restak, 2001).

believed, emerge only after a long period of sensorimotor development. Babies, he said, have no memory of people and objects that are out of sight. Yet we now know that infants begin forming representations of the world very early in life. For example, babies as young as three months of age appear to know that objects are solid and do not disappear when out of view (Baillargeon, 2004).

Why did Piaget fail to detect the thinking skills of infants? Most likely, he mistook babies' limited memory and physical skills for mental immaturity. Piaget's tests required babies to search for objects or reach out and touch them. Newer, more sensitive methods are uncovering abilities that Piaget missed. One such method takes advantage of the fact that babies, like adults, act surprised when they see something "impossible" or unexpected occur. Making use of this effect, psychologist Renee Baillargeon (1991, 2004) puts on little "magic shows" for infants. In her "theater," babies watch as possible and impossible events occur with toys or other objects. Some three-month-old infants act surprised and gaze longer at impossible events, for example, seeing two solid objects appear to pass through each other. By the time that they are eight months old, babies can remember where objects are (or should be) for at least one minute (Figure 3.10).

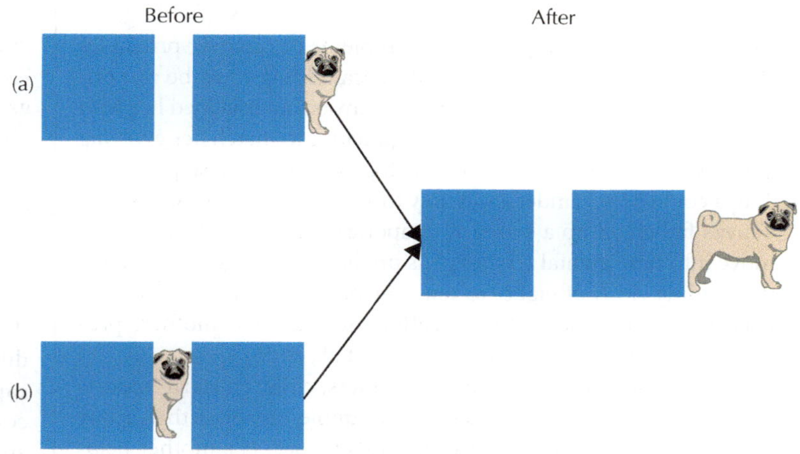

Figure 3.10 Testing for object constancy in infancy. An infant watches as a toy is placed behind the right of two screens (a). After a delay of 70 seconds, a possible event occurs as the toy is brought back into view from behind the right screen. Then the infant watches as the toy is placed behind the left of two screens (b). Now an impossible event occurs, as the toy is again retrieved from behind the right screen. (A duplicate toy was hidden there before testing.) Eight-month-old infants react with surprise when they see the impossible event staged for them. Their reaction implies that they remember where the toy was hidden. Infants appear to have a capacity for memory and thinking that greatly exceeds what Piaget claimed is possible during the sensorimotor period (Baillargeon, Scott, & Bian, 2016). (Adapted from Baillargeon, De Vos, & Graber, 1989.)

Third, Piaget is sometimes criticized for underestimating the impact of culture on mental development. Many psychologists are convinced that Piaget gave too little credit to the effects of the learning environment. For example, children who grow up in villages where pottery is made can correctly answer questions about the conservation of clay at an earlier age than Piaget would have predicted.

While Piaget stressed the role of maturation and the universality of cognitive development, Russian scholar Lev Vygotsky (1896–1934) was focused on the impact of sociocultural factors, stressing that cognitive development was not universal across all children but instead depended heavily on the culture and environment in which the child grew up. More specifically, Vygotsky's (1962, 1978) key insight was that children's thinking develops through dialogues with more capable persons. Let's take a closer look at his ideas.

An Alternative to Piaget: Vygotsky's Sociocultural Theory

So far, no one has published *A Child's Guide to Life on Earth*. Instead, children must learn about life from various "tutors," such as parents, teachers, and older siblings. Even if *A Child's Guide to Life on Earth* did exist, we would need a separate version for every culture. It is not enough for children to learn how to think. They also must learn specific intellectual skills valued by their culture.

Like Piaget, Vygotsky believed that children actively seek to discover new principles. However, Vygotsky emphasized that many of a child's most important "discoveries" are guided by skillful tutors. Psychologists Jay Shaffer and Katherine Kipp (2014) offer the following example:

Tanya, a four-year-old, has just received her first jigsaw puzzle as a birthday present. She attempts to solve the puzzle but gets nowhere until her father comes along, sits down beside her, and gives her some tips. He suggests that it would be a good idea to put together the corners first, points to the pink area at the edge of one corner piece, and says, "Let's look for another pink piece." When Tanya seems frustrated, he places two interlocking pieces near each other so that she will notice them, and when Tanya succeeds, he offers words of encouragement. As Tanya gradually gets the hang of it, he steps back and lets her work more and more independently (page 233).

Interactions like this are most helpful when they take place within a child's **zone of proximal development**. The word *proximal* means "close" or "nearby." Vygotsky realized that at any given time, some tasks are just beyond a child's reach. The child is close to having the mental skills needed to do these tasks, but they are a little too complex to be mastered alone. However, children working within this zone can make rapid progress if they receive sensitive guidance from a skilled partner (Gredler, 2012).

Vygotsky also emphasized a process that he called **scaffolding**. A scaffold is a framework or temporary support. Vygotsky believed

Conservation Piaget's term for the awareness that physical quantities stay constant despite changes in shape or appearance.

Formal operational stage Piaget's fourth stage of cognitive development, characterized by the ability to engage in thinking that includes abstract, theoretical, and hypothetical ideas.

Zone of proximal development A term referring to the range of tasks that a child cannot yet master alone, but that she or he can accomplish with the guidance of a more capable partner.

Scaffolding The process of adjusting instruction so that it is responsive to a beginner's behavior and supports the beginner's efforts to understand a problem or gain a mental skill.

that adults help children learn how to think by "scaffolding," or supporting, their attempts to solve problems or discover principles (Daniels, 2005). To be most effective, scaffolding must be responsive to a child's needs. For example, as Tanya's father helped her with the puzzle, he tailored his hints and guidance to match her evolving abilities. The two of them worked together, step by step, so that Tanya could better understand how to assemble a puzzle. In a sense, Tanya's father set up a series of temporary bridges that helped her move into new mental territory. As predicted by Vygotsky's theory, the reading skills of eight- to ten-year-old children are closely related to the amount of verbal scaffolding that their mothers provided at ages three and four (Dieterich et al., 2006).

During their collaborations with others, children learn important cultural beliefs and values. For example, imagine that a boy wants to know how many baseball cards he has. His mother helps him stack and count the cards, moving each card to a new stack as they count it. She then shows him how to write the number on a slip of paper so that he can remember it. This teaches the child not only about counting, but also that writing is valued in our culture. In other parts of the world, a child learning to count might be shown how to make notches on a stick or tie knots in a cord.

Vygotsky saw that grown-ups play a crucial role in what children know. As they try to decipher the world, children rely on adults to help them understand how things work. Vygotsky further noticed that adults unconsciously adjust their behavior to give children the information that they need to solve problems that interest the child. In this way, children use adults to learn about their culture and society (Gredler, 2012).

Beyond Piaget: Recent Research in Children's Cognitive Development

Much of the work that Piaget and Vygotsky did was aimed at establishing developmental timetables and exploring the role of maturation and environmental contributions to mastering basic cognitive tasks. Though their research was carried out decades ago, developmental psychologists continue to explore these important questions related to children's and adolescents' thinking.

More recent research in cognitive development, however, has expanded to include other areas, many of which are covered in the chapters of this book. For example, there is considerable interest in the executive functions that are described in our discussion of self-regulation (■ see Section 2.5) (Reynolds et al., 2019; Willoughby et al., 2019). Executive functioning relates to how we *control* our thinking in ways that allow us to develop plans and see them through (even when we are tempted to do something else instead!). Because they are so central to academic success and antisocial behavior, psychologists have been working hard to better understand how executive functions develop, and how they can be fostered.

Another area of interest among cognitive developmentalists relates to children's ongoing mastery of academic subjects, including math, science, and languages (Herodotou, 2018; Jirout & Newcombe, 2015; Zippert et al., 2019). Here, researchers have been working to better understand both the maturational and environmental factors that contribute to success in these areas. Greater awareness of how such knowledge evolves can, in turn, inform strategies that parents and teachers can use to promote children's confidence (■ see Section 6.4 for more about school-based learning).

Finally, there have been some exciting studies investigating children's memory, particularly in applied contexts such as the courtroom (Evans et al., 2019). Using the work on theory of mind as a starting point, developmental psychologists are investigating children's ability to truthfully and accurately answer questions about criminal activity, including their own experiences of abuse and mistreatment (■ see Section 7.4 for more about eyewitness testimony).

Cognitive Development in Adulthood

According to Piaget, full adult intellectual ability is attained during the stage of formal operations. Older adolescents are capable of inductive and deductive reasoning, and they can comprehend mathematics, physics, philosophy, psychology, and other abstract systems. They can learn to test hypotheses in a scientific manner. Of course, many adults can think formally about topics on which they are experts, but their thinking becomes concrete when the topic is unfamiliar. This implies that formal thinking may be more a result of culture and learning than maturation.

In any case, after late adolescence, improvements in intellect are based on gaining specific knowledge, experience, and wisdom, rather than on any leaps in basic thinking capacity. Of course, people do experience a gradual loss of *fluid intelligence* (abilities requiring speed or rapid learning) as they age, but this can often be offset by *crystallized intelligence* (abilities involving already learned knowledge and skills), such as vocabulary and stored-up facts, which may actually improve—at least into the sixties (Schaie, 2005). At work, job performance need not suffer as workers grow older (Agrigoroaei & Lachman, 2011). In the professions, wisdom and expertise can usually more than compensate for any loss of mental quickness (Cavanaugh & Blanchard-Fields, 2015).

Moral Development

Consider the following problem:

> A woman was near death from cancer, and there was only one drug that might save her. The druggist who discovered it was charging 10 times what it cost to make the drug. The sick woman's husband, Heinz, could pay only $1,000, but the druggist wanted $2,000. He asked the druggist to sell it cheaper or to let him pay later. The druggist said no. So Heinz became desperate and broke into the store and stole the drug for his wife. (This scenario is adapted from Kohlberg, 1969.)

How do you feel about Heinz's theft? Do you think that the husband should have done what he did? Was it wrong or right? Why? Finally, what would you do if it was up to you? These are *moral* questions, or questions of *ethics* (Haidt, 2012).

Like *attitudes*, morals have emotional and cognitive, as well as behavioral, dimensions (Shaffer & Kipp, 2014). **Moral development** begins in early childhood and continues into adulthood, as we acquire the specific values that, along with appropriate emotions and cognitions, guide responsible behavior (King, 2009). Let's take a brief look at this intriguing aspect of personal development. (■ For more on attitude formation and change, see Chapter 16.)

Moral Emotions and Thinking Across the Lifespan: Kohlberg's Theory

Did you get a "gut feeling" that what Heinz did was right or wrong? According to psychologist Jonathan Haidt (2013), our morals are, first and foremost, immediately and intuitively *felt*. Even infants as young as 15 months of age notice when toys are not being fairly shared, long before they can explain the concept of fairness (Sommerville et al., 2013).

Fundamental moral intuitions, such as the fact that it's wrong to harm others and that it's important to be fair, may be partly innate; part and parcel of our evolved social nature (Hamlin, 2013). Nevertheless, moral intuitions also develop, in part, through our experiences. For example, the children of parents who deal calmly with conflicts are likely to resist playing with a prohibited toy at a younger age (by the age of three) than children of less calm parents (Laible & Thompson, 2002).

Once we begin to experience moral intuitions (those "gut level" feelings that something is right or wrong), we seek to explain them (Nucci & Gingo, 2011). In an influential account of development in this area, psychologist Lawrence Kohlberg (1981) held that we clarify our values through thinking and reasoning. To study moral development Kohlberg posed dilemmas, like the one that Heinz faced, to children of different ages. Each child was asked what action the husband should take. Kohlberg classified the reasons given for each choice and identified three levels of moral development. Each is based not so much on the choices made (that is, steal the drug or not), but rather on the reasoning used to arrive at that choice.

Preconventional Moral Reasoning

At the lowest, **preconventional moral reasoning** level, moral thinking is guided by the consequences of actions (punishment, reward, or an exchange of favors). For example, a person at this level might reason: "The man shouldn't steal the drug because he could get caught and sent to jail" (avoiding punishment). The preconventional level is most characteristic of young children and delinquents (Forney, Forney, & Crutsinger, 2005).

Conventional Moral Reasoning

At the second, **conventional moral reasoning** level, thinking is based on a desire to please others or to follow accepted authority, rules, and values. For example, a person at this intermediate level might say, "He shouldn't steal the drug because others will think he is a thief. His wife would not want to be saved by thievery" (avoiding disapproval), or "Although his wife needs the drug, he should not break the law to get it. Everyone has to obey the law. His wife's condition does not justify stealing" (adhering to authority).

Conventional, group-oriented morals are typical of older children and most adults. Some adults may not reach even the conventional level. For instance, a significant number of men in their first year of college think unwanted sexual aggression is acceptable, even though laws in many countries forbid it (Tatum & Foubert, 2009).

Postconventional Moral Reasoning

At the highest, **postconventional moral reasoning** level, moral behavior is directed by self-chosen ethical principles that tend to be general, comprehensive, or universal. People at this level place a high value on justice, dignity, and equality. For example, a person reasoning at this level might say, "He should steal the drug and then inform the authorities that he has done so. He will have to face a penalty, but he will have saved a human life" (self-chosen ethical principles).

Kohlberg estimated that only about 20 percent of the adult population achieves the self-direction and higher principles of postconventional morality. An important question, though, is whether his theory properly reflects the diversity and complexity that is reflected in people's thinking about ethical behavior. For example, as we mentioned in ■ Section 1.4, Kohlberg's studies suggested that women were morally "immature" compared to men. In response, Carol Gilligan (1982) pointed out that Kohlberg's theory is concerned mainly with *fairness*, or *justice*. Based on studies of women who faced real-life dilemmas, Gilligan argued that there is also a moral ethic of *harm*, or *caring* about others. As one illustration, she presented the following story to 11- to 15-year-old American children:

> Seeking refuge from the cold, a porcupine asked to share a cave for the winter with a family of moles. The moles agreed. But because the cave was small, they soon found they were being scratched each time that the porcupine moved. Finally, they asked the porcupine to leave. But the porcupine refused, saying, "If you moles are not satisfied, I suggest that you leave."

Boys who read this story tended to opt for justice in resolving the dilemma: "It's the moles' house. It's a deal. The porcupine leaves." In contrast, girls tended to look for solutions that reflected caring, and would keep all parties happy and comfortable (for example, "Cover the porcupine with a blanket").

Gilligan's point is that male psychologists have, for the most part, defined moral maturity in terms of fairness, justice, and autonomy. From this perspective, a woman's concern with relationships (that is, a focus on caring) can look like weakness rather than strength. Indeed, a woman who is concerned about what helps or harms others would be placed at the conventional level in Kohlberg's system. But Gilligan believes that caring also is a major element of moral development, and she suggests that males may lag in achieving it (Lambert et al., 2009).

It's worth noting that several studies have found little or no difference in men's and women's overall moral reasoning abilities (Glover, 2001). Both men and women may use caring *and* justice to make moral decisions. The moral yardstick that they use appears to depend on the situation that they face (Wark & Krebs, 1996). Moreover, research exploring human diversity suggests that for some people, concepts beyond caring and justice may be important in guiding our values (Graham, Haidt, & Nosek, 2009; ■ see Section 2.5).

Moral development The development of values that, along with appropriate emotions and cognitions, guide responsible behavior.

Preconventional moral reasoning Moral thinking based on the consequences of one's choices or actions (punishment, reward, or an exchange of favors).

Conventional moral reasoning Moral thinking based on a desire to please others or to follow accepted rules and values.

Postconventional moral reasoning Moral thinking based on carefully examined and self-chosen moral principles.

Reflective Practice

Language, Cognitive, and Moral Development

1. Simple two-word sentences are characteristic of ____________ speech.
2. Noam ____________ advanced the idea that language acquisition is built on innate patterns.

Match each item with one of the following Piagetian stages.

a. Sensorimotor
b. Concrete operational
c. Preoperational
d. Formal operational

3. ____________ egocentric thought
4. ____________ abstract or hypothetical thought
5. ____________ purposeful movement
6. ____________ conservation
7. ____________ reversibility thought
8. ____________ object permanence
9. Vygotsky called the process of providing a temporary framework of supports for learning new mental abilities ____________

THINK CRITICALLY

10. In Western cultures, children as young as age four can understand that other people have mental states that differ from their own. In other words, they have developed a theory of mind. Would you evaluate this ability to be uniquely Western, or would you argue that children from other cultures also develop a theory of mind?
11. Applying what you know about values that can be based on different moral foundations (harm, care, purity, and loyalty), how would you analyze people's different responses (outrage to strong support) to burning an American flag in protest over the treatment of illegal immigrants being held in poor conditions at the border?

SELF-REFLECT

- You have been asked to help a child learn to use a calculator to do simple addition. How would you identify the child's zone of proximal development for this task? How would you scaffold the child's learning?

Answers: 1. telegraphic 2. Chomsky 3. b 4. d 5. a 6. c 7. c 8. a 9. scaffolding 10. All humans need to be able to base their actions on their understanding of the intentions, desires, and beliefs of others. Thus, children from Micronesia, a group of small islands in the Pacific Ocean, also develop a theory of mind at around four years of age (Oberle, 2009). 11. People who reason from different moral "foundations" may view exactly the same behavior in very different ways. For example, people whose values are primarily based on *caring* may feel that it is perfectly acceptable to burn the flag in protest because the most important factor in judging the situation is the fact that immigrants are people and they are being badly treated. However, people whose values are primarily based on *loyalty*, for example, will view flag burning very negatively because, for them, the most important factor in judging the situation is the fact that people burning flags are showing tremendous disloyalty toward their country.

Moral values are especially likely to come into sharper focus during adolescence and the transition to adulthood as the capacity for abstract thinking increases and people begin to establish their own "moral compass" (Hart & Carlo, 2005; Krettenauer et al., 2014). Many of the choices we make every day involve fundamental questions of right and wrong. The ability to think clearly about such questions is essential to becoming a responsible adult, which is why we'll explore this topic further in the section that follows.

3.5 Psychology and Your Skill Set: Ethical Behavior

GATEWAYS LEARNING OUTCOMES:
After reading this section you should be able to:

3.5.1 Create a plan to manage a challenge to your own values

If you follow popular media, you don't have to look far to find a scandal. We regularly see stories about athletes who took illegal drugs to win competitions, Hollywood stars who cheated on their partners, business executives who engaged in illegal practices to ensure larger profits, and politicians who misled people so that they could win elections. This type of behavior isn't just confined to the rich and powerful, either: Individuals download illegal copies of music, movies, and software every day. They also file misleading tax returns and fraudulent insurance claims for items that were never stolen. And at school, roughly two-thirds of students admit to cheating in their courses (McCabe, Butterfield, & Trevino, 2012).

Although our discussion of moral development highlighted the fact that a sense of right and wrong emerges in early childhood, the most important growth in this area doesn't occur until adolescence. It's at that point in the lifespan that we develop the capacity for abstract thought that's so important in guiding our values. This also fits with what we know about self-regulation (■ see Section 2.5). The prefrontal cortex—the part of our brain that's important in guiding our ability to resist temptation—is still developing well into the teens and early twenties. So, how "grown-up" are your ethics?

Check out the following list of behaviors. How much would someone have to pay you to do each of these things *if no one else*

tuaindeed/Shutterstock.com

How "grown-up" are your ethics?

would ever know? Would you do any of them for free? How about a thousand dollars? A million dollars? Is there anything on the list that you simply wouldn't do for any amount of money (adapted from Graham, Haidt, & Nosek, 2009)?

1. Kick a dog in the head, hard.
2. Sign a secret-but-binding pledge to hire only people of your race at your company.
3. Burn your country's flag in private.
4. Give a disrespectful hand gesture to your boss or professor.
5. Get a transfusion of disease-free, compatible blood from a convicted child molester.

Human Diversity and Moral Reasoning

As we saw earlier in this chapter, for years, when psychologists wrote about moral values they focused on ideas related to *caring/harm* and *justice/fairness*. The first two examples on the list above are related to these two values. But as we mentioned, more recently psychologists have expanded their thinking about morality, partly because diverse groups often have very different ideas about what it means to behave ethically in our everyday lives (Haidt, 2007, 2012). In particular, current ideas about ethical behavior go beyond focusing on harm and fairness and emphasize the link between our moral values and both the cultural groups we belong to and our religious beliefs (Graham et al., 2011; Haidt, 2013).

For example, research on morality now includes discussions about how core beliefs can also be shaped by our feelings about *loyalty*. This aspect of morality is focused on our connection to groups that are very important to us, and how we respond to a betrayal of that group (such as burning your country's flag). *Authority or power* also appears to be an important idea that shapes our values. For example, we're very sensitive to signs of social status and can react strongly to people who don't act in line with their "position" in life (say, giving the finger to your boss or disrespecting your elders). Finally, psychologists have also found that our morals can be related to ideas about the *purity/sanctity* of our bodies and environment (which is why some of you will have said that you wouldn't want the blood of a child molester running through your veins for any amount of money).

How to Promote Ethical Behavior

We're all aware that there can be important consequences for behaving in an unethical way. When the actions are illegal, people can be arrested or fined large sums of money. But even when unethical behavior isn't against the law, it can still result in severe consequences. For example, relationships may end, or people can be fired from their jobs or expelled from college. Perhaps more important, though, is how these behaviors affect the way you think about yourself. Research suggests that people want to behave with integrity and make an effort to resist temptation because they place a high value on being ethical. People are also prone to seeing themselves as moral, and are highly motivated to preserve that image because an inability to do so has negative implications for their self-concept (Barkan et al., 2012; Mazar, Amir, & Ariely, 2008).

Ok, so I can see it's important to behave in line with my values, but is there any way that I can increase my chances of doing that? That's a great question, because it focuses attention on an unusual idea suggested by Mary Gentile (2010); namely that behaving ethically ourselves—and promoting ethical behavior in others—is a skill that can be taught. It's important to realize that this doesn't mean you must change your values. Instead, she has outlined several ways in which you can try to create the conditions that will help you speak and behave in ways that are in keeping with your core beliefs, even when the situation is challenging. Her ideas can be summarized as follows:

Recognize Everyday Ethical Challenges

If you consider some of the ethical dilemmas that make headlines in the news, it might be tempting to think that challenges to your integrity will only arise if you're working in very senior positions with large companies, or if you were involved in politics or Hollywood romances. In reality, though, each of us faces moral issues with surprising regularity because they're a very normal part of everyday life. They can arise at school, on sports teams, while working, or in our relationships with friends and family.

For example, at school you may be asked to cheat on a test or let a friend copy your homework assignment. At work you may be asked to "upsell," convincing a client that they ought to purchase more from you than they need. Or imagine a friend asking you to cover for him with his girlfriend while he's on a date with someone else. When we accept how frequently ethical challenges can arise, it allows us to consider, in advance, the possible ethical traps we may find ourselves in and—more importantly—how we might manage them.

Anticipate Conditions That Influence Ethical Responses

Once you have become more aware of situations that are likely to present challenges to your values, ask, "What conditions will either promote ('enablers') or discourage ('inhibitors') behavior that's in line with my values?" For example, people may feel more comfortable speaking up in ethically challenging situations at work when there are enabling forces present, such as having a like-minded colleague who'd be willing to express support for your position. On the flipside, people may have more trouble being true to their values if they feel that there are disabling forces at work. For example, it may be challenging to express your values and beliefs if you have a boss who is disinterested in the views of people she supervises, or if you work at an organization that does not encourage open communication. Being aware of these enabling and inhibiting forces can help you map out a strategy that will help you to behave with integrity.

Plan How to Manage Ethical Challenges

Once you have a handle on the moral dilemmas you might face and the conditions that would enable or inhibit your ability to act in line with your values, you can begin to anticipate how you might manage such situations. But Gentile argues that you should go much further than just thinking about these situations. Instead, she suggests that you should actively imagine possible scenarios in detail, and think about what you would like to say, and how you would say it. She even suggests that it might be valuable to practice what you'd say aloud, or run it by other people so that you can get feedback about your response.

There are at least three reasons why this type of advanced planning can be helpful. First, preparation makes it less likely that you will be put in a position where you need to make a quick decision about what to do, without having time to think things through. Instead, formulating your thoughts (and your words!) ahead of time makes it more likely that you'll be able to speak up and behave in keeping with your values when the time comes. We've already seen that doing so has a positive impact on how you perceive yourself, but another consequence is that behaving with integrity early in a relationship helps to set up other people's expectations about you in a positive way. That's important because if the same situation arises again, people will expect you to behave as you have in the past. More importantly, *you'll* expect yourself to behave as you have in the past.

A second benefit of advance planning for ethically challenging situations is that it allows you to consider how you can best explain the reasons that underlie your value-based decision. The planning you do is likely to mean that you will be more confident when you present your views. Presenting your beliefs in a calm, clear way may be helpful in ensuring that you won't engage in highly emotional "shaming and blaming," and that other people will listen and take you seriously.

A third benefit that arises from practicing how you would manage ethically challenging situations in advance is that it gives you the opportunity to think about your audience. For example, is there any way to make the person you're talking to feel more comfortable, or to improve the chances that she will listen to you with an open mind? What questions are other people likely to ask about your position on this ethical issue, and how you might respond to any arguments that are raised in opposition to your way of thinking?

You should also anticipate how people might try to "explain away" their support of nonethical choices and how you can counteract this tendency. Recently, psychologists have offered three suggestions about how you can reduce the likelihood that those around you will behave unethically (Ayal et al., 2015). The first suggestion is based on the finding that people are prone to justifying unethical behavior by taking advantage of ambiguities or "gray areas" ("It's not really the company's responsibility"; "It's not written down anywhere"; "Everyone does it"; "It may not be right, but it's not really important enough to worry about"). To counteract this tendency, you can offer reminders—even subtle ones—that will make others think about their own moral character before they have the opportunity to make an unethical choice. A teacher whose goal is to reduce the likelihood of cheating during an exam might remind students that she views them as honest people, and that she knows that her students want to behave with integrity.

A second suggestion for minimizing others' unethical behavior involves providing cues that restrict any feelings of anonymity ("No one's going to know"), since people are more likely to violate morals when they believe that their behavior is anonymous. During the exam, then, that same teacher would be walking through the aisles and keeping an eye on each of her students, making eye contact if possible when they look up from their exams.

Finally, unethical behavior often results from the fact that while values and morals are somewhat abstract, ethically questionable behaviors are typically concrete. As a result, it can be easy to avoid connecting the two. The third suggestion, then, is to reduce unethical behavior by creating the necessary connections between abstract moral values and more concrete behaviors. To this end, the teacher might have each of her students do something concrete, such as sign an "honor pledge" before the exam indicating that they understand what's meant by cheating on the test (which can be a somewhat abstract idea).

The Last Word

What you're saying makes sense, but what if I find myself in an ethically challenging situation and I have no time to prepare myself? It's true that you can't always predict when you're going to find yourself in a situation that challenges your values. In those situations, Gentile's best advice is simply to know yourself well, so that if you do find yourself in a difficult situation, you'll be in a stronger position to act with integrity. Consider your strengths and what feels most comfortable for you. Are you most effective in a group or one on one? Orally or in writing? If you have a strong sense of what's most comfortable for you, then when you experience a values conflict, you can try to frame it in such a way as to play to your strengths. Remember, too, that if you feel that you're just one lowly person and that no one will listen to your ethical concerns, it might be worth talking to the people around you to see whether they feel the same way—perhaps others would be willing to stand with you and argue for doing the right thing!

Reflective Practice

Psychology and Your Skill Set: Ethical Behavior

1. Psychologists interested in moral behavior initially focused on ideas about power and loyalty. T or F?
2. "Enablers" are conditions that help you to behave in ways that are in keeping with your values. T or F?
3. Planning in advance what you would do in an ethically challenging situation will help you to be true to your values. T or F?

THINK CRITICALLY

4. Many of the issues confronting the country—abortion, same-sex marriage, stem cell research, and physician-assisted suicide—are often considered to be a matter of ethics, and this is why people are so passionate about them. Evaluate which of the five moral foundations is most likely to be associated with our views on these issues.

SELF-REFLECT

- Which of the five ideas that shape our values—harm, fairness, loyalty, power, and purity—is the most important in guiding your own set of core beliefs?

Answers: 1. F 2. T 3. T 4. Each of these issues is most closely associated with purity/sanctity.

Gateways to Human Development

Summary: Gateways Learning Outcomes

3.1 The Forces That Shape Development: Nature and Nurture

3.1.1 Explain how genes impact human development

Genes reside on deoxyribonucleic acid (DNA) in the nucleus of each cell. The DNA is twisted into chromosomes, and the DNA in each of the body's cells is identical. The genes in each cell carry hereditary instructions. Most characteristics are polygenic and reflect the combined effects of dominant and recessive genes.

3.1.2 Explain how the environment impacts human development

Prenatal development is influenced by intrauterine environmental factors, such as various teratogens, including diseases, drugs, and radiation, as well as the mother's diet, health, and emotions. After birth, a variety of environmental factors (access to good food and health care, schooling, family members, peer groups, media, and so on) contribute to the child's development; environments that are deprived will hamper development while enriched environments will optimize it.

3.1.3 Explain how epigenetic factors impact human development

Though the genetic instructions in every cell are the same, those instructions can be "read" differently depending on epigenetic markers that are the product of environmental influences. For this reason, developmental psychologists say that heredity (nature) and environment (nurture) are interacting forces that are both necessary for human development.

3.2 Physical and Perceptual Development

3.2.1 Describe key aspects of physical development across the lifespan

Physical development tends to look similar across people, as evidenced by common infant reflexes and physical development that proceeds in a cephalocaudal and proximodistal manner. Physical changes that characterize puberty (e.g., development of sex characteristics) and adulthood (e.g., muscle and bone weakness) are also relatively similar across individuals. Though such similarities suggest an important role for "nature" or genetic factors, environmental factors (e.g., opportunities to practice motor skills in infancy; maintaining a healthy lifestyle in adulthood) also contribute to physical development.

3.2.2 Explain key aspects of perceptual development across the lifespan

While most of our senses (hearing, taste, touch, smell) are well developed at birth, infants' vision is not as good as that of older children and adults. However, environmental stimulation and maturation of the visual system lead to rapid improvements, such that babies will see as well as adults by the age of one year. Depending on environmental factors (e.g., reading in poor light; listening to loud music), declines in perception (hearing loss; poor vision) may be seen as early as adolescence, and continue in adulthood.

3.3 Emotional and Social Development

3.3.1 Describe key aspects of emotional development across the lifespan

Basic emotions emerge very early in childhood and include happiness, sadness, fear, anger, surprise, and disgust. In contrast, some complex emotions such as embarrassment, shame, guilt, and pride require a sense of the self as separate from others and thus do not develop until later (approximately 18 months). Emotions are often more intense in adolescence than they were in childhood. Though positive emotions are common, survey data suggest that recent generations of adolescents appear to be managing higher levels of sadness (depression) and fear (anxiety) than has been the case in the past. In terms of adulthood, there is little truth to the common adage that all adults experience an emotional midlife crisis. Instead, adulthood—and particularly older adulthood—is often characterized by high levels of positive emotion that may be related to the positivity effect (the tendency to pay attention to, and remember, more positive than negative information). Aging is also associated with an improved ability to regulate emotions. Some negative emotions, including anger and despair, appear to characterize the response to imminent death, though such responses are by no means universal.

3.3.2 Describe key aspects of social development across the lifespan, including:

(a) the eight psychosocial dilemmas described by Erikson

Erik Erikson identified a series of specific psychosocial dilemmas that occur as we age. Successful resolution of the dilemmas produces healthy development, whereas unsuccessful outcomes make it harder to deal with later crises. In order, the dilemmas are: trust vs. mistrust, autonomy vs. shame/doubt, initiative vs. doubt, industry vs. inferiority, identity vs. role confusion, intimacy vs. isolation, generativity vs. stagnation, and integrity vs. despair.

(b) the importance of temperament and attachment in childhood

While it is clear that parents have an important role in shaping the quality of relationships, infants also make a contribution. In particular, infants' temperament (which can be classed as easy, difficult, or slow-to-warm-up) influences caregivers' responses to them. Research suggests that infants' attachment to their caregivers is associated with their feelings of security and confidence that the caregiver will help them in times of stress. The quality of attachment can be classified as secure, insecure-avoidant, or insecure-ambivalent. Good-quality relationships are promoted when caregivers are sensitive to their babies' signals. Whereas mothers typically emphasize caregiving, fathers tend to function as playmates for infants.

(c) what is known about parenting styles, and how they differ across cultures

Studies suggest that parental styles have a substantial impact on emotional and intellectual development. Three major parental styles are authoritarian, permissive, and authoritative (effective). Authoritative parenting, relying more on management techniques rather than power assertion or withdrawal of love, appears to benefit children the most, though this conclusion is most likely to hold true in Western countries. Other parenting styles may be more advantageous in other cultures.

(d) the characteristics of emerging adults' and older adults' social networks

Relationships outside the family become increasingly important during adolescence, and parents often support their children's identity explorations into their twenties. This extended adolescence is referred to as emerging adulthood, and it is most characteristic of wealthy nations. Social networks expand in middle adulthood but diminish in size in older adulthood. This reduction in size appears to be, at least to some extent, a function of older adults actively choosing to prune their networks and socialize only with people whose company they enjoy.

3.4 Language, Cognitive, and Moral Development

3.4.1 Describe key aspects of language development across the lifespan

Language development proceeds from crying to cooing, then babbling, to the use of single words, and then to telegraphic speech. The underlying patterns of telegraphic speech suggest a biological predisposition to acquire language. However, learning augments this innate tendency. In particular, both prelanguage communication between parent and child (which involves shared rhythms, nonverbal signals, and turn-taking) and motherese/parentese (a simplified, musical style of speaking that parents use with very young children) help with language learning.

3.4.2 Describe key aspects of cognitive development across the lifespan, including

(a) the central ideas that underlie Piaget's theory of development

Piaget believed that children go through a fixed series of cognitive stages. The stages and their approximate age ranges are *sensorimotor* (0–2 years), *preoperational* (2–7 years), *concrete operational* (7–11 years), and *formal operational* (11 years–adult). Several concepts were important in his theory, including assimilation, accommodation, object permanence, egocentrism, and conservation. *Assimilation* refers to a situation in which children encounter something novel and can successfully integrate it with a concept (or schema) that they have already developed. *Accommodation* refers to a situation in which something novel does not fit into an existing schema and a new one must be established.

Object permanence refers to children's ability to understand that people and objects continue to exist even when they are no longer visible. *Egocentrism* refers to children's inability to understand that the world looks different to other people. Egocentrism can relate to the physical world, when children fail to understand that people standing in other locations may not see what they can see from where they are situated. It may also relate to the mental world, when children do not understand that others have thoughts and feelings that differ from their own. When children begin to understand that others have their own unique thoughts and feelings we say that they have acquired a theory of mind. *Conservation* refers to the understanding that physical quantities stay the same even if they change their shape or appearance.

At least three criticisms of Piaget's work have emerged more recently. First, contrary to Piaget's ideas, many psychologists now believe that cognitive development proceeds in a more gradual manner rather than in sharply defined stages. Second, more recent research suggests that children acquire cognitive milestones earlier than Piaget believed. Finally, researchers have suggested that Piaget may have underestimated the role of the environment (including culture) in guiding cognitive development.

(b) the central ideas that underlie Vygotsky's theory of cognitive development

Lev Vygotsky's sociocultural theory places a particular emphasis on the role of culture and the environment in guiding cognitive development. In particular, he stressed that a child's mental abilities are advanced by interactions with more-competent partners. Mental growth takes place in a child's zone of proximal development, where a more skillful person may scaffold the child's progress.

(c) the focus of more recent work concerning cognitive development

More recent work in the area of cognitive development has focused on areas such as executive functions, mastery of academic subjects, memory and intelligence.

3.4.3 Describe key aspects of moral development across the lifespan, including Kohlberg's three stages of moral development and Carol Gilligan's criticism of this theory

Kohlberg's theory included the following stages:

Preconventional: moral thinking is guided by consequences (e.g., reward, punishment).

Conventional: moral thinking is guided by a desire to please others or follow rules.

Postconventional: moral thinking is guided by self-chosen ethical principles.

Young children function at the preconventional level. Most people function at the conventional level of morality, but some never get beyond the preconventional level. Only a minority of people attain the highest, or postconventional, level of moral reasoning. Carol Gilligan distinguished between Kohlberg's fairness (justice) perspective and a harm (caring) perspective. Because Kohlberg's theory placed a high value on justice, she argued that women—who reason more frequently from a caring perspective—wrongly appeared to demonstrate less moral maturity than men. Now, most researchers believe that mature adult morality likely involves reasoning from both perspectives, and cultural research suggests that there may also be other moral foundations that underlie people's values.

3.5 Psychology and Your Skill Set: Ethical Behavior

3.5.1 Create a plan to manage a challenge to your own values

Challenges to your ability to behave ethically can be managed by recognizing the potential for everyday ethical challenges, considering the conditions that will help or hinder ethical behavior in the face of those challenges, creating a plan for managing ethical challenges that are likely to occur, and working to counteract the tendency of others to behave in unethical ways. We hope that after reading this section, you'll be better able to think about how you can use these strategies to help when you need to manage the everyday threats to your values!

4 Sensation, Attention, and Perception

PA Images/Alamy Stock Photo

Gateway Theme We actively construct our perceptions out of the information provided by our senses and our past experience; the resulting perceptions are not always accurate representations of events.

Chapter Outline

Who Wants to Be a Millionaire?

Waterloo Station in London, England is a hectic place. The busiest train station in the United Kingdom, the gates at Waterloo log nearly one hundred million entries and exits each year. How, then, was 3D artist Kurt Wenner able to create a deep pit right in the middle of its 24 platforms? And more importantly, how was he able to move an enormous vault full of money right up to its edge?

It may surprise you to know that the answer to that question has nothing to do with construction equipment. In fact, the only tools needed are your eyes and your brain. The pit and vault that you see—or *think* you see—were actually created over four days using several sticks of chalk. And though your eyes are likely picking up the sensory information needed to recognize that the pit and the open vault door are simply flat surfaces, your brain put the perceptual puzzle together differently: It created a three dimensional image of millions of dollars in free money pouring out of a vault and disappearing into a deep pit.

Information from your senses can be interpreted (and misinterpreted!) in various ways as it arrives at the brain to create our perceptions. It is those perceptions that allow us to take the raw material of sensation and use it to recognize faces, melodies, great beer, the scent of a skunk—and, occasionally, a great deal of money flying around a major transit hub at rush hour. We begin this chapter with the first steps in generating our experiences of the world; that is, *sensation* arising from information picked up by the eyes, ears, nose, tongue, and skin. We then go on to talk about the decisions about which sensory experiences merit our *attention*. Finally, we'll move on to explore the last step in the process—*perception*—as the brain tries to create order from all of the information it receives from the senses.

4.1 Sensation

GATEWAYS LEARNING OUTCOMES:
After reading this section you should be able to:

4.1.1 Define sensation and transduction, and outline what happens in the sensory organs during transduction

4.1.2 Distinguish between absolute threshold and difference threshold

4.1.3 Identify four ways by which the senses reduce the amount of information sent to the brain

If you think about it for a moment, our sensory organs take in a vast amount of information from the environment every minute that we're awake. It's their job to get that information to the brain, but just how does that happen? Let's take a closer look at this amazing process of sensation.

Transduction: The Sense Organs' Primary Job

The primary function of the sensory organs—our eyes, ears, tongue, nose, and skin—is to act as biological **transducers**; that is, devices that convert one kind of energy into another (Fain, 2003; Goldstein & Brockmole, 2017). We saw in ■ Section 2.1 that the brain only works with one type of energy—electrical energy in the form of action potentials. But information that's out in the world comes to us as many different forms of energy and each one needs to be converted into electrical energy so that the brain can understand it.

Our sensory organs can therefore be thought of as translators, converting these different forms of energy into electrical energy so that the brain can understand the information from the outside world. Through the process of **sensation**, then, the eyes convert light energy, the ears translate mechanical energy from sounds, and the nose and tongue translate chemical energy from odors and foods. Information arriving at the brain from the sense organs creates *sensory impressions*.

When sensory organs are damaged and unable to transduce energy, the brain cannot interpret the information from that sense, leading to difficulties with seeing, hearing, smell, and so on. However, new technologies are allowing scientists to bypass damaged sensory organs and artificially restore sight, hearing, or other senses. In one approach, researchers used a miniature television camera to send electrical signals directly to the brain, bypassing damaged eyes and optic nerves (● Figure 4.1) (Dobelle, 2000; Warren & Normann, 2005). Using technologies such as these, people who have lost their vision are now able to "see" letters, words, and some common objects such as knives and forks (Nirenberg & Pandarinath, 2012).

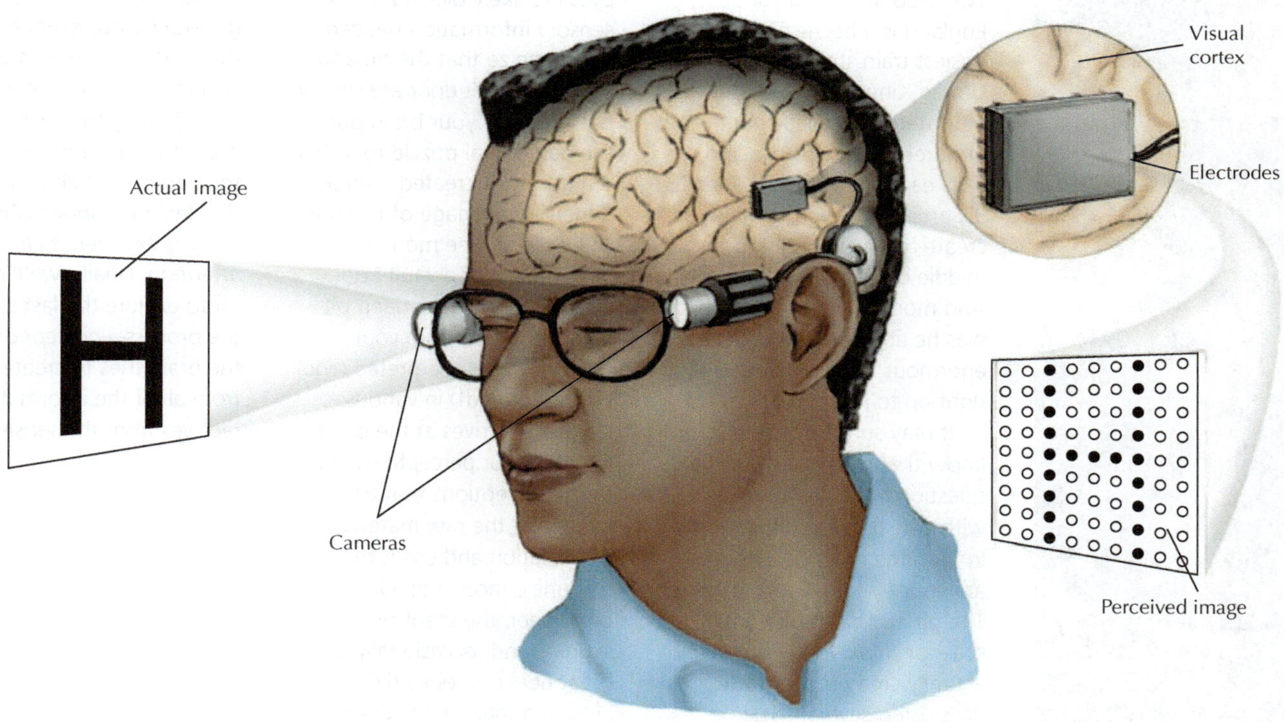

● **Figure 4.1 An artificial visual system.** Video cameras translate light into electrical impulses that directly stimulate the visual cortex, resulting in rudimentary visual experiences. What do you suppose this person would experience if the electrical impulses were sent to the auditory cortex instead?

Brian J. Skerry/National Geographic Image Collection

Absolute thresholds define the sensory worlds of humans and animals, sometimes with serious consequences. The endangered Florida manatee (sea cow) is a peaceful, plant-eating creature that can live for more than 60 years. Every year, many manatees are injured or even killed by boats. The problem? Manatees have poor sensitivity to the low-frequency sounds made by slow-moving boats. Current laws require boats to slow down in manatee habitats, which may actually increase the risk to these gentle creatures (Gerstein, 2002).

Psychophysics: Measuring Sensory Impressions

In the field of **psychophysics**, the physical properties of stimuli (such as sound waves, light waves, or chemical molecules in food) are measured and related to the resulting experiences that our brain constructs (such as the loudness of a sound, the brightness of a light, or the sweetness of a piece of cheesecake …) (Lu & Dosher, 2014).

It was psychophysicists who scientifically demonstrated that energy above a certain minimum intensity is necessary for a sensory impression to arise. The **absolute threshold** for any sensory input is formally defined as the minimum amount of physical energy that can be detected 50 percent of the time. Of course, the absolute threshold can vary between people and species. For example, the sound of a very soft humming noise might fall below the absolute threshold for a man who is partially deaf but be above the absolute threshold for his granddaughter. Moreover, owls, which hunt at night, have much lower absolute thresholds than humans for hearing and can easily hear sounds that we cannot. In a similar way, absolute thresholds exist for other senses, including sight, smell, taste, and so on.

It's also worth noting that not every *difference* between two stimuli is experienced; instead, the difference must be sufficiently large to be noticed. A psychophysicist studying **difference thresholds** will ask, "How different must two stimuli be before the difference becomes noticeable 50 percent of the time?" For example, if you were to put one extra grain of sugar in your coffee, would you notice a difference in its taste? How much would it take? A few grains? A half-spoonful? A spoonful?

Selection: Four Ways to Reduce Sensory Overload

Sensory transduction usually involves some *selection*. Consider, for example, vision, which gives us an amazingly wide window on the world. In one instant, you can view a star that is light years away; in the next, you can peer into the microscopic universe of a dewdrop. Yet psychophysical research has found that vision also narrows what we can possibly observe. Like the other senses, vision acts as a *data selection system*. It selects information in order to code and send to the brain only the most important sensory information for further processing (Goldstein & Brockmole, 2017). There seem to be four ways by which sensory selection takes place. Let's take a closer look at each one.

Lack of Specific Transducers

Considerable selection occurs because human sensory receptors do not transduce all the energies that they encounter. For example, the eye transduces light waves, the ear transduces sound waves, and so on. But many other types of stimuli cannot be sensed directly because we lack sensory receptors to transduce their energy. For example, humans cannot sense the bioelectric fields of living creatures, but sharks have special organs that can (Caputi et al., 2013). (Do they *hear* the fields, *feel* them, or what?) ● See Figure 4.2.

● **Figure 4.2 Electroreceptors in sharks.** Sharks and rays have special receptors called the ampullae of Lorenzini. Researchers suspect that they use this sense to detect the Earth's magnetic field, allowing them to navigate the ocean.

Transducers Devices that convert one kind of energy into another.

Sensation Conversion of energy from the environment into a pattern of response by the nervous system; also, a sensory impression.

Psychophysics Study of how the mind interprets the physical properties of stimuli.

Absolute threshold Minimum amount of physical energy that can be detected 50 percent of the time.

Difference threshold Minimum difference in physical energy between two stimuli that can be detected 50 percent of the time.

Restricted Range of Transducers

Further selection occurs because sense receptors transduce only part of their target energy range (Fain, 2003). For example, your eyes transduce only a tiny fraction of the entire range of electromagnetic energies—the part that we call the *visible spectrum*. The eyes of honeybees can transduce, and therefore see, parts of the electromagnetic spectrum that are invisible to humans. Likewise, bats *shout* at a pitch too high for humans to transduce. But bats can hear their own reflected echoes. This ability, called *echolocation*, allows bats to fly in total darkness, avoid collisions, and catch insects. As you can see, our rich sensory experiences are only a small part of what *could* be sensed and what some animals *can* sense.

Studying the Science: Extrasensory Perception

Doesn't extrasensory perception allow us to override the limits of our five senses? More than a third of the general public believes in the existence of *extrasensory perception* (*ESP*), the purported ability to perceive events in ways that cannot be explained by known sensory capacities (Gray & Gallo, 2016). However, even after over 130 years of research into ESP, few psychologists share this belief (Shermer, 2011). People who think critically when reading the available research will realize that ESP experiments often reveal serious problems of evidence, procedure, and scientific rigor (Alcock, 2010; Alcock, Burns, & Freeman, 2003; Hyman, 2007).

Sensory Adaptation

Think about walking into a house in which fried liver, sauerkraut, and headcheese were just prepared for dinner. (Aren't you glad you were invited?) Although you might pass out at the door, people who had been in the house for some time likely wouldn't be aware of the food odors. Why? Because sensory receptors respond less over time to unchanging stimuli, a process called **sensory adaptation**.

Fortunately, the olfactory (smell) receptors adapt quickly. When exposed to a constant odor, they send fewer and fewer nerve impulses to the brain until the odor is no longer noticed. In terms of touch, adaptation to pressure from a wristwatch, waistband, ring, or glasses is based on the same principle. Because there is usually little reason to keep reminding the brain that a sensory input is unchanged, sensory receptors generally respond best to *changes* in stimulation.

Feature Detection

As the senses collect information, *feature detectors* in the brain also reduce the flow of sensory input by dividing the world into important **perceptual features**, or basic stimulus patterns. A **feature detector** is a cell, or collection of cells, in the cerebral cortex that responds to a specific attribute of an object. As a consequence, the brain need only further process the perceptual feature rather than the underlying sensory pattern.

The visual system, for example, has a set of feature detectors that are attuned to specific stimuli, such as lines, shapes, edges, spots, colors, and other patterns (Hubel & Wiesel, 2005). Look at Figure 4.3 and notice how eye-catching the single vertical line is among a group of slanted lines. This effect, which is called *visual pop-out*, occurs because your visual system is highly sensitive to these perceptual features (Hsieh, Colas, & Kanwisher, 2011).

Similarly, frog eyes are highly sensitive to small, dark, moving spots. In other words, they are "tuned" to detect bugs flying nearby (Lettvin, 1961). But the insect (spot) must be moving, or the frog's "bug detectors" won't work. A frog could starve to death surrounded by dead flies.

Although our sensitivity to perceptual features is an innate characteristic of the nervous system, it also is influenced by experiences early in life. For instance, Colin Blakemore and Graham Cooper of Cambridge University raised kittens in a room with only vertical stripes on the walls. Another set of kittens was raised seeing only horizontal stripes. When returned to normal environments, the "horizontal" cats could easily jump onto a chair, but when walking on the floor, they bumped into chair legs. "Vertical" cats, on the other hand, easily avoided chair legs, but they missed when they tried to jump to horizontal surfaces. The cats raised with vertical stripes were "blind" to horizontal lines, and the "horizontal" cats acted as if vertical lines were invisible (Blakemore & Cooper, 1970). Other experiments show an actual decrease in brain cells that are tuned to the missing features (Grobstein & Chow, 1975).

To summarize, our sensory organs have a remarkable capacity to take in the rich and varied information that exists in the world around us. You may be "sensing" that now is a good time to do a quick check on your understanding of what we've learned so far about the process of sensation generally. After that, we'll take a closer look at the specific sensory systems, and how they transduce this information so that it can be processed in the brain.

Figure 4.3 Visual pop-out. This pop-out is so basic that babies as young as three months respond to it. (Adapted from Adler & Orprecio, 2006.)

Reflective Practice

Sensation

1. Sensory receptors are biological ________________, or devices for converting one type of energy to another.
2. As time passes, nerve endings in the skin under your clothes send fewer signals to the brain and you become unable to feel your clothes. This process is called
   a. transduction c. reverse attention
   b. difference threshold d. sensory adaptation
3. Brain cells that respond to a specific attribute of an object are known as feature
   a. transducers c. pop-outs
   b. detectors d. adapters
4. The minimum amount of physical energy that can be detected 50 percent of the time is called the
   a. difference threshold c. absolute threshold
   b. psychophysical difference d. sensory biasing
5. Rigorous psychological research has confirmed the existence of extrasensory perception. T or F?

THINK CRITICALLY

6. William James once said, "If a master surgeon were to cross the auditory and optic nerves, we would hear lightning and see thunder." Can you explain what James meant?

SELF-REFLECT

- If you had to prioritize the loss of your senses, which one would you prefer to lose first? Which one would you want to hang on to until last?

Answers: 1. transducers 2. d 3. b 4. c 5. F 6. The explanation is based on sensory localization: If a lightning flash caused rerouted messages from the eyes to activate auditory areas of the brain, we would experience a sound sensation. Likewise, if the ears transduced a thunderclap and sent impulses to the visual area, a sensation of light would occur. It is amazing that some people, called synesthetes, naturally experience sensory inputs in terms of other senses. For example, one synesthete experiences the number 37 as lumpy porridge, whereas for another, the taste of beef is blue (Zaraska, 2016).

4.2 Vision

GATEWAYS LEARNING OUTCOMES:
After reading this section you should be able to:

4.2.1 Describe three characteristics of light that are processed by the eye

4.2.2 Outline what is meant by accommodation in the eye, and the conditions that result from problems with accommodation

4.2.3 Describe the process of transduction in the eye, and two problems associated with color vision

4.2.4 Contrast the trichromatic and opponent-process theories of color vision

When you first open your eyes in the morning, you effortlessly become aware of the visual richness of the world around you. But that richness obscures the fact that your eyes transduce only the tiniest fraction of the entire range of electromagnetic energies—the visible spectrum. You cannot "see" the vast majority of the electromagnetic spectrum, such as microwaves, cosmic rays, X-rays, or radio waves (see Figure 4.4). Similarly, the effortlessness with which normally sighted people can *see* obscures incredible complexity. How does sensory transduction in vision actually occur? Let's take a deeper dive into this issue and find out.

Sensory adaptation A decrease over time in sensory response to an unchanging stimulus.

Perceptual features Basic attributes of a stimulus, such as lines, shapes, edges, or colors.

Feature detector Cells in the cortex that respond to a specific attribute of an object.

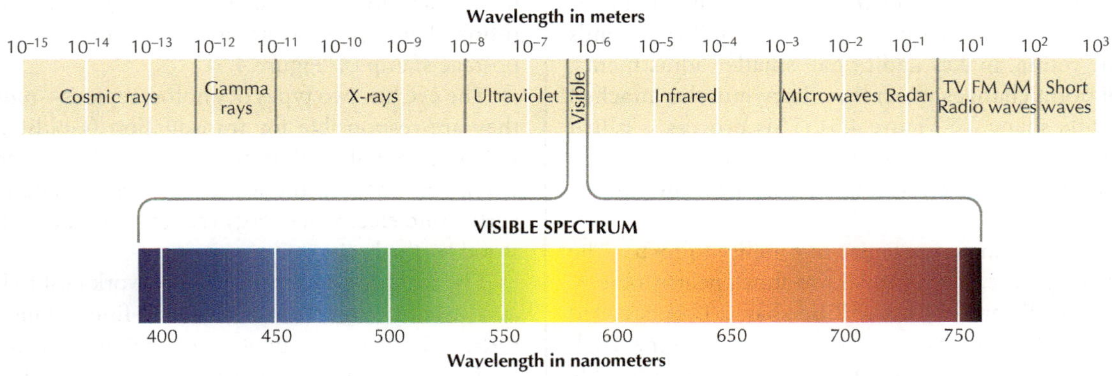

Figure 4.4 The visible spectrum.

Characteristics of Light: What the Eye Sees

The *visible spectrum*—the sliver of electromagnetic energies to which the eyes respond—is made up of a narrow range of wavelengths of electromagnetic radiation. Visible light starts at "short" wavelengths of 400 *nanometers* (nan-OM-et-ers), equal to one-billionth of a meter, which we sense as purple or violet. Successively longer light waves produce blue, green, yellow, orange, and red, which has a wavelength of 700 nanometers (● Figure 4.4).

Three characteristics of light are important. The first—**hue**—refers to the various colors of light: red, orange, yellow, green, blue, indigo, and violet. As just noted, various hues, or color sensations, correspond to the wavelength of the light that reaches our eyes (Goldstein & Brockmole, 2017). White light, in contrast, is a mixture of many wavelengths. The second characteristic is *saturation*. Hues (colors) from a narrow band of wavelengths are very saturated, or pure. (An intense, fire-engine red is more saturated than a muddy, brick red that might include some degree of orange or brown.) A third characteristic of light, *brightness*, corresponds roughly to the amplitude, or height, of light waves. Waves of greater amplitude are taller, carry more energy, and cause the colors that we see to appear brighter or more intense. For example, the same brick red would look brighter in intense, high-energy illumination and more drab in dim light.

So how does the eye actually work? Although the visual system is much more complex than any digital camera, both cameras and eyes have a lens to focus light rays on a light-sensitive surface at the back of an enclosed space, where the image is created. Basically, then, we can think about the structure of the eye as serving two purposes: it begins by *focusing* the light waves coming in from the world, and then it carries out the important work of *transducing* them so that the brain can make sense of the incoming information and create an image. Let's talk about each one of those in turn.

The Process of Accommodation in the Eye: Focus!

In cameras, focusing is done relatively simply—by changing the distance between the lens and the image sensor. In the eye, though, most focusing is done by the **cornea**, a curved, transparent, protective layer at the front of the eye that bends light inward. The **lens**, the clear structure behind the pupil that bends light toward the retina, makes additional, smaller adjustments. Your eye's focal point changes when the ciliary muscles attached to the lens alter its shape (● Figure 4.5). This process is called **accommodation**, and it's what allows you to focus on objects regardless of whether they are several feet away or right in front of your nose.

At least two factors can compromise our ability to focus. The first is the shape of the eye. If your eye is too short, nearby objects will be blurred, but distant objects will be sharp. This is called **hyperopia** (HI-per-OPE-ee-ah), or farsightedness. If your eyeball is too long, images fall short of the retina, and you won't be able to focus on distant objects. This results in **myopia** (my-OPE-ee-ah), or nearsightedness. Further, when the cornea or the lens is misshapen, part of your vision will be focused and part will be fuzzy. In this case, the eye has more than one focal point, a problem called **astigmatism** (ah-STIG-mahtiz-em). All three visual defects can be corrected by placing glasses (or contact lenses) in front of the eye to change the path of light (● Figure 4.6).

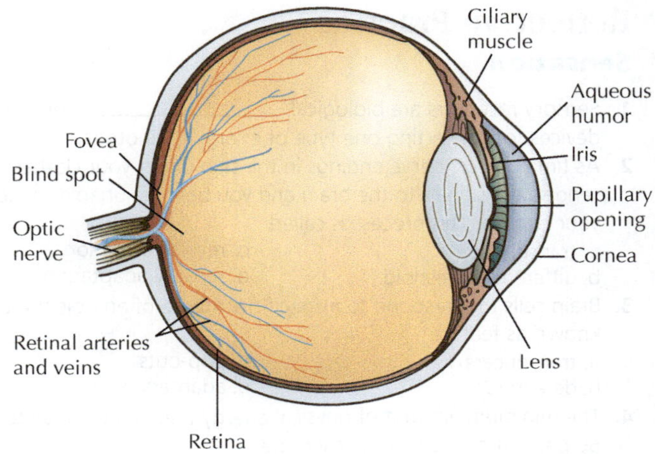

● **Figure 4.5 Anatomy of the eye.**

A second factor that impacts our ability to focus is the flexibility of the lens. As people age, the lens becomes less flexible and accommodating is more difficult. The result is **presbyopia** (prez-bee-OPE-ee-ah), from the Latin for "old vision"—farsightedness due to aging. Perhaps you have seen a grandparent or older friend reading a newspaper at arm's length because of presbyopia. Eventually, many people need bifocals as they age. Bifocal lenses correct near vision *and* distance vision.

The Process of Transduction in the Eye

We mentioned earlier that, similar to a camera, it's the job of the cornea and lens to focus light rays on a *light-sensitive surface at the back of an enclosed space*. In a camera, the light-sensitive surface is a layer of pixels in the digital image sensor. In the eye, it is a layer of light-sensitive cells called *photoreceptors* that are located in the **retina**. The retina has an area about the size and thickness of a postage stamp (● Figure 4.5).

The eye has two types of photoreceptors—*rods* and *cones*—and they are responsible for transduction (Goldstein & Brockmole, 2017). Remember that transduction is the process by which energy out there in the world—in this case, light energy—is converted into electrical energy (action potentials) that can be understood by the brain.

The 5 million **cones** in each eye work best in bright light. They also produce color sensations and fine details. In contrast, the **rods**, numbering about 120 million, can't detect colors (● Figure 4.7). Pure rod vision is black and white. However, rods are much more sensitive to light than cones. Rods therefore allow

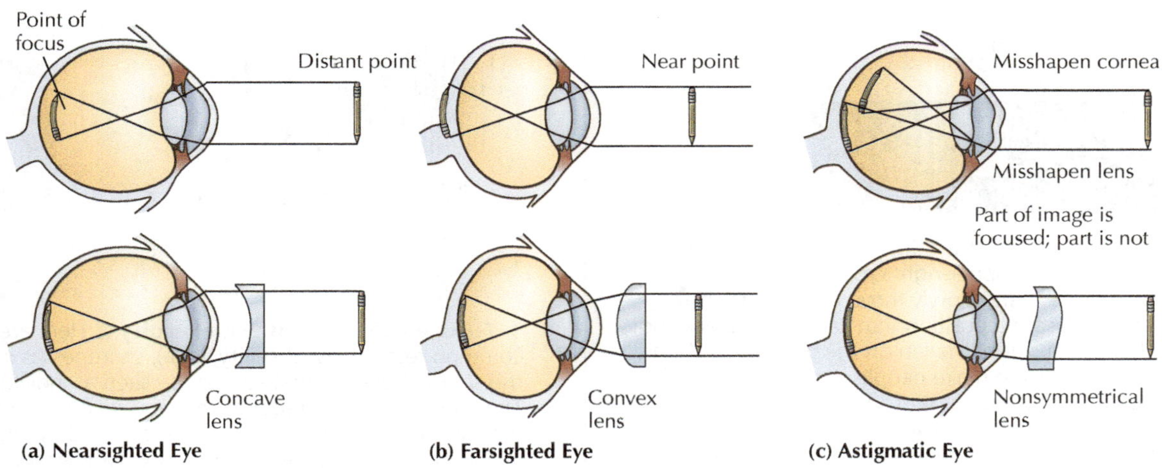

Figure 4.6 Visual defects and corrective lenses. (a) A myopic (longer than usual) eye. The concave lens spreads light rays just enough to increase the eye's focal length. (b) A hyperopic (shorter than usual) eye. The convex lens increases refraction (bending) to focus light on the retina. (c) An astigmatic (lens or cornea that are not symmetrical) eye. In astigmatism, parts of vision are sharp and parts are unfocused. Lenses to correct astigmatism are nonsymmetrical.

us to see in very dim light. Inside the rods and cones is where transduction occurs in the eye, but they also have a role to play in **visual acuity**, or sharpness (Pirson, Ie, & Langer, 2012). Once those photoreceptors have converted light energy into electrical energy, those action potentials travel along a series of *interneurons* to the optic nerve, and then on to the brain.

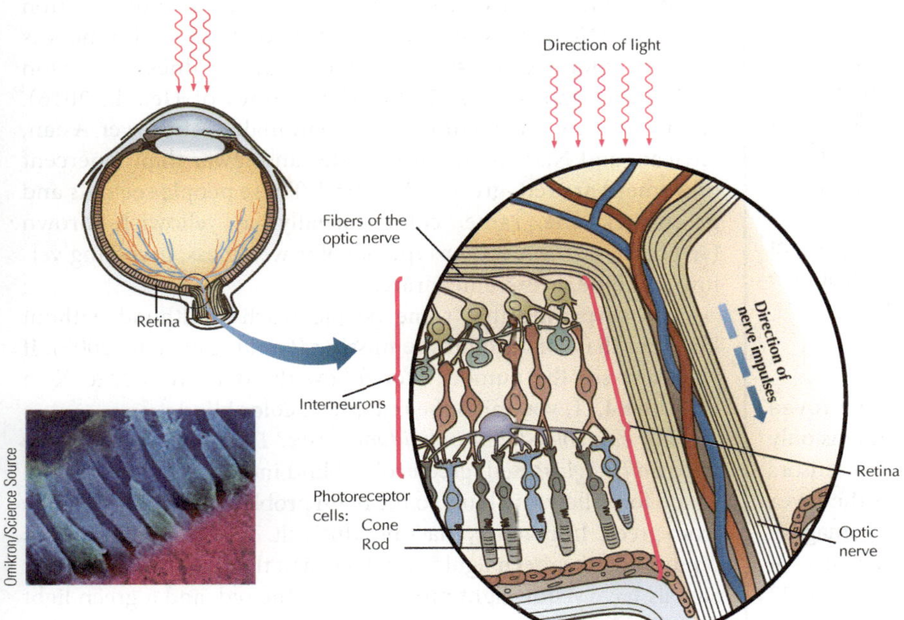

Figure 4.7 Anatomy of the retina. Note that light does not fall directly on the rods and cones. It must first pass through the cornea, the lens, the vitreous humor (a jellylike substance that fills the eyeball), and the outer layers of the retina. Only about half of the light at the front of the eye reaches the rods and cones—testimony to the retina's amazing sensitivity. The lower-left photograph shows rods and cones as seen through an electron microscope. In the photograph, the cones are colored green and the rods blue.

Hue Color of light, as determined by its wavelength.

Cornea Curved, transparent, protective layer through which light enters the eye.

Lens Clear structure behind the pupil that bends light toward the retina.

Accommodation Changes in the shape of the lens of the eye to enable the seeing of close and far objects.

Hyperopia Having difficulty focusing on nearby objects (farsightedness).

Myopia Having difficulty on distant objects (nearsightedness).

Astigmatism Defects in the cornea, lens, or eye that cause some areas of vision to be out of focus.

Presbyopia Farsightedness caused by aging.

Retina Surface at the back of the eye onto which the lens focuses light rays.

Cones Photoreceptors that are sensitive to color.

Rods Photoreceptors for dim light that produce only black and white sensations.

Visual acuity The sharpness of visual perception.

Figure 4.8 Experiencing the blind spot. (a) With your right eye closed, stare at the upper-right cross. Hold the book about 1 foot from your eye and slowly move it back and forth. You should be able to locate a position that causes the black spot to disappear. When it does, it has fallen on the blind spot. With a little practice, you can learn to make people or objects you dislike disappear too (use your new power wisely)! (b) Repeat the procedure described, but stare at the lower cross. When the white space falls on the blind spot, the black bar will appear to be continuous. This may help you understand why you do not usually experience a blind spot in your visual field.

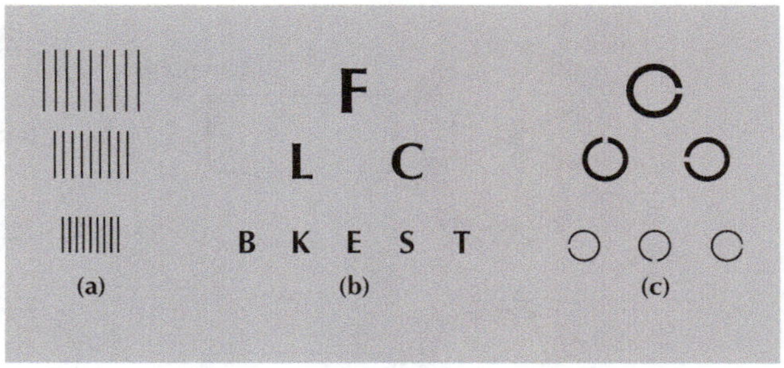

Figure 4.9 Tests of visual acuity. Here are some common tests of visual acuity. In (a), sharpness is indicated by the smallest grating that still can be seen as individual lines. The Snellen chart (b) requires that you read rows of letters of diminishing size until you no longer can distinguish them. The Landolt rings (c) require no familiarity with letters. Simply note which side has a break in it.

Fun fact about the retina: It has a "hole" in it! Each retina has a **blind spot** because there are no photoreceptors at the location where the **optic nerve** exits the eye to convey visual information to the brain, and blood vessels enter (Raman & Sarkar, 2016; Figure 4.8*a*). The blind spot shows that vision depends greatly on the brain. If you close one eye, some of the incoming light will fall on the blind spot of your open eye. Why isn't there a gap in your vision? The answer is that the visual cortex of the brain actively fills in the gap with patterns from surrounding areas (Figure 4.8*b*). By closing one eye, you can visually "behead" other people by placing their images on your blind spot. (Just a hint for some classroom fun.) The brain can also "erase" distracting information. Roll your eyes all the way to the right and then close your right eye. You should clearly see your nose in your left eye's field of vision. Now, open your right eye again, and your nose nearly disappears because your brain disregards its presence.

This trick with the blind spot makes it clear what an important job those photoreceptors are doing. Let's take a closer look at how those cones and rods allow us to see the world around us.

Cones

The cones lie mainly at the center of the eye. In fact, the **fovea** (FOE-vee-ah), a tiny spot in the center of the retina, contains only cones—about 50,000 of them. Like high-resolution digital sensors made of many small pixels, the tightly packed cones in the fovea produce the highest level of acuity (that is, the sharpest images). Normal acuity is designated as 20/20 vision: At a distance of 20 feet, you can distinguish what the average person can see at 20 feet (Figure 4.9). If your vision is 20/40, you can see at 20 feet only what the average person can see at 40 feet. If your vision is 20/200, everything is a blur and you need glasses! Vision that is 20/12 means that you can see at 20 feet what the average person must be 8 feet nearer to see, indicating better-than-average acuity.

The cones are primarily responsible for your color vision, though in some cases individuals are not able to see colors in the normal way. In such cases, we say that they are experiencing color blindness or color weakness. Let's take a look at each one.

Vision in Everyday Life: Color Blindness

Do you know anyone who regularly draws hoots of laughter by wearing clothes of wildly clashing colors? Or someone who sheepishly tries to avoid naming the color of an object? If so, you probably know someone who is color blind.

What is it like to be color blind? What causes color blindness? A person with **color blindness** cannot perceive colors. It is as if the world were a black-and-white movie. The color-blind person either lacks cones or has cones that do not function normally (Neitz & Neitz, 2011). Such total color blindness is rare. In **color weakness**, or partial color blindness, a person can't see certain colors (National Institutes of Health, 2016). Approximately 8 percent of Caucasian males (but fewer Asian, African, and Native-American males and fewer than 1 percent of women) are red–green color blind. These people see reds and greens as the same color, usually a yellowish brown (Figure 4.10). Another type of color weakness, involving yellow and blue, is extremely rare.

It is surprising that some people reach adulthood without knowing that some colors are missing (Gündogan et al., 2005). If you can't see the number 5 or follow the dots from X to X in Figure 4.11, you might be red–green color blind.

How can color-blind individuals drive? Don't they have trouble with traffic lights? Red–green color-blind individuals have normal vision for yellow and blue, so the main problem is telling red lights from green. In practice, that's not difficult. The red light is always on top, and the green light is brighter than the red. Also, red traffic signals have yellow light mixed in with the red, and a green light is really blue-green.

Rods

Areas outside the fovea also get light, creating a large region of **peripheral (side) vision**. This is the area where the rods take over from the cones. The rods are most numerous about 20 degrees from the center of the retina, so much of our peripheral vision is rod vision.

(a) (b) (c)

Figure 4.10 Color blindness and color weakness. (a) Photograph illustrates normal color vision. (b) Photograph is printed in blue and yellow and gives an impression of what a red–green color-blind person sees. (c) Photograph simulates total color blindness. If you are totally color-blind, all three photos will look nearly identical.

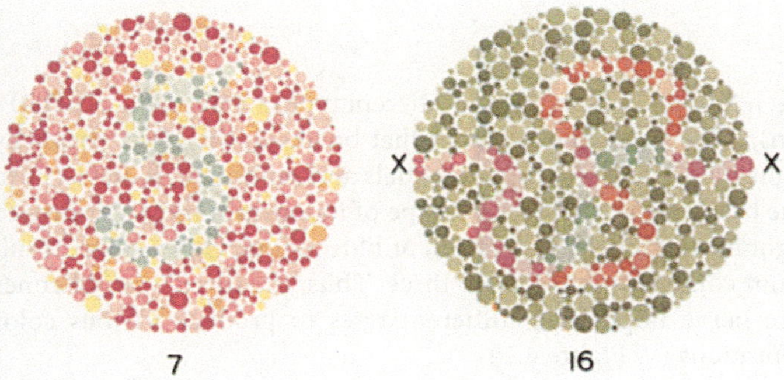

Figure 4.11 Testing for red–green color blindness. A replica of two images from the widely used Ishihara test for red–green color blindness.

Although rod vision is not very high resolution, the rods are quite sensitive to *movement* in peripheral vision (Yamamoto & Philbeck, 2013). To experience this characteristic of the rods, look straight ahead and hold your hand beside your head, at about 90 degrees. Wiggle your finger and slowly move your hand forward until you can detect motion. You will become aware of the movement before you can actually see your finger. Seeing "out of the corner of your eye" is important for sports, driving, and walking down dark alleys. People who suffer from *tunnel vision* (a loss of peripheral vision) feel as if they are wearing blinders (Godnig, 2003).

The rods also are highly responsive to dim light. **Dark adaptation** is the dramatic increase in the eye's sensitivity to light that occurs after a person enters the dark (Goldstein & Brockmole, 2017). Consider walking into a movie theater. If you enter from a brightly lit lobby, you practically need to be led to your seat. Almost immediately, the **pupil**, the opening surrounded by the colored **iris**, begins to open to allow more light to enter the eye. After a short time you can see the entire room in detail (including the couple kissing over in the corner). The retina, however, also becomes more sensitive, taking about 30 to 35 minutes of complete darkness to reach maximum visual sensitivity (Figure 4.12). At that point, your eye will be 100,000 times more sensitive to light.

What causes dark adaptation? Like cones, which contain a pigment called iodopsin, rods contain a light-sensitive visual pigment, *rhodopsin* (row-DOP-sin), which allows them to see in black and white. When struck by light, visual pigments *bleach* (break down) chemically. The afterimages that you see after looking at the explosion of a camera's flash are a result of this bleaching. In fact, a few seconds of exposure to bright white light can completely wipe out dark adaptation. That's why you should avoid looking at oncoming headlights when you are driving at night—especially newer bluish-white xenon lights. To restore light sensitivity, the rhodopsin in the rods must recombine, which takes time.

The rods are *insensitive* to extremely red light. That's why submarines, airplane cockpits, and ready rooms for fighter pilots are illuminated with red light. In each case, people can move quickly from a light place into a dark one without having to adapt. Because the red light doesn't stimulate the rods, it is as if they had already spent time in the dark.

Blind spot Area in the retina where the optic nerve exits that contains no photoreceptor cells.

Optic nerve Structure that conveys visual information away from the retina to the brain.

Fovea Tiny spot in the center of the retina, containing only cones, where visual acuity is greatest.

Color blindness A total inability to perceive color.

Color weakness An inability to distinguish some colors.

Peripheral (side) vision Vision at the edges of the visual field.

Dark adaptation Increased light sensitivity of the eye under low-light conditions.

Pupil The black opening inside the iris that allows light to enter the eye.

Iris Colored structure on the surface of the eye surrounding the pupil.

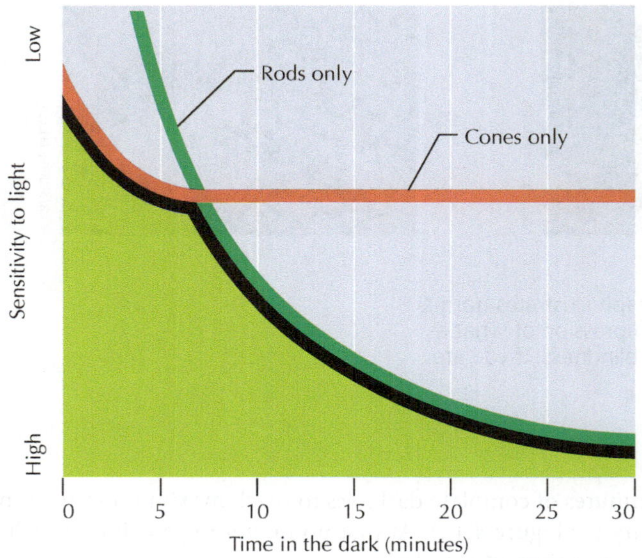

Figure 4.12 Typical time course of dark adaptation. The dark line shows how the threshold for vision lowers as a person spends time in the dark. (A lower threshold means that less light is needed for vision.) The green line shows that the cones adapt first, but they soon cease adding to light sensitivity. Rods, shown by the red line, adapt more slowly. However, they continue to add to improved night vision long after the cones are fully adapted.

Theories of Color Vision

The **trichromatic theory of color vision** (TRY-kro-MAT-ik) holds that there are three types of cones, each most sensitive to either red, green, or blue. Other colors result from combinations of these three. Unfortunately, two basic problems with the trichromatic theory have been identified. The first is that *four* colors of light—red, green, blue, and yellow—seem to be primary. Second, this theory doesn't account for the fact that it's impossible to have a reddish green color, or a yellowish blue.

These problems led to the development of a second view of color vision, known as the **opponent-process theory of color vision**, which states that vision analyzes colors into "either-or" messages (Goldstein & Brockmole, 2017). That is, the visual system can produce messages for either red or green, yellow or blue, or black or white. Coding one color in a pair (red, for instance) seems to block the opposite message (green) from coming through. As a result, a reddish green is impossible, but a yellowish red (orange) can occur.

According to opponent-process theory, fatigue caused by repeatedly having the cones respond to one color produces an afterimage of the opposite color as the system recovers. *Afterimages* are visual sensations that persist after a stimulus is removed—like seeing a spot after a flashbulb goes off. To see an afterimage of the type predicted by opponent-process theory, look at Figure 4.13 and follow the instructions there.

Which color theory is correct? Both! The three-color theory applies to the retina, in which three different types of cones have been found. Each contains a different type of *iodopsin* (i-oh-DOP-sin), a light-sensitive pigment that breaks down when struck by light. This triggers action potentials and sends neural messages to the brain. As predicted, each type of iodopsin is most sensitive to light in roughly the red, green, or blue region. Other colors result from combinations of these three. Thus, the three types of cones fire nerve impulses at different rates to produce various color sensations (Figure 4.14).

Figure 4.13 Negative afterimages. Stare at the dot near the middle of the flag for at least 30 seconds. Then look immediately at a plain sheet of white paper or a white wall. You will see the U.S. flag in its normal colors. Reduced sensitivity to yellow, green, and black in the visual system, caused by prolonged staring, results in the appearance of the complementary colors. Project the afterimage of the flag on other colored surfaces to get additional effects.

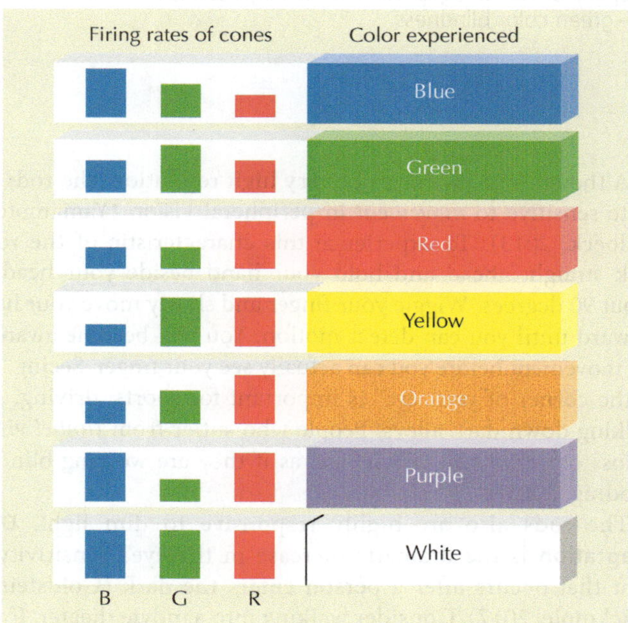

Figure 4.14 Firing rates of blue, green, and red cones in response to different colors. The taller the colored bar, the higher the firing rates for that type of cone. As you can see, colors are coded by differences in the activity of all three types of cones in the normal eye. (Adapted from Goldstein & Brockmole, 2017.)

In contrast, the opponent-process theory better explains what happens beyond the retina—in the optic pathways and the brain—*after* information leaves the cones (Sanes & Masland, 2015). For example, some nerve cells in the brain are excited by the color red and inhibited by the color green. Basically, then, both theories have a role to play in explaining color vision. One explains what happens in the cones. The other explains how color information is analyzed after messages leave the cones (Gegenfurtner & Kiper, 2003).

Reflective Practice

Vision

1. Match:

______ Myopia	**A.** Farsightedness
______ Hyperopia	**B.** Elongated eye
______ Presbyopia	**C.** Misshapen cornea or lens
______ Astigmatism	**D.** Farsightedness due to aging

2. In dim light, vision depends mainly on photoreceptors called the ______________. In brighter light, color and fine detail are produced by photoreceptors called the ______________.

3. The greatest visual acuity is associated with the ______________ and the ______________.
a. fovea, rods
b. periphery, cones
c. fovea, cones
d. periphery, rods

4. Colored afterimages are best explained by
a. trichromatic theory
b. the effects of astigmatism
c. sensory localization
d. opponent-process theory

5. Dark adaptation is directly related to an increase in
a. rhodopsin
b. astigmatism
c. accommodation
d. iodopsin

THINK CRITICALLY

6. Evaluate how color blindness might impact someone who works in an office environment.

SELF-REFLECT

- Think about how your sense of vision interacts with other senses during multimodal integration. Can you think of an event during which vision was combined with two or more other senses to create a particularly rich experience?

Answers: 1. B, A, D, C 2. rods, cones 3. c 4. d 5. a 6. Color blindness sometimes reduces the possibility of doing some jobs (color-blind people who wish to be pilots, for example, may struggle to find training programs that will work with them); however, many people who are color blind are very successful in their careers. Some challenges come along with this condition, though, including difficulties seeing typed text that are in different colors and reading presentation slides that contain specific colors. Another challenge may be dealing with websites for which color is important in navigation or interpreting the information presented.

4.3 Hearing

GATEWAYS LEARNING OUTCOMES:
After reading this section you should be able to:

4.3.1 Describe two characteristics of sound that are processed by the ear

4.3.2 Describe the process of transduction in the ear, and two associated forms of hearing loss

4.3.3 Contrast the frequency and place theory of hearing pitch

Whether it's a great concert or the ocean waves rolling into shore; a child's laugh or a purring cat, the riches of sound have undoubtedly moved you. But hearing is also important in our ability to navigate the world. The ears gather information from all around the body, detecting the direction of approach of an unseen car as well as the voice of your roommate asking if you want a cup of coffee (Yes please!) (Johnstone, Nábělek, & Robertson, 2010).

Characteristics of Sound: What the Ear Hears

If you throw a stone into a quiet pond, a circle of waves spreads in all directions. In much the same way, sound travels as a series of invisible waves of *compression* (peaks) and *rarefaction* (RARE-eh-fak-shun), or valleys, in the air. Any vibrating object—a tuning fork, the string of a musical instrument, or the vocal cords—will produce sound waves (rhythmic movement of air molecules).

The sound wave has a few important characteristics. Two of the most important are its frequency and its amplitude. The *frequency* of sound waves (the number of waves per second) corresponds to the perceived **pitch** (higher or lower tone) of a sound. The *amplitude*, or physical "height," of a sound wave tells how much energy it contains. Psychologically, amplitude corresponds to sensed **loudness** or sound intensity (Figure 4.15).

Trichromatic theory of color vision A theory of color vision based on three cone types: red, green, and blue.

Opponent-process theory of color vision Proposition that color vision is based on coding things as red or green, yellow or blue, or black or white.

Pitch How high or low a tone sounds; related to the frequency of a sound wave.

Loudness The volume of a sound; related to the amplitude of a sound wave.

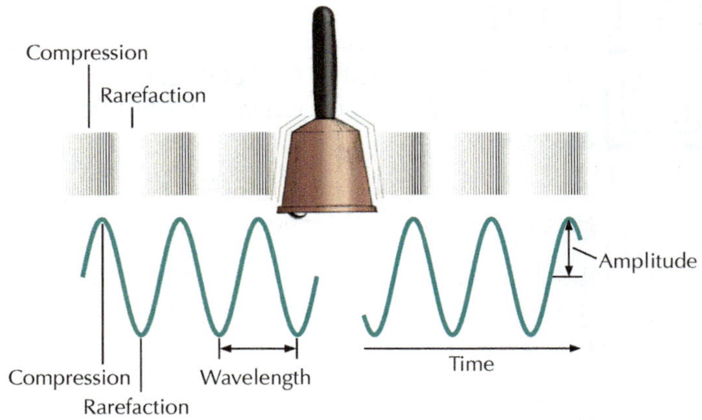

Figure 4.15 Characteristics of sound waves. Waves of compression in the air, or vibrations, are the stimulus for hearing. The frequency (or wavelength) of sound waves determines their pitch. The amplitude determines loudness.

The Process of Transduction in the Ear

Remember that transduction is the process by which a sensory organ—the ear in this case—converts some form of energy into electrical energy (in the form of action potentials) so that the brain can interpret it. In order for us to hear, the ear is responsible for transducing mechanical energy in the form of sound waves.

Hearing involves a chain of events that begins with the *pinna* (PIN-ah), the visible, external part of the ear. In addition to being a good place to hang earrings or balance pencils, the pinna acts like a funnel to focus sounds. After they are guided into the ear canal, sound waves collide with the **eardrum** (*tympanic membrane*), setting it vibrating in response, thus transmitting them inward. This, in turn, causes three small middle ear *ossicles* (OSS-ih-kuls) or bones, the *malleus* (MAL-ee-us) or hammer, *incus* or anvil, and *stapes* (STAY-peas) or stirrup, to vibrate (Figure 4.16). The ossicles link the eardrum with the **cochlea** (KOCK-lee-ah), a

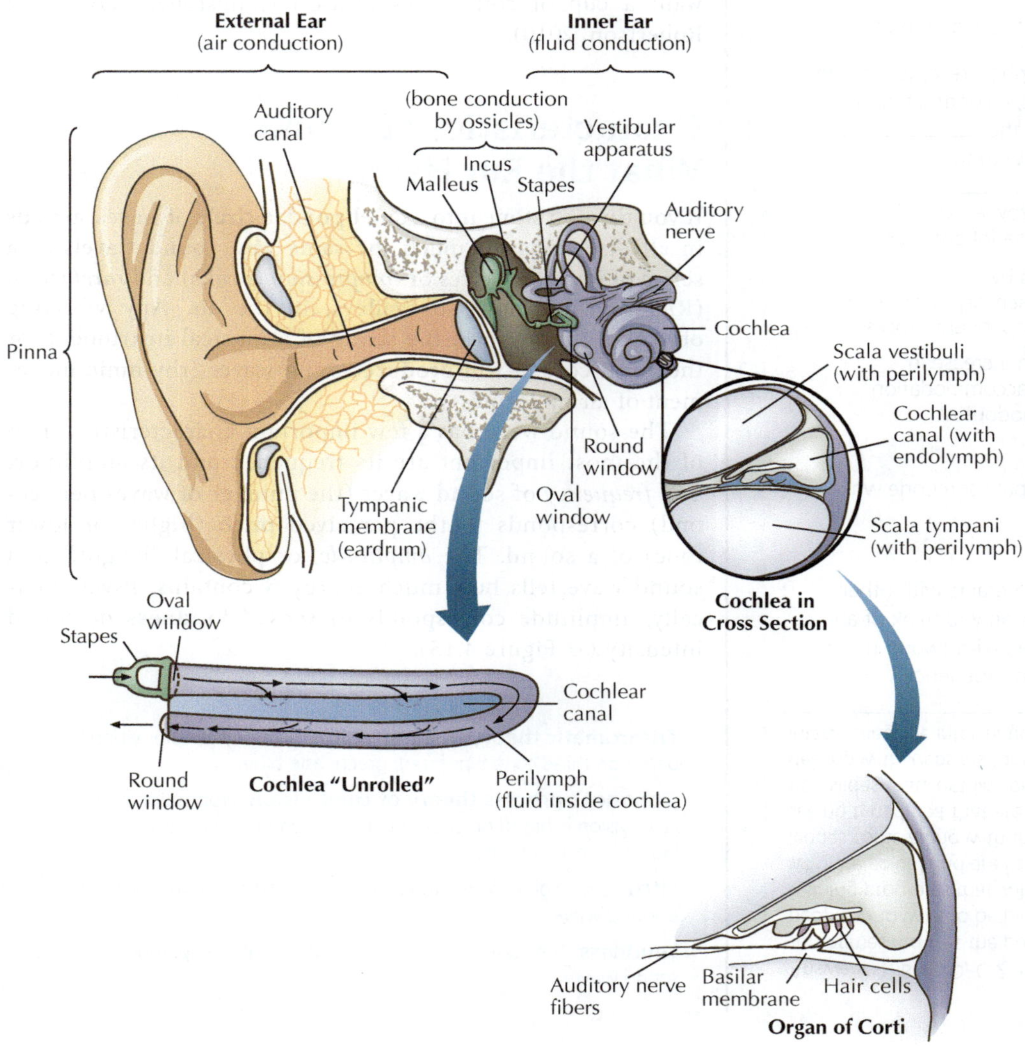

Figure 4.16 Anatomy of the ear. The entire ear is a mechanism for transducing waves of air pressure into nerve impulses. The inset in the foreground ("Cochlea 'Unrolled'") shows that as the stapes moves the oval window, the round window bulges outward, allowing waves to ripple through fluid in the cochlea. The waves move membranes near the hair cells, causing cilia, or "bristles," on the tips of the cells to bend. The hair cells then generate nerve impulses that are carried to the brain. (See an enlarged cross section of the cochlea in Figure 4.17.)

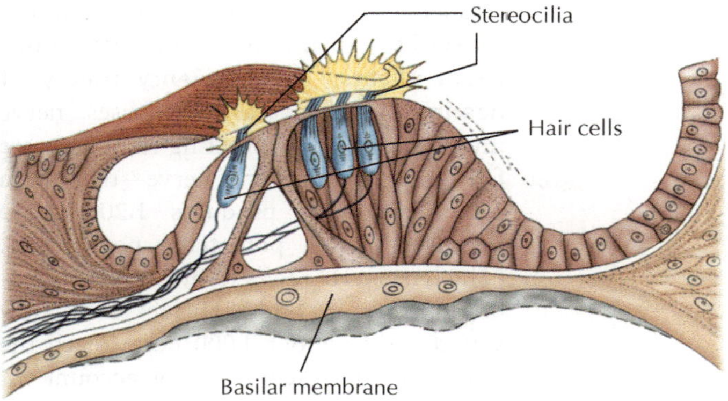

Figure 4.17 Functioning of hair cells. A closer view of the hair cells shows how movement of fluid in the cochlea causes the bristling "hairs," or cilia, to bend, generating a nerve impulse.

snail-shaped organ that makes up the inner ear. The stapes is attached to a membrane on the cochlea called the *oval window*. As the oval window moves back and forth, it makes waves in a fluid inside the cochlea.

Inside the cochlea, the fluid waves trigger vibrations in the **basilar membrane**, the "floor" of the *organ of Corti* (KOR-tee). In turn, tiny **hair cells** embedded in the basilar membrane are pushed up against the *tectorial membrane*. As a consequence, a set of *stereocilia* (STER-ee-oh-SIL-ih-ah), or "bristles," atop each hair cell brush against the tectorial membrane whenever waves ripple through the fluid surrounding the organ of Corti. As the stereo-cilia are bent, action potentials are triggered, which then flow to the brain (Figure 4.17).

Hearing Loss

Are there different types of hearing loss? Hearing loss afflicts about 37.5 million Americans (National Institute on Deafness and Other Communication Disorders, 2016) and 360 million people worldwide (World Health Organization, 2017). There are two common types of hearing loss. **Conductive hearing loss** occurs when the transfer of vibrations from the outer ear to the inner ear weakens. For example, the eardrums or ossicles may be damaged or immobilized by disease or injury. In many cases, conductive hearing loss can be overcome with a hearing aid, which amplifies sounds, making them louder and clearer.

Sensorineural hearing loss is quite different, and results from damage to the inner ear hair cells or the auditory nerve. Many jobs, hobbies, and pastimes can cause **noise-induced hearing loss**, a common subtype of sensorineural hearing loss that occurs when very loud sounds damage fragile hair cells (National Institute on Deafness and Other Communication Disorders, 2017).

If you work in a noisy environment or enjoy loud music, motorcycling, snowmobiling, hunting, or similar pursuits, you may be risking noise-induced hearing loss. Be forewarned: Dead hair cells are never replaced. When you abuse them, you lose them. By the time you are 65, more than 40 percent of them will be gone, mainly those that transduce high pitches (Lin et al., 2011). You may remember from Section 3.2 that this developmental change is the basis for the creation of high-pitched cellphone ringtones: Students can typically hear them, but a teacher with aging ears cannot.

How loud must a sound be to be hazardous? Daily exposure to 85 decibels or more may cause permanent hearing loss (Goldstein & Brockmole, 2017). *Decibels* are a measure of sound intensity. Every 20 decibels increases the sound pressure by a factor of 10. In other words, a rock concert at 120 decibels is 1,000 times stronger than a voice at 60 decibels. Short periods at 120 decibels can cause temporary hearing loss, and even one brief exposure to 150 decibels (a jet airplane nearby) may cause permanent hearing loss. You might find it interesting to check the decibel ratings of some of your activities in Figure 4.18. Be aware that attending loud music concerts, frequent use of earbuds, and cranking up car stereos also can damage your hearing.

Unfortunately, hearing aids are no help in cases of sensorineural hearing loss because auditory messages are being blocked from reaching the brain. In many cases, however, the hair cells are damaged but the auditory nerve is intact. This finding has spurred the development of cochlear implants that bypass hair cells and stimulate the auditory nerves directly (Figure 4.19). Wires from a microphone carry electrical signals to an external coil. A matching coil under the skin picks up the signals and carries them to one or more areas of the cochlea.

The latest implants separate higher and lower tones into separate channels. This has allowed some formerly deaf persons to hear human voices, music, and other higher-frequency sounds. About 60 percent of all multichannel implant patients can understand some spoken words and appreciate music (Leal et al., 2003; Park et al., 2011). Some deaf children with implants learn to speak, and those who receive a cochlear implant before age 2 have the best chance to learn spoken language at a near normal rate (Ertmer & Jung, 2012; Gordon et al., 2011).

Theories of Hearing Pitch

We mentioned earlier that two important characteristics of a sound are its loudness (which comes from the amplitude of the sound wave) and its pitch (which is determined by the wave's

Eardrum Membrane that vibrates in response to sound waves and transmits them inward.

Cochlea Snail-shaped organ in the inner ear that contains sensory receptors for hearing.

Basilar membrane Structure in the cochlea containing hair cells that convert sound waves into action potentials.

Hair cells Receptor cells within the cochlea that transduce vibrations into nerve impulses.

Conductive hearing loss Poor transfer of sounds from the eardrum to the inner ear.

Sensorineural hearing loss Loss of hearing caused by damage to the inner-ear hair cells or auditory nerve.

Noise-induced hearing loss Damage caused by exposing the hair cells to excessively loud sounds.

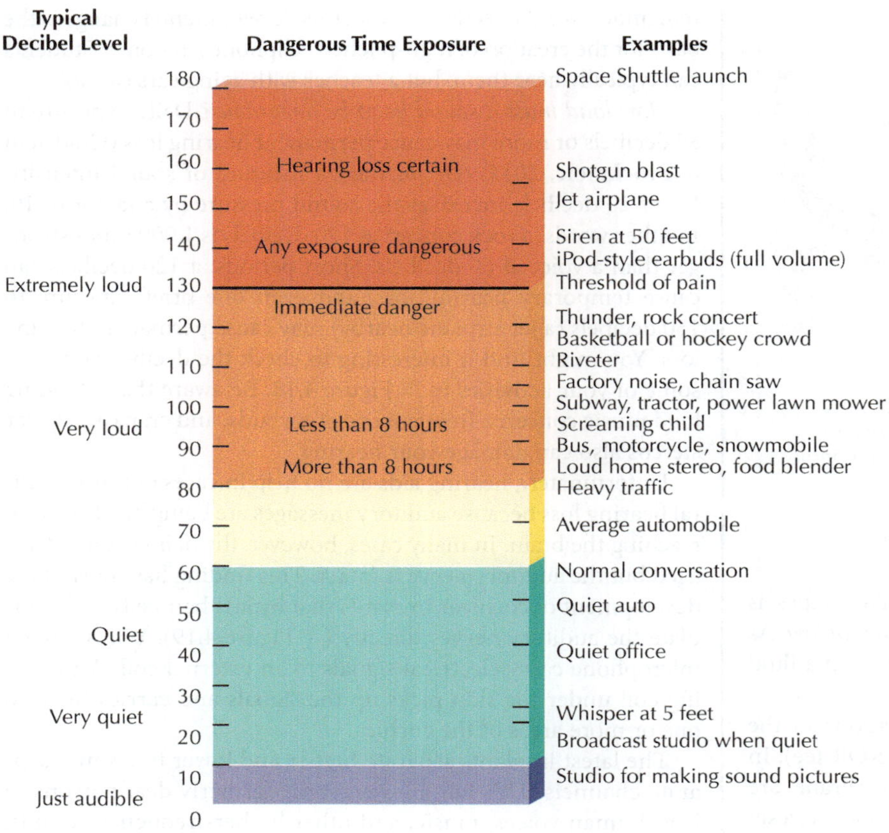

Figure 4.18 Decibel scale. The loudness of sound is measured in decibels. The faintest sound most people can hear is little more than zero decibels. Sounds of 110 decibels are uncomfortably loud. Prolonged exposure to sounds above 85 decibels may damage the inner ear. Some music concerts, which can reach 120 decibels, have caused hearing loss in musicians and may affect audiences as well. Sounds of 130 decibels pose an immediate danger to hearing.

frequency). Two theories have been put forward to explain how we distinguish different pitches. The **frequency theory of hearing** states that as pitch rises, nerve impulses of a corresponding frequency are fed into the auditory nerve—that is, a 1,200-hertz tone produces 1,200 nerve impulses (action potentials) per second. (The term *hertz* refers to the number of vibrations per second.) This explains how sounds up to about 4,000 hertz reach the brain, but the theory cannot account for how we hear pitches (that is, tones) that are higher than that.

To explain how the brain can make out tones higher than 4,000 hertz, we turn to the **place theory of hearing**, which states that higher and lower tones excite specific places in the cochlea. High tones register most strongly at the base of the cochlea (near the oval window). Lower tones, on the other hand, mostly move hair cells near the narrow outer tip of the cochlea (Figure 4.20). Pitch is then signaled by the area of the cochlea that is most strongly activated. Place theory is useful in explaining why hunters sometimes lose their hearing in a narrow pitch range. "Hunter's notch," as this condition is called, occurs when hair cells are damaged in the specific area of the cochlea affected by the pitch of gunfire.

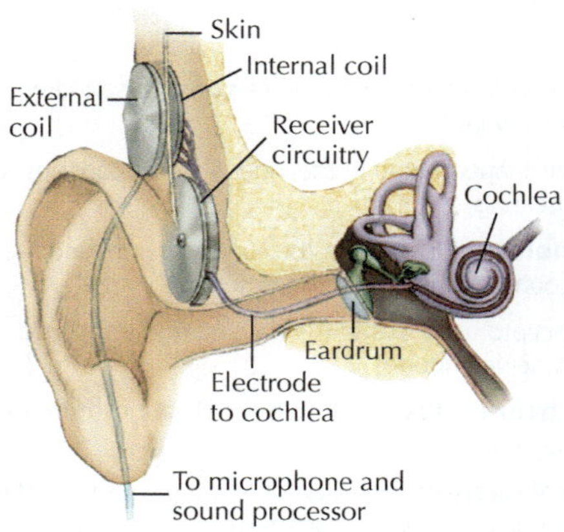

Figure 4.19 A cochlear implant, or "artificial ear."

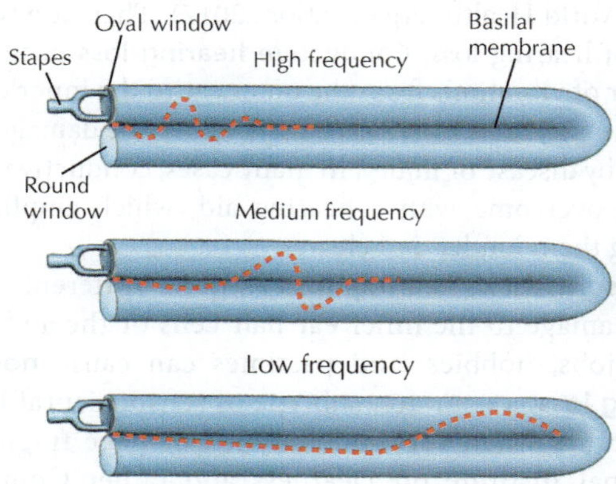

Figure 4.20 Side view of the cochlea "unrolled." The basilar membrane is the elastic "roof" of the lower chamber of the cochlea. The organ of Corti, with its sensitive hair cells, rests atop the basilar membrane. The colored line shows where waves in the cochlear fluid cause the greatest deflection of the basilar membrane. (The amount of movement is exaggerated in the drawing.) Hair cells respond most in the area of greatest movement, which helps identify sound frequency.

Reflective Practice

Hearing

1. The frequency of a sound wave corresponds to how loud it is. T or F?
2. Sensorineural hearing loss occurs when the auditory ossicles are damaged. T or F?
3. Daily exposure to sounds with a loudness of at least ______________ decibels may cause permanent hearing loss.
4. Conductive hearing loss would be treated with a hearing aid. T or F?

THINK CRITICALLY

5. Explain why your voice sounds so different to you when you hear a recording of your speech.

SELF-REFLECT

- Do you enjoy listening to loud music? Why do you think that some people enjoy the sensation of listening to some types of music (or some bands, or songs) at a very high volume? How does it change your experience of the music to listen to it that way?

Answers: 1. F 2. F 3. 85 4. T 5. The answer lies in another question: How else might vibrations from the voice reach the cochlea? Other people hear your voice only as it is carried through the air. You hear not only that sound, but also vibrations conducted by the bones of your skull.

4.4 Chemical and Somesthetic Senses

GATEWAYS LEARNING OUTCOMES:
After reading this section you should be able to:

4.4.1 Name and describe the two chemical senses and three somesthetic senses

4.4.2 Describe the process of transduction in the nose

4.4.3 Describe the process of transduction on the tongue

4.4.4 Describe the process of transduction on the skin, including the function of large and small nerve fibers in the sensation of pain

4.4.5 Describe the process of transduction in the vestibular system

4.4.6 Define multimodal integration

Unless you are a wine taster, a perfume blender, or a gourmet chef, you may think of the *chemical senses*—**olfaction** (smell) and **gustation** (taste)—as minor senses (Di Lorenzo & Youngentob, 2013). But don't be deceived—life without these senses can be difficult (Drummond, Douglas, & Olver, 2007). One person, for instance, almost died because he couldn't smell the smoke when his apartment building caught fire! Besides, olfaction and gustation add pleasure to our lives.

Similarly, many people take for granted the *somesthetic senses*—those that are related to our ability to "feel" the body. But even the most routine activities, such as walking, running, or passing a sobriety test, would be impossible without the **skin senses** (touch), the **kinesthetic senses** (receptors in muscles and joints that detect body position and movement), and the **vestibular senses** (receptors in the inner ear for balance, gravity, and acceleration). Let's see how they work.

Smell

The first of the two chemical senses is smell. Smell receptors respond to chemical molecules that are airborne. When we talk about "chemical molecules" in this situation, we're not just talking about traditional chemicals like ammonia, bleach, or alcohol. Anything that you can smell—from flowers to fudge to formaldehyde—is producing chemical molecules that are picked up by your nose.

The Process of Transduction in the Nose

Remember that transduction refers to the process by which one form of energy that's picked up by the senses (in this case, chemical energy) is converted into electrical energy (in the form of action potentials) that can be interpreted in the brain. As air enters the nose, it flows over roughly 5 million nerve fibers embedded in the lining of the upper nasal passages (● Figure 4.21). Receptor proteins on the surface of the fibers are sensitive to various airborne chemical molecules. When a fiber is stimulated, it creates an action potential that then travels to the brain (Dalton & Lomvardas, 2015).

Theory of Odor Detection

The specific way that different odors are detected is still an unfolding mystery, however. One hint about the process comes from a type of *anosmia* (an-OZE-me-ah), a sort of "smell blindness" to a single odor. Five people out of 100 experience some degree of anosmia, including the total loss of smell (Bramerson et al., 2004). Risks for anosmia include infections, allergies, and blows to the head (which may tear the olfactory nerves).

Frequency theory of hearing Proposition that pitch is decoded from the rate at which hair cells of the basilar membrane are firing.

Place theory of hearing Proposition that higher and lower tones excite specific areas of the cochlea.

Olfaction Sense of smell.

Gustation Sense of taste.

Skin senses The senses of touch, pressure, pain, heat, and cold.

Kinesthetic senses The senses of body movement and positioning.

Vestibular senses Perception of balance, gravity, and acceleration.

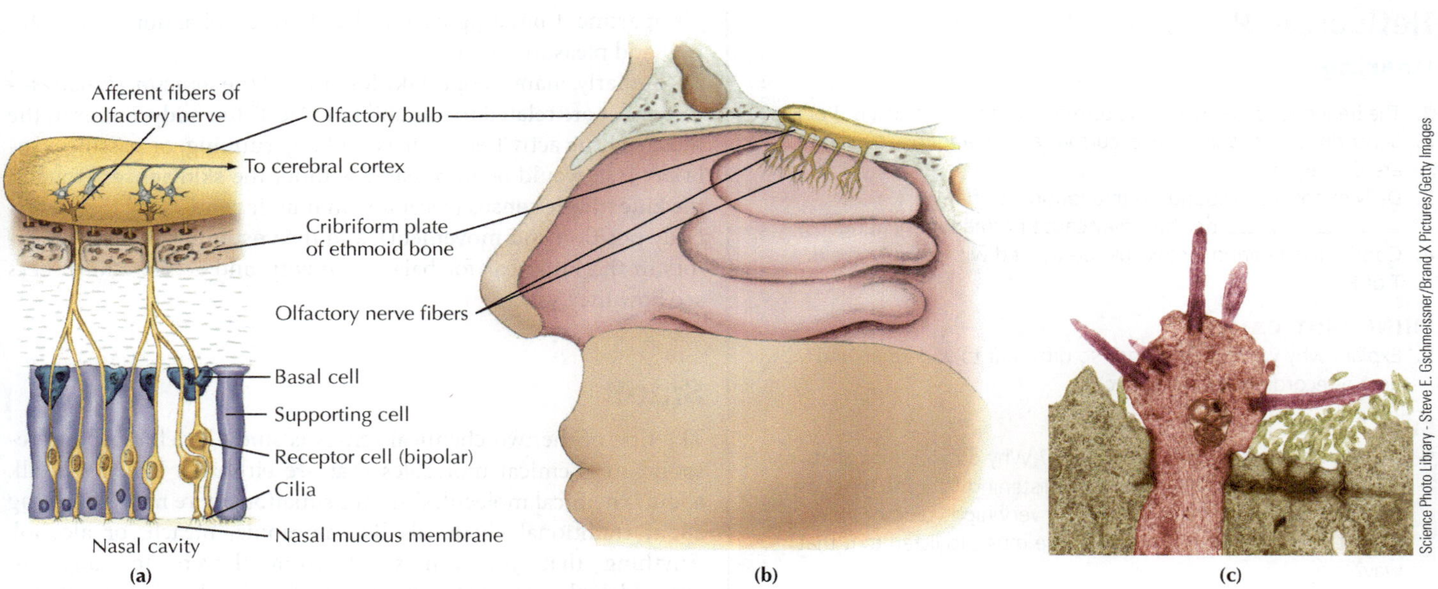

Figure 4.21 Receptors for the sense of smell (olfaction). (a) Olfactory nerve fibers respond to gaseous molecules. Receptor cells are shown in cross section to the left. (b) Olfactory receptors are located in the upper nasal cavity. (c) On the right, an extreme close-up of an olfactory receptor shows fibers that sense gaseous molecules of various shapes.

Repeated exposure to chemicals such as ammonia, paints, solvents, and hairdressing "potions" also can cause anosmia. If you value your sense of smell, be careful what you sniff (Drummond, Douglas, & Olver, 2007)!

Loss of sensitivity to specific types of odors in anosmia suggests the presence of receptors in the nose for specific odors. More specifically, it appears that different-shaped "holes," or "pockets," exist on the surface of olfactory receptors. The **lock-and-key theory of olfaction** suggests that these receptors may bind with airborne chemical molecules that have a matching "shape" to create odors. Like a piece fits into a puzzle, airborne chemical molecules produce odors when part of the molecule matches a hole on the receptor of the same shape (hence the name, "lock and key" theory). Scientists have suggested that many different receptors may exist—in fact; humans carry genes for about 1,000 types of smell receptors, although only about 400 of them are expressed (Sela & Sobel, 2010).

The specific shape of the molecules may produce odors that we perceive as floral, camphoric (like mothballs), musky (like sweat), minty, and etherish (like ether or cleaning fluid). Furthermore, chemical molecules trigger activity in different *combinations* of odor receptors. Thus, humans can detect at least 10,000 different odors. Just as you can make hundreds of thousands of words in English from the 26 letters of the Roman alphabet, there are many combinations of the 400 types of receptors that can be activated, resulting in many different odors.

In addition to the lock and key theory, researchers have noted that scents are also identified, in part, by the *location* of the receptors in the nose that a particular odor activates. And finally, the *number of activated receptors* tells the brain the strength of an odor (Bensafi et al., 2004). The brain uses these distinctive patterns of messages it gets from the olfactory receptors to recognize particular scents (Sela & Sobel, 2010).

Taste

In addition to smell, taste is also a chemical sense. In this case, though, the chemical molecules are found in our food. There are at least five basic taste sensations: *sweet*, *salty*, *sour*, *bitter*, and *umami* (Dalton & Lomvardas, 2015). We are generally most sensitive to bitter and sour. Going back many generations, this may have helped prevent poisonings when most humans foraged for food because bitter and sour foods are more likely to be inedible.

But umami? The Japanese word *umami* (oo-MAH-me) describes a pleasant savory or "brothy" taste associated with certain amino acids in chicken soup, some meat extracts, kelp, tuna, human milk, cheese, and soybeans. The receptors for *umami* are sensitive to glutamate, a substance found in monosodium glutamate (MSG) (Nakamura et al., 2011).

The Process of Transduction on the Tongue

Taste buds, clusters of taste-receptor cells, are located mainly on the top side of the tongue, especially around the edges. However, a few are found elsewhere inside the mouth (Figure 4.22). As food is chewed, it dissolves and the chemical molecules enter the taste buds, where they set off action potentials that travel to the brain (Vandenbeuch et al., 2010).

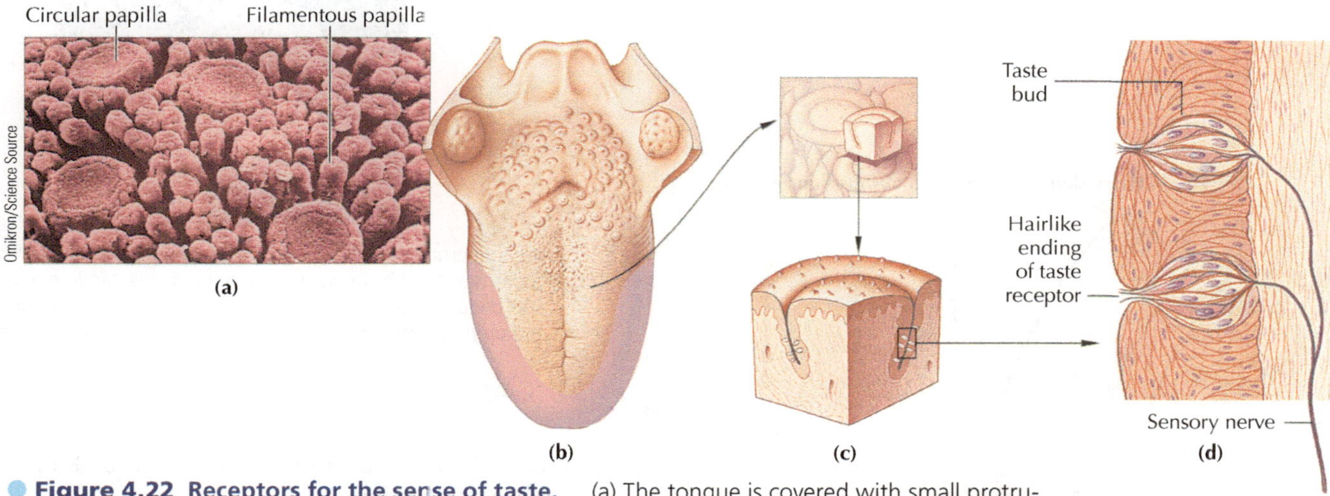

Figure 4.22 Receptors for the sense of taste. (a) The tongue is covered with small protrusions called *papillae.* (b) Most taste buds are found around the top edges of the tongue (shaded area). However, some are located elsewhere, including under the tongue. Stimulation of the central part of the tongue causes no taste sensations. All five primary taste sensations occur anywhere that taste buds exist. (c) An enlarged drawing shows that taste buds are located near the base of papillae. (d) Detail of a taste bud. These receptors also occur in other parts of the digestive system, such as the lining of the mouth.

Theory of Taste Detection

Much like smell, sweet, bitter, and umami tastes appear to be based on a lock-and-key match between the molecules and intricately shaped receptors. Saltiness and sourness, however, are triggered by a direct flow of charged atoms into the tips of taste cells (Dalton & Lomvardas, 2015; Lindemann, 2001).

If there are only five tastes, how can there be so many different flavors? Flavors seem more varied because we include sensations of texture, temperature, pain (think "hot" chili peppers), and smell when we taste things. Smell, in particular, is important in determining flavor (Doty, 2012). If you plug your nose and eat small bits of apple, potato, and onion, they will "taste" almost exactly alike. So do gourmet jellybeans! That's also why food loses its "taste" when you have a cold. It is probably fair to say that subjective flavor is at least half based on smell.

Touch

Touch (the skin senses) is the first of the somesthetic, or body-related, senses. It's difficult to imagine what life would be like without the sense of touch, a condition called *anaphia.* The plight of Ian Waterman gives us a hint, though. After an illness he suffered at 19, Waterman permanently lost all feeling below his neck. Now, in order to know the position of his body, he must be able to see it. If he moves with his eyes closed, he has no idea where he is going. And if the lights go out in a room, he's in big trouble (Gallagher, 2004).

The Process of Transduction on the Skin

Skin receptors produce at least five different sensations: *light touch, pressure, pain, cold,* and *warmth.* Receptors with particular shapes appear to specialize somewhat in various sensations (Figure 4.23). However, free nerve endings alone can produce all five sensations (Carlson, 2013). Altogether, the skin has about 200,000 nerve endings for temperature, 500,000 for touch and pressure, and 3 million for pain.

Does the number of receptors in an area of skin relate to its sensitivity? Yes. Your skin can be "mapped" by applying heat, cold, touch, pressure, or pain to points all over your body (Hollins, 2010). Such testing would show that the number of skin receptors varies and that sensitivity generally matches the number of receptors in a given area. Broadly speaking, important areas such as the lips, tongue, face, hands, and genitals have a higher density of receptors. Of course, what you ultimately feel will depend on brain activity.

Does the number of pain receptors also vary? Yes. About 230 pain points per square centimeter (about a half-inch) are found behind the knee, 180 per centimeter on the buttocks, 60 on the pad of the thumb, and 40 on the tip of the nose. (Is it better, then, to be pinched on the nose or behind the knee? It depends on what you like!)

Pain carried by *large nerve fibers* is sharp, bright, and fast and seems to come from specific body areas (McMahon & Koltzenburg, 2013). This is the body's **warning system**. Give yourself a small jab with a pin and you will feel this type of pain. As you do this, notice that warning pain quickly disappears. Much as we may

Lock-and-key theory of olfaction A theory holding that odors are related to the shapes of chemical molecules.

Taste buds Receptor cells for taste.

Warning system Pain based on large nerve fibers; warns that bodily damage may be occurring.

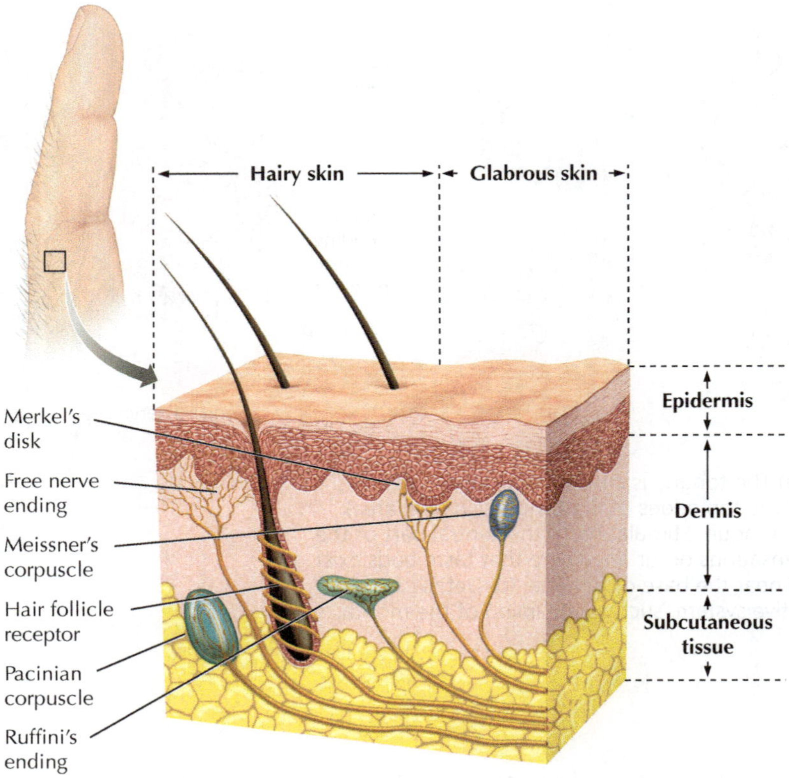

Figure 4.23 Receptors for the skin senses. The skin senses include touch, pressure, pain, cold, and warmth. This drawing shows different forms the skin receptors can take. The functions of these receptors are likely as follows: Merkel's disks sense pressure on the skin; free nerve endings sense warmth, cold, and pain; Meissner's corpuscles sense pressure; hair follicle receptors sense hair movement; Pacinian corpuscles sense pressure and vibration; and Ruffini's endings sense skin stretching (Freberg, 2016; Kalat, 2016). The feeling of being touched is likely made up of a combination of varying degrees of activity in all these receptors.

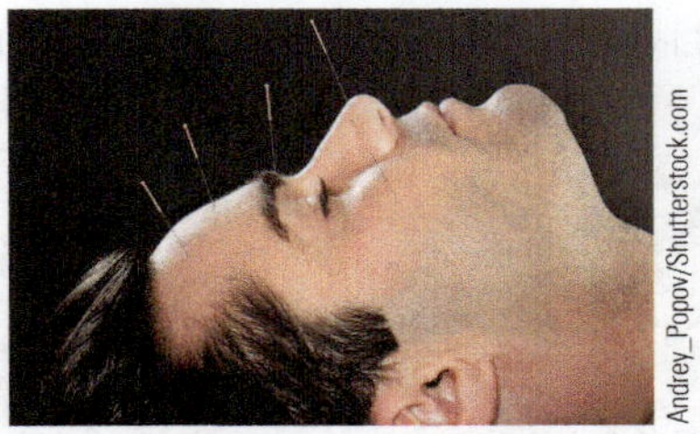

Acupuncture involves inserting thin, stainless steel needles into areas identified by ancient Chinese medicine. Modern research has begun to explain the painkilling effects of acupuncture, although its purported ability to cure diseases is more debatable.

dislike warning pain, it is usually a signal that the body has been, or is about to be, damaged. Without warning pain, we would be unable to detect or prevent injury.

A second type of somatic pain is carried by *small nerve fibers*. This type of pain is slower, nagging, aching, widespread, and very unpleasant (McMahon & Koltzenburg, 2013). It gets worse if the pain stimulus is repeated. This is the body's **reminding system**, which reminds the brain that the body has been injured. For instance, lower-back pain often has this quality. Sadly, the reminding system can cause agony long after an injury has healed, or in terminal illnesses, when the reminder is useless.

The Pain Gate

You may have noticed that one type of pain sometimes cancels another. Ronald Melzack's (1999) **gate control theory** suggests that pain messages from the two different types of nerve fibers pass through the same neural "gate" in the spinal cord. If the gate is "closed" by one pain message, other messages may not be able to pass through (Melzack & Katz, 2006; Moayedi & Davis, 2013).

How is the gate closed? It may depend on what types of nerve fibers are carrying information about the pain. Messages carried by large, fast nerve fibers seem to close the spinal pain gate directly. Doing so can prevent slower, "reminding system" pain from reaching the brain. But messages from small, slow fibers seem to take a different route. After going through the pain gate, they continue to a "central biasing system" in the brain which then sends a message back down the spinal cord, closing the pain gates (Figure 4.24).

Melzack believes that gate control theory may explain the painkilling effects of *acupuncture*, the Chinese medical art of relieving pain and illness by inserting thin needles into the body. As the acupuncturist's needles are twirled, heated, or electrified, they activate small pain fibers. These relay through the biasing system to close the gates to intense or chronic pain. Studies have shown that acupuncture produces short-term pain relief, though its ability to cure illness is much more debatable (Hopton, Thomas, & MacPherson, 2013; Witt et al., 2011).

The Kinesthetic and Vestibular Systems

Along with touch, the kinesthetic and vestibular senses are somesthetic senses and they are primarily concerned with the position of your body in relation to the rest of the world. As we mentioned earlier, the kinesthetic transducers are special receptors that are located in the muscles and joints. They send information to the brain about where your various body parts are located in space, relative to one another. They allow the brain to recognize, for example, if you are bent over at the waist to tie your shoes, if your arm is outstretched to catch a baseball, or where your legs are while you're dancing. (The receptors cannot tell you whether you look ridiculous while you're dancing, though. Only your friends can do that.) The kinesthetic senses also allow you to touch your nose (or any other part of your

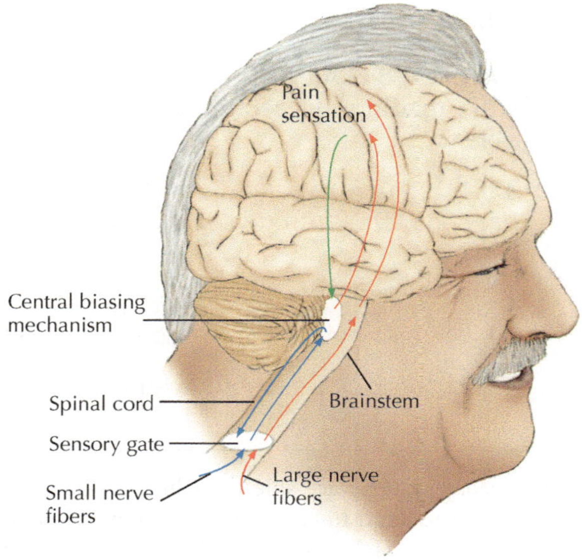

Figure 4.24 A sensory gate for pain. A series of pain impulses going through the gate may prevent other pain messages from passing through. Alternatively, pain messages may relay through a "central biasing mechanism" that exerts control over the gate, closing it to other impulses.

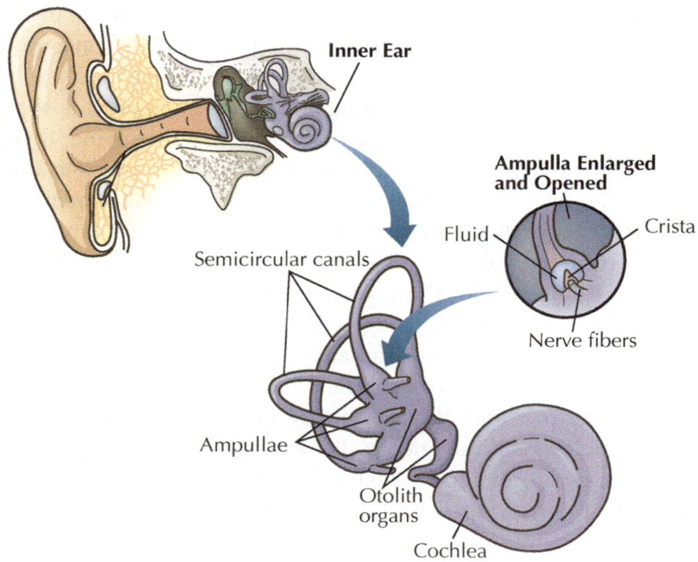

Figure 4.25 The vestibular system.

body) even when your eyes are closed and you cannot see your hand or where it is moving.

The vestibular system is somewhat different. Its primary function is related to the position of the body as a whole in space, and it has an important role to play in the ability to keep our balance.

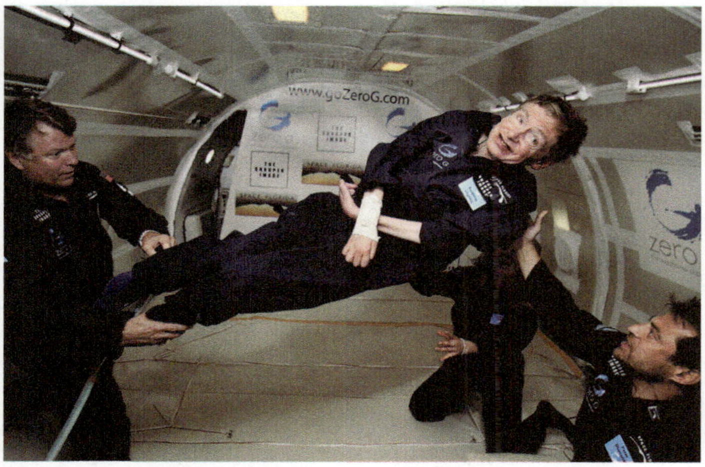

NASA

Weightlessness presents astronauts with a real challenge in sensory adaptation. In 2007, world-famous physicist Stephen Hawking, who lived with amyotrophic lateral sclerosis (ALS, or Lou Gehrig's disease), fulfilled a lifelong dream of experiencing weightlessness. He took a flight on the "Weightless Wonder," the official nickname that the National Aeronautics and Space Administration (NASA) gives to the high-flying airplane that provides short periods of weightlessness to train astronauts. (Its unofficial nickname, which stems from its unfortunate side effects, is the "Vomit Comet.")

The Process of Transduction in the Vestibular System

Transducers for the vestibular system are located in the inner ear. There, fluid-filled sacs called *otolith* (OH-toe-lith) *organs* are sensitive to movement, acceleration, and gravity (Figure 4.25). The otolith organs contain tiny crystals in a soft, gelatinlike mass. The tug of gravity or rapid head movements can cause the mass to shift. This, in turn, stimulates hairlike receptor cells, allowing us to sense gravity, acceleration, and movement through space (Lackner & DiZio, 2005).

Three fluid-filled tubes—called the *semicircular canals*—are the sensory organs for balance. If you could climb inside these tubes, you would find that head movements cause the fluid to swirl about. As the fluid moves, it bends a small "flap," or "float," called the *crista*, that detects movement in the semicircular canals. The bending of each crista again stimulates hair cells and signals head rotation.

Sensation in Everyday Life: Motion Sickness

It's important to note that the information coming from a variety of senses (or "modalities") isn't necessarily processed by the brain separately. Our tendency to integrate, or combine, the sensory impressions from several modalities is referred to as **multimodal**

Reminding system Pain based on small nerve fibers; reminds the brain that the body has been injured.

Gate control theory A theory proposing that pain messages pass through neural "gates" in the spinal cord.

Multimodal integration The process by which the brain combines information coming from multiple senses.

integration. For example, information from the vestibular system, vision, and kinesthesis is often integrated to give you a more complete sense of your body's orientation in space. On solid ground, the information coming from those senses will align. However, in a heaving, pitching boat, or an airplane flying through turbulence, or even playing a video game, a serious mismatch can occur in the sensory input from different modalities. This may cause disorientation and heaving of another kind altogether (Chang et al., 2012). Astronauts also experience this type of sensory mismatch. Although space flight might look like fun, the likelihood of you throwing up during your first experience in orbit is about 70 percent, primarily because weightlessness and space flight create sensory conflict.

You can probably think of many other clear instances that reflect multimodal integration. For example, interpreting speech requires us to combine visual information from the face with auditory information from the voice. Enjoying a gourmet meal involves integration of both smell, taste, and, to some extent, vision (since chefs often spend considerable time making sure the meal looks appetizing). The richness of our environment becomes much more apparent when sensations from different modalities are integrated in a unified way.

Reflective Practice

Chemical and Somesthetic Senses

1. Olfaction appears to be at least partially explained by the ______________ theory of molecule shapes and receptor sites.
2. Which of the following is a somesthetic sense?
   a. gustation
   b. olfaction
   c. rarefaction
   d. kinesthesis
3. Warning pain is carried by ________ nerve fibers.
4. Head movements are detected primarily in the semicircular canals and gravity by the otolith organs. T or F?

THINK CRITICALLY

5. Drivers are less likely to become carsick than passengers. Why do you think that drivers and passengers differ in susceptibility to motion sickness?

SELF-REFLECT

- What is your favorite food aroma? What is your favorite taste? Explain how you are able to sense the aroma and taste of foods.
- Stand on one foot with your eyes closed. Now touch the tip of your nose with your index finger. Which of the somesthetic senses did you use to perform this feat?

Answers: 1. lock-and-key 2. d 3. large 4. T 5. Drivers experience less of a mismatch between their sensory experiences (vision and the somesthetic senses) because they control the car's motion. This allows them to anticipate the car's movements and to coordinate their head and eye movements with those of the car.

4.5 Attention

GATEWAYS LEARNING OUTCOMES:
After reading this section you should be able to:

4.5.1 Explain what research on multitasking has indicated with respect to the limits of attention

4.5.2 Identify four factors that influence whether we will pay attention to a stimulus

4.5.3 Describe the positive and negative effects of mind-wandering

Although sensory systems are able to reduce a flood of sights, sounds, odors, tastes, and touch sensations to more manageable levels (■ see Section 4.1), the result is still too much for the brain to handle. That's why the brain further reduces sensory information through **selective attention**, or our ability to focus on specific sensory input. Selective attention appears to be based on the ability of brain structures to select and divert incoming sensory messages (Isbell et al., 2016). The idea of selective attention suggests that we are able to "tune in" to a single sensory message while excluding others. You might find it helpful to think of selective attention as a *bottleneck*, or a narrowing in the information channel that links the senses to perception.

Demonstrating the Limits of Attention: Multitasking

Many people believe that they can effectively divide their attention and perform two tasks simultaneously. After all, who hasn't attempted to talk on the phone while preparing (and maybe eating) food? But exactly how far can we push things? How many things can we attend to at one time? Psychologists have known for many decades that attentional resources are limited (Goldstein, 2019). Such an observation is never clearer than when we attempt to multitask, or carry out several tasks at the same time.

Searching YouTube, it's not difficult to find humorous videos that demonstrate the perils of multitasking. While talking on cell phones, for example, people can often be seen walking into walls or falling down a flight of stairs. Such instances provide real-life examples of what psychological scientists now understand well: Limits on our attention mean that efforts to divide it can result in poor consequences (and, sometimes, splitting headaches) (Koch et al., 2018). It simply isn't possible to do multiple things at one time when they all require some degree of focus. But clearly multitasking isn't always a problem. After all, most of us are quite capable of folding laundry while talking on the phone or eating an apple while walking to class. So what *are* the limits on dividing our attention?

Many decades of research provide evidence for two findings related to multitasking. The first is that even when we think we're dividing attention to complete multiple things at once, we likely aren't. Instead, what we're doing is *task-switching*—moving our attention rapidly between each of the things that we're working on. The second finding is that we cannot task-switch well among tasks that demand significant attentional resources (Alzahabi, Becker, & Hambrick, 2017). This is why texting while driving in very busy traffic often leads to accidents, and why people don't learn well if they're surfing the web while trying to take notes during a lecture—each of these jobs requires substantial attention. However, when tasks are very well practiced, like folding laundry and eating apples, they become more automatic and require substantially less attention to complete (Willingham & Reiner, 2019). Well-practiced tasks can often be successfully carried out alongside other, more attention-demanding tasks with some success, making it *seem* like we're multitasking.

Good examples of well-practiced, automatic tasks are things like walking and driving under "easy" conditions (provided you have been driving for many years of course). This is why it's often possible to rapidly task-switch between driving the familiar road to work in good weather and having a conversation with a passenger in your car. The same can be said of talking on your phone while walking to class. But challenges to this kind of seamless task-switching emerge when well-practiced tasks become more challenging and require additional attentional resources. For example, driving in bad weather or very busy traffic makes holding a conversation with your passenger much more difficult. Similarly, even walking requires more attention when the area is unfamiliar (and, based on those YouTube videos, when stairs are involved).

Four Factors Influencing Selective Attention

Clearly, attentional resources are limited and we need to allocate them in an effective way. How do we select what we attend to? Several factors impact the likelihood that stimuli will attract our attention. Here, we'll focus on four of them: intensity, contrast, personal importance, and goals.

Many people believe that they are good at multitasking, but psychological research has shown that people of all ages perform more poorly when they try to divide their attention.

Intensity

Very *intense* stimuli usually command attention—we will naturally focus on stimuli that are brighter, louder, larger, or sharper. For example, a gunshot would be hard to ignore. If a brightly colored hot-air balloon ever lands at your college campus, it almost certainly will draw a crowd.

Contrast

ATTENTION ALSO IS **FREQUENTLY** RELATED TO contrast OR *change* IN STIMULATION. The contrasts between **bold**, *italics*, CAPITALS, and lowercase in these sentences draw attention because they are a change from the usual pattern and are *unexpected*.

Personal Importance

Have you ever had the experience of standing in a crowded room, surrounded by voices, and still heard your own name spoken somewhere else in the room (Koch et al., 2011)? This familiar example related to auditory stimuli is referred to as the *cocktail party effect*. Prominent perceptual psychologist Anne Treisman suggested that humans are primed to divert attention toward things that are of importance to us, and the cocktail party effect likely stems from the fact that it's often relevant to know what others are saying about us (especially, perhaps, when they think we're not listening).

Similar examples can be seen with other senses, including vision. For example, in many crimes, victims fall prey to *weapon focus*, fixing all of their attention on the knife, gun, or other weapon that an attacker is holding. Such a response is completely natural, given the importance of that weapon to their personal safety. Unfortunately, in doing so, eyewitnesses will often fail to notice details of appearance, dress, or other clues that might help with identification of the criminal later (Fawcett et al., 2013).

Goals

In early research, Yarbus (1967) demonstrated how our attention can be purposefully directed in ways that allow us to meet our goals. All of the participants in his study were asked to view the same picture—*An Unexpected Visitor* by the artist Ilya Repin—seven times, each time with a different set of instructions. Yarbus' study was one of the first to employ rudimentary *eye-tracking*, a method that allows researchers to record the path of participants' eyes while they complete a task. In Figure 4.26, you can see that participants' attention was purposefully directed to different parts of the painting depending upon the goal outlined in the instructions that they were given.

A somewhat funnier demonstration of the importance of goals comes from a classic study in which participants were shown a film of two basketball teams, one wearing black shirts and the other wearing white. Observers were asked to watch the film closely and count how many times a basketball passed between members of the white team. As observers watched and counted, a person wearing a black gorilla suit walked into the middle of the

Selective attention Giving priority to a particular incoming sensory message.

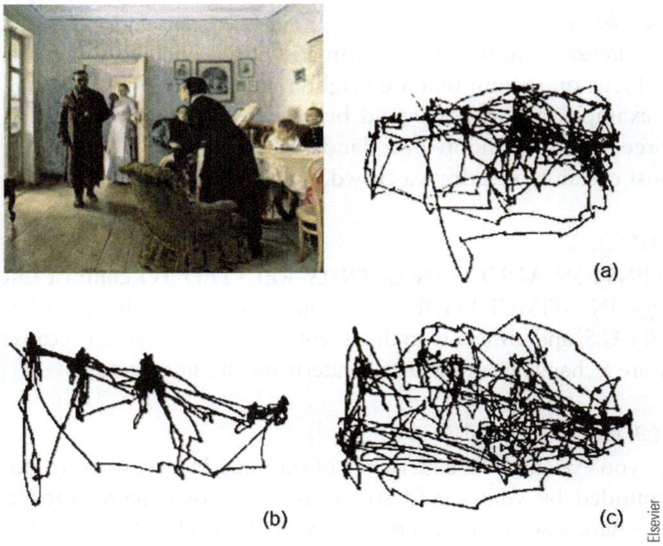

Figure 4.26 Examining a picture (*The Unexpected Visitor*) with different goals in mind. Lines show movement of the eyes when participants were given the following instructions: (a) Estimate the wealth of the family in the picture. (b) Give the ages of the people. (c) Remember the position of the people and objects in the room.

basketball game, faced the camera, thumped his chest, and walked out of view. Shockingly, fully half of the observers failed to notice this rather striking event. In an effort to meet their goal of focusing on the white team they ignored those in black—including the large black gorilla (Simons & Chabris, 1999). (This effect probably explains why fans of opposing sports teams often act as if they had seen two completely different games.)

The "invisible gorilla" study provides a good example of **inattentional blindness**, a failure to notice a stimulus because attention is focused elsewhere (Thakral, 2011). A similar phenomenon—**change blindness**—refers to situations in which we fail to notice that the background in our field of vision is changing because we are focused on one specific element of the scene. Both forms of "blindness" result in us not seeing something that is plainly before our eyes and they occur for two reasons. The first is that our attention is narrowly focused *while we attempt to address a goal,* like counting the number of passes made by a group of basketball players (Bressan & Pizzighello, 2008). The second is that we often miss things—like gorillas in basketball games—that are *not expected* (Chabris & Simons, 2009). That second point is important: We typically assume that we will see things—especially distinctive things—when we are looking right at them. But research has repeatedly demonstrated that this is not the case at all. In fact, it's entirely possible for something quite large (and sometimes hairy) to go completely unnoticed if you aren't looking for it and don't expect to see it.

If this seems like a bit of a silly demonstration, consider a recent real-world adaptation of the "invisible gorilla" study, in which 24 experienced radiologists were asked to scan lung X-rays for evidence of tumors. What these doctors did not know was that one of the X-rays had been altered to include a small picture of a gorilla (no, we're not kidding) (Figure 4.27). The results are somewhat sobering: Only 17% of the radiologists in this study actually noticed that a hairy primate had taken up residence in the patient's lung, *including many of those whose eye tracking results showed that they looked directly at it* (Drew, Vo, & Wolfe, 2013)!

If you're wondering how such a thing could happen to experienced professionals, you needn't look any further than radiologists' goals and expectations: When they examine X-rays, they're checking very specifically for things that resemble a cancerous tumor. Tumors tend to appear in specific locations and have particular features; with experience, radiologists learn to pay attention to regions and objects that are in keeping with their objectives and expectations and are likely to miss those (including gorillas) that aren't.

Attention in Everyday Life: Mind-wandering

Have you ever had this experience? You're sitting in class, listening to a lecture by your favorite instructor. Everything is moving along well—you're focused on the slides and taking notes when all of a sudden—BAM!—you're relaxing on a beach, listening to the

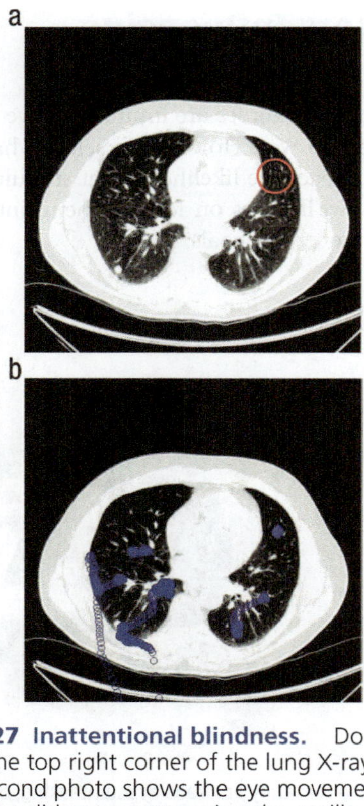

Figure 4.27 Inattentional blindness. Do you see the gorilla in the top right corner of the lung X-ray in the first photo? The second photo shows the eye movements of one of the doctors who did not report seeing the gorilla, even though the eye tracker indicated that this person looked directly at it.

waves crashing in on the shore. No, you haven't been teleported to the sun and surf (sorry!). In fact, your body hasn't even left the lecture hall—it's only your mind that's travelled down to the ocean with its imaginary tube of sunscreen.

Up until now, our discussion of attention has been focused on the external world. In recent years, though, psychologists have become interested in the phenomenon of **mind-wandering**, or the tendency for our attention to stray to things that are internal, and unrelated to stimuli in the environment (Smallwood & Schooler, 2006). One of the reasons for researchers' interest in this area lies in the consequences of mind-wandering. When our attention shifts away from things in the real world and turns inward to focus on our own thoughts, concerns, and wishes (that beach, for example), there are clear implications for our ability to respond to what's going on around us (that lecture, for example).

Early research focused on implications of mind-wandering that are clearly negative, including an increased likelihood of accidents while driving, challenges to reading comprehension, impaired memory, and difficulties in the workplace. However, more recent research on mind-wandering suggests that it may also be beneficial, as it has been associated with increased creativity and relief from boredom. Moreover, because it is typically future-oriented, mind-wandering may allow for planning and goal setting (Mooneyham & Schooler, 2013).

Initially, researchers believed that mind-wandering was unintentional; that is, the assumption was that people always do their best to keep their attention on-task but occasionally fail in their efforts. More recently, though, it has become clear that sometimes mind-wandering is quite intentional and may arise when we believe that the task at hand does not require our full attention (Seli et al., 2018). It probably won't surprise you to know that both intentional and unintentional mind-wandering have been linked to the executive functions that we discussed in ■ Sections 2.5 and 3.4, as they play an important role in our ability to control our thinking.

If your mind hasn't wandered away, let's take a few minutes now to do a bit of reflective practice on the topic of attention.

Reflective Practice

Attention

1. Which of the following influence selective attention?
   a. goals
   b. personal relevance
   c. intensity
   d. all of the above

2. Inattentional blindness refers to a situation in which
   a. you are not being attentive to someone who is legally blind.
   b. you cannot see a stimulus because your eyes are not transducing light energy properly.
   c. you fail to see a stimulus because your attention is directed toward something else.
   d. you fail to see the background of a scene changing because your attention is directed toward something else.

3. Research suggests that it is possible to perform two tasks simultaneously. T or F?

4. Xin is sitting through a presentation but realizes that the speaker is talking about something he's already very familiar with. Deciding that he doesn't really need to listen to this part of the talk, he mentally reviews what he needs to pick up at the grocery store on the way home. Xin is engaged in ________________ mind-wandering.

THINK CRITICALLY

5. Many places allow people to talk on the phone while driving provided that a hands-free unit is being used. Using what you have learned about multitasking, evaluate the likely effectiveness of such a law in preventing accidents.

SELF-REFLECT

- What types of things are most likely to function as distractors for you during your lectures? Are there strategies that you can use in class to maintain your attention for longer periods of time?

Answers: 1. d 2. c 3. F 4. intentional 5. Such laws are likely to have some effect on the number of accidents, but is unlikely to eliminate them. It's obviously important that people not text while driving and having two hands on the wheel may be better than one in trying to prevent an accident. For these reasons, hands-free laws are useful. However, these laws do not address the problems associated with having attention diverted toward a phone conversation rather than paying attention to what's on the road.

4.6 Perception

GATEWAYS LEARNING OUTCOMES:
After reading this section you should be able to:

4.6.1 Describe the relationship between sensation and perception

4.6.2 Contrast bottom-up and top-down processing

4.6.3 Explain how both sensory transduction and experience contribute to similarities and differences in perception

4.6.4 Describe the effects of culture on the perception of the Müller-Lyer illusion

4.6.5 Differentiate between monocular and binocular depth cues, giving examples of each

4.6.6 Explain how depth cues are used in the world of art and by clinical psychologists using virtual reality to treat clients

Inattentional blindness A failure to notice a stimulus because attention is focused elsewhere.

Change blindness A failure to notice that the background is changing because attention is focused elsewhere.

Mind-wandering The process by which attention is withdrawn from the physical environment to focus on internal events.

When the brain organizes and interprets sensory impressions into meaningful patterns, we're speaking about **perception**. Some brain areas receive visual information; others receive auditory information, and still others receive taste or touch information. It is surprising for many people to realize that "seeing" and "hearing" actually take place in your brain, not in your eyes or ears. It is also fascinating to realize that much, if not all, of the sensation-perception process is unconscious; that is, we are usually aware only of the result, the *percept*.

Of course, the brain doesn't get things right all the time, and perceptual *mis*construction is responsible for many illusions. In an **illusion**, information that is sent to the brain from the senses is interpreted in a way that is not consistent with objective reality. The optical illusion discussed at the beginning of this chapter is an excellent example. Though reality involved some very clever artistic effects, the brain interpreted it as an open vault with money falling from it into a deep pit. Though illusions can happen with information from any of the senses, those involving vision are most common. Notice that illusions are distorted perceptions of stimuli that actually exist. In a **hallucination**, though, people perceive objects or events that have no external reality (Moseley, Fernyhough, & Ellison, 2013). For example, they see things that are not there, or hear the voices of people who are not present (Gregory, 2016).

Both illusions and hallucinations are quite distinct from the clinical condition called **synesthesia**. For these individuals, sensory impressions cross normal sensory barriers (Craver-Lemley & Reeves, 2013; Marks, 2014). In some cases, then, a specific sound may bring on the sensation of a particular color, or the taste of a certain food may be linked with the sensation

The Café Wall Illusion was first discovered in 1898, at which time it was called the Kindergarten Illusion. It was rediscovered in 1973 by a British psychologist who observed the effect in the tiles of a café in Bristol, England. In this illusion, the horizontal lines appear to be sloped, even though they are perfectly parallel.

of touch. For example, one person might perceive spiced chicken as tasting "pointy"; another may experience chocolate as smelling pink and stripey (Dixon, Smilek, & Merikle, 2004; Russell, Stevenson, & Rich, 2015). A clearly defined cause of synesthesia has not been determined, though there is evidence for both genetic and epigenetic effects (Baron-Cohen et al., 1996; Bosley & Eagleman, 2015). (■ For a review of genetic and epigenetic influences, see Section 3.1.) Over the years, a number of celebrities have reported experiencing synesthesia, including Stevie Wonder, Eddie van Halen, Vincent van Gogh, Marilyn Monroe, and Duke Ellington.

Visual perception involves finding meaningful patterns in complex stimuli. If you look closely at this pixelated photo, you can see that it is entirely made up of small individual differently colored pixels. An infant or newly sighted person might well see only a jumble of meaningless colors. But because the pixels form a familiar pattern, you should easily see the dog.

That's an interesting point about genetic and epigenetic effects on synesthesia. But is ordinary perception based only on our genes, or is some learning required? As a thought experiment, imagine what it would be like to have your vision restored after many years of blindness. What would your experience be like? It turns out that getting your first look at the world as an adult is likely to be disappointing because the newfound ability to *sense* (see) the world does not guarantee that it can be *perceived*, or understood. Newly sighted persons must learn to identify objects, to read clocks, numbers, and letters, and to judge sizes and distances. For instance, Mr. S. B. was a cataract patient who had been blind since birth. After an operation finally restored his sight at age 52, Mr. S. B. struggled to use his newfound vision (Gregory, 2003).

Mr. S. B. soon learned to tell time from a large clock and to read block letters that he previously had known only from touch. At a zoo, he recognized an elephant from descriptions that he had heard. However, handwriting meant nothing to him for more than a year after he regained sight, and many objects were meaningless until he touched them. Thus, Mr. S. B. slowly learned to organize his *sensations* into meaningful *perceptions*. Cases such as those of Mr. S. B. show that your experiences are **perceptual constructions**, or mental models of external events, that *are actively created by your brain* (Goldstein & Brockmole, 2017). They also reveal how powerfully the brain seeks meaningful patterns in sensory input to create our perceptual experience. Let's take a few minutes now to explore two processes that underlie perceptual construction: bottom-up and top-down processing.

Bottom-Up and Top-Down Processing

Moment by moment, our perceptions are typically constructed in both a *bottom-up* and *top-down* fashion. Think about the process of building a house: Raw materials, such as lumber, doors, tiles, carpets, screws, and nails, must be painstakingly fitted together. At the same time, an overall building plan guides how these raw materials are assembled.

Our brain builds perceptions in similar ways. In **bottom-up processing**, we start constructing at the "bottom" with raw materials—that is, we begin with the sensory impressions we discussed earlier in this chapter and put them together to build a complete perception. But the reverse also occurs: In **top-down processing**, prior knowledge and experience provide an "overall building plan" that is used to rapidly guide the perception of meaningful wholes, without necessarily distinctly processing the individual components that make it up (Goldstein & Brockmole, 2017).

That may sound a bit abstract so let's look at a concrete example. If you put together a picture puzzle that you've never seen before, you are relying mainly on bottom-up processing: you must assemble small pieces until a recognizable pattern begins to emerge. Top-down processing is quite different. Think about what happens when you perceive a face. If you were engaged in bottom-up processing, then you would take stock of individual features: two eyes centered above a nose; mouth centered below the nose; red hair and an ear on each side. Is that how you typically perceive faces? No, of course not. In one single glance, you perceive the face holistically as a complete unit. Moreover, in keeping with this idea of top-down processing, your past experience will guide your perception of that face, providing instant information about its familiarity (it's my favorite psychology professor!), for example, as well as any emotion that is being expressed (she's happy to see me!).

Both types of processing are illustrated by Figure 4.28. The first time that you see this photo, you will probably process it from the bottom-up, picking out features until they become recognizable. The next time you see it, because of your experience, you will engage in top-down processing and you will instantly recognize what's being hidden.

An excellent example of top-down perceptual construction can also be found in Gestalt ideas about **figure-ground organization**. The Gestalt psychologists proposed that the simplest organization involves grouping some sensations into an object, or figure, that stands out against a plainer background. Figure-ground organization is probably inborn because it is the first perceptual ability to appear after cataract patients like Mr. S. B. regain sight. (See Section 1.3 for a brief history of Gestalt psychology.)

Figure 4.28 Bottom-up vs. top-down processing. Check out this abstract design. If you process it "bottom-up," likely all that you will see are three small, dark, geometric shapes near the edges. Would you like to try some top-down processing? Knowing the title of the design will allow you to apply your knowledge and see it in an entirely different way. The title? It's *Special K*. Can you see it now?

In normal figure-ground perception, only one "figure" is easily seen against an obvious (back)ground, though this will not always be the case. Take a moment and look at Figures 4.29 and 4.30. Because camouflage patterns break up figure-ground organization, distinguishing the figure and ground becomes more difficult. Moreover, in *reversible figures,* figure and ground can be switched. In Figure 4.31, it is equally possible to see either a

Synesthesia a perceptual phenomenon in which stimulation of one sensory system creates perceptual experiences in another sensory system.

Perception Selection, organization, and interpretation of sensory input.

Illusion A misleading or misconstructed perception.

Hallucination Perception with no basis in reality.

Perceptual construction A mental model of external events.

Bottom-up processing Organizing perceptions by beginning with low-level features.

Top-down processing Perception guided by prior knowledge or expectations.

Figure-ground organization Organizing a perception so that part of a stimulus appears to stand out as an object (figure) against a less prominent background (ground).

Dr Morley Read/Shutterstock.com

Figure 4.29 A challenging example of perceptual organization. Once the camouflaged insect (a species of stick insect) becomes visible, it is almost impossible to view the picture again without seeing the insect. Go ahead, try!

U.S. Army photo

Figure 4.30 Figure-ground organization in everyday life. Hunters and members of the military make use of camouflage as well.

Figure 4.31 The Rubin vase. Do you see two faces in profile, or a vase?

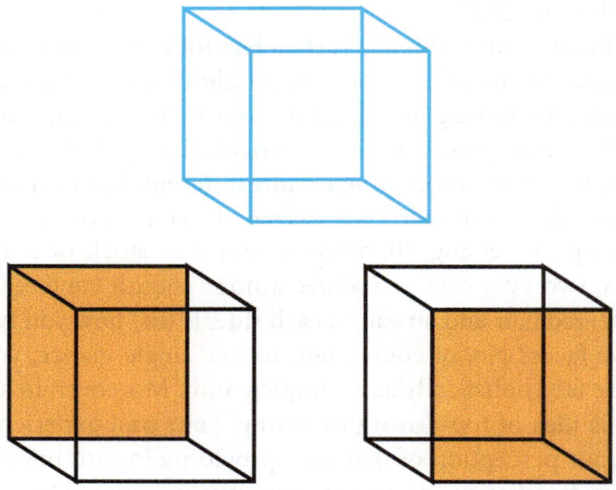

Figure 4.32 The Necker cube.

vase on a dark background or two facial profiles on a light background. As you shift from one pattern to the other, you should get a clear sense of what figure-ground organization means.

The role of top-down perceptual processes is perhaps most apparent for *ambiguous stimuli* (patterns allowing more than one interpretation). Look at the Necker cube in Figure 4.32 if you doubt that perception is an active process. Visualize the top cube as a wire box. If you stare at the cube, its organization will change. Sometimes it will seem to project upward, like the lower-left cube; other times, it will project downward. The difference lies in how your brain interprets the same information. To reiterate, we actively *construct* meaningful perceptions using past experience as a guide; we do not passively record the events and stimuli around us (Intaitė et al., 2013; Rolls, 2008).

In some instances, though, a stimulus may offer such conflicting information that past experience leads us astray. For example, past experience promotes a tendency to interpret the world in three dimensions. However, in Figure 4.33 the tendency to make a three-dimensional (3-D) object out of the "three-pronged widget" is doomed because it is an *impossible figure.* If you cover either end of the drawing in Figure 4.33, it makes sense perceptually. However, a problem arises when you try to organize the entire drawing. Then, the conflicting information that it contains prevents you from constructing a stable perception.

Similarities and Differences in People's Perception

If bottom-up and top-down processes work in the same way for everyone then it might be logical to conclude that when faced with the same stimuli (a sight, sound, or taste, for example) we would all share exactly the same perceptual experience. And while that's sometimes true, it's not always the case—it's entirely possible for two people to see or hear exactly the same thing and perceive it quite differently. Why is that? It turns out that similarities and differences in our perceptions often stem from both our sensory organs (and their ability to transduce) and our past experiences.

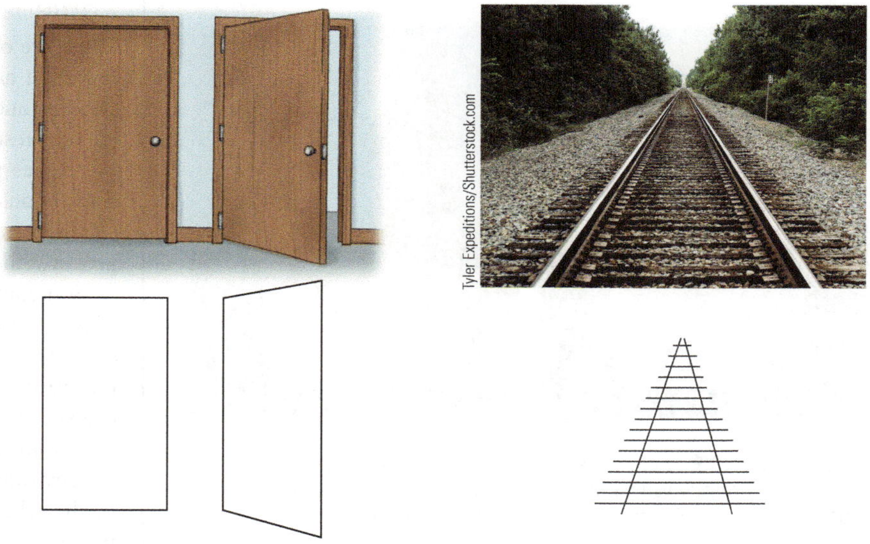

(a) (b)

Figure 4.34 Shape constancy. (a) When a door is open, its image actually forms a trapezoid. Shape constancy is indicated by the fact that it is still perceived as a rectangle. (b) When train tracks disappear into the distance, they appear to converge, forming a triangular shape. Shape constancy allows you perceive them as parallel.

Perceptual Similarities Due to Transduction

Common perceptual experiences are often the result of the fact that normally functioning sensory organs transduce information in the same way. For people with typical vision, then, seeing a daffodil will result in a similar process of transduction unfolding in the eye's photoreceptors. The result will be a shared perception of the daffodil's characteristic "trumpet" shape in the color yellow. Similarly, people who put a few grains of sugar on their tongue will perceive a sweet taste because the transducers in the tongue function in the same way across individuals.

Perceptual Similarities Due to Experience

While similarities in transduction can result in shared perceptions, many perceptual experiences are the same because of *perceptual constancies*—little perceptual "rules of thumb" that the brain develops based on its years of experience interpreting the world. And because many of our experiences are similar to some extent, those rules of thumb operate in the same way and lead to similar perceptions. Let's take a look at some perceptual constancies, with a focus on the visual system.

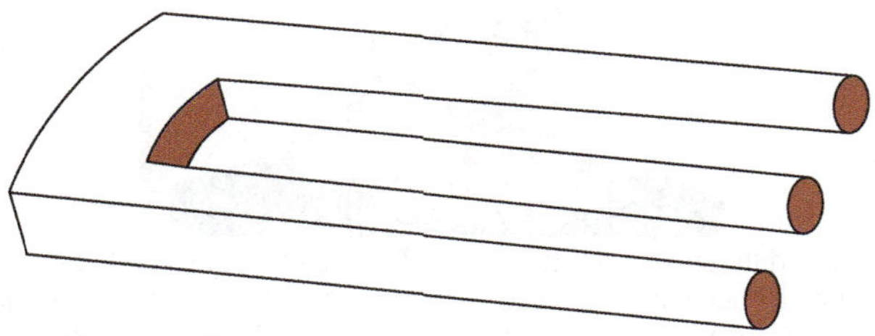

Figure 4.33 An impossible figure. The "three-pronged widget."

Shape Constancy

In **shape constancy**, the shape of an object remains stable, even though the shape of its retinal image changes. For some examples, take a look at Figure 4.34. Most of us have seen lots of doors in our lives, and our brain has used all of that experience to develop some rules for perceiving them. For example, on first glance you—and probably everyone you know—would interpret the door on the right as being a rectangle, similar to the one on the left. But that's not actually what's there on the page—that's not the information your eyes pass along to the brain. In reality, if you look at the outlines on the bottom you can see that the true shape of the door on the right is a trapezoid! (Figure 4.34a). The same is true of the railway tracks in the photo—people who have seen such tracks many times in the past will share the perception that those lines are parallel, even though the raw sensory input suggests that they are converging (Figure 4.34b).

Size Constancy

When Mr. S. B. first regained his vision, he could judge distance only in familiar situations (Gregory, 1990). One day, he was found crawling out of a hospital window to get a closer look at traffic on the street. It's easy to understand his curiosity, but he had to be restrained—his room was on the fourth floor!

Shape constancy The principle that the perceived shape of an object is unaffected by changes in its retinal image.

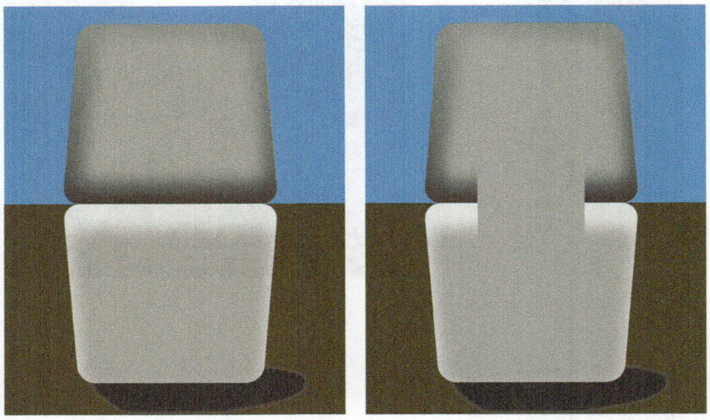

Figure 4.35 Brightness constancy. Because of the brain's experience with light and shadow we perceive the top and bottom of the figure as being two different colors, even though they are the same.

Why would Mr. S. B. try to crawl out of a fourth-story window? Couldn't he at least tell distance from the size of the cars? No. You must be visually familiar with objects to use their size to judge distance. Try holding your left hand a few inches in front of your nose and your right hand at arm's length. Your right hand should appear to be about half the size of your left hand. Still, you know that your right hand did not suddenly shrink because you have seen it many times, at various distances. We call this **size constancy**: The perceived size of an object remains the same, even though the size of its image on the retina changes (Wagner, 2012).

Brightness Constancy

Let's say that you are outside in bright sunlight. Beside you, a friend is wearing a gray skirt and a white blouse. Suddenly a cloud shades the sun. It might seem that the blouse would grow dimmer, but it still appears to be bright white. This happens because the blouse continues to reflect a greater *proportion* of light than nearby objects. **Brightness constancy** refers to the fact that our brains have learned—after a great deal of experience with dark and light—that the relative brightness of objects stays the same even as lighting conditions change.

However, using its many years of experience, your perceptual system is even more sophisticated than that because it will automatically account for different types of lighting *in the same scene*. Take a look at Figure 4.35. If you look at the image on the left, you will likely perceive the top half of the figure to be gray and the bottom to be white. Again, though, that's not what's really on the page—looking at the image on the right, you'll see that both halves are actually the same color. You don't see it that way, though, because your brain is using its past experience with lighting, and it knows that the general rule of thumb is that when light is coming from above (as it seems to be here), the color of objects directly in its path should be interpreted as they appear. Objects that are likely to be in shadow (as the bottom half of the figure would be if the light was above) are likely brighter than they seem because the shadow will put them in a darker light. Knowing that's the case, your brain "corrects" for the shadow and perceives the bottom half to be white.

Perceptual Differences Due to Transduction

While we often perceive things in the same way as those around us, that's not always the case—sometimes the same sensory experience (looking at the same scene, or smelling the same pot of soup for example) can result in very different perceptions. In some cases, differences in people's perception stem from genuine differences in the sensory impressions that come from transducers. So, for example, when sensory organs such as the eyes, ears, nose, tongue, and skin do not work properly, the information that they send to the brain may be faulty.

Sometimes this happens because of *flaws in the genetic code* for the sense organs (for example, color blindness or weakness) or *environmental trauma* (for example, childhood abuse or repeated exposure to very loud music). But we saw in Section 3.2 and earlier in this chapter that sense organs can also show *age-related decline* in ways that compromise their ability to transduce the sights, sounds, and tastes in the environment. Such changes can, to some extent, explain the social media debate a few years ago about an audio recording that some people heard as "Laurel" and others heard as "Yanny" (Pressnitzer et al., 2018). Age-related change is one factor that can impact our ability to hear high-frequency sounds. In the original recording, hearing "Yanny" relies heavily on our ability to perceive those higher frequencies. And though age-related change is not the only factor that influences high-frequency sound perception, it offers one potential reason why older people might be more likely to hear "Laurel" than "Yanny."

Perceptual Differences Due to Experience

Past experience can also shape differences in perception. Take, for example, the infamous dress that broke the Internet (see Figure 4.36). It all started with a photo sent to a bride-to-be by her mom, who wanted her daughter to see the dress that she'd purchased to wear at the wedding. After some disagreement about its color, the daughter posted the photo to social media. But it turned out that her friends couldn't agree on the color either and after considerable online commentary, the question was picked up by an editor at Buzzfeed. The rest, as they say, is history. At the end of 24 hours, #thedress had been the subject of 4.4 million tweets on Twitter.

Perceptual differences sometimes arise because transducers do not work as they should. These problems can result from genetic abnormalities, age-related decline and, sometimes, trauma. Academy Award winning actress Halle Berry is partially deaf because a physically abusive relationship caused damage to the cells in her ear that transduce sound.

Figure 4.36 #thedress Some people saw #thedress as blue and black; others saw it as white and gold. Researchers now know that when a scene's lighting is ambiguous, perceptual differences may result from people's tendency to assume that the light is more yellow (like daylight) or blue (like fluorescent light), based on their past experience. Look at the two circles in this figure. The bars between them help to show that the colors on the two dresses are the same. However if your brain assumed the light on the dress was yellow (left side), you would have concluded the dress was blue and black. If the light was assumed to be blue (right side), the dress would be perceived as white and gold.

But how can the same visual stimulus be perceived so differently, even among people whose eyes are transducing properly? To answer the question, we need to return to our discussion of perceptual constancies. Remember that the brain has a number of rules of thumb that are based on years of experience, and that it will use them to quickly interpret incoming sensory information. One of those constancies—brightness—is governed by our experience with light sources and how colors change depending on the light in which they're viewed. In many instances, the nature of lighting in a scene is clear. We know where the light is, and whether the type of light is twilight, natural daylight, candlelight, fluorescent light, or something else altogether.

In the original photo of the dress, though, the nature of the lighting was somewhat ambiguous. Under such circumstances, our brains seem to rely on a "default" setting for lighting and will interpret what's seen as though it's the default light that's present. But it turns out that people have different default light settings that are likely based on their past experience. People whose default is "bright light" will see the dress as black and blue (its true colors) (Figure 4.36a), but people whose default is "dim light" will see the dress as white and gold (Figure 4.36b) (Wallisch, 2017).

Human Diversity and Perceptual Differences

Perceptual differences can also result from experiences that are cultural in their origin. Consider the drawing in Figure 4.37*a*. This is the familiar **Müller-Lyer illusion** (MEOO-ler-LIE-er) in which the horizontal line with arrowheads appears shorter than the line with Vs. A quick measurement will show that they are the same length. How can we explain this illusion?

Evidence suggests that it is based on a lifetime of experience with the edges and corners of rooms and buildings (Deręgowski, 2013). Richard Gregory (2000) believes that you see the line with the arrowheads as if it were the nearby corner of a room joining two walls receding from it (Figure 4.37a). The line with the Vs (Figure 4.37b), on the other hand, suggests the farther corner of a room or building joining two walls coming closer. (If these two lines were belly buttons, (a) would be an "outie" and (b) would be an "innie.") In other words, cues that suggest a three-dimensional (3-D) space alter our perception of a two-dimensional (2-D) design.

If two objects make images of the same size, the more distant object must be larger. This is known formally as *size-distance invariance* (the size of an object's image is precisely related to its distance from the eyes). Gregory believes that his concept explains the Müller-Lyer illusion. If the V-tipped line looks farther away from you than the arrowhead-tipped line, you must compensate by seeing the V-tipped line as longer. This explanation presumes that you have had years of experience with straight lines, sharp edges, and corners—a pretty safe assumption in our culture. In other words, we misperceive the Müller-Lyer lines because of perceptual habits we acquired while living in a "carpentered world" (Deręgowski, 2013).

If we could test someone who saw only curves and wavy lines as a child, though, we would know if experience with a "carpentered" culture is important. Fortunately, a few San Bushmen, a culture from the Kalahari Desert in Africa, still live a traditional hunting-gathering life in the "round." Traditional San rarely encounter straight lines in their daily lives: their temporary dwellings are semicircular, and the area has few straight roads or square buildings.

What happens if a San looks at the Müller-Lyer design? The typical traditional San does not experience the illusion. At most, she or he sees the V-shaped line as *slightly* longer than the other (Henrich, Heine, & Norenzayan, 2010). This seems to confirm the importance of perceptual habits in determining our view of the world.

Perception in Everyday Life: 3-D Vision

Each of us experiences the benefits of our perceptual system in our everyday lives. In this section, we'll take a deeper dive into depth perception and 3-D vision. More specifically, we'll examine how this perceptual skill is used by artists and movie directors,

Size constancy The principle that the perceived size of an object remains constant, despite changes in its retinal image.

Brightness constancy The principle that the apparent (or relative) brightness of objects remains the same so long as they are illuminated by the same amount of light.

Müller-Lyer illusion Two equal-length lines tipped with inward or outward pointing Vs appear to be of different lengths.

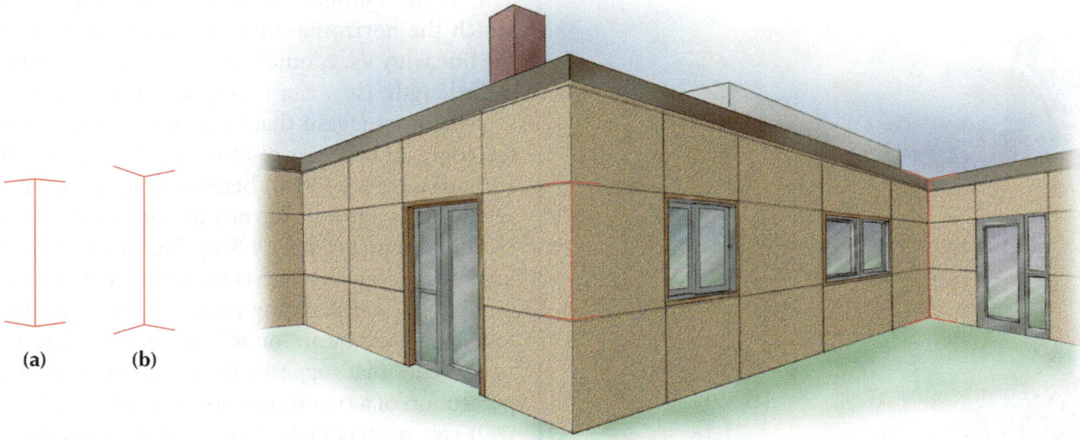

● **Figure 4.37 The Müller-Lyer illusion.** Why does line (b) in the Müller-Lyer illusion look longer than line (a)? Probably because it looks more like a distant corner than a nearer one. Because the vertical lines form images of the same length, the more "distant" line must be perceived as larger. As you can see in the drawing on the right, additional depth cues accentuate the Müller-Lyer illusion.

and by virtual reality software companies that are creating programs to help with everything from training doctors to treating patients with substance abuse.

The Basics of Depth Perception

Depth perception is the ability to see space and to accurately judge distances, allowing us to construct a 3-D experience of the world around us (Howard, 2012). Studies done with infants on a "visual cliff" suggest that depth perception is partly learned and partly innate (Witherington et al., 2005). Basically, a visual cliff is a glass-topped table (● Figure 4.38). On one side, a checkered surface lies directly beneath the glass. On the other side, the checkered surface is 4 feet below the tabletop. This makes the glass look like a tabletop on one side and a cliff, or drop-off, on the other.

To test for depth perception, 6- to 14-month-old infants were placed in the middle of the visual cliff. This gave them a choice of crawling to the shallow side or the deep side. (The glass prevented them from doing any "skydiving" if they chose the deep side.) Most infants chose the shallow side. In fact, most refused the deep side even when their mothers tried to call them toward it (Gibson & Walk, 1960). Though a basic level of depth perception is likely innate, more recent research has shown that depth perception begins to develop as early as two weeks of age and continues to improve up until six months of age (Nawrot, Mayo, & Nawrot, 2009; Yonas, Elieff, & Arterberry, 2002).

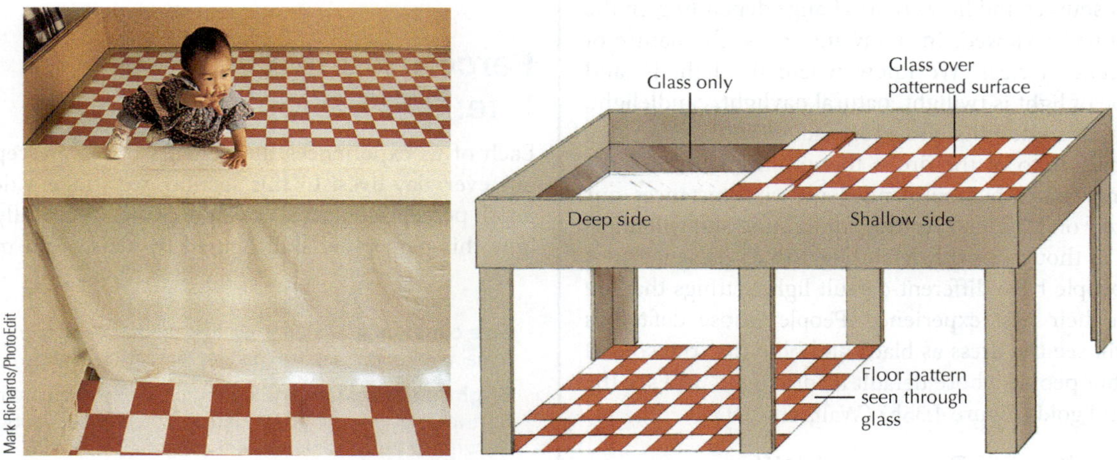

● **Figure 4.38 The visual cliff.** Human infants and newborn animals refuse to go over the edge of the visual cliff.

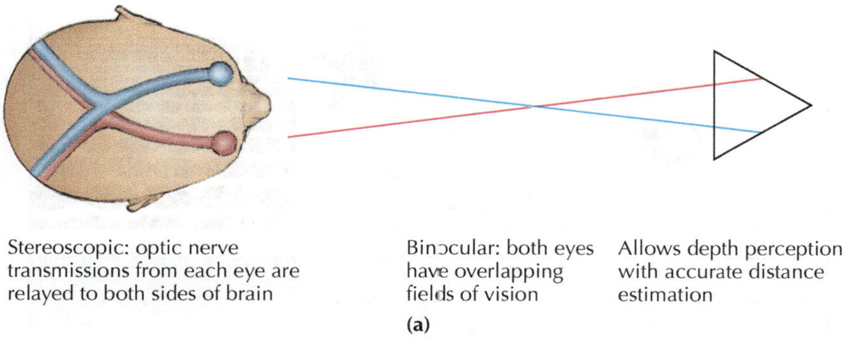

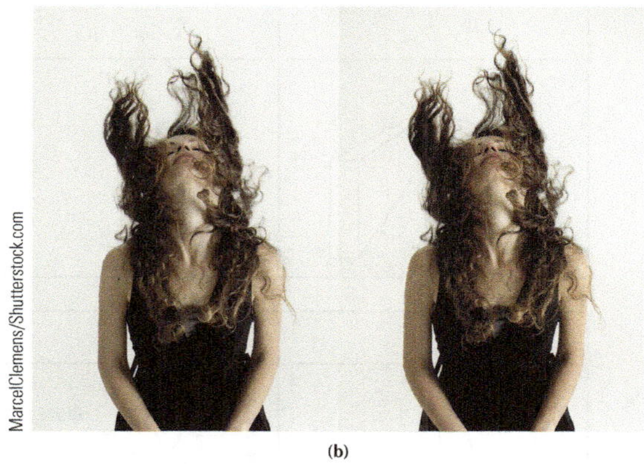

Figure 4.39 Stereoscopic vision. (a) The geometry of stereoscopic vision. (b) The photographs show what the right and left eyes would see when viewing this person. Hold the page about 6 to 8 inches from your eyes. Allow your eyes to cross and focus on the overlapping image between the two photos. Then try to fuse the person into one image. If you are successful, the third dimension will appear like magic.

Depth Perception and the World of Art

But what, exactly, are infants doing as they learn to construct a 3-D world? Essentially, we learn to construct our perception of 3-D space by integrating information from a variety of *depth cues* (Schiller et al., 2011). **Depth cues** are features of the environment and messages from the body that supply information about distance and space, and our visual system makes use of two kinds: binocular and monocular.

Binocular depth cues require two eyes. An example is **retinal disparity**, which is based on the fact that the eyes are about 2.5 inches apart and thus project slightly different images of the world to the retina. When the two different images are fused into one overall image, **stereoscopic vision** (3-D sight) occurs (Harris & Jenkin, 2011). The result is a powerful sensation of depth (Figure 4.39). Another binocular depth cue, **convergence**, is the degree to which the eyes turn in to focus on a close object. When you look at a distant object, the lines of vision from your eyes are almost parallel. You normally are not aware of it, but whenever you estimate a distance under 50 feet (as when you play catch or shoot trash can hoops with the first draft of your essay), you are using convergence. How? Muscles attached to the eyeball feed information on eye position to the brain to help it judge distance (Figure 4.40).

In contrast, **monocular depth cues** can be perceived with just one eye. We learned about one such cue—*accommodation* (bending of the lens to focus on nearby objects)—in our prior discussion of vision. Sensations from muscles attached to each lens flow back to the brain. Changes in these sensations are really only helpful in judging distances within about 4 feet of the eyes, though, so accommodation is more important to a watchmaker or someone threading a needle than it is to a basketball player or someone driving an automobile. Other monocular depth cues are referred to as **pictorial depth cues** (see Figure 4.41).

We regularly make use of these visual cues in our everyday lives, effortlessly perceiving the world in three dimensions.

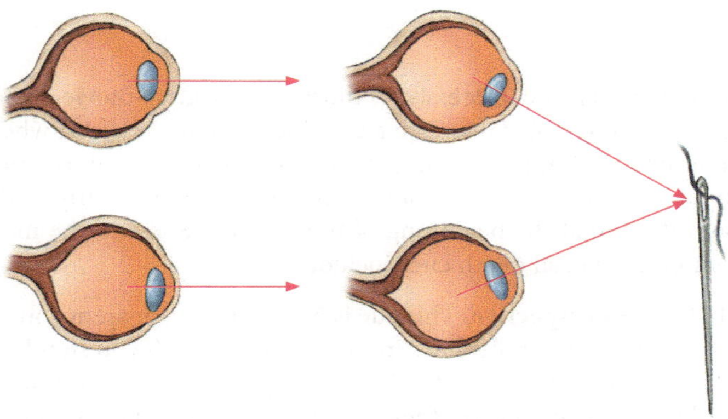

Figure 4.40 Convergence. The eyes must converge, or turn in toward the nose, to focus close objects. The eyes shown are viewed from above the head.

Depth perception The ability to see three-dimensional (3-D) space and to judge distances accurately.

Depth cues Features of the environment and messages from the body that supply information about distance and space.

Binocular depth cues Perceptual features that impart information about distance and three-dimensional (3-D) space that require two eyes.

Retinal disparity Difference between the images projected onto each eye.

Stereoscopic vision Perception of space and depth as a result of each eye receiving different images.

Convergence Degree to which the eyes turn in to focus on a close object.

Monocular depth cues Perceptual features that impart information about distance and three-dimensional (3-D) space that require just one eye.

Pictorial depth cues Monocular depth cues found in paintings, drawings, and photographs that impart information about space, depth, and distance.

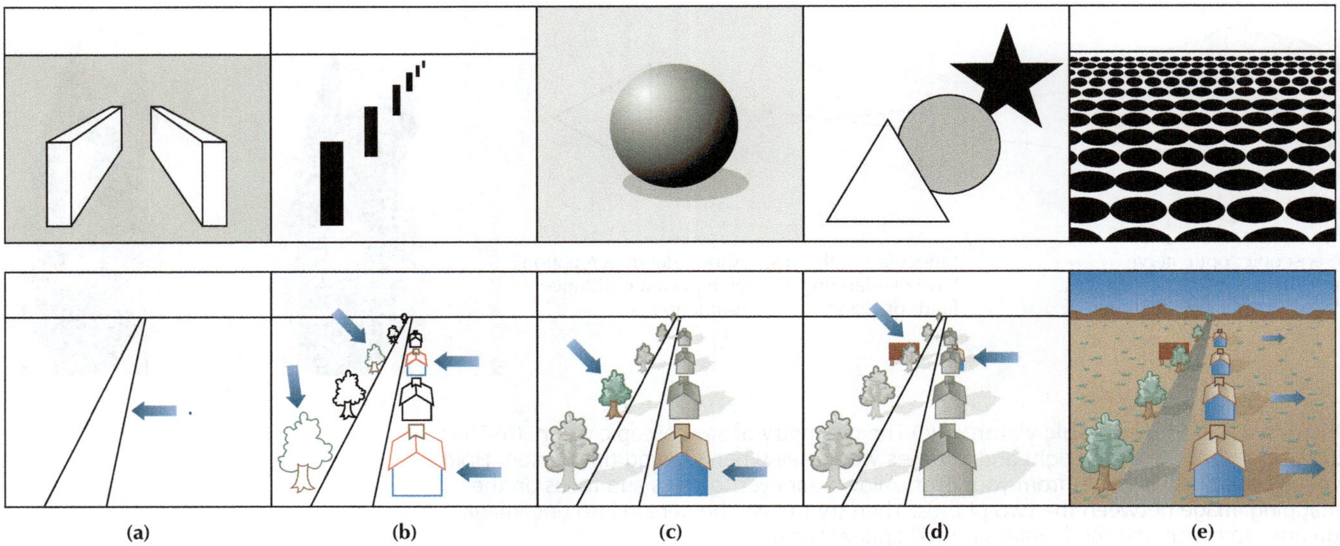

Figure 4.41 Pictorial depth cues. (a) Linear perspective. (b) Relative size. (c) Light and shadow. (d) Overlap. (e) Texture gradients. Drawings in the top row show fairly "pure" examples of each of the pictorial depth cues. In the bottom row, the pictorial depth cues are used to assemble a more realistic scene.

Perhaps even more impressive is the fact that a good movie, painting, or photograph can create a convincing sense of depth where none exists, simply by using these cues to impart information about space, depth, and distance. We saw this quite clearly in the vault illusion at the beginning of this chapter. Some of the more common pictorial depth cues include:

1. **Linear perspective.** This cue is based on the apparent convergence of parallel lines in the environment. If you stand between two railroad tracks, they appear to meet near the horizon, even though they actually remain parallel. Because you know that they are parallel, their convergence implies great distance (see Figure 4.41*a*).
2. **Relative size.** If an artist wants to depict two objects of the same size at different distances, the artist makes the more distant object smaller (see Figure 4.41*b*). Special effects in films create sensational illusions of depth by rapidly changing the image size of planets, airplanes, monsters, or what have you.
3. **Height in the plane.** Objects that are placed higher (i.e., closer to the horizon line) in a drawing tend to be perceived as more distant. In the upper frame of Figure 4.41*b*, the black columns look like they are receding into the distance, partly because they become smaller, but also because they move higher in the drawing.
4. **Light and shadow.** Most objects are lighted in ways that create clear patterns of light and shadow. Copying such patterns of light and shadow can give a 2-D design a 3-D appearance (see Figure 4.41*c*). (Also, see Figure 4.42 for more information on light and shadow.)
5. **Overlap.** Overlap (or *interposition*) occurs when one object partially blocks another object. Hold your hands up and ask a friend across the room which is nearer. Relative size will give the answer if one hand is much nearer to your friend than the other. But if one hand is only slightly closer than the other, your friend may not be able to tell—until you slide one hand in front of the other. Overlap then removes any doubt (see Figure 4.41*d*).
6. **Texture gradients.** Changes in texture also contribute to depth perception. If you stand in the middle of a cobblestone street, the street looks coarse near your feet. However, its texture will get smaller and finer as you look into the distance (see Figure 4.41*e*).
7. **Relative motion.** Relative motion, also known as *motion parallax* (PAIR-ah-lax), can be seen by looking out a window and moving your head from side to side. Notice that nearby

Figure 4.42 Shading and depth. When judging depth we usually assume that light comes mainly from one direction, usually from above. Squint a little to blur the image you see here. You should perceive a collection of globes projecting outward. If you turn this page upside down, the globes should become cavities. (After Ramachandran, 1995.)

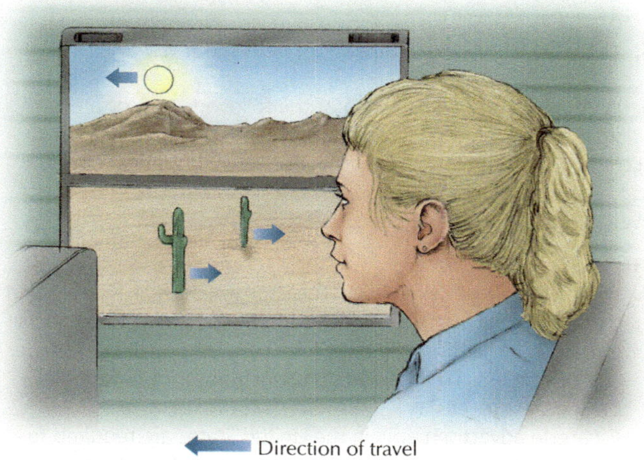

Figure 4.43 Motion parallax. The apparent motion of objects viewed during travel depends on their distance from the observer. Apparent motion can also be influenced by an observer's point of fixation. At middle distances, objects closer than the point of fixation appear to move backward; those beyond the point of fixation appear to move forward. Objects at great distances, such as the sun or moon, always appear to move forward.

objects appear to move a sizable distance as your head moves. Trees, houses, and telephone poles that are farther away appear to move slightly in relation to the background. Distant objects such as hills, mountains, or clouds don't seem to move at all (see Figure 4.43).

While each cue can be important on its own, combining several of them can create a powerful illusion of depth. (See ▲ Table 4.1 for a summary of all the depth cues that we have discussed here.)

Depth Perception and Virtual Reality

Artists have used cues related to depth perception for centuries to create realistic representations of our three-dimensional world on a two-dimensional canvas or screen. Not surprising, then, is the fact that artists and animators are in demand at software companies seeking to develop realistic and immersive worlds using virtual reality technology. **Virtual reality** (VR) is an artificial computer-simulated environment that is perceived in three dimensions through the use of a special headset. Like the real world, VR worlds are dynamic and can be altered by both computer software and the actions of the user.

▲ Table 4.1 Summary of Visual Depth Cues

Binocular Depth Cues
• Retinal disparity • Convergence
Monocular Depth Cues
• Accommodation • Pictorial depth cues (listed below) Linear perspective Relative size Height in the picture plane Light and shadow Overlap Texture gradients Relative motion (motion parallax)

Although most commonly known for its connection to gaming, VR is now being applied in many areas of clinical psychology, including obsessive-compulsive disorder, schizophrenia, pain management, eating disorders, and autism (Maples-Keller, Bunnell, Kim, & Rothbaum, 2017). Addictions are another promising area in which VR has been helpful. For example, therapists treating clients with substance abuse problems are able to use VR to put their clients in the middle of realistic scenes that are likely to trigger drinking or drug use. In this way, people can practice using the skills they've been taught in therapy in a realistic environment, potentially preventing a relapse (Worley, 2019).

Perhaps the most common clinical application of VR technology, though, is in the area of anxiety-related disorders. For example, software now exists to help people who suffer from a paralyzing fear of giving presentations. They simply strap on a VR headset and they are instantly transported into a room full of people. As they begin to give their talk, a psychologist will monitor their anxiety. If it seems as though things are progressing smoothly, the psychologist can gradually change the VR program settings and the virtual audience will begin to change. Now, they're getting a bit restless. Or maybe they begin to look just the slightest bit hostile. The psychologist will monitor what happens as the presentation progresses, ensuring that the speaker continues to sound confident. If anxiety rises, the psychologist can offer reminders about how it can be managed to ensure that the presentation will be successful (Anderson, Zimland, Hodges, & Rothbaum, 2005).

And anxiety over speeches isn't the only application for VR: Psychologists can use it to simulate all kinds of things that provoke crippling fears: high places, turbulence during airplane landings, job interviews—even snakes and spiders. Unlike older treatments that involve visualization, VR is more realistic because perceptual depth cues mimic the real world. For better or worse, you don't have to imagine a spider when you're in treatment—you can actually see a 3-D spider crawling on your hand with your own eyes! Moreover, the technology allows for the experience to be graded, gradually becoming more threatening as the client's fears become better controlled.

Veterans and first responders suffering from post-traumatic stress disorder (PTSD) have also benefitted from VR treatments that allow them to revisit battle sites in Iraq or Afghanistan, or the site of the 9/11 terrorist attacks (Beidel et al., 2019). The realism of a VR headset can even be supplemented with special effects

Virtual reality Environment in which sensory stimuli (such as sights and sounds) are provided by computer software to realistically simulate "real world" events

AP Images/Ted S. Warren

Initially used primarily for gaming, virtual reality technology is now being used in the treatment of psychological disorders, including phobias and post-traumatic stress disorder.

that engage senses other than vision. For example, companies are beginning to experiment with incorporating smell into the VR experience. There are also efforts underway to engage the sense of touch, including the experience of sunlight or rain on your face, and vests that mimic the vibrations sensed by the body during a bomb blast.

Studying the Science: VR Treatments

If you're thinking critically, you'll likely be wondering whether research supports the value of these treatments. The emerging consensus of psychological research on VR is that the answer is a somewhat qualified yes. Studies carried out to date have showed promising results, but a recent review of work done in this area makes it clear that more work needs to be done (Maples-Keller et al., 2017). In particular, future studies need to focus on many of things we learned about in ■ Sections 1.5 and 1.6—larger sample sizes to ensure that findings will replicate, the need to control for extraneous variables and, most importantly, the use of control groups in experimental designs.

Reflective Practice

Perception

1. In top-down processing of information, individual features are analyzed and assembled into a meaningful whole. T or F?
2. In a(n) ____________________, the brain misinterprets information sent from the senses; in a(n) ______________, people perceive sensory events that have no basis in reality.
   a. illusion, perceptual construction
   b. hallucination, illusion
   c. perceptual construction, hallucination
   d. illusion, hallucination
3. The design known as the Necker cube is a good example of an impossible figure. T or F?
4. Which among the following are subject to basic perceptual constancy?
   a. figure-ground organization
   b. size
   c. ambiguity
   d. brightness
   e. continuity
   f. closure
   g. shape
   h. nearness
5. The visual cliff is used to test for infant sensitivity to ______________.
6. Write an *M* or a *B* after each of the following to indicate whether it is a monocular or binocular depth cue.

accommodation _______ convergence _______ retinal disparity _______ linear perspective _______ motion parallax _______ overlap _______ relative size _______

THINK CRITICALLY

7. People who have taken psychedelic drugs, such as lysergic acid diethylamide (LSD) or mescaline, often report that the objects and people that they see appear to be changing in size, shape, and brightness. This suggests that such drugs disrupt which perceptual process?
8. Cigarette advertisements in the United States are required to carry a warning label about the health risks of smoking. How have tobacco companies made these labels less visible?

SELF-REFLECT

- Do you think that it is ethical to use therapeutic techniques involving virtual reality to treat clients when research in this area is still in its infancy?

Answers: 1. F 2. D 3. F 4. b, d, g 5. depth 6. Accommodation (M), convergence (B), retinal disparity (B), linear perspective (M), motion parallax (M), overlap (M), relative size (M) 7. Perceptual constancies (size, shape, and brightness). 8. Advertisers place health warnings in the corners of ads, where they attract the least possible attention. Also, the labels are often placed on „busy" backgrounds so they are partially camouflaged. Finally, the main images in ads are designed to be the primary focus of attention. This further distracts readers from seeing the warnings.

4.7 Psychology and Your Skill Set: Effective Communication

GATEWAYS LEARNING OUTCOMES:
After reading this section you should be able to:

4.7.1 Distinguish between verbal and nonverbal communication

4.7.2 Outline two verbal communication methods and two verbal communication points of view

4.7.3 Create a plan to improve your own communication with others

In this chapter we saw that sensation and perception are important in determining how people see and hear the world around them. For that reason, sensory and perceptual systems play an

nmedia/Shutterstock.com

important role in our ability to communicate with others, both nonverbally and verbally. *Nonverbal communication* refers to our perception of other people's voice, eye contact, and body language. Though humans are very sensitive to nonverbal cues (Siegman & Feldstein, 2014), in this section, we focus on *verbal communication*—the words that people use when they write or speak.

Communication is an important skill because it serves a number of purposes that are valuable in connecting us with others. For example, we use communication to persuade people to give us what we need (or want). We also use it to gather information that we need, or to provide others with information. The information that's exchanged may include facts or explanations, but it can also be more personal, relating to our thoughts, opinions, and feelings.

When you think about using verbal communication skills to meet these goals, there are two things to consider. First, there are two main *communication methods* that we use: oral (or spoken) and written. Second, there are two *communication points of view*: either we're providing information or we're receiving information. If you put those two ideas together, you'll see that there are four communication-based skills that are important to master (▲ Table 4.2).

Mastering these skills also requires an appreciation of the many *channels* we now use for verbal communication, which include more traditional forms (written letters, books, telephone conversations, and lectures) and those that have become popular more recently (email, texting, and social media). These channels differ in terms of the level of formality that is typically considered

▲ Table 4.2 Forms of Communication

	Providing Information	Receiving Information
Oral/spoken communication	Speaking skills	Listening skills
Written communication	Writing skills	Reading skills

acceptable when communicating, as well as the type of information that is appropriate for sharing and discussion.

Given the purposes that it serves, communication is critical in developing and maintaining positive personal and professional relationships. On the personal side, for example, researchers have demonstrated that conflict in marriages and parent–child relationships can often be traced back to difficulties with communication (Flora & Segrin, 2015; Gottman, 1994). In terms of your professional life, many employers are interested in hiring people who have good teamwork and leadership skills, both of which are dependent on being able to communicate well (Lussier & Achua, 2015). Let's take a closer look at how the four verbal communication skills—reading, listening, writing, and speaking—help to create positive home and work environments, and how you can improve on your own abilities in this area.

Receiving Information: Reading and Listening

Good communication depends on our ability to accurately understand the information that other people are providing. We've already spent some time talking about how to improve reading skills in the introduction to this book. But what about listening skills? Aamodt (2016) has summarized a number of things that we should be aware of when listening to others. Some of the most important ones include:

- **Don't interrupt the speaker.** Let her finish speaking,
- **Show the speaker that you are listening through your nonverbal cues.** You should make eye contact and nod your head occasionally, and avoid nonverbal signs of disinterest such as checking your phone for new texts.
- **Keep an open mind while you are listening.** Try to listen without judging and without jumping to conclusions.
- **Ask clarifying questions** to ensure that you understand the point that's being made.
- **Focus on what's being said.** Don't be distracted by the speaker's mannerisms, his hair, his accent, or the movie that you're going to see after dinner.

Providing Information: Writing and Speaking

When you have to convey information to other people, it's important to think carefully about the message that you want to send, and the words that you'll use to make that message clear.

One of the easiest ways to avoid miscommunication is to ensure that you don't use vague language. For example, if a friend says to you that he's just stepping out and won't be long, when would you expect to see him? Actual answers to that question range from 10 minutes to 3 hours, suggesting that written and spoken communication is much less likely to be misinterpreted if you are concrete in your choice of words.

However, even when you carefully choose your words, communication problems can still occur when people are not sensitive to the fact that *communication styles* can differ. Tannen (1995) describes communication style as a person's characteristic speaking (or writing) style, and it can include features such as directness, pacing, and the extent to which we tend to use jokes, questions, or apologies when we write or speak. These styles are learned early in life and are typically guided by two important elements: the need to *demonstrate power* and the need to *foster positive relationships.* But the communication challenges that result from differing styles are not limited to misunderstandings about what has been said. To understand the far-reaching implications of communication styles, consider the following characteristics of our speech and how they can influence people's perceptions of one another and the work that they do:

1. **The Tendency to Say "I" Versus "We"**

People interested in promoting relationships are more likely to speak in terms of the group ("we") rather than themselves ("I"), even when they are describing work that they did for the team *on their own.* When describing work that has been done with others, it may seem trivial whether you have a tendency to use "I" rather than "we." In reality, though, Tannen suggests that this element of conversational style can have important consequences for things such as who gets credit for a job, and whether people are perceived as being "arrogant" or "a team player."

2. **The Tendency to Ask Questions**

In some environments, there's a lot of value placed on asking questions because doing so can stimulate productive discussions and help to ensure that people have a good understanding of the material. In other places, though, asking questions can have more negative consequences, including being taken as a sign of ignorance or being overly dependent.

3. **The Tendency to Apologize or Admit Fault**

For some, apologies of any sort are seen as a demonstration of weakness and something to be avoided at all costs. For others, though, a communication style that demonstrates a willingness to take responsibility is very positive and demonstrates a sign of maturity. It's noteworthy, though, that in some communication styles, "apologies" are really a reflection of concern rather than an admission of guilt. For example, "I'm sorry" can often mean "I'm sorry that happened to you," rather than "I apologize for what I did." While these "ritual apologies" may help to build good relationships, Tannen has noted that people who apologize frequently (even when it is an expression of concern) can be viewed as weaker and less confident than others.

4. **The Tendency to Be Direct**

The extent to which we speak in a direct manner—that is, in a fairly blunt way, without trying to "sugarcoat" things—has important implications for conversations, particularly those that involve making requests or providing criticism or feedback to others. Requests that are presented in an indirect way ("How would you like to help Sue with those reports?") rather than more directly ("Please help Sue with the reports") may be viewed as being more collegial, since they downplay power relationships. However, it's also possible that when a request is framed as a question in this way, people will not understand that they aren't really being given a choice.

Similar issues can arise when feedback is being provided on work that has been done. For example, people whose conversational style is focused more on promoting relationships may feel that it is important to begin a feedback session with praise that's aimed at what was done well, followed by areas for improvement. This approach allows the speaker to buffer the criticism that's to come. Unfortunately, it's possible that if the person receiving this type of feedback has a more direct approach to communicating, she will downplay the need for improvement (since it wasn't offered until the very end) and assume that the main point that's being made is that everything is going well (since that's how the feedback session began).

What's the Best Communication Style?

Having seen that communication styles can have important implications for how people are perceived by others, it's tempting to ask "What's the best communication style?" As you may have guessed from reading this section, though, the answer depends to some extent on the *impression that you're trying to convey.* For example, are you trying to present the impression of being in command, or are you more focused on building relationships? In addition, because communication is always two-sided, you also need to recognize that *the communication style of your partner may differ from your own, and will color his or her interpretation of your communication cues.* As a result, the "best" communication style has to take into account what you know about the person you're speaking with. Will they see your tendency to ask questions as a sign of engagement or incompetence? Will your direct style of speaking be viewed as callous or clear?

An important communication skill, then, is not just the ability to understand our own style, but to recognize that other people will have different tendencies and to consider whether it might be necessary to adjust the way we express ourselves to ensure that our goals can be met. Recognizing and responding to the diverse communication styles of others will help to minimize misunderstandings and ensure that you are being perceived by others in the way that you'd like to be seen.

Reflective Practice

Psychology and Your Skill Set: Effective Communication

1. The two types of communication are __________ and __________.
2. The two methods of verbal communication are __________ and __________.
3. What are the four main verbal communication skills?

THINK CRITICALLY

4. In what situation would the tendency to apologize be beneficial? In what situations would it be less effective?

SELF-REFLECT

- Reflect on your current communication style. Can you think of a situation—either in your personal life or at work—when your communication style has worked well? What about a situation when your communication style has been less effective?
- Can you remember a situation when you have experienced a "communication breakdown" with someone? What happened to cause the miscommunication?

Answers: 1. nonverbal and verbal 2. oral and written 3. speaking, listening, writing, reading 4. It would be beneficial to have the tendency to apologize in a situation that demonstrates you are mature and taking responsibility. It would be less effective if you apologize for something you are not responsible for, which can exhibit weakness and less confidence.

CHAPTER IN REVIEW

Gateways to Sensation, Attention, and Perception

Summary: Gateways Learning Outcomes

4.1 Sensation

4.1.1 Define sensation and transduction, and outline what happens in the sensory organs during transduction

Sensation is the process by which information from the world is gathered by the sensory organs and then sent on to the brain. Transduction is the process by which one form of energy is converted into another. The sense organs (eyes, ears, skin, tongue) transduce various forms of energy found in the environment (e.g., electromagnetic energy from light; mechanical energy from sound) into electrical energy in the form of action potentials so that the brain can understand the information taken in by the senses.

4.1.2 Distinguish between absolute threshold and difference threshold

Absolute threshold refers to the minimum amount of sensory input that must be present for physical energy (light; sound) to be detected 50 percent of the time. In contrast, *difference threshold* refers to the minimum difference that must exist between two stimuli for that difference to be detected 50 percent of the time.

4.1.3 Identify four ways by which the senses reduce the amount of information sent to the brain

The senses act as selective data selection systems to prevent the brain from being overwhelmed by sensory input. Four ways by which this happens are: a lack of specific transducers, the restricted range of transducers, sensory adaptation, and feature detection.

4.2 Vision

4.2.1 Describe three characteristics of light that are processed by the eye

The eye takes in information about hue (associated with the frequency or wavelength of the light wave), saturation (associated with the width of the band of wavelengths), and brightness (associated with the amplitude of the light wave).

4.2.2 Outline what is meant by accommodation in the eye, and the conditions that result from problems with accommodation

Accommodation refers to the eye's ability to focus, and is carried out by the lens. Four common visual defects are myopia, hyperopia, presbyopia, and astigmatism.

4.2.3 Describe the process of transduction in the eye, and two problems associated with color vision

The rods and cones are photoreceptors in the retina of the eye. The rods specialize in peripheral vision, night vision, seeing black and white, and detecting movement. The cones specialize in color vision, acuity, and daylight vision. People may experience *color blindness* (an inability to perceive color) or *color weakness* (an inability to see certain colors).

4.2.4 Contrast the trichromatic and opponent-process theories of color vision

Color vision is explained by the trichromatic theory within the retina itself, where three types of cones (red, blue, green) containing different pigments are responsible for generating action potentials. The opponent-process theory explains color vision beyond the retina, once the information about color is sent to the optic nerve.

4.3 Hearing

4.3.1 Describe two characteristics of sound that are processed by the ear

The ear takes in information about pitch (associated with the frequency of the sound wave) and loudness (associated with the amplitude of the sound wave).

4.3.2 Describe the process of transduction in the ear, and two associated forms of hearing loss

Sound waves are the stimulus for hearing. They are amplified and directed by the eardrum, auditory ossicles, and oval window to the cochlea, where they are transduced by the hair cells to generate action potentials. Two basic types of hearing loss are conductive hearing loss (caused when transfer of vibration from the outer ear to the inner ear weakens) and sensorineural hearing loss (caused when there is damage to the hair cells or auditory nerve). Noise-induced hearing loss is a common form of sensorineural hearing loss caused by exposure to loud noise.

4.3.3 Contrast the frequency and place theory of hearing pitch

Frequency theory (pitch corresponds to frequency of action potentials) explains how we hear tones up to 4,000 hertz; place theory (higher and lower tones are associated with excitation of different parts of the cochlea) explains it for tones above 4,000 hertz.

4.4 Chemical and Somesthetic Senses

4.4.1 Name the two chemical senses and three somesthetic senses

Olfaction (smell) and gustation (taste) are chemical senses that respond to airborne or liquefied molecules. The somesthetic senses include touch, the vestibular senses (responsible for balance), and kinesthetic senses (responsible for detecting the position of your body parts in space).

4.4.2 Describe the process of transduction in the nose

Receptors on nerve fibers in the nose are sensitive to various chemical molecules and create action potentials when they are stimulated. The lock-and-key theory of olfaction suggests different receptors have differently shaped "holes" that can bind with matching chemical molecules, creating the basis for a unique smell. In addition, the location of the olfactory receptors in the nose helps people identify various scents.

4.4.3 Describe the process of transduction on the tongue

There are five basic tastes: sweet, salt, sour, bitter, and umami. Sweet, bitter, and umami tastes are based on a lock-and-key coding of molecule shapes; when there is a match between receptors and the chemical molecules found in food an action potential is activated. Salty and sour tastes are triggered by a direct flow of ions into taste receptors, activating an action potential.

4.4.4 Describe the process of transduction on the skin, including the function of large and small nerve fibers in the sensation of pain

Receptors located on the skin have particular shapes that specialize in activating action potentials for specific sensations, but nerve endings in the skin can also activate action potentials directly. Warning pain (signaled by large nerve fibers) lets the body know that the body is (or is about to be) harmed. Reminding pain (signaled by small nerve fibers) reminds the body of a prior injury.

4.4.5 Describe the process of transduction in the vestibular system

Sacs called otolith organs in the inner ear respond to changes in gravity, acceleration, and movement through space, stimulating hair cells that activate action potentials. Balance is maintained through fluid in the ear's semicircular canals, which stimulates hair cells that create an action potential.

4.4.6 Define multimodal integration

Multimodal integration refers to the brain's ability to integrate the incoming sensory impressions from multiple senses.

4.5 Attention

4.5.1 Explain what research on multitasking has indicated with respect to the limits on attention

Multitasking research suggests that attention is limited and that rather than carrying out two tasks simultaneously, we typically switch rapidly between tasks. Task switching is easier when at least one of the tasks is well-practiced.

4.5.2 Identify four factors that influence whether we will pay attention to a stimulus

We are most likely to attend to stimuli that are intense, that are unexpected, that are personally important, and that help us to address our goals.

4.5.3 Describe the positive and negative effects of mind-wandering

Mind-wandering research has illuminated the fact that when we turn our attention inward from the environment, we are less able to respond to external conditions which can have negative consequences (e.g., traffic accidents; failure to learn from lectures). However, mind-wandering may promote creativity, relief from boredom, and the ability to plan for the future.

4.6 Perception

4.6.1 Describe the relationship between sensation and perception

Sensation is the process by which sensory organs take in information from the environment, while perception is the process by which the brain interprets that information.

4.6.2 Contrast bottom-up and top-down processing

Perceptions are based on simultaneous bottom-up and top-down processing. Complete perceptions can be assembled from small sensory features in "bottom-up" processing. In contrast, preexisting knowledge is applied to sensory information in "top-down" processing to help organize features into a meaningful whole. Top-down processes are at work when we work to separating figure and ground, as well as in the interpretation of reversible and ambiguous figures.

4.6.3 Explain how both sensory transduction and experience contribute to similarities and differences in perception

In many situations, people exposed to the same sensory input will have a similar perceptual experience. Such similarities often arise because sensory transduction typically proceeds the same way across individuals. However, perceptual similarities sometimes result from the fact that we have shared experiences that train the perceptual system in ways that are common across people, resulting in *perceptual constancies*. Perceptual constancies are "rules of thumb" developed by the brain as a product of years of experience interpreting the environment. They help the brain to quickly process incoming sensory information in ways that are usually accurate. Three examples are size, shape, and brightness constancy.

In some cases, though, people exposed to the same sensory input will have different perceptual experiences. These differences may result from transduction; specifically, differences in transduction can be the product of flaws in the genetic code, environmental trauma, and age-related decline. In all cases, transduction may not work in a typical way (or at all), leading to differences in perception. Experience may also play a role in perceptual differences, particularly when characteristics of the stimuli are ambiguous. In the case of #thedress, for example, the lighting was ambiguous, leading people to use their own unique "defaults" about lighting conditions to interpret the dress's color. Cultural differences may also have a role to play in our differing perceptual experiences.

4.6.4 Describe the effects of culture on the perception of the Müller-Lyer illusion

The Müller-Lyer illusion is the effect of seeing two straight lines—one with conventional arrowheads at its ends, and the other with V shapes at its ends—as being different lengths, even though they are actually the same. The effect is believed to stem from Western cultures' experience with the edges and corners of rooms and buildings. Indeed, in cultures that have little experience with straight lines (like the San of the Kalahari desert), individuals do not experience the illusion to the same extent.

4.6.5 Differentiate between monocular and binocular depth cues, giving examples of each

Depth perception depends on binocular cues (those that require two eyes) of retinal disparity and convergence. Depth perception also depends on monocular cues (those requiring one eye) that include accommodation and "pictorial" depth cues (linear perspective, relative size, height in the picture plane, light and shadow, overlap, texture gradients, and motion parallax).

4.6.6 Explain how depth cues are used in the world of art and by clinical psychologists using virtual reality to treat clients

Monocular pictoral depth cues are used by artists to create a sense of three dimensions on flat surfaces such as painting canvases. These same skills with depth cues are now being employed in the creation of realistic virtual reality worlds. Clinicians are now using virtual reality to assist clients with a range of problems, but particularly substance abuse disorders and anxiety disorders. VR technology allows clinicians to simulate real-life conditions for these clients, changing those conditions gradually as therapy progresses.

4.7 Psychology and Your Skill Set: Effective Communication

4.7.1 Distinguish between verbal and nonverbal communication

Two types of communication are nonverbal and verbal. Nonverbal communication refers to the perceptions of other's actions, such as people's tone of voice, body language, and eye contact. Verbal communication refers to words.

4.7.2 Outline two verbal communication methods and two verbal communication points of view

There are two verbal communication methods we use to transmit ideas (oral and written) and two verbal communication points of view (providing information or receiving information). The four verbal communication skills that can be developed depending on your method and point of view are: speaking, listening, writing, and reading.

4.7.3 Create a plan to improve your own communication with others

Being mindful of the speaker and being self-aware of your own cues can improve good listening skills. Writing and speaking skills can be improved by using words that are clear and concrete. When communicating with others, keep in mind that communication styles are guided by the extent to which people want to demonstrate power versus foster positive relationships, and include things such as directness and pacing, as well as the tendency to use jokes, questions, and apologies. We hope that after reading this section, you'll be better able to think about how you can use these strategies to help you communicate with others, but always be mindful of the fact that an optimal communication style involves taking into account the style of the person to whom you are writing or speaking.

5 States of Consciousness

Jamen Percy/Shutterstock.com

Gateway Theme Understanding states of consciousness can promote self-awareness and enhance personal effectiveness.

Chapter Outline

Blown Away

In Iceland, a hiker viewing the aurora borealis enters a fully conscious state of mindfulness.

In Brisbane, Australia, a graduate student drifts into a pleasant daydream while sitting at the back of class.

In Alaska, a long-haul trucker heads to a bar for a few drinks after a particularly stressful day.

In Boston, an aspiring actor is hypnotized to help reduce her stage fright.

In a Dallas hospital, a man lies deep in a coma after falling down a flight of stairs.

At a park in Amsterdam, a group of street musicians smoke a joint and sing for spare change.

In Scotland, a nun living in a convent spends an entire week in silent prayer and contemplation.

In Iowa, a college student downs some Ritalin to help her stay awake while studying for an important exam.

A short drive away from Niagara Falls, one of your authors brews himself another cup of cappuccino.

Each of these people is experiencing a different state of consciousness. Some have no choice, while others are deliberately seeking to alter their state of mind—in different ways, to different degrees, and for different reasons. As these examples suggest, consciousness can take many forms, some "mind blowing" and others … not so much. In this chapter, we'll explore different types of conscious experience ranging from dreams to drugs, and everything in between.

5.1 States of Consciousness—The Many Faces of Awareness

GATEWAYS LEARNING OUTCOMES:
After reading this section you should be able to:

5.1.1 Define consciousness

5.1.2 Distinguish between disordered states of consciousness and altered states of consciousness

To be *conscious* means to be aware. **Consciousness** consists of your awareness of external events in the environment around you, as well as your awareness of your mental processes, including thoughts, memories, and feelings about your experiences and yourself (Morin, 2006; Robinson, 2008). Take, for example, that hiker's profound moment in Iceland. As Donnie absorbed the sheer magnitude of the aurora borealis, he was "blown away" by deep feelings of insignificance and awe. In that instant, he was also fully aware that he *was* experiencing a deeply moving moment.

Although this definition of consciousness may seem obvious, it is based on your own introspective experience and it has limitations. While you may be the expert on *what* it feels like to be you, your subjective experience almost certainly offers no insight into *how* your brain gives rise to your consciousness or *why* you are conscious in the first place (Allen et al., 2013).

If you're thinking critically, you'll realize that a key challenge for psychology is to use objective studies to help us understand the mind and consciousness, which are basically subjective phenomena (Feinberg & Mallatt, 2016). Objectivity makes it possible to identify various states of consciousness and explore the role they play in our lives. This chapter summarizes some of what we have learned about those different states. To begin, let's examine the distinction between *disorders of consciousness* and *altered states of consciousness*. In subsequent sections of this chapter, we'll move on to look at several different ways that people achieve altered states of consciousness, including hypnosis, meditation, sleep, and drug use.

Disorders of Consciousness

We spend most of our lives in **waking consciousness**, a state of clear, organized alertness. In waking consciousness, we perceive times, places, and events as real and can respond to external stimuli. But many other states of consciousness are possible. For example, brain injury can result in anything from a short-lived disorientation to a **disorder of consciousness**—a long-term lack of consciousness and responsiveness (Monti, 2012; Schnakers & Laureys, 2012).

Disorders of consciousness have traditionally been difficult to accurately diagnose (Singh et al., 2013). You simply can't ask someone in a *coma*—a state of total unresponsiveness—if he or she can hear you or feel pain. But does the lack of responsiveness mean that a person is *brain dead* (De Tanti et al., 2016)? What if the person is *locked-in*, like Kate Adamson, whom we met earlier, in Section 2.4? (■ Recall that a damaged brain stem left Kate fully aware but almost totally unresponsive.)

Newer brain imaging methods, such as positron emission tomography (PET) and functional magnetic resonance imaging (fMRI) (■ see Section 2.2), promise to improve the diagnosis of disorders of consciousness while also shedding light on consciousness itself. In one study, normal individuals and patients in a *persistent vegetative state*—a longer-term waking state without any signs of awareness—were administered a mildly painful stimulus. Normal individuals consciously reported feeling pain, while vegetative patients did not, as expected. PET scans revealed brain activity in the midbrain, thalamus, and somatosensory cortex of both normal individuals and vegetative patients. However, only the normal individuals in this study showed activity in the frontal areas of the cortex, implying that these brain regions must be functional in order for someone to have a conscious experience of pain (Laureys et al., 2002).

In light of findings such as these, doctors can be more confident that patients diagnosed in a persistent vegetative state who also show no frontal cortical activity in response to pain are likely feeling no pain. At the same time, results such as these suggest that frontal lobe activity is central to conscious experience. Echoing Kate Adamson's experience of being locked-in, an fMRI investigation of patients in a persistent vegetative state showed varying degrees of frontal cortical activity. Some of them, for example, showed a frontal cortex response to hearing their own names (Bick et al., 2013).

There can be little doubt that studies such as these are beginning to improve diagnostic accuracy while illuminating the complex brain circuitry underlying our conscious experience (Askenasy & Lehmann, 2013; Långsjö et al., 2012).

Altered States of Consciousness

Many other states of conscious also differ from normal awareness, including states of consciousness related to fatigue, delirium, hypnosis, drugs, and euphoria (Chalmers, 2010). Everyone experiences at least some altered states, such as sleep, dreaming, and daydreaming. In everyday life, changes in consciousness may even accompany long-distance running, listening to music, making love, or other circumstances.

How are altered states distinguished from normal awareness? During an **altered state of consciousness (ASC)**, changes occur in the *quality* and *pattern* of mental activity. Typically, distinct shifts happen in our perceptions, emotions, memories, time sense, thoughts, feelings of self-control, and suggestibility (Hohwy & Fox, 2012). Definitions aside, just like our hiker, Donnie, most people know when they have experienced an ASC. In fact, heightened self-awareness is an important feature of many ASCs (Revonsuo, Kallio, & Sikka, 2009).

Human Diversity and Altered States of Consciousness

In some instances, altered states have important cultural meanings. One dramatic example is the regular consumption of a mind-altering potion called ayahuasca. Considered a psychedelic sacrament by members of Uniao do Vegetal (UDV), a Brazilian religion, twice-monthly consumption of ayahuasca is believed to foster a deeper connection with nature, improving physical, emotional, and spiritual well-being. Like Buddhists engaging in meditation practices, Turkish whirling dervishes entranced by their twirling dance, or New Zealand Maori priests performing nightlong rituals to communicate with the mythical period that the Aborigines call "Dreamtime," the ritual use of ayahuasca is meant to cleanse the mind and body. When they are especially intense, such experiences can bring altered awareness and personal revelation (de Rios & Grob, 2005).

People seek some altered states purely for pleasure or escape, as is often true of drug intoxication. Yet as the UDV illustrates, many cultures regard altered consciousness as a pathway to personal enlightenment. Indeed, all cultures and most religions recognize and accept some alterations of consciousness. However, the meaning given to these states varies greatly—from signs of "madness" and "possession" by spirits to life-enhancing breakthroughs. Thus, cultural conditioning greatly affects what altered states we recognize, seek, consider normal, and attain (Cardeña et al., 2011).

What are some of the other causes of ASCs? In addition to the ones mentioned, we could add sensory overload (a rave, Mardi Gras crowd, or mosh pit), monotonous stimulation (such as "highway hypnotism" on long drives), unusual physical conditions (high fever, hyperventilation, dehydration, sleep loss, near-death experiences), restricted sensory input (extended periods of isolation), and many other possibilities. Let's continue with a more detailed look at two interesting altered states, hypnosis and meditation, before turning our attention to sleep, dreams, and drug use in the sections that follow.

John Mitterer

In many cultures, rituals of healing, prayer, meditation, purification, or personal transformation at sites like this Buddhist temple near Hong Kong are accompanied by altered states of consciousness.

5.2 Hypnosis and Meditation: Relax ...

GATEWAYS LEARNING OUTCOMES:
After reading this section you should be able to:

5.2.1 Describe how hypnosis works, distinguishing between state and nonstate theories of hypnosis

5.2.2 Describe how meditation works, distinguishing between mindfulness and concentrative meditation

Many people are familiar with hypnosis and meditation, even if they don't have any personal experience with them. Though they are both considered altered states of consciousness, there are some important differences between them. Let's take a closer look at each one.

Hypnosis

"Your body is becoming heavy. You can barely keep your eyes open. You are so tired you can't move. Relax. Let go. Close your eyes and relax." These are the last words that a textbook should probably ever say to you, but they are among the first that a hypnotist might say.

Interest in hypnosis began in the 1700s with Austrian doctor Franz Mesmer, whose name gave us the term *mesmerize* (to hypnotize). Mesmer believed that he could cure disease with magnets. Mesmer's strange "treatments" are related to hypnosis because they relied on the power of suggestion, not magnetism (Hammond, 2013). Think carefully for a moment and you'll likely see that what Mesmer's patients were demonstrating was the placebo effect (■ see Section 1.6). For a time, Mesmer enjoyed quite a following. In the end, however, his theories of "animal magnetism" were rejected and he was branded a fraud.

Ever since, stage hypnotists have entertained us with a combination of little or no hypnosis and a bit of deception. On stage, people are unusually cooperative because they don't want to "spoil the act." As a result, they readily follow almost any instruction given by the entertainer. After volunteers loosen up and respond to a few suggestions, they find that they are suddenly the stars of the show. Audience response to the antics on stage brings out the "ham" in many people. No hypnosis is required; all the "hypnotist" needs to do is direct the action. It's worth noting that some of this action makes liberal use of deception. One of the more impressive stage tricks is to rigidly suspend a person between two chairs. This is astounding only

Consciousness An organism's awareness of its external environment and internal mental processes.

Waking consciousness A state of clear, organized alertness.

Disorder of consciousness A condition of awareness that is atypical (e.g., coma; persistent vegetative state).

Altered state of consciousness (ASC) A condition of awareness distinctly different in quality or pattern from waking consciousness.

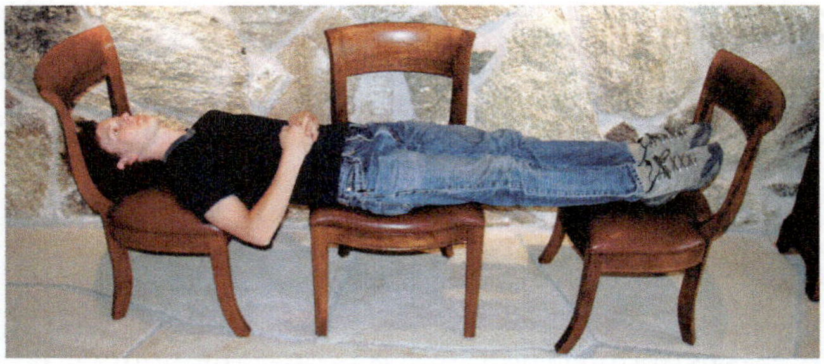

Figure 5.1 The chair suspension trick. Arrange three chairs as shown. Have someone recline as shown. Ask him or her to lift slightly while you remove the middle chair. Accept the applause gracefully! (Concerning hypnosis and similar phenomena, the moral, of course, is "Suspend judgment until you have something solid to stand on.")

because the audience does not question it. Anyone can do it, as is shown in the photographs and instructions in Figure 5.1. Try it!

Entertainment aside, hypnosis is a real phenomenon. The term *hypnosis* was coined by English surgeon James Braid. The Greek word *hypnos* means "sleep," and Braid used it to describe the hypnotic state. Today, we know that hypnosis is *not* sleep. Confusion about this point remains because some hypnotists give the suggestion, "Sleep, sleep." However, brain activity recorded during hypnosis is different from that observed when a person is asleep or pretending to be hypnotized (Del Casale et al., 2012; Kihlstrom, 2013; Santarcangelo & Scattina, 2016).

Theories of Hypnosis

If hypnosis isn't sleep, then what is it? That's a good question. **Hypnosis** is currently defined as a state of consciousness characterized by focused attention, reduced peripheral awareness, and heightened suggestibility (Elkins et al., 2015). Notice that this definition suggests that hypnosis may be a distinct *state* of consciousness.

The best-known *state theory* of hypnosis was proposed by Ernest Hilgard (1904–2001), who argued that hypnosis causes a *dissociative state*, or "split" in awareness. To illustrate, he asked hypnotized participants to plunge one hand into a painful bath of ice water. Participants told to feel no pain said they felt none. The same participants were then asked if any part of their mind did feel pain. With their free hand, many wrote, "It hurts," or "Stop it, you're hurting me," while they continued to act pain-free (Hilgard, 1977, 1994). Thus, one part of the hypnotized person says there is no pain and acts as if there is none. Another part, which Hilgard calls the *hidden observer*, is aware of the pain but remains in the background. The **hidden observer** is a detached part of the hypnotized person's awareness that silently watches events.

Not everyone believes that hypnosis is a distinct state of consciousness. *Nonstate theorists* argue that hypnosis is merely a blend of conformity, relaxation, imagination, obedience, and role-playing (Lynn et al., 2015; Lynn & O'Hagen, 2009). For example, many theorists believe that all hypnosis is really self-hypnosis (*autosuggestion*). From this perspective, a hypnotist merely helps another person follow a series of suggestions. These suggestions, in turn, alter sensations, perceptions, thoughts, feelings, and behaviors (Lynn & Kirsch, 2006). Autosuggestion also plays a role in many forms of self-therapy (Yapko, 2011).

Regardless of which theoretical approach finally prevails, both views suggest that hypnosis works through principles that can be explained.

How Hypnosis Works

How is hypnosis done? Could I be hypnotized against my will? Hypnotists use many different methods. Still, all techniques encourage a person to (1) focus attention on what is being said, (2) relax and feel tired, (3) "let go" and accept suggestions easily, and (4) use a vivid imagination (Barabasz & Watkins, 2005). Basically, you must cooperate to become hypnotized.

What does it feel like to be hypnotized? You might be surprised at some of your actions during hypnosis. You also might have mild feelings of floating, sinking, anesthesia, or separation from your body. Personal experiences vary widely. A key element in hypnosis is the **basic suggestion effect**—a tendency of hypnotized persons to carry out suggested actions as if they were involuntary. Hypnotized persons feel like their actions and experiences are *automatic*—they seem to happen without effort.

To gain insight into autosuggestion, tie a string to a ring and hold the ring at eye level, near your face. Don't intentionally swing the ring. Instead, concentrate and mentally push the ring ever so slightly away from you. Then release it and let it swing back toward you. Continue to mentally push and release the ring until it is swinging freely. If the ring seems to move on its own, you used autosuggestion to influence your own behavior. Suggestions that the ring would swing caused your hand to make tiny micromuscular movements. These, in turn, caused the ring to move.

Contrary to how hypnosis is portrayed in movies, hypnotized people generally remain in control of their behavior and are aware of what is going on. For instance, most people will not act out hypnotic suggestions that they consider immoral or repulsive, such as disrobing in public or harming someone (Kirsch & Lynn, 1995).

Hypnotizability

Can everyone be hypnotized? About 75 percent of people can be hypnotized, but only 40 percent will be good hypnotic participants. People who are imaginative and prone to fantasy are often highly responsive to hypnosis (Hoeft et al., 2012). But people who lack these traits also may be hypnotized. If you are willing to be hypnotized, chances are good that you could be. Hypnosis depends more on the efforts and abilities of the hypnotized person than the skills of the hypnotist. But make no mistake: People who are hypnotized are not merely faking their responses.

Hypnotizability refers to how easily a person can become hypnotized (Elkins et al., 2015). It is measured by giving a series of suggestions and counting the number of times a person responds. The *Stanford Hypnotic Susceptibility Scale*, shown in ▲ Table 5.1, is a typical test of hypnotizability. In the test, various suggestions are made, and the person's response is noted. For instance, you might be told that your left arm is becoming more and more rigid and that it will not bend. If you can't bend your arm during the next 10 seconds, you have shown you are hypnotizable.

▲ Table 5.1 Stanford Hypnotic Susceptibility Scale

Suggested Behavior	Criterion of Passing
1. Postural sway	Falls without forcing
2. Eye closure	Closes eyes without forcing
3. Hand lowering (left)	Lowers at least 6 inches by end of 10 seconds
4. Immobilization (right arm)	Arm rises less than 1 inch in 10 seconds
5. Finger lock	Incomplete separation of fingers at end of 10 seconds
6. Arm rigidity (left arm)	Less than 2 inches of arm bending in 10 seconds
7. Hands moving together	Hands at least as close as 6 inches after 10 seconds
8. Verbal inhibition (name)	Name unspoken in 10 seconds
9. Hallucination (fly)	Any movement, grimacing, acknowledgment of effect
10. Eye catalepsy	Eyes remain closed at end of 10 seconds
11. Posthypnotic (changes chairs)	Any partial movement response
12. Amnesia test	Three or fewer items recalled

Adapted from Weitzenhoffer & Hilgard (1959).

Effects of Hypnosis

What can (and cannot) be achieved with hypnosis? Many abilities have been tested during hypnosis, leading to the following conclusions:

1. **Physical ability.** Hypnosis may improve some physical abilities in some sports (Tramontana, 2011), although it has no more effect on physical strength than instructions that encourage a person to make his or her best effort (Chaves, 2000).
2. **Memory.** Some evidence shows that hypnosis can enhance memory (Wester & Hammond, 2011). However, it frequently increases the number of false memories as well. For this reason, many states now bar persons from testifying in court if they were hypnotized to improve their memory of a crime that they witnessed. (■ Should the police use hypnosis to enhance the memories of witnesses? The evidence generally says no. See Section 7.5.)
3. **Amnesia.** A person told to forget something heard during hypnosis may claim not to remember. In some instances, this may be nothing more than a deliberate attempt to avoid thinking about specific ideas. However, brief memory loss of this type does seem to occur (Barnier, McConkey, & Wright, 2004).
4. **Pain relief.** Hypnosis can relieve pain (Baad-Hansen et al., 2013; Hammond, 2008; Kohen, 2011). It can be especially useful when chemical painkillers are ineffective. For instance, hypnosis can reduce phantom limb pain (Oakley, Whitman, & Halligan, 2002).
5. **Sensory changes.** Hypnotic suggestions concerning sensations are among the most effective. Given the proper instructions, a person can be made to smell a small bottle of ammonia and respond as if it were a wonderful perfume. It also is possible to alter color vision, hearing sensitivity, time sense, perception of illusions, and many other sensory responses.

Generally speaking, hypnosis is more successful at changing subjective experience than it is at modifying behaviors such as smoking or overeating. Nonetheless, like meditation, which we explore next, hypnosis is a valuable tool in a variety of settings (Yapko, 2011). It can help people relax, feel less pain, and make better progress in therapy (Lynn, Kirsch, & Rhue, 2010).

Meditation

Meditation is a mental exercise used to alter consciousness. In general, meditation heightens awareness and produces relaxation by interrupting the typical flow of thoughts, worries, and analysis.

Hypnosis State of consciousness characterized by focused attention, reduced peripheral awareness, and heightened suggestibility.

Hidden observer A detached part of the hypnotized person's awareness that silently watches events.

Basic suggestion effect The tendency of hypnotized persons to carry out suggested actions as if they were involuntary.

Hypnotizability One's capacity for becoming hypnotized.

Meditation Mental exercise for producing relaxation or heightened awareness.

People who use meditation to reduce stress often report less daily physical tension and anxiety (Hosemans, 2014; Vago & Nakamura, 2011). Brain scans (such as PET and fMRI) reveal changes in brain activity during meditation, including the frontal lobes, suggesting that it may be a distinct state of consciousness (Fox et al., 2016; Lutz et al., 2016).

Meditation takes two major forms. **Mindfulness meditation** is "open," or expansive. The aim is to observe your own thoughts, feelings, and sensations without reacting to them. Ultimately, the goal is to achieve a total, nonjudgmental awareness of the world (Hölzel et al., 2011). An example is becoming fully consciousness while walking in the wilderness with a quiet and receptive mind, just like Donnie's aurora borealis experience.

Psychologists interested in positive mental states have begun to study the effects of mindfulness. For example, cancer patients who are taught mindfulness meditation have lower levels of distress and a greater sense of well-being (Jones et al., 2013). Similarly, being mindful makes it easier to quit smoking (Brewer et al., 2011). Such benefits apply to healthy people, too. In general, mindfulness is associated with self-knowledge and well-being (Ameli, 2014; Friese, Messner, & Schaffner, 2012). Anyone who has a tendency to sleepwalk through life—and that's most of us at times—would be wise to be mindful of the value of mindfulness.

In contrast, **concentrative meditation** techniques such as transcendental meditation involve attending to a single focal point, such as an object, a thought, or your own breathing. The basic idea is to sit still and quietly focus on some external object or on a repetitive internal stimulus, such as your own breathing or humming. Alternatively, you can silently repeat a *mantra* (a word used as the focus of attention in concentrative meditation). Typical mantras are smooth, flowing sounds that are easily repeated. A widely used mantra is the word *om*. A mantra also could be any pleasant word or a phrase from a familiar song, poem, or prayer. If other thoughts arise as you repeat a mantra, just return attention to it as often as necessary to maintain meditation.

The Relaxation Response

Researcher Herbert Benson believes that the core of meditation is the **relaxation response**—an innate physiological pattern that opposes your body's fight-or-flight mechanisms (Chang, Dusek, & Benson, 2011). Benson feels, quite simply, that most of us have forgotten how to relax deeply. People in his experiments learned to produce the relaxation response by following instructions such as these:

> Sit quietly and comfortably. Close your eyes. Relax your muscles, beginning at your feet and progressing up to your head. Relax them deeply. Become aware of breathing through your nose. As you breathe out, say a word like "peace" silently to yourself. Don't worry about how successful you are in relaxing deeply. Just let relaxation happen at its own pace. Don't be surprised by distracting thoughts. When they occur, ignore them and continue repeating "peace." (Adapted from Chang, Dusek, & Benson, 2011; Hölzel et al., 2011.)

Meditation may be a good stress-control technique for people who want to bring about the relaxation response but struggle to "turn off" upsetting thoughts. In one study, a group of college students who received just 90 minutes of training in the relaxation response experienced greatly reduced stress levels (Deckro et al., 2002). The physical benefits of meditation include lowered heart rate, blood pressure, muscle tension, and other signs of stress (Zeidan et al., 2010), as well as improved immune system activity (Davidson et al., 2003).

According to Shauna Shapiro and Roger Walsh (2006), meditation has benefits beyond relaxation. Practiced regularly, meditation may foster mental well-being and positive mental skills such as clarity, concentration, and calm. In this sense, meditation may share much in common with psychotherapy. Indeed, research has shown that mindfulness meditation relieves a variety of psychological disorders, from insomnia to excessive anxiety. It also can reduce aggression and the use of psychoactive drugs (Brewer et al., 2011; Shapiro & Walsh, 2006). Regular meditation may even help people develop enhanced attentional control, self-awareness, and creativity (Hodgins & Adair, 2010; Müller, Gerasimova, & Ritter, 2016).

The Relaxation Response and Sensory Deprivation

Imagine floating in a tank of warm water, for a short while, without the least bit of muscle tension. You cannot hear anything, and it is pitch dark. You are experiencing brief *sensory deprivation*, a major reduction in the amount or variety of sensory stimulation.

What happens when stimulation is greatly reduced like this? A hint comes from reports by prisoners in solitary confinement, Arctic explorers, high-altitude pilots, long-distance truck drivers, and radar operators. When faced with limited or monotonous stimulation, people sometimes have bizarre sensations, dangerous lapses in attention, and wildly distorted perceptions. Intense or prolonged sensory deprivation is stressful and disorienting.

Yet, oddly enough, brief periods of sensory restriction can produce a strong relaxation response (Bood et al., 2006). An hour or two spent in a flotation tank can cause a large drop in blood

Pixtal/SuperStock

Psychologists have used small flotation tanks like this one to study the effects of mild sensory deprivation. Participants float in darkness and silence. The shallow, body-temperature water contains hundreds of pounds of Epsom salts, so participants float near the surface. Mild sensory deprivation produces deep relaxation.

pressure, muscle tension, chronic pain, and other signs of stress (Bood et al., 2006; Kjellgren, Buhrkall, & Norlander, 2011). And like other forms of meditation, mild sensory deprivation also may help with more than relaxation. Deep relaxation makes people more open to suggestion, and sensory deprivation interrupts habitual behavior patterns. This can loosen belief systems, making it easier for people to quit smoking, lose weight, and reduce their use of alcohol and drugs (Suedfeld & Borrie, 1999; van Dierendonck & Te Nijenhuis, 2005). Mild sensory deprivation even shows promise as a way to stimulate creative thinking and enhance sports and music performance skills (Norlander, Bergman, & Archer, 1998, 1999; Vartanian & Suedfeld, 2011).

Reflective Practice

States of Consciousness; Hypnosis and Meditation

1. Changes in the quality and pattern of mental activity define a(n) ________________.
   a. EEG
   b. REM
   c. SIDS
   d. ASC
2. In Ernest Hilgard's dissociative state theory of hypnosis, awareness is split between normal consciousness and ________________.
   a. disinhibition
   b. autosuggestion
   c. memory
   d. the hidden observer
3. Which of the following is most likely to be achieved via hypnosis?
   a. unusual strength
   b. pain relief
   c. improved memory
   d. sleeplike brain waves
4. The focus of attention in concentrative meditation is "open," or expansive. T or F?
5. Mantras are words said silently to oneself to end a session of meditation. T or F?
6. The most immediate benefit of meditation appears to be its capacity for producing the relaxation response. T or F?

THINK CRITICALLY

7. Regular meditators report lower levels of stress and a greater sense of well-being. Evaluate the other explanations that we must we eliminate before this effect can be regarded as genuine.

SELF-REFLECT

- Make a quick list of some altered states of consciousness that you have experienced. What do they have in common? How are they different? What conditions caused them?
- How have your beliefs about hypnosis changed after reading the preceding section? Can you think of specific examples in which hypnosis was misrepresented—for example, in movies or on television?
- Various activities can produce the relaxation response. When do you experience states of deep relaxation, coupled with a sense of serene awareness?

Answers: 1. d 2. d 3. b 4. F 5. F 6. T 7. Studies on the effects of meditation must control for the placebo effect and the fact that those who choose to learn meditation may not be a representative sample of the general population.

5.3 Sleep: The Nightly Roller Coaster

GATEWAYS LEARNING OUTCOMES:
After reading this section you should be able to:

5.3.1 Describe the typical pattern of sleeping and waking

5.3.2 Describe NREM (non-REM) sleep, including its function and four stages

5.3.3 Describe REM sleep and its function

5.3.4 Explain why we need to sleep, and the consequences of not sleeping

5.3.5 Name and briefly describe the three theories of dreaming

5.3.6 Outline five sleep disorders

Each of us will spend some 25 years of life asleep. Because sleep is familiar, many people think they know all about it. But many commonsense beliefs about sleep are false. For example, you are not totally unresponsive during sleep. A sleeping mother may ignore a jet thundering overhead but wake at the slightest whimper of her child. Likewise, you are more likely to awaken if you hear your own name spoken instead of another. It's even possible to do simple tasks while asleep. In one experiment, people learned to avoid an electric shock by touching a switch each time a tone sounded, without waking. (This is much like the basic survival skill of turning off your alarm clock without waking.)

Let's begin to explore what we know about sleep (while awake, of course).

Sleep Patterns

You sleep, dream occasionally, and wake up. What's to know? Sleep is not as simple as it might seem—research has revealed that it is a complex phenomenon and it is still not completely understood. Sleep is an innate **biological rhythm** that never can be entirely ignored (Luyster et al., 2012). Rhythms of sleep and waking are usually so steady that they continue for many days, even when clocks and light–dark cycles are removed. However, under such conditions, humans eventually shift to sleep–waking cycles that

Mindfulness meditation Mental exercise based on widening attention to become aware of everything experienced at any given moment.

Concentrative meditation Mental exercise based on attending to a single object or thought.

Relaxation response The pattern of internal bodily changes that occurs at times of relaxation.

Biological rhythm Any repeating cycle of biological activity, such as sleep and waking cycles or changes in body temperature.

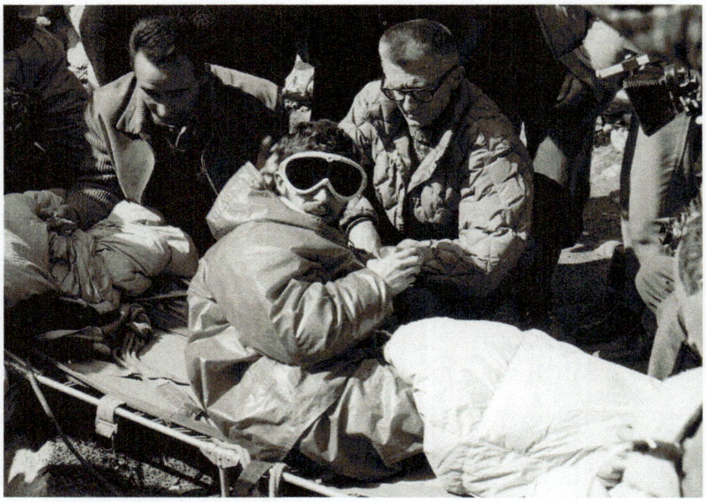

Keystone-France/Getty Images

Frenchman Michel Siffre has spent months at a time living in caves deep underground without the usual external markers of night and day. He found that without these markers, his sleep cycles tended to get longer. During one such stay, he settled into a 48-hour sleep–waking cycle.

average more than 24 hours (Czeisler et al., 1999; Eastman et al., 2012). This suggests that external time markers, especially light and dark, help tie our sleep rhythms to days that are exactly 24 hours long. Otherwise, many of us would drift into our own unusual sleep cycles (Kovrov et al., 2012). (■ Sleep cycles can be disrupted by rapid travel across time zones [jet lag] and by shift work. See Section 10.2 for more information.)

What is the normal range of sleep? The majority of us sleep on a familiar seven-to-eight-hour-per-night schedule. Only a small percentage of the population are *short sleepers*, averaging five hours of sleep or fewer per night. On the other end of the scale, we find *long sleepers*, who doze nine hours or more (Grandner & Kripke, 2004). A few rare individuals can even get by on an hour or two of sleep a night—and feel perfectly fine. Urging everyone to sleep eight hours would be like advising everyone to wear medium-size clothing.

We sleep less as we get older, right? Yes, total sleep time declines throughout life. Infants spend up to 20 hours a day sleeping, usually in two- to four-hour cycles. As they mature, most children go through a nap stage and eventually settle into a steady cycle of sleeping once a day. In contrast, those older than 50 average only six hours of sleep a night. Mid-afternoon sleepiness is a natural part of the sleep cycle. Perhaps we should all continue to take an afternoon siesta. Brief, well-timed naps can help maintain alertness in people such as truck drivers and hospital interns, who often must fight to stay alert (Ficca et al., 2010).

Busy people may be tempted to sleep less. However, people on *shortened* cycles—for example, three hours of sleep to six hours awake—often can't get to sleep when the cycle calls for it. Adapting to *longer*-than-normal days is more promising. Such days can be tailored to match natural sleep patterns, which have a ratio of 2 to 1 between time awake and time asleep (16 hours awake and 8 hours asleep). For instance, one study showed that 28-hour "days" work for some people. Overall, sleep patterns may be bent and stretched, but they rarely yield entirely to human whims (Åkerstedt, 2007; Sallinen et al., 2017).

The Stages of Sleep

Recordings of changes in electrical activity in the brain (brain waves) reveal that sleep also progresses through several stages every night (Pagel, 2012). When you are awake and alert, the **electroencephalograph (EEG)** (eh-LEK-tro-en-SEF-uh-lo-graf) reveals a pattern of small, fast waves called **beta waves** (● Figure 5.2). Immediately before sleep, the pattern shifts to larger and slower waves called **alpha waves**. (Alpha waves also occur when you are relaxed and allow your thoughts to drift.) As the eyes close, breathing becomes slow and regular, the pulse rate slows, and body temperature

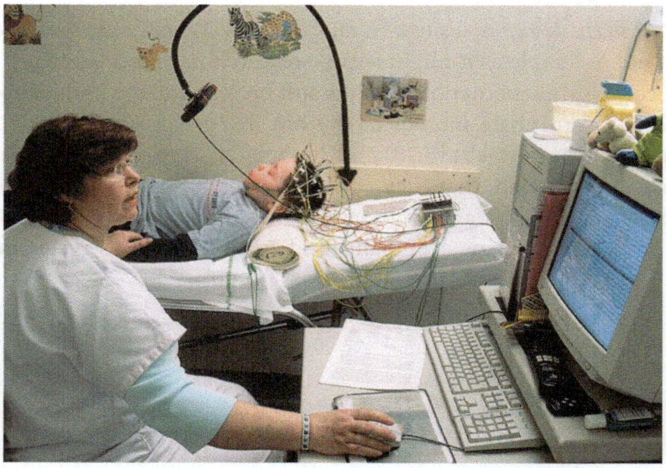

ASTIER-CHRU LILLE/BSIP/Superstock

(a)

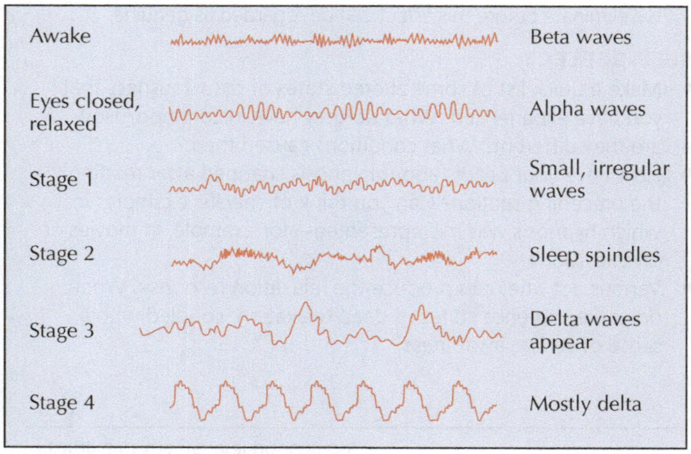

(b)

● **Figure 5.2 Stages of sleep.** (a) Photograph of an EEG recording session. The boy in the background is asleep. (b) Changes in brain-wave patterns associated with various stages of sleep. Most wave types are present at all times, but they occur more or less frequently in various sleep stages.

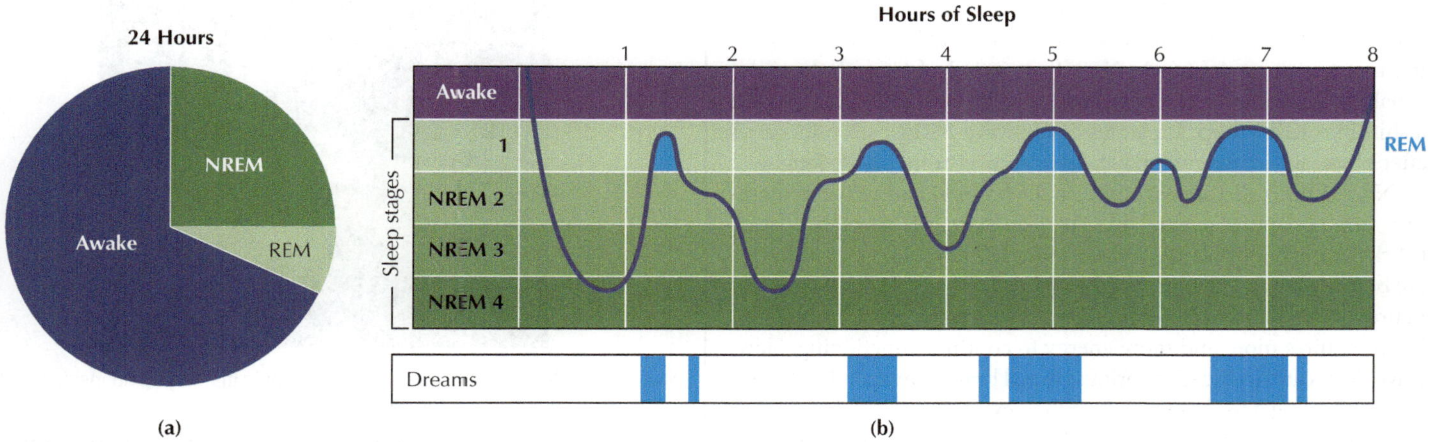

Figure 5.3 REM and NREM sleep. (a) Average proportion of time adults spend daily in REM sleep and NREM sleep. REM periods add up to about 20 percent of total sleep time. (b) Typical changes in stages of sleep during the night. Note that dreams mostly coincide with REM periods.

drops. Soon after, we descend into *slow-wave sleep* through four distinct **sleep stages**.

But your nights involve much more than simply moving through the four stages of deeper, slow-wave sleep. Fluctuations in sleep hormones mean that we also experience periods of lighter sleep as well (Steiger, 2007; Figure 5.3). During these repeated periods of lighter sleep, a curious thing happens: the sleeper's eyes occasionally move under the eyelids. If you ever get a chance to watch a sleeping child, roommate, or spouse, you may see these **rapid eye movements (REMs)**. In addition, **REM sleep** is characterized by dreaming and is marked by a return of high-frequency brain waves similar to Stage 1 sleep. In fact, the brain is so active during REM sleep that it looks as if the person is awake.

The two most basic states of sleep, then, are **non-REM (NREM) sleep**, which occurs during all four sleep stages, and REM sleep, with its associated dreaming (Rock, 2004). Let's take a closer look at each one.

The Four Stages of non-REM Sleep

1. **Stage 1**
   As you enter **light sleep (Stage 1 sleep)**, your heart rate slows even more. Breathing becomes more irregular. The muscles of your body relax. This may trigger a reflex muscle twitch called a *hypnic* (HIP-nik: sleep) *jerk*. (This is quite normal, so have no fear about admitting to your friends that you fell asleep with a hypnic jerk.) In Stage 1 sleep, the EEG is made up mainly of small, irregular waves, with some alpha waves. Persons awakened at this time may or may not say that they were asleep.

2. **Stage 2**
   As sleep deepens, body temperature drops further. Also, the EEG begins to include **sleep spindles**, which are short bursts of distinctive brain-wave activity generated by the thalamus (Caporro et al., 2012). Sleep spindles may help prevent the sleeping brain from being aroused by external stimuli, thus marking the true boundary of sleep (Dang-Vu et al., 2010). Within a few minutes after spindles appear, most people will say they were asleep.

3. **Stage 3**
   In Stage 3, very large and slow **delta waves** begin to appear. They signal a move to deeper slow-wave sleep and a further loss of consciousness.

4. **Stage 4**
   Most people reach **deep sleep (Stage 4 sleep)**—the deepest level of normal sleep—in about an hour. Stage 4 brain waves are almost pure slow-wave delta, and the sleeper is in a state of oblivion. If a sleeper hears a loud noise during Stage 4, he or she will wake up in a state of confusion and may not remember the noise.

Electroencephalograph (EEG) Device that records electrical activity in the brain.

Beta waves Small, fast brain waves associated with being awake and alert.

Alpha waves Large, slow brain waves associated with relaxation and falling asleep.

Sleep stages Levels of sleep identified by brain-wave patterns and behavioral changes.

Rapid eye movements (REMs) Swift eye movements during sleep.

REM sleep Stage of sleep marked by rapid eye movements, high-frequency brain waves, and dreaming.

Non-REM (NREM) sleep Non-rapid eye movement sleep characteristic of sleep Stages 1, 2, 3, and 4.

Light sleep (Stage 1 sleep) Marked by small, irregular brain waves and some alpha waves.

Sleep spindles Distinctive bursts of brain-wave activity that indicate a person is asleep.

Delta waves Large, slow brain waves that occur in deeper sleep (Stages 3 and 4).

Deep sleep (Stage 4 sleep) The deepest form of normal sleep.

So what's the function of non-REM sleep? NREM sleep is dream-free about 90 percent of the time and is deepest early in the night during the first few Stage 4 periods. Your first period of Stage 1 sleep also usually lacks REMs and dreams. Later Stage 1 periods typically include a shift into REM sleep. Dreamless, slow-wave NREM sleep increases after physical exertion and may help us recover from bodily fatigue.

NREM sleep also appears to calm the brain in part to begin memory consolidation during the earlier part of a night's sleep (Diekelmann & Born, 2010; Holz et al., 2012). The basic idea is that we are bombarded by information throughout the day, which causes our neural networks to become more and more active. As a result, your brain requires more and more energy to continue functioning. Slow-wave sleep early in the night brings overall brain activation levels back down, allowing a fresh approach to the next day.

Consider for a moment the rich jumble of events that make up a day. Some experiences are worth remembering (like what you are reading right now, of course), and others are not so important (like which sock you put on first this morning). As slow-wave sleep reduces overall activation in the brain, less important experiences may fade away and be forgotten. If you wake up feeling clearer about what you studied the previous night, it might be because your brain doesn't "sweat the small stuff"!

REM Sleep and Dreaming

The brain areas associated with imagery and emotion become more active during REM sleep, likely owing to the fact that REM sleep is associated with dreaming (Gujar et al., 2011). Although not all people remember their dreams upon awakening in the morning, people awakened during REMs report vivid dreams roughly 85 percent of the time. In fact, "nondreamers" are often surprised by their dreams when first awakened during REM sleep.

REM dreaming is often accompanied by eye movements. Dream that you are watching a tennis match, and you will probably move your eyes from side to side. REM sleep is easy to observe in pets, such as dogs and cats. Watch for eye and face movements and irregular breathing. (You can forget about your pet iguana, though. Reptiles show no signs of REM sleep.)

What else happens to the body when a person dreams? REM sleep is a time of high emotion (Gujar et al., 2011). The heart beats irregularly. Blood pressure and breathing waver. Both males and females appear to be sexually aroused. This occurs for all REM sleep, so it is not strictly related to erotic dreams.

Paradoxically, during REM sleep, your body becomes quite still, as if you were paralyzed. To understand why, imagine for a moment the results of acting out some of your recent dreams. Very likely, REM-sleep paralysis prevents some hilarious—and dangerous—nighttime escapades. When it fails, some people thrash violently, leap out of bed, and may attack their bed partners. A lack of muscle paralysis during REM sleep is called *REM behavior disorder* (Neikrug & Ancoli-Israel, 2012). One patient suffering from the disorder tied himself to his bed every night. That way, he couldn't jump up and crash into furniture or walls (Shafton, 1995).

Sometimes sleep paralysis can go a little too far. While it normally prevents us from moving during REM sleep, it can occur just as you begin to wake up. During such episodes, people sometimes have *hypnopompic* (hip-neh-POM-pik: "upon awakening") hallucinations, including bizarre experiences, such as sensing that an alien being is in your bedroom; feeling something pressing on your chest, suffocating you; or feeling like you are floating out of your body (D'Agostino & Limosani, 2010; Waters et al., 2016).

Swiss artist Henry Fuseli drew on hypnopompic imagery as an inspiration for his famous painting *The Nightmare*.

Although most of us shrug off these weird experiences, some people try to make sense of them. Earlier in history, people interpreted these hallucinated intruders as angels, demons, or witches and believed that their out-of-body experiences were real (Cheyne & Girard, 2009). However, as our culture changes, so do our interpretations of sleep experiences. Today, for example, some people who have sleep-related hallucinations believe they have been abducted by space aliens or sexually abused (McNally & Clancy, 2005).

Superstitions and folklore often develop as attempts to explain human experiences, including some of the stranger aspects of sleep. By studying unusual experiences such as REM behavior disorder and hypnopompic hallucinations, psychologists hope to offer natural explanations for many experiences that might otherwise seem supernatural or paranormal (Cheyne & Girard, 2009).

How important are REM sleep and dreaming? To answer this question, sleep expert William Dement awakened volunteers each time they entered REM sleep. Soon, their need for "dream time" grew more urgent. By the fifth night, many had to be awakened 20 or 30 times to prevent REM sleep. When the volunteers were finally allowed to sleep undisturbed, they dreamed extra amounts. This effect, called an **REM rebound**, explains why alcoholics have horrible nightmares after they quit drinking. Alcohol reduces sleep quality by suppressing REM sleep, thus setting up a powerful rebound when it is withdrawn (Stein & Friedmann, 2005).

What's the function of REM sleep? Whereas NREM sleep may calm the brain, REM sleep appears to sharpen or complete the consolidation of our memories of the previous day's more important experiences (Diekelmann & Born, 2010; Saxvig et al., 2008). During the day, when information is streaming in, the brain may be too busy to efficiently select useful memories. When the conscious brain is "off-line," we may be better able to identify and solidify important new memories. Daytime stress tends to increase REM sleep, which may rise dramatically when there is a death in the family, trouble at work, a marital conflict, or other emotionally charged events. The value of more REM sleep, then, may be that it helps us sort and retain important memories, especially memories about strategies for solving problems (Stickgold, 2013; Walker & Stickgold, 2006). This is why, after studying for a long period, you may remember more if you go to sleep rather than pulling an all-nighter. (REMember to get some REM!)

The Need for Sleep

It has long been thought that sleep helps keep the body, including the brain and immune system, healthy by regulating temperature, conserving energy, and aiding development and repair (Faraut et al., 2011; Ingiosi, Opp, & Krueger, 2013; Irwin, 2015). According to **repair/restorative theories of sleep**, lowering body metabolism and brain activity during sleep may help replenish and conserve energy and lengthen life.

With few exceptions, four days or more without sleep becomes hell for everyone. The world record is held by Randy Gardner, who at age 17 went about 11 days without sleep. As you might expect, he felt the effects of staying awake that long: At various times, Randy's speech was slurred, and he couldn't concentrate, remember clearly, or name common objects (Coren, 1996). Sleep loss also typically causes trembling hands, drooping eyelids, inattention, irritability, staring, increased pain sensitivity, and general discomfort (Doran, Van Dongen, & Dinges, 2001). In addition, most people experience *hypersomnia* (hi-per-SOM-nee-ah), or excessive daytime sleepiness, after even a few hours of sleep loss (Centers for Disease Control, 2012). Hypersomnia is a common problem during adolescence (Carskadon, Acebo, & Jenni, 2004; Kotagal, 2012). Rapid physical changes during puberty increase the need for sleep even though the quality and quantity of sleep time tends to decrease during the teen years.

Given the costs of **sleep deprivation**, or sleep loss, it's interesting that most people who have not slept for a day or two can still do interesting or complex mental tasks. But they have trouble paying attention, staying alert, and doing simple or boring routines (Trujillo, Kornguth, & Schnyer, 2009). They also are susceptible to **microsleeps**, which are brief shifts in brain activity to the pattern normally recorded during sleep. For a pilot or machine operator, this can spell disaster (Hardaway & Gregory, 2005; Sallinen et al., 2017). If a task is monotonous (such as factory work or air traffic control), no amount of sleep loss is safe. Severe sleep loss can even cause a temporary **sleep-deprivation psychosis**—a loss of contact with reality. Confusion, disorientation, delusions, and hallucinations are typical of this reaction. Fortunately, such "crazy" behavior is uncommon (Petrovsky et al., 2014; Szpak & Allen, 2012).

So what happened to Randy? Surprisingly, Randy needed only 14 hours of sleep to recover. As he discovered, most of the symptoms of sleep loss are reversed by a single night's rest (Sallinen et al., 2008).

Pacific Stock-Design Pics/Pacific Stock-Design Pics/Superstock

Not all animals sleep, but, like humans, those that do have powerful sleep needs. For example, dolphins must voluntarily breathe air, which means they face the choice of staying awake or drowning. A dolphin solves this problem by sleeping on just one side of its brain at a time! The other half of the brain, which remains awake, controls breathing.

Dream Theories

Some theorists believe that dreams have deeply hidden meanings. Others regard dreams as nearly meaningless. Yet others hold that dreams reflect our waking thoughts, fantasies, and emotions (Hartmann, 2011). Let's examine all three views.

Psychodynamic Dream Theory

Psychodynamic theories of dreaming emphasize internal conflicts and unconscious forces (Fischer & Kächele, 2009). Interpreting dreams is such an important part of psychoanalysis that Freud referred to them as "the royal road to the unconscious." Sigmund Freud's (1900) landmark book, *The Interpretation of Dreams*, first advanced the idea that many dreams are based on **wish fulfillment**—an expression of unconscious desires.

One of Freud's key proposals was that dreams express unconscious desires and conflicts as disguised **dream symbols**—images that have deeper symbolic meaning. Understanding a dream, then, requires analyzing the dream's **manifest content**, or obvious, visible meaning, to uncover its **latent content**, or hidden, symbolic meaning. For instance, a woman who dreams of stealing her best friend's wedding ring and placing it on her own hand may be unwilling to consciously admit that she is sexually attracted to her best friend's husband. Similarly, a journey might symbolize death, and horseback riding or dancing could symbolize sexual intercourse.

Do all dreams have hidden meanings? Probably not. Freud realized that many dreams are trivial "day residues" or carryovers from

REM rebound The occurrence of extra rapid eye movement sleep following REM sleep deprivation.

Repair/restorative theories of sleep Proposals that lowering body and brain activity and metabolism during sleep may help conserve energy and lengthen life.

Sleep deprivation Being prevented from getting desired or needed amounts of sleep.

Microsleep A brief shift in brain-wave patterns to those of sleep.

Sleep-deprivation psychosis A major disruption of mental and emotional functioning brought about by sleep loss.

Psychodynamic theories Any theory of behavior that emphasizes internal conflicts, motives, and unconscious forces.

Wish fulfillment Freudian belief that many dreams express unconscious desires.

Dream symbols Images in dreams that serve as visible signs of hidden ideas, desires, impulses, emotions, relationships, and so forth.

Manifest content (of dreams) The surface, "visible" content of a dream; dream images as the dreamer remembers them.

Latent content (of dreams) The hidden or symbolic meaning of a dream, as revealed by dream interpretation and analysis.

According to psychodynamic theory, dream imagery often has symbolic meaning. How would you interpret this dreamlike image? The fact that dreams don't have a single unambiguous meaning is one of the shortcomings of Freudian dream theory.

ordinary waking events. On the other hand, dreams do tend to reflect a person's current concerns, so Freud wasn't entirely wrong.

The Activation-Synthesis Hypothesis

Psychiatrists Allan Hobson and Robert McCarley have a radically different view of dreaming, called the **activation-synthesis hypothesis**. They believe that during REM sleep, several lower brain centers are "turned on" (*activated*) in more or less random fashion. However, messages from those centers are blocked from reaching the body (remember sleep paralysis?), so no movement occurs. Nevertheless, the centers continue to tell higher brain areas of their activities. Struggling to interpret this random information, the brain searches through stored memories and manufactures (*synthesizes*) a dream. Because frontal areas of the cortex, which control higher mental abilities, are mostly shut down during REM sleep, the resulting dreams are more primitive and more bizarre than daytime thoughts (Hobson, 2000, 2005).

How does that help explain dream content? According to the activation-synthesis hypothesis, dreams are usually meaningless. Let's use the classic chase dream as an example. In such dreams, we feel that we are running but not going anywhere. This occurs because the brain is told that the body is running, but it gets no feedback from the motionless legs. To try to make sense of this information, the brain creates a chase drama. A similar process probably explains dreams of floating or flying.

So dreams have no meaning? The activation-synthesis hypothesis rejects the idea that dreams are deliberate, meaningful messages from our unconscious. However, it does not rule out the possibility that we can find meaning in some dreams. Because dreams are created from memories and past experiences, parts of dreams can sometimes reflect each person's mental life, emotions, and concerns (Hobson, 2000).

Neurocognitive Dream Theory

Can't dreams just be about everyday stuff? Yes, they can. According to William Domhoff's **neurocognitive dream theory**, dreams have much in common with waking thoughts and emotions. Domhoff believes this is true because many brain areas that are active when we are awake remain active during dreaming (Domhoff, 2003, 2011). From this perspective, our dreams are a conscious expression of REM sleep processes that are sorting and storing daily experiences (Klinger, 2013; Levin & Nielsen, 2009). Speaking very loosely, it's as if the dreaming brain were reviewing messages left on voice mail to decide which are worth keeping. Thus, we shouldn't be surprised if a student who is angry at a teacher dreams of embarrassing the teacher in class, a lonely person dreams of romance, or a hungry child dreams of food. It is not necessary to seek deeper symbolic meanings to understand these dreams.

Which dream theory is the most widely accepted? Each theory has strengths and weaknesses (Hobson & Schredl, 2011; MacDuffie & Mashour, 2010). However, studies of dream content tend to support neurocognitive theory's focus on the continuity between dreams and waking thought. Rather than seeming exotic or bizarre, most dreams reflect everyday events (Domhoff & Schneider, 2008; Pesant & Zadra, 2006). For example, athletes tend to dream about the previous day's athletic activities (Erlacher & Schredl, 2004).

Nevertheless, many psychologists continue to believe that some dreams have deeper meanings (Halliday, 2010; Wilkinson, 2006). A striking example is provided by Dr. Otto Loewi, a Nobel Prize winner. Loewi had spent years studying the chemical transmission of nerve impulses. A tremendous breakthrough in his research came when he dreamed of an experiment three nights in a row. On the third night, he got up after having the dream, went straight to his laboratory, and performed the crucial experiment. Loewi later said that if the experiment had occurred to him while awake, he would have rejected it.

We will now turn our attention to a survey of some sleep problems—if you are still awake.

Sleep Troubles: Some Things That Go Wrong in the Night

Sleep quality has taken a beating in North America. Artificial lighting, frenetic schedules, exciting pastimes, smoking, drinking, overstimulation, and many other factors have contributed to a near epidemic of sleep problems. **Sleep–wake disorders** include difficulties falling asleep, staying asleep, waking up, or any combination of these. They range from daytime sleep attacks to sleepwalking and terrifying nightmares (▲ Table 5.2). Let's explore a few of the sleep problems that some people face.

Insomnia Disorder

No one wants to lie awake staring at the ceiling at 2 a.m. Yet, about 40 million Americans have chronic insomnia, while another 20 million have occasional problems with sleep (National Institute of Neurological Disorders and Stroke, 2014). **Insomnia** includes difficulty in getting to sleep or staying asleep (such as frequent nighttime awakenings or waking too early). Insomnia can harm people's work, health, and relationships (Ebben & Spielman, 2009).

Types and Causes of Insomnia

Worry, stress, and excitement can cause *temporary insomnia* and a self-defeating cycle. First, excess mental activity ("I can't stop turning things over in my mind") and heightened arousal block sleep. Then, frustration and anger over not being able to sleep cause more worry and arousal. This further delays sleep, which

▲ **Table 5.2 Sleep–Wake Disorders**

Insomnia disorder	Difficulty in getting to sleep or staying asleep; also, not feeling rested after sleeping.
Hypersomnolence disorder	Excessive daytime sleepiness. This can result from depression, insomnia, narcolepsy, sleep apnea, sleep drunkenness, periodic limb movements, drug abuse, and other problems.
Narcolepsy	Sudden, irresistible, daytime sleep attacks that may last anywhere from a few minutes to a half-hour. Victims may fall asleep while standing, talking, or even driving.
Breathing-related sleep disorders	Interruption in breathing during sleep. For example, during sleep, breathing stops for 20 seconds or more (sleep apnea) until the person wakes a little, gulps in air, and settles back to sleep; this cycle may be repeated hundreds of times per night.
Circadian rhythm sleep–wake disorders	A mismatch between the sleep–wake schedule demanded by a person's bodily rhythm and that demanded by the environment.
Disorders of arousal	During NREM sleep, a person engages in activities that are normally engaged in while awake, such as sleepwalking; also includes sleep terrors, partial awakenings marked by panic.
Nightmare disorder	Vivid, recurrent nightmares that significantly disturb sleep.
REM sleep behavior disorder	A failure of normal muscle paralysis, leading to violent actions during REM sleep.
Restless legs syndrome	An irresistible urge to move the legs to relieve sensations of creeping, tingling, prickling, aching, or tension.
Substance-induced sleep disorder	Disturbance of sleep because of a particular substance, such as caffeine.

Source: American Psychiatric Association (2013).

causes more frustration, and so on (Sunnhed & Jansson-Fröjmark, 2014). A good way to interrupt this cycle is to avoid fighting it. Get up and do something useful or satisfying when you can't sleep. (Reading a textbook might be a good choice of useful activities). Return to bed only when you begin to feel that you are struggling to stay awake. If sleeping problems last for more than three weeks, then a diagnosis of *chronic insomnia* can be made.

Drug-dependency insomnia (sleep loss caused by withdrawal from sleeping pills) also can occur. There is real irony in the billion dollars a year that North Americans spend on sleeping pills. Many nonprescription sleeping pills have little sleep-inducing effect. Barbiturates are even worse. These prescription sedatives decrease both Stage 4 sleep and REM sleep, drastically lowering sleep quality. In addition, many users become "sleeping-pill junkies" who need an ever-greater number of pills to get to sleep. Victims must be painstakingly weaned from their sleep medicines. Otherwise, terrible nightmares and *rebound insomnia* may drive them back to drug use.

It's worth remembering that although alcohol and other depressant drugs may help a person get to sleep, they greatly reduce sleep quality (Nau & Lichstein, 2005). Even newer drugs which induce sleep have drawbacks. Possible side effects include amnesia, impaired judgment, increased appetite, decreased sex drive, depression, and even sleepwalking, sleep eating, and sleep driving, making these drugs a temporary remedy at best.

Behavioral Remedies for Insomnia

If sleeping pills are a poor way to treat insomnia, what can be done? It is usually better to treat insomnia with lifestyle changes and behavioral techniques (McGowan & Behar, 2013; Montgomery & Dennis, 2004). Treatment for chronic insomnia usually begins with a careful analysis of a patient's sleep habits, lifestyle, stress levels, and medical problems. All the approaches discussed in the following list are helpful for treating insomnia (Ebben & Spielman, 2009; Nau & Lichstein, 2005):

1. **Stimulus control.** Insisting on a regular schedule helps establish a firm body rhythm, greatly improving sleep. This is best achieved by exercising **stimulus control**, which refers to linking a response with specific stimuli. It is important to get up and go to sleep at the same time each day, including weekends (Vincent, Lewycky, & Finnegan, 2008). In addition, insomniacs should avoid doing anything but sleeping when they are in bed. They are not to study, eat, watch television, read, pay the bills, worry, or even think in bed. (Lovemaking is okay, however.) In this way, only sleeping and relaxation become associated with going to bed at specific times.
2. **Sleep restriction.** Even if an entire night's sleep is missed, it is important not to sleep late in the morning, nap more than an hour, sleep during the evening, or go to bed early the following night. Instead, restricting sleep to normal bedtime hours avoids fragmenting sleep rhythms (Vincent, Lewycky, & Finnegan, 2008).
3. **Paradoxical intention.** Another helpful approach is to remove the pressures of trying to go to sleep. Instead, the goal becomes trying to keep the eyes open (in the dark) and

Activation-synthesis hypothesis Proposition that dreams are how brains process the random electrical discharges of REM sleep.

Neurocognitive dream theory Proposal that dreams reflect everyday waking thoughts and emotions.

Sleep–wake disorders Difficulties falling asleep, staying asleep, waking up, or any combination of these, such as insomnia disorder.

Insomnia Difficulty in getting to sleep or staying asleep.

Stimulus control Linking a particular response with specific stimuli.

stay awake as long as possible (Nau & Lichstein, 2005). This allows sleep to come unexpectedly and lowers performance anxiety (Taylor & Roane, 2010).

4. **Relaxation.** Some insomniacs lower their arousal before sleep by using a physical or mental strategy for relaxing, such as progressive muscle relaxation, meditation, or blotting out worries with calming images. It also is helpful to schedule time in the early evening to write down worries or concerns and plan what to do about them the next day in order to set them aside before going to bed. (■ Learning how to achieve deep relaxation is a highly useful skill. See Section 15.2 for more information.)
5. **Exercise.** Strenuous exercise during the day promotes sleep (Brand et al., 2010). However, exercise within three to six hours of sleep is helpful only if it is very light.
6. **Food intake.** What you eat can affect how easily you get to sleep. Eating starchy foods increases the amount of tryptophan (TRIP-tuh-fan: an amino acid) reaching the brain. More tryptophan, in turn, increases the amount of serotonin in the brain, which is associated with relaxation, a positive mood, and sleepiness (Silber & Schmitt, 2010). Thus, to promote sleep, try eating a starchy snack, such as bread, pasta, or dry cereal. If you really want to drop the bomb on insomnia, try eating a baked potato (which may be the world's largest sleeping pill!).
7. **Stimulant avoidance.** Stimulants, such as coffee and cigarettes, should be avoided. It also is worth remembering that alcohol, although not a stimulant, impairs sleep quality.

Disorders of Arousal: Sleepwalking, Sleeptalking, and Sleepsex

Seriously? Sleepsex? As strange as it may seem, many waking behaviors can be engaged in while asleep, such as driving a car, cooking, playing a musical instrument, and eating (Plazzi et al., 2005). The most common, sleepwalking, is eerie and fascinating in its own right (Banerjee & Nisbet, 2011). **Somnambulists** (som-NAM-bue-lists: those who sleepwalk) avoid obstacles, descend stairways, and on rare occasions may step out of windows or in front of automobiles. Sleepwalkers have been observed jumping into lakes, urinating in garbage pails or closets (phew!), shuffling furniture around, and even brandishing weapons (Schenck & Mahowald, 2005).

The sleepwalker's eyes are usually open, but a blank face and shuffling feet reveal that the person is still asleep. If you find someone sleepwalking, you should gently guide the person back to bed. Awakening a sleepwalker does no harm, but it is not necessary.

Does sleepwalking occur during dreaming? No. Remember that people are normally immobilized during REM sleep. EEG studies have shown that somnambulism occurs during NREM Stages 3 and 4 (Kalat, 2016; Stein & Ferber, 2001). *Sleeptalking* also occurs mostly during NREM sleep. The link with deep sleep explains why sleeptalking makes little sense and why sleepwalkers are confused and remember little when awakened.

Oh, yes, you're curious about sleepsex. *Sexsomnia* is not as exciting as it might sound. Just imagine being startled wide awake by your bed partner, who is asleep, attempting to have sex with you (Andersen et al., 2007; Klein & Houlihan, 2010).

Nightmare Disorder and Sleep Terrors

Stage 4 sleep is also the realm of sleep terrors. These frightening episodes are quite different from ordinary nightmares. A **nightmare** is simply a bad dream that takes place during REM sleep. During a Stage 4 **sleep terror** (also known as a **night terror**), a person suffers total panic and may hallucinate frightening dream images into the bedroom. An attack may last 15 or 20 minutes. When it is over, the person awakens drenched in sweat but only vaguely remembers the terror. Because sleep terrors occur during NREM sleep (when the body is not immobilized), victims may sit up, scream, get out of bed, or run around the room. Victims remember little afterward. (Other family members, however, may have a story to tell.) Although sleep terrors are more common in childhood, they are not uncommon in adulthood (Belicki, Chambers, & Ogilvie, 1997; Kataria, 2004).

Is there any way to stop a recurring nightmare? A bad nightmare can be worse than any horror movie. It's easy to leave a theater, but we often remain trapped in terrifying dreams. Frequently occurring nightmares (one a week or more) are associated with higher levels of psychological distress (Levin & Fireman, 2002).

Nevertheless, most nightmares can be banished by following three simple steps. First, write down your nightmare, describing it in detail. Next, change the dream any way you wish, making sure to spell out the details of the new dream. The third step is *imagery rehearsal*, in which you mentally rehearse the changed dream before you fall asleep again (Krakow & Zadra, 2006). Imagery rehearsal may work because confronting upsetting dreams may reduce their impact. Or perhaps it mentally "reprograms" future dream content. In any case, the technique has helped many people (Hansen et al., 2013; Harb et al., 2012).

Sleep Apnea

Some sage once said, "Laugh and the whole world laughs with you; snore and you sleep alone." While frequent snoring is often harmless, it can signal a serious problem. A person who snores loudly, with short silences and loud gasps or snorts, may suffer from *apnea* (AP-nee-ah: interrupted breathing). In **sleep apnea**, breathing stops for periods of 20 seconds to 2 minutes. As the need for oxygen becomes intense, the person wakes a little and gulps in air. She or he then settles back to sleep. But soon, breathing stops again. This cycle is repeated hundreds of times a night. As you might guess, apnea victims are extremely sleepy during the day. They also can have a harder time functioning during the day (Grenèche et al., 2011) and, in the long run, may suffer damage to their oxygen-hungry brains (Joo et al., 2010).

What causes sleep apnea? Central sleep apnea occurs because the brain stops sending signals to the diaphragm to maintain breathing. *Obstructive sleep apnea hypopnea syndrome* is a blockage of the upper air passages. One of the most effective treatments is the use of a continuous positive airway pressure (CPAP) mask to aid breathing during sleep. The resulting improvement in sleep is often followed by improved daytime function (Ferini-Strambi et al., 2013; Tregear et al., 2010). Other treatments include weight loss and surgery for breathing obstructions.

SIDS

Sleep apnea is suspected as one cause of **sudden infant death syndrome (SIDS)**, or "crib death." In the "typical" crib death, a slightly premature or small baby with some signs of a cold or cough is put to bed. A short time later, parents find the child has died. A baby deprived of air will normally struggle to begin breathing again. However, SIDS babies seem to have a weak arousal reflex. This prevents them from changing positions and resuming breathing after an episode of apnea. SIDS is the leading cause of death in children between 1 month and 1 year of age (National Institute of Child Health and Human Development, 2014).

Babies at risk for SIDS must be carefully watched for the first 6 months of life. To aid parents, a monitor may be used that sounds an alarm when breathing or pulse becomes weak. Babies at risk for SIDS are often premature; have a shrill, high-pitched cry; engage in "snoring," breath-holding, or frequent awakening at night; breathe mainly through an open mouth; or remain passive when their face rolls into a pillow or blanket. For this reason, it is wise to avoid bundling newborns or covering them with blankets or pillows.

Sleeping position is another major risk factor for SIDS. Healthy infants are best off sleeping on their backs (sides are not as good, but it's much better than facedown) (Shapiro-Mendoza et al., 2009). (However, premature babies, those with respiratory problems, and those who often vomit may need to sleep facedown. Ask a pediatrician for guidance.) Remember, "*back* to sleep" is the safest position for most infants (Ball & Volpe, 2013).

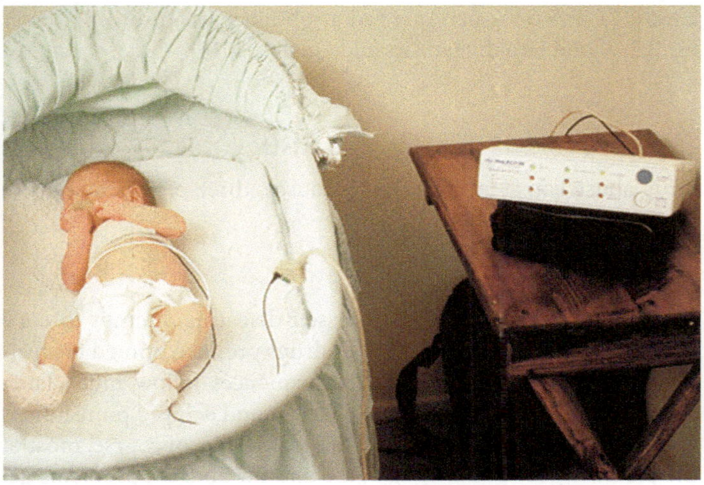

Michael Newman/PhotoEdit

Infants at risk for SIDS are often attached to devices that monitor breathing and heart rate during sleep. An alarm sounds to alert parents if either pulse or respiration falters. SIDS rarely occurs after an infant is 1 year old. Babies, and especially those at risk for SIDS, should be placed on their backs.

Narcolepsy

Narcolepsy (NAR-koe-lep-see), or sudden, irresistible sleep attacks, is one of the most dramatic sleep problems. Victims may fall asleep anywhere for a few minutes to a half-hour, during alert, daytime activities such as standing, talking, or even driving. Emotional excitement, especially laughter, commonly triggers narcolepsy. (Tell an especially good joke and a narcoleptic may fall asleep.) Many victims also suffer from *cataplexy* (CAT-uh-plex-see), a sudden temporary paralysis of the muscles, leading to complete body collapse (Ingravallo et al., 2012). Sleep attacks and paralysis appear to occur when REM sleep intrudes into the waking state (Kalat, 2016). It's easy to understand why narcolepsy can devastate careers and relationships.

Fortunately, narcolepsy is rare. It runs in families, which suggests that it is hereditary (Chabas et al., 2003). This has been confirmed by breeding several generations of narcoleptic dogs. (These dogs, by the way, are simply outstanding at learning the trick "Roll over and play dead.") There is no known cure for narcolepsy, but a variety of drugs help reduce the frequency and intensity of attacks (Ferini-Strambi et al., 2013; Lammers et al., 2010).

Reflective Practice

Sleep: The Nightly Roller Coaster

1. Alpha waves are to pre-sleep drowsiness as ______________ waves are to Stage 4 sleep.
2. Rapid eye movements indicate that a person is in deep sleep. T or F?
3. Sharpening memories and facilitating their storage is one function of ______________
   a. activation-synthesis cycles
   b. REM sleep
   c. deep sleep
   d. NREM sleep
4. Which of the following is *not* a behavioral remedy for insomnia?
   a. daily hypersomnia
   b. stimulus control
   c. progressive relaxation
   d. paradoxical intention
5. Sleep terrors, sleepwalking, and sleeptalking all occur during Stage 1, NREM sleep. T or F?
6. According to the activation-synthesis hypothesis of dreaming, dreams are constructed from ____________ to explain messages received from lower brain centers.

THINK CRITICALLY

7. In addition to helping repair and restore the body, as well as store memories, analyze other biological advantages that sleeping might provide.

SELF-REFLECT

- As a counselor at a sleep clinic, how would you explain the basics of sleep and managing sleep to a new client?
- Do you think your dreams have symbolic meaning or reflect everyday concerns? Can dreams increase self-awareness?
- Almost everyone suffers from insomnia at least occasionally. Which of the techniques for combating insomnia are similar to strategies that you have discovered on your own?
- How many sleep disturbances can you name (including those listed in Table 5.2)? Have you experienced any of them?

Answers: 1. delta 2. F 3. b 4. a 5. F 6. Memories 7. Natural selection may have favored sleep because animals that remained active at night probably had a higher chance of being killed. (We'll bet they had more fun, though.)

Somnambulists People who sleepwalk; occurs during NREM sleep.

Nightmare A bad dream that occurs during REM sleep.

Sleep terror (night terror) A state of panic during NREM sleep.

Sleep apnea Disorder in which a person stops breathing during sleep.

Sudden infant death syndrome (SIDS) The sudden, unexplained death of an apparently healthy infant.

Narcolepsy A sudden, irresistible sleep attack.

5.4 Drug-Altered Consciousness: The High and Low of It

GATEWAYS LEARNING OUTCOMES:
After reading this section you should be able to:

5.4.1 Explain the action of a psychoactive drug, and distinguish between recreational and instrumental drug use

5.4.2 Outline three reasons for drug abuse

5.4.3 Name five common stimulants

5.4.4 Name five common depressants

5.4.5 Name two common hallucinogens

One common way to alter human consciousness is to administer a **psychoactive drug**—a substance capable of altering attention, emotion, judgment, memory, time sense, self-control, or perception. Many psychoactive drugs can be placed on a scale ranging from stimulation to depression (● Figure 5.4). A **stimulant**, or *upper*, is a substance that increases activity in the body and nervous system. A **depressant**, or *downer*, does the reverse.

In general, psychoactive drug use falls into two categories. Using a drug to address a particular issue, such as taking a painkiller for a headache, a cup of coffee to stay awake, or an antidepressant to treat depression is *instrumental* use. In contrast, *recreational* users focus on experiencing the psychoactive effects of a drug. Getting high on heroin, even though you are not in physical pain, is an example. Most, if not all, of the drugs discussed in this chapter have *instrumental* uses (Ksir, Hart, & Black, 2015). Some have been used for centuries in various cultures, in search of insight. Others were developed specifically to treat various mental illnesses. Still others have a variety of health benefits. For example, the main instrumental use for morphine is to control pain.

Most Americans regularly use consciousness-altering drugs (don't forget, caffeine, alcohol, and nicotine are mildly psychoactive). Many musicians have celebrated the use of psychoactive drugs in their music. Other artists, including writers and painters, have even attributed their creativity to drug-induced experiences. While positive images and songs about drug use are commonplace in today's popular culture, they tend to obscure another, darker reality. The problem is that prescription drugs that can ease pain, induce sleep, or end depression have a high potential for *misuse* and *abuse*.

Psychoactive drugs are often misused. Failing to comply with a doctor's prescription, such as overmedicating oneself, is one example. Using a drug recreationally rather than instrumentally, such as using the codeine in a cough medication to get high, is another (Prus, 2014).

So aren't misuse and abuse the same thing? The term *drug abuse* is usually reserved for cases when drug misuse causes some sort of harm. Many recreational users can be classified as *experimental* users (short-term use based on curiosity) or *social-recreational* users

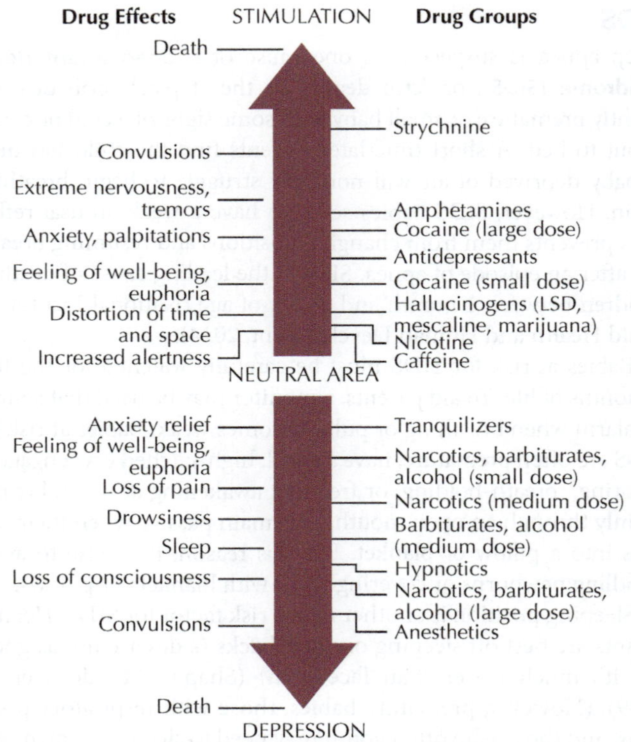

● **Figure 5.4 Spectrum and continuum of drug action.** Many drugs can be rated on a stimulation–depression scale according to their effects on the central nervous system. Although LSD, mescaline, and cannabis are listed here, the stimulation–depression scale is less relevant to these drugs. The principal characteristic of such hallucinogens is their mind-altering quality.

(occasional social use for pleasure or relaxation). While these may be examples of misuse, harm is more typically associated with *intensive* use (daily use with elements of dependence) or *compulsive* use (intense use and extreme dependence), in which case the person may be diagnosed with a **substance use and addictive disorder**. In 2015, almost 21 million Americans had a substance use disorder (Center for Behavioral Health Statistics and Quality, 2016).

Reasons for Drug Abuse

Drug abuse can stem from many causes, three of which seem to be very important.

Coping Efforts

Many abusers turn to drugs in a self-defeating attempt to cope with life. All the frequently abused drugs produce immediate feelings of pleasure. The negative consequences follow much later. This combination of immediate pleasure and delayed punishment allows abusers to feel good on demand. In time, of course, most of the pleasure goes out of drug abuse and the abuser's problems get worse. But if an abuser merely feels better (however briefly) after taking a drug, drug taking can become compulsive (Wood & Rünger, 2016).

Effects on the Brain

Nearly all addictive drugs stimulate the brain's reward circuitry, producing feelings of pleasure (Kalat, 2016; Prus, 2014). In particular, addictive drugs stimulate a brain region called the *nucleus accumbens* to release dopamine (DOPE-ahmeen), a neurotransmitter that results in intensified feelings of pleasure (● Figure 5.5; Floresco, 2015). As a result, the reward pathway signals, "That felt good. Let's do it again. Let's remember exactly how we did it." This creates a compulsion to repeat the drug experience. It's the hook that eventually snares the addict (National Institute on Drug Abuse, 2014).

In the end, the addictive drug physically changes the brain's reward circuitry, making it even harder for the addict to overcome addiction (Henry et al., 2010; Niehaus, Cruz-Bermúdez, & Kauer, 2009). At the same time, addiction may damage the prefrontal cortex, the brain system involved in self-control (Everitt & Robbins, 2016). Adolescents, it should be noted, are especially susceptible to addiction because the prefrontal brain systems that restrain their risk taking are not as mature as those that reward pleasure seeking (Boyd, Harris, & Knight, 2012).

Dependency

A third reason that drug abuse is so common is that taking psychoactive drugs tends to create dependencies. Once you get started, it can be very difficult to stop (Calabria et al., 2010). Drug dependence falls into two broad categories (Maisto, Galizio, & Connors, 2015). When a person compulsively uses a drug to maintain bodily comfort, a **physical dependence (addiction)** exists. Addiction occurs most often with drugs that cause **withdrawal symptoms**—the physical illness and discomfort that follows removal of a drug. Withdrawal from drugs such as alcohol, barbiturates, and opiates can cause violent, flulike symptoms, including nausea, vomiting, diarrhea, chills, sweating, and cramps. Addiction is often accompanied by a **drug tolerance**—a progressive decrease in a person's responsiveness to a drug. This leads users to take larger and larger doses to get the desired effect.

Persons who develop a **psychological dependence** feel that a drug is necessary to maintain their comfort or well-being. Usually, they intensely crave the drug and its rewarding qualities. Psychological dependence can be just as powerful as physical addiction. That's why some psychologists define addiction as any repetitively compulsive pattern. By this definition, a person who has lost control over drug use, for whatever reason, is addicted.

▲ Table 5.3 reveals that the drugs most likely to lead to physical dependence are alcohol, amphetamines, barbiturates, cocaine, codeine, heroin, methadone, morphine, and nicotine (tobacco). Using *most* of the drugs listed in Table 5.3 also can result in psychological dependence. Note also that people who take drugs intravenously are additionally at high risk for developing hepatitis and AIDS. The discussion that follows focuses on the drugs most often abused by students. (■ See Section 11.3 for more information about AIDS.)

Stimulants: Up, Up, and Away

Some of the most common *uppers* are amphetamines, cocaine, MDMA, caffeine, and nicotine.

Amphetamines

Amphetamines are synthetic stimulants. Some common street names for amphetamines are *speed*, *bennies*, *dexies*, *amp*, and *uppers*. These drugs were once widely prescribed for weight loss or depression. Today, the main instrumental medical use of amphetamines is to treat childhood hyperactivity and overdoses of depressant drugs. Illicit use of amphetamines is widespread, however, including among people seeking to stay awake and by those who rationalize that such drugs can improve mental or physical performance (DeSantis & Hane, 2010).

For example, Adderall and Ritalin, two popular "study drugs," are both mixes of amphetamines used to treat **attention deficit hyperactivity disorder (ADHD)**. People with ADHD have difficulty controlling their attention and are prone to displaying hyperactive and impulsive behavior (National Institute of Mental

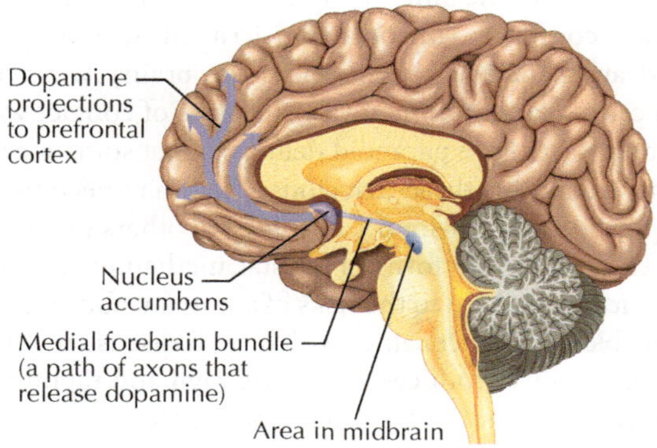

● **Figure 5.5 Addiction and dopamine.** Addictive drugs increase dopamine activity in the medial forebrain bundle and the nucleus accumbens, stimulating the frontal cortex and giving rise to intensified feelings of pleasure.

Psychoactive drug Any substance that can alter a person's state of consciousness.

Stimulant (upper) A substance that increases activity in the body and nervous system.

Depressant (downer) A substance that decreases activity in the body and nervous system.

Substance use and addictive disorder Abuse of, or dependence on, a mood- or behavior-altering drug or equivalent.

Physical dependence (addiction) Compulsive use of a drug to maintain bodily comfort as indicated by the presence of drug tolerance and withdrawal symptoms.

Withdrawal symptoms Physical illness and discomfort after an addict stops taking a drug.

Drug tolerance Progressive decrease in a person's responsiveness to a drug.

Psychological dependence Drug dependence that is based primarily on emotional or psychological needs.

Attention deficit/hyperactivity disorder (ADHD) A behavioral problem characterized by short attention span, restless movement, and impaired learning capacity.

▲ **Table 5.3 Comparison of Psychoactive Drugs**

Name	Classification	Medical Use	Duration of Effect
Alcohol	Sedative-hypnotic	Solvent, antiseptic, sedative	1–4 hours
Amphetamines	Stimulant	Relief of mild depression, control of narcolepsy and hyperactivity	4 hours
Barbiturates	Sedative-hypnotic	Sedation, relief of high blood pressure, anticonvulsant, antianxiety	1–16 hours
Benzodiazepines	Anxiolytic (antianxiety drug)	Tranquilizer	10 minutes–8 hours
Caffeine	Stimulant	Counteract depressant drugs, treatment of migraine headaches	Varies
Cannabis (THC)	Relaxant, euphoriant; in high doses, hallucinogen	Treatment of glaucoma and side effects of chemotherapy	2–4 hours
Cocaine	Stimulant, local anesthetic	Local anesthesia	Varied, 1–4 hours
Codeine	Opioid	Ease pain and coughing	3–6 hours
GHB	Sedative-hypnotic	Experimental treatment of narcolepsy, alcoholism	1–3 hours
Heroin	Opioid	Pain relief	3–6 hours
LSD	Hallucinogen	Experimental study of mental function, alcoholism	8–12 hours
MDMA	Stimulant/hallucinogen	None	4–6 hours
Mescaline	Hallucinogen	None	8–12 hours
Methadone	Opioid	Pain relief	12–24 hours
Morphine	Opioid	Pain relief	3–6 hours
PCP	Anesthetic	None	4–6 hours, plus 12-hour recovery
Psilocybin	Hallucinogen	None	Varies
Tobacco (nicotine)	Stimulant	Emetic (nicotine)	Varies

Question marks indicate conflict of opinion. It should be noted that illicit drugs are frequently mixed with unknown and possibly dangerous substances and thus pose possible hazards to the user.

Health, 2016). Increasing numbers of normal college students are illegally taking these drugs in the hope that they also will be able to focus better while doing schoolwork (Dodge et al., 2012).

Is it true that those drugs actually can help students study? Taking "study drugs" may produce slight improvements in problem-solving performance; however, this may be offset by a slight loss of creativity (Farah et al., 2009). Most important, all amphetamines have side effects that are worrisome, as we will see shortly.

Methamphetamine is a more potent variation of amphetamine. It can be snorted, injected, or eaten. Of the various types of amphetamine, methamphetamine has created the largest drug problem. *Bergs*, *glass*, *meth*, *crank*, or *crystal*, as it is known on the street, can be made cheaply in backyard labs and sold for massive profits. In addition to ruining lives through addiction, it has fueled a violent criminal subculture.

Amphetamines rapidly produce a drug tolerance. Most abusers quickly end up taking ever-larger doses to get the desired effect. Eventually, some users switch to injecting methamphetamine directly into the bloodstream. True "speed freaks" typically go on binges lasting several days, after which they "crash" from lack of sleep and food.

Large doses of amphetamines can cause nausea, vomiting, extremely high blood pressure, fatal heart attacks, and disabling strokes. It is important to realize that amphetamines speed up the use of the body's resources; they do not magically supply energy. After an amphetamine binge, people suffer from crippling fatigue, depression, confusion, uncontrolled irritability, and aggression. Repeated amphetamine use damages the brain. Amphetamines also can cause *amphetamine psychosis*, a loss of contact with reality. Affected users have paranoid delusions that someone is out to get them. Acting on these delusions, they may become violent, resulting in suicide, self-injury, or injury to others (Scott, 2012).

A potent, smokable form of crystal methamphetamine (also known as *ice*) has added to the risks of stimulant abuse. Like *crack*, the smokable form of cocaine (which we'll discuss next), crystal methamphetamine produces an intense high and rapidly leads to compulsive abuse and severe drug dependence.

Cocaine

Cocaine (also known as *coke*, *snow*, *blow*, *snuff*, and *flake*) is a powerful central nervous system stimulant extracted from the leaves of the coca plant. Cocaine produces feelings of alertness, euphoria,

Effects Sought	Long-Term Symptoms	Physical Dependence Potential	Psychological Dependence Potential	Organic Damage Potential
Sense alteration, anxiety reduction, sociability	Cirrhosis, toxic psychosis, neurologic damage, addiction	Yes	Yes	Yes
Alertness, activeness, relieve fatigue	Loss of appetite, delusions, hallucinations, toxic psychosis	Yes	Yes	Yes
Anxiety reduction, euphoria	Addiction with severe withdrawal symptoms, possible convulsions, toxic psychosis	Yes	Yes	Yes
Anxiety relief	Irritability, confusion, depression, sleep–wake disorders	Yes	Yes	No, but can affect fetus
Wakefulness, alertness	Insomnia, heart arrhythmias, high blood pressure	No?	Yes	Yes
Excitation, talkativeness	Depression, convulsions	Yes	Yes	Yes
Euphoria, prevent withdrawal discomfort	Addiction, constipation, loss of appetite	Yes	Yes	No
Intoxication, euphoria, relaxation	Anxiety, confusion, insomnia, hallucinations, seizures	Yes	Yes	No?
Euphoria, prevent withdrawal discomfort	Addiction, constipation, loss of appetite	Yes	Yes	No*
Insightful experiences, exhilaration, distortion of senses	May intensify existing psychosis, panic reactions	No	No?	No?
Relaxation; increased euphoria, perceptions, sociability	Possible lung cancer, other health risks	Yes	Yes	Yes?
Excitation, euphoria	Personality change, hyperthermia, liver damage	No	Yes	Yes
Insightful experiences, exhilaration, distortion of senses	May intensify existing psychosis, panic reactions	No	No?	No?
Prevent withdrawal discomfort	Addiction, constipation, loss of appetite	Yes	Yes	No
Euphoria, prevent withdrawal discomfort	Addiction, constipation, loss of appetite	Yes	Yes	No*
Euphoria	Unpredictable behavior, suspicion, hostility, psychosis	Debated	Yes	Yes
Insightful experiences, exhilaration, distortion of senses	May intensify existing psychosis, panic reactions	No	No?	No?
Alertness, calmness, sociability	Emphysema, lung cancer, mouth and throat cancer, cardiovascular damage, loss of appetite	Yes	Yes	Yes

*Persons who inject drugs under nonsterile conditions run a high risk of contracting AIDS, hepatitis, abscesses, or circulatory disorders.

well-being, power, boundless energy, and pleasure (Julien, 2011). At the turn of the 20th century, dozens of nonprescription potions and cure-alls contained cocaine. It was during this time that Coca-Cola was indeed the "real thing." From 1886 until 1906, when the U.S. Pure Food and Drug Act was passed, Coca-Cola contained cocaine (since then, it has been replaced with caffeine).

How does cocaine differ from amphetamines? The two are very much alike in their effects on the central nervous system. The main difference is that amphetamine effects typically last longer than those of cocaine, which is more quickly metabolized.

Cocaine's capacity for abuse and social damage rivals that of heroin. Rats and monkeys given free access to cocaine find it irresistible. Many, in fact, end up dying of convulsions from self-administered overdoses of the drug. Even casual or first-time users risk having convulsions, a heart attack, or a stroke. Cocaine increases the neurotransmitters *dopamine* and *norepinephrine*. Norepinephrine arouses the brain, and dopamine produces a "rush" of pleasure. This combination is so powerfully rewarding that cocaine users run a high risk of becoming compulsive abusers (Ridenour et al., 2005).

A person who stops using cocaine does not experience heroin-like withdrawal symptoms. Instead, the brain adapts to cocaine abuse in ways that upset its chemical balance, causing depression when cocaine is withdrawn. First, there is a jarring "crash" of mood and energy. Within a few days, the person enters a long period of fatigue, anxiety, paranoia, boredom, and **anhedonia** (an-he-DAWN-ee-ah), an inability to feel pleasure. Before long, the urge to use cocaine becomes intense. So, although cocaine does not fit the classic pattern of addiction, it is ripe for compulsive abuse. Even a person who gets through withdrawal may crave cocaine months or years later (Washton & Zweben, 2009). If cocaine were cheaper, nine out of ten users would progress to compulsive abuse. In fact, rock cocaine (*crack*, *rock*, or *roca*), which is cheaper, produces very high abuse rates.

Anyone who thinks she or he has a cocaine problem should seek advice at a drug clinic or a Cocaine Anonymous meeting. Although quitting cocaine is extremely difficult, three out of four abusers who remain in treatment succeed in breaking their dependence

Anhedonia An inability to feel pleasure.

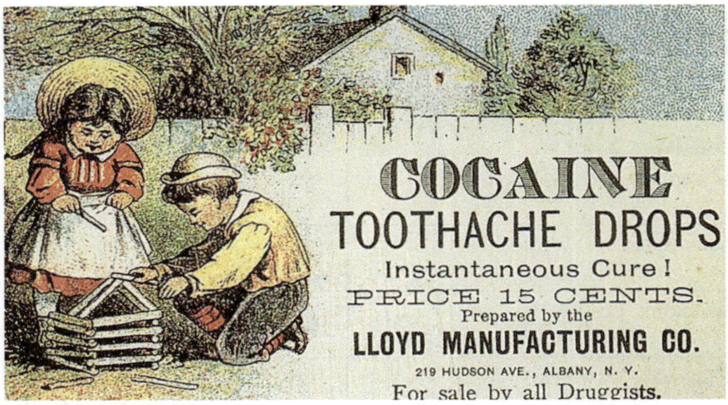

National Library of Medicine

Cocaine was the main ingredient in many nonprescription elixirs before the turn of the 20th century. Today, cocaine is recognized as a powerful and dangerous drug. Its high potential for abuse has damaged the lives of countless users.

(Sinha et al., 2006). Hope also is on the horizon in the form of a vaccine currently undergoing clinical trials that prevents cocaine from stimulating the nervous system (Kosten et al., 2012).

MDMA

The drug *MDMA* (methylenedioxymethamphetamine; also known as *ecstasy* or *molly*) also is chemically similar to amphetamine. While MDMA is technically a stimulant, it is sometimes classified as a hallucinogen since it can produce hallucinations (Prus, 2014). It also produces a rush of energy, and users say it makes them feel closer to others and heightens sensory experiences.

MDMA causes brain cells to release extra amounts of dopamine (resulting in euphoria and increased energy), epinephrine (resulting in increased heart rate, blood pressure, and body temperature), and serotonin (resulting in changes in many bodily functions, such as loss of appetite and increased sexual arousal; National Institute on Drug Abuse, 2016b). Although MDMA increases sexual pleasure, it actually *diminishes* sexual performance, impairing erection in 40 percent of men and delaying orgasm in both men and women (Zemishlany, Aizenberg, & Weizman, 2001).

On an annual basis, more than 2,000,000 Americans use MDMA (Center for Behavioral Health Statistics and Quality, 2016). Every year, emergency room doctors see many MDMA cases, including MDMA-related deaths. Some of these incidents are caused by elevated body temperature, which can lead to collapse. MDMA users at "rave" parties try to prevent overheating by drinking water to cool themselves. This may help to a small degree, but MDMA overheating can cause kidney, heart, or liver failure, which can be fatal (National Institute on Drug Abuse, 2016b).

In addition, MDMA users are more likely to abuse alcohol and other drugs, to neglect studying, to party excessively, and to engage in risky sex (Strote, Lee, & Wechsler, 2002). Ironically, MDMA use does intensify the impact of the music. We say "ironically" because the end result is often overstimulation of the brain, which can lead to a rebound depression (Iannone et al., 2006).

MDMA use also has long-term effects. Feelings of anxiety or depression can persist for months after a person stops taking MDMA. In addition, heavy users typically do not perform well in tests of learning and memory and show some signs of underlying brain damage (Quednow et al., 2006).

Caffeine

Caffeine is the most frequently used psychoactive drug in North America. (Goodnight, Seattle!) Many people have a hard time starting a day (or writing another paragraph) without a cup of coffee or tea because caffeine suppresses drowsiness and increases alertness, especially when combined with sugar (Adan & Serra-Grabulosa, 2010; Smith, Christopher, & Sutherland, 2013). Physically, caffeine can cause sweating, talkativeness, tinnitus (ringing in the ears), and hand tremors (Nehlig, 2004). Caffeine stimulates the brain by blocking chemicals that normally inhibit or slow nerve activity (Maisto, Galizio, & Connors, 2015). Its effects become apparent with doses as small as 50 milligrams, the amount found in about one-half cup of brewed coffee.

How much caffeine did you consume today? It is common to think of coffee as the major source of caffeine, but there are many others. Caffeine is found in tea, many soft drinks (especially colas and so-called "energy drinks"), chocolate, and cocoa. Thousands of nonprescription drugs also contain caffeine, including stay-awake pills, cold remedies, and many name-brand aspirin products.

Are there any serious drawbacks to using caffeine? Overuse of caffeine may result in an unhealthy dependence known as *caffeinism*. Insomnia, irritability, loss of appetite, chills, racing heart, and elevated body temperature are all signs of caffeinism. Many people with these symptoms drink 15 or 20 cups of coffee a day. However, as few as 2.5 cups of coffee a day (or the equivalent) can intensify anxiety and other psychological problems (Hogan, Hornick, & Bouchoux, 2002). People who consume even such modest amounts may experience anxiety, depression, fatigue, headaches, and flulike symptoms during withdrawal (Juliano & Griffiths, 2004).

Caffeine poses a variety of other health risks. Caffeine encourages the growth of breast cysts in women, and it may contribute to bladder cancer, heart problems, and high blood pressure. Pregnant women who consume as little as 2 cups of coffee a day increase the risk of having a miscarriage (Cnattingius et al., 2000). It is wise to remember that caffeine *is* a drug and to use it in moderation.

Nicotine

Next to caffeine and alcohol, *nicotine* is the most widely used psychoactive drug (Julien, 2011). A natural stimulant found mainly in tobacco, nicotine is so toxic that it is sometimes used to kill insects! In large doses, it causes stomach pain, vomiting and diarrhea, cold sweats, dizziness, confusion, and muscle tremors. In very large doses, nicotine may cause convulsions, respiratory failure, and death. For a nonsmoker, 50 to 75 milligrams of nicotine taken in a single dose could be lethal. (Chain-smoking a pack of cigarettes can produce this dosage.) Most first-time smokers get sick on one or two cigarettes. In contrast, regular smokers build a tolerance for nicotine. A heavy smoker may inhale several packs a day without feeling ill.

A vast array of evidence confirms that nicotine is very addictive (Dani & Balfour, 2011). Most smokers begin when they are teenagers, which is unfortunate because young people are even more vulnerable to addiction than are adults (Counotte et al., 2011). Although 35 million Americans each year want to quit smoking, more than 85 percent of them relapse, many within a week (National Institute on Drug Abuse, 2012). As humorist Mark Twain once whimsically lamented, "Giving up smoking is the easiest thing in the world. I know because I've done it thousands of times."

This should come as no surprise because withdrawal from nicotine causes headaches, sweating, cramps, insomnia, digestive upset, irritability, and a sharp craving for cigarettes. These symptoms may last from two to six weeks and may even be worse than heroin withdrawal. Just a few puffs will make that all go away until the next time the smoker works up the courage to quit.

Smoking is the leading cause of preventable deaths worldwide. Every year, 6 million people around the globe, including about 440,000 Americans, die from tobacco use (National Institute on Drug Abuse, 2012; World Health Organization, 2013). Tens of millions more live diminished lives because they smoke.

A burning cigarette releases a large variety of potent *carcinogens* (car-SIN-oh-jins: cancer-causing substances). Smoking causes widespread damage to the body, leading to an increased risk of many cancers (such as lung cancer), cardiovascular diseases (such as stroke), respiratory diseases (such as chronic bronchitis), and reproductive disorders (such as decreased fertility). Together, these health risks combine to reduce the life expectancy of the average smoker by 10 to 15 years.

By the way, urban cowboys and Skoal bandits, the same applies to chewing tobacco and snuff. A 30-minute exposure to one pinch of smokeless tobacco is equivalent to smoking three or four cigarettes. Along with all the health risks of smoking, users of smokeless tobacco also run a higher risk of developing oral cancer (Oral Cancer Foundation, 2017).

Smokers don't just risk their own health; they also endanger those who live and work nearby. Secondhand smoke causes about 7,300 lung cancer deaths and as many as 34,000 heart disease deaths each year in the United States alone. It is particularly irresponsible of smokers to expose young children, who are especially vulnerable, to secondhand smoke (American Lung Association, 2017).

If it's so hard to quit, how do some people manage to succeed? Whatever approach is taken, quitting smoking is not easy. It is especially difficult to try quitting alone, without any support. Many people find that using nicotine patches or gum and/or other medications, such as *bupropion*, helps them suppress their cravings during the withdrawal period (Bolt et al., 2012). The best chance of success comes when the smoker combines the desire to quit with both medication and some sort of counseling (Centers for Disease Control, 2017b).

Many smokers succeed in quitting by quitting abruptly (Lindson-Hawley et al., 2016). However, going "cold turkey" may work best only for those completely committed to quitting since it makes quitting an all-or-nothing proposition. Smokers who smoke even one cigarette after "quitting forever" tend to feel they've failed. Many figure they might just as well resume smoking. Others succeed by tapering down gradually. Those who quit gradually accept that success may take many attempts, spread over several months. Either way, you will have a better chance of success if you decide to quit *now* rather than at some time in the future, and don't delay your quit date too often (Hughes & Callas, 2011).

If you choose to taper off, the best way is *scheduled gradual reduction* (Riley et al., 2002). The key is to deliberately schedule and then gradually stretch the length of time between cigarettes. For example, the smoker might (1) delay having a first cigarette in the morning and then try to delay a little longer each day or (2) gradually reduce the total number of cigarettes smoked each day.

Marc Bruxelle/Shutterstock.com

E-cigarettes are electrical devices that look and feel like cigarettes because they vaporize a smokeless mist that can mimic tobacco smoke. When they deliver no nicotine, or a reduced dose, they may help people quitting smoking by allowing the smoker to enjoy the ritual of smoking while withdrawing from nicotine. However, when they are glamorized as a smokeless way to deliver the usual dose, they become just another delivery device that must be medically regulated (Cobb & Abrams, 2011). Moreover, a rash of deaths associated with vaping in 2019 has called the safety of e-cigarettes into question.

It is also worth noting that smoking is more than a nicotine delivery system for most smokers. The entire ritual of smoking has become a positive experience. Just holding a cigarette, dangling it between the lips, or even seeing a favorite smoking chair can give a smoker pleasure. For this reason, behavioral self-management techniques can be very useful for breaking habits such as smoking. In recent years, e-cigarettes have become popular, and vaping is used as a way to simulate smoking (sometimes without delivering any nicotine). Unfortunately, vaping has become very popular among adolescents and young people, in spite of the fact that it is illegal for minors to use e-cigarettes. Perhaps even more concerning is the fact that vaping is now being investigated for a potential connection to lung injuries (Shmerling, 2019).

Clearly, anyone trying to quit smoking should be prepared to make several attempts before succeeding. But the good news is that tens of millions of people *have* quit—with the right motivation and support, you can clearly "leave the pack behind." (■ Behavioral self-management techniques can be very useful for breaking habits such as smoking. See Section 6.6.)

Depressants: Down and Out

While opioids, like *heroin* and *morphine*, may be more powerful, both as drugs of abuse and as painkillers, the most widely used depressants are alcohol, barbiturates, gamma-hydroxybutyric acid (GHB), and benzodiazepine (ben-zoe-die-AZ-eh-peen) tranquilizers. Depressants are much alike in their effects. In fact, barbiturates and tranquilizers are sometimes referred to as "solid alcohol." Let's examine the properties of each.

Opioids

Raw *opium*, secreted by poppy seedpods, has been used for centuries to produce sleep and pain relief (Dikotter, Laamann, & Xun, 2008). For this reason, opium and the family of chemically related drugs,

Popular music icon Prince died of an accidental fentanyl overdose, as did legendary rock star Tom Petty. They are among the more high-profile casualties of a drug 50 times more powerful than heroin.

such as *heroin (big H, dope, horse)*, *morphine*, *codeine*, *oxycodone*, and *fentanyl*, are now referred to as *opioids*. Also commonly referred to as *narcotics*—drugs that produce a numbing effect—the opioids are among the most addictive of all drugs. Opioids can produce a powerful feeling of euphoria ("rush") accompanied by a reduction of anxiety, relaxation, and, of course, pain relief. At higher doses, breathing can be impaired, leading to death.

Opioid addiction has become depressingly common; more than 47,000 Americans die of opioid overdoses annually (Centers for Disease Control, 2017a; Kolodny et al., 2015). Heroin remains one of the most lethal opioids, and abuse of prescription painkillers such as oxycodone (Oxycontin) is also very prevalent in the United States. Worse still, newer synthetic opioids, especially fentanyl, are emerging as particularly deadly. Fentanyl is about 50 times more powerful than heroin; using even tiny amounts can result in death (National Institute on Drug Abuse, 2016a).

Another opioid, *methadone*, also bears mentioning. Opioid addicts are often treated with methadone, which reduces an opioid's "rush," making it much easier to go through withdrawal. Methadone is often freely given to addicts as part of a **harm-reduction strategy** meant to reduce the negative consequences of addiction without requiring drug abstinence (McKeganey, 2012). Harm-reduction programs are controversial because it can seem as if they merely support substance abusers in their addiction (supplying clean needles for drug injections is another example). In reality, they are often the only hope for addicts who would otherwise cause more harm to themselves and to others (Centre for Addiction and Mental Health, 2012).

Barbiturates

Barbiturates are sedative drugs that depress brain activity. Common barbiturates include amobarbital, pentobarbital, secobarbital, and tuinal. On the street, they are known as *downers*, *blue devils*, *yellow jackets*, *lows*, *goofballs*, *reds*, *pink ladies*, *rainbows*, or *tooies*. Medically, barbiturates are used to calm patients or to induce sleep. At mild dosages, barbiturates have an effect similar to alcohol intoxication. Higher dosages can cause severe mental confusion or even hallucinations. Barbiturates are often taken in excess amounts because an initial dose may be followed by others, as the user becomes uninhibited or forgetful. Overdoses first cause a loss of consciousness followed by severe depression of the brain centers that control heartbeat and breathing. The result is often death (Grilly & Salamone, 2012).

GHB

Would you swallow a mixture of degreasing solvent and drain cleaner to get high? Apparently, a lot of people would. A mini-epidemic of GHB use has taken place in recent years, especially at nightclubs and raves. GHB (also known as *goop*, *scoop*, *max*, and *Georgia Home Boy*) is a central nervous system depressant that relaxes and sedates the body. Users describe its effects as similar to those of alcohol (Johnson & Griffiths, 2013). Mild GHB intoxication tends to produce euphoria, a desire to socialize, and a mild loss of inhibition. GHB's intoxicating effects typically last a few hours, depending on the dosage.

At lower dosages, GHB can relieve anxiety and produce relaxation. However, as the dose increases, its sedative effects may result in nausea, a loss of muscle control, and either sleep or a loss of consciousness. Potentially fatal doses of GHB are only three times the amount typically taken by users. This narrow margin of safety has led to numerous overdoses, especially when GHB was combined with alcohol. An overdose causes coma, breathing failure, and death. GHB also inhibits the gag reflex, so some users choke to death on their own vomit.

In 2000, the U.S. government classified GHB as a controlled substance, making possession a felony. Evidence increasingly suggests that GHB is addictive and a serious danger to users. Two out of three frequent users have lost consciousness after taking GHB. Chronic use leads to brain damage (Pedraza, García, & Navarro, 2009). Heavy users who stop taking GHB have withdrawal symptoms that include anxiety, agitation, tremor, delirium, and hallucinations (Miotto et al., 2001).

Tranquilizers

Tranquilizers lower anxiety and reduce tension. Doctors prescribe benzodiazepine tranquilizers to alleviate nervousness and stress. Valium is the best-known drug in this family; others are Xanax, Halcion, and Librium. Even at normal dosages, these drugs can cause drowsiness, shakiness, and confusion. When used at too high a dosage or for too long, benzodiazepines are addictive (McKim, 2013).

A drug sold under the trade name Rohypnol (ro-HIP-nol) has added to the problem of tranquilizer abuse. This drug, which is related to Valium, is cheap and 10 times more potent. It lowers inhibitions and produces relaxation or intoxication. Large doses induce short-term amnesia and sleep. *Roofies*, as they are known on the street, are odorless and tasteless. They have occasionally been used to spike drinks, which are given to the unwary. Victims of this "date rape" drug are then sexually assaulted or raped while they are unconscious (Nicoletti, 2009). (Be aware, however, that drinking too much alcohol is by far the most common prelude to date rape.)

Repeated use of barbiturates can cause physical dependence. Some abusers suffer severe emotional depression that may end in suicide. Similarly, when tranquilizers are used at too high a dosage or for too long, addiction can occur. Many people have learned the hard way that their legally prescribed tranquilizers are as dangerous as many illicit drugs (Goldberg, 2014).

Alcohol

Alcohol is the common name for ethyl alcohol, the intoxicating element in fermented and distilled liquors. Contrary to popular belief, alcohol is not a stimulant. The noisy animation at drinking parties is due to alcohol's effect as a *depressant*. Small amounts of alcohol reduce inhibitions, consequently producing feelings of relaxation and euphoria. Larger amounts cause greater impairment of the brain until the drinker loses consciousness. Alcohol also is not an aphrodisiac. Rather than enhancing sexual arousal, it usually impairs performance, especially in males. As William Shakespeare observed long ago, drink "provokes the desire, but it takes away the performance."

Some people become relaxed and friendly when they are drunk. Others become aggressive and want to argue or fight. How can the same drug have such different effects? Some people drink for pleasure. Others drink to cope with negative emotions, such as anxiety and depression. That's why alcohol abuse increases with the level of stress in people's lives. People who drink to relieve bad feelings are at great risk of becoming alcoholics (Roberto & Koob, 2009).

When a person is drunk, thinking and perception become dulled or shortsighted, a condition that has been called **alcohol myopia** (my-OH-pea-ah) (Giancola et al., 2010). Only the most obvious and immediate stimuli catch a drinker's attention. Worries and "second thoughts" that would normally restrain behavior are banished from the drinker's mind. That's why many behaviors become more extreme when a person is drunk. On college campuses, drunken students tend to have accidents, get into fights, sexually assault others, or engage in risky sex. They also destroy property and disrupt the lives of students who are trying to sleep or study (Brower, 2002).

More than 20 million people in the United States and Canada have serious drinking problems. One American dies every 20 minutes in an alcohol-related car crash. Significant percentages of Americans of all ages abuse alcohol (Figure 5.6).

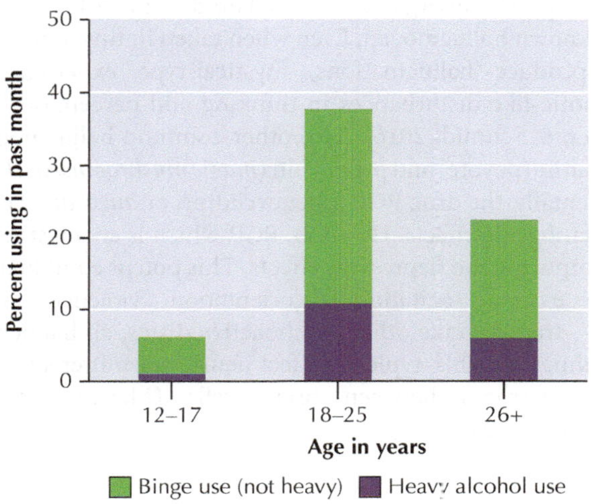

Figure 5.6 Alcohol use in the United States. Many Americans of all ages abuse alcohol. According to this 2015 survey, almost 50 percent of young adults aged 18–25 admitted to heavy alcohol use or binge drinking in the month before the survey was administered (Center for Behavioral Health Statistics and Quality, 2016).

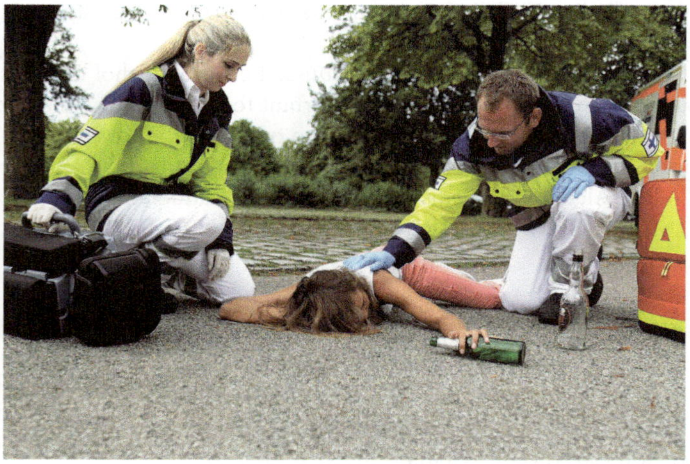

riopatuca/Shutterstock.com

Binge drinking and alcohol abuse have become serious problems among college students (National Institute on Alcohol Abuse and Alcoholism, 2015).

In addition, children of alcoholics and those who have other relatives who abuse alcohol are at greater risk for becoming alcohol abusers themselves. The increased risk appears to be partly genetic (Starkman, Sakharkar, & Pandey, 2012). This is based on the fact that some people have stronger cravings for alcohol after they drink (Hutchison et al., 2002). Women also face some special risks. For one thing, alcohol is absorbed faster and metabolized more slowly by women's bodies. As a result, women get intoxicated from less alcohol than men. Women who drink also are more prone to liver disease, osteoporosis, and depression. Each extra drink per day adds 7 percent to a woman's risk of breast cancer (Aronson, 2003).

It is especially worrisome to see binge drinking among adolescents and young adults. **Binge drinking** is usually defined as downing five or more drinks (four drinks for women) in a short time. Apparently, many students think it's entertaining to get completely wasted and throw up on their friends (Norman, Conner, & Stride, 2012). However, binge drinking is a serious sign of alcohol abuse (Beseler, Taylor, & Leeman, 2010). It is responsible for 1,800 U.S. college student deaths each year and thousands of trips to the emergency room (Mitka, 2009).

Binge drinking is of special concern for adolescents because the brain continues to develop into the early twenties. Research has shown that teenagers and young adults who drink too much may lose as much as 10 percent of their brain power—especially their memory capacity (Brown et al., 2000; Goldstein et al., 2016). Such losses can have a long-term impact on a person's chances for

Harm-reduction strategy A treatment approach to drug addiction that seeks to reduce the negative consequences of addiction without necessarily requiring drug abstinence.

Tranquilizer A drug that lowers anxiety and reduces tension.

Alcohol myopia Shortsighted thinking and perception that occurs during alcohol intoxication.

Binge drinking Consuming five or more drinks in a short time (four for women).

success in life. In short, getting drunk is a slow but sure way to get stupid (Le Berre et al., 2012).

What are the signs of alcohol abuse? Because alcohol abuse is such a common problem, it is important to recognize the danger signals. If you can answer yes to even one of the following questions, you may have a problem with drinking (adapted from the College Alcohol Problems Scale, revised, in Maddock et al., 2001):

AS A RESULT OF DRINKING ALCOHOLIC BEVERAGES, I . . .

1. engaged in unplanned sexual activity.
2. drove under the influence.
3. did not use protection when engaging in sex.
4. engaged in illegal activities associated with drug use.
5. felt sad, blue, or depressed.
6. was nervous or irritable.
7. felt bad about myself.
8. had problems with appetite or sleeping.

Almost everyone has been to a party spoiled by someone who drank too much too fast. Those who avoid overdrinking have a better time, and so do their friends. But how do you avoid drinking too much? After all, as one wit once observed, "The conscience dissolves in alcohol." It takes skill to regulate drinking in social situations, where the temptation to drink can be strong. If you choose to drink, here are some guidelines that may be helpful (adapted from Doumas, Miller, & Esp, 2017; Miller & Munoz, 2005; National Institute on Alcohol Abuse and Alcoholism, 2016):

MODERATED DRINKING GUIDELINES

1. Be reflective about your drinking beforehand, plan how you will manage it, and keep track of how much you drink.
2. Drink slowly (no more than one drink an hour), eat while drinking or drink on a full stomach, and make every other drink (or more) a nonalcoholic beverage.
3. Limit drinking primarily to the first hour of a social event or party.
4. Practice how you will politely but firmly refuse drinks.
5. Learn how to relax, meet people, and socialize without relying on alcohol.

Also remember that research has shown that you are likely to overestimate how much your fellow students are drinking (Maddock & Glanz, 2005). So don't let yourself be lured into overdrinking just because you have the (probably false) impression that other students are drinking more than you. Limiting your own drinking may help others as well. When people are tempted to drink too much, their main reason for stopping is that "other people were quitting and deciding they'd had enough" (Johnson, 2002).

Treatment for alcohol dependence begins with cutting off the supply and sobering up the person. This phase is referred to as **detoxification** (literally, "to remove poison"). It frequently produces all the symptoms of drug withdrawal and can be extremely unpleasant. The next step is to try to restore the person's health. Heavy abuse of alcohol usually causes severe damage to body organs and the nervous system. After alcoholics have "dried out" and some degree of health has been restored, they may be treated with tranquilizers, antidepressants, or psychotherapy. Unfortunately, the success of these procedures has been limited.

One mutual-help approach that has been fairly successful is Alcoholics Anonymous (AA). AA takes a spiritual approach while acting on the premise that it takes a former alcoholic to understand and help a current alcoholic. Participants at AA meetings admit that they have a problem, share feelings, and resolve to stay "dry" one day at a time. Other group members provide support for those struggling to end dependency (Teresi & Haroutunian, 2011). (Other "12-step" programs, such as Cocaine Anonymous and Narcotics Anonymous, use the same approach.)

Other groups offer a rational, nonspiritual approach to alcohol abuse that better fits the needs of some people. Examples include Rational Recovery and Secular Organizations for Sobriety (SOS). Other alternatives to AA include medical treatment, group therapy, mindfulness meditation, and individual psychotherapy (Huebner & Kantor, 2011; Jacobs-Stewart, 2010). There is a strong tendency for abusive drinkers to deny that they have a problem. The sooner they seek help, the better.

Hallucinogens: Tripping the Light Fantastic

Although a **hallucinogen** (hal-LU-sin-oh-jen) is generally a mild stimulant, its main effect is to stimulate perceptions at odds with reality. The most common hallucinogens include LSD, PCP, mescaline, psilocybin, and cannabis. In fact, *cannabis* is by far the most popular illicit drug in America (Center for Behavioral Health Statistics and Quality, 2016).

LSD and PCP

The drug LSD (lysergic acid diethylamide, or *acid*) is perhaps the best-known hallucinogen. Even when taken in tiny amounts, LSD can produce hallucinations, mystical-type experiences, and psychotic-like disturbances in thinking and perception (Liechti, Dolder, & Schmid, 2016). Two other common hallucinogens are mescaline (peyote) and psilocybin (*magic mushrooms*, or *shrooms*). Incidentally, the drug PCP (phencyclidine, or *angel dust*) can have hallucinogenic effects. However, PCP, which is an anesthetic, also has stimulant and depressant effects. This potent combination can cause extreme agitation, disorientation, violence, and—too often—tragedy. Like other psychoactive drugs, all hallucinogens, including cannabis, typically affect neurotransmitter systems that carry messages between brain cells (Maisto, Galizio, & Connors, 2015).

Cannabis

Cannabis and hashish are derived from the hemp plant *Cannabis sativa*. Cannabis (also called *marijuana*, *pot*, *grass*, *reefer*, and *MJ*) consists of the dried leaves and flowers of the hemp plant. Hashish is a resinous material scraped from cannabis buds. The two main psychoactive chemicals in cannabis are THC (*tetrahydrocannabinol*), and CBD (*cannabidiol*).

Artists have tried at times to capture the effects of hallucinogens. Here, the artist depicts visual experiences he had while under the influence of LSD.

Cannabis's psychological effects include a sense of euphoria or well-being, relaxation, altered time sense, and perceptual distortions. At very high dosages, however, paranoia, hallucinations, and delusions can occur (Ksir, Hart, & Black, 2015). All considered, cannabis intoxication is relatively subtle by comparison to drugs such as LSD or alcohol. Despite this, driving a car while high on cannabis can be hazardous (National Institute on Drug Abuse, 2017). As a matter of fact, driving under the influence of any intoxicating drug is dangerous.

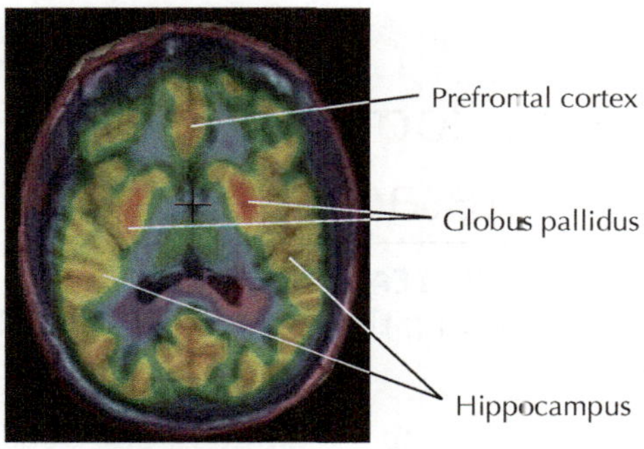

Figure 5.7 Endocannabinoid receptors. The red and yellow areas in this PET scan show some of the areas where the brain is rich in endocannabinoid receptors. The prefrontal cortex plays a role in human consciousness, the globus pallidus is involved in the control of coordinated movement, and the hippocampus plays a role in memory. This may explain why cannabis use negatively affects memory and coordination.

How does cannabis work? Researchers have recently discovered the *endocannabinoid system*, which is widely distributed throughout the brain (Julien, 2011). Neurons in this system communicate via neurotransmitters (such as *anandimide*) called *endocannabinoids* (the prefix *endo-* means *endogenous*, or "originating from within"). It turns out that THC and CBD, the main cannabinoids in cannabis, can also activate neurons with endocannabinoid receptors (Figure 5.7).

Understanding how the endocannabinoid system affects behavior, then, may well help us better understand the effects of cannabis. Conversely, understanding the effects of cannabis may also help us better understand the functioning of the endocannabinoid system (Piomelli, 2014).

Does cannabis produce physical dependence? Yes, according to recent studies (Filbey et al., 2009; National Institute on Drug Abuse, 2017). Frequent users of cannabis can find it very difficult to quit, so dependence is a risk (Hasin et al., 2016). But cannabis's potential for abuse lies primarily in the realm of psychological dependence, not physical addiction.

It's worth noting that although no overdose deaths from cannabis have been reported, cannabis cannot be considered harmless. For about a day after a person smokes cannabis, his or her attention, coordination, and short-term memory are impaired. Frequent cannabis users show small declines in learning, memory, attention, and thinking abilities (Solowij et al., 2002). Accordingly, they score lower on IQ tests (Kuehn, 2012). In fact, many people who have stopped using cannabis say that they quit because they were bothered by short-term memory loss and concentration problems. Fortunately, IQ scores and other cognitive measures rebound about a month after a person quits using cannabis (Grant et al., 2001).

When surveyed, nonusers are healthier, earn more, and are more satisfied with their lives than people who smoke cannabis regularly (Allen & Holder, 2013; Ellickson, Martino, & Collins, 2004). In fact, cannabis use is associated with a variety of mental health problems (Buckner, Ecker, & Cohen, 2010; National Institute on Drug Abuse, 2017). For example, chronic cannabis users are more prone to develop psychosis (Castle et al., 2012).

Cannabis's long-term effects include a number of health risks. THC may interfere with menstrual cycles and ovulation, as well as cause a higher rate of miscarriages. It also can reach the developing fetus: children whose mothers smoked cannabis during pregnancy show a lowered ability to succeed in challenging, goal-oriented activities (National Institute on Drug Abuse, 2017; Noland et al., 2005). As is true for so many other drugs, cannabis should be avoided during pregnancy.

Detoxification In the treatment of drug abuse, including alcoholism, the withdrawal of the patient from the drug(s) in question.

Hallucinogen A substance that alters or distorts sensory impressions.

Medical Cannabis

Is cannabis a dangerous drug or not? On the one hand, as we have just read, cannabis appears to pose a range of health risks. The U.S. government has long labeled cannabis a *Schedule 1 prohibited substance*. Classified in the most dangerous category, along with drugs such as heroin and LSD, cannabis was assumed to pose serious potential for abuse, while offering no medical benefits.

On the other hand, as of this writing, more than half of all states have legalized some instrumental uses of cannabis as a medicine, and more than a dozen have even legalized recreational use. While the legal status of cannabis is a social policy matter best addressed by governments, it can nevertheless be helpful to examine the relevant scientific evidence that cannabis can be medically useful.

Okay, what does the evidence tell us? While the endocannabinoid system is not yet fully understood, it has been shown to influence the impact of stress and pain (Piomelli, 2014). Understandably, then, recent evidence suggests that THC is helpful in treating some forms of pain due to surgery or trauma to the body, reducing vomiting and nausea due to chemotherapy for cancer, promoting weight gain, and even lessening immune system inflammation (National Academies of Sciences, Engineering, and Medicine, 2017; Prus, 2014). Although evidence such as this may suggest that the case in favor of medical cannabis is beyond question, it is worth briefly considering the role cannabis plays in the treatment of post-traumatic stress disorder (PTSD).

PTSD is a debilitating stress reaction to traumatic events that can leave an affected person unable to function normally. Every year, over a million Americans will suffer from PTSD, including many military veterans (National Center for PTSD, 2017). We already know that the amygdala plays a key role in PTSD (Lamprecht et al., 2009) and that the endocannabinoid system moderates the functioning of the amygdala (Piomelli, 2014). It follows, then, that cannabis may help people with PTSD.

But the actual link may not be so straightforward, as suggested by research showing that people with PTSD may be vulnerable to developing a *cannabis use disorder* (Cornelius et al., 2010). In other words, while casual use may make coping with PTSD easier in the short term, it may leave a person's PTSD untreated while adding a drug abuse problem over the long term.

Fortunately, other research suggests that the key to overcoming PTSD is facing your fear (what behavior therapists call *extinction*). Cannabis makes it easier to face those fears and desensitize them in the long run (Rabinak et al., 2013). Combining existing therapies with cannabis use may turn out to be the most effective approach to treating PTSD. (■ See Section 14.4 for more information about PTSD, and ■ Section 15.2 for more information about extinction therapies.)

In summary, cannabis is just like any other drug. Used indiscriminately, it may do more harm than good. Used in medically appropriate circumstances, it may do more good than harm. Hopefully, research will continue to point the way to additional effective medical uses of cannabis.

Reflective Practice

Drug-Altered Consciousness: The High and Low of It

1. Addictive drugs stimulate the brain's reward circuitry by affecting ____________.
   a. neurotransmitters
   b. alpha waves
   c. tryptophan levels
   d. delta spindles
2. Which of the following drugs are known to cause physical dependence?
   a. heroin
   b. morphine
   c. codeine
   d. methadone
   e. barbiturates
   f. alcohol
   g. cannabis
   h. amphetamines
   i. nicotine
   j. cocaine
   k. GHB
3. Amphetamine psychosis is similar to extreme ________________, in which the individual feels threatened and suffers from delusions.
4. Cocaine is very similar to which of the following in its effects on the central nervous system?
   a. alcohol
   b. codeine
   c. cannabis
   d. amphetamine
5. MDMA and GHB are classified as depressants. T or F?
6. College students may overdrink as they try to keep up with how much they falsely imagine that their peers drink. T or F?

THINK CRITICALLY

7. Evaluate why there is such a contrast between the laws regulating cannabis and those regulating alcohol and tobacco.

SELF-REFLECT

- What legal drugs did you use in the last year? Did any have psychoactive properties?
- How do psychoactive drugs differ from other substances in their potential for abuse?

Answers: 1. a 2. All of them 3. paranoia 4. d 5. T 6. T 7. Drug laws in Western societies reflect cultural values and historical patterns of use. Consequently inconsistencies in the law often cannot be justified solely on the basis of pharmacology, health risks, or abuse potential.

5.5 Psychology and Your Skill Set: Metacognition

GATEWAYS LEARNING OUTCOMES:
After reading this section you should be able to:

5.5.1 Define metacognition and describe its three elements

5.5.2 Create a plan to improve your own metacognitive skills

For years, millions of Americans watched as men and women have tried to achieve fame on reality shows such as *America's Got Talent*. Some of the people who auditioned were outstanding and went on to successful careers in show business (such as Season 13 semifinalist, mentalist Aaron Crow Trent, pictured here). But some of the auditions were truly awful. What were these people thinking when they decided to perform in public? Some of them were obviously just having fun and were well aware of their inability to carry a tune, or be funny, or juggle. But others seemed genuinely unaware of their lack of talent or how to interpret audience reactions. Psychologists would likely say that these people were lacking a skill called *metacognition* (as well as talent).

Metacognition is the ability to "think about thinking" (note that psychologists often refer to thoughts as *cognitions*). It includes the ability to monitor and evaluate your thought processes, understanding, and performance across different situations. In this respect it's related to *consciousness*, which was described at the beginning of this chapter as "your sensations and perceptions of external events as well as your self-awareness of mental events, including thoughts, memories, and feelings about your experiences and yourself" (Morin, 2006; Robinson, 2008).

Metacognition is also closely connected to the self-regulation skills that were discussed in Chapter 2, particularly the *executive functions* (Roebers & Feurer, 2015). Recall that executive functions are important in helping people to reach their goals, and one key element in that process is being able to make plans.

Aaron Crow at the "America's Got Talent" Live Show Red Carpet at the Dolby Theater in Los Angeles, CA.

Metacognition is critical in helping you to develop effective plans and in evaluating progress as you carry them out. As a result, it's a skill that's important in helping people to achieve both personal and professional goals.

Do You Know What You Don't Know?

Psychology has a long history of examining how accurate people are when they try to assess their thinking and behavior (Zell & Krizan, 2014). Unfortunately, the news from researchers isn't too good: In general, people are quite poor at evaluating the quality of their thinking, their understanding of material, and their skill level. To make matters worse, this inability to properly monitor what we know and how we're doing is far-reaching, influencing everything from assessments about our social, academic, and athletic skills to our judgments about how much we have understood from a textbook chapter or how long it will take to complete a task (Dunning, Heath, & Suls, 2004).

You may be asking yourself how people could be so poor at evaluating their own thinking. In tackling this question, researchers have shown that there are many things that get in the way of the ability to carry out an accurate self-assessment. According to Serra and Metcalfe (2009), the problems that we face are related to each of the three elements of metacognition: *Knowledge*, *monitoring*, and *control.*

Knowledge

We think about a lot of things every day. Our thought processes can include things that are as diverse as forming an impression of a new acquaintance, considering an essay you have to write, or comparing two options on a restaurant menu. Serra and Metcalfe (2009) describe metacognitive knowledge as the information we consult when considering our thought processes. It can include what you know about your *abilities*, the *biases* you have, and what you know about the *strategies* that will help you achieve your goals.

For example, let's say that you were thinking about an essay on sleep deprivation that's due next week. Your metacognitive knowledge might include the idea that you need to get online and search for journal articles, because you understand that this general "paper-writing strategy" is more likely to result in an essay that meets your instructor's standards than simply reviewing Wikipedia pages. Metacognitive knowledge might also involve an understanding that you find the topic complicated, or the idea that you have a bias toward spending too much time reading when preparing to do a paper (because that part seems easy, and you can convince yourself that you're making progress) and that you tend to procrastinate on actually writing papers (because that task is more difficult).

Metacognitive knowledge can also be important in your personal life. For example, if you want to have good relationships with others, it would be helpful for you to be aware that you have a tendency to talk too much when you're nervous, that you're very quick to judge other people, or that you have trouble seeing things from

Metacognition The conscious experience of thinking about your own thinking and performance.

other people's points of view. These types of strategies, biases, and abilities (and many others) are important in determining relationship quality, so it's important that you use this metacognitive knowledge when you're interacting with others.

Wow. I really should give more thought to my own thinking! It's true! Actively accessing metacognitive knowledge about how you relate to other people or perform work-related tasks is important because an awareness of this information can help as you work toward building good relationships, or plan the work that's needed to complete a school project or write a test (Zhang Zepeda et al., 2015). Of course, simply considering metacognitive knowledge isn't enough. Once you've got that information, you need to work with it, and that's where metacognitive monitoring and control come in.

Monitoring and Control

Metacognitive monitoring refers to the idea that you need to track your thought processes and behaviors as they unfold, and evaluate whether they're going to allow you to meet your goals. In contrast, metacognitive control refers to a situation in which you alter or redirect your thinking and behavior because metacognitive knowledge and monitoring suggests that your current path will not allow you to meet your goals.

If we return to the sleep deprivation paper you're supposed to be writing, for example, you might ask whether you're moving too slowly with reading the research (monitoring) and might need to alter your work schedule in order to finish on time (control). Or perhaps you catch yourself when you seem to be making a snap judgment about someone you have just met (monitoring), and recognize that perhaps you should investigate their personal characteristics further (control). And if you were planning to audition for a reality show, you should be able to assess your own performance relative to a reasonable standard (monitoring), and recognize that if you're doing poorly, you may need additional practice time (control) before you go on television.

Thinking About Thinking

You may be wondering at this point whether poor metacognitive skills are really a big deal. In fact, difficulties with metacognition can lead to problems in many areas of your academic, personal, and professional life. For example, consider how Aysha might plan out her studying when she's preparing for a major exam. What strategies should she use to ensure that she learns the material? At what point should she leave the chapter she's working on and move on to study the next one?

The answers to these questions are important in securing a good result on the exam, and they rely on Aysha's metacognitive skills (Zhang Zepeda et al., 2015). In all likelihood, she'll use study strategies that she *thinks* will be helpful, and she'll move on when she *thinks* she's mastered the material in the chapter she's currently studying. But what if she's wrong? What if her metacognitive skills are poor, and she doesn't know that her study strategies aren't as effective as those outlined in the introduction to this book? What if she's doesn't recognize that she has a very limited understanding of the textbook material?

You can probably see where this type of poor metacognitive awareness leads: Aysha will be using strategies that are not helpful when studying, and will be likely to think—incorrectly!—that she has mastered the material that will be tested. As a result, she won't feel the need to spend any additional time studying and is likely to be very disappointed with her results.

Poor metacognitive skills have important consequences for our personal relationships as well (Myers & Wells, 2015). At one time or another, you have likely met people who don't seem to have any sense of how their behavior is impacting others. These are the people who often wind up either frustrating or intimidating those that they interact with because they don't seem able to monitor the thinking that is behind their actions, or the signals that others are sending them. A lack of self-awareness makes it difficult to forge close and supportive relationships with family, friends, and co-workers because positive interactions with others require that you consider how your thinking impacts your behavior, and assess social cues so that you can alter your thinking and behavior if it seems necessary (Rivers et al., 2012).

So if metacognitive skills are that important, how can I improve on mine? There are several things that you can do to develop your metacognitive awareness. Some of the most effective strategies include the following:

- **Develop your metacognitive knowledge.** Try to become more aware of the strategies, assumptions, and biases that guide your thinking and decision making at school, work, and in your relationships with others. Think carefully about how these tendencies can influence your behavior in particular situations, and whether there might be better ways of responding. Make sure that your thinking and decision making make use of all the information that you have available. Just as important, however, is that you carefully consider the information you *don't* have, but that would be useful for the task at hand. Remember that understanding what you know is only one half of the story—understanding the *limits* of what you know is the other half.
- **Develop your metacognitive monitoring processes.** When your metacognitive knowledge suggests that you're in a situation that is connected to particular strategies, biases, or assumptions, take care to monitor your thought processes and behaviors to ensure that they aren't interfering with the goals you've set for yourself.
- **Develop metacognitive control strategies.** When your metacognitive monitoring suggests that you're not on track to meet your goals, change course by altering your thought processes or your behavior.

We've seen lots of evidence to suggest that metacognition can be important across many areas of our lives. And although the psychological research demonstrates that people aren't always very good at evaluating their own thinking, the positive news is that metacognition is a skill that we can improve on with practice. There are several chapters in this book that offer insight into the biases and situations that are likely to hamper the ability to judge our thinking and behavior. As you read, try to take note of them and incorporate them into your metacognitive knowledge base so that you'll be aware of them in the future. After all, no one needs more information about you than, well . . . you.

Reflective Practice

Psychology and Your Skill Set: Metacognition

1. People are good at evaluating their own thinking. T or F?
2. What are the three self-assessment elements within metacognition?
3. Label the following examples as metacognitive knowledge, monitoring, or control.
   a. You set aside additional time for studying after recognizing that you won't have enough time to get through all the chapters before your test next week.
   b. You know that you find it difficult to write tests without sufficient sleep.
   c. You notice that people tend to disengage from conversations with you when you begin complaining about how much you hate work.

THINK CRITICALLY

4. A friend who experiences social anxiety has just begun using an online dating website in the hopes of meeting a partner. However, after a few dates, he has had little success, but feels that it must be because of the dating site he is using. Using the tips for developing better metacognitive abilities, identify ways you could help your friend approach this problem.

SELF-REFLECT

- Reflect on your current metacognitive abilities. What are some ways you could improve these abilities in your personal and professional life?
- Do you have any current habits that may be holding you back from academic success?
- Are there any areas in your personal relationships that require more metacognitive thought?

Answers: 1. F 2. knowledge, monitoring, and control 3. a) control b) knowledge c) monitoring 4. There might be several steps that you could take to help your friend, including helping him to become more knowledgeable about his social anxiety and what triggers it (metacognitive knowledge). You might also help him to consider how important it is to be aware of how the anxiety may be affecting his dating experiences (metacognitive monitoring); for example, the people he dates may notice his anxiety and respond poorly to it. Finally, you could also help him to consider how to respond to his anxiety on a date (metacognitive control); for example, if he begins to feel anxious, he could excuse himself and practice some breathing exercises in a quiet place to calm down.

CHAPTER IN REVIEW

Gateways to Consciousness

Summary: Gateways Learning Outcomes

5.1 States of Consciousness: The Many Faces of Awareness

5.1.1 Define consciousness

Consciousness is a core feature of mental life consisting of sensations and perceptions of external events as well as self-awareness of mental events, including thoughts, memories, and feelings about experiences and the self.

5.1.2 Distinguish between disordered states of consciousness and altered states of consciousness

Disordered (non-normal) states of consciousness include comas and persistent vegetative states. Altered states of consciousness (ASCs) are characterized by changes in the quality and pattern of mental activity (e.g., perceptions, emotions, time sense). ASCs are especially associated with sleep and dreaming, hypnosis, meditation, and psychoactive drugs. Cultural norms affect what ASCs a person recognizes, seeks, considers normal, and attains.

5.2 Hypnosis and Meditation: Relax …

5.2.1 Describe how hypnosis works, distinguishing between state and nonstate theories of hypnosis

Although not all psychologists agree, hypnosis is usually defined as a state characterized by narrowed attention, reduced peripheral awareness, and increased suggestibility. It is *not* the same as being asleep. Hypnotists have individuals focus attention on the hyponotist's words, asking them to relax, let go and accept suggestions, and use their imagination. Feelings that accompany hypnosis include floating, sinking, and a separation from the body. Hypnosis may improve physical abilities, enhance memory, induce amnesia, relieve pain, and alter sensory experiences. Actions of the hypnotized person feel involuntary, but they are aware of what is happening and remain in control.

The most common state theory of hypnosis suggests it is a dissociative state characterized by a "split" in our awareness, one part of which is a "hidden observer" that is detached from the hypnotized person's awareness and silently watches what is happening. In contrast, nonstate theories suggest hypnosis is simply a blend of conformity, relaxation, imagination, obedience, and role-playing characterized by autosuggestion.

5.2.2 Describe how meditation works, distinguishing between mindfulness and concentrative meditation

Meditation is a mental exercise to alter consciousness. Meditation is thought to work by bringing about the relaxation response, a calming physiological response. The major benefits of meditation are its ability to calm the body and mind, improve mental clarity, relieve some psychological disorders, and improve self-awareness and creativity.

Mindfulness meditation involves observing your own thoughts and feelings without judgment. In contrast, concentrative meditation requires individuals to focus on something specific (word, mantra, breathing) to focus attention.

5.3 Sleep: The Nightly Roller Coaster

5.3.1 Describe the typical pattern of sleeping and waking

Humans' sleep–wake cycles usually work on a 24-hour clock, though in the absence of typical light/dark patterns this cycle will shift to one that averages more than 24 hours. Most people sleep for approximately 7–8 hours, though there can be significant variation in the amount of sleep that people need and there appears to be a developmental shift, with older adults sleeping less.

5.3.2 Describe NREM (non-REM) sleep, including its function and four stages

During NREM sleep, brain waves become longer and slower, pulse rate drops, and body temperature drops. NREM sleep occurs in four stages. Stage 1 is light sleep, and Stage 4 is deep sleep. The sleeper alternates between Stages 1 and 4 (passing through Stages 2 and 3) several times each night. In terms of function, NREM sleep helps the body to recover from fatigue and calms the brain to allow the process of memory consolidation to begin.

5.3.3 Describe REM sleep and its function

Periods of REM (rapid eye movement) sleep are strongly associated with high emotion, aroused physiology, dreaming, and sleep paralysis. With respect to function, REM sleep is important for completing the consolidation of memories.

5.3.4 Explain why we need to sleep, and the consequences of not sleeping

Lowered body metabolism and brain activity during sleep may help conserve energy and lengthen life. Moderate sleep loss affects mainly vigilance and performance on routine or boring tasks. Higher animals and people deprived of sleep experience involuntary microsleeps. Extended sleep loss can (somewhat rarely) produce a temporary sleep-deprivation psychosis.

5.3.5 Name and briefly describe the three theories of dreaming

- The *Freudian, or psychodynamic, view* is that dreams express unconscious wishes, frequently disguised by dream symbols.
- The *activation-synthesis model* portrays dreaming as a random physiological process.
- The *neurocognitive view* of dreams holds that dreams are continuous with waking thoughts and emotions. Supporting the neurocognitive view, most dream content is about familiar settings, people, and actions.

5.3.6 Outline five sleep disorders

1. Insomnia is defined by difficulties getting to sleep and/or staying asleep. It may be temporary or chronic. It is often caused by worry, stress, or excitement but can also be brought on by withdrawal from sleeping pills.
2. Disorders of arousal, including sleepwalking, sleeptalking, and sleepsex (which occur during NREM sleep)
3. Sleep terrors (which occur in NREM sleep) and nightmares (which occur in REM sleep)
4. Sleep apnea (interrupted breathing), which is suspected to be one cause of SIDS
5. Narcolepsy and cataplexy (which are caused by a sudden shift to Stage 1 REM patterns during normal waking hours)

5.4 Drug-Altered Consciousness: The High and Low of It

5.4.1 Explain the action of a psychoactive drug, and distinguish between recreational and instrumental drug use

Psychoactive drugs affect the brain in ways that alter consciousness. Most psychoactive drugs can be placed on a scale ranging from stimulant to depressant.

Instrumental use of drugs refers to situations when drugs are used to address a specific issue. Recreational use of drugs refers to situations when drugs are used to experience the psychoactive effects of a drug. Recreational use may be experimental, social-recreational, intensive, or compulsive. Drug abuse is most often associated with the last two recreational uses.

5.4.2 Outline three reasons for drug abuse

Psychoactive drugs are abused as a *coping mechanism*, to achieve the *rewarding experience* that drugs generate in the brain, and because the user has developed a *dependency*.

5.4.3 Name five common stimulants

- Amphetamines, or synthetic stimulants (e.g., methamphetamine and "study drugs" such as Adderall and Ritalin)
- Cocaine; a natural stimulant extracted from cocoa
- MDMA/Ecstasy
- Caffeine
- Nicotine

5.4.4 Name five common depressants

- Opioids, or narcotics (e.g., opium, heroin, morphine, codeine, oxycodone, methadone. and fentanyl)
- Barbiturates, or sedatives
- GHB
- Tranquilizers (e.g., benzodiazapines such as Valium, Xanax)
- Alcohol

5.4.5 Name two common hallucinogens

- LSD/PCP
- Cannabis

5.5 Psychology and Your Skill Set: Metacognition

5.5.1 Define metacognition, and describe its three elements

Metacognition is the ability to think about our thinking, understanding, and performance. In general, people have poor metacognitive judgments. The three elements of metacognition are knowledge (about skills, biases, and strategies), monitoring (through tracking and evaluating thoughts and behaviors), and control (changing or redirecting thoughts and behaviors).

5.5.2 Create a plan to improve your own metacognitive skills

Developing metacognitive knowledge, monitoring processes, and control strategies are important in personal and professional settings, and can help you with such things as building relationships or assessing how you might best study for exams or complete a big project. We hope that after reading this section, you'll be better able to use what you know about the three elements of metacognition to help you improve your awareness about your skills and knowledge in areas that are important to you.

6 Conditioning and Learning

Robert Alexander/Archive Photos/Getty Images

Gateway Theme There are many different ways to learn, and the principles of learning can be used to understand and manage behavior.

Chapter Outline

Just Learn It

Over the years, sports apparel giant Nike has used its advertising campaigns to push important—and sometimes polarizing—social issues. Their ads have prominently featured athletes who were older, physically disabled, and openly HIV-positive, as well as those who have faced anger and discrimination in the United States and other countries.

You might wonder why Nike would be interested in having their products linked with controversial athletes like former NFL quarterback Colin Kaepernick or transgender triathlete Chris Mosier. Or perhaps even with distance runner Walt Stack who, at 80 years of age, was featured prominently in the very first "Just Do It" advertising campaign.

In this chapter we'll explore this question by talking about several different types of learning, including *classical conditioning*—a type of learning that stems from the associations that are created when two things are repeatedly paired together. We'll see how these various types of learning work, and how they have important implications for our everyday behavior—including the likelihood that we'll purchase a pair of Nikes the next time we need new running shoes.

6.1 The Basics of Learning

GATEWAYS LEARNING OUTCOMES:
After reading this section you should be able to:

6.1.1 Define learning

6.1.2 Outline four types of learning

6.1.3 Define associative learning and identify two types of associative learning

Imagine you suddenly lost everything you had ever learned. What would you still be able to do? You definitely wouldn't be able to read, write, or speak. You couldn't feed yourself, find your way home, tie your shoes, or play the clarinet (assuming, of course, that you knew how to play a clarinet in the first place). Needless to say, you would likely be totally incapacitated.

Types of Learning

Learning is a relatively permanent change in knowledge and/or behavior that results from experience (Powell, Honey, & Symbaluk, 2017). Notice that this definition excludes both temporary changes and more permanent changes caused by motivation, fatigue, maturation, disease, injury, or drugs. Each of these can alter our understanding or behavior, but none qualifies as learning.

Further, there are different types of learning (Abrahamse et al., 2016; Milton et al., 2017; Vadillo & Luque, 2013). **Associative learning** occurs whenever a person or an animal forms a simple association among various stimuli, behaviors, or both. Associative learning requires little or no awareness or thought (Everitt & Robbins, 2016). For early psychologists, such as Ivan Pavlov, John Watson, and Edward Thorndike (■ see Section 1.3), associative learning was a fairly mechanical process of "stamping in" associations between objective stimuli and objective responses, or behaviors (Hergenhahn & Henry, 2014).

In this chapter, we'll talk about two types of associative learning: classical conditioning and operant conditioning. We'll also discuss other ways by which people learn, including observational learning and cognitive learning.

Reflective Practice

The Basics of Learning

1. In which of the following situations would you say learning had **not** taken place?
   a. Charmi's piano skills improved as a result of taking lessons for many years.
   b. Tariq no longer eats hamburgers because he became very ill after eating one at a county fair many years ago.
   c. Two-year-old Esme figured out how to open the back door of her house after watching her brother do it.
   d. Michael became much more aggressive as his dementia became more severe.
2. The two forms of associative learning are
   a. punishment and reinforcement
   b. discrimination and generalization
   c. classical and operant conditioning
   d. imitation and modeling
3. Associative learning involves making associations between stimuli, behaviors, or both with little or no awareness. T or F?

Answers: 1. d 2. c 3. T

6.2 Classical Conditioning: Pair Up!

GATEWAYS LEARNING OUTCOMES:
After reading this section you should be able to:

6.2.1 Explain how classical conditioning works

6.2.2 Distinguish between extinction and spontaneous recovery

6.2.3 Differentiate between stimulus generalization and stimulus discrimination

6.2.4 Name four instances of classical conditioning in everyday life

At the beginning of the 20th century, something happened in the lab of Russian physiologist Ivan Pavlov that gained him the Nobel Prize: His subjects drooled at him. By itself this wasn't too surprising—after all, Pavlov was studying digestion by putting dogs in harnesses and placing food on their tongues. By arranging for a tube to carry saliva from the dogs' mouths to a lever that activated a recording device, he was able to objectively measure the resulting flow of saliva (see ● Figure 6.1).

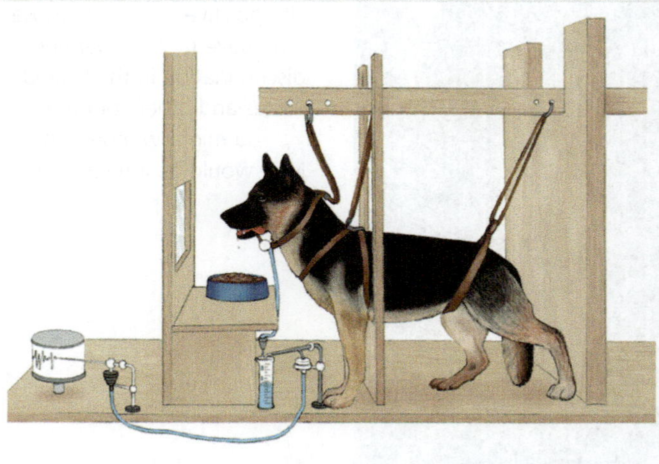

● **Figure 6.1 An apparatus for Pavlovian conditioning.** A tube carries saliva from the dog's mouth to a lever that activates a recording device (*far left*). During conditioning, various stimuli can be paired with a dish of food placed in front of the dog. The device pictured here is more elaborate than the one that Pavlov used in his early experiments.

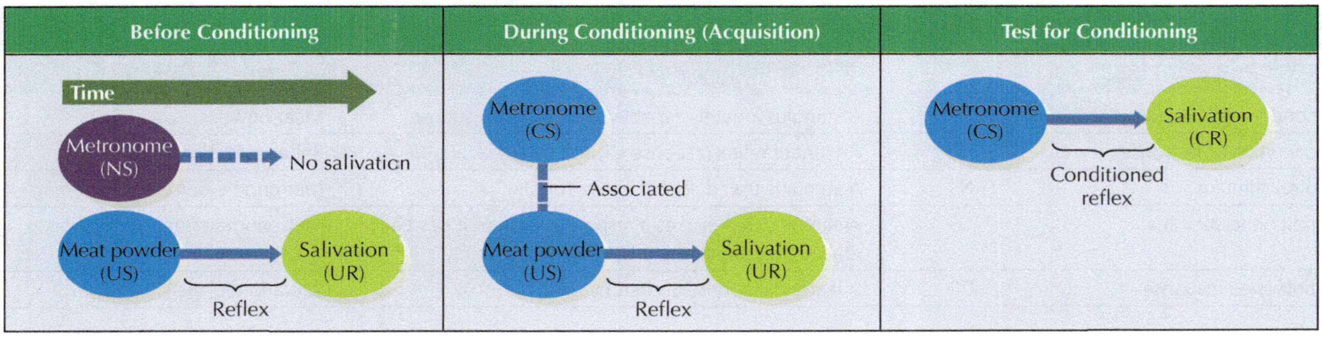

Figure 6.2 The classical conditioning procedure.

However, after repeating his procedure many times, Pavlov noticed that his dogs began salivating *before* the food reached their mouths. Later, the dogs even began to salivate when they saw Pavlov enter the room. Now, Pavlov believed that salivation is an automatic, inherited reflex. It really shouldn't change from one day to the next. His dogs were *supposed* to salivate when he put food in their mouths, but they were *not* supposed to salivate when they merely saw him. This was a change in behavior due to experience—in other words, the dogs were learning! Because of its place in history, this form of associative learning is now called **classical conditioning** (also known as *Pavlovian conditioning* or *respondent conditioning*) (Schultz & Schultz, 2016). Pavlov was fascinated by it and began the process of determining how this type of conditioning worked.

How Classical Conditioning Works

So how did Pavlov study conditioning? Pavlov's work started with a metronome, which is a small device often used by musicians because it can be set to produce a steady beat. To begin, he set the metronome going with a steady, constant rhythm—let's say it was one beat per second. At first, the sound of the metronome was neutral (the dogs did not respond to it by salivating). Immediately after starting the metronome, though, he placed meat powder on the dogs' tongues, which caused reflexive salivation. This sequence was repeated a number of times: metronome, meat powder, salivation; metronome, meat powder, salivation. Eventually, as classical conditioning took place, the dogs began to salivate as soon as they heard the metronome (Figure 6.2). Through its association with food, the metronome—which before was neutral had no effect—began to evoke the same response as food. Pavlov demonstrated this by sometimes starting the metronome *without* providing food. The dogs still salivated, even though no food had been placed in their mouths.

Psychologists use several terms to describe these events (▲ Table 6.1). The meat powder is an **unconditioned stimulus (US)**—a stimulus that elicits a response without any prior experience (salivation in this case). Notice that the dog did not have to learn to respond to the US—its salivation response is based on reflexes. Because a reflexive response like salivation is innate, or "built in," it is called an **unconditioned response (UR)**—a response to a stimulus that requires no previous experience. Reflex salivation was the UR in Pavlov's experiment.

The metronome starts out as a **neutral stimulus (NS)**—one that does not produce a specific response. In time, though, this neutral stimulus becomes a **conditioned stimulus (CS)**—a stimulus that, through repeated pairing with an unconditioned stimulus like meat powder, comes to elicit a learned response. When hearing Pavlov's metronome also produced salivation, the dog was making a new response. Thus, salivation also had become a **conditioned response (CR)** or learned reaction. One thing that's really important to remember is that conditioning will be most rapid if the US (meat powder) follows *immediately* after the CS (the metronome). With most classical conditioning, the optimal delay between CS and US is from ½ second to about 5 seconds (Olson & Hergenhahn, 2013).

But the CR and the UR are the same thing—salivation. If that's the case, then why do they have different names? That's a great question! The answer is that although the UR and CR are the same in this example, that isn't always the case (Kaulich et al., 2010). And sometimes even when the UR and CR seem to be the same, there are often small differences between them that are only

Learning Any relatively permanent change in knowledge or behavior that can be attributed to experience.

Associative learning The formation of simple associations between various stimuli and responses.

Classical conditioning A form of learning in which reflex responses are associated with new stimuli.

Unconditioned stimulus (US) Something that elicits a response without any prior experience.

Unconditioned response (UR) Response to a stimulus that requires no previous experience.

Neutral stimulus (NS) A stimulus that does not evoke a response.

Conditioned stimulus (CS) Neutral stimulus that, through pairing with an unconditioned stimulus, comes to elicit a learned response.

Conditioned response (CR) Learned reaction elicited by pairing an originally neutral stimulus with an unconditioned stimulus.

▲ Table 6.1 Elements of Classical Conditioning

Element	Symbol	Description	Example
Unconditioned stimulus	US	A stimulus innately capable of eliciting a response	Meat powder
Unconditioned response	UR	An innate reflex response elicited by a US	Reflex salivation *to the US*
Neutral stimulus	NS	A stimulus that does not evoke the UR	Metronome *before conditioning*
Conditioned stimulus	CS	A stimulus that evokes a response because it has been repeatedly paired with a US	Metronome *after conditioning*
Conditioned response	CR	A learned response elicited by a CS	Salivation *to the CS*

noticeable if you're looking very closely. For example, the amount of saliva produced in response to the metronome (CR) may be slightly less than the amount produced in response to the meat powder (UR).

It's important to note that it's not just dogs that can be classically conditioned—people can learn this way as well. Let's take an example that may be familiar to some of you: If you have ever been to have your eyes checked, you may have experienced a test in which the optometrist blew a puff of air into each eye. People respond to this test with a reflexive reaction: blinking. In classical conditioning terms, a puff of air into the eye (US) will automatically cause you to blink (UR). But what if we took a neutral stimulus—say, a horn—and paired it with the puff of air going into the eye. After repeating this pairing several times, the horn (NS) would become a conditioned stimulus (CS) and it would elicit an eyeblink (CR), even when the horn was no longer paired with the puff of air. Here's a summary of what's happened in this example:

Before Conditioning	**Example**
US → UR (reflexive response)	Puff of air → eye blink
NS → no effect	Horn → no effect

During Conditioning	**Example**
Repeatedly pair US with NS	Sound horn then deliver puff of air to eye

After Conditioning	**Example**
CS → CR	Horn → eye blink

Here's another example: Suppose a scientist named Leonard wants to condition his friend Sheldon. To observe conditioning, he could ring a bell and squirt lemon juice into Sheldon's mouth. Because lemon juice (US) reflexively causes people to salivate (UR), he could condition Sheldon to salivate to the bell (NS) by repeating this procedure several times. The bell would then become a CS that resulted in a CR (salivation). We can use this example as a way of looking at other important aspects of classical conditioning such as extinction, spontaneous recovery, generalization, and discrimination.

Extinction and Spontaneous Recovery

Once an association has been classically conditioned, will it ever go away? If the US stops following the CS, conditioning will fade away, or extinguish. Let's return to Sheldon. If Leonard rings the bell many times and does not follow it with lemon juice, Sheldon's learned expectation that "bell precedes lemon juice" will weaken. As it does, he will lose his tendency to salivate when he hears the bell. Thus, **extinction (in classical conditioning)** occurs by weakening the connection between the conditioned and the unconditioned stimulus.

One thing to remember, though, is that it may take several extinction sessions to completely reverse conditioning. Let's say that Leonard rings the bell until Sheldon quits responding. It might seem that extinction is complete. However, Sheldon will probably respond to the bell again on the following day, at least at first. The return of a learned response after its apparent extinction is called **spontaneous recovery** (Revillo, Paglini, & Arias, 2014; Thanellou & Green, 2011).

Generalization

After conditioning, other stimuli that are similar to the CS may also trigger a response. This is called **stimulus generalization**. In Pavlov's experiment with the dogs, he observed this quite clearly. Remember that the CS was a metronome that was set to a very specific rhythm (one beat per second). However, Pavlov found that after classical conditioning had occurred, the dogs would salivate to the metronome even when the rhythm was a bit faster or slower than that. Similarly, Leonard might find that Sheldon salivates to the sound of a doorbell—even though it was never used as a conditioning stimulus, the doorbell sounds enough like the bell that it can bring about the same response.

It is easy to see the value of stimulus generalization. Consider the child who burns her finger while playing with matches. Most likely, a lighted match will become a conditioned stimulus for her. Because of stimulus generalization, she also may have a healthy fear of flames from lighters, fireplaces, stoves, and so forth. As you may have guessed, though, stimulus generalization has limits. As stimuli become less like the original CS, responding decreases. If you condition a person to blink each time you play a particular note on a piano, blinking will decline as you play higher or lower notes. If the notes are *much* higher or lower, the person will not respond at all (● Figure 6.3).

Discrimination

Let's consider one more idea related to classical conditioning by returning to Pavlov's lab. While the dogs may have initially salivated to the sound of the metronome regardless of its rhythm (owing to generalization), Pavlov was able to teach them to be more selective in their responses. To do this, he would need to pair food with the metronome sound only when it was set to one

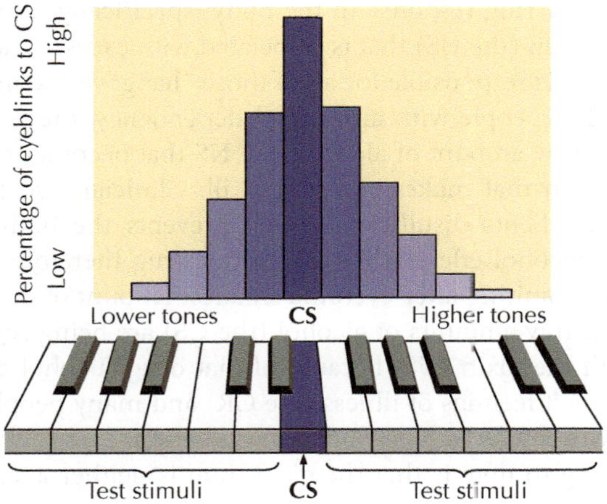

Figure 6.3 Stimulus generalization. After conditioning someone to blink (CR) in response to a note on the piano keyboard (CS), stimuli similar to the CS also elicit a response.

beat per second. Any faster or slower, and the dogs would receive no food. Eventually, the dogs would become very sensitive to the rhythm being produced and would only salivate when it was one beat per second. **Stimulus discrimination**, then, is the learned ability to respond differently to a variety of similar stimuli.

We might also observe discrimination with Sheldon. Suppose Leonard again conditions Sheldon with a bell as the CS. As an experiment, he also occasionally plays the sound of a ringing telephone instead of the bell. However, the ringing telephone is never followed by the US (lemon juice). At first, Sheldon salivates when he hears the telephone (because of generalization). But after Leonard sounds the telephone several times more without any lemon juice, Sheldon will stop responding to it. Why? In essence, Sheldon's generalized response to the telephone has extinguished. As a result, he has learned to *discriminate*, or respond differently, to the bell and the telephone.

Classical Conditioning in Everyday Life

Evidence of classical conditioning is all around us. Let's take a look at some common examples.

Food Aversions

Food aversions provide a good example of classical conditioning in everyday life: People who have become ill after eating a particular food will often refuse to eat that food again. Here's a common example: *E. coli* is a common bacteria (US) that causes severe abdominal pain and vomiting (UR), among other less-than-pleasant symptoms. If you were to eat a burger (initially an NS) that was undercooked and contained the *E. coli* bacteria, the bacteria (US) would be paired with the burger (NS that becomes a CS), bringing about those nasty stomach problems (UR). It's not uncommon in such cases to find that people will avoid eating burgers (CS) in the future because just looking at one makes them feel sick (CR). One thing that you should note about this example is how powerful classical conditioning can be: In many cases of food aversion, effective conditioning happens after just one pairing of the US and NS!

Celebrity Endorsements

Corporations' use of celebrities to promote their products also draws on the principles of classical conditioning. For example, Nike has paid famous athletes such as Serena Williams, Tiger Woods, and LeBron James to appear in their ad campaigns. Each of these athletes (US) has a strong natural association with hard work, talent, and success (UR). What Nike wanted when they signed contracts with them was the opportunity to associate their products (NS that becomes CS) repeatedly with these athletes (US). Doing so would bring about similar positive thoughts of hard work, talent, and success (CR) whenever people saw the Nike swoosh. Even athletes who have generated some controversy like Colin Kaepernick and Chris Mosier appear prominently in Nike ads. From the company's point of view, these individuals are associated with all of those positive qualities as well as an ability to stand behind their values and overcome obstacles. Who *wouldn't* want to walk in those shoes?

Conditioned Emotional Responses

So far, we've talked about situations when learned responses are behavioral (e.g., blinking your eyes in response to a puff of air), cognitive (e.g., thoughts of athletic success), or physical experiences (e.g., feeling sick to your stomach). But learned responses can also be emotional (e.g., feelings of happiness or anxiety). In a very early example of this phenomenon, pioneering psychologist John B. Watson reported conditioning a young child named Little Albert to fear a white rat by pairing the white rat with a loud noise (Beck, Levinson, & Irons, 2009). Loud noise (US) is reflexively associated with fear (UR), but when that noise was repeatedly associated with the rat (the NS that became the CS) Albert began to show fear (CR) in response to the rat.

Since then, it has been widely accepted that many human phobias (FOE-bee-ahs) begin as a **conditioned emotional response (CER)**, or a learned emotional reaction to a previously neutral stimulus (Ollendick & Muris, 2015; Vriends et al., 2012) (Figure 6.4). A *phobia* is a fear that persists even when no realistic danger exists. Fears of animals, water, heights, thunder, fire, bugs, elevators, and the like are common.

Extinction (classical conditioning) Weakening of a learned response by repeatedly presenting the conditioned stimulus without the unconditioned stimulus.

Spontaneous recovery Reappearance of a learned response after its apparent extinction.

Stimulus generalization Tendency to respond to stimuli similar to a conditioned stimulus.

Stimulus discrimination The learned ability to respond differently to similar stimuli.

Conditioned emotional response (CER) An emotional response that has been linked to a previously nonemotional stimulus by classical conditioning.

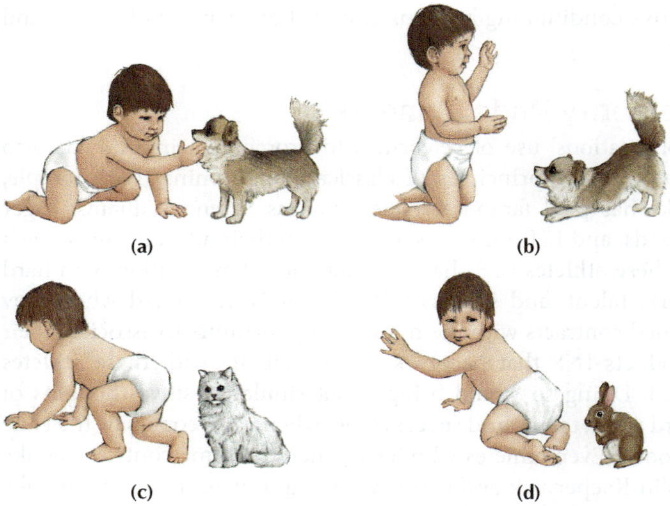

Figure 6.4 Hypothetical example of a CER becoming a phobia. A child approaches a dog (a) and is frightened by it (b). This fear generalizes to other household pets (c) and later to virtually all furry animals (d).

Of course, sometimes a CER can also be positive. Consider Himari, who comes from a close family and has a very good relationship with her mother. Her mother (US) is strongly associated with feelings of happiness (UR) for Himari. Together, the two of them spent many happy hours in the kitchen making shokupan bread while Himari was growing up. Eventually, for Himari the bread (NS) came to be strongly associated with her mom. When Himari grew up and went away to college, she found that even the smell of shokupan bread in a store made her feel happy and comforted. The bread (NS that became a CS) brought about those positive feelings (CR) because of its association with her mom. You may have had a similar experience: Particular smells or songs (NS that becomes CS), for example, bring about conditioned emotional responses (CERs) because they have been paired with people or situations (US) from your past.

Aversion Therapy

Finally, let's take a look at a situation in which conditioning is used by clinicians who are providing assistance to clients. A good example is aversion therapy, in which classical conditioning is used to help individuals overcome bad habits. Aversion therapy involves taking a US that naturally (or reflexively) elicits an aversive, or negative response (the UR). The US is then regularly paired with a negative behavior that the client is trying to eliminate (the NS that becomes the CS). Eventually that behavior begins to elicit the negative response (CR) and clients are less inclined to engage in the behavior.

One common example of aversion therapy is the use of the drug disulfiram for people with alcohol dependency. Here's how it works: Many people have experienced the downside caused by drinking too much alcohol: feelings of nausea, often accompanied by vomiting. This none-too-pleasant experience is based on a naturally occurring response in the body; specifically, a particularly nasty toxin (the US) that is associated with excessive alcohol consumption is responsible for all of those "hangover" symptoms (the UR). For people with an alcohol dependency, the key is to pair even a tiny amount of alcohol (the NS that becomes the CS) with the toxin that makes you feel so ill. Clinicians do this by giving their clients disulfiram, which prevents the body from processing alcohol effectively—taking the drug therefore causes nausea and vomiting after even the smallest amount of drinking. When even tiny amounts of alcohol (the CS) are being regularly paired with the toxin (US) because of that drug, alcohol quickly begins to elicit feelings of illness (the CR) and many people who struggle with alcoholism give up their addiction.

One thing to note is that the disulfiram is neither a stimulus nor a response here. Its importance in this example of conditioning is simply that it allows the pairing of the alcohol (NS) and the toxin (US) to happen very quickly, thus allowing the NS to become the CS. Remember that the effectiveness of classical conditioning depends to a large extent on how quickly the US (toxin) follows the CS (alcohol). Under normal circumstances (that is, without the drug being present) it would take considerable time (and a large amount of alcohol that will probably be coupled with some positive feelings!) for the toxin to build up and cause feelings of illness. For the therapy to be most effective, then, it's important that drinking becomes associated with a negative UR (feelings of illness) very quickly—disulfiram makes that possible.

Reflective Practice

Classical Conditioning: Pair Up!

1. Eating homemade cookies will naturally cause people to salivate. If your mom often bakes cookies that you get to eat, your mouth will eventually start to water as soon as you smell the odor of cookies being baked. Apparently, the odor of cookies is a __________ and your salivation is a __________.
   a. CR, CS
   b. CS, CR
   c. CS, US
   d. UR, CS
2. The ________________ stimulus is repeatedly paired with the unconditioned stimulus and eventually becomes a conditioned stimulus.
3. After you have acquired a conditioned response, it may be weakened by
   a. spontaneous recovery
   b. stimulus generalization
   c. repeated presentation of the CS without the US
   d. repeated presentation of the CS followed by the US
4. Stimulus discrimination is the learned ability to respond differently to a variety of similar stimuli. T or F?
5. Psychologists theorize that many phobias begin when a CER generalizes to other, similar situations. T or F?

THINK CRITICALLY

6. Lately, you have been getting a shock of static electricity every time you touch a door handle. Now, you hesitate before you approach a door handle. Can you analyze this situation in terms of classical conditioning?

SELF-REFLECT

- US, CS, UR, CR—How will you remember these terms? First, note that we are interested in either a stimulus (S) or a response (R). Each S or R can be either conditioned (C) or unconditioned (U). If a stimulus provokes a response before any learning, then it's a US. If you have to learn to respond, then it's a CS. Does a response occur without being learned? Then it's a UR. If it has to be learned, then it's a CR.

Answers: 1. b 2. neutral 3. c 4. T 5. T 6. Electric shocks (the unconditioned stimulus) naturally cause people to reflexively withdraw (unconditioned response). In this case, the door handles are initially a neutral stimulus, but as they are paired repeatedly with the unconditioned stimulus (shocks), door handles become the conditioned stimulus, capable of causing the conditioned response (hesitating to touch with your hand).

6.3 Operant Conditioning: Shape Up!

GATEWAYS LEARNING OUTCOMES:
After reading this section you should be able to:

6.3.1 Explain how operant conditioning works, including how positive and negative reinforcement and punishment will impact the likelihood that a behavior will be repeated

6.3.2 Distinguish between generalization and discrimination in operant conditioning

6.3.3 Explain how shaping works

6.3.4 Name three factors that impact the effectiveness of reinforcement and punishment

6.3.5 Differentiate between continuous and partial schedules of reinforcement and name the four types of partial reinforcement schedules

6.3.6 Contrast primary and secondary reinforcers

6.3.7 Name two instances of operant conditioning in everyday life

Classical conditioning, the subject of the previous section, is one form of associative learning. A second form of associative learning, **operant conditioning** (sometimes called ***instrumental conditioning***), is based on the *consequences* of responding. The basic principle is simple: Acts that are followed by a positive consequence tend to be repeated (Lefrançois, 2012). A dog is much more likely to keep searching for food under a pillow if it finds food there (positive consequence). The dog will likely stop looking there if it fails to find food (no consequence) or finds something frightening (negative consequence). Pioneer learning theorist Edward L. Thorndike called this the **law of effect**—the probability of a response is altered by the effect that it has had (Benjafield, 2015).

You may recall that classical conditioning is passive. It is based on naturally occurring reflexive responses, and simply "happens to" the learner when an unconditioned stimulus repeatedly follows a neutral stimulus (the neutral stimulus then becomes a conditioned stimulus). In contrast, operant conditioning requires that the learner actively "operate on" the environment; in other words, the learner needs to voluntarily emit, or produce, some kind of behavior. Thus, operant conditioning refers mainly to learning *voluntary* responses. For example, pushing buttons on a television remote control is a voluntary behavior that has the potential to become a learned operant response. When you push a particular button on the remote and gain the consequence you desire (changing channels and finding a good program or muting an obnoxious commercial), that behavior will be reinforced and become a learned response. (See ▲ Table 6.2 for a further comparison of classical and operant conditioning.)

Operant (instrumental) conditioning Learning based on the positive or negative consequences of responding.

Law of effect Responses that lead to desirable effects are repeated; those that produce undesirable results are not.

▲ Table 6.2 Comparison of Classical and Operant Conditioning

	Classical Conditioning	Operant Conditioning
Nature of response	Involuntary, reflex	Spontaneous, voluntary
Timing of learning	Occurs *before* response (CS paired with US)	Occurs *after* response (response is followed by reinforcing stimulus or event)
Role of learner	Passive (response is *elicited* by US)	Active (response is emitted)
Nature of learning	Neutral stimulus becomes a CS through association with a US	Probability of making a response is altered by consequences that follow it
Learned expectancy	US will follow CS	Response will have a specific effect

How Operant Conditioning Works

Many early studies of operant conditioning in animals used an **operant conditioning chamber (Skinner box)**, which was developed by B. F. Skinner in the 1930s (Skinner, 1938; Figure 6.5). The walls are bare except for a metal bar and a tray into which food pellets can be dispensed. Two things increase the chances that a subject—usually a rat—will voluntarily emit the desired behavior, which is pressing the bar. First, there's not much to do in a Skinner box. Second, hunger keeps the animal motivated to seek food and actively *emit* a variety of responses.

Let's take a closer look at how operant conditioning works by considering what happens when Einstein—a smart and hungry rat—is placed in an operant conditioning chamber. For a while, Einstein walks around, grooms, sniffs at the corners, or stands on his hind legs—all typical rat behaviors. Then it happens. He places his paw on the bar to get a better view of the top of the cage. *Click!* The bar depresses, and a food pellet drops into the tray. Einstein scurries to the tray, eats the pellet, and then grooms himself. Up and exploring the cage again, he leans on the bar. *Click!* After another trip to the food tray, he returns to the bar and sniffs it, and then puts his paw on it. *Click!* Soon Einstein settles into a smooth pattern of frequent bar pressing.

Notice that Einstein did not acquire a new skill, or response, in this situation. He was already able to press the bar. In operant conditioning, the probability that various responses (like pressing a bar) will be made is influenced by the *consequences* of those responses. Two types of consequences are important in operant learning: reinforcement and punishment.

Reinforcement

As a practical rule of thumb, psychologists define a **reinforcer** as any event that follows a response and increases its probability of occurring again (Figure 6.6). Usually, when people think about reinforcement they think about **positive reinforcement**, which occurs when a reward or other positive event follows a response. For example, giving a child praise for helping with the dishes would be an example of positive reinforcement. Similarly, providing employees with a bonus when they exceed a sales target would also serve as positive reinforcement.

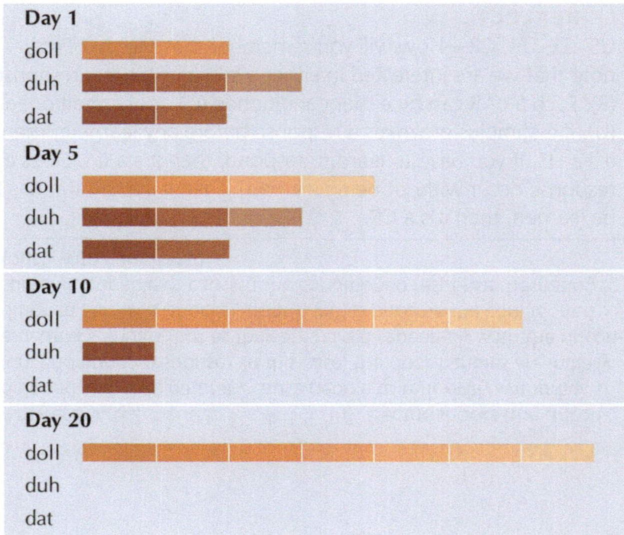

Figure 6.6 Reinforcing language use. Assume that a child who is learning to talk points to her favorite doll and says either "doll," "duh," or "dat" when she wants it. Day 1 shows the number of times the child uses each word to ask for the doll (each block represents one request). At first, she uses all three words interchangeably. To hasten learning, her parents decide to give her the doll only when she names it correctly. Notice how the child's behavior shifts as reinforcement is applied. By day 20, saying "doll" has become the most probable response.

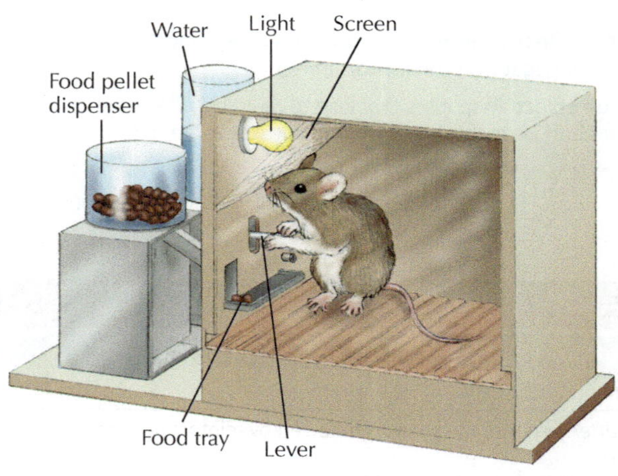

Figure 6.5 The Skinner box. This simple device, invented by B. F. Skinner, allows careful study of operant conditioning. When the rat presses the bar, a pellet of food or a drop of water is automatically released.

So isn't reinforcement *just another term for* reward? Not exactly, because rewards do not always increase responding. For example, imagine that Matteo works in sales and at the end of the year he is given something—maybe a steak dinner or a small plaque—to acknowledge his work. Such rewards do not necessarily guarantee increased responding (that is, Matteo working harder the next year), which *must* happen if a reward is to be considered positive reinforcement. Put another way, all positive reinforcers are rewarding, but not all rewards are positively reinforcing.

Operant learning can also be reinforced through **negative reinforcement**, which occurs when making a response is followed by removing something unpleasant from the environment of the organism. Don't be fooled by the word *negative*. Negative reinforcement also increases responding. However, it does so by ending (*negating*, or taking away) discomfort.

Let's say that you have a headache and take a Tylenol. This behavior—taking the painkiller—will be negatively reinforced if the headache stops, and you will be more likely to repeat that behavior the next time you have a headache. Likewise, a rat could be given a continuous mild shock (through the floor of its cage)

Photographee.eu/Shutterstock.com

Punishers are consequences that lower the probability that a response will be made again. Receiving a traffic citation is directly punishing because the driver is delayed and reprimanded. Paying a fine and higher insurance rates add to the punishment in the form of response cost.

that stops if the rat presses a bar. In this case, the bar press is negatively reinforcing.

Punishment

A **punisher** is an event or consequence that follows a response and makes that response less likely to happen in the future. A good example would be a young woman who drives her car very fast and receives a speeding ticket from a less-than-impressed police officer. In this situation, the voluntary behavior (or operant response)—fast driving—has been followed by an *aversive* (unpleasant) punisher (the speeding ticket). This situation is known as **positive punishment** (but usually we just say **punishment**). Again, don't be fooled by the word *positive.* Positive punishment *decreases* the likelihood that the response will occur again. However, it does so by initiating (*adding*) discomfort or other negative consequences.

Many people mistake negative reinforcement for (positive) punishment. The difference between negative reinforcement and punishment can be shown in a hypothetical example: Let's say that you live in an apartment and your neighbor's stereo is blasting so loudly that you can't concentrate on reading this book. If you pound on the wall and the volume suddenly drops (something negative has been removed) then you will have been negatively reinforced, and you will be more likely to pound on the wall if the same thing happens again. Remember, any form of reinforcement makes a behavior more likely to happen in the future.

In contrast, if you pound on the wall and the volume increases (you have been positively punished) or if the neighbor comes over and pounds on you (more positive punishment), your wall-pounding behavior becomes less likely to happen if the loud music starts again. Any form of punishment makes a behavior less likely to happen in the future.

Isn't it also punishing to have privileges, money, or other positive things taken away for making a particular response? Yes. Punishment also occurs when a reinforcer or positive state of affairs is removed, such as losing privileges. This second type of punishment is called **negative punishment (response cost)**. Negative punishment also decreases responding. However, it does so by ending (*negating*, or taking away) something pleasant.

The best-known form of negative punishment is the *time-out*, in which children are removed from situations that normally allow them to gain reinforcement (Donaldson et al., 2013). When your parents put you in time-out by sending you to your room, they denied you the reinforcement of being with the rest of your family or hanging out with your friends. Another example might be parents taking away a child's allowance for poor behavior. For your convenience, ▲ Table 6.3 summarizes five basic consequences of making a response.

But what if the consequences for a behavior changed over time? Would Einstein the rat stop pressing the bar if no more food arrived? Yes, but not immediately. Through **extinction (in operant conditioning)**, learned responses that are not reinforced gradually

Operant conditioning chamber (Skinner box) An apparatus designed to study operant conditioning in animals.

Reinforcer Any event that reliably increases the probability or frequency of responses it follows.

Positive reinforcement Occurs when a response is followed by a reward or other positive event.

Negative reinforcement Occurs when a response is followed by an end to discomfort or by the removal of an unpleasant event.

Punisher Any event that decreases the probability or frequency of responses that it follows.

Positive punishment (punishment) Any event that follows a response and *decreases* its likelihood of occurring again; the process of suppressing a response.

Negative punishment (response cost) Removal of a positive reinforcer after a response is made.

Operant extinction The weakening or disappearance of a nonreinforced operant response.

▲ Table 6.3 Behavioral Effects of Various Consequences

	Consequence of Making a Response	Example	Effect on Response Probability
Positive reinforcement	Good event begins	Food given	Increase
Negative reinforcement	Bad event ends	Pain stops	Increase
Positive punishment	Bad event begins	Pain begins	Decrease
Negative punishment (response cost)	Good event ends	Food removed	Decrease
Nonreinforcement	Nothing	N/A	Decrease

weaken. Just as acquiring an operant response takes time, so does operant extinction. For example, if a television program that you initially enjoyed watching (that is, watching was reinforced because the show was enjoyable) begins to bore you as it moves into its eighth season, then your "watching behavior" will likely be extinguished over time.

Learning the Boundaries of Reinforcement and Punishment: Generalization, Discrimination, and Shaping

As the previous section made clear, operant conditioning depends on the consequences of a voluntarily emitted behavior. When the consequences are reinforcing, there's an increased likelihood that a behavior will occur again; when the consequences involve punishment the likelihood of the behavior happening again decreases. However, researchers interested in operant conditioning have also noticed that even after the consequences of a specific behavior have been established, additional learning can still take place. For example, it's possible to "test the boundaries" to learn whether other, similar behaviors will bring about the same consequences, a concept referred to as *generalization*. Alternately, it's possible to discover that only a very specific behavior will generate that consequence—this is referred to as *discrimination*. The ability to discriminate exactly what behaviors will bring about particular consequences can be further used to learn more complicated sets of behaviors in a process called *shaping*. Each of these three terms—generalization, discrimination, and shaping—are discussed next.

Generalization

Is generalization the same in operant conditioning as it is in classical conditioning? Basically, yes. We know that reinforcement and punishment will result in behavior occurring more or less frequently, respectively. However, over time it's also possible that an emitted behavior will begin to happen in situations that are similar (but not identical) to those that have been reinforced in the past. This is called **operant stimulus generalization** (but usually just **generalization**).

Assume, for instance, that your dog has begun to jump up at you whenever you are eating dinner at the kitchen table. (Bad dog!) Mind you, that's because you have been positively reinforcing its behavior with table scraps. (Bad owner!) The dog has learned that reinforcement tends to occur when you are at the kitchen table. With a bit of time, though, you may find that your dog begins to jump up at you when you're sitting at the dining room table as well. Because the tables are similar, your dog will likely jump up because this response has *generalized* to other tables.

Examples of generalization can also be seen in humans. Imagine a toddler who responds with a temper tantrum when told by his father that he cannot have a chocolate bar that he has seen while waiting in a line at the grocery store. To avoid embarrassment, the father gives in and buys the chocolate bar. If temper tantrums are reinforced in this way, it's entirely possible that we will begin to see this behavior generalize to other situations, and with other people. For example, the child may have a temper tantrum at the store a few days later when told by his grandmother that he can't have a chocolate bar.

Discrimination

In the previous example we saw that because jumping up at the kitchen table signaled the availability of reinforcement (table scraps) to your dog, it also began jumping up while you sat at a different table in the dining room (generalization). But if you do not feed your dog while sitting at the dining room table, the jumping response that originally generalized to it will extinguish because of *nonreinforcement*. In other words, if your dog's jumping response is consistently rewarded only in the presence of a specific table (the one in the kitchen), jumping at other tables will eventually be extinguished. Through **operant stimulus discrimination** (usually just referred to as **discrimination**), your dog has learned to differentiate between antecedent stimuli (in this case, the two tables) that signal reward and nonreward. Similarly, if the child's temper tantrum is never reinforced by the grandmother, he will quickly learn through discrimination that this behavior will only be reinforced under certain conditions (in this case, when he's with his dad).

Discrimination is aptly illustrated by the training of "sniffer" dogs like URL (pronounced *earl*, aka "smut mutt") that work alongside law enforcement agents investigating criminal activity (Concha et al., 2014). URL is one of an elite handful of dogs trained to detect electronic devices such as USB drives that are used to store pornography (Cabrera, 2016). Similarly trained dogs are widely used to search for a variety of odors, such as those given off by drugs, blood, explosives, currency, animals, animal parts, and even human remains. Discrimination was used to teach URL to recognize the scent of electronic devices, distinguishing the smell of the specific chemical found in cell phones, thumb drives, and microSD cards from other chemicals. During his initial training, then, he was reinforced with food only for approaching containers baited with electronic devices.

Shaping

Ultimately, people who train dogs like URL want to have the dogs go even further than just finding the device. For example, in one case an electronic sniffer dog named Iris learned to sit once she had found a device; when the handler then said, "Show me," Iris would put her nose as close as possible to its location.

It seems pretty unlikely that a dog like Iris would just spontaneously show all those behaviors in the correct order. How would she ever get reinforced and learn what she was supposed to do? That's a great question. When it comes to learning behaviors that are rare or complex, the answer lies in a process called **shaping**, which is the reinforcement of behaviors that are increasingly close approximations to a desired response. Shaping depends heavily on discrimination, as the dog (or human!) begins to recognize slight changes in the way their behaviors are reinforced.

To take a closer look at shaping, let's return to our favorite rat, Einstein. Even in a barren Skinner box, it could take a long time for a rat (even one as smart as Einstein) to accidentally press the bar and get a food pellet. And that bar-pressing behavior is pretty simple—we might wait forever for more complicated chains of responses to occur. For example, you would have to wait a long time for a duck to accidentally walk out of its cage, turn on a light, play a tune on a toy piano, turn off the light, and walk back to its cage. If this is what you wanted to reward, it's entirely possible that you would never get the chance.

Yale Joel/The LIFE Picture Collection/Getty Images

Figure 6.7 Pigeon ping-pong. Operant conditioning principles were used to train these pigeons to play ping-pong.

belizar/Shutterstock.com

This trainer is using operant shaping to teach tricks to these seals. Fish from a cup hanging from her waist serve as reinforcers. Notice that she is using a whistle and hand signals as discriminative stimuli to control the performance.

Instead of waiting to reinforce Einstein for pressing the bar spontaneously, we could have shaped his behavior. In general, shaping refers to a process in which a complex or rare behavior is broken down into a series of smaller steps. In the beginning, subjects (either animal or human) are reinforced for achieving a relatively simple first step. However, once they successfully achieve the second step, they are no longer reinforced for the first. Once they manage the third step in the series, they will no longer be reinforced for the second. This process continues until all of the steps have been mastered and the desired behavior has been achieved.

In the case of Einstein pressing a bar, shaping would look something like this: Assume that Einstein has not yet learned to press the bar, but our goal is to get him to do so. At first, we settle for just getting him to face the bar. Any time he turns toward the bar, he is reinforced with a bit of food. Soon Einstein spends much of his time facing the bar. Next, we reinforce him every time he takes a step toward the bar. At this point, if he is just facing the bar (the first step), nothing happens. But when he faces the bar and takes a step forward (the second step), he would be reinforced with food. By gradually changing the rules about what makes a successful response, we can eventually train Einstein to approach the bar and press it. In other words, *successive approximations* (ever-closer matches) to a desired response are reinforced during shaping. Believe it or not, Skinner once taught two pigeons to play ping-pong in this way (Figure 6.7)!

You should be able to see how this process of shaping depends on discrimination: Einstein needs to learn what behaviors are being reinforced at each stage, but he also needs to learn how the conditions for reinforcement change when we move from one step to another. In other words, he needs to learn how to discriminate between past behaviors that were rewarded in previous steps and those that are now being rewarded in the current step of the process.

Of course, human behavior can also be shaped (Lamb et al., 2010). Let's say that you want to exercise more often, and your ultimate goal is to run for 30 minutes three nights each week. If you were to employ shaping, you'd start by breaking this bigger goal down into a series of manageable steps. For example, during the first week, you might begin by reinforcing yourself for just going out for a walk three times. During the second week you'd up the ante, and you'd only get your reinforcement if you ran for five minutes at the beginning of each of the three walks. In the third week, there would only be a reinforcer if you ran for 10 minutes each time you went out. This process would continue until, eventually, reinforcement would only come if you were running for the full 30 minutes on each of the three nights (Watson & Tharp, 2014). In Section 6.6 we'll explore ways to use operant conditioning to change our behaviors in positive and productive ways.

Factors Influencing the Effectiveness of Reinforcement and Punishment

Several factors influence how effective reinforcement and punishment are during operant learning. Three of the most important factors are *intensity, timing,* and *contingency*. Let's take a closer look at each one.

Intensity

In the case of reinforcers, those that are more intense (that is, powerful) will be more likely to result in behaviors being repeated in the future. For example, recreational drugs that provide a powerfully positive high (that is, more intense positive reinforcement) are more likely to be used again than are those that produce only mildly pleasant feelings. Similarly, when working with a child who has been diagnosed with autism, therapists will often save the most powerful positive reinforcers (the ones that the child loves the most) for rewarding the behaviors that they consider most important for that child to learn.

Operant stimulus generalization The tendency to respond to stimuli similar to those that preceded reinforcement.

Operant stimulus discrimination The tendency to make an operant response when stimuli previously associated with reward are present and to withhold the response when stimuli associated with nonreward are present.

Shaping Gradually molding responses to a final desired pattern.

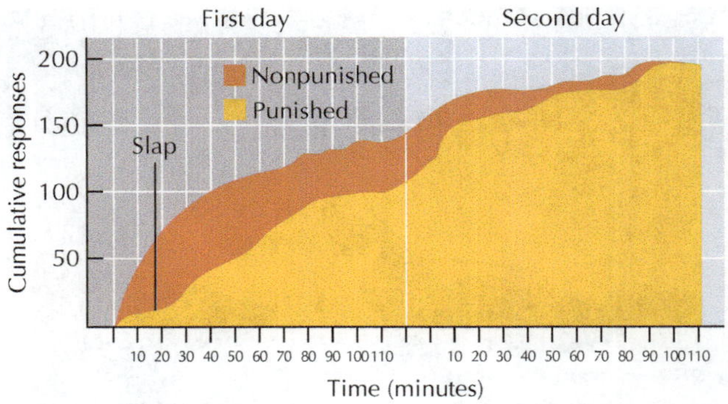

Figure 6.8 The effect of punishment on extinction. Immediately after punishment, the rate of bar-pressing is suppressed, but by the end of the second day, the effects of punishment have disappeared. (After B. F. Skinner, 1938.)

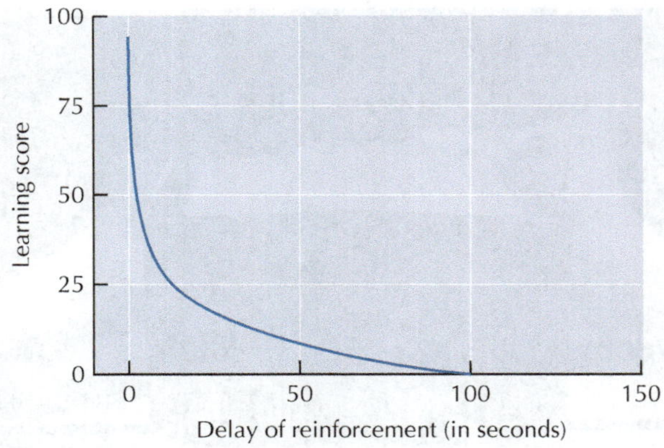

Figure 6.9 The effect of delay of reinforcement. Notice how rapidly the learning score drops when reward is delayed. Animals learning to press a bar in a Skinner box showed no signs of learning if the food reward followed a bar press by more than 100 seconds.

The story is similar when it comes to punishment. Severe positive punishment (that is, following a response with an intensely aversive or unpleasant stimulus) can be extremely effective in stopping behavior. If 10-year-old Yuri sticks his finger in a light socket and gets a severe shock, that may be the last time he *ever* tries it. Intense punishment can permanently suppress responding, even for actions as basic as eating. However, mild punishment only temporarily *suppresses* a response. And if the response is still reinforced on occasion, mild punishment may be particularly ineffective. This fact was demonstrated in an experiment with two groups of well-trained rats who were placed in a Skinner box. Prior to the study, the rats in both groups had learned to press the bar to obtain food. As the study unfolded, one group was mildly punished with a gentle slap for each bar press, and the other group was not. It might seem that the slap would cause bar-pressing to extinguish more quickly. Yet, this was not the case, as you can see in Figure 6.8. Punishment temporarily slowed bar pressing, but it did not cause extinction. Mild punishment such as gently slapping the paws of rats or children has little permanent effect on a reinforced response.

Timing

Reinforcement and punishment are most effective when they rapidly follow a response (Powell, Honey, & Symbaluk, 2017). For rats in a Skinner box, little or no learning occurs if the delay between bar pressing and receiving food exceeds 100 seconds (Figure 6.9). In general, you will be most successful if you present a reinforcer *immediately* after a response you want to change. Similarly, punishment works best when it occurs as the response is being made, or *immediately* afterward. Thus, if simply refusing to feed your dog table scraps is not enough to stop it from jumping at you when you sit at a table, you could effectively (and humanely) punish it by spraying water on its nose immediately, each time it jumps up.

Consistency

It might seem that reinforcement and punishment would work best when they are *response contingent* (kon-TIN-jent); that is, given *only* after a desired response has occurred, and when they are given *consistently*. While these things are both true, the story is somewhat more complicated than that, especially when it comes to reinforcement. Given that's the case, we'll take some time to unpack consistency in reinforcement in more detail.

Until now, we have treated reinforcement as if it were always continuous. **Continuous reinforcement** means that a reinforcer follows every correct response. At the start, continuous reinforcement is useful for learning new responses (Chance, 2014). To teach your dog to come to you, it is best to reinforce your dog every time that it comes when called. Curiously, once your dog has learned to come when called, it is best to shift to **partial reinforcement**, in which reinforcers do *not* follow every response. Responses acquired by partial reinforcement are highly resistant to extinction, a phenomenon known as the **partial reinforcement effect** (Horsley et al., 2012; Powell, Honey, & Symbaluk, 2017).

Partial reinforcement can be given on different schedules. A **schedule of reinforcement** is a protocol for determining how often and under what conditions responses will be rewarded (Chance, 2014). Let's consider the four most basic schedules: fixed ratio, variable ratio, fixed interval, and variable interval. Typical responses to each of these schedules are shown in Figure 6.10. Results such as these are obtained when a recorder is connected to a Skinner box. Rapid responding results in a steep line; a horizontal line indicates no response. Small tick marks on the lines show when a reinforcer was given.

In a **fixed ratio (FR) schedule**, the number of correct responses that a subject must give to receive reinforcement is predetermined (that is, fixed). For example, FR-3 means that every third response is reinforced; FR-10 means that 10 responses must be made to obtain a reinforcer. Fixed ratio schedules produce *very high response rates*. A hungry rat on an FR-10 schedule will quickly run off 10 responses, pause to eat, and then run off 10 more. A similar situation occurs when factory employees or farmworkers are paid on a piecework basis. When a fixed number of items must be produced for a set amount of pay, work output is high.

In a **variable ratio (VR) schedule**, a varying number of correct responses must be made to get a reinforcer. Instead of reinforcing

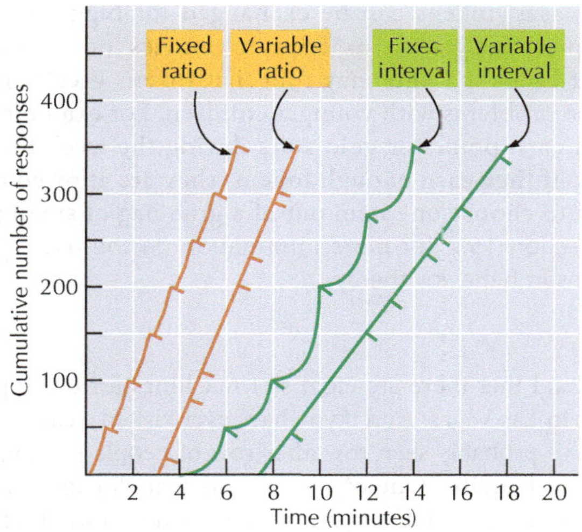

Figure 6.10 Typical response patterns for partial reinforcement schedules.

every fourth response (FR-4), for example, a person or animal on a VR-4 schedule gets rewarded every fourth response *on average*. Sometimes two responses must be made to obtain a reinforcer; sometimes it's five; sometimes four; and so on. The actual number varies, but it averages out to four (in this example). VR schedules also produce high response rates.

In another pattern, called a **fixed interval (FI) schedule**, reinforcement is given only when a correct response is made *after a set amount of time has passed*. This time interval is measured from the last reinforced response. Responses made during the time interval are not reinforced. Thus, a rat on an FI-30-second schedule has to wait 30 seconds after the last reinforced response before a bar press will pay off again. The rat can press the bar as often as it wants during the interval, but it will not be rewarded. FI schedules produce *moderate response rates*. Animals working on an FI schedule seem to display a keen sense of the passage of time (Zentall, 2010). Few responses occur just after a reinforcement is delivered, and a spurt of activity occurs just before the next reinforcement is due.

A **variable interval (VI) schedule** is a variation on a fixed interval schedule. Here, reinforcement is given for the first correct response made after a varying time period. On a VI-30-second schedule, reinforcement is available after an interval that *averages* 30 seconds. VI schedules produce *slow, steady response rates* and tremendous resistance to extinction (Lattal, Reilly, & Kohn, 1998). If you check your text messages every now and then for an important message, your reward (getting that message) is on a VI schedule. You may have to wait a few minutes or hours. If you are like most people, you will doggedly check over and over until you get your message.

Operant Conditioning in Everyday Life

In this section we've tried to give you lots of examples of how operant conditioning is relevant in our everyday lives. From training animals to time-outs; from traffic tickets to Tylenol, operant conditioning is happening around us all the time. In this section, we'll discuss two additional examples: the use of token economies to reinforce young children's positive behavior and the clever use of reinforcement schedules in gambling meccas like Las Vegas.

Token Economies: Not a Token Gesture

For humans, learning may be reinforced by anything from a candy bar to a word of praise. In categorizing reinforcers, a useful distinction can be made between *primary reinforcers* and *secondary reinforcers*. A **primary reinforcer** produces comfort, ends discomfort, or fills an immediate physical need: It is natural, unlearned, and rooted in biology. Food, water, and sex are obvious examples, but psychoactive drugs such as cocaine, caffeine, and alcohol also fall in this category because they stimulate the pleasure pathways in the brain. Every time you open the refrigerator, walk to a drinking fountain, turn up the heat, or order a double latte, your actions reflect primary reinforcement (Lazenka, Legakis, & Negus, 2016; Prus, 2014).

But humans also respond to other reinforcers that are *not* rooted in biology—instead, they gain their power through learning. Money, praise, attention, approval, success, affection, grades, and the like can each serve as a learned **secondary reinforcer**. Some secondary reinforcers gain their value because they can be *exchanged* for primary reinforcers (Powell, Honey, & Symbaluk, 2017). For example, printed money obviously has little or no value of its own. You can't eat it, drink it, or sleep with it. However, it can be exchanged for food, water, lodging, and other necessities.

Continuous reinforcement A pattern in which a reinforcer follows every correct response.

Partial reinforcement A pattern in which only a portion of all responses are reinforced.

Partial reinforcement effect Responses acquired with partial reinforcement are more resistant to extinction.

Schedules of reinforcement Rules or plans for determining which responses will be reinforced.

Fixed ratio (FR) schedule An arrangement where a set number of correct responses must be made to get a reinforcer. For example, a reinforcer is given for every four correct responses.

Variable ratio (VR) schedule An arrangement where a varied number of correct responses must be made to get a reinforcer. For example, a reinforcer is given after three to seven correct responses; the actual number changes randomly.

Fixed interval (FI) schedule An arrangement where a reinforcer is given only when a correct response is made after a set amount of time has passed since the last reinforced response. Responses made during the time interval are not reinforced.

Variable interval (VI) schedule An arrangement where a reinforcer is given for the first correct response made after a varied amount of time has passed since the last reinforced response. Responses made during the time interval are not reinforced.

Primary reinforcers Nonlearned reinforcers; usually those that satisfy physiological needs.

Secondary reinforcer A learned reinforcer; often one that gains reinforcing properties by association with a primary reinforcer.

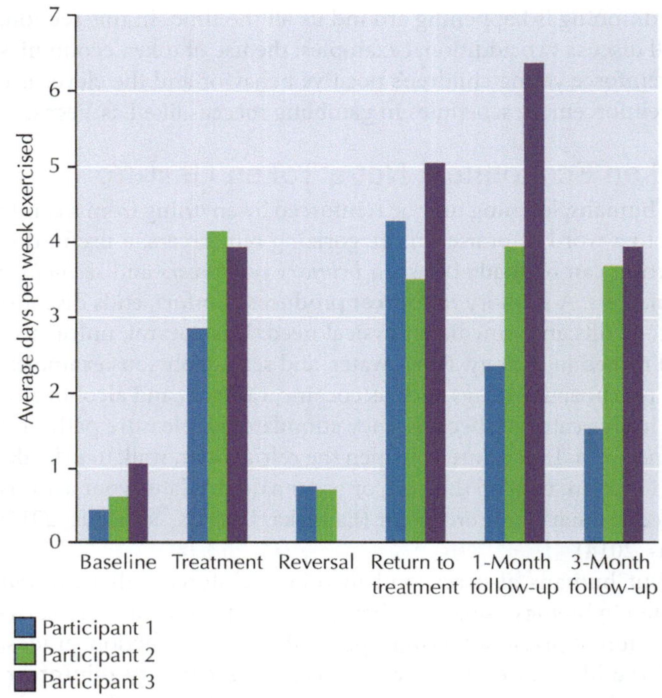

Figure 6.11 Reinforcement in a token economy. Children with cystic fibrosis (a hereditary lung disease) benefit from exercise that clears blocked airways. This graph shows the effects of using tokens to reward aerobic exercise in three children with cystic fibrosis. The number of minutes of aerobic exercise each day was measured. Tokens earned could be exchanged for rewards such as going to see a movie or staying up past bedtime. The graph shows that all three children exercised relatively infrequently without the reinforcement (*baseline* and *reversal* phases) and relatively more when the reinforcement was in place (*training* and return to *treatment* phases). It is encouraging to note that exercise rates remained heightened for months after the token economy was first implemented. (Adapted from Bernard, Cohen, & Moffett, 2009.)

Secondary reinforcement is at the heart of many programs to change children's (and sometimes adults') behaviors. Such programs often rely on **token reinforcers**, which are tangible secondary reinforcers such as money, a gold star, or a poker chip. Tokens are routinely used in educational settings to promote learning, particularly with individuals who have developmental delays. For instance, tokens are often used as reinforcers to decrease undesirable behaviors (biting and self-injurious behavior) and increase desirable ones (appropriate use of speech) among children with autism. Later, the child can exchange tokens for candy, toys, or other treats.

Token economies, systems for managing and altering behavior through reinforcement of selected responses, have also been used with troubled children, adults with special needs, and even in ordinary school classrooms (Alberto & Troutman, 2013; Maggin et al., 2011; Figure 6.11). In each case, the goal is to provide an immediate reward for learning. In such cases, tokens can be exchanged for bigger items or special privileges, such as trips to movies or amusement parks. At home, parents may find that tokens greatly reduce discipline problems with younger children. For example, children can earn points or gold stars during the week for good behavior. If they earn enough tokens, they are allowed on the weekend to choose one item out of a grab bag of small prizes (see Section 15.2 for more information on the use of token economies in behavior therapy).

Casinos

It's been said that there are eight slot machines for every person who lives in Las Vegas. And if you have ever visited a casino in Sin City, you've probably seen row after row of people playing those "one-armed bandits." One of the reasons that slot machines are such a lucrative part of the casinos' business lies in what we know about reinforcement schedules. To understand why, start by imagining that you put a dollar in a slot machine and pull the handle. A light flashes, a bell rings and—voila!—$10 spills into the tray in front of you. Now let's say that this pattern continues for several minutes. Every pull is followed by a payoff. Because you are being reinforced on a continuous schedule, you quickly "get hooked" (and begin to plan your retirement). But, alas, suddenly each pull is followed by nothing. Obviously, you would respond several times more before giving up, because extinction isn't immediate. However, when continuous reinforcement is followed by extinction, the message quickly becomes clear: No more payoffs (or early retirement).

Of course, slot machines don't work on a schedule of continuous reinforcement—the casinos would never make money if they did. Instead, the schedule of reinforcement looks more like this: You put a dollar in a slot machine five times without a payoff. You are just about to quit but decide to play once more. Bingo! The machine returns $20. Payoffs will continue on a partial reinforcement schedule; some pulls will bring a payout and others won't.

The key point with partial reinforcement is that the timing of all payouts is variable and unpredictable. Sometimes you hit two in a row, and sometimes 20 or 30 pulls go unrewarded. Under

RK Studio/Monashee Frantz/Getty Images

The one-armed bandit (slot machine) is a dispenser of partial reinforcement.

these circumstances, how many times do you think you would continue to pull that handle before your behavior is extinguished? Because you have developed the expectation that any play may be "the one," it will be hard to resist just one more play . . . and then one more . . . and one more. Also, because partial reinforcement might include long periods of nonreward, it will be harder to distinguish between periods of reinforcement and extinction. It is no exaggeration to say that the clever use of partial reinforcement in casinos has left many people penniless, because such schedules make behavior very *resistant to extinction* (Horsley et al., 2012).

Reflective Practice

Operant Conditioning: Shape Up!

1. Changing the rules in small steps so that an animal (or person) is gradually trained to respond as desired is called ____________________.
2. The schedule of reinforcement associated with playing slot machines and other types of gambling is
   a. fixed ratio
   b. variable ratio
   c. fixed interval
   d. variable interval
3. Positive reinforcers increase the rate of responding, and negative reinforcers decrease it. T or F?
4. Partial reinforcement increases resistance to extinction. T or F?
5. If you eat a pizza to satisfy your hunger pangs, pizza will serve as a:
   a. partial reinforcer
   b. primary reinforcer
   c. secondary reinforcer
   d. positive reinforcer
6. A behavior therapist at a treatment center is working with a young girl diagnosed with autism and trying to teach her to use more verbal language so that others will know what she wants. Using reinforcement, the therapist eventually gets the girl to say "food" when she wants to eat, rather than just taking food. Next, though, the therapist's goal is to get the girl to use the word "food" at home with her parents, and not just at the treatment center. The therapist wants to achieve:
   a. shaping
   b. extinction
   c. discrimination
   d. generalization

THINK CRITICALLY

7. Using the concept of partial reinforcement, can you analyze why inconsistent punishment is especially ineffective?

SELF-REFLECT

- See if you can think of at least one everyday example of the five basic schedules of reinforcement (continuous reinforcement and the four types of partial reinforcement).

Answers: 1. shaping 2. b 3. F 4. T 5. b 6. d 7. An inconsistently punished response will continue to be reinforced on a partial schedule, which can make it even more resistant to extinction.

6.4 Observational Learning: Watch It!

GATEWAYS LEARNING OUTCOMES:
After reading this section you should be able to:

6.4.1 Name the three steps involved in observational learning

6.4.2 Describe three characteristics of models we are most likely to imitate

6.4.3 Explain the connection between observational learning and operant conditioning

6.4.4 Name two instances of observational learning in everyday life

6.4.5 Outline three reasons why exposure to violent media may be associated with later aggression among children and adolescents, and what the research actually says about this association

While it's possible to learn many things through classical and operant conditioning, Stanford psychologist Albert Bandura (1971) called attention to the power of **observational learning**—watching and imitating the actions of another person. We humans share the capacity for observational learning with many mammals (Tennie et al., 2010; Zentall, 2011).

How Observational Learning Works

The value of learning by observation is obvious: Imagine trying to learn how to perform a complex behavior such as tying a shoe or playing a piano by having someone verbally explain the steps to you, or by engaging in shaping (as described in the previous section). A far more effective way to learn is by observing a **model**—someone who serves as an example—and then copying their actions.

What kind of responses do we learn from observing others? Bandura indicated that anything that can be learned from direct experience can also be learned by observation. So we can learn to perform specific actions (how to throw a football, fix a leaky faucet, or make a cake) by watching others, but our attitudes and emotional responses (whether men and women are equally

Token reinforcer A tangible secondary reinforcer such as money, gold stars, poker chips, and the like.

Observational learning (modeling) Learning achieved by watching and imitating the actions of another or noting the consequences of those actions.

Model (in learning) A person who serves as an example in observational learning.

Observational learning often imparts large amounts of information that would be difficult to obtain by reading instructions or memorizing rules.

capable of effective parenting; a fear of dogs) can also be influenced by watching the actions of others.

The Three Steps of Observational Learning

Observational learning involves three steps: paying attention, remembering the model's behavior, and reproducing (or imitating) that behavior. Here's a bit more detail about each one:

Paying Attention

We know from ■ Section 4.5 that the world is full of stimuli and that we aren't capable of attending to everything, or everyone, that we see and hear. So what determines whether we will attend to a model and learn from their behavior?

One important factor is the *characteristics of the model.* We are more likely to pay attention to models who are in a position of authority over us, as well as those that we admire (e.g., people who have high social status, such as people who are famous or well respected). We're also more likely to attend to models who are similar to us in terms of age, sex, and interests (Bandura, 1971).

Another factor that motivates us to attend to models relates to the *characteristics of the situation.* We're more likely to watch and learn from others when we find ourselves in situations that are unfamiliar and ambiguous, or in situations when we're uncertain about our knowledge and abilities.

Remembering

The second step of observational learning is that the learner must *remember* what the model did. While a beginning surgeon might be interested enough to pay close attention to an operation (the first step in observational learning), she may be unable to remember all of the steps afterward. Her inability to remember everything that she watched means that observational learning is not yet complete, since remembering allows for the third step in observational learning: imitating or reproducing the model's actions.

Reproducing

The final step in observational learning is that the learner must be able to *reproduce,* or *imitate,* the modeled behavior. Sometimes accurate imitation will require practice, but it's also possible that even after many hours of trying the learner will never be able to perform the behavior as well as the model. We may admire the feats of world-class musicians or athletes, for example, but most of us could never reproduce them no matter how much we practiced.

The Three Steps in Action

In a classic experiment, Bandura had children watch an adult attack a large blow-up "BoBo the Clown" doll. Some children saw an adult sit on the doll, punch it, hit it with a hammer, and kick it around the room. Others saw a movie of an adult performing these same actions. A third group saw a cartoon version of the aggression. Later, the children were frustrated by having some attractive toys taken away from them. Then they were allowed to play with the BoBo doll. Most of the children imitated the adult's attack, demonstrating behaviors that were very much the same as those carried out by the model (● Figure 6.12). It is interesting that the cartoon was only slightly less effective in encouraging aggression than the live adult model and the filmed model (Bandura, Ross, & Ross, 1963). The children's actions demonstrated that they had successfully completed each of the three steps of observational learning: They had paid attention to the model's behavior, remembered it, and then were able to reproduce it at a later time.

Bandura's study teaches us two other important points about observational learning and imitation. The first is that *not all of the behaviors that can be learned from models are positive.* In addition to the aggressive behaviors learned in this study, we know, for example, that adolescents are much more likely to

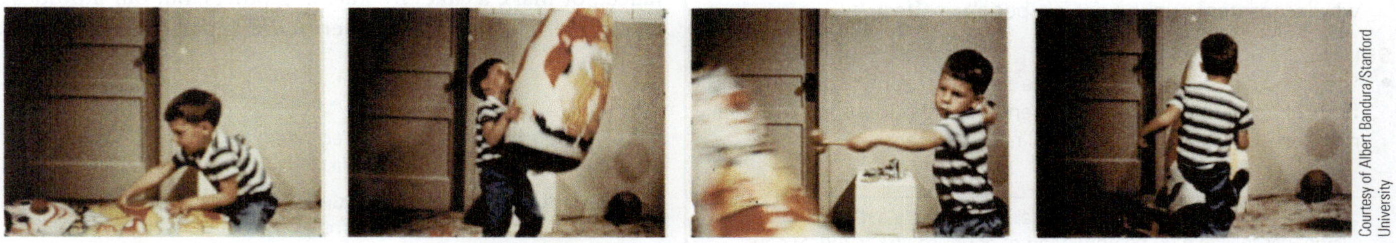

● **Figure 6.12 Imitating aggression.** A nursery school child imitates the aggressive behavior of an adult model he has just seen in a movie.

begin smoking if their parents, siblings, and friends smoke (Wilkinson & Abraham, 2004).

The second lesson to take away from Bandura's study is that *learning may take place even when the model wasn't intentionally trying to teach anything.* For example, children can learn something about managing anger—including the aggressive responses seen in Bandura's study—by watching how parents deal with their frustrations over time. This can happen even though that parent isn't aware that the child is paying attention to their actions, and in spite of the parent not consciously attempting to communicate any particular message about anger management. Similarly, research has suggested that many excellent managers credit their success to managers that they themselves have had, and simply watching how those individuals handled particular situations that emerged at work (Koch & Binnewies, 2015).

The Role of Operant Conditioning in Observational Learning

Will people always reproduce, or imitate, the behaviors learned by observation? The short answer is no. In a follow-up study, Bandura (1965) recreated his original study, but in this case the children observed the model being either rewarded, punished, or receiving no consequences for their aggressive behavior toward the Bobo doll. When the children were themselves frustrated afterward, those who saw the model either being rewarded or experiencing no consequences were far more likely to imitate the model's aggressive acts than those who saw the model being punished.

According to the results of this study, then, we learn more than just responses when we watch others: We also learn something about whether it would be a good idea to imitate what we've observed. What these findings tell us is that *observational learning only prepares us to duplicate a response.* Whether that response is actually imitated may depend on the consequences experienced by the model that we're observing. In this way, the operant learning principles that we discussed in Section 6.3 appear to play a role in observational learning as well. Just as the consequences of our own actions determine the likelihood of us performing those same actions again, so too is our behavior influenced by the consequences experienced by others from whom we learn.

Observational Learning in Everyday Life

Observational learning is very common in everyday life; you can probably think of a number of examples yourself. Children clearly learn a number of skills by watching others, from simple things like doing up zippers and brushing hair to more complex behaviors like using a knife and fork or tying their shoes. But people continue to learn in this way as they move through adolescence and adulthood as well. For example, teenagers learn how to drive by watching their parents or a driving instructor. After leaving school, adults can learn how to perform their jobs by observing others; in fact, observational learning is at the heart of most apprenticeships and other "hands-on" experiential learning opportunities.

Monkey Business Images/Shutterstock.com

It's not just children who learn by observing others—adolescents and adults also watch others to gain new knowledge and skills.

Workplace Behavior

People also learn about acceptable standards of behavior in the workplace by watching how their co-workers behave. This became particularly apparent as the #metoo movement gained momentum and highlighted work environments in which harassment and disrespectful behavior were commonplace. In many instances, it appeared that newer workers had learned their poor behavior from those who were more experienced. The fact that these actions were tolerated rather than punished meant that they continued to happen. In contrast, those individuals who may have wanted to report what was happening in these work environments quickly learned from watching other "whistle blowers" that doing so would be ignored or punished. As a result, many individuals tolerated harassment and other poor working conditions for the sake of preserving their jobs.

Media Coverage of Real-Life Tragedies

Another everyday example of the power of observational learning can be seen in the recent scrutiny of media coverage following tragedies such as high-profile suicides and mass shootings. A number of studies have now connected such events to an increased likelihood of other, similar occurrences in the weeks and months that follow, a phenomenon that is sometimes referred to as "copycat" behavior. According to researchers, when the media provides widespread, in-depth coverage of such events, they glorify both the act and the person who committed it. Others who are watching things unfold on TV or via the Internet may then be inspired to do something similar as a way of gaining the same type of attention (Bridge et al., 2019; Lankford & Madfis, 2018).

Media Violence

One of the most controversial examples of observational learning relates to our increasing consumption of media. Specifically, there is considerable interest in what people learn from violent media (e.g., violent shows, movies, and video games). Earlier in this chapter we said that the likelihood that people will imitate behavior depends on the model's characteristics, including the extent to which they are seen as having prestige. Because this type of status is often associated with fame, and because children tend to imitate what they observe in all media (Kirsh, 2010), psychological researchers have invested a great deal of time examining the impact of media-based role models.

We know that today's children and young adults spend less time in the classroom than they do engaging with various media, including the Internet, video games, movies, television, music, and print (Rideout, Foehr, & Roberts, 2010). From social media (Anderson & Jiang, 2018) to rap music (Wingood et al., 2003) to video games (Carnagey & Anderson, 2004), children have plenty of opportunities to observe and imitate both the good and the bad (and the ugly?) that they see in the media. Of particular concern to many people is media-based exposure to self-harm and aggression.

Studying the Science: Media and Self-Harm

A clear example of concern related to self-harm can be seen with the Netflix adaptation of Jay Asher's book, *Thirteen Reasons Why*. Concerns about the depiction of a young woman's suicide in the show's first season prompted an outcry from parents, teachers, and mental health workers. Their general feeling was that the show glorified suicide and depicted potential support people, like counselors, as ineffective. As it turned out, there was good reason to be wary: Data gathered by researchers at the National Institutes of Health found that suicides among 10- to 17-year-olds rose by nearly one-third in the month following release of the first season, and that the trend was most pronounced for young boys (Bridge et al., 2020). In response, Netflix quickly moved to cut the controversial suicide scene from the show.

Collection Christophel/Alamy Stock Photo

Psychological research has demonstrated that some negative effects may arise from watching media-based violence, but newer studies have shown that the relationship between media violence and negative outcomes is more complex than first believed.

Studying the Science: Media and Aggression

In addition to concerns about exposure to material that glorifies self-harm and suicide, the Internet is also of concern because it allows children to vicariously experience violence and to directly engage in *electronic aggression* through bullying or harassment of others (Centers for Disease Control, 2016b). It should come as no surprise, then, that many parents and educators have concerns about the effects of experiencing high levels of media violence, fed in part by early studies that suggested that children who watch a great deal of televised violence are more prone to behave aggressively (Anderson, Gentile, & Buckley, 2007; Miller et al., 2012).

When describing Bandura's famous studies with the Bobo doll, we suggested that observing violence (including media violence) may teach people new antisocial actions, as well as disinhibiting dangerous impulses that viewers already have. **Disinhibition**—the removal of inhibition—results in acting out behavior that normally would be restrained. Another possibility is that repeated exposure to media violence may result in **desensitization**—a reduction in emotional sensitivity—making people less likely to react negatively to violence and, hence, more prone to tolerate this behavior in others and engage in it themselves (Carnagey, Anderson, & Bushman, 2007; Krahé et al., 2011).

Does the same conclusion apply to video games? Many reviews have concluded that violent video games increase aggressive behavior in children and young adults (Krahé & Möller, 2010; Miller et al., 2012). As with television, younger children appear to be especially susceptible to fantasy violence in video games (Anderson et al., 2003; Bensley & Van Eenwyk, 2001). In fact, the more personalized, intimate experience of video games may heighten their impact (Fischer, Kastenmüller, & Greitemeyer, 2010).

Ok, but aren't these studies correlational? I thought that meant we couldn't make claims about cause and effect. Good job thinking like a psychological scientist! It's worth noting that much of the early research *was* correlational (see ■ Section 1.7). One of the most important things to remember about correlational research is that we cannot infer causation. It's difficult to know, then, whether more exposure to violence causes an increase in aggression, or whether a tendency to be more aggressive causes people to seek out violent media content.

Moreover, we now know that much of the early research may have led to overly strong conclusions (Adachi & Willoughby, 2011a; Valadez & Ferguson, 2012). For example, in one of these earlier studies, college students played a violent (*Mortal Kombat*) or nonviolent (*PGA Tournament Golf*) video game. Next, they competed with another "student" (who was actually an actor) in a task that allowed aggression and retaliation to take place. Students who played the violent game were much more likely to aggress by punishing their competitor (Bartholow & Anderson, 2002).

It's important to note, though, that these two games differed not only in their degree of violence, they also differed in degree of competitiveness, difficulty, and pace of action. Thinking like a psychological scientist, then, we realize that when we find differences in aggression for people watching violent versus nonviolent

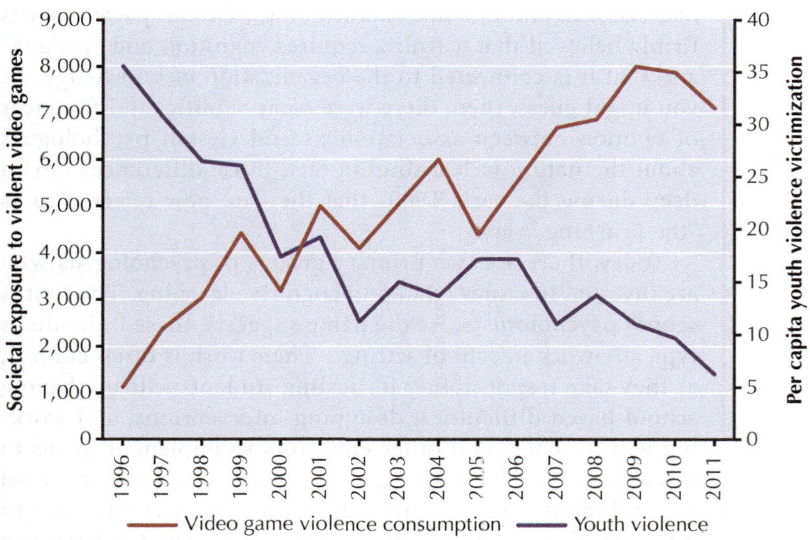

Figure 6.13 Video game violence and youth violence rates. This graph shows that the rate of violent crimes among youth declined between the years 1996 and 2011. Yet, during the same period, exposure to violent video games increased. While correlational data such as these are not by themselves conclusive, they do help us put the issue of violence in video games into a broader perspective. (Adapted from Ferguson, 2015.)

games in this experiment, we don't really know whether the difference in aggression stemmed from the fact that the games differed in violent content or one of the other variables (e.g., competitiveness or difficulty). Going back to terms you learned in Chapter 1, competitiveness, difficulty, and pace are *extraneous variables*, and we need to control for them if we want a clear picture of whether violent content (the independent variable) causes aggressive behavior (the dependent variable).

Two more recent studies have attempted to address this concern. In the first, researchers compared a violent action game (*Conan*) and a nonviolent racing game (*Fuel*) that were assessed as equally competitive, difficult, and fast-paced. In a subsequent task, college students who played the violent game were no more likely to be aggressive than those who played the nonviolent game (Adachi & Willoughby, 2011b). Taking experimental control one step further, researchers conducting the second study modified *the same game* so that it was more or less violent (Hilgard et al., 2019). Their results also suggested no effect of game violence on participants' aggression.

Taken together, these newer studies suggest that we should not be too hasty in jumping to the conclusion that video game violence has any significant effect on aggressive behavior. Of course, it's possible that the relationship between violent video games and aggressiveness may be more complicated. For example, maybe playing violent video games only makes aggression more *likely*, but other factors (e.g., personality characteristics, family conflict, depression, and negative peer influences) ultimately affect whether hostile thoughts will be turned into actions (Ferguson & Dyck, 2012; Ferguson, Miguel, & Hartley, 2009; Valkenburg, Peter, & Walther, 2016). More research is clearly needed before we have a full understanding of this relationship.

Parents and educators who worry that violent media are turning young people into a generation of sadistic criminals can also take heart from the correlational data shown in Figure 6.13. In recent years, the violent crime rate among youth has declined, even as sales of violent video games have risen. However, none of this is to say that we should be unconcerned about the long-term effects of experiencing violent media, including imitation, disinhibition, and desensitization. This is especially true for younger children, who are more likely to be influenced because they don't always fully recognize that media characters and stories are fantasies (McKenna & Ossoff, 1998).

Reflective Practice

Observational Learning: Watch It!

1. Through observational learning we can learn
   a. behaviors
   b. attitudes
   c. emotional responses
   d. all of the above
2. Which of the following is not one of the three steps of observational learning?
   a. remembering the model's behavior
   b. judging the model's behavior
   c. paying attention to the model's behavior
   d. reproducing the model's behavior
3. The name of the researcher who carried out the studies in which children watched a model interact with a Bobo doll is ________.
4. Children only learn positive behaviors from observing others. T or F?
5. If a model is successful, or rewarded, the model's behavior is
   a. less difficult to reproduce
   b. less likely to be attended to
   c. more likely to be imitated
   d. more subject to positive transfer

Disinhibition The removal of inhibition; results in acting out that normally would be restrained.

Desensitization A reduction in emotional sensitivity to a stimulus.

6. Children who observed a live adult behave aggressively became more aggressive; those who observed movie and cartoon aggression did not. T or F?

THINK CRITICALLY

7. A young college student secures an excellent internship working in an advertising office. During his first team meeting, the intern observes the manager ridicule one member of the team for questioning the manager's decision about how to proceed with an ad campaign. Applying what you know about observational learning, predict what the intern is likely to learn by observing what happened in that meeting.

SELF-REFLECT

- Who are some of the most powerful models for young people on social media, in your opinion? What characteristics do these models possess that make others want to imitate them? Are the models likely to be the same for males versus females?

Answers: 1. d 2. b 3. Bandura 4. F 5. c 6. F 7. The intern is likely to learn to keep quiet if he has concerns about the manager's decisions and not to question them, for fear of also being subject to ridicule in front of the team.

6.5 Cognitive Learning: Think!

GATEWAYS LEARNING OUTCOMES:
After reading this section you should be able to:

6.5.1 Define cognitive learning, and name two groups of psychologists who are interested in cognitive learning

6.5.2 Outline the two main dimensions of Bloom's taxonomy

6.5.3 Describe four factors that affect cognitive learning

6.5.4 Name some instances of cognitive learning in everyday life

One of the most common ways that we learn new things is through instruction. **Cognitive learning** refers to humans' ability to acquire behaviors, skills, and information in ways that are heavily dependent on memory, thinking, and problem solving (we'll learn more about all of these things in Chapters 7 and 8). The emphasis on cognitive processes in this type of learning makes it very different from the associative learning described in ■ Sections 6.2 and 6.3.

The earliest psychologists who concentrated on the cognitive aspects of learning were Gestalt theorists (■ see Section 1.3). Unlike associationists (who focused on associative learning like classical and operant conditioning), Gestalt psychologists firmly believed that learning requires cognition and "insight," and that it is connected to the organization of knowledge. As you might guess, then, there were some significant differences of opinion between associationists and Gestalt psychologists about the nature of learning. In fact, those differences ran so deep during the early 1900s that they are now referred to as "the Learning Wars."

Today, there are two primary groups of psychologists who are invested in issues related to cognitive learning. The first is **school psychologists**. As the name suggests, these individuals typically work in school settings. Their work is often clinical, as they take responsibility for testing students who are having school-based difficulties, designing interventions, and working with teachers and other educators to implement plans to assist students. The second group is referred to as **educational psychologists**, and they are primarily researchers who seek to understand how people best learn and how teachers can improve instruction in the classroom and online (Snowman & McCown, 2015). In addition to carrying out research relevant to children in schools, educational psychologists might also work on research projects related to adult learners, including the most effective ways to provide training to people in the workforce.

Psychologists interested in cognitive learning focus on a number of topics. Classic early research in this area focused on basic questions related to classifying what we learn, and the processes by which we learn (Bloom, 1956). More recently, though, researchers have examined questions related to the factors that impact learning (Hattie & Donoghue, 2016). We'll take a look at both of these areas of research in the sections that follow.

Bloom's Taxonomy: What We Learn and How We Learn It

Back in the late 1940s, many men and women who had just returned from the Second World War were interested in going to college. A special government stipend had been set up to help them with the costs, and campuses across the country were suddenly flooded with new students. Benjamin Bloom, then at the University of Chicago, found himself charged with trying to create a system of testing the educational standing of these men and women so that they could be placed in classes that were appropriate to their current level of knowledge. The exam questions that his team developed could then be shared with colleges across the country so that these young adults would be tested in a consistent way.

But Bloom's team did much more than just design a set of questions—they developed a system for thinking about cognitive learning, which is commonly referred to as **Bloom's taxonomy** (see ● Figure 6.14). A taxonomy is a system of classification—in this case a method of classifying knowledge and learning. His team's ideas proved to be enormously successful and the initial taxonomy has now been updated to reflect ongoing thinking about the field of education

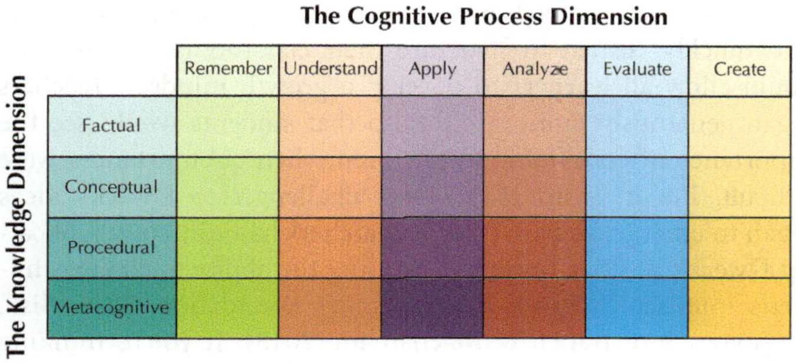

Figure 6.14 Bloom's taxonomy. The two dimensions of Bloom's taxonomy—knowledge and cognitive processes—can be considered together when instructors design classroom activities and assessments.

(Anderson, 2003; Krathwohl, 2002). The most recent version underscores the importance of different types of knowledge (what we learn) as well as different cognitive processes (how we learn).

What We Learn: Types of Knowledge

The newest version of Bloom's taxonomy describes four types of knowledge. The first is *factual knowledge* or an understanding of basic units of information (facts). An example of factual knowledge might be an understanding of the idea that associative learning includes both classical and operant conditioning.

The second type of knowledge is *conceptual*. Concepts are typically abstract ideas that often have multiple parts. Mastering conceptual knowledge requires learners to understand not just the parts, but how they fit together. Classical conditioning, described in ■ Section 6.2, is a good example of a concept. It's an abstract idea that has several components (e.g., unconditioned stimulus and response; conditioned stimulus and response) and to really understand it, you'd need to not only know those four components but how they work together to foster that particular kind of learning.

The third type of knowledge is *procedural knowledge*, or knowing how to do something. An example of procedural knowledge might include how to use the principles of classical conditioning to help an alcoholic stop drinking (■ see Section 6.2).

The last type of knowledge is *metacognitive knowledge*. You may remember that we looked at metacognition in ■ Section 5.5—it refers to our ability to think about and understand the limits of our own knowledge (knowing what you know and don't know!) and what learning strategies work best for us. For example, metacognitive knowledge would allow you to recognize that you sometimes struggle to understand the difference between the unconditioned and conditioned responses in classical conditioning. This type of knowledge is important to learning because it allows us to accurately assess our current understanding or skill level (and consequently know the areas in which we might need to learn more), to know what is helpful (and unhelpful!) for our learning, and what we can do to improve our learning when things aren't going well.

How We Learn: Cognitive Processes

In addition to the types of knowledge that we can acquire, the newest version of Bloom's taxonomy also addresses six ways in which we can work with that knowledge. The first is *remembering*, or simply being able to retrieve information from memory. The second is *understanding*, which refers to the ability to decode or establish the meaning of that information. The third process is *applying*, or using knowledge to carry out a given procedure, and the fourth is *analyzing* (working to understand the various parts that comprise a whole, and how they relate to one another). The fifth is *evaluating*, which involves using a set of criteria to judge skills and knowledge, and the sixth is *creating*, which involves using knowledge to create something totally original. If you look closely, you'll see that the learning outcomes at the beginning of each section of this book draw from the different cognitive processes outlined in Bloom's taxonomy, as do the questions in the *Reflective Practice* at the end of every section.

The six processes are often presented as a hierarchy, based on the idea that higher-level processes (evaluating; creating) are more complex and challenging than lower-level ones (remembering and understanding). Presenting things this way has had the unfortunate consequence that teachers often feel that their lessons aren't valuable if they are focused on "lower-level" processes like remembering, and that they should consistently be designing activities that push students toward more sophisticated processes like evaluating and creating. More recently, though, educational psychologists have suggested that the higher levels are more difficult to achieve without mastery of the lower levels (Hirsch, 2016). For example, it's difficult to evaluate or create something truly novel unless you first know a great deal about the subject (in other words, unless you have acquired a great deal of basic factual and conceptual knowledge that you remember and truly understand).

Factors That Influence Cognitive Learning

More recent research in educational psychology has moved beyond Bloom's taxonomy to look at questions related to improving learning. In a very large-scale analysis of 80,000 studies that investigated 300 million learners, John Hattie (2017) has organized the factors that influence learning into several categories. We discuss four that have been investigated by many educational psychologists: learner characteristics, learning strategies, type of instruction, and the learning environment.

Cognitive learning Higher-level learning involving thinking, knowing, understanding, and anticipation.

School psychologists Psychologists who work in schools and design interventions for students who are having difficulties.

Educational psychologists Psychologists who carry out research to better understand how people best learn and how teachers can improve instruction.

Bloom's taxonomy A system for classifying knowledge and learning.

Learner Characteristics

A number of learner characteristics have been investigated to establish which ones might be helpful in promoting learning. Some of those that appear to be important across many studies include working memory (■ see Section 7.2), clinical diagnoses (e.g., ADHD, anxiety, or learning disabilities; ■ see Section 14.4), persistence or "grit" (■ see Section 14.5), motivation (■ see Section 10.3), and self-efficacy (■ see Section 12.1). In this section we'll explore research related to two others—mindset and learning styles—in a bit more detail.

Studying the Science: Mindset

In a widely viewed TED talk, Carol Dweck of Stanford University talks about her decades-long interest in how children respond to setbacks and failure at school. Some, she argues, will push on in the face of obstacles and are determined to overcome them. In contrast, others will shrink back and simply give up. Over many years, she came to see these different response patterns as stemming from two different *mindsets* that guide our response to challenge (Dweck, 2008; 2017).

A **growth mindset** is associated with the belief that our intelligence and talents can be developed through hard work and effort. This belief system has important consequences, including increased persistence in the face of obstacles and greater success in school and at work. In contrast, a **fixed mindset** is linked to the idea that intelligence and talents are inborn and cannot easily be changed. Someone with such a belief system is more likely to give up when the going gets rough, so it likely won't surprise you that a fixed mindset is associated with greater struggles at school and less success in the workforce. What was most exciting about Dweck's research, though, was her finding that mindset could be changed using particular classroom techniques, and that it was possible to move from having a fixed mindset to one that was more linked to growth (Dweck, 2012).

LumiNola/E+/Getty Images

People with a growth mindset believe that characteristics like intelligence can be changed with effort and practice. In contrast, those who have a fixed mindset believe that such characteristics are stable and not amenable to change.

Dweck's ideas proved to be immensely popular with educators who quickly rushed to structure their classrooms in ways that would allow all learners to develop a growth mindset. Teachers began generously praising effort so that students would see the importance of continuing to try, even when circumstances were difficult. But it wasn't long before challenges to Dweck's ideas began to emerge. In particular, researchers had difficulty replicating Dweck's positive findings regarding the ability to change children's mindset (Education Endowment Foundation, 2019; Sisk, Burgoyne, Sun, Butler, & Macnamara, 2018). If you're thinking critically, you'll remember that it's important for researchers to establish the validity of their findings through replication (■ see Section 1.5). The fact that others were unable to find the same pattern of results began to cast some doubt on whether fostering a growth mindset works in the classroom, or whether it even exists.

In response, Dweck has recently spoken out in an effort to clarify her views about mindset, and the ways in which her research has been misunderstood and misused in schools (Dweck, 2016). In particular, she points to two common misconceptions that have become popular since her initial work was published:

1. *People have a "pure" mindset that is either fixed or growth.* Given the results of the early research, it seemed clear that having a growth mindset was a good thing, and having a fixed mindset was not. Unfortunately, there was a worrying trend for teachers to use mindsets to explain why students weren't succeeding ("Oh, he has a fixed mindset—that's why he's not doing well in math."). In reality, Dweck argues, everyone displays fixed and growth mindsets in different circumstances, and all of us have "triggers" that will bring on a fixed mindset. For example, how do you react when someone is much better than you at something that you really value? And how do you react to failure in different circumstances? Are there feelings of defensiveness, anger, or anxiety in some situations but not others? A sense of being incompetent or defeated? Do you find yourself looking for excuses? Identifying those specific challenges that bring on a fixed mindset in particular situations will put you on a path toward a growth mindset.
2. *Developing a growth mindset among students is just about praising effort.* Too often, Dweck argues, teachers took her research to mean that one simply needed to praise students' efforts and a growth mindset would emerge. This approach of praising effort—*even when students were not learning*—is not productive in the long run for two reasons. First, students need to know when they are not meeting a standard, and if the teacher's sole focus is on praising effort then that feedback about their learning will be absent. Second, Dweck argues that effort alone will never be enough for learning to take place—students still need to be taught a variety of strategies that they can use when things aren't going well, including the value of seeking help. Ultimately, it's using these strategies (even if you have to try a number of them!) that will help students to see the value of persisting in the face of challenge. In other words, focusing students' attention on the *process* by which learning happens—not just the effort they expend—is critical in promoting a growth mindset.

Jose Luis Pelaez Inc./DigitalVision/Getty Images

The idea that people learn best using their preferred "learning style" has not been supported by psychological research.

Studying the Science: Learning Styles

Another learner characteristic that has generated considerable interest among educators is *learning styles*, or the idea that people have a preferred means of receiving and processing information. Though many different types of learning styles have been proposed over the years, one of the most popular relates to the idea that people can be classified as visual, auditory, or kinesthetic learners, depending on the sensory input through which they prefer to receive new information (Willingham, 2009). Intuitively, this model has a lot of appeal. After all, we've all met people who seem to have a remarkable ability to visualize material that they've seen previously, or a remarkable "ear" for languages or music. Some people also note that they think better on their feet (literally!) or while they are moving, a preference that is associated with the kinesthetic sense (■ see Section 4.4).

Researchers and educators who subscribe to the idea of learning styles indicate that if we take note of people's preferred style and teach material to them in that way, learning will be enhanced. Many studies have investigated this claim and, like many other theories in learning research, the results concerning learning styles have been somewhat mixed. To try to settle the matter, researchers examined the results of many studies to obtain a larger and more diverse sample (Pashler, McDaniel, Rohrer, & Bjork, 2008). These authors observed two things: First, the vast majority of studies attempting to test the utility of learning styles often did not use research methods that would allow them to draw clear conclusions (for example, they often did not control for extraneous variables; ■ see Section 1.6). Second, in the studies that they assessed, learning styles did *not* appear to have any significant effect on most measures of learning, such as test results. A more recent review of both correlational and experimental findings also concluded that more rigorous studies (that is, experimental studies with a control group) provide no evidence that adjusting teaching to suit student learning styles affects students' performance at school (Cuevas, 2015).

Cognitive psychologist Dan Willingham (2009) has attempted to explain why the results have been so disappointing when the idea of learning styles seems to make so much sense. He argues that while it's true that some people do have a superior memory for visual images or for sounds that they hear, it's unlikely to matter for most types of cognitive learning. Why? Because the majority of information that we learn isn't stored in memory as visual images, sounds, or movements. Instead, much of what we learn—including how to add numbers, do laundry, drive a car, and cook spaghetti—is stored in memory as abstract ideas and concepts. Put another way, our memories are *usually* stored on the basis of meaning, rather than as a collection of pictures, sounds, and movements (■ see Section 7.3). Given that this is the case, having an excellent visual or auditory memory, or having a strong kinesthetic sense, will not be of any great help when you have to retrieve the learned information from your memory. Of course, when you're learning information that *is* stored in memory as an image (for example, what the Mona Lisa painting looks like) or as a sound (how to properly pronounce the name of the Welsh town Llanfairpwllgwyngyllgogerychwyrndrobwllllantysiliogogogoch), then people with particularly good visual or auditory memory may have an advantage when they're being tested on that material. Unfortunately, that's just not likely to be the case most of the time.

Learning Strategies

When it comes to learning, one of the most important things that educational psychologists have studied is the strategies that learners adopt when they try to master new material. Many of the most effective strategies were introduced to you in other chapters (especially the introduction to this book!), and they include:

- *Spacing out your learning* over several days or weeks, rather than trying to cram everything into one session
- *Being reflective* about your learning. For example, it's important to think carefully about how the to-be-learned material "fits in" with things that you already know, and to ask yourself lots of "wh" questions as you learn (e.g., Why might that be true? When might this result not hold up? Which of these two things is likely to be more effective?)
- *Testing yourself* on the material you're learning, doing your best to mimic the exam conditions if you're going to be evaluated in a formal way
- *Using metacognitive strategies*. Remember in ■ Section 5.5 we spoke about the need to be aware of your own knowledge, as well as your strengths and weaknesses when it comes to learning new things. It's also important to actively monitor your progress during learning and make adjustments (e.g., putting in more time, or spending your time differently) if your learning isn't progressing as you had hoped or planned.

Growth mindset The belief that intelligence and talents can be developed through hard work and effort.

Fixed mindset The belief that intelligence and talents are inborn and cannot easily be changed.

Weekend Images Inc./E+/Getty Images

Students can adopt a number of effective strategies to improve their learning, including self-testing.

Type of Instruction

There is little doubt that teachers can greatly affect student interest, motivation, and creativity. But what type of instruction is likely to be effective? To answer this question, psychologists have examined many methods of teaching. Two of the most basic are *direct instruction* and *discovery learning.*

Studying the Science: Direct Instruction Versus Discovery Learning

In **direct instruction**, information is presented by lecture or demonstration, and students often learn through rote practice. In **discovery learning**, teachers create conditions that encourage students to discover or construct knowledge for themselves (Dean & Kuhn, 2007). Figure 6.15 illustrates the difference. Two groups of students were taught to calculate the area of a parallelogram by multiplying the height by the length of the base. Some were encouraged to see that a "piece" of a parallelogram could be "moved" to create a rectangle. Later, they were better able to solve unusual problems in which the height times base formula didn't seem to work. In this study, students who simply memorized a rule were confused by similar problems, suggesting that discovery can lead to a better understanding of new or unusual problems (Wertheimer, 1959).

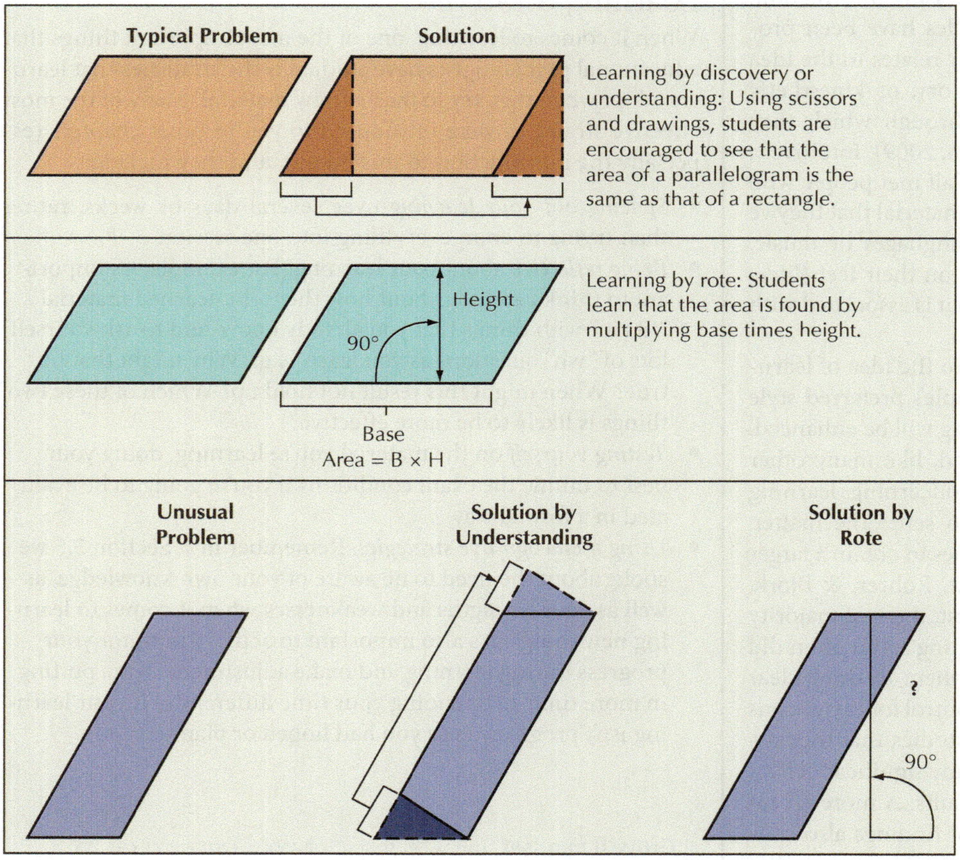

Figure 6.15 Learning by understanding and by rote. Though learning by discovery sometimes yields better results for students, there are also situations when rote learning is superior. (After Wertheimer, 1959.)

Such findings initially led researchers to believe that direct instruction techniques led to *passive learning* (that is, students are provided with knowledge by someone who has expertise) and that a better approach to teaching was the use of techniques like discovery learning that promote *active learning* (in which students work to construct knowledge for themselves). And as was the case with research on mindset and learning styles, many educators embraced the idea of active learning and moved quickly to design class lessons that revolved around students asking their own questions and solving problems without explicit instruction. Unfortunately, later research demonstrated that, in some cases, students taught *only* using discovery-based active learning techniques (including, for example, problem-based learning) fared *worse* on later assessments than those taught using direct instruction (Kirschner, Sweller, & Clark, 2006).

Educational psychologists have more recently tried to explain the finding that active learning techniques are not always superior, in spite of the fact that they have a great deal of appeal. After all, who doesn't like the image of students working excitedly on interesting "real-world" problems in the classroom instead of passively listening to a lesson or lecture? The difficulty with discovery learning is that it's sometimes very difficult to solve problems effectively or generate good questions about a topic when you aren't an expert. And putting students who know very little about a topic into a situation where they are trying to engage in the higher-level cognitive processes of Bloom's taxonomy can be much more frustrating than rewarding. Of course, once students have developed a good working knowledge of a particular topic—usually through listening to and reading the work of experts—they will be in a much better position to solve those challenging problems and generate creative ideas.

What this research tells us is that students shouldn't be asked to stumble around trying to discover for themselves the principles of math, physics, or any other subject for that matter. The best teaching strategies are much more likely to be based on *guided discovery,* in which students are given enough guidance through direct instruction that they gain a solid understanding of foundational facts and concepts. Such instruction can certainly include active learning components, such as using clickers to answer in-class questions or engaging in small group discussions. Ensuring that students have a good base of knowledge, though, will put them in a very strong position to engage in inquiry and think productively about problems that need to be solved (Mayer, 2011; Mukherjee, 2015).

Learning Environment

Aside from the type of instruction that a teacher uses, there are other elements of the learning environment that can be important in guiding learning. Two that have received considerable attention from educational psychologists are the use of feedback and technology.

Feedback

Feedback is an important contributor to student learning, and research from the workforce suggests that feedback continues to be important in terms of driving workers' on-the-job learning and success (Harms & Roebuck, 2010). Providing feedback that is maximally effective, though, requires a good understanding of what feedback is (and what it isn't!).

One of the most important aspects of feedback is that it provides information about progress toward a goal (Lefrançois, 2012). If you're a comedian and your goal is to make people laugh, then feedback would come from whether your audience greets your jokes with side-splitting laughter or stony silence. If you are a tennis player and your goal is to improve your backhand, then feedback would come from whether your backhand shots cross the net and how accurately you can place them on the other side of the court.

The most helpful feedback will be delivered soon after the performance. This is why we encourage you to work through the *Reflective Practice* questions at the end of each module and then check your answers—we want to provide you with some immediate feedback about how well you've mastered the basic ideas presented in each section, so that you have a good sense of what to do next (move on to the next section, or go back and re-read some of the material related to questions you got wrong).

Good feedback will also be based on patterns of responses over time, rather than a single instance. Some of the exercises in *Mindtap*, the online resource that accompanies this book, work on this principle by tracking your responses to similar questions over many trials and providing greater practice with concepts that are giving you trouble.

Sometimes, of course, it's not always easy to pick up on feedback because you're so focused on the task at hand (Wiggins, 2012). New teachers, for example, are often so absorbed with delivering a lesson effectively that they may fail to register student behaviors (engaged faces or lost looks) that would provide them with valuable information about their performance. This is why recorded feedback can be very helpful, regardless of whether you are learning to teach, play a musical instrument, sing, speak a second language, or deliver a speech. In sports, video replays are routinely used to provide feedback on everything from tennis serves to pick-off moves in baseball.

It's important to note that feedback is not the same thing as *advice*, even though we often use the terms interchangeably (Wiggins, 2012). The difference lies in the fact that advice doesn't provide any information about your progress toward a goal. Statements like "You should give more examples in your paper," "You need to keep your eye on the ball," or "You need to pull your shoulders back when you sing" are all good examples of advice. Though they can be helpful, they're usually much more beneficial when they're provided along with feedback, because then you'll understand *why* the advice is being given.

Studying the Science: Educational Technology

In addition to feedback, educational technology ("ed tech") can be another important component of the learning environment. Over the past two decades, technology has become very common in schools and other environments that foster cognitive learning. In general, two things have contributed to this rise of technology in the learning domain. The first is people's creative use of the Internet to promote cognitive learning. For example, the rise of YouTube has provided a new kind of "informal classroom," where people can learn about subjects that range from Renaissance literature to replacing the radiator in your car. The Internet has also paved the way for more formal classes to be offered online, allowing students who are working toward certificates, diplomas, or degrees to have greater flexibility to pursue their credits at a time and place that is convenient for them. And even when courses are offered in a more conventional classroom, it's common for both instructors and students to make use of the web's vast resources to easily gather information for lessons and projects and to communicate with others in the class.

The second thing that has contributed to the rise of technology in education is the development of hardware and software that can aid in teaching and learning. For example, some technology has been designed to support students with issues that

Direct instruction A method of instruction in which information is presented by lecture or demonstration, and students often learn through rote practice.

Discovery learning Learning based on insight and understanding.

Feedback Information returned to people about their progress toward a goal.

previously limited access to education (e.g., being blind or deaf). Smartboards, clickers, and PowerPoint are also examples of technological tools that, when used properly, can support learning.

The literature related to the utility of such technology has been mixed, with some studies suggesting significant benefits while others indicate little value or, worse, declines in learning (Hattie, 2017). One reason that might help to explain such mixed findings is the fact that technology isn't a substitute for good teaching. To be effective, technology needs to be used in such a way that it enhances well-informed teaching practice. Using it simply to "jazz up" a lesson will not be helpful—good teaching is at the heart of successful learning.

One area related to technology that has generated controversy concerns the use of laptops in the classroom for note-taking. On the one hand, people argue, laptops can make taking notes more effective since people can usually type faster than they can write (and some have indicated that their typed notes are far more legible than their written ones!). This might lead to a more complete set of notes that will be of greater value when studying. On the other hand, concerns have been raised that using laptops may lead to less active information processing during a lesson, with students simply transcribing the teacher's words without really thinking about them.

So how do those competing claims stand up in the research? Two well-controlled experiments have demonstrated that taking notes on a laptop does tend to lead to more notes, and notes that more closely resemble a "transcription" of the lecture (Morehead, Dunlosky, & Rawson, 2019; Mueller & Oppenheimer, 2014). What's less clear is the impact of taking notes in this way: While one study demonstrated that taking notes on a laptop led to poorer test results than taking notes by hand, the other suggested that this was not the case. Clearly more research will be needed to settle this issue, and it may well be the case that the answer is more complex. For example, laptops may indeed be more beneficial as a note-taking strategy, but only for certain subjects or particular people.

Nejron Photo/Shutterstock.com

Using laptops to take notes in class appears to have both costs and benefits for students.

Of course, the quality of the notes isn't the only issue. Some educators have expressed concern that allowing laptops in the classroom creates a distraction, since students often confess that they will use their laptops during class to check social media, send texts, and check out the latest offerings on Amazon. If that's the case, then there's good reason to be concerned that allowing laptops in the classroom will compromise learning because of the distraction that they pose, not only for the student with the computer but also for those who are sitting around them (Sana, Weston, & Cepeda, 2013).

Cognitive Learning in Everyday Life

We've spent quite a lot of time discussing cognitive learning in relation to conventional "school" settings where teachers provide instruction to learners. But cognitive learning happens in all kinds of settings in our everyday lives outside of formal education. For example, it can occur when you learn something new by watching videos or reading magazines, books, newspapers, websites, or blog posts. It can also happen when you engage in everyday conversations with others, gaining new information from listening to them share their insights.

One of the messages that you should take away from the research on teaching and cognitive learning, though, is that the media will routinely make claims about research that demonstrates "the one thing" that will improve learning and help everyone reach their potential. Educators saw this with the research on mindset and learning styles, as well as the studies concerned with discovery learning and excitement about the possibilities posed by new technology.

If you read of any such claims concerning miraculous educational interventions, you would be wise to be cautious. Over the years, education has witnessed many "revolutions" that have failed to produce consistently positive results over time (Chew & Cerbin, 2017). In some respects, this shouldn't come as much of a shock: More than ever before, educators face an increasingly diverse mix of students: "regular" students, adult learners, students who have disabilities and mental health challenges, students who speak English as a second language, and students who are juggling multiple responsibilities aside from school (Bowe, 2000). Faced with such diversity, it really shouldn't be surprising that there is no "one size fits all" miracle approach to teaching that will work for everyone. Instead, we need to recognize that *almost all teaching strategies work some of the time* to enhance cognitive learning. The challenge for educational psychologists is to establish which strategies work for whom, and under what conditions (Bernstein, 2018).

Remember, though, that learning is a relatively *permanent* change in knowledge or behavior. This means that in order for learning to take place, the information that you gather needs to be stored in memory. In the next chapter we'll talk more about memory, and the process by which new information moves from perceptual processes like seeing and hearing to permanent storage in our memory.

Reflective Practice

Cognitive Learning: Think!

1. Which of the following is ***not*** one of the types of knowledge included in Bloom's taxonomy?
   a. conceptual
   b. metacognitive
   c. factual
   d. implicit
2. People who respond to challenge by persisting and working hard to overcome the obstacles they face are said to have:
   a. a growth mindset
   b. a fixed mindset
   c. an optimal learning style
   d. poor metacognition
3. The strong disagreement between associationists and Gestalt psychologists about how learning happens has been referred to as "The Learning Wars" T or F?
4. ________________ is a type of instruction that recognizes the importance of providing students with fundamental information about a topic and then allowing them to work on solving problems related to that topic.
5. Research related to note-taking during lectures suggests that
   a. using a laptop is superior to taking notes by hand
   b. taking notes by hand is superior to using a laptop
   c. using a laptop leads to notes that look more like a transcription of the lecture
   d. students never use laptops to check social media or send texts during lecture
6. Most educational "revolutions" have failed to produce consistently positive results over time. T or F?

THINK CRITICALLY

7. Imagine that you're studying for your psychology exam. How could you apply the well-established learning strategies outlined in this module to create a plan that will ensure your success?

SELF-REFLECT

- Think about a subject you know a lot about, or a skill at which you really excel. Try to apply Bloom's four types of knowledge to your learning. What kind of factual knowledge is necessary to master this subject or skill? What conceptual knowledge is important? What procedural knowledge can come from learning about this subject or skill? What sort of metacognitive knowledge would someone need to consider to become an expert in this area?

Answers: 1. d 2. a 3. T 4. guided discovery 5. c 6. T 7. The first strategy involves spacing out your studying, so ideally you'd begin your studying early, and create a timetable that will allow you to work away at the material in small chunks over a period of time. The second strategy is to be reflective. For all of the material you study, think about how the various pieces "fit together" and how they fit in with material that you have already studied (or things that you already know). If it helps, try drawing a diagram to show how things are connected. The third strategy is self-testing, using methods that mimic what you'll have to do on the exam. If the exam will include multiple choice questions then you should practice with multiple choice questions (try Mindtap!). And don't use the textbook to help during your practice test (unless it's going to be an open-book exam!). Finally, try to employ metacognitive strategies to monitor your progress and understand the gaps in your own knowledge. The self-testing from the previous step can be incredibly useful in this regard—make sure you leave yourself with enough time to go back over the areas in which you are struggling the most.

6.6 Psychology and Your Skill Set: Behavioral Self-Management

GATEWAYS LEARNING OUTCOMES:
After reading this section you should be able to:

6.6.1 Name four strategies that can help you to change bad habits

6.6.2 Distinguish between covert sensitization and covert reinforcement

6.6.3 Create a plan to change your own behavior

Chuck used to be out of shape. Worse, he was having a tough time motivating himself to exercise. Now he is back on track, at least as far as his fitness is concerned. How did he do it?

Chuck began by targeting the number of hours per week he spent exercising. For the first week, he tracked how many hours per day he exercised (almost none, as it turned out). With this baseline in place, he set the goal of exercising an hour a week the first week, and an additional hour every week afterward until he reached his final goal of exercising five hours a week. His fitness tracker let him easily keep track of the time spent exercising, along with the number of steps he took and calories he burned. For every hour he spent exercising, Chuck rewarded himself by watching an hour of videos on YouTube. When he didn't stick to his exercise schedule, he gave up his morning coffee at Starbucks the next day. Within a month, Chuck reached his exercise goal. (Now if only he could spend more time studying.)

Chuck's path to success relied heavily on operant conditioning. For example, he was reinforced for actions that were in line with his goals (and punished for those that were not!). But how can you take those principles of operant conditioning and actually use them to change your behavior? Let's take a look.

Mariday/Shutterstock.com

The Basics of Behavioral Self-Management

This is an invitation to use the principles of operant conditioning to carry out a self-management project of your own—one that can help you with any behavior that's important in your relationships or the work that you do. Let's explore how to identify, track, and modify the behaviors that you want to reduce or increase in frequency (Miltenberger, 2016; Watson & Tharp, 2014).

Create a Management Plan

It is best to begin with a little reflective planning. Before getting started, you would be wise to review the basic principles of classical and operant conditioning we explored in this chapter (■ and also to look ahead to Sections 15.4 and 15.5, which discuss some uses of conditioning principles in therapy). Once you're ready to proceed, you can create your own behavioral management plan, which includes the following steps:

1. **Specify a Behavioral Goal** In many ways, behavioral self-management is connected to the idea of *self-regulation* (■ which was discussed in Section 2.9). Recall that self-regulation is related to the ability to achieve our goals, and involves both internal mental processes and control of external observable behaviors. Is there a behavior you want to eliminate altogether, such as quitting smoking or biting your nails? Perhaps you just want to *decrease* a behavior, such as watching less television. Or maybe you want to *increase* a behavior, such as exercising more or studying longer.

   Most of us find it quite difficult to suddenly completely change our behavior (hence so many broken New Year's resolutions). (■ Remember the principle of shaping—the reinforcement of increasingly close approximations of a desired response; see Section 6.4.) Instead, set realistic goals for gradual improvement over a number of successive weeks. Also, set daily goals that add up to the weekly goal for any given week.

   To increase the likelihood of meeting your goals, consider creating a **behavioral contract**. Write down the specific behavioral goal you want to achieve. Also state the rewards you will receive, privileges you will forfeit, or punishments you must accept. The contract should be signed by you and a person you trust.
2. **Record a Baseline** Once you have targeted a behavior, spend a week or so recording how much time you currently spend performing the target behavior. Or count the number of desired or undesired responses you make each day. You will be able to evaluate your progress against your baseline.
3. **Choose Reinforcers** If you meet your daily goal, what reward will you allow yourself? Daily rewards might be watching Netflix, eating a candy bar, socializing with friends, listening to your iPod, or whatever you enjoy. Also establish a weekly reward. A movie? A dinner out? Some time playing a computer game? A weekend hike? If you have trouble thinking of rewards, remember that anything you like to do can serve as reinforcement. This is known as the **Premack principle**, named after David Premack, the psychologist who popularized its use.

   For example, suppose you like to watch television every night and want to study more. All you need to do is to make television watching contingent (dependent) on whether or not you meet your daily goal (study more). You might make it a rule not to watch anything until (and unless!) you have studied for an hour (or whatever length of time you choose).
4. **Record Your Progress** Keep accurate records of the amount of time spent each day on the target behavior, or the number of times you exercise, arrive late to class, eat vegetables, smoke a cigarette, study, watch television, drink a cappuccino, swear, or whatever behavior you have targeted.

   Even if you find it difficult to give and withhold rewards, **self-recording**—keeping records of response frequencies, a form of feedback—can make a difference all by itself. Reflective record-keeping helps break habits (Wood & Rünger, 2016). Also, feedback can be motivating as you begin to make progress. In general, when you systematically (and honestly) observe yourself, you are more likely to engage in desired behaviors and less likely to perform undesired behaviors (Fireman, Kose, & Solomon, 2003; Watson & Tharp, 2014). As you may have noticed, this is the basic idea behind modern fitness trackers such as the Fitbit or goal-setting apps such as stickK.com.
5. **Reward Successes** If you meet your daily goal, collect your reward. If you fall short, be honest with yourself and skip the reward. Do the same for your weekly goal.
6. **Adjust Your Plan as You Learn More About Your Behavior** Overall progress will reinforce your attempts at self-management, so don't be dismayed by the occasional setback. Attempting to manage or alter your own behavior may be more difficult than it sounds. If you feel you need more information, have a look at *Self-directed behavior: Self-modification for personal adjustment* (Watson & Tharp, 2014). If you do try a self-modification project but find it impossible to reach your goals, be aware that professional advice is available.

Extra Techniques to Break Bad Habits

Are there any extra tips for breaking stubborn bad habits? Breaking bad habits may be especially difficult to do. Here are some additional strategies you can add to your behavioral management plan to help you change bad habits.

Look for Alternate Behaviors

A good strategy for change is to try to get the same reinforcement with a new behavior. For example, Marta often tells jokes at the expense of others. Her friends sometimes feel hurt by her sharp-edged humor. Marta senses this and wants to change. What can she do? Usually, Marta's joke telling is reinforced by attention and approval. She could just as easily get the same reinforcement by giving other people praise or compliments. Making a change in her behavior should be easy because she will continue to receive the reinforcement that she seeks.

Break Up Response Chains

Breaking up response chains that precede an undesired behavior will help break the bad habit. The key idea is to scramble the chain of events that leads to an undesired response (Watson & Tharp,

2014). For example, Ignacio often comes home from work, logs in to his favorite role-playing game, and eats a whole bag of cookies or chips. He then takes a shower and changes clothes. By dinnertime, he has lost his appetite. Ignacio realizes he is substituting junk food for dinner. Ignacio could solve the problem by breaking the response chain that precedes dinner. For instance, he could shower immediately when he gets home or delay logging in until after dinner.

Reduce Cues and Antecedents

Try to avoid, narrow down, or remove stimuli that elicit the bad habit.

Example: Brent wants to cut down on smoking. He can take many smoking cues out of his surroundings by removing ashtrays, matches, and extra cigarettes from his house, car, and office. Drug cravings are strongly related to cues conditioned to the drug, such as the odor of cigarettes. Brent can narrow antecedent stimuli even more. He could begin by smoking only in the lounge at work, never in his office or in his car. He could then limit his smoking to home. Then to only one room at home. Then to one chair at home. If he succeeds in getting this far, he may want to limit his smoking to only one unpleasant place, such as a bathroom, basement, or garage (Riley et al., 2002).

Use Covert Sensitization and Reward

In *covert sensitization,* aversive imagery is used to reduce the occurrence of an undesired behavior, such as smoking or overeating (Kearney, 2006; Watson & Tharp, 2014). Suppose, for example, you want to quit smoking. Every time you get the urge, repeatedly and vividly imagine yourself painfully coughing up blood or having to tell the most important person in your life that you have untreatable lung cancer and have only three months left to live. The scenes you imagine should be so *disturbing* or *disgusting* that thinking about them would temporarily make you very uncomfortable about indulging in the habit.

Covert reinforcement—the use of positive imagery—can also be used to reinforce desired behavior (Kearney, 2006; Watson & Tharp, 2014). To make use of covert reinforcement, rehearse your target behavior mentally. Then follow each rehearsal with a vivid, rewarding image. For example, suppose that your target behavior is not smoking. Imagine that you are at a bar with your friends. You are offered a cigarette and politely refuse. Next, imagine a pleasant, reinforcing scene: Picture yourself nicotine-free. Someone you really like says to you, "Gee, you just played your best tennis ever. I've never seen you so healthy."

While actual direct self-reinforcement is the best way to alter behavior, covert or "visualized" reinforcement can have similar effects. So while covert sensitization and reinforcement may sound as if you are "playing games with yourself," it can be a great help if you want to cut down on a bad habit (Kearney, 2006).

Reflective Practice

Psychology and Your Skill Set: Behavioral Self-Management

1. After a target behavior has been selected for reinforcement, it's a good idea to record a baseline so that you can set realistic goals for change. T or F?
2. Self-recording, even without the use of extra rewards, can bring about desired changes in target behaviors. T or F?
3. The Premack principle states that behavioral contracting can be used to reinforce changes in behavior. T or F?
4. A self-management plan should use the principle of shaping by setting a graduated series of goals. T or F?
5. Like covert sensitization, covert reinforcement of desired responses also is possible. T or F?

THINK CRITICALLY

6. Apply what you know from this chapter to explain why setting daily goals in a behavioral self-management program helps maximize the effects of reinforcement.

SELF-REFLECT

- Even if you don't expect to carry out a self-management project right now, outline a plan for changing your own behavior. Be sure to describe the behavior that you want to change, set goals, and identify reinforcers.
- How could you use covert sensitization and covert reinforcement to change your behavior?

Answers: 1. T 2. T 3. F 4. T 5. T 6. Daily performance goals and rewards reduce the delay of reinforcement, which maximizes the impact of the reinforcement.

Behavioral contract A formal agreement stating behaviors to be changed and consequences that apply.

Premack principle Any high-frequency response can be used to reinforce a low-frequency response.

Self-recording Self-management based on keeping records of response frequencies.

Gateways to Learning and Conditioning

Summary: Gateways Learning Outcomes

6.1 The Basics of Learning

6.1.1 Define learning

Learning is a relatively permanent change in knowledge or behavior due to experience.

6.1.2 Outline four types of learning

Four types of learning include classical conditioning, operant (or instrumental) conditioning, observational learning, and cognitive learning.

6.1.3 Define associative learning and identify two types of associative learning

Associative learning is a simple type of learning that occurs when we form associations between stimuli, behaviors, or both. Classical conditioning and operant conditioning are two basic types of associative learning.

6.2 Classical Conditioning: Pair Up!

6.2.1 Explain how classical conditioning works

Classical conditioning, studied by Pavlov, is based on a naturally occurring association between an unconditioned stimulus (US) and an unconditioned, reflexive response (UR) that occurs in response to that US. If a neutral stimulus (NS) is consistently paired with the US, an association between the two will be established. The NS will become a conditioned stimulus (CS) that is capable of producing a conditioned response (CR).

6.2.2 Distinguish between extinction and spontaneous recovery

When the CS is repeatedly presented without the US, the CR will be weakened or inhibited, and *extinction* will occur. After extinction seems to be complete, a rest period may lead to the temporary reappearance of a CR. This is called *spontaneous recovery*.

6.2.3 Differentiate between stimulus generalization and stimulus discrimination in classical conditioning

Through stimulus generalization, stimuli similar to the CS also will produce a response. Generalization gives way to stimulus discrimination when an organism learns to respond to one stimulus, but not to similar stimuli.

6.2.4 Name four instances of classical conditioning in everyday life

Food aversions can stem from classical conditioning, and *celebrity endorsements* for products are also usually based on classical conditioning. Emotional responses can also be the product of classical conditioning. These are referred to as *conditioned emotional responses* (CERs). Finally, clinicians also use classical conditioning in *aversion therapy* as a way to get clients to give up bad habits such as alcohol dependency.

6.3 Operant Conditioning: Shape Up!

6.3.1 Explain how operant conditioning works, including how positive and negative reinforcement and punishment will impact the likelihood that a behavior will be repeated

Operant conditioning occurs when a voluntary action is followed by a reinforcer (which increases the frequency of the action) or a punisher (which decreases the frequency of the action). Both positive reinforcement and negative reinforcement *increase* the likelihood that a response will be repeated. Positive and negative punishment *decrease* the likelihood that the response will occur again.

6.3.2 Distinguish between generalization and discrimination in operant conditioning

In generalization, an operant response tends to occur when stimuli similar to those preceding reinforcement are present. In discrimination, responses are given in the presence of discriminative stimuli associated with reinforcement and withheld in the presence of stimuli associated with nonreinforcement.

6.3.3 Explain how shaping works

By rewarding successive approximations to a particular response, behavior can be shaped into desired patterns.

6.3.4 Name three factors that impact the effectiveness of reinforcement and punishment

The effectiveness of reinforcement and punishment is dependent upon their *intensity* (typically they will be more effective when they are more intense), *timing* (typically they will be more effective when they are delivered very soon after a behavior), and *how consistently they are administered* (punishment is more effective when it is administered consistently, after every behavior; however, the effectiveness of reinforcement depends on its schedule).

6.3.5 Differentiate between continuous and partial schedules of reinforcement and name the four types of partial schedules of reinforcement

Two basic schedules of reinforcement are continuous (after every response) or partial (only a portion of responses are reinforced). Continuous reinforcement is useful in the early stages of learning; partial reinforcement is effective after a behavior has been learned and produces greater resistance to extinction. The four most basic partial schedules of reinforcement are *fixed ratio, variable ratio, fixed interval,* and *variable interval.* Each produces a distinct pattern of responding.

6.3.6 Contrast primary and secondary reinforcers

Operant learning may be based on primary reinforcers (which are rooted in biology) and secondary reinforcers (such as tokens and social reinforcers). Primary reinforcers are "natural," physiologically based rewards. Secondary reinforcers are learned and sometimes gain their reinforcing value because they can be exchanged for primary reinforcers. Tokens and money gain their reinforcing value in this way.

6.3.7 Name two instances of operant conditioning in everyday life

Operant conditioning can be seen in the use of token economies and in the partial reinforcement schedules that govern slot machines in casinos.

6.4 Observational Learning: Watch It!

6.4.1 Name the three steps involved in observational learning

Through observational learning, we can learn to perform particular actions (e.g., how to tie your shoes) as well as specific attitudes and emotional responses. Observational learning involves three steps: *paying attention* to the model, *remembering* what the model did, and being able to *reproduce (imitate)* the model's behavior.

6.4.2 Describe three characteristics of models we are most likely to imitate

We are more likely to pay attention to models that we *admire*, who are *authority* figures, or who are *similar* to us. However, not all behaviors, attitudes, and emotions that are learned through observation are positive, and observational learning can occur even when the model did not intend to teach anything.

6.4.3 Explain the connection between observational learning and operant conditioning

Whether we imitate a model's behavior depends on whether we have seen the model rewarded or punished for their actions. In this way, operant learning principles play a role in observational learning.

6.4.4 Name two instances of observational learning in everyday life

Observational learning is important in the *workplace*, where people learn acceptable standards of behavior by watching their co-workers. In addition, the *media*—including television, the Internet, and video games—provides powerful models from which kids can learn through observation.

6.4.5 Outline three reasons why exposure to violent media may be associated with later aggression among children and adolescents, and what the research actually says about this association

Young people may *learn new and aggressive and antisocial behaviors* from models in the media. However, aggressive behavior may also be increased if media serves to *disinhibit viewer's impulses to control aggression*, or if it *desensitizes people to violence*. Early research suggested that playing violent video games promotes aggression; however, more recent research has suggested a more complex relationship between these two factors. It's also important to remember that much of the early research was correlational, and we cannot establish cause-and-effect relationships under such circumstances.

6.5 Cognitive Learning: Think!

6.5.1 Define cognitive learning, and name two groups of psychologists who are interested in cognitive learning

Cognitive learning refers to our ability to acquire skills and information using thinking, memory, and problem solving. Two groups of psychologists who study issues related to cognitive learning are school psychologists and educational psychologists.

6.5.2 Outline the two main dimensions of Bloom's taxonomy

Bloom's taxonomy is a classification system that organizes information about *types of knowledge* (factual, conceptual, procedural, and metacognitive) and the *cognitive processes* (remembering, understanding, applying, analyzing, evaluating, creating) that are involved in learning.

6.5.3 Describe four factors that affect cognitive learning

Cognitive learning is influenced by *learner characteristics* (working memory, clinical diagnoses, persistence, motivation, self-efficacy, and mindset, but not learning styles), *learning strategies* (use of self-testing and metacognitive strategies), *type of instruction* (direct instruction, discovery learning, guided discovery), and the *learning environment* (use of feedback and technology).

6.5.4 Name some instances of cognitive learning in everyday life

In addition to traditional "school" settings, cognitive learning happens in many other settings (e.g., while reading for pleasure, watching a video, or engaging in everyday conversations).

6.6 Psychology and Your Skill Set: Behavioral Self-Management

6.6.1 Name four strategies that can help you to change bad habits

Four strategies that can help change bad habits are reinforcing alternative responses, breaking response chains, avoiding antecedent cues, and using covert sensitization and reinforcement.

6.6.2 Distinguish between covert sensitization and covert reinforcement

In covert sensitization, aversive images are used to discourage unwanted behavior. Covert reinforcement is a way to encourage desired responses by mental rehearsal.

6.6.3 Create a plan to change your own behavior

We hope that after reading this section, you'll be better able to think about how you can use these strategies to help develop a plan to manage any bad habit that you want to change!

7 Memory

Carl Wagner/Tribune News Service/Newscom

Gateway Theme It is important to understand how our memories are affected as they are encoded, stored, and retrieved since what we remember and what we forget shape who we are.

Chapter Outline

A Case of Mistaken Identity

Penny Beernsten was out running in a Wisconsin state park when a man grabbed her and dragged her into the woods. As he tried to rape her, she fought back. He responded by pressing on her windpipe, and she quickly lost consciousness. Eventually, she was rescued by two strangers who took her to the hospital. While she was recovering, police officers asked if she could identify her attacker. Looking over the photographs they provided, Penny selected the man she remembered seeing during the assault. Later faced with a live police lineup, she selected the same man—Steven Avery.

At the trial, Penny's eyewitness testimony was instrumental in securing a conviction. In spite of the fact that he had 14 people willing to provide alibis, Steve Avery was sentenced to 32 years in prison for the rape. There was just one problem—DNA evidence later made it clear that Steven Avery wasn't guilty at all. As it turned out, Penny Beernsten's memories of the events that fateful day in the park were faulty, and Steven Avery had spent 17 years in prison for a crime he didn't commit.

In this chapter we examine memory, including how our memories are stored and retrieved. We'll look at its power, which allows us to recall events from moments ago as well as those from years in the past. But we'll also examine the weaknesses of human memory, including those that can lead to false and inaccurate memories such as the one reported by Penny Beernsten. We'll finish the chapter with some practical advice about improving your ability to remember important information, and applying what we know about memory to give unforgettable presentations.

7.1 A General Model of Memory

GATEWAYS LEARNING OUTCOMES:
After reading this section you should be able to:

7.1.1 Define memory

7.1.2 Describe the types of memory and memory processes that are outlined in the Atkinson-Shiffrin model of memory

Take a moment to answer the following questions (adapted from Hard, 2018):

What is the 10th word in the American national anthem?
What is the capital of France?
What did you eat for breakfast?
How many rooms are there in the house or apartment where you grew up?

If you think about it, answering each of these questions required you to draw on your memory. And yet, we'd be willing to bet that trying to answer all of them probably felt quite different for you. Some questions—such as the one about the number of rooms in the place where you grew up—may have required you to create a mental image and wander through it. In contrast, coming up with the 10th word of the national anthem likely involved you "hearing" the song in your head. Other memory-related questions may require you to mentally "roll back" events in your life to answer questions about things that occurred in your past (what you ate for breakfast). And still others are more similar to "looking up" information, just as you would in a book or on a computer (the capital of France).

Types of Memory

Clearly, **memory** is not simply a passive library of facts. Instead, it's a series of active systems that receive, store, organize, alter, and recover information (Sternberg, 2017). For information to be stored for a long time it must pass through several types of memory: *sensory memory*, *short-term memory* (or *working memory*), and *long-term memory*.

For information to pass through each of these three types of memory, you need to engage in different memory processes. Let's say, for example, that you're trying to remember all of the new terms in this chapter for your next psychology exam. The information will enter sensory memory by way of your vision, but then you must *pay attention* to that sensory memory (that is, the sensory image of the words on the page) sufficiently to move them through to short-term (working) memory. You can keep the information active in short-term memory briefly by using a process called *maintenance rehearsal*, but if you want to move it into the more permanent storage in long-term memory then you will need to engage in **encoding** and **storage** of the information. When you need that information to answer a question on the exam, you'll have to engage in **retrieval** to get it from long-term memory back into short-term memory. The different types of memory, and the processes associated with them, are summarized by a modified version of the *Atkinson-Shiffrin model of memory*, shown in Figure 7.1 (Atkinson & Shiffrin, 1968; Sternberg, 2017). We'll take a closer look at each part of the model in the sections that follow.

Reflective Practice

A General Model of Memory

Match: A. paying attention B. rehearsal C. retrieval D. encoding

1. _______ The process of moving information from long-term memory to short-term memory
2. _______ The process of moving information from sensory memory to short-term memory
3. _______ The process of moving information from short-term memory to long-term memory
4. _______ The process by which you can keep information active in short-term memory
5. The three types of memory represented in the Atkinson-Shiffrin model are:
   a. Creative memory, sensory memory, long-term memory
   b. Visual memory, short-term memory, long-term memory
   c. Creative memory, visual memory, long-term memory
   d. Sensory memory, short-term memory, long-term memory

THINK CRITICALLY

6. How is long-term memory helping you read this sentence: The man made bread by mixing flour, water, and yeast and then baking the dough in an oven.

SELF-REFLECT

- Think about how you've used your memory in the last hour. Can you identify an example of each of the following: retrieving a memory from long-term memory? Rehearsing information to keep it in short-term memory? Trying to store, or encode, information in long-term memory?

Answers: 1. C 2. A 3. D 4. B 5. D 6. If your understanding of the meanings of the words wasn't already stored in LTM, could you read at all?

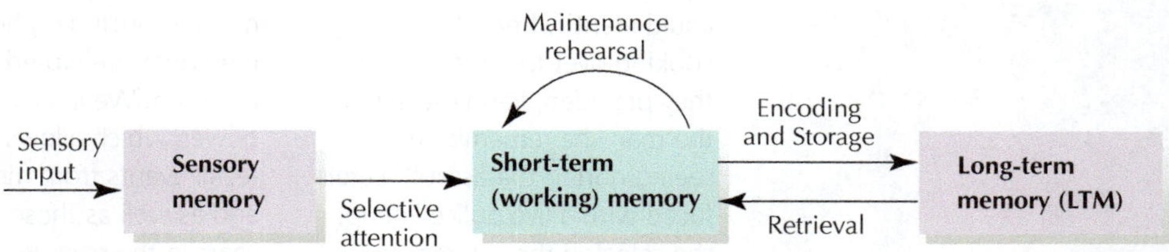

Figure 7.1 Modified Atkinson-Shiffrin model. Successful long-term remembering involves three memory systems (that is, three types of memory). Sensory memory stores sensory information for a second or two. Selectively attending to that information allows it to move into short-term/working memory, where it is processed. Any resulting meaningful information may be encoded in long-term memory, where it is stored until it is needed, at which time it may be retrieved. It is worth noting that this is a useful, but highly simplified, *model* of memory; it may not be literally true regarding what happens in the brain.

7.2 Sensory and Short-Term (Working) Memory

GATEWAYS LEARNING OUTCOMES:
After reading this section you should be able to

7.2.1 Describe sensory memory, including its capacity and duration

7.2.2 Describe short-term (working) memory, including its capacity and duration

7.2.3 Explain what is meant by "chunking," and how it helps to expand the capacity of working memory

7.2.4 Distinguish between rote rehearsal (rote learning) and elaborative rehearsal (elaborative encoding)

The first two types of memory are sensory and short-term, or working, memory. Let's do a deeper dive on each one.

Sensory Memory

We saw in ■ Section 4.1 that we can gather information from the world through a variety of senses. This information enters **sensory memory**. The capacity of sensory memory is thought to be very, very large, but its duration is very short (that is, the information that enters sensory memory cannot be held there for very long). It's important to note that we are typically not aware of sensory memory (Radvansky, 2017).

To get an idea of what sensory memory is like, look at the next words in this paragraph and then quickly close your eyes. If you are lucky, a fleeting "photocopy" of the letters will persist. **Iconic** (eye-KON-ick) **memory** typically stores visual sensory images for about a half second (Clarke & Mack, 2015). Similarly, when you hear information, sensory memory stores it for up to two seconds as an **echoic memory**, a brief flurry of activity in the auditory system (Cheng & Lin, 2012).

If you are *selectively attending* to sensory input, such as the words on this page, then it can move into temporary storage in short-term memory. Background events that receive very little attention, such as a voice on the television announcing a new season of your favorite show, likely will not. Similarly, if you are just looking at the words on this page but not paying attention (maybe because you are also watching television!) it is unlikely that information will get past sensory memory (see ■ Section 4.5 for more on the factors that impact attention).

Short-Term (Working) Memory

Short-term memory (STM) is thought to be storage that has a small capacity (that is, it holds a small amount of information) and a relatively short duration of about a dozen seconds or so (Jonides et al., 2008). But since the Atkinson-Shiffrin model in Figure 7.1 was proposed, psychologists have realized that STM is not just a temporary storage space. Instead, it's better conceived of as a kind of mental "workbench" where the information we're currently thinking about is subject to lots of mental activity. For example, information in STM can be evaluated or compared with other things we know (Will this shirt look good on me? Is it nicer than the one in the other store?). We can mentally imagine how that information in STM might change under other circumstances (Would it look better in red?), or we can perform operations on it (The shirt is on sale for 50% off, so it will cost me 25 dollars.).

As a result of all the activity that happens here, STM has been re-named **working memory** to emphasize the "work" that goes on there (Chein & Fiez, 2010; Nevo & Breznitz, 2013). Working memory is the only type of memory that is conscious: Whenever you read a book, do mental arithmetic, put together a puzzle, plan a meal, or follow directions, you are using working memory (Baddeley, 2012; Prime & Jolicoeur, 2010). Moreover, all of the questions that were asked at the beginning of ■ Section 7.1 required you to consciously operate on information in your working memory.

Stephen Kosslyn, Thomas Ball, and Brian Reiser (1978) provided a good demonstration of the fact that mental operations are being carried out in working memory. Participants first memorized a map like the one shown in ● Figure 7.2*a*. They were then asked to picture a black dot moving from one object, such as one of the trees, to another, such as the hut at the top of the island. Did people really form a working memory image to do this task? It seems that they did. As shown in ● Figure 7.2*b*, the time that it took to "move" the dot was directly related to actual distances on the map.

Here's another example, this time with sounds: Read the following two numbers out loud and add them together in your head: 1,874 + 3,326. Come on, give it a try. Regardless of how well you did, notice that you had to encode and store the two numbers, likely by the sound of their number names, along with any carries or other intermediate calculations, as you carried out the addition.

Memory Mental system for receiving, encoding, storing, organizing, altering, and retrieving information.

Encoding (in memory) Converting information into a form to be retained in memory.

Storage (in memory) Holding information in memory for later use.

Retrieval (in memory) Recovery of stored information.

Sensory memory Fleeting storage system for sensory impressions.

Iconic memory A mental image or visual representation.

Echoic memory A brief continuation of sensory activity in the auditory system after a sound is heard.

Short-term memory (STM) Storage system used to hold small amounts of information in conscious awareness for about a dozen seconds.

Working memory Another name for *short-term memory*, especially as it is used for thinking and problem solving.

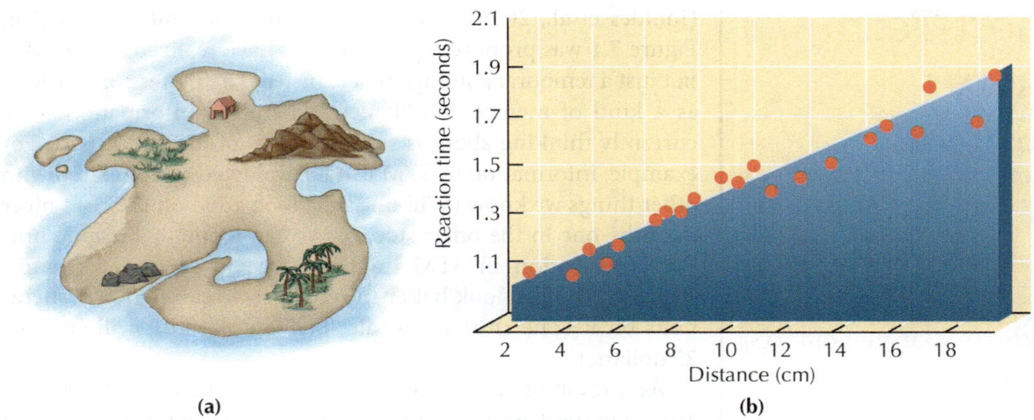

Figure 7.2 Scanning mental images. (*a*) "Treasure map" similar to the one used by Kosslyn, Ball, and Reiser (1978) to study images in memory. (*b*) This graph shows how long it took participants to move a visualized spot various distances on their mental images of the map. (See text for explanation.)

The Capacity of Working Memory

How much information can be held in working memory? It depends on whether the information is comprised of sounds, mental images, or a combination of the two. Read the following numbers once, and then turn away from this book and write down as many as you can, in the correct order.

8 5 1 7 4 9 3

This is called a *digit-span* test—a measure of attention and working memory (Bowden et al., 2013). Most adults can correctly repeat about seven digits. Now try to memorize the following list, again reading it only once.

7 1 8 3 5 4 2 9 1 6 3 4

This series was likely beyond the capacity of your working memory. Psychologist George Miller (1920–2012) found that working memory is limited to the "magic number" of seven plus or minus two (so, five to nine) **information bits** (Miller, 1956). A bit is a single meaningful "piece" of information, such as a digit or letter. More conservative psychologists believe that working memory may actually hold only four items (Jonides et al., 2008; Mathy & Feldman, 2012). Basically, then, it is as if working memory has somewhere between four and nine "slots" or "bins" into which separate bits of information can be placed. When all of the slots are filled, there is no room for new information.

Hacking the Capacity of Working Memory: Chunking

Before we continue, let's test your working memory again, this time with letters. Read the following letters once, and then look away and try to write them down in the proper order.

L O L B T W O M G I D K

Notice that there are 12 letters, or "bits" of information. If you studied the letters one at a time, this should be beyond the upper limit of working memory. However, you may have noticed that the letters can be organized, or *chunked,* together. For example, you may have realized that LOL is the abbreviation used in texting for "laugh out loud." If so, the three bits L, O, and L became one chunk. **Chunking**, then, is the process of grouping similar or meaningful information together. Put another way, chunking recodes or reorganizes information into units that are already in long-term memory.

In classic experiments that have used lists like this one, people remembered best when the letters were read as familiar meaningful chunks; in this case the familiar texting abbreviations LOL, BTW, OMG, IDK (Bower & Springston, 1970). If you recoded the letters this way, you will have reorganized 12 letters—more than the capacity of working memory—into four *chunks* of information, which is well within its limits. Each chunk of three letters is now the equivalent of one "bit" of information that can fit into a single "slot" or "bin" in working memory. As a result, chunking has allowed you to expand the capacity of your working memory. Instead of being limited to between four and seven individual letters, you probably easily remembered the entire list of 12.

Chunking suggests that working memory holds about four to seven of whatever units we are using, for example, letters, numbers, words or, in this case, texting short forms. Picture working memory as a workbench again. Through chunking, we actively combine several individual items into one "stack" of information. This allows us to place approximately seven stacks on the workbench, whereas before, there was room for only seven separate items.

The clear message is that creating information chunks is the key to making the most efficient use of the limited space in your working memory (Jones, 2012). This means, for example, that it is well worthwhile to find or create meaningful chunks when you need to remember something. While you are studying, try to find ways to link two, three, or more separate facts or ideas into larger chunks, and your working memory will improve.

Working Memory Processes

For how long is information stored in working memory? That depends, because you can keep sounds active in working memory by repeating them over and over, a process called **maintenance rehearsal** (see Figure 7.1). You have probably used maintenance rehearsal to keep a phone number active in your mind while looking at your cellphone and dialing it. In a sense, rehearsing information (whether silently or out loud) allows you to "hear" it many times, not just once (Jarrold & Hall, 2013).

But what if rehearsal is prevented? Without maintenance rehearsal, individual memories rapidly *decay*, or fade, from working memory. This prevents our minds from more permanently storing useless names, dates, telephone numbers, and other trivia. For example, in one experiment, participants heard meaningless syllables such as "xar," followed by a number such as 67. As soon as participants heard the number, they began counting backward by threes (to prevent them from rehearsing the syllable). After a delay of between 12 and 18 seconds, their memory for the syllables fell to zero (Peterson & Peterson, 1959). The results of this study demonstrate that information in working memory is very sensitive to interruption and can easily be displaced. You've probably experienced something like this yourself: A friend gives you a phone number to call, say to order a pizza. As you start to dial, your friend suddenly asks you a question. You answer and return to dialing, only to find that answering the question displaced your memory for the phone number. Because working memory can handle only small amounts of information, it can be difficult to do more than one task at a time (Mercer & McKeown, 2010).

Isn't saying stuff to yourself over and over, like you do during maintenance rehearsal, also a way of studying? It *is* true that the more times information in working memory is rehearsed, the greater its chances of being encoded in long-term memory (Goldstein, 2015; refer to Figure 7.1). This is **rote rehearsal (rote learning)**—encoding by simple repetition. But studies related to memory have continuously demonstrated that rote learning is not a very effective way to encode information into long-term memory particularly when the information being learned is complex.

In contrast, **elaborative rehearsal** (or **elaborative encoding**), which makes information more meaningful, is a far better way to encode lasting memories. When encoding information for the first time, it is best to elaborate on the meaning of the information, especially by forming links between that information and memories that are already in long-term memory (Raposo, Han, & Dobbins, 2009). As you read, try to reflect frequently. Ask yourself "why" questions, such as, "Why would that be true?" (Toyota & Kikuchi, 2005). Also, try to relate new ideas to your own experiences and prior knowledge (Karpicke & Smith, 2012). If you do not already recognize this advice, consider (re?)reading the introduction to this book, *Psychology and Your Skill Set—Reflective Studying*, if only to elaborate on your concept of elaborative rehearsal.

Reflective Practice

Sensory and Short-Term (Working) Memory

1. Iconic memory refers to
a. sensory memory associated with the kinesthetic system
b. sensory memory associated with the auditory system
c. sensory memory associated with the somesthetic system
d. sensory memory associated with the visual system

2. Working memory is
a. the same as sensory memory
b. considered to be like a "mental workbench"
c. unconscious
d. shorter in duration than sensory memory

3. Early research on short-term memory suggested that its capacity was seven information bits, plus or minus two. T or F?

4. One method for increasing the capacity of working memory is:
a. chunking c. encoding
b. retrieval d. imagining

5. Which form of rehearsal is most effective for moving information from short-term to long-term memory?
a. maintenance rehearsal c. elaborative rehearsal
b. rote rehearsal d. basic rehearsal

THINK CRITICALLY

6. If you were attempting to study this section of the textbook for a test, what might you do to ensure that the information was stored in long-term memory?

SELF-REFLECT

- What kinds of information are you good at remembering? Why do you think your memory is better for those topics?

Answers: 1. D 2. B 3. T 4. A 5. C 6. Your goal should be to engage in elaborative rehearsal, attempting to connect the information you've learned about sensory and short-term memory to things that you already know. You might think about instances when you've been aware of using the "mental workbench" of working memory, for example, or you might ask yourself questions to elaborate on the material (e.g., "Do blind people have iconic sensory memory?").

7.3 Long-Term Memory

GATEWAYS LEARNING OUTCOMES:
After reading this section you should be able to:

7.3.1 Describe long-term memory, including its duration, capacity, and organization

7.3.2 Define the terms retrieval cue and redintegration, and explain their relation to spreading activation in the memory network

7.3.3 Distinguish between implicit and explicit memory

7.3.4 Distinguish between episodic and semantic memory

Information bits Meaningful units of information, such as numbers, letters, words, or phrases.

Chunking Process of grouping similar or meaningful information together.

Maintenance rehearsal Repeating information over and over to keep it active in short-term memory.

Rote rehearsal (rote learning) Learning by simple repetition.

Elaborative rehearsal (elaborative encoding) Making memories more meaningful through processing that encodes links between new information and existing memories and knowledge, either at the time of the original encoding or on subsequent retrievals.

7.3.5 Name the parts of the brain that are important in memory

7.3.6 Outline two reasons why it's helpful to have information stored in long-term memory

Information that is important or meaningful is encoded in **long-term memory (LTM)**, a storage system that can hold a great deal of information over lengthy periods of time. Though we are not generally aware of information that is stored in LTM, it contains everything you know about the world—from aardvark to zebra, math to operating your cellphone, facts to fantasy. Yet, there appears to be no danger of running out of room because it's generally believed that LTM can store nearly limitless amounts of information. In fact, we'll see in this section that the more you know, the easier it becomes to add new information to memory. This is the reverse of what we would expect if LTM could be "filled up" (Goldstein, 2015). In this section we'll take a closer look at LTM and how it works.

Storage and Organization of Information in Long-Term Memory

How is information stored and organized in LTM? This is a challenging question. One of the first answers came from studies such as the one described in this short passage:

> An electrode touched the patient's brain. Immediately, she said, "Yes, sir, I think I heard a mother calling her little boy somewhere. It seemed to be something happening years ago. It was somebody in the neighborhood in which I live." A short time later, the electrode was applied to the same spot. Again, the patient said, "Yes, I hear the same familiar sounds. It seems to be a woman calling, the same lady" (Penfield, 1958).

A woman made these statements while she was undergoing brain surgery. The brain has no pain receptors, so the patient was awake while her brain was electrically stimulated (● Figure 7.3). When activated, some brain areas seemed to produce vivid memories of long-forgotten events (Jacobs, Lega, & Anderson, 2012).

Results such as these led neurosurgeon Wilder Penfield to propose that LTM records the past like a "strip of movie film, complete with soundtrack" (Penfield, 1957). However, as you already know, this is an exaggeration because many events never get past sensory or working memory. Also, as we'll see later in this chapter, many memories are clearly distorted or false. But if information isn't saved in LTM as something similar to a movie and its soundtrack, then how is it stored and organized?

Storage Based on Meaning

Most psychologists agree that at least some long-term memories *are* encoded as images or sounds. If you were asked to think about Albert Einstein, for example, chances are that there's an image of him stored somewhere in your LTM. Similarly, if you were asked to think about your phone, you might remember the sound of its ringtone. In ■ Section 6.5, though, we discussed the fact that most information is stored in LTM on the basis of *meaning*. If you make an error in recalling something from LTM on an exam, then, it probably will be related to meaning. For example, if you are trying to recall the phrase *test anxiety*, you are more likely to mistakenly write down *test nervousness* or *test worry* than *text anxiety* or *tent anxiety*—the first two are much closer in meaning to the original phrase than the second two.

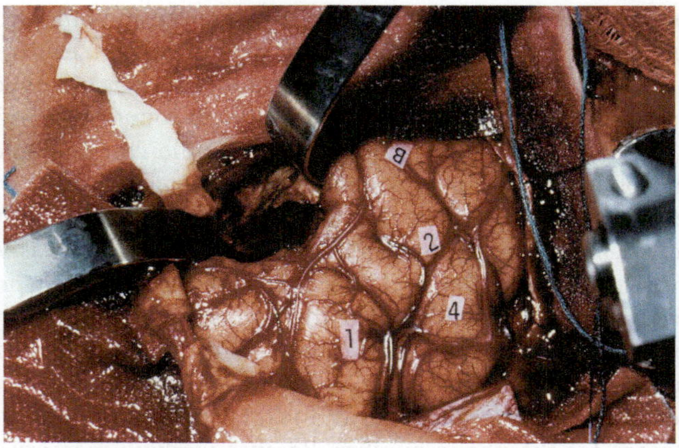

Southern Illinois University/Science Source

● **Figure 7.3 Exposed cerebral cortex of a patient undergoing brain surgery.** While operating on the brains of wide-awake patients, Wilder Penfield would sometimes deliver a mild electric "shock" to the surface of the exposed cortex. In response, patients would often experience vivid memories. A critical evaluation of such reports suggests that they are more like dreams than memories. This fact raises questions about claims that long-term memories are permanent.

But the idea that organization in LTM is "meaning-based" doesn't only refer to the meaning of individual words. In the case of LTM, meaning-based also refers to the idea that information is being stored as a set of abstract concepts and properties based on what that information means to you. For example, some of the information in LTM about your best friend might include the fact that she's a great cook, she's totally trustworthy, and she can make you laugh even when you feel as though everything is going wrong. All of these ideas that are based on what your best friend means to you will be stored together in your LTM. Similarly, if you happen to be enthusiastic about motorcycles and have a great deal of information on the subject in your LTM, then "meaning" might refer to information being stored according to what you know about the reliability of different models, how powerful their engines are, and how much they cost. Again, that information will be grouped together in your LTM.

Human Diversity and Meaning-Based Storage

Because it has an important impact on the meaning that people attribute to various concepts, culture also affects the encoding of information into the LTM network, and the structure of the network itself (Ross & Wang, 2010). For example, American culture emphasizes individuals, whereas Chinese culture emphasizes membership in groups. Put another way, the two cultures give different meaning to the importance of individuals versus groups.

In one study, European-American and Chinese adults were asked to recall 20 memories from any time in their lives. As expected, American memories tended to be self-centered: Most people remembered surprising events and what they did during the events. Chinese adults, in contrast, remembered important social or historical events and their own interactions with family members, friends, and others (Wang & Conway, 2004). Thus, in the United States, personal memories tend to be about "me"; in China they tend to be about "we" (Wang, 2013).

Organization Based on Networks

It makes sense that memories that are linked in terms of their meaning will be stored together. But how is all of that information that you've acquired organized more broadly in LTM? Psychologists have established that a **network model** best explains the structure, or organization, of our long-term memories (see Figure 7.4). Those networks can be quite extensive or quite sparse, depending on how much information we have stored about a topic in LTM. For example, Figure 7.5 shows the LTM networks of two students, Erica and Jerry, on the subject of reinforcement in relation to operant conditioning (described in Section 6.3). You can see that Erica has much more information in her LTM about the topic than Jerry; consequently, her network is much more complex. On a test question about this topic, Erica will have a much better chance of being successful.

Keith Dannemiller/Alamy Stock Photo

After going for a walk in nature, could you remember the locations, appearances, and names of all of the plants you saw along the way? Unless you are a botanist, doing so would be quite a feat of memory. However, for indigenous peoples, such as this Piaroa Indian shaman from Venezuela, it would be easier. Plants are very important (that is, *meaningful*) to indigenous peoples as sources of food and medicine (Kimmerer, 2013). Since a shaman's power is strongly influenced by his knowledge of plants and because memory is organized primarily around meaning, the shaman can encode and store information about plants and their uses that would be difficult for most other people to remember.

Here's another thing that's worth noting about memory networks: Because memories are stored based on their meaning, you'll often see points in the network where a single concept is linked to two very different meanings. For example, take a look at Jerry's network. The concept of reinforcement is connected to operant conditioning (he knows that events followed by reinforcement will be more likely to recur), but it's also connected to another, quite different meaning (sending more soldiers during a battle). Similarly, in your own LTM network, the concept "apple" might have one series of meaning-based connections related to the fruit (Granny Smith, seeds, orchards, worms) and a completely separate set of connections that are related to the company (iPhones, the App Store, Steve Jobs, and Siri).

With this type of memory network in mind, assume that Erica was given two statements to which she must quickly answer yes or no: (1) *Classical conditioning was developed by Pavlov.* (2) *Classical conditioning is due to experience.* Which will she answer more quickly? Erica most likely will say yes to the statement *Classical conditioning was developed by Pavlov* faster (Collins & Quillian, 1969).

To explain why, think about the following example: Imagine finding a picture taken on your sixth birthday. The photo serves as a **retrieval cue**, triggering the retrieval of memories of that day. Then, one memory links to another associated memory, which links to another, and another. Soon you have triggered a stream of seemingly forgotten details as link after link is activated. This process is called *spreading activation* in the memory network, and it is associated with **redintegration** (reh-DIN-tuh-GRAY-shun)—the process by which a complete memory can be retrieved from partial cues or reminders.

For Erica, the retrieval cue was the question about classical conditioning. When she saw it, redintegration would have set off a chain, activating lots of things in her memory network related to this topic. But the distance between the retrieval cue and other items in the network matters for retrieval. When ideas are "farther apart" in the network, it takes a longer chain of associations to connect them during the process of spreading activation. The

Long-term memory (LTM) Unlimited capacity storage system that can hold information over lengthy periods of time.

Network model (of memory) A model of memory that views it as an organized system of linked information.

Retrieval cue Any information that can prompt or trigger the retrieval of particular memories. Retrieval cues usually enhance memory.

Redintegration Process by which memories are reconstructed or expanded by starting with one memory and then following chains of association to other, related memories.

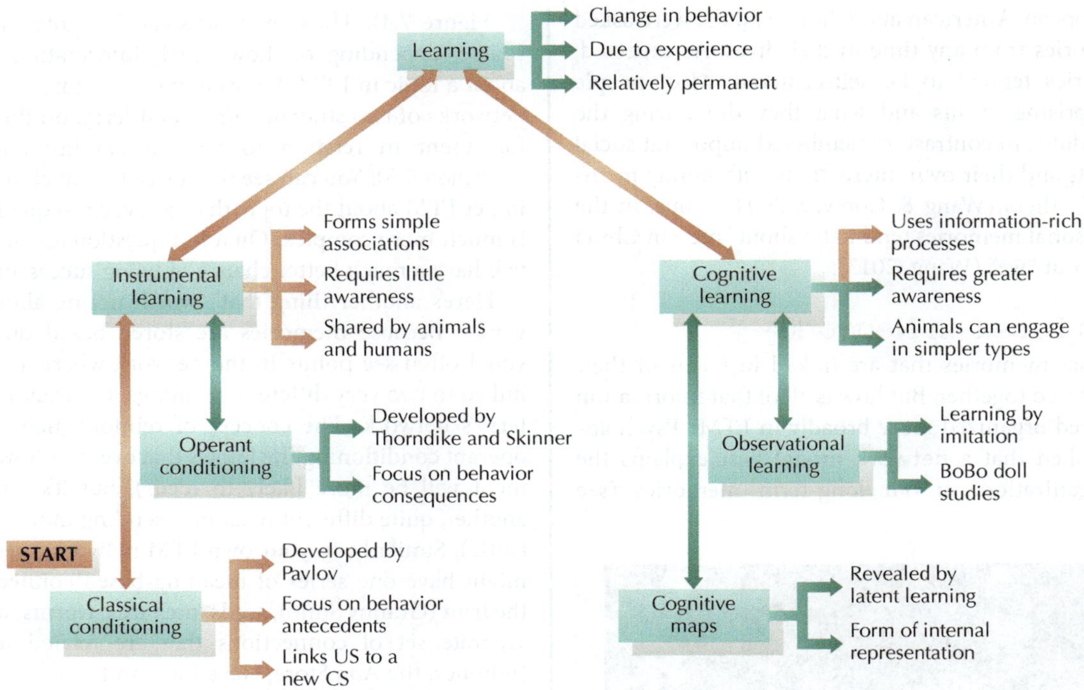

Figure 7.4 A network model of student learning. Erica, a first-year psychology major, has just finished studying for an exam on conditioning and learning. This figure presents a hypothetical network model of a part of what she just learned. Small networks of ideas such as this are probably organized into larger and larger units and higher levels of meaning.

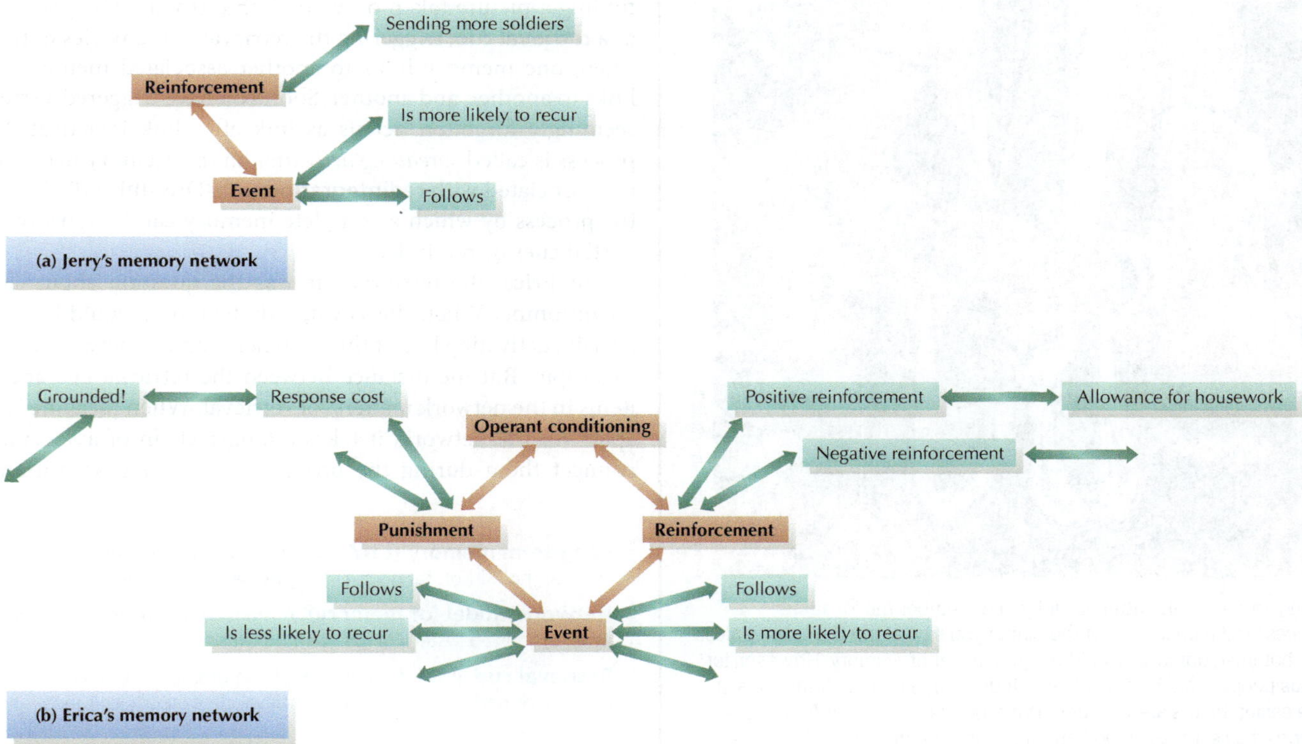

Figure 7.5 Hypothetical networks of two students' concepts of reinforcement. Jerry is in trouble, while Erica is not. Only part of her more elaborate network is shown here. See if you can connect this fragment of Erica's network to her other fragment, shown in Figure 7.4.

Figure 7.6 The Tower of Hanoi puzzle. All the colored disks must be moved to the right-hand post without ever placing a larger disk on a smaller one. Only one disk may be moved at a time, and a disk must always be moved from one post to another (it cannot be held aside). An amnesic patient learned to solve the puzzle in 31 moves, the minimum possible. Even so, each time he began, he protested that he did not remember ever solving the puzzle before and that he did not know how to begin. Evidence such as this suggests that memories for skills are distinct from memories for facts.

more two items are separated in the network, then, the longer it takes to connect them and the further something is from the original cue, the less likely it is to be remembered.

Types of Long-Term Memory

A curious thing happens to many people who develop amnesia. Amnesic patients may be unable to remember a telephone number, an address, or a person's name. Yet, the same patients can use their memory to learn the solutions to complex puzzles in a normal amount of time (Cavaco et al., 2004; Figure 7.6). These and other observations have led many psychologists to conclude that LTM is comprised of at least two categories (Lum & Bleses, 2012). One is called *implicit memory*; the other is *explicit memory*. Moreover, there are two types of explicit memory: semantic and episodic (Figure 7.7).

Implicit Memory

Implicit memory refers to memories that lie outside of awareness. That may sound a bit strange at first—after all, how can you have a memory and not be aware of it? But if you think about your

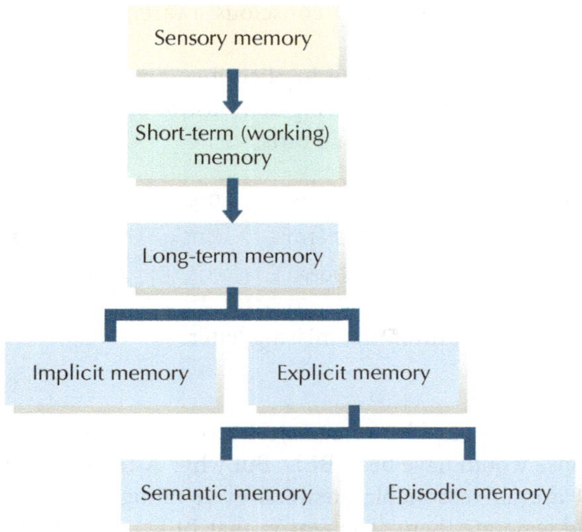

Figure 7.7 Types of memory. In the model shown, long-term memory is divided into implicit memory and explicit memory. Implicit memory includes skill-based learning, conditioned responses, and primed responses. Explicit memory can be divided into semantic (fact-based knowledge) or episodic (personal experiences associated with specific times and places) memory.

everyday life, you'll realize there are actually several examples of memories like this. We'll discuss three of them here: memory for skills, learning through conditioning, and priming.

The first type of implicit memory concerns our long-term memories for how to do things that require motor or performance *skills*, such as typing, driving, or swinging a golf club. You may sometimes hear the expression "muscle memory," but it's worth noting that the information you need to carry out these tasks isn't stored in your muscles—it resides in LTM. A second type of implicit memory is related to classical and instrumental *conditioning* (see Sections 6.2 and 6.3)—again, once this type of learning has occurred, it's stored in LTM and we draw on those memories

Implicit memory A recollection that a person does not know exists and is retrieved unconsciously.

Can you label the letter keys on this blank keyboard? If you can, you probably used implicit memory to do it.

automatically, without any conscious awareness (Freberg, 2016; Lum & Bleses, 2012).

A third and final type of implicit memory is perhaps best understood through the following demonstration: Take a moment to look at the following list of words:

snooze	dream	blanket	doze	pillow	nap
snore	mattress	alarm	clock	rest	slumber
nod	sheet	bunk	cot	cradle	groggy

Quickly now, fill in the missing letter:

B__D

If you are like the vast majority of people, your immediate response would have been BED. But why? After all, BAD, BID, or BUD are all reasonable answers, even though very few people would generate them. The reason that BED is the most common answer relies on a third type of implicit memory called **priming**. In this example, reading the list would have activated, or primed, the concept of sleeping in your memory network. Because LTM is organized according to meaning, the process of spreading activation would then have made BED much more accessible to you when you were asked to fill in the blank.

Explicit Memory

Explicit memory stores information from your personal life, as well as specific factual information, such as names, faces, words, dates, and ideas. Explicit memory can be further divided into *semantic memory* and *episodic memory* (Irish & Piguet, 2013; Tulving, 2002).

Semantic Memory

Much of our basic factual knowledge about the world is almost totally immune to forgetting. The names of objects, the days of the week or months of the year, simple math skills, the seasons, words and language, and other general facts are all quite lasting. Such impersonal knowledge makes up our **semantic memory**, which serves as a mental dictionary or encyclopedia of basic knowledge.

Episodic Memory

Semantic memory typically has no connection to times or places. It would be rare, for instance, to remember when and where you first learned the names of the seasons. In contrast, **episodic memory** (ep-ih-SOD-ik) stores an "autobiographical" record of personal experiences. It stores life events (or episodes) day after day, year after year. Can you remember your seventh birthday? Your first date? What you did yesterday? All are episodic memories about the "what," "where," and "when" of our lives. More than simply storing information, they allow us to mentally travel back in time and reexperience events (Moscovitch et al., 2016; Philippe, Koestner, & Lekes, 2013).

Are episodic memories as lasting as semantic memories? Either type of memory can last indefinitely. However, unless episodic memories are important, they are easily forgotten. In fact, it is the forgetting of episodic information that can result in the formation of semantic memories. For example, at first you likely did remember when and where you were when you learned the names of the seasons. ("Mommy, Mommy, guess what I learned in preschool today!") Over time, you forgot the episodic details, but you will likely remember the names of the seasons as a semantic memory for the rest of your life.

Long-Term Memory and the Brain

It's clear that LTM contains a great deal of information—somewhere within the 3-pound mass of the human brain lies all we know. But where is this information? According to neuroscientists, many parts of the brain become active when we form and retrieve long-term memories, but some areas are more important for different types of memory and memory processes (Squire & Wixted, 2011).

For example, brain imaging studies reveal that frontal areas of the cerebral cortex (the wrinkled outer layer of the brain, see ■ Section 2.3) are more important in processing episodic memory. In contrast, side and back areas of cortex are more important in processing semantic memory (LePort et al., 2012; Shimotake et al., 2015; Tulving, 1989, 2002; see ● Figure 7.8). As another example, different parts of the cortex are activated when we are engaging in memory retrieval as opposed to memory suppression (Mecklinger, 2010).

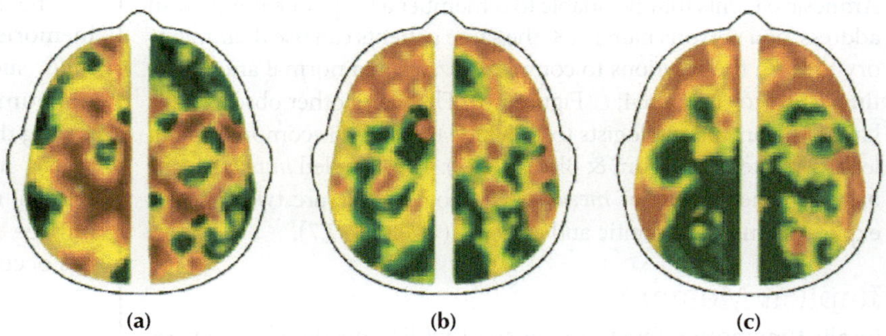

● **Figure 7.8 Cortical areas involved in semantic and episodic memory.** Patterns of blood flow in the cerebral cortex (wrinkled outer layer of the brain) change as areas become more or less active. Thus, blood flow can be used to draw "maps" of brain activity. This drawing, which views the brain from the top, shows the results of measuring cerebral blood flow while people were thinking about a semantic memory (*a*) or an episodic memory (*b*). In the map, green indicates areas that are more active during semantic thinking. Red shows areas of greater activity during episodic thinking. The brain in view (*c*) shows the difference in activity between views (*a*) and (*b*). The resulting pattern suggests that the front of the cortex is related to episodic memory. Areas toward the back and sides of the cortex, especially the temporal lobes, are more associated with semantic memory (Tulving, 1989, 2002). Copyright © Tulving, E. (1989). "Remembering and knowing the past." *American Scientist*, 77(4), 361–367. Reprinted by permission.

But the brain also plays an important role in solidifying information to create memories in the first place. This process is referred to as **consolidation** (Nadel et al., 2012), and it deserves a closer look.

Consolidation

You can think of consolidation as being somewhat like writing your name in wet concrete. Once the concrete is set, the information (your name) is fairly lasting. But while the concrete is setting, the information that needs to be stored is quite vulnerable.

Sleep assists in the process of consolidation (see ■ Section 5.3), but other factors are also important, including shocks to the brain. Consider a classic experiment in which a rat is placed on a small platform. The rat steps down to the floor and receives a painful electric shock. After one shock, the rat can be returned to the platform repeatedly, but it will not step down. Obviously, the rat remembers the shock (just as you remember the principles of operant conditioning!). Would it remember if memory consolidation were disturbed?

Curiously, one way to prevent consolidation is to give a different kind of shock called *electroconvulsive shock* (*ECS*). ECS is a mild electric shock to the brain. It does not harm the animal, but it does destroy any memory that is being formed. If each painful shock (the one the animal remembers) is followed by ECS (which wipes out memories during consolidation), the rat will step down over and over. Each time, ECS erases the memory of the painful shock. (■ ECS has been used with humans as a psychiatric treatment for severe depression. Used in this way, electroshock therapy also causes memory loss. See Section 15.4.)

What would happen if ECS was given several hours after the learning? Recent memories are more easily disrupted than older memories. If enough time is allowed to pass between learning and ECS, the memory will be unaffected because consolidation is already complete. That's why people with mild head injuries (another type of shock) lose only memories from just before the accident, whereas older memories remain intact (Baddeley, Eysenck, & Anderson, 2009).

While many parts of the brain are responsible for memory, the **hippocampus** is particularly important in consolidation (Squire & Wixted, 2011). The hippocampus, part of the limbic system, acts as a sort of "switching station" between working and long-term memory (Moscovitch et al., 2016). The hippocampus does this, in part, by growing new neurons and by making new connections within the brain (Pan, Storm, & Xia, 2013; Zammit et al., 2017).

Why Long-Term Memory Matters (or, Why You Can't Just Google Everything)

It's not uncommon now to hear people talk about the fact that we've entered a time when it's no longer necessary to work at encoding information into LTM. After all, why do you need to work at storing information when you can just Google the answer on your phone?

There are two reasons why you don't want to rely on Googling everything you don't know rather than trying to commit information to LTM. The first is the most obvious—in many situations, it's just too slow. Think about a lifeguard who needs to be able to administer CPR if someone has a heart attack and stops breathing. Do you think that swimmers would prefer to be saved by a lifeguard who can instantly access that information from LTM, or one who needed to dig around for their phone and look it up? Enough said.

But even mundane everyday tasks are made much more efficient when information is already stored in LTM. For example, if you go to buy coffees for six people and they cost two dollars each, it's helpful to know from your memorized multiplication tables that you're going to pay 12 dollars, rather than having to check your calculator app.

The second reason that you should work on storing information in LTM rather than relying on Googling everything is less obvious, so we'll begin with a demonstration:

Are you a baseball fan? If you are, chances are good that you have a reasonable amount of knowledge about the game stored in LTM. If that's the case, then as you read the paragraph below, that knowledge will be activated and will allow you to very quickly summarize the passage in two words.

> Duncan hit a ground ball to Fernandez, the shortstop, who threw it to Alomar, the second baseman. Alomar stepped on the bag, forcing out Dykstra, who was running from first, and then threw the ball to Olerud, the first baseman. Duncan failed to beat the throw (adapted from Willingham, 2009).

Someone who understands baseball—that is, someone with lots of knowledge stored in their LTM about the game—would very quickly think: *double play*. Someone who wasn't much of a baseball fan and doesn't really understand the game (that is, has much less knowledge in LTM) would probably still be able to understand the paragraph but it would take longer, and chances are that it would be very difficult to come up with a short summary.

This demonstration helps to illustrate the second reason that you want a well-developed memory network in LTM: That information stored in LTM—we call it prior knowledge—helps you to quickly and efficiently *understand* new information. Furthermore, when you are better able to understand new information, there is also a greater likelihood that you will find it easy to encode it in LTM and *remember* it later.

Priming Facilitating the retrieval of an implicit memory by using cues to activate hidden memories.

Explicit memory A recollection that a person is aware of having or is consciously retrieved.

Semantic memory A subpart of declarative memory that records impersonal knowledge about the world.

Episodic memory A subpart of declarative memory that records personal experiences that are linked with specific times and places.

Consolidation Process by which relatively permanent memories are formed in the brain.

Hippocampus Part of the limbic system associated with storing memories.

This demonstration of how prior knowledge aids in encoding and remembering was at the heart of a clever study carried out by Recht and Leslie (1988). The researchers began by dividing 12-year-old participants into four groups: good readers with high prior knowledge of baseball, good readers with low prior knowledge of baseball, poor readers with high prior knowledge, and poor readers with low prior knowledge. They then had students sit down in front of a small model of a baseball diamond, complete with small wooden figures that represented players on each team.

Participants were asked to read a series of passages about a baseball game and then demonstrate their memory for the passage by re-enacting what had been described using the model diamond and figures. Passages that the students saw might have looked like the one that you just read in the previous demonstration. The researchers repeated this procedure many times, with participants reading different passages each time and then setting up the figures on the diamond to correspond to the action described in the paragraph.

Which group do you think was most effective at remembering the passages and setting up the model diamond accurately? Somewhat surprisingly, the researchers found that reading ability mattered little in predicting participants' performance, as shown in ● Figure 7.9. But prior knowledge about baseball turned out to be *very* important. In fact, weak readers who had a good working understanding of baseball were able to perform almost as well as strong readers. Why? Prior knowledge helped them to very quickly extract the meaning of each passage. What this tells us, then, is that the more extensive and elaborate your LTM network is (that is, the more prior knowledge you have), the better able you will be to understand, encode, and remember new information that comes your way. Basically, when it comes to information, those who have more knowledge will find it easier to acquire more knowledge: It's a classic case of the rich getting richer.

If you want to see the effect of prior knowledge in action, take a moment to read this passage (adapted from Willingham, 2009):

> Borax, or sodium borate, comes from a natural mineral that has been mined from California lakes for hundreds of years. It is commonly used to supplement other cleaning products in the house, including chemicals like chlorine bleach. For example, it can be used in the laundry to whiten clothes and eliminate odors caused by fungi and bacteria. It can also be used to remove stains from sinks and appliances, and it enhances the power of carpet and upholstery cleaners. Of course, even though it is a natural product, it's still wise to be cautious about its use. For example, borax should always be kept away from children and pets, since ingesting even a small amount can be fatal. There is also some concern about the health effects of borax exposure on an unborn fetus; as a result, pregnant women should avoid it.

Now read this one:

> Nuclear control rods are made from a variety of elements including silver, cadmium, boron, and indium. Their primary purpose is to absorb neutrons during the fission process in nuclear chain reactions, so the material used in the rod is dependent on the energy spectrum of the neutrons found in the reactor. For example, boiling water reactors have thermal neutron energies that are well served by rods made of boron carbide. Pressurized water reactors, however, may have rods made of a cadmium-silver-indium alloy. While they are very effective, there are several safety-related issues related to the use of control rods in nuclear reactors. For example, scientists have learned that using the right materials in the rod is very important in preventing nuclear explosions. The number of rods in the reactor is also important for ensuring safety, since more rods can contain the nuclear chain reaction more quickly.

If you look closely, the two paragraphs are of approximately equal length and they are structured very similarly. Each one begins with an introductory sentence that is followed by a very general statement about function (that is, what borax and control rods are used for). Specific examples are then provided, and the paragraph concludes with some safety-related issues.

What is completely different about the two paragraphs is their subject matter: the first is about borax and the second is control rods. We're guessing that most of you have relatively little experience with the finer details of how a nuclear reactor works and how control rods are important to their safe operation. However, many of you will have a good working understanding of cleaning and doing laundry. Put another way, you have some prior knowledge about one topic but not the other.

Now think about how easy it would be to have to remember material like this for a test tomorrow. Again, we'd bet that most of

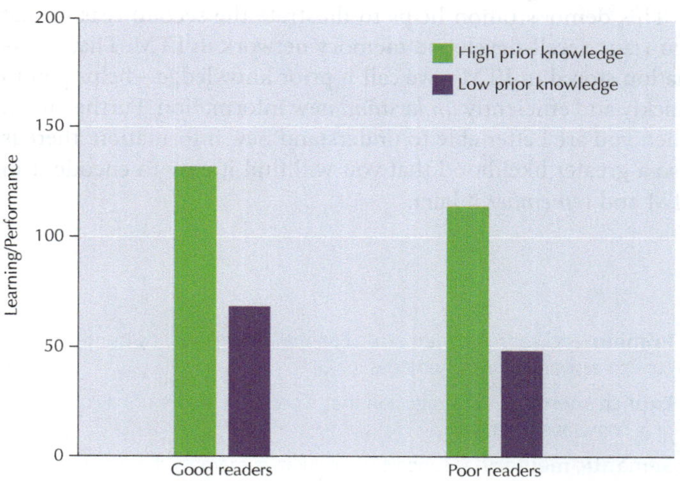

● **Figure 7.9 The impact of prior knowledge on learning.** In a study that examined the effects of prior knowledge on learning, researchers found that reading ability had little impact on students' performance, but prior knowledge was very important.

(Adapted from Effect of Prior Knowledge on Good and Poor Readers' Memory of Text, by Recht and Leslie, Journal of Educational Psychology, 1988, Vol. 80, No. 1, 16–20.)

you would find it easier to remember the first paragraph than the second, but why? The answer lies in the memory networks created by prior knowledge. When you already have a lot of background knowledge (as you do about cleaning), your memory network will be quite extensive—there will be lots of concepts and ideas represented there, and lots of links between them (see Figure 7.5). In a complex network like that, it's much easier to encode new information (like the material about borax) in relation to what's already there, because there are lots of places in the network to create associations and make the new material meaningful. Once the new information is embedded there in the network, it's much more likely to be remembered at a later time.

Reflective Practice

Long-Term Memory

1. Though some long-term memories are stored as images or sounds, most of the information in LTM is stored based on meaning. T or F?
2. Long-term memory can be divided into
   a. episodic and syntactic memory
   b. implicit and episodic memory
   c. explicit and semantic memory
   d. explicit and implicit memory
3. Which of the following parts of the brain does ***not*** appear to have a major role to play in memory?
   a. cortex
   b. hippocampus
   c. basal ganglia and cerebellum
   d. corpus collosum
4. Semantic memory is associated with memory for
   a. our past experiences
   b. skills
   c. facts
   d. associations learned through conditioning
5. Priming is used to reveal which type of memories?
   a. explicit
   b. sensory
   c. episodic
   d. implicit

THINK CRITICALLY

6. When asked to explain why they may have failed to recall some information, people often claim it must be because the information is no longer in their memory. Why does the existence of implicit memories challenge this explanation?

SELF-REFLECT

- Recht & Leslie's study demonstrated how a great deal of prior knowledge about a topic (baseball, in this case) can be helpful in understanding and remembering new information. Can you think of a topic for which you have a great deal of prior knowledge? Have you noticed that you are better able that others (who know less about the topic) to quickly make sense of new material on that subject?

Answers: 1. T 2. d 3. d 4. c 5. d 6. It is possible to have an implicit memory that cannot be consciously recalled. Such memories are available even though they are not consciously accessible (Voss, Lucas, & Paller, 2012).

7.4 Remembering and Forgetting

GATEWAYS LEARNING OUTCOMES:
After reading this section you should be able to:

7.4.1 Describe two factors that improve encoding and two factors that do *not* improve encoding

7.4.2 Name three ways that we can measure memory

7.4.3 Name five factors that contribute to forgetting

7.4.4 Distinguish between active and passive forgetting

We don't expect information in sensory and working memories to remain with us for long—they fade away or are displaced by incoming information. But when you want to retain information in LTM so that you can remember it later, two processes are important: encoding and retrieval. As we've seen earlier in this chapter, the first is all about getting information into LTM, and the second is about getting information out. Let's take a closer look at each one.

Encoding Information into Long-Term Memory

Information in working memory is moved into the more permanent storage of LTM through a process of encoding. Given that encoding is key to creating durable memories, it's worth learning more about the things that do (and do not!) influence it.

Factors That Improve Encoding

Here, we'll consider two factors that do seem to enhance encoding: emotion and deep processing.

Emotion

Research suggests that there is a positive correlation between the intensity of the emotion experienced during an event and people's ability to remember that event. In other words, the more intense the emotion, the more vivid the memory. This is true regardless of whether the emotion being experienced is positive or negative (McGaugh, 2018). No doubt you have experienced this phenomenon firsthand. Do you find that you have particularly clear memories of your first kiss or your prom night, for example? How about a time you when had to speak in front of a large audience? Or maybe a car accident that you were in, or witnessed? This is not to say that those memories are always recalled accurately, mind you—it's just that they're relatively easy to retrieve.

What about events that are very, very stressful—are they easier to remember? Many adults can still remember when they first

Joseph Sohm/Shutterstock.com

The 2016 presidential election was a very emotional one for many Americans. Do you have a flashbulb memory for that day? You do if you were at all involved and can still remember it like it happened yesterday. You even do if you saw the news on TV and you have clear memories of how you reacted.

learned about the terrorist attacks on New York City's World Trade Center in 2001. They can even recall lots of detail, including how they reacted. Psychologists have a special name for a memory like this: it's called a **flashbulb memory** (Paradis et al., 2004).

The term flashbulb memory was first used to describe recollections that seemed to be unusually vivid and permanent at times of emotionally significant personal or public events (Brown & Kulik, 1977; Lanciano, Curci, & Semin, 2010). Depending on their age, people may also have a flashbulb memory for the assassinations of John F. Kennedy or Martin Luther King, Jr., or the deaths of Princess Diana or George Floyd (Curci & Luminet, 2006).

Does the brain handle flashbulb memories differently? Powerfully exciting or stressful experiences activate the limbic system, a part of the brain that processes emotions. Heightened activity in the limbic system, in turn, appears to intensify memory consolidation (LaBar, 2007). It has become clear, however, that flashbulb memories are not particularly accurate (Tinti et al., 2013). More than anything else, what sets flashbulb memories apart is that we tend to place great *confidence* in them—even when they are wrong (Niedzwienska, 2004). Perhaps that's because we review emotionally charged events over and over and tell others about them. Also, public events such as wars, earthquakes, and elections reappear many times in the news, which highlights them in memory. Over time, flashbulb memories tend to crystallize into consistent, if not entirely accurate, landmarks in our lives (Lanciano, Curci, & Semin, 2010).

Unfortunately, some memories go beyond flashbulb clarity and become so intense that they may haunt a person for years. Extremely traumatic experiences, such as military combat or maltreatment as a child, can produce so much limbic system activation that the resulting memories and "flashbacks" leave a person emotionally handicapped (Bergstrom et al., 2013; Goodman, Quas, & Ogle, 2010). [■ To read more about post-traumatic stress disorder (PTSD), see Section 14.4.]

Deep Processing

A second factor that improves encoding is thinking deeply about the to-be-remembered information. In a classic experiment, Hyde and Jenkins (1973) asked participants to read a list of words that were presented one at a time. One group was told to read the words and determine whether or not each one contained either the letter *a* or *q*. The second group was asked to rate the pleasantness of each word on a scale. Though they had not been informed about it at the outset, participants were then given a test to determine how many words they could recall. Which group do you think performed better on the memory test?

The results of this experiment were very clear: On average, participants in the group that rated the pleasantness of each word had much higher scores than those who were searching for the letters *a* and *q*. In explaining their findings, the researchers indicated that the improved performance of the "pleasantness" group was due to the fact that their task forced them to process the words in a deep (rather than shallow) manner. Put another way, in order to decide whether something is pleasant or not, you need to think about the object and its meaning, and to do so you would have had to consider the connections to it in your memory network. In contrast, the search for letters in a word requires only shallow processing of the word.

This finding has been replicated many times, and is referred to as the *levels of processing* effect: Information that is processed at a deeper level—that is, information that we work to connect to the network in our LTM—is much more likely to be encoded than information that is processed in a superficial way. This is the reason why, when you are studying, it's important that you think carefully about the *meaning* of the ideas that you're reading about. As we discussed earlier, information in LTM is organized in a network that is largely based on meaning. To ensure that encoding is effective, then, you should work to connect ideas in your text and notes to each other (and what you already know), thinking carefully about relationships between the ideas, for example, and similarities and differences to other concepts. Psychologists refer to this process as elaborative rehearsal (or elaborative encoding). Elaborative encoding offers an important way to gain meaning, by linking new information currently in working memory to knowledge already stored in LTM. This makes it easier to encode in LTM and, hence, remember.

Factors That Do Not Improve Encoding

In addition to factors like emotion and deep processing that enhance encoding, there are also some things that do *not* help us with this process and can lead to **encoding failure**. Here, we'll examine two of them: intention to remember information and repeated exposure.

Intention to Remember Information

You might wonder whether the results of Hyde and Jenkins' study would have been different if the participants had known that they were going to be tested. After all, if they had been told about the test then surely even the group that was looking for letters would have performed better.

As it happens, Hyde and Jenkins actually tested that possibility themselves in a follow-up study. The results might surprise you though: It turned out that the "letter search" group still performed much more poorly than the "pleasantness" group, even when they knew about the test (and presumably intended to remember the words they saw). It's not a big leap to see how this finding applies to studying for exams in college: Just because you intend to remember material for a test does not ensure that you will actually encode that material. One of the best ways to ensure that encoding takes place is to engage in elaborative encoding and work to connect new information to prior knowledge in LTM.

Repeated Exposure to Information

Whose head is on a U.S. penny? Which way is it facing? What is written at the top of a penny? Can you accurately draw and label a penny? In an interesting experiment, Ray Nickerson and Marilyn Adams (1979) tested recall memory by asking a large group of students to draw a penny. Few could. In fact, few could even recognize a drawing of a real penny situated among several fakes (Figure 7.10). In an example that may surprise you even more, very few college students were able to accurately recall the logo associated with Apple computers, iPads, and iPhones (Blake, Nazarian, & Castel, 2015). Moreover, fewer than 50 percent of the participants were able to recognize the logo in a set of eight possibilities.

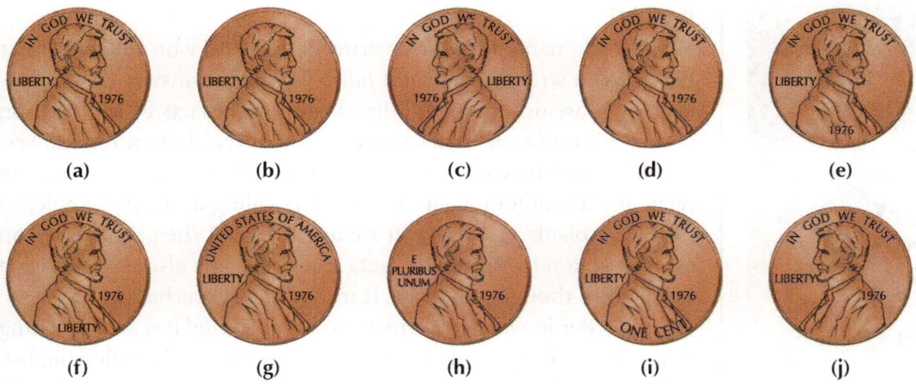

Figure 7.10 Find the real penny. Penny A is correct but was seldom recognized. Pennies G and J were popular wrong answers. (Adapted from Nickerson & Adams, 1979.)

What's going on here? After all, most adults have seen thousands of pennies and many see the Apple logo almost daily. As it turns out, though, the most obvious reason for forgetting is also the most commonly overlooked. The reality is that repeated exposure to information (even across thousands of repetitions!) is not enough to ensure that encoding will happen. For students facing exams, then, it's not going to be enough to read (and re-read) the textbook and your notes. If you really want to remember something in the future, you'll need to engage in active strategies like elaborative encoding.

In a clever study, researchers asked undergraduate students to recall the Apple logo—something that most of them had seen thousands of times before. Putting aside their sometimes poor drawing skills, it was clear that many of them could not remember even basic aspects of the logo, such as which direction the leaf pointed, or where the "bite" should be. The drawings you see here are based on a replication that was carried out by a web-based design company. They obtained similar findings, and discovered that we're equally poor at remembering other logos, including Starbucks and Dominos Pizza.

Retrieving Information from LTM

Aside from encoding, the other key process associated with LTM is retrieval. Whereas encoding is concerned with getting information into LTM, retrieval is the process by which information is pulled out and returned to the conscious thinking that happens in working memory. Retrieval begins with a retrieval cue—something in the environment that prompts us to remember material that's stored in LTM. Sometimes those cues can be explicit directives to actively remember information, like a question on a test, or your friend asking whether you saw his ex-girlfriend at the party last night. Sometimes, though, the cues trigger remembering simply by virtue of the fact that they are associated with something in your LTM network. For example, as you walk down the aisle in a grocery store, packages of spaghetti might serve as a retrieval cue for your grandmother, who used to make pasta for you every time you went to visit.

Of course, sometimes retrieval cues fail to bring about remembering. It's worth noting, though, that remembering isn't an all-or-nothing phenomenon—"remembered" versus "forgotten." Whether we successfully remember something depends to some extent on how we measure memory. There are a number of different ways that we can assess our ability to remember, and we'll unpack them a bit in the section that follows.

Flashbulb memory Especially vivid and detailed recollection of an emotional event.

Encoding failure Failure to store sufficient information to form a useful memory.

dcwcreations/Shutterstock.com

External cues such as those found in a photograph, in a scrapbook, or during a walk through an old neighborhood often aid recall of seemingly lost memories. For this veteran, visiting the final resting place of a fallen comrade unleashed a flood of memories.

Measuring Our Ability to Retrieve Information

You either remember something or you don't, right? Wrong. *Partial memories* are common. For instance, students writing exams sometimes find themselves stuck in a **tip-of-the-tongue (TOT) state**. This is the feeling that you cannot locate or retrieve a complete memory that is stored in LTM (Brown, 2012). Perhaps you, too, have had this experience. You read an exam question and immediately the answer is there but just out of reach—on the "tip of your tongue." You know what often happens next, right? As soon as you leave the exam, the answer "pops" into your head.

Déjà vu, the feeling that you have already experienced a situation that you are experiencing for the first time, may be another example of partial memory (Brown & Marsh, 2010). If a new experience triggers vague memories of a past experience, without yielding *any* details at all, you might be left saying to yourself, "I feel like I've seen it before." The new experience seems familiar, even though the older memory is too weak to rise to the level of awareness.

Because memory is not an all-or-nothing event, it can be measured in several ways. Three commonly-used methods of measuring memory are *recall*, *recognition*, and *relearning*. Let's see how they differ.

Recall

What is the name of your favorite song? Who won the last Super Bowl? Who wrote *Romeo and Juliet*? If you can answer these questions, you are using **recall**, a direct retrieval of facts or information with a minimum of retrieval cues. Tests of recall often require *verbatim* (word-for-word) memory. If you study a poem until you can recite it without looking at it, you are recalling it. If you complete a fill-in-the-blank question, you are using recall. When you answer an essay question by providing facts and ideas, you also are still using recall, even though you didn't learn your essay verbatim.

The order in which information is memorized has an interesting effect on recall. To experience it, try to memorize the following list, reading it only once:

bread,	apples,	soda,	ham,	cookies,	rice,
lettuce,	beets,	mustard,	cheese,	oranges,	
ice cream,	crackers,	flour,	eggs		

If you are like most people, it will be hardest for you to recall items from the middle of the list. Figure 7.11 shows the results of a similar test. Notice that most errors occur with middle items of an ordered list. This is the **serial position effect** (Bonk & Healy, 2010; Gavett & Horwitz, 2012). You can remember the last items on a list because they are still in STM. The first items also are remembered well because they entered an "empty" STM. This allows you to rehearse the items so that they move into long-term memory. The middle items are neither held in short-term memory nor moved to long-term memory, so they are often lost.

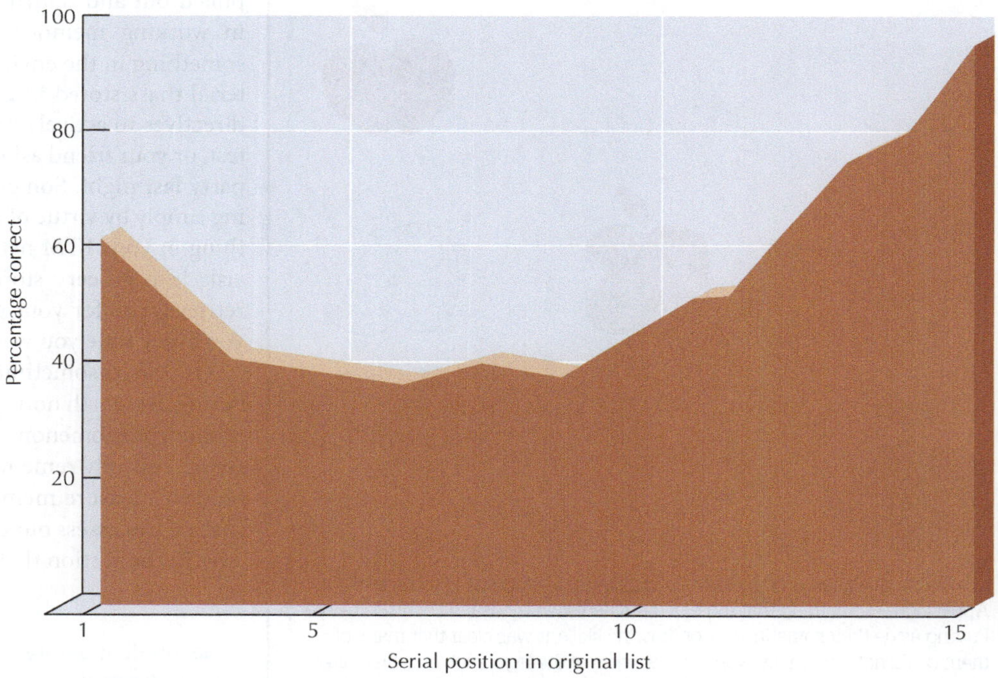

Figure 7.11 The serial position effect. The graph shows the percentage of participants correctly recalling each item in a 15-item list. Recall is best for the first and last items. (Data from Craik, 1970.)

Recognition

Try to write down everything that you can remember from a class you took last year. If you actually did this, you might conclude that you had learned very little. However, a more sensitive test based on recognition could be used. In **recognition**, previously learned material is correctly identified from material that is presented to you. For instance, you could take a multiple-choice test on facts and ideas from the course. Because you would have to recognize only correct answers, you probably would find that you had learned a lot.

Recognition can be amazingly accurate for pictures and photographs (Oates & Reder, 2011). In one classic study, people viewed 2,560 photographs at a rate of one every 10 seconds. Each person was then shown 280 pairs of photographs. Each pair included an "old" picture (from the first set of photos) and a similar "new" image. Participants could tell 85 to 95 percent of the time which photograph they had seen before (Haber, 1970). This finding may explain why we rarely need to see our friends' vacation photos more than once.

When memory is assessed via recognition, then, the results are usually superior to what we would see with recall. That's why people so often say, "I may forget a name, but I never forget a face." (You can't recall the name but can recognize the face.) That's also why police departments use photographs or a lineup to identify criminal suspects. Witnesses who disagree when they try to recall a suspect's height, weight, age, or eye color often agree completely when they merely need to recognize the person.

Relearning

In a classic experiment, a psychologist read a short passage in Greek to his son every day when the boy was between 15 months and 3 years of age. At age 8, the boy was tested to see if he remembered the Greek passage. He showed no evidence of recall or recognition. Had the psychologist stopped, he might have concluded that no memory of the Greek passage remained. However, the child was then asked to memorize the original passage and others of equal difficulty. This time, his earlier learning became evident. The boy memorized the passage he had heard in childhood 25 percent faster than the others (Burtt, 1941). As this classic experiment suggests, **relearning** is typically the most sensitive measure of memory.

When a person is tested by relearning, how do we know a memory still exists? As with the boy described, relearning is measured by a *savings score* (the amount of time saved when relearning information). Let's say that it takes you 60 minutes to memorize all the names in a telephone book. (It's a small town.) Two years later, you relearn them in 45 minutes. Because you "saved" 15 minutes, your savings score would be 25 percent (15 divided by 60 times 100). Savings of this type are a good reason for studying a wide range of subjects. It may seem that learning algebra, history, or a foreign language is wasted if you don't use the knowledge immediately. But when you do need such information, you will be able to relearn it quickly.

Rich Legg/E+/Getty Images

Police lineups make use of the sensitivity of recognition memory. However, unless great care is taken, false identifications are still possible (Wells, 2001). Is this a fair or an unfair lineup? What problems may be created with this lineup?

Forgetting

Why do we forget long-term memories? Most forgetting tends to occur quickly, before memories have been consolidated. Herman Ebbinghaus (1885) famously tested his own memory at various intervals after learning. To be sure that his memory would not be influenced by prior knowledge in LTM, he memorized nonsense syllables—meaningless three-letter combinations such as *cef*, *wol*, and *gex*.

By waiting various lengths of time before testing himself, Ebbinghaus plotted a *curve of forgetting*. This graph shows the amount of information remembered after varying lengths of time (Figure 7.12). Notice that forgetting is rapid at first and is followed by a slow decline (Hintzman, 2005; Sternberg, 2017). The same result applies to meaningful information, but the forgetting curve is stretched over a longer time. As you might expect, recent events are recalled more accurately than those from the more distant past. Thus, you are more likely to remember what you had for dinner last night than what you ate for lunch a week ago last Tuesday.

The Ebbinghaus curve shows that less than 30 percent of what is learned is remembered after only two days have passed. Is forgetting really that rapid? No, not always. Meaningful information that is well connected in your LTM network is not lost nearly as quickly as nonsense syllables, which are difficult to link to anything you have previously stored in memory. Still, we're all familiar with the frustration that comes when we can't pull information we need out of LTM. Why does that happen?

Tip-of-the-tongue (TOT) state The feeling that a memory is available but not quite retrievable.

Recall Retrieval of information with a minimum of external cues.

Serial position effect When remembering an ordered list, the tendency to make the most errors with middle items.

Recognition Ability to correctly identify previously learned information.

Relearning Learning again something that was previously learned. Used to measure memory of prior learning.

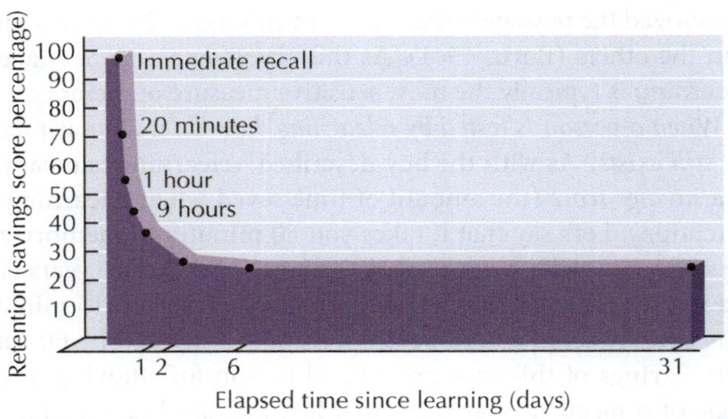

Figure 7.12 The curve of forgetting. This graph shows the amount remembered (measured by relearning) after varying lengths of time. Notice how rapidly forgetting occurs. The material learned was nonsense syllables. Forgetting curves for meaningful information also show early losses followed by a long gradual decline, but overall, forgetting occurs much more slowly. (After Ebbinghaus, 1885.)

Explaining Why Forgetting Happens

Although the Ebbinghaus curve gives a general picture of forgetting from long-term memory, it doesn't explain it. But then, forgetting doesn't have a single explanation—there are several potential reasons for retrieval failures. For example, pick a card from the six shown here in Figure 7.13. Look at it closely, and be sure that you can remember which card is yours.

Now, snap your fingers and look at the cards in Figure 7.14. Poof! Only five cards remain, and the card you chose has disappeared. Obviously, you could have selected any one of the six cards in Figure 7.13. How did we know which one to remove?

Figure 7.13

Figure 7.14

This trick demonstrates the first, and most basic, reason that we sometimes fail to retrieve information: the information was never encoded in the first place. Recall that you were asked to concentrate on one card among the six original cards in Figure 7.13. That prevented you from paying attention to the other cards, so they weren't encoded in your memory (Unsworth, Brewer, & Spillers, 2012). The five cards you see in Figure 7.14 are all new (none is shown in Figure 7.13). Because you couldn't find it in the "remaining five," your card seemed to disappear. This is similar to our earlier demonstration with the pennies and corporate logos—information has to be encoded in order to be retrieved.

Of course, sometimes even if memories are *available* (that is, they have been encoded in your memory), you may still experience **retrieval failure** (Della Sala, 2010; Guerin et al., 2012). There are several circumstances that may bring about retrieval failure. We'll look at five of them in greater detail, including atypical brain function, cue-dependent forgetting, state-dependent learning, interference, and motivated forgetting.

Atypical Brain Function

Sometimes the basis for retrieval failures lies in the fact that the brain is not functioning as it should. For example, brain injuries resulting from head trauma can also impact our ability to retrieve information. Conditions such as *Alzheimer's disease* and other *dementias* will also slowly strangle the brain's ability to process and store information (Hanyu et al., 2010; Verma & Howard, 2012). In the early stages of Alzheimer's, more recent memories may be forgotten, while older ones are intact. So at the same time that your Uncle Oscar's recent memories are fading, he may have vivid memories of trivial and long-forgotten events from the past. "Why, I remember it as clearly as if it were yesterday," he will say, forgetting that the story he is about to tell is one he told earlier the same day (twice).

Another explanation for retrieval failures is **amnesia**, an inability to form or retrieve memories of events due to an injury or trauma to the brain (Papanicolaou, 2006). **Retrograde amnesia** involves forgetting events that occurred *before* an injury or trauma (MacKay & Hadley, 2009), whereas **anterograde amnesia** is characterized by forgetting information that *follows* an injury or trauma. Anterograde amnesia has been associated with damage to the hippocampus; as a result, patients show a striking inability to consolidate new memories. A man described by Brenda Milner (1965) provides a dramatic example. Two years after an operation damaged his hippocampus, the 29-year-old H. M. continued to give his age as 27 and reported that the operation had just taken place. His memory of events before the operation remained clear, but he found forming new long-term memories almost impossible. When his parents moved to a new house a few blocks away on the same street, he could not remember the new address. Month after month, he read the same magazines over and over without finding them familiar. If you had met this man, he would have seemed fairly normal because his short-term, or working, memory was intact. But if you were to leave the room and return 15 minutes later, he would have acted as if he had never seen you before. Lacking the ability to form new lasting memories, he lived eternally in the present until his death in 2008 at the age of 82 (Bohbot & Corkin, 2007).

Cue-Dependent Forgetting

A second reason why retrieval may fail is that good retrieval cues are missing when the time comes to access the information. For instance, if you were asked, "What were you doing on Monday afternoon of the third week in May, two years ago?" your reply might very reasonably be, "Come on, how should I know?" However, if you were given a good retrieval cue such as, "That was the day the courthouse burned down" or "That was the day your mom had her car accident," you might immediately remember what you were doing that day.

The presence of appropriate cues almost always enhances memory retrieval. As we saw previously, more elaborately encoded memories—that is, those that are embedded in a complex LTM network—are more likely to be remembered because there will be more retrieval cues that are associated with any particular piece of information.

Though it's not always possible, note that memory will tend to be even better if you are retrieving information in the same room where you remembered it in the first place. This effect stems from the fact that you have the same cues available at retrieval that were present during encoding. Think about this when you study: To enhance your memory during the test, try to visualize the room where you will be tested while you're learning the material (Jerabek & Standing, 1992). Similarly, people remember better if the same odor (such as lemon or lavender) is present both when they study and are tested (Parker, Ngu, & Cassaday, 2001). In fact, odors are among the most powerful retrieval cues for emotional memories (Arshamian et al., 2013).

State-Dependent Learning

Have you heard the one about the drunk who misplaced his wallet and had to get drunk again to find it? This is not too far-fetched. The bodily state that exists during learning also can be a strong retrieval cue for later memory, an effect known as **state-dependent learning** (Radvansky, 2017). Being very thirsty, for instance, might prompt you to remember events that took place another time when you were thirsty. Because of such effects, information learned under the influence of a drug is best remembered when the drugged state occurs again (Koek, 2011; Mariani et al., 2011). (Note that this is a laboratory finding. In school, it's far better to study with a clear head!)

A similar effect applies to emotional states (Wessel & Wright, 2004; Yang & Ornstein, 2011). For instance, Gordon Bower (1981) found that people who learned a list of words while in a happy mood recalled them better when they were again happy. People who learned while they felt sad remembered best when they were sad (Figure 7.15). Similarly, if you are in a happy mood, you are more likely to remember recent happy events. If you are in a bad mood, you will tend to have unpleasant memories. Such links between emotional cues and memory could explain why couples who quarrel often end up remembering—and rehashing—old arguments.

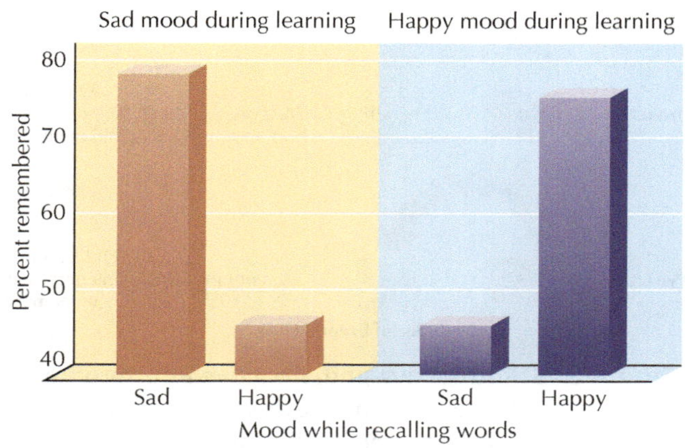

Figure 7.15 The effect of mood on memory. Participants best remembered a list of words when their mood during testing was the same as their mood when they learned the list. (Adapted from Bower, 1981.)

Interference

Interference refers to the tendency for new memories to impair retrieval of older memories (and the reverse). It seems to apply to both short-term and long-term memory (Radvansky, 2017; Rodríguez-Villagra et al., 2012). There are two types of interference: retroactive and proactive. **Retroactive interference** (RET-ro-AK-tiv) refers to the tendency for new learning to inhibit retrieval of old learning. Avoiding new learning prevents retroactive interference. This doesn't exactly mean that you should hide in a closet after you study for an exam. However, you should, if possible, avoid studying other subjects until the exam. Reading or writing about other topics, or even watching television, may cause retroactive interference.

Retrieval failure Failure to access (locate) memories even though they are available (stored in memory).

Amnesia Inability to form or retrieve memories of events due to an injury or trauma.

Retrograde amnesia Inability to retrieve memories of events that occurred before an injury or trauma.

Anterograde amnesia Inability to form or retrieve memories of events that occur after an injury or trauma.

State-dependent learning Memory influenced by one's physical state at the time of learning and at the time of retrieval. Improved memory occurs when the physical states match.

Interference The tendency for new memories to impair retrieval of older memories, and the reverse.

Retroactive interference The tendency for new memories to interfere with the retrieval of old memories.

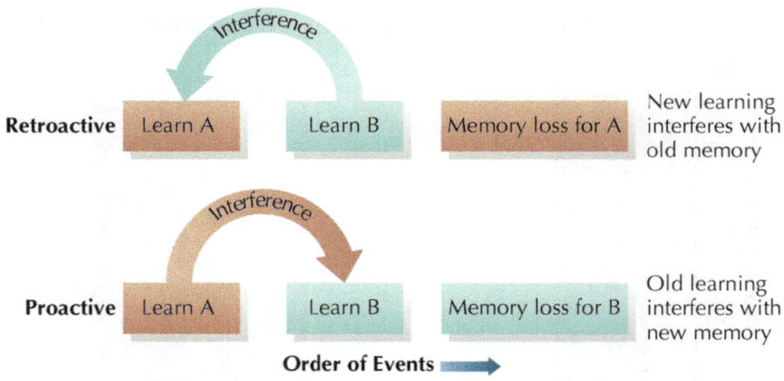

Figure 7.16 Retroactive and proactive interference. The order of learning and testing shows whether interference is retroactive (backward) or proactive (forward). (Source: Adapted from Bower, 1981.)

Retroactive interference is easily demonstrated in the laboratory by this arrangement:

Experimental group:	Learn Task A	Learn Task B	Test Task A
Control group:	Learn Task A	Rest	Test Task A

Imagine yourself as a member of the experimental group. In Task A, you learn a list of telephone numbers. In Task B, you learn a list of Social Security numbers. How do you score on a test of Task A (the telephone numbers)? If you do not remember as much as the control group that learns *only* Task A, then retroactive interference has occurred. The second thing learned (the Social Security numbers in Task B) interfered with memory of the first thing learned; the interference went "backward," or was "retroactive" (Figure 7.16).

In contrast, **proactive interference** (pro-AK-tiv) occurs when prior learning inhibits recall of later learning. A test for proactive interference would take this form:

Experimental group:	Learn Task A	Learn Task B	Test Task B
Control group:	Rest	Learn Task B	Test Task B

Let's assume that the experimental group remembers less than the control group on a test of Task B. In that case, learning Task A interfered with remembering Task B.

How could anyone lose something as large as a car? If you park your car in a different place every day, you may have experienced forgetting caused by proactive interference. Today's memory about your car's location is easily confused with memories from yesterday, and the day before, and the day before that.

Here, proactive interference goes "forward." For instance, if you cram for a psychology exam and then, later the same night, cram for a history exam, your memory for the second subject studied (history) will be less accurate than if you had studied only history. (Because of retroactive interference, your memory for psychology also would probably suffer.) The greater the similarity in the two subjects studied, the more interference takes place. The moral, of course, is don't procrastinate in preparing for exams. The more you can avoid studying competing information one after another, the more likely you are to recall what you want to remember (Wixted, 2004).

One interesting point to note here: The interference effects that we have described apply primarily to memories of verbal information, such as the contents of this chapter. When you are learning a skill, though, similarity can sometimes be beneficial, rather than disruptive.

Motivated Forgetting

Take a moment and scan the events of the last few years of your life. What kinds of things most easily come to mind? As we discussed earlier, when asked that question many people will report events that are associated with intense emotions, both positive and negative (McGaugh, 2018). Sometimes, though, memories that are intensely negative are not recalled at all. This tendency is called **repression**, or motivated forgetting. Through repression, distressing, threatening, or embarrassing memories are kept buried in the unconscious, unavailable for retrieval. An example is provided by soldiers who have repressed some of the horrors that they saw during combat (Anderson & Huddleston, 2012).

If I try to forget a test I failed, am I repressing it? Probably not. Repression can be distinguished from **suppression**, an active, conscious attempt to put something out of mind (Anderson et al., 2011). By not thinking about the test, you have merely suppressed a memory. If you choose, you can remember the test. Clinicians consider true repression an *unconscious* event and one of the major psychological defenses we use against emotional threats. When a memory is repressed, we may be unaware that forgetting has even occurred.

An Updated View of Forgetting

For many years, psychological scientists who studied memory focused their attention on retrieval, and how to improve its success. The study of forgetting remained squarely on the sidelines until recently. Recent research has shed more light on forgetting and two things are becoming clear. The first is that forgetting comes in two varieties: passive and active (Carey, 2015). The second is that while we often talk about forgetting as though it was the enemy of memory and something to avoid, this isn't the case at all. Let's check out what psychological scientists have to say about forgetting.

Active Versus Passive Forgetting

One view of forgetting, **decay theory**, holds that **memory traces**—changes in neurons or brain activity—passively decay or weaken over time, making them more difficult to retrieve. Earlier in this chapter we saw that decay is a factor in the early stages of the Atkinson-Shiffrin model (see Figure 7.1), as information in sensory and working memory can quickly be lost. But early researchers suggested that this type of passive decay was also relevant to LTM. In some of his classic writings, learning theorist Edward

Thorndike (see Section 6.3) described the **Law of Disuse**—the idea that, over time, memories in LTM that were not often used (that is, retrieved) would eventually decay and be forgotten. We now know that disuse likely is important in our ability to retrieve information, though Thorndike's conception of passive decay was probably somewhat oversimplified (Bjork & Bjork, 2013).

But while forgetting can be a passive process in which memories degrade over time, newer research is shedding light on the fact that some forgetting is necessary and is done actively as a means of managing the enormous volume of information that we encounter every day (Gravitz, 2019). Rather than being a bug in the memory system, then, forgetting is actually an integral part of the system. To understand why, let's look at two examples.

Jill Price has an exceptional episodic memory system (also known as *highly superior autobiographical memory*): "Whenever I see a date flash on the television (or anywhere else for that matter) I automatically go back to that day and remember where I was, what I was doing, what day it fell on and on and on and on and on." (Parker, Cahill, & McGaugh, 2006, pp. 35–36; Price & Davis, 2009). Before you get too jealous, here's a bit more of what Jill Price has to say about her "perfect" episodic memory: "My memory has ruled my life ... It is nonstop, uncontrollable, and totally exhausting ... Most have called it a gift, but I call it a burden. I run my entire life through my head every day and it drives me crazy!!!" (Parker, Cahill, & McGaugh, 2006, pp. 35–36; Price & Davis, 2009).

Other people like Mr. S. have remarkable semantic memory. As a professional memorizer, he regularly wowed audiences with his ability to memorize, with equal ease, long strings of digits, meaningless consonants, mathematical formulas, and poems in foreign languages. Once again, though, don't be too quick to envy Mr. S.'s abilities. He described living his life "as if in a haze" and had to devise ways to *forget* unimportant information—such as writing it on a piece of paper and then burning it (Luria, 1968).

The cases of Jill Price and Mr. S. make clear why some forgetting is done actively, as the brain's way of keeping the flow of information at a level that is manageable. If the brain was not set up to purposefully forget information, we would find ourselves overwhelmed by the trivial details of our day-to-day lives.

Reflective Practice

Remembering and Forgetting

1. Two factors that improve encoding into long-term memory are ________________ and ________________.
2. Essay tests require ________________ of facts or ideas.
3. As a measure of memory, a savings score is associated with
   a. recognition
   b. priming
   c. relearning
   d. reconstruction
4. You are asked to memorize long lists of telephone numbers. You learn a new list each day for 10 days. When tested on list three, you remember less than a person who learned only the first three lists. Your larger memory loss is probably caused by
   a. disuse
   b. retroactive interference
   c. regression
   d. proactive interference
5. If you consciously succeed at putting a painful memory out of mind, you have used
   a. redintegration
   b. suppression
   c. negative rehearsal
   d. repression

THINK CRITICALLY

6. Based on state-dependent learning, why do you think music often strongly evokes memories?

SELF-REFLECT

- Have you observed a savings effect while relearning information you studied in the past (such as in high school)?
- What things do you do that are based on implicit memories? For instance, how do you know which way to turn various handles in your house, apartment, or dorm? Do you have to explicitly think, "Turn it to the right," before you act?

Answers: 1. emotion and deep processing 2. recall 3. c 4. b 5. b 6. Music tends to affect a person's mood, and moods tend to affect memory (Barrett et al., 2010).

7.5 The Accuracy of Long-Term Memory

GATEWAYS LEARNING OUTCOMES:
After reading this section you should be able to:

7.5.1 Explain the origins of false and inaccurate memories

7.5.2 Describe three factors that might improve confidence in eyewitness testimony

We mentioned earlier that the neuroscientist Wilder Penfield once surmised that memories were passively recorded and stored like a video, complete with soundtrack. This image of LTM would suggest that anything you want to recall can simply be retrieved and

Proactive interference The tendency for old memories to interfere with the retrieval of newer memories.

Repression Keeping distressing thoughts and feelings buried in the unconscious.

Suppression A conscious effort to put something out of mind or to keep it from awareness.

Decay theory Proposition that the strength of memories weakens over time, making them harder to retrieve.

Memory traces Physical changes in neurons or brain activity that take place when memories are stored.

Law of Disuse (in memory) Proposition that memory traces weaken when memories are not periodically used or retrieved.

"played" on some type of internal DVD player, providing you with a faithful copy of what happened.

Psychologists now know that this idea is far from the truth. In fact, the processes of encoding and retrieval are active, and we often "edit" events as they are retrieved and re-stored repeatedly over time. In addition, gaps in memory—which are common—may be filled in by prior knowledge *each time a memory is retrieved* (Schacter, 2012). In this section, we'll explore the accuracy of our memories, and the consequences of remembering slightly altered versions of past events. Before we get started, though, we'd like to return to a list that we showed you earlier. Take a look at it again, and then carry on reading.

snooze	dream	blanket	doze	pillow	nap
snore	mattress	alarm	clock	rest	slumber
nod	sheet	bunk	cot	cradle	groggy

Remembering Something That Didn't Happen

In a classic early experiment that demonstrated how memories can be altered, Elizabeth Loftus and John Palmer (1974) showed people a filmed car accident. Afterward, one group of participants was asked to estimate how fast the cars were going when they "smashed" into one another. For other groups, the words "bumped," "contacted," or "hit" replaced "smashed."

The researchers observed that changing the wording in this way had an important impact on participants' estimates of the speed at which the car was traveling, suggesting that asking "leading" questions can have an effect on our memory. Moreover, one week later, each person in the study was asked, "Did you see any broken glass in the film?" Those asked earlier about the cars that "smashed" into one another were much more likely to say yes, *even though no broken glass was shown in the film*. The phrasing of the question ("smashed") had been incorporated into the original memories, elaborating those memories and producing a **false memory**. Such "memories" can seem accurate, in spite of the fact that they never happened (Loftus, 2003; Weinstein & Shanks, 2010). In another study, people who had visited a Disney resort were shown several fake ads for Disney that featured Bugs Bunny. Later, about 16 percent of the people who saw these fake ads claimed that they had met Bugs at Disneyland. This is impossible, of course, because Bugs Bunny is a Warner Brothers character that would never show his face at Disneyland (Braun, Ellis, & Loftus, 2002).

You may be thinking to yourself that these examples only demonstrate that memory can be manipulated by asking leading questions or showing people false advertisements. Perhaps when left to remember without the manipulation of other people, we'd be better at remembering things accurately? Unfortunately, the scientific research has repeatedly demonstrated that this is not the case, and nowhere is this clearer than in the many studies that have investigated eyewitness testimony.

Studying the Science: Eyewitness Testimony

False memories are a common problem in police work. For example, a witness may select a photo of a suspect from police files or see a photo in the news. Later, the witness identifies the suspect in a photo lineup. Did the witness really remember the suspect from the scene of the crime? Or was the memory distorted in some way? The question is an important one, because in the courtroom eyewitness testimony can be a key to proving guilt or innocence. The claim "I saw it with my own eyes" still carries a lot of weight with a jury, as we saw in the case of Steve Avery at the beginning of this chapter. While highly confident witnesses are generally more accurate than those who are less confident, even eyewitnesses who are completely certain are frequently wrong (Lindsay et al., 2013).

Unfortunately, memories that are formed when a person is surprised, threatened, or under stress are especially prone to distortion (Yuille & Daylen, 1998). One study of eyewitness cases found that the wrong person was chosen from police lineups 25 percent of the time (Levi, 1998). Since DNA testing became available, more than 330 people who were convicted in the United States of major crimes have been exonerated after serving an average of over 13 *years* in prison. About 75 percent of these innocent people were convicted mainly on the basis of eyewitness testimony (Innocence Project, 2016).

Adding to the problem is the fact that too many jurors tend to assume that eyewitness testimony is nearly infallible (unless, of course, they have taken a psychology class) (Odinot, Wolters, & van Giezen, 2013). Even U.S. judges have shown unwarranted optimism about the accuracy of eyewitness testimony (Wise et al., 2010; Wise & Safer, 2010). Fortunately, psychologists are gradually convincing lawyers, judges, and police that eyewitness errors are common (Yarmey, 2010).

What about the victim of a crime? Wouldn't that person remember events more accurately than a mere witness? Not necessarily. A classic study found that eyewitness accuracy is virtually the same for witnessing a crime (seeing a pocket calculator stolen) as it is for being a victim (seeing one's own watch stolen) (Hosch & Cooper, 1982). Placing more weight on the testimony of victims may be a serious mistake.

Now let's do a check on *your* eyewitness memory. Without looking back to the list of words you read a few minutes ago, see if you can tell which of the following are "old" words (items from the list you read) and which are "new" words (items that weren't on the list). Mark each of the following words as old or new:

sofa	sleep	lamp	kitchen

If you're like most people, you'll say that "sleep" is the only word from the original list, and that all the others are new. But contrary to what you may think you remembered, *all* of the listed words are new. None was on the original list! If you thought you remembered that "sleep" was on the original list, you had a false memory. In your memory network, the word *sleep* is likely associated with the words on the original list because they are related in their meaning. This helps to create a strong impression that you saw it earlier (Roediger & McDermott, 1995; Schacter, 2012).

The Recovered Memory/False Memory Debate

Another area of forensic psychology that demonstrates the challenges of memory concerns *recovered memories*. Many sexually abused children develop psychological and behavioral problems that persist into adulthood. In some instances, they repress all memory of the abuse. According to some psychologists, uncovering these hidden memories can be an important step toward regaining emotional health (Colangelo, 2007; Haaken & Reavey, 2010).

Although the preceding may be true, the search for repressed memories of sexual abuse has itself been a problem. Families have been torn apart by accusations of sexual abuse that later turned out to be completely false. For example, when Meredith Maran thought that she had recovered vivid memories of being molested by her father, she withdrew herself and her children from any further contact with him. It was not until nine years later that she realized that her "memories" were not true and finally apologized to her father (Maran, 2010). Things have gotten much worse for other people, as some cases have gone to court, some innocent people have gone to jail, and some actual sexual abuse victims have been accused of making false claims about their very real memories.

Why would anyone have false memories about such disturbing events? Several popular books and a few misguided therapists have actively encouraged people to find repressed memories of abuse. Hypnosis, guided visualization, suggestion, age regression, administering the so-called truth drug Amytal, and similar techniques can elicit fantasies that are mistaken for real memories (Weinstein & Shanks, 2010).

In an effort to illustrate how easy it is to create false memories, and to publicize *false memory syndrome*, memory expert Elizabeth Loftus once deliberately implanted a false memory in actor Alan Alda. As the host of the television series *Scientific American Frontiers*, he was scheduled to interview Loftus. Before the interview, Alda was asked to fill out a questionnaire about his tastes in food. When he arrived, Loftus told Alda that his answers revealed that he must once have gotten sick after eating hard-boiled eggs (which was false). Later that day, at a picnic, Alda would not eat hard-boiled eggs (Loftus, 2003).

Certainly, some memories of abuse that return to awareness are genuine and must be dealt with. However, there is little doubt that some "recovered" memories are pure fantasy. No matter how real a recovered memory may seem, it could be false, unless it can be verified by others or by court or medical records (Bernstein & Loftus, 2009; Otgaar & Smeets, 2010). The saddest thing about such claims is that they deaden public sensitivity to actual abuse. Childhood sexual abuse is widespread, and awareness of its existence must not be repressed.

Explaining Inaccuracies in Memory

The work on eyewitness testimony and repressed memories provide some evidence that our memories cannot always be trusted. But inaccurate memories are not just confined to situations that involve criminal behavior—they happen to all of us on a regular basis, even in very ordinary everyday situations. Why is that?

To understand inaccurate and false memories, we need to return to our general model of memory in Figure 7.1. Let's revisit what happens during the process of remembering: Faced with a retrieval cue, you seek to pull relevant information from LTM back onto the mental workbench of working memory where conscious thinking happens. But this process isn't like a passive search for information in LTM that ends with you depositing a faithful copy of "the facts" into working memory. Instead, remembering is an active process of reconstructing information. Because your memory network is organized based on meaning, and because retrieval initiates a process of spreading activation in LTM, *lots* of information related to the retrieval cue can make its way back into working memory. Some of that information will be relevant to what you want to remember, and some of it will be related but more peripheral. If the relevant information that you want to remember is incomplete, then gaps in your memory can be "filled in" with other material that seems to fit with that incomplete information. Retrieval should therefore be considered an *active* process of constructing and reconstructing our memories, and one which can lead to memories that are not entirely accurate (Scoboria et al., 2012).

Let's take a look at how this active construction process might play out in real life. Say you're at a family reunion and your cousin Jake brings up the speech that your Uncle Alex gave at your sister's wedding. Jake's comment is the retrieval cue and spreading activation will bring lots of information from your network in LTM into working memory. Some of the information that arrives in working memory will be directly related to the speech itself, but other, related information will come along too. That other information might include your general impressions about Uncle Alex (he usually smells bad, drinks too much, and says really inappropriate things) and several details about the wedding (it was unseasonably hot, your sister was really nervous, your dress was itchy, and the food was amazing).

Chances are good that you don't remember the speech word-for-word, so there will be some gaps in your memory. These gaps are likely to be "filled" with other information that seems to fit with what you might reasonably expect to have happened during the speech. You might, for example, remember that Uncle Alex made a comment about the weather (since you remember it was very hot), that he seemed to slur his words (since that fits with your impression that he drinks too much), or that he made an off-color comment and no one laughed (since that would fit with your belief that he often says inappropriate things). It's possible, though, that none of those things actually happened during the speech—instead, in an effort to construct a relatively complete memory of the event, you've simply filled in a few blanks using information that's reasonably reliable based on your knowledge, experience, beliefs, and stereotypes. None of this "gap filling" is conscious of course—it's a completely seamless process that happens almost instantly, which is why the memory *feels* accurate.

A second kind of memory inaccuracy has to do with the source of information in our LTM. Sometimes a new memory is merely

False memory A memory that can seem accurate but is not.

stored in LTM alongside a similar but older memory. In this case, the two memories can potentially be confused. This can make us vulnerable to **source confusion**, which occurs when the origins of a memory are misremembered (Fandakova, Shing, & Lindenberger, 2012; Rosa & Gutchess, 2011). For example, a witness to a crime might inappropriately "remember" a face when they accidentally retrieve the *wrong* memory (Ruva, McEvoy, & Bryant, 2007). One famous example involved memory expert Donald Thomson. After appearing live on Australian television, he was accused of rape. It turns out that the victim was watching him on television when the actual rapist broke into her apartment (Schacter, 1996). She correctly remembered Thomson's face, but attributed it to the wrong *source*. Many tragic cases of mistaken identity occur this way.

Of course, memories are not always distorted during recall and slight distortions in our memories don't always result in serious, life-altering consequences. Most of the time, inaccuracies that result from the active reconstruction of our memories are quite benign. Moreover, it's important to note that the process itself stems from the brain's understandable desire to create an orderly world using information and impressions that it deems reliable. The take-home message is that we should continually remind ourselves that memories are typically "works in progress." When important consequences hang on their accuracy, it's always worth checking your memories against those of someone else that was present at the time.

Improving Eyewitnesses' Memory

We've seen that there are numerous problems that can arise when we rely on the memories of people who experience or witness a crime. In this section we examine two things that seem to improve witnesses' memory for events (changing procedures for police lineups and using cognitive interviews) and one that does not (hypnosis).

Police Lineups

We've already seen that many hundreds of people have been put in jail on the basis of mistaken eyewitness memories (Lampinen, Neuschatz, & Cling, 2012; Wade, Green, & Nash, 2010). In some instances, witnesses have described a criminal as black, tall, or young. Then a police lineup was held in which a suspect was the only African American among whites, the only tall suspect, or the only young person. In such cases, a false identification is very likely (Steblay, 2013). To avoid tragic mistakes, it's better to have *all* the distractors (that is, people in the lineup) look like the person witnesses described. Also, to reduce false positives, witnesses should be warned that the culprit *may not be present*. It may also be better to show witnesses one photo at a time (a sequential lineup). For each photo, the witness must decide whether the person is the culprit before another photo is shown (Mickes, Flowe, & Wixted, 2012; Wells & Olsen, 2003).

Eyewitness memories are notoriously inaccurate. By the time that witnesses are asked to testify in court, information they learned after an incident may blend into their original memories.

The Cognitive Interview

To help police detectives, R. Edward Geiselman and Ron Fisher created the **cognitive interview**, a technique that uses *redintegration* to improve the memory of eyewitnesses (Fisher & Geiselman, 1987; Ginet, Py, & Colomb, 2014). The key to this approach is recreating the crime scene. Witnesses revisit the scene in their imaginations or in person. That way, aspects of the crime scene, such as sounds, smells, and objects, provide helpful retrieval cues (stimuli associated with a memory). Back in the context of the crime, the witness is encouraged to recall events in different orders and from different viewpoints. Every new memory, no matter how trivial it may seem, can serve as a cue to trigger the retrieval of yet more memories.

When used properly, the cognitive interview produces 35 percent more correct information than standard questioning (Centofanti & Reece, 2006; Geiselman et al., 1986). This improvement comes without adding to the number of false memories elicited, as occurs with hypnosis (Holliday et al., 2012). The result is a procedure that is more effective in actual police work, even across cultures (Memon, Meissner, & Fraser, 2010; Stein & Memon, 2006).

What about hypnosis—can that help with eyewitness memory? In one case, 26 children were abducted from a school bus and held captive for ransom. Under hypnosis, the bus driver recalled the license plate number of the kidnappers' van. This memory helped break the case. Such successes seem to imply that hypnosis can improve memory. But does it?

Research has shown that hypnosis increases false memories more than it reveals true ones. In one experiment, 80 percent of the new memories produced by hypnotized subjects were *incorrect* (Dywan & Bowers, 1983). This is in part because a hypnotized person is more likely than normal to use imagination to fill in gaps in memory. Also, if a questioner asks misleading or suggestive questions, hypnotized persons tend to elaborate the questioner's information into their memories (Scoboria et al., 2002). To make matters worse, even when a memory is totally false, the hypnotized person's confidence in it can be unshakable (Burgess & Kirsch, 1999).

Thus, hypnosis sometimes uncovers more information, as it did with the bus driver (Wester & Hammond, 2011). However, in the absence of corroborating evidence, there is no sure way to tell which memories are false and which are true (Mazzoni, Heap, & Scoboria, 2010).

Reflective Practice

The Accuracy of Long-Term Memory

1. Eyewitness testimony is typically very accurate. T or F?
2. Police lineups could be improved by
   a. presenting photographs of at least 20 different people for the eyewitness to choose from
   b. having the officer in charge of the case provide cues if the eyewitness is struggling with identification
   c. presenting photographs to the eyewitness sequentially instead of in a single array
   d. having the eyewitness identify the perpetrator while under hypnosis
3. The cognitive interview helps people remember more by providing
   a. retrieval cues
   b. a serial position effect
   c. phonetic priming
   d. massed practice

THINK CRITICALLY

4. What can be done to ensure that juries are aware of the limitations of human memory?

SELF-REFLECT

- Have you ever found yourself disagreeing with someone about exactly what happened during a situation for which both of you were present? Given what you now know about the reconstructive process of memory, do you think it's possible that you may have filled in "gaps" in your memory with plausible but inaccurate information?

Answers: 1. F 2. c 3. a 4. One method for trying to ensure that juries are aware of the limitations of eyewitness memory is to have memory researchers appear in court as an expert witness. However, bringing in expert witnesses to educate juries about the problems associated with human memory can be expensive and time-consuming for attorneys (and the expert witnesses, who need to develop a deep understanding of the case). More recently, psychologists have advocated for educating judges about the pitfalls of memory so that they can educate the jury before deliberations begin.

7.6 Improving Your Memory

GATEWAYS LEARNING OUTCOMES:
After reading this section you should be able to:

7.6.1 Name up to eight ways that could be helpful in ensuring that you will be able to encode and remember information

7.6.2 Define mnemonics, and provide four examples of mnemonic devices

In keeping with the (mistaken) idea that forming a memory is like snapping a photo, many students assume that encoding and retrieval *should be effortless*—nothing could be further from the truth. For example, in an early study that was designed to test the original "seven plus or minus two" limit on short-term memory, researchers were able to train a student volunteer named Steve to listen to 80 digits and then repeat them back without making a mistake (Ericsson & Chase, 1982). Impressive? Sure. But easy? Not at all. Steve, a student volunteer who could initially remember only seven digits, spent 20 months (!) practicing memorizing ever-longer lists of digits. But Steve is no exception to the rule. A Chinese man named Lu Chao once held the world record for reciting from memory the first 67,890 digits of the number *pi* (Hu et al., 2009). Like other people with exceptional semantic memories, Lu Chao does not have a photographic memory. Instead he spent many years practicing, competing against other "pi memorizers," and making use of memory techniques anyone can use to improve their memories (Hu & Ericsson, 2012).

While you may never need to remember strings of 80 (or 67,890!) digits, one way to improve your memory is to ensure that you fully encode information. There are a number of strategies you can use to improve memory encoding—let's take a look at some of them (Fry, 2012; McDaniel, Maier, & Einstein, 2002).

Use Chunking to Organize Information

The ability to organize information into chunks underlies expertise in many fields (Gilchrist, Cowan, & Naveh-Benjamin, 2009; Gobet, 2005). For example, Steve practiced chunking digits into meaningful groups containing three or four digits each. Steve's avid interest in long-distance running helped greatly. When a string of numbers such as 928 came up, he'd think "9 minutes and 28 seconds—a good time for a 2-mile run." When running times wouldn't work, Steve used other associations, such as ages or dates, to chunk digits (Ericsson & Chase, 1982). In your everyday life, be open to searching for good ways to better chunk customer's orders if you are a restaurant server, the playbook if you are on a football team, sections of speeches if you are a public speaker, and so on.

Use Elaborative Rehearsal

Let us reiterate: The more you *rehearse* (mentally review) information as you read, the better you will remember it. Even repeatedly thinking about facts helps link them together in memory. But remember that maintenance rehearsal alone is not very effective. Elaborative rehearsal (or elaborative encoding), in which you rehearse by looking for connections to existing knowledge, is far better. For example, students in one classic study had the daunting task of trying to recall a list of 600 words. As they read the list (which they did not know they would be tested on), the students gave three other words closely related in meaning to each listed word. Remember that LTM is organized according to meaning, so coming up with those cues naturally created connections between the words in the list and the ideas already in the LTM network. In

Source confusion (in memory) Occurs when the origins of a memory are misremembered.

Cognitive interview Use of various cues and strategies to improve the memory of eyewitnesses.

a test given later, the words each student supplied were used as cues to jog memory. The students recalled an astounding 90 percent of the original word list (Mantyla, 1986).

The same principles hold for more conventional exams. Figure 7.5 shows the differences in memory networks for two students: one who used rote rehearsal to study the concept of reinforcement in operant conditioning and another who used elaborative rehearsal. Rote rehearsal (simple repetition) typically results in memory networks that are quite sparse. In contrast, using elaborative rehearsal involves thinking deeply about the concepts, such as comparing operant and classical conditioning. You might also ask yourself how reinforcement and punishment differ and note the distinguishing characteristics of positive and negative reinforcement and punishment. Elaborative rehearsal also involves trying to make material personally meaningful; in this case that might mean coming up with examples of each kind of reinforcement and punishment from your own life.

The preceding examples show, once again, that encoding is hard work, but that it often helps to *elaborate* on information as you learn. To make information meaningful when you study, try to use new names, ideas, or terms in several sentences. Your goal should be to knit meaningful retrieval cues into your memory at encoding to help you remember information when you need it.

Use Spaced Practice

To keep boredom and fatigue to a minimum, try alternating short study sessions with brief rest periods. This pattern, called **spaced practice**, is generally superior to **massed practice**, in which little or no rest is given between learning sessions (Dunlosky & Rawson, 2015). By improving attention and consolidation, three 20-minute study sessions can produce more learning than one hour of continuous study.

Perhaps the best way to use spaced practice is to *schedule* your time. To make an effective schedule, designate times during the week before, after, and between classes when you will study particular subjects. Then treat these times just as if they are classes that you have to attend.

Use Mental Images

Mental images, especially vivid ones, are particularly memorable (Worthen & Hunt, 2010). According to the *multimedia principle*, which we will encounter at the end of this chapter, it is also better to mix words and images than to rely on words alone (Overson, 2014). According to the multimedia principle, supplementing words with images generally improves memory. Make these images as vivid, and even bizarre, as possible (Soemer & Schwan, 2012). Bizarre images make stored information more *distinctive* and therefore easier to retrieve (Worthen & Hunt, 2010). Do note, however, that bizarre images help improve mainly immediate memory, and they work best for fairly simple information (Fritz et al., 2007). Nevertheless, they can be a first step toward learning. For example, suppose that you have to learn the names of all the bones and muscles in the human body. To remember that the jawbone is the *mandible,* you can associate it to a *man nibbling,* or maybe you can picture a *man dribbling* a basketball with his jaw (make this image as ridiculous as possible).

Exaggerated mental images can link two words or ideas in ways that aid memory. Here, the keyword method is used to link the English word *letter* with the Spanish word *carta.*

Consider Whole Versus Part Learning

If you have to memorize a speech, is it better to try to learn it from beginning to end or in smaller parts like paragraphs? It depends. For fairly short, organized information, it is usually better to practice whole packages of information rather than smaller parts (*whole learning*). Learning parts is usually better for extremely long, complicated information. In *part learning,* subparts of a larger body of information are studied (such as sections of a textbook chapter). To decide which approach to use, remember to study the *largest meaningful amount of information* you can at one time.

For very long or complex material, try the *progressive-part method,* by breaking a learning task into a series of short sections. At first, you study part A until it is mastered. Next, you study parts A and B; then A, B, and C; and so forth. This is a good way to learn the lines of a play, a long piece of music, or a poem (Ash & Holding, 1990). After the material is learned, you also should practice by starting at points other than A (at C, D, or B, for example). This helps prevent getting "lost" or going blank in the middle of a performance.

Beware of the Serial Position Effect!

Whenever you must learn something in *order,* remember the serial position effect. As you will recall, this is the tendency to make the most errors in remembering the middle of a list. If you are introduced to a long line of people, the names you are likely to forget will be those in the middle, so you should make an extra effort to attend to them. You also should give extra practice to the middle of a list, poem, or speech.

Overlearn

Numerous studies have shown that memory is greatly improved when you *overlearn* or continue to study beyond bare mastery. After you have learned material well enough to remember it once without error, you should continue studying. Overlearning is your best insurance against going blank on a test because of nervousness.

Use Mnemonics

Imagine the poor biology or psychology student who is required to learn the names of the 12 cranial nerves (in order, of course). Although the spinal nerves connect the brain to the body through the spinal cord, the cranial nerves do so directly. Just in case you want to know, the names are olfactory, optic, oculomotor, trochlear, trigeminal, abducens, facial, vestibulocochlear, glossopharyngeal, vagus, spinal accessory, and hypoglossal.

As you might imagine, most of us find it difficult to successfully encode this list. In the absence of any obvious meaningful relationship among these terms, it is difficult to apply the memory strategies that we discussed in the previous section and tempting to resort to *rote* learning (learning by simple repetition). Fortunately, there *is* an alternative. Use a **mnemonic device** (nee-MON-ik)—a strategy for enhancing memory—to impose an artificial organization on material if none is naturally present. The superiority of mnemonic learning as opposed to rote learning has been demonstrated many times (Carney & Levin, 2014; Worthen & Hunt, 2010).

Here are some examples:

Create Acrostics

In an *acrostic*, the first letters of the word in a target list are used to create a sentence. Generations of students have learned the names of the spinal nerves by memorizing the sentence "**O**n **O**ld **O**lympus' **T**owering **T**op **A** **F**amous **V**ocal **G**erman **V**iewed **S**ome **H**ops." This mnemonic device, which uses the first letter of each of the cranial nerves to generate a nonsense sentence, indeed produces better recall of the cranial nerves. Similarly, **S**ome **P**eople **C**an **F**ly! helps psychology students remember Piaget's stages of cognitive development: sensorimotor, pre-operational, concrete operational, formal operational. Such acrostics are even more effective if you make up your own (Fry, 2012). (Try making them rhyme for an added memory boost.)

Tyler Olson/Shutterstock.com

Mnemonics can be an aid in preparing for tests. However, because mnemonics help most in the initial stages of storing information, it is important to follow through with other elaborative learning strategies.

The Keyword Method

Let's say that you have some new vocabulary words to memorize in Spanish. You can use the **keyword method**, in which a familiar word or image is used to link two other words or items (Campos, Camino, & Pérez-Fabello, 2011; Fritz et al., 2007). To remember that the word *pajaro* (pronounced PAH-hah-ro) means "bird," you can link it to a "key" word in English: *pajaro* sounds a bit like "parked car-o." Therefore, to remember that *pajaro* means "bird," you might visualize a parked car jam-packed with birds. You should try to make this image as vivid and exaggerated as possible, with birds flapping and chirping and feathers flying everywhere. Similarly, for the word *carta* (which means "letter"), you might imagine a shopping *cart* filled with postal letters.

If you link similar keywords and images for the rest of the list, you may not remember them all, but you will get most without much more practice. As a matter of fact, if you have formed the *pajaro* and *carta* images, it will be almost impossible for you to see these words again without remembering what they mean. The keyword method is also superior when you want to work "backward" from an English word to a foreign word (Campos, Rodríguez-Pinal, & Pérez-Fabello, 2013).

Create Stories or Chains

How can mnemonic devices be used to remember things in order? To remember lists of ideas, objects, or words in order, try forming an exaggerated association (mental image) connecting the first item to the second and then the second to the third, and so on. To remember the following short list in order—elephant, doorknob, string, watch, rifle, oranges—picture a full-size *elephant* balanced on a *doorknob* playing with a *string* tied to him. Picture a *watch* tied to the string, and a *rifle* shooting *oranges* at the watch. This technique can be used quite successfully for lists of 20 or more items. In one test, people who used a linking mnemonic did much better at remembering lists of 15 and 22 errands (Higbee et al., 1990). Try it next time you go shopping and leave your list at home. Another helpful strategy is to make up a short story that links all the items on a list that you want to remember (McNamara & Scott, 2001; Worthen & Hunt, 2010).

Ancient Greek orators had another interesting way to remember ideas in order when giving a speech: the *method of loci* (locations). They took a mental "walk" along a familiar path. As they did, they associated topics with the images of statues found along the walk. You can do the same thing by "placing" objects or ideas along the way as you mentally take a familiar walk (Radvansky, 2017).

Spaced practice A practice schedule that alternates study periods with brief rests.

Massed practice A practice schedule in which studying continues for long periods, without interruption.

Mental images Mental pictures or visual depictions used in memory and thinking.

Mnemonic device A strategy for enhancing memory.

Keyword method As an aid to memory, using a familiar word or image to link two items.

Reflective Practice

Improving Memory

1. As new information is encoded, it is helpful to elaborate on its meaning and connect it to other information. T or F?
2. Overlearning refers to
   a. using retrieval cues to learn more about the concept of "over"
   b. learning information beyond basic mastery
   c. learning information in locations that overlook where you will be tested
   d. studying (that is, "going over") the concept of learning
3. Which of the following is least likely to improve a memory in the long term?
   a. using exaggerated mental images
   b. forming a chain of associations
   c. turning visual information into verbal information
   d. associating new information to information that is already known or familiar

THINK CRITICALLY

4. What are the advantages of taking notes as you read a textbook, as opposed to underlining words in the text?
5. How are elaborative processing and mnemonic devices alike?

SELF-REFLECT

- Review the techniques for improving memory, and think of a specific example of how you could use each technique at school, at home, or at work.
- The best mnemonic devices are your own. As an exercise, see if you can create a better acrostic for the 12 cranial nerves. One student generated **O**ld **O**tto **O**ctavius **T**ried **T**rigonometry **A**fter **F**acing **V**ery **G**rim **V**irgin's **S**ad **H**usbands (Bloom & Lamkin, 2006).

Answers: 1. T 2. b 3. c 4. Properly done, note-taking is a form of elaborative processing; it encourages active reflection and facilitates the organization and selection of important ideas, and your notes can be used for review. 5. Both attempt to relate new information to information already stored in LTM that is familiar or already easy to retrieve.

7.7 Psychology and Your Skill Set: Giving Memorable Presentations

GATEWAYS LEARNING OUTCOMES:
After reading this section you should be able to:

7.7.1 Define the multimedia principle

7.7.2 Create a plan that will make your multimedia presentation more memorable

Did you ever sit through a presentation overflowing with words or complicated diagrams? Overwhelmed by listening and reading, you probably noticed that you didn't remember (or care to remember) very much at all. By the same token, you may also have experienced presentations that kept you on the edge of your seat, and that you remembered many months—or even years—later.

AP Images/J. Scott Applewhite

In an effort to explain the U.S. Forces strategy in Afghanistan, members of the American military prepared a very complex Microsoft PowerPoint slide for General Stanley McChrystal. The general, who was in charge of North Atlantic Treaty Organization (NATO) forces in the region, had just one thing to say about it: "When we understand that slide, we'll have won the war."

These days, it's common to give presentations at school or work that involve videos or slides made using PowerPoint, Prezi, or Keynote. Clearly, there are important technology-related skills needed to create this type of presentation. Giving a *memorable* presentation, however, requires a different set of skills altogether—skills that depend on a solid understanding of how human memory works.

So far in this chapter we have described human memory, including the three memory systems (sensory memory, short-term or working memory, and long-term memory) and some of the factors that contribute to remembering and forgetting. In this final closing section, we make use of what we know about memory to describe how to give an effective multimedia presentation—that is, a presentation that includes both words (either spoken or text) and graphics (including pictures, animations, charts, or video).

The Multimedia Principle

One of the reasons that multimedia presentations can be so useful in conveying information is that people process words and mental images together better than they do words alone, a finding referred to as the **multimedia principle**. There are three important assumptions associated with this principle (Overson, 2014). The first is that people process multimedia information through two sensory channels—visual (the eyes) and verbal (the ears).

The second assumption is that people can only process a limited amount of information through either of these channels at any moment in time. For example, if you present an image or a video on the screen, the audience can only hold a portion of that graphic in working memory at one time. Similarly, when you are speaking during your presentation, the audience is only able to keep a few words in working memory.

Finally, the third assumption is that people remember information best when they *select* important information from sensory memory, *organize* it in a meaningful way in working memory, and *integrate* it with other information in the long-term memory network (Mayer, 2014). A memorable presentation is one that promotes active processing by helping the audience with the tasks of selecting, organizing, and integrating information.

Speak to Your Audience's Memory

Multimedia presentations are common in workplaces ranging from business to education to health care. Part of your success in the workplace, then, may rest on your ability to give a presentation that is persuasive, informative, and above all, memorable.

OK. How do I do that? Begin by noting the characteristics of your audience, such as their age and background knowledge. Understanding your audience is important because it will guide the complexity of the ideas that you present, the language that you use, and the pace at which you provide information. Audiences that are extremely knowledgeable require much less in the way of background information and will not be left behind if you move through your material at a somewhat faster pace. On the other hand, a less experienced audience will need you to move more slowly, explaining the background more thoroughly and providing examples where appropriate. If you're presenting on ideas in a field that uses a specialized professional vocabulary, it will be important to explain each term and how it relates to the main points that you're trying to make.

In terms of the multimedia part of your presentation, recall that people have a limited ability to process information through their visual and verbal channels. Remember, too, that they remember information best when they *select* information that's important from the material that enters sensory memory, *organize* it in a meaningful way while it is in working memory, and *integrate* it with other information that is in long-term memory. Let's look at how to create presentations that meet these goals (Atkinson & Mayer, 2004).

Help the Audience Select Important Information

- *Eliminate distractions.* Critically evaluate the slide design template that you have selected, as well as other features that you are using. Does the template have a very busy pattern with wild colors? Is the font easy to read? You should also ask yourself whether any animations you've selected will be distracting for the audience. For example, do you have points that are zooming onto the screen from the side, or text that bounces up and down? What about humorous GIFs that repeat over and over? These kinds of animations will consume your audience's valuable processing capacity unnecessarily. Always remember that just because these features *can* be used doesn't mean that they *should* be used.
- *Eliminate anything on the slide that does not support the main point.* On individual slides, the things that you cut out may include unnecessary graphics, such as logos, backgrounds or watermarks (the images that can be seen "behind" the text), or any text that does not support the main point being made on the slide.
- *Limit yourself to a few main points per slide.* This will help limit the amount of text that's up on the screen for people to process. You can also limit the amount of text by avoiding points that are paragraphs—use the minimum number of words necessary to convey your point clearly. If you do find yourself with a large amount of text on your slide, consider splitting it into two (or more) slides.
- *Highlight the main points you want to make on each slide.* There are many ways that you can draw the audience's attention to the central point being made on a slide. One is to use italics and colored font to draw attention to key words or phrases on the slide (but make sure that there aren't too many!). If you are contrasting two ideas, another way to visually highlight points is to use a table format that places them side-by-side, rather than two sets of bullet points.
- *Instead of a title at the top of the slide, use a headline.* A headline is written in the active voice and contains a noun and verb. Its primary purpose is to summarize, in a very limited number of words, the single overarching idea that is being conveyed by the information or graphics on the slide. People—especially those who are not very familiar with the material that you are presenting—have a better chance of remembering a short summary rather than all of the text that's on the slide. Instead of a title such as "Mnemonics," then, you may want to consider the headline "Mnemonics Help Improve Memory."

Help the Audience Organize Information

- *Keep your eye on the whole story.* As you create individual slides, it's very easy to get caught up in what information you should include on each one. Remember, though, that the entire presentation is intended to tell your audience a story. The best presentations don't begin with the creation of slides—PowerPoint or Keynote—they begin when you map out the story's beginning (What does your audience already know?) and end (What do you want them to know by the time you're finished?), and then carefully plot the points you need to make

Multimedia principle The idea that people process words and mental images together better than they do words alone.

to bridge that gap. To ensure that your story is developing smoothly, you should regularly check on the flow of the presentation as a whole by using features such as Slide Sorter in PowerPoint or Light Table in Keynote.

- *Make the structure of your points clear.* You will have noticed that each chapter in this book has a clear structure. The main topics have titles in very large print; if there are smaller points being made within these main topics, then their titles are written in smaller print. Using fonts of different sizes in this way helps to signal the overall structure of the information to the reader and helps them to organize it in their minds. When you create a slide that includes text, you can do the same thing: Use points and subpoints to help the audience see the underlying structure of your talk. And if you really want to emphasize structure, consider a single opening or closing slide that summarizes only the main points being made.
- *Talk over pictures.* The multimedia principle tells us that people learn better from pictures and words than they do from words alone. Because most presenters don't realize this, slides are often filled only with words. This verbal information has to be processed by the visual channel, which can quickly become overloaded when there is a lot of text on the screen. This problem is made worse when the presenter is also speaking, because the audience's attention is then trying to process the same type of information through both the visual and auditory channels! A better strategy is to use carefully selected (and high-quality) visuals that can make the point, and to narrate the text out loud for your audience (Fenesi et al., 2014). By "talking over pictures" in this way, you can capitalize on people's ability to process visual and auditory information at the same time.

Help the Audience Integrate Information

- *Help the audience make connections.* Whenever possible, help the audience to see how the information you're presenting is related to material that is already in their long-term memory. For example, you might draw their attention to how the material is similar or different to things they have seen before, how it extends what they already know, or how your topic is connected to their own personal experiences.

Practice, Practice, Practice

The final thing to remember if you want to deliver a good presentation is simple: practice, practice, practice! Practicing your talk will confirm whether you will be able to stick to the time you've been given and will help to develop your confidence. That confidence will help you to speak without stumbling over your words and present the image of someone who really understands the material. And what could be more memorable than that?

Reflective Practice

Psychology and Your Skill Set: Giving Memorable Presentations

1. People learn more from words alone than from words and graphics. T or F?
2. We can process unlimited multimedia information through our visual and verbal sensory channels. T or F?
3. People will remember information best when they ___________ information that they consider important, ___________ it in a meaningful way, and ___________ it with other long-term information.

THINK CRITICALLY

4. You are asked to give a presentation to a group of Grade 1 students on how to study. Now, what if you were asked to present the same topic to a group of university students? How would you tailor your presentations to suit each audience?

SELF-REFLECT

- Think of a time you sat in a lecture and found yourself disengaged because of the professor's presentation style, tone of voice, or layout of information. Now think of a really great lecture you attended. What was it about the presentation that made this lecture engaging? How can you apply these techniques to your own presentations in the future?

Answers: 1. F 2. F 3. Select, organize, and integrate. 4. Considering the demographics of each audience, you could tailor language, pace of information, background knowledge, and visuals. For the Grade 1 class you should use simple language, move at a slower pace, provide less information, assume little background knowledge, and keep visuals simple and age-appropriate.

CHAPTER IN REVIEW

Gateways to Memory

Summary: Gateways Learning Outcomes

7.1 A General Model of Memory

7.1.1 Define memory

Memory is an active system that encodes, stores, and retrieves information.

7.1.2 Describe the types of memory and memory processes that are outlined in the Atkinson-Shiffrin model of memory

The Atkinson-Shiffrin model of memory includes three types of memory (sensory memory, short-term or working memory, and long-term memory) that hold information for increasingly longer periods. Moving information between sensory and short-term memory requires that we pay attention to information. Moving information from short-term to long-term memory requires the process of encoding; getting information back into short-term memory from long-term memory requires the process of retrieval.

7.2 Sensory and Short-Term (Working) Memory

7.2.1 Describe sensory memory, including its capacity and duration

We are normally unaware of sensory memory, which takes in the information provided by the sense organs (see Section 4.1). Though its capacity is very large, information is stored in sensory memory for a very short time (2 seconds or less). Two common types of sensory memory are iconic and echoic memory. Iconic memory is a type of sensory memory that stores information coming in from the visual system. Echoic memory is sensory memory devoted to information coming into the auditory system.

7.2.2 Describe short-term (working) memory, including its capacity and duration

We are conscious of the contents of short-term memory, which can function as a "mental workbench" where information is subjected to mental operations. Initially, STM was believed to have a capacity of about seven bits of information (plus or minus two), but more recent researchers have suggested the number may be as low as four. Information can be held in STM for about a dozen seconds, though longer timeframes are possible when maintenance rehearsal is used.

7.2.3 Explain what is meant by "chunking," and how it helps to expand the capacity of working memory

Chunking is the process by which meaningfully similar information is grouped (or "chunked") together, increasing the capacity of STM

7.2.4 Distinguish between rote rehearsal (rote learning) and elaborative rehearsal (elaborative encoding)

Rote rehearsal refers to simple repetition of information; elaborative rehearsal is the process by which we try to make information more meaningful by connecting it to things that are already stored in long-term memory. For transferring information to LTM, rote rehearsal is less effective than elaborative rehearsal.

7.3 Long-Term Memory

7.3.1 Describe long-term memory, including its duration, capacity, and organization

We are not generally conscious of long-term memories. Long-term memories are relatively permanent, and LTM seems to have an almost unlimited storage capacity. It is organized as a network of information that is organized based on meaning.

7.3.2 Define the terms retrieval cue and redintegration, and explain their relation to spreading activation in the memory network

Retrieval cues refer to external prompts to remember information that has been stored in LTM. The cue causes relevant information to be retrieved from LTM and returned to working memory. Through a process of spreading activation in the LTM network, one memory then links to another associated memory, which links to another, and another, bringing more information that is meaningfully related to the cue into working memory. This process is associated with redintegration (the process by which a complete memory can be retrieved from partial cues or reminders).

7.3.3 Distinguish between implicit and explicit memory

Implicit memory refers to long-term memories of which we are unaware. Some examples of implicit memories include those that stem from well-learned skills, conditioned responses (classical and instrumental responses), and priming. Explicit memories are those that are associated with our personal lives as well as factual knowledge that we have learned. Explicit memory can be further divided into semantic and episodic memory.

7.3.4 Distinguish between episodic and semantic memory

Episodic memory stores information about our personal, or autobiographical experiences. In contrast, semantic memory contains information about the world that is not connected to the time or place that information was learned.

7.3.5 Name the parts of the brain that are important in memory

Parts of the brain that are important in memory include the hippocampus (where consolidation occurs), the cortex (where long-term memories are often stored), and the basal ganglia and cerebellum (where memory for motor skills appears to be localized).

7.3.6 Outline two reasons why it's helpful to have information stored in long-term memory

Storing information in LTM is helpful because it's more time-efficient to retrieve information from LTM than it is to look information up. In addition, stored information helps us to understand (and therefore remember) incoming information.

7.4 Remembering and Forgetting

7.4.1 Describe two factors that influence encoding and two factors that do ***not*** influence encoding

Two factors that influence encoding are emotion and whether information is processed in a deep or shallow way. Two factors that do not appear to affect encoding are the intention to remember information and repeated exposure to information.

7.4.2 Name three ways that we can measure memory

Memories may be revealed by recall, recognition, relearning. In recall, memories are retrieved without explicit cues, as in an essay exam. A common test of recognition is the multiple-choice question. In relearning, material that seems to be forgotten is learned again, and memory is revealed by a savings score (the amount of time saved when relearning information). Recall, recognition, and relearning mainly measure explicit memories.

7.4.3 Name five factors that contribute to forgetting

Five factors that contribute to forgetting include atypical brain function (e.g., dementia; amnesia), cue-dependent forgetting, state-dependent learning, interference (proactive and retroactive), and motivated forgetting.

7.4.4 Distinguish between active and passive forgetting

Active forgetting refers to purposeful forgetting that is carried out to keep the amount of information we process reasonable, and to avoid creating memories of trivial things that are unlikely to be helpful over the long term. Passive forgetting is characterized as the decay that occurs when memories are not retrieved often.

7.5 The Accuracy of Long-Term Memory

7.5.1 Explain the origins of false and inaccurate memories

False and inaccurate memories emerge as a result of the fact that memories are actively reconstructed each time they are retrieved from LTM. During this process, gaps in memory can be unconsciously "filled in" with prior knowledge, expectations, beliefs, and stereotypes, resulting in memories that may be inaccurate or false, but that seem accurate.

7.5.2 Describe three factors that might improve confidence in eyewitness testimony

Things that might improve confidence in eyewitness testimony include changing the way police lineups are carried out, using cognitive interviews when interviewing suspects, and eliminating consideration of eyewitness or victim's memories that emerge only through hypnosis.

7.6 Improving Your Memory

7.6.1 Name up to eight ways that could be helpful in ensuring that you will be able to encode and remember information

Memory can be improved through chunking, elaborative rehearsal (or elaborative encoding), spaced practice, using mental images, whole (versus part) learning, considering the serial position effect, overlearning, and the use of mnemonics.

7.6.2 Define mnemonics, and provide four examples of mnemonic devices

Mnemonic devices use bizarre or exaggerated verbal associations and mental images to link new information with familiar memories already stored in LTM. Some examples of mnemonic devices include acrostics, the keyword method, and stories or chains (including the method of loci).

7.7 Psychology and Your Skill Set: Giving Memorable Presentations

7.7.1 Define the multimedia principle

Multimedia presentations involve both visual and auditory information; however, we can process only very limited amounts of information through the auditory and visual channels at a specific time. The multimedia principle states that people learn more from words and graphics together than they do from words alone.

7.7.2 Create a plan that will make your multimedia presentation more memorable

The audience will remember information from a presentation best when you *select* important information, *organize* it in a meaningful way, and *integrate* it with other existing information. You can help the audience *select* important information by eliminating irrelevant background distractions and information from slides, putting a few main points per slide and highlighting them, and using headlines rather than titles for each slide. You can help your audience *organize* information by outlining your presentation as a story, clearly structuring points, and making complementary use of the auditory and visual channels. You can help the audience *integrate* information by highlighting connections between information and external knowledge.

8 Cognition, Language, and Creativity

AP Images/Taylor Jewell

Gateway Theme The origins of intelligent behavior lie in thinking, language, problem solving, and creativity.

Chapter Outline

Capturing the Wind

William Kamkwamba grew up in a rural village in Malawi. The second eldest of seven children, he had to leave school at the age of 14 because his parents were unable to afford the $80 fee. Rather than sitting idle, though, William borrowed books from the village library and set about continuing his education at home. One of the books he brought home was an 8th grade American physics textbook with a picture of a wind turbine on its cover. William was fascinated and imagined how he could use the book's ideas to build a windmill that would provide power to the family home. Using plans from the book as his guide, his first windmill was constructed from a broken bicycle, a tractor fan blade, a pulley, and blue gum trees. And though people in the village initially thought he was crazy, they quickly changed their minds when they realized that the windmill was powering four light bulbs and two radios.

William's story, told in the book *The Boy Who Harnessed the Wind*, is a testament to the power of human cognition (or thinking), problem solving, and creativity. But William's success also raises important questions for psychological scientists. How do we think? How do we make decisions, and how are we able to solve problems? How do people create works of art, science, and literature? In this chapter, we'll attempt to answer these questions by exploring a broad range of human cognition, from detail-oriented decision-making to innovative creative visions.

8.1 The Basic Units of Cognition: Mental Imagery, Concepts, and Language

GATEWAYS LEARNING OUTCOMES:
After reading this section you should be able to:

8.1.1 Distinguish between experiential and reflective processing

8.1.2 Explain how imagery is used in thinking

8.1.3 Explain how concepts are used in thinking

8.1.4 Explain how language is used in thinking

Cognition is the process of thinking, gaining knowledge, and dealing with knowledge. At its most basic, cognition refers to processing a *mental representation* (internal subjective expression) of a problem or situation (Sternberg, 2017). Human cognition can take many forms, from experiential daydreaming to more reflective problem solving and reasoning.

Let's do some more experiential and reflective thinking while looking at Figure 8.1. On the left (*a*), is this face happy or sad? Chances are that you *knew* the answer just by looking at the photo.

(a) (b)

Figure 8.1 Experiential versus reflective processing. (a) An experiential processing task; (b) a reflective processing task. See the text for an explanation. (After Kahneman, 2011.)

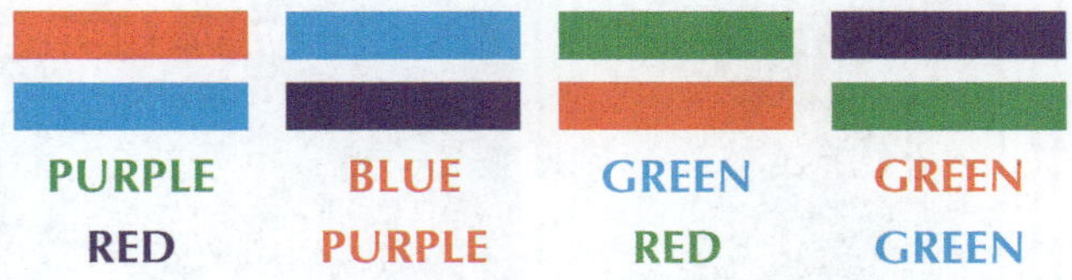

Figure 8.2 The Stroop interference task. Test yourself by naming out loud the colors in the top two rows as quickly as you can. Then name out loud the colors of the ink used to print the words in the bottom two rows. (Do not read the words themselves.) Was it harder to name the ink colors in the bottom rows?

You were engaging in more or less unconscious, effortless, and automatic **experiential processing.**

Now looking at (*b*), what is the sum of these numbers? This time, experiential processing likely was not enough; you likely had to deliberately concentrate and engage in **reflective processing** (Kahneman, 2011; Norman, 1994). (■ The difference between these two types of cognition is relevant to how well you understand and remember what you are learning; see the introduction to this book, *Psychology and Your Skill Set—Reflective Studying.*)

What do you mean when you say that experiential processing is "automatic"? To answer that question, begin by trying the activity shown in Figure 8.2, which is commonly referred to as the Stroop Task.

Fluent readers of English usually have difficulty quickly naming the color of ink used to print the words in the bottom two rows of this figure. But why? When fluent readers look at words, they normally read them automatically (Moors, 2016). In this case, the task is *not* to read the words; instead, it is to name the ink color used to print the words. But reading words is so automated that fluent readers cannot help themselves. Sooner or later, when fluent readers work through lists like these, they are likely to make some mistakes, reading out loud, for example, the word *purple* instead of naming the ink color (*green* in this example).

At the very least, fluent readers cannot speed through such lists since the *automatic* processing of word meanings is just too strong to ignore and interferes with color naming. To avoid making mistakes, fluent readers having to engage in some reflective cognition, deliberately checking responses to make sure they are not reading the color words aloud. Oddly enough, nonfluent readers do not have as much trouble in the Stroop interference task since they cannot (yet) automatically read the color words (Protopapas, Archonti, & Skaloumbakas, 2007).

But it's also possible to see experiential and reflective processes at work in more everyday sorts of problems. Consider this question (Trémolière & De Neys, 2014): A Rolls Royce and a Ferrari are being sold together for \$190,000. The Rolls Royce costs \$100,000 more than the Ferrari. How much does the Ferrari cost?

Most people rely on fast experiential processing to manage this question. They will very quickly generate an answer—the Ferrari costs \$90,000—and move on without ever realizing that they're wrong. If you engage slower reflective processing, though, you'll see the error: If the Ferrari costs \$90,000 and the Rolls Royce costs \$100,000 more than that, then the Rolls Royce must cost \$190,000. Together, then, the two cars would cost \$280,000 (\$190,000 + \$90,000).

These examples indicate that there are some clear limitations to human cognition. However, there are also great strengths in our ability to think and reason. The power of human cognition is dramatically illustrated by chess grand master Miguel Najdorf, who once simultaneously played 45 chess games while blindfolded. How did Najdorf do it? Like most people, he effectively used three of the basic units of thought: mental images, concepts, and language (or symbols). Mental images are picture-like mental representations. A concept is a mental category for classifying things based on common features or properties. Language consists of words or symbols and rules for combining them. Thinking often involves all three units. For example, blindfolded chess players rely on visual images, concepts ("Game 2 has started with a strategy called an English opening"), and the notational system, or "language," of chess.

In this section we'll take a closer look at these three basic units of cognition. You should be aware, though, that many of the ideas that you've seen previously in this book are also involved in cognition, including attention, pattern recognition, and memory (Goldstein, 2015).

Mental Imagery

Most of us use images to think, remember, and solve problems. For instance, we may use **mental images** to do the following:

- Make a decision or solve a problem (choose what clothes to wear; figure out how to arrange furniture in a room)
- Change feelings or behaviors (think of pleasant images to get out of a bad mood; imagine yourself as thin to stay on a diet)
- Improve a skill or prepare for some action (use images to improve a tennis stroke; mentally rehearse how you will ask for a raise)
- Aid memory (picture Mr. Cook wearing a chef's hat, so you can remember his name)

To better understand our capacity to create and use mental images, let's tackle three of their characteristics.

First, mental images are *not flat like photographs*. Researcher Stephen Kosslyn showed this by asking people, "Does a frog have lips and a stubby tail?" Unless you often kiss frogs, you'll probably tackle this question by using mental images. Most people picture a frog, "look" at its mouth, and then mentally "rotate" the frog in mental space to check its tail (Kosslyn, 1983). Mental rotation is partly based on imagined movements (Figure 8.3). That is, we can mentally "pick up" an object and turn it around or even fold it (Harris, Hirsh-Pasek, & Newcombe, 2013; Wraga, Boyle, & Flynn, 2010).

Second, mental images often *approximate what is true in the "real world."* Our ability to create images that are in keeping with our environment becomes clear when we zoom in and out of mental images. To demonstrate this, let's try two tasks. In the first, picture a cat sitting beside a housefly. Now try to "zoom in" on the cat's ears so you see them clearly. How quickly could you do that? In the second task, picture a rabbit sitting beside an elephant, then try to "zoom in" on the rabbit's front feet. How quickly were you able to do that? Did it take longer than zooming in on the cat's ears?

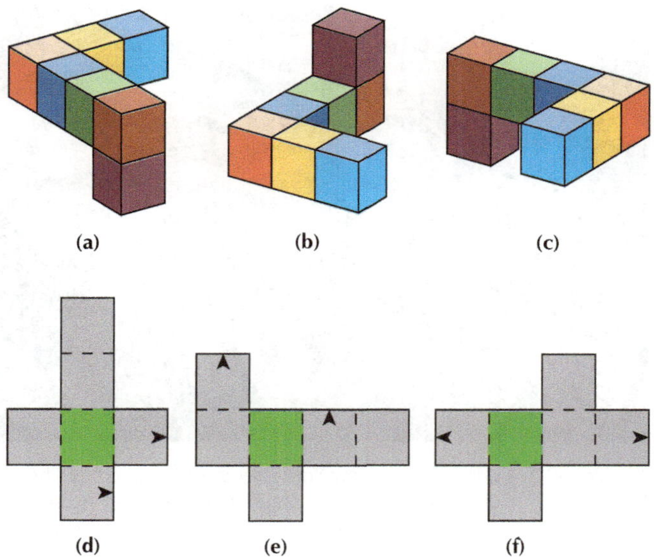

Figure 8.3 Imagery in thinking. (*Top*) Participants were shown a drawing similar to (a) and drawings of how (a) would look in other positions, such as (b) and (c). Participants could recognize (a) after it had been "rotated" from its original position. However, the more (a) was rotated in space, the longer it took to recognize it. This result suggests that people formed a three-dimensional image of (a) and rotated the image to see if it matched (Shepard, 1975). (*Bottom*) Try your ability to manipulate mental images: Picture each of these shapes as a piece of paper that can be folded to make a cube. After they have been folded, on which cubes do the arrow tips meet (Kosslyn, 1985)?

Typically, the second task takes longer because the mental images we create mirror what's true in the world. When a rabbit is pictured with an elephant, the rabbit's image must be small because the elephant is large. Using such tasks, Stephen Kosslyn (1985) found that the smaller an image is, the harder it is to "see" its details. To put this finding to use when studying, try forming oversize images of things you want to think about. For example, to understand synaptic transmission, picture the synapse as a canal with neurotransmitter molecules the size of small rowboats moving across the canal; to understand the human ear, explore it (in your mind's eye) like a large cave; and so forth.

Third, mental images are *held in short-term, or working, memory* and when they're active in our thinking, they reside in a part of working memory called the *visuospatial sketch pad* (Baddeley, 2012).

Cognition Process of thinking, gaining knowledge, and dealing with knowledge.

Experiential processing Thought that is passive, effortless, and automatic.

Reflective processing Thought that is active, effortful, and controlled.

Mental images Mental picture or visual depiction used in memory and thinking.

The Vessel in Hudson Yards, New York City, was designed by Thomas Heatherwick. Could a person lacking mental imagery design such a masterpiece? Most artists, architects, designers, sculptors, and filmmakers have excellent visual imagery.

Where in the brain is the visuospatial sketch pad located? Different psychological processes, like rotating a mental image in working memory, are not always easy to localize in the brain because they may actually be carried out by an interconnected collection of brain areas. Roughly speaking, though, seeing something in your "mind's eye" is similar to seeing real objects. Information from the eyes normally activates the brain's primary visual area, creating an image (● Figure 8.4). Other brain areas then help us recognize the image by relating it to prior knowledge that is stored in long-term memory.

When you form a mental image, the system works in reverse. Brain areas in which memories are stored send signals back to the visual cortex, where once again an image is created (Borst & Kosslyn, 2010; Zvyagintsev et al., 2013). For example, if you visualize a friend's face right now, the area of your brain that specializes in perceiving faces will become more active (Prochnow et al., 2013).

Kinesthetic Imagery

In a sense, we think with our bodies as well as our brains. *Kinesthetic (motor) images* are created from muscular sensations (Grangeon, Guillot, & Collet, 2011; Olshansky et al., 2015). Such images help us think about movements and actions.

As you think and talk, kinesthetic sensations can guide the flow of ideas. For example, if a friend calls and asks you the combination of a lock you lent her, you may move your hands as if twirling the dial on the lock. Or, try answering this question: Which direction do you turn the hot-water handle in your kitchen to shut off the water? If you haven't memorized the words "leftie loosie" and "rightie tightie," you may "turn" the faucet in your imagination before answering. You may even make a turning motion with your hand before answering.

Kinesthetic images are especially important in movement-oriented skills such as music, sports, dance, skateboarding, and martial arts. An effective way to improve such skills is to practice by rehearsing kinesthetic images of yourself performing flawlessly (Anema & Dijkerman, 2013).

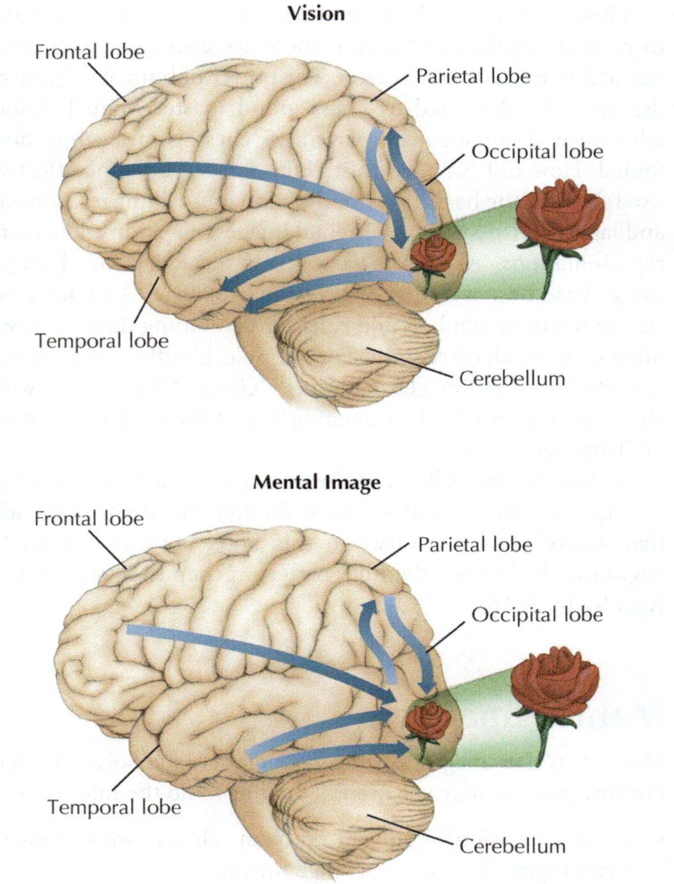

● **Figure 8.4 Imagery in the brain.** *(Top)* When you see a flower, its image is represented by activity in the primary visual area of the cortex at the back of the brain. Information about the flower also is relayed to other brain areas. *(Bottom)* If you form a mental image of a flower, information follows a reverse path. The result, once again, is activation of the primary visual area.

Concepts

As noted previously, a **concept** is an idea that represents a category of objects or events. Concepts help us identify important features of the things that we encounter in the world. That's why experts in various areas of knowledge are good at classifying objects. Bird watchers, tropical fish fanciers, five-year-old dinosaur enthusiasts, and others all learn to look for identifying details that beginners tend to miss. If you are knowledgeable about a topic, such as horses, flowers, or football, you literally see things in those conceptual categories differently than less well-informed people do (Harel et al., 2010; Ross, 2006). Connecting this to what we learned in ■ Section 7.3, the long-term memory networks for concepts will be more elaborate for experts than nonexperts.

Forming Concepts

Concept formation is the process of classifying information into meaningful categories (Ashby & Maddox, 2005; Newell, 2012). At its most basic, concept formation is based on experience with *positive* and *negative instances* (examples that belong, or do not belong, to the concept category). However, concept formation is

Gavriel Jecan/AGE Fotostock

Rock climbers use kinesthetic imagery to learn climbing routes and to plan their next few moves (Boyd & Munroe, 2003).

not as simple as it might seem, as we discovered in ■ Section 3.4. Recall that the cognitive developmental psychologist Jean Piaget documented that children acquire concepts through the complex and ongoing processes of *assimilation* (working new information into existing concepts) and *accommodation* (creating new concepts when information does not fit within existing ones). Imagine a child learning the concept of *dog*:

> A father pushes his young child down the street in a stroller. At a neighbor's house, they see a medium-sized dog. The father says, "See the dog." As they pass the next yard, the child sees a cat and says, "Dog!" Her father corrects her, "No, that's a *cat*." The child now thinks, "Aha, dogs are large and cats are small." In the next yard, she sees a Pekingese and says, "Cat!" "No, that's a dog," replies her father.

The child's confusion is understandable. At first, she might even mistake a Pekingese for a dust mop. However, with more positive and negative instances, the child will eventually recognize everything from Great Danes to Chihuahuas as members of the same category—dogs.

As adults, we often acquire concepts by learning or forming *conceptual rules*, guidelines for deciding whether objects or events belong to a concept class. For example, a triangle must be a closed shape with three sides made of straight lines. Trying to develop rules for concepts won't always work, though—for example, it's unlikely that memorizing rules would allow a new listener to accurately categorize *rhythm and blues*, *hip-hop*, *rock*, *salsa*, *reggae*, *country*, and *rap* music. Clearly, while rules are an efficient way to learn concepts, concrete examples remain important.

● **Figure 8.5 Identifying prototypes.** When does a cup become a bowl or a vase? Deciding if an object belongs to a conceptual class is aided by relating it to a prototype, or ideal example. Participants in one experiment chose number 5 as the "best" cup. (After Labov, 1973.)

To get a sense of the importance of concrete examples in learning about concepts, consider what happens when you think about the concept *bird*. Do you mentally list the features of birds? Probably not. In addition to rules and features, we might use a **prototype**, or a concrete example of an "ideal model," to identify concepts (Rosch, 1977; Tunney & Fernie, 2012). A robin, for example, is a prototypical bird; an ostrich is not. In other words, some things are better examples of a concept than others (Smith, 2013). Now it's your turn: Which of the drawings in ● Figure 8.5 best represents a cup? At some point, as a cup grows taller or wider, it becomes a vase or a bowl. How do we know when the line is crossed? Probably, we mentally compare objects to an "ideal" cup, like number 5. That's why it's hard to identify concepts when we can't come up with relevant prototypes—we have nothing to use as a comparison (Minda & Smith, 2011).

Faulty Concepts

One of the challenges associated with concepts relates to the fact that they do not always accurately reflect reality. Using such faulty concepts often leads to thinking errors. For example, *social stereotypes* are oversimplified concepts of groups of people that do not properly account for the diversity of people within that category (Le Pelley et al., 2010). (■ Stereotypes have a major impact on social behavior and frequently contribute to prejudice and discrimination. See Section 17.3 for more information.) A related problem is all-or-nothing thinking (one-dimensional thought). In this case, we classify things as absolutely right or wrong, good or bad, fair or unfair, black or white, honest or dishonest. Thinking this way prevents us from appreciating the subtleties of most of the problems we'll confront in everyday life (Alberts, Thewissen, & Raes, 2012).

Concept Mental category for classifying things based on common features or properties.

Prototype An ideal model used as a prime example of a particular concept.

Michelangelo Gratton/Shutterstock.com

Wine tasting illustrates the encoding function of language. To communicate their experiences to others, wine connoisseurs must put taste sensations into words. The wine you see here is "Marked by deeply concentrated nuances of plum, blackberry, and currant, with a nice balance of tannins and acid, building to a spicy oak finish." (Don't try this with a soda!)

Language

As we have seen, thinking may occur without **language**. Everyone has searched for a word to express an idea that exists as a vague image or feeling. Nevertheless, most thinking relies heavily on language, because words *encode* (translate) the world into symbols that are easy to manipulate.

The Structure of Language

What does it take to make a language? First, a language must provide *symbols* that stand for objects and ideas (Harley, 2014). The symbols we call words are built out of **phonemes** (FOE-neems), basic speech sounds; and **morphemes** (MOR-feems), speech sounds collected into meaningful units, such as syllables. For instance, in English, the sounds *m*, *b*, *w*, and *a* cannot form the syllable *mbwa*. In Swahili, they can. (Also see ● Figure 8.6.)

Next, a language must have a **grammar**, or set of rules for making sounds into words and words into sentences (Reed, 2013). One part of grammar, known as **syntax**, concerns rules for word order. Syntax is important because rearranging words almost always changes the meaning of a sentence: Consider the difference between "Dog bites man" versus "Man bites dog."

John Mitterer

Albanian	mak, mak
Chinese	gua, gua
Dutch	rap, rap
English	quack, quack
French	coin, coin
Italian	qua, qua
Spanish	cuá, cuá
Swedish	kvack, kvack
Turkish	vak, vak

● **Figure 8.6 "Vak, Vak."** Animals around the world make pretty much the same sounds. Notice, however, how various languages use slightly different morphemes to express the sound that a duck makes.

Traditional grammar is concerned with "surface" language—the sentences we actually speak. In contrast, linguist Noam Chomsky has focused on the *un*spoken rules that we use to change core ideas into various sentences. Chomsky (1986) believes that we do not learn all the sentences we might ever say. Rather, we actively *produce* them by applying **transformation rules** to universal, core patterns. We use these rules to change a simple declarative sentence to other voices or forms (past tense, passive voice, and so forth). For example, the core sentence "Man rides horse" can be transformed to these patterns (and others):

Past: The man rode the horse.
Passive: The horse was ridden by the man.
Negative: The man did not ride the horse.
Question: Did the man ride the horse?

Children seem to be using transformation rules when they say things such as "I runned home." That is, the child applied the normal past tense rule (added "ed" to the end of the word) to the irregular verb *to run*.

A true language is, therefore, *productive*—it can generate new thoughts or ideas. In fact, words can be rearranged to produce a nearly infinite number of sentences. Some are silly: "Please don't feed me to the chipmunk." Some are profound: "We hold these truths to be self-evident, that all men are created equal." In either case, the productive quality of language makes it a powerful tool for thinking.

Semantics

The study of meaning in words and language is known as **semantics** (Youn et al., 2016). It is here that the link between language and thought becomes most evident. Generally speaking, words have two types of meaning. The **denotative meaning** of words is their exact, or dictionary, definition. The **connotative meaning** is the emotional or personal meaning of words. The denotative meaning of the word *naked* (having no clothes) is the same for a nudist as it is for a movie censor, but we could expect their connotations to differ.

Connotative meaning can be measured with a technique called the *semantic differential*, as shown in ● Figure 8.7. When we rate words or concepts, most of their connotative meaning boils down to the dimensions *good/bad*, *strong/weak*, and *active/passive*. A good example comes from the following three words that have very different connotations, even though their denotative meanings are similar: We are *conscientious*, she is *careful*, and he is *nitpicky*! (We know this because we are conscientious—not nitpicky, right?)

Connotative differences can influence how we think about issues. Would you rather eat *rare prime beef* or *bloody slab of dead cow*? The arts of *political spin* and *propaganda* often amount to manipulating connotations (Aly et al., 2017; Sussman, 2011). For example, as a combatant in a war, would you rather be described as a *terrorist* or a *freedom fighter* (Payne, 2009)?

Semantics and Context

Word meanings also depend on context. To see what we mean by that, circle the word that does not belong in this series:

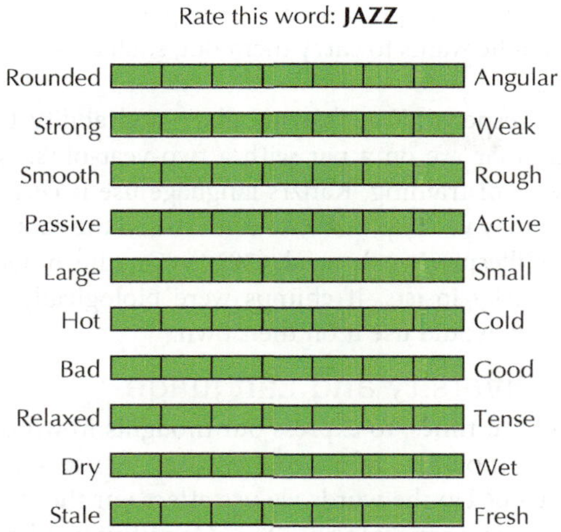

Figure 8.7 Osgood's semantic differential. Osgood's semantic differential. The connotative meaning of the word *jazz* can be established by rating it on the scales. Mark your own rating by placing dots or *X*'s in the spaces. Connect the marks with a line; then, have a friend rate the word and compare your responses. It might be interesting to do the same for *rock and roll, classical,* and *hip-hop.* You also might want to try the word *psychology.* (Adapted from Osgood, 1952.)

SKYSCRAPER CATHEDRAL TEMPLE PRAYER

If you circled *prayer,* you answered as most people do. Now try again to circle the odd item:

CATHEDRAL PRAYER TEMPLE SKYSCRAPER

Did you circle *skyscraper* this time? The new order subtly alters the meaning of the last word. This occurs because words get much of their meaning from *context.* For example, the word *shot* means different things depending on whether we are thinking of marksmanship, bartending, medicine, photography, or golf (Harley, 2014).

Language also plays a major role in defining ethnic communities and other social groups. Thus, language can be a bridge or a barrier between cultures. Translating languages can cause a rash of semantic problems. Perhaps a hotel in Acapulco, Mexico, can be excused for attempting to reassure tourists that their water is safe to drink by posting a sign reading, "The Manager Has Personally Passed All the Water Served Here." However, in more important situations, such as in international business and diplomacy, avoiding semantic confusion may be vital.

Alternative Languages

Contrary to commonsense belief, language is not limited to speech and text, nor is it restricted to humans. In this section, we explore gestural languages such as American Sign Language and animals' use of language.

Gestural Languages

Take a moment to consider the case of Ildefonso, a young man who was born deaf. At age 8, Ildefonso had never communicated with another human, except by mime. Then, at last, Ildefonso had a breakthrough: after much hard work with a sign language teacher, he understood the link between a cat and the gesture for it. At that magic moment, he grasped the idea that "cat" could be communicated to another person, just by signing the word.

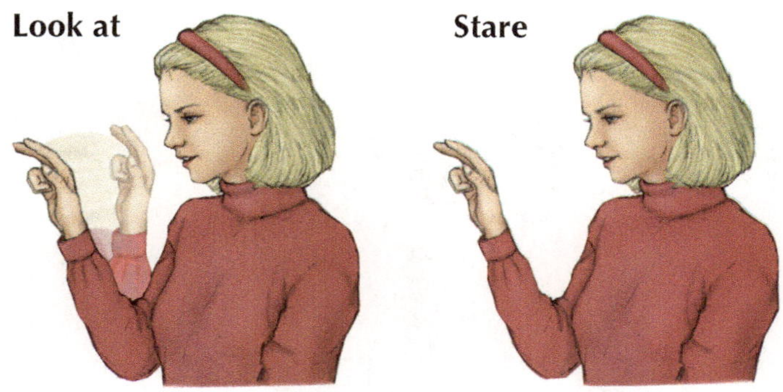

Figure 8.8 American Sign Language. ASL has only 3,000 root signs, compared with roughly 600,000 words in English. However, variations in signs make ASL a highly expressive language. For example, the sign LOOK-AT can be varied in ways to make it mean "look at me," "look at her," "look at each," "stare at," "gaze," "watch," "look for a long time," "look at again and again," "reminisce," "sightsee," "look forward to," "predict," "anticipate," "browse," and many more variations.

American Sign Language (ASL), a gestural language, made Ildefonso's breakthrough possible. ASL is a true language, like German, Spanish, or Japanese (Liddell, 2003; Shaw & Delaporte, 2011). In fact, people who use other gestural languages, such as French Sign, Mexican Sign, or Old Kentish Sign, may not easily understand ASL (Lucas & Bayley, 2011).

Although ASL has a *spatial* grammar, syntax, and semantics all of its own (Figure 8.8), both speech and signing follow similar universal language patterns. Signing children pass through the stages of language development at about the same age as speaking children. Some psychologists now believe that speech evolved from gestures, far back in human and primate history (Gillespie-Lynch et al., 2014; Kendon, 2016). Do you ever make hand gestures when you are speaking on the phone? If so, you may

Language Words or symbols, and rules for combining them, that are used for thinking and communication.

Phonemes Basic speech sounds of a language.

Morphemes Smallest meaningful units in a language, such as syllables or words.

Grammar A set of rules for combining language units into meaningful speech or writing.

Syntax Rules for ordering words when forming sentences.

Transformation rules Rules by which a simple declarative sentence may be changed to other voices or forms (past tense, passive voice, and so forth).

Semantics The study of meanings in words and language.

Denotative meaning The exact, dictionary definition of a word or concept; its objective meaning.

Connotative meaning The subjective, personal, or emotional meaning of a word or concept.

Infants can express the idea "pick me up" in gestures before they can make the same request in words. Their progression from gestures to speech may mirror the evolution of human language abilities (Genty et al., 2009).

be displaying a remnant of the gestural origins of language. Perhaps that's also why the same brain areas become more active when a person speaks or signs (Enrici et al., 2011).

Sign languages naturally arise out of a need to communicate visually. But they also embody a personal identity and define a distinct community. Those who "speak" sign share not just a language but a rich culture as well (West & Sutton-Spence, 2012).

Animal Language

Do animals use language? Animals in the wild definitely communicate. The cries, gestures, and mating calls of animals have broad meanings immediately understood by other animals of the same species (Bradbury & Vehrencamp, 2011). For the most part, however, natural animal communication is quite limited. Even apes and monkeys make only a few dozen distinct cries, which carry messages such as "attack," "flee," or "food here." More important, animal communication lacks the productive quality of human language. For example, when a monkey gives an "eagle distress call," it always means something like, "I see an eagle." The monkey has no way of saying, "I don't see an eagle," or "Thank heavens that wasn't an eagle," or "That sucker I saw yesterday was some huge eagle" (Pinker & Jackendoff, 2005).

What about trying to teach language to animals? To this point, numerous chimps and gorillas, as well as an assortment of dolphins, sea lions, and parrots, have been taught to communicate with word symbols of various kinds (Pepperberg, 2016). The "champion" is probably a pygmy chimpanzee named Kanzi, who was taught to communicate by pushing buttons on a computer keyboard. Researchers Duane Rumbaugh and Sue Savage-Rumbaugh marked each of the 250 buttons with a *lexigram*, or geometric word-symbol. Some of the lexigrams that Kanzi has learned are quite abstract, like symbols for "bad" and "good" (Lyn, Franks, & Savage-Rumbaugh, 2008). Using the lexigrams, Kanzi can create primitive sentences several words long. He also can understand about 650 spoken sentences.

Kanzi's sentences consistently follow correct word order. Like a child learning language, Kanzi picked up some rules from his caregivers (Segerdahl, Fields, & Savage-Rumbaugh, 2005). However, he has developed other patterns on his own (Gillespie-Lynch et al., 2011). For example, Kanzi usually places action symbols in the order that he wants to carry them out, such as "chase tickle" or "chase hide."

In these respects, Kanzi's vocabulary and ability to invent a simple grammar are on a par with a two-year-old's. After more than 30 years of training, Kanzi's language use is certainly noteworthy and may yet help us better understand the roots of human language (Gillespie-Lynch et al., 2014). On the other hand, as Noam Chomsky insists, if chimps were biologically capable of language, they would use it on their own.

Human Diversity and Language

Our struggle, at times, to express our thoughts in words makes it clear that our thoughts influence the words we use. But might the reverse be true? Do the words we use affect our thoughts and actions? The answer appears to be "Yes." Cognitive psychologist Lera Boroditsky has reported that aboriginal children from Cape York, a remote part of northeastern Australia, can accurately point to any compass direction as early as age 5. In contrast, most Americans cannot do this even as adults (Boroditsky, 2011).

But why? According to Boroditsky, unlike English, Kuuk Thaayorre, the language of the Cape York Australian aboriginals, relies exclusively on *absolute* directional references. Like English, Kuuk Thaayorre has words for *north*, *south*, and so on. Unlike English, Kuuk Thaayorre lacks words for *relative* directional references, such as *left* and *right*.

For long distances, an English speaker might say, "Chicago is north of here." But for short distances, the same speaker will shift to a relative reference and might say, "My brother is sitting to my right." In contrast, a speaker of Kuuk Thaayorre always uses absolute directional references, saying things like "My friend is sitting southeast of me" and "The spoon is west of the cup."

Another interesting consequence for speakers of Kuuk Thaayorre is how they arrange time. In one study, English speakers given a set of cards depicting a series of events (for example, a person getting older or a meal being cooked and eaten) and asked to put them in

Kanzi's language learning has been impressive. He can comprehend spoken English words. He can identify lexigram symbols when he hears corresponding words. He can use lexigrams when the objects to which they refer are absent, and he can, if asked, lead someone to the object. All these skills were acquired through observation, not conditioning (Segerdahl, Fields, & Savage-Rumbaugh, 2005).

order usually arranged them from left to right. Hebrew speakers usually arranged the cards from right to left, presumably because this is the direction in which Hebrew is written. In contrast, speakers of Kuuk Thaayorre arrange temporal sequences from east to west. If the sorter is facing north, the cards are arranged from right to left, but if the sorter is facing south, the cards are arranged from left to right, and so on (Boroditsky & Gaby, 2010).

Findings like these lend support to the **linguistic relativity hypothesis**, the idea that the words we use not only reflect our thoughts but can shape them as well (Lucy, 2016). So the next time you think that your future is "ahead" of you and your past is "behind," think again. For speakers of Aymara, a South American language, it is the past that is "ahead" (Miles et al., 2010).

Bilingualism

Wouldn't it be better to be able to speak more than one language? It would certainly reduce the likelihood of miscommunication across cultures if each of us could speak numerous languages. However, such abilities can bring personal benefits as well. Consider, for example, **bilingualism**, the ability to speak two languages. Though recent large-scale studies suggest that bilingualism is not directly associated with executive functions or other cognitive abilities (■ see Section 2.5), being able to speak another language may help with employment opportunities and expands on our opportunities to interact with other people (Nichols et al., 2020).

Unfortunately, millions of minority American children who do not speak English at home experience *subtractive bilingualism.* Immersed in English-only classrooms, in which they are expected to "sink or swim," they usually end up losing some of their native language skills. Such children risk becoming less than fully competent in *both* their first and second languages. In addition, they tend to fall behind educationally. As they struggle with English, their grasp of arithmetic, social studies, science, and other subjects also may suffer. In short, English-only instruction can leave them poorly prepared to succeed in the majority culture (Durán, Roseth, & Hoffman, 2010; Matthews & Matthews, 2004).

For the majority of children who speak English at home, the picture can be quite different because learning a second language is almost always beneficial and poses no threat to the child's home language. This has been called *additive bilingualism* because learning a second language adds to a child's overall competence (Hermanto, Moreno, & Bialystok, 2012).

Reflective Practice

The Basic Units of Cognition: Mental Imagery, Concepts, and Language

1. Reflective processing is automatic and effortless. T or F?
2. Our reliance on imagery in thinking means that problem solving is impaired by the use of language or symbols. T or F?
3. Humans can form three-dimensional images that can be moved or rotated in mental space. T or F?
4. Stereotyping is an example of oversimplification in thinking. T or F?
5. True languages are ____________ because they can be used to generate new possibilities.
6. The basic speech sounds are called ____________; the smallest meaningful units of speech are called ____________.
7. Noam Chomsky believes that we can create an infinite variety of sentences by applying ____________ to universal language patterns.

THINK CRITICALLY

8. A Democrat and a Republican are asked to rate the word *democratic* on the semantic differential. Under what conditions would their ratings be most alike?

SELF-REFLECT

- Name some ways that you have used imagery in the thinking that you have done today.
- Just for fun, see if you can illustrate the productive quality of language by creating a sentence that no one has ever before spoken.

Answers: 1. F 2. F 3. T 4. T 5. productive 6. phonemes, morphemes 7. transformation rules 8. If they both assume that the word refers to a form of government, not a political party or a candidate.

8.2 Problem Solving

GATEWAYS LEARNING OUTCOMES:
After reading this section you should be able to:

8.2.1 Distinguish between four methods of problem solving: algorithms, understanding, heuristics, and insight

8.2.2 Outline the barriers that can interfere with problem solving

8.2.3 Compare the problem solving of experts and novices

We all solve problems every day. Problem solving can be as commonplace as figuring out how to make a nonpoisonous meal out of leftovers or as significant as developing a cure for cancer. How do we solve such problems? A good way to start is to solve a problem. Give this one a try:

> Santiago got the surprise of his life. He had anchored his little motorboat 10 miles from an island and gone snorkeling. He returned to the boat, only to discover that two seals had settled in for a quick nap. He climbed into his boat and immediately began to cruise toward the island at 7 miles per hour. Just then the two

Linguistic relativity hypothesis The idea that the words we use not only reflect our thoughts but can shape them as well.

Bilingualism The ability to speak two languages.

seals woke up, indignantly jumped into the water, and also swam toward the island. At the same instant, Santiago's friend left the island in a sailboat at 3 miles per hour, coming out to rendezvous with the motorboat. The seals swam back and forth between the motorboat and sailboat at a speed of 12 miles per hour. How far will the seals have swum when the two boats meet?

If you didn't immediately see the answer to this problem, try it again. (The answer is revealed in the "Insight" section later in this chapter.)

Methods of Problem Solving

No matter what form a problem takes, it is usually best faced *mindfully* (Hayes, Strosahl, & Wilson, 2012). However, there are a number of methods that people can use to successfully solve problems. In the sections that follow we'll outline four of them: algorithms, understanding, heuristics, and insight.

Algorithms

For routine problems, an **algorithmic solution**—achieved by following a series of step-by-step rules—may be enough to solve the problem (Goldstein, 2015). A simple example of an *algorithm* is the steps that you used to add up the numbers in Figure 8.1 (whether you did it in your head or by using a calculator). Here's another example: if you forget the combination to your bike lock, you will be able to discover it if you systematically try all the possible combinations (this could take some time, though …).

Algorithmic thinking is an example of **logical thought**—proceeding from given information to new conclusions on the basis of *explicit rules*. To this, we can add that logical thought may be **inductive thought**—going from specific facts or observations to general principles—or **deductive thought**—going from general principles to specific situations. Becoming a problem-solving expert in any particular field involves, at a minimum, becoming familiar with the algorithms available in that field. If you have a good background in math, you may have found an algorithmic solution to the problem of the seals and the boats. (We hope you didn't. There is an easier solution.)

Understanding

Many problems cannot be solved algorithmically. In such cases, **understanding** (deeper comprehension of a problem) is necessary. Try this problem:

> A person has an inoperable stomach tumor. A device is available that produces rays that at high intensity will destroy tissue (both healthy and diseased). How can the tumor be destroyed while minimizing damage to the surrounding tissue? (Also see the sketch in Figure 8.9.)

German psychologist Karl Duncker gave college students this problem in a classic series of studies. Duncker asked them to think aloud as they worked. He found that successful students first had to discover the general properties of a correct solution. A **general solution** defines the requirements for success but not in enough detail to guide further action. This phase was complete when students realized that the intensity of the rays had to be lowered on their way to the tumor. Then, in the second phase, they proposed a number of **functional solutions**, or workable solutions, and selected the best one (Duncker, 1945). (One solution is to focus weak rays on the tumor from several angles. Another is to rotate the person's body to minimize exposure of healthy tissue.)

Heuristics

Imagine that you are traveling to Washington, DC, and decide to look up an old FBI friend, Penelope Garcia. You search an online directory and find dozens of P. Garcias listed. Of course, you could follow an algorithm such as dialing each number in alphabetical order until you found the right one.

Alternatively, you could use a **heuristic** (hew-RIS-tik)—a shortcut or "rule of thumb" for finding a solution to a problem. Typically, a heuristic *reduces the number of alternatives* that thinkers must consider (Benjafield, Smilek, & Kingstone, 2010). You could, for example, simplify the problem of looking up Penelope by randomly choosing just a few, plausible-looking entries. In this case, you would be using a **random search strategy**. This is an example of trial-and-error thinking in which some possibilities are tried, more or less randomly. "Forget it," you say to yourself. "Is there a better way I can narrow the search?" "Oh, yeah! I remember hearing that Penelope lives near work." Then you Google a map and call only the numbers with addresses in southern Washington, nearer to Quantico.

Here's another example. Amateur naturalists usually begin painfully identifying the birds, butterflies, mammals, and plants they find by mechanically (i.e., by rote) searching through published field guides until they find the correct species name and description. In time, those who persist begin to identify more and more

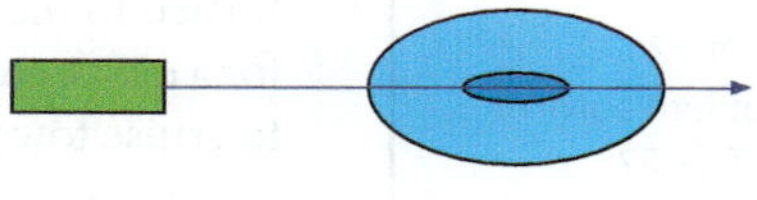

Figure 8.9 The tumor problem. A schematic representation of Duncker's tumor problem. The dark spot represents a tumor surrounded by healthy tissue. How can the tumor be destroyed without injuring surrounding tissue? (Adapted from Duncker, 1945.)

Water lilies

Problem: Water lilies growing in a pond double in area every 24 hours. On the first day of spring, only one lily pad is on the surface of the pond. Sixty days later, the pond is entirely covered. On what day is the pond half-covered?

Twenty dollars

Problem: Jessica and Blair both have the same amount of money. How much must Jessica give Blair so that Blair has $20 more than Jessica?

How many pets?

Problem: How many pets do you have if all of them are birds except two, all of them are cats except two, and all of them are dogs except two?

Between 2 and 3

Problem: What one mathematical symbol can you place between 2 and 3 that results in a number greater than 2 and less than 3?

One word

Problem: Rearrange the letters NEWDOOR to make one word.

● **Figure 8.10 Some insight problems.**

species from memory and others based on the general properties that they have learned through experience. With enough practice, this is exactly how novices become experts in a wide variety of fields.

Expert problems solvers are good at using heuristic strategies like these:

- Try to identify how the current state of affairs differs from the desired goal. Then find steps that will reduce the difference.
- Try working backward from the desired goal to the starting point or current state.
- If you can't reach the goal directly, try to identify an intermediate goal or subproblem that at least gets you closer.
- Represent the problem in other ways—with graphs, diagrams, or analogies, for instance.
- Generate a possible solution and test it. Doing so may eliminate many alternatives, or it may clarify what is needed for a solution.

One important point to remember about heuristics, though, is that although they raise the odds of success, they do not guarantee a solution.

Insight

A thinker who suddenly solves a problem has experienced **insight** (Cushen & Wiley, 2012). Insights are usually based on reorganizing a problem. This allows us to see problems in new ways and makes their solutions seem obvious (Hélie & Sun, 2010).

Let's return now to the problem of the boats and the seals that was outlined earlier. The best way to solve it is by insight. Because the boats will cover the 10-mile distance in exactly one hour, and the seals swim 12 miles per hour, the seals will have swum 12 miles when the boats meet. Very little math is necessary if you have insight into this problem. ● Figure 8.10 lists some additional insight problems that you may want to try (the answers can be found in ▲ Table 8.1).

▲ Table 8.1 Solutions to Insight Problems

Water lilies:	Day 59
Twenty dollars:	$10
How many pets?:	Three (one bird, one cat, and one dog)
Between 2 and 3:	A decimal point
One word:	ONE WORD (You may object that the answer is two words, but the problem called for the answer to be "one word," and it is.)

Algorithmic solution A problem solution achieved by following a series of step-by-step rules.

Logical thought Drawing conclusions on the basis of formal principles of reasoning.

Inductive thought Thinking in which a general rule or principle is gathered from a series of specific examples; for instance, inferring the laws of gravity by observing many falling objects.

Deductive thought Thought that applies a general set of rules to specific situations; for example, using the laws of gravity to predict the behavior of a single falling object.

Understanding (in problem solving) A deeper comprehension of the nature of a problem.

General solution A solution that correctly states the requirements for success, but not in enough detail for further action.

Functional solution A detailed, practical, and workable solution.

Heuristic Shortcut or rule of thumb for finding a solution to a problem.

Random search strategy Trying possible solutions to a problem in a more or less random order.

Insight A sudden mental reorganization of a problem that makes the solution obvious.

Psychologist Janet Davidson (2003) believes that insight involves three abilities. The first is *selective encoding*, which refers to selecting information that is relevant to a problem while ignoring distractions. For example, consider the following problem:

> If you have white socks and black socks in your drawer, mixed in the ratio of 4 to 5, how many socks will you have to take out to ensure that you have a pair of the same color?

A person who recognizes that "mixed in a ratio of 4 to 5" is irrelevant will be more likely to come up with the correct answer of three socks.

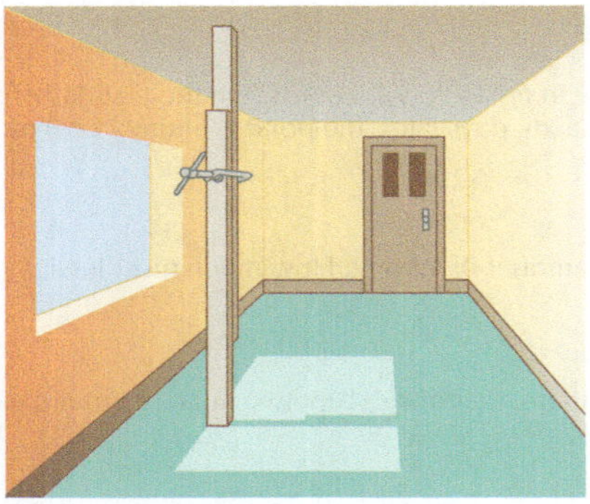

Figure 8.11 A solution to the hat rack problem.

Second, insight relies on *selective combination,* or bringing together seemingly unrelated bits of useful information. Try this sample problem:

> With a 7-minute hourglass and an 11-minute hourglass, what is the simplest way to time boiling an egg for 15 minutes?

The answer requires using both hourglasses in combination. First, the 7-minute and the 11-minute hourglasses are started. When the 7-minute hourglass runs out, it's time to begin boiling the egg. At this point, 4 minutes remain on the 11-minute hourglass. Thus, when it runs out, it is simply turned over. When it runs out again, 15 minutes will have passed.

A third source of insights is *selective comparison*. This is the ability to compare new problems with old information or with problems already solved. A good example is the hat rack problem, in which participants must build a structure that can support an overcoat in the middle of a room. Each person is given only two long sticks and a C-clamp to work with. The solution, shown in Figure 8.11, is to clamp the two sticks together so that they are wedged between the floor and ceiling. If you were given this problem, you would be more likely to solve it if you first thought of how pole lamps are wedged between floor and ceiling.

Human Diversity and Insight

The culture that we grow up in affects our ability to use selective comparison to solve problems. See if you can solve this problem:

> A treasure hunter wanted to explore a cave, but he was afraid that he might get lost. Obviously, he did not have a map of the cave; all that he had with him were some common items such as a flashlight and a bag. What could he do to make sure he did not get lost trying to get back out of the cave later? (Adapted from Chen, Mo, & Honomichl, 2004.)

To solve his problem, the man could leave a trail of small objects, such as pebbles or sand, while traveling through the cave, and then follow this trail out to exit.

A total of 75 percent of American college students, but only 25 percent of Chinese students, were able to solve the cave problem. Why was there such a difference in the two groups? It seems that American students benefited from having heard the story of Hansel and Gretel when they were growing up. As you may recall, Hansel and Gretel were able to find their way out of the woods because Hansel made a trail of pebbles that led back home (Chen, Mo, & Honomichl, 2004).

Now try this problem:

> In a village by a river, the chief of a tribe guards a sacred stone statue. Every year, the chief goes downriver to the next village to collect taxes. There, he places the statue in a tub at one end of a hanging balance. To pay their taxes, the villagers have to fill a tub at the other end of the scale with gold coins until the scale balances. This year, the chief forgot to bring his balance scale. How can he figure out how much gold to collect to match the statue's weight? (Adapted from Chen, Mo, & Honomichl, 2004.)

To solve this problem, the chief could put a tub in the river, and place the statue in the tub. Then he could mark the water level on the outside of the tub. To pay their taxes, the villagers would have to put gold coins in the tub until it sank to the same level as it did when the statue was in it.

With this problem, 69 percent of Chinese students, but only 8 percent of American students, were able to solve it. Again, it seems that being exposed to a similar problem in the past was helpful. Most Chinese are familiar with a traditional tale about weighing an elephant that is too big to put on a scale. In the story, the elephant is placed in a boat and the water level is marked. After the elephant is removed, the boat is filled with small stones until the water again reaches the mark. Then, each of the stones is weighed on a small scale and the total weight of the elephant is calculated (Chen, Mo, & Honomichl, 2004).

Every culture prepares its members to solve some types of problems more easily than others (Boroditsky, 2011). As a result, learning about other cultures can make us more flexible and resourceful thinkers—and that's no fairy tale.

Barriers to Problem Solving

Just as there are many methods to solve problems, there are also numerous factors that can interfere with successful problem solving. Let's take a closer look at some of them.

Fixations

One of the most important barriers to problem solving is **fixation**, or the tendency to get "hung up" on wrong solutions or to become blind to alternatives (Sternberg, 2017). This usually occurs when, without giving it any thought, we place unnecessary restrictions on our thinking (McCaffrey, 2012). How, for example, could you plant four small trees so that each is an equal distance from all the others? (The answer is shown in Figure 8.12.)

A prime example of restricted thinking is **functional fixedness**, a tendency to perceive an item only in terms of its most common use (Bernstein & Lucas, 2008). If you have ever used a dime as a screwdriver, you've overcome functional fixedness.

Figure 8.12 The four trees problem. Four trees can be placed equidistant from one another by piling dirt into a mound. Three of the trees are planted equal distances apart around the base of the mound. The fourth tree is planted on the top of the mound. If you were fixated on arrangements that involve level ground, you may have been blind to this three-dimensional solution.

How does functional fixedness affect problem solving? Karl Duncker once asked students to mount a candle on a vertical board so that the candle could burn normally. He gave each student three candles, some matches, some cardboard boxes, some thumbtacks, and other items. Half of Duncker's participants received these items *inside* the cardboard boxes. The others were given all the items, including the boxes, spread out on a tabletop.

Duncker found that when the items were in the boxes, solving the problem was very difficult. Why? If students saw the boxes as *containers*, they didn't realize the boxes might be part of the solution (if you haven't guessed the solution, check Figure 8.13). Undoubtedly, we could avoid many fixations by being more flexible in categorizing

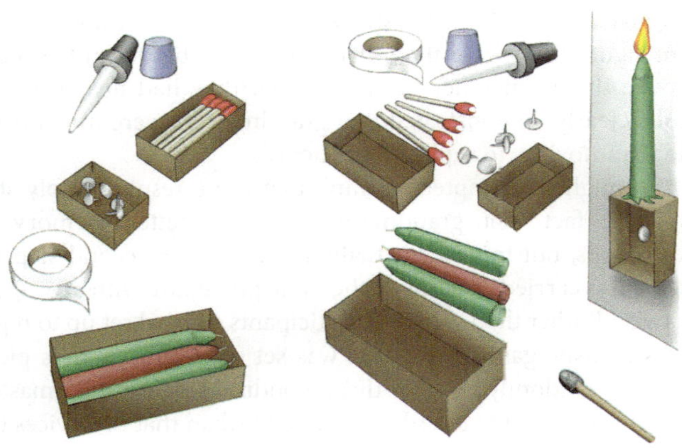

Figure 8.13 The candle problem. Materials for solving the candle problem were given to participants in boxes (*a*) or separately (*b*). Functional fixedness caused by condition (*a*) interfered with solving the problem. The solution to the problem is shown in (*c*).

the world (Kalyuga & Hanham, 2011; McCaffrey, 2012). For instance, creative thinking could be facilitated in the container problem by saying "This *could be* a box," instead of "This *is* a box."

When tested with the candle problem, five-year-old children show no signs of functional fixedness. Apparently, this is because they have had less experience with the use of various objects. It is sometimes said that to be more creative, you should try to see the world without preconceptions, as if through the eyes of a child. In the case of functional fixedness, that may be true (German & Defeyter, 2000).

Other Common Barriers to Problem Solving

Functional fixedness is just one of the mental blocks that prevent insight (Reed, 2013). Here's an example of another: A $5 bill is placed on a table and a stack of objects is balanced precariously on top of the bill. How can the bill be removed without touching, moving, or toppling the objects? A good answer is to split the bill on one of its sides. Gently pulling from opposite ends will tear the bill in half and remove it without toppling the objects. Many people fail to see this solution because they have learned not to destroy money (Adams, 2001). Notice again the impact of placing something in a category—in this case, "things of value" (which should not be destroyed). Other common mental blocks can hinder problem solving:

1. **Emotional barriers:** Inhibition and fear of making a fool of oneself, fear of making a mistake, inability to tolerate ambiguity, excessive self-criticism

   Example: An architect doesn't try an unconventional design because she fears that other architects will think it is frivolous.

2. **Cultural barriers:** Values that hold that fantasy is a waste of time; that playfulness is for children only; that reason, logic, and numbers are good; that feelings, intuitions, pleasure, and humor are bad or have no value in the serious business of problem solving

   Example: A corporate manager wants to solve a business problem but becomes stern and angry when members of his marketing team joke playfully about possible solutions.

3. **Learned barriers:** Conventions about uses (functional fixedness), meanings, possibilities, taboos

   Example: A cook doesn't have any clean mixing bowls and fails to see that she could use a pot as a bowl.

4. **Perceptual barriers:** Habits leading to a failure to identify important elements of a problem

   Example: A beginning artist concentrates on drawing a vase of flowers without seeing that the "empty" spaces around the vase are part of the composition, too.

Fixation (in problem solving) The tendency to repeat wrong solutions or faulty responses, especially as a result of becoming blind to alternatives.

Functional fixedness Tendency to perceive an item only in terms of its most common use.

The Problem Solving of Experts Versus Novices

It's probably not surprising that experts can typically generate solutions to a problem much more quickly than novices and that they are better able to come up with solutions to problems that are slightly outside the boundaries of their expertise. How does expertise help to explain these differences in problem solving?

You might think that experts just exhibit very different cognitive processes than novices, but this doesn't seem to be the case (Willingham & Riener, 2019). Instead, an important key to experts' superior performance seems to reside in the amount of prior knowledge held in their long-term memory, and the way that knowledge is organized (see Section 7.3 for a discussion of the importance of prior knowledge). Let's take a look at each of these.

Differences in Amount of Prior Knowledge

To understand why having a great deal of prior knowledge is important to problem solving, let's start by looking at two problems:

> A woman has been given the responsibility of putting grass seed down on a football field. The field measures 300 yards long by 160 yards wide. She goes online to order the grass seed and sees that one large bag of seed will cover 10 square yards. How many bags does she need to seed the field?

> Students in a high school art class have decided to paint a large mural on the back wall of their gym. Before they can begin painting the mural, though, they need to paint the wall white. The wall measures 100 feet long by 18 feet high. A large bucket of white paint will cover 900 square feet and costs $100. How much money will they spend to paint the wall?

Researchers have noted that there are two key elements of any problem (Chi, Feltovich, & Glaser, 1981; Willingham, 2009). The first has been called the *surface structure* of a problem, and refers to the problem's superficial features. Here, the surface structure of the first problem would be football fields and grass seed; in the second it would be walls and paint. The second element is *deep structure*, which refers to the problem's fundamentals. If you look closely at the two problems above, you might notice that while their surface structure is quite different, the deep structure is the same. Stripping away the superficial surface features of the problems, people who have some experience with high school math will quickly recognize that solving both problems requires that you begin by calculating the area of a rectangle (the football field or the wall) to determine an amount that needs to be purchased (grass seed or paint).

It probably won't surprise you to know that while surface structure is always easy to see, deep structure typically is not (Gick & Holyoak, 1980). Our attention is often captured by the superficial aspects of a problem while its underlying fundamentals are harder to spot. However, as our understanding of a particular topic increases (that is, as prior knowledge accumulates), the ability to see a problem's deep structure improves considerably. Evidence for experts' ability to better recognize deep structure comes from a classic study carried out with novices (undergraduate physics students) and experts (physics graduate students and professors) (Chi et al., 1981). These participants read a series of physics problems and were asked to determine how to best sort them. The basis for the groupings of novices and experts showed important differences: Novices were clearly focused on the surface structure of the problems, typically sorting based on the objects pictured in the problem (e.g., springs, inclined planes, pulleys). In contrast, experts were much more likely to sort the problems using deep structure as a guide. Specifically, their categories focused on the laws of physics that were relevant to the solution (e.g., conservation of energy, Newton's second law), regardless of the objects that were described in the problem.

There are at least two helpful consequences that stem from experts' ability to see the deep structure of a problem (Willingham, 2009). The first is that a better understanding of a problem's fundamentals allows experts to focus on the most relevant aspects of the problem, ignoring details that are unlikely to be helpful. The second is that a good understanding of deep structure allows experts to *transfer* their knowledge; that is, they are better able to see fundamental similarities between problems that look different on the surface. Recognizing similarities in deep structure thus allows experts to recognize when solutions developed for one problem might effectively be used to manage another. Fixated on the more superficial elements of a problem, novices are unlikely to see how two problems that appear different on the surface are related, and how the solution to one might transfer to another.

Differences in Organization of Prior Knowledge

It makes sense that experts have more prior knowledge than novices in a particular area. However, research also suggests that this prior knowledge is organized differently in the long-term memories of experts as compared to novices. Consider the results of early research carried out by de Groot (1946/1978) and later replicated by Chase and Simon (1973). In these studies, chess grandmasters and novices were shown a chessboard with the pieces set up to represent the middle of a realistic game. The participants were given a few minutes to study the board before it was removed from sight. They were then given an empty board and asked to recreate the arrangement of pieces that they had just seen. The results clearly demonstrated that grandmasters were much better able than novices to replicate the board.

You might be tempted to think that these results simply stem from the fact that grandmasters have a better memory for chessboards, but this isn't actually the case. In a second step, the researchers carried out exactly the same procedure with an important twist: Rather than showing participants a board set up to represent a realistic game, the board was set up with the chess pieces arranged randomly. Under these conditions, the grandmasters' ability to recreate the board was no better than that of novices (see Figure 8.14).

How do we explain these findings? The answer seems to lie in the way that information is organized in long-term memory. Specifically, grandmasters' prior knowledge about the position of chess pieces appears to be organized in chunks that represent strategies regularly employed in a game (Willingham & Riener, 2019). When they look at a mid-game board, then, they

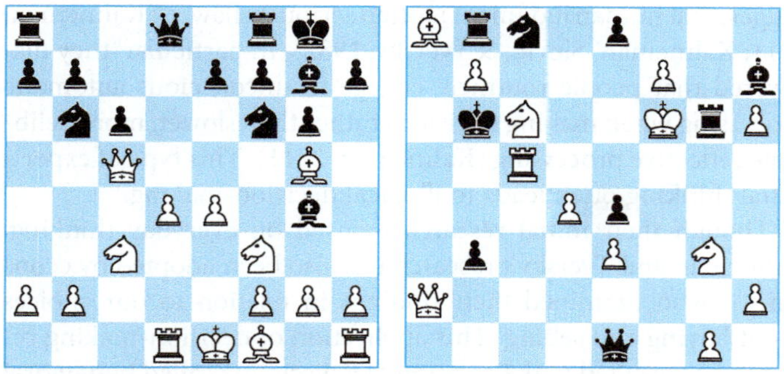

Figure 8.14 Memory for chess positions. The left chessboard shows a realistic game. The right chessboard is a random arrangement of pieces. Expert chess players can memorize the left board at a glance, yet they are no better than beginners at memorizing the random board (Ross, 2006). Expert performance at most thinking tasks is based on acquired strategies and knowledge. If you want to excel at a profession or a mental skill, plan on adding to your knowledge every day (Reed, 2013).

automatically take in clusters of pieces that form functional units that will impact a player's likelihood of winning. Put another way, what really sets experts apart is their ability to recognize how groups (or chunks) of pieces represent typical *patterns* in a game of chess (Gorman, Abernethy, & Farrow, 2013). (Remember from Section 7.2 that chunking single bits of information together like this allows people to draw more information back into the limited space of working memory where problem solving happens; Kalyuga, Renkl, & Paas, 2010).

This research also makes it clear that experts aren't consistently thinking reflectively. Instead, just the opposite seems to be true. Expertise involves lots of automatic processing, or fast, effortless thinking based on experience with similar problems. At the highest skill levels, experts' actions become rapid, fluid, and insightful (Hélie & Sun, 2010). Thus, when a chess master recognizes a pattern on the chessboard, the most desirable tactic comes to mind almost immediately.

The abilities displayed by experts come at a price of time and effort. Expert chess players can automatically recognize 50,000 to 100,000 patterns, a level of skill that takes about 10 years of mindful, reflective processing to build up (Ross, 2006). Throw into the mix that experts learn thousands of patterns and practice solving many problems and you can see that developing expertise involves years of hard work (Ericsson & Pool, 2016). Think about that the next time someone says of an expert, "She makes it look easy."

Reflective Practice

Problem Solving

1. Insight refers to rote, or trial-and-error, problem solving. T or F?
2. The first phase in problem solving by understanding is to discover the general properties of a correct solution. T or F?
3. Problem-solving strategies that guide the search for solutions are called ______________.
4. A common element underlying insight is that information is encoded, combined, and compared ______________.
   a. algorithmically
   b. by rote
   c. functionally
   d. selectively
5. Functional fixedness is a major barrier to ______________.
   a. insightful problem solving
   b. using random search strategies
   c. algorithmic problem solving
   d. achieving fixations through problem solving
6. Human expertise is characterized by a considerable amount of knowledge held in long-term memory. T or F?

THINK CRITICALLY

7. Do you think that it is true that "a problem clearly defined is a problem half solved"?
8. In captivity, white-handed gibbons (a type of ape) have been observed building swings to swing on. Does this qualify as thinking?

SELF-REFLECT

- Identify at least one problem that you have solved algorithmically. Now identify a problem that you solved by understanding. Did the second problem involve finding a general solution, a functional solution, or both? What heuristics did you use to solve the problem?
- Can you think of a time when you overcame functional fixedness to solve a problem?

Answers: 1. F 2. T 3. heuristics 4. d 5. a 6. T 7. Although this might be an overstatement, it is true that clearly defining a starting point and the desired goal can serve as a heuristic in problem solving. 8. It certainly involves tool use. Thinking also may be implicated because the actions appear to be planned with an awareness of likely results (Bentley-Condit & Smith, 2010).

8.3 Intuition, Decision-Making, and Cognitive Biases

GATEWAYS LEARNING OUTCOMES:
After reading this section you should be able to:

8.3.1 Distinguish between four common biases that can lead to errors in decision-making: framing, availability, representativeness, and ignoring the odds

8.3.2 Explain what is meant by choice overload

You don't have to be a genius to experience flashes of insight. In fact, most people frequently experience **intuition**—quick, impulsive thought that is connected to the automatic (or experiential) processing we discussed at the beginning of this chapter (Henry, Penner, & Eggly, 2016).

Intuition Quick, impulsive thought that does not use formal logic or clear reasoning.

For example, think back to your least favorite teacher. (Not your psychology instructor, of course!) How long did it take you to figure out that he or she wasn't going to make your list of star teachers? Psychologist Nalini Ambady once asked people to watch video clips of teachers they did not know. After watching three 10-second segments, participants were asked to rate the teachers. Amazingly, their ratings correlated highly with year-end course evaluations made by actual students (Ambady & Rosenthal, 1993). Ambady obtained the same result when she presented an even thinner "slice" of teaching behavior, just three 2-second clips. A mere 6 seconds is all that participants needed to form intuitive judgments of the instructors' teaching!

Malcolm Gladwell (2005) argues this is not a case of hurried irrationality. Instead, it is *thin-slicing*, or quickly making sense of thin slivers of experience. Such immediate, intuitive reactions are a testament to the power of the cognitive unconscious, which is a part of the brain that does automatic, experiential processing (Bar-Anan, Wilson, & Hassin, 2010; Wilson, 2004). Far from being irrational, intuition may be an important part of how we think (Ritter, van Baaren, & Dijksterhuis, 2012).

Sometimes, then, rapid intuitive judgments can be as accurate as more reflective, rational consideration. The trick, of course, is figuring out when thin-slicing can be trusted and when it can't. After all, first impressions aren't always right. Have you ever had a teacher you came to appreciate only after the course was over? In many circumstances, quick impressions are most valuable when you take the time to verify them through more reflective observation (Tom, Tong, & Hesse, 2010). Let's take a closer look at some of the ways in which intuition and experiential processing can lead us astray when we're making decisions.

Errors and Biases in Intuition and Decision-Making

Research suggests at least two factors that contribute to poor decision-making. The first is "hot cognition," or *thinking that is driven by emotions* (Lerner et al., 2015). Our emotional reactions to various possibilities can determine what intuitively seems to be the right answer. Emotions such as fear, hope, anxiety, liking, or disgust can either eliminate possibilities from consideration or promote them to the top of the list (Rolls, 2014).

For many people, choosing which political candidate to vote for is a good example of how emotions can cloud clear thinking. Rather than comparing candidates' records and policies, it is tempting to vote for the person we like rather than the person who is most qualified for the job. Indeed, it's also usually better to cool down a bit before deciding to pick that bar fight, running off and eloping, or immediately declining that daunting job offer (Johnson, Batey, & Holdsworth, 2009). Personal rituals such as counting to 10 or meditating for a moment can be calming in the moment, paving the way for more reflective consideration of the alternatives that are before you (Damisch, Stoberock, & Mussweiler, 2010).

A second factor that contributes to poor decision-making is rooted in the fact that *automatic processing can sometimes lead to irrational choices*. Two noted psychologists, Daniel Kahneman and Amos Tversky, have studied how we manage information and make decisions in the face of uncertainty. Their findings strongly suggest that human judgment is often seriously flawed (Kahneman, 2011; Kahneman, Slovic, & Tversky, 1982). In particular, they discovered that people routinely engage in unconscious automatic processing when making decisions rather than slower, more deliberate reflective processing (Kahneman, 2011). This type of experiential thinking often leads to illogical decision-making.

Though their initial research focused on everyday thinking, Kahneman and Tversky's research has also been adopted by economists, who examined their findings in relation to our choices about buying and selling. This application of decision-making research has resulted in the creation of a discipline called **behavioral economics** (Thaler & Ganser, 2015). Traditional economic theories assumed that decisions about buying and selling were based on a careful weighing of the available options. This very deliberate decision-making, they reasoned, should lead to rational and logical decisions that properly reflected costs and benefits. However, applying Kahneman and Tversky's findings, research by behavioral economists has made it clear that how we think about money, and our decisions about what to spend it on, are not rational at all (Thaler, 2016). Indeed, Kahneman received the Nobel Prize in economics in 2002 to recognize the contribution of this research to improving our understanding of consumer behavior.

Let's explore a few of Kahneman and Tversky's common decision-making errors so that you will be better prepared to avoid them. We'll focus on four: framing effects, availability, representativeness, and ignoring the odds.

Framing

The most general conclusion about intuition is that the way a problem is stated, or **framed**, affects decisions (Kahneman, 2011; Tversky & Kahneman, 1981). To gain some added insight into framing, try thinking about this problem:

A couple is divorcing. Both parents seek custody of their only child, but custody can be granted to just one parent. If you had to make a decision based on the following information, to which parent would you award custody of the child?

Parent A: Average income, average health, average working hours, reasonable rapport with the child, relatively stable social life

Parent B: Above-average income, minor health problems, lots of work-related travel, very close relationship with the child, extremely active social life

Most people choose to award custody to Parent B, the parent who has some drawbacks but also several advantages (such as above-average income). That's because people tend to look for *positive qualities* that can be *awarded* to the child.

However, who would you choose if you were asked this question: Given exactly the same characteristics, which parent should be denied custody? In this case, most people choose to deny custody to Parent B. Why is Parent B a good choice one moment and a poor choice the next? It's because the second question was framed differently than the first, asking who should be *denied* custody. To answer this question, people tend to look for *negative qualities* that would *disqualify* a parent. As you can see, the way a question is framed can channel us down a narrow path so that we attend to only part of the information provided, rather than reflectively weighing all the pros and cons.

Usually, the broadest way of framing or stating a problem produces the best decisions. However, people often state problems in increasingly narrow terms until a single, seemingly "obvious" answer emerges. For example, to select a career, it would be wise to consider pay, working conditions, job satisfaction, needed skills, future employment outlook, and many other factors. Instead, such decisions are often narrowed to thoughts such as, "I like to write, so I'll be a journalist," "I want to make good money and law pays well," or "I can be creative in photography." Framing decisions so narrowly greatly increases the risk of making a poor choice. If you would like to think more critically and analytically, it is important to pay attention to how you are defining—that is, framing—problems before you try to solve them. Remember that shortcuts to answers often short-circuit clear thinking.

Availability

If we were to ask you which is more frequent—gun-related homicides or gun-related suicides—what would you say? When faced with this question, most people would say homicides, and they would be wrong. In fact, suicides involving guns have exceeded homicides for more than two decades in the United States, and not by a small margin. Why, then, are so many people prone to estimate incorrectly? The answer lies in a decision-making bias called the **availability heuristic** (Braga et al., 2018; Schwarz et al., 1991). Essentially, when asked to estimate the likelihood or frequency of an event, we begin with a search of our long-term memory. If we can readily bring many instances of the event to mind, we assume that it must occur often and be quite likely.

Now you might be thinking that biases related to the availability heuristic probably don't matter much—after all, does anyone really care whether you know the statistics on gun violence? But consider another example, this one closer to home (literally). In a well-known study, couples were asked to estimate their contribution to household work, including things like taking out the garbage, cleaning the house, and caring for young children (Ross & Sicoly, 1979). Consistently, partners' estimates of their own contributions totaled more than 100%, while estimates of their partners' efforts were much less. Why would that be?

Using what we know about the availability heuristic, it seems likely that people in the study were very conscious of the work that they had done. As a result, instances of their own contributions to the household chores were quickly and easily retrieved from memory. Recalling situations in which the partners had done work, however, was likely more difficult (sometimes because they weren't always there to see it!). The lesson to take away, then, is that when you're involved with any sort of team it's always worth stepping back if you feel as though you're doing more than your fair share—chances are good that members of the team are doing work that you haven't noticed, and there's a reasonable chance that many of them are feeling just as overworked as you are!

Representativeness

Another common pitfall in decision-making is illustrated by Kahneman and Tversky's classic "Linda problem" (Tversky & Kahneman, 1983). Here is a short description of her:

> Linda is 31 years old, single, outspoken, and very bright. She majored in philosophy. As a student, she was deeply concerned with issues of discrimination and social justice, and also participated in antinuclear demonstrations.

Given what you know about Linda, which alternative is more probable?

A. Linda is a bank teller.

B. Linda is a bank teller and is active in the feminist movement.

People routinely see B as more probable than A, and the tendency to do so is a powerful one. According to Tversky and Kahneman (1982), this conclusion is based on the **representativeness heuristic**—that is, we tend to give a choice greater weight if it seems to be similar to what we already know. In this case, Linda certainly *seems* like she could be involved in the feminist movement—her actions are representative of other people we know who endorse feminism. Therefore, B might seem more likely than A, even though it logically can't be.

Consider now that this tendency to make a decision based on representativeness leads to completely illogical conclusions; namely, the intuitive answer B overlooks an important fact: The likelihood of two events occurring together (this *and* that) must be lower than the probability of either one alone. For example, the probability of getting one head when flipping a coin (one half, or 0.5) is higher than the probability of getting one head *and* another head, or two heads in a row (one fourth, or 0.25). Logically, then, A (Linda is a bank teller) must be more likely than B (Linda is a bank teller *and* she is active in the feminist movement).

When decision-making is unknowingly based on representativeness, the results can be disastrous. In courtrooms, for example, jurors are more likely to think that a defendant is guilty if the person appears to fit the profile of a person likely to commit a crime (Davis & Follette, 2002). For example, a young, single man from a poor neighborhood would be more likely to be judged guilty of theft than a middle-aged, married father from an affluent suburb.

Ignoring the Odds

Another common error in intuitive judgment involves ignoring the **base rate**, or underlying probability of an event. People in one experiment were told that they would be given descriptions of 100 people—70 lawyers and 30 engineers. Participants were then

behavioral economics a branch of economics that applies psychology to the study of economic decision-making

Framing In thought, the terms in which a problem is stated or the way that it is structured.

Availability heuristic Mental shortcut that relies on how quickly examples come to mind when evaluating a topic or making a decision.

Representativeness heuristic Mental shortcut of judging if something belongs in a given class based on similarity to other members.

Base rate The basic rate at which an event occurs over time; the basic probability of an event.

asked to guess, without knowing anything about a person, whether she or he was an engineer or a lawyer. All correctly stated the probabilities as 70 percent for lawyer and 30 percent for engineer. Participants were then given this description:

> Eric is a 30-year-old man. He is married with no children. A man of high ability and high motivation, he promises to be quite successful in his field. He is well liked by his colleagues.

Quickly now, what are the odds Eric is a lawyer or an engineer? Notice that the description gives no new information about Eric's occupation. He could still be either an engineer or a lawyer. Therefore, the odds should again be estimated as 70–30. However, most people changed the odds to 50–50. Intuitively, it seems that Eric has an equal chance of being either an engineer or a lawyer. But this guess completely ignores the underlying odds, or base rate.

Perhaps it is fortunate that we do ignore underlying odds at times. Were this not the case, how many people would get married in the face of a 50 percent divorce rate? Or how many would start high-risk businesses? On the other hand, people who smoke, drink and then drive, take drugs, or skip wearing seatbelts, ignore rather high odds of injury or illness. In many high-risk situations, ignoring base rates is the same as thinking that you are an exception to the rule (which is very rarely the case).

Decision-Making in Everyday Life: Choice Overload

More recently, psychology has also been applied to consumer decision-making in more everyday settings, including big-box retailers such as Costco. Specifically, researchers have begun to examine a phenomenon that is referred to as the *paradox of choice* (Schwartz, 2004). It's not uncommon, for example, to be standing in your local Starbucks and hear someone say, "Venti, double-shot, sugar-free, peppermint, nonfat, double-cupped, extra hot, please." Overhearing the order while standing in line, you can possibly imagine an older woman remarking to her husband, "Don't you miss the days when all you could order was a coffee with cream and sugar?" In response, a young man might whisper in his friend's ear, "Poor old people!" One stereotype of elderly people is that they have trouble coping with modern life that includes numerous options—after all, isn't the freedom of having a wide variety of choices a good thing (Leotti, Iyengar, & Ochsner, 2010)?

Maybe not. According to consumer psychologist Alexander Chernev (Chernev, Böckenholt, & Goodman, 2015), too much choice can lead to **choice overload**—difficulty making a decision in the face of many alternatives. In one study, for example, consumers were given an option to purchase jam. Half of them could choose from six different flavors; the other half had 24 flavors from which to choose. Although consumers with more choice expressed more interest, they were 10 times *less* likely to purchase *any* jam (Iyengar & Lepper, 2000). Similarly, restaurants with menus that feature a broader variety of choices often find that patrons are more likely to order from a smaller number of familiar choices (Soman, 2010). Apparently, businesses that increase the variety of their product offerings are not guaranteed increased sales (Gourville & Soman, 2005; Greifeneder, Scheibehenne, & Kleber, 2010).

A more recent overview of the research suggests that choice overload does not always occur—after all, there are lots of people who appreciate having dozens of different ways to order a coffee. The pressing question now is to establish the conditions under which having numerous options is helpful versus harmful to decision-making. While it may be faintly amusing that people have trouble exercising choice in a coffee shop, choice overload isn't at all funny when more important issues are involved, such as choosing the best medical procedure or selecting how to invest your retirement savings (Sethi-Iyengar, Huberman, & Jiang, 2004).

Why are more complex choices so tough to make? Researchers have identified a number of factors, such as the complexity of the set of choices, the difficulty of the decision task, uncertainty about one's preferences, and the goal of the decision (Chernev, Böckenholt, & Goodman, 2015). Although the growing complexity of modern life may increase our freedom, our choices may be expanding beyond our capacity to cope. It's OK to order a coffee with cream and sugar sometimes.

Reflective Practice

Intuition, Decision-Making, and Cognitive Biases

1. The tendency to judge the likelihood of an event based on how quickly you can bring similar instances to mind is called the
   a. representative heuristic
   b. availability heuristic
   c. similarity heuristic
   d. trial-and-error heuristic
2. Experiential processing refers to our tendency to think slowly and deliberately about information that we are given. T or F?
3. Behavioral economics is a field of study that combines economics with psychological research about how people make decisions. T or F?
4. It is not always optimal to make decisions when we are feeling very emotional. T or F?
5. Our decisions are greatly affected by the way that a problem is stated, a process called
   a. framing
   b. base rating
   c. induction
   d. selective encoding

THINK CRITICALLY

6. A coin is flipped four times with one of the following results: (a) H T T H, (b) T T T T, (c) H H H H, (d) H H T H. Which sequence would most likely precede getting a head on the fifth coin flip?

SELF-REFLECT

- Make up a question that would require convergent thinking to answer. Now, do the same for divergent thinking.
- On which of the tests of creativity described in the text do you think you would do best? (Look back if you can't remember them all).
- Explain in your own words how base rates, framing, and representativeness contribute to thinking errors.

Answers: 1. b 2. F 3. T 4. T 5. a 6. None of them; the chance of getting heads on the fifth flip is the same in each case. Each time that you flip a coin, the chance of getting a head is 50 percent, no matter what happened before. However, many people intuitively think that b is the answer because a head is "overdue," or that c is correct because the coin is "on a roll" for heads.

8.4 Creative Thinking

GATEWAYS LEARNING OUTCOMES:
After reading this section you should be able to:

8.4.1 Describe the nature of creative thinking and how it is measured

8.4.2 Outline the five stages of creative problem solving

8.4.3 Describe five characteristics associated with a creative personality

Original ideas have changed the course of human history. Much of what we now take for granted in art, medicine, music, technology, and science was once regarded as radical or impossible. What is it that defines creative thinkers?

The Nature of Creativity

We saw earlier in this chapter that problem solving may be based on algorithms, understanding, or insight. Routine problem solving usually requires logical **convergent thinking**, where lines of thought converge on the answer. There is one correct answer and the problem is to find it. In contrast, **creativity** is the ability to combine mental elements in new and useful ways. Let's take a closer look at two characteristics of creative individuals—divergent thinking and problem finding. (See ▲ Table 8.2 for some examples of convergent and divergent problems.)

Divergent Thinking

Creative ideas are usually best achieved through **divergent thinking**, in which many possibilities are developed from one starting point. We can purposefully try to engage in divergent thinking when we try to solve problems, but it is also a characteristic of daydreams (vivid waking fantasies that are often associated with greater mental flexibility or creativity; Langens & Schmalt, 2002).

Divergent thought tends to be *intuitive and associative*. Whereas problem solving is usually a consciously reflective processing activity, creativity more likely involves apparently unconscious experiential processing (Ritter, van Baaren, & Dijksterhuis, 2012).

▲ Table 8.2 Convergent and Divergent Problems

Convergent Problems

- What is the area of a triangle that is 3 feet wide at the base and 2 feet tall?
- Erica is shorter than Zoey but taller than Carlo, and Carlo is taller than Jared. Who is the second tallest?
- If you simultaneously drop a baseball and a bowling ball from a tall building, which will hit the ground first?

Divergent Problems

- What objects can you think of that begin with the letters *BR*?
- How could discarded aluminum cans be put to use?
- Write a poem about fire and ice.

walter_g/Shutterstock.com

Whimsical creations such as this eyeball light bulb make it clear that in addition to being original or novel, a creative solution must be high quality and relevant to the problem.

In addition, divergent thinking involves *fluency*, *flexibility*, and *originality*. For example, let's say that you would like to find creative uses for the billions of plastic containers that are discarded each year. The creativity of your suggestions could be rated in this way: **Fluency** is defined as the total number of suggestions that you are able to make. **Flexibility** is the number of times that you shift from one class of possible uses to another. **Originality** refers to how novel or unusual your ideas are. By counting the number of times that you showed fluency, flexibility, and originality, we could rate your capacity for creative, divergent thinking (Runco, 2012; Runco & Acar, 2012).

Isn't creativity more than divergent thought? What if a person comes up with a large number of useless answers to a problem? Good question. Divergent thinking is an important part of creativity, but there is more to it. To be creative, the solution to a problem must be more than novel, unusual, or original. It also must be *high-quality* and *relevant* to solving the original problem (Kaufman & Sternberg, 2010). This is the dividing line between a "harebrained scheme" and a "stroke of genius." In other words, creative people bring reasoning and critical thinking to bear on new ideas once they are produced (Runco, 2012).

Choice overload Difficulty making a decision in the face of many alternatives.

Convergent thinking Thinking directed toward discovery of a single established correct answer; conventional thinking.

Creativity Ability to combine mental elements in new and useful ways.

Divergent thinking Thinking that produces many ideas or alternatives; a major element in original or creative thought.

Fluency In tests of creativity, fluency refers to the total number of solutions produced.

Flexibility In tests of creativity, flexibility is indicated by how many different types of solutions are produced.

Originality In tests of creativity, originality refers to how novel or unusual solutions are.

Gary Miller/FilmMagic/Getty Images

Fluency is an important part of creative thinking. Thomas Edison held over 1,000 patents. Bob Dylan published over 500 musical compositions. Not all of these works were masterpieces. However, a fluent outpouring of ideas fed the creative efforts of each of these geniuses.

Problem Finding

Problem finding is a second characteristic of creative thinkers. Many of the problems we solve are "presented" to us—by employers, teachers, circumstances, or life in general. **Problem finding** involves actively seeking problems to solve. When you are thinking creatively, a spirit of discovery prevails: you are more likely to find unsolved problems and *choose* to tackle them. Thus, problem finding may be a more creative act than the convergent problem solving that typically follows it (Runco, 2015).

Measuring Creativity

Divergent thinking can be measured in several ways (Kaufman, 2009; Runco & Acar, 2012). In the *Unusual Uses test*, you would be asked to think of as many uses as possible for some object, such as the plastic containers mentioned previously. In the *Consequences test*, you would list the consequences that would follow a basic change in the world. For example, you might be asked, "What would happen if everyone suddenly lost their sense of balance and could no longer stay upright?" People try to list as many reactions as possible. If you were to take the *Anagrams test*, you would be given a word, such as *creativity*, and asked to make as many new words as possible by rearranging the letters. Each of these tests can be scored for fluency, flexibility, and originality. (For an example of other tests of divergent thinking, see Figure 8.15.)

Stages of Creative Thought

Does creative thinking have a pattern? Typically, five stages occur during creative problem solving:

1. **Orientation.** As a first step, the person defines the problem and identifies its most important dimensions.
2. **Preparation.** It helps to be prepared *in general*, as an expert might be when first confronting a problem, but it also helps to become saturated with as much information about the *specific* problem as possible (Klein, 2013).
3. **Incubation.** Most major problems will have a period during which all attempted solutions are futile. At this point, problem solving may proceed on a subconscious level: Although the problem seems to have been set aside, it is still "cooking" in the background.
4. **Illumination.** The incubation stage is often ended by a rapid insight or series of insights. These produce the "Aha!" experience, often depicted in cartoons as a light bulb appearing over the thinker's head.
5. **Verification.** The final step is to test and critically evaluate the solution obtained during the illumination stage. If the solution proves faulty, the thinker reverts to the stage of incubation.

Perhaps the greatest misconception of the creative process is that it is all about that flash of illumination. But as inventor Thomas Edison once remarked, "Genius is one percent inspiration and ninety-nine percent perspiration." Many hours of *orientation* and *preparation* can be overshadowed by the brilliance of the "Aha" *illumination*. Also, much creative problem solving is *incremental*. That is, it is the end result of many small steps. This is certainly true of many inventions, which build on earlier ideas.

Some psychologists believe that truly exceptional creativity requires a rare combination of thinking skills, personality, and a supportive social environment. This mix, they believe, accounts for creative giants such as Leonardo DaVinci, Sigmund Freud, Wolfgang Amadeus Mozart, Pablo Picasso, and others (Robinson, 2010; Simonton, 2009).

The Creative Personality

What makes a person creative? According to the popular stereotype, highly creative people are eccentric, introverted, neurotic, socially inept, unbalanced in their interests, and on the edge of madness. After all, isn't there a "fine line between genius and insanity"? In general, direct studies of creative individuals suggest that such characteristics are something of a stereotype (Hennessey & Amabile, 2010; Robinson, 2010). However, research has offered the following findings with respect to creativity:

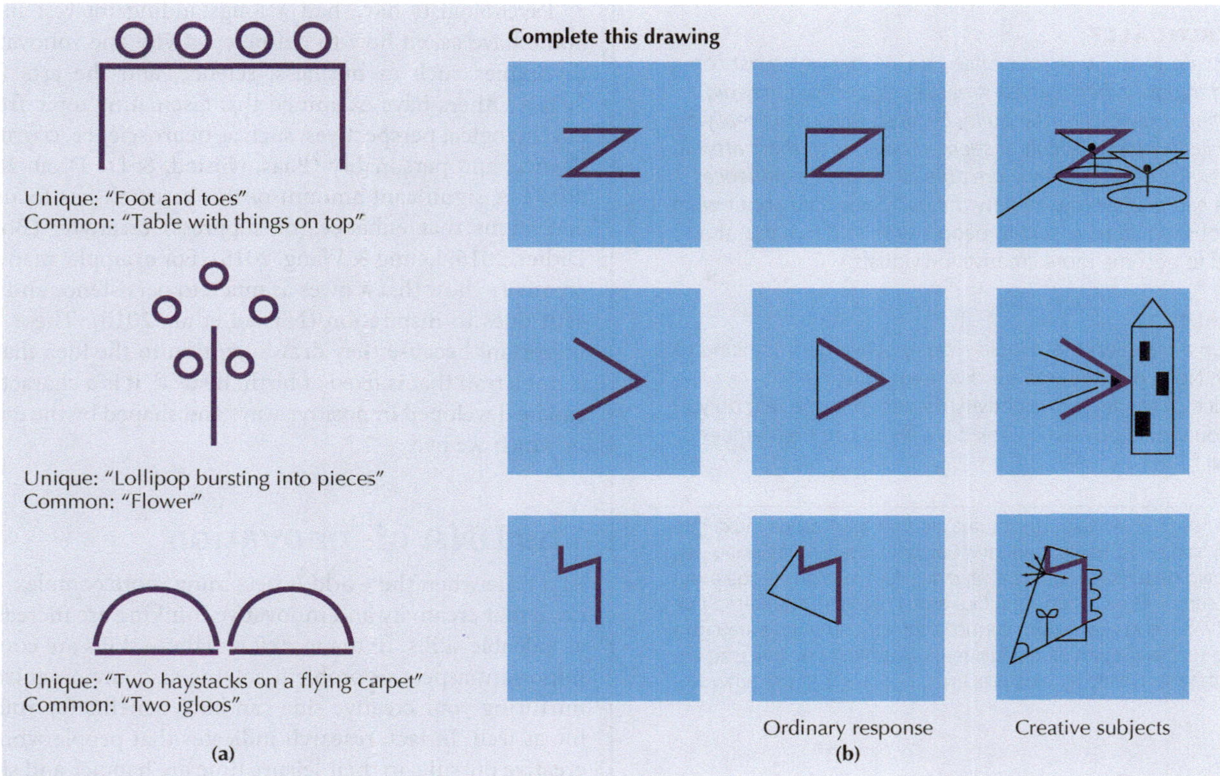

Figure 8.15 Some tests of divergent thinking. Creative responses are more original and more complex.
(*a*) Adapted from Wallach & Kogan, 1965; (*b*) adapted from Barron, 1958.

1. Creativity test scores (which measure divergent thinking) and IQ test scores (which measure convergent thinking) are weakly correlated with one another (Kim, Cramond, & VanTassel-Baska, 2010; Silvia, 2015). Highly creative people are not necessarily highly intelligent (using the operational definition that is assessed with IQ tests) and vice versa.
2. Creative people usually have a greater-than-average range of knowledge and interests, and they are more fluent in combining ideas from various sources. They also are good at using mental images and metaphors in thinking (Riquelme, 2002).
3. Creative people are open to a wide variety of experiences. They accept irrational thoughts and are uninhibited about their feelings and fantasies. They tend to use broad categories, question assumptions, and break mental sets, and they find order in chaos. They also experience more unusual states of consciousness, such as lucid dreams and mystical experiences (Zink & Pietrowsky, 2013).
4. Creative people enjoy symbolic thought, ideas, concepts, and possibilities. They tend to be interested in truth, form, and beauty, rather than in fame or success. Their creative work is an end in itself (Robinson, 2010).
5. Creative people value their independence and prefer complexity. However, they are unconventional and nonconforming primarily in their work; otherwise, they do not have unusual, outlandish, or bizarre personalities.

Can creativity be learned? It is beginning to look as if some creative thinking skills can be learned. In particular, you can become more creative by practicing divergent thinking and by taking risks, asking unusual questions, analyzing ideas, and seeking odd connections between ideas (Bucher, 2011; Sternberg, 2017). To learn more about developing your creative side, take a look at this chapter's *Psychology and Your Skill Set*.

Reflective Practice

Creative Thinking

1. Fluency, flexibility, and originality are characteristics of
a. convergent thought
b. deductive thinking
c. creative thought
d. trial-and-error solutions

2. To be creative, an original idea also must be high-quality and relevant. T or F?

3. Intelligence and creativity are highly correlated; the higher a person's IQ, the more likely he or she is to be creative. T or F?

4. Which of the following is ***not*** one of the stages of creative thinking?
a. incubation
b. orientation
c. verification
d. consultation

Problem finding The active discovery of problems to be solved.

THINK CRITICALLY

5. Apple co-founder Steve Jobs once said: "*Creativity is just connecting things. When you ask creative people how they did something, they feel a little guilty because they didn't really do it, they just saw something. It seemed obvious to them after a while. That's because they were able to connect experiences they've had and synthesize new things.*" Speculate about what Steve Jobs would have said to people who told him that they wanted to become more creative individuals.

SELF-REFLECT

- Make up a question that would require convergent thinking to answer. Now, do the same for divergent thinking.
- On which of the tests of creativity described in the text do you think you would do best? (Look back if you can't remember them all.)

Answers: 1. c 2. T 3. F 4. d 5. He likely would have indicated that the best way to foster their creativity would be to seek out diverse experiences that put you into contact with a variety of new people and different situations. These might include joining groups to learn more about subjects they knew little about, traveling to places they had never seen, and interacting with people whose values, beliefs, and experiences were very different from their own.

8.5 Psychology and Your Skill Set: Creativity and Innovation

GATEWAYS LEARNING OUTCOME:
After reading this section you should be able to:

8.5.1 Create a plan to enhance your creativity and innovation skills

Struck by a boat propeller while waterskiing, college student Van Phillips had his leg severed just below the knee. His prosthetic limb (basically, a pink foam foot on the end of an aluminum tube) came with a piece of medical advice: Get used to your new "best friend." But Phillips hated his awkward artificial limb. So he set out to build a better prosthetic, one that would allow users to run, jump, and rebound. He considered the benefits associated with the C-shape of a cheetah's hind leg, but eventually settled on an L-shape that provided spring when weight was applied to the "heel." He tested hundreds of prototypes on himself before founding Flex-Foot, a company that produces high-quality prosthetic limbs for amputees, including Paralympic athletes. Not content to stop there, Phillips has now turned to the problem of reducing costs, so that artificial limbs can be made more widely available to landmine victims in developing countries.

You might think that people like Van Phillips are born with innovative minds, but research suggests that this isn't the case. In fact, we all have the skills that are needed to be creative—all it takes is a willingness to practice them.

Psychologists have had a longstanding interest in creativity. Some have asked how to define creativity and innovation across disciplines such as business, science, and the arts (Simonton, 2016). Others have examined this fascinating topic from diverse psychological perspectives, such as neuroscience, cognition, intelligence, and personality (Baas, Nijstad, & De Dreu, 2015; Silvia, 2015). A significant amount of this research has focused on the conditions that enhance (or suppress) creativity (Bonnardel & Didier, 2016; Leung & Wang, 2015). For example, many studies of creativity show that it owes as much to persistence and dedication as it does to inspiration (Nijstad et al., 2010). These studies are important because they draw attention to the idea that creativity is not a trait that is fixed at birth. Instead, it is a characteristic that can be developed in positive ways and shaped by the environment in which we live.

The DNA of Innovation

At a time when the world is becoming more complex, it's no surprise that creativity and innovative thinking are increasingly seen as valuable skills. In the workforce, these skills are considered an important aspect of problem solving at many organizations. But nurturing your creative side can have benefits for your personal life as well. In fact, research indicates that people who engage in creative pursuits in their leisure time are happier and show higher levels of well-being (Cameron et al., 2013).

How can creative, innovative thinking be fostered? This is exactly what an international team of researchers asked when they spent six years interviewing some of the most innovative people in the world (Dyer, Gregersen, & Christensen, 2013). They found that these people demonstrated four key "discovery skills," which they describe in *The Innovator's DNA* project. The good news? These discovery skills can be cultivated by anyone who's willing to practice them. Let's take a closer look at what those skills are.

Make Associations

Associating refers to our ability to connect ideas, questions, or concepts that, at first glance, seem to be completely unrelated. Dyer, Gregersen, and Christensen (2013) pointed out that such

filrom/iStock/Getty Images

unusual connections are easier to make when you've had diverse experiences or when you work with people who have had diverse experiences. (■ Note that the value of diversity is also discussed in Section 17.4.)

Steve Jobs, the cofounder of Apple, understood this intuitively. He once noted that creativity was simply the process of connecting things, adding, "If you're gonna make connections which are innovative ... you have to not have the same bag of experiences as everyone else does, or else you're going to make the same connections [as everybody else]." Remember, creativity requires *divergent* thinking. To make creative associations, then, you might attempt to shift your mental "prospecting" to new areas. Try relating a problem to random words from the dictionary, for example, or to novel objects or photos. Imagine how another person would view the problem. What would a child, engineer, professor, mechanic, artist, psychologist, judge, or minister ask about it? Also, don't be afraid to ask "silly" or playful questions such as: If the problem were alive, what would it look like? If the problem were edible, how would it taste? Is any part of the problem pretty? Ugly? Stupid? Friendly? (de Bono, 1992; Michalko, 2006; Simonton, 2009).

You can also improve your ability to make novel connections by exploring a range of interests and hobbies. Finally, creative associations can be fostered when you engage with new people whose values and life experiences differ from your own. You may choose to do this by traveling to other countries, but in many American cities and towns, it's easy to find diverse others close to home or where you work. J. K. Rowling, for example, noted in a speech to the graduating class at Harvard that her experience working with a wide range of individuals at Amnesty International was valuable in the process of bringing Harry Potter to life in her books.

Ask Questions

Being creative also includes a willingness to challenge conventions and a refusal to accept the status quo. This means that you should often be asking questions such as "Why?," "Why not?," and "What if?" Van Phillips provides a good example of someone who understands the value of pushing back against conventional wisdom. He didn't accept, for example, that existing prosthetics were as good as they could be. And he was willing to ask unconventional questions such as, "What if a prosthetic leg didn't have to look like a human's, but instead could look more like a cheetah's?"

Questions that force people to consider constraints can also spur innovative thinking. For example, creative solutions can sometimes emerge when we consciously work toward eliminating mental sets. A **mental set** is the tendency to perceive a problem in a way that blinds us to possible solutions. Mental sets are a major barrier to creative thinking. They usually trap us "in a box," leading us to see a problem in preconceived terms that impede our problem-solving attempts (Thurson, 2008). (Fixations and functional fixedness, which were described earlier in this chapter, are specific types of mental sets.) Try the problems pictured in ● Figure 8.16. If you have difficulty, try asking yourself what assumptions you are making. The problems are designed to demonstrate the limiting effects of a mental set. (The answers to these problems, along with an explanation of the mental sets that prevent their solution, are found in ● Figure 8.17.)

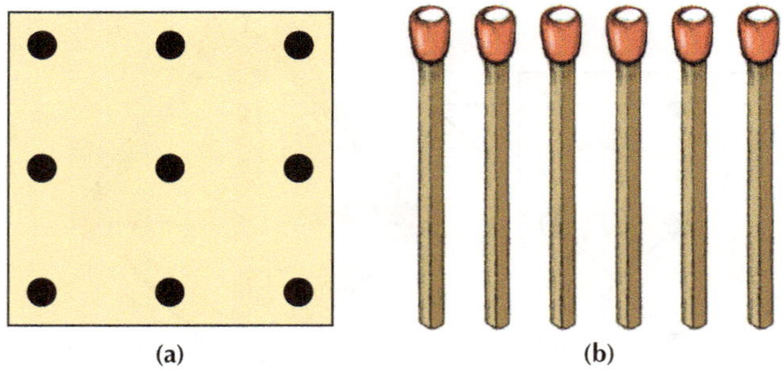

● **Figure 8.16 Mental set problems.** (a) Nine dots are arranged in a square. Can you connect them by drawing four continuous straight lines without lifting your pencil from the paper? (b) Six matches must be arranged to make four triangles. The triangles must be the same size, with each side equal to the length of one match. (The solutions to these problems appear in Figure 8.17.)

An effective way to break mental sets is to frame the problem broadly (Reed, 2013; Thurson, 2008). For instance, assume that your problem is to design a better doorway. This is likely to lead to ordinary solutions. Why not change the problem to design a better way to get through a wall? Now your solutions will be more original. Best of all might be to state the problem as follows: Find a better way to define separate areas for living and working. This could lead to truly creative solutions.

But while it's clear that it can be useful to ask questions that will help you recognize (and avoid!) the constraints imposed by mental sets, it's interesting to note that sometimes creative ideas can also be fostered by *imposing* constraints on your thinking. For example, at a time when one company found itself in a very challenging and competitive business environment, the CEO asked the following questions: "What if we were legally prohibited from

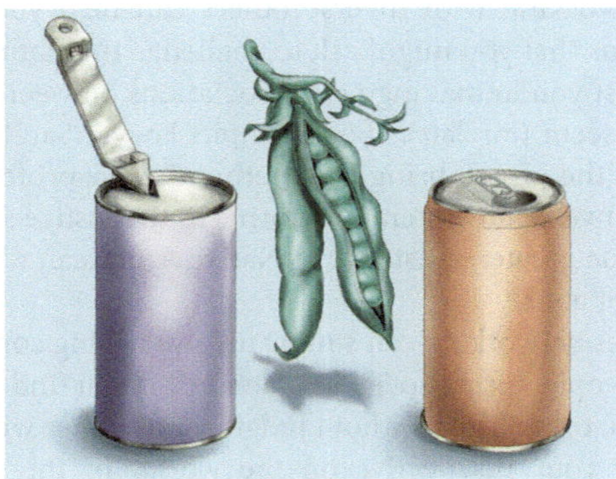

Let's say that you are leading a group that's designing a new can opener. Wisely, you ask the group to think broadly about opening in general, rather than about can openers. This was just the approach that led to the pop-top can. As the design group discussed the concept of opening, one member suggested that nature has its own openers, such as the soft seam on a pea pod. Instead of a new can-opening tool, the group invented the self-opening can (Stein, 1974).

Mental set A predisposition to perceive or respond in a particular way.

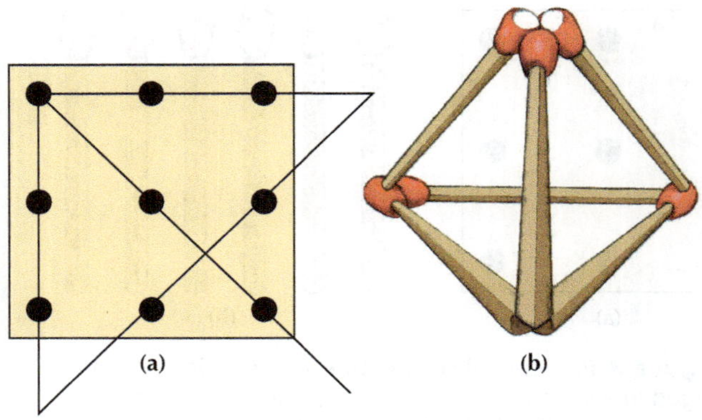

Figure 8.17 Mental set problem solutions.
(a) The dot problem can be solved by extending the lines beyond the square formed by the dots. Most people assume incorrectly that they may not do this. (b) The match problem can be solved by building a three-dimensional pyramid. Most people assume that the matches must be arranged on a flat surface. If you remembered the four-tree problem from earlier in the chapter, the match problem may have been easy to solve.

selling to our existing customers next year? How would we make money?" Thinking in terms of restrictions like this forced people at the company to think about new possibilities they might not previously have considered. Thinking in terms of restrictions is also valued at Google, where one of the nine principles of innovation is "*Creativity loves constraint.*"

Seek Varied Input Through Networking

If making associations and questioning are important in boosting creativity, then it's worth noting that both of these skills can be enhanced when you regularly exchange ideas with a wide range of people. Networking with diverse others can help you consider new questions that you might ask to challenge the status quo, and can also assist you in making new associations between ideas that at first may seem unrelated. For example, lawyer Sarah Deer has championed the idea of bringing together diverse professionals in an effort to investigate potential reforms to the justice system that would provide greater assistance to Native American women who are victims of abuse.

Sometimes networking can simply involve having conversations with other people during social interactions. If you find yourself in this situation, try to listen without judging, but rather with the goal of widening your perspective on the world. In the workplace, though, you may find yourself working with a team to complete a project that requires creative thought. If this is the case, you may find it useful to encourage team members to use their diversity to best advantage through a process called *brainstorming*.

The essence of **brainstorming** is that producing and evaluating ideas are kept separate. This encourages the kind of divergent thinking that is promoted when you work with people who have had different experiences. In group problem solving, each person is encouraged to produce as many ideas as possible without fear of criticism (Henningsen & Henningsen, 2013). Only at the end of a brainstorming session are ideas reconsidered and evaluated. As ideas are freely generated, an interesting **cross-stimulation effect** takes place in which one participant's ideas trigger ideas from others (Brown et al., 1998; Laughlin, 2011).

Can brainstorming be applied to individual problem solving as well? Absolutely! The essential point to remember is to *suspend judgment.* Creative ideas should first be produced without regard for logic, organization, accuracy, practicality, or any other evaluation. In writing an essay, for instance, you would begin by writing ideas in any order, the more the better, just as they occur to you. Later you can go back and reorganize, rewrite, and criticize your efforts.

The basic rules for successful brainstorming are (Kaufman, 2009; Michalko, 2006; Scannell & Mulvilhill, 2012):

1. Absolutely do not criticize ideas until later in the session.
2. Modify or combine ideas freely. Don't worry about giving credit for ideas or keeping them neat. Mix them up!
3. Try to generate lots of ideas. In the early stages of brainstorming, quantity is more important than quality.
4. Let your imagination run amok! Seek unusual, remote, or wild ideas.
5. Record ideas as they occur.
6. Elaborate or improve on the most promising ideas.

Observe and Experiment

Creative individuals practice their observation skills by watching the behavior of people in their everyday lives, taking note of what they do and say, what frustrates them, and what makes them happy. Often, this type of observation is combined with the questioning skills that were described earlier. After watching people, then, you might be inclined to ask yourself, "Why do they do that?," "What if they did it this way instead?," or "How does what I'm seeing differ from what I expected?" Of course, you may also want to think about taking your observations one step further. For example, Richard Branson, the CEO of Virgin, isn't just a keen observer of what's going on around him: He is well-known for taking notes about everything that he sees, and every conversation that's of interest.

After observing something interesting and asking questions, you might then attempt to answer those questions in a process of experimentation. ■ Recall from Section 1.5 that people interested in psychological experiments begin with questions and then develop hypotheses about what they believe will happen. Consider approaching the world with this type of hypothesis-testing mindset, which encourages you to examine your questions and hypotheses out in the world and watch to see whether the results conform to expectations. It's important to recognize that "experimenting" in this sense isn't necessarily something that's happening in a laboratory—anyone can test an idea that he or she has by simply implementing it and then evaluating the consequences.

An important thing to remember, though, is that experimenting with ideas can truly be a process of trial and error—don't be afraid to fail! When your ideas don't work or your hypotheses aren't confirmed, try to establish whether there's anything to be learned from the experience and then consider how you might use that information as you move forward. As Thomas Edison once remarked, "I haven't failed. I have simply found 10,000 ways that do not work."

Psychological Science and Creativity

In promoting the importance of these four "discovery skills," the authors of *The Innovator's DNA* highlight the value of a psychology degree in fostering creativity and innovative thinking. As a discipline that places a great deal of value on observing human behavior, asking questions, testing hypotheses, and promoting engagement with diverse others, studying psychology will put you in a stronger position to live creatively both at work and at play.

Reflective Practice

Psychology and Your Skill Set: Creativity and Innovation

1. Creativity has been linked to many areas of psychology, including personality and intelligence. T or F?
2. The four "discovery skills" outlined in the *Innovator's DNA* are making associations, asking questions, networking with diverse others, and observing/experimenting. T or F?
3. Creativity is diminished when we place constraints on our thinking. T or F?

THINK CRITICALLY

4. Do you think there is any connection between your mood and your creativity?

SELF-REFLECT

- Review the preceding pages and note which methods you could use more often to improve the quality of your thinking. Now, mentally summarize the points that you especially want to remember.

Answers: 1. T 2. T 3. F 4. In general, more intense moods are associated with higher creativity (Davis, 2009).

Brainstorming Method of creative thinking that separates the production and evaluation of ideas.

Cross-stimulation effect In group problem solving, the tendency of one person's ideas to trigger ideas from others.

CHAPTER IN REVIEW

Gateways to Cognition, Language, and Creativity

Summary: Gateways Learning Outcomes

8.1 The Basic Units of Cognition: Mental Imagery, Concepts, and Language

8.1.1 Distinguish between experiential and reflective processing

Experiential processing refers to thinking that occurs quickly and automatically, outside of awareness. Reflective processing refers to effortful, conscious thought that requires attention and concentration.

8.1.2 Explain how imagery is used in thinking

Mental images aid thinking by allowing us to imagine processes or outcomes in an effort to improve upon them. They can also assist with memory. The same brain areas are involved in both vision and visual imagery, and the mental images that are created are three-dimensional and can be mentally rotated. They can also be made larger or smaller in our "mind's eye." Kinesthetic images are a special type of mental imagery and are used to represent movements and actions.

8.1.3 Explain how concepts are used in thinking

Concepts are categories of objects or events. When faced with novel stimuli, we try to classify them using conceptual rules (which provide "boundaries" about the things that fall into that category) and prototypes (ideal models of that category). Concepts such as stereotypes can be faulty, though, leading to thinking that is overly simplistic.

8.1.4 Explain how language is used in thinking

Language encodes stimuli and events into symbols for easy mental manipulation during thinking. The linguistic relativity hypothesis holds that just as thought shapes language, so too, language shapes thought. Language carries meaning by combining a set of symbols according to a set of rules (grammar), which includes rules about word order (syntax). The study of word meaning in language is called *semantics*, and semantics are influenced by context. Words have denotations (dictionary definitions) and connotations (personal or emotional meanings). True languages (including complex gestural systems like ASL) are productive and can be used to generate new ideas or possibilities during thinking.

8.2 Problem Solving

8.2.1 Distinguish between four methods of problem solving: algorithms, understanding, heuristics, and insight

Algorithmic solutions are derived by employing rule-based strategies (which might well be time-consuming). Algorithms may be inductive (from the specific to more general) or deductive (from more general to specific). Solutions by understanding usually begin with discovery of the general properties of an answer, followed by a functional solution. Problem solving using heuristics refers to the use of "shortcuts" to narrow the search for solutions. Finally, solutions derived using insight usually involve reorganizing a problem in such a way that a rapid solution follows. Three elements of insight are selective encoding, selective combination, and selective comparison.

8.2.2 Outline the barriers that can interfere with problem solving

Problem solving can be blocked by fixations, or a tendency to get "stuck" on wrong solutions. Functional fixedness is a common fixation, and refers to a tendency to see items only in terms of their most common uses. Emotional blocks, cultural values, learned conventions, and perceptual habits can also be barriers to problem solving.

8.2.3 Compare the problem solving of experts and novices

Compared to novices, experts' solutions are of higher quality and are generated more quickly. Cognitive psychologists have suggested that one reason that explains these findings is that experts have more prior knowledge than novices. More prior knowledge means that experts are better able to see the deep structure of problems rather than being distracted by their surface structure, and this allows them to focus on the most relevant aspects of the problem. A second reason that explains the better problem solving of experts relates to the organization of prior knowledge in long-term memory. Specifically, experts' knowledge is chunked, allowing them to draw a greater amount of information back into the limited space of working memory where problem solving happens.

8.3 Intuition, Decision-Making, and Cognitive Biases

8.3.1 Distinguish between four common biases that can lead to errors in decision-making: framing, availability, representativeness, and ignoring the odds

Framing errors occur when we respond to how a problem is worded instead of focusing on the problem's fundamentals. The availability heuristic refers to our tendency to estimate the likelihood of an event based strictly on how easily similar events can be called to mind from long-term memory. The representativeness heuristic influences decisions by guiding us to give greater weight to options that seem to be similar to what we already know. Finally, when making decisions people often fail to consider the base rate, or probability, of events—this is referred to as ignoring the odds.

8.3.2 Explain what is meant by choice overload

Choice overload refers to situations in which having many options is not beneficial because we feel overwhelmed and unable to make a decision. It stems from a phenomenon called the paradox of choice, which suggests that although we usually like to have many options so that we can select something that is "just right," sometimes being presented with so many alternatives has the paradoxically opposite effect, preventing us from choosing anything at all.

8.4 Creative Thinking

8.4.1 Describe the nature of creative thinking and how it is measured

Creative thinking requires divergent thought, characterized by fluency, flexibility, and originality. Problem finding, or actively seeking out problems to solve, is another characteristic of creative thinkers. Creativity is often measured using tests of divergent thinking, such as the Unusual Uses test and the Consequences test.

8.4.2 Outline the five stages of creative problem solving

Five stages often seen in creative problem solving are orientation, preparation, incubation, illumination, and verification.

8.4.3 Describe five characteristics associated with a creative personality

Studies suggest that the creative personality has a number of characteristics, most of which contradict popular stereotypes. First, only a very small correlation exists between IQ and creativity; creative people are not necessarily "intelligent," as defined by standardized tests. Second, creative people have a broad range of experiences and interests. Third, they are open to new experiences and question assumptions. Fourth, they enjoy abstract ideas and symbolic thought. Fifth, creative individuals value independence and complexity.

8.5 Psychology and Your Skill Set: Creativity and Innovation

8.5.1 Create a plan to enhance your creativity and innovation skills

There are several things that you can do to boost your creativity and innovation skills, including making associations between unrelated ideas, asking good questions, seeking input from others, and engaging in observation and experimentation. We hope that after reading this section, you'll be better able to think about how you can use these strategies to help boost your creative juices!

9 Intelligence

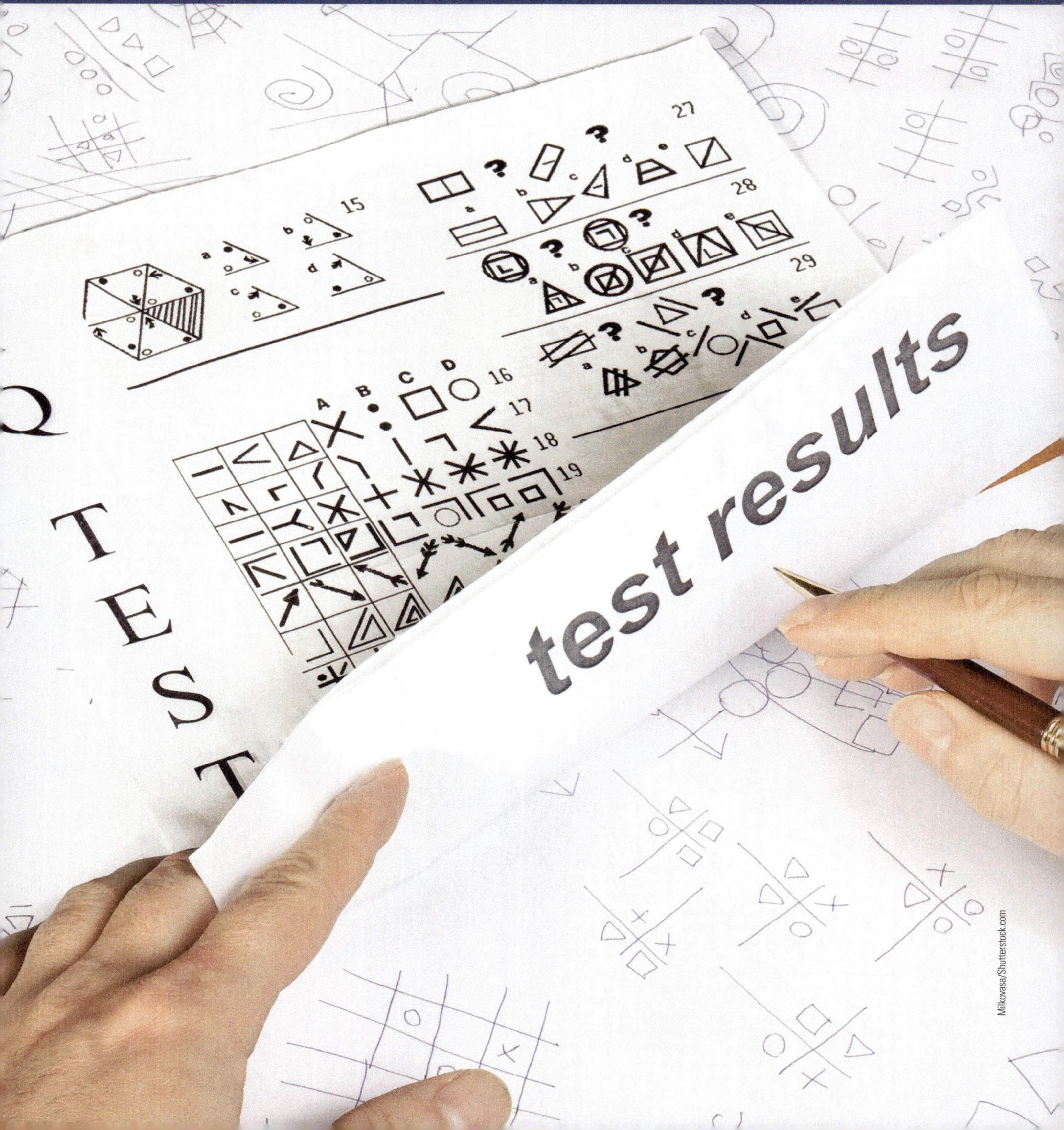

Gateway Theme Measuring intelligence is worthwhile, but tests provide a narrow definition of intelligent behavior.

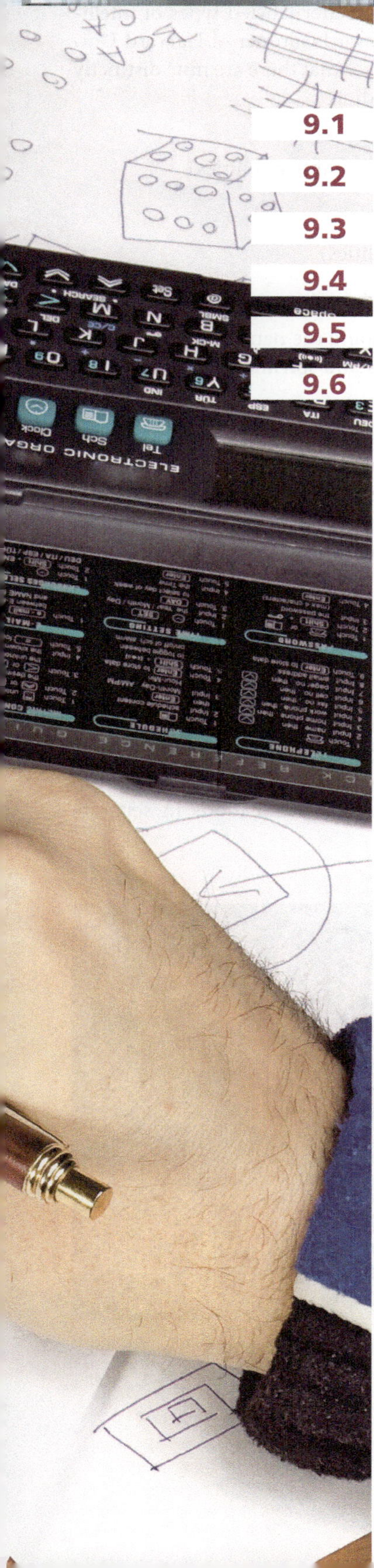

Chapter Outline

Good or Evil?

Darryl Lester and Dawn Harris Sherling have never met. Yet there's an invisible thread that links them, and millions of other Americans, together. Both Darryl and Dawn were required to take an intelligence test during the course of their education. In Darryl's case, the test was the first step down a rocky road that saw him falsely labeled as "mentally retarded." He was subjected to long days at school, during which time people rarely tried to educate him. But no one bothered to inform Darryl's mother, who was furious when she found out. She responded by launching a lawsuit, the effects of which are still being felt today. The verdict? Owing to their cultural bias, intelligence tests are not to be administered to any Black child in the state of California.

It's tempting to think of intelligence testing in purely negative terms when you hear Darryl's story. But Dawn Harris Sherling helps to shed light on why the issue is not so simple. Raised by a single immigrant father, she says that her excellent performance on an intelligence test—the SAT exam—was an important factor in her admission to a good college, followed by medical school at Yale. While acknowledging the test's flaws, she argues "the SAT afforded me, as it has thousands of others, a way to prove that a poor, public-school kid who never had any test prep can do just as well as, if not better than, her better-off peers."

What, then, are we to make of this concept of "intelligence" and our ways of measuring it? In this chapter we take a closer look at what psychological scientists have learned, and what is still being debated.

9.1 Defining Human Intelligence

GATEWAYS LEARNING OUTCOMES:
After reading this section you should be able to:

9.1.1 Define what is meant by the g-factor in intelligence

9.1.2 Describe some of the challenges associated with defining intelligence

In broad terms, we typically think about **intelligence** as being the overall capacity to think rationally, to act purposefully, and to adapt to one's surroundings (Barber, 2010; Flynn, 2012). Beyond this, however, there is much debate about the details. According to one popular theory in psychology, the core of intelligence is an overall mental ability called the **g-factor**, where the "g" denotes the idea that it represents a *general* level of intelligence. The term was introduced in the early 1900s by Charles Spearman, who believed that g was an overarching construct encompassing several specific *mental abilities* like those we have been exploring in the last two chapters: working memory, reasoning, problem solving, and representing knowledge (Kan et al., 2013; Ziegler et al., 2011).

High levels of g involve both **fluid intelligence** (the ability to solve novel problems involving perceptual speed or rapid insight) and **crystallized intelligence** (the effective use of prior knowledge). You may recall that we talked about prior knowledge in our discussion of long-term memory (■ see Section 7.3). By way of summarizing this view, intelligence is a complex capacity comprised of a general ability (g-factor), that is strengthened by both fluid and crystallized intelligence. In turn, fluid and crystallized intelligence are each comprised of a larger set of specific mental abilities (Keith & Reynolds, 2010).

Here's how the g-factor might look in the real world: While trying to figure out how long it will take to get to a street address you have never visited before, you might draw on your working memory, visual-spatial skills, and some basic knowledge of math and geography. During the journey, you might need to rely upon your knowledge of languages and an ability to reason about unfamiliar situations as you stop to help people at a traffic accident that you come across. In everyday life, you never know just what demands life will place upon you from one moment to the next, but people high in g-factor (intelligence) are good at bringing the right intellectual resources to bear on the variety of challenges that life throws our way.

Challenges in Defining Intelligence

As comprehensive as it may seem, this definition of intelligence leaves many unanswered questions. How does the g-factor work to coordinate more specific mental abilities? Just which specific mental abilities together constitute intelligence? Is there really a g-factor or do we all possess very different, unconnected "intelligences" (Hampshire et al., 2012)? After all, there may be many ways to be smart. For example, consider William, a grade-school student who is two years behind in reading, but who shows his teacher how to solve a difficult computer-programming problem. Or what about his classmate, Malika, who is also a poor reader but plays intricate pieces of piano music? Both of these children show clear signs of what have sometimes been called **aptitudes**, yet there are some psychologists who feel that they are better labeled types of intelligence. One such psychologist is Howard Gardner of Harvard University. Gardner (2008, 2011) theorizes that there are nine distinctly different kinds of intelligence, including:

1. *Linguistic* (language abilities)
2. *Logical-mathematical* (logic and number abilities)
3. *Visual* (pictorial abilities)
4. *Musical* (music abilities)
5. *Bodily-kinesthetic* (physical abilities)
6. *Intrapersonal* (self-knowledge)
7. *Interpersonal* (social abilities)
8. *Naturalist* (an ability to understand the natural environment)
9. *Existential* (an ability to understand spirituality and existence)

If Gardner's theory of **multiple intelligences** is correct then traditional views really only capture a small part of real-world intelligence, namely linguistic, logical-mathematical, and spatial abilities (Roberts & Lipnevich, 2012). Instead, Gardner would argue that a student like Malika should also be considered highly intelligent owing to her skill with music.

Human Diversity and Definitions of Intelligence

In addition to the question of how many types of intelligence exist, there's a second issue that has concerned psychologists. To understand it, consider this example: Imagine you have been asked to sort some objects into categories. Wouldn't it be smart to put the clothes, containers, implements, and foods in separate

Aspen Photo/Shutterstock.com

According to Howard Gardner's theory, bodily-kinesthetic skills reflect one of nine distinct types of intelligence.

piles? Not necessarily. When individuals from the Kpelle people in Liberia were asked to sort objects, they grouped them together by function. For example, a potato (food) would be placed with the knife needed to cut it up for cooking (implement). When the Kpelle were asked why they grouped the objects this way, they often said that was how a wise man would do it. The researchers finally asked the Kpelle, "How would a fool do it?" Only then did they sort the objects into the nice, neat categories that Westerners prefer.

This anecdote, related by cultural psychologist Patricia Greenfield (1997), raises serious questions about general definitions of intelligence. For example, among the Cree of Northern Canada, "smart" people are those who have the skills needed to find food on the frozen tundra (Darou, 1992). For the Puluwat people in the South Pacific, "smart" means having the oceangoing navigation skills necessary to get from island to island. Such a view of intelligence is central to the ideas put forward by Robert Sternberg, who argues that an important component of intelligence is related to our ability to demonstrate skills that are practical or useful in the environment where we live (Sternberg, 2004).

Each of these examples makes it clear that defining what it means to be intelligent is a challenging task. On the one hand, Gardner and Sternberg's models have an intuitive appeal. In both cases the central ideas seem to make sense, and they are particularly attractive if you believe in the value of human diversity and the fact that being successful in life may require that we be "smart" in very different ways.

On the other hand, there is relatively little support in the research for either of these models. More importantly, though, if we're going to say that being "intelligent" can refer to many, many things, each of which is very different, then the term itself becomes somewhat meaningless and impossible to study. Moreover, studies consistently demonstrate that using the initial definition—that is, intelligence defined as g—has some value because it's a characteristic that correlates with many outcomes that our culture views as important, such as better educational success, health, and financial security (Deary, Harris, & Hill, 2019).

For these reasons, most psychologists opt to operationally define intelligence in terms of g, and the mental abilities that it includes. Adopting this definition does *not* mean that psychologists doubt that there are other ways to be smart or talented; in fact, psychologists study many of the factors on Gardner's list precisely because they *do* understand the value of those characteristics.

Psychologists are also very sensitive to the values that Western society attaches—rightly or wrongly—to the idea of intelligence defined as g. Those who study it often work hard to report on their research in a way that properly represents its complexity and the limits of their findings. Unfortunately, the popular press does not always follow suit, and has been known to misrepresent and oversimplify the findings of psychological studies related to intelligence. It's important, then, to think critically when you encounter reports about research on this topic—take the time to look past sensational headlines and ensure that reporters are not telling a story that distorts the researchers' claims.

Reflective Practice

Defining Human Intelligence

1. The g-factor refers to
   a. a *generic* intelligence factor that refers to being "smart" in any domain, including academics, music, and working with mechanical items.
   b. a *general* intelligence factor that includes several cognitive domains such as working memory, reasoning, and problem solving.
   c. a *good* intelligence factor that includes measures of kindness toward others.
   d. a *gross* intelligence factor that is very, very large.
2. How many different types of intelligence did Gardner's theory of multiple intelligences include?
   a. four
   b. six
   c. nine
   d. twelve
3. According to Howard Gardner's theory, which of the following is ***not*** measured by traditional IQ tests?
   a. interpersonal skills
   b. spatial skills
   c. logical skills
   d. linguistic skills

THINK CRITICALLY

4. Knowing that "intelligence" is defined by most psychologists as a g-factor coordinating a large number of more specific mental abilities, would you predict that human intelligence is controlled by relatively few or relatively many genes?

SELF REFLECT

- Thinking forward, what would you predict might be some of the major concerns about trying to measure g?

Answers: 1. b 2. c 3. a 4. Most complex human qualities are controlled by many genes (i.e., they are polygenic), each having a small impact on its own. This is definitely true of human intelligence (Plomin & Deary, 2015).

Intelligence Capacity for rational thought, purposeful action, and effective adaptation.

g-factor Measure of an individual's overall intelligence as opposed to specific abilities.

Fluid intelligence The ability to solve novel problems involving perceptual speed or rapid insight.

Crystallized intelligence The ability to solve problems using already acquired knowledge.

Aptitude A capacity for learning certain abilities.

Multiple intelligences Howard Gardner's theory that there are several specialized types of intellectual ability.

9.2 Measuring Intelligence

GATEWAYS LEARNING OUTCOMES:
After reading this section you should be able to:

9.2.1 Name and describe four characteristics of a good psychometric test

9.2.2 Explain the need for "culture-fair" intelligence tests

9.2.3 Explain the difference between general intelligence (g) tests and aptitude tests

9.2.4 Name two well-established intelligence tests, and some of the main cognitive abilities that they test

9.2.5 Explain how the results of intelligence tests are expressed, and how the scores are distributed in the population

Whether it is an intelligence test or any other kind of psychometric test, there will always be questions that you should ask if you want to take its results seriously. Let's take a look at four that are very important.

Studying the Science: Characteristics of Good Intelligence Tests

The first question we should always ask about a **psychometric test** is, "Is it *reliable*?," which refers to the test's ability to deliver consistent results. The second is, "Is it *valid*?," a question that gets at whether the test actually measures what it claims to measure. Third, we want to ask about whether the test can accurately assess a diverse group of people. We can be a bit more certain of this if the test has been *standardized*. Finally, we'd also want to know whether the test was *objective*; in other words, that the results would be interpreted the same way by many people.

It's important to note that the vast majority of "IQ tests" that you can find on the Internet would not meet the bar that's set by these standards—these tests may have some entertainment value, but don't make the mistake of thinking that your score on them will be a good measure of your intelligence. Let's do a deeper dive into these four elements of a good psychometric test (that is, one that doesn't try to measure your intelligence by asking you what celebrities you'd most like to have lunch with).

Reliability

If you weigh yourself several times in a row, a reliable bathroom scale gives more or less the same weight each time. Likewise, a **reliable** psychometric test must give approximately the same score each time a person takes it (Kaplan & Saccuzzo, 2018). In other words, the scores should be *consistent* each time the test is taken. It is easy to see why unreliable tests have little value. Imagine a medical test for pregnancy or breast cancer, for instance, which gave positive and negative responses for the same woman on the same day.

To check the reliability of a test, we could give it to a large group of people. Then each person could be tested again a week later to establish *test–retest reliability*. We also might want to know whether scores on one half of the test items match scores on the other half (*split-half reliability*). If two versions of a test are available, we could compare scores on one version to scores on the other (*equivalent-forms reliability*). In all cases, if the test is reliable then the scores being compared should be similar, or highly correlated with one another (■ see Section 1.7 for a refresher on correlations).

Validity

Just because a psychometric test is reliable, however, does not mean that it should be trusted; test *validity* is also important. To see why this is the case, try creating an IQ test with 10 questions that only you could possibly answer. Your test would be very reliable: Each time you give the test, everyone scores zero, except you, who scores 100 percent (apparently, you're a genius!). Even though we all have days when it seems we *are* the only smart person left on the planet, it should be obvious this wouldn't be a great intelligence test. A test must also have **validity**; in other words, it should measure what it claims to measure (Neukrug & Fawcett, 2015). By no stretch of the imagination could a test of intelligence be valid if the person who wrote it is the only one who can pass it.

How is validity established? Great question! Validity is usually demonstrated by comparing test scores to actual performance on some other measure (or criterion) that is known to assess the construct you're trying to measure. This is called *criterion validity*. Scores on a test of math ability, for example, might be compared to grades in high school math (the criterion). If high test scores correlate with high grades, or some other standard (criterion) of success, the test is more likely to be valid.

Human Diversity and Culture-Fair Intelligence Tests

Early intelligence tests have been roundly criticized as being valid only for Western cultures. As we mentioned earlier, cultural values, as well as knowledge, language patterns, and traditions, can greatly affect performance on tests designed for Western cultures (Nisbett et al., 2012; Sternberg & Grigorenko, 2005). Psychologist Jerome Kagan once remarked, "If the Wechsler and Binet intelligence scales were translated into Spanish, Swahili, and Chinese and given to every 10-year-old in Latin America, East Africa, and China, the majority would obtain IQ scores in the intellectually disabled range."

Certainly, we cannot believe that children of other cultures are all intellectually disabled. Instead, the problem resides with the fact that the test isn't providing a valid measure of their intelligence (Castles, 2012).

In view of such problems with validity, psychologists have tried to create "culture-fair" intelligence tests that do not disadvantage certain groups. A **culture-fair test** is designed to minimize the importance of skills and knowledge that may be more common in some cultures than in others. (For a sample of culture-fair test items, see ● Figure 9.1.) The value of creating such tests lies not just

Keren Su/Getty Images

How important do you think the mental abilities assessed in modern intelligence tests are to this Dani hunter in Papua New Guinea?

in testing people from other cultures. They also are useful for testing children in the United States who come from poor communities, rural areas, or ethnic minority families (Stephens et al., 1999).

Unfortunately, no intelligence test can be entirely free of cultural influences. For instance, our culture is very "visual" because children are constantly exposed to television, movies, video games, and the like. Thus, compared with children in developing countries, a child who grows up in the United States may be better prepared to take both nonverbal tests and traditional IQ tests.

Objectivity and Standardization

Let's return to your "I'm the Smartest Person in the World IQ Test" for a final point. Is your test *objective*? Actually, it might be. If your IQ test is given the same score when evaluated by different people, it is an **objective test**. However, objectivity is not enough to guarantee a fair test. Useful tests must also be *standardized* (Neukrug & Fawcett, 2015).

Test standardization refers to two things. First, it means that standard procedures are used in giving the test. The instructions, answer forms, amount of time to work and so forth are the same for everyone. Second, it means finding the **norm**, or average score, for a large group of people similar to those for whom the test was designed. Without standardization, we couldn't fairly compare the scores of people taking the test at different times. And without norms, there would be no way to tell whether a score is high, low, or average. For many tests, including intelligence tests, developers will establish norms for a variety of groups, including different age groups, sexes, or races.

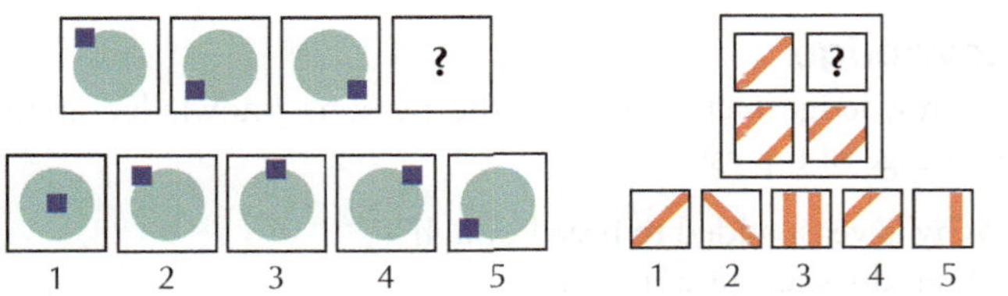

(a) Sample series problem **(b) Sample matrix problem**

Figure 9.1 Sample items like those often found on culture-fair intelligence tests. (a) Sample series problem. Which pattern correctly continues the series of patterns shown at the top left? (Number 4.) (b) Sample matrix problem. Which pattern best completes the matrix of patterns shown at the top right? (Number 1.) The idea is that the ability to read and the mastery of culturally relevant knowledge should not be necessary to do well on these questions. Nevertheless, do you think that illiterate street orphans from São Paulo, Brazil, or aboriginals living in the desert of the Australian outback would find the items as easy to complete as you did? If not, can you think of any other truly culture-fair way to test intelligence across different cultures?

Ways to Measure Intelligence

Intelligence can be measured in a number of different ways. In this section, we'll examine three of them: *general aptitude* tests, the *Stanford-Binet* test, and the *Wechsler Scales.*

General Aptitude Tests

As a child, Hedda displayed an aptitude for art. Today, Hedda is a successful graphic artist. How does an aptitude like Hedda's differ from general intelligence? An aptitude is a capacity for learning certain abilities. Persons with mechanical, artistic, or musical aptitudes are likely to do well in careers involving mechanics, art, or music, respectively.

Are there tests for general aptitudes? How are they different from intelligence tests? Aptitude tests measure a narrower range of abilities than do intelligence tests (Kaplan & Saccuzzo, 2018). For example, **special aptitude tests** predict whether you will succeed in a single area, such as clerical work or computer programming (Figure 9.2).

Multiple aptitude tests measure two or more types of ability. These tests tend to be more like intelligence tests, and it's possible that you've taken one yourself. For example, the *Scholastic Assessment Test* (SAT), the *American College Test* (ACT), and the *College Qualification Test* (CQT) all fall in this category, as do the tests for entry into graduate schools of law, medicine, business, and dentistry. Each of these group tests is designed to predict your chances for success in college programs. Because the tests measure general knowledge and a variety of mental aptitudes (language, math, and reasoning), each can also be used to estimate intelligence.

Psychometric test Any measurement of a person's mental functions.

Reliability The ability of a test to yield the same score, or nearly the same score, each time it is given to the same person.

Validity The ability of a test to measure what it purports to measure.

Culture-fair test A test (such as an intelligence test) designed to minimize the importance of skills and knowledge that may be more common in some cultures than in others.

Objective test A test that gives the same score when different people correct it.

Test standardization Establishing standards for administering a test and interpreting scores.

Norm An average score for a designated group of people.

Special aptitude test A test to predict a person's likelihood of succeeding in a particular area of work or skill.

Multiple aptitude test A test that measures two or more aptitudes.

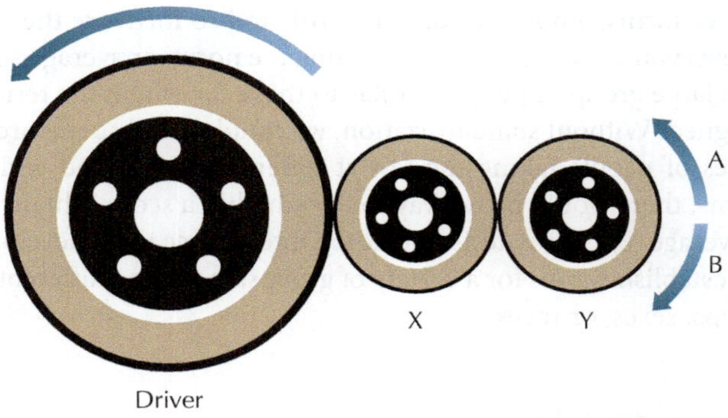

1. If the driver turns in the direction shown, which direction will wheel Y turn? A B

2. Which wheel will turn the slowest? Driver X Y

Figure 9.2 Testing mechanical aptitude. Sample questions like those found on tests of mechanical aptitude. (The answers are A and the Driver.)

The broadest aptitude measures are **general intelligence tests**, which assess a wide variety of intellectual abilities (Kaplan & Saccuzzo, 2018). (Psychologists use a variety of aptitude tests to select people for employment and to advise people about choosing careers. For more information, see Section 18.1.) We'll discuss two of the most common intelligence tests—the Stanford Binet and the Wechsler tests—in more detail.

Stanford Binet Intelligence Test

Like many important concepts in psychology, intelligence is an abstract concept that cannot be observed directly. So how can it be measured? Let's compare two children:

> When she was 14 months old, Anne wrote her own name. She taught herself to read at age 2. At age 5, she astounded her kindergarten teacher by bringing an iPad to class—on which she was reading an encyclopedia. At 10, she breezed through an entire high school algebra course in 12 hours.

> Billy, who is 10 years old, can write his name and can count, but he has trouble with simple addition and subtraction problems and finds multiplication impossible. He has been held back in school twice and is still incapable of doing the work his 8-year-old classmates find easy.

Anne is considered a genius; Billy, a slow learner. There seems little doubt that they differ in intelligence.

Wait! Anne's ability is obvious, but how do we know that Billy isn't just unmotivated? That's the problem Alfred Binet faced in 1904 (Benjafield, 2015; Cicciola, Foschi, & Lombardo, 2014). The French Minister of Education wanted to find a way to distinguish slower students from the more capable (or the capable but lazy). In a flash of brilliance, Binet and an associate created a test made up of "intellectual" questions and problems. Next, they learned which questions an average child could answer at each age. By comparing test scores of individual children to the average score for their ages, they could tell whether a child was performing up to his or her potential (Kaplan & Saccuzzo, 2018). Binet's approach gave rise to modern intelligence tests but, at the same time, it launched an ongoing debate about the basic difficulty of defining intelligence (Sternberg et al., 2011).

American psychologists quickly saw the value of Alfred Binet's test. By 1916, Lewis Terman and others at Stanford University had revised it for use in North America. After more revisions, the *Stanford-Binet Intelligence Scales, Fifth Edition* (SB5), continues to be widely used. The SB5 primarily is made up of age-ranked questions that get a little harder at each age level. The SB5 is appropriate for people from age 2 to 85+ years, and scores on the test are very reliable (Roid & Pomplun, 2012).

The SB5 measures five cognitive factors, or mental abilities, thought to make up general intelligence: fluid reasoning (roughly related to fluid intelligence), knowledge (roughly related to crystallized intelligence), quantitative reasoning, visual-spatial processing, and working memory. Each factor is measured with verbal questions (those involving words and numbers) and nonverbal questions (items that use pictures and objects). If you were to take the SB5, you would be assessing your general intelligence (g-factor, or the overall score), verbal intelligence (the score on the verbal questions), nonverbal intelligence (the score on the nonverbal questions), and each of the five cognitive factors (Roid & Pomplun, 2012). Let's see what each factor looks like:

Fluid Reasoning

Verbal questions like the following are used to test fluid reasoning, the ability to reason in unfamiliar situations:

> How are an apple, a plum, and a banana different from a beet?
> An apprentice is to a master as a novice is to (an) ________.
> "I knew my bag was going to be in the last place I looked, so I looked there first." What is silly or impossible about that?

Other nonverbal items ask people to fill in the missing shape in a group of shapes and to tell a story that explains what's going on in a series of pictures.

Knowledge

The knowledge factor assesses the person's knowledge about a wide range of topics:

> Why is yeast added to bread dough?
> What does "cryptic" mean?
> What is silly or impossible about this picture? (For example, a bicycle has square wheels.)

Quantitative Reasoning

Test items for quantitative reasoning measure a person's ability to solve problems involving numbers. Here are some samples:

> If I have six marbles and you give me another one, how many marbles will I have?
> Given the numbers 3, 6, 9, 12, what number would come next?
> If a shirt is being sold for 50 percent of the normal price, and the price tag is $60, what is the cost of the shirt?

Bob Daemmrich/The Image Works

Modern intelligence tests are widely used to measure cognitive abilities. When properly administered, such tests provide one potential operational definition of intelligence.

Visual-Spatial Processing

People who have strong visual-spatial skills are good at putting picture puzzles together and copying geometric shapes (such as triangles, rectangles, and circles). Nonverbal visual-spatial processing questions ask test takers to reproduce patterns of blocks and choose pictures that show how a piece of paper would look if it were folded or cut. Verbal questions also can require visual-spatial abilities:

> Suppose that you are going east, then turn right, then turn right again, then turn left. In what direction are you facing now?

Working Memory

The working memory part of the SB5 measures the ability to use short-term memory. Some typical memory tasks include the following:

> Correctly remember the order of colored beads on a stick.
> After hearing several sentences, name the last word from each sentence.
> Repeat a series of digits (forward or backward) after hearing them once.

The Wechsler Tests

Is the Stanford-Binet the only intelligence test? No. One widely used alternative is the *Wechsler Adult Intelligence Scale—Fourth Edition* (WAIS-IV). A version for children is called the *Wechsler Intelligence Scale for Children—Fifth Edition* (WISC-V). Like the Stanford-Binet, the Wechsler tests yield a single overall intelligence (g-factor) score. In addition, these tests also have separate scores for **performance (nonverbal) intelligence**, and **verbal intelligence**—language- or symbol-oriented intelligence (Neukrug & Fawcett, 2015). The abilities measured by the Wechsler tests and some sample test items are listed in ▲ Table 9.1.

The Results of Intelligence Tests: Intelligence Quotients

What is an IQ? Imagine that a child named Yuan can answer intelligence test questions that an average 7-year-old can answer. We could say that 7 is her **mental age** (average cognitive ability displayed by 7-year-olds). How intelligent is Yuan? We can't say yet, because we don't know how old she is. If she is 10, her intelligence would be lower. If she's 5, though, her intelligence would be quite high. To estimate a child's intelligence, then, we need to compare her mental age and her *chronological age* (age in years). When the Stanford-Binet was first used, MA (mental age) was divided by CA (chronological age). The resulting *quotient* was then multiplied by 100 to give a whole number, rather than a decimal, yielding an **intelligence quotient (IQ)**:

$$\frac{\text{MA}}{\text{CA}} \times 100 = \text{IQ}$$

"The five candles represent his mental age."

Kes/CartoonStock Ltd

General intelligence test A test that measures a wide variety of intellectual abilities.

Performance (nonverbal) intelligence Intelligence measured by solving puzzles, assembling objects, completing pictures, and other nonverbal tasks.

Verbal intelligence Intelligence measured by answering questions involving vocabulary, general information, arithmetic, and other language- or symbol-oriented tasks.

Mental age In intelligence testing, the average cognitive ability displayed by people of a given age.

Intelligence quotient (IQ) Mental age divided by chronological age times 100.

▲ Table 9.1 Sample Items Similar to Those Used on the WAIS-IV

Verbal Comprehension	Sample Items or Descriptions
Similarities	In what way are a wolf and a coyote alike? In what way are a screwdriver and a chisel alike?
Vocabulary	The test consists of asking, "What is a(n) ________?" or "What does ________ mean?" The words range from more to less familiar and difficult.
Information	How many wings does a butterfly have? Who wrote *Romeo and Juliet?*
Perceptual Reasoning	
Block design	Copy designs with blocks (as shown at right).
Matrix reasoning	Select the item that completes the matrix.
Visual puzzles	Choose the pieces that go together to form a figure.
Working Memory	
Digit span	Repeat from memory a series of digits, such as 8 5 7 0 1 3 6 2, after hearing it once.
Arithmetic	Four girls divided 28 jellybeans equally among themselves. How many jellybeans did each girl receive? If 3 peaches take 2 minutes to find and pick, how long will it take to find and pick a dozen peaches?
Processing Speed	
Symbol search	Match symbols appearing in separate groups.
Coding	Fill in the symbols:

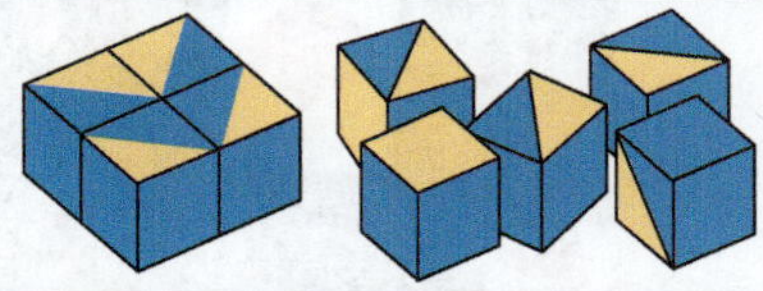

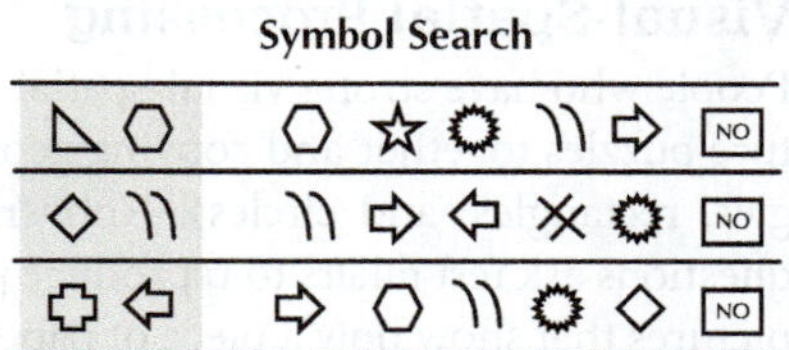

1	2	3	4
X	III	I	0

3	4	1	3	4	2	1	2

Items similar to those in Wechsler (2008).

In this way, children with different chronological and mental ages can be easily compared. For instance, 10-year-old Justin has a mental age of 12. Thus, his IQ is 120 ($12/10 = 1.2 \times 100 = 120$). Justin's friend Suke also has a mental age of 12. However, Suke's chronological age is 12, so his IQ is 100. The IQ shows that 10-year-old Justin is brighter than his 12-year-old friend Suke, even though their intellectual skills are about the same. Notice that a person's IQ will be 100 whenever mental age equals chronological age. This is why an IQ score of 100 is defined as average intelligence.

Then, does a person with an IQ score below 100 have below average intelligence? Not unless the IQ is well below 100. Average intelligence is usually defined as any score from 90 to 109. The important point is that IQ scores will be over 100 when mental age is higher than age in years. IQ scores below 100 occur when a person's age in years exceeds his or her mental age.

IQ scores from the WAIS-IV are classified as shown in ▲ Table 9.2. A look at the percentages reveals a definite pattern.

▲ Table 9.2 Distribution of Adult IQ Scores on the WAIS-IV

IQ	Description	Percent
Above 130	Very superior	2.2
120–129	Superior	6.7
110–119	Bright normal	16.1
90–109	Average	50.0
80–89	Dull normal	16.1
70–79	Borderline	6.7
Below 70	Intellectually disabled	2.2

Derived from Wechsler (2008).

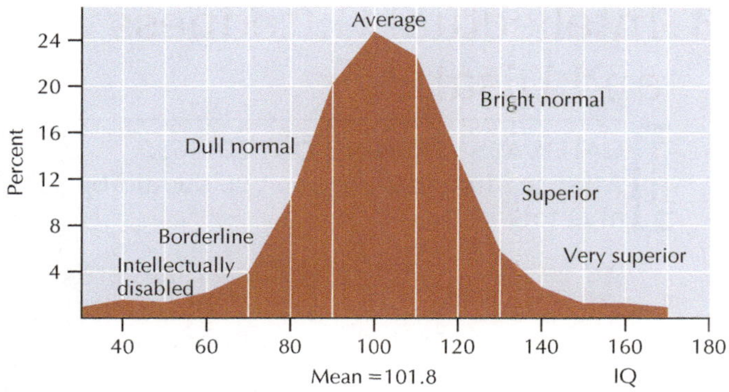

Figure 9.3 The bell curve. Distribution of Stanford-Binet Intelligence Test scores for 3,184 children. (Adapted from Terman & Merrill, 1937/1960.)

The distribution (or scattering) of IQ scores approximates a bell-shaped or **normal distribution**. That is, most scores fall close to the average and very few are found at the extremes. Figure 9.3 shows this characteristic of measured intelligence.

Deviation IQs

Although the preceding discussion may give you some insight into IQ scores, it's no longer necessary to directly calculate IQs. Instead, modern tests use **deviation IQs**. Tables supplied with the test are used to convert a person's relative standing in the group to an IQ score—that is, they tell how far above or below average the person's score falls. For example, if you score at the 50th percentile, half the people your age who take the test score higher than you and half score lower. In this case, your deviation IQ score is 100.

Predicting Achievement from IQ Scores

How do IQ scores relate to success in school, jobs, and other things we do? IQ differences of a few points are unlikely to be helpful in predicting differences between people, such as their performance in college. But if we look at people with a broader range of scores, the differences do become meaningful, adding support for the validity of the tests. For example, a person with an IQ of 80 might struggle with college, whereas one with an IQ of 120 would do just fine.

The correlation between IQ and school grades is about .50—a sizable association (Calvin et al., 2010; Mayes et al., 2009). However, research clearly demonstrates that academic performance may depend even more on motivation than it does on intelligence. No matter how smart you are, you likely won't do well at school if you simply don't care about your grades (see Section 14.5 for more information about perseverance). The same is true of "real-world" success beyond school (Strenze, 2007). Although the correlation between IQ and job performance ranges between .27 and .53, the correlations are higher for jobs that really emphasize the factors that are measured on an IQ test.

As you might expect, though, skills that are unrelated to IQ scores also predict positive career outcomes. Many of them are the focus of our *Psychology and Your Skill Set* sections; for example, self-regulation (Section 2.5), ethical behavior (Section 3.5), and the ability to work with diverse others (see Section 17.4). Moreover, IQ is *not* the best predictor of success in art, music, writing, dramatics, science, and leadership. Tests of creativity are much more strongly related to achievement in these areas (Runco, 2012; Zenasni et al., 2016).

Group Differences in IQ

Psychologists who measure IQ have noted that differences sometimes emerge on the scores obtained by different groups. Of greatest interest have been those related to age, sex, and race. We consider age and sex differences here; racial differences are discussed later in this chapter.

IQ and Age

The IQ scores of young children are not very reliable (that is, stable or consistent). In other words, knowing a child's IQ at age 3 tells us very little about what his or her IQ will be in adulthood. However, IQs do become more reliable as children grow older. Knowing a child's IQ at age 11 is a good predictor of his or her IQ later in life (Gow et al., 2010; Schneider, Niklas, & Schmiedeler, 2014).

After middle childhood, IQ scores usually change very little from year to year, with a small, gradual increase until about age 40 and a small, slow decline thereafter (Larsen, Hartmann, & Nyborg, 2008). This trend, of course, is an average; actual IQs also reflect a person's education, maturity, and experience. Some people make fairly large gains in IQ, whereas others have sizable losses. In general, those who gain in IQ are exposed to intellectual stimulation during early adulthood. Those who decline typically suffer from chronic illnesses, drug or alcohol abuse, or unstimulating lifestyles (Nisbett, 2009).

After middle age, the picture gets a bit more complex. Intellectual skills involved in fluid intelligence—solving novel problems involving perceptual speed or rapid insight—slowly decline after middle age. By way of compensation, crystallized intelligence-solving problems using already acquired knowledge—can actually increase or, at least, decline very little until older adulthood (Agbayani & Hiscock, 2013). In other words, younger people are generally "quick learners" (fluid intelligence) but tend to be "wet behind the ears" (lack experience or crystallized intelligence). Older people might be a little "slower on the uptake" but tend to "know the ropes." Since IQ tests such as the SB5 and WAIS test for components of both fluid intelligence and crystallized intelligence,

Normal distribution Bell-shaped curve of scores with a large number in the middle and very few on the high and low ends.

Deviation IQ An IQ obtained statistically from a person's relative standing in his or her age group—that is, how far above or below average the person's score is relative to other scores.

overall, age-related losses are small for most healthy, well-educated individuals (Agbayani & Hiscock, 2013; Rindermann, Flores-Mendoza, & Mansur-Alves, 2010).

IQ and Sex

While males and females do not appear to differ in *overall* intelligence, general intelligence tests allow us to compare the patterns of men and women on the different factors (Hyde & Else-Quest, 2013). For decades, women, as a group, performed best on items that require verbal ability, vocabulary, and rote learning. Men, in contrast, were best at items that require spatial visualization and math (Calvin et al., 2010; Clements et al., 2006). Today, such male–female differences have almost disappeared among children and young adults. The small differences that remain appear to be based on a tendency for parents and educators to encourage males, more than females, to learn math and spatial skills (Ceci & Williams, 2010).

Reflective Practice

Measuring Intelligence

1. The WAIS-IV, SB5, and SAT are all culture-fair intelligence scales. T or F?
2. Apply what you know about psychometric tests by placing an R or a V after each operation to indicate whether it would be used to establish the reliability (R) or the validity (V) of a test.
   a. Compare the score on one half of test items to the score on the other half. ( )
   b. Compare scores on test to grades, performance ratings, or other measures. ( )
   c. Compare scores from the test after administering it on two separate occasions. ( )
   d. Compare scores on alternate forms of the test. ( )
3. The WAIS-IV is an intelligence test for children. T or F?
4. IQ was originally defined as ________________ times 100.
5. The distribution of IQs approximates a ________________ (bell-shaped) curve.
6. Scores on modern intelligence tests are based on one's deviation IQ (relative standing among test takers), rather than on the ratio between mental age and chronological age. T or F?

THINK CRITICALLY

7. Assume that a test of memory for words is translated from English to Spanish. Would the Spanish version of the test be equal in difficulty to the English version?

SELF-REFLECT

- Do you think it would be possible to create an intelligence test that is universally culture-fair? What would its questions look like? Can you think of any type of question that wouldn't favor the mental skills emphasized by some culture, somewhere in the world?

Answers: 1. F 2. a. R, 2. b. V, 2. c. R, 2. d. R 3. F 4. MA/CA 5. Normal 6. T 7. Probably not, because the Spanish words might be longer or shorter than the same words in English. The Spanish words might also sound more or less alike than words on the original test. Translating an intelligence test into another language can subtly change the meaning and difficulty of test items.

9.3 Intellectual Giftedness and Disability

GATEWAYS LEARNING OUTCOMES: After reading this section you should be able to:

9.3.1 Outline how gifted individuals are identified, and the outcomes that are typically associated with giftedness

9.3.2 Outline how people with intellectual disabilities are identified, and the outcomes that are typically associated with this diagnosis

9.3.3 Outline some of the causes of intellectual disability, and name some of the resulting conditions

IQs that are extreme—below 70 or above 130—are very unusual; only about 4 percent of the population falls in these ranges. Nevertheless, that still translates to millions of people who have exceptionally high or low IQs. Let's take a closer look at what it means to live on the outer edges of the IQ test.

Intellectual Giftedness

Just as our understanding of the concept of intelligence is not yet fully settled, so too the definitions of terms like *genius* or *gifted* are still open to debate (Carman, 2013; Zenasni et al., 2016). Of course, the simplest definition is to reserve these terms for people with high IQs. Using this method, people who score above 130 on IQ tests (2 out of 100) are usually described as "gifted." Only one person in 1,000 scores above 145. These people are certainly gifted, or perhaps even "geniuses." However, some psychologists reserve the term *genius* for people who are exceptionally creative (Hallahan, Kauffman, & Pullen, 2015).

One of the questions that has interested psychological scientists is whether high IQ scores in childhood predict success in life beyond academic ability. In a classic attempt to answer this question, Lewis Terman followed a gifted group of 1,500 children with IQs of 140 or more (the "Termites," as he called them) from childhood to adulthood. Most were quite successful. A majority finished college, earned advanced degrees, or held professional positions, and many had written books or scientific articles (Terman & Oden, 1959). It's worth noting, though, that some had also committed crimes, were unemployable, or were unhappy misfits. Remember that a high IQ reveals *potential*. It does not guarantee success. Nor does a lower IQ guarantee failure.

How did Terman's more successful Termites differ from the less successful ones? Most of them had educated parents who valued learning and encouraged them to do the same. In general, successful gifted persons tend to have strong *intellectual determination*—a desire to know, to excel, and to persevere. As we indicated earlier, all signs point to the fact that, gifted or not, most people

It is wise to remember that a child may be gifted in many ways. Many schools now offer Gifted and Talented Education programs for students who have a variety of special abilities—not just for those who score well on IQ tests.

who go on to be successful tend to be persistent and motivated to learn—no one is paid to sit around being capable of achievement (Reis & Renzulli, 2010; Winner, 2003). That's why a child's talents are most likely to blossom when she or he is nurtured with support, encouragement, education, and effort (Reis, 2016).

Results from a recent large-scale European study are consistent with much of what Terman originally found: In general, children with higher IQs grow up into adults with higher IQs, more advanced educational achievements, and greater socioeconomic success (Fischbach et al., 2013; Schalke et al., 2013). At the same time, personality characteristics in childhood, such as optimism, studiousness, and attentiveness, are also related to adult success (Spengler et al., 2015).

Identifying Gifted Children

The National Association for Gifted Children notes that intellectual strengths are only one type of giftedness. In their definition, **giftedness** can also include other aptitudes, such as music or languages (Kreger Silverman, 2013). The following signs may reveal that a child is gifted: a tendency to seek out older children and adults; an early fascination with explanations and problem solving; perceptiveness and quick-wittedness, a tendency to challenge traditions or norms, an early interest in books, along with early reading (often by age 3), development of a strong vocabulary and the ability to talk in complete sentences at an early age, an unusually good memory, and a precocious talent in art, music, or number skills (Dai, 2010; Distin, 2006).

Programs for Gifted Children

Being exceptionally bright is not without its problems. Usually, parents and teachers must make adjustments to help gifted children make the most of their talents (Jolly et al., 2011). The gifted child may become bored in classes designed for average children. This can lead to misbehavior or clashes with teachers who think the gifted child is a show-off or smart aleck. Extremely bright children may also find classmates less stimulating than older children or adults. In recognition of these problems, many schools now provide special classes for gifted children. Such programs combine classroom enrichment with fast-paced instruction to satisfy the gifted child's appetite for intellectual stimulation (Dai, 2010; Moon, 2016; Reis & Renzulli, 2010). (■ All children benefit from enriched environments. For a discussion of enrichment and some guidelines for parents, see Section 3.1.)

Intellectual Disability

Just as some children have exceptionally high IQs, so other children have exceptionally low IQs. A person with cognitive abilities far below average is termed *intellectually disabled* (the former term, *mentally retarded*, is now regarded as offensive).

Identifying Individuals with Intellectual Disabilities

According to the definition listed in the American Psychiatric Association's *Diagnostic and Statistical Manual of Mental Disorders* (DSM-5), **intellectual disability (intellectual developmental disorder)** begins at an IQ of approximately 70 or below and is classified as shown in ▲ Table 9.3 (American Psychiatric

▲ Table 9.3 Levels of Intellectual Disability

IQ Range	Degree of Intellectual Disability	Educational Classification	Required Level of Support
55–70	Mild	Educable	Intermittent
40–55	Moderate	Trainable	Limited
25–40	Severe	Dependent	Extensive
Below 25	Profound	Life support	Pervasive

Adapted from American Psychiatric Association (2013).

Giftedness The possession of either a high IQ or special talents or aptitudes.

Intellectual disability (intellectual developmental disorder) The presence of a developmental disability, a formal IQ score below 70, and a significant impairment of adaptive behavior.

Association, 2013). The listed IQ ranges are approximate because IQ scores normally vary a few points if you take the test multiple times. The terms in the right-hand columns are listed only to give you a general impression of each IQ range.

It's important to recognize that in diagnoses of intellectual disability, a person's ability to perform *adaptive behaviors* (basic skills such as dressing, eating, communicating, shopping, and working) is more important than IQ (American Psychiatric Association, 2013). After all, why label someone with fairly good adaptive skills "severely intellectually disabled" just because his or her IQ falls within a prescribed range? The end result of such labels is, too often, a placing of needless limitations on the educational goals of intellectually disabled persons (Kirk, Gallagher, & Coleman, 2015; Murray et al., 2013).

Are the intellectually disabled usually placed in institutions? No. Total care is usually necessary only for the *profoundly* disabled (IQ below 25). Many of these individuals live in group homes or with their families. Those who are *severely* disabled (IQ of 25–40) and *moderately* disabled (IQ of 40–55) are capable of mastering basic language and self-help skills. Many become self-supporting by working in sheltered workshops (special, simplified work environments). The *mildly* disabled (IQ of 55–70) make up about 85 percent of all those affected. This group can benefit from carefully structured education. As adults, these persons, as well as the *borderline disabled* (IQ 70–85), can successfully marry or live alone. However, they tend to have difficulties with many of the demands of adult life (Danielsson et al., 2010; van Duijvenbode et al., 2013).

As is the case with *all* people, there is more to intellectually disabled people than what is revealed by the results of IQ testing (Treffert, 2014). In particular, they have no handicap concerning feelings. They are easily hurt by rejection, teasing, or ridicule. Likewise, they respond warmly to love and acceptance. They have a right to self-respect and a place in the community (Montreal Declaration on Intellectual Disabilities, 2004). This is especially important during childhood, when support from others adds greatly to each person's chances of becoming a well-adjusted member of society.

In addition, people who fall under the broad umbrella of intellectual disabilities can be very diverse. For example, some intellectually disabled individuals display a remarkable mixture of brilliance alongside their intellectual disability. They have **savant syndrome**, a limited general intelligence accompanied by exceptional mental ability in one or more narrow areas, such as mental arithmetic, calendar calculation, art, or music (Crane et al., 2010; Young, 2005).

For example, Kim Peek, who died in 2009, could recite from memory more than 9,000 books. The model for Dustin Hoffman's character in the Academy Award-winning film *Rain Man*, Kim knew all the ZIP codes and area codes in the United States and could give accurate travel directions between any two major US cities. He also could discuss hundreds of pieces of classical music in detail and could play most of them quite well. Amazingly, though, for someone with such skills, Kim had difficulty with abstract thinking and tests of general intelligence. He was poorly coordinated and couldn't button his own clothes (Treffert, 2010; Treffert & Christensen, 2005).

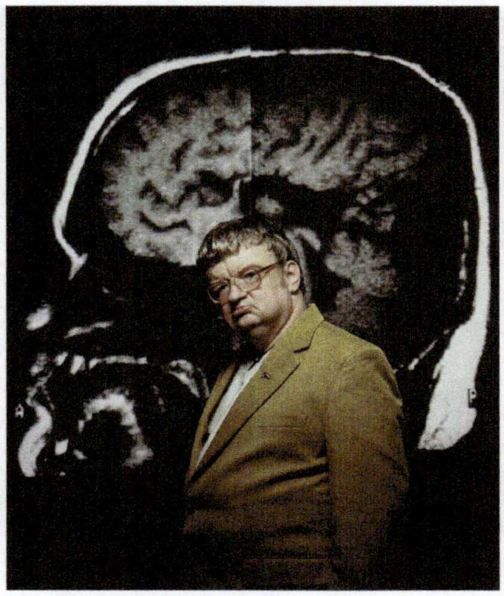

Ethan Hill/Contributor/Getty Images

Once, four months after reading a novel, Kim was asked about a character. He immediately named the character, gave the page number on which a description appeared, and accurately recited several paragraphs about the character (Treffert & Christensen, 2005).

The cause of savant syndrome is not clearly understood. According to one theory, many savants have suffered some form of damage to their left hemispheres, freeing them from the "distractions" of language, concepts, and higher-level thought. This allows them to focus with crystal clarity on music, drawing, prime numbers, license plates, television commercials, and other specific information (Young, 2005). Another theory holds that the performances of many savants result from intense practice (Snyder et al., 2006; Treffert, 2014).

Causes of Intellectual Disability

In 30 to 40 percent of cases, no known biological or intellectual disability can be identified. In many such instances, the degree of disability is mild (in the 50–70 IQ range). Often, other family members are also mildly disabled. **Familial intellectual disability**, as this is called, occurs mostly in very poor households, where nutrition, intellectual stimulation, medical care, and emotional support may be inadequate. This suggests that familial intellectual disability is largely a result of impoverished environments, and that it could be prevented by better nutrition, education, and early childhood enrichment programs could prevent many cases of intellectual disability (Harris, 2010).

About half of all cases of intellectual disability are *organic*, or related to physical disorders (Das, 2000). These include *birth injuries* (such as lack of oxygen during delivery), and *fetal damage* (prenatal damage from disease, infection, or drugs, including maternal alcoholism or drug use). (■ Fetal alcohol syndrome is the leading preventable cause of intellectual disability. See Section 3.1, for more details.) *Metabolic disorders*, which affect energy production and use in the body, also cause intellectual disability. Some forms of intellectual disability are linked to *genetic abnormalities*, such as missing genes, extra genes, or defective genes. Malnutrition and exposure to lead, polychlorinated biphenyls (PCBs), and other toxins early in childhood can also cause organic intellectual disability (Kalat, 2016). In many cases, no known biological problem can be identified.

Let's briefly look at several distinctive problems:

Down Syndrome

In 1 out of 800 babies, the disorder known as **Down syndrome** causes moderate to severe intellectual disability and a shortened life expectancy of around 49 years. It is now known that Down syndrome children have an extra 21st chromosome. This condition, which is called *trisomy-21,* results from flaws in the parents' egg or sperm cells (National Down Syndrome Society, 2017). Thus, while Down syndrome is *genetic,* it is not usually *hereditary* (that is, it doesn't "run in the family").

The age of biological parents (especially mothers) is a major factor in Down syndrome. As people age, their reproductive cells are more prone to errors during cell division. This raises the odds that an extra chromosome will be present. As you can see in the following table, the older a woman is, the greater the risk (National Down Syndrome Society, 2017):

Mother's Age	Incidence of Down Syndrome
25	1/1,200
35	1/350
49	1/10

Fathers, and possibly especially older fathers, also add to the risk; in about 5 percent of cases, the father is the source of the extra chromosome. Older adults who plan to have children should carefully consider the odds shown here.

There is no "cure" for Down syndrome. However, these children are usually loving and responsive, and they make progress in a caring environment. At a basic level, Down syndrome children can do most of the things that other children can, only slower. The best hope for Down syndrome children, therefore, lies in specially tailored educational programs that enable them to lead fuller lives.

Fragile X Syndrome

The second most common form of genetic intellectual disability (after Down syndrome) is **fragile X syndrome**. Unlike Down syndrome, fragile X syndrome is hereditary—it *does* run in families. The problem is related to a thin, frail-looking area on the *X* (female) chromosome. Fragile X is sex-linked (like color blindness); boys are usually more affected, at a rate of about 1 out of every 5,000 (Centers for Disease Control, 2016e).

Fragile X males generally have long, thin faces and big ears. Physically, they are usually larger than average during childhood, but smaller than average after adolescence. Up to three-fourths of all fragile X males suffer from hyperactivity and attention disorders. Many also have a tendency to avoid eye contact with others.

While fragile X males are only mildly intellectually disabled during early childhood, they are often severely or profoundly intellectually disabled as adults (Schneide, Ligsay, & Hagerman, 2013). When learning adaptive behaviors, they tend to do better with daily living skills than with language and social skills (Hallahan, Kauffman, & Pullen, 2015).

Phenylketonuria (PKU)

Another genetic disorder called **phenylketonuria (PKU)** (FEN-ul-KEET-uh-NURE-ee-ah) plagues children who lack an important enzyme. This causes phenylpyruvic (FEN-ul-pye-ROO-vik) acid (a destructive chemical) to collect within their bodies. PKU is also linked to very low levels of dopamine, an important chemical messenger in the brain. If PKU goes untreated, severe intellectual disability typically occurs (Kalat, 2016).

PKU can be detected in newborn babies by routine medical testing. Affected children are usually placed on a diet low in phenylalanine, the substance that the child's body can't handle. Carefully following this diet will usually minimize the degree of intellectual disability (Palermo et al., 2017). (Phenylalanine is present in many foods, including aspartame—the artificial sweetener in diet colas.)

Microcephaly

The word **microcephaly** (MY-kro-SEF-ah-lee) means "small-headedness." The microcephalic person suffers a rare abnormality in which the skull is extremely small or fails to grow. This forces the brain to develop in a limited space, causing severe intellectual disability (Centers for Disease Control, 2016g). Although they are typically institutionalized, microcephalic persons are usually affectionate, well behaved, and cooperative.

This young woman exhibits the classical features of Down syndrome, including almond-shaped eyes, a slightly protruding tongue, a stocky build, and stubby hands with deeply creased palms. Although she is mildly intellectually disabled, she is very loving and has a right to self-respect and a place in the community.

Savant syndrome The possession of exceptional mental ability in one or more narrow areas, such as mental arithmetic, calendar calculation, art, or music, by a person of limited general intelligence.

Familial intellectual disability Mild intellectual disability associated with homes that are intellectually, nutritionally, and emotionally impoverished.

Down syndrome A genetic disorder caused by the presence of an extra chromosome; results in intellectual disability.

Fragile X syndrome A genetic form of intellectual disability caused by a defect in the *X* chromosome.

Phenylketonuria (PKU) A genetic disease that allows phenylpyruvic acid to accumulate in the body.

Microcephaly A disorder in which the head and brain are abnormally small.

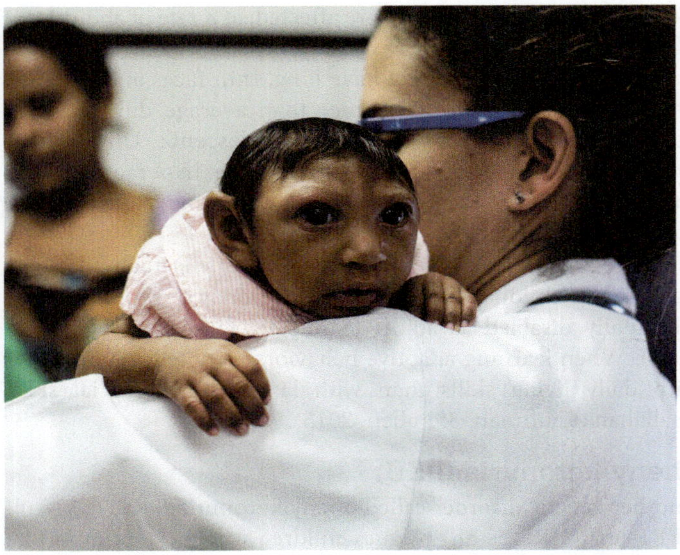

Barcroft Media/Barcroft Media/Getty Images

Unfortunately, over the last few years the prevalence of microcephaly has spiked. This is because pregnant women who are bitten by a mosquito infected with the Zika virus are at risk for transmitting the virus to their fetuses, leading to microcephaly and other brain malformations (Ahrens et al., 2017).

Hydrocephaly

Hydrocephaly (HI-dro-SEF-ah-lee), which means "water on the brain," is caused by a buildup of cerebrospinal fluid within brain cavities. Pressure from this fluid can damage the brain and enlarge the head. Hydrocephaly is not uncommon—about 10,000 hydocephalic babies are born each year in the United States and Canada. However, thanks to well-established medical procedures, many of these infants will lead nearly normal lives. A surgically implanted tube drains fluid from the brain into the abdomen and minimizes brain damage. Although affected children often score below average on mental tests, severe intellectual disability usually can be prevented (Tully et al., 2016).

Congenital Hypothyroidism

Congenital hypothyroidism is another type of intellectual disability that appears in infancy. It results from an insufficient supply of thyroid hormone. In some parts of the world, this disorder is caused by a lack of iodine in the diet (the thyroid glands require iodine to function normally). Iodized salt has made this source of intellectual disability rare in developed nations. Congenital hypothyroidism causes stunted physical and intellectual growth that cannot be reversed. Fortunately, it is easily detected in infancy and can be treated with thyroid hormone replacement before permanent damage occurs.

Reflective Practice

Intellectual Giftedness and Disability

1. Diagnoses of intellectual disability incorporate adaptive behaviors as well as IQ scores. T or F?
2. The association between IQ and high-status professional jobs proves that such jobs require more intelligence. T or F?
3. Only about 6 percent of the population scores above 140 on IQ tests. T or F?
4. An IQ score below 90 indicates intellectual disability. T or F?
5. Many cases of intellectual disability without known organic causes appear to be ____________________.

THINK CRITICALLY

6. Lewis Terman took great interest in the lives of many of the "Termites." He even went so far as to advise them about what kinds of careers they should pursue. Evaluate his actions and indicate what error of observation Terman made.

SELF-REFLECT

- Do you think that giftedness should be defined by high IQ or having special talents (or both)?
- As a psychologist you are asked to assess a child's degree of intellectual disability. Will you rely more on IQ or the child's level of adaptive behavior? Would you be more confident in your judgment if you took both factors into account?

Answers: 1. T 2. F 3. F 4. F 5. familial 6. Terman may have unintentionally altered the behavior of the people he was studying. Although Terman's observations are generally regarded as valid, he did break a basic rule of scientific observation.

9.4 Genetic and Environmental Contributions to Intelligence

GATEWAYS LEARNING OUTCOMES:
After reading this section you should be able to:

9.4.1 Describe the general results of research investigating the role of genes in intelligence

9.4.2 Describe the general results of research investigating the role of the environment in intelligence

Like the vast majority of our traits, psychologists agree that intelligence is a product of both genes and environment. The question of how much each contributes, however, can be contentious. Some psychologists believe that intelligence is strongly affected by heredity. Others feel that environment is dominant. Let's examine the evidence for each view.

Hereditary Influences

In a classic study of genetic factors in learning, Tryon (1929) managed to breed separate strains of "maze-bright" and "maze-dull" rats (animals that were extremely good or poor at learning mazes). After several generations of breeding, even the slowest "bright" rat outperformed the best "dull" rat This and other studies of *eugenics*, selective breeding for desirable characteristics, suggest that some traits are highly influenced by heredity.

That may be true, but is maze-learning really a good operational definition of intelligence? You may remember from ■ Section 1.3 that when we're trying to study psychological characteristics that can't be seen, we need to find ways to define those characteristics in terms of observable behaviors—these are considered to be operational definitions. Many people would agree that maze running isn't a great operational definition—while Tryon's study seemed to show that intelligence is inherited, later researchers found that the "bright" rats were simply more motivated by food and less easily distracted during testing. When they weren't chasing after rat chow, the bright rats were no more intelligent than the supposedly dull rats. Thus, Tryon's study did demonstrate that behavioral characteristics like motivation and distractibility can be influenced by heredity (at least among rats); however, it was inconclusive concerning intelligence. What do more recent human studies have to say?

Most people are aware of a moderate similarity in the intelligence of parents and their children or brothers and sisters. As ● Figure 9.4 shows, the closer two people are on a family tree, the more alike their IQs are likely to be. At first glance, that might seem to suggest that intelligence is inherited. If you're thinking critically, though, you'll see a problem with that logic: Siblings and their parents share similar environments, as well as similar genes (Grigorenko, 2005; Kaplan, 2012). How do we know which one is causing the similarities between people who are related?

Twin Studies

To separate the effects of nature and nurture on intelligence, a **twin study** may be done. Such studies compare the IQs of twins who were either raised together or separated at birth. This allows us to better estimate how much heredity and environment affect intelligence. Notice in ● Figure 9.4 that the IQ scores of fraternal twins are more alike than the IQs of ordinary brothers and sisters. **Fraternal twins** come from two separate eggs that are fertilized at the same time. They are no more genetically alike than ordinary siblings. Why, then, should the twins' IQ scores be more similar? The reason is environmental: Parents likely treat fraternal twins more alike than ordinary siblings, resulting in a closer match in IQs.

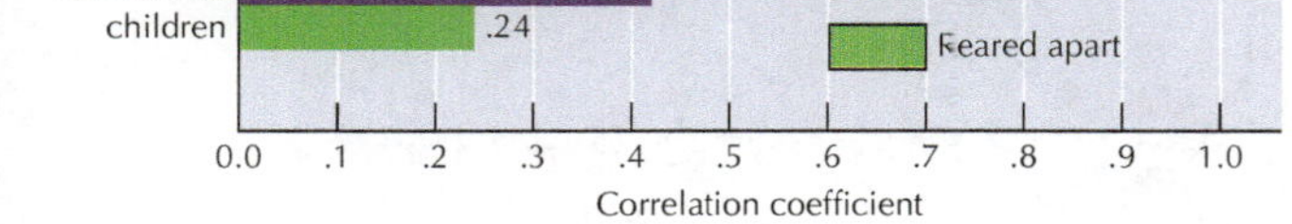

● **Figure 9.4 IQ as a function of genetic relatedness.** Approximate correlations between IQ scores for persons with varying degrees of genetic and environmental similarity. Notice that the correlations grow smaller as the degree of genetic similarity declines. Also, note that a shared environment increases the correlations in all cases. (Adapted from McGue et al., 1993.)

More striking similarities are observed with **identical twins**, who develop from a single egg and have identical genes. At the top of Figure 9.4, you can see that identical twins who grow up in the same family have highly correlated IQs. This is what we would expect with an identical genome and very similar environments. Now, let's consider what happens when identical twins are reared apart. As you can see, the correlation drops, but only from .86 to .72. Figures like these show that differences in adult intelligence are roughly 50 percent hereditary (Jacobs et al., 2008; Nisbett et al., 2012). (■ Identical twins also tend to have similar personality traits. This suggests that heredity contributes to personality as well as intelligence. For more information, see Section 12.4.)

There's an interesting twist on the heritability of intelligence, though: It has a developmental component. What this means is that the importance of genes as contributors to intelligence changes as we move through the lifespan. What's more, their importance changes in a way that is the *opposite* of what people typically expect. We've noted that heritability estimates are approximately 50 percent, but that number is much lower in childhood, and it gets higher as we age. Put another way, genes make less of a contribution to measures of intelligence in childhood, but they have an increasing influence as we move into adulthood (Sauce and Matzel, 2018).

Studying the Science: Genes and Intelligence

Let's dig a bit deeper on those twin studies that have contributed to our understanding of heritability. Specifically, it's worth mentioning a subtle point about identical twins reared apart: Separated identical twins are often placed in adoptive homes that are socially and educationally similar. These similar environments would tend to inflate apparent genetic effects by making the separated twins' IQs more alike. Another frequently overlooked fact is that twins grow up in the same environment before birth (in the womb). Taking these post-adoption and prenatal environmental effects into account, it's possible that intelligence may be less than

Hydrocephaly A buildup of cerebrospinal fluid within brain cavities.

Congenital hypothyroidism Stunted growth and intellectual disability caused by an insufficient supply of thyroid hormone.

Twin study A comparison of the characteristics of twins who were raised together or separated at birth; used to identify the relative impact of heredity and environment.

Fraternal twins Twins conceived from two separate eggs.

Identical twins Twins who develop from a single egg and so share the same genes.

50 percent heritable (Nisbett et al., 2012; Turkheimer et al., 2003); however, arriving at a specific number is likely to be impossible. What's clear from these twin studies is that genes *do* make an important contribution to the cognitive abilities that are measured by IQ tests. Remember, though, that when you encounter such numbers in the popular press, they represent scientists' best guess as to what is likely to be true in the *population*—for any individual pair of related people, similarities in intelligence due to genes may be higher or lower. Put another way, heritability estimates are useful when we think about groups, not individual people.

Intelligent Genes?

After the human genome was fully mapped, some scientists went in search of specific genes that might be responsible for intelligence, and early studies nominated a small number of "candidate genes" that seemed to be particularly critical. Importantly, this research suffered from many of the problems that accompany small samples and, like other studies in the medical sciences, they have failed to replicate (Chabris et al., 2012; ■ see Section 1.4 for a refresher on the importance of replication in science and why small samples make replication unlikely). Indeed, the view that is emerging now from larger-scale studies is that virtually all psychological characteristics—including intelligence—are the products of dozens, if not hundreds, of genes, each of which contributes only a very, very small amount to a person's score on a measure of intelligence (Chabris et al., 2015). Though cognitive biases push us toward seeking simple stories to explain the world, all of the evidence points to the fact that the story of genes and IQ is a very long and complex one, and cannot be understood simply by looking at a small number of genes.

How Genes Influence Intelligence

If genes have a role to play in intelligence then it's reasonable to ask where and how they exert their effects. It probably won't surprise you to know that the types of tasks included on an IQ test depend heavily on the central nervous system (the brain and spinal cord). But what, exactly, are those genes coding for? What's different about the nervous system of someone who can do well on an IQ test? We'll explore two related possibilities here: the first is that the genes may contribute to differences in the *structure* of the nervous system; the second is that differences in structure may result in corresponding changes to its *functioning*.

Effects on the Structure of the Nervous System

Your genome makes an important contribution to human development, including development of the brain. You may recall from ■ Section 2.3 that the brain's frontal lobes are related to more complex behaviors (Colom et al., 2013). They appear to be responsible for our *executive functions*, the higher-level mental processes that allow us to regulate and coordinate our own thought processes (■ see Section 2.5 for more information about executive functions).

While brain imaging studies confirm the role that the frontal lobes, and especially prefrontal area, play in intelligence, there is more to the story (Langeslag et al., 2013). First, the degree to which the frontal cortex is interconnected with the rest of the brain also appears to be important (Cole et al., 2012; Penke et al., 2012). That makes sense; our executive functions by themselves are not the sum total of our intelligence. Instead they are more likely the g-factor, *regulating* and *coordinating* other parts of our brain.

Second, as you can see in ● Figure 9.5, while these brain images reveal that parts of the frontal cortex are larger in people with higher IQs, the same is true for other parts of the cortex (Haier et al., 2004). Again, perhaps we shouldn't be surprised that a function as complex as intelligence relies on activity in many different brain areas.

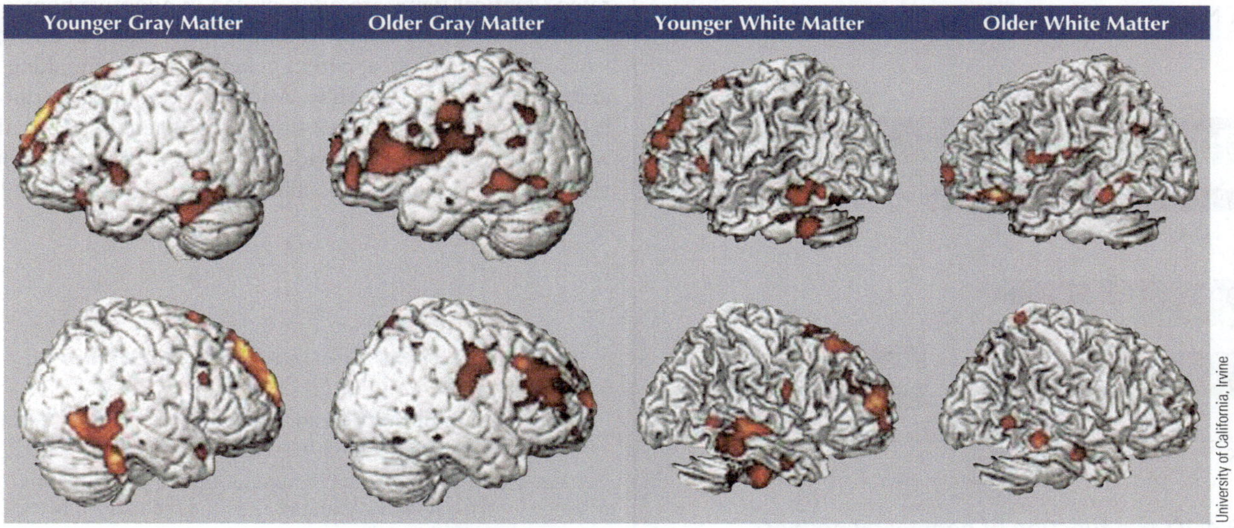

● Figure 9.5 Magnetic resonance imaging (MRI) identification of cortical areas whose size is correlated with IQ. Brain areas pictured in red and yellow are larger in people with higher IQs. Size differences were found in both gray matter (nuclei, or clumps of neuron cell bodies) and white matter (tracts, or bundles of myelinated axons). The left hemisphere is shown in the top row; the right is on the bottom. Two groups were studied: Younger and older participants. (From Haier et al., 2004.)

Effects on the Functioning of the Nervous System

In addition to structural differences, researchers are investigating differences in the functioning of the nervous system. One possibility is that intelligent people have brains that work more efficiently (Haier, 2017). Another is that they have nervous systems that respond more quickly. To investigate this possibility, researchers measure how fast people process various kinds of information (Coyle et al., 2011; Doebler & Scheffler, 2016). For example, psychologists have looked at people's **reaction time**, or the time that it takes to respond to a stimulus (see Figure 9.6). The flurry of brain activity that follows exposure to a stimulus can also be recorded. Such studies attempt to measure a person's **speed of processing**, which is assumed to reflect the brain's speed and efficiency (Madison et al., 2016; Waiter et al., 2009).

In general, people higher in measured IQ perform faster on reaction time tasks like that shown in Figure 9.6 (McCrory & Cooper, 2005). In addition, brain areas that control higher mental abilities usually become more active during reaction time testing (Waiter et al., 2009). Such observations suggest that having a quick nervous system is part of what it means to be smart, swift, or brainy.

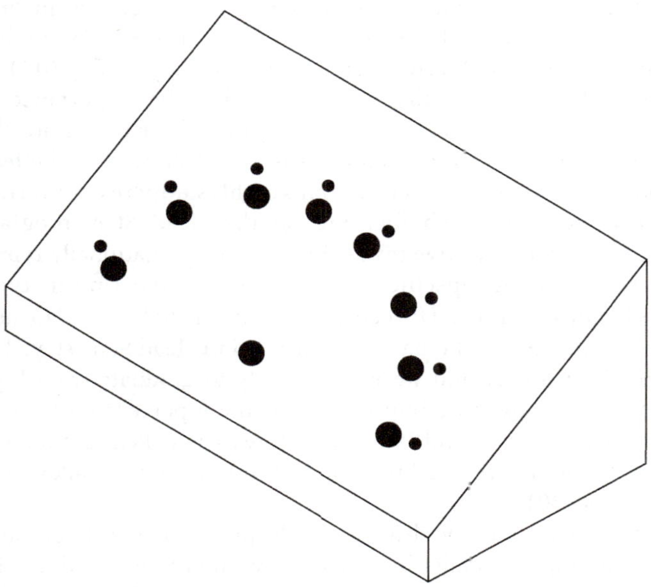

Figure 9.6 Jensen box for measuring reaction time. The large circles are buttons and the small circles are lights. The button without a light is the home button. Simple reaction time is measured using only one light. Research participants press the home button until that light comes on, at which time the corresponding button must be pressed as soon as possible. More complex reaction times can be measured by having the research participant press the home button until one of the lights comes on, at which time the correct button must be pressed as soon as possible. As the number of alternatives increases (say from 2 to 4 or even 8), the decision becomes more complex, resulting in longer and longer reaction times (Doebler & Scheffler, 2016).

In addition to speed, though, much intelligent behavior is an expression of the quality of our thinking skills. Cognitive psychologist David Perkins believes that how smart you are depends on three factors:

- Relatively fixed **neural intelligence** (the speed and efficiency of the nervous system)
- **Experiential intelligence** (specialized knowledge and skills acquired over time)
- **Reflective intelligence** (an ability to become aware of one's own thinking habits)

Little can be done to change neural intelligence. However, by adding to experiential intelligence (that is, personal knowledge), people can become more intelligent (Perkins, 1995; Ritchhart & Perkins, 2005). Recall in Section 7.3 we discussed the value of prior knowledge stored in long-term memory, and its value in learning. Essentially, years of research suggest that the more you know, the more quickly you'll be able to process new information.

Moreover, by applying reflective intelligence, it is possible to develop **metacognitive skills**. *Meta* means "about," so metacognitive skills are skills about cognition, or how you think about your own thinking. Such skills involve an ability to manage your own thinking and problem solving. Typically, this means learning about breaking problems into parts, establishing goals and subgoals, monitoring your progress, and making corrections. Learning metacognitive skills is an important component in becoming more intelligent (Ku & Ho, 2010). (Look back at Section 5.5 to remind yourself about how to sharpen your metacognitive skills.)

Environmental Influences

Of course, genes' contribution to brain development is only part of the story. Data suggesting that the environment has a role to play in intelligence have emerged in several areas of study. Here, we'll address three of them: adoption studies, long-term studies of the Flynn effect, and research investigating formal education.

Reaction time The amount of time that a person must look at a stimulus to make a correct judgment about it.

Speed of processing The speed with which a person can mentally process information.

Neural intelligence The innate speed and efficiency of a person's brain and nervous system.

Experiential intelligence Specialized knowledge and skills acquired through learning and experience.

Reflective intelligence An ability to become aware of one's own thinking habits.

Metacognitive skills An ability to manage one's own thinking and problem-solving efforts.

Adoption Studies

Some evidence for an environmental view of intelligence comes from adoption studies that investigate children who are adopted out of environments characterized by low socioeconomic status (SES). Dutch developmental psychologist Marinus van IJzendoorn carried out two large meta-analyses that specifically addressed this issue (■ recall from Section 1.6 that a meta-analysis involves pulling together data from a large number of studies to increase the sample size and bolster confidence in the results). The first included 62 studies and 18,000 children, and found that IQ scores of adopted children were, on average, 17.6 points higher than those children who were not adopted. The second meta-analysis investigated 3,800 children in 19 countries and found that, on average, children who were adopted out of orphanages had IQ scores that were 16.5 points higher than those who were not adopted. Further adding to the argument for environmental effects, this IQ difference was slightly smaller when the orphanage was located in countries that are higher on the Human Development Index (11.9 points) than those that are lower (21 points). (Countries with a high Human Development Index have lower mortality, better rates of literacy and education, and a higher quality of life; van IJzendoorn et al., 2008.)

The Flynn Effect

Many psychologists now agree that IQ scores in Western, industrialized nations have risen over the last 50 or so years (Flynn, 2012; Williams, 2013). Not by a little bit, mind you. If our grandparents scored an IQ of 100 (average, remember?) 50 years ago, they might score as low as about 70 on today's IQ tests. Conversely, if your IQ is 100 today, 50 years ago you might have scored as much as 130 on the old IQ tests. This rapid rise in IQ, referred to as the *Flynn effect* after the discoverer, New Zealand psychologist James Flynn, has occurred in far too short a time to be explained by genetics. Instead, it is more likely that the gains reflect environmental factors (Flynn, 2012; Rindermann, Becker, & Coyle, 2017).

But which factors? Flynn (2012) credits modern society, which is becoming ever more complex, demanding ever more abstract, "scientific" skills of its members. If you've ever tried to fill out an online tax form or set up a wireless network in your home, you'll understand why people may be getting better at answering IQ test questions. Video games, the Internet, and even television programming are also becoming more complex. As a result, everyday living demands greater abstract cognitive effort from us. In the end, popular culture may well be inviting us to read, reflect, and problem solve more than ever before (Jaeggi et al., 2008).

Does this mean that my grandparents were intellectually disabled or that I am a genius? No, but your grandparents likely depended less on abstract reasoning than you do. For example, Flynn gives the following question that you might find on a modern IQ test: "How are dogs and rabbits alike?" (Crist & Requarth, 2012). While you might abstractly answer (correctly, according to the IQ test) that "They are both mammals," your grandparents were more likely to give a concrete, functional answer like "Dogs hunt rabbits" (which modern IQ tests are likely to score as wrong).

Just like people from other cultures, your grandparents did not automatically value the abstract reasoning prized in today's more complex society. Nevertheless, had they been born today, they undoubtedly would have developed abstract reasoning skills just as well as you have. Alternatively, had you been born into their world, you undoubtedly would have, in the end, answered IQ test questions more like them. The takeaway point is that our intelligence, along with the ways we measure it, cannot easily be separated from the social and cultural context of the particular places and times in which we grow up.

Formal Education

If the Flynn effect is real, then it suggests that life experiences can result in raised IQ scores. It's reasonable to wonder, then, whether formal education can boost intelligence. Consider, for example, **early childhood education (ECE) programs**, such as Head Start, which are designed to provide disadvantaged preschool children with high-quality educational experiences to better prepare them for the regular school system.

Initial findings did not look promising: It appeared, for example, that there were academic gains for children in the program, but that they did not persist (Shager et al., 2013). In contrast, a more recent meta-analysis that was restricted to high-quality experimental and quasi-experimental studies suggested that early childhood education did have benefits, including lower rates of placement in special education classes and higher rates of high school graduation (McCoy et al., 2017). If you're thinking critically, you'll remember the importance of experimental studies from ■ Section 1.6: Experiments are the only type of research that allow us to establish cause and effect, and consequently the positive results of this study are noteworthy. Other recent research focusing on the Head Start program found similarly positive results in a very large, nationally representative sample. Specifically, economists at the University of Michigan examined US census data from 2000 to 2013 and found that adults who had been enrolled in Head Start stayed in school for longer and were more likely to graduate from high school. Perhaps more impressive was the 9 percent increase in college enrolments and 19 percent increase in college graduation rates for adults who had participated in Head Start (Bailey, Sun, & Timpe, 2018).

It's not completely clear how ECE programs like Head Start work to improve adults' lives. The early studies suggested that it's *not* the result of improving their academic skills like reading and math. However, it may be that these programs help children with other skills that allow them to be successful, such as self-regulation (■ see Section 2.5), problem solving (■ see Section 8.2), or emotional stability (■ see Section 10.4). Given the importance of the environment on children's development more generally (■ see Section 3.1), benefits to children may also stem from the fact that ECE programs allow parents to work, thus improving the family's standard of living (Chaudry et al., 2011).

Reflective Practice

Genetic and Environmental Contributions to Intelligence

1. The closest similarity in IQs would be observed for
   a. parents and their children
   b. identical twins reared apart
   c. fraternal twins reared together
   d. siblings reared together
2. Most psychologists believe that intelligence is 90 percent hereditary. T or F?
3. The claim that heredity accounts for racial differences in average IQ ignores environmental differences and the cultural bias inherent in standard IQ tests. T or F?
4. Reaction time has been used as a measure of ________________ intelligence.
   a. experiential
   b. neural
   c. reflective
   d. analytical

THINK CRITICALLY

5. Some people treat IQ as if it were a fixed number, permanently stamped on the forehead of each child. Evaluate this view in light of what you have learned in this section, and suggest why it is in error.

SELF-REFLECT

- Why do you think that studies of hereditary and environmental influences on intelligence have provoked such emotional debate? Which side of the debate would you expect each of the following people to favor: teacher, parent, school administrator, politician, medical doctor, liberal, conservative, bigot?

Answers: 1. b 2. F 3. T 4. b 5. Because one's IQ depends on the intelligence test used to measure it, change the test and you will, to some extent, change the score. Also, heredity establishes a range of possibilities; it does not automatically preordain a person's intellectual capacities.

9.5 Thinking Ethically About Intelligence

GATEWAYS LEARNING OUTCOMES:
After reading this section you should be able to:

9.5.1 Identify two problems associated with the claim that genetic differences between groups explain group-based differences in intelligence

9.5.2 Define artificial intelligence, and explain some of the ethical concerns raised by its use

To understand why IQ tests are so controversial, we need only look at their history. Seen through the lens of our current knowledge, for example, it's clear that early versions of IQ tests had very significant limitations, and that they disadvantaged particular groups of people. You need look no further than Darryl Lester, described at the beginning of this chapter, for evidence of this fact. Poor psychometric tests of intelligence still exist of course—as we mentioned earlier, you don't have to look very far on the Internet to find them. But if we limit ourselves to talking about legitimate IQ testing by psychologists and other qualified professionals, the controversy often centers on how these tests can still be misused and misinterpreted.

Scores on an IQ test aren't innocuous in the same way as those you'll get from the *Buzzfeed* quiz that classifies you as an introvert or extrovert based on the potato-based foods you like (yes, that one's for real). Every day, IQ tests contribute to decision making with important implications for people's lives: which people get into which colleges, which people will receive additional resources in school, which people are deemed criminally insane by the justice system, and which people will be hired for particular jobs. Before eugenics laws were struck down in the 1970s, IQ scores were even used to justify forced sterilization so that people deemed intellectually "inferior" could not have children.

Perhaps it's just as important to consider the value that we place on the characteristic we call intelligence. People classed as intelligent tend to command respect; people listen carefully to their opinions and are inclined to follow their directions without the scrutiny they might give to others who are thought to be less intelligent. For all of these reasons, it's critical that we continually examine the IQ tests we use and look for ways to make them better. It's also important that we use intelligence tests with care, and that we're sensitive to their effects. Finally, we need to respect the boundaries of interpreting the IQ score, and what it can and cannot tell us about people.

In this section, we tackle two current ethical challenges related to the concept of intelligence. The first concerns interpretations of race-based differences in IQ scores. The second is a more unusual challenge that is emerging as computing becomes more sophisticated; namely, managing the technology that is associated with artificial intelligence. Let's dig a bit deeper to explore these two issues in more detail.

IQ Scores and Race

One of the most persistent misinterpretations related to IQ tests concerns their connection with race. Historically, African American children in the United States scored an average of about 15 points lower on standardized IQ tests than European American children (although this gap has been reduced by one-third since 1972; Nisbett et al., 2012). Conversely, as a group, Japanese American children scored above average in IQ.

In light of this information, a question that repeatedly emerges concerns whether these differences are genetic. After all, if IQ has a genetic basis, and race has a genetic basis, then shouldn't some of the group differences in IQ be based on genes? The question is

Early childhood education program A program that provides stimulating intellectual experiences, typically for disadvantaged preschoolers.

more important than it may at first seem: Some people feel that a genetic explanation for group IQ differences would be sufficient reason to deny resources to a particular group. Their reasoning is that a genetic basis for lower IQ scores would suggest that providing additional resources "won't change anything." For example, one persistent, but disputed, claim is that African Americans score below average in IQ because they are genetically incapable of climbing out of poverty (Ossorio, 2011; Rushton & Jensen, 2005). Consequently, the argument goes, there is no point in providing enriched daycare experiences or other supports for African American children—their genes have already determined that these resources won't help.

Psychologists (and geneticists) have responded to such claims with several counterarguments that make clear the problems with this assertion. To begin, it is no secret that, as a group, African Americans are more likely than European Americans to live in environments that are physically, educationally, and intellectually impoverished. When unequal education is part of the equation, IQs may tell us little about how heredity affects intelligence (Sternberg et al., 2011; Suzuki & Aronson, 2005). Indeed, we have already explored how powerful adoption can be on IQ: One study found that placing poor African American children into European American adoptive families increased the children's IQs by an average of 13 points, bringing them into line with those of European American children (Nisbett, 2005, 2009). In other words, providing African American children with the same environmental experiences—including education—available to European American children erased IQ differences.

Moreover, researchers have concluded that there is no scientific evidence that group differences in average IQ have *any* basis in genetics. This is not to say that those group IQ differences are completely based in the environment. Instead, it's a statement to the effect that, *at this time, there is simply no way to put a simple number on the importance of genes versus the environment in understanding the root of those group differences in IQ* (Nisbett, Harden, & Turkheimer, 2017). There are two reasons why this is the case.

The first relates to newer research, described earlier, indicating that there are likely hundreds of genes that contribute in very small ways to intelligence. What's important to note about that work is that virtually all of the studies are based on the DNA of European Americans. At this time, we know very little about the extent to which those findings about "intelligence genes" will hold in other populations, but the work thus far suggests substantial differences often exist between groups and so generalizing from one group to another may not be valid (1000 Genomes Consortium, 2015).

The second reason that we cannot make any claims about the relationship between IQ, race, and genetics has to do with the very imperfect relationship between race and genetics. Old measures of race were crude, including "race" questions on a census form. Most scientists now agree that these self-identified categories are not helpful because they tell us nothing about a person's *ancestry* (that is, what proportion of their genes reflect African, European, Asian, or American ancestral backgrounds). Skin color, which was often used as the obvious marker of race, has much less to do with genetic differences than does ancestral background (Bonham, Warshauer-Baker, & Collins, 2005; Sternberg, 2007). Newer studies that measure genetic ancestry have the potential to provide a much clearer picture of how genes impact many characteristics, including intelligence, but as yet we cannot say whether genes play any role at all in explaining group differences in IQ.

After testing her DNA, author Anita Foeman discovered, to her surprise, that her ancestry includes British, Scandinavian, and Asian genes, as well as those from Africa.

Intelligence in Everyday Life: Artificial Intelligence

Many Americans now take for granted how easy it is to tell the personal assistant on their phone or in their home to take care of a task. Asking Siri what song is playing on the radio or telling Alexa to order a pizza is now commonplace. Many people also appreciate the fact that online shopping and streaming services can now anticipate what they might want to buy or watch, and make helpful suggestions. These examples demonstrate just how deeply artificial intelligence has moved into our everyday lives.

While most research on intelligence has focused on humans, a group of psychologists and computer scientists have immersed themselves in furthering **artificial intelligence (AI)**. AI fundamentally refers to computer programs that demonstrate the ability to do things such as reason and solve problems—tasks that are associated with an intelligent human mind (Müller, 2012; Russell & Norvig, 2014).

In the early days, computers were most successful in specific situations where complex skills could be converted into clearly stated rules that a computer can follow. The resulting *expert systems* can already predict the weather, analyze geological formations, diagnose disease, play chess, read, tell when to buy or sell stocks, harmonize music, and perform many other tasks better than humans (Giarratano & Riley, 2004; Mahmoodabadi et al., 2010). Consider, for example, IBM's "Watson," which outperformed expert humans at playing the television game *Jeopardy* (Markoff, 2011). Another example is Deep Blue, which beat world chess champion Garry Kasparov in 1997. For fans of Go, AlphaGo finished off world Go champion, Lee Se-dol, in 2016.

Source: YouTube

This robot recently held the robot world record for solving the Rubik's Cube, taking less than 1 second. What did it take the fastest human, you ask? About 5.25 seconds! To what extent is the way this robot comes up with solutions helpful for understanding how humans do it?

While these expert systems may perform some impressive feats, their intelligence was generally limited by that of their programmers: They had to be programmed and could not learn on their own. However, a new field of artificial intelligence, *machine learning*, has sought to overcome this limitation by creating programs that gain information through learning, rather than programming (Jordan & Mitchell, 2015).

How do they do that? By mimicking the human brain. ■ Recall from Section 2.1 that the brain is a massive interconnected network of neurons and that the strength of the connection between any two neurons depends on how frequently the synaptic connection between those neurons is activated (Hebb's rule; Sporns, 2011). Using variations of these two general principles, computer scientists have created neural network-like computers and computer programs that learn in much the same way that human brains do. The results systems have shown remarkable promise in overcoming the limitations of programmed expert systems in a wide variety of applications (Christensen et al., 2016; Mangos & Hulse, 2017; Steele et al., 2017).

Machine learning is proving to be powerful in many ways. For example, it's critical to the technology behind driverless cars and is now being used in health care to diagnose medical cases and provide a "voice" to people who have lost the ability to speak. But troubling ethical issues are also beginning to emerge. For example, the new race to build "smart cities" has begun. In such communities, data about resources and people will be gathered and analyzed by machines to optimize everything from garbage pick-ups to transportation routes. But ethical concerns have been raised about how the data gathered from residents will be used, and whether collecting such data violates people's right to privacy (Braun et al., 2018).

Similar concerns about privacy have been raised over the use of images to improve facial recognition programs. Using millions of photos gathered from the Internet and cameras in the community, AI researchers have compiled datasets of faces that have been shared around the world, allowing companies to develop increasingly powerful software that continues to learn and refine itself. The technology has proven useful to law enforcement officials, who use it to identify criminals in a variety of settings, including airports and sporting events like the Super Bowl. But the ethical challenges of using intelligent machines in this way are just beginning to be understood (Bowyer, 2004; Kitchin, 2016). In many instances, for example, it's not made clear to people that they are being "watched" by AI. Moreover, some Americans have become alarmed at how these programs are being used for racial profiling by governments in other countries. It's particularly troubling given how poorly the software performs with identifying members of visible minorities.

We will undoubtedly become able to build more and more powerful computers designed to learn from experience, like the human brain. Perhaps one day such artificial "brains" will even help us solve some of the most pressing problems that confront us (Resnick, 2017). In the meantime, though, we would be wise to use our considerable *human* intelligence to continually evaluate our progress, always asking whether "we should" just because "we can."

Reflective Practice

Thinking Ethically About Intelligence

1. The controversy surrounding intelligence tests comes from past misuses and misinterpretations of the test results. T or F?
2. Eugenics laws
   a. resulted in forced sterilizations for people deemed intellectually inferior.
   b. were abolished by 1900.
   c. were based on IQ testing that was culture-fair.
   d. All of the above are true.
3. At this point in time, genetic research tells us that the IQ gap between different cultures is
   a. entirely based on genes.
   b. entirely based on environmental causes.
   c. evenly split between genetic and environmental causes.
   d. Research is not currently able to tell us about the relative importance of genetics and environment.
4. Defining race in terms of single categories is less accurate than examining DNA to establish a person's ancestry. T or F?

THINK CRITICALLY

5. Is it ever accurate to describe a machine as "intelligent"?

SELF-REFLECT

- Funding for schools in some states varies greatly in rich and poor neighborhoods. Imagine that a politician opposes spending more money on disadvantaged students because she believes it would "just be a waste." Applying what you have learned in this chapter, what arguments can you offer against her assertion?

Answers: 1. T 2. a 3. d 4. T 5. Rule-driven expert systems may appear "intelligent" within a narrow range of problem solving. However, they are idiots at everything else. In contrast, machine learning has the potential to produce true intelligence.

Artificial intelligence (AI) Any artificial system (often a computer program) that is capable of humanlike problem solving or intelligent responding.

9.6 Psychology and Your Skill Set: Emotional Intelligence

GATEWAYS LEARNING OUTCOMES:
After reading this section you should be able to:

9.6.1 Define emotional intelligence, including its four components

9.6.2 Create a plan to respond in more emotionally intelligent ways in your everyday life

Time magazine once ran an article titled "Why Americans Are So Angry About Everything." That anger is clearly visible each time we look at news headlines, as people express their frustration about everything from racism and immigration to climate change, and from health care to the growing income gap between the rich and poor. In communities from coast to coast, strong emotions about the state of the country sometimes erupt into hard-fought arguments and, occasionally, violent clashes.

The Greek philosopher Aristotle had a recipe for handling relationships smoothly: "be angry with the right person, to the right degree, at the right time, for the right purpose, and in the right way." Put another way, people who excel in life tend to be emotionally "intelligent." They seem to know the right way. They are people who know how to offer a toast at a wedding, tell a joke at a roast, comfort the bereaved at a funeral, add to the fun at a party, or calm a frightened child.

What about you? Do you find it easy to recognize your own emotions or the emotions of others? And when is it good to express your emotions? What are the best ways to do so? Are there consequences for being unable to understand and manage your emotions? These questions provide a good starting point for thinking about **emotional intelligence**, the ability to perceive, use, and understand emotions in ourselves and others, as well as the ability to manage those feelings effectively (Caruso, Salovey, & Mayer, 2015). Being emotionally skilled can make us more flexible, adaptable, agreeable, and emotionally mature (English et al., 2012; Johnson, Batey, & Holdsworth, 2009).

Andrew Lichtenstein/Corbis News/Getty Images

But how do psychologists think about emotional intelligence? While some researchers view it as a stable trait that people possess to a greater or lesser extent (Gugliandolo et al., 2015), others see emotional intelligence as a collection of skills that can be learned (Campo, Laborde, & Weckemann, 2015). The idea that we can improve upon our emotional intelligence is an important one. After all, there is ample evidence for circumstances when this characteristic may need development. For example, in ■ Chapter 14, we'll focus on various types of psychopathology, including common forms of psychoses, as well as mood and anxiety disorders. Difficulties with emotional intelligence have been connected with a number of these, including schizophrenia (Frajo-Apor et al., 2016; Tabak et al., 2015) and depression (Abdollahi & Talib, 2015). ■ Moreover, in Chapter 15, we will devote time to a discussion of psychological therapies. Clinical and counseling psychologists draw heavily on emotional intelligence. They rely on such skills when listening to their clients discuss their emotional issues, as well as to understand and manage their own emotions so that they can deliver therapy effectively (Linsley, Digan, & Nugent, 2016).

Psychologists have also found that emotional intelligence is associated with other psychological concepts that we discuss in this book, including prosocial and antisocial behavior in ■ Chapter 17 (Kahn et al., 2016; Martin-Raugh, Kell, & Motowidlo, 2016) and leadership in ■ Section 12.5 (Cavazotte, Moreno, & Hickmann, 2012). Emotional intelligence is also closely connected to nonverbal communication skills (■ see Section 4.7), which depend on the ability to understand people's emotional states—and communicate your own—even when words aren't being used.

Given its importance in everyday life, let's take a closer look at how we might improve our emotional intelligence.

The Four Elements of Emotional Intelligence

It is natural to welcome positive emotions, such as joy, while avoiding negative emotions, such as anger. But make no mistake—being able to recognize and effectively manage negative emotions can be valuable and constructive. For example, recognizing feelings of persistent distress in yourself may help you to see that it's time to seek help or find a new direction in life (Izard, 2011). Recognizing those emotions in others can let you know that you need to mend a relationship or provide support.

At the same time, positive emotions are not just a pleasant side effect of happy circumstances. Emotions such as joy, interest, and contentment create an urge to play, to be creative, to explore, to savor life, to seek new experiences, to integrate, and to grow. This opens up new possibilities and encourages personal growth and social connection (Izard, 2011). Often, the experience of positive emotions can also provide a natural buffer against misfortune and help people live more positive, genuinely happy lives (Compton & Hoffman, 2013; Ong, Zautra, & Reid, 2010).

In addition to recognizing emotions in yourself and others, being emotionally intelligent is associated with understanding how to manage your emotions appropriately, a necessary skill in an increasingly social world. The challenges associated with poor emotion regulation skills can be high (Sheppes, Suri, & Gross, 2015). They range from problems with health and achievement problems to poor relationships at home and difficulties at work (Joseph et al., 2015; Zampetakis & Moustakis, 2011; Zeidner, Matthews, & Roberts, 2012). Perhaps the greatest toll falls on children and teenagers (Alegre, 2011; Frederickson, Petrides, & Simmonds, 2012). For them, having poor emotional management skills can contribute to depression, eating disorders, unwanted pregnancy, aggression, violent crime, and poor academic performance.

You mentioned that four specific skills make up emotional intelligence. What are they? Many elements contribute to emotional intelligence (Deutschendorf, 2009). A description of four of the most important skills follows.

Perceiving Emotions

The foundation of emotional intelligence is the ability to perceive emotions in yourself and others. Emotionally intelligent people are tuned in to their own feelings (Taylor & Taylor-Allan, 2007). They are able to recognize quickly if they are angry, envious, feeling guilty, or depressed. This is valuable because many people have disruptive emotions without being able to pinpoint why they are uncomfortable. At the same time, emotionally intelligent people have *empathy* (Engelen & Röttger-Rössler, 2012). They accurately perceive emotions in others and sense what others are feeling. They are good at "reading" facial expressions, tone of voice, and other signs of emotion.

Using Emotions

People who are emotionally intelligent use their feelings to enhance thinking and decision making. For example, if you can remember how you reacted emotionally in the past, it can help you react better to new situations. You also can use emotions to promote personal growth and improve relationships with others. For instance, you may have noticed that helping someone else makes you feel better, too. Likewise, when good fortune comes their way, people who are emotionally smart share the news with others. Almost always, doing so strengthens relationships and increases emotional well-being (Gable et al., 2004).

Understanding Emotions

Emotions contain useful information. For instance, anger is a cue that something is wrong; anxiety indicates uncertainty; embarrassment communicates shame; depression means we feel helpless; and enthusiasm tells us we're excited. People who are emotionally intelligent know what causes various emotions, what they mean, and how they might affect behavior (Hoerger et al., 2012).

Managing Emotions

Emotional intelligence involves an ability to manage your own emotions and those of others. For example, you know how to calm down when you are angry, and you also know how to calm others. As Aristotle noted so long ago, people who are emotionally intelligent have an ability to amplify or restrain emotions, depending on the situation (English et al., 2012).

While most discussions about intelligence focus on IQ, this section is intended to make clear that emotional intelligence can be just as important in our everyday lives. The ability to "read" our own emotions and those of others—and manage them effectively—can enhance your self-awareness and improve your ability to foster positive relationships with people in your personal life and at work. Taking the time to develop your skills in this area, then, is just the (emotionally) intelligent thing to do!

The Last Word

In the final analysis, intelligence reflects development as well as potential, nurture as well as nature (Richardson, 2013). Moreover, the fact that intelligence is partly determined by heredity tells us little of any real value. Genes are fixed at birth, but improving the environments in which children learn and grow is one important way we can ensure that they reach their full potential (Ormrod, 2014; Roberts & Lipnevich, 2012).

It is also well worth remembering that intelligence tests are a double-edged sword; our opening story about Darryl Lester and Dawn Harris Sherling shows us that they can be very beneficial in some cases, yet they also have the potential to do great harm. That story highlights the fact that IQ is not *equivalent* to intelligence; instead, it is simply one *index* of intelligence that is narrowly defined by a particular test. As Howard Gardner has pointed out, creativity, motivation, physical health, mechanical aptitude, artistic ability, and numerous other qualities not measured by intelligence tests contribute to the achievement of life goals (Neukrug & Fawcett, 2015).

Perhaps most important of all, people can be intelligent without being wise. In many areas of human life, wisdom represents a mixture of convergent thinking, intelligence, and reason, spiced with creativity and originality (Meeks & Jeste, 2009). Perhaps just as important is the fact that people who are wise approach life with openness and tolerance, thinking often about the long-term consequences of their actions for themselves and those around them (Le, 2011). To us, that sounds like a pretty smart way to live your life.

Emotional intelligence The ability to perceive, use, understand, and manage emotions.

Reflective Practice

Psychology and Your Skill Set: Emotional Intelligence

1. People who rate high in emotional intelligence tend to be highly aware of their own feelings and unaware of emotions experienced by others. T or F?
2. Using the information imparted by emotional reactions can enhance thinking and decision-making. T or F?
3. Positive emotions may be pleasant, but they tend to limit personal growth and the range of possible actions that we are likely to consider. T or F?
4. Which of the following is ***not*** a skill associated with emotional intelligence?
   a. managing emotions
   b. using emotions
   c. perceiving emotions
   d. minimizing emotions

THINK CRITICALLY

5. You are angry because a friend borrowed money from you and hasn't repaid it. What would be an emotionally intelligent response to this situation?

SELF-REFLECT

- Think of a person you know who is smart cognitively (that is, has a high IQ) but low in emotional intelligence. Think of another person who is smart cognitively *and* emotionally. How does the second person differ from the first? Which person do you think would make a better parent, friend, supervisor, roommate, or teacher?

Answers: 1. F 2. T 3. F 4. d 5. There's no single right answer. Rather than being angry, it might be better to reflect on whether friendship or money is more important in life. If you appreciate your friend's virtues, accept that no one is perfect, and reappraise the loan as a gift, you could save a valued relationship and reduce your anger at the same time. Alternatively, if you become aware that your friend persistently manipulates other people with emotional appeals for support, it may be worth reappraising your friendship.

CHAPTER IN REVIEW

Gateways to Intelligence

Summary: Gateways Learning Outcomes

9.1 Defining Human Intelligence

9.1.1 Define what is meant by the g-factor in intelligence

Intelligence refers to the general capacity (or g-factor) to act purposefully, think rationally, and adapt to the environment. g-factor, in turn, can be divided into fluid and crystallized intelligence.

9.1.2 Describe some of the challenges associated with defining intelligence

Challenges associated with defining intelligence include establishing which aptitudes ought to qualify as being central to intelligence, taking into account cultural differences in what it means to be "smart," and the many different ways in which people can demonstrate themselves to be talented.

9.2 Measuring intelligence

9.2.1 Name and describe four characteristics of a good psychometric test

To be of any value, a psychological test must be *reliable* (give consistent results). A worthwhile test must also have *validity*, meaning that it measures what it claims to measure. Widely used intelligence tests are also *objective* (they give the same result when scored by different people) and *standardized* (the same procedures are always used in giving the test, and norms have been established so that scores can be interpreted).

9.2.2 Explain the need for "culture-fair" intelligence tests

Early tests of intelligence were biased against members of other cultural groups, members of minority groups and people who were poor. The bias stemmed from questions that tested knowledge not common in these groups and a scoring system that assumed implicitly that European-American ways of thinking were more "intelligent" than those adopted by other groups.

9.2.3 Explain the difference between general intelligence (g) and aptitude tests

Special aptitude tests and multiple aptitude tests are used to assess a person's capacities for learning various abilities (e.g., music; interpersonal skills). Aptitude tests measure a narrower range of abilities than general intelligence tests do. Many psychologists have suggested that Gardner's "multiple intelligences" actually reflect a number of aptitudes rather than various forms of intelligence.

9.2.4 Name two well-established intelligence tests, and some of the main cognitive abilities that they test

One intelligence test is the Stanford-Binet Intelligence Scales, Fifth Edition (SB5). A second major intelligence test is the Wechsler Adult Intelligence Scale—Fourth Edition (WAIS-IV). The children's version of this test is the Wechsler Intelligence Scale for Children—Fifth Edition (WISC-V). The SB5, WAIS-IV, and WISC-V measure both verbal and performance intelligence through tests of working memory, quantitative reasoning, and visual-spatial processing, for example.

9.2.5 Explain how the results of intelligence tests are expressed, and how the scores are distributed in the population

Intelligence is expressed as an intelligence quotient (IQ), defined as mental age divided by chronological age and then multiplied by 100. The distribution of IQ scores approximates a normal distribution. Modern IQ tests no longer calculate IQs directly. Instead, the final score reported by the test is a deviation IQ.

9.3 Intellectual Giftedness and Disability

9.3.1 Outline how gifted individuals are identified, and the outcomes that are typically associated with giftedness

People considered gifted tend to score above 130 on IQ tests. Intellectually gifted children often have difficulties in average classrooms and benefit from special accelerated programs. Research tends to support the ideas that gifted children are successful in their personal and professional lives, though the correlation is not perfect.

9.3.2 Outline how people with intellectual disabilities are identified, and the outcomes that are typically associated with this diagnosis

The term *intellectually disabled* is applied to those whose IQ falls below 70 and who lack various adaptive behaviors. Current classifications of intellectual disability are as follows: mild (50–55 to 70), moderate (35–40 to 50–55), severe (20–25 to 35–40), and profound (below 20–25). Chances for educational success are related to the degree of intellectual disability; however, those individuals who are able to demonstrate adaptive behaviors can make contributions to their communities and lead fulfilling lives.

9.3.3 Outline some of the causes of intellectual disability, and name some of the resulting conditions

Many cases of intellectual disability are thought to be the result of familial intellectual disability, a generally low level of educational and intellectual stimulation in the home, and poverty and poor nutrition. About 50 percent of the cases of intellectual disability are organic, being caused by birth injuries, fetal damage, metabolic disorders, or genetic abnormalities. The remaining cases are of undetermined cause.

Six distinct forms of organic intellectual disability are Down syndrome, fragile X syndrome, phenylketonuria (PKU), microcephaly, hydrocephaly, and congenital hypothyroidism.

9.4 Genetic and Environmental Contributions to Intelligence

9.4.1 Describe the general results of research investigating the role of genes in intelligence

Studies of twins demonstrate clearly that intelligence is partially determined by heredity. Heritability estimates tend to suggest that intelligence is approximately 50 percent heritable, but this is an average for the population as a whole. For any given pair of relatives, it may be higher or lower. Moreover, the importance of genes changes across the lifespan: they are less important earlier in life, but are more important contributors to intelligence as we move into adulthood. Newer studies suggest that there are likely hundreds of genes that contribute to intelligence, each one having a very small effect.

It is possible that genes code for a larger frontal cortex area in the brain, as this is the area that is most active when we carry out the type of tasks that are included on IQ tests. Another possibility is that genes code for a central nervous system (brain and spinal cord) that responds more quickly in intelligent people, or one that allows for better metacognitive thinking.

9.4.2 Describe the general results of research investigating the role of the environment in intelligence

Both adoption studies and the Flynn effect strongly suggest that the environment makes an important contribution to intelligence. Results of studies examining the effect of formal education (early childhood education, or ECE, in particular) have been mixed. While early gains in intelligence associated with ECE are typically not sustained over the long term, research does suggest other advantages may be associated with ECE programs like Head Start. These include higher high school and college graduation rates, suggesting that even if school-based programming does not improve intelligence, it may affect other characteristics that allow children to persist in school.

9.5 Thinking Ethically About Intelligence

9.5.1 Identify two problems associated with the claim that genetic differences between groups explain group-based differences in intelligence

The first problem stems from the fact that what is currently known about the human genome is largely based on the DNA of people of European descent, and there is evidence to suggest that there may be substantial differences in the genomes of different racial groups. It's not clear, then, whether the genes traditionally associated with intelligence in European Americans will be the same for other groups, including African Americans. The second problem has to do with the fact that past research has relied on a very crude measure of race: identification using a limited number of options on a form, or obvious characteristics such as skin color. In reality, genetics are more closely aligned with ancestry, which reveals how one's DNA may be influenced by many races over several generations. Using ancestry to obtain more precise measures of genetic inheritance going forward may be useful in shedding more light on whether genes have any role to play in group-based differences in IQ.

9.5.2 Define artificial intelligence, and explain some of the ethical concerns raised by its use

Artificial intelligence (AI) refers to any artificial system that can perform tasks that require intelligence when done by people. Two principal areas of AI research on particular human skills are expert systems and machine learning. Increased use of AI has raised ethical concerns about violations of people's right to privacy, and the possibility of racial profiling.

9.6 Psychology and Your Skill Set: Emotional Intelligence

9.6.1 Define emotional intelligence, including its four components

Emotional intelligence is the ability to recognize and understand emotions in ourselves and others, as well as the ability to manage those feelings effectively. Recognizing emotions in yourself and others can be helpful in terms of directing your behavior in ways that will promote your own growth and positive relationships with others. Similarly, being able to control your emotions appropriately has important consequences for health, achievement, and relationships. People who are "smart" emotionally are able to make use of each of the four components of emotional intelligence: perceiving emotions, using emotions, understanding emotions, and managing emotions.

9.6.2 Create a plan to respond in more emotionally intelligent ways in your everyday life

Skillfully managing the emotional responses of ourselves and others requires that we think carefully about the four components of emotional intelligence. We hope that after reading this section, you'll be better able to think about how you can use these components to help when you need to handle difficult emotions in your everyday life!

10 Motivation and Emotion

John Parra/Getty Images Entertainment/Getty Images

Gateway Theme Our motives and emotions energize and direct many types of behavior.

Chapter Outline

Modelling Motivated Behavior

Halima Aden's rise to the top of the modeling world was an emotional ride that repeatedly tested her motivation to succeed. For example, when she told her mother that she wanted to enter the Miss Minnesota USA pageant, her mother felt somewhat concerned that it would distract Halima from her college courses. After all, it wasn't the kind of thing that Somali women typically did. But Halima was determined to move forward with her plans, even though doing so caused her to feel more than a little anxiety. For example, as a Muslim woman, she needed to move past her fears and inform the pageant staff that she wasn't prepared to remove her hijab, and that she wouldn't go onstage in a conventional bathing suit. Her anxiety turned to relief when it became clear that neither of those things posed a problem for pageant staff.

Feelings of disappointment emerged when Halima didn't win the Miss Minnesota contest, but they were quickly replaced by excitement when she landed a major modeling contract soon afterward. And these days she's not just motivated to be a great model—she's also determined to be a great *role* model. By supporting other Muslim models and working as an ambassador for UNICEF, Halima is showing young people everywhere that they can be true to their values and still be successful.

The words emotion and motivation both have their roots in the Latin word *movere*, which means "to move." This makes sense when you consider how each of them can "move" our behavior in everyday life. Let's begin with a discussion about what motivates us, and then we'll move on to explore how our emotions affect our actions.

10.1 The Basics of Motivation

GATEWAYS LEARNING OUTCOMES:
After reading this section you should be able to:

10.1.1 Explain the role played by needs, drives, responses, goals, and incentives in shaping our motives

10.1.2 Distinguish between intrinsic and extrinsic motivation

10.1.3 Distinguish between Maslow's basic needs and growth needs

10.1.4 Distinguish between biological, stimulus, and learned motives

What are your goals? Why do you pursue them? When are you satisfied? When do you give up? These are all questions about motivation, or why we act as we do. Psychologists believe that **motivation** refers to the dynamics of behavior—the ways in which our actions are *aroused*, *maintained*, and *guided* (Deckers, 2014; Petri & Govern, 2013). Imagine that Li Na is studying biology in the college library. Her stomach begins to growl. She can't concentrate. She grows restless and decides to go to the cafeteria. Closed. Li Na drives to a nearby fast-food outlet, where she finally eats. Her hunger satisfied, she resumes studying. Notice how Li Na's food seeking was *aroused* by a physical need for food. Her search was *maintained* because her need was not immediately met, and her actions were *guided* by possible sources of food.

A Model of Motivation

Many motivated activities begin with a **need**, or internal deficiency. The need that aroused Li Na's search was a shortage of key nutrients in her body. Needs cause a **drive** (state of bodily tension that arises from an unmet need) to develop. In Li Na's case, the drive was hunger. Drives activate a **response** (an action or series of actions) designed to push us toward a **goal** (the target of motivated behavior). Reaching a goal that satisfies the need ends the chain of events. Thus, a simple model of motivation can be shown in this way:

NEED → DRIVE → RESPONSE → GOAL
(NEED REDUCTION)

Aren't needs and drives the same thing? No. The strength of needs and drives can differ (Deckers, 2014). For example, it is not unusual for older people to suffer from dehydration (a physical *need* for water) despite experiencing a lack of thirst (the *drive* to drink) (Begg, Sinclair, & Weisinger, 2012).

Now, let's observe Li Na again. It's a holiday weekend, and she's traveled home to Chicago from college. For dinner, Li Na has soup, salad, a large steak, a baked potato, two pieces of cheesecake, and three cups of coffee. After dinner, she complains that she is "too full to move." Soon after, Li Na's aunt arrives with a pie. Li Na exclaims that pie is her favorite dessert and eats three large pieces! Is this hunger?

Certainly, Li Na's dinner had already satisfied her biological needs for food. Li Na's "pie lust" illustrates that motivated behavior isn't only energized by the "push" of internal needs. It's also possible for motivated behavior to emerge from the "pull" of an external **incentive**—a reward or other stimulus that motivates behavior. Some goals are so desirable (a delicious pie, for example) that they can motivate behavior in the absence of an internal need. Other goals offer such a low incentive that they may be rejected even if they could meet an internal need. Roasted grasshoppers, for instance, are nutritious. However, it is doubtful that you would eat one, unless you were a contestant on a reality show that had you foraging for food in the wilderness.

Usually, our actions are energized by a mixture of internal needs *and* external incentives. That's why a strong need may change an unpleasant incentive into a desired goal. Perhaps you've never eaten a grasshopper, but we'll bet you've eaten some pretty horrible leftovers when the refrigerator was empty. The incentive

Figure 10.1 Drive strength. Needs and incentives interact to determine drive strength (*above*). (a) Moderate need combined with a high-incentive goal produces a strong drive. (b) Even when a strong need exists, drive strength may be moderate if a goal's incentive value is low. It is important to remember, however, that incentive value lies "in the eye of the beholder." No matter how hungry, few people would be able to eat the pictured roasted grasshoppers. (Does it help that they are garnished with tomato, onions, and lime?)

value of external goals also helps to explain motives that don't seem to come from internal needs, such as drives for success, status, or approval (● Figure 10.1).

Classifying Motives

Over the years, psychologists have come up with a number of ways to classify, or group, human motives. Classifying motives can be useful for predicting how people will behave under certain conditions; however, the classification systems differ in their focus. In this section, we'll look at three systems. The first stems from self-determination theory. The second is a more complex model developed by humanist Abraham Maslow, whose work we explored briefly in ■ Section 1.3. Finally, we'll consider a simplified model of classifying motives that fits with both self-determination theory and Maslow's work.

Self-Determination Theory

According to **self-determination theory**, we are all motivated by three innate motives: *competence* (our desire to experience mastery over our environment), *autonomy* (our desire to control our own lives), and *relatedness* (our desire to be connected to, and care for other people).

Self-determination theory stresses the importance of freedom of choice, and classifies motives depending on whether you are doing something because it inherently brings you pleasure, or because there are outside forces that are compelling you to act (Olafsen et al., 2015; Ryan, Curren, & Deci, 2013). For example, some people cook for a living and consider it hard work. Others cook for pleasure and dream of opening a restaurant. For some people, gardening is gratifying and a wonderful way to relax. For others, it's the equivalent of having to do housework outdoors.

Intrinsic motivation occurs when we act based on internal rewards without any obvious external rewards. We simply enjoy an activity or see it as an opportunity to explore, learn, and actualize our potentials. In contrast, **extrinsic motivation** stems from factors outside of the person, such as pay, grades, rewards, obligations, and approval. Most of the activities we think of as "work" are extrinsically rewarded (Murayama et al., 2017).

It's important to note that although salaries and bonuses may increase the amount of work done, people are not motivated solely by external rewards such as money. A chance to do challenging, interesting, and intrinsically rewarding work is often just as important. Work *quality* is affected more by intrinsic factors, such as personal interest and freedom of choice (Moneta, 2012; Murayama et al., 2015). Moreover, when extrinsic motivation is stressed, people are less likely to solve tricky problems and come up with innovative ideas (Hennessey & Amabile, 2010). While some popular press reports have suggested that younger adults are more motivated by intrinsic factors than older adults when selecting and persisting in a job, large-scale studies in the United States and elsewhere indicate that this is not the case (Heyns & Kerr, 2018; Twenge et al., 2010). Apparently, finding value and intrinsic reward in your career path is important at any age.

Extrinsic Motivation in Everyday Life: Turning Play into Work

I thought rewards were a good thing. Don't extrinsic incentives like high salaries strengthen motivation? Yes, they can, but not always. In fact, *excessive* rewards can decrease intrinsic motivation and spontaneous interest. For instance, in one classic study, children who were lavishly rewarded for drawing with felt-tip pens later showed little interest in playing with the pens again (Greene & Lepper, 1974). Apparently, "play" can be turned into "work" by *requiring* people to do something that they would otherwise enjoy (Patall, Cooper, & Robinson, 2008). When we are coerced or "bribed" to act, we tend to feel as if we are "faking it." Employees who lack initiative and teenagers who reject school and learning are good examples of those who have such a reaction (Olafsen et al., 2015).

Should extrinsic motivation be avoided then? No, but extrinsic motivation shouldn't be overused, especially with children.

AUGUST Image, LLC

Intrinsically motivated people like James Cameron feel free to explore creative solutions to problems. Best known as the director of blockbuster films such as *Titanic* and *Avatar*, Cameron has also codeveloped digital 3D cameras and remote vehicles to explore the ocean's depths.

Motivation A process that arouses, maintains, and guides behavior toward a goal.

Need An internal deficiency that may energize behavior.

Drive A state of bodily tension, such as hunger or thirst, that arises from an unmet need.

Response Any action, glandular activity, or other identifiable behavior.

Goal The target or objective of motivated behavior.

Incentive A reward or other stimulus that motivates behavior.

Self-determination theory Proposes that needs for competence, autonomy, and relatedness are critical motivational needs.

Intrinsic motivation Desire to engage in a behavior based on internal rewards.

Extrinsic motivation Motivation that comes from outside of the person.

In general, (1) if there's no intrinsic interest in an activity to begin with, you have nothing to lose by using extrinsic rewards, (2) if basic skills are lacking, extrinsic rewards may be necessary at first, (3) extrinsic rewards can focus attention on an activity so that real interest will develop, and (4) if extrinsic rewards are used, they should be small and phased out as soon as possible (Buckworth et al., 2007; Cameron & Pierce, 2002).

Maslow's Hierarchy of Needs

One of the limitations of self-determination theory is that it does not focus on more "basic" biological motives such as eating, drinking, and sex. A more comprehensive classification system that accounts for such motives was proposed by Abraham Maslow. Specifically, Maslow proposed that we humans experience a **hierarchy of needs**, in which some needs are more basic or powerful than others.

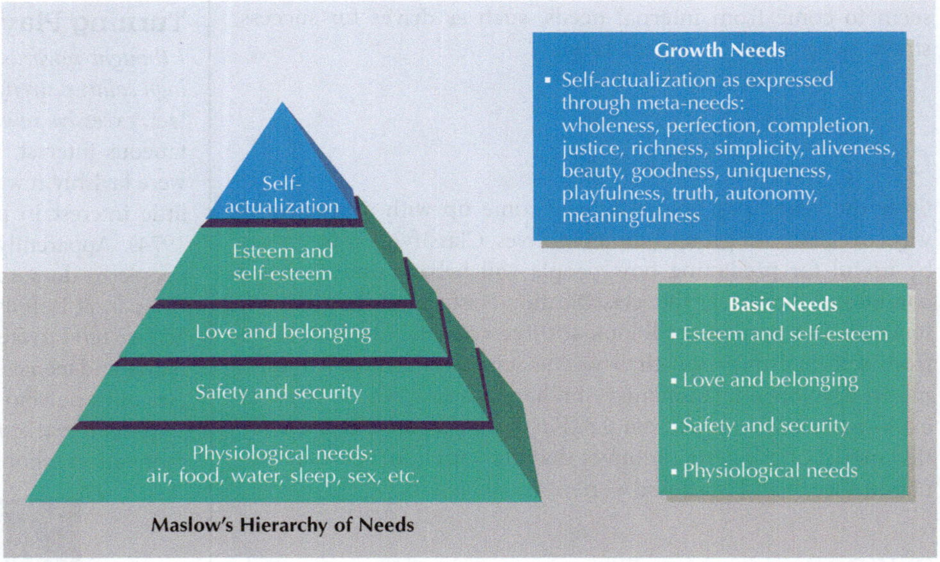

Figure 10.2 Maslow's hierarchy of needs. Although the pyramid illustration was originally developed by management theorist Keith Davis, it so well expressed the kernel of truth at the heart of Maslow's theory that it immediately became associated with Maslow himself (Bridgman, Cummings, & Ballard, 2019). Maslow believed that lower needs in the hierarchy are dominant. Basic needs must be satisfied before growth motives are fully expressed.

Maslow's hierarchy is often represented as a pyramid that shows basic, biological needs at the bottom and higher-level needs for personal fulfillment at the top (Figure 10.2). It's worth noting that historians have suggested that representing the hierarchy of needs as a pyramid was not Maslow's idea, but instead became very popular when his theory was applied to the issue of managing employees in a business setting (Bridgman, Cummings, & Ballard, 2019). Along the way, some of Maslow's ideas have been misrepresented and oversimplified, so let's take a closer look at what he had to say.

Maslow believed that **basic needs** related to our physical survival (physiological needs; safety and security) must be met for us to live, and consequently they tend to be prepotent, or dominant, in our everyday lives. Other basic needs are for love and belonging (family, friendship, caring) and esteem and self-esteem (recognition and self-respect). All the basic needs are *deficiency* motives—that is, they are activated by a *lack* of food, water, security, love, esteem, and so on.

At the top of the hierarchy, we find **growth needs**, which are expressed as a need for self-actualization (see Sections 1.3 and 12.1 for a discussion of self-actualization). If our basic needs are met, he said, we tend to move on to actualizing our potential (Tay & Diener, 2011). For instance, a person who is starving (physiological needs not met) or feeling threatened (safety needs not met) might have little interest in writing poetry or even talking with friends as a way of meeting higher-level needs (Noltemeyer et al., 2012). The need for self-actualization is not based on deficiencies; rather, it is a positive, life-enhancing force for personal growth (D'Souza & Gurin, 2016).

There is some intuitive appeal in the idea that we are motivated to manage fundamental needs that ensure survival prior to addressing higher-level needs that may bring greater self-actualization. We routinely see evidence of this kind of prioritization in everyday life. For example, college students who are concerned primarily with money, personal appearance, and social recognition (all basic needs) score lower than average on growth needs such as vitality, self-actualization, and general well-being (Kasser, 2016; Nickerson, Diener, & Schwarz, 2011).

It is important to realize, however, that Maslow was clear on the point that the dominance of basic needs is not absolute. Instead, his original work was sensitive to the fact that culture and circumstances might lead to needs emerging in a different order than the one outlined in the pyramid. For example, think of a person who fasts as part of a social protest, or someone who engages in humanitarian work in a dangerous war zone because their efforts bring them a sense of personal fulfillment and satisfaction. In both cases, growth needs are being addressed while basic needs for food and safety are not (Bridgman et al., 2019).

Maslow's hierarchy is not well documented by research, and studies that have been carried out raise questions about his definition of self-actualization and the applicability of the model in other cultures. Despite such objections, though, Maslow's work was important in raising awareness about the rich interplay of very diverse human motives (Peterson & Park, 2010).

Three-Way Classification of Motives

A third and final method for classifying motives groups them into three major categories:

1. **Biological motives** are based on innate needs that must be met for survival. The most important biological motives are hunger, thirst, pain avoidance, and the needs for air, sleep, elimination of wastes, and regulation of body temperature.

Michaelpuche/Shutterstock.com

Wheelchair athletes engage in vigorous competition. Maslow considered such behavior an expression of the need for self-actualization.

2. **Stimulus motives** express our needs for stimulation and information. Examples include activity, curiosity, exploration, manipulation, and physical contact. Although such motives also appear to be innate, they are not strictly necessary for survival.
3. **Learned motives** are based on learned needs, drives, and goals. Often social in nature, learned motives help explain many human activities, such as running for office or auditioning for a reality show. Many learned motives are related to learned needs for power, achievement, affiliation (the need to be with others), approval, status, and security.

In the next two sections of this chapter, we use this three-way classification system to explore motives in greater detail.

Reflective Practice

The Basics of Motivation

1. Motives ________________, maintain, and ________________ activities.
2. Needs provide the ________________ of motivation, whereas incentives provide the ________________.
3. Desirable goals are motivating because they are high in
   a. secondary value
   b. stimulus value
   c. homeostatic value
   d. incentive value
4. The highest level of Maslow's hierarchy of needs involves
   a. the need for self-actualization
   b. needs for safety and security
   c. needs for love and belonging
   d. extrinsic needs
5. Intrinsic motivation is often undermined in situations in which obvious external rewards are applied to a naturally enjoyable activity. T or F?

THINK CRITICALLY

6. A mom wants to get her preschool son interested in playing the piano and is thrilled when she sees him climb up on the bench and start banging away at the keys. She enthusiastically tells him he's doing a wonderful job and gives him some candy as a reward. After rewarding him a few times for his efforts to "play," she finds that he no longer has any interest in the instrument and refuses all of her efforts to coax him onto the piano bench. What happened?

SELF-REFLECT

- See if you can think of something that you do that illustrates the concepts of need, drive, response, and goal. Does the goal in your example vary in incentive value? What effects do high and low incentive-value goals have on your behavior?
- Which levels of Maslow's hierarchy of needs occupy most of your time and energy?
- Name an activity that you do that is intrinsically motivated and another that is extrinsically motivated. How do they differ?

Answers: 1. arouse, guide 2. push, pull 3. d 4. a 5. T 6. When intrinsically rewarding activities (like the boy's piano playing at the outset) are rewarded, they may become less interesting and intrinsically motivating over time. This, in turn, means that these activities are less likely to be carried out for pleasure.

10.2 Biological Motives

GATEWAYS LEARNING OUTCOMES:
After reading this section you should be able to:

10.2.1 Explain what is meant by the term sex drive, and how hormones are related to the sex drive of human and nonhuman animals

10.2.2 Explain what is meant by the term circadian rhythms, and how these rhythms impact human sleep cycles

10.2.3 Outline why pain is considered an episodic drive, and how our responses to pain are shaped

10.2.4 Distinguish between intracellular and extracellular thirst, and how each is best managed

10.2.5 Outline the internal and external factors that impact hunger

10.2.6 Distinguish between anorexia nervosa and bulimia nervosa, and outline the causes of these eating disorders

How important is air in your life? Water? Sleep? Food? Temperature regulation? Finding a restroom? For most of us, satisfying biological needs is so routine that we overlook the extent to which they guide

Hierarchy of needs Maslow's classification of human motivations by order of importance from basic biological function to self-actualization.

Basic needs The first four levels of needs in Maslow's hierarchy; lower needs tend to be more potent than higher needs.

Growth needs In Maslow's hierarchy, the higher-level needs associated with self-actualization.

Biological motives Innate motives based on biological needs.

Stimulus motives Innate needs for stimulation and information.

Learned motives Motives based on learned needs, drives, and goals.

our behavior. But exaggerate any of these needs through famine, shipwreck, poverty, near drowning, bitter cold, or drinking 10 cups of coffee, and their powerful grip on behavior becomes evident.

Biological drives are essential because they maintain *homeostasis* (HOE-me-oh-STAY-sis), or bodily equilibrium (Cooper, 2008). The term **homeostasis** means "standing steady" or "steady state." Optimal levels exist for body temperature, chemicals in the blood, blood pressure, and so forth (Goel, 2012; Petri & Govern, 2013). When the body deviates from these "ideal" levels, automatic reactions begin to restore equilibrium (Deckers, 2014). Thus, it might help to think of homeostasis as similar to a thermostat set at a particular temperature.

A (Very) Short Course on Thermostats

The thermostat in your house constantly compares the actual room temperature to a *set point*, or ideal temperature, which you can control. When room temperature falls below the set point, the heat is automatically turned on to warm the room. When the heat equals or slightly exceeds the set point, it is automatically turned off or the air conditioning is turned on. In this way, room temperature is kept in a state of equilibrium hovering around the set point.

The first reactions to disequilibrium in the human body are also automatic. For example, if you become too hot, more blood will flow through your skin and you will begin to perspire, thus lowering body temperature. We are often unaware of such changes, unless continued disequilibrium drives us to seek shade, warmth, food, or water.

In the next few sections, we'll dig more deeply into five specific biological motives: sex, sleep, pain, thirst, and hunger.

Sex

Human sexual behavior and attitudes are discussed in detail in ■ Section 11.3. For now, it is worth noting that sex is unlike most other biological motives because (contrary to anything your personal experience might suggest) it is not necessary for *individual* survival. It is necessary, of course, for *group* survival.

The term **sex drive** refers to the strength of one's motivation to engage in sexual behavior. In lower animals, the sex drive is directly related to hormones. Female mammals (other than humans) are interested in mating only when their fertility cycles are in the stage of **estrus**, or "heat." Estrus is caused by a release of **estrogen** (one of several types of female sex hormone) into the bloodstream. Hormones are important in males as well. But in contrast to females, the normal male animal is almost always ready to mate. His sex drive is aroused primarily by the behavior and scent of a receptive female. Therefore, in many species, mating is closely tied to female fertility cycles.

How much do hormones affect human sex drives? Hormones affect the human sex drive, but not as directly as in animals (Rosenthal, 2013). The sex drive in men is related to the amount of **androgens** (male hormones such as testosterone) provided by the testes. When the supply of androgens dramatically increases at puberty, so does the male sex drive. Likewise, the sex drive in women is related to their estrogen levels (Hyde & DeLamater, 2014). However, "male" hormones also affect the female sex drive. In addition to estrogen, a woman's body produces small amounts of androgens. Testosterone levels decline with age, and various medical problems can lower sexual desire. In some instances, taking testosterone supplements can restore the sex drive in both men and women (Crooks & Baur, 2017).

Perhaps the most interesting fact about the sex drive is that it is largely **non-homeostatic**—relatively independent of body need states. In humans, the sex drive can be aroused at virtually any time by almost anything. Therefore, it shows no clear relationship to deprivation (the amount of time since the drive was last satisfied). Certainly, an increase in desire may occur as time passes. But recent sexual activity does not prevent sexual desire from occurring again. Notice, too, that people may seek to arouse the sex drive as well as to reduce it. This unusual quality means that the sex drive is capable of motivating a wide range of behaviors. (It also explains why sex is used to sell almost everything imaginable.)

The non-homeostatic quality of the sex drive is illustrated by the fact that a male animal that is allowed to copulate until it seems to have no further interest in sexual behavior will cease sexual activity. However, if a new sexual partner is provided, the animal will often resume sexual activity immediately. This pattern is called the *Coolidge effect*, after former US president Calvin Coolidge. What, you might ask, does Calvin Coolidge have to do with the sex drive? The answer is found in the following story:

While touring an experimental farm, Coolidge's wife reportedly asked if a rooster mated just once a day. "No, ma'am," she was told, "he mates dozens of times each day." "Tell that to the president," she said, with a faraway look in her eyes. When President Coolidge reached the same part of the tour, his wife's message was passed along to him. His reaction was to ask if the dozens of matings were with the same hen. No, he was told, different hens were involved. "Tell *that* to Mrs. Coolidge," the president is said to have replied.

Sleep and Circadian Rhythms

Our needs and drives can often change from moment to moment. For example, after eating our motivation to eat more food tends to diminish, and just a few minutes in the hot sun can leave us feeling thirsty. But our motivation also can vary over longer cycles, guided by internal "biological clocks."

Every 24 hours, your body undergoes a cycle of changes called a **circadian rhythm** (SUR-kay-dee-AN; *circa*: about; *diem*: a day) (Abbott, Reid, & Zee, 2015; Goel, 2012). Throughout the day, activities in the liver, kidneys, and endocrine glands undergo large changes. Body temperature, blood pressure, and amino acid levels also shift from hour to hour. These activities, and many others, peak once a day (● Figure 10.3). People are usually more motivated and alert at the high point, or peak, of their circadian rhythms (Bass & Takahashi, 2010; Chipman & Jin, 2009). People with early peaks in their circadian rhythms are "day people," who wake up alert, are energetic early in the day, and fall asleep early in the evening. People with later peaks are "night people," who wake up groggy, are lively in the afternoon or early evening, and stay up late (Martynhak et al., 2010).

Circadian rhythms are most noticeable after a major change in time schedules. When you take a long flight, have a late shift at

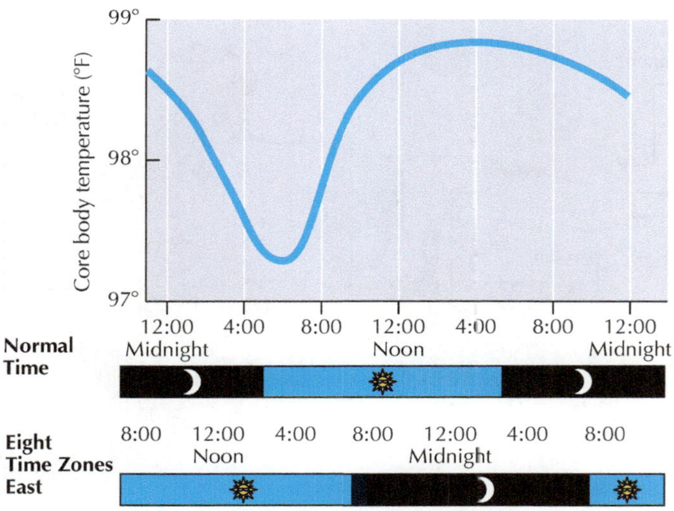

Figure 10.3 Circadian rhythms. Core body temperature is a good indicator of a person's circadian rhythm. Rapid travel to a different time zone, shift work, depression, and illness can throw sleep and waking patterns out of synchronization with the body's core rhythm. Mismatches of this kind are very disruptive (Reinberg & Ashkenazi, 2008). Most people reach a low point two to three hours before their normal waking time. It's no wonder that both the Chernobyl and Three-Mile Island nuclear power plant accidents occurred around 4 a.m.

work, or engage in an all-night study session, your circadian rhythms can fall "out of sync" with day–night cycles. In the case of flying, this is most likely if you travel great distances east or west. If the peaks and valleys of your circadian rhythms fall out of phase with the sun and clocks, sleep difficulties are likely to follow (Iskra-Golec, 2016; Lazar et al., 2013). For example, you might be wide awake at midnight and feel like you're sleepwalking during the day (return to Figure 10.3). When body rhythms are disturbed like this, performance often suffers as well, due to the accompanying fatigue, irritability, upset stomach, and depression (Teff & Silva, 2015; Wright, Bogan, & Wyatt, 2013).

What can be done to cope with circadian rhythm disturbances? Circadian rhythms are partially controlled by variations in levels of *melatonin*, a hormone produced by the pineal gland. Normally, when light levels fall in the evening, melatonin levels rise; conversely, when light levels rise in the morning, melatonin levels fall (hence the nickname "Dracula hormone"). Because of this, taking small doses of melatonin just before bedtime for a few evenings may help synchronize circadian rhythms to the day–night cycle. (■ Changes in melatonin levels are thought to partly explain seasonal affect disorder that occurs when people endure several months of long dark days. See Section 14.3.)

Light exposure can also help. Bright light affects the timing of body rhythms by reducing the amount of melatonin produced by the pineal gland. For this reason, a few intermittent five-minute periods of exposure to bright light early in the morning are helpful for resetting your circadian rhythm (Dodson & Zee, 2010). In contrast, even dim light at night can upset circadian rhythms, reducing sleep quality and causing weight gain (Fonken et al., 2013).

In general, if you can anticipate an upcoming body rhythm change, it is best to *preadapt* by gradually matching your sleep–waking cycle to a new time schedule. Before traveling, for instance, you should go to sleep one hour later (or earlier) each day until your sleep cycle matches the time at your destination. But if you are simply planning to "burn the midnight oil," remember that departing from your regular schedule may cost more than it's worth. You may be motivated to do as much during one hour in the morning as you could have done in three hours of work after midnight. You might just as well go to sleep two hours earlier.

Pain

Not all drives are governed by circadian rhythms. While hunger, thirst, and sleepiness come and go in a fairly regular cycle each day, pain avoidance is an *episodic drive*: It occurs in distinct episodes when bodily damage takes place or is about to occur. Most drives prompt us to actively seek a desired goal (food, drink, warmth, and so forth). Pain prompts us to *avoid* or *eliminate* sources of discomfort.

Some people feel that they must be "tough" and not show any pain or distress. Others complain loudly at the smallest ache. The first attitude raises pain tolerance, and the second lowers it. As this

Sivaram V/Reuters

Tolerance for pain and the strength of a person's motivation to avoid discomfort are greatly affected by cultural practices and beliefs, such as the self-infliction of pain by this penitent at a Hindu festival.

Homeostasis The steady state of body equilibrium.

Sex drive The strength of one's motivation to engage in sexual behavior.

Estrus Changes in the sexual drives of animals that create a desire for mating; particularly used to refer to females in heat.

Estrogen Any of a number of female sex hormones.

Androgen Any of a number of male sex hormones, especially testosterone.

Non-homeostatic drive A drive that is relatively independent of physical deprivation cycles or body need states.

Circadian rhythm A 24-hour biological cycle found in humans and many other species.

suggests, the drive to avoid pain is partly learned. That's why members of some societies endure cutting, burning, whipping, tattooing, and piercing of the skin that would agonize most people (Chang, 2009). (Apparently, devotees of piercing and "body art" can relate.) In general, we learn how to react to pain by observing family members, friends, and other role models (McMahon & Koltzenburg, 2013).

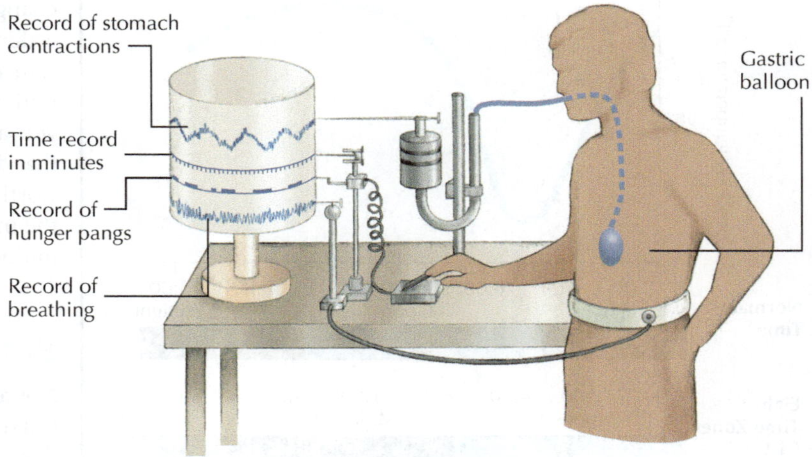

Figure 10.4 Measuring hunger. In Walter Cannon's early study of hunger, a simple apparatus was used to simultaneously record hunger pangs and stomach contractions. (Adapted from Cannon, 1934.)

Thirst

Thirst is regulated by separate *thirst* and *thirst satiety* systems in a small subcortical area of the brain called the hypothalamus. However, you may be surprised to learn that thirst is only partially controlled by dryness of the mouth. If you were to take a drug that made your mouth constantly wet or dry, for example, your water intake would remain normal.

Moreover, there are two different kinds of thirst (Thornton, 2010). **Extracellular thirst** occurs when water is lost from the fluids surrounding the cells of your body. Bleeding, vomiting, diarrhea, sweating, and drinking alcohol cause this type of thirst (Petri & Govern, 2013). When a person loses both water and minerals in any of these ways—especially by perspiration—a slightly salty liquid such as Gatorade may be more satisfying than plain water.

A second type of thirst occurs when you eat a salty meal. In this instance, your body does not lose fluid. Instead, excess salt causes fluid to be drawn out of your body's cells. As the cells "shrink," **intracellular thirst** is triggered. Thirst of this type is best quenched by plain water (Thornton, 2010).

Hunger

Like almost every other human motive, our hunger levels are affected by both internal bodily factors and external environmental and social ones. Let's explore each of these more closely.

Internal Factors That Control Eating

If asked, many people would likely say that hunger originates in the stomach. To find out, Walter Cannon and A. L. Washburn (1912) decided to see whether stomach contractions cause hunger. In an early study, Washburn trained himself to swallow a balloon, which could be inflated through an attached tube. (You, too, would do anything for science, right?) This allowed Cannon to record the movements of Washburn's stomach (Figure 10.4). When Washburn's stomach contracted, he reported that he felt "hunger pangs." In view of this, the two scientists concluded that hunger is nothing more than the contractions of an empty stomach. (This, however, proved to be an "inflated" conclusion ...)

Of course, eating *does* slow when the stomach is stretched or distended (full). (Remember last Thanksgiving?) However, for many people hunger produces feelings of weakness or shakiness (rather than a "growling" stomach), and we now know that the stomach is not essential for feeling hunger. Even if the nerve carrying information between your stomach and brain were severed, you would still feel hungry and eat regularly (Petri & Govern, 2013).

Then what does cause hunger? Many different factors combine to promote and suppress hunger (Young, 2012). Although no single "hunger thermostat" exists, the **hypothalamus** (HI-po-THAL-ahmus) is especially important in managing hunger, just as it is in the control of thirst (Young, 2012). (See Figure 10.5.) (For more information about the role of the hypothalamus in controlling behavior, see Section 2.4.)

The hypothalamus receives neural messages from the tongue and digestive system, and is sensitive to levels of a variety of substances in the blood, such as sugar. For example, as the levels of blood sugar (glucose) drop, the liver responds by sending nerve impulses to the brain. When combined, these signals provide an indication about your level of hunger (Freberg, 2016; Woods & Ramsay, 2011). (Incidentally, the hypothalamus also responds to a chemical in cannabis that can produce intense hunger, sometimes known as the "munchies" [Koch et al., 2015].)

Three parts of the hypothalamus seem to have a role in hunger and eating. The first is the lateral hypothalamus, which acts as a

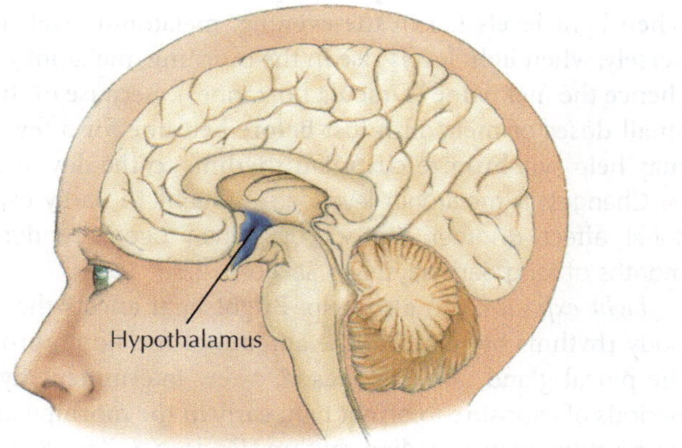

Figure 10.5 The hypothalamus. Location of the hypothalamus in the human brain.

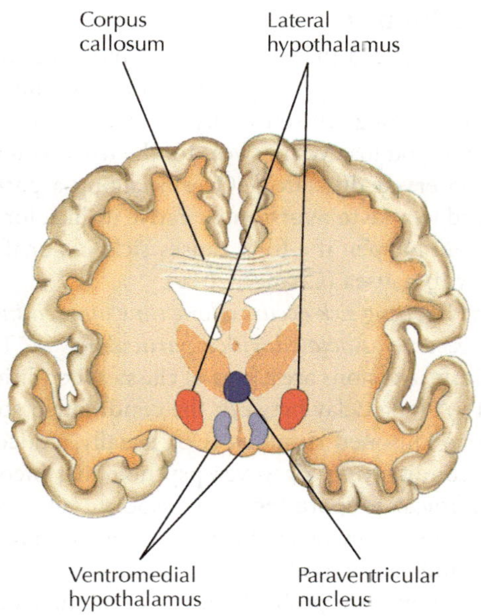

Figure 10.6 Hypothalamic areas that control eating. This is a cross section through the middle of the brain (viewed from the front). Indicated areas of the hypothalamus are associated with hunger and the regulation of body weight.

feeding "start button" and can be activated in a variety of ways. (The term *lateral* simply refers to the *sides* of the hypothalamus. See Figure 10.6.) If the lateral hypothalamus is "turned on" with an electrified probe, even a well-fed animal immediately begins eating. If the same area is destroyed (hence no "start button"), the animal may never eat again.

A second area in the hypothalamus—the *ventromedial* (VENT-ro-MEE-dee-al) *hypothalamus*—functions as a "stop button" (Ribeiro et al., 2009). (*Ventromedial* refers to the bottom middle of the hypothalamus.) Research has demonstrated that if the ventromedial hypothalamus is destroyed, dramatic overeating results.

Finally, the *paraventricular* (PAIR-uh-ven-TRICK-you-ler) *nucleus* of the hypothalamus also affects hunger (see Figure 10.6). This area helps keep blood sugar levels steady by both starting and stopping eating. It's worth noting that it takes at least 10 minutes for the hypothalamus to respond after you begin eating. That's why you are less likely to overeat if you eat slowly and give your brain time to get the message that you've had enough (Liu et al., 2000).

Damage to the hunger satiety system in the hypothalamus can produce a very fat rat, a condition called *hypothalamic hyperphagia* (hi-per-FAGE-yah), which means "overeating." This rat weighs 1,080 grams. (The pointer has gone completely around the dial and beyond.)

Internal Factors and the Long-Term Control of Weight

In addition to determining when to start eating and when meals are over, your brain also controls your weight over long periods of time. Like a thermostat, your brain maintains a **set point** in order to control your weight over the long term. It does this by monitoring the amount of fat stored in your body in specialized *fat cells* (Gloria-Bottini, Magrini, & Bottini, 2009; Vieira & Valentine, 2009).

Your set point is the weight that you maintain when you are not trying to gain or lose weight. When your body weight goes below its set point, you will feel hungry most of the time. On the other hand, fat cells release a substance called *leptin* when your weight climbs above the set point and your "spare tire" is well inflated. Leptin is carried in the bloodstream to the hypothalamus, where it tells us to eat less (Woods & Ramsay, 2011).

Can you change your fat set point? Your leptin levels are partly under genetic control. In rare cases, mice (and we humans) inherit a genetic defect that reduces leptin levels in the body, leading to obesity. In such cases, taking leptin can help (Berman et al., 2013). For the rest of us, the news is not so encouraging. Currently, there is no known way to lower your set point for fat because the number of fat cells remains unchanged throughout adult life (Spalding et al., 2008). To make matters worse, radical diets do not help; in fact, they may even raise the set point for fat (Ahima & Osei, 2004). The good news is that while you may not be able to lose weight by resetting your hypothalamus, psychologists have studied more effective approaches to weight loss. We examine some later in this chapter.

Extracellular thirst Thirst caused by a reduction in the volume of fluids found between body cells.

Intracellular thirst Thirst triggered when fluid is drawn out of cells due to an increased concentration of salts and minerals outside the cells.

Hypothalamus A small area of the brain that regulates emotional behaviors and basic biological needs.

Set point (for fat) The proportion of body fat that tends to be maintained by changes in hunger and eating.

External Factors That Control Eating

As we have seen, "hunger" is affected by more than just the "push" of our biological needs for food. In fact, if internal needs alone controlled eating, fewer people would overeat (Stroebe, Papies, & Aarts, 2008). Nevertheless, roughly 72 percent of adults in the United States are currently overweight or obese (extremely overweight) (Centers for Disease Control, 2020; Figure 10.7). Childhood obesity has also reached epidemic proportions in the United States, having tripled in prevalence since 1980 (Ogden et al., 2010). Let's consider some external influences on hunger and their role in obesity, a major health risk and, for many, a source of social stigma and low self-esteem.

External Eating Cues

Most of us are sensitive to the "pull" of *external eating cues*, signs and signals linked with food. In cultures like ours, in which food is plentiful, eating cues add greatly to the risk of overeating (Casey et al., 2008). Many college freshmen gain weight rapidly during their first three months on campus (the famous "Frosh 15"). All-you-can-eat dining halls in the dorms and night-time snacking appear to be the culprits (Kapinos & Yakusheva, 2011). The presence of others also can affect whether people overeat (or undereat), depending on how much everyone else is eating and how important it is to impress them (Pliner & Mann, 2004).

Cultural Factors

Learning to think of some foods as desirable and others as revolting has a large impact on what we eat. In North America, we would never consider eating the eyes out of the steamed head of a monkey, but in some parts of the world, they are considered a delicacy. By the same token, vegans and vegetarians shun eating any kind of meat. In short, cultural values greatly affect the *incentive value* of foods.

Taste and Plenty

You may have noticed that if you eat too much of any particular food, it becomes less appealing. For example, if you are well fed, leptin dulls the tongue's sensitivity to sweet tastes (Domingos et al., 2011). If you lose your "sweet tooth" when you are full, you may have observed this effect. Overindulging a particular food can even lead to a **taste aversion**, or active dislike, for a particular food. This can happen if a food causes sickness or if it is merely associated with nausea (Chance, 2014).

But what if getting sick occurs a long time after eating? How does the nausea become associated with a particular food? That's a good question. Taste aversions are a type of classical conditioning (see Section 6.1). A long delay between the conditioned stimulus (CS) and the unconditioned stimulus (US) usually reduces the effectiveness of conditioning. However, psychologists theorize that we have a **biological preparedness** to associate an upset stomach with foods eaten previously. Such learning usually protects us from eating unhealthy foods.

These shifts in taste probably help us maintain variety in our diets and even avoid severe nutritional imbalances. For example, if you go on a fad diet and eat only grapefruit, you eventually will begin to feel ill. In time, associating your discomfort with grapefruit may create an aversion to it and restore some balance to your diet.

In our society of plenty, unfortunately, shifts in taste may end up encouraging obesity. The availability of a variety of tasty foods means that we can easily shift what we eat. If you overdose on hamburgers or French fries, moving on to some cookies or chocolate cheesecake certainly won't do your body much good (Pinel, Assanand, & Lehman, 2000).

Dieting

A diet is *not* just a way to lose weight. Your current diet is defined by the types and amounts of food you regularly eat. Some diets actually tend to encourage overeating, especially those that are high in sugar and fat (Dobson & Gerstner, 2010). Unfortunately, North American culture provides the worst kinds of foods for people who suffer from obesity. For example, restaurant and fast food tend to be higher in fat and calories than meals made at home (Kessler, 2009). "Super-sized" meals are another problem. Food portions at restaurants in the United States are 25 percent larger, or more, than they are in France. Far fewer people are obese in France, most likely because they simply eat less. The French also take longer to eat a meal, which discourages overeating (Rozin et al., 2003).

Because of the prevalence of obesity in our culture, hundreds of new diets are published each year. Many of them are "fad" diets that will have you eating only grapefruit and protein, for example. Although you will lose weight on most of these diets, you will likely gain it back when you stop dieting. In fact, many people end up weighing even

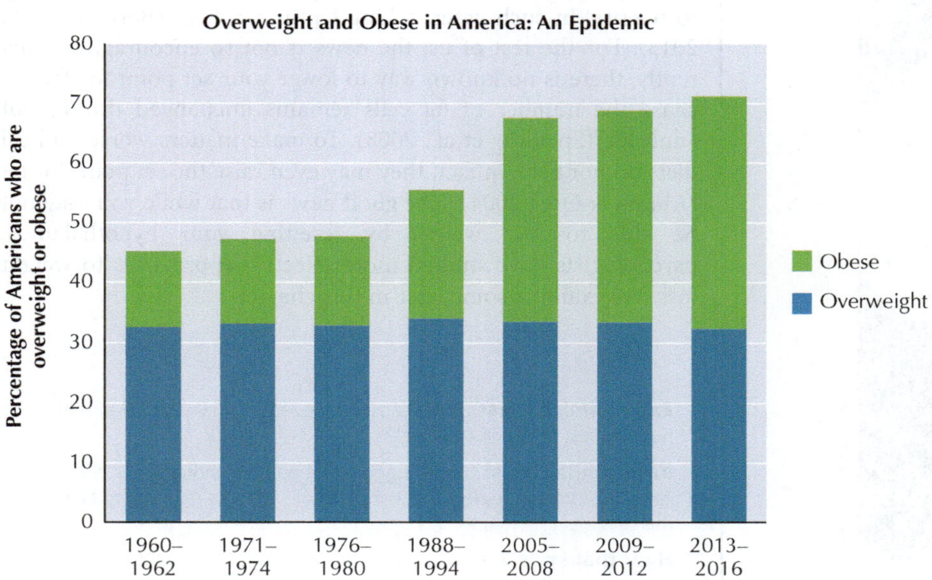

Figure 10.7 The obesity epidemic. A near-epidemic of obesity has occurred in the United States during the last 30 years, with almost three quarters of all Americans now classified as overweight or obese. (Adapted from Centers for Disease Control, 2020.)

more than before they dieted (Freedman, 2011). Why should this be so? Dieting (starving) slows the body's rate of metabolism (the rate at which energy is used). In effect, a dieter's body becomes highly efficient at *conserving* calories and storing them as fat (Pinel, Assanand, & Lehman, 2000).

Apparently, evolution prepared us to save energy when food is scarce and to stock up on fat when food is plentiful. Briefly starving yourself, therefore, may have little lasting effect on weight. "Yo-yo dieting," or repeatedly losing and gaining weight, is especially dangerous. Frequent changes in weight can dramatically slow the body's metabolic rate. As noted earlier, this may raise the body's set point for fat, making it harder to lose weight each time a person diets and easier to regain weight when the diet ends. Frequent weight changes also increase the risk for heart disease and premature death (Wang & Brownell, 2005).

To avoid bouncing between feast and famine, a *permanent* change in eating habits and exercise is required. Such an approach is called **behavioral dieting** (Freedman, 2011; Kiernan et al., 2013), and emphasizes actions such as recording food intake in a "diet diary," thinking carefully about your personal eating cues (e.g., establishing when and where you do most of your eating and avoiding those situations), and developing techniques to control eating (e.g., smaller portions, eating slowly, and putting food away before leaving the kitchen). Such approaches also stress the need to develop a balanced, healthy diet that you can stick with over the long term (that is, one that includes foods that you like and doesn't make you feel as though you are being starved) and committing to regular exercise.

Hunger in Everyday Life: Eating Disorders

Anorexia nervosa (AN-uh-REK-see-yah ner-VOH-sah: self-starvation) is a type of **feeding and eating disorder**—a problem managing food intake that manifests itself in forms such as a life-threatening failure to maintain sufficient body weight. Although a compulsive attempt to lose weight causes them to not seek or desire food, anorexics usually still feel physical hunger. Often, anorexia starts with "normal" dieting that slowly begins to dominate the person's life. In time, anorexics suffer debilitating health problems, including the highest mortality rates of all the mental illnesses (Krantz et al., 2012). ▲ Table 10.1 lists the symptoms of anorexia nervosa.

Bulimia nervosa (bue-LIHM-ee-yah) is a second major eating disorder (de Vries & Meule, 2016; Dryer, Tyson, & Kiernan, 2013). Bulimic persons gorge on food, and then vomit or take laxatives to avoid gaining weight (see Table 10.1). Bingeing without purging is a separate disorder called *binge eating disorder* (American Psychiatric Association, 2013). Bingeing and purging seriously damage health. Typical risks include sore throat, hair loss, muscle spasms, kidney damage, dehydration, tooth erosion, swollen salivary glands, menstrual irregularities, loss of sex drive, and even heart attack.

About 1 percent of all adults suffer from anorexia, along with 3 percent who are bulimic. But these are only the most serious cases. As many as 14 to 22 percent of all adolescents experience some form of disordered eating (Swanson et al., 2011).

Pascal Le Segretain/Getty Images News/Getty Images

Anorexia nervosa is far more dangerous than many people realize. This haunting Italian anti-anorexia poster shows 68-pound model Isabelle Caro, who suffered from anorexia for years up until her death in 2010 at age 28. Many celebrities have struggled with eating disorders, including Karen Carpenter (who died of starvation-induced heart failure), Paula Abdul, Kirstie Alley, Fiona Apple, Victoria Beckham, Princess Diana, Tracey Gold, Janet Jackson, and Mary-Kate Olsen.

▲ Table 10.1 Recognizing Eating Disorders

Anorexia Nervosa

- Refusal to maintain body weight in normal range. Body weight at 85 percent or less of normal for one's height and age.
- Intense fear of becoming fat or gaining weight, even though underweight.
- Disturbance in one's body image or perceived weight. Self-evaluation is unduly influenced by body weight. Denial of seriousness of abnormally low body weight.
- Purging behavior (vomiting or misuse of laxatives or diuretics).

Bulimia Nervosa

- Recurring binge eating. Eating—within an hour or two—an amount of food that is much larger than most people would consume. Feeling a lack of control over eating.
- Purging behavior (vomiting or misuse of laxatives or diuretics). Excessive exercise to prevent weight gain. Fasting to prevent weight gain.
- Self-evaluation is unduly influenced by body weight.

Adapted from American Psychiatric Association (2013).

Taste aversion An active dislike for a particular food.

Biological preparedness (to learn) Organisms are more easily able to learn some associations (e.g., food with illness) than others (e.g., flashing light with illness). Evolution, then, places biological limits on what an animal or person can easily learn.

Behavioral dieting Weight reduction based on changing exercise and eating habits, rather than temporary self-starvation.

Anorexia nervosa An eating disorder characterized by a distorted body image and maintenance of unusually low body weight.

Feeding and eating disorder A problem managing food intake that manifests itself in forms such as a life-threatening failure to maintain sufficient body weight.

Bulimia nervosa A disorder marked by excessive eating followed by inappropriate methods of preventing weight gain.

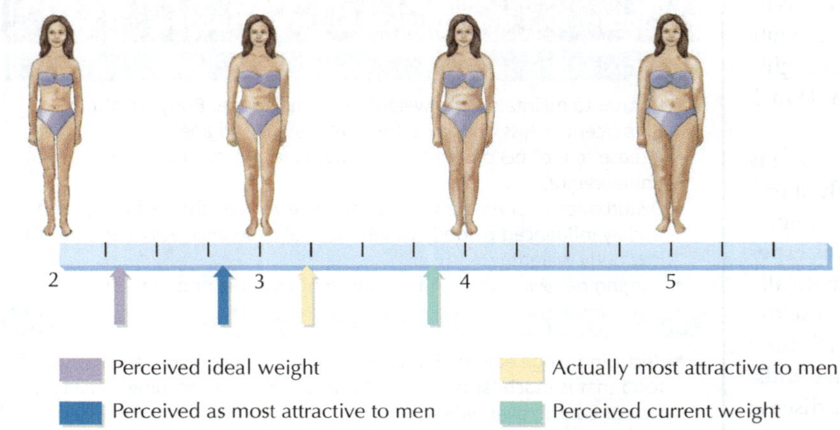

Figure 10.8 Rating body shape. Women with abnormal eating habits were asked to rate their body shape on a scale similar to the one you see here. As a group they chose ideal figures much thinner than what they thought their current weights were. (Most women say they want to be thinner than they currently are, but to a lesser degree than women with eating problems.) Notice that the women with eating problems chose an ideal weight that was even thinner than what they thought men prefer. This is not typical of most women. In this classic study, only women with eating problems wanted to be thinner than what they thought men find attractive (Zellner, Harner, & Adler, 1989).

While women are more prone to develop them, eating disorders are on the rise among men. More and more men also are experiencing *muscle dysmorphia*, or excessive worry about not being muscular enough (Fang & Wilhelm, 2015; Nieuwoudt et al., 2012). Currently, one-third of men say they want less body fat and another third want more muscles. As a result, many men are altering what they eat and exercising excessively (Hartmann, Greenberg, & Wilhelm, 2013). Some are going too far: About 25 percent of anorexics and bulimics are now males (Jones & Morgan, 2010; Wooldridge & Lytle, 2012).

Causes of Eating Disorders

What causes anorexia and bulimia? People who suffer from eating disorders are extremely dissatisfied with their bodies (Trentowska, Bender, & Tuschen-Caffier, 2013). Usually, they have distorted views of themselves. Women have low self-esteem and exaggerated fears of becoming fat. Many overestimate their body size by 25 percent or more. As a result, they think they are disgustingly "fat" when in reality they are wasting away (Figure 10.8) (Polivy & Herman, 2002). Men generally think they are not muscular enough if they are not "cut" or do not have a "six-pack" (Jones & Morgan, 2010).

Many of these problems are related to the idealized body images presented in the media (Hausenblas et al., 2013). Some websites even go so far as to celebrate anorexia and bulimia (referred to by "fans" as "Ana" and "Mia"; Borzekowski et al., 2010; Juarez, Soto, & Pritchard, 2012). Girls who spend a lot of time reading fashion magazines or visiting these websites are more likely to have distorted body images and unrealistic ideas about how they compare with others (Bauer et al., 2017; Martinez-Gonzalez et al., 2003).

The popularity of fitness, exercise, and sports also has contributed to eating disorders. Today, more people are changing their diets in search of a lean, muscular look. People engaged in sports that require low body fat or extreme weight loss (such as wrestling, gymnastics, pole vaulting, high jumping, and even cycling) are particularly likely to develop eating disorders (Weltzin et al., 2005).

People with eating disorders appear to be trying to gain some measure of control. Anorexic teen girls are usually described as "perfect" daughters—helpful, considerate, conforming, and obedient. They seem to be rewarded by seeking perfect control in their lives by being perfectly slim (Keating, 2010; Slof-Op't Landt, Claes, & van Furth, 2016). People suffering from bulimia also are concerned with control (Bardone-Cone et al., 2008). Typically, they are obsessed with thoughts of weight, food, eating, and ridding themselves of food. As a result, they feel guilt, shame, self-contempt, and anxiety. Vomiting reduces their anxiety, which makes purging highly reinforcing.

Treatment for Eating Disorders

Most people suffering from eating disorders do not seek help on their own. This is especially true for men because eating disorders are often perceived to be a female problem (Jones & Morgan, 2010; Weltzin et al., 2005). Typically, it takes strong urging by family or friends to get victims into treatment.

Treatment for anorexia usually begins with giving drugs to relieve obsessive fears of gaining weight. Then, a medical diet is used to restore weight and health. Next, a counselor may help patients work on the emotional conflicts that led to weight loss. For bulimia, behavioral counseling may include self-monitoring of food intake. A related cognitive behavioral approach focuses on changing the thinking patterns and beliefs about weight and body shape that perpetuate eating disorders (Galsworthy-Francis & Allan, 2014; Waller et al., 2014).

Human Diversity and Body Image

Women with eating disorders are not alone in having body image problems. In Western cultures, many women learn to see themselves as "objects" that are evaluated by others. As a result, they try to shape their bodies to the cultural ideal of slimness through dieting (Fredrickson et al., 1998).

Just looking at a fashion magazine tends to leave women less satisfied with their weight and anxious to be thinner (Simpson, 2002). However, women from some cultural backgrounds appear to be less susceptible to the glorification of slimness. For example, Asian-American college students are only half as likely to diet as other college women are (Tsai, Hoerr, & Song, 1998). Within the African-American and Pacific-Islander communities, there is a general preference for a fuller and shapelier figure. In these groups, a larger body size is still associated with high social status, health, and beauty (Becker et al., 2010; Flynn & Fitzgibbon, 1998). Clearly, what constitutes an attractive body style is a matter of opinion, and is influenced by cultural values.

Reflective Practice

Biological Motives

1. The maintenance of bodily equilibrium is called thermostasis. T or F?
2. The term *jet lag* is commonly used to refer to disruptions of
   a. the inverted-U function
   b. circadian rhythms
   c. any of the episodic drives
   d. the body's set point
3. Maintaining your body's set point for fat is closely linked with the amount of ______________ in the bloodstream.
   a. hypothalamic factor-1
   b. ventromedial peptide-1
   c. NPY
   d. leptin
4. People who diet frequently tend to benefit from practice: They lose weight more quickly each time they diet. T or F?
5. In addition to changing eating habits, a key element of behavioral dieting is
   a. exercise
   b. well-timed snacking
   c. better eating cues
   d. commitment to "starving" every day
6. Bingeing and purging are most characteristic of people who have
   a. taste aversions
   b. anorexia
   c. bulimia
   d. strong sensitivity to external eating cues
7. Thirst may be either intracellular or ______________.
8. Pain avoidance is a(n) ______________ drive.
9. Sexual behavior in animals is largely controlled by estrogen levels in the female and the occurrence of estrus in the male. T or F?

THINK CRITICALLY

10. Kim, who is overweight, is highly sensitive to external eating cues. How might her wristwatch contribute to her overeating?

SELF-REFLECT

- Think of the last meal you ate. What caused you to feel hungry? What internal signals told your body to stop eating? How sensitive are you to external eating cues? How were you influenced by portion size? Have you developed any taste aversions?
- A friend of yours seems to be engaging in yo-yo dieting. Can you explain to her or him why such dieting is ineffective? Can you summarize how behavioral dieting is done?

Answers: 1. F 2. b 3. d 4. F 5. a 6. c 7. extracellular 8. episodic 9. F 10. The time of day can influence eating, especially for externally cued eaters, who tend to get hungry at mealtimes, regardless of their internal needs for food.

10.3 Stimulus and Learned Motives

GATEWAYS LEARNING OUTCOMES:
After reading this section you should be able to:

10.3.1 Explain the central idea that underlies arousal theory

10.3.2 Describe the relationship between arousal and performance, as outlined in the Yerkes-Dodson law

10.3.3 Outline what is meant by the need for achievement (nAch) and need for power

10.3.4 Explain the central idea that underlies opponent-process theory

You don't have to look far to realize that human behavior stems from many things beyond biological motives. In this section, we look at two other types of motives: stimulus motives and learned motives.

Stimulus Motives

Most people enjoy a steady "diet" of external stimuli such as new movies, novels, music, fashions, games, news, websites, and adventures. Yet, *stimulus motives*, which reflect needs for information, exploration, manipulation, and sensory input, go beyond mere entertainment. Stimulus motives also help us survive. As we scan the external environment, we constantly identify stimuli such as sources of food, danger, shelter, and other key details. The drive for stimulation is already present during infancy. By the time a child can walk, few things in the home have not been tasted, touched, viewed, handled, or, in the case of toys, destroyed!

Harlow Center for Biological Psychology

Monkeys happily open locks that are placed in their cage. Because no reward is given for this activity, it provides evidence for the existence of stimulus needs.

Stimulus motives are readily apparent in animals as well as humans. For example, monkeys will quickly learn to solve a mechanical puzzle made up of interlocking metal pins, hooks, and latches (Butler, 1954). No food treats or other external rewards are needed to get them to explore and manipulate their surroundings. The monkeys seem to work for the sheer fun of it.

Arousal Theory

Are stimulus motives homeostatic? Yes. According to **arousal theory**, we try to keep the arousal that stems from external stimuli at an optimal level (Güçlütürk, Jacobs, & van Lier, 2016; Petri & Govern, 2013). *Arousal* refers to the activation of the body and nervous system. Arousal is zero at death, low during sleep, moderate during normal daily activities, and high at times of excitement, intense emotion, or panic.

More importantly, the level of arousal that people experience is closely linked with their motivation. Arousal theory assumes that we become uncomfortable when arousal is too low ("I'm bored") or too high ("We're ready to begin your root canal now"). In other words, when your level of arousal is too low or too high, you will seek ways to raise or lower it to achieve homeostasis. The right mix of activities prevents boredom *and* overstimulation (Csikszentmihalyi, Abuhamdeh, & Nakamura, 2005).

Human Diversity and Arousal: Sensation Seekers

Do people vary in their needs for stimulation? Arousal theory suggests that people learn to seek particular levels of arousal (Lynne-Landsman et al., 2011). Where would you prefer to go on your next summer vacation? Your backyard? How about a week with your best friends at a cottage on a nearby lake? Or a shopping and museum trip to New York City? How about scuba diving with sharks?

If the shark adventure attracts you, you are probably high in *sensation seeking*, a trait of people who prefer high levels of stimulation (Lynne-Landsman et al., 2011). Whether you are high or low in sensation seeking is probably based on how your body responds to new, unusual, or intense stimulation (Cservenka et al., 2013; Harden, Quinn, & Tucker-Drob, 2012). Low sensation seekers are orderly, nurturant, and giving, and enjoy the company of others. In contrast, people high in sensation seeking tend to be bold, independent, and value change. Exciting lives aside, though, sensation seeking does have a dark side (Dunlop & Romer, 2010). For example, high sensation seekers are more likely to engage in high-risk behaviors such as smoking, substance abuse, and casual unprotected sex (Drane, Modecki, & Barber, 2017; Harden, Quinn, & Tucker-Drob, 2012).

Mauricio Graiki/Shutterstock.com

Sensation seeking is a trait of people who prefer high levels of stimulation.

Arousal and Peak Performance

If we set aside individual differences, most people perform best when their arousal level is *moderate*. Let's say that you have to take an essay exam. If you are feeling sleepy, lazy, or bored (arousal level too low), your performance will suffer. If you are in a state of anxiety or panic about the test (arousal level too high), you also will perform below par. Thus, the relationship between arousal and performance usually forms an *inverted, or upside-down, U function*, a relationship referred to as the **Yerkes-Dodson law** (● Figure 10.9) (Petri & Govern, 2013).

The inverted *U* tells us that at very low levels of arousal, you're not sufficiently energized to perform well. Performance will improve as your arousal level increases, up to the middle of the curve. Then, performance begins to drop off as arousal continues to increase and you become anxious, emotional, frenzied, or disorganized.

Is performance always best at moderate levels of arousal? No. According to the original theory advanced by Yerkes and Dodson, the ideal level of arousal depends on the complexity of a task. If a task is very simple and well-practiced, it is best for arousal to be high, and this high level of arousal will not compromise

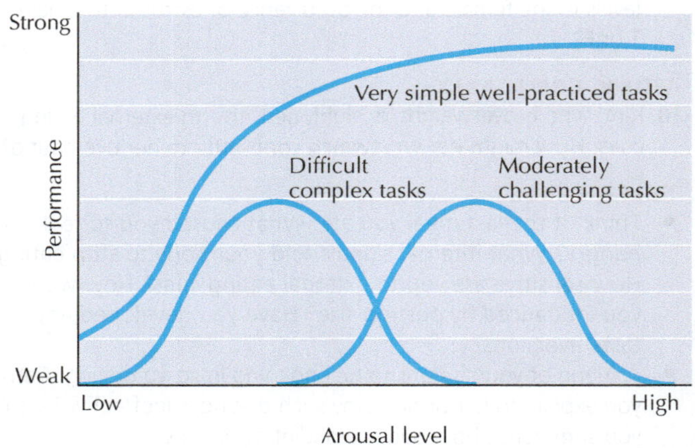

● **Figure 10.9 Yerkes-Dodson law.** The Yerkes-Dodson law shows the relationship between arousal and performance. Performance on very simple tasks is not compromised, even at high levels of arousal. The relationship takes the form of an inverted-U for moderately challenging and very difficult tasks. As difficulty of the task increases, the curve moves to the left such that the optimal level of arousal for a strong performance becomes lower.

performance (see the top line in Figure 10.9). When a task is moderately complex, you begin to see the inverted U shape (see the right-hand curve in Figure 10.9), and as tasks become even more complex your best performance will occur at lower and lower levels of arousal (see the left-hand curve in Figure 10.9).

To make these ideas more concrete, let's consider an example. Imagine that Yingfang is a manager at an advertising company. She's getting ready to make a big presentation to potential clients, after which she'll spend about 30 minutes answering any questions they might have about the ad campaign she's developed. Just before the presentation she has three things to do: set up the projector before everyone arrives for the presentation, give the presentation, and manage the questions afterward. As the presentation draws closer, Yingfang begins to feel the pressure and her arousal level starts to rise.

The first task is a very simple one for Yingfang. She's a wizard with technology, and she's set the projector up for presentations hundreds of times. For well-practiced tasks like this, rising arousal will help to focus her attention. Even if her arousal level before the presentation was very high, it likely wouldn't affect her ability to perform a task that she finds very easy. Put another way, we don't see performance decline for simple tasks, even when arousal is high.

The second task—giving the presentation—is certainly more complex and challenging. Yingfang has given a number of presentations during her career, though, and she's reasonably confident in her abilities. For moderately challenging tasks like this, we would likely see the inverted-U relationship between arousal and her performance during the presentation. A reasonable amount of arousal will be helpful in terms of her performance, but if it becomes too great then her presentation will likely suffer.

Yingfang considers the final task—answering the client's questions—to be the most difficult of all. Though she has given a number of presentations to clients in the past, her boss has typically handled the questions afterward. Moreover, she knows that the questions can be unpredictable, and she'll need to be able to think well on her feet. For very complex tasks like this one, especially those that have been practiced less often, the inverted-U function still applies, but the optimal level of arousal for peak performance is lower than it would be for less challenging tasks like giving the presentation. In other words, as arousal rises, we'll see Yingfang's performance on the question session begin to decline earlier than we would on the less-challenging presentation. On the graph in Figure 10.9, this means that as task difficulty increases, the inverted-U curve moves to the left and peak performance is achieved at lower levels of arousal.

Arousal in Everyday Life: Coping with Test Anxiety

In school, most students have had experience with "test anxiety," a familiar example of how too much arousal can lower performance. You might initially think that a person could do better on tests by simply learning to calm down. Sometimes that is the case, but not always. To begin with, we've just seen that some arousal is healthy; it focuses us on the task at hand. It is only when arousal *interferes* with performance that we refer to anxiety. **Test anxiety** is a mixture of *heightened physiological arousal* (nervousness, sweating, pounding heart) and *excessive worry*. This combination—arousal plus worry—tends to distract students with a rush of upsetting thoughts and feelings (Putwain & Aveyard, 2016; Sparfeldt et al., 2013). Here are some suggestions for coping with test anxiety:

1. **Preparation**
   Hard work is the most direct antidote for test anxiety. Many test-anxious students simply study too little, too late. That's why improving your study skills is a good way to reduce test anxiety (Cassady, 2004). Not studying while remaining calm simply means that you will calmly fail the test.
   The best solution is to *overprepare* by studying long before the "big day." Well-prepared students score higher, worry less, and are less likely to panic (Santrock & Halonen, 2013). (■ If test anxiety is a problem for you, it would be wise to return to the introduction in this book, *Psychology and Your Skill Set—Reflective Studying*, and review the learning and test-taking skills described there.)

2. **Relaxation**
   Learning to relax is another way to lower test anxiety (Bradley et al., 2010; Mowbray, 2012). (■ You can learn self-relaxation skills by looking at Sections 5.2 and 15.2, where relaxation techniques are described.) Emotional support also helps (Stöber, 2004). If you are test anxious, discuss the problem with your professors or study for tests with a supportive classmate.

3. **Rehearsal**
   To reduce nervousness, rehearse how you will cope with upsetting events. Before taking a test, imagine yourself going blank, running out of time, or feeling panicked. Then, calmly plan how you will handle each situation—by keeping your attention on the task, by focusing on one question at a time, and so forth (Watson & Tharp, 2014).

4. **Restructuring Thoughts**
   Another helpful strategy involves listing the upsetting thoughts that you have during exams. Then you can learn to combat these worries with calming, rational replies (Olpin & Hesson, 2016). (■ These are called *coping statements*; see Section 13.5 for more information.) Let's say you think, "I'm going to fail this test and everybody will think I'm stupid." A good reply to this upsetting thought would be to say, "If I prepare well and control my worries, I will probably pass the test. Even if I don't, it won't be the end of the world. My friends will still like me, and I can try to do better on the next test." You can also try working on your *explanatory style*, as described in the *Psychology and Your Skill Set* section at the end of this chapter.

Arousal theory Assumes that people prefer to maintain ideal, or comfortable, levels of arousal.

Yerkes-Dodson law A summary of the relationships among arousal, task complexity, and performance.

Test anxiety High levels of arousal and worry that seriously impair test performance.

Students who cope well with exams usually try to do the best they can, even under difficult circumstances. Becoming a more confident test-taker can actually increase your scores because it helps you remain calm. With practice, most people can learn to be less testy at test-taking time.

Learned Motives

Learned motives are not as closely linked to survival as biological and stimulus motives. Instead, their power comes from learned needs that are associated with concepts that humans value. For example, you will have no doubt recognized that some of your friends are more motivated than others by success, achievement, competition, money, possessions, status, love, approval, grades, dominance, power, or belonging to groups. All of these are *social motives* or goals. We acquire **social motives** through learning, including socialization and cultural conditioning (Deckers, 2014). The behavior of many newsworthy individuals is best understood in terms of such learned social motives, particularly the need for achievement and the need for power, which we explore in the next two sections.

Need for Achievement

To many people, being "motivated" means being interested in achievement (Petri & Govern, 2013; van de Pol & Kavussanu, 2012). The **need for achievement (nAch)** is a drive to excel in one's endeavors (McClelland, 1961). People with high nAch strive to do well any time they are evaluated (Steinmayr & Spinath, 2009).

Venus and Serena Williams possess high achievement motivation. They have become professional tennis champions by playing with perseverance, passion, and self-confidence.

When people high in nAch tackle a task, they do so with perseverance, passion, and self-confidence (Duckworth et al., 2007; Munroe-Chandler, Hall, & Fishburne, 2008). They tend to complete difficult tasks, they earn better grades, and they tend to excel in their occupations. College students high in nAch attribute success to their own ability; they attribute failure to insufficient effort. Thus, high-nAch students are more likely to renew their efforts when they perform poorly. When the going gets tough, high achievers get going.

Is that like the aggressive businessperson who strives to make a lot of money? Not necessarily. It's true that nAch may lead to wealth and prestige, but people who are high achievers in art, music, science, or amateur sports may excel without seeking riches. Such people typically enjoy challenges and relish a chance to test their abilities. Put another way, they are driven by intrinsic, rather than extrinsic, motives.

Need for Power

The need for achievement differs from the **need for power**, which is a desire to have impact or control over others (Lammers et al., 2016; McClelland, 1975). People with a strong need for power want their importance to be visible: They buy expensive possessions, wear prestigious clothes, and exploit relationships. In some ways, the pursuit of power and financial success is the dark side of the American dream. People whose main goal in life is to make lots of money tend to be poorly adjusted and unhappy (Kasser, 2016).

Connecting Motivation and Emotion: Opponent Process Theory

It is easy enough to see that praise, money, success, pleasure, and similar reinforcers affect our goals and desires. But how do people learn to enjoy activities that are at first painful or frightening? Why do people climb rocks, jump out of airplanes, run marathons, take saunas, or swim in frozen lakes?

Psychologist Richard L. Solomon (1980) offers an intriguing explanation for learned motives of this kind. According to his **opponent-process theory**, if a stimulus causes a strong emotion, such as fear or pleasure, the opposite emotion tends to occur when the stimulus ends. For example, if you are in pain and the pain ends, you will feel a pleasant sense of relief. If a person feels pleasure, as in the case of drug use, and the pleasure ends, it will be followed by craving or discomfort (Vargas-Perez, Ting-AKee, & van der Kooy, 2009). If you are in love and feel good when you are with your lover, you will be uncomfortable when she or he is absent.

Solomon also assumes that when a stimulus—even a painful or frightening one—is repeated, our response to it gets weaker. Many first-time hang gliders, for example, are likely terrified during their first solo flight. But with repeated flights, fear decreases, until finally the hang glider feels a "thrill" instead of terror. While the initial emotions diminish with repetition, the emotional aftereffects get stronger. After a first flight, beginners feel a brief but exhilarating sense of relief. After many such experiences, though, seasoned hang gliders can get a "rush" of euphoria that lasts for hours. Put another way, with repetition the pleasurable aftereffect gets stronger and the initial "cost" (pain or fear) gets weaker. The opponent-process theory thus explains how skydiving, rock climbing, ski jumping, and other hazardous pursuits become reinforcing. If you are a fan of horror movies, carnival rides, or bungee jumping, your motives may be based on the same effect.

Notice the strong link between motivation and emotion in these examples related to opponent-process theory. In the next few sections of this chapter, we turn to the subject of emotion and examine its effects on our thinking and behavior.

Reflective Practice

Stimulus and Learned Motives

1. Exploration, manipulation, and curiosity provide evidence for the existence of ____________________ motives.
2. Complex tasks, such as taking a classroom test, tend to be disrupted by high levels of arousal, an effect predicted by
   a. sensation seeking
   b. the Yerkes-Dodson law
   c. studies of circadian arousal patterns
   d. studies of nAch
3. According to opponent-process theory, when a stimulus is repeated, our response to it gets stronger. T or F?
4. People high in nAch show high levels of perseverance, passion, and ____________________.
   a. control
   b. intelligence
   c. self-confidence
   d. sensation seeking

THINK CRITICALLY

5. Many US college freshmen say that "being well-off financially" is an essential life goal and that "making more money" was a very important factor in their decision to attend college. Which needs are fulfilled by "making more money"?

SELF-REFLECT

- Think of at least one time when your performance could have been predicted by the Yerkes-Dodson law; that is, your performance was impaired by arousal that was too low or too high.
- Do you have a high or low need for stimulation? Are you a sensation seeker?
- Do you think you are high or low in nAch? When faced with a challenging task, are you high or low in perseverance? Passion? Self-confidence?

Answers: 1. stimulus 2. b 3. F 4. c 5. None of them.

10.4 The Four Basic Aspects of Emotion

GATEWAYS LEARNING OUTCOMES:
After reading this section you should be able to:

10.4.1 Outline the four basic aspects of an emotion

10.4.2 Explain what is meant by emotional experience, and how it differs from mood

10.4.3 Describe the physiological responses that are associated with emotions

10.4.4 Outline the various ways in which an emotion can be expressed and regulated

10.4.5 Describe two types of cognition that are relevant to emotions

Now that we have looked at motivation, let's turn our attention to emotion. For many years, philosophers and psychologists focused most of their attention on cognition, assuming that rational thinking was a window into the best of human functioning. Emotion was seen as interfering with cognition, and was therefore something that needed to be controlled. More recently, though, psychologists have embraced the value of our emotional lives, and noted that there is a tight coupling between cognition and emotion. Indeed, it's generally accepted that cognition and emotion are often so tightly intertwined that it's impossible to distinguish where one begins and the other ends.

An **emotion** is a state that's characterized by four basic components: *experience* (that is, subjective feelings), *physiology*, *expression* (facial expressions, gestures, and tone of voice, for example), and *cognitions* (for example, attributions and appraisals). In this section, we'll take a closer look at each one.

Experience

A person's private emotional experiences are the most obvious component of emotions; they are the part of emotion with which we are usually most familiar. For example, we all seem to have an

Social motives Learned motives acquired as part of growing up in a particular society or culture.

Need for achievement (nAch) The drive to excel in one's endeavors.

Need for power The desire to have social impact and control over others.

Opponent-process theory States that strong emotions tend to be followed by the opposite emotional state; also the strength of both emotional states changes over time.

Emotion A feeling state that has physiological, cognitive, and behavioral components.

intuitive understanding of what emotions such as anger, sadness, and happiness "feel like," and we know how to recognize and label these subjective emotional feelings when we experience them. As a result, people often tend to imagine that each emotion produces a "signature" experience that is exactly the same in all people and completely different from other emotions. Researchers, however, have not had much success in finding evidence to support this idea that there are discrete categories of emotional experience that are totally distinct from one another and experienced the same way by all people. Instead, the story seems to be more complex, as we will see later in this section.

Emotional Experience Versus Moods

A **mood** is a specific type of emotional state (● Figure 10.10). While the words *emotion* and *mood* tend to be used interchangeably in everyday language, psychologists make two important distinctions between these two terms. First, emotions tend to be *shorter in duration* than moods. While emotional states tend to be brief, lasting seconds or minutes, moods can last for many hours, days, or even months. Second, emotions tend to *have a target*; that is, they are caused by something that's identifiable. When we experience emotions like anger, sadness, or excitement, for example, we are typically mad, sad, or excited about something (or someone) specific. In contrast, moods tend to be more general and are not necessarily directed at anyone or anything in particular.

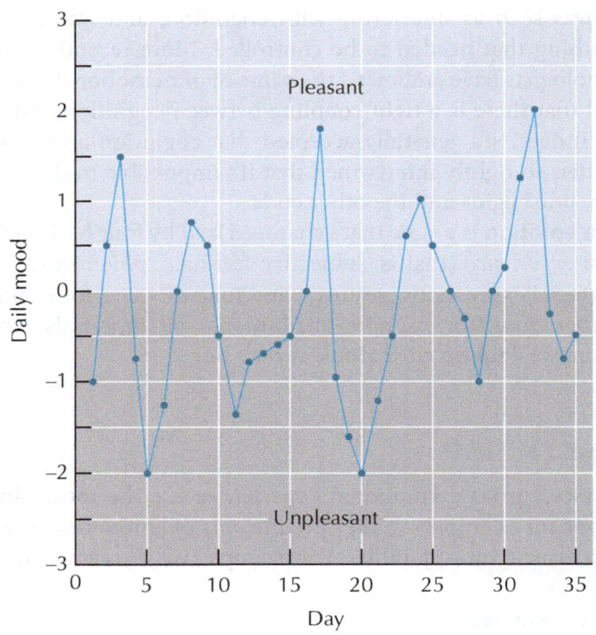

● **Figure 10.10 Moods by the week.** Folklore holds that people who work or attend school on a weekly schedule experience their lowest moods on "Blue Monday." Actually, moods generally tend to be lower for *most* weekdays than they are on weekends. The graph shown here plots the average daily moods of a group of college students over a five-week period. As you can see, many people find that their moods rise and fall on a seven-day cycle. For most students, a low point tends to occur around Monday or Tuesday and a peak on Friday or Saturday. In other words, moods are shaped by weekly schedules. (Adapted from Larsen & Kasimatis, 1990.)

Like our motives, moods are closely tied to circadian rhythms. When your body temperature is at its daily low point, for example, you are more likely to feel "down" emotionally. When body temperature is at its peak, your mood is likely to be positive—even if you missed a night of sleep (Boivin, Czeisler, & Waterhouse, 1997; McClung, 2011).

Physiology

An African Bushman is frightened by a lion. A city dweller is frightened by someone walking behind them in a dark alley. Though these two scenarios might look quite different on the surface, the emotion aroused—fear—is likely to cause very similar physiological reactions. Whether the encounter happens in the heart of the Kalahari Desert or the streets of New York, it will produce muscle tension, a pounding heart, dryness of the throat and mouth, sweating, butterflies in the stomach, trembling, and numerous other body changes.

Strong emotional reactions often generate activity in the **autonomic nervous system (ANS)**—the part of the peripheral nervous system that connects the brain with internal organs and glands (Freberg, 2016). (■ As you may recall from Section 2.1, activity of the ANS is *automatic*, rather than voluntary.) The ANS has two divisions: the sympathetic branch and the parasympathetic branch. Both branches are active at all times; whether you are relaxed or aroused at any moment depends on the relative balance of activity in the two branches.

What does the ANS do during emotion? In general, the sympathetic branch activates the body for emergency action—for "fighting or fleeing"—and consequently is often active when we experience emotions such as anger or fear. The sympathetic nervous system arouses some body systems and inhibits others (● Figure 10.11). For example, sugar is released into the bloodstream for quick energy, the heart beats faster to supply blood to the muscles, digestion is temporarily slowed, blood flow in the skin is restricted to reduce bleeding, and so forth. Such reactions improve the chances of surviving an emergency.

The parasympathetic branch reverses emotional arousal, calming and relaxing the body (Figure 10.11). After a period of high emotion, the heart is eventually slowed, the pupils return to normal size, blood pressure drops, and so forth. In addition to restoring balance, the parasympathetic system helps build up and conserve the body's energy. The parasympathetic system responds much more slowly than the sympathetic system. That's why a pounding heart, muscle tension, and other signs of arousal don't fully settle down for 20 or 30 minutes after you feel an intense emotion such as anger or fear. Moreover, after a strong emotional shock, the parasympathetic system may overreact and lower blood pressure too much. This can cause you to become dizzy or faint after seeing something shocking, such as a horrifying accident.

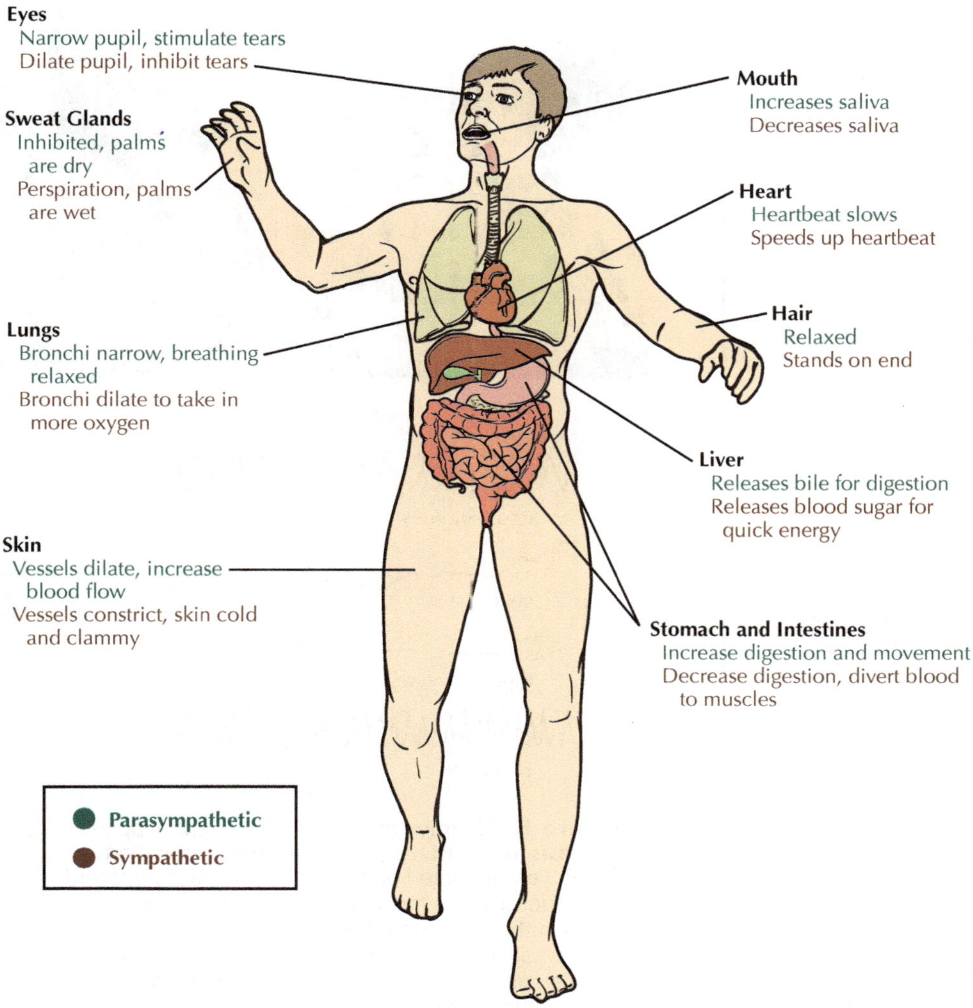

Figure 10.11 The autonomic nervous system. The parasympathetic branch of the ANS calms and quiets the body. The sympathetic branch arouses the body and prepares it for emergency action.

Emotion Physiology and the Brain

Imagine this test: Go to a zoo and place your face close to the glass in front of a rattlesnake display. Suddenly, the rattlesnake strikes at your face. Do you flinch? Even though you know that you are safe, psychological scientist Joseph LeDoux predicts that you will not be able to avoid recoiling from the attack (LeDoux, 2000, 2012). According to LeDoux, this basic fear response is automatic and not under the control of higher brain centers; instead, it is a form of experiential processing (see Section 8.1). Specifically, the **amygdala**, a part of the *limbic system*, receives sensory information directly, before the cortex (Figure 10.12). (See Section 2.4 for more information.)

This subcortical circuit through the amygdala allows us to respond quickly to potential danger before we really know what's happening (Martínez-Alvarez et al., 2016). However, though an emotion like fear is first managed in the limbic system, most emotions are eventually processed in the cortex (Saarimäki et al., 2016). This additional cortical processing can be much more elaborate, giving rise to rich emotional experiences that reflect the complexity of our lives.

Emotion Physiology in Everyday Life: Lie Detectors

You undoubtedly know that criminals are not always truthful. But what you may not know is that up to 25 percent of all wrongful convictions include false confessions as evidence (Kassin, 2005). The most popular method for detecting falsehoods measures the bodily changes that accompany emotion. Unfortunately, the accuracy of "lie detector" tests is doubtful, and they can be a serious invasion of privacy (Bunn, 2012; Meijer & Verschuere, 2010).

How do lie detectors work? The lie detector is more accurately called a **polygraph**, a word that means "many writings" (Figure 10.13). The polygraph was invented in 1915 by psychologist William Marston, who also created the comic book character Wonder Woman, a superhero whose "magic lasso" could force people to tell the truth (Grubin & Madsen, 2005). Although popularly known as a lie detector because the police use it for that purpose, in reality, the polygraph is not a lie detector at all. A suspect is questioned while "hooked up" to a polygraph, which typically records changes in heart rate, blood pressure, breathing, and the galvanic skin response (GSR). The GSR is recorded from the hand by electrodes that measure skin conductance, or, more simply, sweating. Because the device records only general emotional arousal, it can't tell the difference between lying and fear, or anxiety and excitement (Iacono, 2008).

Couldn't an innocent but nervous person fail a polygraph test? Absolutely. To minimize this problem, skilled polygraph examiners might use the **guilty knowledge test** (Hakun et al., 2009). A series

Mood A low-intensity, long-lasting emotional state.

Autonomic nervous system (ANS) The system of nerves carrying information to and from the internal organs and glands.

Amygdala A part of the limbic system associated with the rapid processing of emotions; especially fear.

Polygraph A device for recording heart rate, blood pressure, respiration, and galvanic skin response; commonly called a "lie detector."

Guilty knowledge test A polygraph procedure involving testing people with facts that only a guilty person could know.

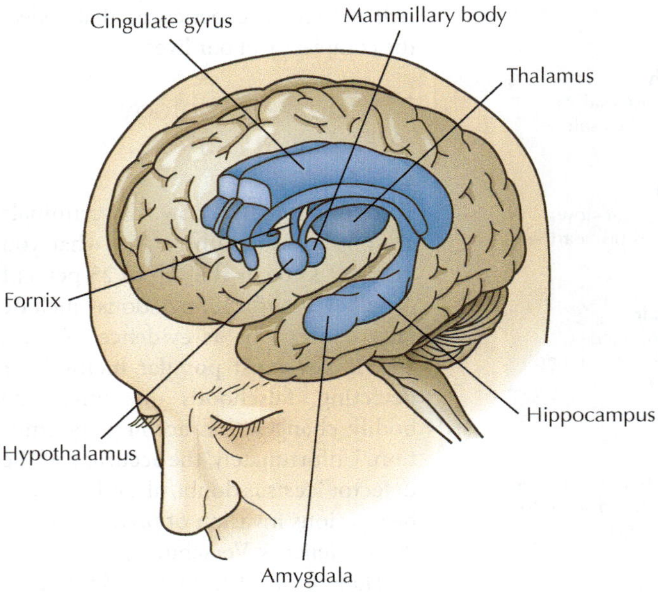

Figure 10.12 Parts of the limbic system. An amygdala can be found buried beneath the temporal lobes on each side of the brain (■ see Section 2.4. The subcortical limbic system is a sort of "primitive core" of the brain strongly associated with emotion). The amygdala appears to provide "quick and dirty" processing of emotional stimuli that allows us to react involuntarily to danger.

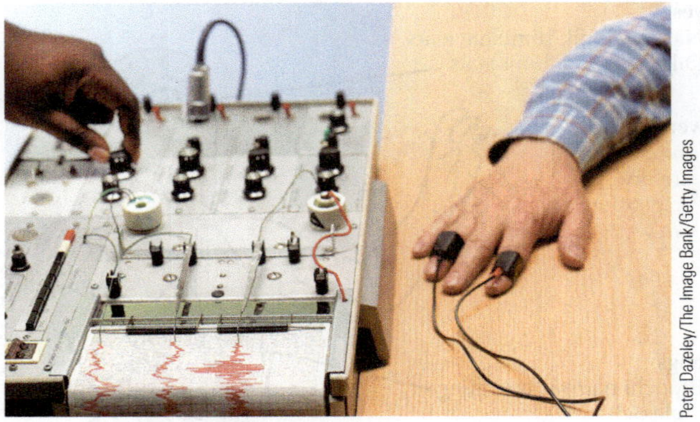

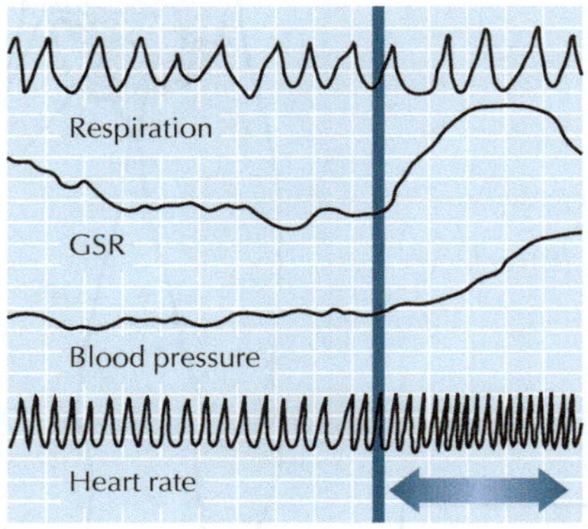

Figure 10.13 Polygraph. *(photo)* A typical polygraph measures heart rate, blood pressure, respiration, and GSR. Pens mounted on the top of the machine record bodily responses on a moving strip of paper *(graph)*. Changes in the area marked by the arrow indicate emotional arousal. If such responses appear when a person answers a question, he or she may be lying, but arousal may have other causes.

of multiple-choice questions are asked; one answer is correct. For example, one question might be: "Was the gun that killed Hensley a (a) Colt; (b) Smith & Wesson; (c) Walther PPK; or (d) Luger?" A guilty person who knew which gun she had used may show an elevated response to the correct answer. Because an innocent person couldn't know which gun was involved, she could only respond similarly to all four alternatives (Iacono, 2011).

Although proponents of lie detection claim it is 95 percent accurate, errors may occur even when questioning is done properly (Bunn, 2012). In one study, accuracy was dramatically lowered when people thought about past emotional experiences as they answered irrelevant questions (Ben-Shakhar & Dolev, 1996). Similarly, the polygraph may be thrown off by self-inflicted pain, tranquilizing drugs, or people who can lie without anxiety. Worst of all, the test is much more likely to label an innocent person guilty rather than a guilty person innocent (Nahari, 2012). In studies involving real crimes, an average of one innocent person in five was rated as guilty by the lie detector (Lykken, 2001). For such reasons, the National Academy of Sciences (2003) has concluded that polygraph tests should not be used to screen employees.

Despite the lie detector's flaws, you may be tested for employment or for other reasons. Should this occur, the best advice is to remain calm; afterward, you may decide to actively challenge the results if the machine wrongly questions your honesty.

Isn't there a better way to detect lies? Possibly. Brain scans like fMRI directly measure brain activity, thus bypassing the traditional approach of measuring indirect signs of emotional arousal (Hakun et al., 2009; Lefebvre et al., 2007) (■ see Section 2.2 for more information about fMRI imaging). For example, researchers have found that different brain areas are involved in telling a lie. Psychiatrist Daniel Langleben (2008) theorizes that a liar must inhibit telling the truth in order to lie. Thus, extra brain areas must be activated to tell a lie, which can be seen in brain images when people are lying.

Even if new methods are used, the key problem remains: How can we avoid falsely classifying liars as truth tellers and truth tellers as liars? Until that can be done with acceptable accuracy, any new technique may have no more value than the polygraph (Choi, 2015).

Expression

When we experience emotions, there are many ways in which we can display those feelings. In some cases, emotions can be expressed in maladaptive ways. For example, stage fright, or performance anxiety, can spoil performances. Similarly, expressions of hate, anger, contempt, disgust, and fear can disrupt relationships.

Figure 10.14 Simplified faces. When shown groups of simplified faces (without labels), the angry and scheming faces "jumped out" at people before the sad, happy, and neutral faces. An ability to rapidly detect threatening expressions probably helped our ancestors survive. (Adapted from Tipples, Atkinson, & Young, 2002.)

More often, though, emotions aid survival by promoting **adaptive behaviors** such as attacking, fleeing, seeking comfort, helping others, and reproducing. Such behaviors help us adjust to changing conditions. Moreover, as social animals, it would be impossible for humans to live in groups, cooperate in raising children, and defend one another without emotion-related expressions and behavior (Buss, 2015).

When most people think about emotional expressivity, they immediately think about *facial expressions*. Psychologists believe that emotional expressions evolved to communicate our feelings to others, which aids survival. The idea that facial displays have evolutionary significance dates back to Charles Darwin (1872), who observed that angry tigers, monkeys, dogs, and humans all bare their teeth in the same way. And there is evidence to suggest that we are quite good at interpreting these signals in others: For instance, in one study, people were able to detect angry and scheming faces faster than happy, sad, or neutral faces (Figure 10.14). Presumably, we are especially sensitive to threatening faces because they warn us of possible harm and provide valuable hints about what other people are likely to do next (Adolphs, 2008; Kalat & Shiota, 2012).

More recently, though, psychological scientists have recognized that emotional expressivity goes well beyond facial expressions. One modality that seems to be important is **kinesics**, or body language. In particular, researchers have explored how body language related to *touch* may be important in the expression of emotion. For example, researchers have demonstrated that even very brief touches of a half second can reliably communicate information about emotions such as gratitude, sadness, anger, love, and disgust (Cowen et al., 2019; Hertenstein et al., 2009). Beyond touch, body language related to *posture* and *eye gaze* can also be useful in signaling particular types of emotion. Self-conscious emotions such as shame, embarrassment, and pride, for example, are associated with very specific body language: Most of us can easily recognize the slumped posture and downward gaze that is associated with shame (Keltner et al., 2019).

In addition to facial expressions and body language such as touch, posture, and gaze, emotions are also expressed through the human *voice*. Prosidy—the tone and rhythm of our speech—is particularly helpful in communicating how we feel. In one study, an international group of researchers had people from five nations try to express several very different emotions—anger, contempt, shame, fear, happiness, lust, pride, relief, and sadness, for example—while saying the same, emotionally neutral sentence ("Let me tell you something"). In keeping with many other studies, these psychological scientists discovered that people listening to these sentences were able to reliably judge differences in the emotion being conveyed. Though their words were exactly the same, tone of voice provided a useful gauge of the differing emotions being signaled by the speaker (Laukka et al., 2016). But speech is not the only way we communicate emotion vocally: Psychologists have also noted that short vocal bursts such as shrieks, growls, sighs, oooohs, and aahhhs can be valuable in terms of understanding others' emotional states (Keltner et al., 2019).

Emotional Expression in Everyday Life: Emotion Contagion

Typically, our emotional expressions are tightly connected to our own circumstances and emotional experiences. In some cases, though, they can also be governed by the emotions of those around us. *Emotion contagion* is a process by which our own short-term emotions become more similar to those of other people that we interact with face-to-face or via the Internet (Goldenberg & Gross, 2020).

One example of emotion contagion is *behavioral mimicry*, which refers to unconsciously imitating the postures, mannerisms, and facial expressions of other people as we interact with them (Dalton, Chartrand, & Finkel, 2010). Psychologist Tanya Chartrand has found that if another person copies your gestures and physical postures to some extent, you are more inclined to like them (Chartrand & Lakin, 2013). If that person goes too far, however, you are more likely to be "creeped out" (Leander, Chartrand, & Bargh, 2012).

Eviled/Shutterstock.com

Emotions are often unconsciously revealed by gestures and body positioning.

Adaptive behaviors Actions that aid attempts to survive and adapt to changing conditions.

Kinesics Study of the meaning of body movements, posture, hand gestures, and facial expressions; commonly called *body language*.

More recently, increased attention has been directed at online sources of emotion contagion. It's no secret that much of the content on social media, for example, is steeped in emotions, both positive and negative. There is evidence to suggest that content that is more emotional is more likely to be shared online (Guadagno et al., 2013). Moreover, exposure to the emotions of others online can have an important impact on our own emotions. Companies—particularly social media companies—understand this and actively manage the content that users see in ways that ensure maximum engagement with their platforms (Kramer et al., 2014).

Such findings have led to a growing number of ethical questions about the way that companies such as Facebook, YouTube, and Twitter operate, particularly when the emotional content being shared falls in the category of misinformation or hoaxes. While some people are calling for greater regulation of social media, others counter with reminders about the value of free speech. One way or another, two skills are important when engaging with others online about topics that pull for strong emotional responses: The first is the importance of digital literacy, a topic that we discussed in detail in ■ Section 1.8. The other, though, is the ability to manage, or *regulate*, your emotions—a topic to which we turn now.

Regulating Emotional Expression

We regularly work to change, or *regulate*, our emotional expressions so that they differ from our emotional experience. Maybe you've concealed your anger with a boss, or put a lid on your happiness about a good test grade after finding out that your best friend had failed. There are many times in our lives when it makes sense to express *less* emotion than we really feel.

Of course, sometimes we may also work to express *more* emotion than we actually feel. At one time or another, for example, you may have tried to express greater enthusiasm than you actually felt for your brother's performance in a concert, or you may have "played up" your sadness at hearing some news that was clearly upsetting to a colleague.

Regardless of whether you're trying to show more or less emotion than you feel, in such instances psychological scientists would say that we're engaging in **emotion regulation,** or the active management of emotion-related expressions. Though any emotion can be regulated, it's probably most common to do so when we feel negative emotions and are trying not to show them. In such circumstances, people can be quite good at suppressing outward signs of emotion.

Unfortunately, restraining negative emotion in this way can actually increase activity in the sympathetic nervous system. In other words, hiding emotion requires a lot of effort. Suppressing emotions also can impair thinking and memory as you devote energy to self-control. Thus, although suppressing emotion allows us to appear calm and collected on the outside, this cool appearance comes at a high cost (Gross, 2013).

Though suppression may sometimes be necessary, it's usually better to manage emotions using other strategies (Gross, 2013). Effective emotion regulation strategies may include any of the following:

- *Situation selection* involves managing emotions by controlling the circumstances in which you find yourself. You can choose, for example, to seek out situations (and people) who make you feel happy and minimize the times you find yourself in situations that create significant stress or unhappiness. If interacting with your great aunt Tabitha always frustrates you because she complains a lot and criticizes your lifestyle, you may simply choose not to attend family functions when you know she'll be there.
- *Situation modification* refers to efforts aimed at altering unavoidable situations to make them more palatable. For example, if you can't avoid great aunt Tabitha because she's going to be at your family's Thanksgiving celebration, then perhaps you make sure you're seated at the far end of the table so that you don't have to speak with her.
- *Redirecting attention* means that you shift your focus in ways that allow you to avoid negative emotions and increase the likelihood of positive ones. For example, at Thanksgiving you may direct most of your attention to conversations that you find interesting and rewarding, rather than attending to great aunt Tabitha's rants that make you feel edgy and annoyed.
- *Cognitive reappraisal* refers to the idea that you can sometimes change the way you interpret events that are going on around you. For example, maybe when great aunt Tabitha starts complaining about how her neighbor's dogs bark all the time and prevent her from enjoying her favorite soap operas, you can re-frame the situation as a great opportunity for you to practice your ability to listen empathically (which, as you know from Section 4.7, is a great skill that will serve you well in both your personal and professional life!).
- *Response modulation* is what people most often think about when they consider emotion regulation, and it involves controlling our outward signs of emotion. This might involve maintaining a neutral or pleasant expression on your face, and making sure your body language doesn't convey your frustration when great aunt Tabitha starts criticizing the shoes you're wearing.

Human Diversity and Emotional Expression

It is common to think of emotion as an individual event; however, emotion is also shaped by cultural ideas, values, and practices (Boiger & Mesquita, 2012). For example, how many times have you expressed anger this week? If it was more than once, you're not unusual. In Western cultures, expressing anger is widely viewed as a "natural" reaction to feeling that you have been treated unfairly. Very likely this is because our culture emphasizes personal independence and free expression of individual rights and needs. In contrast, many Asian cultures place a high value on group harmony. In Asia, expressing anger in public is less common and anger is regarded as less "natural" because anger tends to separate people. Thus, for many Asians, being angry is at odds with a culture that values cooperation. These same cultural values can also influence the expression of positive emotions. In the United States, we tend to have positive feelings such as pride, happiness, and superiority, which emphasize our role as *individuals.* In Japan, positive feelings are more often linked with membership

Alfredo Estrella/AFP/Getty Images

The expression of emotion is strongly influenced by learning. As you have no doubt observed, women cry more often, longer, and more intensely than men. Men begin learning early in childhood to suppress crying—possibly to the detriment of their emotional health (Williams & Morris, 1996). Many men are especially unwilling to engage in public displays of emotion.

in groups (friendly feelings, closeness to others, and respect) (Markus et al., 2006).

It's also worth noting that the specific expressions used to convey emotions can differ across cultures. Among the Chinese, for example, sticking out the tongue is a gesture of surprise, not of disrespect or teasing. Similarly, what do you think it means if you touch your thumb and first finger together to form a circle? In North America, it means "Everything is fine" or "A-okay." In some Middle Eastern cultures it's a symbol that can represent the evil eye. In other parts of the world, it can have more negative connotations that refer to sex, or the idea that something (or someone) is worth nothing, or zero. When interacting with a person from another culture, then, it is wise to remember that you may easily misunderstand his or her expressions (Carroll & Russell, 1996; Kalat & Shiota, 2012).

What about sex differences in emotional expression? Women have a reputation for being "more emotional" than men—is that true? Compared with women, men in Western cultures are more likely to have difficulty expressing their emotions (Pérusse, Boucher, & Fernet, 2012). In fact, Western men are more likely than women to experience **alexithymia** (a-LEX-ih-THIGH-me-ah), from the Latin for "can't name emotions."

According to psychologist Ronald Levant and his colleagues (2006, 2009), although male babies start out life more emotionally expressive than female babies, little boys soon learn to "toughen up," beginning in early childhood. As a result, men have learned to curtail the expression of most of their emotions. Whereas girls are encouraged to express sadness, fear, shame, and guilt, boys are more likely to be allowed to express only anger and hostility (Fischer et al., 2004).

But does this mean that men experience emotions less than women? Levant believes that men who fail to express emotions over time become less aware of their own emotions and, hence, less able to name them (Levant, Allen, & Lien, 2014; Reker et al., 2010). For many men, a learned inability to express feelings or to even be aware of them is a major barrier to having close, satisfying relationships with others and also can lead to health problems, such as depression or addictive behaviors (Ogrodniczuk, Piper, & Joyce, 2011; Vanheule et al., 2010). Blunted emotions may even contribute to tragedies such as all-too-common school shootings. For many young males, anger is the only emotion they can freely feel and express.

Cognitions

As mentioned at the outset of this section, cognition and emotion are closely connected to one another—the way that we think can have an important impact on how we feel, and vice versa. At least two types of cognition are relevant to emotions: *appraisals* and *attributions*. Let's dig a bit deeper into each one.

Appraisals

Psychologists know that the way that we think about—or *appraise*—our environment can give rise to the emotions that we experience. According to Richard Lazarus (1991a, 1991b), the emotions you experience are greatly influenced by your **emotional appraisal**, or how you evaluate the personal meaning of a stimulus: Do you think of it as good/bad, threatening/supportive, relevant/irrelevant (León & Hernández, 1998)? Emotional appraisals can be fast and automatic, as with startling fear stimuli, or they can be slower and more reflective (Bunk & Magley, 2013).

It's important to note that there can be significant differences in the way that people appraise the same event. For example, imagine that Jasmeet and Daisha have arrived at an amusement park for the day, and each of them has just caught their first glimpse of the site's largest roller coaster. It's 300 feet tall and the almost-vertical drop allows riders to reach speeds of more than 90 miles per hour. Even though they're looking at exactly the same thing, their appraisals of the roller coaster couldn't be more different. Jasmeet's appraisal is one of threat, and it's associated with emotions such as fear and uneasiness. But Daisha's appraisal of that same roller coaster is entirely different—she's curious about the experience and can't wait to climb aboard for the ride. As a result, her emotional response is also distinct from Jasmeet's: She's feeling interest, excitement, and anticipation, even as she waits in line (without Jasmeet, who's now riding the merry-go-round). (■ These differing emotional appraisals also have a major impact on the ability to cope with threats and stress, which may ultimately affect your health. See Section 13.2.)

Emotion regulation Altering expression such that the emotion being displayed does not accurately reflect the one that is being experienced.

Alexithymia A learned difficulty expressing emotions, more common in men.

Emotional appraisal Evaluating the personal meaning of a stimulus or situation.

Attributions

A second type of cognition—**attributions**—can also influence the type of emotions we experience. Attributions refer to our explanations about why things happen (■ see Section 16.1 for more information). Research suggests that in the very same situation, one attribution might lead us to feel a particular emotion (say, anger) while another attribution would lead to an emotion that is completely different. For example, imagine that a father watched his daughter poke her younger brother. Psychological research suggests that when parents attribute this type of bad behavior to children's failure to control their temper (implying that the cause of the situation was within the child's control), they respond with anger. But what if it turned out that the daughter had been sick for a week with the flu and was feeling tired and unwell? Suddenly the father's attribution for her behavior might be quite different, and his emotional response might be quite different as well (Grusec & Hastings, 2007).

Reflective Practice

The Four Basic Aspects of Emotion

1. Many of the physiological changes associated with emotion are caused by secretion of the hormone
   a. atropine c. attributine
   b. adrenaline d. insulin
2. Emotional ____________ often serve to communicate a person's emotional state to others.
3. A formal term for "body language" is ____________.
4. Preparing the body for "fighting or fleeing" is largely the job of the ________ branch of the ____________.
   a. parasympathetic; autonomic nervous system
   b. sympathetic; autonomic nervous system
   c. parasympathetic; peripheral nervous system
   d. sympathetic; peripheral nervous system
5. What body changes are measured by a polygraph?

THINK CRITICALLY

6. Can you explain why people "cursed" by shamans or "witch doctors" sometimes actually die?

SELF-REFLECT

- How did your most emotional moment of the past week affect your emotional experience, expressions, physiology, and cognitions? Could you detect both sympathetic and parasympathetic effects?
- What did you think about lie detectors before reading this chapter? What do you think now?

Answers: 1. b 2. expressions 3. kinesics 4. b 5. heart rate, blood pressure, breathing rate, galvanic skin response 6. In cultures where there is deep belief in superstitions like magic or voodoo, a person who thinks that she or he has been cursed may become uncontrollably emotional. After several days of intense terror, the stress of sympathetic arousal may produce a heart attack. Alternatively, a *parasympathetic rebound* is possible, as the parasympathetic system struggles to calm down. If the rebound is severe enough, it can lead to the heart stopping.

10.5 Connecting the Four Aspects of Emotion: Theories of Emotion

GATEWAYS LEARNING OUTCOMES:
After reading this section you should be able to:

10.5.1 Outline the similarities and differences between the James-Lange, Cannon-Bard, and Schachter-Singer theories of emotion

10.5.2 Explain the central idea that underlies basic emotion theories (BETs), and the strengths and weaknesses of Ekman's BET

Over the years, psychologists have put forward many theories to explain how the four components of emotions are related to one another. We'll begin by exploring two early theories of emotion: the James-Lange and Cannon-Bard theories. What's noteworthy about these early ideas about emotion is that they focused on just three of the four aspects of emotion: experience (or feelings), physiology, and behavior. It wasn't until later that cognitions were incorporated into researchers' thinking, as we'll see when we look at a more recent theory advanced by Schachter and Singer. Finally, we'll conclude this section by examining current ideas about how we can account for the complexity of human emotional experience, including basic theories of emotion.

James-Lange Theory

Imagine you're hiking in the woods and a bear steps onto the trail right in front of you. It snarls in a menacing way and bares its teeth at you. What will happen next? Common sense tells us that we then will feel fear, become physiologically aroused, and demonstrate appropriate behavior (we're thinking that running, yelling, and an expression of terror will be high on the list). But is this the true order of events? Is this how emotion-related experience, physiology, and expressive behavior fit together?

In the 1880s, William James and Carl Lange (LON-geh) proposed that common sense had it backward (Kardas, 2014). According to the **James-Lange theory**, physiological arousal (such as increased heart rate) does not follow a feeling such as fear. Instead, they argued, the *subjective experience follows physiological arousal and expression (behavior)*. Thus, we see a bear, run, are aroused, and *then* feel fear as we become aware of our body reactions (● Figure 10.15).

In support, James pointed out that we frequently fail to experience an emotion until after reacting. For example, imagine that you are driving. Suddenly, a car pulls out in front of you. You swerve and skid to an abrupt halt. Only then do you notice your pounding heart, rapid breathing, and tense muscles—and recognize your fear.

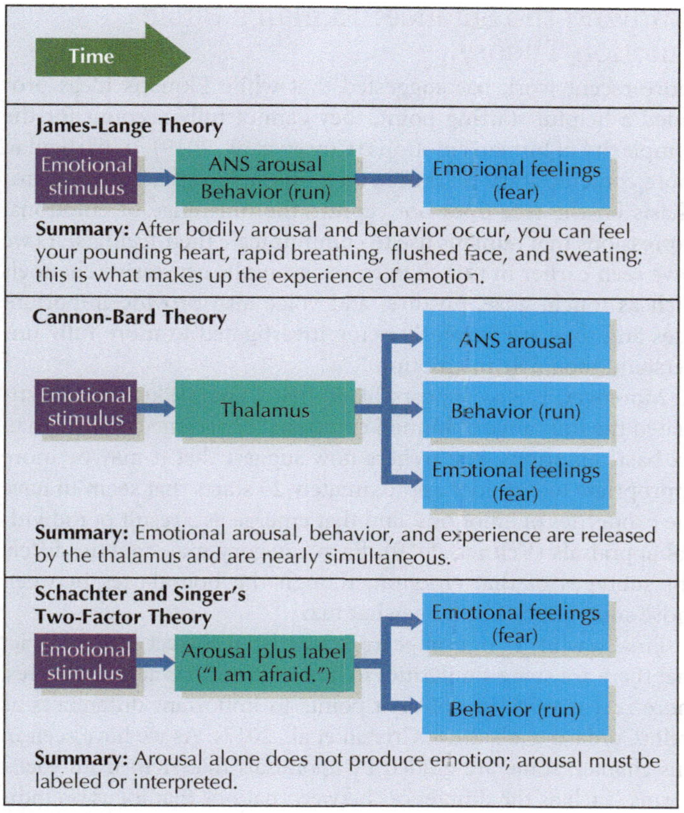

Figure 10.15 **Early theories of emotion.**

Cannon-Bard Theory

Walter Cannon (1932) and Phillip Bard disagreed with the James-Lange theory. According to the **Cannon-Bard theory**, emotional experience, expression (or behavior), and physiological arousal *occur at the same time* (Cannon, 1932; Schultz & Schultz, 2016). Seeing a bear activates limbic structures in the brain, such as the amygdala, thalamus, and hypothalamus. They, in turn, alert the peripheral nervous system for action and the cortex for further reflection. The peripheral nervous system triggers a chain of events that arouses the body. The cortex produces our emotional experience and emotional behavior simultaneously. Thus, if you see a dangerous-looking bear, brain activity produces body arousal, running, and a feeling of fear all at once (Figure 10.15).

Schachter and Singer's Two-Factor Theory

As mentioned previously, early theories of emotion were concerned mostly with emotional experience, physiological arousal, and behavioral changes. It was Stanley Schachter who, along with Jerome Singer, realized that cognitive factors are also important to emotion and should be incorporated into psychologists' theories (Schachter & Singer, 1962). According to **Schachter and Singer's two-factor theory**, emotions come about when we experience general physiological arousal (the first factor) and then use cognitive processes to label its cause (the second factor) (Figure 10.15). These researchers believed that we choose the appropriate label through a process of attribution, by deciding which source is leading to the arousal (León & Hernández, 1998; Marian & Shimamura, 2012).

Imagine, for instance, that someone sneaks up behind you on a dark street and says, "Boo!" Your body is now experiencing the general physiological arousal (pounding heart, sweating palms, and so on)—the first factor described by Schachter and Singer. The second factor requires that you examine the environment and make a determination about the cause of that arousal. If you attribute your arousal to the fact that you've just been tapped on the shoulder by a total stranger, you'd likely label your arousal as fear. If, however, you attribute your arousal to the fact that you've just been tapped on the shoulder by a close friend, you may label the arousal as surprise or delight. The label you give to this general physiological response (such as anger, fear, or happiness) determines what emotion is experienced as well as the behaviors that will follow, and this two-step process can be influenced by your past experiences, the situation, and the reactions of others.

Some support for this theory comes from an experiment in which people watched a slapstick movie (Schachter & Wheeler, 1962). Before viewing the movie, everyone got an injection, but no one was told what the injection contained. One-third of the people received an arousing injection of adrenaline, one-third got a placebo (saltwater) injection, and one-third were given a tranquilizer. People who received the adrenaline rated the movie funniest and laughed the most while watching it. In contrast, those given the tranquilizer were least amused. The placebo group fell in-between. According to Schachter and Singer, individuals who received adrenaline had a stirred-up body that they then attributed to the movie, leading them to label their arousal as happiness and amusement. This and similar experiments make it clear that emotion is about much more than just physiological arousal. Perception, experience, attitudes, judgment, and many other mental factors also affect the emotions that we feel.

There is, of course, no guarantee that we always make the correct attributions about our responses. In fact, *misattributions* are more common than you might think. As an example, let's shift from a fear of bear bodies to an appreciation of bare bodies. In a now-classic study, male college students viewed a series of

Attribution The act of assigning cause to behavior.

James-Lange theory The proposition that bodily arousal leads to subjective feelings.

Cannon-Bard theory The proposition that thalamus activity causes emotions and bodily arousal to occur simultaneously.

Schachter-Singer two-factor theory A theory stating that emotions occur when physical arousal is labeled or interpreted on the basis of experience and situational cues.

photographs of nude females while listening to an amplified heartbeat that each student believed was his own (Valins, 1967). In reality, students were listening to a recorded heartbeat carefully designed to beat *louder* and *stronger* when some (but not all) of the photos were shown. After watching the photos, each student was asked to say which was most attractive. Students who heard the false heartbeat consistently rated photos paired with a "pounding heart" as the most attractive. In other words, when a student saw a photo and heard his heart beat louder, he (falsely) attributed his "emotion" to the photo.

The preceding example is not as far-fetched as it may seem. For another example, consider a study in which a female psychologist interviewed men in a park. Some were interviewed on a swaying suspension bridge, 230 feet above a river. The rest were on a solid wooden bridge just 10 feet above the ground. After the interview, the psychologist gave each man her telephone number, so he could "find out about the results" of the study. Men interviewed on the suspension bridge were much more likely to give the "lady from the park" a call (Dutton & Aron, 1974). Apparently, these men experienced heightened arousal while swaying 20 stories above the ground, which they misinterpreted as attraction to the experimenter—a clear case of love at first fright! (■ Love is one basis for interpersonal attraction, but there are others, such as similarity and proximity. To learn more about what brings people together, see Section 17.1.)

Contemporary Ideas About Emotion: Basic Emotion Theories

Many contemporary theories of emotion fall under the broad umbrella of basic emotion theories (BETs). Though there are a number of different BETs, they each acknowledge that an emotion is a brief state that arises after cognitive appraisals of events, and involves broadly distinct expressions, physiology, and behavior. In BETs, then, emotions tend to fall into broad categories (Keltner, 2019), though not all researchers share this view (Barrett, 2017).

One of the earliest and most influential BETs was put forward by Paul Ekman, who suggested that there were six **basic emotions** that are sometimes referred to as the "Big Six": surprise, happiness, sadness, anger, disgust, and fear (Ekman & Friesen, 1971). Ekman argued that basic emotions appear early in infancy, suggesting they are relatively unlearned (Ekman & Cordaro, 2011; Izard, 2011; Panksepp & Watt, 2011). Moreover, in keeping with this view that emotions are deeply rooted in our evolution, Ekman's early research suggested that expression of the six basic emotions is common across all people, regardless of culture. For example, Ekman's research indicated that facial expressions of the Big Six are well recognized around the world (Dailey et al., 2010). In some very interesting research supporting Ekman's ideas, psychologists examined the facial expressions of children who are born blind, and therefore have little opportunity to learn emotional expressions from others. In general, these children were found to display basic expressions in much the same way as sighted people (Galati, Scherer, & Ricci-Bitti, 1997).

Studying the Science: Ekman's Basic Emotion Theory

More recent work has suggested that while Ekman's ideas provided a helpful starting point, they cannot fully account for the complexity of human emotions (Cowen et al., 2019). In particular, more contemporary BETs are based on the idea that Ekman's emphasis on the face does not capture the full range of emotional expressions that humans use to communicate their feelings. As we have seen earlier in this chapter, for example, expressive channels such as touch, gaze, posture, and voice also provide important cues and they are currently being investigated to more fully understand their role in emotion.

Moreover, it also appears likely that Ekman likely underestimated the full range of human emotional experience. Rather than six basic emotions, researchers now suggest that it may be more appropriate to consider approximately 25 states that seem to have the properties of emotions, and that emerge as a result of individual appraisals (Keltner, 2019). Each category may contain different subtypes of that emotion, though the boundaries between those subtypes can be somewhat fuzzy.

Finally, while Ekman appears to have been correct about the fact that there are some similarities in human emotions across cultures, more recent work in this area points to important differences as well (Cordaro et al., 2018; Crivelli et al., 2017). As we have seen in this chapter, some are guided by appraisals that stem from social norms (such as the differences between nations that focus on individuals versus groups, discussed in the previous section), while others seem to stem from the unique and complex language that various countries have developed to describe their emotional lives (Elfenbein, 2013). If emotions do indeed color the rhythms of our lives, as we suggested at the outset of this chapter, then it would appear that they allow for a full rainbow of possibilities.

Pepe Baeza/Shutterstock.com

Is happiness expressed the same way in different cultures? Masks that are meant to show happiness are strikingly similar around the world. Most have an open, upward-curved mouth and rising cheeks, with downturned outer eyebrows. Obviously, the smile mask shown here is not meant to be angry or frightening. Your ability to "read" its emotional message suggests that basic emotional expressions have universal biological roots (Adolphs, 2008).

Reflective Practice

Connecting the Four Aspects of Emotion: Theories of Emotion

1. According to the James-Lange theory, emotional experience precedes physical arousal and emotional behavior. (We see a bear, are frightened, and run.) T or F?
2. The Cannon-Bard theory of emotion says that bodily arousal and emotional experience occur ________________.
3. The idea that labeling arousal helps define what emotions we experience is associated with ________________.
   a. the James-Lange theory
   b. Schachter and Singer's two-factor theory
   c. the Cannon-Bard theory
   d. Darwin's theory of innate emotional expressions
4. Subjects in Valins's false heart rate study attributed increases in their heart rate to the action of a placebo T or F?
5. Basic emotions theories suggest that
   a. emotions fall into broad categories
   b. emotions are brief in duration
   c. emotions involve distinct expressions, physiology, and behavior
   d. all of the above

THINK CRITICALLY

6. People with high spinal injuries may feel almost no signs of physiological arousal from their bodies. Nevertheless, they still feel emotion, which can be intense at times. What theory (or theories) of emotion does this observation contradict?

SELF-REFLECT

- Write a list of basic emotions that you think you can accurately detect from facial expressions. How many did you come up with?
- Which theory seems to best explain your own emotional experiences?

Answers: 1. F 2. simultaneously 3. b 4. F 5. d 6. The James-Lange theory and Schachter and Singer's two-factor theory.

10.6 Psychology and Your Skill Set: Positivity and Optimism

GATEWAYS LEARNING OUTCOMES:
After reading this section you should be able to:

10.6.1 Outline what is meant by the terms positive psychology, subjective well-being, and optimism

10.6.2 Outline the three elements of explanatory style

10.6.3 Create a plan that will allow you to be more positive and optimistic about an issue that you find challenging

Michael J. Fox was only 29 years old and at the height of his acting career when he found out he had Parkinson's disease. A diagnosis like this would be devastating to many people. Not Fox. Instead, he chose to focus on the positive and the things that he *could* control, rather than those he couldn't. He has continued to act. He founded the Michael J. Fox Foundation to fund research into Parkinson's disease. He even wrote two books: *Lucky Man* and *Always Looking Up: Adventures of an Eternal Optimist*. When asked about his condition, he said: "I see possibilities in everything. For everything this disease has taken away, something of greater value has been given."

Stephen Lovekin/MJF/Getty Images

You've likely met people like Fox—relentlessly hopeful, even when the deck seems stacked against them. How do they do it? While optimism is, to some extent, part of your natural disposition, even the most pessimistic people can work toward becoming more optimistic. If you're optimistic about becoming more optimistic, read on!

Psychologists have always paid attention to the negative side of human behavior. This is easy to understand because of the pressing need to solve human problems. More recently, psychologists have also become interested in **positive psychology**, the study of human strengths, virtues, and positive emotions (Compton & Hoffman, 2013). Many topics from positive psychology can be found in this book including empathy and helping behavior (■ Section 17.2), creativity (■ Section 8.4), effective coping strategies (■ Section 13.8), and emotional intelligence (■ Section 9.6).

For researchers who are interested in positive psychology, positive emotions such as joy, hopefulness, contentment, and happiness are of particular interest. Optimism and positive emotions are both closely connected to feelings of **subjective well-being** (Diener, 2013), which occur when people are generally satisfied with their lives, have frequent positive emotions, and relatively few negative emotions (Diener, Scollon, & Lucas, 2009; Tay & Diener, 2011).

So good and bad events predict feelings of subjective well-being? Life events themselves are not as important as a person's *explanatory style*—the way that he or she interprets those events (Seligman, 1998). And that interpretation is, in turn, influenced by many factors, such as culture, goals, values, and personality (Scollon, Koh, & Au, 2011). Most importantly, people like Michael J. Fox, who have an optimistic explanatory style, tend to have positive emotions

Basic emotions Theories that suggest emotions are brief states arising from cognitive appraisals and involve distinct expressions, physiology, and behavior.

Positive psychology The study of human strengths, virtues, and effective functioning.

Subjective well-being General life satisfaction, combined with frequent positive emotions and relatively few negative emotions.

about events—even the bad ones. As a result, they are happier and seem to negotiate life's demands more smoothly (Wong, 2011).

Ok, but sometimes things actually are *bad—surely it's not good to assume that everything will always get better!* You're right. Optimism can have negative consequences when people fail to ground their thinking in reality. Specifically, people who demonstrate *unrealistic optimism* and refuse to see risks may not take appropriate action to deal with their problems (Weinstein, 1989). The end result is often that their difficulties worsen because they have not been addressed (Dillard, Midboe, & Klein, 2009). For example, people who always expect that things will turn out well may fail to address challenging issues that arise in their relationships, or may fail to seek early treatment for health-related concerns. As Michael J. Fox will tell you, there's an important line that needs to be drawn between *hopeful* thinking and *wishful* thinking. His latest book, written after living with Parkinsons disease for three decades, provides a look at how more recent health challenges caused him to re-examine what it means to be a "realistic optimist" during very difficult circumstances.

Is optimism part of your personality? To a degree, some people are more temperamentally disposed to be upbeat and hopeful, a characteristic that researchers refer to as *dispositional optimism* (Carver & Scheier, 2014; Wrosch, Jobin, & Scheier, 2016). However, psychologist Martin Seligman has clearly established that anyone can work toward cultivating an optimistic view of life events (Seligman, 1998). In other words, optimism isn't necessarily a stable personality trait—it's a skill that you can improve upon, with a little practice. Let's take a closer look at why that might be important, and how you can do it.

Facing Adversity

Good and bad events occur in all lives. What separates optimists and pessimists is largely a matter of attitude. Hopeful, positive people tend to see their lives in more positive terms, even when trouble comes their way. For example, optimistic people tend to find humor in disappointments. They look at setbacks as challenges. They are strengthened by losses (Lyubomirsky & Tucker, 1998).

Optimists also tend to expect that things will turn out well. In general, this motivates them to actively cope with adversity. They are less likely to be stymied by temporary setbacks and more likely to tackle problems head on. In general, pessimists are more likely to ignore or deny problems. The result of such differences can be seen both at work and in people's personal lives. At home, optimists have relationships that last longer and are more satisfying (Neff & Geers, 2013). They also tend to do well at work, especially in jobs where setbacks are a common occurrence (Forgeard & Seligman, 2012). In terms of health, optimists are less stressed and anxious than pessimists, and are physically healthier (Carver & Scheier, 2014). In general, optimists tend to take better care of themselves, because they believe that their efforts to stay healthy will succeed (Peterson & Chang, 2003; Taylor, 2011).

Becoming More Optimistic

Sometimes I find it hard to be optimistic. Can I get better at thinking this way? Definitely. Psychological research has tested a few different ways to increase optimistic thinking. For example, simply imagining your best possible self for five minutes each day can lead to greater feelings of optimism (Meevissen, Peters, & Alberts, 2011; Peters, Meevissen, & Hanssen, 2013).

It is also helpful to better understand your *explanatory style* (Seligman, 1998). As we just discussed, what's important is not so much whether you experience negative or positive life events but rather how you interpret those experiences. For example, imagine that you have just received a poor midterm grade. As you try to make sense of this negative event, there are likely to be three key components of your explanation:

- **Pervasiveness**. The first relates to the *pervasiveness* of the event, or the extent to which you believe the event will impact other aspects of your life. Reacting to your poor midterm grade with the pessimistic thought "My whole life is ruined" is very different from reacting with a more optimistic one, such as "This is just one grade; the rest of my grades will be better."
- **Permanence**. A second relates to the *permanence* of the event—that is, how long you expect the conditions will last. A pessimist might look at a poor grade and think that the next exam will likely be just as bad, while an optimist may think that the next exam will likely be much better.
- **Personal**. The third component of explanatory style relates to the extent to which you think that the event is due to something *personal* about you, as opposed to something related to your situation. A pessimist is more likely to see negative events as stemming from something unchangeable about his or her personality ("I'm just so stupid"), while an optimist is more likely to consider circumstances that can be changed ("I didn't study enough for that test").

To summarize, optimists view negative events as being limited in their effects, short term, and the result of circumstances that can be changed. Conversely, pessimists view positive events as being broader in their effects, long term, and the result of stable aspects of their personality. Upon doing well on an exam, an optimist is more likely to think, "Things are going well," "I'm on a roll, exam-wise," and "I'm smart enough."

Challenging Pessimistic Explanations

So, do you have an optimistic or pessimistic explanatory style? To reflect on this, take a look at the following four events (two positive and two negative) and imagine that each one has happened to you. Ask yourself why this might have happened, and if you come up with multiple reasons, then try to narrow them down to the single most important one (from Peterson et al., 1982).

Your boyfriend/girlfriend has been treating you more lovingly.

You can't get all the work done that others expect of you.

You meet a friend for lunch and he or she is behaving in a hostile way toward you.

You apply for a position that you want very badly and you get it.

Now consider the reasons you thought would lead to these events and ask yourself: Are they likely to be short or long term? Limited or far-reaching in their effects? The result of stable personality traits or temporary circumstances?

If you find that your explanatory style is somewhat pessimistic, challenge your thinking. If you can, ensure that your beliefs about the causes of events—whether positive or negative—are accurate. For example, before accepting that a poor midterm grade is the result of your intelligence, look carefully at all of the available evidence and ask yourself whether this is really true. In all likelihood it isn't, because there are bound to be many other skills that you possess, and many other times when you have been successful.

It may not always be easy to change the way that you think about the world, but psychological research has demonstrated that it is possible to change your explanatory style (Barber et al., 2005). And it's likely to be well worth the effort: Thinking carefully about the explanations that you make about events has important consequences for your health, relationships, and well-being. Clearly we should all take heed of the advice that Henry Ford passed along way back in 1947: "Whether you believe you can do a thing or not, you are right."

Reflective Practice

Psychology and Your Skill Set: Positivity and Optimism

1. Optimism is only influenced by heredity. T or F?
2. People with an optimistic explanatory style view negative events as being short term and limited in their effects. T or F?
3. Subjective well-being refers to the idea that people are generally satisfied with their lives, have very few positive emotions, and have many negative emotions. T or F?
4. Optimism can have negative consequences when people fail to ground their thinking in reality. T or F?
5. What are the three components of explanatory style?

THINK CRITICALLY

6. Scenario 1: You just failed a test, but you think to yourself that it will be okay, because you will try harder next time. As a result, you study much harder and receive a better grade. Scenario 2: You feel nauseous and feverish, but are trying not to think about it because you have too much schoolwork to do. You tell yourself that you can't be sick right now—if you don't think about it and avoid it, it might go away. Which of these scenarios represents the concept of "unrealistic optimism"? Why?

SELF-REFLECT

- Reflect on your own explanatory style. Do you think you are more pessimistic or optimistic? What could you do in your personal and professional life to try to become more optimistic?

Answers: 1. F 2. T 3. F 4. T 5. Pervasiveness, permanence, personal 6. The second scenario is using unrealistic optimism. Ignoring or avoiding the fact that you are sick could actually make the problem worse because you may fail to take appropriate action (e.g., see a doctor, rest in bed). In contrast, if you addressed the problem appropriately, you are likely to prevent your illness from getting worse and will recover much faster.

CHAPTER IN REVIEW

Gateways to Motivation and Emotion

Summary: Gateways Learning Outcomes

10.1 The Basics of Motivation

10.1.1 Explain the role played by needs, drives, responses, goals, and incentives in shaping our motives

Motives arouse, maintain, and guide behavior and typically involve the following sequence: need, drive, goal, and goal attainment (need reduction). Needs are internal deficiencies (things we lack), while a drive is a state of bodily tension that arises when needs are not met. Drives activate a response that pushes us toward a goal (usually, to address the unmet need). Incentives are rewards that can motivate behavior.

10.1.2 Distinguish between intrinsic and extrinsic motivation

According to self-determination theory, competence, autonomy, and relatedness are the highest needs and are closely related to intrinsic motivation (motivation that is based on internal, rather than external, rewards). In contrast, extrinsic motivation stems from factors outside the person (e.g., money, rewards, obligations, approval).

10.1.3 Distinguish between Maslow's basic needs and growth needs

Maslow's hierarchy of needs categorizes needs as either basic or growth-oriented. Basic needs are lower in the hierarchy and are assumed to be prepotent (dominant). Basic needs include those required for physical survival (e.g., food and shelter), as well as those related to love, acceptance, and belonging. Growth needs include the drive toward self-actualization, or the need to fulfill our potential.

10.1.4 Distinguish between biological, stimulus, and learned motives

In the three-way classification of motives, biological motives refer to those that must be met for survival. Stimulus motives relate to the need for stimulation. Learned motives are based on needs that we develop as a result of interacting with others (e.g., the need for power or achievement).

10.2 Biological Motives

10.2.1 Explain what is meant by the term sex drive, and how hormones are related to the sex drive of human and nonhuman animals

The sex drive refers to the strength of our motivation to engage in sexual behavior. It is unusual in that it is non-homeostatic (independent of body need states). The sex drive is influenced primarily by estrogen in females. In humans, androgens, such as the hormone testosterone, impact the sex drive of men and, to a lesser extent, women.

10.2.2 Explain what is meant by the term circadian rhythms, and how these rhythms impact human sleep cycles

Circadian rhythms refer to the cycles that are governed by the body's internal clock. People with early peaks in their circadian rhythm are usually early risers, while those with later peaks are more likely to be night owls. Time zone travel, shift work, and pulling all-nighters can seriously disrupt sleep and circadian rhythms.

10.2.3 Outline why pain is considered an episodic drive, and how our responses to pain are shaped

Pain avoidance is unusual because it is an episodic drive (one that occurs in distinct episodes when there is damage to the body) as opposed to cyclic. Pain avoidance and pain tolerance are partially learned through interactions with the people and culture that surround us.

10.2.4 Distinguish between intracellular and extracellular thirst, and how each is best managed

Intracellular thirst is caused by the consumption of salt, causing fluid to move out of your cells. It is best managed by consuming water. In contrast, extracellular thirst results from water being lost from the body through bleeding, sweating, vomiting, and diarrhea. This type of thirst is best managed by drinking something that contains salt and minerals (e.g., Gatorade or other sports drinks).

10.2.5 Outline the internal and external factors that impact hunger

Hunger is influenced by a complex interplay of internal factors that include the body's set point, fullness of the stomach, blood sugar levels, metabolism in the liver, and fat stores in the body. The hypothalamus exerts the most direct internal control of eating, through areas that act like feeding and satiety systems. The hypothalamus is sensitive to both neural and chemical messages, which affect eating. External factors influencing hunger include external eating cues, the attractiveness and variety of diet, emotions, learned taste preferences and taste aversions, and cultural values.

10.2.6 Distinguish between anorexia nervosa and bulimia nervosa, and outline the causes of these eating disorders

Anorexia nervosa and bulimia nervosa are two prominent eating disorders. Anorexia involves a reduction in food consumption (though hunger is still experienced) that results in significant weight loss. Bulimia is a disorder in which people gorge on food and then purge by vomiting or taking laxatives to eliminate waste, which allows them to prevent weight gain. Both tend to involve conflicts about self-image, self-control, and anxiety.

10.3 Stimulus and Learned Motives

10.3.1 Explain the central idea that underlies arousal theory

Drives for stimulation are partially explained by arousal theory, which states that an ideal level of bodily arousal will be maintained if possible. The desired level of arousal or stimulation varies from person to person.

10.3.2 Describe the relationship between arousal and performance, as outlined in the Yerkes-Dodson law

Optimal performance on a task usually occurs at *moderate* levels of arousal, though the relationship between arousal and performance depends on the difficulty of the task. For very simple tasks that are well-practiced, performance is not impacted even when arousal becomes quite high. However, for tasks that are moderately or very difficult, the relationship between arousal and performance is described by an inverted-U function. Using this inverted-U function, the Yerkes-Dodson law states that for moderately challenging tasks, the ideal arousal level is higher, but as tasks become more complex or less well-practiced, it is lower.

10.3.3 Outline what is meant by the need for achievement (nAch) and need for power

In the three-way classification of motives (biological, stimulus, and learned), learned motives include social motives. Social motives such as nAch and the need for power relate to our relationships with others, and are learned through socialization and cultural conditioning.

10.3.4 Explain the central idea that underlies opponent-process theory

Opponent-process theory explains the operation of some learned motives. Essentially, the theory proposes that when a stimulus generates a strong emotion, the opposite emotion will occur when the stimulus is removed, or ends. However, when the stimulus is repeated many times, our initial response to it will weaken and will be replaced with its opposite. However, the emotional aftereffects will strengthen.

10.4 The Four Basic Aspects of Emotion

10.4.1 Outline the four basic aspects of an emotion

The four basic aspects of an emotion are experience (feelings), physiology, expression, and cognitions.

10.4.2 Explain what is meant by emotional experience, and how it differs from mood

Emotion experience refers to our subjective emotion-related feelings. Emotions differ from moods because they are shorter in duration than moods, and because emotions typically have a target (that is, they are directed at something identifiable).

10.4.3 Describe the physiological responses that are associated with emotions

Physical changes associated with emotion are caused by activity in the autonomic nervous system (ANS). The sympathetic branch of the ANS is primarily responsible for arousing the body, the parasympathetic branch for quieting it. The amygdala provides a "quick and dirty" pathway for the arousal of fear, bypassing the cerebral cortex.

10.4.4 Outline the various ways in which an emotion can be expressed and regulated

Emotions can be expressed through multiple channels, or modalities. The most obvious one is the face, but researchers have established that body language (including touch, posture, and eye gaze) is also important. The formal study of body language is known as kinesics. In addition to facial expressions and body language, psychologists have also found that the human voice (including prosidy and vocal bursts) is important in expressing emotion.

In terms of emotion regulation, strategies include *suppression* (clamping down on emotional experiences), *situation selection* (controlling the circumstances in which you find yourself), *situation modification* (altering unavoidable situations to make them more palatable), *redirecting attention* (shifting your focus in ways that allow you to avoid negative emotions and increase the likelihood of positive ones), *cognitive reappraisal* (changing the way you interpret events that are going on around you), and *response modulation* (controlling outward signs of emotion like facial expressions and body language).

10.4.5 Describe two types of cognition that are relevant to emotions

Two types of cognitions that are relevant to emotions are attributions and appraisals.

10.5 Connecting the Four Aspects of Emotion: Theories of Emotion

10.5.1 Outline the similarities and differences between the James-Lange, Cannon-Bard, and Schachter-Singer theories of emotion

Contrary to common sense, the James-Lange theory says that emotional experience follows bodily reactions. In contrast, the Cannon-Bard theory says that bodily reactions and emotional experiences occur at the same time. However, these theories are similar in the sense that they focus only on three of the four aspects of emotion (experience, physiology, and behavior/expression). Schachter and Singer's two-factor theory also brings in the cognitive aspect of emotion, and emphasizes that emotion emerges when we experience physiological arousal (first factor) and then use cognitive attributions to label the bodily arousal (second factor) as a particular emotion.

10.5.2 Explain the central idea that underlies basic emotion theories (BETs), and the strengths and weaknesses of Ekman's BET

BETs share a common belief that emotions are brief states that arise after cognitive appraisals of events, and involve broadly distinct expressions, physiology, and behavior; as a result, they believe that emotions fall into broad categories. Paul Ekman argued that there are at least six basic emotions: surprise, happiness, sadness, anger, disgust, and fear. Basic emotions are fast and automatic, they appear early in infancy, they are universal among humans, and they are shared with other mammals.

While current BETs share the idea that emotions fall into categories, they differ from Ekman's in complexity. Specifically, unlike Ekman, they argue that the face does not capture the full range of emotional expressions, and that other channels (touch, gaze, posture, and voice) also provide important cues. Moreover, current BETs suggest that there may be as many as 25 states that seem to have the properties of emotions, rather than the six proposed by Ekman. Finally, while Ekman appears to have been correct about the fact that there are some similarities in human emotions across cultures, more recent work in this area points to important differences as well.

10.6 Psychology and Your Skill Set: Positivity and Optimism

10.6.1 Outline what is meant by the terms positive psychology, subjective well-being, and optimism

The field of positive psychology focuses on people's experience of positive emotions, optimism (seeing the positive side of events that occur), and subjective well-being (people's views about the quality of their lives). Optimism can help you overcome and grow from negative events; however, "unrealistic optimism" can cause people to ignore preventable risks. To some extent, optimism is a stable characteristic (dispositional optimism), but it is also considered a skill that can be developed.

10.6.2 Outline the three elements of explanatory style

Your explanatory style (the way that you evaluate the events that you experience) has three components: *pervasiveness* (the extent to which you believe the event can impact other areas of your life), *permanence* (the extent to which you believe the conditions will last), and the extent to which the events reflect things that are *personal* (that is, how much they reflect your unchanging characteristics versus changeable circumstances).

10.6.3 Create a plan that will allow you to be more positive and optimistic about an issue that you find challenging

Developing an explanatory style that allows for optimistic assessments about the permanence, pervasiveness, and role of personal factors in events that you experience is important in both personal and professional settings. Specifically, a positive explanatory style can help you with such things as building relationships and maintaining a resilient attitude in the face of challenges. We hope that after reading this section, you'll be better able to use what you know about the three elements of explanatory style to help you tackle all of the things—both positive and negative—that life sends your way.

11 Sex, Gender, and Sexuality

Michael Nagle/The New York Times/Redux

Gateway Theme It is important to draw a distinction between a person's sex and gender. Sexuality is a normal and healthy part of human behavior.

Chapter Outline

Either/Or; Neither/Nor

Chris Mosier is a remarkable athlete. He has completed three Ironman competitions, each time pushing himself hard through the grueling 2.5-mile swim, 112-mile bike race, and 26-mile run. By comparison, then, you might think that competing the New York City triathlon wouldn't be much of a challenge for Chris. The distances are much shorter than an Ironman, after all, and he'd completed that same race two years earlier. But things had been different then. You see, at that time Chris Mosier had been competing as a woman.

After coming out as a transgender man, Chris Mosier continued breaking down barriers that prevented LGBTQ athletes from fully participating in sports. He became the first openly transgender member of the US men's sprint duathlon team, competing at multiple World Championships. He has advocated—successfully—for changes to international rules, making sports more inclusive for all people. But perhaps most importantly, he continues to coach young athletes so that each of them can reach their full potential.

Chris Mosier's story is a lesson in how traditional ideas about sex and gender are changing in our society. We used to think strictly in terms of "either/or"—either male or female; masculine or feminine. Now, though, people are increasingly comfortable identifying as "neither/nor," rejecting binary categories in favor of being more fluid. To understand why, let's take a deeper dive into this fascinating area of psychology.

11.1 Sexual Development and Orientation

GATEWAYS LEARNING OUTCOMES:
After reading this section you should be able to:

11.1.1 Describe the four basic dimensions of biological sex, including the role of hormones in shaping sexual development prenatally and postnatally

11.1.2 Define sexual orientation and outline its causes

The term **sex** refers to whether you are biologically female or male. But contrary to common belief, classifying a person's sex is not a simple either/or proposition. To understand why, we'll begin by examining the various dimensions of biological sex.

Dimensions of Biological Sex

At the very least, classifying a person as biologically female or male requires that we consider four dimensions: (1) **genetic sex** (*XX* or *XY* chromosomes), (2) **hormonal sex** (predominance of estrogens or androgens), (3) **gonadal sex** (ovaries or testes), and (4) **genital sex** (clitoris and vagina in females, penis and scrotum in males). To see why each of these four dimensions is important, let's trace the events involved in becoming female or male.

Genetic Sex

Becoming male or female may seem simple enough. Genetic sex is determined at the instant of conception: Two ***X* chromosomes** initiate female development; an *X* chromosome plus a ***Y* chromosome** produces a male. The mother's ovum always provides an *X* chromosome because she has two *X*s in her own genetic makeup. In contrast, one-half of the father's sperm carry *X* chromosomes and the other half carry *Y*s.

Even at conception, however, variations may occur because some individuals begin life with too many or too few sex chromosomes (Crooks & Baur, 2017). For example, in *Klinefelter's syndrome*, a boy is born *XXY*, with an extra *X* chromosome. As a result, when he matures, he may appear feminine, have undersized sexual organs, and be infertile. In *Turner's syndrome*, a girl is born with only one *X* chromosome and no *Y* chromosome. As an adolescent, she may appear boyish and she also will be infertile.

Hormonal and Gonadal Sex

While genetic sex stays the same throughout life, it alone does not determine biological sex. In general, sexual characteristics are also related to the effects of sex hormones before birth. (Hormones are chemical substances secreted by endocrine glands. See ■ Section 2.4.) The **gonads** (or sex glands) affect sexual development and behavior by secreting *estrogens* (female hormones) and *androgens* (male hormones). The gonads in the male are the testes; the female gonads are the ovaries. The adrenal glands (located above the kidneys) also supply sex hormones.

Most people produce both estrogens and androgens. Sex differences, then, are related to the *proportion* of these hormones found in the body. In fact, prenatal development of male or female anatomy is largely due to the presence or absence of **testosterone** (tes-TOSS-teh-rone), one of the androgens, secreted mainly by the testes (LeVay, Baldwin, & Baldwin, 2015). For the first six weeks of prenatal growth, genetically female and male embryos look identical. However, if a *Y* chromosome is present, testes develop in the embryo and supply testosterone (Knickmeyer & Baron-Cohen, 2006). This stimulates growth of the penis and other male structures (● Figure 11.1). In the absence of testosterone, the embryo will develop female reproductive organs and genitals, regardless of genetic sex (LeVay, Baldwin, & Baldwin, 2015).

Prenatal growth does not always match genetic sex. For both genetic females and males, hormonal problems before birth may produce an **intersex person** (one who has ambiguous sexual anatomy). (The former term, *hermaphrodite*, is now regarded as offensive.) For example, a genetic male won't develop male genitals if too little testosterone is available. Even if testosterone is present, an inherited *androgen insensitivity syndrome* (unresponsiveness to testosterone) may exist. Again, the result is female development (Cadet, 2011).

Similarly, androgens must be at low levels or absent for an *XX* embryo to develop as a female. For instance, a biologically female fetus may be masculinized by the anti-miscarriage drug progestin, or by a problem known as *congenital adrenal hyperplasia*. In this syndrome, the child's body produces estrogen, but a genetic abnormality causes the adrenal glands to release too much androgen. In such cases, a female child may be born with genitals that are more male than female (Kalat, 2016).

Hormonal and Gonadal Sex in Everyday Life: Intersex Athletes

Recently, intersex conditions have received greater recognition in the media, partly in response to controversies over the participation of intersex athletes in elite sporting competitions such as the

Hanne Gaby Odiele is a Belgian model who was born intersex as a result of an insensitivity to androgens while developing in the womb. All of her cells contain an *X* and *Y* chromosome, but she identifies as a woman in spite of having internal testes and no uterus or ovaries.

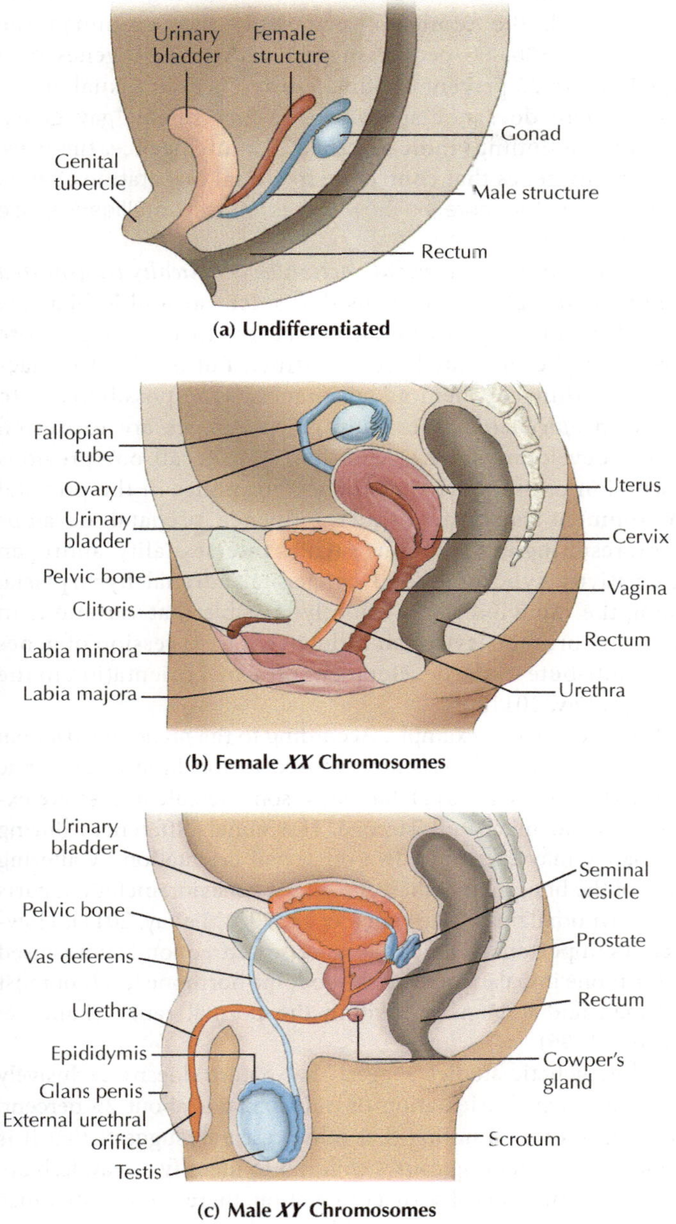

Figure 11.1 Prenatal development of the reproductive organs. Early development of ovaries or testes affects hormonal balance and alters sexual anatomy. (a) At first, the sex organs are the same in the human female and male. (b) When androgens are absent, female structures develop. (c) Male sex organs are produced when androgens are present.

Olympics. In particular, there has been considerable debate about whether intersex persons who are genetically male, but whose bodies appear female, should be allowed to compete with other women.

At issue is the fact that such athletes often have significantly higher levels of testosterone than those who are genetically female, a situation that some people argue confers an unfair advantage (Harper et al., 2018). Chris Mosier, whose story appears at the beginning of this chapter, represents the opposite situation—a genetic female competing with men. In general, there has been less controversy over his participation in the men's category because he is not perceived to have an undue advantage over athletes who are biologically male.

On the other side of the controversy are people who point out that we have never, in the past, restricted the participation of people in sports where their genes might confer an advantage (Katwala, 2019). People who are particularly tall, for example, are not banned from playing basketball in the Olympics. Nor are runners from East Africa prevented from competing in middle- and long-distance running, in spite of the fact that there is some consensus that genes play a role in their overwhelming success in those events.

Regardless of where people's opinions lie with respect to the controversy, one thing is very evident: Efforts to resolve this ethical issue highlight the limitations of taking a binary approach to biological sex. A more nuanced approach is clearly needed, along with an open-minded evaluation of the arguments on both sides.

Genital Sex

Mature males and females also differ in both *primary* and *secondary* sexual characteristics. **Primary sexual characteristics** refer to the sexual and reproductive organs themselves: the vagina, ovaries, and uterus in females; and the penis, testes, and scrotum in males. **Secondary sexual characteristics** are more

Sex One's physical, biological classification as female or male.

Genetic sex Sex as indicated by the presence of *XX* (female) or *XY* (male) chromosomes.

Hormonal sex Sex as indicated by a preponderance of estrogens (female) or androgens (male) in the body.

Gonadal sex Sex as indicated by the presence of ovaries (female) or testes (male).

Genital sex Sex as indicated by the presence of male or female genitals.

***X* chromosome** The female chromosome contributed by the mother; produces a female when paired with another *X* chromosome and a male when paired with a *Y* chromosome.

***Y* chromosome** The male chromosome contributed by the father; produces a male when paired with an *X* chromosome. Fathers may give either an *X* or a *Y* chromosome to their offspring.

Gonads The primary sex glands—the testes in males and ovaries in females.

Testosterone A male sex hormone, secreted mainly by the testes and responsible for the development of many male sexual characteristics.

Intersex person A person who has genitals suggestive of both sexes.

Primary sexual characteristics Sex as defined by the genitals and internal reproductive organs.

Secondary sexual characteristics Sexual features other than the genitals and reproductive organs—breasts, body shape, facial hair, and so forth.

superficial physical features that appear at puberty. These features develop in response to hormonal signals from the pituitary gland. In females, secondary sexual characteristics include breast development, broadening of the hips, and other changes in body shape. Males grow facial and body hair, and the voice deepens.

These changes signal that a person is biologically ready to reproduce. Reproductive maturity is especially evident in the female *menarche* (MEN-are-kee), the onset of menstruation. Soon after menarche, monthly ovulation begins. *Ovulation* refers to the release of ova (eggs) from the ovaries. From the first ovulation until **menopause**—the stage of life when a female stops menstruating—women can bear children.

Sexual Orientation

Aside from biological sex, another aspect of sexual development is **sexual orientation**, your enduring pattern of emotional and erotic attraction. Just as biological sex does not fall neatly into two categories—male or female—sexual orientation is also more complicated than simply classifying people as gay or straight (Carroll, 2016). People who are **heterosexual**, or straight, are romantically and erotically attracted to members of the opposite sex. Men and women who are attracted to members of the same sex are **gay** or **lesbian**, respectively. **Bisexual** individuals are attracted to both men and women.

According to a growing number of psychologists, though, *asexuality*—a lack of attraction to both men and women—constitutes a fourth type of sexual orientation. While people who are *celibate* choose not to act on their sexual attractions, **asexual** individuals experience little or no sexual attraction in the first place, although they can experience sexual desire (Bogaert, 2012; Brotto et al., 2010).

About 3.5 percent of all adults regard themselves as gay, lesbian, or bisexual (Conron, Mimiaga, & Landers, 2010). Those who are asexual account for about 1 percent of adults (Bogaert, 2015). This means that over 12 million people in the United States alone are gay, lesbian, bisexual, or asexual. Millions more have a family member who is not heterosexual. It also is worth remembering that these figures are likely on the low side because many nonheterosexuals are unwilling to identify themselves as such (Bogaert, 2006). There's clearly a tremendous amount of variation in Americans' preferences regarding sexual partners, and this diversity is showing itself in families across the country.

Origins of Sexual Orientation

Why are some people attracted to the opposite sex, whereas others prefer members of the same sex, or both sexes? One possibility is that sexual orientation is partly hereditary (LeVay, 2011). For example, one study found that if one identical twin identifies as gay, lesbian, or bisexual, there is a 50 percent chance that the other twin is, too. Though there was initial speculation that a handful of genes might influence sexual orientation, more recent work suggests this might not be the case. Indeed, the results of one study that examined the genomes of 500,000 people suggested that while genes may explain up to 25 percent of human differences in sexual orientation, there does not appear to be any single "gay gene." Instead, the findings indicated that, like intelligence, there are likely many genes that contribute to sexual orientation (Ganna et al., 2019; for more on how genes impact intelligence, see ■ Section 9.4).

But how could same-sex attraction be genetically transmitted at all? At first glance, it seems that since gay and lesbian sex doesn't result in genes being passed on to offspring, those genes would eventually become extinct. But maybe it is inaccurate to think of them as "gay genes." One possibility is to focus on *epigenetics*, the study of how genes are expressed during development (see ■ Section 3.1). Recall our previous discussion of how variations in sex hormones in the prenatal environment can dramatically influence prenatal development, resulting in conditions such as intersexuality, androgen insensitivity syndrome, and congenital adrenal hyperplasia. Along the same lines, it is entirely possible that variations in prenatal hormone levels can influence the expression of genes that contribute to the development of sexual orientation in the fetus (LeVay, 2011).

Here's a concrete example: According to the *prenatal hormonal theory*, some male fetuses are exposed to too little testosterone (Bogaert & Skorska, 2011). Similarly, some female fetuses are exposed to too much testosterone. Hormonal differences during pregnancy may exert an effect on sexual orientation by altering areas of the brain that orchestrate sexual behavior, including parts of the hypothalamus (Kinnunen et al., 2004; LeVay, 2011). However, it's important to note that same-sex attraction is not caused by hormone imbalances in adulthood; the hormone levels of most gay men and lesbians are within the normal range (Banks & Gartrell, 1995).

While genetic studies suggest that nature doesn't exclusively determine sexual orientation (it only explains about 25 percent, after all), it's worth noting that other research suggests that it is unlikely that parenting causes children to identify as gay, lesbian, or bisexual. In terms of sexual orientation, there is little difference between the development of children with same- or opposite-sex parents (Farr, 2017; Hart, Mourot, & Aros, 2012). Indeed, most lesbians and gay men were raised by heterosexual parents, and most children raised by gay or lesbian parents become heterosexual.

Taken together, these findings tend to discredit myths about parents' contribution to sexual orientation, as well as those indicating that identifying as gay, lesbian, or bisexual is strictly a choice. Instead, the available evidence seems to suggest that sexual orientation has a genetic and hormonal component, although social, cultural, and psychological influences are also involved (LeVay, 2011; LeVay, Baldwin, & Baldwin, 2015). In view of this, discriminating against gay, lesbian, and bisexual individuals is much like rejecting a person for other characteristics that are partially determined by genes, such as being extroverted or left-handed (Smith et al., 2011).

Research has repeatedly suggested that the children of same-sex parents are no more likely to grow up to be gay or lesbian than children of heterosexual parents.

Stability of Sexual Orientation

Sexual orientation is a deep part of personal identity and is usually quite stable. Starting with their earliest erotic feelings, most people remember being attracted to either the opposite sex or the same sex. The chances are practically nil of a person being "converted" from one orientation to another, which is why conversion therapy has not been supported by research and has been banned in some parts of the world (Mock & Eibach, 2012; Savin-Williams, Joyner, & Rieger, 2012). If you are heterosexual, you are probably certain that nothing could ever make you have homoerotic feelings. If so, then you know how gay and lesbian individuals feel about the prospects for changing their sexual orientation.

But what about people who have had both same-sex and other-sex relationships? The fact that sexual *orientation* is usually quite stable doesn't rule out the possibility that for some people, sexual *behavior* may change during the course of a lifetime. However, many such instances involve gay or lesbian individuals who date or marry members of the opposite sex because of pressures to fit into heterosexual society. When these people realize that they are not being true to themselves, their identity and relationships may shift. Other apparent "shifts" in orientation probably involve people who would be more accurately described as bisexual (Mock & Eibach, 2012).

Current Views on Sexual Orientation

Psychologists have, for some time, accepted that homosexuality, bisexuality, and asexuality all fall within a normal range of variations in sexual orientation (Silverstein, 2009). Gay men, lesbians, and bisexuals encounter hostility because they are members of minority groups, not because there is anything inherently wrong with them (American Psychological Association, 2008b).

The problems faced by lesbians and gay men can include rejection by family and friends, as well as discrimination in hiring and housing. Such unfair treatment is based on homophobia and heterosexism in our society (Murray, 2009; Stefurak, Taylor, & Mehta, 2010). *Homophobia* refers to prejudice, fear, and dislike directed at gay and lesbian individuals. *Heterosexism* is the belief that heterosexual relationships are better or more "natural" than those of same-sex couples.

The presence of homophobia and heterosexism means that most gay and lesbian people have at one time or another suffered verbal abuse—or worse—because of their sexual orientation (Doyle & Molix, 2016; Fine, 2011). Much of this rejection is based on false stereotypes. The following points are a partial reply to such stereotypes. Gay and lesbian people:

- do not try to "convert" others to a same-sex lifestyle
- are no more likely to molest children than heterosexuals
- are no more likely to be mentally ill than heterosexuals
- do not hate persons of the opposite sex
- do not, as parents, make their own children gay
- do have long-term, caring, monogamous relationships
- are no less able to contribute to society than heterosexuals

Understandably, social rejection tends to produce higher rates of anxiety, depression, and suicidal thinking (Bostwick et al., 2014; Lester, 2006). However, anyone—regardless of sexual orientation—facing discrimination and stigma would react in much the same way (DeBord et al., 2017; Greene & Britton, 2012). When such stresses are factored out, gay and lesbian persons are no more likely to have emotional problems than heterosexual people (Goldfried, 2001; Meyer et al., 2011).

Gay, lesbian, bisexual, and asexual people are found in all walks of life, at all social and economic levels, and in all cultural groups. They are as diverse in terms of race, ethnicity, age, parenthood, relationships, careers, health, education, politics, and sexual behavior as the heterosexual community. Perhaps as more people come to see gay and lesbian people in terms of their humanity, rather than their sexuality, the prejudices that they have faced will wane (American Psychological Association, 2008b; Silverstein, 2009).

Menopause The stage of life when a female stops menstruating.

Sexual orientation Enduring pattern of attraction to members of the same and/or other sex.

Heterosexual A person romantically and erotically attracted to members of the opposite sex.

Gay/Lesbian A man/woman (respectively) who is romantically and erotically attracted to same-sex persons.

Bisexual A person romantically and erotically attracted to both men and women.

Asexual A person not romantically or erotically attracted to either men or women.

Reflective Practice

Sexual Development and Orientation

1. The four basic dimensions of biological sex are the following: ______, ______, ______, ______
2. All individuals normally produce both androgens and estrogens, although the proportions differ in females and males. T or F?
3. Whether a person has erotic fantasies about women or men is a strong indicator of his or her sexual orientation. T or F?
4. Sexual orientation is determined by:
   a. the environment
   b. genetics
   c. both the environment and genetics
   d. neither the environment nor genetics

THINK CRITICALLY

5. Why might reaching puberty and developing secondary sexual characteristics be a mixed blessing for some adolescents?

SELF-REFLECT

- Which of your prior beliefs about sexual orientation were true? Which were false?
- In 2007, the American Medical Association changed its antidiscrimination policies to include transgender people. This means, for example, that doctors no longer can refuse medical treatment to transgender patients. Do you agree or disagree with this change? Why?

Answers: 1. genetic sex, gonadal sex, hormonal sex, genital sex 2. T 3. T 4. c 5. When girls reach puberty early, they may experience heightened social anxiety about their new bodies and increased sexual pressure (Deardorff et al., 2007). When boys reach it late, they may also experience social anxiety.

11.2 Gender Identities and Roles

GATEWAYS LEARNING OUTCOMES:
After reading this section you should be able to:

11.2.1 Outline what is meant by gender identity, including the factors that influence it and what it means for an individual to be gender variant

11.2.2 Explain what is meant by the term gender role

11.2.3 Define psychological androgyny and explain its advantages

While the term *sex* refers to your biological maleness or femaleness, **gender** is culturally determined and refers to the characteristics that are associated with masculinity and femininity (Crooks & Baur, 2017). **Gender identity**, then, is your subjective sense of being male or female as expressed in appearance, behavior, and attitudes.

Gender Identity

Just as biological sex is not binary, gender identity also comes in shades of masculine and feminine. You will probably not be surprised, then, to learn that the relationship between sex and gender is also a rainbow of possibility (Carroll, 2016). By adulthood, most biological males have a gender identity that is more or less masculine, and most biological females have a gender identity that is more or less feminine. At the same time, some males are quite feminine and some females are quite masculine. In the most extreme cases, people may be **gender variant**, in that their preferred gender does not correspond to traditional masculine or feminine norms (Veale, Clarke, & Lomax, 2010). In some cases, gender-variant individuals will identify as **transgender**. Transgender individuals do not identify with the biological sex assigned at birth; however, they do not always identify with the opposite sex either. It's important to note, though, that these variations in the relationship between sex and gender should *not* be confused with variations in sexual orientation. Many feminine men and masculine women are, nonetheless, heterosexual.

Many transgender individuals experience a disconnect between their biological sex and gender identity from an early age. Consider the case of Elena, who, when asked about her early life as a boy remarked, "I have always known I was a girl. . . . In first grade, I avoided boys like the plague. Boys called me 'sissy' and 'crybaby' and beat me up." As an adult, she decided to become the woman she always felt she was. As Elena put it, "I was determined to transition. Of course, I was terrified the changes would leave me destitute and friendless, that I would wind up dead in a ditch somewhere, victim of someone else's fist. . . . Lucky for me, I had nothing to fear at work. When I came out to our company president, he sent an email to the whole organization (with my permission) stating that I was transitioning from male to female, and that I was to be treated with the same respect and dignity [as] any other woman. My 650 co-workers fully accepted me, as did most of my family" (Kelly, 2010).

Is gender variance a psychological disorder? Gender variance was once considered a form of psychiatric illness. Today, though, an individual usually is considered for a diagnosis of **gender dysphoria** only if he or she is experiencing extreme distress because of his or her gender variance (American Psychiatric Association, 2013). Take note, though: it's not the gender variance that is considered problematic in this diagnosis, it's the distress that emerges as a result.

In this way of thinking, the suffering of many transgender individuals stems not from their gender variance, but from the prejudice, hostility, and stigmatization of mainstream society. Gender-variant individuals deserve our understanding and support (Diamond, 2009; Meadow, 2011). When it comes to children, many parents of gender-variant children try to encourage what they see as gender-appropriate behavior. Others wait and see if their children will develop a gender identity that is in keeping with their biological sex. Still others seek to accept and support their children's experiences. If there is a trend in the United States today, it is toward greater acceptance and support (Gray et al., 2016; Zeiler & Wickström, 2009).

When treatment is requested, it may include psychotherapy and, in more clear-cut cases, *sex reassignment surgery* (Imbimbo et al., 2009). Surgery can reconfigure the external appearance of the genitals, while hormone treatments shift the chemical balance in the body, and a deliberate effort can be made to transform the person's sense of sexual identity. Adults who deliberately seek sex reassignment are generally happy with the results (Imbimbo et al., 2009).

Sex reassignment surgery is also sometimes carried out with young people. Supporters of early sex reassignment argue that the benefits usually outweigh the long-term psychological costs (Zeiler & Wickström, 2009). However, others believe that it is better to wait until adulthood, when transgender individuals are in a better position to make an informed choice about whether or not to have surgery and whether to live as a man or a woman (Thyen et al., 2005). In such cases, doctors may prescribe puberty-blocking medication that will delay the sex-related changes that typically accompany adolescence. In this way, transgender individuals have additional time to consider their options and consult with professionals about their feelings and concerns. Because the relationship between sex and gender is complex, though, the best course of treatment needs to be determined on a case-by-case basis (Rathus, Nevid, & Fichner-Rathus, 2013).

Origins of Gender Identity

Is your gender identity also biologically determined, or is it learned? That's a good question—let's explore the evidence for each of these possibilities.

The Role of Biology

In animals, clear links exist between prenatal hormones and male or female behaviors. In humans, abnormal levels of prenatal androgens and estrogens can also strongly influence the development of the body, nervous system, and later behavior patterns, such as sexual preference. Slight variations in the levels of sex hormones may subtly "sex-type" the brains of most of us before birth, altering our chances of developing feminine or masculine traits (Berenbaum, Blakemore, & Beltz, 2011). Evidence for this **biological biasing effect** is provided by females exposed to small increases in androgens before birth. After birth, their hormones shift to female, and they are raised as girls. Nevertheless, prenatal exposure to male hormones has a relatively slight masculinizing effect. During childhood, such girls are typically "tomboys" who prefer the company of boys to girls.

At the risk of getting mired in the "battle of the sexes," let's consider the belief that the biological biasing effect imparts different thinking abilities in women and men. The left side of the brain, you may recall, is largely responsible for language and rote learning. The right side is superior at spatial reasoning. Some psychologists have suggested that different patterns of brain activation may explain why men (as a group) do slightly better on "right side" activities such as spatial tasks and math, and why women (as a group) are slightly better at "left side" activities such as language skills (Clements et al., 2006; Sommer, 2010). Others, however, reject this theory, claiming it is based on shaky evidence and sexist thinking (Fine, 2010). The most telling evidence on this point may be that female and male scores on the SAT Reasoning Test (SAT) are rapidly becoming more alike. The same applies to tests of math ability (Ceci & Williams, 2010). The narrowing gap is probably explained by a growing similarity in male and female interests, experiences, and educational goals.

The most important point to take away from this debate is that the differences that do exist between women and men are based on *averages* (● Figure 11.2). Many women are better at math than most men. Likewise, many men are better at verbal skills than most women. Scores for women and men overlap so much that it is impossible to predict whether any one person will be good or bad at math or language skills simply from knowing his or her sex. When we do see larger male–female performance gaps, they can often be traced to differences in the socialization, opportunities, and power given to men and women (Reilly, Neumann, & Andrews, 2016). Unequal power tends to exaggerate differences between men and women and then makes these artificial differences appear to be real.

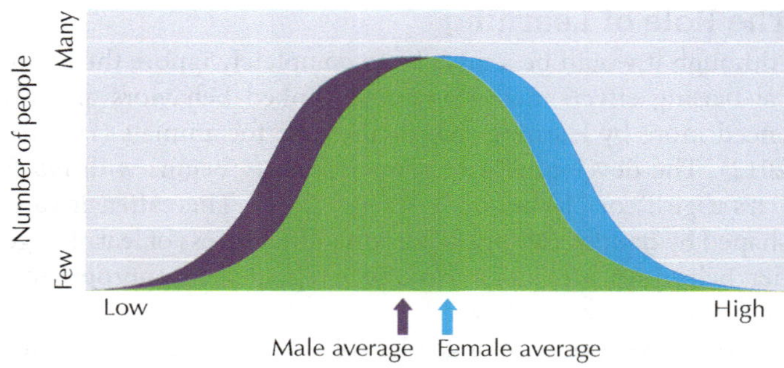

Figure 11.2 Distribution of male–female differences. Recorded differences in various abilities that exist between women and men are based on *averages*. For example, if we were to record the number of men and women who have low, medium, or high scores on tests of language ability, we might obtain graphs like those shown. For other abilities, men would have a higher average. However, such average differences are typically small. As a result, the overlap in female abilities and male abilities (shown in green) is very large (Eliot, 2009; Fine, 2010).

Gender Culturally constructed distinctions between male and female characteristics.

Gender identity One's personal, private sense of maleness or femaleness.

Gender variant (transgender) A condition in which a person's biological sex does not match his or her preferred gender.

Gender dysphoria Distress that may occur when gender identity does not match a person's physical sex.

Biological biasing effect The hypothesized effect that prenatal exposure to sex hormones has on development of the body, nervous system, and later behavior patterns.

The Role of Learning

Although it would be a mistake to completely ignore the biological biasing effect, most human sex-linked behaviors are influenced more by learning than is the case for animals (Helgeson, 2012). The development of gender identity begins with *labeling* ("It's a girl!" or "It's a boy!") (Eagly, 2009). Thereafter, it can be shaped by **gender role socialization**—the process of learning gender behaviors (stereotyped or not) regarded as appropriate for one's sex in a given culture.

We can see evidence of gender role socialization in many areas. For example, stereotyped gender roles are the norm in various media including TV commercials, children's picture books, and video games (Kahlenberg & Hein, 2010; Oppliger, 2007). But parents themselves can also subtly (or not-so-subtly) reinforce traditional ideas about gender: Infant girls are held more gently and treated more tenderly than boys. Both parents play more roughly with sons than with daughters (who are presumed to be more "delicate"). Later, boys are allowed to roam over a wider area without special permission. They also are expected to run errands earlier than girls. Though things are changing somewhat, daughters are still told that they are pretty and that "nice girls don't fight." Boys are told to be strong and that "tough guys don't cry." Sons are more often urged to control their emotions, except for anger and aggression, which parents tolerate more in boys than in girls. Overall, then, parents and other adults in Western countries like the United States have tended to encourage boys to engage in goal-directed, or **instrumental behaviors**, to be directly aggressive, to hide their emotions, and to prepare for the world of work. Girls, on the other hand, have often been encouraged in emotion-oriented, or **expressive behaviors**, and, to a lesser degree, have been socialized for indirect aggression and for motherhood (Eagly, 2009).

Pat Byrnes/The New Yorker Collection/Cartoonbank.com

wavebreakmedia/Shutterstock.com

One study found that the mothers interacted differently with their infant sons and daughters as they played with gender-neutral toys. Mothers of girls engaged in more interpretation and conversation, whereas mothers of boys commented more and offered more instructions (Clearfield & Nelson, 2006).

In addition, toys, sports, and play are strongly sex-typed (Hardin & Greer, 2009). Parents buy dolls for girls; they buy trucks, tools, and sports equipment for boys. Fathers, especially, tend to encourage their children to play with "appropriate" sex-typed toys (Freeman, 2007). Beginning around age 3, boys start to play mostly with boys and girls play with girls. Girls tend to play indoors and near adults. They like to cooperate by playing house and other games that require lots of verbal give and take. Boys prefer superhero games and rough-and-tumble play outdoors. Thus, from an early age, males and females tend to grow up in different, gender-defined cultures (Oppliger, 2007; Shaffer & Kipp, 2014).

Gender role socialization reflects all the pressures from parents, peers, and cultural forces that urge boys to "act like boys" and girls to "act like girls" (Orenstein, 2011). The outcome is not surprising: By the time they are 30 months of age, children are aware of gender role differences (Martin & Ruble, 2009). At 3 or 4 years of age, gender identity is usually well formed (Martin, 2011).

When parents are told that they treat boys and girls differently, many explain that the sexes are just "naturally" different. But what comes first, "natural differences" or the gender-based expectations that create them? In our culture, "male" seems to sometimes be defined simply as "not female"; that is, parents often have a vague fear of expressive and emotional behavior in male children. To them, such behavior implies that a boy is effeminate or a sissy. Many parents who would not be troubled if their daughters engaged in "masculine" play might be upset if their sons played with dolls or imitated "female" mannerisms (Wiseman & Davidson, 2012).

Gender Roles

A person's gender identity usually conforms to the **gender role**, or favored pattern of behavior, expected of each sex. Traditionally, in our culture, boys are encouraged to be strong, fast, aggressive, dominant, and achieving, and females are expected to be sensitive, intuitive, passive, emotional, and "naturally" interested in child-rearing.

A look at other cultures shows that our gender roles are by no means "natural" or universal. For example, in some cultures, women do the heavy work because men are considered too weak for it (Best, 2002). In Russia, roughly 75 percent of all medical doctors are women, and women make up a large portion of the workforce. Such cross-cultural variability makes it clear that a man is no less a man if he cooks, sews, or cares for children. A woman is no less a woman if she excels in sports, succeeds in business, or works as an auto mechanic.

Despite much progress in the last 40 years, gender role stereotypes continue to have a major impact on women and men. **Gender role stereotypes** are oversimplified beliefs about what men and women are actually like. While gender roles influence how we act, gender role stereotypes, in contrast, turn gender roles into false beliefs about what men and women can and can't do.

Of course, many people find traditional gender roles acceptable and comfortable. They may even enrich many lives. Others, however, may find traditional gender roles, especially gender role stereotypes, burdensome. If you are, for example, a fiercely independent woman or a deeply emotional man, you may experience **gender role strain**—stress associated with a conflict between your personal "reality" and the expectations associated with a gender role (Levant, 2011; Levant & Powell, 2017).

But isn't it possible to feel as though you have both traditionally masculine and feminine qualities? Great question! Imagine that Sharmila describes herself as being ambitious, competitive, decisive, and independent (all "masculine" traits), as well as affectionate, compassionate, loyal, and sympathetic (traditionally "feminine" traits). When someone like Sharmila feels that she is characterized by both masculine and feminine traits, psychologists would say that she is *androgynous.*

John Mitterer

Is this South American less of a man because he sews? Behaviors that are considered typical and appropriate for each sex (gender roles) vary a great deal from culture to culture. Undoubtedly, some cultures magnify sex differences more than others (Carroll, 2016).

Psychological Androgyny

The characteristics Sharmila used to describe herself come from the seminal work of psychologist Sandra Bem (1974). By combining 20 traditionally "masculine" traits (like self-reliant, assertive), 20 traditionally "feminine" traits (like affectionate, gentle), and 20 neutral traits (like truthful, friendly), Bem created the *Bem Sex Role Inventory* (BSRI). (Some psychologists prefer to use the term *sex role* instead of gender role.) Next, she and her associates gave the BSRI to thousands of people, asking them to say whether each trait applied to them. Of those surveyed, 50 percent fell into traditional feminine or masculine categories, 15 percent scored higher on traits of the opposite sex, and 35 percent were androgynous, getting high scores on both feminine and masculine items.

The word **androgyny** (an-DROJ-ih-nee) literally means "man-woman" and refers to having both masculine and feminine traits (Helgeson, 2012). Bem was convinced that our complex society requires flexibility with respect to gender roles. She believed that it was necessary for men to also be gentle, compassionate, sensitive, and yielding and for women to also be forceful, self-reliant, independent, and ambitious—*as the situation requires.*

One of the advantages of androgyny is that it is associated with greater adaptability and higher levels of emotional intelligence, since androgynous individuals are less hindered by traditional images of "feminine" or "masculine" behavior. (Remember ■ Section 9.6; Dean & Tate, 2016.) In general, androgynous persons are more flexible when it comes to coping with difficult situations, and they can use both instrumental and emotionally expressive capacities to enhance their lives and relationships

Gender role socialization The process of learning gender behaviors considered appropriate for one's sex in a given culture.

Instrumental behaviors Actions directed toward the achievement of some goal.

Expressive behaviors Actions that express or communicate emotion or personal feelings.

Gender role Pattern of behaviors regarded as "male" or "female" within a culture.

Gender role stereotypes Oversimplified and widely held beliefs about the basic characteristics of men and women.

Gender role strain Stress associated with any conflict between personal identity and the expectations associated with a gender role.

Androgyny The presence of both "masculine" and "feminine" traits in a single person (as masculinity and femininity are defined within one's culture).

Androgynous individuals adapt more easily to both traditionally "feminine" and "masculine" situations.

(see Figure 11.3). As a consequence, androgynous persons tend to experience less gender role strain and be more satisfied with their lives.

In contrast, Bem concluded that masculine males have great difficulty expressing warmth, playfulness, and concern—even when they are appropriate (Bem, 1975, 1981). Masculine men, it seems, tend to view such feelings as unacceptably "feminine." Masculine men also find it hard to accept emotional support from others, particularly women (Levant, 2003). They tend to be interested in sports, have mostly male friends, and dislike feminists. Problems faced by highly feminine women are the reverse of those faced by masculine men. Such women have trouble being independent and assertive, even when these qualities are desirable.

Over the years, the concept of androgyny has been variously supported, attacked, and debated. In the final analysis, it is worth repeating that many people remain comfortable with traditional views of gender. Nevertheless, there are clear advantages in our society to possessing both "feminine" and "masculine" traits (Dean & Tate, 2016; Lefkowitz & Zeldow, 2006).

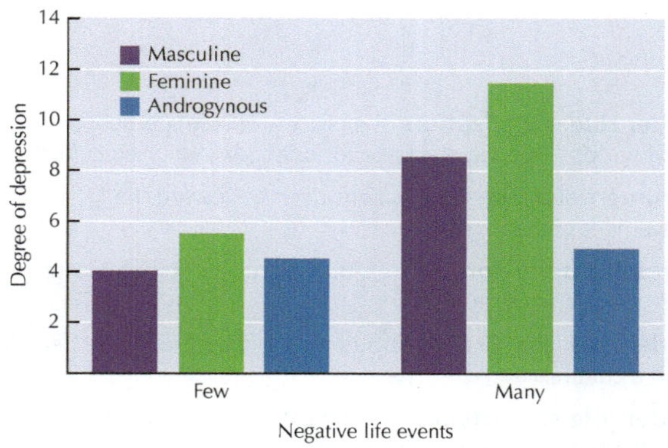

Figure 11.3 Androgyny and stress. Another indication of the possible benefits of androgyny is found in a study of reactions to stress. When confronted with an onslaught of negative events, strongly masculine or feminine persons become more depressed than androgynous individuals do. (Adapted from Roos & Cohen, 1987.)

Reflective Practice

Gender Identities and Roles

1. One's private sense of maleness or femaleness is referred to as ____________.
2. Traditional gender role socialization encourages ____________ behavior in males.
   a. instrumental
   b. emotional
   c. expressive
   d. dependent
3. A person who is androgynous scores high on ratings of traits usually possessed by the opposite sex. T or F?
4. Gender dysphoria will be diagnosed whenever someone feels as though their biological sex does not align with their preferred gender. T or F?

THINK CRITICALLY

5. Could a person be androgynous in a culture where "masculine" and "feminine" traits differ greatly from those on Bem's list?

SELF-REFLECT

- As a child, do you think that you were encouraged to engage more in instrumental behaviors or expressive behaviors?
- Think of three people you know, one who is androgynous, one who is traditionally feminine, and one who is traditionally masculine. What advantages and disadvantages do you see in each collection of traits?

Answers: 1. Gender identity 2. a 3. T 4. F 5. Yes. Being androgynous means having both masculine and feminine traits *as they are defined within one's culture.*

11.3 Sexual Responses, Attitudes, and Behaviors

GATEWAYS LEARNING OUTCOMES:
After reading this section you should be able to:

11.3.1 Contrast females and males in terms of their sexual responses

11.3.2 Explain how sexual attitudes and behaviors have changed over time

In 1934, Cole Porter's musical, *Anything Goes,* opened on Broadway. The lyrics of the title song started like this: "In olden days a glimpse of stocking was looked on as something shocking now heaven knows, anything goes." In his music, Porter was announcing a sexual revolution. The openness of the 1930s would indeed have shocked a person from the Victorian era. And yet the revolution didn't stop there. If a woman and a man living in the year 1934 could be transported to the present, they would, in turn, be stunned by today's North American sexual values and practices. Unmarried couples (or anyone, for that matter) having explicit sex on television; advertisements for provocative undergarments, tampons, and cures for "jock itch"; near-nudity at the beach; sexually explicit movies, hook-up culture, and, of course, the wide-open Internet—these and many other elements of contemporary culture would shock our time travelers from 1934.

So has there been a "sexual revolution"? The word "revolution" suggests rapid change. Although human *sexual responding* (that is, the human sex drive and the act of sex) has not changed over the years, many people would agree that *attitudes* toward sexuality have evolved very quickly. For example, in 1959, 88 percent of those interviewed agreed that premarital sex is wrong. More recent polls suggest that among young men and women, that number is less than 30 percent (Wilke & Saad, 2013). Similar shifts have occurred in attitudes toward same-sex relationships, sex education, having a baby outside of marriage, and related issues. Changes in attitudes have brought with them changes in *behavior,* as we will see in this section.

Even just 40 years ago, provocative clothing and sex were relatively rare in the media. Today, however, it's quite common to see portrayals of nudity, bluntly explicit sex, and even sexual violence.

Human Sexual Response

There is no question that the human **sex drive**—the strength of one's motivation to engage in sexual behavior—is extraordinarily powerful. Although it is modulated by factors such as cultural values, attitudes toward sex, and sexual experience, it is, in the end, a basic biological drive.

In lower animals, **castration** (surgical removal of the testicles or ovaries) tends to abolish sexual activity in inexperienced animals. In humans, the effects of male and female castration vary. At first, some people experience a loss of sex drive; in others, there is no change. (That's why castration of sex offenders does not necessarily curb their behavior.) However, after several years, almost all subjects report a decrease in sex drive unless they take hormone supplements.

The preceding observations have nothing to do with **sterilization** (surgery to make a man or woman infertile). The vast majority of women and men who choose surgical birth control (such as a tubal ligation or a vasectomy) do not lose interest in sex. If anything, they may become more sexually active when pregnancy is no longer a concern.

A capacity for sexual arousal is apparent at birth or soon after. One of the most basic sexual behaviors is **masturbation**—self-stimulation that causes sexual pleasure or orgasm. Self-stimulation has been observed in infants under one year of age. Researcher Alfred Kinsey even verified instances of orgasm in boys as young as five months old and girls as young as four months (Kinsey & Pomeroy, 1953; Kinsey, Pomeroy, & Martin, 1948). Kinsey also found that 2- to 5-year-old children spontaneously touch and exhibit their genitals. Although various sexual behaviors continue throughout childhood, the human sex drive normally doesn't "kick in" until the early teens. That's when the hormonal changes of puberty promote rapid physical growth and sexual maturity.

As discussed at the beginning of this chapter, a male's sex drive is related to the amount of androgens (especially testosterone) supplied by the testes (Crooks & Baur, 2017). The connection can be very direct: When a man chats with a woman he finds attractive, his testosterone levels actually increase (Roney, 2003). While the sex drive in females is related to estrogen levels, testosterone also plays a role (Rosenthal, M., 2013). A woman's sex drive is closely related to the testosterone level in her bloodstream. Of course, women produce much smaller amounts of testosterone than men. But that doesn't mean their sex drive is weaker.

Sex drive The strength of one's motivation to engage in sexual behavior.

Castration Surgical removal of the testicles or ovaries.

Sterilization Medical procedures such as vasectomy or tubal ligation that make a man or a woman infertile.

Masturbation Producing sexual pleasure or orgasm by directly stimulating the genitals on your own body.

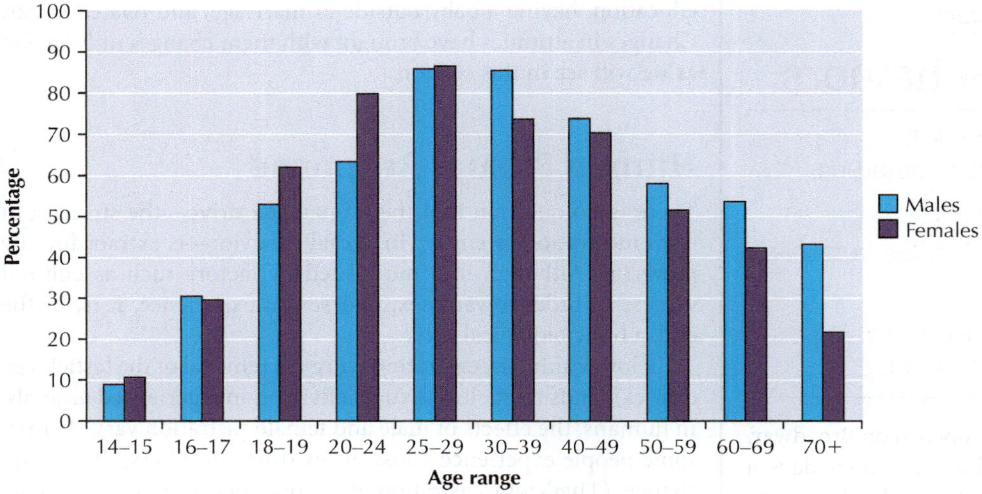

Figure 11.4 Sexual intercourse across age groups. Percentage of men and women of various ages who experienced vaginal intercourse during the last month. Although percentages decline beginning as adults enter their forties, significant percentages of older people remain sexually active. (Data adapted from Herbenick et al., 2010a.)

Women's bodies are more sensitive to testosterone, and their sex drive is comparable to males.

One way to gauge the strength of the human sex drive is to chart its expression as sexual behavior. As you can see, many sexually mature men and women are sexually active at every age (see Figure 11.4).

What about masturbation? As Figure 11.5 shows, masturbation is also a regular feature of the sex lives of many people. Masturbation is an important part of the psychosexual development of most adolescents. Among other things, it provides a healthy substitute for sexual involvement at a time when young people are maturing emotionally. Approximately 70 percent of married women and men masturbate at least occasionally. Generally speaking, masturbation is valid at any age and usually has no effect on marital relationships (Herbenick et al., 2010b). Contrary to popular myths, people are not always compelled to masturbate because they lack a sexual partner (Kott, 2011). Masturbation is often just "one more item on the menu" for people with active sex lives.

Does alcohol increase the sex drive? In general, no. Alcohol is a *depressant* (see Section 5.4); however it may stimulate erotic desire by lowering inhibitions. This effect no doubt accounts for alcohol's reputation as an aid to seduction. (Humorist Ogden Nash once summarized this bit of folklore by saying "Candy is dandy, but liquor is quicker.") However, in larger doses, alcohol suppresses orgasm in women and erection in men. Getting drunk decreases sexual desire, arousal, pleasure, and performance (Sobczak, 2009).

Numerous other drugs are reputed to be *aphrodisiacs* (af-ruh-DEEZ-ee-aks); that is, substances that increase sexual desire or pleasure. However, like alcohol, many other drugs do not enhance—and may even actually impair—sexual response (McKay, 2005; Shamloul, 2010). Some examples are amphetamines, amyl nitrite, barbiturates, cocaine, Ecstasy, lysergic acid diethylamide (LSD), and cannabis. (It is worth noting that, around the world, many other substances are believed to be aphrodisiacs, such as oysters, chocolate, powdered rhinoceros horn, and so on. In general, these are, at best, superstitions that might produce a placebo effect.) (Crooks & Baur, 2017).

What happens to the sex drive in old age? A natural decline in sex drive typically accompanies aging. This is related to a reduced output of sex hormones, especially testosterone (Carroll, 2016). However, sexual activity need not come to an end. Some people in their eighties and nineties continue to have active sex lives. The crucial factor for an extended sex life appears to be regularity and opportunity. ("Use it or lose it.") In some instances, taking testosterone supplements can restore the sex drive in both men and women (Rosenthal, M., 2013).

Sexual Arousal

Human sexual arousal is complex. It may, of course, be produced by direct stimulation of the body's **erogenous zones** (eh-ROJ-eh-nus), which means "productive of pleasure or erotic desire."

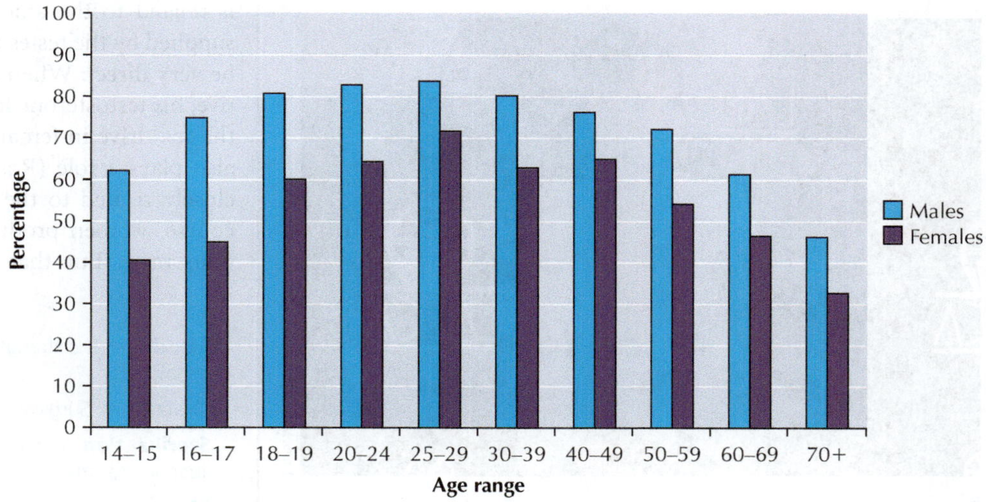

Figure 11.5 Masturbation across age groups. Percentage of women and men of various ages who masturbated alone during the last year. (Data adapted from Herbenick et al., 2010a.)

Human erogenous zones include the genitals, mouth, breasts, ears, anus, and, to a lesser degree, the entire surface of the body. It is clear, however, that more than physical contact is involved: A urological or gynecological exam rarely results in any sexual arousal. Likewise, an unwanted sexual advance may produce only revulsion. Human sexual arousal obviously includes a large mental element.

The pioneering work of gynecologist William Masters and psychologist Virginia Johnson greatly expanded our understanding of sexual responses, regardless of how they are triggered (Masters & Johnson, 1966, 1970). In a series of experiments, interviews, and controlled observations, Masters and Johnson directly studied sexual intercourse and masturbation in nearly 700 males and females. This objective information has given us a much clearer picture of human sexuality.

According to Masters and Johnson, sexual response can be divided into four phases: (1) *excitement*, (2) *plateau*, (3) *orgasm*, and (4) *resolution* (Figures 11.6 and 11.7). These four phases, which are the same for people of all sexual orientations (Carroll, 2016), can be described as follows:

- **Excitement phase** The first level of sexual response, indicated by initial signs of sexual arousal
- **Plateau phase** The second level of sexual response, during which physical arousal intensifies
- **Orgasm** A climax and release of sexual excitement
- **Resolution** The final level of sexual response, involving a return to lower levels of sexual tension and arousal

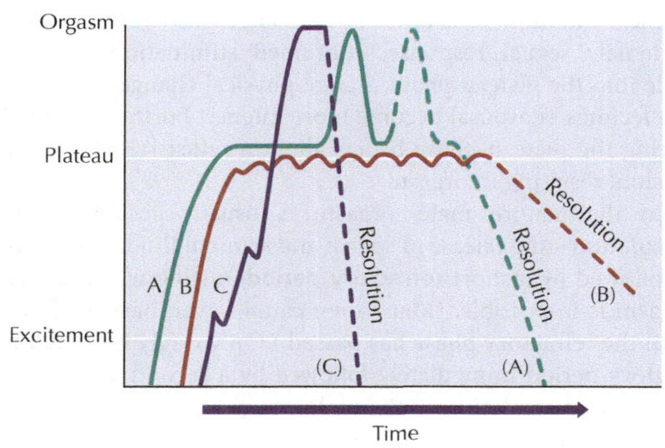

Figure 11.6 Female sexual response cycle. The green line shows that sexual arousal rises through the excitement phase and levels off for a time during the plateau phase. Arousal peaks during orgasm and then returns to pre-excitement levels. In pattern A, arousal rises from excitement through the plateau phase and peaks in orgasm. Resolution may be immediate, or it may first include a return to the plateau phase and a second orgasm (dotted line). In pattern B, arousal is sustained at the plateau phase and slowly resolved without sexual climax. Pattern C shows a fairly rapid rise in arousal to orgasm. Little time is spent in the plateau phase, and resolution is fairly rapid. (Adapted from Carroll, 2016.)

Female Response

In women, the excitement phase is marked by a complex pattern of changes in the body. The vagina is prepared for intercourse, the nipples become erect, pulse rate rises, and the skin may become flushed or reddened. When sexual stimulation ends, the excitement phase gradually subsides. If a woman moves into the plateau phase, physical changes and subjective feelings of arousal become more intense. Sexual arousal that ends during this phase tends to ebb more slowly, which may produce considerable frustration. Sometimes women skip the plateau phase (see Figure 11.6).

During orgasm, 3 to 10 muscular contractions of the vagina, uterus, and related structures discharge sexual tension. Orgasm is usually followed by resolution, a return to lower levels of sexual tension and arousal. After orgasm, about 15 percent of all women return to the plateau phase and may have one or more additional orgasms (Mah & Binik, 2001).

Before the work of Masters and Johnson, theorists debated whether "vaginal orgasms" are different from those derived from stimulation of the clitoris, a small, sensitive organ located above the vaginal opening. Sigmund Freud claimed that a "clitoral orgasm" is an "immature" form of female response. Because the clitoris is the female structure comparable to the penis, Freud believed that women who experienced clitoral orgasms had not fully accepted their femininity.

Masters and Johnson exploded the Freudian myth by showing that physical responses are the same no matter how an orgasm is produced (Carroll, 2016; Mah & Binik, 2001). As a matter of fact, the inner two-thirds of the vagina is relatively insensitive to touch. Most sensations during intercourse come from stimulation of the clitoris and other external areas. For most women, the clitoris is an important source of pleasurable sensations. Apparently, sensations from many sources are fused into the total experience of orgasm. Thus, to downgrade the "clitoral orgasm" ignores basic female biology (Prause, 2012).

Male Response

Sexual arousal in the male is signaled by erection of the penis during the excitement phase. A rise in heart rate, increased blood flow to the genitals, enlargement of the testicles, erection of the

Erogenous zones Areas of the body that produce pleasure, provoke erotic desire, or both.

Excitement phase The first phase of sexual response, indicated by initial signs of sexual arousal.

Plateau phase The second phase of sexual response, during which physical arousal is further heightened.

Orgasm A climax and release of sexual excitement.

Resolution (in sexual response) The fourth phase of sexual response, involving a return to lower levels of sexual tension and arousal.

nipples, and numerous other body changes also occur. As is true of female sexual response, continued stimulation moves the male into the plateau phase. Again, physical changes and subjective feelings of arousal become more intense. Further stimulation during the plateau phase brings about a reflex release of sexual tension, resulting in orgasm.

In the mature male, orgasm is usually accompanied by **ejaculation**—the release of sperm and seminal fluid. Afterward, it is followed by a short **refractory period**, during which a second orgasm is impossible. (Many men cannot even have an erection until the refractory phase has passed.) Only rarely is the male refractory period immediately followed by a second orgasm. Both orgasm and resolution in the male usually do not last as long as they do for females (see Figure 11.7).

Comparing Male and Female Responses

Although male and female sexual responses are generally quite similar, the differences that do exist can affect sexual compatibility. For example, women typically go through the sexual phases more slowly than do men. During lovemaking, 10 to 20 minutes is often required for a woman to go from excitement to orgasm. Males may experience all four stages in as little as 3 minutes. However, there is much variation, especially in women. (Note that these times refer only to intercourse, not to an entire arousal sequence.) Such differences should be kept in mind by couples seeking sexual compatibility (Carroll, 2016).

OK, so I have a bunch of questions. First of all, does that mean that a couple should try to time lovemaking to promote simultaneous orgasm? Simultaneous orgasm (both partners reaching sexual climax at the same time) can undoubtedly be satisfying (Brody & Weiss, 2011). But it is usually a mistake to make it the "goal" of lovemaking because "failure" may reduce sexual enjoyment. It is more advisable for couples to seek mutual satisfaction through a combination of intercourse and erotic touching (*foreplay*) than it is to inhibit spontaneity, communication, and pleasure.

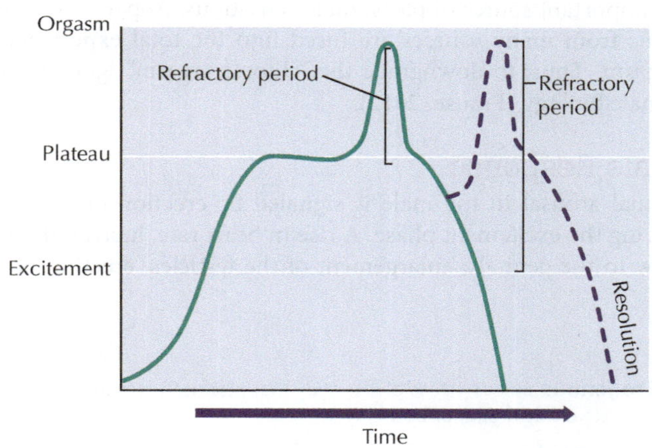

Figure 11.7 Male sexual response cycle. The green line shows that sexual arousal rises through the excitement phase and levels off for a time during the plateau phase. Arousal peaks during orgasm and then returns to pre-excitement levels. During the refractory period, immediately after orgasm, a second sexual climax is typically impossible. However, after the refractory period has passed, there may be a return to the plateau phase, followed by a second orgasm (*dotted line*). (Adapted from Carroll, 2016.)

Alright, but does the slower female response mean that women are less sexual than men? Definitely not. During masturbation, 70 percent of females reach orgasm in 4 minutes or less. This casts serious doubt on the idea that women respond more slowly. Slower female response during intercourse probably occurs because stimulation to the clitoris is less direct. It might be said that men simply provide too little stimulation for more rapid female response, not that women are in any way inferior.

Asking for a friend: Does penis size affect female response? Contrary to popular belief, there is no relationship between penis size and male sexual potency. Think about it. If a woman's sexual satisfaction is related to her partner's attention to clitoral stimulation and foreplay, then why would his penis length matter? Besides, Masters and Johnson found that the vagina adjusts to the size of the penis and that subjective feelings of pleasure and intensity of orgasm are not related to penis size. They also found that although individual differences exist in flaccid penis size, there tends to be much less variation in size during erection. That's why erection has been called the "great equalizer." Lovemaking involves the entire body. Preoccupation with the size of a woman's breasts, a man's penis, and the like are based on myths that undermine genuine caring, sharing, and sexual satisfaction (Hyde & DeLamater, 2014).

Men almost always reach orgasm during intercourse, but many women do not. Doesn't this indicate that women are less sexually responsive? Again, the evidence argues against any lack of female sexual responsiveness. It is true that about one woman in three does not experience orgasm during the first year of marriage, and only about 30 percent regularly reach orgasm through intercourse alone. However, this does not imply lack of physical responsiveness, because 90 percent of all women reach orgasm when masturbating (Conley et al., 2011). However, women tend to place more emphasis on emotional closeness with a lover than men (Peplau, 2003). Many women also want to be active partners in lovemaking, and they want their needs and preferences to be acknowledged (Benjamin & Tlusten, 2010).

In another regard, women are clearly more responsive. Only about 5 percent of males are capable of multiple orgasms (and then only after an unavoidable refractory period). Most men are limited to a second orgasm at best. In contrast, Masters and Johnson's findings suggest that most women who regularly experience orgasm are capable of multiple orgasms (Herbenick et al., 2010a). Remember though, that only about 15 percent regularly have multiple orgasms. A woman should not automatically assume that something is wrong if she isn't orgasmic or multiorgasmic. Many women have satisfying sexual experiences even when orgasm is not involved (Komisaruk, Beyer-Flores, & Whipple, 2006; Zietsch et al., 2011).

Regardless, male and female sexual patterns are rapidly becoming more alike. Figure 11.8 presents some of the data on sexual behavior from a major national health survey of American men and women ages 25 to 44. As you can see, in any given year, men and women do not differ in their average number of

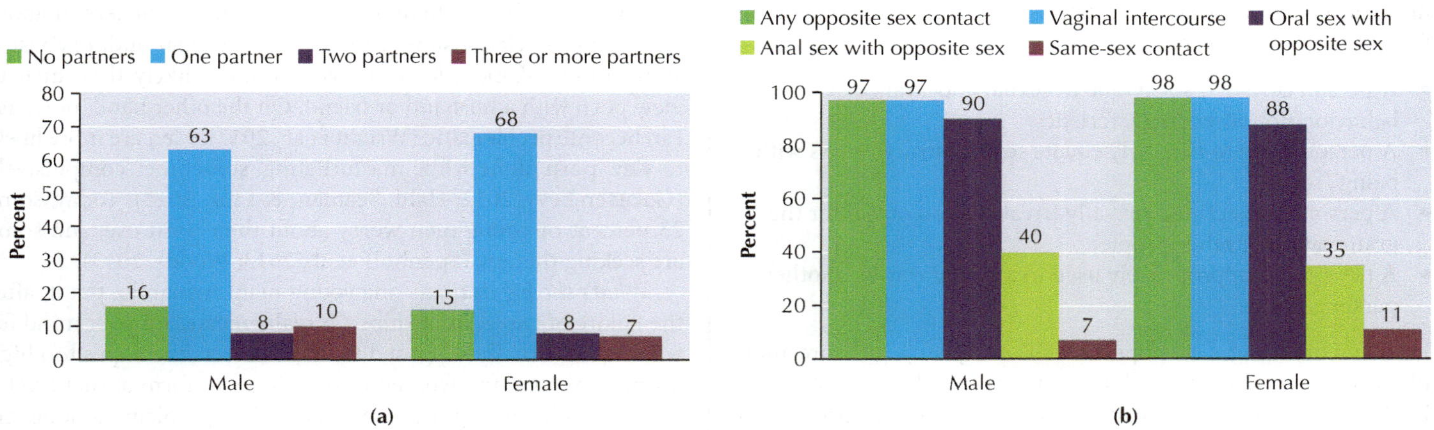

Figure 11.8 Pattern of sexual behavior of American adults. Men and women do not differ (a) in their average number of sexual partners or (b) in their overall pattern of sexual activity. (Adapted from Mosher, Chandra, & Jones, 2005.)

opposite-sex partners or in their overall pattern of sexual activity (Mosher, Chandra, & Jones, 2005). Exaggerating the differences between male and female sexuality is not only inaccurate, it can also create artificial barriers to sexual satisfaction (Conley et al., 2011; Wiederman, 2001). For example, assuming that men should always initiate sex denies the fact that women have comparable sexual interests and needs.

Sexual Attitudes and Behavior

Changes in sexual attitudes over the years have brought about parallel changes in Americans' sexual behavior. Let's take a look at several trends.

Greater Tolerance

One notable change is that there is greater *tolerance* for sexual activity, especially activity that is engaged in by others. For example, a 1970s magazine poll found that 80 percent of all readers considered extramarital sex acceptable under some circumstances (Athenasiou, Shaver, & Tavris, 1970). But another poll found that, in practice, only about 30 percent of married persons actually had extramarital sexual experience themselves (Rubenstein & Tavris, 1987). These are older studies, but the percentages have not changed greatly over the last 50 years (Mark, Janssen, & Milhausen, 2011). Perhaps more importantly, faithfulness in marriage remains a widely shared value. In any given year, only about 4 percent of married people have sex partners other than their spouse. Americans actually seem to live up to the norm of marital fidelity quite well (Mosher, Chandra, & Jones, 2005).

Abandoning the Double Standard

Another major change that has occurred in sexual attitudes and behavior is the growing rejection of the **double standard**, or the use of different rules to judge the appropriateness of male and female sexual behavior. In the past, for example, males were largely forgiven for engaging in premarital sex. Young males who "sowed some wild oats" were widely tolerated. In fact, many were tacitly encouraged to seek casual sex as a step toward manhood. On the other hand, women who were sexually active before marriage ran the risk of being labeled "easy," "bad," or "promiscuous."

On the one hand, the ability of women (and men) to more freely to express their sexuality is another positive side of changing sexual attitudes and values. As the gap between female and male sexual patterns continues to close, it is increasingly likely that an end to the double standard is in sight (Kreager & Staff, 2009; Sakaluk & Milhausen, 2012; Schleicher & Gilbert, 2005). On the other hand, liberalized attitudes can lead to individuals feeling pressured into sexual behavior (Judson, Johnson, & Perez, 2013). Greater sexual freedom is a positive development only for those ready for it (Hatch, 2011). There is, for example, a growing recognition that young girls are being oversexualized by influences such as beauty pageants, the sexual antics of female singers during concerts, and the availability of consumer goods such as padded bras for girls as young as six (Durham, 2009; Lerum & Dworkin, 2009).

Pressures to engage in sexual behaviors probably come as much from the individual as from others. Regardless, for a greater acceptance of sexuality to be constructive, people must feel that they have the right to say no, as well as the right to choose when, where, how, and with whom they will express their sexuality. As is true elsewhere, freedom must be combined with responsibility, commitment, and caring if it is to have meaning. According to the American Psychological Association (2010), unhealthy sexualization can be

Ejaculation The release of sperm and seminal fluid by the male at the time of orgasm.

Refractory period A short period after orgasm during which males are unable to again reach orgasm.

Double standard (in sexual behavior) Applying different standards for judging the appropriateness of male and female sexual behavior.

distinguished from healthy sexuality when one or more of the following conditions occurs:

- A person is valued solely due to sexual appearance or behavior, not other characteristics.
- A person is led to narrowly equate sexual attractiveness with being "sexy."
- A person is objectified sexually (treated as an object for the gratification of other people).
- A person is inappropriately used in a sexual way by another person.

From media images to popular fashions, young girls are more likely to be oversexualized than are young boys (Roberts & Zurbriggen, 2013). Oversexualization leads young girls to see themselves as having value only as sexual objects. This results in low self-esteem, eating disorders, depression, and feelings of shame (Ward, 2004). Some studies have even shown that sexualized girls perform more poorly on intellectual activities (Hebl, King, & Lin, 2004). Most worrisome is an increasing tendency for young girls to engage in risky sexual behaviors, such as unprotected oral sex (Atwood, 2006; Hatch, 2011).

According to the American Psychological Association (2010), parents, educators, and others should encourage young girls to develop relationships based on their personalities and interests, rather than on how they look.

Number of Partners

A third trend is the fact that people today spend as much of their adult lives (on average) alone as they do in marriage. As a result, many people are involved in nonmarried sexual relationships, and this tends to increase the number of sexual partners that adults encounter (Lau, 2012). Men now report having an average of seven female sexual partners in their lifetimes, while women report four. Further, in any given year, about 17 percent of men (and 10 percent of women) reported having two or more sexual partners (Fryar et al., 2007).

All in all, there is ample evidence that sexual behavior in the United States has generally increased in the last 50 years. Although this trend has brought problems, it does not seem to represent a wholesale move toward sexual promiscuity. Even premarital intercourse does not appear to represent a major rejection of traditional values and responsible behavior. The connection between sexuality and love or affection remains strong for most people. Both premarital sex and cohabitation are still widely viewed as preludes to marriage or as temporary substitutes for it. Likewise, other changes in attitudes and behavior appear to reflect a greater acceptance of sexuality rather than a total rejection of earlier values (Crooks & Baur, 2017).

Internet Pornography

A fourth trend in sexual behavior is directly related to the spread of pornography via the Internet. With the liberalization of sexual attitudes has come a glut of free pornography, always just a few clicks away. As a consequence, it is getting harder and harder (no pun intended) to find individuals who haven't at least taken a curious peek, as public attitudes toward porn have become more accepting (Carroll, 2016).

On the one hand, there is little reason to be concerned about spicing up a relationship with some occasional auditory/visual stimulation. Women, for example, are more likely than men to view porn with a husband or friend. On the other hand, porn use can become problematic (Wright et al., 2017). Men are more likely to view porn alone while masturbating, sometimes compulsively (Galatzer-Levy, 2012; Hald, Seaman, & Linz, 2014). Today, some 25 percent of young men worry about their porn use, and some are seeking therapy (Spenhoff et al., 2013; Woods, 2013).

What's the big deal? As one young man, Armando, put it, after the failure of two relationships, "It really messes up your mind for what sex is actually supposed to be. . . . It sets the hopes too high for normal men and women to be able to perform at that level. I believe that's causing a lot of relationship problems among my peers" (McMahon, 2014).

One way to think about porn is as a **supernormal stimulus**, which is more potent than the natural stimuli we have evolved to encounter (Ward, 2013). Idealized women and men, along with their idealized sexual encounters, may well be the processed sugar or crack cocaine of sex. In other words, porn can be so exciting that normal sex seems to pale by comparison. With excessive use, desensitization sets in. What starts out as a curiosity can, over time, become a compulsion (Griffiths, 2012).

STDs and Safer Sex

Finally, changes in sexual attitudes and behavior have led to an increased risk of acquiring a **sexually transmitted disease (STD)**, an infection passed from one person to another by intimate physical contact. Sexually active people run higher risks for human papillomavirus (HPV), chlamydia (klah-MID-ee-ah), gonorrhea, hepatitis B, herpes, syphilis, and other STDs (▲ Table 11.1). Over 1.9 million new cases of chlamydia, gonorrhea, and syphilis were reported in the United States in 2015 (Centers for Disease Control, 2016f).

Despite such statistics, many sexually active people underestimate their risk for a variety of reasons. One study of sexually active teenage girls engaging in risky sex is a case in point. Nearly 90 percent of the girls thought that they had virtually no chance of getting an STD. In reality, over the next 18 months, one in four got chlamydia or gonorrhea (Ethier et al., 2003).

Ollyy/Shutterstock.com

Is too much access to online pornography a problem? What do you think?

▲ Table 11.1 Common Sexually Transmitted Diseases

STD	Male Symptoms	Female Symptoms	Prevention	Treatment
Gonorrhea	Milky discharge from urethra; painful, frequent urination	Vaginal discharge and inflammation; painful urination	Condom/safer sex practices	Antibiotics
Chlamydia	Painful urination; discharge from urethra	Painful urination; discharge from vagina; abdominal pain	Condom/safer sex practices	Antibiotics
Syphilis	Painless sores on genitals, rectum, tongue, or lips; skin rash; fever; headache; aching bones and joints	Same as male	Condom/safer sex practices	Antibiotics
Genital herpes	Pain or itching on the penis; water blisters or open sores	Pain or itching in the genital area; water blisters or open sores	Condom/safer sex practices	Symptoms can be treated but not cured
Human papillomavirus (HPV)	Warty growths on genitals; some cancers	Same as male	Condom/safer sex practices	Wart removal by surgery or laser, HPV vaccine for prevention
HIV/AIDS	Prolonged fatigue; swollen lymph nodes; fever lasting more than 10 days; night sweats; unexplained weight loss; purplish lesions on skin; persistent cough or sore throat; persistent colds; persistent diarrhea; easy bruising or unexplained bleeding	Same as male	Condom/safer sex practices	Can be treated with various drugs but cannot be cured
Hepatitis B	Mild cases may have no symptoms, but infection can cause chronic liver disease, cirrhosis of the liver, or liver cancer	Same as male	Vaccination	None available
Pelvic inflammatory disease	Does not apply	Intense pain in lower back, abdomen, or both; fever	Condom/safer sex practices	Antibiotics

One reason for underestimating sexual risk is that people who are sexually active may have indirect contact with many other people. One study of sexual relationships at a high school in a Mid-western city found long chains of sexual contact between students. Thus, a student at the end of the chain might have had sex with only one person, but in reality, she or he had indirect contact with dozens or even hundreds of others (Bearman, Moody, & Stovel, 2004).

Another reason people underestimate their risk is that many individuals who carry STDs remain *asymptomatic* (a-SIMP-tehmat-ik), or lacking obvious symptoms. It is easy to have an infection without knowing it. Likewise, it is often impossible to tell whether a sexual partner is infectious.

Also, because most of the more common STDs are treatable, it is easy to dismiss their impact on health. But STDs such as chlamydia or gonorrhea produce a variety of painful and embarrassing symptoms. Chlamydia can even "silently" (without symptoms) damage a woman's reproductive organs, resulting in infertility. Gonorrhea can damage the fertility of both men and women (Centers for Disease Control, 2016f).

Of course, one of the most serious threats to human health comes from the human immunodeficiency virus (HIV). Whereas most other STDs are treatable, HIV infections disable the immune system, leading to acquired immune deficiency syndrome (AIDS), which can be lethal. As the immune system weakens, other "opportunistic" diseases invade the body.

The first symptoms of AIDS may show up as few as two months after HIV infection, but they typically don't appear for 10 years. Because of this long incubation period, infected persons often pass the HIV virus on to others without knowing it. Medical testing can detect an HIV infection. However, for at least the first six months after becoming infected, a person can test negative while carrying the virus. Even a negative test result, therefore, is

Supernormal stimulus Any stimulus (often artificial) that is more potent than the natural stimuli that we have evolved to encounter.

Sexually transmitted disease (STD) A disease that is typically passed from one person to the next by intimate physical contact; a venereal disease.

no guarantee that a person is a "safe" sex partner. In fact, 25 percent of HIV-infected individuals are unaware of their infections (Nguyen et al., 2008).

HIV infections are spread by direct contact with body fluids—especially blood, semen, and vaginal secretions. The HIV virus cannot be transmitted by casual contact. People do not get HIV from shaking hands, touching or using objects touched by an HIV-infected person, eating food prepared by an infected person, or from social kissing, touching sweat or tears, sharing drinking glasses, sharing towels, and so forth.

HIV can be spread by all forms of sexual intercourse, and it has affected persons of all sexual orientations. In North America, those who remain at greatest risk for HIV infection remain men who have had sex with other men (gay and bisexual men), people who have shared needles (for tattoos or for intravenous drug use), sexual partners of people in the preceding groups, and heterosexuals with a history of multiple partners. Thus, the vast majority of people are not at *high* risk of HIV infection. Regardless, HIV could potentially affect anyone.

What should you take away from this discussion about STDs? First and foremost, be aware that sexually active people can do a great deal to protect their own health. Remember that it is risky to engage in the behaviors listed here with a person who has an STD:

- Unprotected (without a condom) vaginal, oral, or anal sex with an infected partner
- Having two or more sex partners (additional partners further increase the risk)
- Sex with someone you don't know well, or with someone you know has had several partners
- Sex with someone you know injects drugs or shares drug needles and syringes (HIV/AIDS)

It's important to remember that you can't tell from external appearances if a person is infected. Many people would be surprised to learn that their partners have engaged in behavior that places them both at risk. The preceding list of high-risk behaviors can be contrasted with the following list of safer sexual practices. (Note, however, that unless a person completely abstains, sex can be made safer, but it's not risk-free).

- Not having sex at all
- Having sex with one mutually faithful, uninfected partner
- Using a condom
- Discussing contraception with your partner
- Discussing your partner's sexual health prior to engaging in sex
- Being selective regarding sexual partners
- Reducing the number of sexual partners
- Not engaging in sex while intoxicated
- Not injecting drugs (HIV/AIDS)

Sexually active persons should practice safer sex until their partner's sexual history and/or health has been clearly established. Unfortunately, this message is not always getting through to those who most need to hear it. The HIV/AIDS epidemic initially triggered a sharp decrease in risky sex and an increase in monogamous relationships among gay men. Unfortunately, this trend has begun to reverse. Once again, rates for many STDs are rising among gay men. In part, this may be because new medical treatments are helping people with HIV live longer. Many victims simply do not look or act sick. This gives a false impression about the dangers of HIV infection and encourages foolish risk taking (Stevens, Bernadini, & Jemmott, 2013). Regardless, about 15 percent of new HIV infections in the United States are transmitted through heterosexual sex (Centers for Disease Control, 2016h). The focus on HIV/AIDS prevention may also have deemphasized the health impact of the other STDs.

Isn't it possible that practicing safer sex would be interpreted as a sign that you mistrust your lover? Those who do not ensure their own safety, or that of their partners, are gambling with their health. As is the case with other behavioral risk factors, taking precautions could, instead, be defined as a way of showing that you really care about your own health, as well as that of your partner (Essien et al., 2010).

Sexual Attitudes and Behavior Among Young People

When we examine sexual attitudes and behavior among young people, current trends reveal some interesting contrasts. On the one hand, young people today are growing more conservative when it comes to engaging in sexual intercourse at a young age. The social upheaval that began in the 1960s led to an especially sharp rise in sexual activity among teenagers. This increase continued into the 1980s but has begun to reverse in recent years. In 1988, 60 percent of teenage males and 51 percent of teenage females had intercourse by age 19. By 2015, the rates had dropped to 43 percent for teenage males and 39 percent for teenage females. The drop is especially pronounced among younger teens (Centers for Disease Control, 2016f). This change has been accompanied by higher rates of contraceptive use and declining rates of teen pregnancy and abortion (Kost & Maddow-Zimet, 2016). By 2010, the rate of teen births reached a historic low (Centers for Disease Control, 2017c). [Nevertheless, the United States still has the highest teenage pregnancy rates among all industrialized nations (Kearney & Levine, 2012)]. Apparently as young people learn more about their sexuality they become more likely to *delay* the age at which they first engage in sexual intercourse (Ballonoff Suleiman & Brindis, 2014; Kohler, Manhart, & Lafferty, 2008).

On the other hand, younger Americans continue to shift toward more liberal *sexual scripts* favoring casual sex (Lyons et al., 2013; Stephens, 2012; Wentland & Reissing, 2011). A **sexual script** is a mental plan that guides sexual behavior. Such scripts influence when and where we are likely to express sexual feelings and with whom (McCormick, 2010; Ryan, 2011). They provide a "plot" for the order of events in lovemaking and they outline "approved" actions, motives, and outcomes.

According to one survey, more than half of all college students have followed a *friends with benefits* script to have sex without romantic involvement (Mongeau et al., 2013). Also common and even more casual is the *hook-up* script, in which two people having sex are more or less strangers (Bradshaw, Kahn, & Saville, 2010; Holman & Sillars, 2012). In contrast, traditional sexual scripts stress courtship, romance, and marriage. Sex in such relationships might be premarital, but it is still romantic (Roese et al., 2006).

As casual sexual scripts become more common, the traditional focus on intercourse is fading in favor of oral sex, which tends to be seen as less risky, more acceptable, and "not a big deal." Casual sexual scripts are also spreading to younger children. One study found that 20 percent of American ninth graders have already had oral sex and more than 30 percent intend to try it soon (Halpern-Felsher et al., 2005).

Casual sex is often viewed as easier than facing the challenges of romantic attachment and finding a lifelong partner. However, it is not without its own risks. Casual sex is usually associated with alcohol use and unsafe sexual behaviors, such as unprotected sex (Fortunato et al., 2010). Although oral sex is safer than intercourse, a significant chance of getting a sexually transmitted disease (STD) remains (Boskey, 2016). Another downside of casual sex is the letdown that can occur when one person follows a romantic script and the other follows a casual script ("He [or she] just isn't that into you"). Psychological distress is also often involved (Bersamin et al., 2014). For example, young women who are having casual sex are more likely to be depressed (Grello, Welsh, & Harper, 2006).

On balance, adolescents and young adults have always engaged in experimentation and exploration. Most young people emerge unscathed if they clearly understand that their encounters are casual and if they practice safe sex.

Human Diversity and Sexual Behavior

A survey of 59 nations found that a "sexual revolution" has not occurred in most other countries (Wellings et al., 2006). People from the United States and other industrialized nations are more likely to have had two or more recent sexual partners; most people from developing countries have had only one recent sexual partner. On average, though, teenagers around the world have their first sexual experience at the same age as American teenagers. One finding of particular note concerns Africa, the epicenter of the AIDS epidemic. Contrary to popular opinion elsewhere, Africans are not promiscuous. They report fewer sexual partners than their counterparts in developed countries. Instead, it's likely that high rates of sexually transmitted diseases in Africa result from a lack of knowledge and access to condoms.

Reflective Practice

Sexual Responses, Attitudes, and Behavior

1. Masturbation is problematic sexual behavior. T or F?

2. The sexual response of males is quite different than that of females. T or F?

3. The term ______________ ______________ describes the tendency for the sexual behavior of women and men to be judged differently.

4. A sexual script refers to
- a. a script for a movie that includes a lot of sexual content
- b. a doctor's prescription for medication to improve sexual intercourse
- c. a mental plan that guides sexual behavior
- d. none of the above

5. The HIV virus is spread
- a. only when gay men have sex
- b. only by direct contact with the semen of an infected individual
- c. through day-to-day contact like kissing and shaking hands
- d. through many kinds of bodily fluids (blood, semen, vaginal secretions) as well as infected needles

THINK CRITICALLY

6. Which do you think would be better suited to reducing STDs and unwanted pregnancies among adolescents: abstinence-only education programs or more comprehensive sex education programs?

SELF-REFLECT

- Based on your own observations of attitudes toward sex and patterns of sexual behavior, do you think that there has been a sexual revolution?

Answers: 1. F 2. F 3. double standard 4. c 5. d 6. More comprehensive programs are actually more effective at reducing STDs and unwanted pregnancies among adolescents (Kirby, 2008).

11.4 Sexual Relationships

GATEWAYS LEARNING OUTCOMES:
After reading this section you should be able to:

11.4.1 Outline the factors that contribute to healthy sexual relationships

11.4.2 Outline the most common sexual dysfunctions

11.4.3 Define what is meant by a paraphilic disorder, and provide some examples

11.4.4 Define what is meant by sexual harassment, and provide some examples

11.4.5 Define what constitutes rape, and what is meant by "rape myths"

No matter the age, sex, gender, or sexual orientation, intimate sexual relationships are an important part of most people's lives. In some cases, though, challenges can arise. While new lovers might assume their passion will burn brightly forever, most couples find that their sexual interest and passion decline over time (Impett et al., 2008, 2010). In some cases, sexual discomfort or dysfunction will test couples' relationship. In others, managing issues related to consent or sexually transmitted diseases will create difficulties. Let's take a look at each of these factors that contribute to satisfaction in sexual relationships.

Sexual script An unspoken mental plan that defines a "plot," dialogue, and actions expected to take place in a sexual encounter.

Fostering Positive Sexual Relationships

Nurturing passion does take effort, plus a willingness to resolve other types of problems in a relationship (Strong, DeVault, & Cohen, 2011). For example, conflict or anger about other issues frequently takes a toll on sexual adjustment. Conversely, couples who share positive experiences and satisfying relationships also tend to have satisfying sex lives (Algoe, Gable, & Maisel, 2010). Sex is not a performance or a skill to be mastered like playing tennis. It is a form of communication within a relationship. Couples with strong and caring relationships can usually remain passionate (Impett et al., 2010; Joel et al., 2013). Conversely, a couple with a satisfactory sex life but a poor relationship rarely stays together for long.

When disagreements arise over issues such as frequency of lovemaking, who initiates lovemaking, or what behavior is appropriate, the rule should be, "Each partner must accept the other as the final authority on his or her own feelings." Partners are urged to give feedback about their feelings by following what therapists call the "touch and ask" rule: Touching and caressing should often be followed by questions such as, "Does that feel good?" "Do you like that?" and so forth. Satisfying erotic relationships focus on enhancing sexual pleasure for both partners, not on selfish interest in one's own gratification (Carroll, 2016; Strong, DeVault, & Cohen, 2011).

When problems do arise, partners are urged to be *responsive* to each other's needs at an *emotional* level and to recognize that all sexual problems are *mutual.* "Failures" should always be shared without placing blame. It is particularly important to avoid the "numbers game"—that is, couples should avoid being influenced by statistics on the average frequency of lovemaking, by stereotypes about sexual potency, and by the media. It is especially important not to be overly influenced by the superhuman sexual exploits portrayed in pornographic media.

According to sex therapist Barry McCarthy, four elements are necessary for a continuing healthy sexual relationship:

1. *Sexual anticipation.* Looking forward to lovemaking can be inhibited by routine and poor communication between partners. It is wise for busy couples to set aside time to spend together. Unexpected, spontaneous lovemaking should also be encouraged.
2. *Valuing one's sexuality.* This is most likely to occur when you develop a respectful, trusting, and intimate relationship with your partner. Such relationships allow both partners to deal with negative sexual experiences when they occur.
3. *Believing that you deserve sexual pleasure.* As previously noted, the essence of satisfying lovemaking is the giving and receiving of pleasure.
4. *Valuing intimacy.* A sense of closeness and intimacy with one's partner helps maintain sexual desire, especially in long-term relationships (McCarthy, 1995; McCarthy & Fucito, 2005).

The last point—valuing intimacy—suggests that a good sex life requires couples to work hard at maintaining the relationship more generally. Indeed, a study that compared happy couples with unhappy couples found that, in almost every regard, the happy couples showed superior *communication* skills.

Good communication leads to good sex; poor communication leads to …

If you really want a good relationship, then, you can foster intimacy and communication by doing the following (Driver & Gottman, 2004; Gottman & Krokoff, 1989; Haas et al., 2007; Joel et al., 2013):

- **Be Open About Feelings.** Always be ready to talk with your partner. Happy couples not only talk more, they also convey more personal feelings and show greater sensitivity to their partners' feelings. Persistent negative feelings especially need to be expressed. Avoid *gunnysacking*—saving up feelings and complaints to use as ammunition in a fight. Gunnysacking is very destructive to a relationship.
- **Don't Be Defensive.** Own your s--t. Get comfortable with saying, "I'm sorry" when it's your fault. Whenever possible, expressions of negative feelings should be given as statements of one's own feelings, not as statements of blame. It is far more constructive to say, "It makes me angry when you leave things around the house," than it is to say, "You're a slob!" Remember, too, that if you use the words *always* or *never*, you are probably mounting a character attack.
- **Don't Be a "Right Fighter."** Constructive fights are aimed at resolving shared differences, not at establishing who is right or wrong, superior or inferior.
- **Recognize That Constructive Anger Is Appropriate.** A fight is a fight. As is the case with any other emotion in a relationship, anger should be expressed. However, it should be expressed constructively by sticking to the real issues. Destructive anger, such as "hitting below the belt" or resorting to threats, such as announcing, "This relationship is over," is damaging to relationships.
- **Try to See Things Through Your Partner's Eyes.** Marital harmony is closely related to the ability to put yourself in another person's place. When a conflict arises, always pause to try to take your partner's perspective. Seeing things through your partner's eyes can be a good reminder that no one is ever totally right or wrong in a personal dispute.

- **Don't Be a Mind-Reader.** The preceding suggestion should not be taken as an invitation to engage in mind-reading. Assuming that you know what your partner is thinking or feeling can muddle or block communication. Hostile or accusatory mind-reading, as in the following examples, can be very disruptive: "You're just looking for an excuse to criticize me, aren't you?" "You don't really want my mother to visit, or you wouldn't say that." Rather than *telling* your partner what she or he thinks, *ask* her or him.

If it seems to you that following these guidelines requires expending some serious energy, you are right. Falling in love may be as easy as falling off a log; staying in love is more challenging, but well worth the effort.

Sexual Dysfunctions

Even the best-intentioned couples who work hard at staying intimate may nevertheless experience **sexual dysfunctions**, which are far more common than many people realize. In general, people who seek sexual counseling have one or more of the following types of problems (American Psychiatric Association, 2013; Crooks & Baur, 2017):

1. **Desire disorders:** The person has either little or no sexual motivation or desire, or has too much.
2. **Arousal disorders:** The person desires sexual activity but does not become sexually aroused.
3. **Orgasm disorders:** The person does not have orgasms or experiences orgasm too soon or too late.
4. **Sexual pain disorders:** The person experiences pain that makes lovemaking uncomfortable or impossible.

There was a time when people suffered such problems in silence. However, in recent years, effective treatments have been found for many complaints (Carroll, 2016). Medical treatments or drugs (such as Viagra for men) may be helpful for sexual problems that clearly have physical causes. In other cases, counseling or psychotherapy may be the best approach. Let's briefly investigate the nature, causes, and treatments of sexual dysfunctions.

Desire Disorders

Desire disorders, like most sexual problems, must be defined in relation to a person's age, sex, partner, expectations, and sexual history. It is not at all unusual for a person to briefly lose sexual desire. Typically, erotic feelings return when anger toward a partner fades, or fatigue, illness, and similar temporary problems end. Under what circumstances, then, is loss of desire a dysfunction? First, the loss of desire must be *persistent.* Second, the person must be *troubled by it.* When these two conditions are met, **hypoactive sexual desire** is said to exist. Diminished desire can apply to both sexes. However, it is somewhat more common in women (Bitzer, Giraldi, & Pfaus, 2013; Segraves & Woodard, 2006).

Some people don't merely lack sexual desire; they are *repelled* by sex and seek to avoid it. A person who suffers from a *sexual aversion* feels fear, anxiety, or disgust about engaging in sex. Often, the afflicted person still has some erotic feelings. For example, he or she may still masturbate or have sexual fantasies. Nevertheless, the prospect of having sex with another person causes panic or revulsion. People with sexual aversions may be diagnosed with a *sexual dysfunction not otherwise specified* (American Psychiatric Association, 2013).

Sexual desire disorders are common. Possible physical causes include illness, fatigue, hormonal difficulties, and the side effects of medicines. Desire disorders also are associated with psychological factors such as depression, fearing loss of control over sexual urges, strict religious beliefs, fear of pregnancy, marital conflict, fear of closeness, and simple loss of attraction to one's partner (King, 2012).

Isn't it possible for someone to experience too much sexual desire? Yes it is. Some psychologists consider *hypersexual disorder*—an excess of sexual desire—to be a legitimate diagnosis, although it is not included in the manual that clinicians use to diagnose psychological disorders (Reid et al., 2012). Again, the excess must be *persistent* and the person must be *troubled by it.* Plagued by intense and recurrent sexual fantasies, urges, and/or behaviors, people with hypersexual disorder are sometimes described as *sex addicts* (Kafka, 2010).

In terms of treatment, it's important to note that desire disorders are complex. Unless they have a straightforward physical cause, they are difficult to treat. Desire disorders are often deeply rooted in a person's childhood, sexual history, personality, and relationships. In such instances, counseling or psychotherapy is recommended (King, 2012).

Arousal Disorders

A person with an arousal disorder experiences little or no physical arousal. Both men and women can experience arousal disorder—let's take a look at each one separately.

Erectile Disorder

Most men with an arousal disorder usually have an inability to maintain an erection but nevertheless desire sex, a condition referred to as **erectile disorder**. This problem, which also is known as *erectile dysfunction*, was once referred to as *impotence.* However, psychologists now discourage use of the term impotence because of its many negative connotations.

Erectile disorders can be primary or secondary. Men suffering from primary erectile dysfunction have never had an erection. Those who previously performed successfully but then developed a problem suffer from secondary erectile dysfunction. Either way, persistent erectile difficulties tend to be very disturbing to the man and his sexual partner (Gambescia & Weeks, 2015).

It is important to recognize that occasional erectile problems are normal. In fact, "performance demands" or overreaction to the temporary loss of an erection may generate fears and doubts that contribute to a further inhibition of arousal (Thompson &

Sexual dysfunctions Problems with sexual desire, arousal, or response.

Hypoactive sexual desire A persistent, upsetting loss of sexual desire.

Erectile disorder An inability to maintain an erection for lovemaking.

Barnes, 2012). At such times, it is particularly important for the man's partner to avoid expressing anger, disappointment, or embarrassment. Patient reassurance helps prevent the establishment of a vicious cycle.

How often must a man experience failure for a problem to exist? Erectile disorder involves a persistent difficulty of at least six months' duration, although ultimately, only the man and his partner can make this judgment (American Psychiatric Association, 2013). Repeated erectile dysfunction should therefore be distinguished from *occasional* erectile problems. Fatigue, anger, anxiety, and drinking too much alcohol can cause temporary erectile difficulties in healthy males. True erectile disorders typically persist for months or years (Rowland, 2007).

What causes erectile disorders? Roughly 40 percent of all cases are *organic*, or physically caused. The origin of the remaining cases is **psychogenic** (a result of emotional factors). Even when erectile dysfunction is organic, however, it is almost always made worse by anxiety, anger, and dejection. If a man can have an erection at times other than lovemaking (during sleep, for instance), the problem probably is not physical.

Organic erectile problems have many causes. Typical sources of trouble include alcohol or drug abuse, diabetes, vascular disease, prostate and urological disorders, neurological problems, and reactions to medication for high blood pressure, heart disease, or stomach ulcers. Erectile problems also are a normal part of aging. As men grow older, they typically experience a decline in sexual desire and arousal and an increase in sexual dysfunction (Albersen, Orabi, & Lue, 2012).

Secondary erectile disorders may be related to anxiety about sex in general, guilt because of an extramarital affair, resentment or hostility toward a sexual partner, fear of inability to perform, concerns about STDs, and similar emotions and conflicts. Often the problem starts with repeated sexual failures caused by drinking too much alcohol or by premature ejaculation. In any event, initial doubts soon become severe fears of failure—which further inhibit sexual response.

In terms of treatment, drugs or surgery may be used in medical treatment of organic erectile disorders. The drug Viagra is successful for about 70 to 80 percent of men with erectile disorders. However, fixing the "hydraulics" of erectile problems may not be enough to end the problem. Effective treatment should also include counseling to remove fears and psychological blocks (Gambescia & Weeks, 2015). It is important for the man to also regain confidence, improve his relationship with his partner, and learn better lovemaking skills. To free him of conflicts, the man and his partner may be assigned a series of exercises to perform. This technique, called **sensate focus**, directs attention to natural sensations of pleasure and builds communication skills (Weeks & Gambescia, 2009).

In sensate focus, the couple is told to take turns caressing various parts of each other's bodies. They are further instructed to carefully avoid any genital contact. Instead, they are to concentrate on giving pleasure and on signaling what feels good to them. This takes the pressure to perform off the man and allows him to learn to give pleasure as a means of receiving it. For many men, sensate focus is a better solution than depending on an expensive drug to perform sexually.

Over a period of days or weeks, the couple proceeds to more intense physical contact involving the breasts and genitals. As inhibitions are reduced and natural arousal begins to replace fear, the successful couple moves on to mutually satisfying lovemaking.

Female Sexual Interest/Arousal Disorder

Because most women with sexual arousal problems also experience a lack of sexual desire, they are usually diagnosed with **female sexual interest/arousal disorder**. Such women respond with little or no physical arousal to sexual stimulation (American Psychiatric Association, 2013). As in the male, female sexual arousal disorder may be primary or secondary. Also, it is again important to remember that all women occasionally experience inhibited arousal. In some instances, the problem may reflect nothing more than a lack of sufficient sexual stimulation before attempting lovemaking (King, 2012).

The causes of inhibited arousal in women are similar to those seen in men. Sometimes the problem is medical, being related to illness or the side effects of medicines or contraceptives. Psychological factors include anxiety, anger or hostility toward one's partner, depression, stress, or distracting worries (Basson & Brotto, 2009). Some women can trace their arousal difficulties to frightening childhood experiences, such as molestations, incestuous relations, a harsh religious background in which sex was considered evil, or cold, unloving childhood relationships. Also common are a need to maintain control over emotions, deep-seated conflicts over being female, and extreme distrust of others, especially males.

For women, treatment for arousal disorder typically includes sensate focus, genital stimulation by the woman's partner, and "nondemanding" intercourse controlled by the woman (Segraves & Althof, 2002). With success in these initial stages, full, mutual, intercourse is gradually introduced. As sexual training proceeds, psychological conflicts and dynamics typically appear, and as they do, they are treated in separate counseling sessions.

Orgasm Disorders

A person suffering from an orgasm disorder either fails to reach orgasm during sexual activity or reaches orgasm too soon or too late (Regev, Zeiss, & Zeiss, 2006). Notice that such disorders are very much based on expectations. For instance, if a man experiences delayed orgasm, one couple might define it as a problem, but another might welcome it. It also is worth noting again that some women rarely or never have orgasm and still find sex pleasurable (King, 2012).

Female Orgasmic Disorder

The most prevalent sexual complaint among women is a persistent inability to reach orgasm during lovemaking (McCabe, 2015). It is often clear in **female orgasmic disorder** that the woman is not completely unresponsive. Rather, she is unresponsive in the context of a relationship—she may easily reach orgasm by masturbation but not during lovemaking with her partner.

Then, couldn't the woman's partner be at fault? Sex therapists try to avoid finding fault or placing blame. However, it is true that the woman's partner must be committed to ensuring her gratification. Roughly two-thirds of all women need direct stimulation of the clitoris to reach orgasm. Therefore, some apparent instances of female orgasmic disorder can be traced to inadequate stimulation or faulty technique on the part of the woman's partner. Even when this is true, sexual adjustment difficulties are best viewed as a problem the couple shares, not just as "the woman's problem," "the man's problem," or "her partner's problem."

If we focus only on the woman, the most common source of orgasmic difficulties is overcontrol of the sexual response. Orgasm requires a degree of abandonment to erotic feelings. It is inhibited by ambivalence or hostility toward the relationship, by guilt, by fears of expressing sexual needs, and by tendencies to control and intellectualize erotic feelings. The woman is unable to let go and enjoy the flow of pleasurable sensations (Segraves & Althof, 2002).

In treatment, anorgasmic women (those who do not have orgasms) are first trained to focus on their sexual responsiveness through masturbation or vigorous stimulation by a partner. As the woman becomes consistently orgasmic in these circumstances, her responsiveness is gradually transferred to lovemaking with her partner. Couples also typically learn alternative positions and techniques of lovemaking designed to increase clitoral stimulation. At the same time, communication between partners is stressed, especially with reference to the woman's expectations, motivations, and preferences (Kelly, Strassberg, & Turner, 2006).

Delayed Ejaculation

Among males, delay or absence of orgasm was once considered a rare problem. But milder forms of **delayed ejaculation** account for increasing numbers of clients seeking therapy (Foley & Gambescia, 2015). Typical background factors are strict religious training, fear of impregnating, lack of interest in the sexual partner, symbolic inability to give of oneself, unacknowledged same-sex attraction, or the recent occurrence of traumatic life events. Power and commitment struggles within relationships may be important added factors.

Treatment for delayed ejaculation consists of sensate focus, manual stimulation by the man's partner (which is designed to orient the male to his partner as a source of pleasure), and stimulation to the point of orgasm followed by immediate intercourse and ejaculation. Treatment also focuses on resolving personal conflicts and marital difficulties underlying the problem (Waldinger, 2009).

Premature (Early) Ejaculation

Premature ejaculation exists when it occurs reflexively or the man cannot tolerate high levels of excitement at the plateau stage of arousal. Basically, ejaculation is premature if it consistently occurs before the man and his partner want it to occur (McMahon et al., 2013).

Do many men have difficulties with premature ejaculation? Approximately 50 percent of young adult men have problems with premature ejaculation. Theories advanced to explain it have ranged from the idea that it may represent hostility toward the man's sexual partner (because it deprives the partner of satisfaction) to the suggestion that most early male sexual experiences (such as those taking place in the backseat of a car and masturbation) tend to encourage rapid climax. Excessive arousal and anxiety over performance are usually present. Also, some men simply engage in techniques that maximize sensation and make rapid orgasm inevitable.

Ejaculation is a reflex. To control it, a man must learn to recognize the physical signals that it is about to occur. Some men have simply never learned to be aware of these signals. Whatever the causes, premature ejaculation can be a serious difficulty, especially in the context of long-term relationships (King, 2012).

The most common treatment for premature ejaculation is a "stop–start" procedure called the **squeeze technique** (Grenier & Byers, 1995). The man's sexual partner stimulates him manually until he signals that ejaculation is about to occur. The man's partner then firmly squeezes the tip of his penis to inhibit orgasm. When the man feels that he has control, stimulation is repeated. Later, the squeeze technique is used during lovemaking. Gradually, the man acquires the ability to delay orgasm sufficiently for mutually satisfactory lovemaking. During treatment, skills that improve communication between partners are developed, along with a better understanding of the male's sexual response cues (McCarthy & Fucito, 2005).

Sexual Pain Disorders

Pain in the genitals before, during, or after sexual intercourse, called *dyspareunia* (DIS-pah-ROO-nee-ah), is rare in males. In females, this problem is often related to *vaginismus* (VAJ-ih-NIS-mus), a condition in which muscle spasms of the vagina prevent intercourse (Binik, 2010). Together, these disorders constitute the major symptoms of **genito-pelvic pain/penetration disorder** (American Psychiatric Association, 2013).

Genito-pelvic pain/penetration disorder is often accompanied by obvious fears of intercourse, and where fear is absent, high levels of anxiety are present (Cherner & Reissing, 2013). This disorder, therefore, appears to often be a phobic response to intercourse. Predictably, its causes include experiences of painful intercourse, rape or other brutal and frightening sexual encounters, fear of men and of penetration, misinformation about sex (belief that it is injurious), fear of pregnancy, and fear of the specific male partner (Borg et al., 2012).

Psychogenic Having psychological origins, rather than physical causes.

Sensate focus A form of therapy that directs a couple's attention to natural sensations of sexual pleasure.

Female sexual interest/arousal disorder A lack of interest in sex, lack of physical arousal to sexual stimulation, or both.

Female orgasmic disorder A persistent inability to reach orgasm during lovemaking.

Delayed ejaculation A persistent delay or absence of orgasm during lovemaking.

Premature ejaculation Ejaculation that consistently occurs before the man and his partner want it to occur.

Squeeze technique A method for inhibiting ejaculation by compressing the tip of the penis.

Genito-pelvic pain/penetration disorder A sexual pain disorder in women involving dyspareunia (genital pain before, during, or after sexual intercourse), usually accompanied by vaginismus (muscle spasms of the vagina).

Treatment of genito-pelvic pain/penetration disorder is similar to what might be done for a nonsexual phobia. It includes extinction of conditioned muscle spasms by progressive relaxation of the vagina, desensitization of fears of intercourse, and masturbation or manual stimulation to associate pleasure with sexual approach by the woman's partner (Bergeron & Lord, 2003). Hypnosis also has been used successfully in some cases (Roja & Roja, 2010).

Atypical Sexual Behavior

Though some people still have fairly strict ideas about what sex "should" be like, these standards are often at odds with our society's private behavior. Just as the hunger drive is expressed and satisfied in many ways, the sex drive also leads to an immense range of behaviors. In this section, we'll take a closer look at *paraphilia*, or sexual arousal that comes about in response to atypical people, situations, objects, or behaviors. Some people refer to these as fetishes.

I just read Fifty Shades of Grey *after seeing the movie and really liked it. Is something wrong with me?* For those of you who might not know, this is a wildly successful novel (and film) about bondage/discipline, dominance/submission, and sadism/masochism (BDSM) (Bloom & Bloom, 2012). At one time, engaging in unusual sexual behaviors such as *sadism* (deriving sexual pleasure from inflicting pain, humiliation, or both) and *masochism* (desiring pain, humiliation, or both as part of the sex act) was viewed as evidence of a psychiatric disorder. More recently, however, we have witnessed a growing social consensus that a person who is aroused by, or engages in, unusual sexual practices like BDSM does not automatically suffer from a psychiatric disorder (American Psychiatric Association, 2013).

Today, people are usually diagnosed with a **paraphilic disorder** (PAIR-eh-FIL-ick) only if it involves engaging in sexual practices *that typically cause guilt, anxiety, or discomfort for one or more participants.* For example, most sadists and masochists voluntarily associate with people who share their sexual interests. Thus, their behavior may not harm anyone, except when it is extreme. While some people may see even casual experimentation with deviant sexual behaviors as immoral or odd, and while local laws may criminalize such behaviors, psychologically, the mark of true sexual disorders is that they are compulsive, destructive, and/or cause people to feel guilt or anxiety.

The paraphilic disorders listed in ▲ Table 11.2 cover a wide variety of behaviors (Balon, 2016b). Two of the most common are pedophilia and exhibitionism.

Pedophilia/Child Molestation

The psychiatric label for child molestation is *pedophilic disorder* (American Psychiatric Association, 2013; Strickland, 2015). Child molesters, or pedophiles, are usually males, most are married, and two-thirds are fathers. Many molesters are rigid, passive, puritanical, or religious. They are often consumers of child pornography (Seto, Cantor, & Blanchard, 2006). As children, child molesters themselves were often witnesses to or victims of sexual abuse (Cohen et al., 2010; Nunes et al., 2013). Molesters also are often thought of as child rapists, but most molestations rarely exceed fondling (Seto, 2008, 2009).

Child molesters are sometimes pictured as "grabbers," despicable perverts lurking in dark alleys, seeking their prey. In fact, most are "groomers," gradually insinuating themselves into the trust of children and their families (van Dam, 2006). As such, they are usually friends, acquaintances, or relatives of the child (Abel, Wiegel, & Osborn, 2007).

How serious are the effects of a molestation? The impact varies widely. It is affected by how long the abuse lasts, the identity of the abuser, and whether genital sexual acts are involved. Many authorities believe that a single incident of fondling by a relative stranger is unlikely to cause severe emotional harm to a child. For most children, the event is frightening but not a lasting trauma (Rind, Tromovitch, & Bauserman, 1998). That's why parents are urged not to overreact to such incidents or to become hysterical. Doing so only further frightens the child. This by no means

▲ Table 11.2 Paraphilic Disorders

Focus of Paraphilia	Paraphilic Disorder	Primary Symptom
Nonhuman objects	Fetishistic disorder	Sexual arousal associated with inanimate objects
	Transvestic disorder	Achieving sexual arousal by wearing clothing of the opposite sex
Nonconsenting people	Exhibitionistic disorder	"Flashing," or displaying the genitals to unwilling viewers
	Voyeuristic disorder	"Peeping," or viewing the genitals of others without their permission
	Frotteuristic disorder	Sexually touching or rubbing against a nonconsenting person, usually in a public place such as a subway
	Pedophilic disorder	Sex with children or child molesting
Pain or humiliation	Sexual masochism disorder	Desiring pain, humiliation, or both as part of the sex act
	Sexual sadism disorder	Deriving sexual pleasure from inflicting pain, humiliation, or both

Adapted from the American Psychiatric Association (2013); Sue et al. (2016).

implies, however, that parents should ignore hints from a child that a molestation may have occurred.

Parents should watch for the following hints of trouble:

1. Unusual avoidance of, or interest in, sexual matters
2. Secretiveness (including about Internet access)
3. Emotional disturbances such as depression, irritability, or withdrawal from family, friends, or school
4. Nightmares or other sleep problems
5. Misbehavior, such as unusual aggressiveness, suicidal behavior, or unusual risk-taking, such as riding a bicycle dangerously in traffic
6. Loss of self-esteem or self-worth

(Adapted from American Academy of Child and Adolescent Psychiatry, 2014)

How can children protect themselves? Children should be taught to shout "No!" if an adult tries to engage them in sexual activity. If children are asked to keep a secret, they should reply that they don't keep secrets. Parents and children also need to be aware that the Internet gives pedophiles an easy way to make contact with children. If an adult suggests to a child online that they could meet in person, the child should immediately tell his or her parents.

It also helps if children know the tactics typically used by molesters. Interviews with convicted sex offenders revealed the following (Elliott, Browne, & Kilcoyne, 1995; van Dam, 2006):

1. Most molesters act alone.
2. Most assaults take place in the abuser's home.
3. Many abusers gain access to the child through caretaking.
4. Children are targeted at first through bribes, gifts, and games.
5. The abuser tries to lull the child into participation through talking about sex and through persuasion. (This can take place through email or chat rooms on the Internet.)
6. The abuser then uses force, anger, threats, and bribes to gain continued compliance.

Repeated molestations, those that involve force or threats, those that are perpetuated by trusted caregivers, and incidents that exceed fondling can leave lasting emotional scars. As adults, many victims of incest or molestation develop sexual phobias. For them, lovemaking may evoke vivid and terrifying memories of the childhood victimization. Serious harm is especially likely to occur if the molester is someone whom the child deeply trusts. Molestations by parents, close relatives, teachers, priests, youth leaders, and similar persons can be quite damaging. In such cases, professional counseling is often needed (American Academy of Child and Adolescent Psychiatry, 2014).

Exhibitionism

The psychiatric label for exhibitionism is *exhibitionistic disorder* (American Psychiatric Association, 2013). Exhibitionism, or indecent exposure, is a common disorder (Sue et al., 2016). Between one-third and two-thirds of all sexual arrests are for "flashing." Exhibitionists also have high repeat rates among sexual offenders. Although it was long thought that exhibitionists are basically harmless, research has shown that many exhibitionists go on to commit more serious sexual crimes and other offenses (Bader et al., 2008; Firestone et al., 2006).

Exhibitionists are typically male and married, and most come from strict and repressive backgrounds. Most of them feel a deep sense of inadequacy, which produces a compulsive need to prove their "manhood" by frightening women (Murphy & Page, 2008). In general, a woman confronted by an exhibitionist can assume that his goal is to shock and alarm her. By becoming visibly upset, she actually encourages him (Sue et al., 2016).

Sexual Harassment

Sexual harassment has been defined as a situation in which unwanted sexual comments, gestures, or actions are directed at people because of their biological sex, expression of their gender identity, or sexual orientation (Burn, 2019). Researchers have noted that there are three main behaviors associated with sexual harassment: unwanted *sexual attention* (inappropriate touching, making suggestive comments), *sexual coercion* (requiring sexual favors in exchange for benefits or rewards), and *gender harassment* (insulting or degrading behaviors that focus on a person's gender expression or sexual orientation) (Fitzgerald, Swan, & Magley, 1997).

The #metoo movement brought the prevalence of sexual harassment into sharp relief. In the workplace and online, for example, nationally representative surveys suggest that 22 percent of women and 8 percent of men have been victims of sexual harassment, and numbers are higher among vulnerable groups such as minorities (Duggan, 2017; Parker & Funk, 2017). And it's clear that adults are not the only targets: A large proportion of high-school and college students have also reported such experiences (Hill & Kearl, 2011; Wolff, Rospenda, & Colaneri, 2017). Unfortunately, given that some people are reluctant to report harassing behaviors, these numbers may underestimate the problem.

Victims of sexual harassment experience a number of consequences (Burn, 2019). Some are emotional, including feelings of embarrassment, stress, frustration, and fear. Sexual harassment can also diminish people's confidence, making it difficult for them to achieve their full potential at work or at school. Mental health issues are also common, including disordered eating, depression, and anxiety. But it's worth noting that not all of the consequences are experienced by individuals. Organizations revealed to have a culture of sexual harassment will also experience costs, including the loss of revenue and reputation (Quick & McFadyen, 2017).

What can be done? Burn (2019) reviews a number of possibilities, including changing organizational culture through training, clear anti-harassment policies, and reporting processes for victims that prevent retaliation. Unfortunately, policies on their own cannot stop the problem: Effective control of sexual harassment in the workplace also requires the support of senior managers who understand the severity of the problem and the importance of controlling it. At the individual level, researchers have suggested training programs that focus on changing social norms, developing empathy for victims, and promoting bystander intervention.

Paraphilic disorders Deviations in sexual behavior such as pedophilia, exhibitionism, fetishism, voyeurism, and so on.

In the end, sexual harassment is not something that must be confronted only by its victims—it's a societal issue for which we all have some responsibility.

Sexual Consent and the Crime of Rape

It is estimated that nearly 20 percent of all American women will be raped in their lifetimes. The rate is much lower among men, but the crime is no less serious or traumatic when the victim is a man (Coxell & King, 2010). Although it is commonly believed that rapists are usually strangers to their victims, nothing could be further from the truth—rape is much more likely to happen in the context of relationships (Breiding et al., 2014; Martin, Taft, & Resick, 2007). It has been found that 85 percent of American women who have been sexually or physically assaulted reported that the perpetrator was a husband, intimate partner, or acquaintance. Similarly, about one-half of rapes committed against college students can be classified as **acquaintance (date) rape**, forced intercourse that occurs in the context of a date or other voluntary encounter. In other words, they were carried out by first dates, casual dates, or romantic acquaintances (Fisher, Cullen, & Daigle, 2005).

The laws that govern rape can differ by state, and some have done away with the term rape, instead using terms such as *sexual assault*. The FBI defines rape as "penetration, no matter how slight, of the vagina or anus with any body part or object, or oral penetration by a sex organ of another person, without the consent of the victim." It's worth noting that more recently, the definition of rape has become broader, such that it now includes unwanted sex that results from perpetrator threats to harm the victim (or the victim's family or friends), as well as situations in which victims cannot provide consent because they are unconscious or impaired in some way. Previously, the primary focus was on **forcible rape**, which is rape that results in bodily injury. Most psychologists no longer think of forcible rape as a primarily sexual act. Rather, it is an act of brutality or aggression based on the need to control others.

Typical aftereffects for rape victims include rage, guilt, depression, loss of self-esteem, shame, sexual adjustment problems, and, in many cases, a lasting mistrust of male–female relationships (Littleton & Breitkopf, 2006). The impact is so great that victims continue to report fear, anxiety, and sexual dysfunction a year or two after being raped. Even years later, rape survivors are more likely to suffer from depression, alcohol or drug abuse, and other emotional problems.

Rape Myths

Rape is related to traditional gender role socialization. Traditional feminine stereotypes include the idea that women should not show direct interest in sex. Traditional masculine stereotypes, on the other hand, include the ideas that a man should take the initiative and persist in attempts at sexual intimacy—even when the woman says no. In general, research has confirmed a link between acceptance of rape myths and sexual violence toward women (Chapleau & Oswald, 2010; Ryan, 2011).

In a classic experimental confirmation of the hypothesis that stereotyped images contribute to rape, male college students were classified as either high or low in gender role stereotyping. Each student then read one of three stories: The first described voluntary intercourse; the second depicted stranger rape; and the third described date rape. As predicted, college males high in gender role stereotyping were more aroused by the rape stories.

Further, because of these stereotypes, men who commit marital or date rape often believe that they have done nothing wrong. One study of college men found that many tend to blame *women* for date rape. According to them, women who are raped by an acquaintance actually wanted to have sex. A typical explanation is, "Her words were saying no, but her body was saying yes." This is just one example of several widely held beliefs that qualify as **rape myths** (Hayes, Abbott, & Cook, 2016; Suarez & Gadalla, 2010). All of these statements are also myths:

- A woman who appears alone in public and dresses attractively is "asking for it."
- When a woman says no, she really means yes.
- Many women who are raped actually enjoy it.
- If a woman goes home with a man on a first date, she is interested in sex.
- If a woman is sexually active, she is probably lying if she says she was raped.

Men who believe rape myths are more likely to misread a woman's resistance to unwanted sexual advances, assuming that she really means yes when she says no (Forbes, Adams-Curtis, & White, 2004). Men who believe rape myths and who have been drinking are especially likely to ignore signals that a woman wants sexual advances to stop (Chapleau & Oswald, 2010).

In view of such findings, perhaps the time has come for our culture to make it crystal clear that no means *no*. Educating men about rape myths has been one of the most successful ways of preventing sexual assault (King, 2012).

Reflective Practice

Sexual Relationships

1. Rape myths are related to ______ ______ ______ ______.
2. Sensate focus is the most common treatment for premature ejaculation. T or F?
3. Sexual adjustment is best viewed as a relationship issue, not just one partner's problem. T or F?
4. The term *gunnysacking* refers to the constructive practice of hiding anger until it is appropriate to express it. T or F?
5. A person is usually diagnosed with a paraphilic disorder only if he or she is engaging in an illegal sexual act. T or F?
6. Wanting to practice safe sex is an insult to your lover. T or F?

THINK CRITICALLY

7. Who would you expect to have the most frequent sex and the most satisfying sex, hook-up couples or committed couples?

SELF-REFLECT

- To what extent do movies, music videos, and video games contribute directly to the perpetuation of rape myths? What about indirectly, by portraying gender role stereotypes?
- In plain language, sexual disorders can be summarized this way: The person doesn't want to do it. The person wants to do it but can't get aroused. The person wants to do it, gets aroused, but has problems with orgasm. The person wants to do it and gets aroused, but lovemaking is uncomfortable. What are the formal terms for each of these situations?

Answers: 1. traditional gender role stereotypes 2. F 3. T 4. F 5. F 6. F 7. Contrary to mass-media portrayals of sexy hook-ups, committed couples have better sex and overall well-being (Bersamin et al., 2014). Greater opportunity, plus familiarity with a partner's needs and preferences, probably accounts for these findings.

11.5 Psychology and Your Skill Set: Civic Engagement

GATEWAYS LEARNING OUTCOMES:
After reading this section you should be able to:

11.5.1 Explain what is meant by civic engagement

11.5.2 Outline the individual and societal benefits associated with civic engagement

11.5.3 Create a plan to become more civically engaged

Some of you will know of Laverne Cox. She starred in a popular Netflix series, and was the first openly transgender person of color to appear on the cover of *Time* magazine. Perhaps just as importantly, though, she joins Lady Gaga, Harry Hay, and Harvey Milk (portrayed by Sean Penn in the movie *Milk*) as an advocate who has worked hard to advance the rights of the LGBTQ community. The efforts of these individuals and millions of others have moved the United States past the period when same-sex relationships were defined as both illegal and deviant. And while there is still much work to do in terms of equality, millions of Americans—both gay and straight—have already demonstrated that they are willing to step up and contribute to advancing this cause.

Being Civic-Minded

The gay rights movement is just one of many social issues that groups of Americans have come together to support. Historically, we are all familiar with the work of those who understood the importance of civil rights and equality for women. More recently, Americans have joined forces to raise awareness about other important problems, including racial disparities faced by people of color, global warming

Lev Radin/Alamy Stock Photo

and the challenges faced by our war veterans. But the initiatives that Americans support aren't always global, or even national, in their reach: Local contributions such as participation in a religious community, volunteering at a school's breakfast program, or helping to rebuild a church destroyed by fire also bring people together to support the greater good.

Participation in these types of activities is commonly referred to as **civic engagement**, which is defined as "individual and collective actions designed to identify and address issues of public concern" (American Psychological Association, 2017a). In other words, it refers to people coming together to support an issue of importance to them, with the goal of improving communities either at the local, state, or federal level. Acts of civic engagement include those that raise awareness, as well as organizing or participating in fundraising activities. In some cases, people will also provide "hands on" help to build or create something, as is the case for those working for organizations such as Habitat for Humanity. In many instances, people are not paid for their efforts; instead, they volunteer their time because the cause is one that aligns with their values.

But civic engagement can also include political behavior. It involves everything from marching in rallies to support issues that you care about, to writing letters to elected officials at the federal, state, or local levels. An excellent example is the support demonstrated for the Black Lives Matter movement during the lead-up to

Acquaintance (date) rape Forced intercourse that occurs in the context of a date or other voluntary encounter.

Forcible rape Sexual intercourse carried out against the victim's will, under the threat of violence or bodily injury.

Rape myths False beliefs about rape that tend to blame the victim and increase the likelihood that some men will think that rape is justified.

Civic engagement Individual and collective actions designed to identify and address issues of public concern.

the 2020 election. In cases where the issue is one of great importance to you, this type of engagement might even mean becoming involved in politics yourself! At its most basic level, though, political engagement refers to Americans' right to vote in free elections, indicating their support for issues and political candidates whose platforms are in keeping with their own values.

Benefits of Civic Engagement

The struggle to advance important causes is often difficult and can sometimes require many years of sustained effort. Is it worth it? Researchers from psychology and other disciplines suggest that the answer is yes (Pancer, 2015). At the broader level of both countries and communities, research suggests that the benefits of civic engagement include greater overall health and well-being of citizens, lower rates of crime, greater economic prosperity, and more effective government. But there are also individual psychological benefits that can be derived from social and political involvement. For example, young people who are civically engaged are more likely to have higher self-esteem and better relationships with others. They are also less likely to engage in risky behaviors (e.g., smoking, excessive drug and alcohol use, unprotected sex), or delinquent behaviors such as vandalism or theft. The benefits of community and political engagement that are experienced by young people often carry over into adulthood: Adults who are actively involved in causes that matter to them have similarly high self-esteem and positive social relationships, and they also appear to experience better physical and mental health as they grow older.

Skilled Civic Engagement

It's clear that civic engagement has positive benefits for individuals in terms of their health and well-being. But it's also the case that contributing to important causes can enhance your professional life as well. Employers often see volunteering as a positive sign that you are prepared to act on your values and make a commitment to working with others toward a positive goal (Hirst, 2001). Not surprisingly, these are the same kinds of behaviors that they hope to see in their employees.

But volunteering and political action can be helpful above and beyond simply "looking good on a resume." Given the broad scope of activities that we've been discussing, it probably won't surprise you to learn that there's a broad set of skills associated with civic engagement (Bussell & Forbes, 2002; Kirlin, 2002). For example, people need to take the time to inform themselves about causes and key issues so that they can make informed choices when voting, or when making decisions about the organizations that they will support through donations or volunteering. This requires the kinds of critical thinking skills that were discussed in Sections 1.5 and 1.8, and it pushes people to think about the issues in relation to their own personal values (■ Section 3.5). Helping to persuade others about the importance of a cause also requires good communication skills (■ Section 4.7); working with others on such projects requires a good understanding of diversity (■ Section 17.4), teamwork (■ Section 16.4), and, in some cases, leadership skills (■ Section 12.5).

Generation Me or We?

Given all of its personal and professional benefits, it's interesting that much has been written about the decline of civic engagement among adolescents and young adults (Putnam, 2000). Some have described this current cohort of high school and college students as "Generation Me." For example, Twenge (2014) has claimed that they are more lazy, self-entitled, and narcissistic than any generation that has come before. Others have strongly disagreed, suggesting that this group of young people is *more* engaged than older adults were at the same age, and have correspondingly referred to them as "Generation We."

It turns out that the picture may be somewhat more complicated than either one of these alternatives. In general, it does seem to be true that young people are showing up in increasingly smaller numbers to vote in elections (though the 2004, 2008, and 2020 presidential elections were an exception to this trend). However, though young adults do seem less inclined than their parents and grandparents to go to the polls, they are still very active in social causes that matter to them, and they report volunteering more than their parents' generation (Twenge, Campbell, & Freeman, 2012).

Arnett (2010) has suggested that this may reflect the fact that the current generation of young adults demonstrates less prejudice with respect to characteristics such as race and sexual orientation. Others have noted that newer technologies including social media have led teenagers and young adults to think about both "engagement" and "community" in a different way (Nelson et al., 2016). While previous generations typically associated the idea of community with the physical location where they lived, easy access to the Internet means that today's communities can be virtual and might include people who share similar beliefs but live in countries around the world.

The increasing use of social media by young adults to communicate with others means that they can contribute to initiatives much further from home, and demonstrate social responsibility in ways that are very different from those available to older adults when they were young. A good example was the movement to raise awareness about climate change, which took root when Swedish teen Greta Thunberg forcefully criticized governments across the world for failing to curb greenhouse gases. Speaking at

Matthew Kaplan/Alamy Stock Photo

conferences and the United Nations, she called for young people to demand action—and they responded.

In cities across the United States, twitter hashtags and numerous Facebook pages began to spring up as students learned more about the issue. Effective use of web-based resources helped to mobilize other young people (as well as some older ones!) across the globe. The result was the Global Climate Strike—7.6 million people marching in the streets of 185 countries over 7 days to protest government inaction on this very important issue. Generation We? Sounds more like Generation We Can Do It.

Reflective Practice

Psychology and Your Skill Set: Civic Engagement

1. Civic engagement includes both volunteering and political actions, such as voting. T or F?
2. Civic engagement benefits individuals, but has no effect on communities or nations. T or F?
3. Civic engagement helps with skill development. T or F?
4. All of the evidence to date suggests that young adults today demonstrate less civic engagement than their parents or grandparents. T or F?

THINK CRITICALLY

5. We saw that civic engagement is correlated with better physical and mental health for both younger and older individuals. What factors might contribute to this correlation?

SELF-REFLECT

- Which particular issues are important to you? Have you considered how you might act on this issue to bring about positive change?

Answers: 1. T 2. F 3. T 4. F 5. It might be tempting to slip into causal thinking here, and assume that activities like volunteering cause you to be healthier, but we know that we can't infer causality from correlations. It's also possible that the relationship might be exactly the opposite: Healthier people are more likely to be civically engaged—does this seem plausible?

CHAPTER IN REVIEW

Gateways to Sex, Gender, and Sexuality

Summary: Gateways Learning Outcomes

11.1 Sexual Development and Orientation

11.1.1 Describe the four basic dimensions of biological sex, including the role of hormones in shaping sexual development prenatally and postnatally

The four dimensions of biological sex are genetic sex, gonadal sex, hormonal sex, and genital sex. Sexual development begins with genetic sex (*XX* or *XY* chromosomes) and is then influenced by prenatal hormones, particularly androgens (male sex hormones) and estrogens (female sex hormones). One type of androgen, testosterone, is needed for a male embryo to develop male structures such as a penis and testicles. Sexual development in utero may be atypical when hormones are not present at the usual levels, or when the embryo is not sensitive to those hormones. For example, androgen insensitivity syndrome, exposure to progestin, congenital adrenal hyperplasia, and similar problems may result in the development of an intersex individual. Postnatally, estrogens and androgens influence the development of different primary and secondary sexual characteristics in males and females.

11.1.2 Define sexual orientation and outline its causes

Sexual orientation refers to one's degree of emotional and erotic attraction to members of the opposite sex, the same sex, both sexes, or neither sex. All four sexual orientations are part of the normal range of human variability. Sexual orientation tends to be stable over time even if sexual behaviors change. Similar factors (heredity, biology, and socialization) underlie all sexual orientations.

11.2 Gender Identities and Roles

11.2.1 Outline what is meant by gender identity, including the factors that influence it and what it means for an individual to be gender variant

Gender identity is the subjective sense of being male or female, irrespective of your biological sex. Many researchers believe that prenatal hormones exert a biological biasing effect that combines with social factors to influence gender identity. However, *gender role socialization* (that is, raising children to assume characteristics and roles that are seen as "appropriate" for their biological sex) seems to account for most observed female–male gender differences. Gender-variant individuals experience a persistent mismatch between their biological sex and their experienced gender.

11.2.2 Explain what is meant by the term gender role

The term gender role refers to a society's favored pattern of behavior for each sex. Traditionally, in Western culture, boys are encouraged to behave in ways that are strong and aggressive, while females are expected to behave in ways that are more gentle and caring. These gender roles may not be applicable in other cultures.

11.2.3 Define psychological androgyny and explain its advantages

People who possess both masculine and feminine traits are androgynous. In our society, androgyny allows for greater adaptability to a range of situations. This flexibility is helpful in relationships and is related to greater life satisfaction.

11.3 Sexual Responses, Attitudes, and Behaviors

11.3.1 Contrast females and males in terms of their sexual response

Sex is a powerful biological motive that finds expression in both men and women through various sexual behaviors, such as masturbation and intercourse. The similarities between female and male sexual responses and behaviors far outweigh the differences. For example, sexual arousal for both sexes is related to the body's erogenous zones, but mental and emotional reactions are the ultimate source of sexual responsiveness. In addition, the sexual response of both men and women can be divided into four phases: excitement, plateau, orgasm, and resolution, though women move through the stages more slowly than men. Finally, men and women are similar in the average number of partners they have, and in their overall pattern of sexual activity. The frequency of sexual behavior gradually declines for both sexes with increasing age. However, many elderly persons remain sexually active, and large variations exist at all ages.

11.3.2 Explain how sexual attitudes and behaviors have changed over time

Research suggests that people's attitudes about sex, including premarital sex, have become more tolerant. There is less of a double standard around the sexual behaviors of men and women, and people now report having more sexual partners. Young people, in particular, are more likely now than in the past to engage in casual sex. People have greater access to pornography through online websites. More liberal attitudes and behaviors related to sex mean that people increasingly must deal with sexually transmitted diseases such as HIV. Other industrialized nations have followed the same pattern while the developing nations remain more conservative.

11.4 Sexual Relationships

11.4.1 Outline the factors that contribute to healthy sexual relationships

Although solutions exist for many sexual adjustment problems, good communication and a healthy relationship are the real keys to sexual satisfaction. This includes being honest about your feelings, avoiding defensiveness, arguing constructively, trying to take your partner's perspective, and avoiding the tendency to know what your partner is thinking or feeling if you haven't asked.

11.4.2 Outline the most common sexual dysfunctions

Problems with sexual function can involve desire, arousal (e.g., erectile disorder, female arousal disorder), orgasm (female orgasmic disorder, delayed ejaculation, premature ejaculation), or pain. Behavioral methods and counseling techniques have been developed to alleviate many sexual problems.

11.4.3 Define what is meant by a paraphilic disorder, and provide some examples

Paraphilic disorders are compulsive sexual behaviors that tend to emotionally handicap people. The paraphilic disorders include pedophilia, exhibitionism, voyeurism, frotteurism, fetishism, sexual masochism, sexual sadism, and transvestic fetishism. The most common paraphilic disorders are pedophilia and exhibitionism.

11.4.4 Define what is meant by sexual harassment, and provide some examples

Sexual harassment refers to unwanted sexual comments, gestures, or actions that are directed at people because of their biological sex, gender identity, or sexual orientation. It may include unwanted sexual attention, sexual coercion, and gender harassment.

11.4.5 Define what constitutes rape, and what is meant by "rape myths"

Rape refers to situations that involve penetration of the vagina or anus without the consent of the victim. Rape includes unwanted sex that results from perpetrator threats to harm the victim (or the victim's family or friends), as well as situations in which victims cannot provide consent because they are unconscious or impaired in some way. Rape myths are false beliefs grounded in traditional gender role stereotypes. One example is the (false) belief that a man should persist in attempts at sexual intimacy—even when the woman says no.

11.5 Psychology and Your Skill Set: Civic Engagement

11.5.1 Explain what is meant by civic engagement

Civic engagement refers to individual and collective actions designed to identify and address issues of public concern. Acts of civic engagement include working to raise awareness about an issue, fundraising, providing labor or expertise to a cause, as well as political behaviors such as marching in rallies, writing letters to government officials, and voting.

11.5.2 Outline the individual and societal benefits associated with civic engagement

A society with civically engaged citizens is typically healthier, more economically prosperous, and has a lower crime rate. Individuals who are civically engaged have higher self-esteem, more positive social relationships, and better mental and physical health.

11.5.3 Create a plan to become more civically engaged

Being civically engaged begins with making sure that you are informed about the issues that are important in your community, state, and the country more broadly. Exercise your right to vote to demonstrate your commitment to those issues. Of course, civic engagement also includes helping with causes you feel are important. Today, young adults often use technology as a means of engaging with causes they care about, and this means that they can become involved with issues on a global scale. However, it's also effective to direct your energy toward more local causes by connecting with community agencies, charities, and churches. Regardless of which route you choose, we hope that after reading this section, you'll be better able to imagine how you can use your talents to help others.

12 Personality and Individual Differences

Rosem Morton/The New York Times/Redux

Gateway Theme Personality refers to the consistency we see in patterns of thinking, feeling, and behavior. Measures of personality reveal individual differences and help predict future behavior.

Chapter Outline

Stable or Changing?

Maurice Smith grew up in Harlem. At the time, crack and cocaine were the drugs of choice, and in his neighborhood you could find them on every corner. By the time he reached his early teens, he'd been arrested for possessing and selling drugs. When he was 19 years old, he shot and killed a man who was breaking into a friend's house in Baltimore. He pleaded guilty to a first-degree murder charge and was sentenced to 27 years in prison.

As you mull over this information, chances are good that you're beginning to form some impressions about Maurice Smith's personality. Do you imagine him to be impulsive? Aggressive? Quick-tempered? But what if we now told you that during his years in prison Maurice completed a college degree, and that two months after his release he graduated magna cum laude? Do you think that his personality changed during his incarceration? Or is it more the case that nothing at all had changed, but rather—as Maurice himself says—people could now "see what I always knew I was."

Without doubt, personality is an important part of our everyday lives. Falling in love, getting along with co-workers, coping with your zaniest relatives and, yes, earning a degree while serving time for murder, all shine a spotlight on our personalities. But what is personality? Can we measure it? Is it stable, or can it change? We'll address these questions and more in this chapter, so let's get started.

12.1 Theories of Personality

GATEWAYS LEARNING OUTCOMES:
After reading this section you should be able to:

12.1.1 Define the term personality and distinguish it from temperament, self-concept, and self-esteem

12.1.2 Describe how psychoanalytic theories explain personality

12.1.3 Describe how behaviorists and social learning theorists explain personality

12.1.4 Describe how humanistic theories explain personality

Psychologists regard **personality** as a person's unique long-term pattern of thinking, emotions, and behavior (Schultz & Schultz, 2017). In other words, personality refers to the consistency in who you are, have been, and will become. It also refers to the special blend of talents, values, hopes, loves, hates, and habits that makes each of us a unique person. Personality is believed to develop out of infants' **temperament**, the general pattern of attention, arousal, and mood that is evident from birth, including biological predispositions to be sensitive, irritable, and distractible and to display a typical mood (Shiner et al., 2012).

While personality is intended to be a somewhat objective assessment of your characteristics, **self-concept** is more of a subjective appraisal and consists of all your ideas, perceptions, stories, and feelings about who you are. It is the mental "picture" that you have of your own personality (Fite et al., 2017; Ritchie et al., 2011). We creatively build our self-concepts out of daily interactions, and slowly revise them as we have new experiences.

Once a stable self-concept exists, it tends to guide what we pay attention to, remember, and think about. Because of this, self-concepts can greatly affect our behavior and personal adjustment. Self-concepts also impact our **self-esteem**: positive self-concepts are associated with high levels of self-esteem while more negative self-concepts are linked to low levels of self-esteem. A person with high self-esteem is confident, proud, and self-respecting. One who has low self-esteem is insecure, lacking in confidence, and self-critical (Baumeister et al., 2003; Coelho, Marchante, & Jimerson, 2017).

Human Diversity and Self-Esteem

Psychological scientists have noted that the reasons for having high self-esteem can vary across cultures. For example, imagine that you and some friends are playing soccer. Your team wins, in part because you make some good plays. After the game, you bask in the glow of having performed well. You don't want to brag about being a hotshot, but your self-esteem gets a boost from your personal success.

Now let's imagine a slight twist on this example: In Japan, Shinobu and some of his friends are playing soccer. His team wins, in part because he makes some good plays. After the game, Shinobu

ZUMA Press, Inc./Alamy Stock Photo

Joe Giddens/AFP/Getty Images

We see individual differences in people's personalities and self-concepts every day. How would you describe the personalities of Kim Kardashian and Catherine, Duchess of Cambridge? What do you think their self-concepts would be like? What about their self-esteem?

▲ Table 12.1 Comparison of Personality Theories

	Trait Theories	Psychoanalytic Theory	Humanistic Theories	Behaviorist and Social Learning Theories
Role of inheritance (genetics)	Maximized	Stressed	Minimized	Minimized
Role of environment	Recognized	Recognized	Maximized	Maximized
View of human nature	Neutral	Negative	Positive	Neutral
Is behavior free or determined?	Determined	Determined	Free will	Determined
Principal motives	Depends on one's traits	Sex and aggression	Self-actualization	Drives of all kinds
Personality structure	Traits	Id, ego, superego	Self	Habits, expectancies
Role of unconscious	Minimized	Maximized	Minimized	Practically nonexistent
Conception of conscience	Traits of honesty, etc.	Superego	Ideal self, valuing process	Self-reinforcement, punishment history
Developmental emphasis	Combined effects of heredity and environment	Psychosexual stages	Development of self-image	Critical learning situations, identification, and imitation
Barriers to personal growth	Unhealthy traits	Unconscious conflicts, fixations	Conditions of worth, incongruence	Maladaptive habits, unhealthy environment

is happy because his team did well. However, Shinobu also dwells on the ways in which he let his team down. He thinks about how he could improve, and he resolves to be a better team player.

These sketches illustrate a basic difference in Eastern and Western psychology. In individualistic cultures such as the United States, self-esteem is often based on personal success and outstanding performance (Buss, 2012; Ross et al., 2005). For us, the path to higher self-esteem lies in self-enhancement. We are pumped up by our successes and tend to downplay our faults and failures.

Asian cultures place a greater emphasis on collectivism or interdependence among people. For them, self-esteem is based on a secure sense of belonging to social groups. As a result, people in Asian cultures are more apt to engage in self-criticism (Kitayama, Markus, & Kurokawa, 2000; Tafarodi et al., 2011). By correcting personal faults, they add to the well-being of the group. And, when the *group* succeeds, individual members feel better about themselves, which raises their self-esteem.

Clearly self-esteem is still based on success in both Eastern and Western cultures (Brown et al., 2009). However, it is fascinating that cultures define success in such different ways (Buss, 2012; Schmitt & Allik, 2005).

The study of personality has a long history in psychological science, and researchers and clinicians have developed an array of theories designed to help us understand how it emerges and develops. A **personality theory** is a system of concepts, assumptions, ideas, and principles proposed to explain personality (Burger, 2015). In this section, we'll take a close look at several different theories of personality, including psychoanalytic theories, behavioral and learning theories, humanistic theories, and genetic theories. ▲ Table 12.1 provides an overview of these theoretical approaches to personality.

Psychoanalytic Theory

As we discussed in ■ Section 1.3, **psychoanalytic theory** was the first (and best-known) psychodynamic approach. It grew out of the work of Sigmund Freud, a Viennese physician who was fascinated by patients whose problems seemed to be more emotional than physical. From about 1890 until his death in 1939, Freud developed a theory of personality that has deeply influenced modern thought (Schultz & Schultz, 2017; Tauber, 2010). Let's consider some of its main features.

Personality Structure

Freud's model portrays personality as a dynamic system directed by three mental structures: the *id*, the *ego*, and the *superego*. According to Freud, most behavior involves activity of all three systems.

Personality A person's unique and relatively stable patterns of thinking, emotions, and behavior.

Temperament General pattern of attention, arousal, and mood that is evident from birth.

Self-concept The perception of one's own personality traits.

Self-esteem Regarding oneself as a worthwhile person; a positive evaluation of oneself.

Personality theory A system of concepts, assumptions, ideas, and principles used to understand and explain personality.

Psychoanalytic theory Freudian theory of personality that emphasizes unconscious forces and conflicts.

Rykoff Collection/Corbis Historical/Getty Images

Freud considered personality an expression of two conflicting forces, life instincts and the death instinct. Both are symbolized in this drawing by Allan Gilbert. (If you don't immediately see the death symbolism, move farther away from the drawing.)

The Id

The **id** contains primitive drives present at birth. The id operates on the **pleasure principle**—that is, it seeks to avoid pain and freely express pleasure-seeking urges of all kinds. It is self-serving, irrational, impulsive, and totally unconscious. If we were solely under control of the id, the world would be chaotic beyond belief.

Freud believed that the id acts as a power source for the entire **psyche** (SIGH-key), or personality. This energy, called **libido** (lih-BEE-doe), flows from **Eros**, the life instincts. According to Freud, libido underlies our efforts to survive, as well as our sexual desires and pleasure seeking. Freud also described **Thanatos**, the "death" instinct—although today it is more often thought of as an impulse toward aggression and destructive urges. Most id energies, then, are aimed at discharging tensions related to sex and aggression.

The Ego

The **ego** is sometimes described as the "executive" because it is a system of thinking, planning, and problem solving that makes decisions about how to direct energies supplied by the id. The ego is guided by the **reality principle**, which means that it tries to accommodate the desires of the id in ways that are realistic, given the external realities of the world. It is in conscious control of the personality and often delays action until it is practical or appropriate.

The Superego

The **superego** represents moral conscience by acting as a judge or censor for the thoughts and actions of the ego. The superego acts as an "internalized parent" to bring behavior under control. In Freudian terms, a person with a weak superego will be a delinquent, criminal, or antisocial personality. In contrast, an overly strict or harsh superego may cause inhibition, rigidity, or unbearable guilt.

Personality Dynamics

How do the id, ego, and superego interact? Just to be clear, Freud didn't picture the id, ego, and superego as parts of the brain or as "little people" running the human psyche. Instead, they are conflicting mental processes. Freud theorized a delicate balance of power among the three. For example, let's say that you are sexually attracted to an acquaintance. The id clamors for immediate satisfaction of its sexual desires but is opposed by the superego (which, in Freud's day, would have found the very thought of sex shocking). The id says, "Go for it!" The superego icily replies, "Never even think that again!" And what does the ego say? The ego says, "Hold on—I have a plan!" To reduce tension, the ego could begin actions leading to friendship, romance, courtship, and marriage—strategies that would satisfy both the id and superego to some extent.

Is the ego always caught in the middle? Basically, yes, and the pressures on it can be intense. In addition to meeting the conflicting demands of the id and the moralizing superego, the overworked ego must deal with external reality. According to Freud, you feel anxiety when your ego is threatened or overwhelmed. Each person develops habitual ways of calming these anxieties, and many resort to using *ego-defense mechanisms* to lessen internal conflicts. Defense mechanisms are mental processes that deny, distort, or otherwise block out sources of threat and anxiety. Two common examples are *repression* and *denial*, both of which

Sidney Harris/www.CartoonStock.com

▲ Table 12.2 Freud's Psychosexual Stages

Stage	Age	Erogenous Zone	Consequences of Fixation for Personality
Oral	Birth–1 year	Mouth	• Oral dependent (gullible, passive, needs attention) • Oral aggressive (exploitative, manipulative)
Anal	1–3 years	Anus	• Anal retentive (stingy, orderly, compulsively clean) • Anal expulsive (disorderly, destructive, cruel, messy)
Phallic	3–6 years	Genitals	• Unresolved Oedipal complex (attraction to opposite-sex parent) results in underdeveloped superego, leading to vanity, pride, narcissism (self-love)
Latency	6–12 years	None	• Lack of sexual fulfillment
Genital	12–adulthood	Genitals	• Unsatisfying adult relationships

prevent disturbing thoughts or events from being consciously considered. Other examples include *sublimation* and *displacement*, which involve satisfying an unacceptable impulse (grabbing that acquaintance that the id is attracted to and kissing him senseless) with something that's considered more acceptable, like exercise or a very cold shower. (■ The ego-defense mechanisms that Freud identified are used as a form of protection against stress, anxiety, and threatening events. See Section 13.4)

Levels of Awareness

Like other psychodynamic theorists, Freud believed that our behavior often expresses unconscious (or hidden) forces. The **unconscious** holds repressed memories and emotions, plus the instinctual drives of the id. It is interesting that modern scientists have found brain circuits that do, in fact, seem to underlie defense mechanisms such as repression and the triggering of unconscious emotions and memories (Berlin, 2011; Stevens, 2016).

Are the actions of the ego and superego also unconscious, like the id? At times, yes, but they also operate on two other levels of awareness (● Figure 12.1). The **conscious** level includes everything that you are aware of at a given moment, including thoughts, perceptions, feelings, and memories. The **preconscious** lies between the unconscious and conscious parts of the mind and contains material that can be easily brought to awareness. If you stop to think about a time when you felt angry or rejected, you are moving this memory from the preconscious to the conscious level of awareness.

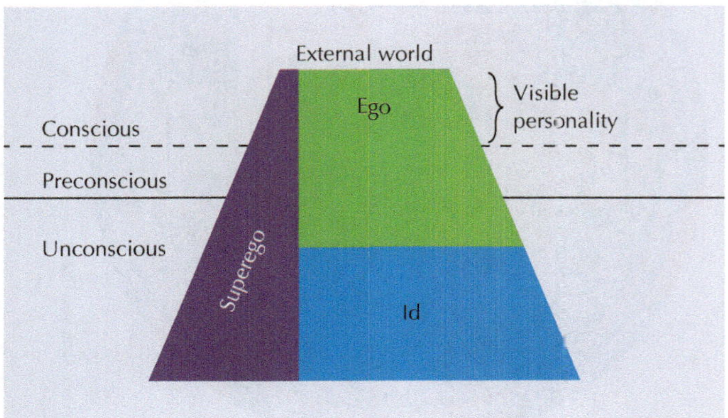

● Figure 12.1 Freud's levels of consciousness. The approximate relationship between the id, ego, and superego, and the levels of awareness.

Personality Development

How does psychoanalytic theory explain personality development? Freud believed that erotic urges in childhood have lasting effects on development, and that the core of personality develops before age 6 in a series of **psychosexual stages** (Ashcraft, 2015) (▲ Table 12.2). As you might expect, this is a controversial idea. However, Freud used the terms *sex* and *erotic* very broadly to refer to many physical sources of pleasure.

Id Component of Freud's personality theory containing primitive drives present at birth.

Pleasure principle According to Freud, the id's drive to avoid pain and seek what feels good.

Psyche The mind, mental life, and personality as a whole.

Libido In Freudian theory, the force, primarily pleasure oriented, that energizes the personality.

Eros Freud's name for the "life instincts."

Thanatos The death instinct postulated by Freud.

Ego According to Freud, the decision-making part of personality that operates on the reality principle.

Reality principle Delaying action (or pleasure) until it is appropriate.

Superego According to Freud, the part of personality that represents moral conscience

Unconscious Contents of the mind that are beyond awareness, especially impulses and desires.

Conscious The region of the mind that includes all mental contents that a person is aware of at any given moment.

Preconscious An area of the mind containing information that can be voluntarily brought to awareness.

Psychosexual stages How Freud classifies a period of development.

Was Freud's ever-present cigar a sign of an oral fixation? Was it a phallic symbol? Was it both? Or was it neither? Once, when he was asked, Freud himself apparently replied, "Sometimes a cigar is just a cigar." An inability to say for sure is one of the shortcomings of psychoanalytic theory.

Freud identified five psychosexual stages, *oral*, *anal*, *phallic*, *latency*, and *genital*. At each stage except latency, a different part of the body becomes a child's primary **erogenous zone**—an area capable of producing pleasure. Each area then serves as the main source of pleasure, frustration, and self-expression. Freud believed that many adult personality traits can be traced to **fixations**—unresolved conflicts caused by overindulgence or frustration—in one or more of the stages.

Expansion of Psychoanalytic Theory

Freud's ideas quickly attracted a brilliant following. Some, like Freud's daughter, Anna Freud, and Otto Rank, focused on further developing his ideas. Others, known as neo-Freudians (*neo* means "new"), created theories that stressed the role of cultural and social factors in the development of the personality. Let's take a look at three of the more influential neo-Freudians: Alfred Adler, Karen Horney, and Carl Jung.

Alfred Adler (1870–1937)

Adler broke away from Freud because he disagreed with Freud's emphasis on the unconscious, on instinctual drives, and on the importance of sexuality. He believed that we are social creatures governed by social urges, not by biological instincts (Carlson & Maniacci, 2012).

In Adler's view, the main driving force in personality is a **striving for superiority** that stems from feelings of inferiority. These feelings occur mainly because we begin life as small, weak, and relatively powerless children surrounded by larger and more powerful adults. Feelings of inferiority may also come from our personal limitations. This striving, then, is a struggle to overcome imperfections, an upward drive for competence, and mastery of shortcomings. Failure of this struggle can lead to an **inferiority complex**, characterized by a chronic lack of self-worth along with self-doubt (Schultz & Schultz, 2017).

Karen Horney (1885–1952)

Karen Horney (HORN-eye) remained faithful to most of Freud's theory, but she resisted his more mechanistic, biological, and instinctive ideas. For example, Horney rejected Freud's claim that males are dominant or superior to females, challenging the male bias that characterized the social norms of that era (Eckardt, 2005).

Horney also disagreed with Freud about the causes of neurosis. Freud held that neurotic (anxiety-ridden) individuals are struggling with forbidden id drives that they fear they cannot control. Horney's view was that a core of **basic anxiety** occurs when people feel isolated and helpless in a hostile world (Engler, 2014). These feelings, she believed, are rooted in childhood. Trouble occurs when an individual tries to control basic anxiety by exaggerating one of three ways to interact with others: moving *toward* others (by depending on them for love, support, or friendship), moving *away* from others (by withdrawing, acting like a "loner," or being "strong" and independent), or moving *against* others (by attacking, competing with, or seeking power over them). Horney believed that emotional health reflects a balance in moving toward, away from, and against others. In her view, emotional problems tend to lock people into overuse of one of the three modes—an insight that remains valuable today (Engler, 2014; Mitchell, 2015).

Carl Jung (1875–1961)

Like Freud, Jung (pronounced *Yoong*) was interested in the conscious and unconscious aspects of the mind and called the conscious part of the personality the *ego*. However, he further noted that a *persona*, or "mask," exists between the ego and the outside world. The **persona** is the "public self" presented to others. It is most apparent when we adopt particular roles or hide our deeper feelings.

Was Jung's view of the unconscious the same as Freud's? Jung used the term *personal unconscious* to refer to what Freud simply called the unconscious. The **personal unconscious** is a mental storehouse for a single individual's experiences, feelings, and memories. But Jung also described a **collective unconscious**, a deeper mental storehouse for unconscious ideas and images shared by all humans. Jung believed that, from the beginning of time, all humans have had experiences with birth, death, power, god figures, mother and father figures, animals, the earth, energy,

Jung regarded mandalas as symbols of the self-archetype and representations of unity, balance, and completion within the personality.

evil, rebirth, and so on. According to Jung, such universals create **archetypes** (ARE-keh-types): original ideas, images, or patterns that are common to all people, but show themselves differently across cultures in art, religion, myths, and dreams (Rutter & Singer, 2015). Let's say, for instance, that a man dreams of dancing with his sister. To Freud, this would probably be a sign of hidden incestuous feelings. To Jung, universal archetypes related to masculinity and femininity might better explain the dream. Specifically, the image of the sister might represent an unexpressed feminine side of the man's personality, and the dream might represent the cosmic dance that intertwines "maleness" and "femaleness" in all lives.

Current Views on Psychoanalytic Theory

Is Freudian theory still widely accepted? Although few psychologists wholeheartedly embrace Freud's theory today, it remains influential for several reasons. First, it pioneered the general idea of unconscious processes. Contemporary psychodynamic theorists generally agree that some part of the human mind is unconscious and yet plays an important role in shaping human behavior, even if they do not share Freud's (over?)focus on the motivating power of sex and death (Epstein, 2003). Other motives and cognitive factors are today seen as having equal importance.

Second, the general idea that critical events during the first years of life help shape adult personality remains widely accepted. For example, the importance of early experiences has played a role in the development of modern-day attachment theory. In addition, Freud was among the first to propose that development proceeds through a series of stages. In this respect, Erik Erikson's *psychosocial* stages, which cover development from birth to old age, are a modern offshoot of Freud's ideas. (■ See Section 3.3.)

However, when it comes to the details, Freud clearly was often wrong. His portrayal of the elementary school years (latency) as free from sexuality and unimportant for personality development has been discredited, as have his more specific ideas about the role of parenting in children's development. In addition, Freud's ideas on the development of women have been thoroughly discredited (Hyde & Else-Quest, 2013). For example, Freud has been heavily criticized for his views of patients who believed that they were sexually molested as children (Marcel, 2005). Freud assumed that such events were merely childhood fantasies, and led to a long-standing tendency to disbelieve children and women who had been sexually assaulted (Brannon, 2011).

A final important criticism is that Freud's concepts are almost impossible to verify scientifically. His ideas provide numerous ways to explain almost any thought, action, or feeling *after* it has occurred. However, they lead to few predictions, which makes his claims difficult to test.

Learning Theories

Behavioral personality theories emphasize that personality is no more (or less) than a collection of relatively stable learned behavior patterns. Personality, like other learned behavior, is acquired through classical and operant conditioning, observational learning, reinforcement, extinction, generalization, and discrimination. (See ■ Sections 6.1 to 6.3.)

Freud believed that aggressive urges are instinctual. In contrast, behavioral theories assume that personal characteristics such as aggressiveness are learned. Is this boy's aggression the result of observational learning, harsh punishment, or prior reinforcement?

If his parents consistently reward little Sanjay for honesty, for example, he is more likely to become an honest adult. If his parents are less scrupulous, Sanjay might well grow up differently (Schultz & Schultz, 2017).

Personality Structure and Dynamics

The behavioral view of personality can be illustrated with an early theory proposed by John Dollard and Neal Miller (1950). In their view, learned behavior patterns, or **habits**, make up the structure of personality. As for the dynamics of personality, habits are governed by four elements of learning: *drive*, *cue*, *response*, and *reward*. A *drive* is any stimulus strong enough to move a person to

Erogenous zone Any body area that produces pleasurable sensations.

Fixation A lasting conflict developed as a result of frustration or overindulgence.

Striving for superiority According to Alfred Adler, this basic drive propels us toward perfection.

Inferiority complex Arises when feelings of inferiority become overwhelming; negative pattern characterized by a chronic lack of self-worth along with self-doubt.

Basic anxiety A primary form of anxiety that arises from living in a hostile world.

Persona The "mask" or public self presented to others.

Personal unconscious A mental storehouse for an individual's unconscious thoughts.

Collective unconscious According to Carl Jung, a mental storehouse for unconscious ideas and images shared by all humans.

Archetype According to Carl Jung, a universal idea, image, or pattern found in the collective unconscious.

Behavioral personality theory Any model of personality that emphasizes learning and observable behavior.

Habit A deeply ingrained, learned pattern of behavior.

action (such as hunger, pain, lust, frustration, or fear). *Cues* are signals from the environment. These signals guide *responses* (actions) so that they are most likely to bring about *reward* (positive reinforcement).

Let's see how these ideas would play out in a real-world example. Say that a child named Amina is frustrated by her older brother, Kelvin, who takes a toy from her. Amina could respond in several ways: She could throw a temper tantrum, hit Kelvin, tell her mother, and so forth. The response that she chooses is guided by available cues and the previous effects of each response. If telling her mother has paid off in the past, and her mother is present, telling may be Amina's immediate response. If a different set of cues exists (if her mother is absent, or if Kelvin looks particularly menacing), Amina may select some other response. To an outside observer, Amina's actions seem to reflect her personality. To a learning theorist, they simply express the combined effects of drive, cue, response, and reward. (■ Behavioral theories have contributed greatly to the creation of therapies for various psychological problems and disorders. See the discussion of behavior therapy in Section 15.2.)

The concept of environmental cues in the previous example emphasizes the fact that learning theorists also consider the **situational determinants** of our actions (Mischel & Shoda, 2010; Mischel, Shoda, & Smith, 2008). Knowing that someone is honest, for example, does not automatically allow us to predict whether that person will be honest in a very specific situation (Carter, 2013). For example, in one study people were intentionally overpaid for doing an assigned task. Under normal circumstances, 80 percent kept the extra money without mentioning it. But as few as 17 percent did so if the situation was altered: Specifically, if people thought the money was coming out of the pocket of the person running the study, participants were much more likely to return the overpayment (Bersoff, 1999).

It's important at this point to return to the idea that when we talk about personality, we're still focused on the idea of relatively *consistent* patterns of responding. So while situations clearly have some impact on our behavior, researchers would argue that true characteristics of our personality reveal themselves across a variety of situations. If we want to make the claim that Annabelle is lazy, for example, then we'd be saying that she shows that trait across many situations in which people might be expected to differ on laziness. But if Annabelle only seems to be lazy when it comes to cleaning up her room and is hardworking in the majority other situations (completing homework, working at her part-time job, doing the gardening), a personality psychologist would be unlikely to say that she's lazy.

Expansion of Learning Theories

Learning theorists originally set out to provide a simple, clear model of personality, but they eventually had to face a fact that they previously tended to set aside: People think. Contemporary behavioral psychologists— whose interests include perception, thinking, expectations, and other mental events—are called *social learning theorists.* Learning principles, modeling, thought patterns, perceptions, expectations, beliefs, goals, emotions, and social relationships are combined in **social learning theory** to explain personality (Brauer & Tittle, 2012; Mischel, Shoda, & Smith, 2008).

Digital Vision/Photodisc/Getty Images

Seventy-five percent of American college students admit that they have been academically dishonest in one way or another. What can be done about these high rates of dishonesty? The behavioral perspective holds that honesty is determined as much by circumstances as it is by personality. In line with this, simple measures such as announcing in classes that integrity codes will be enforced can significantly reduce cheating. Using multiple forms of exams and web-based plagiarism software and educating students about plagiarism also tend to deter dishonesty (Altschuler, 2001; McKeever, 2006).

Social Learning Theory

The "cognitive behaviorism" of social learning theory can be illustrated by three classic concepts proposed by Julian Rotter: the *psychological situation*, *expectancy*, and *reinforcement value* (Rotter & Hochreich, 1975). Let's examine each one.

Someone trips you. How do you respond? Your reaction probably depends on whether you think it was planned or an accident. It is not enough to know the setting in which a person responds. We also need to know the person's **psychological situation** (how the person interprets or defines the situation). As another example, let's say that you score low on an exam. Do you consider it a challenge to work harder, a sign that you should drop the class, or an excuse to get drunk? Again, your interpretation is important.

These examples make clear that our actions are affected by an **expectancy**, or anticipation, that making a response will lead to reinforcement. To continue the example, if working harder has paid off in the past, then more studying is a likely reaction to a low test score. But to really predict your response, we also would have to know if you expect your efforts to pay off in the *present* situation. In fact, expected reinforcement may be more important than actual past reinforcement.

Albert Bandura believes that one of the most important expectancies we develop concerns **self-efficacy** (EF-uh-keh-see)—the belief in our capacity to produce a desired result. Believing that our actions will produce desired results influences the activities and environments that we choose (Bandura, 2001; Schultz & Schultz, 2017). You're attracted to someone in your anthropology class. Will you ask him or her out? You're beginning to consider a career in psychology. Will you take the courses that you need to get into graduate school? You'd like to exercise more on the weekends. Will you join a hiking club? In these and countless other situations, expectancies about our self-efficacy play a key role in shaping our lives (Byrne, Barry, & Petry, 2012; Prat-Sala & Redford, 2012).

And what about the *value* you attach to grades, school success, or personal ability? The third concept, **reinforcement value**, states that we attach different subjective values to various activities or rewards. You will likely choose to study harder if passing your courses and obtaining a degree is highly valued.

With respect to reinforcement, one additional idea deserves mention. At times, we all evaluate our actions and may reward ourselves with special privileges or treats for "good behavior." With this in mind, social learning theory adds the concept of self-reinforcement to the behaviorist view. **Self-reinforcement** refers to praising or rewarding yourself for having made a particular response (such as completing a school assignment). Thus, habits of self-praise and self-blame become an important part of personality (Schultz & Schultz, 2017).

Personality Development

Learning theorists tend to agree with Freud that the first six years are crucial for personality development, but for different reasons. Rather than thinking in terms of psychosexual urges and fixations, they believe that childhood is a time of urgent drives, powerful rewards and punishments, and crushing frustrations. These forces combine to shape the core of personality (Shaffer, 2009).

Social reinforcement, which is based on praise, attention, or approval from others, is especially important (Brauer & Tittle, 2012). One obvious example involves learning socially defined "male" and "female" gender roles—which, in turn, affects personality (Cervone & Pervin, 2013). For example, from birth onward, children are labeled as boys or girls and encouraged to learn appropriate **gender roles**—the pattern of behaviors regarded as "male" or "female" within a culture (Fine, 2011; Orenstein, 2011; see ■ Section 11.2).

According to social learning theory, identification and imitation contribute greatly to personality development and to sex training. **Identification** refers to the child's emotional attachment to admired adults, especially those who provide love and care. Identification typically encourages **imitation**, a desire to act like the admired person. Many "male" or "female" traits come from children's attempts to imitate a same-sex parent with whom they identify (Helgeson, 2012).

If children are around parents of both sexes, why don't they imitate behavior typical of the opposite sex as well as of the same sex? You may recall from ■ Section 6.3 that observational learning allows us to learn without direct reward by simply observing and remembering the actions of others. But the actions that we choose to imitate depend on the outcomes that models experience. For example, boys and girls have equal chances to observe adults and other children acting aggressively. However, girls are less likely than boys to imitate *directly* aggressive behavior (shouting at or hitting another person). Instead, girls are more likely to rely on *indirectly* aggressive behavior (excluding

John Mitterer

We can reward ourselves through self-reinforcement for personal achievements and other "good" behavior. (At least that's the theory, right?)

Situational determinants External conditions that strongly influence behavior.

Social learning theory A theory that combines learning principles with cognitive processes, socialization, and modeling, to explain behavior, including personality.

Psychological situation A situation as it is perceived and interpreted by an individual, not as it exists objectively.

Expectancy Anticipation about the effect that a response will have, especially regarding reinforcement.

Self-efficacy Belief in your capacity to produce a desired result.

Reinforcement value The subjective value that a person attaches to a particular activity or reinforcer.

Self-reinforcement Praising or rewarding oneself for having made a particular response (such as completing a school assignment).

Social reinforcement Praise, attention, approval, and/or affection from others.

Gender roles Pattern of behaviors regarded as "male" or "female" within a culture.

Identification Feeling emotionally connected to a person and seeing oneself as like him or her.

Imitation An attempt to match one's own behavior to another person's behavior.

Adult personality is influenced by identification with parents and imitation of their behavior.

others from friendship, spreading rumors). This could be because girls do not as often see direct female aggression rewarded or approved (Field et al., 2009). In other words, "girlfighting" is likely a culturally reinforced pattern (Brown, 2005). It is intriguing that over the last few years, girls have become more willing to engage in direct aggression as popular culture presents more and more images of directly aggressive women (Artz, 2005; Taylor & Ruiz, 2013).

Humanistic Theory

At the beginning of this chapter, you met Maurice Smith. While in prison, he opted to pursue a college degree and graduated just after his release. Where do such desires for personal growth come from? **Humanism** focuses on human experience, problems, potentials, and ideals. As we saw in ■ Section 1.3, the core of humanism is a positive image of humans as creative beings capable of **free will**—an ability to choose that is not determined by genetics, learning, or unconscious forces. In short, humanists seek ways to encourage our potentials to blossom.

Humanism is sometimes called a "third force" in that it is opposed to both psychodynamic and learning (behaviorist) theories of personality. Humanism is a reaction to the pessimism of psychoanalytic theory. It rejects the Freudian view of personality as a battleground for instincts and unconscious forces. Instead, humanists view **human nature—**the traits, qualities, potentials, and behavior patterns most characteristic of the human species— as inherently good. Humanists also oppose the machinelike overtones of the behaviorist view of human nature. We are not, humanists say, merely a bundle of moldable responses.

To a humanist, the person you are today is largely the product of all the choices that you have made, both good and bad. Humanists also emphasize immediate **subjective experience**—private perceptions of reality—rather than prior learning. They believe that there are as many "real worlds" as there are people. To understand behavior, we must learn how a person subjectively views the world—what is "real" for her or him.

Key Theorists

Many psychologists have added to the humanistic tradition. Of these, the best known are Abraham Maslow (1908–1970) and Carl Rogers (1902–1987). Let's take a closer look at their ideas.

Maslow and Self-Actualization

Abraham Maslow became interested in people who were living unusually effective lives (Hoffman, 2008). How were they different? To find an answer, Maslow began by studying the lives of great men and women from history, such as Albert Einstein, William James, Jane Addams, Eleanor Roosevelt, Abraham Lincoln, John Muir, and Walt Whitman. From there, he moved on to study living artists, writers, poets, and other creative individuals.

Along the way, Maslow's thinking changed radically. At first, he studied only people of obvious creativity or high achievement. However, it eventually became clear that anyone could live a rich, creative, and satisfying life (D'Souza & Gurin, 2016). Maslow referred to the process of fully developing personal potentials as **self-actualization** (Maslow, 1954). The heart of self-actualization is a continuous search for personal fulfillment (Ivtzan et al., 2013; Peterson & Park, 2010).

Although Maslow tried to investigate self-actualization empirically, his choice of people to study was subjective and therefore somewhat limiting. Having said that, Maslow made an important contribution to humanistic theories by drawing our attention to the possibility of lifelong personal growth (Peterson & Park, 2010). He found no magic formula for leading a more creative life; instead, Maslow emphasized that self-actualization is primarily a *process,* not a goal or an end point. As such, it requires hard work, patience, and commitment. Nevertheless, some helpful suggestions can be gleaned from his writings (Maslow, 1954, 1967, 1971). Here are some ways to begin your own journey of self-actualization:

1. **Be willing to change.** Continually ask yourself, "Am I living in a way that is deeply satisfying to me and that truly expresses me?" If not, be prepared to make changes in your life.
2. **Take responsibility.** You can become an architect of self by acting as if you are personally responsible for every aspect of your life. Avoid the habit of blaming others for your own shortcomings.
3. **Examine your motives.** Self-discovery involves an element of risk. If your behavior is restricted by a desire for safety or security, it may be time to test some limits.
4. **Experience honestly and directly.** Wishful thinking is another barrier to personal growth. Self-actualizers trust themselves enough to accept all kinds of information without distorting it to fit their fears and desires. Try to see yourself as others do.
5. **Use your positive experiences.** Maslow considered *peak experiences* temporary moments of self-actualization. Therefore, you might actively repeat activities that have caused feelings of awe, amazement, exaltation, renewal, reverence, humility, fulfillment, or joy in you.
6. **Be prepared to be different.** Maslow felt that everyone has a potential for "greatness," but most fear becoming everything that they might become. As part of personal growth, be prepared to trust your own impulses and feelings; don't automatically judge yourself by the standards of others.
7. **Get involved.** With few exceptions, self-actualizers tend to have a mission or "calling" in life. For these people, "work" is not done just to fill deficiency needs, but to satisfy higher yearnings for truth, beauty, community, and meaning. Turn your attention to problems outside yourself.

8. **Assess your progress.** There is no final point at which one becomes self-actualized. It's important to gauge your progress frequently and to renew your efforts. If you feel bored at school, at a job, or in a relationship, consider it a challenge. Have you been taking responsibility for your own personal growth?

Rogers and Self Theory

Another well-known humanist, Carl Rogers, also emphasized the human capacity for inner peace and happiness (Elliott & Farber, 2010). The **fully functioning person**, he said, lives in harmony with his or her deepest feelings and impulses. Such people are open to their experiences, and they trust their inner urges and intuitions (Rogers, 1961). Rogers believed that this attitude is most likely to occur when a person receives ample amounts of love and acceptance from others.

Rogers's theory emphasizes the **self**, a flexible and changing perception of personal identity. Much behavior can be understood as an attempt to maintain consistency between our *self-image* and our actions. Your **self-image** is a total subjective perception of your body and personality. For example, people who think of themselves as kind tend to be considerate in most situations.

Let's say that I know a person who thinks she is kind, but she really isn't. How does that fit Rogers's theory? According to Rogers, we allow into awareness experiences that match our self-image, and they gradually change the self. Information or feelings inconsistent with the self-image are said to be incongruent. Thus, a person who thinks she is kind but really isn't is in a state of **incongruence**. In other words, there is a discrepancy between her experiences and her self-image. As another example, it would be incongruent to believe that you are a person who "never gets angry" if you spend much of each day seething inside.

Experiences that are seriously incongruent with the self-image can be threatening and are often distorted or denied conscious recognition. Blocking, denying, or distorting experiences prevents the self from changing. This creates a gap between the self-image and reality (Ryckman, 2013). As the self-image grows more unrealistic, the *incongruent person* becomes confused, vulnerable, dissatisfied, or seriously maladjusted (● Figure 12.2). In line with Rogers's observations, a study of college students confirmed that being *authentic* is vital for healthy functioning—that is, we need to feel that our behavior accurately expresses who we are (Human et al., 2014; Wenzel & Lucas-Thompson, 2012). Please note, however, that being authentic doesn't mean that you can do whatever you want. Being true to yourself is no excuse for acting irresponsibly or ignoring the feelings of others (Kernis & Goldman, 2005).

When your self-image is consistent with what you really think, feel, do, and experience, you are best able to actualize your potential. Rogers also considered it essential to have congruence between the self-image and the **ideal self**, or the image of the person that you would most like to be (Przybylski et al., 2012). (■ Rogers and other humanistic theorists believe that some psychological disorders are caused by a faulty or incongruent self-image. See Section 14.4.)

According to psychologists Hazel Markus and Paula Nurius (1986), our current ideal self is only one of a number of **possible selves**—persons that we could become or are afraid of becoming.

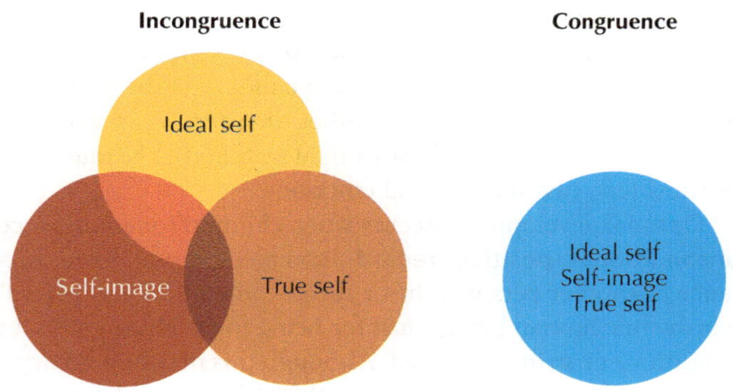

● **Figure 12.2 Incongruence versus congruence.** Incongruence occurs when there is a mismatch between any of these three entities: the ideal self (the person you would like to be), your self-image (the person you think you are), and the true self (the person you actually are). Self-esteem suffers when there is a large difference between one's ideal self and self-image. Anxiety and defensiveness are common when the self-image does not match the true self.

Consider Maurice Smith, for example. While in prison, he clearly imagined that he could become a successful college graduate. At the same time, he might well have feared the possibility that he'd be unable to complete his college courses, or perhaps that he'd wind up reoffending once he was paroled.

How does development of the self contribute to later personality functioning? Rogers believed that positive and negative evaluations by others cause children to develop internal standards of evaluation called **conditions of worth**. In other words, we learn

Humanism An approach that focuses on human experience, problems, potentials, and ideals.

Free will The ability to freely make choices that are not controlled by genetics, learning, or unconscious forces.

Human nature Those traits, qualities, potentials, and behavior patterns most characteristic of the human species.

Subjective experience Reality as it is perceived and interpreted, not as it exists objectively.

Self-actualization The process of fully developing personal potentials.

Fully functioning person A person living in harmony with her or his deepest feelings, impulses, and intuitions.

Self A continuously evolving conception of one's personal identity.

Self-image Total subjective perception of one's body and personality (another term for *self-concept*).

Incongruence A state that exists when there is a discrepancy between one's experiences and self-image or between one's self-image and ideal self.

Ideal self An idealized image of oneself (the person that one would like to be).

Possible selves A collection of thoughts, beliefs, feelings, and images concerning the person that one could become.

Conditions of worth Internal standards used to judge the value of one's thoughts, actions, feelings, or experiences.

that some actions win our parents' love and approval, whereas others are rejected. More important, parents may label some *feelings* as bad or wrong. For example, a child might be told that it is wrong to feel angry toward a brother or sister—even when anger is justified. Likewise, a little boy might be told that he must not cry or show fear, two very normal emotions.

Optimal development occurs when children (or adults) receive **unconditional positive regard**—complete, unqualified acceptance of another person as he or she is—when they are "prized" as worthwhile human beings, just for being themselves, without any conditions or strings attached. Although this may be a luxury that few people enjoy, Rogers believed that it leads to a later capacity for self-esteem, positive self-evaluation, or **positive self-regard** (Drigotas, 2002; Righetti, Rusbult, & Finkenauer, 2010).

Reflective Practice

Theories of Personality

1. Freud stated that the mind functions on three levels: the conscious, the unconscious, and the
   a. psyche
   b. preconscious
   c. superego
   d. subconscious
2. List the three divisions of personality postulated by Freud: ______________, ______________, and ______________.
3. Humanists view human nature as basically good, and they emphasize the effects of subjective learning and unconscious choice. T or F?
4. According to Rogers, a close match between the self-image and the ideal self creates a condition called incongruence. T or F?
5. Learning theorists believe that personality "traits" really are ______________ that are acquired through prior learning. They also emphasize ______________ determinants of behavior.
6. To explain behavior, social learning theorists include mental elements, such as ______________ (the anticipation that a response will lead to reinforcement).

THINK CRITICALLY

7. What role would your "possible selves" play in the choice of a college major?
8. Rotter's concept of *reinforcement value* is closely related to a motivational principle discussed in Chapter 10. Can you name it?

SELF-REFLECT

- Try to think of at least one time when your thoughts, feelings, or actions seemed to reflect the workings of each of the following: the id, the ego, and the superego.
- Do you know anyone who seems to be making especially good use of his or her personal potential? Does that person fit Maslow's profile of a self-actualizer?
- Some people love to shop; others hate it. How have the psychological situation, expectancy, and reinforcement value affected your willingness to "shop 'til you drop"?

Answers: 1. b 2. id, ego, superego 3. F 4. F 5. habits; situational 6. expectancies 7. Career decisions almost always involve, in part, picturing oneself occupying various occupational roles. Such possible "future selves" play a role in many of the major decisions we make (Masters & Holley, 2006). 8. Incentive value

12.2 Traits: The Building Blocks of Personality

GATEWAYS LEARNING OUTCOMES:
After reading this section you should be able to:

12.2.1 Describe what is meant by a personality trait

12.2.2 Outline the history of the trait approach to understanding personality, including the work of Allport and Cattell

12.2.3 Contrast the Big Five and HEXACO models of personality

12.2.4 Explain what is meant by a personality type, and the weaknesses associated with this approach to classifying personality

The *trait approach* is currently the dominant approach to studying personality. A **personality trait** refers to differences among individuals in their thoughts, feelings, and behavior that are relatively stable over a variety of situations and a fairly long period of time (Ashton, 2018). Trait theorists, then, seek to describe personality with a small number of key traits or factors.

There are at least two reasons why this is such an important area of study. The first is that examining traits helps us to make sense of **individual differences**; that is, the ways in which humans show their diversity with respect to cognition, emotion, and behavior. The second is that a good understanding of traits can be helpful in predicting how people will react in particular circumstances. If you see Daryl talking in an animated way to strangers—first at a supermarket and later at a party—you might infer that he is sociable. Noting this about Daryl will allow you to comfortably predict that if you took him home to meet your family at Thanksgiving, you wouldn't have to worry about him feeling uncomfortable around your family and sitting alone in a corner. This kind of predictive power extends to other, more significant life outcomes too: For example, certain traits can be used to predict health-related behaviors, as well as marital and occupational success (Donnellan et al., 2012; Strickhouser, Zell, & Krizan, 2017).

Traits: Stable or Situation-Dependent?

It's important to emphasize that psychological scientists view traits as *stable* dispositions that a person shows in most situations (Mõttus, Johnson, & Deary, 2012). For example, if you are usually friendly, optimistic, and cautious, these qualities are traits of your personality.

But what if I am also sometimes shy, pessimistic, or uninhibited? The original three qualities are still traits so long as they are most *typical* of your behavior. Let's say that Lin's old boyfriend Winston approaches most situations with optimism but tends to expect the worst each time he applies for a job. If his pessimism is limited to this situation or just a few others, it is still accurate and useful to describe him as an optimistic person. What this example demonstrates, though, is that traits *interact* with situations to determine how we will act (Mischel, 2004).

In a **trait–situation interaction**, external circumstances influence the expression of a personality trait. For instance, imagine what would happen if a shy person moved from a church to a classroom to a party to a football game. As the setting changed, he would probably become somewhat louder and more boisterous. At the same time, though, his more stable personality traits also would be apparent: If he's more shy than other people in church and in class, he will probably be quieter than average in the other settings like a football game, too. Put another way, though your behavior can change somewhat across situations, your standing on a particular trait *relative to other people* likely won't change very much.

What about extreme situations? Wouldn't they impact how personality traits are expressed? If you think about Maurice Smith, whom you met at the beginning of this chapter, you'll know that this is an important question. Maurice's behavior before his incarceration might well have led you to believe that he was impulsive and aggressive, with little interest in education. And yet, when discussing his remarkable educational achievements (which surely required traits such as patience, perseverance, and dedication to his studies) he seemed happy that people would now see the person he had always believed himself to be. So what happened?

Personality researchers typically believe that while situations might have some impact on behavior, over the long term, traits will prove to be better predictors of what to expect from people. When the situational influences are extreme and prolonged, though, it's possible that they may override a person's natural traits (Asendorpf, 2009). Such situations might include those that Maurice experienced—living in a dangerous neighborhood with constant exposure to threat—but they might also include situations such as prolonged abuse or neglect, or living in extreme poverty. In such cases, the natural tendencies governed by our traits might be overtaken by more immediate concerns with protecting ourselves and staying safe.

Classifying Traits

To get a better sense of how psychologists think about traits, start by taking a moment to read through ▲ Table 12.3 and check the traits that describe your personality. Once you're done, ask yourself: Are the traits you checked of equal importance? Are some stronger or more basic than others? Do any overlap? For example, if you checked "dominant," did you also check "confident" and "bold"?

To better understand personality, trait theorists consider how traits relate to one another in just this sort of way. For many years, they have attempted to classify traits into a small number of groups to simplify our understanding of individual differences. Let's take a closer look at what this research can teach us.

Early Approaches to Classifying Traits

Are there different types of traits? Yes. Psychologist Gordon Allport (1897–1967) distinguished between *central traits* and *secondary traits*. **Central traits** are the basic building blocks of personality.

▲ Table 12.3 Adjective Checklist

Check the traits that you feel are characteristic of your personality. Are some more basic than others?

Aggressive	Organized	Ambitious	Clever
Confident	Loyal	Generous	Calm
Warm	Bold	Cautious	Reliable
Sensitive	Mature	Talented	Jealous
Sociable	Honest	Funny	Religious
Dominant	Dull	Accurate	Nervous
Humble	Uninhibited	Visionary	Cheerful
Thoughtful	Serious	Helpful	Emotional
Orderly	Anxious	Conforming	Good-natured
Liberal	Curious	Optimistic	Kind
Meek	Neighborly	Passionate	Compulsive

A surprisingly small number of central traits can capture the essence of a person. For instance, just six traits would provide a good description of Jacintha's personality: dominant, sociable, honest, cheerful, intelligent, and optimistic. When college students were asked to describe someone they knew well, they mentioned an average of seven central traits (Allport, 1961).

Secondary traits are more superficial personal qualities, such as food preferences, attitudes, political opinions, musical tastes, and so forth. In Allport's terms, a personality description might therefore include the following items:

Name: Jane Doe
Age: 22
Central traits: Possessive, autonomous, artistic, dramatic, self-centered, trusting
Secondary traits: Prefers colorful clothes, likes to work alone, politically liberal, always late

How can you tell whether a personality trait is central or secondary? Raymond B. Cattell (1906–1998) tried to answer this question by directly studying the traits of a large number of

Unconditional positive regard Complete, unqualified acceptance of another person as he or she is.

Positive self-regard Thinking of oneself as a good, lovable, worthwhile person.

Personality trait Stable quality that a person shows in most situations.

Individual differences Study of the variation that exists between people.

Trait–situation interaction The influence that external settings or circumstances have on the expression of personality traits.

Central traits The core traits that characterize an individual personality.

Secondary traits Traits that are inconsistent or relatively superficial.

people. Cattell began by measuring a large number of observable traits but soon noticed that they often appeared together in groups. In fact, some traits clustered together so often that they seemed to represent a single, more basic trait. Cattell called these deeper characteristics, or dimensions, **source traits (factors)** and considered them to be the core of an individual's personality.

How do source traits differ from Allport's central traits? That's a great question. Allport classified traits subjectively (that is, based on his own opinion), and it's possible that he was wrong at times. To look for connections among traits, Cattell used **factor analysis**, a more objective statistical technique used to correlate multiple measurements and identify general underlying factors. For example, he found that imaginative people are almost always inventive, original, curious, creative, innovative, and ingenious. If you are an imaginative person, we automatically know that you have several other traits. Thus, *imaginative* is a source trait, or factor. Figure 12.3 shows one of the first trait theories of personality, developed by Hans Eysenck, that was composed of two factors: introversion–extroversion and emotionally stable–unstable.

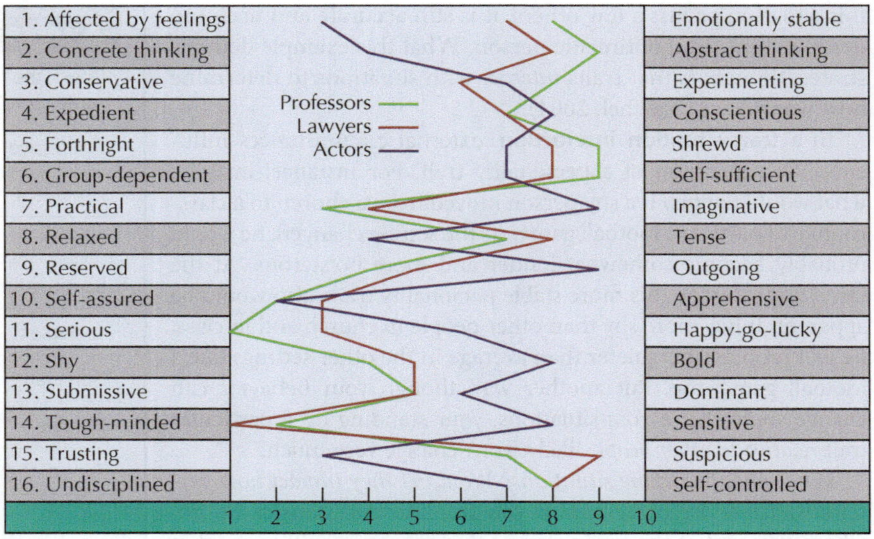

Figure 12.4 Hypothetical 16 PF profiles. The 16 source traits measured by Cattell's (1973) 16 PF are listed beside the graph. Scores can be plotted as a profile for an individual or a group. The hypothetical profiles shown here are group averages for college professors, lawyers, and professional actors. Notice the similarities between professors and lawyers and the differences between these two groups and professional actors. (Of course, your authors may only be expressing the common stereotype that professors and lawyers are more reserved abstract thinkers than actors or that actors are less emotionally stable and more happy-go-lucky than professors and lawyers. What do you think?)

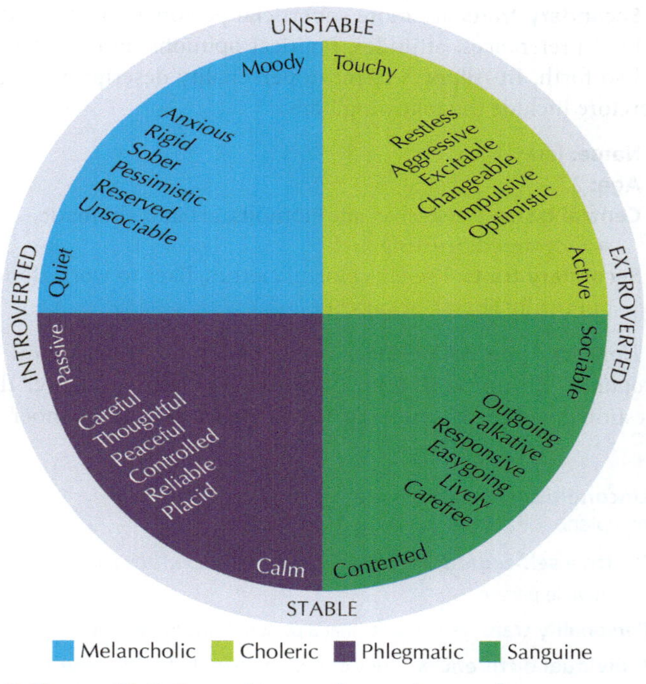

Figure 12.3 Eysenck's two-factor theory of personality. English psychologist Hans Eysenck (1916–1997) proposed that many personality traits are related to whether you are mainly introverted or extroverted and whether you tend to be emotionally stable or unstable (highly emotional). These characteristics, in turn, are related to four basic types of temperament first recognized by the early Greeks. The types are *melancholic* (sad, gloomy), *choleric* (hot-tempered, irritable), *phlegmatic* (sluggish, calm), and *sanguine* (cheerful, hopeful). (Adapted from Eysenck, 1981.)

Cattell (1973) identified 16 source traits, or dimensions of personality. According to him, all 16 are needed to fully describe a personality. Source traits are measured by the *Sixteen Personality Factor Questionnaire* (often referred to as the *16 PF*). Like many personality tests, the 16 PF can be used to produce a *trait profile*, a graph of a person's score on each trait. Trait profiles draw a "picture" of individual personalities, which makes it easier to compare them (Figure 12.4).

Recent Approaches to Classifying Traits

More recent approaches to identifying the key factors that underlie personality have been aimed at simplification. Specifically, psychologists have focused on whether it is possible to accurately describe personality using something fewer than Cattell's 16 factors. Two well-established models suggest that it is: The first, and best-known, is called the Big Five model; the second is referred to as the HEXACO model.

The Big Five Model

Noel is outgoing and friendly, conscientious, even-tempered, and curious. His brother Joel is reserved, hostile, irresponsible, temperamental, and uninterested in ideas. You will be spending a week in a space capsule with either Noel or Joel. Who would you choose? If the answer seems obvious, it's because Noel and Joel were described with the **Big Five personality traits**, a theory that only a handful of characteristics account for most individual differences in personality.

The "Big Five" traits shown in Figure 12.5 attempt to reduce Cattell's 16 factors to just five factors, or source traits (McCrae &

Costa, 2013; Noftle & Fleeson, 2010). If you would like to compare the personalities of two people, try rating them informally on the five dimensions shown in ● Figure 12.5. For *extroversion*, rate how introverted or extroverted each person is. *Agreeableness* refers to how friendly, nurturant, and caring a person is, as opposed to cold, indifferent, self-centered, or spiteful. A person who is *conscientious* is self-disciplined, responsible, and achieving. People low on this factor are irresponsible, careless, and undependable. *Neuroticism* refers to negative, upsetting emotions. People who are high in neuroticism tend to be anxious, emotionally "sour," irritable, and unhappy. Finally, people who rate high on *openness to experience* are creative and open to new ideas.

The Big Five traits have been related to different brain systems and chemicals (DeYoung et al., 2010; Nettle, 2008). They also predict how people will act in various circumstances (Heidemeier & Göritz, 2016; Sutin & Costa, 2010). For example, people who score high in conscientiousness tend to perform well at work, do well in school, and rarely have automobile accidents (Brown et al., 2011; Chamorro-Premuzic & Furnham, 2003). They are healthier and even live longer (Hampson et al., 2013; Martin, Friedman, & Schwartz, 2007).

Extroversion										
Loner Quiet Passive Reserved	**Low**	1	2	3	4	5	6	7	**High**	Joiner Talkative Active Affectionate

Agreeableness										
Suspicious Critical Ruthless Irritable	**Low**	1	2	3	4	5	6	7	**High**	Trusting Lenient Soft-hearted Good-natured

Conscientiousness										
Negligent Lazy Disorganized Late	**Low**	1	2	3	4	5	6	7	**High**	Conscientious Hard-working Well-organized Punctual

Neuroticism										
Calm Even-tempered Comfortable Unemotional	**Low**	1	2	3	4	5	6	7	**High**	Worried Temperamental Self-conscious Emotional

Openness to Experience										
Down-to-earth Uncreative Conventional Uncurious	**Low**	1	2	3	4	5	6	7	**High**	Imaginative Creative Original Curious

● **Figure 12.5 The Big Five.** According to the five-factor model, basic differences in personality can be "boiled down" to the dimensions shown here. Rate yourself on each factor. The five-factor model answers these essential questions about a person: Is she or he extroverted or introverted? Agreeable or difficult? Conscientious or irresponsible? Emotionally stable or unstable? Curious or uncreative? These dimensions cover a large measure of what we might want to know about someone's personality. (Trait descriptions adapted from McCrae & Costa, 2001.)

Human Diversity and Personality Traits: The HEXACO Model

More recently, personality psychologists have demonstrated the existence of a sixth dimension of personality. This new factor—honesty/humility—was discovered after researchers noted that many studies related to the Big Five had been carried out exclusively with samples from Western countries. In the earliest studies to examine whether the five factors could be seen in other cultures, researchers translated an established Big Five questionnaire

Thomas Barrat/Shutterstock.com

Knowing where a person stands on the "Big Five" personality factors helps predict his or her behavior. For example, people who score high on conscientiousness tend to be attentive drivers who are unlikely to have automobile accidents.

Source traits (factors) Basic underlying traits, or dimensions, of personality; each source trait is reflected in a number of surface traits.

Factor analysis A statistical technique used to correlate multiple measurements and identify general underlying factors.

Big Five personality traits Theory that only a handful of characteristics account for most individual differences in personality.

into Korean and asked a large sample of people in Seoul, South Korea to complete it.

Like Cattell, factor analysis was used to establish how many dimensions (factors) could be seen in the Korean data. Factors that corresponded well with the Big Five were clearly represented in the results, but there was also a sixth factor—one that had never been reported in previous research. This sixth factor contained traits such as *truthful*, *frank*, *honest*, *unassuming*, and *sincere*, and on its opposing side were adjectives such as *calculating*, *sly*, *hypocritical*, *conceited*, *pompous*, and *pretentious* (Lee & Ashton, 2012).

While it was somewhat surprising to find such a large and clear sixth factor representing honesty/humility in the Korean results, subsequent studies have demonstrated that this "H factor" can be reliably found in data from many European countries as well (Ashton et al., 2004). The result of this work is the HEXACO model of personality, which represents an extension of the Big Five (Ashton & Lee, 2001). It's a convenient name, since the prefix "hexa" means six and the letters represent each of the factors: **H**onesty/Humility, **E**motionality (which is the equivalent of Neuroticism), e**X**traversion, **A**greeableness, **C**onscientiousness, and **O**penness to Experience.

Few Factors, Many Personalities

If you think about just how diverse people can be, it may seem a bit strange to think that something as complex as personality can be reduced to just five or six factors. To understand how that can be, take a moment to think about using a questionnaire to rate your best friend's personality. For each of the six factors in the HEXACO model, then, let's say you could rate your friend on a 5-point scale. If we were talking about the Agreeableness factor, then, we might rate that person as being either "very disagreeable," "disagreeable," "neutral," "agreeable," or "very agreeable."

According to Ashton (2018), if we did that for each of the six factors, we could describe $5 \times 5 \times 5 \times 5 \times 5 \times 5 = 16,625$ kinds of people. If you could accurately rate people on a 7-point scale instead of one with only 5 points, you would be able to describe close to 118,000 kinds of people. Clearly, a small number of factors can take you a long way in understanding the wide diversity that we can see in people's personalities.

a katz/Shutterstock.com

Psychologists and employers are especially interested in the personality traits of individuals who hold high-risk, high-stress positions concerning public safety, such as police, firefighters, air traffic controllers, and nuclear power plant employees.

Are some trait scores better than others? Interesting question. To answer it, start by rating yourself on the factors that make up the Big Five (see Figure 12.5). Now, when you were rating yourself, did you think that some of the traits didn't seem very attractive? After all, who would want to score low in *extroversion?* What could be good about being a quiet, reserved loner? In other words, aren't some personality patterns better than others?

You might be surprised to learn that there is no single "best" personality pattern. For example, extroverts tend to earn more during their careers than introverts, and they have more sexual partners. But they also are more likely to take risks than introverts (and to land in the hospital with an injury). Extroverts also are more likely to divorce. Because of this, extroverted men are less likely to live with their children. In other words, extroversion tends to open the doors to some life experiences, and introversion opens doors to others (Cain, 2012; Nettle, 2005).

The same is true for *agreeableness.* Agreeable people attract more friends and enjoy strong social support from others. But agreeable people often put the interests of friends and family ahead of their own. This can leave such people at a disadvantage. To do creative, artistic work or to succeed in the business world often involves putting your own interests first sometimes (Nettle, 2008).

How about conscientiousness? That seems like it would always be a good trait. Up to a point, conscientiousness is associated with high achievement. However, having impossibly high standards, a trait called *perfectionism*, can be a problem. As you might expect, college students who are perfectionists tend to get good grades. Yet some students cross the line into maladaptive perfectionism, which typically *lowers* performance at school and elsewhere (Weiner & Carton, 2012). Authentic Navajo rugs always have a flaw in their intricate designs. Navajo weavers intentionally make a "mistake" in each rug as a reminder that humans are not perfect. There is a lesson in this: It is not always necessary, or even desirable, to be "perfect." To learn from your experiences, you must feel free to make mistakes. Success, in the long run, is more often based on seeking "excellence" rather than "perfection" (Enns, Cox, & Clara, 2005).

Except for very extreme personality patterns, which are often maladaptive, most personality dimensions involve a mix of costs and benefits (Turiano et al., 2013). We all face the task of pursuing life experiences that best suit our own unique personality patterns (Nettle, 2008).

Personality Traits in Everyday Life: Cruelty, Sadism, and Psychopathy

In 2002, psychologist Delroy Paulhus and his student Kevin Williams published an influential paper in which they described three personality traits—a dark triad—that seemed to predict some of the worst of human behavior (Paulhus & Williams, 2002). The first of these traits, *narcissism,* is marked by a grandiose

▲ **Table 12.4 The Dirty Dozen**

		Strongly disagree			Strongly agree	
1	I tend to manipulate others to get my way.	1	2	3	4	5
2	I have used deceit or lied to get my way.	1	2	3	4	5
3	I have used flattery to get my way.	1	2	3	4	5
4	I tend to exploit others toward my own end.	1	2	3	4	5
5	I tend to lack remorse.	1	2	3	4	5
6	I tend to be unconcerned with the morality of my actions.	1	2	3	4	5
7	I tend to be callous or insensitive.	1	2	3	4	5
8	I tend to be cynical.	1	2	3	4	5
9	I tend to want others to admire me.	1	2	3	4	5
10	I tend to want others to pay attention to me.	1	2	3	4	5
11	I tend to seek prestige or status.	1	2	3	4	5
12	I tend to expect special favors from others.	1	2	3	4	5

self-concept, as well as feelings of entitlement and superiority. The second trait is *subclinical psychopathy* (psychopathy that is still considered within the range of "normal"), which is associated with thrill seeking paired with low anxiety and empathy. The third trait is *Machiavellianism*, a term which gets its name from an Italian political advisor named Machiavelli who, in the 1500s, wrote a book called *The Prince*, in which he seemed to glorify immoral behavior. Those who score high on Machiavellianism tend to be cold and manipulative (Furnham, Richards, & Paulhus, 2013).

In the years since Paulhus and Williams' original paper was published, psychologists have examined how the dark triad can help us to predict some of the most disturbing types of behavior. For example, those who score higher on the dark triad are more prone to endorse prejudice toward immigrants (Hodson, Hogg, & MacInnis, 2009) and take revenge in romantic relationships (Rasmussen & Boon, 2014). Moreover, there are links between all three elements of the dark triad and bullying among adults (Baughman, Dearing, Giammarco, & Vernon, 2012).

As you might expect, dark personalities tend to be men who are risk takers and are more likely to smoke, drink, and do drugs (Jonason, Koenig, & Tost, 2010). Although these "bad boys" also tend to be promiscuous and indiscriminate in their choice of sex partners, women find them strangely attractive (Aitken, Lyons, & Jonason, 2013; Carter, Campbell, & Muncer, 2014). (It is worth noting that some women also have dark triad personalities [Jonason & Lavertu, 2017].)

Do you think you know someone like this? Try using the "Dirty Dozen" in ▲ Table 12.4 to rate that person. A high score on the first four questions is associated with the trait of Machiavellianism, a high score on the middle four questions is associated with the trait of psychopathy, and a high score on the last four questions is associated with the trait of narcissism (Furnham, Richards, & Paulhus, 2013).

Paulhus' more recent research suggests that a fourth personality characteristic—*subclinical sadism*—is also a good predictor of the antisocial behaviors associated with the dark triad, leading him to propose a "dark tetrad." While sadism is typically associated with extreme levels of sexual and criminal deviance, "everyday sadism"—the enjoyment of cruelty that can be observed in our day-to-day life—is very common in our society. We see it, for example, in police and military brutality, Ultimate Fighting Championship events, and the way people eagerly engage with video games that depict graphic and sometimes savage scenes of rape and torture.

In his research, Paulhus and his students have found that when aggressive acts could be easily committed, all four elements of the dark tetrad were associated with unprovoked aggression toward an innocent victim. Only those who scored high on sadism, however, were willing to *work* for the opportunity to harm an innocent person (Buckels, Jones, & Paulhus, 2013). Similarly, a study of Internet behavior revealed that each aspect of the dark tetrad predicts Internet trolling (deceptive and destructive behavior in a social setting on the web), though everyday sadism was the best predictor of the four (Buckels, Trapnell, & Paulhus, 2014). Clearly there's some wisdom in the web-based warning "Don't feed the trolls."

Aren't these traits signs of mental illness? In Section 14.3, we will discuss personality disorders such as narcissistic personality disorder. Individuals with these disorders typically express dark triad traits, *but to the extreme*. In contrast, these traits are **subclinical** in many dark triad personalities, and hence not extreme enough to qualify for a diagnosis.

Subclinical (traits) Qualities of individuals that are not extreme enough to merit a psychiatric diagnosis.

Traits Versus Types

Have you ever asked the question, "What type of person is she (or he)?" A **personality type** refers to people who have *several traits in common* (Larsen & Buss, 2014). Informally, your own thinking might include categories such as the executive type, the athletic type, the motherly type, the techno geek, and so forth. If you tried to define these informal types, you would probably list a different collection of traits for each one.

Over the years, psychologists have proposed many ways to categorize personalities into types. One of the most common is the Myers-Briggs Type Indicator (MBTI), which is based on the work of Carl Jung (McCaulley, 2000). The MBTI has four scales: Introversion/Extroversion (I vs. E), Sensing/Intuition (S vs. N), Thinking/Feeling (T vs. F), and Judging/Perceiving (J vs. P). The questionnaire requires that respondents read numerous pairs of statements and, in each case, choose which one best describes them. After completing the MBTI, people are assigned to a "type" based on their scores for the four scales. For example, someone whose answers suggest that they are Introverted (I), Intuitive (N), Thinking (T), and Judging (J) would be classified as an INTJ "type."

Weaknesses of Type Models

Unlike questionnaires that assess the HEXACO or Big Five models of personality, the MBTI assigns people to one end of a scale or the other. If we take Introversion/Extroversion as an example, a questionnaire based on the Big Five would allow for people to be classed as extremely extroverted, extremely introverted, or anywhere in between. Earlier, we saw how allowing for this type of variation on the Big Five dimensions can be helpful in explaining the vast diversity we see in personality.

In contrast, the MBTI would classify each person as being either introverted or extroverted, with no middle ground possible. In some cases, the answer to a *single question* on the MBTI might tip the balance in terms of a person being classified as "I" or "E" on this scale. As a result, one of the great weaknesses of type models in general, and the MBTI in particular, is the lack of precision that comes from trying to reduce individual differences in personality to the point where people must be grouped into one of two discrete categories (Ashton, 2018). Doing so oversimplifies the reality that we observe every day when we interact with our friends, family, and coworkers: differences on the dimensions of personality are often subtle, and cannot realistically be viewed in either/or terms.

Strengths of Type Models

Even though types tend to oversimplify personality, they do have value, especially in the clinical domain. Most often, types are a shorthand way to label people who have several key traits in common. For example, in the next chapter, we discuss hardy personalities. Hardy people are unusually resistant to stress (see ● Figure 12.6). Similarly, in ■ Section 14.3, you will read about unhealthy personality types such as the paranoid personality, the dependent personality, and the antisocial personality. Each problem type is defined by a specific collection of traits that are not adaptive.

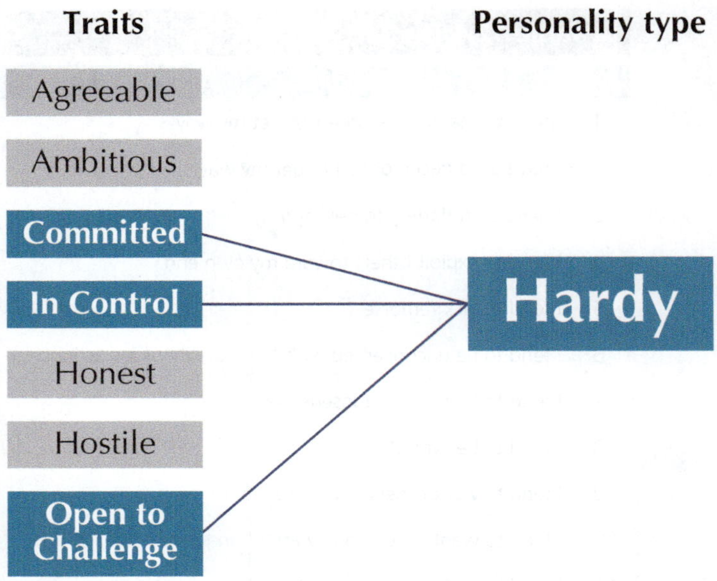

● **Figure 12.6 Personality types.** Personality types are defined by the presence of several specific traits. For example, several possible personality traits are shown in the left column. A person who has a hardy personality typically possesses all or most of the highlighted traits. Hardy persons are especially resistant to stress (■ see Section 13.1).

Reflective Practice

Traits: The Building Blocks of Personality

1. Eysenck's early trait theory was composed of two factors, emotional stability–instability and ________________.
2. Traits are stable dispositions that a person shows in most ________________.
3. Central traits are those shared by most members of a culture. T or F?
4. Cattell believes that ________________ traits are at the core of people's personality.
5. Which of the following is ***not*** one of the Big Five personality traits?
   a. submissiveness
   b. agreeableness
   c. extroversion
   d. neuroticism
6. The unique factor that defines the HEXACO model of personality is ________________.

THINK CRITICALLY

7. Can you think of a Big Five trait besides conscientiousness that might be related to academic achievement?

SELF-REFLECT

- List six or seven traits that best describe your personality. Which system of traits seems to best match your list, Allport's, Cattell's, the Big Five, or the HEXACO model?

Answers: 1. introversion–extroversion 2. situations 3. F 4. source 5. a 6. honesty/humility 7. In one study, conscientiousness was positively related to academic performance, as you might expect. Students high in neuroticism also were better academic performers, but only if they were not too stressed (Kappe & van der Flier, 2010).

12.3 Personality Assessment

GATEWAYS LEARNING OUTCOME:
After reading this section you should be able to:

12.3.1 Outline four ways in which personality can be measured

Measuring personality can help predict how people will behave at work, at school, and in therapy. However, painting a detailed picture can be a challenge. Psychologists use a number of methods to assess personality, each of which has strengths and weaknesses (Engler, 2014). For this reason, they are often used in combination. Let's take a deeper dive into four of the most common ways to assess personality and individual differences: interviews, observation, personality inventories, and projective tests.

Interviews

In an **interview**, direct questioning is used to learn about a person's life history, personality traits, or current mental state (Craig, 2013; Murphy & Dillon, 2015). In an **unstructured interview**, conversation is informal, and topics are taken up freely as they arise. In a **structured interview**, information is gathered by asking a planned series of questions.

How are interviews used? Interviews are used to select people for jobs, college, or special programs; to study the dynamics of personality; and to identify personality disturbances that may be helpful for counseling or therapy. In addition to providing information, interviews make it possible to observe a person's tone of voice, hand gestures, posture, and facial expressions. Such "body language" cues are important because they may radically alter the message sent, as when a person claims to be "completely calm" but trembles uncontrollably.

Interviews can give rapid insight into personality, but they have limitations. For one thing, interviewers can be swayed by preconceptions. A person identified as a "housewife," "college student," "high school athlete," "punk," "geek," or "ski bum" may be misjudged because of an interviewer's personal biases about those categories (Forgas, 2011). Second, an interviewer's own personality, gender, or ethnicity may influence a client's behavior. When this occurs, it can accentuate or distort the person's apparent traits (Kaplan & Saccuzzo, 2018). A third problem is that people sometimes try to deceive interviewers. For example, a person accused of a crime might try to avoid punishment by pretending to be mentally unfit to stand trial. Finally, a fourth problem is the **halo effect**, which is the tendency to generalize a favorable (or unfavorable) impression to an entire personality (Hartung et al., 2010). Because of the halo effect, a person who is likable or physically attractive may be rated more mature, intelligent, or mentally healthy than she or he actually is.

Even with their limitations, interviews are a respected method of assessment. In many cases, interviews are the first step in evaluating personality and an essential prelude to therapy. Nevertheless, interviews are usually not revealing enough and are often supplemented by other measures and tests (Murphy & Dillon, 2015; Meyer et al., 2001).

Direct Observation

Do you often find yourself surveying people's actions when you're in airports, bus depots, parks, taverns, subway stations, or other public places? Many people relish a chance to observe the actions of others. When used for assessment, looking at behavior by **direct observation** is a simple extension of this natural interest in "people watching." For instance, a psychologist might arrange to observe a disturbed child as she plays with other children. Is the child withdrawn? Does she become hostile or aggressive without warning? Through careful observation, the psychologist can identify the girl's personality traits and clarify the nature of her problems.

Unfortunately, direct observations have limitations similar to those of interviews. For example, the misperceptions and biases of observers can be a problem. Moreover, the people who are being observed may not behave as they normally would if they know they are being watched. For this reason, alternative forms of observation have been developed. We'll discuss two of them: rating scales and situational testing.

g-stockstudio/Shutterstock.com

What is your impression of this person awaiting a job interview? If you think that he looks friendly, attractive, or neat, your other perceptions of him might be altered by that impression. Interviewers are often influenced by the halo effect (see text).

Personality type A style of personality defined by a group of related traits.

Interview (personality) A face-to-face meeting held for the purpose of gaining information about an individual's personal history, personality traits, current psychological state, and so forth.

Unstructured interview An interview in which conversation is informal and topics are taken up freely as they arise.

Structured interview An interview that follows a prearranged plan, usually a series of planned questions.

Halo effect The tendency to generalize a favorable or unfavorable particular impression to unrelated details of personality.

Direct observation Assessing behavior through direct surveillance.

Rating Scales and Behavioral Assessment

A **rating scale** is a list of personality traits or aspects of behavior that can be used to evaluate a person during observations (Siefert, 2010) (● Figure 12.7). Rating scales limit the chance that some traits will be overlooked by observers while others are exaggerated (Synhorst et al., 2005).

An alternative approach is to do a **behavioral assessment** by counting the frequency of specific behaviors (Cipani & Schock, 2010). In this case, observers record *actions*, not what traits they think a person has. For example, a psychologist working with hospitalized psychiatric patients might note the frequency of a patient's aggression, self-care, speech, and unusual behaviors. Behavioral assessments also can be used to probe thought processes. In one study, for example, couples were assessed while talking with each other about their sexuality. Couples with sexual difficulties were less likely to be receptive to discussing their sexuality and more likely to blame each other than were couples with no sexual difficulties (Kelly, Strassberg, & Turner, 2006).

Situational Testing

In a **situational test**, real-life conditions are simulated during an observation so that a person's spontaneous reactions can be observed. Such tests assume that the best way to learn how people react is to put them in realistic situations and watch what happens. Situational tests expose people to frustration, temptation, pressure, boredom, or other conditions capable of revealing personality characteristics (De Leng et al., 2016). Some popular reality TV programs bear some similarity to situational tests—which may account for their ability to attract millions of viewers.

Larry St. Pierre/Shutterstock.com

A police special tactics team undergoes a judgmental firearms training exercise to protect students from a school shooter. Variations on this situational test are used by many police departments. All officers must score a passing grade.

How are situational tests done? An interesting example of situational testing is the *judgmental firearms training* provided by many police departments. At times, police officers must make split-second decisions about using their weapons. A mistake could be fatal. In a typical shoot–don't shoot test, actors play the part of armed criminals. As various high-risk scenes are acted out live or online, officers must decide to shoot or hold their fire.

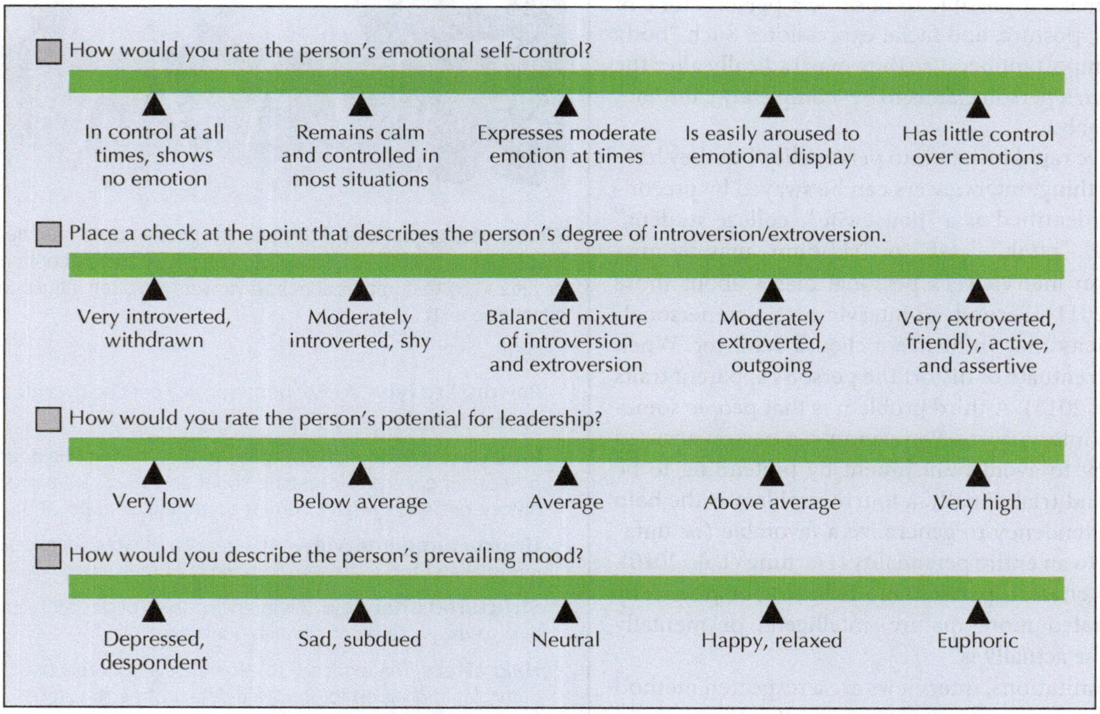

● **Figure 12.7 Sample rating scale items.** To understand how the scale works, imagine someone you know well. Where would you place check marks on each of the scales to rate that person's characteristics?

Personality Inventories

A **personality inventory** (or questionnaire) is a paper-and-pencil test designed to reveal personality characteristics. Personality inventories are more objective than interviews or observation. (An **objective test** gives the same score when different people take it.) The questions, administration, and scoring of personality inventories are all standardized, so that scores are unaffected by any biases that an examiner may have. In addition, a good personality test must also be reliable and valid (Kaplan & Saccuzzo, 2018). A test has **reliability** if it yields stable scores over time—that is, if it yields close to the same score each time that it is given to the same person. A test has **validity** if it measures the traits it was designed to assess. Unfortunately, many personality tests that you will encounter, such as those in magazines or on the Internet, have little or no validity. Finally, an objective test benefits from extensive **norms**, which are standards used to compare an individual's performance on a test with that of others. (■ Reliability and validity are important characteristics of all psychological tests, especially intelligence tests. See Section 9.2.)

Dozens of personality tests are available, including the *California Psychological Inventory* (CPI), the *Eysenck Personality Questionnaire* (EPQ), the *Sixteen Personality Factor Questionnaire* (16 PF), and the *Neuroticism, Extraversion, Openness Personality Inventory* (NEO-PI). One of the best-known and most widely used standardized tests is the **Minnesota Multiphasic Personality Inventory** (MMPI). The current version (MMPI-2) is composed of 567 items to which a test taker must respond "true" or "false" (Butcher, 2011). Items include statements such as the following:

Everything tastes the same.
I am very normal, sexually.
I like birds.
I usually daydream in the afternoon.
Mostly, I stay away from other people.
Someone has been trying to hurt me.
Sometimes I think strange thoughts.*

At first, these items may seem like a strange way to assess someone's personality. (Liking birds? Seriously?) However, the creators of inventories such as the MMPI-2 understand that any single item tells us very little about personality. It is only through *patterns* of responses to many items that personality dimensions are revealed.

The MMPI-2 measures 10 major aspects of personality (listed in ▲ Table 12.5). After the MMPI-2 is scored, results are charted graphically as an *MMPI-2 profile* (● Figure 12.8). By comparing a person's profile with scores produced by typical adults, a psychologist can identify various personality disorders. Additional scales can identify substance abuse, eating disorders, repression, anger, cynicism, low self-esteem, family problems, inability to function in a job, and other problems (Butcher, 2011).

How accurate is the MMPI-2? Personality questionnaires are accurate only if people tell the truth about themselves. Because of this, the MMPI-2 has additional *validity scales* that reveal whether a person's scores should be discarded. The validity scales detect attempts by test-takers to "fake good" (make themselves look good) or "fake bad" (make it look like they have problems) (Scherbaum et al., 2013). Other scales uncover defensiveness or tendencies to exaggerate shortcomings and troubles. When taking the MMPI-2, it is best to answer honestly and not try to second-guess the test.

In spite of its strengths, a clinical psychologist trying to decide whether a person has emotional problems would be wise to take more than the MMPI-2 into account. Test scores are informative, but they can incorrectly label some people (Kaplan & Saccuzzo, 2018). Fortunately, clinical judgments usually rely on information from interviews, tests, and other methods of assessment. Also, despite their limitations, it is reassuring to note that psychological assessments are at least as accurate as commonly used medical tests (Neukrug & Fawcett, 2015).

*MMPI-2 statements themselves cannot be reproduced, to protect the validity of the test.

▲ Table 12.5 MMPI-2 Basic Clinical Subscales

1. **Hypochondriasis** (HI-po-kon-DRY-uh-sis). Exaggerated concern about one's physical health.
2. **Depression.** Feelings of worthlessness, hopelessness, and pessimism.
3. **Hysteria.** The presence of physical complaints for which no physical basis can be established.
4. **Psychopathic deviate.** Emotional shallowness in relationships and a disregard for social and moral standards.
5. **Masculinity/femininity.** One's degree of traditional "masculine" aggressiveness or "feminine" sensitivity.
6. **Paranoia.** Extreme suspiciousness and feelings of persecution.
7. **Psychasthenia** (sike-as-THEE-nee-ah). The presence of obsessive worries, irrational fears (phobias), and compulsive (ritualistic) actions.
8. **Schizophrenia.** Emotional withdrawal and unusual or bizarre thinking and actions.
9. **Mania.** Emotional excitability, manic moods or behavior, and excessive activity.
10. **Social introversion.** One's tendency to be socially withdrawn.

Rating scale A list of personality traits or aspects of behavior on which a person is rated.

Behavioral assessment Recording the frequency of various behaviors.

Situational test Simulating real-life conditions so that a person's reactions may be directly observed.

Personality inventory A paper-and-pencil test consisting of questions that reveal aspects of personality.

Objective test A test that gives the same score when different people take it.

Reliability Stability of test scores over time.

Validity Degree to which a test measures the trait that it was designed to.

Norm Standard used to compare an individual's performance on a test with that of others.

Minnesota Multiphasic Personality Inventory A standardized test designed to identify problem areas of functioning in an individual's personality.

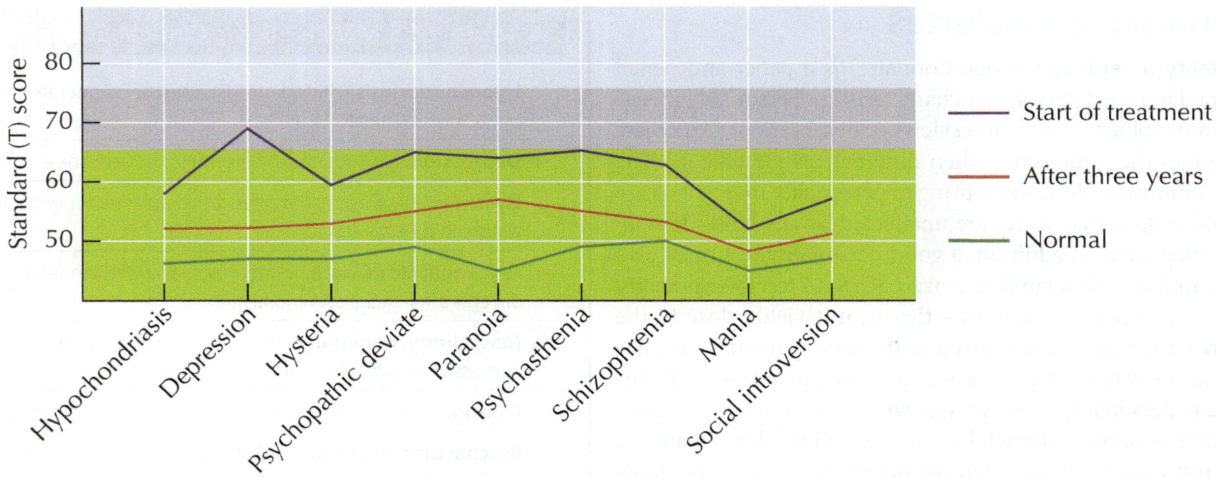

Figure 12.8 MMPI-2 profiles. The MMPI-2 can even track progress in therapy. At the start of treatment, the scores of a group of severely troubled individuals were elevated on most of the individual scales. (Note that the masculinity/femininity scores are not included.) After three years of therapy, their scores have declined significantly and are much more similar to normal scores, which usually fall in the 45–50 range. An unusually low score (40 and below) also may reveal personality characteristics or problems. (Adapted from Gordon, 2001.)

Projective Tests

Projective tests take a different approach to personality. Interviews, observation, rating scales, and inventories try to directly identify overt, observable traits. By contrast, projective tests seek to uncover deeply hidden or *unconscious* wishes, thoughts, and needs (Burger, 2015; McGrath & Carroll, 2012).

As a child, you may have delighted in finding faces and objects in cloud formations. Or perhaps you have learned something about your friends' personalities from their reactions to movies or paintings. If so, you have some insight into the rationale for projective tests. In **projective tests**, a person is asked to describe ambiguous or unstructured stimuli or make up stories about them. Describing an unambiguous stimulus (a picture of an automobile, for example) tells little about your personality. But when you are faced with an unstructured stimulus, you must organize what you see in terms of your own life experiences. Everyone sees something different in a projective test, and what is perceived can reveal the inner workings of personality.

Projective tests have no right or wrong answers, which makes them difficult to fake. Moreover, projective tests can be a rich source of information because responses are not restricted to simple true/false or yes/no answers. There are several types of projective tests; two of the most common are the Rorschach Inkblot Test and the Thematic Apperception Test.

Rorschach Inkblot Test

Is the inkblot test a projective technique? The **Rorschach Inkblot Test** (ROAR-shock) is one of the oldest and most widely used projective tests. Developed by Swiss psychologist Hermann Rorschach in the 1920s, it consists of 10 standardized inkblots forming complex, irregular shapes.

How does the test work? First, a person is shown each blot and asked to describe what she or he sees in it (Figure 12.9). Later,

Figure 12.9 The Rorschach. Inkblots similar to those used on the Rorschach. What do you see?

the psychologist may return to a blot, asking the person to identify specific sections of it, to expand previous descriptions, or to give new impressions about what it contains. Obvious differences in content—such as "blood dripping from a dagger" versus "flowers blooming in a basket"—are important for identifying personal conflicts and fantasies. But surprisingly, content is less important than what parts of the inkblot are used to organize images. These factors allow psychologists to detect emotional disturbances by observing how a person perceives the world (Bornstein, 2012; Kishimoto et al., 2016). (■ Schizophrenia and other psychotic disorders are associated with severe disturbances in thinking and perception. See Section 14.5.) Such disturbances are usually readily apparent during projective testing (Moore et al., 2013).

Thematic Apperception Test

Another popular projective test is the **Thematic Apperception Test (TAT)**, developed by personality theorist Henry Murray (1893–1988).

How does the TAT differ from the Rorschach? The TAT consists of 20 sketches depicting various scenes and life situations (● Figure 12.10). During testing, a person is shown each sketch and asked to make up a story about the people in it. Later, the person looks at each sketch a second or a third time and elaborates on previous stories or creates new stories.

To score the TAT, a psychologist analyzes the content of the stories. Interpretations focus on how people feel, how they interact, what events led up to the incidents depicted in the sketch, and how the story will end. For example, TAT stories told by bereaved college students typically include themes of death, grief, and coping with loss (Balk et al., 1998).

● **Figure 12.10 The Thematic Apperception Test.** This is a picture like those used for the TAT. If you wish to simulate the test, tell a story that explains what led up to the pictured situation, what is happening now, and how the action will end.

A psychologist might also count how many times the central figure in a TAT story is angry, overlooked, apathetic, jealous, or threatened. A student wrote the following story to describe Figure 12.10:

> The girl has been seeing this guy her mother doesn't like. The mother is telling her that she better not see him again. The mother says, "He's just like your father." The mother and father are divorced. The mother is smiling because she thinks she is right. But she doesn't really know what the girl wants. The girl is going to see the guy again, anyway.

As this example implies, the TAT is especially good at revealing feelings about social situations and relationships (Jenkins, Dobbs, & Leeper, 2015; Serfass & Sherman, 2013).

Limitations of Projective Testing

Although projective tests have been popular, their validity is open to question (Ackerman, Lewis, & Taylor, 2014; Bornstein, 2012). Objectivity and reliability (consistency) also are low for different users of the TAT and Rorschach. Note that after a person interprets an ambiguous stimulus, the scorer must interpret the person's (sometimes) ambiguous responses. In a sense, the interpretation of a projective test may be a projective test for the scorer!

Despite their drawbacks, clinicians feel that projective tests still have value (McGrath & Carroll, 2012). This is especially true when they are used as part of a *test battery* (collection of assessment devices and interviews). In the hands of a skilled clinician, projective tests can be a good way to detect major conflicts, to get clients to talk about upsetting topics, and to set goals for therapy (Garcia-Barrera et al., 2013; Teglasi, 2010).

Reflective Practice

Personality Assessment

1. All personality tests have strengths and weaknesses, which is why it's best to use them in combination. T or F?
2. The halo effect can be a serious problem in accurate personality assessment that is based on ______.
   a. projective testing
   b. behavioral recording
   c. interviewing
   d. the TAT
3. Doing a behavioral assessment requires direct observation of the person's actions or a direct report of the person's thoughts. T or F?
4. A test is considered valid if it consistently yields the same score when the same person takes it on different occasions. T or F?

Projective tests Personality tests that use ambiguous or unstructured stimuli.

Rorschach Inkblot Test Projective test that consists of complex, irregular monochromatic shapes.

Thematic Apperception Test (TAT) A projective test consisting of 20 different scenes and life situations about which respondents make up stories.

5. Which of the following is considered the most objective measure of personality?
   a. rating scales
   b. personality questionnaires
   c. projective tests
   d. TAT
6. The use of ambiguous stimuli is most characteristic of
   a. interviews
   b. projective tests
   c. personality inventories
   d. direct observation

THINK CRITICALLY

7. Projective testing would be of greatest interest to which type of personality theorist?

SELF-REFLECT

- How do *you* assess the personality of your friends, family and coworkers? Do you informally use any of the methods described in this section of the chapter?

Answers: 1. T 2. c 3. T 4. F 5. b 6. b 7. Psychodynamic, because projective testing is designed to uncover unconscious thoughts, feelings, and conflicts.

12.4 Factors Influencing Personality

GATEWAYS LEARNING OUTCOME:
After reading this section you should be able to:

12.4.1 Describe the results of behavioral genetics studies with regard to the role of genetic and environmental influences on personality

Like many other human characteristics, personality is influenced by both genes and the environment. However, personality theorists have long grappled with the relative contributions of nature and nurture in shaping personalities. Some approaches, such as trait theory and psychoanalytic theory, stress the role of inherited biological predispositions, whereas others, including humanist and behavioral theories, stress the role of learning and life experiences.

To understand the effect of genetics and environment on personality, psychologists often turn to the field of **behavioral genetics**, the study of inherited behavioral traits. We know that facial features, eye color, body type, and many other physical characteristics are inherited, but so are many of our behavioral dispositions (Kalat, 2016). For example, behavioral genetic studies have shown that intelligence, language, and some psychological disorders are influenced by heredity. (See ■ Sections 9.4 and ■ 14.2.) What about personality?

It probably won't surprise you to learn that research clearly indicates that genes affect personality as well (Briley & Tucker-Drob, 2017). Much of the work in this area has focused on the Big Five personality dimensions, and is aimed at trying to establish the extent to which our genes contribute to individual differences. To answer such questions, psychological scientists examine the personalities of people who vary in terms of the amount of genetic material they share. In particular, they often focus on identical twins (who share 100 percent of their genes), fraternal twins and other non-twin siblings (who share, on average, 50 percent of their genes), and adopted siblings (who share 0 percent of their genes).

For several decades, psychologists at the University of Minnesota have studied identical twins who grew up in different homes. Medical and psychological tests reveal that reunited twins are very much alike, even when they are reared apart (Bouchard, 2004; Segal, 2012). If one twin excels at art, music, dance, drama, or athletics, the other is likely to as well—despite wide differences in childhood environment. They may even be similar in voice quality, facial gestures, hand movements, and nervous tics, such as nail biting.

Many reunited twins in the Minnesota study (the Minnesota Twins?) have displayed similarities far beyond what would be expected on the basis of heredity (Segal, 2012). The "Jim twins," James Lewis and James Springer, are one famous example. Both Jims had married and divorced women named Linda. Both had undergone police training. One named his firstborn son James Allan—and the other named *his* firstborn son James Alan. Both drove Chevrolets and vacationed at the same beach each summer. Both listed carpentry and mechanical drawing among their hobbies. Both had built benches around trees in their yards (Holden, 1980).

But not all twins are so similar. Consider identical twins Carolyn Spiro and Pamela Spiro Wagner who, unlike the "Jim twins," lived together throughout their childhood. While in sixth grade, they found out that President Kennedy had been assassinated. Carolyn wasn't sure why everyone was so upset. Pamela heard voices announcing that she was responsible for his death. After years of hiding her voices from everyone, Pamela tried to commit suicide while the twins were attending Brown University. She was later diagnosed with schizophrenia. Though never cured, she nonetheless went on to write award-winning poetry. In contrast, Carolyn eventually became a Harvard psychiatrist (Spiro Wagner & Spiro, 2005).

Clearly, some twins reared apart can appear very similar while some who are reared together appear rather different. What, then, can we say about the role of genes in personality overall? It turns out that examining a large number of twins suggests that personality *is* influenced by genes, and that each of the Big Five dimensions shows a similar degree of heritability—about 50 percent (Loehlin, McCrae, Costa, & John, 1998).

Of course, this figure implies that personality is shaped as much by environment as it is by biological predispositions (Johnson et al., 2009). Each personality, then, is a unique blend of heredity and environment, nature and nurture, biology and culture. We are not— thank goodness!—genetically programmed robots whose behavior and personality traits are "wired in" for life (Funder, 2010).

If personality is shaped by the environment as well as genes, then does that mean it will change over time as we get older and have

new experiences? Good question. To answer it, we need to know whether, on average, younger, middle-aged, and older adults look similar with respect to personality traits, or whether personality changes as we move through the lifespan. Researchers have investigated this question, and it appears that the answer is yes, there are indeed age-related changes in the levels of various traits. For example, across large groups of people, assertiveness and confidence tend to increase across adulthood, as does agreeableness, conscientiousness, self-regulation, and honesty/humility. In contrast, anxiety tends to be much higher among young adults than those that are older, on average (Ashton, 2018).

What these findings tell us is that even though any one person's level of a particular trait may go up or down over the course of their lifetime, *on average*, across many people, there is a general tendency for levels of some traits to rise or fall. Moreover, some researchers do believe that these trends may reflect the experiences that adulthood brings with it. Such experiences may include beginning a career, settling into a stable romantic relationship, becoming a parent, or providing care for aging relatives. The *social roles hypothesis* suggests that as we rise up to meet these new life experiences, personality traits will change in a way that allows us to be successful (Vandewater, 1997).

Reflective Practice

Factors Influencing Personality

1. The study of inherited behavioral traits is called ______________________.
2. Research suggests that the environment does not impact personality. T or F?
3. Studies indicate that when identical twins are reared apart, their personalities are
   a. not at all similar
   b. just as similar as identical twins reared together
   c. more similar than identical twins reared together
   d. difficult to evaluate
4. Studies examining personality across the lifespan indicate an overall decrease in trait-level ________________ as people get older.
   a. honesty/humility
   b. agreeableness
   c. self-regulation
   d. anxiety

CRITICAL THINKING

5. Why might major life experiences like getting married or starting a new job lead to changes in personality traits?

SELF-REFLECT

- To what extent do you think that your personality is similar to your parents? What about your siblings?

Answers: 1. Behavioral genetics 2. F 3. b 4. d 5. Both getting married and starting a new job require young adults to build relationships that are likely to last many years, and from which they cannot easily disengage. Ensuring that such relationships are positive and productive means that people need to foster those personality traits that contribute to successful relationships, including self-regulation, honesty/humility, and agreeableness.

12.5 Psychology and Your Skill Set: Leadership

GATEWAYS LEARNING OUTCOME:
After reading this section you should be able to:

12.5.1 Create a plan to improve your leadership abilities

Jonathan Ferrar is a true leader. That much was already clear when he was growing up in Brooklyn's Sunset Park. As a teenager, he recognized that his low-income neighborhood was home to significant environmental risks: three power plants, a sludge transfer facility, dozens of industrial sites, and a major highway carrying 200,000 cars and trucks each day. He also learned about the effects on residents' health—above-average rates of lung cancer and respiratory illnesses.

Some people might resign themselves to accepting the situation, but not Jonathan. Instead, he worked for Uprose, an environmental not-for-profit agency. He testified in front of the Environmental Protection Agency about the risk of storm surges brought on by climate change. He warned that they could unleash toxic waste into the air and water from the industrial waterfront

Photo Courtesy The Barron Prize

Are people like Jonathan Ferrar born leaders, or can each of us develop these skills?

Behavioral genetics The study of inherited behavioral traits and tendencies.

in his community. Sadly, he was proven right when Hurricane Sandy smashed into the New York coastline 18 months later. Jonathan has also organized the annual New York City Climate Justice Youth Summit so that young people can have a voice in political discussions about the environment.

Are people born leaders, or can each of us develop these skills? If you want to know the answer, we'll lead you there.

Are Good Leaders Born or Built?

Most early leadership research focused on the personality of the successful leader. It was generally accepted that good leaders possessed certain personality traits that enabled them to effectively manage teams (Northouse, 2016). Psychologists focused on traits such as self-confidence, intelligence, extroversion, persistence, and responsibility, although they also examined traits that are more closely connected to building relationships, such as sociability, cooperativeness, and emotional intelligence.

Does that mean people are either "born leaders" or they are not? Just as with early theories of personality, early *trait-based approaches* to leadership assumed that traits were inborn. More recently, however, psychologists studying leadership have begun to think of traits as relatively stable learned behavior patterns. (■ The same is true of personality psychologists. See Section 12.3.) This *behavioral approach* to leadership refocused research on leadership behaviors, the role of environmental circumstances, and how to "learn" leadership.

The behavioral approach examines what successful leaders actually say and do. In general, two groups of behaviors appear to be important. The first is related to *managing tasks*. Here, the focus is on the extent to which leaders can manage time, define responsibilities, and delegate appropriately. The second group of behaviors relates to *managing people*, and involves actions that build a sense of trust, respect, and liking among members of a team (Northouse, 2016).

Studying leadership behaviors is also connected to an interest in the leadership environment and the extent to which different leadership behaviors are more or less effective under different circumstances. For example, more recent research has examined how different leadership characteristics are more or less helpful when working in different cultures, or in different types of organizations (Aktas, Gelfand, & Hanges, 2016).

Most importantly, the behavioral approach to leadership also suggests the possibility that people can be taught to be good leaders. After all, if leadership traits are relatively stable learned behavior patterns, it should be possible to learn those patterns, or skills, and how to identify which skills are most appropriate for various leadership situations (Day et al., 2014; Middlehurst, 2015). What are the skills that people should develop to improve their leadership abilities? Read on so that you can lead on. . . .

Becoming a Good Leader—Learning to Lead

Employers value employees with leadership potential because these individuals can take the initiative and advance projects of importance to an organization. Good leaders also help to develop the skills of their team members, thus developing a strong pool of talent. But leadership skills can be helpful in your personal life as well. For example, maybe you'll become active in community-based causes that matter to you (like Jonathan Ferrar). Or perhaps you will take on a mentoring role by coaching or teaching others. Taking a leadership role in this way helps to build strong and healthy communities, and often provides a great deal of personal satisfaction.

In spite of their importance, employers have noted that graduating students have weak leadership skills (Radermacher & Walia, 2013). Similarly, graduating students often don't feel as confident about their leadership abilities as they do about other skills. This may be because leadership skills are not readily developed through course assignments, unlike many of the other skills described in this book. Instead, students often indicate that leadership abilities are fostered through extracurricular activities, such as clubs, varsity sports, and student government. Students may also hone their leadership skills through work that they perform either for pay or as volunteers (Desmarais et al., 2013).

What are the leadership skills that I should consider developing while completing my studies? There is no simple answer since different leadership skills may be more or less effective, depending on the situation. In their research with effective college student leaders, however, Kouzes and Posner (2014) identified the following abilities as being important.

Be Inspiring and Commit to a Shared Vision

Getting others to support your leadership requires that you have a clear sense of the values that guide you (■ see Section 3.5), and that you work toward understanding the values of other members of the group. Values are important in promoting commitment, because people will always work harder on projects that appeal to their fundamental beliefs (Kouzes & Posner, 2014). As a result, good leaders will work toward finding common ground among the values of the people they work with so that all members of the team feel dedicated to the work that needs to be done. Establishing shared values for the group is a process that requires input from all members. It may take some time to achieve consensus and considerable skill in negotiating to find compromises. Ultimately, though, it's a good use of time because group members will feel as though they have been heard, and are more likely to buy into the approach that's being adopted to move a project forward.

Ultimately, though, defining the shared values of a group is unhelpful unless a leader acts in ways that are in keeping with those values (Northouse, 2016). People will be unlikely to follow someone who "talks the talk" but isn't prepared to "walk the walk." For this reason, it's important to pay close attention to your own behavior: Are your actions in keeping with the group's goals and shared values? It's also important that you seek feedback about how your actions are affecting the team's performance. Though it isn't always easy to hear what others have to say about your performance, keep in mind that good leadership is promoted through self-awareness and metacognition (■ see Section 5.5), which are both enhanced when you solicit the views of other people.

Be Innovative and Challenge the Process

The skills associated with creativity and innovation are an important part of a leader's toolbox, as is the ability to recognize when those skills are necessary to bring about change (■ see Section 8.5). It's important to note that leadership isn't about changing things just because you can—it's about creating change that will improve the situation.

To determine whether change is necessary, good leaders continually ask why things are done in a particular way, and whether doing things differently would lead to improvement. Moreover, they recognize and draw upon the strengths and insights of other group members, who often have had diverse experiences that can help to fuel the creative process needed for change (■ see Section 17.4 for the benefits associated with diversity).

When a team faces big challenges, wise leaders break the problem down into smaller, more manageable pieces. This lessens the chances that group members will be overwhelmed and lose the motivation needed to continue. Generating "small wins" can also be helpful in building momentum behind the effort to bring about change. People are more likely to get behind an effort that is heading in the right direction.

Of course, challenging the process may also result in failures. When they happen, try to learn from the experience rather than being defeated by it. Good leaders are active learners and have a strong belief in the idea that things can be turned around (Burbach, Matkin, & Fritz, 2004). They are also optimistic and show great resilience in the face of setbacks. What's more, they will work to develop these characteristics among other group members, so that they can provide each other with support when necessary.

Promote Strong Relationships and Individual Talent

A group's success is enhanced when leaders work to foster positive relationships and a sense of responsibility for one another (Kouzes & Posner, 2014). Leaders can do this by listening carefully, showing an interest in others' concerns and circumstances, and by trusting team members to do their job rather than continually trying to take control and micromanage. Efforts to build a team can also be advanced when leaders create a climate in which members can get to know one another as individuals, and when tasks are structured in such a way that the goals allow people to work together cooperatively, rather than in isolation.

It's important, too, to recognize the unique talents of people on the team and to help them develop these abilities. Encouraging self-confidence through effective coaching can be extremely helpful in this regard. Good mentoring involves setting clear goals for people on your team and providing clear and consistent feedback. Providing feedback can be challenging, since people will sometimes take it as criticism. For this reason, it's useful to consider the following tips when providing assessments to people that you work with:

- Give feedback that focuses on the person's behaviors rather than their character.
- Whenever possible, provide concrete examples that provide some basis for your comments so that people can see how you have drawn your conclusions.
- Be selective—a few well-chosen suggestions are more likely to be acted upon than a very large number, which people may find overwhelming.
- Present your suggestions so that they will invite a dialogue by stating your thoughts and asking for their reaction.
- Pay careful attention to people's responses to your feedback, including nonverbal cues that might provide insight into their reactions to your suggestions.

Finally, it's important to make sure that, as a leader, you take time to note and celebrate the team's successes. Celebrations don't need to be big and expensive; sometimes they can simply take the form of a congratulatory email that recognizes a job well done. And always remember that a leader can go a long way with team members by remembering two small words: thank you.

Reflective Practice

Psychology and Your Skill Set: Leadership

1. Different people, cultures, and organizations benefit from different leadership styles. T or F?
2. Employers value leadership because they prefer one person to do the work of many. T or F?
3. Employers report recent graduates to be deficient in leadership abilities. T or F?

THINK CRITICALLY

4. In the following scenario, identify effective and ineffective leadership practices and provide suggestions to improve ineffective strategies: You are evaluating your peer following a presentation she gave. You tell her that the pace of her speech could have been slower. You add that the presentation was unclear, and because you want to save time, you offer to email a list of other suggestions to her later on.

SELF-REFLECT

- Consider the recommended skills that can increase your leadership ability. Are there any areas in which you perform particularly well? Are there areas you could improve upon? How could improving these skills benefit your personal and professional life?

Answers: 1. T 2. F 3. T 4. Effective: Focusing on speech as behavioral criticism instead of framing comment toward the peer's character. Ineffective: Giving vague criticism such as "unclear," and emailing a list of suggestions. Emailing a list could be overwhelming and does not encourage dialogue from your peer. Improvements: Give concrete examples of a part of your peer's presentation that was unclear, make notes that outline a few important criticisms, and welcome her feedback in person so you can respond to her reactions and feelings about your comments.

Gateways to Personality and Individual Differences

Summary: Gateways Learning Outcomes

12.1 Theories of Personality

12.1.1 Define the term personality and distinguish it from temperament, self-concept, and self-esteem

Personality refers to a person's consistent and unique patterns of thinking, emotion, and behavior. It is believed to emerge from infants' *temperament*, which is the general pattern of attention, arousal, and mood that is evident from birth. Behavior is influenced by *self-concept*, which is a perception of one's own personality traits. *Self-esteem* (our evaluation of ourselves) stems directly from our self-concept: A positive self-concept leads to high self-esteem. Low self-esteem results from a negative self-concept and is associated with stress, unhappiness, and depression.

12.1.2 Describe how psychoanalytic theories explain personality

Like other psychodynamic approaches, Sigmund Freud's psychoanalytic theory emphasizes unconscious forces and conflicts within the personality. In Freud's theory, personality is made up of the id, ego, and superego. The personality operates on three levels: the conscious, preconscious, and unconscious. The Freudian view of personality development is based on a series of psychosexual stages: the oral, anal, phallic, latency, and genital stages. According to Freud, fixation at any stage can leave a lasting imprint on personality. Neo-Freudian theorists accepted the broad features of Freudian psychology, but developed their own views.

12.1.3 Describe how behaviorists and social learning theorists explain personality

Behavioral theories of personality emphasize learning, conditioning, and immediate effects of the environment (situational determinants). Learning theorists Dollard and Miller consider habits the basic core of personality. Habits express the combined effects of drive, cue, response, and reward. Social learning theory adds cognitive elements, such as perception, thinking, and understanding to the behavioral view of personality. Social learning theory is exemplified by Julian Rotter's concepts of the psychological situation, expectancies, and reinforcement value.

12.1.4 Describe how humanistic theories explain personality

Humanistic theories stress subjective experience, free will, self-actualization, and positive models of human nature. Abraham Maslow found that self-actualizers share characteristics that range from efficient perceptions of reality to frequent peak experiences. Carl Rogers viewed the self as an entity that emerges from personal experience. We tend to become aware of experiences that match our self-image and exclude those that are incongruent with it. The incongruent person has a highly unrealistic self-image, a mismatch between the self-image and the ideal self, or both. The congruent or fully functioning person is flexible and open to experiences and feelings. Like the ideal self, possible selves help us become the person we would like to become. As parents apply conditions of worth to children's behavior, thoughts, and feelings, children begin to do the same. Internalized conditions of worth then contribute to incongruence that disrupts the organismic valuing process.

12.2 Traits: The Building Blocks of Personality

12.2.1 Describe what is meant by a personality trait

Traits are characteristics related to thoughts, feelings, and behavior that differ among people and are relatively stable over a variety of situations and a fairly long period of time. Though they are assumed to be quite stable, traits can sometimes interact with the environment (situations) to explain our behavior.

12.2.2 Outline the history of the trait approach to understanding personality, including the work of Allport and Cattell

Trait theories identify qualities that are most lasting or characteristic of a person. Allport made a useful distinction between central and secondary traits. Cattell's theory defines the existence of 16 underlying source traits (or dimensions) that are central to personality. Source traits are measured by the *Sixteen Personality Factor Questionnaire* (16 PF).

12.2.3 Contrast the Big Five and HEXACO models of personality

The five-factor model (Big Five) attempted to reduce the number of personality dimensions outlined in Cattell's research. Specifically, the Big Five model identifies five universal dimensions of personality: extroversion, agreeableness, conscientiousness, neuroticism, and openness to experience. Work in cultures outside of the West supported the existence of the Big Five but also identified a sixth dimension of personality—honesty/humility. The HEXACO model of personality thus extends the Big Five to include this sixth factor.

12.2.4 Explain what is meant by a personality type, and the weaknesses associated with this approach to classifying personality

Personality types group people into categories on the basis of shared traits. One significant weakness of this approach is that it oversimplifies people's personalities because it classifies people as having/not having a particular trait instead of acknowledging that people may possess traits to a greater or lesser extent.

12.3 Personality Assessment

12.3.1 Outline four ways in which personality can be measured

Techniques typically used for personality assessment are *interviews*, *observation*, *questionnaires*, and *projective tests*. Structured and unstructured interviews provide much information, but they are subject to interviewer bias and misperceptions. The halo effect may also reduce the accuracy of an interview. Direct observation, sometimes involving situational tests, behavioral assessment, or the use of rating scales, allows evaluation of a person's actual behavior. Personality questionnaires, such as the *Minnesota Multiphasic Personality Inventory-2 (MMPI-2)*, are objective and reliable, but their validity is open to question. Projective tests ask a person to project thoughts or feelings onto an ambiguous stimulus or unstructured situation. Two well-known examples are the *Rorschach Inkblot Test* and the *Thematic Apperception Test (TAT)*. Projective tests are low in validity and objectivity. Nevertheless, they are considered useful by many clinicians, particularly as part of a test battery.

12.4 Factors Influencing Personality

12.4.1 Describe the results of behavioral genetics studies with regard to the role of genetic and environmental influences on personality

Behavioral genetics and studies of identical twins suggest that both heredity and environment contribute significantly to adult personality traits. Heredity appears to impact each of the Big Five factors approximately equally.

12.5 Psychology and Your Skill Set: Leadership

12.5.1 Create a plan to improve your leadership abilities

Leadership skills are beneficial in the workplace because they can be used to promote organizational goals. Leadership skills also benefit your personal life, because taking on leadership roles can bring great personal satisfaction. To improve upon your leadership abilities, you need to help your team commit to shared values, ask questions of your team members, seek feedback, welcome innovation, be a creative problem solver, be optimistic, and promote team success and individual talents. We hope that after reading this section, you'll be better able to think about how you can use these strategies to help when you find yourself in a leadership position!

13 Health Psychology

Gateway Theme Health is affected greatly by thinking and behavior patterns, especially those patterns related to stress.

Chapter Outline

Doing Justice to Diabetes

Sonia Sotomayor was only seven years old when the doctor diagnosed her with type 1 diabetes. Fortunately, she had recently learned how to tell time—it was a skill that came in handy when she was learning how to properly sterilize her insulin needles in boiling water. She preferred to do the injections herself, she has said, because her mother was often working and her father's hands shook whenever he tried to help.

Diabetes is one of many diseases that can have serious implications for Americans' health and well-being. However, the work of health psychologists suggests that many illnesses can be either prevented or managed in ways that allow people to lead meaningful and rewarding lives. If you're not convinced about that, you can always ask Sonia Sotomayor: Her diabetes certainly didn't stop her graduating from Princeton with honors. Or from becoming the first Hispanic and Latina member of the US Supreme Court, for that matter.

Health psychology is a relatively new domain, but one that is growing quickly. In part, its popularity stems from its clear application to improving the quality of people's everyday lives. In the first two sections of this chapter, we'll explore how our health is affected by a variety of biological, psychological, social, and behavioral factors, including stress. After that, we'll look at how both treatments and coping strategies can be used to manage health-related challenges. We'll conclude this chapter with a look at how you can best manage stress in an effort to stay healthy.

13.1 Biopsychosocial and Behavioral Contributions to Health

GATEWAYS LEARNING OUTCOMES:
After reading this section you should be able to:

13.1.1 Distinguish between the medical and biopsychosocial models in terms of their conceptions of health

13.1.2 Explain the biological, psychological, and social factors that influence health

13.1.3 Outline the main behavioral risk factors that contribute to poor health

13.1.4 Describe three strategies that help to minimize behavioral risk factors

Health psychology is a subfield of psychology that aims to use cognitive and behavioral principles to prevent and treat illness, and to promote well-being (Hales, 2015). Health psychologists may work with doctors in the allied field of **behavioral medicine**, which brings together experts in the biological, psychological, and social sciences to manage medical problems such as diabetes or asthma. Their interests include helping people cope with pain and chronic illness, stress-related diseases, self-screening for diseases (such as breast cancer), and finding ways to encourage people to seek—and adhere to—treatments when they are unwell (Brannon, Feist, & Updegraff, 2014; Davis et al., 2015).

As the definition suggests, though, health psychologists are not just concerned with managing illness—they are also interested in getting people to increase behaviors that promote good health. For these psychologists, health is not just an absence of disease (Diener, 2013; Diener & Chan, 2011). Instead, they believe that people who are truly healthy enjoy a positive state of *subjective well-being*. People who attain subjective well-being are both physically and psychologically healthy (Wrosch, Jobin, & Scheier, 2016). They are happy, optimistic, self-confident individuals who can bounce back emotionally from adversity. People who enjoy a sense of well-being also have supportive relationships with others and do meaningful work. (■ Many of these aspects of subjective well-being are addressed elsewhere in this book. For example, see ■ Section 10.6 for more on positivity and optimism.)

In this section we examine some of the factors that impact our health. We begin with a small history lesson on this topic, and then move on to talking about biological, psychological, and social factors that influence health. We conclude with a look at health-related behaviors that are both helpful and harmful.

Human Diversity and Historical Conceptions of Health

Western medicine was dominated by the *medical model* for centuries (Engel, 2012; Middleton, 2015). From this perspective, the body is a complex biological machine. When it functions well, it is healthy; when it breaks down it becomes ill (and takes *you* down with it). Moreover, in the medical model, physical illnesses call for physical treatments ("Got a cold? Take your medicine") and any impact of the mind on health is dismissed as a mere placebo effect. (■ To remind yourself about placebo effects, see Section 1.6.)

In contrast, other cultures have historically adopted a broader model of health. For example, rather than defining health as the absence of disease, Chinese culture stresses the importance of balancing yin and yang, the two main forces in the universe. In India, people who practice Ayurveda emphasize the body, senses, mind, and soul. Members of other cultural groups, including American Indians and Alaska Natives, place a similar value on psychological and spiritual health, in addition to physical well-being (Gurung, 2019).

Most American psychologists now reject the medical model as too simplistic, preferring instead the more holistic *biopsychosocial model* that we first encountered in ■ Section 1.4. From the biopsychosocial perspective, both disease and health are better understood as being influenced by biological, psychological, *and* social processes (Lane, 2014; Saxbe, 2017). While some medical practitioners may still undervalue the effect the mind has on health and illness, health psychologists accept that health is a state of physical *and* psychological well-being that is impacted by our environment

Monkey Business Images/Shutterstock.com

Adherents of the medical model historically focused only on physiology when considering health. Now, psychologists adopt a more holistic approach to health that also emphasizes the importance of psychological, spiritual, and social factors, in keeping with the biopsychosocial model.

and social world (Oakley, 2004). In keeping with the importance of the biopsychosocial model, let's take a closer look at the biological, psychological, and social contributions to health.

Biological Factors That Influence Health

It probably goes without saying that biological factors have an important role to play in human health. Health psychologists may focus on any one of a number of physiological systems, as well as their interactions with one another, in their efforts to better understand and promote overall good health. Here, we briefly outline six of them.

First, *genetic factors* are at the root of many health-related concerns. Our genetic code may include instructions, inherited from our parents, that either provide protection from, or susceptibility to, a variety of illnesses (Xavier et al., 2019). Health psychologists have an important role to play in this regard, particularly in terms of educating people about genetic risks and the behaviors that can help reduce those risks. Health psychologists are also involved in genetic counseling, helping individuals to make wise choices about genetic screening for themselves and, in some cases, an unborn child. They can also assist with interpreting test results, as well as providing guidance about available options and counseling to manage anxiety or distress (Taylor, 2021).

Second, the various branches of the *nervous system* and *endocrine system* that were outlined in Chapter 2 are at the root of many health concerns. Disorders of the nervous system include epilepsy, Parkinson's disease, multiple sclerosis, and cerebral palsy, while diabetes is an increasingly common disease that is associated with a malfunctioning endocrine system (Gurung, 2019).

Third, a considerable amount of attention has recently been directed toward the *immune system*, which is responsible for generating a temporary inflammation response that provides protection against short-term assaults on the body. These threats include things like bacteria and viruses, some of which are quite serious (think, COVID-19), as well as minor problems such as blisters and mosquito bites (Taylor, 2021). However, more chronic problems associated with the immune system, such as lupus and lymphoma, have long been of interest to healthcare providers.

More recently, researchers have increasingly stressed that when the immune system does generate chronic, low-level inflammation, other serious health-related challenges may result. Problems associated with this type of chronic inflammation include a diverse range of concerns, including Alzheimer's disease, osteoporosis, asthma, arthritis, and a variety of cancers (Furman et al., 2019).

The remaining three physiological systems are associated with key organs in the body. For example, the *cardiovascular* and *respiratory systems* are of interest to health psychologists for their role in common problems such as heart disease and heart attacks, high blood pressure, asthma, and emphysema. The *digestive system* is concerned with the metabolism of food and disorders include hepatitis, ulcers, and acid reflux. Finally, the *reproductive system* also has an important role to play in maintaining our good health: disorders of interest to health psychologists include sexually transmitted diseases (■ see Section 11.3), fertility problems, and prostate problems in men (Taylor, 2021).

Psychological Factors That Influence Health

Psychological scientists have spent considerable time investigating the relationship between various psychological characteristics and health, including attention and perceptions, cognitions, emotions, and motivation. In particular, considerable attention has been paid to the role of *personality*. Here we look at two specific lines of research that relate to health: the Type A personality and the hardy personality.

Type A Personalities

There has been a lot of publicity around the possible existence of a "cardiac personality"—a person at high risk for heart disease. In an early study of heart problems, two cardiologists, Meyer Friedman and Ray Rosenman, classified people as either a *Type A personality*, someone who runs a high risk for heart attack, or a *Type B personality*, someone who is unlikely to have a heart attack. (Health researchers have also identified the Type D personality, someone who is worried, expresses many negative emotions, and is disease-prone; Meyer, 2014.)

According to Friedman and Rosenman, Type A people are hard driving, ambitious, highly competitive, achievement oriented, and striving. Type A people believe that with enough effort they can overcome any obstacle, and they push themselves accordingly. Perhaps the most telltale signs of a Type A personality are time urgency and chronic anger or hostility. Type As hurry from one activity to another, racing the clock in self-imposed urgency. As they do, they feel a constant sense of frustration and anger. In an eight-year follow-up, these researchers found that the rate of heart disease among Type As was more than twice that found among Type Bs (Friedman & Rosenman, 1983).

Though the initial research appeared to support the idea of a "cardiac personality" subsequent research has not, leading to skepticism about the distinction between Types A, B, and D personalities (Kastytis et al., 2015; Petticrew, Lee, & McKee, 2012). Specifically, some researchers have found that it's really only feelings of anger and hostility that are reliably related to an increased risk for heart attack (Brydon et al., 2010; Bunde & Suls, 2006); other characteristics of the Type A personality do not seem to matter nearly as much.

In particular, the most damaging health outcomes may occur in hostile persons who keep their anger "bottled up." Such people seethe with anger but don't express it outwardly. This increases their pulse rate and blood pressure and puts a tremendous strain on the heart (Bongard, al'Absi, & Lovallo, 1998; Lemogne et al., 2010; Smith & Traupman, 2011).

Health psychology Study of how cognitive and behavioral principles can be used to prevent illness and promote physical well-being.

Behavioral medicine A medical specialty focused on the study of nonbiological factors influencing physical health and illness.

Donald Reilly/The New Yorker Collection/Cartoon Bank

Hardy Personalities

In addition to research on Type A personalities, a second line of research also bears mentioning. Psychologist Salvatore Maddi has studied people who have a **hardy personality**. Such people seem to be unusually resistant to stress (Maddi, 2013; Sandvik et al., 2013). The first study of hardiness began with two groups of managers at a large utility company. All the managers held high-stress positions, yet some tended to get sick after stressful events, whereas others were rarely ill.

How did the people who were thriving differ from their "stressed-out" colleagues? The main difference was that the hardy group seemed to hold a worldview that consisted of three traits (Maddi, 2013; Maddi et al., 2009):

1. They had a sense of personal *commitment* to self, work, family, and other stabilizing values.
2. They felt that they had *control* over their lives and their work.
3. They had a tendency to see life as a series of *challenges* rather than as a series of threats or problems.

How do such traits protect people from the effects of stress? Persons strong in terms of commitment find ways to turn whatever they are doing into something that seems interesting and important. They tend to get involved rather than feeling alienated. Persons strong in terms of control believe that more often than not, they can influence the course of events around them. This prevents them from passively seeing themselves as victims of circumstance. Finally, people strong in terms of challenge find fulfillment in continual growth. They seek to learn from their experiences rather than accept easy comfort, security, and routine. Indeed, many "negative" experiences can enhance personal growth—if you have support from others and the skills needed to cope with challenge (Garrosa et al., 2008; Stix, 2011).

Research into hardy personalities has indicated an important connection between hardiness and *optimism* (■ see Section 10.6). Optimists tend to expect that things will turn out well, which helps them to feel in control, and to view events as challenges rather than threats (two of the three traits that characterize hardy personalities). This worldview motivates them to actively cope with adversity. They are less likely to be stopped by temporary setbacks and more likely to deal with problems head-on. Pessimists are more likely to ignore or deny problems. The result of such differences is that optimists are less stressed and anxious than pessimists. Moreover, optimists tend to take better care of themselves because they believe that their efforts to stay healthy will succeed (Kok et al., 2013; Taylor, 2011).

Similar to optimism, *happiness* has also been associated with hardy individuals. Happy people tend to see their lives in more positive terms, even when trouble comes their way. For example, happier people tend to find humor in disappointments. They also look at setbacks as challenges. They are strengthened by losses (Cohn et al., 2009; Maddi et al., 2009).

Why is there a connection between hardiness and happiness? As psychologist Barbara Fredrickson has pointed out, positive emotions tend to broaden our mental focus. Emotions such as joy, interest, and contentment create an urge to play, to be creative, to explore, to savor life, to seek new experiences, to integrate, and to grow. When you are stressed, experiencing positive emotions can make it more likely that you will find creative solutions to your problems. Positive emotions also tend to reduce the bodily arousal that occurs when we are stressed, possibly limiting stress-related damage (Diener & Chan, 2011; Fredrickson, 2003).

Social Factors That Influence Health

There is no question that the social environment in which we live has an important influence on our health. Researchers have investigated a number of factors that appear to be important; here, we take a close look at two of them: *social networks* and *poverty*.

Social Networks

Would you like to eat better, exercise more, or quit smoking? Researchers Nicholas Christakis and James Fowler believe that they know why it can be difficult to alter unhealthy behaviors: Often, it's social factors that are a barrier to change. Unhealthy behaviors such as overeating or smoking seem to spread almost like a "mental virus" among people who spend time together (Christakis & Fowler, 2009; Lyons, 2011).

One study of this type of social contagion found that people were 57 percent more likely to become obese if they had a friend who became obese first (Christakis & Fowler, 2007). Similarly, smokers tend to "hang out" with other smokers (Christakis & Fowler, 2008). Another study found that spending time with drinkers increases alcohol consumption (Ali & Dwyer, 2010). Apparently, we tend to flock together with like-minded people and adopt many of their habits (Barnett et al., 2013; Miller & Prentice, 2016).

Does that mean I am doomed to be unhealthy if my family and friends have unhealthy habits? Not necessarily. Social networks also can spread healthy behaviors (Fowler & Christakis, 2010). If one smoker in a group of smokers quits, others are more likely to follow suit. If your spouse quits smoking, you are 67 percent more likely to quit. If a good friend quits smoking, your chances of abandoning tobacco go up by 6 percent (Christakis & Fowler, 2008). The

Tony Arruza/The Image Bank Unreleased/Getty Images

If you are a smoker, do your friends also smoke? Are your family members fast-food junkies just like you? Are your friends all drinkers?

growing social unpopularity of smoking may be the best explanation of why fewer and fewer American adults (now only 15 percent) still smoke (Centers for Disease Control, 2016a).

The implication? Don't wait for your friends or family to adopt healthier habits. Instead, take the lead and inspire them to join you. Failing that, start hanging out with a crowd that prizes their well-being. You might catch something healthy!

Poverty

It probably won't surprise you to learn that poverty isn't good for your health and is linked to lower life expectancy (Fuller-Rowell, Evans, & Ong, 2012). According to the World Bank (2020), 734 million people around the world lived in *absolute poverty*, surviving on less than the international poverty line of $1.90 per day. And while that number had been declining over the past 30 years, the worldwide COVID-19 pandemic will reverse that trend because of its disproportionate effect on the world's poorest people.

Human Diversity: Poverty and COVID-19

Even in a wealthy country such as the United States, COVID-19 infections and deaths were far more likely to occur among those with the fewest financial resources. In part, these statistics reflect the way health care is administered in the United States: In the absence of universal health care, poor people are less likely to have a family doctor and are far more likely to be uninsured or underinsured. During the pandemic, this meant that poor people were unlikely to seek treatment because they simply didn't have the money to pay for a visit to the doctor, or for a test. Moreover, poorer Americans also live in much smaller dwellings, so if one member of the family became sick then it was difficult to quarantine them to protect other members of the household (Vesoulas, 2020).

But the association between COVID-19 and poverty is more complex than that, and it underscores the importance of the social aspect of the biopsychosocial model (Vesoulas, 2020). For example, many low-income earners simply could not afford to stop working and self-isolate at home: Their jobs were much less likely than those of higher earners to provide them with sick days, and if money was needed for rent and food then they needed to go out to work. In many cases their work could not be done remotely, but even if their jobs could be done from home, these individuals likely would have struggled to afford high-speed Internet or the potential child care costs. And there were other effects as well: For instance, school closures meant the end of free and reduced-cost breakfasts and lunches for low-income children, often a critical element of their ability to maintain a healthy diet. A lack of fast and reliable Internet also made it difficult for these children to keep up with their lessons.

Presumably, we need not go on about how the trickle-down effects of poverty can have important health-related consequences. But money is clearly not the whole story when it comes to health. The phenomenon of *relative poverty* is a good example of how changing how you view things can also be important. For example, physician Stephen Bezruchka has shown that Greeks earn, on average, less than half of what Americans earn and yet they have a longer life expectancy (Bezruchka as cited in Sapolsky, 2005).

How could this be? One possibility is suggested by a study that found poorer women in California are more likely to die if they live in better-off neighborhoods than if they live in poorer neighborhoods (Winkleby, Ahn, & Cubbin, 2006). Apparently, being constantly reminded that you are relatively poor piles on an extra measure of stress (Bjornstrom, 2011; Fritzell et al., 2015).

But relative poverty is not the whole story either, since even better-off Americans are not as healthy as their counterparts in other developed countries (Weir, 2013). Instead, income inequality itself may prove to be a chronic social stressor (Cushing et al., 2015). *Income inequality* refers to a situation in which a large proportion of the country's wealth is held by a very small proportion of the population. Currently, the United States has the largest income inequality in the developed world. Of course, no one should pretend that relative poverty in the United States is anywhere near as big a problem as absolute poverty around the world. Nevertheless, it is a growing problem in the United States as the gap between the rich and poor continues to widen (Emerson, 2009; Oishi, Kesebir, & Diener, 2011).

ULU_Bird/Shutterstock.com

Although being poor in the United States may mean living above an absolute poverty level, it also means constantly living with the stress of dramatic income inequality (Wilkinson & Pickett, 2009).

Hardy personality A personality style associated with superior stress resistance.

What should I do if I always feel poor? We would never want to diminish the challenges that come with living in difficult financial circumstances, and we recognize that making changes can be difficult when that's the case. Nevertheless, the data are clear about the positive correlation between education and income, so if you're in school (and reading this book!), you've already taken an important step toward an improved financial future. If at all possible, remain committed to changing your circumstances through education and hard work. In the meantime, note that something is a stressor only if you *think* it is one. Remember Michael J. Fox's optimistic assessment regarding his diagnosis of early-onset Parkinson's disease (■ see Section 10.6)? Whenever possible, try to focus on the positives and find the good things in your life. Doing so may reveal that you are "richer" than you think.

Behaviors That Influence Health

Up to this point we have considered some of the biological, psychological, and social factors that underpin good health. Each of these factors has a role to play in determining our health-related behaviors. While many behaviors can promote good health, there are just as many that compromise it; indeed, many diseases and well over half of all deaths in North America each year can be traced to unhealthy behaviors (Danaei et al., 2009). A century ago, most people died primarily from external factors, such as infectious diseases and unavoidable injuries. Today, more people than ever are dying from **lifestyle diseases** that involve risky, health-damaging behaviors (Kozica et al., 2012). Examples include heart disease, stroke, HIV/AIDS, and lung cancer (● Figure 13.1).

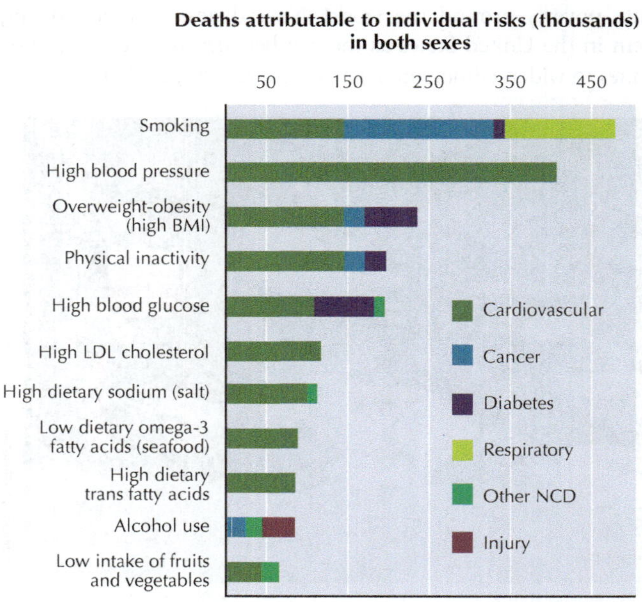

● **Figure 13.1 Causes of preventable deaths in the United States.** The leading causes of preventable deaths in the United States are tobacco and alcohol consumption, along with poor diet and exercise habits. Together, they account for over half of all premature deaths and cause no end of day-to-day health problems. (Data adapted from Kann et al., 2015. NCD = noncommunicable diseases.)

Behavioral Risk Factors

Behavioral risk factors are actions people choose to take that increase the chances of disease, injury, or early death. For example, about 480,000 Americans die every year from smoking-related diseases—about 20 percent of all deaths, regardless of the cause (Centers for Disease Control, 2016a). Similarly, almost three-quarters of all American adults are overweight. Of those, a large proportion are extremely overweight, or *obese* (Flegal et al., 2010). In terms of health consequences, a person who is overweight at age 20 can expect to lose 5 to 20 years of life expectancy (Fontaine et al., 2003). In fact, being overweight may soon overtake smoking as the main cause of preventable death (Danaei et al., 2009).

▲ Table 13.1 outlines a number of other factors that often stem from behavioral choices and create significant health risks

In the long run, behavioral risk factors and lifestyles do make a difference in health and life expectancy.

▲ Table 13.1 Major Health-Promoting Behaviors

Source	Desirable Behaviors
Tobacco	Do not smoke; do not use smokeless tobacco.
Nutrition	Eat a balanced, low-fat diet; have appropriate caloric intake; maintain a healthy body weight.
Exercise	Engage in at least 30 minutes of aerobic exercise, 5 days per week.
Blood pressure	Lower blood pressure with diet and exercise or medicine if necessary.
Alcohol and drugs	Drink no more than two alcoholic drinks per day; abstain from using drugs.
Sleep and relaxation	Avoid sleep deprivation; provide for periods of relaxation every day.
Sex	Practice safer sex; avoid unplanned pregnancy.
Injury	Curb dangerous driving habits; use seat belts; minimize sun exposure; forgo dangerous activities.
Stress	Learn stress management; lower hostility.

(Brannon, Feist, & Updegraff, 2014): high levels of stress, untreated high blood pressure, cigarette smoking, abuse of alcohol or other drugs, inadequate exercise, unsafe sexual behavior, exposure to toxic substances, violence, excess sun exposure, reckless driving, and disregarding personal safety (that is, avoidable accidents).

About 70 percent of all medical costs are related to just six of these factors—smoking, alcohol abuse, drug abuse, poor diet, insufficient exercise, and risky sexual practices (Brannon, Feist, & Updegraff, 2014; Orleans, Gruman, & Hollendonner, 1999). (■ Risky sex is discussed in Section 11.3.) Moreover, the risky behaviors that you engage in when you are 18 or 19 greatly affect your health, happiness, and life expectancy years later (Gurung, 2019). ▲ Table 13.2 shows the percentage of American high school students who engaged in a variety of risky behaviors during the previous year. (It is worth noting that these percentages were the lowest recorded since this particular record-keeping program was first instituted in 1991.)

On the flip side of these behavioral risk factors are health-promoting behaviors, which include obvious practices such as getting regular exercise, controlling smoking and alcohol use, maintaining a balanced diet, getting good medical care, and managing stress (Zarcadoolas, Pleasant, & Greer, 2006). In one study, the risk of dying during a 10-year period was cut by 65 percent for adults who were careful about diet, alcohol, exercise, and smoking (Knoops et al., 2004).

It's important to note that these health-promoting behaviors don't have to be restrictive or burdensome. For instance, maintaining a healthy diet doesn't mean surviving on tofu and wheatgrass. The healthiest people in the study just mentioned ate a tasty "Mediterranean diet" higher in fruit, vegetables, and fish and lower in red meat and dairy products. Likewise, you don't need to exercise like an Olympic athlete to benefit from physical activity (Portugal et al., 2013). All you need is 30 minutes of exercise (the equivalent of a brisk walk) three or four times a week. Almost everyone can fit this type of "lifestyle physical activity" into his or her schedule (Pescatello, 2001).

What about alcohol? Moderation in drinking doesn't mean that you must be a teetotaler. Consuming one or two alcoholic drinks per day is generally safe for most people, especially if you remain alcohol free two or three days a week. A glass of red wine daily may even be healthy (Anekonda, 2006). However, having three or more drinks a day greatly increases the risk for stroke, cirrhosis of the liver, cancer, high blood pressure, heart disorders, and other diseases (Knoops et al., 2004; Lamont et al., 2011).

To summarize, a small number of behavior patterns account for many common health problems (Kann et al., 2015; Straub, 2012). Nevertheless, health psychologists have contributed to research that suggests it's possible to change behaviors that compromise health, and move people toward healthier lifestyles. We'll take a look at some of them in the next section.

▲ Table 13.2 Percentage of US High School Students Who Engaged in Health-Endangering Behaviors

Risky Behavior	Percentage
Rode with drinking driver (previous 30 days)	20.0
Were in a physical fight (previous 12 months)	22.6
Carried a weapon (previous 30 days)	16.2
Drank alcohol (previous 30 days)	32.8
Used cannabis (previous 30 days)	21.7
Engaged in sexual intercourse (previous 90 days)	30.1
Did not use condom (during last sexual intercourse)	43.1
Smoked cigarettes (previous 30 days)	10.8
Did not have any fruit (previous 7 days)	5.2
Did not have any vegetables (previous 7 days)	6.7
Played 3 or more hours of video games (average school day)	41.7

Source: Kann et al., 2015.

Minimizing Behavioral Risk Factors

If some behaviors are so damaging to our long-term health and well-being, then what can we do to minimize them, or give them up completely? Research has investigated three possibilities that show promise: making *lifestyle changes*, working toward *early prevention*, and employing *community-health and social media campaigns*. Let's dig deeper into each of these possibilities.

Make Lifestyle Changes

To prevent disease, health psychologists first try to reduce behavioral risk factors. In many cases, lifestyle diseases can be prevented by making specific, minor changes in behavior. For example, small adjustments in how food is prepared—especially using less salt—can greatly influence hypertension (high blood pressure), which can be deadly. Losing weight, using alcohol sparingly, and getting more exercise will also help (Edenfield & Blumenthal, 2011).

None of these changes need be enacted quickly, or in an all-or-nothing manner. Instead, slow but steady alterations to lifestyle often mean that the changes are less noticeable and are therefore less likely to make people feel as though they are being deprived of something they like. Over the longer term, though, these incremental changes can add up to a significant improvement in overall health.

You probably won't be surprised to learn that many people fail to engage in health-promoting behaviors until ill health forces it upon them. A friend of one of your authors commented about his recent heart attack, "I guess that's my wake-up call. Time to lose some weight, exercise more, and eat healthier. I want to be around while my grandchildren grow up." To address this problem, health

Lifestyle disease A disease related to health-damaging personal habits.

Behavioral risk factors Behaviors that increase the chances of disease, injury, or premature death.

psychologists have tried using early prevention programs and community health campaigns, which are described below.

Early Prevention

Given that changing behavior is so hard, it makes sense that a better strategy would be to try to avoid developing poor health habits in the first place. A great example of the utility of preventative measures can be seen with smoking, which is the largest preventable cause of death and the single most lethal contributor (Centers for Disease Control, 2016a).

What have health psychologists done to help prevent people from taking up smoking? When humorist Mark Twain said, "Giving up smoking is the easiest thing in the world. I know because I've done it thousands of times," he stated a basic truth—only 1 smoker in 10 has long-term success at quitting (Krall, Garvey, & Garcia, 2002; García-Rodríguez et al., 2013). Thus, the best way to deal with smoking is to prevent it before it becomes a lifelong habit. Attempts to "immunize" youths against pressures to start smoking are a good example: Prevention programs in schools discourage smoking with quizzes about smoking, multimedia presentations, antismoking art contests, poster and T-shirt giveaways, antismoking pamphlets for parents, and questions for students to ask their parents (Flynn et al., 2011; Prokhorov et al., 2010). Such efforts are designed to persuade kids that smoking is dangerous and "uncool."

Some antismoking programs also include **refusal skills training.** In such training, youths learn to resist pressures to begin smoking (or using other drugs). For example, junior high students can role-play ways to resist smoking pressures from peers, adults, and cigarette ads. Similar methods can be applied to other health risks, such as sexually transmitted diseases and teen pregnancy (Wandersman & Florin, 2003; Witkiewitz et al., 2011).

Many health programs also teach students general life skills that will help them cope with day-to-day stresses. That way, they will be less tempted to escape problems through drug use or other destructive behaviors. **Life skills training** includes practice in stress reduction, self-protection, decision-making, goal setting, self-control, and social skills (Allen & Williams, 2012; Corey & Corey, 2014).

Community Health and Social Media Campaigns

In addition to early prevention, health psychologists have had some success with **community health campaigns.** These are community-wide education projects designed to lessen major risk factors, and they may be carried out with the help of community psychologists (see Section 18.3 for more information about community psychology) (Hawe, 2015; Lounsbury & Mitchell, 2009).

Community health campaigns inform people of risks such as stress, alcohol abuse, high blood pressure, high cholesterol, smoking, sexually transmitted diseases, or excessive sun exposure. This is followed by efforts to motivate people to either change their behavior, or to avoid engaging in the behavior in the first place (Miller & Prentice, 2016). Campaigns sometimes provide *role models* (positive examples) who show people how to improve their own health. They also direct people to services for health screening, advice, and treatment.

Community health campaigns draw on a wide range of media and can be helpful in raising awareness about important health-related issues.

Health campaigns may reach people through mass media, public schools, fairs, workplaces, or self-help programs. Recently, however, *social media* platforms have become increasingly important as tools for bringing cost-effective health information to large numbers of people, as well as fostering behavioral change (Moller et al., 2017). (See Section 18.2 for a discussion of *social norms marketing* and *personalized normalized feedback*, two promising social media approaches to fostering effective behavioral change.)

Reflective Practice

Biopsychosocial and Behavioral Contributions to Health

1. The __________ model sees health as connected to the physical body, while the __________ model views health more holistically, and includes psychological and social factors.
2. With respect to health, which of the following is *not* a major behavioral risk factor?
   a. overexercise
   b. cigarette smoking
   c. stress
   d. high blood pressure
3. Lifestyle diseases related to just six behaviors account for 70 percent of all medical costs. The behaviors are smoking, alcohol abuse, drug abuse, poor diet, insufficient exercise, and
   a. driving too fast
   b. excessive sun exposure
   c. unsafe sex
   d. exposure to toxins
4. The "cardiac personality" described by Friedman and Rosenman describes someone who is hard driving, ambitious, competitive, achievement-oriented, striving, and chronically __________.
5. Both absolute and relative poverty can make an important contribution to health. T or F?
6. Behavioral risk factors can be minimized through
   a. early prevention
   b. community health programs that may include social media
   c. lifestyle changes
   d. all of the above

THINK CRITICALLY

7. The general public is increasingly well informed about health risks and healthy behavior. Can you apply the concept of reinforcement to explain why so many people fail to act on this information?

SELF-REFLECT

- Make a list of the major behavioral risk factors that apply to you. Are you laying the foundation for a lifestyle disease?
- Which of the health-promoting behaviors listed in Table 13.1 would you like to increase?
- If you were designing a community health campaign, who would you use as role models of healthy behavior?

Answers: 1. medical; biopsychosocial 2. a 3. c 4. angry/hostile 5. T 6. d 7. Many unhealthy behaviors result in immediate reinforcement, while the benefits of healthy behaviors may be delayed by months or years, greatly lessening the immediate rewards for healthful behavior (Watson & Tharp, 2014).

13.2 Stress and Health

GATEWAYS LEARNING OUTCOMES:
After reading this section you should be able to:

13.2.1 Distinguish between two types of stressors: life events and hassles

13.2.2 Differentiate between primary and secondary appraisals, and outline the four factors that guide them

13.2.3 Describe the three stages of general adaptation syndrome

13.2.4 Describe three consequences of prolonged stress

Health psychology pays special attention to the effect that stress has on health and illness. Although stress can be a major risk factor if it is prolonged or severe, it isn't always bad. As Canadian stress research pioneer Hans Selye (SEL-yay) (1976) observed, "To be totally without stress is to be dead." That's because **stress** is the pressure or demand placed on an organism to adjust or adapt. Unpleasant events such as work pressures, marital problems, or financial woes are naturally stressful. But so are travel, sports, a new job, rock climbing, dating, and other positive activities. Even if you aren't a thrill seeker, a healthy lifestyle may include a fair amount of *eustress* (good stress). Activities that provoke "good stress" are usually challenging, rewarding, and energizing.

Types of Stressors

A **stressor** is a specific condition or event that challenges or threatens a person. From major life events, such as getting married or moving to another country, to minor hassles, such as getting cut off by the car in front of you or having too many things to do, almost anything can become a stressor under the right circumstances. Let's look at two classes of stressors—*life events* and *hassles*—in more detail.

Life Events

We know that disaster, depression, and sorrow often precede illness (Harrington, 2013). More surprising is the finding that major *life changes*—both good *and* bad (*and* ugly?)—can increase susceptibility to illness. These changes in our surroundings or routines require us to be on guard and ready to react. Over long periods, this can be quite stressful.

How can I tell if I am experiencing too much stress from major life events? Psychiatrist Thomas Holmes and graduate student Richard Rahe developed the first rating scale to estimate the health hazards we face when stresses add up (Holmes & Rahe, 1967). Still widely used today, a version of the **Social Readjustment Rating Scale (SRRS)** is reprinted in ▲ Table 13.3 (Miller & Rahe, 1997; Woods, Racine, & Klump, 2010). Notice that the impact of life events is expressed in *life change units (LCUs)* (numerical values assigned to each life event).

Halfpoint/Shutterstock.com

Marriage is usually a positive life event. Nevertheless, the many changes that it brings can be stressful.

Refusal skills training A program that teaches youths how to resist pressures to begin smoking (also can be applied to other drugs and health risks).

Life skills training A program that teaches stress reduction, self-protection, decision-making, self-control, and social skills.

Community health campaign A community-wide education program that provides information about how to lessen risk factors and promote health.

Stress Pressure or demand placed on an organism to adjust or adapt.

Stressor Specific condition or event that challenges or threatens a person.

Social Readjustment Rating Scale (SRRS) A scale that rates the impact of various life events on the likelihood of illness.

▲ **Table 13.3 Social Readjustment Rating Scale (SRSS)**

Rank	Life Event	Life Change Units	Rank	Life Event	Life Change Units
1.	Death of spouse or child	119	23.	Mortgage or loan greater than $10,000	44
2.	Divorce	98	24.	Change in responsibilities at work	43
3.	Death of close family member	92	25.	Change in living conditions	42
4.	Marital separation	79	26.	Change in residence	41
5.	Fired from work	79	27.	Begin or end school	38
6.	Major personal injury or illness	77	28.	Trouble with in-laws	38
7.	Jail term	75	29.	Outstanding personal achievement	37
8.	Death of close friend	70	30.	Change in work hours or conditions	36
9.	Pregnancy	66	31.	Change in schools	35
10.	Major business readjustment	62	32.	Christmas	30
11.	Foreclosure on a mortgage or loan	61	33.	Trouble with boss	29
12.	Gain of new family member	57	34.	Change in recreation	29
13.	Marital reconciliation	57	35.	Mortgage or loan less than $10,000	28
14.	Change in health or behavior of family member	56	36.	Change in personal habits	27
15.	Change in financial state	56	37.	Change in eating habits	27
16.	Retirement	54	38.	Change in social activities	27
17.	Change to different line of work	51	39.	Change in number of family get-togethers	26
18.	Change in number of arguments with spouse	51	40.	Change in sleeping habits	26
19.	Marriage	50	41.	Vacation	25
20.	Spouse begins or ends work	46	42.	Change in church activities	22
21.	Sexual difficulties	45	43.	Minor violations of the law	22
22.	Child leaving home	44			

Source: Reprinted from Miller & Rahe (1997).

It seems weird that going on vacation is on the list. As we noted earlier, positive life events can be stressful as well. (For example, marriage rates a 50 and Christmas a 30, even though they usually are happy events.) Even a change in social activities rates 27 LCUs, whether the change is due to an improvement or a decline. A stressful adjustment may be required in either case. To use the SRRS, add up the LCUs for all the life events you have experienced during the last year and compare the total to the following standards:

0–150: No significant problems

150–199: Mild life crisis (33 percent chance of illness)

200–299: Moderate life crisis (50 percent chance of illness)

300 or more: Major life crisis (80 percent chance of illness)

You have a higher chance of illness or accident when your LCU total exceeds 300 points. Other stressful events—such as entering college, changing majors, or experiencing a breakup in a steady relationship—can affect the health of college students more specifically.

Since people differ greatly in their reactions to the same event, stress scales like the SRRS at best provide a rough index of stress. Nevertheless, research has shown that if your stress level is too high, an adjustment in your activities or lifestyle may be needed. In one classic study, people were deliberately exposed to the virus that causes common colds. The results were nothing to sneeze at: If a person had a high stress score, she or he was much more likely to actually get a cold (Cohen, Tyrrell, & Smith, 1993). In view of such findings, higher levels of stress should be taken seriously (Hales, 2015).

Hassles

There must be more to stress than major life changes. Isn't there a link between ongoing minor stresses and health? In addition to having a direct impact, major life events spawn countless daily frustrations and irritations (Henderson, Roberto, & Kamo, 2010). Also, many of us face ongoing stresses at work or at home that do not involve major life changes (Pett & Johnson, 2005). Such minor but frequent stresses are called **hassles (microstressors).** Some common hassles faced by college students include too many things to do, people making "jokes" that are discriminatory, communication problems with friends, driving to school in heavy traffic every day, finding a work–life balance, getting into shape, and parents' expectations (Pett & Johnson, 2005).

In a year-long study, 100 men and women recorded the daily hassles they endured. Participants also reported on their physical and mental health. Frequent and severe hassles turned out to be better predictors of day-to-day health than major life events. However, major life events did predict changes in health one or two years after the events took place. It appears that daily hassles are closely linked to immediate health and psychological well-being while major life changes have more of a long-term impact, exacerbating the effects of daily hassles (Crowther et al., 2001; Woods, Racine, & Klump, 2010).

Responding to Stressors

Akihito, an acquaintance of one of your authors, would find it stressful to listen to five of his son's hip-hop albums in a row. His son Takashi would find it stressful to listen to *one* of his father's opera albums. But our responses to stressors, both major and minor, depend on how you interpret, or appraise, those events. As we will see in a moment, whenever a stressor is appraised as a threat, a powerful stress reaction follows (Lazarus, 1991a,b; Smith & Kirby, 2011). (■ See Section 10.4 for a discussion of how appraisal influences emotions.) Psychological scientists have established that two specific types of appraisals are important in determining stress responses: *primary* and *secondary* appraisals. Those appraisals are important in governing a broader physiological response to stress that is referred to as *general adaptation syndrome*. In the sections that follow, we'll do a deeper dive on both appraisals and general adaptation syndrome.

Primary and Secondary Appraisals

Imagine that you have been selected to give a speech to 300 people. Or a doctor tells you that you must undergo a dangerous and painful operation. Or the one true love of your life walks out the door. What would be your response to these events?

According to Richard Lazarus (1991a, b), there are two important steps in dealing with a stressor. The first is **primary appraisal**, during which you make a very basic decision about whether a situation is relevant or irrelevant; positive or threatening. In essence, this step answers the question, "Am I okay or in trouble?" Next, you engage in **secondary appraisal**, during which you assess your resources, establish whether they are sufficient to deal with the stressor, and choose a way to meet the threat or challenge. ("What can I do about this situation?")

Thus, the way a situation is "sized up" greatly affects our ability to cope with it (● Figure 13.2; Gomes, Faria, & Lopes, 2016). Public speaking, for instance, can be appraised as an intense potential threat to self-esteem or as a great opportunity to build your skill set. Emphasizing the threat—by imagining failure, rejection, or embarrassment during your speech—will obviously result in a strong stress response (Tripp et al., 2011). In contrast, viewing the talk as a challenge and a valuable opportunity to practice your communication skills is likely to provoke a very different reaction, and significantly less stress.

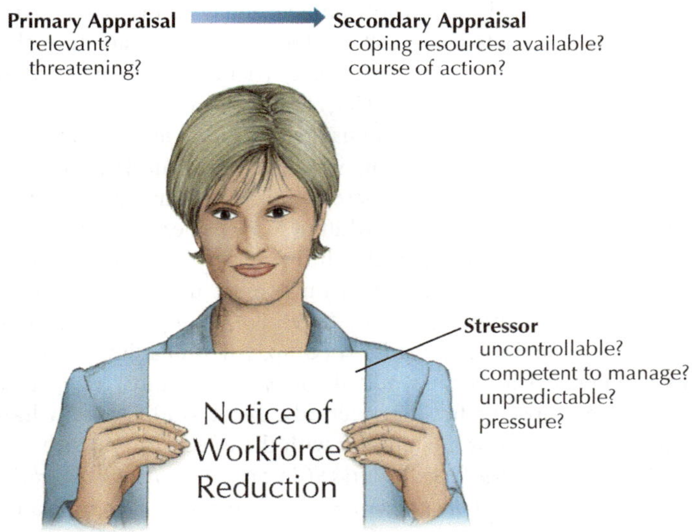

● **Figure 13.2 The origins of stress.** Stress is the product of an interchange between a person and the environment.

At least four factors contribute to our primary and secondary appraisals. First, in most day-to-day situations, perceived threat is connected with the idea of control. We are particularly prone to feel stressed when we can't—or think we can't—control our immediate environment. In short, a *perceived lack of control* is just as threatening as a real lack of control. For example, college students who feel overloaded will experience stress even though their workload may not be any heavier than that of their classmates (Jacobs & Dodd, 2003).

Second, our appraisals are guided by beliefs about whether we can reach desired goals. Specifically, it is more threatening to feel that we lack *competence* to manage life's demands, and this will lead to greater feelings of stress (Bandura, 2001; Leiter, Gascón, & Martínez-Jarreta, 2010). Again, though, perceptions are important: What really drives our appraisals is whether we feel competent, rather than any objective measure of our abilities.

Unpredictability is a third important factor that can influence appraisals. Police officers, for instance, suffer from a high rate of stress-related diseases. The threat of injury or death—plus occasional confrontations with angry, drunk, or hostile citizens—takes a toll. A major factor is the unpredictable nature of police work. An officer who stops a car to issue a traffic ticket never knows whether a cooperative citizen or an armed gang member is waiting inside.

Hassle (microstressor) Any distressing, day-to-day annoyance.

Primary appraisal Deciding if a situation is relevant to oneself and if it is a threat.

Secondary appraisal Deciding how to cope with a threat or challenge.

A revealing study shows how unpredictability adds to stress. In a series of one-minute trials, college students breathed air through a mask. On random (i.e., unpredictable) trials, the air contained 20 percent more carbon dioxide (CO_2) than normal. If you were to inhale this air, you would feel anxious, stressed, and a little like you were suffocating. Students tested this way hated the "surprise" doses of CO_2. They found it much less stressful to be told in advance which trials would include a choking whiff of CO_2 (Lejuez et al., 2000).

A fourth and final factor that influences appraisals is *pressure*. Pressure occurs when a person must meet urgent external demands or expectations (Szollos, 2009). For example, we feel pressured when activities must be sped up, when deadlines must be met, when extra work is added, or when we must work near maximum capacity for long periods. Most students who have survived final exams are familiar with the effects of pressure.

What if I set deadlines for myself instead of someone else doing it? Does the source of the pressure make a difference? It can certainly help when the pressure is self-imposed, since that would tend to increase your sense of self-control (Brough, Drummond, & Biggs, 2017; Leiter, Gascón, & Martínez-Jarreta, 2010). In one study, nurses with a high sense of control (e.g., over the pacing of work and the physical arrangement of the working environment) were less likely to get sick, either physically or mentally, than nurses with a low sense of control (Ganster, Fox, & Dwyer, 2001).

To summarize, our primary and secondary appraisals of life events and hassles are often guided by the extent to which those stressors seem *controllable,* the extent to which we see ourselves as *competent* to address them, how *predictable* they seem, and how much *pressure* we are experiencing.

General Adaptation Syndrome

Regardless of whether it is triggered by a pleasant or an unpleasant event, appraisals of threat generate a *stress reaction* that begins with the same autonomic nervous system (ANS) arousal that occurs during emotion. For example, imagine that you are standing at the top of a wind-whipped ski jump for the first time. Internally, you experience a rapid surge in your heart rate, blood pressure, respiration, muscle tension, and other ANS responses. *Short-term* stressors of this kind can be uncomfortable, but they rarely do any damage. (Your landing might, however.) *Long-term* stressors are another matter entirely.

The impact of long-term stressors can be understood by examining the body's defenses against stress, a pattern known as **general adaptation syndrome** (GAS). GAS is a series of three stages that occur in response to prolonged stress. Selye (1976) noticed that the first symptoms of almost any disease or trauma (poisoning, infection, injury) are almost identical. The body responds in much the same way to any stress, be it infection, failure, embarrassment, a new job, trouble at school, or a stormy romance. The GAS consists of three stages: an alarm reaction, a stage of resistance, and a stage of exhaustion (Figure 13.3; Selye, 1976).

In the **alarm reaction**, your body mobilizes its resources to cope with added stress. The pituitary gland signals the adrenal glands to produce more adrenaline, noradrenaline, and cortisol. As these stress hormones are dumped into the bloodstream, some bodily processes speed up and others are slowed. This allows bodily resources to be applied where they are needed.

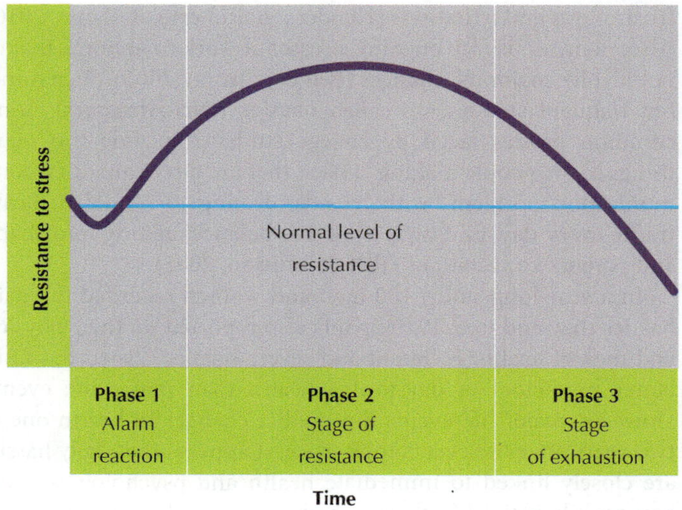

Figure 13.3 General adaptation syndrome (GAS). During the initial alarm reaction to stress, resistance falls below normal. It rises again as body resources are mobilized, and it remains high during the stage of resistance. Eventually, resistance falls again as the stage of exhaustion is reached. (Based on Selye, 1976.)

We should all be thankful that our bodies automatically respond to emergencies in this way. But brilliant as this emergency system is, it also can cause problems. In the first phase of the alarm reaction, people have symptoms such as headache, fever, fatigue, sore muscles, shortness of breath, diarrhea, upset stomach, loss of appetite, and a lack of energy. Notice that these also are the symptoms of being sick, of stressful travel, of final exams week, and (possibly) of falling in love!

During the **stage of resistance**, bodily adjustments to stress stabilize. As the body's defenses come into balance, symptoms of the alarm reaction disappear. Outwardly, everything seems normal. However, this appearance of normality comes at a high cost. The body is better able to cope with the original stressor, but its resistance to other stresses is lowered. For example, animals placed in extreme cold become more resistant to the cold but more susceptible to infection. It is during the stage of resistance that the first signs of psychosomatic disorders (genuine physical disorders triggered by psychological factors) begin to appear.

Continued stress leads to a **stage of exhaustion**, in which the body's resources are drained and stress hormones are depleted. Some of the typical signs or symptoms of impending exhaustion include the following (Friedman, 2002; Gurung, 2019):

Emotional signs: Anxiety, apathy, irritability, mental fatigue; excessive worry about illness

Behavioral signs: Avoidance of responsibilities and relationships, extreme or self-destructive behavior, self-neglect, poor judgment

Physical signs: Frequent illness, exhaustion, overuse of medicines, physical ailments and complaints

GAS may sound melodramatic if you are young and healthy, or if you've never endured prolonged stress. However, do not take stress lightly. When Selye examined animals in the later stages of

Subbotina Anna/Shutterstock.com

Stress and negative emotions lower immune system activity and increase inflammation. This, in turn, raises our vulnerability to infection, worsens illness, and delays recovery.

GAS, he found that their adrenal glands were enlarged and discolored. Intense shrinkage of internal organs, such as the thymus, spleen, and lymph nodes, was evident, and many animals had stomach ulcers. In addition to such direct effects, stress can disrupt the body's immune system. Let's take a closer look at some of the consequences that people experience when they're exposed to stress for a long period of time.

Consequences of Stress

Stress responses, especially those that persist over the long term, can have a number of negative consequences. We'll explore three of them in detail: *illness and psychosomatic disorders*, *learned helplessness*, and *burnout*.

Illness and Psychosomatic Disorders

Can stress actually result in a physical illness? An answer can be found in your body's immune system, which mobilizes defenses (such as white blood cells) against invading microbes and other disease agents. The immune system is regulated, in part, by the brain. Because of this link, stress and upsetting emotions can affect the immune system in ways that increase susceptibility to disease (Janusek, Cooper, & Mathews, 2012; Zachariae, 2009). The study of links among behavior, stress, disease, and the immune system is called **psychoneuroimmunology** (Clark & Fessler, 2014; Daruna, 2012).

Studies show that students' immune systems are weakened during major exam times (as you may already have unfortunately discovered). Why? Stress causes the body to release substances that increase inflammation. This is part of the body's natural self-protective response to threats, but it can prolong infections and delay healing (Kiecolt-Glaser, 2010). Immunity is also lowered by divorce, bereavement, a troubled marriage, job loss, poor sleep, depression, and similar stresses (Motivala & Irwin, 2007; Segerstrom & Miller, 2004). Lowered immunity explains why it's so common to experience the "double whammy" of getting sick when you are trying to cope with prolonged or severe stress (Pedersen, Bovbjerg, & Zachariae, 2011).

Prolonged stress reactions are closely related to a large number of psychosomatic (SIKE-oh-so-MAT-ik) illnesses. In **psychosomatic disorders** (*psyche*: mind; *soma*: body), psychological factors contribute to actual bodily damage or to damaging changes in bodily functioning (Bourgeois et al., 2009; Fava, 2016). Psychosomatic problems, therefore, are not the same as *somatic symptom disorders*. People with somatic symptom disorders *imagine* that they have diseases. (■ The term *hypochondriac* refers to a person who imagines illness, or mistakes normal bodily processes for illness; see Sections 13.3 and 14.4 for more details.)

The most common psychosomatic problems are gastrointestinal and respiratory (stomach pain and asthma, for example), but many others exist, including eczema (skin rash), hives, migraine headaches, rheumatoid arthritis, hypertension (high blood pressure), colitis (ulceration of the colon), and heart disease. If you consider this list carefully, it should not surprise you that severe psychosomatic disorders can be fatal. But many lesser health complaints are also stress related. Typical examples include sore muscles, headaches, neckaches, backaches, indigestion, constipation,

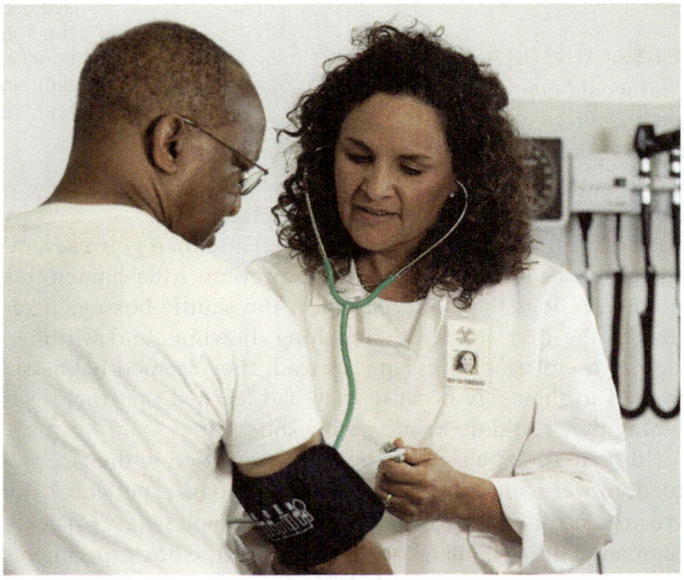

Ariel Skelley/The Image Bank/Getty Images

It is estimated that at least half of all patients who see a doctor have a psychosomatic disorder or an illness that is complicated by psychosomatic symptoms.

General adaptation syndrome Three-stage model of stress response, consisting of alarm, resistance, and exhaustion.

Alarm reaction The first stage of the general adaptation syndrome, during which body resources are mobilized to cope with a stressor.

Stage of resistance The second stage of the general adaptation syndrome, during which the body adjustments to stress stabilize, but at a high physical cost.

Stage of exhaustion The third stage of the general adaptation syndrome, at which time the body's resources are exhausted and serious health consequences occur.

Psychoneuroimmunology Study of the links among behavior, stress, disease, and the immune system.

Psychosomatic disorders Illnesses in which psychological factors contribute to bodily damage or to damaging changes in bodily functioning.

chronic diarrhea, fatigue, insomnia, premenstrual problems, and sexual dysfunctions (Taylor, 2012).

Could reducing stress help prevent illness then? Yes, absolutely. Various psychological approaches, such as support groups, relaxation exercises, guided imagery, and stress-management training, can actually boost immune system functioning (Kottler & Chen, 2011). For example, stress management reduced the severity of cold and flu symptoms in a group of university students (Reid, Mackinnon, & Drummond, 2001). There is even evidence that stress management can improve the chances of survival in people with life-threatening diseases, such as cancer, heart disease, and HIV/AIDS. With some successes to encourage them, psychologists are now searching for the best combination of treatments to help people resist disease (Phillips et al., 2012; Schneiderman et al., 2001). For more detail about how to manage your stress, see the *Psychology and Your Skill Set* section at the end of this chapter.

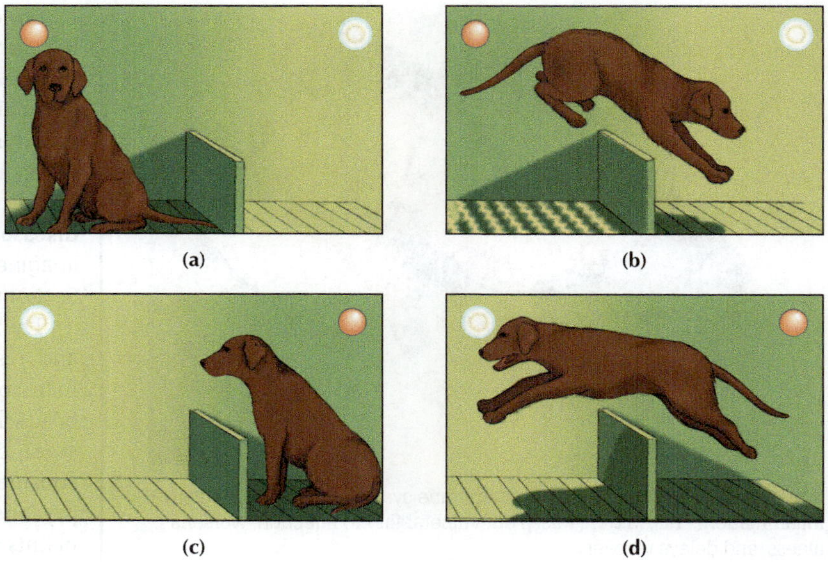

Figure 13.4 Learned helplessness. In the normal course of escape and avoidance learning, a light dims shortly before the floor is electrified (a). Because the light does not yet have meaning for the dog, the dog receives a shock (non-injurious, by the way) and leaps the barrier (b). Dogs soon learn to watch for the dimming of the light (c) and to jump before receiving a shock (d). Dogs made to feel "helpless" rarely even learn to escape shock, much less to avoid it.

Learned Helplessness

What would happen if a person appraised a threatening situation as hopeless? Some of the first clues to answering this question came from studies carried out with dogs that were tested in a shuttle box (Figure 13.4). The dog was first placed in a harness (from which it could not escape) and then given several painful shocks that it was helpless to prevent. After having this experience, dogs that were placed in the shuttle box again reacted to the first shock by crouching, howling, and whining. None of them tried to escape. Instead, they seemed helplessly resigned to their fate because they had learned that there was nothing they could do about getting shocked.

This pattern of behavior—showing resignation in the face of a situation over which you believe (based on past experience) you have no control—has been termed **learned helplessness** (Maier & Seligman, 2016; Seligman, 1989). As the shuttle box experiments suggest, helplessness is a psychological state that occurs when an appraisal suggests that events *do not appear to be controllable* (Maier & Seligman, 2016).

Jason Patterson/The New Yorker Collection/Cartoonbank.com

Helplessness also afflicts humans, and it is a common reaction to repeated failure and to unpredictable or unavoidable punishment (Domjan, 2015; Reivich et al., 2013). Indeed, Martin Seligman and others have pointed out the similarities between learned helplessness and **depression**. Both are marked by feelings of despondency, powerlessness, and hopelessness. For example, Seligman (1972) described the fate of Archie, a 15-year-old boy: For Archie, school is an unending series of shocks and failures. Other students treat him as if he's stupid; in class, he rarely answers questions because he doesn't know some of the words. He feels knocked down everywhere he turns. These may not be electric shocks, but they are certainly emotional "shocks," and Archie has learned to feel helpless to prevent them. Research suggests that when he leaves school, Archie's chances of success are poor, but Archie is not alone in this regard. Hopelessness is almost always a major element of depression, which is now one of the most common mental health concerns in America (Durand & Barlow, 2016; Reivich et al., 2013).

Does Seligman's research give any clues about how to "unlearn" helplessness? With dogs, an effective technique is to forcibly drag them away from shock into the "safe" compartment. After this is done several times, the animals regain "hope" and feelings of control over the environment. Just how this can be done with humans is a question that psychologists are exploring. It seems obvious, for instance, that someone like Archie would benefit from an educational program that would allow him to learn strategies that would help him to "succeed" repeatedly.

In **mastery training**, responses that lead to mastery of a threat or control over one's environment are reinforced. Animals that undergo such training become more resistant to learned helplessness (Volpicelli et al., 1983). For example, animals that first learn to escape shock become more persistent in trying to flee inescapable shock. In effect, they don't give up, even when the situation really is "hopeless." Such findings suggest that we might be able to "immunize" people against helplessness and depression by allowing them to master difficult challenges (Miltenberger, 2016).

The value of hope should not be overlooked. As fragile as this emotion seems, it is a powerful antidote to depression and helplessness (Weingarten, 2010). As an individual, you may find hope in religion, nature, human companionship, or even technology. Wherever you find it, remember its value: Hope is among the most important of all human emotions and is closely related to overall well-being (Diener & Chan, 2011).

Burnout

When workers are physically, mentally, and emotionally drained, they may experience **burnout** (Leiter, Gascón, & Martínez-Jarreta, 2010). (See ▲ Table 13.4 for a list of the most common sources of stress at work.) When people become burned out, they experience emotional exhaustion, cynicism or detachment, and feelings of reduced personal accomplishment.

Burnout may occur in any job, but it is a special problem in emotionally demanding helping professions, such as nursing, teaching, social work, childcare, counseling, or police work (Ray et al., 2013). Also, people who are more passionate about their work are more vulnerable to burnout (Turgoose et al., 2017; Vallerand, 2010). If we wish to keep caring people in the helping professions, it may be necessary to adjust workloads, rewards, and the amount of control people have in their jobs (Leiter & Maslach, 2005).

Can college students experience burnout? Yes, they can (Parker & Salmela-Aro, 2011). If you have a negative attitude toward your studies and feel that your college workload is too heavy, you may be vulnerable to burnout (Jacobs & Dodd, 2003). On the other hand, if you have a positive attitude toward your studies, take a course load that appropriately reflects your other commitments, participate in extracurricular activities, and enjoy good social support from your friends, burnout becomes much less likely.

▲ Table 13.4 The Top 10 Work Stresses

Work Stress	Rank
Low salary	1
Lack of opportunity for growth	2
Workload too heavy	3
Hours too long	4
Job expectations uncertain	5
Job expectations unrealistic	6
Work interferes with personal time	7
Job insecurity	8
Lack of participation in decision making	9
Inflexible hours	10

Source: Data from American Psychological Association (2012).

Reflective Practice

Stress and Health

1. According to Richard Lazarus, choosing a way to meet a threat or challenge takes place during the
a. primary stress reaction
b. secondary stress reaction
c. primary appraisal
d. secondary appraisal

2. Stress tends to be greatest when a situation is appraised as a(n) ____________ and a person does not feel ____________ to cope with the situation.

3. The first signs of psychosomatic disorders begin to appear during the GAS stage of
a. alarm
b. exhaustion
c. resistance
d. appraisal

4. The SRRS appears to predict long-range changes in health, whereas the frequency and severity of daily microstressors are closely related to immediate ratings of health. T or F?

5. Students taking stressful final exams are more susceptible to the cold virus, a pattern best explained by the concept of
a. the disease-prone personality
b. psychoneuroimmunology
c. emotion-focused coping
d. reaction formation

6. Hives, migraine headaches, and stomach pain are all examples of common psychosomatic disorders. T or F?

7. Learned helplessness occurs when events appear to be
a. frustrating
b. in conflict
c. problem-focused
d. uncontrollable

THINK CRITICALLY

8. Mindy complains about her health all the time, but she seems to be just fine. An acquaintance of Mindy's dismisses her problems by saying, "Oh, she's not really sick. It's just psychosomatic." What's wrong with this use of the term *psychosomatic* in this situation?

SELF-REFLECT

- Are you experiencing any signs of GAS? (Not a joke, guys ☺.) What are they?
- Do you think there is more of a connection between major life events and your health? Or have you observed more of a connection between microstressors and your health?

Answers: 1. d 2. threat, competent 3. c 4. T 5. b 6. T 7. d 8. The term psychosomatic illness refers to situations in which psychological factors, including stress, cause *actual* damage to the body and its functioning, thus compromising health. It is important to distinguish this term from somatic symptom disorders (or hypochondriasis), in which people like Mindy *imagine* that they have an illness.

Learned helplessness Belief that one cannot control the outcome of events.

Depression A state of despondency marked by feelings of powerlessness and hopelessness.

Mastery training Reinforcement of responses that lead to mastery of a threat or control over one's environment.

Burnout A work-related condition of mental, physical, and emotional exhaustion.

13.3 Improving Health with Treatment

GATEWAYS LEARNING OUTCOMES:
After reading this section you should be able to:

13.3.1 Outline the main features of somatic symptom disorder

13.3.2 Describe how biological, psychological, and social factors contribute to our ability to recognize illness

13.3.3 Outline four factors that influence people's decision to seek treatment

13.3.4 Define what is meant by the term complementary and alternative medicine, and outline one main concern associated with this type of treatment

13.3.5 Identify the forms that treatment noncompliance can take, describe four factors that contribute to treatment noncompliance, and outline the key to minimizing treatment noncompliance

An important contribution made by health psychologists is their role in working with other healthcare professionals to ensure that, when illness does occur, it is managed in the most effective way possible. This means contributing to what is known about how to help people *recognize when they're sick* (and when they're not!), ensuring that people *seek treatment* in a timely way and, most importantly, confirming that people *comply with treatments* suggested by healthcare providers. In this section, we examine each of these three issues more closely.

Recognizing Illness

When it comes to recognizing illness, people demonstrate a wide range of cognitions, emotions, and behaviors. At one end of the spectrum are people who deny or ignore the very real symptoms of illness, persuading themselves that nothing is wrong and refusing to seek medical attention until it is too late for effective treatments to be administered. At the other end are those who believe that they are experiencing the symptoms of disease, even though they are not.

Psychologists and psychiatrists refer to this latter condition as **somatic symptom disorder**, though a more commonly used term is hypochondriasis. Often rooted in anxiety, people who are hypochondriacs may convert more general concerns and distress—about work or relationships, for example—into a persistent and excessive worry that they are seriously ill or dying. They become convinced that they are experiencing all of the symptoms of a particular disease, and their concerns often persist even in the face of medical reassurances that there is nothing wrong. Charles Darwin is among the most well-known suspected hypochondriacs, with his ongoing concerns about stomach ailments, headaches, and heart palpitations. Other hypochondriacal symptoms may include back pain, joint pain, and "allergies" to particular foods or environmental conditions.

In between hypochondriacs and those who deny real health problems are people who realistically evaluate their health and seek appropriate treatment when necessary. Health psychologists have helped to illuminate some of the factors that contribute to individuals' ability to recognize and interpret the signs of illness, many of which fit within the biopsychosocial model.

Biological Factors

On the biological side of the biopsychosocial model, people are more likely to recognize and take seriously those symptoms that *affect parts of the body that are highly valued*, such as the eyes or the heart, or those that limit a person's ability to move around with ease (Eifert et al., 1996). Perhaps unsurprisingly, people are also more likely to concern themselves with *symptoms that cause them pain*, in contrast with those that do not (Taylor, 2021).

Psychological Factors

With respect to the psychological element of the biopsychosocial model, health psychologists have noted that some *personality* variables, particularly neuroticism (and the anxiety that often accompanies it), are associated with people's tendency to notice and respond to symptoms of illness (Rosmalen et al., 2007). Moreover, the psychological experience of *stress* can amplify people's attention to their body, possibly because they understand that stress makes them more vulnerable to becoming sick (Ewart et al., 2014). Finally, *mood* and *emotion* also appear to play a role in our ability to recognize and properly interpret physical symptoms. Negative emotions, and feelings of depression in particular, are correlated with a greater likelihood of reporting symptoms and more concerns that treatments will be ineffective (Howren et al., 2009; Leventhal et al., 1996).

Social Factors

Finally, at least two variables related to the social aspect of the biopsychosocial model appear to be important to people's tendency to notice signs of illness. First, Taylor (2021) has pointed out the importance of people's *lay referral network* in shaping their interpretation of symptoms. The term lay referral network was first articulated by sociologist Eliot Freidson (1960), and refers to your informal web of friends and relatives, many of whom will be more than happy to comment on any health-related issues or concerns that you share with them. These comments may take the form of interpreting what the symptoms likely mean, whether or not it's wise to seek treatment, and suggestions about possible treatments that you could try for yourself at home.

Second, *the Internet* is also an important source of information that impacts people's recognition and interpretation of symptoms. A large, representative sample of American adults indicated that, depending on whether they lived in a rural or urban area, between one-third and one-half of respondents had used the Internet as a means of helping them to identify and understand disease-related symptoms (Centers for Disease Control, 2015).

While it may be beneficial that so much information is now readily available to people who are interested in better recognizing and understanding their symptoms, a major challenge stems from the fact that not all of the information that's posted on the web is current and reliable. Information literacy skills, such as those discussed in ■ Section 1.8, are particularly important when evaluating health websites, and it is critical to monitor yourself for signs of confirmation bias when you undertake a search. (■ Recall from Section 1.1 that confirmation bias refers to a tendency to seek out and believe only that information that conforms with what you already believe, or what you want to be true.)

Studying the Science: Web-based Information About COVID-19

The COVID-19 pandemic presented an excellent example of the perils that can be associated with health-related misinformation on the Internet. In the earliest weeks of the pandemic, web-based searches for information spiked as news stories began to appear, with people initially seeking out information about symptoms, in particular (Bento et al., 2020). Unfortunately, in the weeks that followed, it quickly became apparent that much of the information about the virus that was circulating on the web was misleading, and often reflected opinion rather than evidence based on sound research from reputable scientists. The health implications of following such advice were sometimes simply unhelpful; for example, people who believed sites telling them they could avoid being infected by staying away from 5G networks, eating garlic, or living in a hot climate were bound to be disappointed. At worst, though, this misinformation—including the outrageous claim that people should try drinking bleach, alcohol, or hand sanitizer to protect themselves—proved tragic in terms of its consequences.

The general rule of thumb about health information on the web is that you need to carefully screen your sources, relying only on those that are known to be evidence based and reputable. (Hint: Hollywood celebrities and professional athletes often don't fall into this category when it comes to health.) Here are a few websites that will always be a good starting point in your search for reliable healthcare information:

- Centers for Disease Control and Prevention (www.cdc.gov)
- National Institutes of Health (www.nih.gov)
- Mayo Clinic (www.mayoclinic.org)
- Cleveland Clinic (www.clevelandclinic.org)

Seeking Treatment

The decision to seek treatment is often one that is made with great care, but health psychologists have noted that some people are more likely to use healthcare services than others. In this section, we examine four factors—sex, age, income, and culture—that seem to influence whether people will pursue treatment when they are feeling unwell, as well as some of the remedies that are available to them.

Factors Influencing Decisions to Seek Treatment

Psychological scientists have outlined at least four factors that seem to be important in the decision to seek help for health concerns. First, *sex* differences have been observed, with women being more likely than men to seek out health care (Bertakis et al., 2000). This difference is likely due in part to their experiences with pregnancy and childbirth, but it may also reflect differing gender norms related to the acceptability of acknowledging pain or physical limitations (Novak et al., 2019).

Not surprisingly, *income* is a second factor that influences medical help-seeking (Lusardi, Schneider, & Tufano, 2015). As previously noted, poor Americans are far less likely to have insurance or the financial resources to pay for such services, though some government initiatives, such as Medicaid, help to alleviate this problem. It has also long been recognized that poor people have access to fewer high-quality healthcare options, such as reputable specialists and clinics. Finally, low-income Americans are less likely than those who are more wealthy to make use of alternatives that help to prevent disease in the first place, including vaccinations and screening for treatable conditions such as high blood pressure (Fox & Shaw, 2014; Murimi & Harpel, 2010).

Age is a third factor that influences the use of healthcare resources. In particular, the very youngest and the very oldest members of society are the largest consumers of health care because of the unique needs associated with their stages of life (Meara, White, & Cutler, 2004). Very young children, for example, often require regular visits to the doctor for vaccinations. They are also more likely to become sick because they are susceptible to illness while their immune systems are developing.

Older adults are also more likely than adolescents and younger adults to use the healthcare system, and they are less likely to delay seeking help. For the most part, this trend reflects the fact that aging is associated with a greater number of potential health concerns. Some of these problems, such as heart disease and osteoporosis, are preventable because they are typically the result of lifestyle choices (Malhotra et al., 2017). Other diseases may be more clearly connected to genetic factors: Some of these, including specific forms of kidney disease and breast cancer, are connected to the inheritance of particular genes that confer risk (Ford et al., 1994). However, genes also play a role in the diseases of adulthood because genetic mutations accumulate over a lifetime, increasing the chances of illness (Zhaurova, 2008). And, of course, epigenetic forces can also be at play when the environment and genetics interact, leading to disease. Many diseases that are common among older adults are likely to have epigenetic origins, including diabetes, many forms of cancer, and various forms of dementia, including Alzheimer's disease (Brunet & Berger, 2014). (■ See Section 3.1 for a discussion of epigenetics.)

A fourth and final factor that impacts help seeking for medical issues is *culture* (Gurung, 2019). For cultures that adopt more collectivist values (that is, belief systems that prioritize the importance of the group over the individual), in particular,

Somatic symptom disorder (hypochondriasis) A disorder in which people convert general distress into excessive worry that they are seriously ill or dying.

the extended family is likely to play an important role in decisions to seek treatment. This is appropriate, since the family will often assume considerable responsibility in helping to care for members who are unwell. In some cases, a decision may be made to consult with other group members who are believed to have appropriate expertise, such as spiritual healers or shamen, before turning to "Western-style" medical options. Moreover, in some cultures, treatment will not be sought at all if the disabilities or health challenges are believed to bring shame to the family or compromise other family members' ability to find a spouse (Purnell, 2003).

Types of Treatment

Having decided that healthcare treatment is needed, what options are available to people? If the problem is thought to be mild, then sometimes the answer is a trip to the pharmacy to purchase an *over-the-counter medication*. More serious concerns, however, often result in an appointment with a *medical professional*. In some cases, this will mean being seen by a physician trained at a traditional medical school. More recently, though, Americans also have the opportunity to seek treatment from nurses with advanced training, such as nurse practitioners. For more targeted treatments, people may follow up with specialized healthcare professionals, such as physiotherapists (for mobility concerns), occupational therapists (for assistance with completion of everyday tasks), or audiologists (for hearing-related issues), for example.

In some cases, though, people may elect to make use of **complementary and alternative medicine** (CAM) to treat their illness, either instead of, or in addition to, more traditional forms of medicine (Wagner, 2020). CAMs encompass a wide range of treatments, including homeopathy and dietary supplements, acupuncture, chiropractic services, massage, yoga, and many others. Such approaches are more often in line with the full biopsychosocial model, and emphasize the idea that restoring good health requires holistic attention to the mind, spirit, and environment, as well as the body. CAMs are sometimes rooted in the healing practices of other cultures; good examples include traditional Chinese medicine and Ayurvedic medicine, which has its origins in India (Taylor, 2021).

While CAM treatments are often praised by those who use them, a significant problem is that there have been relatively few large-scale studies evaluating their effectiveness (Lee et al., 2019). For this reason, it's difficult to say with certainty whether people's positive experiences reflect the treatment itself or placebo effects that are similar to those observed in more traditional medical treatments (Friesen, 2019). Of course, many people would argue that even if a positive outcome results from the placebo effect, it may not matter—the end result is still improved health and well-being. Moreover, at least some CAMs, such as massage and yoga, are enjoyable and intrinsically motivating, so even if they do not have a medical effect they may still improve people's quality of life.

At present, CAMs are increasing in popularity among Americans and are becoming an increasingly visible component of the American healthcare system (Frass et al., 2012). While many of them seem to offer benefits to those who use them, it would be beneficial to further examine their effectiveness through large-scale studies carried out by scientists without clear conflicts of interest (that is, people who have nothing to gain if the results of the study are positive; Friesen, 2019). Stronger evidence concerning the potential benefits of CAMs would be useful because it would strengthen the argument for their inclusion in healthcare insurance plans, allowing greater access to them. In the meantime, though, you should always do a thorough investigation of any CAM you are considering using, making sure to deploy all of the information literacy tools that you learned in ■ Section 1.8.

Complying with Treatments

Many healthy choices—such as eating a balanced diet or quitting smoking—certainly don't require a visit to the doctor. Most people have heard these messages from family, friends, and the media often enough to know the truth of them. However, earlier in this chapter we noted the difficulty of getting people to change these types of behaviors in ways that would improve their health.

In a similar way, people may sometimes fail to act on the recommendations provided by healthcare professionals, including suggestions for prescription medications or specific therapeutic programs. This situation referred to as **treatment noncompliance** (or treatment nonadherence). Why does this happen? And what are the consequences of this type of noncompliance? Let's take a closer look at these issues.

Treatment noncompliance can take several different forms. In some cases, patients simply *ignore* the suggestions being provided by healthcare professionals. However, noncompliance can also result when people *misunderstand*, *forget*, or *carry out treatments incorrectly* (Martin et al., 2005). The extent to which these things

Mr. Exen/Shutterstock.com

Too many people diagnosed with lifestyle illnesses, such as this smoker with severe emphysema, fail to comply with their doctor's instructions. Changing long-standing risky behaviors usually involves more than just telling people what they need to do differently. One major goal of health psychology is to find ways to increase compliance with doctors' advice.

happen varies depending on the treatment that has been prescribed. In one study of American adults, average noncompliance was estimated at approximately 40 percent, though it was as low as 15 percent for some treatments and as high as 93 percent for others (DiMatteo et al., 2002).

In some respects, these numbers are surprising, given the benefits that often follow from adhering to the suggestions made by healthcare professionals. Why don't people comply with these treatments? Large-scale studies and meta-analyses suggest that there are many reasons (Martin et al., 2005). The first—and one of the most important—relates to *cognitive factors*. Following a treatment plan requires that people be able to read at a basic level, and that they be able to understand written instructions. Language barriers and limited access to formal education can compromise these skills, which is why physicians are now encouraged to check people's ability to comprehend instructions before issuing a treatment plan.

A second key factor that influences adherence is *memory* (Martin et al., 2005). It goes without saying that for someone to be able to follow the instructions laid out by a healthcare professional, they need to be able to remember it. Researchers have noted that this may be an important reason for noncompliance among older adults (Dong et al., 2017; Myers & Midence, 1998). However, even among young people memory can be an issue. This is especially true when the treatment is complex, with many steps or components. Given what you know about the limits of working memory (■ see Section 7.2), it probably won't surprise you to find out that much of what a healthcare provider says during an appointment is forgotten before people arrive home unless instructions are written down.

A third variable that can affect compliance relates to the *relationship between care providers and recipients* (Martin et al., 2005). In the United States, people are far more likely to stick to a treatment plan when they feel that the professionals have given them a chance to be actively involved in its development, and have created a sense that they are partners in the process of getting well. Adherence also improves when people trust their care provider, and view them as an empathic person with a good "bedside manner."

Fourth and finally, patient emotions, particularly *anxiety and depression*, also influence compliance with treatment (DiMatteo et al., 2000; Martin et al., 2005). Anxiety is important because it can compromise people's ability to remember instructions and inhibit their willingness to ask questions if they do not understand. Anxiety about the treatment itself, including potentially undesirable side effects or unmanageable costs, may also play a role. Depression, on the other hand, is often associated with pessimism about whether a treatment will work and a lower likelihood of seeking social support during treatment, both of which have been linked to the chances that people will follow the directions outlined by their healthcare provider.

Addressing Noncompliance

Failure to comply with prescribed treatments comes with an enormous cost. Some estimates suggest that more than 125,000 Americans die prematurely each year because they did not follow a recommended treatment plan. Economically, data suggest that the cost of nonadherence in the United States may be as high as $300 billion dollars, largely the result of extra visits to healthcare professionals and additional hospitalizations (IMS Institute for Healthcare Informatics, 2013).

Given these costs, it makes sense to ask what healthcare providers can do to improve the chances that people will follow through with their recommendations. In this respect, two key skills are important: good *communication* (■ see Section 4.7) and strong *interpersonal skills* (including an understanding of how to work well with diverse others; ■ see Section 17.4) (Iuga & McGuire, 2014). Good communication and interpersonal skills help to foster the trust that will encourage people to assume a partnership role in their own treatment and feel a sense of ownership for the plan that is developed (Martin et al., 2005).

In some cases, building trust means encouraging people to "tell their story," thus giving healthcare providers information about the reality of their life circumstances and the potential barriers to following through with treatment. If child care or transportation is likely to affect the ability to get to a clinic, for example, then it's important to know that up front, and to have the opportunity to consider solutions and alternatives (Haskard-Zolnierek et al., 2017). A trusting relationship also makes it more likely that providers can carry out a realistic assessment of their patients' or clients' ability to understand the treatment, and that patients or clients will ask questions and be candid about how the treatment progresses over time.

At the end of the day, the most important aspect of gaining compliance is to ensure that the treatment plan reflects the individual for whom it has been designed. For healthcare providers, this means fully acknowledging all aspects of the biopsychosocial model. The biological side of the model involves selecting a treatment that will be effective in addressing the specific physiological system of concern to the patient or client. The psychological aspect means giving due consideration to such things as the attitudes, personality, memory, emotions, and motivation of the person seeking help. Finally, the social element of the model requires that the healthcare provider consider the cultural background of their clients and patients, given that cultural beliefs may have an important impact on their willingness to ask questions or their desire to assume a partnership role in treatment. Considering other elements of the social environment that characterize the patient's life, such as family responsibilities, the presence of social support, and financial resources is also critical. When it comes to adherence, then, a holistic approach means that treatments will always be unique—just like the people for whom they're designed!

Complementary and alternative medicine A range of treatments that emphasize importance of attention to the mind, spirit, and environment, as well as the body.

Treatment noncompliance Failure to comply with a treatment recommended by a healthcare provider.

Reflective Practice

Improving Health with Treatment

1. In terms of biological factors, people are more likely to recognize illness when
   a. they have never been sick before
   b. the illness is related to the internal organs
   c. their parents were often ill
   d. the illness impairs their mobility
2. The lay referral network
   a. refers to informal friends and family
   b. may be influential in making suggestions about interpreting symptoms you have
   c. may make suggestions about potential treatments
   d. all of the above
3. Which of the following factors does *not* appear to be influential in determining whether someone will seek treatment?
   a. sex
   b. income
   c. culture
   d. marital status
4. Complementary and alternative medicine
   a. contradicts the biopsychosocial model
   b. is a relatively recent "invention" in health care
   c. has not been well validated in large-scale studies
   d. works for only a very small number of people
5. Treatment noncompliance only happens when people ignore the instructions provided by healthcare workers. T or F?
6. The best way to minimize treatment noncompliance is to
   a. build a trusting relationship with the client or patient
   b. call the patient or client every day
   c. threaten not to continue with treatment if instructions aren't followed
   d. none of the above

THINK CRITICALLY

7. You have a friend who has started seeing a homeopath who has prescribed a special diet to address your friend's problems with digestion. After a few weeks, your friend tells you that the diet has worked wonders and she feels like a new person. All of her symptoms have disappeared! Based on your knowledge of research, would you conclude that the diet was effective?

SELF-REFLECT

- Do you feel that you have a good relationship with your healthcare provider? If so, what did this person do to help foster a trusting relationship? If not, what do you think has contributed to a less positive relationship?
- Have you ever tried complementary and alternative medicines? Which ones? What was your experience like—did the CAM help you?

Answers: 1. d 2. d 3. d 4. c 5. F 6. a 7. Probably not. While it's possible that the diet worked, it's also possible that your friend is experiencing a placebo effect. To properly establish whether the diet works, we'd need to run a study with experimental controls. In other words, our study would include randomly assigning people with similar digestion problems to either a treatment group (those who would go on the diet) or a control group (those who would follow another diet that was not expected to have any effect on the digestive symptoms). If the treatment group experienced significantly better outcomes than the control group, then we could be certain that the diet actually works.

13.4 Improving Health Through Coping

GATEWAYS LEARNING OUTCOMES:
After reading this section you should be able to:

13.4.1 Distinguish between problem-focused, emotion-focused, and relationship-focused coping

13.4.2 Explain the effects of traumatic stress, and some strategies for coping with it

13.4.3 Identify the four main patterns of coping with acculturation, and the level of acculturative stress associated with each one

13.4.4 Describe some of the factors that contribute to the "college blues," and some strategies for coping with this problem

In ■ Sections 13.1 and 13.2, we explored a number of variables associated with illness and poor health, including both behavioral risk factors and stressors. In ■ Section 13.3, we looked at managing disease through medical and CAM treatments. But what about our own efforts to manage health concerns and other stressors? Is there anything we can do ourselves to manage these problems when they occur?

In this section, we explore research related to **coping**, or the tendency to change cognitions and behaviors in an effort to manage illness, as well as the more general demands that life places upon us (Lazarus & Folkman, 1984). We begin by examining three different methods of coping. We then move on to discuss common examples of coping in everyday life, including the management of traumatic stress, acculturative stress, and the "college blues."

Strategies for Coping

Psychological scientists have outlined three major forms of coping, each of which involves thinking and acting in ways that help us handle illness and other challenges that life throws our way (Gardner et al., 2017; Smith & Kirby, 2011). These three strategies are referred to as problem-focused, emotion-focused, and relationship-focused coping. Let's take a look at each one.

Problem-focused Coping

Problem-focused coping aims to manage or correct the distressing situation, or the problem at hand. In general, problem-focused coping tends to be especially useful when you are facing a controllable stressor—that is, a situation you can actually do something about.

Broadly speaking, problem-focused strategies are aimed at changing either the situation or ourselves (Stephenson et al., 2016). Efforts to *change the situation* may include things like eliminating conditions that are causing the stress (e.g., quitting a stressful job or leaving a bad relationship), or altering your response to those conditions (e.g., making a plan of action to bring about change). In contrast, efforts to *change ourselves* reflect coping that alters your abilities or characteristics in ways that will make you better able to manage the stressor. This might include learning new skills or acquiring new knowledge that will improve your ability to cope with the challenges that are facing you.

Emotion-focused Coping

In **emotion-focused coping**, we try to control our emotional reactions to the situation and minimize distress. For the most part, emotion-focused efforts seem best suited to managing your reaction to stressors you cannot control (Folkman & Moskowitz, 2004; Smith & Kirby, 2011). For example, a distressed person may *distract* herself by listening to music, taking a walk to relax, or seeking emotional support from others. Other strategies that fall under the umbrella of emotion-focused coping include *cognitive reappraisal*; that is, changing the way that you view or appraise the situation (■ see Section 2.5), and *relaxation* strategies such as meditation (■ see Section 5.2).

In addition, psychodynamic psychologists have noted that people may use specific types of emotion-focused coping that are referred to as *defense mechanisms*. Defense mechanisms allow us to reduce the anxiety caused by stressful situations or our own shortcomings (Sue et al., 2016). Many of the defenses were first identified by Sigmund Freud, who assumed they operate unconsciously. Often, defense mechanisms create large blind spots in awareness, making it difficult for people to realize that they're in use (and that they might need some help to correct their behavior). Some of the most common defense mechanisms are outlined in ▲ Table 13.5 (Sue et al., 2016).

▲ Table 13.5 Psychological Defense Mechanisms

Compensation	Counteracting a real or imagined weakness by emphasizing desirable traits or seeking to excel in the area of weakness or in other areas
Denial	Protecting oneself from an unpleasant reality by refusing to acknowledge or perceive it
Displacement (sublimation)	Diverting a thought or behavior from its natural target toward a less threatening one
Fantasy	Fulfilling unmet desires in imagined achievements or activities
Identification	Taking on some of the characteristics of an admired person, usually as a way to compensate for perceived personal weaknesses or faults
Intellectualization	Separating emotion from a threatening or anxiety-provoking situation by talking or thinking about it in impersonal "intellectual" terms
Isolation	Separating contradictory thoughts or feelings into "logic-tight" mental compartments so that they do not come into conflict
Projection	Attributing one's own feelings, shortcomings, or unacceptable impulses to others
Rationalization	Creating false but plausible excuses to justify unacceptable behavior
Reaction formation	Preventing dangerous impulses from being expressed in behavior by exaggerating opposite behavior
Regression	Retreating to an earlier level of development or to earlier, less demanding habits or situations
Repression	Keeping distressing thoughts and feelings buried in the unconscious

Relationship-focused Coping

A third type of coping explored by psychological scientists concerns relational approaches to managing stress (Gurung, 2019). **Relationship-focused coping** (or relational coping) begins with the idea that our relationships with others are key to a rewarding life and that maintaining them is an important goal. Specific strategies that are associated with relationship-focused coping include *demonstrating empathy*, working toward *compromise*, and providing *social support*. The term social support is a broad one that captures the many different forms of help that people provide to one another. Included among them are instrumental support (material assistance, such as the loan of a car or helping to pack moving boxes, that helps to solve a problem), informational support (that is, advice), and emotional support (Cohen & Wills, 1985).

Couldn't problem-, emotion-, and relationship-focused coping occur together to manage illness and other stressors? Yes. In fact, sometimes these three different types of coping aid one another. Say, for example, that you feel anxious as you step in front of your classmates to give a presentation. If you receive a pep talk from your friend before class (relationship-focused coping) and then take a few deep breaths to reduce your anxiety (emotion-focused coping), you will be better able to glance over your notes to improve your delivery (problem-focused coping).

Of course, it is also possible for coping efforts to clash. For instance, if you have to make a difficult decision about a treatment for cancer, you may suffer intense emotional distress. In such circumstances, it is tempting to make a quick, unreflective choice just to end the suffering (Arnsten, Mazure, & Sinha, 2012). Doing

Coping A tendency to change cognitions and behaviors to manage illness and more general life demands.

Problem-focused coping Directly managing or remedying a stressful or threatening situation.

Emotion-focused coping Managing or controlling one's emotional reaction to a stressful or threatening situation.

Relationship-focused coping Using relationships as a means of managing a stressful or threatening situation.

so may allow you to avoid coping with your emotions, but it short-changes problem-focused coping.

Coping in Everyday Life

We use the kinds of coping strategies described in this chapter every day, to greater and lesser degrees. In this final section, we discuss three examples of circumstances that can benefit from the effective use of problem, emotion, and relationship-focused coping: *traumatic stress*, *acculturative stress*, and the *college blues*.

Managing Traumatic Stress

Traumatic experiences produce psychological injury or intense emotional pain. Victims of **traumatic stresses**, such as war, torture, rape, assassination, plane crashes, natural disasters, and street violence, may suffer from nightmares, flashbacks, insomnia, irritability, nervousness, grief, emotional numbing, and depression (Durand & Barlow, 2016; Sue et al., 2016).

People who personally witness or survive such distressing experiences are most affected by traumatic stress. For instance, 20 percent of the people who lived close to the World Trade Center in New York City suffered serious stress disorders after the 9/11 terrorist attack (Galea et al., 2002). Yet even those who experience horror at a distance may be traumatized (Galea & Resnick, 2005). In fact, 44 percent of US adults who only saw the 9/11 attacks on television had at least some stress symptoms (Schuster et al., 2001). For example, Americans faced elevated risks of hypertension and heart problems for three years after 9/11 (Holman et al., 2008). Indirect exposure to such terrorist attacks, coupled with the ongoing risk of more attacks, has ensured that many people will suffer ongoing stress into the foreseeable future (Marshall et al., 2007).

Traumatic stress produces feelings of helplessness and vulnerability. Victims realize that disaster could strike again without warning. In addition to feeling threatened, many victims sense that they are losing control of their lives (Fields & Margolin, 2001; Ford, 2012).

There can be no doubt that Malala Yousafazi experienced a trauma. When she was a 15-year-old student in northwest Pakistan, she was shot in the head by a religious extremist who believed that girls should not be educated. She not only survived, she has thrived as a global symbol of the power of education and received a Nobel Peace Prize for her efforts to improve access to schooling in developing nations.

When traumatic stresses are severe or repeated, some people have even more serious symptoms (Durand & Barlow, 2016). They suffer from crippling anxiety or become emotionally numb. Typically, they can't stop thinking about the disturbing event, they anxiously avoid anything associated with the event, and they are constantly fearful or nervous. Such reactions can leave victims emotionally handicapped for months or years after a disaster. The consequences can last a lifetime for children who are the victims of trauma (Gillespie & Nemeroff, 2007; Salloum & Overstreet, 2012). If you feel that you are having trouble coping with a severe emotional shock, consider seeking help from a psychologist or other professional (American Psychological Association, 2017b; Bisson et al., 2007). (■ These are the symptoms of *stress disorders,* which are discussed in Section 14.4.)

What can people do to cope with such reactions? Psychologists recommend the following strategies, which draw on problem-, emotion-, and relationship-focused coping:

- Identify what you are feeling and talk to others about your fears and concerns.
- Think about the skills that have helped you overcome adversity in the past and apply them to the present situation.
- Continue to do the things that you enjoy and that make life meaningful.
- Get support from others. This is a major element in recovery from all traumatic events.
- Give yourself time to heal. Fortunately, most people are more resilient than they think.

Human Diversity and Coping: Managing Acculturative Stress

One way to guarantee that you will experience a large number of both major life changes and more minor hassles is to live in a foreign culture. Around the world, an increasing number of immigrants and refugees must adapt to dramatic changes in language, dress, values, and social customs. For many, the result is a period of culture shock or **acculturative stress**—stress caused by adapting to a foreign culture. Typical reactions to acculturative stress are anxiety, hostility, depression, alienation, physical illness, or identity confusion (Castañeda et al., 2015). For many young immigrants, acculturative stress is a major source of mental health problems (Claudat, White, & Warren, 2016; Sirin et al., 2013).

The severity of acculturative stress is related in part to how a person adapts to a new culture. Here are four main patterns (Fox, Thayer, & Wadhwa, 2017; Sam & Berry, 2010):

Integration: Maintain your old cultural identity but participate in the new culture.

Separation: Maintain your old cultural identity and avoid contact with the new culture.

Assimilation: Adopt the new culture as your own and have contact with its members while avoiding contact with your old cultural identity.

Marginalization: Reject your old culture, but suffer rejection by members of the new culture.

One of the best antidotes for acculturative stress is a society that tolerates or even celebrates ethnic diversity. While some people find it hard to accept new immigrants, the fact is, nearly everyone's family tree includes people who, like this Syrian family, had the courage to become strangers in a strange land.

To illustrate each pattern, let's consider a family that has immigrated to the United States from the imaginary country of Heinleinia:

- The father favors *integration*. He is learning English and wants to get involved in American life. At the same time, he is a leader in the Heinleinian-American community and spends much of his leisure time with other Heinleinian Americans. His level of acculturative stress is low.
- The mother's approach reflects *separation*. She speaks only the Heinleinian language and interacts only with other Heinleinian Americans. She remains almost completely separate from American society. Her stress level is high.
- The teenage daughter prefers *assimilation*. She is annoyed by hearing Heinleinian spoken at home, by her mother's serving only Heinleinian food, and by having to spend her leisure time with her extended Heinleinian family. She would prefer to speak English and to be with her American friends. Her stress level is moderate.
- The son is experiencing *marginalization*. He doesn't particularly value his Heinleinian heritage, yet his schoolmates reject him because he speaks with a Heinleinian accent. He feels trapped between two cultures. His stress level is high.

As you can see, integration and assimilation are the best options. However, a big benefit of assimilating is that people who embrace their new culture experience fewer social difficulties. For many, this justifies the stress of adopting new customs and cultural values (Gurung, 2014; Sam & Berry, 2010).

Managing the College Blues

During the school year, many college students suffer symptoms of depression, which can exert a toll on academic performance (Lindsey, Fabiano, & Stark, 2009). In one study, students diagnosed with depression scored half a grade point below nondepressed students (Hysenbegasi, Hass, & Rowland, 2005). Why do students get "blue"? Various problems contribute to depressive feelings. Here are some of the most common (Aselton, 2012; Gonzalez, Reynolds, & Skewes, 2011; Tran & Rimes, 2017):

1. Stresses from college work and pressures to choose a career can leave students feeling that they are missing out on fun or that all their hard work is meaningless.
2. Isolation and loneliness are common when students leave their support groups behind. Before they went to college, family, a circle of high school friends, and often a boyfriend or girlfriend could be counted on for support and encouragement.
3. Problems with studying and grades frequently trigger depression. Many students start college with high aspirations and little prior experience with failure. At the same time, many lack the basic skills necessary for academic success and are afraid of failure.
4. Depression can be triggered by the breakup of an intimate relationship, either with a former boyfriend or girlfriend or with a newly formed college romance.
5. Students who find it difficult to live up to their idealized images of themselves are especially prone to depression.
6. An added danger is that depressed students are more likely to abuse alcohol, which is a depressant.

Bouts of the college blues are closely related to stressful events. Learning to manage college work and to challenge self-critical thinking can help alleviate mild school-related depression (Halonen & Santrock, 2013). For example, if you don't do well on a test or a class assignment, how do you react? If you appraise it as a small, isolated setback, you probably won't feel too bad. However, if you feel like you have "blown it" in a big way, depression may follow. Students who strongly link everyday events to long-term goals (such as a successful career or high income) tend to overreact to day-to-day disappointments (McIntosh, Harlow, & Martin, 1995; Halonen & Santrock, 2013).

How should students cope with the college blues? It's important to take daily tasks one step at a time and chip away at them (Watson & Tharp, 2014). That way, you are less likely to feel overwhelmed, helpless, or hopeless. Problem-focused approaches can be particularly helpful. For example, when you feel "blue," you should make a daily schedule for yourself (Pychyl, 2013). Try to schedule activities to fill up every hour during the day. It is best to start with easy activities and progress to more difficult tasks. Check off each item as it is completed. That way, you will begin to break the self-defeating cycle of feeling helpless and falling further behind. (Depressed students spend much of their time sleeping.) A series of small accomplishments, successes, or pleasures may be all that you need to get going again. However, if you are lacking skills needed for success in college, ask for help in getting them. Don't remain "helpless."

Emotion-focused efforts at coping can also be useful. Feelings of worthlessness and hopelessness are usually supported by self-critical or negative thoughts. Consider writing down such thoughts as they occur, especially those that immediately precede feelings of sadness (Pennebaker & Chung, 2007). After you have collected these thoughts, write a rational answer to each. For example, the thought "No one loves me" should be answered with a list of those who do care about you. One more point to keep in

Traumatic stresses Extreme events that cause psychological injury or intense emotional pain.

Acculturative stress Stress caused by the many changes and adaptations required when a person moves to a foreign culture.

mind is this: When events begin to improve, try to accept it as a sign that better times lie ahead. Positive events are most likely to end depression if you view them as stable and continuing rather than temporary and fragile.

Attacks of the college blues are common and should be distinguished from more serious cases of depression. Severe depression is a serious problem that can lead to suicide or a major impairment of emotional functioning. In such cases, it would be wise to deploy relationship-focused coping strategies, seeking both social support and professional help rather than simply trying to cope on your own (Cuijpers et al., 2016). As you will see in the next section, it's rarely wise to suffer in silence.

Reflective Practice

Improving Health Through Coping

1. Which of the following is *not* a common form of coping?
   a. stress-based coping
   b. emotion-focused coping
   c. problem-based coping
   d. relationship-based coping
2. Stress is always better dealt with through problem-focused coping. T or F?
3. A specific type of emotion-focused coping in which people try to reduce the anxiety that is caused by stressful situations or our own shortcomings is called
   a. anxiety defenses
   b. unconscious defenses
   c. defense mechanisms
   d. threat mechanisms
4. The pattern of managing acculturative stress that involves adopting the new culture as your own and breaking ties with the old culture is called
   a. separation
   b. assimilation
   c. marginalization
   d. integration
5. Symptoms of traumatic stress include
   a. nightmares and insomnia
   b. depression
   c. flashbacks
   d. grief
   e. all of the above

THINK CRITICALLY

6. How might learned helplessness play a role in contributing to the "college blues?"

SELF-REFLECT

- Suppose that you moved to a foreign country. How much acculturative stress do you think you would face? Which pattern of adaptation do you think you would adopt in order to cope?
- What type of coping do you tend to use when you face a stressor such as public speaking or taking an important exam?
- Imagine that a friend of yours is suffering from the college blues. What advice would you give your friend?

Answers: 1. a 2. F 3. c 4. b 5. e 6. College students who have a rough start and experience a number of stressors (poor grades, trouble making friends) may begin to feel as though they are not in control of the college experience. For example, receiving a poor grade after they feel they have studied hard may lead to an impression that it doesn't matter what they do, they won't be successful. This type of learned helplessness is associated with depressive symptoms similar to those seen among students experiencing the college blues.

13.5 Psychology and Your Skill Set: Stress Management

GATEWAYS LEARNING OUTCOMES:
After reading this section you should be able to:

13.5.1 Name three effects that are triggered by stress

13.5.2 Create a plan to manage each of these stress-induced effects

Abandoned backpacks—1,100 of them—were scattered across the grass on campus, and college students who were passing stopped to look. They didn't need to ask where the owners were, though. The signs next to the bags told them everything they needed to know.

Send Silence Packing is a travelling art exhibition that has moved between more than 200 campuses in the United States since 2008. Each of the backpacks represents a student who takes his or her life at an American college each year. Many of these students commit suicide because they are overwhelmed by the pressure that comes with the desire to succeed at school, to be liked by their peers, and to manage other responsibilities, including work. They may feel unable to cope with the stress they experience, but are often reluctant to speak up and seek help for fear of appearing weak. But the message that the backpacks provide is clear: Suffering in silence when you are feeling stressed and overwhelmed is not the answer. And while dealing with stress is not easy, there are things that you can do to make things more manageable. Let's take a closer look.

Stress management is the use of cognitive and behavioral strategies to reduce stress and improve coping skills. In this chapter we have seen that working to minimize stress is helpful, given that psychologists have provided considerable evidence of its

Richard Levine/Alamy Stock Photo

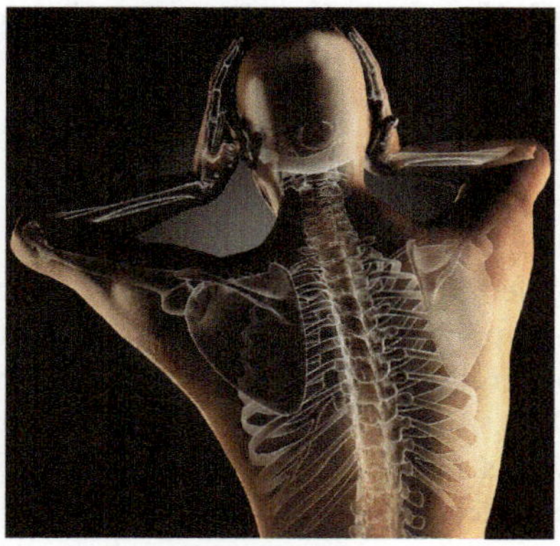

Bodily Reactions	Ineffective Behavior	Upsetting Thoughts
• Fight-or-flight response	• Too fast-paced	• Negative self-statements
• Tight muscles	• Too disorganized	• Fearful
• Pounding heart	• Too unbalanced	• Worried
• Shallow breathing	• Unrealistic	• Distracted
• Poor sleep	• Indecisive	• Obsessive
• Tiredness	• Avoidant	• Excessively body aware
• Stress-based illness	• Inefficient	• Health fears
• Poor digestion	• Aggressive	• Self-doubt

Figure 13.5 Effects of stress on body, behavior, and thought.

negative effects. Psychological research has gone much further in terms of promoting our understanding of stress, though. For example, psychologists have begun to document the unique effects of different kinds of stress, such as the acculturative stress demonstrated by new immigrants (Suh et al., 2016) and the post-traumatic stress experienced after events such as natural disasters, rape, terrorist attacks, and military deployment (Post et al., 2015). They have also examined how the effects of stressors change across the lifespan (Jamieson & Mendes, 2016) and as a function of our genes and physiology (Belsky et al., 2015). Finally, newer research has begun to examine whether stressful events can have positive consequences (e.g., post-traumatic growth; Tsai et al., 2015), as well as the effectiveness of alternative forms of treating stress-related responses, such as virtual reality, drugs that blunt the emotions associated with traumatic memories, and Internet-based therapy (Lane et al., 2015; Morina et al., 2015).

De-Stress!

Stress can have a number of negative consequences that are likely to affect your own life, as well as your relationships with others. In addition to doing physical damage to your body (e.g., increased risk of cardiovascular problems), stress can also be at the root of psychological issues such as anxiety and depression. But the effects of stress aren't restricted to your physical and psychological well-being. Stress can also prove damaging to your relationships, both at home and at work. People under stress can appear more unmotivated, defensive, short tempered, or withdrawn than they would be otherwise. Such behaviors can create tension between people, resulting in strained relationships.

I can't help feeling stressed—I have three midterms next week! Is there anything I can do to manage my stress better? Obviously, the simplest way of coping with stress is through problem-focused coping (that is, modifying or removing the source of the stress)—that might mean leaving a stressful job or a bad relationship, for example. As you point out, though, this is often impossible; there's simply no way to avoid those midterms!

You can begin to manage your stress by recognizing that stress triggers *bodily effects, ineffective behavior,* and *upsetting thoughts* (Figure 13.5). All of these effects are important, but each one may require different techniques to effectively manage the stressor. Of course, not all techniques will be effective for all people, but you should try them out to see what works for you.

Managing Bodily Effects

Much of the immediate discomfort of stress is caused by fight-or-flight emotional responses. The body is ready to act, with tight muscles and a pounding heart. If action is prevented, we merely remain "uptight." A sensible remedy is to learn a reliable, drug-free way to relax.

Exercise

Stress-based arousal can be dissipated by using the body. Any full-body exercise can be effective. Swimming, dancing, jumping rope, yoga, most other sports, and especially walking are additional valuable outlets. Regular exercise alters hormones, circulation, muscle tone, and several other aspects of physical functioning. Together, such changes can reduce anxiety and lower the risks for disease (Brannon, Feist, & Updegraff, 2014; Edenfield & Blumenthal, 2011).

Be sure to choose activities that are vigorous enough to relieve tension, yet enjoyable enough to be done repeatedly. Exercising for stress management is most effective when it is done daily. As little as 30 minutes of total exercise per day, even if it occurs in short 10- to 20-minute sessions, can improve mood and energy (Hansen, Stevens, & Coast, 2001).

Meditation

Many stress counselors recommend meditation for quieting the body and promoting relaxation. Meditation is one of the most effective ways to relax, and many free apps are now available to help you learn this skill (Sears & Kraus, 2009; Zeidan et al., 2010). Be aware that listening to or playing music, taking nature walks, enjoying hobbies, and the like can be meditative. Anything that reliably interrupts upsetting thoughts and promotes relaxation can be helpful. For now, it is enough to state that meditation is easy to

Stress management The application of cognitive and behavioral strategies to reduce stress and improve coping skills.

learn—taking an expensive commercial course is unnecessary. (■ To learn more about meditation and its effects, read Section 5.3.)

Progressive Relaxation

It is possible to relax systematically, completely, and by choice. The basic idea of **progressive relaxation** is to tighten all the muscles in a given area of your body (the arms, for instance) and then voluntarily relax them. By first tensing and relaxing each area of the body (also called the *tension-release method*), you can learn what muscle tension feels like. Then, when each area is relaxed, the change is more noticeable and more controllable. In this way, it is possible, with practice, to greatly reduce tension. (■ To learn the details of how this is done, consult Section 15.4.)

Guided Imagery

In a technique called **guided imagery**, people visualize images that are calming, relaxing, or beneficial in other ways. Relaxation, for instance, can be promoted by visualizing peaceful scenes. Pick several places where you feel safe, calm, and at ease. Typical locations might be a beach or lake, the woods, floating on an air mattress in a warm pool, or lying in the sun at a quiet park. To relax, vividly imagine yourself in one of these locations. In the visualized scene, you should be alone and in a comfortable position. It is important to visualize the scene as realistically as possible. Try to feel, taste, smell, hear, and see what you would experience in the calming scene. Practice forming such images several times a day for about five minutes each time. When your scenes become familiar and detailed, they can be used to reduce anxiety and encourage relaxation.

Modifying Ineffective Behavior

Stress is often made worse by our misguided responses to it. The following suggestions may help you deal with stress more effectively.

Slow Down

Remember that stress can be self-generated. Try to deliberately do things at a slower pace—especially if your pace has speeded up over the years. Tell yourself, "What counts most is not if I get there first, but if I get there at all," or "My goal is distance, not speed."

Strike a Balance

Work, school, family, friends, interests, hobbies, recreation, community, church—a satisfying life has many important elements. Damaging stress often comes from letting one element—especially work or school—get blown out of proportion. Your goal should be quality in life, not quantity. Try to strike a balance between challenging "good stress" and relaxation. Remember, when you are "doing nothing," you are doing something very important: set aside time for "me acts" such as loafing, browsing, puttering, playing, and napping.

Recognize and Accept Your Limits

Many of us set unrealistic and perfectionist goals. Given that no one can ever be perfect, this attitude leaves many people feeling inadequate, no matter how well they have performed. Set gradual, achievable goals for yourself. Also, set realistic limits on what you try to do on any given day. Learn to say no to added demands or responsibilities.

Seek Social Support

Social support—close, positive relationships with others—facilitates good health and morale (Ai et al., 2013; Winfree & Jiang, 2010). People with close, supportive relationships have better immune responses and better health (Smith, Ruiz, & Uchino, 2004; Taylor & Master, 2011). Apparently, support from family, friends, and even pets serves as a buffer to cushion the impact of stressful events (Allen, Blascovich, & Mendes, 2002).

Write About Your Feelings

If you don't have someone you can talk to about stressful events, you might try expressing your thoughts and feelings in writing. Several studies have found that students who write about their upsetting experiences, thoughts, and feelings are better able to cope with stress. They also experience fewer illnesses, and they get better grades (Smyth & Pennebaker, 2008). Writing about your feelings tends to leave your mind clearer. This makes it easier to pay attention to life's challenges and come up with effective coping strategies. Thus, after you write about your feelings, it helps to make specific plans for coping with upsetting experiences (Klein & Boals, 2001; Smyth, Pennebaker, & Arigo, 2012).

As an alternative, you might want to try writing about positive experiences. In one study, college students who wrote about intensely positive experiences had fewer illnesses over the next three months. Writing just 20 minutes a day for three days improved the students' moods and had a surprisingly long-lasting effect on their health (Burton & King, 2004).

Counteracting Upsetting Thoughts

Assume that you are taking a test. Suddenly you realize that you are running short of time. If you say to yourself, "Oh no, this is terrible, I've blown it now," your body's response will probably be sweating, tenseness, and a knot in your stomach. On the other hand, if you say, "I should have watched the time, but getting upset won't help; I'll just take one question at a time," your stress level will be much lower.

As stated previously, stress is greatly affected by the views that we take of events. Physical symptoms and a tendency to make poor decisions are increased by negative thoughts or "self-talk." In many cases, what you say to yourself can mean the difference between coping and collapsing (Smith & Kirby, 2011).

Coping Statements

Psychologist Donald Meichenbaum has popularized a technique called **stress inoculation**. In it, clients learn to fight fear and anxiety with an internal monologue of positive coping statements. First, clients learn to identify and monitor **negative self-statements**—self-critical thoughts that increase anxiety. Negative thoughts are a problem because they tend to directly elevate physical arousal. To counter this effect, clients learn to replace negative statements with coping statements from a supplied list. Eventually, they are encouraged to make their own lists (Meichenbaum, 2009).

How are coping statements applied? **Coping statements** are reassuring and self-enhancing. They are used to block out, or counteract, negative self-talk in stressful situations. Before giving a short speech, for instance, you would replace "I'm scared," "I can't do this," "My mind will go blank and I'll panic," or "I'll sound stupid and boring" with "I'll give my speech on something I like," or "I'll breathe deeply before I start my speech," or "My pounding heart just means I'm psyched up to do my best." Additional examples of coping statements follow.

Preparing for Stressful Situations

I'll just take things one step at a time.
If I get nervous, I'll just pause a moment.
Tomorrow, I'll be done with it.
I've managed to do this before.
What exactly do I have to do?

Confronting Stressful Situations

Relax, this can't really hurt me.
Stay organized; focus on the task.
There's no hurry; take it step by step.
Nobody's perfect; I'll just do my best.
It will be over soon; just be calm.

Meichenbaum cautions that saying the "right" things to yourself may not be enough to improve stress tolerance. You must practice this approach in actual stress situations. Also, it is important to develop your own personal list of coping statements by finding what works for you. Ultimately, the value of learning this, and other stress-management skills, ties back into the idea that much stress is self-generated. Knowing that you can manage a demanding situation is in itself a major antidote for stress. In one study, college students who learned stress inoculation not only had less anxiety and depression, but better self-esteem as well (Schiraldi & Brown, 2001).

Lighten the Mood

It's also worth noting again the value of positive emotions. Happiness, laughter, and delight tend to strengthen immune system response. Doing things that make you happy also can protect your health (Diener & Chan, 2011; Rosenkranz et al., 2003).

Humor is especially worth cultivating as a way to reduce stress. A good sense of humor can lower your distress/stress reaction to difficult events (Morrison, 2012). In addition, an ability to laugh at life's ups and downs is associated with better immunity to disease (Earleywine, 2011). Don't be afraid to laugh at yourself and at the many ways that we humans make things difficult for ourselves. You've probably heard the following advice about everyday stresses: "Don't sweat the small stuff" and "It's all small stuff." Humor is one of the best antidotes for anxiety and emotional distress because it helps put things into perspective (Crawford & Caltabiano, 2011; Kuiper & McHale, 2009). The vast majority of events are only as stressful as you allow them to be. Have some fun. It's perfectly healthy.

Reflective Practice

Psychology and Your Skill Set: Stress Management

1. Exercise, meditation, and progressive relaxation are considered effective ways to counter negative self-statements. T or F?
2. A person using progressive relaxation for stress management is most likely trying to control which component of stress?
   a. bodily reactions
   b. upsetting thoughts
   c. ineffective behavior
   d. the primary appraisal
3. Research shows that social support from family and friends has little effect on the health consequences of stress. T or F?
4. While taking a stressful classroom test, you say to yourself, "Stay organized, focus on the task." It's obvious that you are using a
   a. guided image
   b. coping statement
   c. defense mechanism
   d. guided relaxation

THINK CRITICALLY

5. Steve always feels extremely pressured when the due date arrives for his major term papers. How could he reduce stress in such instances?

SELF-REFLECT

- If you were going to put together a "toolkit" for stress management, what items would you include?

Answers: 1. F 2. a 3. F 4. b 5. The stress associated with doing term papers can be almost completely eliminated by breaking up a long-term assignment into many small daily or weekly assignments (Anderson, 2014; Ariely & Wertenbroch, 2002). Students who habitually procrastinate are often amazed at how pleasant college work can be once they renounce pushing things off to the limits of tolerance.

Progressive relaxation A method for producing deep relaxation of all parts of the body.

Guided imagery Intentional visualization of images that are calming, relaxing, or beneficial in other ways.

Social support Close, positive relationships with other people.

Stress inoculation Use of positive coping statements to control fear and anxiety.

Negative self-statements Self-critical thoughts that increase anxiety and lower performance.

Coping statements Reassuring, self-enhancing statements that are used to stop self-critical thinking.

Gateways to Health Psychology

Summary: Gateways Learning Outcomes

13.1 Biopsychosocial and Behavioral Contributions to Health

13.1.1 Distinguish between the medical and biopsychosocial models in terms of their conceptions of health

The *medical model* emphasizes that the body is like a biological machine, and that physical illness requires a physical treatment (i.e., medicine). The mind, spirit, and social context are not considered important to health in this model. The *biopsychosocial model* adopts a more holistic approach and assumes that good health is a function of biological, psychological, and social factors.

13.1.2 Explain the biological, psychological, and social factors that influence health

Biological factors influencing health include genetic (and epigenetic) factors, as well as the functioning of a number of bodily systems including the nervous, endocrine, cardiovascular, respiratory, digestive, reproductive, and immune systems. *Psychological factors* include attention and perceptions, cognitions, emotions, and motivation. Particular attention has been paid to personality characteristics, especially those that characterize the Type A and hardy personalities. Finally, two *social* environmental factors that have received attention include our social networks and poverty.

13.1.3 Outline the main behavioral risk factors that contribute to poor health

The main behavioral factors contributing to poor health include smoking, alcohol abuse, drug abuse, poor diet, insufficient exercise, and risky sex.

13.1.4 Describe three strategies that help to minimize behavioral risk factors

Three strategies that can be used to reduce the risk posed by these behavioral risk factors are making healthy *lifestyle changes*, engaging in *early prevention*, and engaging in *community health and social media campaigns*.

13.2 Stress and Health

13.2.1 Distinguish between two types of stressors: life events and hassles

Stress is the mental and physical condition that occurs when we adjust or adapt to the environment. A stressor is a condition or event that challenges or threatens a person. *Life events* refer to stressors (both good and bad) that are larger scale, such as getting married or divorced, losing your job, or getting organized for a major holiday. *Hassles* (or microstressors) refer to stressors that are smaller in scope but ongoing, including a difficult commute to work or regularly having to deal with people making discriminatory remarks or inappropriate jokes at your expense. Research indicates that multiple life events tend to increase *long-range* susceptibility to health problems. However, one's *current* health is more closely related to the intensity and severity of daily hassles.

13.2.2 Differentiate between primary and secondary appraisals, and outline the four factors that guide them

Primary appraisal is broad-based and involves a basic decision about whether the stressor is positive, neutral, or a threat. Stress is intensified when a situation is appraised as a threat. During a *secondary appraisal*, we examine stressors in relation to our resources and select a way to manage stress. Appraisals are guided by beliefs about *perceived control* and *competence* to cope with the stressor, *unpredictability* of the stressor, and *pressure*.

13.2.3 Describe the three stages of general adaptation syndrome

The body reacts to stress in a series of stages called *general adaptation syndrome (GAS)*. The stages of GAS are *alarm*, *resistance*, and *exhaustion*. Bodily reactions in GAS follow the pattern observed in the development of psychosomatic disorders.

13.2.4 Describe three consequences of prolonged stress

Prolonged stress can be associated with *illness and psychosomatic disorders* (in which psychological factors contribute to genuine bodily damage), *learned helplessness*, and *burnout*.

13.3 Improving Health with Treatment

13.3.1 Outline the main features of somatic symptom disorder

Somatic symptom disorder, also known as hypochondriasis, is rooted in anxiety about general concerns; people convert this anxiety into a belief that something is wrong with them physically.

13.3.2 Describe how biological, psychological, and social factors contribute to our ability to recognize illness

In terms of *biological factors*, people are more likely to take symptoms seriously if they affect highly valued parts of the body, limit mobility, or cause pain. With respect to *psychological factors*, some personality variables (e.g., neuroticism), stress, and emotion all contribute to people's ability to recognize illness. Finally, important *social factors* include the lay referral network (that is, informal social network) and the Internet.

13.3.3 Outline four factors that influence people's decision to seek treatment

Four factors that influence decisions to seek treatment include *sex*, *income*, *age*, and *culture*.

13.3.4 Define what is meant by the term complementary and alternative medicine, and outline one main concern associated with this type of treatment

The term complementary and alternative medicine (CAM) refers to treatment approaches that tend to be more holistic in their approach and are often rooted in long-standing cultural traditions (e.g., traditional Chinese medicine; Ayurvedic medicine). They include homeopathy and dietary supplements, acupuncture, chiropractic services, massage, biofeedback, and yoga. The one main concern with these forms of treatment stems from a lack of good research evaluating their effectiveness.

13.3.5 Identify the forms that treatment noncompliance can take, describe four factors that contribute to treatment noncompliance, and outline the key to minimizing treatment noncompliance

Treatment noncompliance results when people ignore, misunderstand, forget, or carry out treatments incorrectly. Four factors that contribute to noncompliance include *cognitive factors*, *memory*, the *relationship between care providers and recipients*, and *emotions* (particularly anxiety and depression). Minimizing noncompliance requires that healthcare providers use good *communication* and *interpersonal skills* to build a trusting relationship with patients and clients. Doing so will increase the likelihood that they are able to ensure that patients understand the treatment, promote a willingness to abide by it, and will improve the ability to properly assess clients' ability to follow through with it.

13.4 Improving Health Through Coping

13.4.1 Distinguish between problem-focused, emotion-focused, and relationship-focused coping

Problem-focused coping involves directly managing or remedying a stressful or threatening situation. *Emotion-focused coping* relies on managing or controlling one's emotional reaction to a stressful or threatening situation. Defense mechanisms are a specific type of emotion-focused coping, and they are used to avoid, deny, or distort sources of threat or anxiety, including threats to one's self-image. *Relationship-focused coping* is based on the idea that our relationships are important and that we are motivated to preserve them by engaging in strategies such as demonstrating empathy, compromising, and providing social support.

13.4.2 Explain the effects of traumatic stress, and some strategies for coping with it

Traumatic stress can have wide-ranging effects that are both physical (e.g., hypertension) and psychological (anxiety, feelings of vulnerability). Strategies to manage it rely on problem-, emotion-, and relationship-based coping, including talking to others (including professionals), engaging in enjoyable activities, and giving yourself time to heal.

13.4.3 Identify the four main patterns of coping with acculturation, and the level of acculturative stress associated with each one

Acculturative stress arises during adaptation to a foreign culture. Four acculturative patterns are *integration* (associated with low acculturative stress), *separation* (associated with high acculturative stress), *assimilation* (associated with moderate acculturative stress), and *marginalization* (associated with high acculturative stress).

13.4.4 Describe some of the factors that contribute to the "college blues," and some strategies for coping with this problem

The college blues are a relatively mild form of depression that stem from such things as pressure to find a career, isolation and loneliness, problems with grades, relationship problems, and challenges living up to expectations. Coping with the college blues may include problem-focused strategies (e.g., creating a schedule and working steadily at tasks to avoid being overwhelmed), emotion-focused strategies (e.g., challenging self-critical and negative emotions), and relationship-focused strategies (e.g., seeking social support and professional help as needed).

13.5 Psychology and Your Skill Set: Stress Management

13.5.1 Name three effects that are triggered by stress

Three effects triggered by stress include: *bodily effects*, *ineffective behavior*, and *upsetting thoughts*.

13.5.2 Create a plan to manage each of these stress-induced effects

All of the following are good ways to manage *bodily reactions* to stress: Exercise, meditation, progressive relaxation, and guided imagery. To minimize *ineffective behavior* when you are stressed, you can slow down, get organized, balance work and relaxation, accept your limits, seek social support, and write about your feelings. Learning to use coping statements is a good way to combat *upsetting thoughts*. We hope that after reading this section, you'll be better able to think about how you can use these strategies to help manage the stressful events that confront each of us in our daily lives!

14 Psychological Disorders

gary718/Shutterstock.com

Gateway Theme Judgments of abnormality are relative, but psychological disorders clearly exist and need to be classified, explained, and treated.

Chapter Outline

Break In or Break Down?

James was busted trying to break into the Federal Bureau of Investigation (FBI). This account of the episode makes it clear he had suffered another breakdown: "James said he was overwhelmed lately with feelings of apprehension and fear that he and someone important were about to be harmed. He could not specify why he felt this way, but he was sure he had special information that the president of the United States was going to be harmed soon and that he, James, would also be harmed because he knew of the plot. These feelings eventually became so strong that James felt he had to leave his apartment and warn someone at the FBI office. James said he thought the police were going to kill him because they were agents responsible for the plot against the president" (Kearney & Trull, 2018, p. 360).

The statistics are grim. The direct cost of treating people who seek help for mental illness is almost $60 billion a year. Add the indirect costs, such as lost earnings and business productivity, and the total exceeds $315 billion a year. Hidden behind the dollar signs is the immense human cost. James's case is but one hint of the magnitude of mental health problems. In any given year, almost 18 percent of American adults suffer from a diagnosable mental disorder and more than 42,000 Americans commit suicide (Kessler, 2010; National Institute of Mental Health, 2017).

To draw the line between normal behavior and a mental disorder, we must weigh some complex issues. We'll explore some of those issues in this chapter, as well as an array of psychological problems.

14.1 Psychopathology: Classification and Causes

GATEWAYS LEARNING OUTCOMES:
After reading this section you should be able to:

14.1.1 Describe four things to consider when deciding whether behavior is abnormal

14.1.2 Explain how psychological disorders are classified and diagnosed

14.1.3 Describe the causes of mental disorders and the importance of the stress-vulnerability model

A **mental disorder** is a significant impairment in psychological functioning, such as schizophrenia or major depression. The scientific study of mental disorders is known as **psychopathology**, although the term can also refer to mental disorders themselves and to behavior patterns that make people unhappy and impair their personal growth (Sue et al., 2017).

Defining Abnormality

To seriously classify people as mentally unhealthy raises a complex and age-old question: What's abnormal? In this section, we'll talk about four things we might consider when answering that question: statistical abnormality, nonconformity, subjective discomfort, and the degree to which behaviors are maladaptive.

Statistical Abnormality

Let's begin with the idea of statistical abnormality, which some psychologists use to define normality more objectively. **Statistical abnormality** refers to scoring very high or low on some dimension, such as intelligence, anxiety, or depression. Anxiety, for example, is a feature of several psychological disorders. To measure it, we could create a test to learn how many people show low, medium, or high levels of anxiety. Usually, the results of such tests will form a *normal* (bell-shaped) *curve*. (*Normal* here refers only to the shape of the curve.) Notice that most people score near the middle of a normal curve; very few have extremely high or low scores (● Figure 14.1). A person who deviates from the average by being highly anxious is, by definition, statistically abnormal. So, too, is a person who never feels anxiety.

But what if a statistically abnormal person is functioning well? If people with statistically abnormal levels of anxiety are nevertheless functioning well in their lives, why label them mentally ill? This is one limitation of defining abnormality this way. Statistical definitions also can't tell us *where to draw the line* between normality and abnormality. For example, we could obtain the average frequency of sexual intercourse for persons of a particular age, sex, sexual orientation, and marital status. Clearly, a person who feels driven to have sex dozens of times a day has a problem. But as we move back toward the norm, we face the problem of drawing lines. How often does a normal behavior have to occur before it becomes abnormal? As you can see, statistical boundary lines tend to be somewhat arbitrary (Comer, 2013).

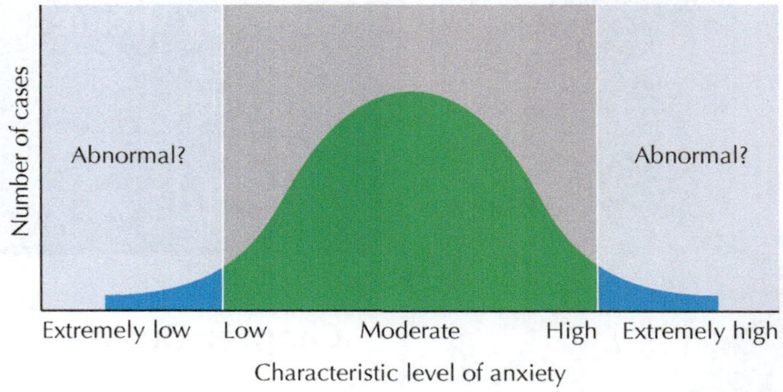

● **Figure 14.1 The normal curve and abnormality.** The number of people displaying a personal characteristic may help define what is statistically abnormal.

Nonconformity

A second approach to defining abnormality is to focus on the nonconformity that may be associated with some disorders. **Social nonconformity** refers to disobeying public standards for acceptable conduct. Extreme nonconformity can lead to destructive, self-destructive, or illegal behavior (think, for instance, of a drug abuser or a vandal). Once again, though, we must be careful to separate unhealthy nonconformity from creative lifestyles. Many eccentric "characters" are charming and emotionally stable. Note, too, that strictly following social norms is no guarantee of mental health. In some cases, psychopathology involves rigid conformity.

Eugenio Marongiu/Shutterstock.com

Performing a mildly abnormal behavior is a good way to get a sense of how social norms define "normality." Here's your assignment: Do something strange in public and observe how people react. (Please don't do anything dangerous or offensive—and don't get arrested!) Try walking around campus on a sunny day carrying an open umbrella. Or stick one finger in your nose and another in your ear and walk through a shopping mall. Better yet, wear an animal mask for a day (no, not Halloween!). As we have noted, social nonconformity is just one facet of abnormal behavior. Nevertheless, actions that are regarded as "strange" within a particular culture are often the first sign to others that a person has a problem.

Furthermore, before we can even begin to judge a behavior as abnormal or nonconforming, we must also consider the *situational context* (social situation, behavioral setting, or general circumstances) in which it occurs. Is it abnormal to stand outside and water a lawn with a hose? It depends on whether it is raining. Is it nonconforming for a grown man to remove his pants and expose himself to another man or woman in a place of business? It depends on whether the other person is a bank clerk or a doctor. Almost any imaginable behavior can be considered normal in some contexts. For example, some years back, a man sawed off his own arm. Mind you, Aaron Ralston had been rock climbing and fell into a crevasse, trapping his arm between two boulders. After five days of trying to free his arm, and nearing unconsciousness, he did what he needed to do to survive (Ralston, 2004).

Culture is one of the most influential contexts in which behavior is judged as normal or not (Kirmayer & Ryder, 2016; Whitbourne & Halgin, 2013). In some cultures, it is considered normal to defecate or urinate in public or to appear naked in public. In our culture, such behaviors would be considered unusual or abnormal. In some Muslim cultures, women who remain completely housebound are considered normal, even virtuous. In some Western cultures, they might be suspected of suffering from a disorder called *agoraphobia.* (Agoraphobia is described later in this chapter.) Thus, *cultural relativity* (the idea that judgments are made relative to the values of one's culture) can affect the definitions of psychological disorders. Still, some things are universally seen as atypical: for example, *all* cultures classify people as abnormal if they fail to communicate with others or are consistently unpredictable in their actions.

Julio Cesar Aguilar/AFP/Getty Images

Social nonconformity does not automatically indicate psychopathology. For example, meet Maria Jose Cristerna, a mother of four and a former lawyer. She is the current *Guinness Book of World Records* record holder for the most body piercings and tattoos. Nonconformist? You bet. Mentally ill? Definitely not.

Subjective Discomfort

Yet another approach to defining abnormality is to consider *subjective discomfort* (private feelings of pain, unhappiness, or emotional distress).

But couldn't a person experience serious distress without psychopathology, and couldn't someone be seriously disturbed without feeling discomfort? Yes on both counts. People who have, for example, lost a loved one or lived through a natural disaster such as a massive wildfire normally take some time to overcome their distress. Such distress is often not considered abnormal, or a sign of psychopathology.

Conversely, genuine psychopathology doesn't always cause personal anguish. A person suffering from mania might feel elated and "on top of the world." A *lack* of discomfort may actually reveal a problem. For example, if you showed no signs of grief or distress after the violent death of a close friend, we might suspect psychopathology. In practice, though, subjective discomfort explains most instances in which people voluntarily seek professional help.

Maladaptive Behavior

If abnormality is so hard to define, how are judgments of psychopathology made? As you can see, categorizing someone as mentally ill is far from "cut and dried." The three criteria for defining abnormality that we have discussed thus far are *relative,* but psychopathological behavior does have a fourth defining feature that applies in all cases: it is **maladaptive**. Rather than helping people cope successfully, maladaptive behavior arises from an underlying psychological or biological dysfunction that makes it more difficult for them to meet the demands of day-to-day life (American Psychiatric Association, 2013). Maladaptive behavior most often results in serious psychological discomfort, disability, and/or loss of control of thoughts, behaviors, or feelings, such as James's overwhelming sense of impending doom.

Mental disorder A significant impairment in psychological functioning.

Psychopathology The scientific study of mental, emotional, and behavioral disorders; the term is also used to refer to maladaptive behavior.

Statistical abnormality Abnormality defined on the basis of an extreme score on some dimension, such as IQ or anxiety.

Social nonconformity Failure to conform to societal norms or the usual minimum standards for social conduct.

Maladaptive (behavior) Behavior arising from an underlying psychological or biological dysfunction that makes it difficult to adapt to the environment and meet the demands of day-to-day life.

For example, gambling is not a problem if people bet for entertainment and can maintain self-control. However, compulsive gambling is maladaptive, and a sign of psychopathology. Hearing uncontrollable voices is a prime example of what it means to lose control of one's thoughts. In the most extreme cases, people become a danger to themselves or others, which is clearly maladaptive.

In practice, deciding that people need help usually occurs when they do something (assault a person, hallucinate, stare into space, collect too many old pizza cartons, and so forth) that annoys or gains the attention of a person in a position of power in their lives (an employer, teacher, parent, spouse, or the person himself or herself). The person may voluntarily seek help, the person may be urged to see a psychologist, a police officer may be called, or a relative may start commitment proceedings.

Classifying Mental Disorders: The DSM-5

Mental disorders are classified by using the most recent version of the *DSM*, the *Diagnostic and Statistical Manual of Mental Disorders (5th Edition)*. The DSM-5 influences most activities in mental health settings—from diagnosis to therapy to insurance company billing (American Psychiatric Association, 2013). As even a quick scan of the DSM-5 makes clear, a wide variety of psychological disorders are currently diagnosed and treated; hundreds of specific disorders are organized into over 20 major categories.

It is worth noting that, using the DSM categories, it's possible for a person to be **comorbid**—that is, they can suffer from more than one disorder at the same time. One way that comorbidity develops is when a *primary* problem causes *secondary* problems. For example, someone experiencing a prolonged and deep depression might start taking drugs (legal or otherwise) for treatment and become addicted, complicating the primary mood disorder with a secondary substance use disorder (Fenton et al., 2012). According to sociologist Ronald Kessler, more than 40 percent of all people with mental disorders are comorbid (Kessler, 2010). Unfortunately, not only does comorbidity increase suffering, it also makes it much more difficult for healthcare providers to provide accurate diagnoses and appropriate treatment.

A partial list of major categories and specific disorders from the DSM-5 can be found in ▲ Table 14.1. Many of the disorders on this list are described in detail in the next three sections. Others are discussed elsewhere in this book, including sleep–wake disorders (■ in Section 5.3), problems with drug abuse and

▲ Table 14.1 Major DSM-5 Categories of Psychopathology

Problem	Primary Symptom	Typical Signs of Trouble	Examples
Neurodevelopmental disorders	Impairment of nervous system development before adulthood	You have intellectual, communication, attentional, or motor problems that emerge early in your life	Intellectual developmental disorder, Autism spectrum disorder, Attention deficit/hyperactivity disorder
Schizophrenia spectrum and other psychotic disorders	Loss of contact with reality	You hear or see things that others don't; your mind has been playing tricks on you	Delusional disorder, Schizophrenia, Brief psychotic disorder
Bipolar and related disorders	Alternating mania and depression	You feel depressed, or you talk too loud and too fast and have a rush of ideas and feelings that others think are unreasonable	Cyclothymic disorder, Bipolar I disorder, Bipolar II disorder
Depressive disorders	Depression	You feel sad and hopeless.	Persistent depressive disorder (dysthymia), Major depressive disorder, Postpartum depression, Seasonal affective disorder
Anxiety disorders	High anxiety or anxiety-related distortions of behavior	You have anxiety attacks and feel like you are going to die; or you are afraid to do things that most people can do	Generalized anxiety disorder, Panic disorder, Agoraphobia, Specific phobia, Social phobia
Obsessive-compulsive and related disorders	Unnecessarily repetitious behavior	You spend unusual amounts of time doing things such as washing your hands or counting your heartbeats	Obsessive compulsive disorder, Hoarding disorder
Trauma- and stressor-related disorders	Difficulty dealing with a traumatic or stressful event	You persistently reexperience a traumatic event; you have an exceptionally strong negative reaction to a traumatic event such as becoming highly anxious, depressed, or, being unable to sleep	Adjustment disorder, Acute stress disorder, Post-traumatic stress disorder
Dissociative disorders	Amnesia, feelings of unreality, multiple identities	There are major gaps in your memory of events; you feel like you are a robot or a stranger to yourself; others tell you that you have done things that you don't remember doing	Dissociative amnesia, Dissociative identity disorder

▲ **Table 14.1** Major DSM-5 Categories of Psychopathology (*Continued*)

Problem	Primary Symptom	Typical Signs of Trouble	Examples
Somatic symptom disorders	Body complaints without an organic (physical) basis	You feel physically sick, but your doctor says nothing is wrong with you; you suffer from pain that has no physical basis; or you are preoccupied with thoughts about being sick	Somatic symptom disorder, Factitious disorder, Conversion disorder
Feeding and eating disorders	Disturbance of food intake into the body	You eat nonfood items (pica) or have difficulty eating enough food to remain healthy	Anorexia nervosa, Bulimia nervosa, Binge eating disorder
Elimination disorders	Disturbance of waste elimination from the body	You have trouble controlling the elimination of urine (enuresis) or feces (encopresis)	Enuresis, Encopresis
Sleep–wake disorders	Trouble falling asleep, staying asleep, or waking up	You have difficulty getting a healthy night's sleep; you snore, have nightmares, or fall asleep inappropriately (narcolepsy)	Insomnia disorder, Hypersomnolence disorder, Narcolepsy, Nightmare disorder
Sexual dysfunctions	Problems in sexual adjustment	You have problems with sexual desire, arousal, orgasm, or pain	Erectile disorder, Female sexual interest/arousal disorder, Genito-pelvic pain/penetration disorder, Male hypoactive sexual desire disorder
Gender dysphoria	Disturbed gender identity	You feel that you are a man trapped in a woman's body (or the reverse)	Gender dysphoria
Disruptive, impulse control and conduct disorders	Difficulties of self-control	You are defiant and aggressive; you set fires (pyromania) or are a chronic thief (kleptomania)	Oppositional defiant disorder, Intermittent explosive disorder, Pyromania, Kleptomania
Substance use and addictive disorders	Disturbances related to drug abuse or dependence as well as other addictive behaviors	You have been drinking too much, using illegal drugs, taking prescription drugs more often than you should, or gambling too much	Opioid use disorder, Stimulant use disorder, Alcohol use disorder, Tobacco use disorder, Gambling disorder
Neurocognitive disorders	Impairment of nervous system development while in adulthood	Your ability to think and remember has suffered a dramatic decline in adulthood	Delirium, Neurocognitive disorder due to Alzheimer's disease, Neurocognitive disorder due to Parkinson's disease, Neurocognitive disorder due to HIV infection
Personality disorders	Unhealthy personality patterns	Your behavior patterns repeatedly cause problems at work, at school, and in your relationships with others	Antisocial personality disorder, Borderline personality disorder
Paraphilic disorders	Deviant sexual behavior	You can gain sexual satisfaction only by engaging in highly atypical sexual behavior	Pedophilic disorder, Exhibitionistic disorder, Voyeuristic disorder, Fetishistic disorder

Sources: American Psychiatric Association, 2013; Sue et al., 2017.

dependence (■ in Section 5.4), eating disorders in (■ Section 10.2), sexual dysfunctions (■ in Section 11.4), and paraphilic disorders (■ in Section 11.4).

As you begin to explore some of these disorders, we urge you to avoid falling prey to "medical student's disease." Medical students, it seems, have a predictable tendency to notice in themselves the symptoms of each dreaded disease they study. As a psychology student, you may notice what seem to be abnormal tendencies in your own behavior. If so, don't panic. In most instances, this shows only that pathological behavior is an *exaggeration* of normal defenses and reactions, not that your behavior is abnormal. Keep this in mind as you read on.

Classification Using Symptoms

Like physical illness, mental illness is typically diagnosed by establishing the presence and/or absence of a number of symptoms, assessing how long the client has experienced those symptoms, and the extent to which the symptoms are interfering with their everyday life (Durand & Barlow, 2016).

Clinicians attempting to make a diagnosis will distinguish between positive and negative symptoms (Rollins et al., 2010).

Comorbid (in mental disorders) The simultaneous presence in a person of two or more mental disorders.

Positive symptoms, such as delusions and hallucinations, are excesses or exaggerations compared to normal behavior. In contrast, *negative symptoms* are absences or deficiencies compared to normal behavior. For example, sometimes patients may be apathetic or display a lack of emotion—flat affect—a condition in which the face is frozen in a blank expression.

As an example of using symptoms for classification, consider the diagnosis of a *major depressive episode.* Of course, one of the symptoms is being in a depressed (sad, empty, or hopeless) mood. But almost everybody gets a little depressed from time to time. This symptom won't qualify for this diagnosis unless the mood is unusually intense and has gone nearly all day, every day, for at least two weeks. Furthermore, there are eight additional main symptoms to consider, such as loss of interest or pleasure, difficulties with sleep, fatigue or loss of energy, and thoughts of suicide. At least five of these nine main symptoms must have occurred nearly all day, every day, for at least two weeks.

Unfortunately, some symptoms may go unnoticed by the person being diagnosed, only to be uncovered by the diagnosing clinician (such symptoms are sometimes referred to as *signs*). For example, Jasper complained to a clinical psychologist about feeling depressed and suicidal but made no mention of sleep problems or fatigue, which were added to Jasper's symptom list only after the clinician completed a careful assessment. Further, a good clinician seeking to make a diagnosis of major depressive episode will have to establish the absence of particular symptoms. For example, Jasper's clinician would need to determine that there weren't any manic episodes (or else this may be *bipolar disorder*) or drug use (or this may be a *substance use disorder*).

A further complicating factor is the potential presence of other symptoms not usually part of the diagnosis under consideration. Although depressed people do not typically report psychotic symptoms such as *hallucinations,* it is not unheard of and may indicate comorbidity. In reality, establishing an accurate clinical diagnosis is substantially more complicated than we have portrayed here, and it takes a skilled practitioner to make accurate diagnoses. Clearly, though, arriving at the right diagnosis is critical because developing an appropriate treatment plan depends on it (Sue et al., 2017).

The Evolution of Diagnostic Categories

Published in 2013, the DSM-5 reflects the most recent scientific advances and culturally accepted norms (American Psychiatric Association, 2013; Birgegård, Norring, & Clinton, 2012). If you look back at previous editions of the DSM, though, you might be surprised to see how much the definitions of mental disorders have changed over time. For example, when the DSM was first published in 1952, *neurosis* was included. The term was dropped in later editions because it is too imprecise. Even though *neurosis* is an outdated term, you may still hear it used to loosely refer to problems involving excessive anxiety. Similarly, *homosexuality* was omitted as a disorder in 1974.

The DSM-5 continues to reflect the evolution of researchers' and clinicians' thinking about mental illness. For example, after considerable debate, the now-outdated term *gender identity disorder* appears in the DSM-5 as *gender dysphoria* (American Psychiatric Association, 2013; De Cuypere, Knudson, & Bockting, 2011). Opponents of the old terminology argued that many people whose physical sex does not match their gender identity are well adjusted and should not be labeled as "disordered" (Hein & Berger, 2012). The new label better reflects this idea because it applies only to individuals who are deeply troubled by their gender variance.

Having said that, the process leading up to the publication of the DSM-5 was controversial (Frances, 2012; Marecek & Gavey, 2013). Perhaps the most important, (and certainly the most contentious) change has been the proliferation of disorders. The original DSM contained about 100 disorders; today, it contains more than 350. As a consequence, critics charge that more and more previously "normal" people are being categorized as "mentally ill" (Frances, 2012; Lane, 2009). For example, *attention deficit hyperactivity disorder (ADHD)* was not a disorder in the original DSM. Since its inclusion, it has become one of the most widely diagnosed disorders among young boys, prompting critics to decry the disorder as "pathologizing boyhood" (Bruchmüller, Margraf, & Schneider, 2012). A related concern is that psychiatric labels are getting easier and easier to apply. For example, changes to the DSM-5 make it easier to label someone whose husband died as suffering from *major depressive disorder* rather than simply experiencing grief (Frances, 2012).

Human Diversity and Diagnostic Categories

As you might well imagine, different cultures around the world have identified their own *culture-bound syndromes* that you won't find in the DSM-5 (Barlow, Durand, & Hofmann, 2018; López & Guarnaccia, 2000; Teo & Gaw, 2010). For example, men in some parts of Asia sometimes run *amok* after they have been insulted. After a period of brooding, they erupt into an outburst of violent, aggressive, or homicidal behavior randomly directed at people and objects. (Yes, this is the origin of the familiar expression "to run amok.") Can *amok* be understood within the framework of the DSM-5 as a *brief psychotic disorder* or not?

As another example, in Japan, adolescents or young adults who refuse to leave their parents' homes for months at a time are experiencing *hikikomori,* an extreme form of social withdrawal. Is *hikikomori* a variation of the DSM-5 disorder *agoraphobia* or something else entirely?

It is clear that people everywhere have a need to label and categorize troubled behavior. With some cultural sensitivity, it is often possible to understand these unusual experiences (Flaskerud, 2009; Ross, Schroeder, & Ness, 2013). By the way, culture-bound syndromes occur in all societies, including our own. For example, psychologists Pamela Keel and Kelly Klump believe that the eating disorder *bulimia nervosa* is primarily a syndrome of Western cultures such as the United States (Keel & Klump, 2003).

Stigma Associated with Diagnostic Labels

A significant concern associated with psychiatric labeling is that it can lead to prejudice and discrimination—that is, the mentally ill in our culture are often stigmatized and rejected. People who have been labeled mentally ill (at any time in their lives) are less likely to be hired, for example. They also tend to be denied housing and are more likely to be falsely accused of crimes. Sadly, the fear of stigmatization, including self-stigmatization, is one major reason many people do not seek help for their mental illness (Mojtabai et al., 2011). Thus, people who are grappling with mental illness may be harmed by social stigma as well as by their immediate psychological problems (Oexle et al., 2017).

Can you give an example? Sure. In the mid-1800s, slaves who tried to escape were sometimes labeled as suffering from "drapetomania," a mental "disorder" that caused slaves to run away (Wakefield, 1992). The "cure"? Amputation of the toes. As this example suggests, psychiatric terms are easily abused. Historically, some labels have also been applied to culturally disapproved behaviors that are not mental disorders—the long-outdated diagnosis of "anarchia," for example, was once considered a form of insanity that led people to seek a more democratic society (Brown, 1990). In more recent times, critics have noted that the practice of labeling homosexuality as a deviant form of sexuality amounted to nothing more than using medical labels as a way to justify prejudice.

Because biases and prejudices can influence perceptions of disorder and normality, it is worth being extra cautious before you leap to conclusions about, or label, the mental health of others (American Psychiatric Association, 2013).

Psychiatric Classification in Everyday Life: The Insanity Defense

Commitment proceedings are legal proceedings that may result in the finding of **insanity**, which is a legal, not a psychological, term (Fuller, 2012). It refers to an inability to manage one's affairs or foresee the consequences of one's actions. People who are declared insane are not legally responsible for their actions. If necessary, they can be involuntarily committed to a psychiatric hospital.

Legally, insanity is established by testimony from *expert witnesses* (psychologists and psychiatrists) recognized by a court of law as qualified to give opinions on a specific topic. Involuntary commitments happen most often when people are brought to emergency rooms or are arrested for committing a crime. People who are involuntarily committed are usually judged to be a danger to themselves or to others, or they are severely intellectually disabled.

What is the insanity defense? Someone accused of a crime may argue that he or she is *not guilty by reason of insanity.* In contrast, someone with brain damage or an intellectual disability such as autism could plead *not guilty by reason of diminished responsibility* (Jones et al., 2013). In practice, this means that the accused, due to a diagnosable mental disorder, was unable to realize that what he or she did was wrong (Gowensmith, Murrie, & Boccaccini, 2013). Of course, such verdicts raise important questions. Should people be set free in spite of their crimes? Should their sentences be reduced? What happens if a clinical intervention is successful and the person is "cured"—should a sentence be served then?

You may be surprised to learn that being diagnosed with a mental disorder does not automatically imply a successful insanity defense. For example, someone diagnosed with, say, an anxiety disorder who commits murder might nevertheless be well aware that murder is against the law. In fact, very few criminal trials end with this verdict (Fuller, 2012; Martin & Weiss, 2010).

Causes of Mental Illness

Like different physical diseases, different mental illnesses undoubtedly have a variety of underlying causes, including those that are biological and psychosocial.

Pima County Sheriff's Forensic Unit/Getty Images News/Getty Images

In 2011, Jared Lee Loughner went on a shooting rampage in Tucson, Arizona, severely injuring his intended target, U.S. Representative Gabrielle Giffords. Of the other 18 people he shot, 12 died of their wounds. Diagnosed with paranoid schizophrenia, he was nevertheless found competent to stand trial. He was convicted and sentenced to life in prison.

Biological Factors

Mental illnesses are directly associated with biological factors that impact the brain. Some of these biological factors are *organic*, such as tumors or hormonal influences. A second group of factors are *environmental*, such as head injuries sustained during accidents or exposure to toxic chemicals or drugs. Poisoning by chemicals such as lead or mercury can damage the brain, causing intellectual disability, hallucinations, delusions, and a loss of emotional control (Kern et al., 2012). That is why the lead poisoning crisis centered in Flint, Michigan, was so frightening to parents. On a much larger scale, "poisoning" of another type, in the form of drug abuse, also can produce deviant behavior and psychotic symptoms (American Psychiatric Association, 2013).

Third and finally, some disorders seem to be connected to *genetics*. For example, one recent study identified 128 gene variations associated with schizophrenia (Schizophrenia Working Group of the Psychiatric Genomics Consortium, 2014). In addition, genes appear to play a role in atypical development across the lifespan, including *neurodevelopmental* and *neurocognitive* disorders.

In general, problems directly related to nervous system damage that arise before adulthood are termed **neurodevelopmental disorders**. For example, Down syndrome, a form of intellectual

Insanity A legal term that refers to a mental inability to manage one's affairs or to be aware of the consequences of one's actions.

Neurodevelopmental disorders Psychopathologies due to various forms of damage to the nervous system arising before adulthood.

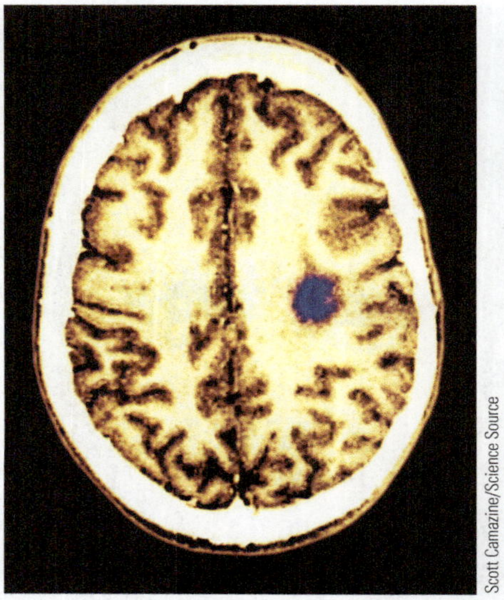

This MRI scan of a human brain (viewed from the top) reveals a tumor (dark spot). Mental disorders sometimes have organic causes of this sort. However, in many instances, no obvious organic damage can be found.

The Mad Hatter, from Lewis Carroll's *Alice's Adventures in Wonderland*, was modeled after an occupational disease of the 18th and 19th centuries. In that era, hat makers were heavily exposed to mercury used in the preparation of felt. Consequently, many suffered brain damage and became psychotic, or "mad" (Kety, 1979). Such environmental exposure to toxic chemicals remains a problem to this day. For example, unacceptably high concentrations of lead in water supplies are currently plaguing the mostly poor families living in cities such as Flint, Michigan.

disability, is caused by a genetic defect. It is also known as trisomy 21 because the defect involves an extra 21st chromosome (■ see Section 9.3). Autism is another neurodevelopmental disorder that appears to have a genetic basis, at least in some cases.

Problems not arising until adulthood, such as *Parkinson's disease*, are termed **neurocognitive disorders**. These are often serious mental impairments in old age caused by deterioration of the brain. In these disorders, we see major disturbances in memory, reasoning, judgment, impulse control, and personality (Treves & Korczyn, 2012). This combination usually leaves people confused, suspicious, apathetic, or withdrawn. Some common causes of neurocognitive disorders are circulatory problems, repeated strokes, or general shrinkage and atrophy of the brain.

Alzheimer's disease (ALLS-hi-merz) is the most common neurocognitive disorder. Alzheimer's victims slowly lose the ability to work, cook, drive, read, write, or do arithmetic. Eventually, they are mute and bedridden. Alzheimer's disease appears to be related to unusual webs and tangles in the brain that damage areas important for memory and learning (Hanyu et al., 2010; Irish et al., 2017). Genetic factors can increase the risk of developing this devastating disease (Treves & Korczyn, 2012).

Discovering that genes play a role in mental illness still leaves researchers with many questions (Sharma et al., 2016). How do particular genes, once they are identified, affect the brain? Do they modify brain structure? Do they alter neurotransmitter function? Most importantly, how can this information help with the development of new therapies?

Psychosocial Factors

Psychosocial factors also are associated with a variety of mental illnesses. Relevant psychological factors include stress, psychological trauma, learning disorders, and a lack of knowledge, control, or mastery. Contributing family factors include parents who are immature, criminal, or abusive; severe marital strife; extremely poor child discipline; and disordered family communication patterns. Relevant social conditions include poverty, stressful living conditions, homelessness, social disorganization, and overcrowding. Of these, the most important are stress and early **psychological trauma**—a psychological (not physical) injury or shock.

The Stress-Vulnerability Model

Most psychologists now accept that many mental illnesses are caused by a blend of environmental and psychosocial stressors, as well as inherited vulnerability (Jones & Fernyhough, 2007; Yim et al., 2015). This type of explanation is in keeping with our discussion of a *biopsychosocial approach* to psychology (■ see Section 1.4)—in the context of mental illness, taking a biopsychosocial approach leads to the **stress-vulnerability model** (or the *diathesis-stress* model). (See ● Figure 14.2.) In the sections that follow, you will

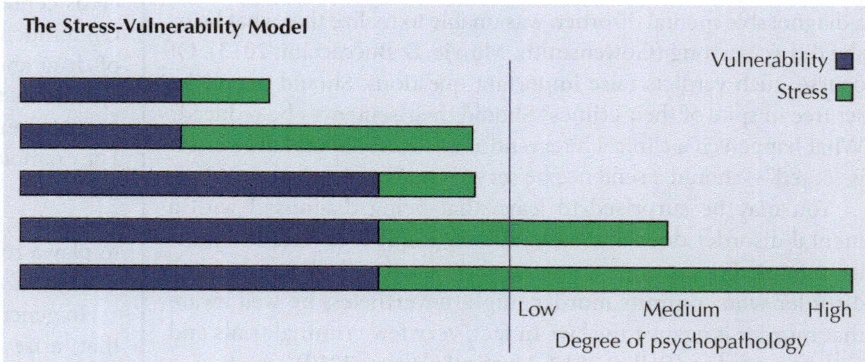

● **Figure 14.2 Stress-vulnerability model.** Various combinations of vulnerability and stress may produce psychological problems. The top bar shows low vulnerability and low stress. The result? No problem. The same is true of the next bar down, in which low vulnerability is combined with moderate stress. Even high vulnerability (third bar) may not lead to problems if stress levels remain low. However, when high vulnerability combines with moderate or high stress (bottom two bars), the person "crosses the line" and suffers from psychopathology.

see that the stress-vulnerability model has been applied to several mental illnesses. We divide our discussion of them into three groups: psychotic disorders, mood and personality disorders, and anxiety disorders.

Reflective Practice

Psychopathology: Classification and Causes

1. One of the most powerful contexts in which judgments of normality and abnormality are made is
   a. the family
   b. occupational settings
   c. religious systems
   d. culture
2. The core feature of abnormal behavior is that it is
   a. statistically unusual
   b. maladaptive
   c. socially nonconforming
   d. a source of subjective discomfort
3. Which of the following is a *legal* concept?
   a. neurosis
   b. psychosis
   c. drapetomania
   d. insanity
4. *Comorbidity* is said to occur when a person suffers from ________________.
5. Mental illness is typically diagnosed by confirming the
   a. absence of symptoms
   b. presence of symptoms
   c. presence of atypical symptoms
   d. all of the above
6. According to the stress-vulnerability model, mental illness is caused by a blend of
   a. environmental stress and lack of knowledge
   b. inherited susceptibility and environmental or psychosocial stressors
   c. brain damage and lack of knowledge
   d. none of the above

THINK CRITICALLY

7. Many states began to restrict the use of the insanity defense after John Hinckley, Jr., who tried to assassinate President Ronald Reagan in 1981, was found not guilty by reason of insanity. What does this trend reveal about insanity?

SELF-REFLECT

- Think of an instance of abnormal behavior that you have witnessed. By what formal standards would the behavior be regarded as abnormal? In every society? Was the behavior maladaptive in any way?
- How are the mentally ill stigmatized in movies and television dramas? Can you think of any positive portrayals (such as John Nash in the film *A Beautiful Mind*)? How do you think such portrayals affect attitudes about mental disorders?

Answers: 1. d 2. b 3. d 4. more than one disorder 5. d 6. b 7. It emphasizes that insanity is a legal concept, not a psychiatric diagnosis. Laws reflect community standards. When those standards change, lawmakers may seek to alter definitions of legal responsibility.

*From Fundamentals of Behavior Pathology by R. M. Suinn. Copyright © 1975. Reprinted by permission of John Wiley & Sons, Inc.

14.2 Psychotic Disorders

GATEWAYS LEARNING OUTCOMES:
After reading this section you should be able to:

14.2.1 Describe the general characteristics of psychotic disorders

14.2.2 Outline the specific characteristics of delusional disorders

14.2.3 Outline the specific characteristics of schizophrenia

14.2.4 Describe the causes of schizophrenia

Psychoses (psycho*sis*, singular; psycho*ses*, plural) involve a loss of contact with shared views of reality, making them among the most dramatic and serious of all mental problems (Durand & Barlow, 2016). Psychoses are characterized by one or more of the following: delusions, hallucinations, disturbed thought and/or speech, disturbed motor behavior, or social/emotional isolation. For example, consider this small excerpt from Edna's intake interview:

"*Dr.:* Tell me, how do you feel?

Patient: London's bell is a long, long dock. Hee! Hee! *(Giggles uncontrollably).*

Dr.: Do you know where you are now?

Patient: D______n! S______t on you all who rip into my internals! The grudgerometer will take care of you all! *(Shouting)* I am the Queen, see my magic, I shall turn you all into smidgelings forever!

Dr.: Your husband is concerned about you. Do you know his name?

Patient: (Stands, walks to and faces the wall) Who am I, who are we, who are you, who are they *(turns)* I . . . I . . . I . . . I! *(Makes grotesque faces).*" (Suinn, 1975*).

Edna is suffering from an extreme form of schizophrenia marked by silliness, laughter, and bizarre or obscene behavior.

Neurocognitive disorders Psychopathologies due to various forms of damage to the nervous system not arising until adulthood.

Alzheimer's disease Age-related condition characterized by memory loss, confusion, and increasing loss of mental abilities.

Psychological trauma A psychological injury or shock, such as that caused by violence, abuse, neglect, separation, etc.

Stress-vulnerability (diathesis-stress) model A model that attributes mental illness to a combination of environmental stress and inherited susceptibility.

Psychosis A withdrawal from reality marked by hallucinations and delusions, disturbed thoughts and emotions, and personality disorganization.

▲ Table 14.2 DSM-5 Classification of Schizophrenia Spectrum and Other Psychotic Disorders

Problem	Typical Signs of Trouble
Delusional disorder	You have some deeply held and bizarre but false beliefs.
Schizophrenia	Your personality has disintegrated; you have hallucinations, delusions, or both.
Brief Psychotic Disorder	You suffer a sudden, but short-lived loss of contact with reality.

Sources: American Psychiatric Association, 2013; Sue et al., 2017.

While not all of the psychotic disorders are this extreme, psychotic patients often cannot control their thoughts, emotions, or actions, which makes psychotic disorders severely disabling. They also are among the most difficult to treat. Drug therapies offer some hope; however, many psychotic individuals end up in prison or committed to a psychiatric hospital.

Psychosis can also occur in a variety of other mental illnesses including Alzheimer's disease, bipolar disorder, and drug use disorder. In this section and the next, however, we will focus on just two major types of **schizophrenia spectrum and other psychotic disorders**: *delusional disorders* and *schizophrenia* (see ▲ Table 14.2). These diagnoses are usually applied only after psychotic disturbances are evident for weeks or months (American Psychiatric Association, 2013; Sue et al., 2017).

Delusional Disorders

People with delusional disorders usually do *not* suffer from **hallucinations** (perceptions with no basis in reality), disturbed motor behavior, emotional excesses, or personality disintegration. Even so, their break with reality is unmistakable. The main symptom of a **delusional disorder** is the presence of deeply held false beliefs called **delusions**. While many different delusions are possible, some of the most common types of delusions are (American Psychiatric Association, 2013; Sue et al., 2017):

- **Erotomanic type:** In this disorder, people have erotic delusions that they are loved by another person, especially by someone famous or of higher status. As you might imagine, some celebrity stalkers suffer from erotomania.
- **Grandiose type:** In this case, people suffer from the delusion that they have some great, unrecognized talent, knowledge, or insight. They also may believe that they have a special relationship with an important person or with God, or that they are a famous person. (If the famous person is alive, the deluded person regards her or him as an imposter.)
- **Jealous type:** An example of this type of delusion would be having an all-consuming, but unfounded, belief that your spouse or lover is unfaithful.
- **Persecutory type:** Delusions of persecution involve the belief that you are being conspired against, cheated, spied on, followed, poisoned, maligned, or harassed.
- **Somatic type:** People suffering from somatic delusions typically believe that their bodies are diseased or rotting, infested with insects or parasites, or that parts of their bodies are defective.

Although false and sometimes far-fetched, these delusions tend to be about experiences that could conceivably occur in real life. For example, people may believe that someone is trying to steal their money, that they are being deceived by a lover, or that the FBI is watching them. However, in other types of psychosis, such as Edna's schizophrenia, delusions tend to be more bizarre and unrealistic, such as the belief that space aliens have replaced one's internal organs with electronic monitoring devices (Brown & Barlow, 2017).

Paranoid Psychosis

The most common delusional disorder, **paranoid psychosis**, centers on persecutory-type delusions. Many self-styled reformers, crank letter writers, conspiracy theorists, and the like suffer paranoid delusions. Paranoid individuals often believe that they are being cheated, spied on, followed, poisoned, harassed, or plotted against. Usually, they are intensely suspicious, believing that they must be on guard at all times.

The evidence that such people find to support their beliefs generally fails to persuade others. Every detail of the paranoid person's existence is woven into a private version of "what's really going on." For instance, buzzing during a telephone conversation may be interpreted as "someone listening," or a stranger who comes to the door asking for directions may be seen as "really trying to get information."

It is difficult to treat people suffering from paranoid delusions because it is almost impossible for them to accept that they need help. Anyone who suggests that they have a problem is quickly incorporated into the "conspiracy" to "persecute" them. Consequently, paranoid people frequently lead lonely, isolated lives that are dominated by constant suspicion and hostility.

Although paranoid people are not necessarily dangerous to others, they can be. People who believe that the Mafia, government agents, terrorists, or a street gang is slowly closing in on them may be moved to violence by their irrational fears. Imagine that a stranger comes to the door to ask a paranoid person for directions. If the stranger has his hand in his coat pocket, he could become the target of a paranoid attempt at "self-defense."

Schizophrenia

In any given year, one person in 100 has **schizophrenia** (SKIT-soh-FREN-ee-uh), a disorder characterized by disturbances in thought, perceptions, emotions, and behavior (National Institute of Mental Health, 2017). In schizophrenia, these disturbances are so severe that a person's thoughts, actions, and emotions are no longer coordinated, resulting in *personality disintegration* along with a consequent break with reality.

Do people with schizophrenia have two personalities? No. How many times have you heard people say something like, "Laurence was so warm and friendly yesterday, but today he's as cold as ice.

Schizophrenia has no bearing on a person's ability to make a contribution to society. Mathematician John Nash was diagnosed with paranoid schizophrenia while teaching at MIT and later earned a Nobel Prize in Economics.

He's so schizophrenic that I don't know how to react." Such statements show how often the term *schizophrenic* is misused. As we will shortly see, a person who displays two or more *integrated* personalities has a *dissociative disorder* and does *not* have schizophrenia. Neither, of course, is a person like Laurence, whose behavior is merely inconsistent.

Symptoms of Schizophrenia

Schizophrenia is characterized by a number of symptoms. Let's take a closer look at four of them: disturbed thinking, disturbed perception, disturbed emotion, and disturbed behavior.

Disturbed Thinking

Many schizophrenic symptoms appear to be related to problems with *selective attention.* In other words, it is hard for people with schizophrenia to focus on one item of information at a time. Having an impaired "sensory filter" in their brains may be why they are overwhelmed by a jumble of thoughts, sensations, images, and feelings (Cellard et al., 2010; Heinrichs, 2001).

Other symptoms such as delusions also frequently occur in schizophrenia. Paranoid delusions are especially common. As in paranoid delusional disorders, **paranoia** in schizophrenia centers on delusions of grandeur and persecution. However, people with paranoid schizophrenia also hallucinate, and their delusions are generally more bizarre and unconvincing than those in a delusional disorder (Corcoran, 2010; Freeman & Garety, 2004). Schizophrenic delusions may include the idea that the person's thoughts and actions are being controlled, that thoughts are being broadcast so others can hear them, that thoughts have been "inserted" into the person's mind, or that thoughts have been removed. When paranoia is the predominant symptom experienced by people with schizophrenia, this is sometimes referred to as *paranoid schizophrenia.*

Disturbed Perception

Hallucinations are also characteristic of schizophrenia. While the most common hallucinations center on hearing voices, psychotic people may feel "insects crawling under their skin," taste "poisons" in their food, or smell "gas" that their "enemies" are using to "get them." Sensory changes, such as anesthesia (numbness, or a loss of sensation) or extreme sensitivity to heat, cold, pain, or touch also can occur.

Unfortunately, thinking that God, the government, or "cosmic rays from space" are controlling their minds, or that someone is trying to poison them, people suffering from paranoid schizophrenia may feel forced to commit violence to "protect" themselves. An example is James Huberty, who in 1984 brutally murdered 21 people at a McDonald's restaurant in San Ysidro, California. Huberty, who had paranoid schizophrenia, felt persecuted and cheated by life. Shortly before he announced to his wife that he was "going hunting humans," Huberty had been hearing *command hallucinations* (Birchwood et al., 2014).

Disturbed Emotions

During a psychotic episode, the emotions of a person with schizophrenia may also become very inappropriate or blunted. For instance, if a person with schizophrenia is told his mother just died, he may smile, giggle, or become wildly elated or hyperemotional. But sometimes psychotic patients may be depressed or apathetic, displaying no emotion at all (*flat affect*).

Disturbed Behavior

Schizophrenia also often involves withdrawal from contact with others, apathy, loss of interest in external activities, a breakdown of personal habits, and an inability to deal with daily events (Neufeld et al., 2003; Ziv, Leiser, & Levine, 2011).

People with schizophrenia may also display **catatonia**, remaining *mute* (not speaking) while holding odd postures for hours or even days at a time (Tandon et al., 2013). These periods of stupor may be similar to the tendency to "freeze" at times of great emergency or panic. Catatonic individuals appear to be struggling desperately to control their inner turmoil (Fink, 2013). One sign of this is the fact that stupor may occasionally give way to agitated outbursts or violent behavior.

Schizophrenia spectrum and other psychotic disorders Severe mental disorders characterized by delusions, hallucinations, disturbed thought and/or speech, disturbed motor behavior, and/or retreat from reality.

Hallucination Perception with no basis in reality.

Delusional disorder A psychosis marked by severe delusions of grandeur, jealousy, persecution, or similar preoccupations.

Delusion Strongly held thought or belief that is at odds with reality.

Paranoid psychosis A delusional disorder centered especially on delusions of persecution.

Schizophrenia Severe disorder characterized by disturbances in thought, perceptions, emotions, and behavior.

Paranoia A symptom marked by a preoccupation with delusions related to a single theme, especially grandeur or persecution.

Catatonia A disorder marked by stupor, rigidity, unresponsiveness, posturing, mutism, and sometimes agitated, purposeless behavior.

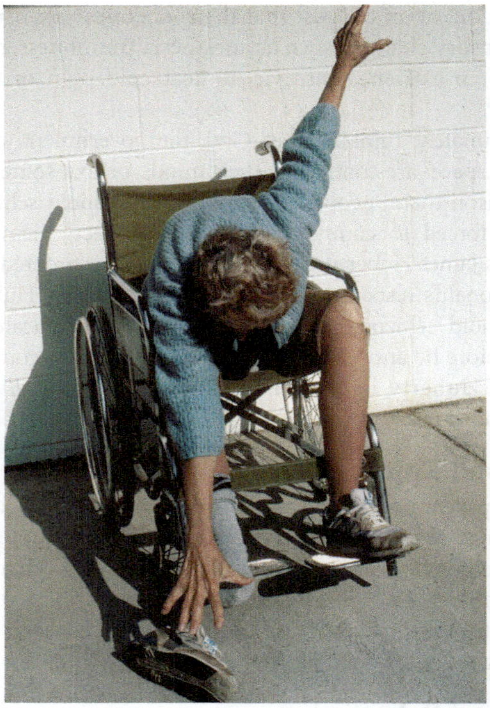

Grunnitus Studio/Science Source

In the DSM-5, catatonia, with its rigid postures and stupor, is associated with a number of disorders including schizophrenia, bipolar disorder, depression, and several other conditions, including drug abuse (Tandon et al., 2013).

Causes of Schizophrenia

An increased risk of developing schizophrenia may begin at birth or even before. Women who are exposed to the influenza (flu) virus or to rubella (German measles) during the middle of pregnancy have children who are more likely to develop schizophrenia (Barlow, Durand, & Hofmann, 2018; Vuillermot et al., 2010). Malnutrition during pregnancy and complications at the time of birth can have a similar impact. Such events likely disturb brain development, leaving people more vulnerable to a psychotic break with reality (Walker et al., 2004).

Psychosocial Factors

Often the victims of schizophrenia were exposed to a psychological trauma, such as sexual abuse, death, divorce, separation, or other stresses in childhood (Walker et al., 2004). Living in a troubled family is a related risk factor. In a disturbed family setting, stressful relationships, communication patterns, and negative emotions prevail. Deviant communication patterns cause anxiety, confusion, anger, conflict, and turmoil. Typically, disturbed families interact in ways that are laden with guilt, prying, criticism, negativity, and emotional attacks (Bressi, Albonetti, & Razzoli, 1998; Davison & Neale, 2006).

Although they may seem intuitive, psychosocial explanations alone are not enough to account for schizophrenia. For example, when the children of parents who have schizophrenia are raised away from their chaotic homes, they still are more likely to become psychotic than someone selected from the general population (Walker et al., 2004). A more complete understanding of schizophrenia requires that we also consider biological factors, including genetics.

Genetics

There is now little doubt that heredity is a factor in schizophrenia (Gejman, Sanders, & Duan, 2010). More specifically, it appears that some individuals inherit a *potential* for developing schizophrenia. They are, in other words, more *vulnerable* to the disorder (Levy et al., 2010; Walker et al., 2004).

How has that been shown? If one identical twin develops schizophrenia (remember, identical twins have identical genes), then the other twin has a 48 percent chance of also developing schizophrenia (Insel, 2010; Lenzenweger & Gottesman, 1994). The figure for twins can be compared with the risk of schizophrenia for the population in general, which is 1 percent. (See Figure 14.3 for other relationships.) In general, schizophrenia is clearly more common among close relatives and tends to run in families. There's even a case on record of *four* identical quadruplets *all* developing schizophrenia (Mirsky et al., 2000). In light of such evidence, researchers are beginning to search for specific genes related to schizophrenia (Curtis et al., 2011; Schwab & Wildenauer, 2013).

A problem exists with current genetic explanations of schizophrenia though: Very few people with schizophrenia have children (Bundy, Stahl, & MacCabe, 2011). How could a genetic defect be passed from one generation to the next if afflicted people don't reproduce? One possibility is suggested by the fact that the older a man is (even if he doesn't suffer from schizophrenia) when he fathers a child, the more likely it is that the child will develop schizophrenia (Helenius, Munk-Jørgensen, & Steinhausen, 2012).

Genetic relatedness	Relationship	Risk
100%	Identical twin	48%
—	Offspring of two patients	46%
50%	Fraternal twin	17%
50%	Offspring of one patient	17%
50%	Sibling	9%
25%	Nephew or niece	4%
0%	Spouse	2%
0%	Unrelated person in the general population	1%

Figure 14.3 Lifetime risk of developing schizophrenia. The risk of developing schizophrenia over a person's lifetime is associated with how closely the person is genetically related to a patient with schizophrenia. A shared environment also increases the risk. (Estimates from Lenzenweger & Gottesman, 1994.)

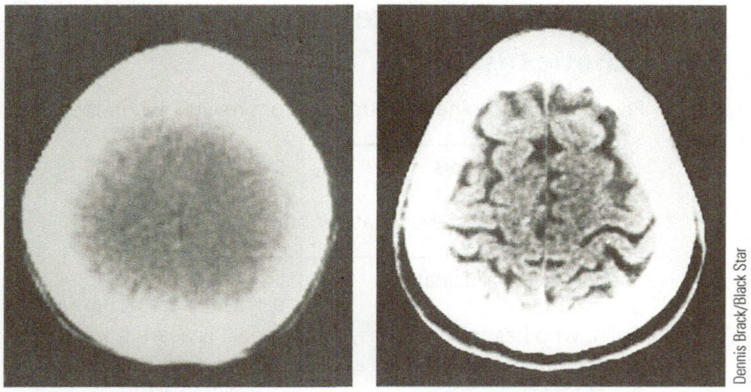

Figure 14.4 Brain fissures and schizophrenia. (*Left*) A CT scan of a normal 25-year-old's brain. In most young adults, the surface folds of the brain are pressed together too tightly to be seen. (*Right*) A CT scan of would-be presidential assassin John Hinckley, Jr., taken when he was 25. The image shows widened fissures in the wrinkled surface of Hinckley's brain. As a person ages, the surface folds of the brain normally become more visible. Pronounced brain fissuring in young adults may be a sign of schizophrenia, chronic alcoholism, or other problems.

Apparently, genetic mutations occur in aging male reproductive cells and increase the risk of disturbed brain development, leading to schizophrenia (as well as other medical problems) (Sipos et al., 2004).

Brain Functioning

Research has demonstrated that the brains of patients with schizophrenia differ from other people in important ways. For example, structural brain imaging methods have revealed that the brains of people with schizophrenia are shrunk, or atrophied (Bora et al., 2011). Figure 14.4 shows a computed tomography (CT) scan of the brain of John Hinckley, Jr., who shot President Ronald Reagan and three other men in 1981. In the ensuing trial, Hinckley was declared insane. As you can see, his brain had wider-than-normal surface fissuring.

Positron emission tomography (PET) scans that reveal brain activity have demonstrated that activity tends to be abnormally low in the frontal lobes of the schizophrenic brain (Barlow, Durand, & Hofmann, 2018; Roffman et al., 2011) (Figure 14.5). Similarly, magnetic resonance imaging (MRI) scans indicate that people who have schizophrenia tend to have enlarged ventricles (fluid-filled spaces within the brain), again suggesting that surrounding brain tissue has withered (Andreasen et al., 2011; Barkataki et al., 2006). (See Section 2.2 for more information about PET and MRI scans.)

What causes these brain differences? One possible explanation is that the schizophrenic brain may be unable to continually create new neurons to replace old ones that have died. In contrast, normal brains continue to produce new neurons throughout life (a process referred to as neurogenesis; see Section 2.1). It is telling that the affected areas are crucial for regulating motivation, emotion, perception, actions, and attention (DeCarolis & Eisch, 2010; Inta, Meyer-Lindenberg, & Gass, 2011; Kawada et al., 2009).

What are the consequences of these brain differences? One consequence of atypical brain development may be the disruption of normal neurotransmitter functions. One likely candidate is *dopamine* (DOPE-ah-meen), an important neurotransmitter naturally found in the brain (Figure 14.6). In schizophrenia, dopamine receptors in one part of the brain appear to become super-responsive to normal amounts of dopamine, triggering a flood of unrelated thoughts, feelings, and perceptions, which may

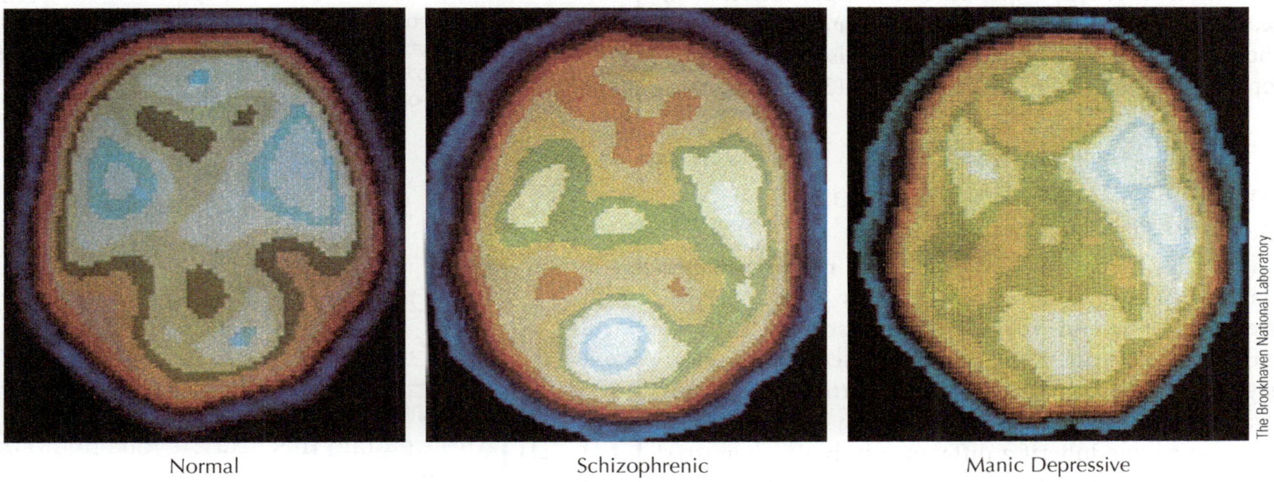

Figure 14.5 Patterns of activity in normal and abnormal brains. In the PET scans of the human brain shown here, red, pink, and orange indicate lower levels of brain activity; white and blue indicate higher activity levels. Notice that activity in the schizophrenic brain is quite low in the frontal lobes (top area of each scan; Velakoulis & Pantelis, 1996). Activity in the manic-depressive brain is low in the left-brain hemisphere and high in the right-brain hemisphere. The reverse is more often true of the schizophrenic brain. Researchers are trying to identify consistent patterns like these to aid the diagnosis of mental disorders.

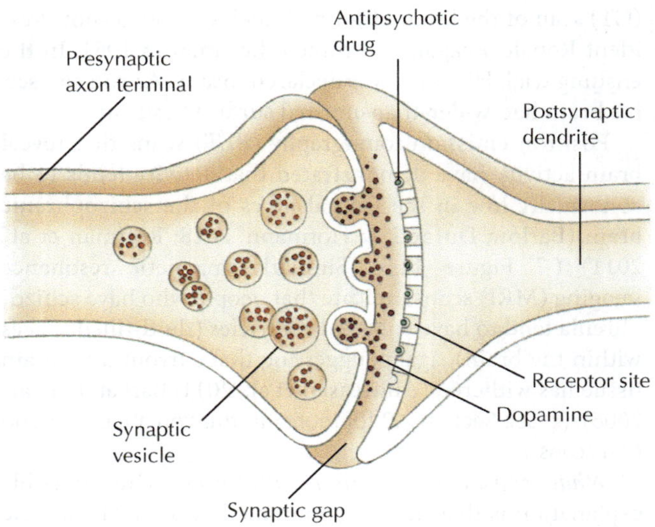

Figure 14.6 Dopamine and schizophrenia. Dopamine normally crosses the synapse between two neurons, activating the second cell. Antipsychotic drugs bind to the same receptor sites as does dopamine, blocking its action. In people suffering from schizophrenia, a reduction in dopamine activity can quiet a person's agitation and psychotic symptoms.

account for the symptoms (voices, hallucinations, and delusions) of schizophrenia (Citrome, 2011; Madras, 2013).

The neurotransmitter *glutamate* also appears to be related to schizophrenia. People who take the hallucinogenic drug phencyclidine (PCP, or angel dust) have symptoms that closely mimic schizophrenia (Javitt et al., 2012). This occurs because PCP affects glutamate levels, which in turn influence brain activity in areas that control emotions, cognition, and sensory information (Citrome, 2011; Volk et al., 2015). Another tantalizing connection is the fact that stress alters glutamate levels, which in turn alters dopamine systems (Holloway et al., 2013; Moghaddam, 2002).

Putting Causes Together: The Stress-Vulnerability Model

In keeping with a biopsychosocial approach, most psychologists today accept that the *stress-vulnerability model* best fits our current understanding of psychotic disorders such as schizophrenia. It takes this form: Anyone subjected to enough stress may be pushed to a psychotic break. (*Battlefield psychosis* among war veterans is an example of such a phenomenon.) However, some people inherit a difference in brain chemistry or brain structure/function that makes them more susceptible to developing psychotic disorders, even when experiencing normal life stresses. Thus, the right mix of environmental or psychosocial stress and inherited potential brings about mind-altering changes in the brain (Pruessner et al., 2017; Walker et al., 2004).

Reflective Practice

Psychotic Disorders

1. People are said to have "retreated from reality" when they suffer from ______.
   a. psychotic disorders
   b. schizophrenia
   c. delusional disorder
   d. all of the above
2. Angela wrongly believes that her body is "rotting away." She is suffering from ______.
   a. depressive hallucinations
   b. a delusion
   c. flat affect
   d. Alzheimer's disease
3. Colin, who has suffered a psychotic break, is hearing voices. This symptom is referred to as ______.
   a. flat affect
   b. a hallucination
   c. a word salad
   d. an organic delusion
4. Hallucinations and personality disintegration are principal features of schizophrenia. T or F?
5. Psychosocial explanations of schizophrenia emphasize emotional trauma and
   a. manic parents
   b. schizoaffective interactions
   c. psychedelic interactions
   d. disturbed family relationships
6. Biochemical explanations of schizophrenia have focused on disturbed functioning of ______ in the brain.
   a. radioactive sugar
   b. webs and tangles
   c. PCP
   d. dopamine and glutamate

THINK CRITICALLY

7. Enlarged surface fissures and ventricles are frequently found in the brains of people with chronic schizophrenia. Why is it a mistake to conclude that such features cause schizophrenia?

SELF-REFLECT

- If you were asked to play the role of a paranoid person for a theater production, what symptoms would you emphasize?
- You have been asked to explain the causes of schizophrenia to the parents of a teenager with schizophrenia. What would you tell them?

Answers: 1. d 2. b 3. b 4. T 5. d 6. d 7. Correlation does not confirm causation. Structural brain abnormalities are merely correlated with schizophrenia. They could be additional symptoms, rather than causes, of the disorder. Alternately, they could emerge as a result of the disorder.

14.3 Mood and Personality Disorders

GATEWAYS LEARNING OUTCOMES:
After reading this section you should be able to:

14.3.1 Describe the general characteristics of mood disorders

14.3.2 Outline the specific characteristics of depression and bipolar disorders

14.3.3 Describe the causes of mood disorders, including their risk factors

14.3.4 Outline some of the factors that lead people to commit suicide

14.3.5 Describe the general characteristics of personality disorders, and the specific features of antisocial personality disorder

Though not considered as serious as psychoses, mood and personality disorders can nonetheless be very debilitating. Let's do a deeper dive into these two types of psychopathology.

Mood Disorders

Psychologists have come to realize that *mood disorders*—the presence of unusual disturbances in the emotions—are among the most serious of all psychological conditions. In any given year, roughly 9.5 percent of the US population suffers from a mood disorder (National Institute of Mental Health, 2017). Two general types of mood disorder are *depressive disorders* and *bipolar disorders* (see ▲ Table 14.3)—let's take a closer look at each one.

Depressive Disorders

In **depressive disorders**, sadness and despondency are exaggerated, prolonged, or unreasonable. Signs of a depressive disorder are dejection, hopelessness, and an inability to feel pleasure or to take interest in anything. Other common symptoms are fatigue, disturbed sleep and eating patterns, feelings of worthlessness, a very negative self-image, and thoughts of suicide.

Some depressive disorders are long-lasting but relatively moderate. If a person is mildly depressed for at least two years, the problem is called a **persistent depressive disorder (dysthymia)** (dis-THY-mee-ah). Even at this level, depressive disorders can be debilitating. However, major depression is much more damaging.

In **major depressive disorder**, the depression is much deeper. Everything looks bleak and hopeless. The person has feelings of failure, worthlessness, and total despair. In serious cases of depression, it is impossible for a person to function at work or at school. Sometimes, depressed individuals cannot even feed or dress themselves. The suffering is intense, and the person may become extremely subdued, withdrawn, or intensely suicidal. Suicide attempted during the depths of a major depression is rarely a "cry for help." Usually, the person intends to succeed and may give no prior warning.

Eakachai Leesin/Shutterstock.com

In major depressive disorders, suicidal impulses can be intense and despair is often overwhelming.

Image Point Fr/Shutterstock.com

An hour or more of bright white or blue light a day can dramatically reduce the symptoms of SAD. Treatment is usually necessary from fall through spring. Light therapy is best done early in the morning, when it simulates dawn in the summer (Avery et al., 2001).

Seasonal Affective Disorder (SAD)

Unless you have experienced "cabin fever" in the far north during winter, you may be surprised to learn that the rhythms of the seasons underlie **seasonal affective disorder (SAD)**, or depression that occurs only during the fall and winter months (in DSM-5, it is now known as *major depressive disorder with seasonal pattern*). Almost anyone can get a little depressed when days are short, dark, and cold. But when a person's symptoms are lasting and disabling, the problem may be SAD.

Starting in the fall, people with SAD sleep longer, but more poorly. During the day they feel tired and drowsy, and they tend to overeat. With each passing day, they become more sad, anxious, irritable, and socially withdrawn (Rosenthal, N. E., 2013). Although their depressions are usually not severe, many victims of SAD face each winter with a sense of foreboding. SAD is especially prevalent in northern latitudes (think of countries such as Sweden and Canada), where days are very short during the winter.

Depressive disorders Class of disorders marked by chronic feelings of sadness and despondency.

Persistent depressive disorder (dysthymia) Moderate depression that persists for two years or more.

Major depressive disorder Mood disorder in which the person has suffered one or more intense episodes of depression.

Seasonal affective disorder (SAD) Depression that occurs only during fall and winter; presumably related to decreased exposure to sunlight.

▲ Table 14.3 DSM-5 Classification of Mood Disorders

Problem	Typical Signs of Trouble
Depressive Disorders	
Persistent depressive disorder (dysthymia)	You feel down and depressed more days than not; your self-esteem and energy levels have been low for many months.
Major depressive disorder	You feel extremely sad, worthless, fatigued, and empty; you are unable to feel pleasure; you are having thoughts of suicide.
Bipolar and Related Disorders	
Cyclothymic disorder	You have been experiencing upsetting emotional ups and downs for many months.
Bipolar I disorder	At times, you have little need for sleep, you can't stop talking, your mind races, and everything you do is of immense importance; at other times, you feel extremely sad, worthless, and empty.
Bipolar II disorder	Most of the time, you feel extremely sad, worthless, fatigued, and empty; however, at times, you feel unusually good, cheerful, energetic, or "high."

Sources: American Psychiatric Association, 2013; Sue et al., 2017.

For instance, 9 percent of those who live in Alaska experience SAD compared to 1 percent in Florida (Melrose, 2015).

Seasonal depressions are related to the release of more melatonin during the winter. This hormone, which is secreted by the pineal gland in the brain, regulates the body's response to changing light conditions (Delavest et al., 2012). That's why 80 percent of SAD patients can be helped by a remedy called **phototherapy**, which involves exposing them to one or more hours of very bright, fluorescent light each day. This is best done early in the morning, where it simulates dawn in the summer (Rosenthal, N. E., 2013; Vandewalle et al., 2011). For many SAD sufferers, a hearty dose of morning "sunshine" appears to be the next best thing to vacationing in the tropics. (■ In addition to its role in producing SAD, melatonin regulates normal circadian rhythms. See Section 10.1.)

Bipolar and Related Disorders

When depression alternates with periods of *mania*, one of the **bipolar and related disorders** is involved (American Psychiatric Association, 2013; Ellison-Wright & Bullmore, 2010). During a **manic episode**, the person is loud, elated, hyperactive, grandiose, and agitated.

A long-lasting but relatively moderate alternation between depression and mania is a **cyclothymic disorder** (SIKE-lo-THY-mik). Like depressive disorders, however, major bipolar disorders are much more severe. In a **bipolar I disorder**, people experience both extreme mania and deep depression. During periods of depression, the person is deeply despondent and possibly suicidal.

In a **bipolar II disorder**, the person is mostly sad and guilt-ridden but has had one or more mildly manic episodes (called *hypomania*). That is, in a bipolar II disorder, both mania and depression occur, but the person's mania is not as extreme as in a bipolar I disorder. Bipolar II patients who are hypomanic usually just manage to irritate everyone around them. They are excessively cheerful, aggressive, or irritable, and they may brag, talk too fast, interrupt conversations, or spend too much money (Nolen-Hoeksema, 2011).

Causes of Mood Disorders

Psychological theories put forth different explanations for mood disorders. Psychoanalytic theory, for instance, holds that depression is caused by repressed anger turned inward as self-blame and self-hate. As discussed in ■ Section 13.2, behavioral theories of depression emphasize learned helplessness (Durand & Barlow, 2016; Reivich et al., 2013). Cognitive psychologists believe that self-criticism and negative, distorted, or self-defeating thoughts underlie many cases of depression. (■ This view is further discussed in Section 15.3.)

Recently, researchers have made important progress in uncovering how several other factors may play a role in mood disorders, particularly depression. Let's take a closer look.

Biology and Depression

Heredity is one biological factor that appears to be important in mood disorders, particularly bipolar disorder (Ciobanu et al., 2016; Curtis et al., 2011). As a case in point, if one identical twin is depressed, the other has a 67 percent chance of suffering depression, too. For fraternal twins, the probability is 19 percent. This difference may be related to the finding that people who have a particular version of a gene (or genes) are more likely to become depressed when they are stressed (Halmai et al., 2013). As we have noted, psychological causes are important in many cases of depression. But for major mood disorders, biological factors seem to play a larger role.

Other scientists have focused their attention on disturbed *neurotransmitter function*, with a particular focus on serotonin, noradrenaline, and dopamine levels. The findings are incomplete, but progress has been made. For example, the chemical lithium carbonate—which influences the levels of several neurotransmitters—can be effective for treating some cases of bipolar depression (Malhi & Outhred, 2016).

Gender and Depression

Overall, women are about twice as likely as men to experience depression (Kuehner, 2017). Hormonal fluctuations likely play a role in cases of depression involving pregnancy, menstruation, and menopause (Lokuge et al., 2011). Nevertheless, researchers believe that social and environmental conditions are the main reason for this difference (Jack & Ali, 2010; McGuinness, Dyer, & Wade, 2012).

Psychosocial factors that contribute to women's greater risk for depression include conflicts about birth control and pregnancy, work and parenting, and the strain of providing emotional support for others. Marital strife, sexual and physical abuse, and poverty also are factors. Nationwide, women and children are most likely to live in poverty. As a result, poor women frequently suffer the stresses associated with single parenthood, loss of control over their lives, poor housing, and dangerous neighborhoods (Estefan, Coulter, & VandeWeerd, 2016; Grant et al., 2011; Stoppard & McMullen, 2003).

One particular source of women's depression is fairly easy to identify. After pregnancy and childbirth, many women face an elevated risk of becoming depressed (Phillips et al., 2010). An estimated 25 to 50 percent of women experience *maternity blues*, a mild depression that usually lasts from one to two days after childbirth. For most women, brief, mild bouts of crying, fitful sleep, tension, anger, and/or irritability are a normal part of adjusting to childbirth.

For some women, though, maternity blues can be the beginning of a persistent depressive disorder or even major depressive disorder. Roughly 13 percent of all women who give birth develop **postpartum depression**, a moderately severe depression that begins within three months following childbirth. Typical signs of postpartum depression are mood swings, despondency, feelings of inadequacy, an inability to cope with the new baby, and an increased risk of self-harm (Healey et al., 2013; National Institute of Mental Health, 2013). Unlike other types of depression, postpartum depression also features unusually high levels of restlessness and difficulty concentrating (Bernstein et al., 2008). Depression of this kind may last anywhere from two months to about a year. Women are not the only ones to suffer when postpartum depression strikes. A depressed mother can seriously affect her child's development (Cooper & Murray, 2001; Tikotzky et al., 2012).

Stress and anxiety before birth and negative attitudes toward child-rearing increase the risk of postpartum depression (Phillips et al., 2010; Yim, 2015). A troubled marriage and lack of support from the father also are danger signs. Part of the problem may be hormonal: After a woman gives birth, her estrogen levels can drop, altering her mood (Fernandez, Grizzell, & Wecker, 2013). Educating new parents about the importance of supporting one another may reduce the risk of depression. Groups where new mothers can discuss their feelings also are helpful. If depression is severe or long lasting, new mothers should seek professional help.

Mood Disorders in Everyday Life: Suicide

Is it mostly depressed people who attempt suicide? A diagnosable mental disorder (usually depression or substance use disorder) is a factor in 90 percent of all suicides. However, suicide is complex and may be the result of many risk factors, including a family history of suicidal behavior; the availability of a firearm; feelings of hopelessness or worthlessness; antisocial, impulsive, or aggressive behavior; and severe anxiety, panic attacks, shame, humiliation, failure, or rejection (Burón et al., 2016; Joiner, 2010; National Alliance on Mental Illness, 2016).

Anyone may temporarily reach a state of depression severe enough to impulsively attempt suicide. Most dangerous for the average person are times of divorce, separation, rejection, failure, and bereavement. Among ethnic adolescents, loss of face, acculturative stress, racism, and discrimination have been identified as additional risk factors (Goldston et al., 2008).

Such situations can seem intolerable and motivate an intense desire to escape, obtain relief, or die. Typically, people isolate themselves from others; they feel worthless, helpless, and misunderstood (Britton et al., 2008; Heisel, Flett, & Hewitt, 2003).

Factors Affecting Suicide Rates

Suicide rates in the United States reveal some general patterns:

- **Sex.** Although four times as many men die by suicide, women make more attempts. While men typically use a gun or an equally fatal method, women most often attempt a drug overdose, so there's a better chance of help arriving before death occurs (Denney et al., 2009; National Institute of Mental Health, 2017).
- **Ethnicity.** Caucasians generally have higher suicide rates than non-Caucasians (National Institute of Mental Health, 2017). Sadly, though, the suicide rate among Native Americans is by far the highest in the country (Goldston et al., 2008).
- **Age.** Although most suicide victims are white males over 45, suicide rates among younger people are of special concern. Suicide is the second-leading cause of death among 10- to 34-year-olds (National Institute of Mental Health, 2017). School is a factor in some youth suicides, as are illegal drug or alcohol use, chronic health problems, and interpersonal difficulties (Barlow, Durand, & Hofmann, 2018; Garlow, Purselle, & Heninger, 2007).
- **Marital status.** Married individuals have lower suicide rates than divorced, widowed, or single persons, at least among men (Denney et al., 2009).

Phototherapy A treatment for SAD that involves exposure to bright, full-spectrum light.

Bipolar and related disorders Mood disorders characterized by alternating periods of mania and depression.

Manic episode Period of abnormally excessive energy and elation.

Cyclothymic disorder Moderate manic and depressive behavior that persists for two years or more.

Bipolar I disorder A mood disorder in which a person has episodes of mania (excited, hyperactive, energetic, or grandiose behavior) and also periods of deep depression.

Bipolar II disorder A mood disorder in which a person is mostly depressed (sad, despondent, guilt-ridden) but also has had one or more episodes of mild mania (hypomania).

Postpartum depression A mild to moderately severe depression that begins within three months following childbirth.

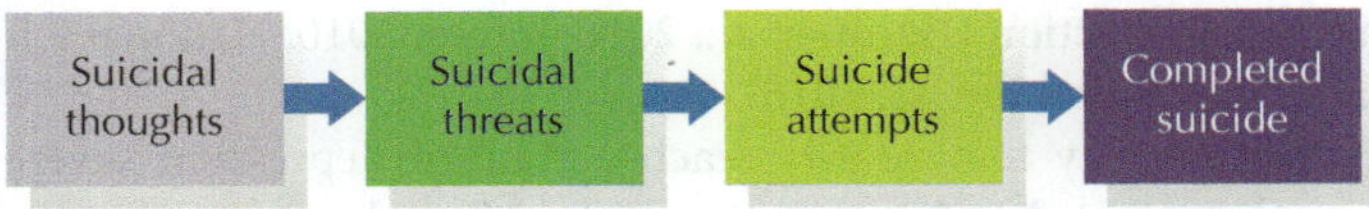

Figure 14.7 The slippery slope of suicide. Suicidal behavior usually progresses from suicidal thoughts, to threats, to attempts. A person is unlikely to make an attempt without first making threats. Thus, suicide threats should be taken seriously (Leenaars, Lester, & Wenckstern, 2005).

Suicide Threats

Is it true that people who talk about or threaten suicide are rarely the ones who try it? Actually, all suicide threats should be taken seriously. Eighty percent of potential suicides give warning beforehand (see Figure 14.7). Some warning signs, especially if they are observed in combination, are: direct threats to take one's own life, preoccupation with death, depression/hopelessness, rage/anger or seeking revenge, aggressive risk taking, alcohol/drug use, withdrawal from contact with others, no sense of purpose in life, sudden swings in mood, personality change, gift-giving of prized possessions, and recent occurrence of a life crisis or an emotional shock (Centers for Disease Control, 2015a; Leenaars, Lester, & Wenckstern, 2005).

How to Help

What should I do if someone hints that he or she is thinking about suicide? People who consider suicide often feel misunderstood. You should offer support, acceptance, and legitimate caring. Try to accept and understand the feelings the person is expressing. It is completely acceptable to ask, "Are you thinking of suicide?" Establishing communication with suicidal persons may be enough to carry them through a difficult time. You also may find it helpful to get day-by-day commitments from them to meet for lunch, share a ride, and the like. Such small commitments can be enough to tip the scales when a person is alone and thinking about suicide.

If a suicide attempt seems to be imminent, remember that most cities have mental health crisis intervention teams or centers for suicide prevention that allow suicidal persons to obtain support over the phone (Spencer-Thomas & Jahn, 2012). Give a person who seems to be suicidal the number of one of these services. Urge the person to call you or the other number if she or he becomes frightened or impulsive. Better yet, help the person make an appointment to get psychological treatment (Kleiman, Miller, & Riskind, 2012; Weishaar, 2006). If the person shares a specific, workable plan, and the means to carry it out, you should accompany that person to the emergency department of a hospital.

Needless to say, you should call for the police or a rescue unit immediately if a person is in the act of attempting suicide. The majority of suicide attempts come at temporary low points in a person's life and may never be repeated. Get involved—you may save a life!

Personality Disorders

Personality disorders are long-standing, inflexible ways of behaving that create a variety of problems. For example, people with a *paranoid personality disorder* are suspicious, hypersensitive, and wary of others. *Narcissistic persons* need constant admiration and are lost in fantasies of power, wealth, brilliance, beauty, or love. Celebrities appear more likely to be narcissistic than noncelebrities, perhaps because they receive so much attention (Young & Pinsky, 2006). The *dependent personality* suffers from extremely low self-confidence. Dependent persons allow others to run their lives, and they place everyone else's needs ahead of their own. People with a *histrionic personality disorder* constantly seek attention by dramatizing their emotions and actions. Individuals diagnosed with a condition called *borderline personality disorder* are very dramatic and impulsive, frequently binging on drugs, sex, or food. Violent mood swings make for turbulent relationships with other people.

Typically, patterns such as the ones just described begin during adolescence or even childhood. Thus, personality disorders are deeply rooted and usually span many years. The list of personality disorders is long (▲ Table 14.4), so let's focus on one that gets significant attention from the media and popular press: antisocial personality disorder.

Antisocial Personality Disorder

A person with an **antisocial personality disorder** displays unusual remorselessness, a lack of empathy, or disregard for social conventions. Simply put, he or she lacks a conscience. Such people are impulsive, selfish, dishonest, emotionally shallow, and manipulative (Visser et al., 2010). They are poorly socialized and seem to be incapable of feeling guilt, shame, fear, loyalty, or love (American Psychiatric Association, 2013). Antisocial persons are sometimes called *psychopaths,* although it may be more accurate to think of psychopathy as an extreme form of antisocial personality disorder (Riser & Kosson, 2013).

Are psychopaths dangerous? Psychopaths tend to have a long history of conflict with society. Many are delinquents or criminals

Many prison inmates have been diagnosed with antisocial personality disorder (Bateman & Fonagy, 2012).

▲ Table 14.4 DSM-5 Classification of Personality Disorders

Type of Personality Disorder	Typical Signs of Trouble
Paranoid	You deeply distrust others and are suspiciousness of their motives, which you perceive as insulting or threatening.
Schizoid	You feel very little emotion and can't form close personal relationships with others.
Schizotypal	You are a loner, you engage in extremely odd behavior, and your thought patterns are bizarre, but you are not actively psychotic.
Antisocial	You are irresponsible, lack guilt or remorse, and engage in antisocial behavior, such as aggression, deceit, or recklessness.
Borderline	Your self-image, moods, and impulses are erratic, and you are extremely sensitive to any hint of criticism, rejection, or abandonment by others.
Histrionic	You are dramatic and flamboyant; you exaggerate your emotions to get attention from others.
Narcissistic	You think that you are wonderful, brilliant, important, and worthy of constant admiration.
Avoidant	You are timid and uncomfortable in social situations and fear evaluation.
Dependent	You lack confidence, and you are extremely submissive and rely on others excessively (clinging).
Obsessive-compulsive	You demand order, perfection, control, and rigid routine at all times.

Sources: American Psychiatric Association, 2013; Sue et al., 2017.

who may be a threat to the general public (Bateman & Fonagy, 2012; Lobbestael, Cima, & Arntz, 2013). However, psychopaths are rarely the crazed murderers that you may have seen portrayed in the media. In fact, many psychopaths are charming at first. Their friends only gradually become aware of the psychopath's lying and self-serving manipulation. Many successful businesspersons, entertainers, politicians, and other seemingly normal people have psychopathic leanings, though they may not meet the threshold for a clinical diagnosis. Basically, antisocial persons, who are usually men, coldly use others and cheat their way through life (Alegria et al., 2013).

Causes of Antisocial Personality Disorder

Typically, people with antisocial personalities showed similar problems in childhood (then usually referred to as *conduct disorder*; Burt et al., 2007). Adult psychopaths also display subtle neurological problems (● Figure 14.8). For example, they have unusual brainwave patterns that suggest underarousal of the brain. This may explain why psychopaths tend to be thrill seekers. Quite likely, they are searching for stimulation strong enough to overcome their chronic underarousal and feelings of "boredom" (Hare, 2006; Pemment, 2013).

In a revealing study, psychopaths were shown extremely grisly and unpleasant photographs of mutilations. The photos were so upsetting that they visibly startled normal people. The psychopaths, however, showed no startle response to the photos (Levenston et al., 2000). Those with antisocial personalities might therefore be described as emotionally cold. They simply do not feel normal pangs of conscience, guilt, or anxiety, perhaps explaining their ability to calmly lie, cheat, steal, or take advantage of others (Blair et al., 2006).

Can psychopathy be treated? Antisocial personality disorders are rarely treated with success (Bateman & Fonagy, 2012). All too often, psychopaths manipulate therapy, just like any other situation. If it is to their advantage to act "cured," they will do so. However, they return to their former behavior patterns as soon as possible. On a more positive note, antisocial behavior does tend to decline somewhat after age 40, even without treatment (Black, 2015).

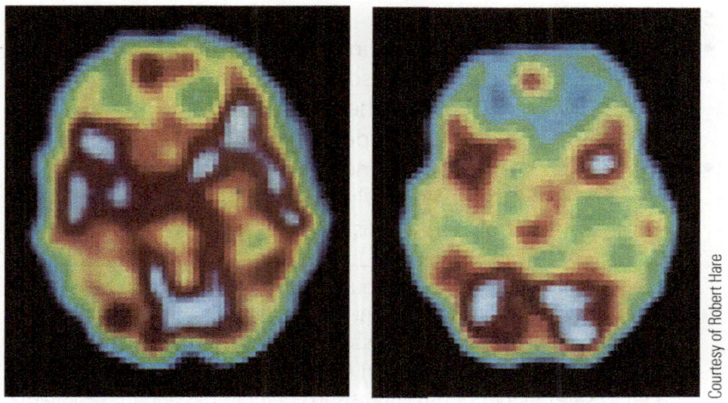

● **Figure 14.8 The psychopathic brain.** Using PET scans, Canadian psychologist Robert Hare found that the normally functioning brain (*left*) lights up with activity when a person sees emotion-laden words such as "maggot" or "cancer." But the brain of a psychopath (*right*) remains inactive, especially in areas associated with feelings and self-control. When Dr. Hare showed the right image to several neurologists, one asked, "Is this person from Mars?"

Personality disorders Long-standing, inflexible ways of behaving that create a variety of problems.

Antisocial personality disorder Unusual remorselessness, lack of empathy, or disregard for social conventions.

Reflective Practice

Mood and Personality Disorders

1. Dysthymic disorder is to depression as cyclothymic disorder is to bipolar disorder. T or F?
2. Learned helplessness is emphasized by ______________ theories of depression.
   a. humanistic c. behaviorist
   b. biological d. psychoanalytic
3. The drug lithium carbonate has been shown to be an effective treatment for personality disorders. T or F?
4. The *maternity blues* and *postpartum depression* are the same thing. T or F?
5. The risk that a person may attempt suicide is greatest if the person has
   a. a concrete, workable plan c. withdrawn from contact with others
   b. had a recent life crisis d. frustrated psychological needs
6. People with antisocial personality disorders react to highly unpleasant photographs with ______________ brain activity compared to normal people.
   a. more c. equal
   b. less d. different

THINK CRITICALLY

7. How might relationships contribute to the higher rates of depression experienced by women?

SELF-REFLECT

- Many of the qualities that define personality disorders exist to a minor degree in normal personalities. Try to think of a person you know who has some of the characteristics described for each type of personality disorder.
- You're working a suicide hotline, and you take a call from a very distressed young man. What risk factors will you look for as he tells you about his anguish?

Answers: 1. T 2. c 3. F 4. F 5. a 6. b 7. Women tend to be more focused on relationships than men are. When listing the stresses in their lives, depressed women consistently report higher rates of relationship problems, such as loss of a friend, spouse, or lover; problems getting along with others; and illnesses suffered by people they care about. Depressed men tend to mention issues such as job loss, legal problems, and work problems (Cambron, Acitelli, & Pettit, 2009).

14.4 Anxiety and Anxiety-Related Disorders

GATEWAYS LEARNING OUTCOMES:
After reading this section you should be able to:

14.4.1 Describe the general characteristics of anxiety disorders

14.4.2 Explain how psychological theories account for anxiety disorders

14.4.3 Name and briefly describe some important anxiety-related disorders

Imagine that you are waiting to take an extremely important test, to give a speech to a large audience, or to find out whether you or a loved one has a serious illness. You've almost certainly felt *anxiety*—feelings of apprehension, dread, or uneasiness—in similar situations.

But now consider a college student named Jian, who became unbearably anxious when he took exams. By the time Jian went to see a counselor, he had skipped several tests and was in danger of flunking out of school. In general, people with anxiety problems like Jian's display the following characteristics:

- High levels of anxiety, restrictive, self-defeating behavior patterns, or both
- A tendency to use elaborate defense mechanisms or avoidance responses to get through the day
- Pervasive feelings of stress, insecurity, inferiority, and dissatisfaction with life

That definitely doesn't seem "normal." So how do you know when normal worry becomes something that requires a diagnosis? That's a great question—let's take a closer look.

Anxiety Disorders

Anxiety becomes a problem when it is so intense that it prevents people from doing what they want or need to do. Usually their anxieties are out of control—they simply cannot stop worrying. People with anxiety disorders feel threatened and don't know what to do about it. They struggle to control themselves but remain ineffective and unhappy (Cisler et al., 2010; Sheppes, Suri, & Gross, 2015).

Some **anxiety disorders** involve feelings of *panic*. Others take the form of *phobias* (irrational fears) or just overwhelming anxiety and nervousness. In all anxiety disorders, though, distress seems greatly out of proportion to a person's circumstances. To deepen your understanding, let's directly examine three of the most common anxiety disorders: generalized anxiety disorder, panic disorder, and phobias (▲ Table 14.5).

Generalized Anxiety Disorder

A person with a **generalized anxiety disorder** experiences nearly constant exaggerated worries. He or she has been extremely anxious and worried for at least six months. Sufferers typically complain of sweating, a racing heart, clammy hands, dizziness, upset stomach, rapid breathing, irritability, and poor concentration. Overall, more women than men have these symptoms (Brown & Barlow, 2017).

Panic Disorder

In a **panic disorder**, people are highly anxious and also feel sudden, intense, unexpected panic. During a *panic attack*, victims experience chest pain, a racing heart, dizziness, choking, feelings of unreality, trembling, or fears of losing control. Many believe that they are having a heart attack, are going insane, or are about to die. Needless to say, this pattern leaves victims unhappy and uncomfortable much of the time. Again, the majority of people who suffer from panic disorder are women (Cannon et al., 2013).

▲ **Table 14.5 DSM-5 Classification of Anxiety Disorders**

Type of Disorder	Typical Signs of Trouble
Anxiety Disorders	
Generalized anxiety disorder	You have been extremely anxious or worried for six months.
Panic disorder	You are anxious much of the time and have sudden panic attacks. You are afraid that your attacks might occur in public places, so you rarely leave home.
Agoraphobia	You fear that something extremely embarrassing will happen if you leave home (but you don't have panic attacks).
Specific phobia	You have an intense fear of particular objects, activities, or locations.
Social anxiety disorder	You fear social situations in which people can watch, criticize, embarrass, or humiliate you.

Sources: American Psychiatric Association, 2013; Sue et al., 2017.

Phobias

According to the DSM-5, **phobias** are persistent, excessive, and unrealistic fears that are triggered by specific objects or situations. In this section, we'll focus on three of the most common phobias: agoraphobia, social anxiety disorder, and specific phobia.

Agoraphobia

Agoraphobia (ah-go-rah-FOBE-ee-ah) is an excessive, irrational fear of being in public places. It usually involves the *fear that something extremely threatening will happen in public*, such as a panic attack, dizziness, diarrhea, or shortness of breath. Going outside the home alone, being in a crowd, standing in line, crossing a bridge, or riding in a car can be impossible for an agoraphobic person. As a result, some agoraphobics are prisoners in their own homes (American Psychiatric Association, 2013).

Although they are considered to be separate disorders, agoraphobia and panic attacks can occur together in the same individual. About 4 percent of all adults suffer from agoraphobia (with or without panic) during their lifetime (Grant et al., 2006).

Social Anxiety Disorder

In **social anxiety disorder** (formerly *social phobia*), people fear situations in which they can be scrutinized, evaluated, or humiliated by others. This leads them to avoid certain social situations, such as eating, writing, using the restroom, or speaking in public. When such situations cannot be avoided, people endure them with intense anxiety or distress. It is common for them to have uncomfortable physical symptoms, such as a pounding heart, shaking hands, sweating, diarrhea, mental confusion, and blushing. Social anxiety disorder greatly impairs a person's ability to work, attend school, and form personal relationships (American Psychiatric Association, 2013). About 7 percent of all adults are affected by social phobias in a given year (National Institute of Mental Health, 2017).

Specific Phobia

In a **specific phobia**, the person's fear, anxiety, and avoidance are focused on specific objects, activities, or situations (Ipser, Singh, & Stein, 2013). Specific phobias can be linked to nearly any object or situation (Stinson et al., 2007). People affected by phobias recognize that their fears are unreasonable, but they cannot control them. For example, a person with a spider phobia would find it impossible to ignore a picture of a spider, even though a photograph can't bite anyone (Lipka, Miltner, & Straube, 2011). About 9 percent of all adults have a specific phobic disorder in any given year (National Institute of Mental Health, 2017).

The most common specific phobias among Americans are phobias of insects, birds, snakes, or other animals, including, of course, arachnophobia (fear of spiders) and zoophobia (fear of all animals). Other "popular" phobias, in descending order of prevalence, are acrophobia (fear of heights), astraphobia (fear of storms, thunder, lightning), aquaphobia (fear of being on or in water), aviophobia (fear of airplanes), and claustrophobia (fear of enclosed spaces).

By combining the appropriate root word with the word "phobia," any number of fears can be named. Some include triskaidekaphobia (fear of the number 13), xenophobia (fear of people or things that are foreign), and hematophobia (fear of blood). One of your authors' favorites is coulrophobia (fear of clowns).

Almost everyone has a few mild phobias, such as fear of heights, enclosed spaces, or bugs and crawly things. True phobias, however, may lead to overwhelming fear, vomiting, wild climbing and running, or fainting. For a phobic disorder to exist, the person's fear must disrupt his or her daily life. Phobic persons are so threatened that they will go to almost any length to avoid the feared object or situation, such as driving 50 miles out of the way to avoid crossing a bridge.

Theoretical Approaches to Anxiety Disorders

Anxiety disorders may be best explained by the stress-vulnerability model which, as we mentioned earlier, is in keeping with a biopsychosocial approach to understanding psychopathology.

Anxiety disorders Class of disorders marked by feelings of excessive apprehension and worry.

Generalized anxiety disorder Psychological disorder characterized by nearly constant, exaggerated worries.

Panic disorder Chronic state of anxiety, with brief moments of sudden, intense, unexpected panic.

Phobia Persistent, excessive, and unrealistic fear that is triggered by specific objects or people.

Agoraphobia The fear that something extremely embarrassing will happen if one leaves the house or enters an unfamiliar situation; excessive, irrational fear of being in public places.

Social anxiety disorder An intense, irrational fear of being observed, evaluated, embarrassed, or humiliated by others in social situations.

Specific phobia Persistent fear and avoidance of a specific object or situation.

Susceptibility to anxiety disorders appears to be partly inherited (Rachman, 2013). Studies show that being high-strung, nervous, or emotional runs in families. For example, 60 percent of children born to parents suffering from panic disorder have a fearful, inhibited temperament. Such children are irritable and wary as infants, shy and fearful as toddlers, and quiet and cautious introverts in elementary school. By the time they reach adulthood, they are at high risk for anxiety problems, such as panic attacks (Barlow, 2000; Barlow, Durand, & Hofmann, 2018).

There are at least four major psychological perspectives on the causes of anxiety disorders. These are (1) the *psychodynamic* approach, (2) the *humanistic-existential* approach, (3) the *behavioral* approach, and (4) the *cognitive* approach. We'll take a closer look at each of these in the sections that follow.

Psychodynamic Approach

The term psychodynamic refers to internal motives, conflicts, unconscious forces, and other dynamics of mental life. Freud was the first to propose a psychodynamic explanation for what he called "neurosis." According to Freud, disturbances like those we have described represent a raging *conflict among subparts of the personality*—the id, ego, and superego.

Freud emphasized that intense anxiety can be caused by forbidden id impulses for sex or aggression that threaten to break through into behavior. The person constantly fears doing something "crazy" or forbidden. She or he also may be tortured by guilt, which the superego uses to suppress forbidden impulses. Caught in the middle, the ego is eventually overwhelmed. This forces the person to use rigid defense mechanisms and misguided, inflexible behavior to prevent a disastrous loss of control.

Humanistic Approaches

Humanistic theories emphasize *subjective experience, human problems, and personal potentials.* Humanistic psychologist Carl Rogers regarded disorders of emotion, including anxiety disorders, as the result of a faulty self-image (Rogers, 1959). Rogers believed that anxious individuals have built up unrealistic mental images of themselves. This leaves them vulnerable to contradictory information. Let's say, for example, that an essential part of Cheyenne's self-image is that she is highly intelligent. If Cheyenne does poorly in school, she may begin to deny or distort her perceptions of herself and the situation. Should Cheyenne's anxiety become severe, she may resort to using defense mechanisms. Anxiety attacks, or similar symptoms, also may result from threats to her self-image. These symptoms, in turn, might become new threats that provoke further distortions. Soon, she could fall into a vicious cycle of maladjustment and anxiety that feeds on itself.

Behavioral Approach

Behaviorist approaches emphasize overt, observable behavior and the effects of *learning and conditioning.* Behaviorists assume that the "symptoms" of anxiety disorders are learned, just as other behaviors are learned. You might recall from ■ Section 6.2, for instance, that phobias can be acquired through classical conditioning. Similarly, panic attacks may reflect conditioned emotional responses that generalize to new situations. One point on which all theorists agree is that disordered behavior is ultimately self-defeating because it makes the person more miserable in the long run, even though it temporarily lowers anxiety.

But if the person becomes more miserable in the long run, how does the pattern get started? The behavioral explanation is that self-defeating behavior begins with operant conditioning (■ see Section 6.3). More specifically, this type of behavior begins when people realize that making a response (usually a response that allows them to avoid something unpleasant) delays or prevents the onset of a painful or unpleasant stimulus. Here's a quick example:

> An animal is placed in a special cage. After a few minutes a light comes on, followed a moment later by a painful shock. Quickly, the animal escapes into a second chamber. After a few minutes, a light comes on in this chamber, and the shock is repeated. Soon the animal learns to avoid pain by moving before the shock occurs. Once an animal learns to avoid the shock, it can be turned off altogether. A well-trained animal may avoid the nonexistent shock indefinitely if the light keeps turning on.

The same analysis can be applied to human behavior. A behaviorist would say that the powerful reward of immediate relief from anxiety is negatively reinforcing, and keeps self-defeating avoidance behaviors alive. This view, known as the **anxiety reduction hypothesis**, seems to explain why the behavior patterns that we have discussed often look very counterproductive to outside observers.

Cognitive Approach

The cognitive view is that *distorted thinking* causes people to magnify ordinary threats and failures, leading to anxiety and distress (Steinman et al., 2013). For example, Bonnie, who is socially phobic, constantly has upsetting thoughts about being evaluated at school. Like other social phobics, Bonnie is a perfectionist and is excessively concerned about making mistakes. She also perceives criticism when none exists. If Bonnie expects that a social situation will focus too much attention on her, she avoids it (Brown & Barlow, 2017). Even when socially phobic persons are successful, distorted thoughts lead them to believe they have failed. In short, changing the thinking patterns of anxious individuals like Bonnie can greatly lessen their fears (Arch et al., 2013).

Anxiety-Related Disorders

Let's now turn our attention to four disorders that are in some way related to anxiety, including obsessive-compulsive and related disorders, trauma- and stressor-related disorders, dissociative disorders, and somatic symptom and related disorders (▲ Table 14.6).

Obsessive-Compulsive and Related Disorders

While the DSM-5 now categorizes obsessive-compulsive and related disorders separately from the anxiety disorders, they do involve coping with anxiety. The **obsessive-compulsive and related disorders** involve extreme preoccupations with certain thoughts and compulsive performance of certain behaviors.

▲ Table 14.6 DSM-5 Classification of Anxiety-Related Disorders

Type of Disorder	Typical Signs of Trouble
Obsessive-Compulsive Disorders	
Obsessive-compulsive disorder	Your thoughts make you extremely nervous, and you rigidly repeat certain actions or routines.
Hoarding disorder	You collect things and have difficulty throwing or giving them away.
Trauma- and Stressor-Related Disorders	
Adjustment disorder	A normal life event has triggered troublesome anxiety, apathy, or depression.
Acute stress disorder	You are tormented for less than a month by the emotional aftereffects of horrible events that you have experienced.
Post-traumatic stress disorder	You are tormented for more than a month by the emotional aftereffects of horrible events that you have experienced.
Dissociative Disorders	
Dissociative amnesia	You can't remember your name, address, or past. In extreme (fugue) cases, you took a sudden, unplanned trip and are confused about who you are.
Dissociative identity disorder	You have two or more separate identities or personality states.
Somatic Symptom and Related Disorders	
Somatic symptom disorder	You are preoccupied with bodily functions and disease.
Factitious disorder (Munchausen syndrome)	You are deliberately faking medical problems to gain attention.
Conversion disorder	You are "converting" severe emotional conflicts into symptoms that closely resemble a physical disability.

Sources: American Psychiatric Association, 2013; Sue et al., 2017.

People who suffer from **obsessive-compulsive disorder (OCD)** are preoccupied daily with distressing, repetitive thoughts and urges to perform certain rituals. You have probably experienced a mild obsessional thought, such as a song or stupid commercial jingle that repeats over and over in your mind. This may be irritating, but it's usually not terribly disturbing. True obsessions are images or thoughts that force their way into awareness against a person's will. They are so disturbing that they cause intense anxiety. The main types of obsessions are (1) about being "dirty" or "unclean," (2) about whether one has performed some action (such as locking the door), (3) about putting things "in order," and (4) about taboo thoughts or actions (such as one's spouse being poisoned or committing immoral acts). A related disorder, **hoarding disorder**, is about excessively collecting various things (Rasmussen, Eisen, & Greenberg, 2013).

Roger Bamber/Alamy Stock Photo

Hoarders are obsessive about collecting things, which they also have great difficulty discarding (Hayward & Coles, 2009).

The traditional view of OCD (let's call it *OCD theory*) is that *obsessions* give rise to *compulsions*, irrational acts that a person feels driven to repeat. The idea is that compulsive acts help control or block out anxiety caused by an obsession. For example, a minister who finds profanities popping into her mind might start compulsively counting her heartbeat. Doing this would prevent her from thinking "dirty" words. Some compulsive people are *checkers* or *cleaners*. For instance, a young mother who repeatedly

Anxiety reduction hypothesis Explains the self-defeating nature of avoidance responses as a result of the reinforcing effects of relief from anxiety.

Obsessive-compulsive and related disorders Extreme preoccupations with certain thoughts and compulsive performance of certain behaviors.

Obsessive-compulsive disorder (OCD) An extreme preoccupation with certain thoughts and compulsive performance of certain behaviors.

Hoarding disorder Excessively collecting various things.

pictures a knife plunging into her baby might check once an hour to make sure that all the knives in her house are locked away.

Of course, not all obsessive-compulsive disorders are so dramatic. Many simply involve extreme orderliness and rigid routine. Compulsive attention to detail and rigid following of rules help keep activities totally under control and make the highly anxious person feel more secure (Challacombe, Oldfield, & Salkovskis, 2011).

Trauma- and Stressor-Related Disorders

If a situation causes distress, anxiety, or fear, we tend to "put it behind us" and avoid it in the future. This is a normal survival instinct. But what happens if we experience traumas or stresses outside our ability to cope? **Trauma- and stressor-related disorders** are behavior patterns that are associated with high levels of fear or anxiety brought on by experiencing traumatic stresses.

How is this different from an anxiety disorder? The outward symptoms are similar. However, people suffering from anxiety disorders seem to generate their own misery, regardless of what's happening around them. They feel that they must be on guard against *future threats* that could happen at any time (Butcher, Mineka, & Hooley, 2010). In contrast, trauma- and stressor-related disorders are caused by a person's *specific life circumstances* and symptoms may improve as life circumstances improve (Kramer et al., 2010).

Do stress and trauma problems cause a "nervous breakdown"? People suffering from trauma- and stressor-related disorders may be miserable, but they rarely experience a "breakdown." Actually, the term *nervous breakdown* has no formal meaning. Nevertheless, a problem known as an *adjustment disorder* does come close to what people mean when they talk about a breakdown.

An **adjustment disorder** occurs when ordinary stresses push people beyond their ability to cope with life. Examples of such stresses are a job loss, intense marital strife, and chronic physical illness. People suffering from an adjustment disorder may be extremely irritable, anxious, apathetic, or depressed. They also have trouble sleeping, lose their appetite, and suffer from various physical complaints. Often their problems can be relieved by rest, sedation, supportive counseling, and a chance to "talk through" their fears and anxieties (Ben-Itzhak et al., 2012).

More extreme reactions can occur when traumas or stresses fall outside the range of normal human experience, such as floods, tornadoes, earthquakes, or horrible accidents. They affect many political hostages; combat veterans; prisoners of war; victims of terrorism, torture, violent crime, child molestation, rape, or domestic violence; and people who have witnessed a death or serious injury (Hughes et al., 2011; Polusny et al., 2011).

Symptoms of more extreme stress disorders include repeated reliving of the traumatic event, avoidance of reminders of the event, and blunted emotions. Also common are insomnia, nightmares, wariness, poor concentration, irritability, and explosive anger or aggression. If such reactions last *less* than a month after a traumatic event, the problem is called an **acute stress disorder**. If they last *more* than a month, the person is suffering from **post-traumatic stress disorder (PTSD)** (Gupta, 2013; Sue et al., 2017).

Anton Oparin/Alamy Stock Photo

Natural disasters, like those that accompany the annual US tornado season, kill many people and upset the lives of many more. In the aftermath of such disasters, many survivors suffer from acute stress reactions. For some, the flare-up of anxiety and distress occurs months or years after the stressful event, an example of a post-traumatic stress reaction.

About 3.5 percent of American adults suffer from PTSD in any given year (National Institute of Mental Health, 2017). Sadly, up to 20 percent of military veterans returning from wars develop PTSD, including soldiers involved in combat in the Middle East (Rosen et al., 2012; Salisbury & Burker, 2011). The constant threat of death and the gruesome sights and sounds of war take a terrible toll.

Dissociative Disorders

A person with one of the **dissociative disorders** experiences a disintegration of consciousness, memory, or self-identity. He or she may have temporary amnesia or multiple personalities. Also included in this category are frightening episodes of depersonalization, in which people feel like they are outside their bodies, are behaving like robots, or are lost in a dream world. In *dissociative disorders*, we see striking episodes of *amnesia*, *fugue*, or *multiple identity*.

Dissociative amnesia is an inability to recall one's name, address, or past. In extreme cases, a person with dissociative amnesia may experience a **dissociative fugue** (pronounced "fewg"), which involves sudden, unplanned travel away from home and confusion about personal identity. In such cases, forgetting personal identity and fleeing unpleasant situations appear to be defenses against intolerable anxiety. A person suffering from a **dissociative identity disorder** has two or more separate identities or personality states. (Don't forget that identity disorders are not the same as schizophrenia. Schizophrenia, which is a psychotic disorder, was discussed previously.)

One famous and dramatic example of multiple identities is described in the book *Sybil* (Schreiber, 1973). Sybil reportedly had 16 different personality states. Each identity had a distinct voice, vocabulary, and posture. One personality could play the piano, but the others (including Sybil herself) could not.

When an identity other than Sybil was in control, Sybil experienced a "time lapse," or memory blackout. Sybil's amnesia and alternate identities first appeared during childhood. As a girl, she was beaten, locked in closets, perversely tortured, sexually abused, and almost killed. Sybil's first dissociations allowed her to escape by creating another person who would suffer torture in her place. Identity disorders often begin with unbearable childhood experiences, like those that Sybil endured. A history of childhood trauma, especially sexual abuse, is found in a high percentage of persons whose personalities split into multiple identities (McLewin & Muller, 2006).

Flamboyant cases such as Sybil's have led some experts to question the existence of multiple personalities (Boysen & VanBergen, 2013; Piper, 2008). However, a majority of psychologists continue to believe that multiple identity is a real, if rare, problem (Boysen, 2011; Dell, 2009).

Somatic Symptom and Related Disorders

Have you ever known someone who appeared healthy but seemed to constantly worry about disease? These people are preoccupied with bodily functions, such as their heartbeat, breathing, or digestion. Minor physical problems—even a small sore or an occasional cough—may convince them that they have cancer or some other dreaded disease. Typically, they can't give up their fears of illness, even if doctors find no medical basis for their complaints (Dimsdale, 2011). **Somatic symptom and related disorders** occur when a person has physical symptoms that mimic disease or injury (e.g., paralysis, blindness, illness, chronic pain) for which there is no identifiable physical cause. In such cases, psychological factors appear to explain the symptoms. Here, we'll take a look at three diagnoses that fall under this category: *somatic symptom disorder*, *factitious disorder*, and *conversion disorder*.

Somatic Symptom Disorder

People with **somatic symptom disorder** typically display some combination of the following: (1) interpreting normal bodily sensations as proof that they have a terrible disease (hypochondria), (2) expressing their anxieties through various bodily complaints, and (3) experiencing disabling pain that has no identifiable physical basis. Such individuals may suffer from problems such as vomiting or nausea, shortness of breath, difficulty swallowing, or painful menstrual periods. Typically, the person feels ill much of the time and visits doctors repeatedly. Most sufferers take medicines or other treatments, but no physical cause can be found for their distress. (■ Don't confuse somatic symptom disorders with psychosomatic illnesses, which occur when stress causes real physical damage to the body. See Section 13.2.)

Factitious Disorder

At 14, Ben was in the hospital again for his sinus problem. Since the age of 8, he had undergone 40 surgeries. In addition, he had been diagnosed at various times with bipolar disorder, oppositional defiant disorder, and ADHD. Ben was taking 19 different medications, and his mother said that she desperately wanted him to be "healed." She sought numerous tests and never missed an appointment. But at long last, it became clear that there was nothing wrong with Ben. Left alone with doctors, Ben revealed that he was "sick of being sick."

In reality, it was Ben's mother who was sick. She was eventually diagnosed as suffering from **factitious disorder** (Awadallah et al., 2005). Factitious disorder can be either *imposed on self* (in *Munchausen syndrome*) if the person fakes his or her own medical problems, or *imposed on another* (in *Munchausen by proxy syndrome*) if the person fakes the medical problems of someone in his or her care. As in Ben's case, most people with Munchausen by proxy syndrome are mothers who fabricate their children's illnesses (Day & Moseley, 2010; Ferrara et al., 2013). Sometimes they even deliberately harm their children to create a medical issue. For example, one mother injected her son with 7-Up (Reisner, 2006).

But why? People who suffer from factitious disorder appear to have a pathological need to seek attention and sympathy from medical professionals. They also may win praise for being health conscious or a good parent (Day & Moseley, 2010).

Conversion Disorder

In another rare disorder, **conversion disorder**, severe emotional conflicts are "converted" into symptoms that actually disturb physical functioning or closely resemble a physical disability. For instance, a soldier might become deaf or lame or develop "glove anesthesia" just before a battle.

Trauma- and stressor-related disorders Behavior patterns brought on by traumatic stresses.

Adjustment disorder Emotional disturbance caused by ongoing stressors within the range of common experience.

Acute stress disorder A psychological disturbance lasting up to one month following stresses that would produce anxiety in anyone who experienced them.

Post-traumatic stress disorder (PTSD) Pattern of unwanted memories, nightmares, and flashbacks following a traumatic event for more than a month.

Dissociative disorders Class of psychological disorders involving disintegration of consciousness, memory, or self-identity.

Dissociative amnesia Loss of memory (partial or complete) for important information related to personal identity.

Dissociative fugue Sudden travel away from home, plus confusion about one's personal identity.

Dissociative identity disorder Presence of two or more distinct personalities (multiple personality).

Somatic symptom and related disorders Physical symptoms that mimic disease or injury (e.g., paralysis, blindness, illness, or chronic pain) for which there is no identifiable physical cause.

Somatic symptom disorder Exhibiting the characteristics of a disease or injury without an identifiable physical cause.

Factitious disorder (Munchausen syndrome) To gain attention, an affected person fakes his or her medical problems or those of someone in his or her care.

Conversion disorder A bodily symptom that mimics a physical disability but is actually caused by anxiety or emotional distress.

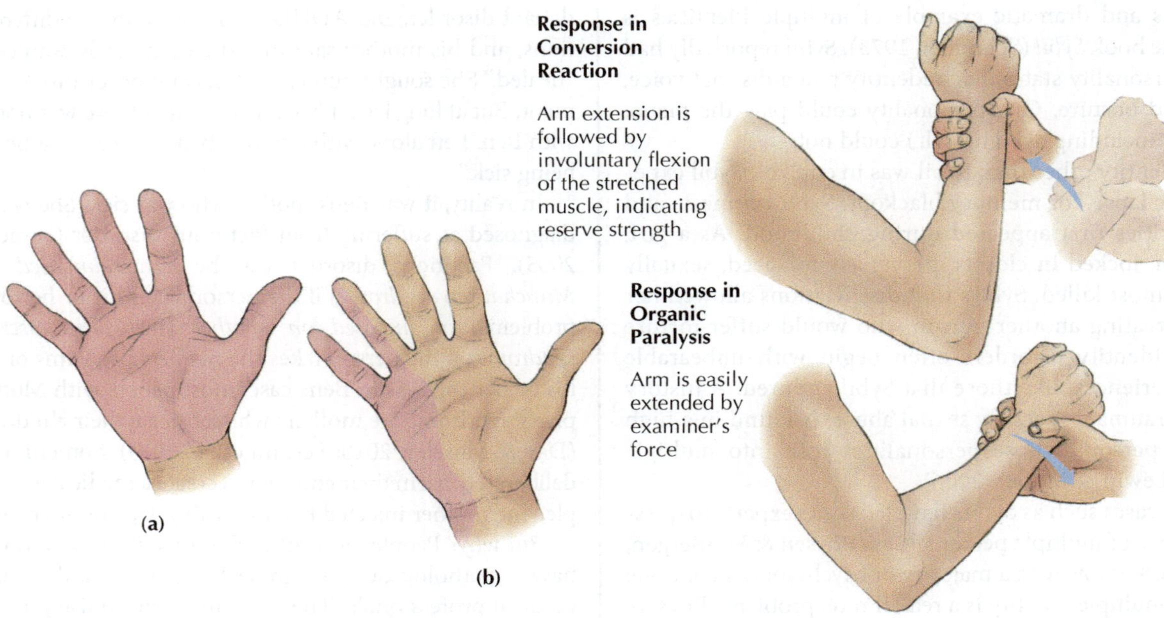

Figure 14.9 Glove anesthesia. (*Left*) "Glove anesthesia" is a conversion reaction involving loss of feeling in areas of the hand that would be covered by a glove (a). If the "anesthesia" were physically caused, it would follow the pattern shown in (b). (*Right*) To test for organic paralysis of the arm, an examiner can suddenly extend the arm, stretching the muscles. A conversion reaction is indicated if the arm pulls back involuntarily. (Adapted from Weintraub, 1983.)

Glove anesthesia? Glove anesthesia is a loss of sensitivity in the areas of the skin that would normally be covered by a glove. Glove anesthesia shows that conversion symptoms often contradict known medical facts. The system of nerves in the hands does not form a glovelike pattern and could not cause such symptoms (Figure 14.9).

If symptoms disappear when a victim is asleep, hypnotized, or anesthetized, a conversion reaction must be suspected (Russo et al., 1998). Another sign to note is that victims of conversion reactions are strangely unconcerned about suddenly being disabled.

A Look Ahead

Treatments for psychological problems range from counseling and psychotherapy to mental hospitalization and drug therapy. Because they vary greatly, a complete discussion of therapies is found in the next chapter. For now, it's worth noting that many milder mental disorders can be treated successfully. Even major disorders may respond well to drugs and other techniques. It is wrong to fear former psychiatric patients, or to exclude them from work, friendships, and other social situations. A struggle with major depression or a psychotic episode does not inevitably lead to lifelong dysfunction. Too often, however, it does lead to unnecessary rejection based on groundless fears (Elkington et al., 2012; Sarason & Sarason, 2005).

Let's conclude by noting that, like many other things in life, overcoming mental illness is challenging and requires a tremendous amount of determination. What can you do to improve your ability to persevere when things get difficult? Consider reading the upcoming *Psychology and Your Skill Set* section for some answers.

Reflective Practice

Anxiety and Anxiety-Related Disorders

1. Disabling anxiety over ordinary life stresses is characteristic of which of the following disorders?
   a. PTSD
   b. agoraphobia
   c. hypochondriasis
   d. adjustment disorder
2. Panic disorder can occur with or without agoraphobia, but agoraphobia cannot occur alone, without the presence of a panic disorder. T or F?
3. According to the ______________ view, anxiety disorders are the end result of a loss of meaning.
   a. psychodynamic
   b. humanistic
   c. behaviorist
   d. cognitive
4. The symptoms of acute stress disorders last less than one month; post-traumatic stress disorder (PTSD) lasts more than one month. T or F?
5. Amnesia, multiple identities, and depersonalization are ______________.
   a. mood disorders
   b. somatic symptom disorders
   c. psychoses
   d. dissociative disorders
6. Which of the following is *not* a dissociative disorder?
   a. fugue
   b. amnesia
   c. conversion disorder
   d. identity disorder

THINK CRITICALLY

7. In this section, we met Ben's mother, who was deliberately faking her son's "illnesses." How did she get away with it? Wouldn't doctors figure out that something was fishy with Ben long before he had 40 surgeries for a faked sinus disorder?

SELF-REFLECT

- Which of the anxiety disorders would you *least* want to suffer from? Why?
- Which of the psychological explanations of anxiety disorders do you find most convincing?

Answers: 1. d 2. F 3. b 4. T 5. d 6. c 7. No one doctor tolerates false symptoms for long. Once a doctor refuses further treatment, the factitious disorder sufferer moves on to another. Also, more than one doctor is often being seen.

14.5 Psychology and Your Skill Set: Perseverance

GATEWAYS LEARNING OUTCOME:
After reading this section you should be able to:

14.5.1 Create a plan to improve your "grit" and perseverance

At first, there may not seem to be much that's similar about these two photos. One shows a group of new cadets at West Point, the elite training academy for officers in the US military. The other is a photo of contestants in the Scripp's National Spelling Bee. Competitors move through eight stressful rounds, spelling words such as "pipsissewa," "sprachgefühl," and "myrmo therene" before a winner emerges.

If you look past the obvious differences in the pictures, though, you'll discover that there's an important similarity between these two groups: In both cases, successful individuals are very likely to possess a characteristic that psychologist Angela Duckworth refers to as "grit"—having the passion and perseverance to pursue a very long-term goal (Duckworth, Peterson, Matthews, & Kelly, 2007).

As we've seen throughout this chapter, overcoming mental health challenges is typically a long journey that requires a great deal of commitment, and perseverance is likely to be a key component of success. But there are many other aspects of our personal and professional lives that also require the ability to "stick to it" when the going gets tough. Surprisingly, Duckworth has found in multiple studies that grit is often a better predictor of success than intelligence (■ see Section 9.1), or the kind of natural ability that inspires awe whenever we watch someone who seems to be a "gifted" athlete, musician, artist, or mathematician. Even better, Duckworth argues that grit isn't a characteristic that's fixed; instead, she makes the case that it's a skill that anyone can work at. How gritty are you? And how can you develop true grit? Read on!

Measuring Grit

Grit can be measured with rating scales that are composed of statements like:

- New ideas and projects sometimes distract me from previous ones.
- Setbacks don't discourage me. I don't give up easily.

The above two statements are the first two items from Angela Duckworth's 10-item *Grit Scale*. (Go to http://angeladuckworth.com/grit-scale/ to complete the entire scale and have it automatically scored. Higher scores indicate higher levels of grit.)

My grit score wasn't very high. Can I get grittier? Given how important grit is in predicting success, it's good to know that it's a skill that anyone can work on. Psychological research suggests that "gritty" individuals possess four important characteristics: *interest*, *practice*, *purpose*, and *hope*. Working at them will help you to develop your passions and improve your performance over the long term, so let's take a closer look.

Interest

Individuals who score high on the grit scale have very well-developed interests that have evolved over a long period of time. This passion may start as a hobby, or as a pastime to which people just devote a

Drew Angerer/Getty Images News/Getty Images

Alex Wong/Getty Images News/Getty Images

few hours each week. Over time, though, as they become more knowledgeable and experienced, a real interest in this activity develops and this drives the desire to keep working at it.

But I haven't really developed a passion like that for anything . . . . According to Duckworth, for most young adults that's likely to be true, and it's nothing to worry about. In fact, she has taken issue with people who casually suggest that everyone should just "follow their passion." The trouble with framing it that way, she argues, is that it might lead you to believe that your passion exists out there in the world and that your job is to just go out, discover its location, and bring it home with you.

Clearly this isn't the way people develop strong interests. A better approach is to open yourself up to trying new things that have some appeal for you. You need to give yourself permission to explore things that are of interest, try them for a period of time and, if they don't really grab you, move on and try something else. The key thing is balance: While exploration is not a bad thing, it's important to keep in mind the human tendency toward novelty. Left to their own devices, people experience a strong pull toward the next fad, or the newest craze. To really improve your level of grit, there will be times when you'll need to think hard about leaving behind something in which you've developed some expertise. To improve the chances of persevering, one strategy is to "substitute nuance for novelty."

What this means is that instead of dropping an activity that you're getting good at to pursue the latest craze, you may want to ask yourself whether it might be better to work at improving your ability to perform smaller elements of that activity. For example, an artist who had developed some expertise in making stained glass might decide that he was going to work a little harder on one very specific element of his technique—perhaps his ability to solder the pieces of glass together with smooth seams—rather than just packing up and moving on to doing something completely different.

Practice

After developing a keen interest in something, the second stage of developing grit is *deliberate practice*. According to Anders Ericsson, deliberate practice is focused on gathering useful feedback to help you recognize your weaknesses and then using that information to improve specific aspects of your performance. Ericsson also wrote about the three F's: *focus, feedback*, and *fix it*. The first of these, focus, refers to the idea that practice will only be helpful if you're really concentrating on what you're doing. According to Ericsson, amateurs tend to daydream or think about more pleasant things when they're practicing—especially when that practice is physically strenuous or mentally challenging. But unless you're using the practice time to very consciously think about what you're doing (and how closely you're approximating your best work), you won't improve very much. It's far better to practice in a very focused way for a shorter period of time than to work longer while expending less effort.

The second F—feedback—emphasizes the importance of having an expert watch your performance and provide advice about what you can do to improve. These days it's not unusual for people to learn to do something by reading a book or watching videos on YouTube. In some cases, we may take classes with others in our efforts to get better at something. These things will all help, but none of them is a substitute for having someone who is very skilled focus specifically on you and explain what it is you need to do to move your performance to the next level.

Finally, Ericsson emphasized the importance of taking the feedback and fixing your weaknesses. In some cases, this will require you to try different methods until you find something that will help you to address those things that need improvement.

Truthfully, deliberate practice is really, really challenging. It involves putting a lot of time and energy into improving your technique, and even people with a great deal of passion and interest will tell you that it's incredibly effortful. Duckworth once asked US Olympic gold-medal swimmer Rowdy Gaines whether he loved to practice, and his answer will sound familiar to anyone who has committed themselves to improving on a skill they care about: "Are you asking me if I love getting up at four in the morning, jumping into a cold pool, and swimming laps looking at a black line on the bottom, at the very edge of my physical ability where my lungs are screaming for oxygen and my arms feel like they're about to fall off? No, I don't, but I love the whole thing. You know, I have a passion for the whole sport."

Purpose and Hope

The final two aspects of grit, purpose and hope, draw on the idea that truly committing to something that's of interest to you—and all of the deliberate practice that's required to improve—is much easier when you see a greater purpose in your actions, and when you possess a sufficient level of hope to carry you through setbacks. When Duckworth talks about feeling a sense of purpose, she's referring to a strong sense that what you're doing matters to others, as well as yourself. Someone committed to playing the piano may feel that their music will bring pleasure to others who listen, while gritty hockey players might believe that their efforts on the ice matter to both their teammates and the people who come to watch the games. And while hope is the last of Duckworth's four characteristics of grit, she emphasizes that it's the one that's necessary throughout the process of developing your passions. Without it, she argues, people would simply give up on their efforts at improvement whenever they encountered an obstacle or felt that they weren't getting better.

The moral of the story? Continue looking for the things that inspire you to work hard and feel satisfied. And when you feel frustrated and want to give up, think about what basketball great Michael Jordan had to say about "true grit": *I have failed over and over and over again in my life. And that is why I succeed.*

Reflective Practice

Psychology and Your Skill Set: Perseverance

1. Grit has been shown to be a better predictor of success than other things, including intelligence and "natural ability." T or F?
2. It's better to practice for longer periods of time—even if you aren't fully focused on the task—than it is to practice for shorter periods while concentrating carefully. T or F?
3. Which of the following is *not* a characteristic of "gritty" individuals?
   a. interest
   b. unbiased thinking
   c. practice
   d. hope
4. People who love what they're doing will always enjoy deliberate practice. T or F?
5. What are the three F's of deliberate practice?
   a. focus, feedback, fervor
   b. feedback, faith, focus
   c. faith, focus, fix it
   d. focus, feedback, fix it

THINK CRITICALLY

6. These days there are lots of different ways that you can learn to do something. What are the limitations of classes and online video training when you're trying to develop expertise in a particular skill?

SELF-REFLECT

- What activities have you tried out of genuine interest? Have you persevered with any of them, engaging in the kind of deliberate practice that Ericsson discusses? If you haven't yet discovered a passion for something, can you think of anything that you'd like to try?

Answers: 1. T 2. F 3. b 4. F 5. d 6. These learning techniques can be very helpful when you're first beginning to learn a skill; however, as you get better you will eventually need to seek out individualized feedback from a true expert who will be able to provide very specific, detailed information about your technique, and how you might improve.

CHAPTER IN REVIEW

Gateways to Psychological Disorders

Summary: Gateways Learning Outcomes

14.1 Psychopathology: Classification and Causes

14.1.1 Describe four things to consider when deciding whether behavior is abnormal

When deciding whether behavior is abnormal, we can consider statistical abnormality, nonconformity, subjective discomfort, and the extent to which the behavior may be considered maladaptive

14.1.2 Explain how psychological disorders are classified and diagnosed

Psychological problems are classified by using the *Diagnostic and Statistical Manual of Mental Disorders (5th Edition) (DSM-5)*, and it is possible for people to be comorbid (i.e., exhibiting symptoms that fit more than one disorder). The DSM is updated regularly, and categories can be added, deleted, or changed based on an evolving understanding of disorders and changes in social norms.

Mental illness is typically diagnosed by confirming the presence and/or absence of a number of symptoms. Symptoms can be divided into those that are positive (i.e., exaggeration compared to normal behavior) and those that are negative (i.e., deficit compared to normal behavior).

14.1.3 Describe the causes of mental disorders and the importance of the stress-vulnerability model

Mental disorders may be due to genetic factors, known injuries, or diseases of the brain. Psychosocial factors that contribute to psychopathology include psychological factors, family factors, and social conditions. A promising explanation for many mental illnesses is the stress-vulnerability model, which emphasizes a combination of inherited susceptibility and environmental or social stress.

14.2 Psychotic Disorders

14.2.1 Describe the general characteristics of psychotic disorders

Psychosis is a break in contact with reality that is marked by delusions, hallucinations, sensory changes, disturbed emotions, disturbed communication, and personality disintegration.

14.2.2 Outline the specific characteristics of delusional disorders

Delusional disorders are almost totally based on the presence of deeply held false beliefs of grandeur, persecution, infidelity, romantic attraction, or physical disease. Paranoid psychosis is the most common delusional disorder. Paranoid persons may be violent if they believe that they are threatened.

14.2.3 Outline the specific characteristics of schizophrenia

Schizophrenia spectrum disorder involves varying degrees of abnormal cognition (delusions, paranoia), perceptions (hallucinations), abnormal mood (flat or inappropriate affect), abnormal behavior (inability to cope, catatonia), and a disintegrated personality.

14.2.4 Describe the causes of schizophrenia

Environmental factors that increase the risk for schizophrenia include viral infection or malnutrition during the mother's pregnancy and birth complications. Psychosocial factors include early psychological trauma and a disturbed family environment. Heredity is a major factor in schizophrenia. Recent biochemical studies have focused on the neurotransmitters glutamate and dopamine and their receptor sites. The stress-vulnerability model currently offers the best general explanation for schizophrenia.

14.3 Mood and Personality Disorders

14.3.1 Describe the general characteristics of mood disorders

Mood disorders primarily involve disturbances of mood or emotion, producing manic or depressive states. Severe mood disorders may include psychotic features.

14.3.2 Outline the specific characteristics of depression and bipolar disorders

In a persistent depressive disorder (dysthymia), depression is long-lasting but moderate. In contrast, major depressive disorder involves extreme sadness and despondency. One specific type of depression, seasonal affective disorder (SAD), occurs during the winter months, and is typically treated with phototherapy. Bipolar disorders combine mania and depression. In a cyclothymic disorder, people suffer from long-lasting, though moderate, swings between depression and elation. In a bipolar I disorder, the person fluctuates between severe mania and severe depression. In a bipolar II disorder, the person is mostly depressed but has had periods of mild mania.

14.3.3 Describe the causes of mood disorders, including their risk factors

Mood disorders are partially explained by genetic vulnerability and changes in brain chemistry. Mood disorders also are partially explained by psychological factors such as loss, anger, learned helplessness, stress, and self-defeating thinking patterns. Gender is one important risk factor. Women are more likely than men to become depressed owing to hormonal fluctuations and stressful social and environmental conditions (including childbirth, which can lead to postpartum depression).

14.3.4 Outline some of the factors that lead people to commit suicide

In individual cases, the potential for suicide is best identified by a desire to escape, unbearable psychological pain, and frustrated psychological needs. Suicide is statistically related to such factors as sex, ethnicity, age, and marital status.

14.3.5 Describe the general characteristics of personality disorder, and the specific features of antisocial personality disorder

Personality disorders are persistent, maladaptive personality patterns. Antisocial personalities seem to lack a conscience. They are emotionally unresponsive, manipulative, shallow, and dishonest. Psychopathy may be an extreme form of antisocial personality disorder.

14.4 Anxiety and Anxiety-Related Disorders

14.4.1 Describe the general characteristics of anxiety disorders

Anxiety disorders are characterized by high levels of anxiety, rigid defense mechanisms, and self-defeating behavior patterns. Anxiety disorders include generalized anxiety disorder, panic disorder, and a variety of phobias.

14.4.2 Explain how psychological theories account for anxiety disorders

The psychodynamic approach emphasizes unconscious conflicts as the cause of disabling anxiety. The humanistic approach emphasizes the effects of a faulty self-image. The behaviorists emphasize the effects of previous learning, particularly avoidance learning. Cognitive theories of anxiety focus on distorted thinking and being fearful of others' attention and judgments.

14.4.3 Name and briefly describe some important anxiety-related disorders

The obsessive-compulsive and related disorders include obsessive-compulsive disorder and hoarding disorder. Trauma- and stressor-related disorders include adjustment disorder, acute stress disorder, and post-traumatic stress disorder. Dissociative disorders may take the form of amnesia, fugue, or multiple identities. Somatic symptom and related disorders center on physical complaints that mimic disease or disability. Three examples are somatic symptom disorder, factitious disorder (Munchausen syndrome and Munchausen by proxy), and conversion disorder.

14.5 Psychology and Your Skill Set: Perseverance

14.5.1 Create a plan to improve your "grit" and perseverance

In psychology, "grit" refers to having the passion and perseverance to pursue a long-term goal, and is associated with four characteristics: interest, (deliberate) practice, purpose, and hope. Improving your level of grit requires that people engage in deliberate practice when you are pursuing a goal. Deliberate practice involves staying focused during training, seeking feedback from experts, and then working to correct problems that have been identified. Fostering a sense of hope will allow you to overcome the obstacles that inevitably occur when we are working toward important goals. We hope that after reading this section, you'll be better able to think about how you can use these strategies to help enhance your "grittiness"!

15 Therapies

Photo 12/Alamy Stock Photo

Gateway Theme Psychotherapies are based on a common core of therapeutic principles. Medical therapies treat the physical causes of psychological disorders. In many cases, these approaches are complementary.

Chapter Outline

Just Say Shhhhhh....

Consider this list: Lizzo, Angelina Jolie, Owen Wilson, Adele, Daniel Radcliffe, Eminem, Ariana Grande, Robert Downey Jr., and Ellen DeGeneres. What do all these people have in common? If you said that it's a list of famous people who have been praised for their acting and music, you'd only be partly correct. It's also a list of A-list celebrities who have talked openly about their struggles with mental health issues, including depression, anxiety, eating disorders, post-traumatic stress disorder, and addictions. Many of them have also been upfront about the treatments that have helped them to deal with those difficult issues. Some, like singer Ellie Goulding, have opted for medication. Others, like Ke$ha, have sought counseling. And even Captain America—actor Chris Evans—has reported that he uses a form of *thought stopping*, silently saying "Shhhh" to himself when things get overwhelming.

This chapter discusses the methods used to alleviate a variety of mental health concerns. We will begin with a look at the origins and varieties of modern therapy before going on to discuss *behavioral therapies*, which directly change troublesome actions. After that, we will describe *cognitive* and *humanistic psychotherapies* that emphasize the value of viewing personal problems with insight and changing thought patterns. Finally, we will explore *medical therapies*, which are based on psychiatric drugs and other physical treatments. In our *Psychology and Your Skill Set* section, we look at how you can address mental health issues in everyday life, offering suggestions that may be helpful either for yourself or for those that you care about.

15.1 The Origins and Effectiveness of Psychotherapy

GATEWAYS LEARNING OUTCOMES:
After reading this section you should be able to:

15.1.1 Briefly describe how mental health problems were treated before the 1900s

15.1.2 Describe the main elements of psychoanalysis

15.1.3 Outline five characteristics that distinguish different psychotherapies

15.1.4 Name four features of effective psychotherapy

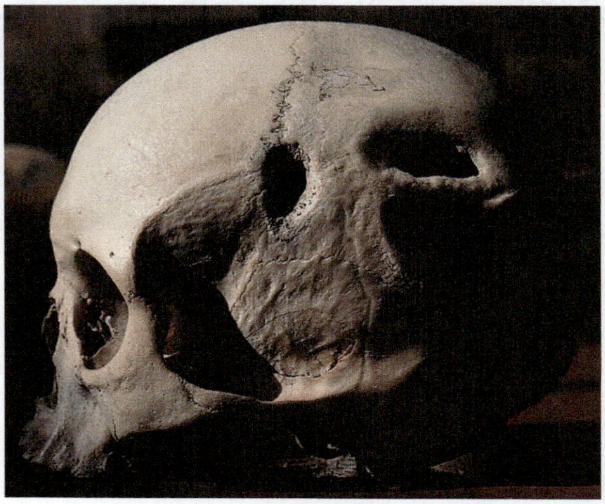

Primitive "treatment" for mental disorders sometimes took the form of boring a hole in the skull. This example shows signs of healing, which means the patient actually survived the treatment. Many didn't.

Estimates suggest that approximately 50 percent of Americans will be diagnosed with a mental health problem at some point during their lifetime (Centers for Disease Control and Prevention, 2020). If this happened to you, what help would be available? In most cases, it would be some form of **psychotherapy**, which is defined as any psychological technique that can bring about positive changes in personality, behavior, or personal adjustment. It might also include some type of medical therapy. Let's begin this chapter with a brief history of mental health care, including a discussion of psychoanalysis, the first fully developed psychotherapy. We'll then move on to talk about the important aspects of therapy, how it can be delivered, and how psychological scientists evaluate its effectiveness.

A Brief History of Psychotherapy

Early treatments for mental illness give good reasons to appreciate modern therapies (Sharf, 2016). Archeological findings dating to the Stone Age suggest that most premodern approaches were marked by fear and superstitious belief in spirits, demons, witchcraft, and magic (McNamara, 2011). If someone had been unlucky enough to be born with a mental health issue several thousand years ago, his treatment might have left him feeling "bored": One of the more dramatic "cures" practiced by primitive "therapists" was a process called *trepanning* (treh-PAN-ing), also sometimes spelled *trephining* (Terry, 2006). In modern usage, trepanning is any surgical procedure in which a hole is bored in the skull. In the hands of primitive therapists, it meant boring, chipping, or bashing holes in the skull. Presumably, this was done to relieve pressure or release the spirits that were possessing the patient.

People were not much better off during the Middle Ages. Then, treatments for mental illness in Europe focused on *demonology*, the study of demons and persons plagued by them. Medieval "therapists" commonly blamed abnormal behavior on supernatural forces, such as possession by the devil, or on curses from witches and wizards. As a cure, they used exorcism to "cast out evil spirits." For the fortunate, exorcism was a religious ritual. More often, physical torture was used to make the body an inhospitable place for the devil to reside.

Modern analyses of "demonic possession" suggest that many victims may have been suffering from epilepsy, schizophrenia, dissociative disorders, Tourette's syndrome, and depression (McNamara, 2011; Mirsky & Duncan, 2005; Thase, 2006; van der Hart, Lierens, & Goodwin, 1996). Thus, many people who were "treated" by demonologists may have been doubly victimized.

An important turning point occurred in 1793 when a French doctor named Philippe Pinel changed the Bicêtre Asylum in Paris from a squalid "madhouse" into a psychiatric hospital by unchaining the inmates (Schuster, Hoertel, & Limosin, 2011). Finally, the emotionally disturbed were regarded as "mentally ill" and given more compassionate treatment.

Though Pinel's views of mental illness represented a radical departure from earlier times, the first true psychotherapy did not come about until much later. In fact, it was Sigmund Freud who first developed a form of psychotherapy in the early 1900s (Borch-Jacobsen & Shamdasani, 2011). As a physician in Vienna, Freud was intrigued by cases of *hysteria*. People suffering from hysteria have physical symptoms (such as paralysis or numbness) for which no physical causes can be found. (■ Such problems are now called somatic symptom disorders, as discussed in Section 14.4.) Freud slowly became convinced that hysteria was related to deeply hidden unconscious conflicts and developed *psychoanalysis*, his "talking cure," to help patients gain insight into those conflicts (Strenger, 2016).

Psychoanalysis

Isn't psychoanalysis the therapy where the patient lies on a couch? Freud's patients usually reclined on a couch during therapy, while Freud sat out of sight taking notes and offering interpretations. This procedure was supposed to encourage a free flow of thoughts

Science Source

Bettmann/Getty Images

(*Left*) Many early asylums were no more than prisons, with inmates held in chains. (*Right*) One late-19th-century "treatment" was based on swinging the patient in a harness—presumably to calm the patient's nerves.

and images from the unconscious. However, the couch was the least important element of psychoanalysis, and many modern analysts have abandoned it.

So what are the most important aspects of psychoanalysis? Freud's theory stressed that neurosis and hysteria were caused by repressed memories, motives, and conflicts—particularly those stemming from instinctual drives for sex and aggression. Although they are hidden, these forces remain active in the personality and cause some people to develop rigid ego defenses and compulsive, self-defeating behavior. Thus, the main goal of **psychoanalysis** is to reduce internal conflicts that lead to emotional suffering (Aron & Starr, 2013).

Freud developed four basic therapeutic techniques to uncover the unconscious roots of neurosis (Freud, 1949): *free association*, *dream analysis*, *analysis of resistance*, and *analysis of transference*.

Prisma Bildagentur AG/Alamy Stock Photo

Freud's original couch is now at the Freud Museum in London, England. Lying down during therapy is not currently considered to be an essential component of psychotherapy.

Free Association

The basis for **free association** is saying whatever comes to mind without worrying whether ideas are painful, embarrassing, or illogical. Thoughts are simply allowed to move freely from one idea to the next, without self-censorship. The purpose of free association is to lower defenses so that unconscious thoughts and feelings can emerge (Lavin, 2012; Spence et al., 2009).

Dream Analysis

Freud believed that dreams disguise consciously unacceptable feelings and forbidden desires (Fischer & Kächele, 2009; Klösch & Holzinger, 2014). The psychoanalyst can use this "royal road to the unconscious" to help the patient work past the obvious, visible meaning of the dream (its *manifest content*) to uncover the hidden, symbolic meaning (its *latent content*). This is achieved by analyzing *dream symbols* (images that have personal or emotional meanings).

For example, suppose that a young man dreams of pulling a pistol from his waistband and aiming at a target as his wife watches. The pistol repeatedly fails to discharge, and the man's wife laughs at him. Freud might have seen this as an indication of repressed feelings of sexual impotence, with the gun serving as a disguised image of the penis. (■ See Section 5.3 for more information about understanding dreams.)

Analysis of Resistance

A central concern of psychoanalysis is the fact that patients who come to analysis for help nevertheless often *resist* changing when it is necessary to become healthier (Levenson, 2012). For example, when free associating or describing dreams, patients may resist talking about or thinking about certain topics. Such **resistances**—blockages in the flow of insights and ideas—reveal particularly important unconscious conflicts. As analysts become aware of resistances, they bring them to the patient's awareness so the patient can deal with them realistically. Rather than being roadblocks in therapy, resistances can be clues and challenges (Plakun, 2012).

Analysis of Transference

Transference is the tendency to "transfer" feelings to a therapist similar to those that the patient had for important persons in his or her past. At times, for example, the patient may act as if the

Psychotherapy Any psychological technique used to facilitate positive changes in a person's personality, behavior, or adjustment.

Psychoanalysis Freudian approach to psychotherapy emphasizing exploration of the unconscious using free association, dream interpretation, resistances, and transference to uncover unconscious conflicts.

Free association The psychoanalytic technique of encouraging a patient to say whatever comes to mind without censoring.

Resistance Blockage in the flow of free association around topics the client avoids thinking or talking about.

Transference The tendency of patients to transfer to a therapist feelings that correspond to those the patient had for important persons in his or her past.

analyst is a rejecting father, an unloving or overprotective mother, or a former lover. As the patient reexperiences repressed emotions, the therapist can help the patient recognize and understand them. Troubled persons often provoke anger, rejection, boredom, criticism, and other negative reactions from others. Effective therapists learn to avoid reacting like others and playing the patient's habitual resistance and transference games. This, too, contributes to therapeutic change (Aron & Starr, 2013).

Current Views About Psychotherapy

Psychoanalysis made a major contribution to modern therapies by highlighting the importance of unconscious conflicts (Borch-Jacobsen & Shamdasani, 2011). Since the development of psychoanalysis, however, psychotherapy has undergone dramatic changes that began with Freud's own followers, the neo-Freudians (■ see Section 12.1). Today, traditional psychoanalysts are relatively hard to find (Cortina, 2016), but a wide variety of other psychotherapeutic options are now available; we will discuss a number of them later in this chapter.

Four Characteristics That Distinguish Psychotherapies

Psychotherapy began as a form of one-on-one dialogue between therapists and their clients that was meant to yield insight. Today, therapists have many approaches from which to choose and, as we will see, each therapy emphasizes different concepts and methods. For this reason, the best approach for a particular person or problem may vary. The terms in the list that follows describe some basic characteristics that distinguish the different types of psychotherapies that we discuss in this chapter (Corsini & Wedding, 2014; Prochaska & Norcross, 2014; Sharf, 2016):

- **Insight versus action therapy:** Does the therapy aim to bring clients to a deeper understanding of their thoughts, emotions, and behavior? Or is it designed to bring about direct changes in troublesome thoughts, habits, feelings, or behavior without seeking insight into their origins or meanings?
- **Nondirective versus directive therapy:** Does the therapist provide strong guidance and advice? Or does the therapist assist clients, who are responsible for solving their own problems?
- **Individual versus group therapy:** Does the therapy involve one therapist with one client? Or can several clients participate at the same time?
- **Face-to-face versus distance therapy:** Will the therapist and client meet face-to-face, or will they communicate over the telephone or the Internet?

Notice that more than one characteristic can apply to a particular therapy. For example, it is possible to have an action, directive, open-ended group therapy meeting via the Internet or an insight, nondirective, individual, time-limited therapy meeting face-to-face. In the sections that follow, we explore these four characteristics of therapies in a bit more detail.

Insight Versus Action Therapy

Freud's initial intent in developing psychoanalysis was to provide patients with an **insight therapy** that could resolve psychological problems by gaining a conscious understanding of previously unconscious psychodynamic conflicts. For example, a psychoanalyst might use free association and dream analysis to enable a client named Stanley to realize that his anxieties originate, say, in an unconscious fear of dying. Perhaps Stanley was approaching the age at which his namesake uncle Stanley died prematurely of a heart attack 22 years ago. Psychoanalysts expect this insight will "discharge" Stanley's unconscious pressures and alleviate his general sense of anxiety. Today, humanistic therapies are also focused on helping clients achieve insight.

In contrast, **action therapies** generally focus on directly changing troubling thoughts and behaviors. We will shortly explore some extreme action therapies, which are referred to as behavioral therapies. A behavioral therapist would spend little time on *why* Stanley felt anxious; rather she might help Stanley learn some relaxation techniques to directly relieve his anxieties whenever they get too strong.

Directive Versus Nondirective Therapy

Psychoanalysis is a **directive therapy**, in which the therapist leads the patient through the therapeutic process. Based on his analysis of Stanley's free associations and dreams, his psychoanalyst might *direct* Stanley's awareness toward his unconscious fear of dying. Without this direction, Stanley might resist gaining the insight needed to overcome his anxiety.

In a **nondirective therapy** the role of the therapist is to create the conditions under which the client can resolve his or her psychological issues. For example, using a humanist technique called client-centered therapy (which we will explore later in this chapter), it would be assumed that Stanley must articulate his own problems and actively seek to resolve them himself. His nondirective therapist's role is to support him in his growing understanding, not to tell Stanley what is "wrong" with him or how to "fix it."

Individual Versus Group Therapy

Many psychotherapies can be adapted for use in groups (Corey, 2016). Surprisingly, **group therapy**—psychotherapy done with several unrelated clients—has turned out to be just as cost-effective as individual therapy and even has some special advantages (Burlingame, Fuhriman, & Mosier, 2003; Wroe & Wise, 2012).

What are the advantages of group therapy? In group therapy, a person can act out or directly experience problems. Doing so often produces insights that might not occur from merely talking about an issue. In addition, other group members with similar problems can offer support and useful input. Group therapy is especially good for helping people understand their personal relationships (Corey, 2016; McCluskey, 2002). For reasons such as these, several specialized groups have emerged, including Alcoholics Anonymous (AA) and Marriage Encounter. Here, we share two approaches that can be used in group therapy: psychodrama and family and couples therapy.

A group therapy session. Group members offer mutual support while sharing problems and insights.

Psychodrama

One of the first group therapies was developed by Jacob Moreno (1953), who called his technique *psychodrama*. In **psychodrama**, clients act out personal conflicts with others who play supporting roles (McVea, Gow, & Lowe, 2011; Schermer, 2015). Through role-playing, the client reenacts incidents that cause problems in real life. For example, Don, a disturbed teenager, might act out a typical family fight, with the therapist playing his father and with other clients playing his mother, brothers, and sisters. Moreno believed that insights gained in this way transfer to real-life situations.

Therapists using psychodrama often find that role reversals are helpful. A **role reversal** involves taking the part of another person to learn how he or she feels. For instance, Don might role-play his father or mother to better understand *their* feelings. A related method is the **mirror technique**, in which a client observes another person reenact his or her behavior. Thus, Don might briefly join the group and watch as another group member plays his role. This would allow him to see himself as others see him. Later, the group may summarize what happened and reflect on its meaning.

Family and Couples Therapy

Family relationships are the source of great pleasure and, all too often, great pain. In **family therapy**, a group of related individuals focuses on improving interpersonal dynamics and communication to resolve the problems of each family member. This is called *couples therapy* when children are not involved (Scheinkman, 2008). Family and couples therapy tends to be time-limited and focused on specific problems, such as frequent fights or a depressed teenager. For some types of problems, family therapy may be superior to other approaches (Eisler et al., 2007; Wiebe & Johnson, 2016).

Family therapists believe that a problem experienced by one family member is the whole family's problem (Teyber & McClure, 2011). If the entire pattern of behavior in a family doesn't change, improvements in any individual family member may not last. Family members, therefore, work together to improve communication, change destructive patterns, and see themselves and each other in new ways (Goldenberg & Goldenberg, 2013; Griffin, 2002).

Does the therapist work with the whole family at once? Family therapists treat the family as a unit, but they may not meet with the entire family at each session (Eisler et al., 2007). If a family crisis is at hand, the therapist may first try to identify the most resourceful family members who can help solve the immediate problem.

Face-to-Face Versus Distance Therapy

While it is generally preferable to meet with a therapist face to face, it is not always possible. Today, psychological services are available in the home through radio, television, telephone, and the Internet (Silverman, 2013). Indeed, during the COVID-19 pandemic, psychologists often used distance therapy to "meet" with their clients. Not only is this approach generally less expensive, it also makes therapy available to people who, for a variety of reasons, cannot easily attend a traditional face-to-face session. Let's look at two ways of delivering distance therapy: mass media and using the telephone or Internet.

Mass Media Therapists

By now, you have probably heard a phone-in radio psychologist or watched one on television. Participants typically describe problems ranging from child abuse to phobias and sexual adjustment to depression. The media psychologist then offers reassurance, advice, or suggestions for getting help. Such programs may seem harmless, but they raise some important questions. For instance,

Insight therapy Any therapy that stresses the importance of understanding the origins of a psychological disorder, usually unresolved unconscious conflicts.

Action therapy Any therapy that stresses directly changing troublesome thoughts and/or behaviors without regard for their origins, unconscious or otherwise.

Directive therapy Any therapy that stresses the need for the therapist to lead the patient toward a resolution of his or her psychological distress.

Nondirective therapy Any therapy in which the therapist supports the client while the client gains insight into his or her own problems and their resolution.

Group therapy Psychological treatment involving several unrelated clients.

Psychodrama A therapy in which clients act out personal conflicts and feelings in the presence of others who play supporting roles.

Role reversal Taking the role of another person to learn how one's own behavior appears from the other person's perspective.

Mirror technique Observing another person reenact one's own behavior, like a character in a play; designed to help persons see themselves more clearly.

Family therapy Treatment of a group of related individuals that focuses on interpersonal dynamics and communication.

AF archive/Alamy Stock Photo

Popular TV psychologist Phillip McGraw was awarded a President's Citation from the APA for his work in publicizing mental health issues (Meyers, 2006). Media psychologists have been urged to educate without actually doing therapy on the air. Some overstep this boundary, however. Do you think Dr. Phil ever goes too far?

is it reasonable to give advice without knowing anything about a person's background? Could the advice do harm? What good can a psychologist do in three minutes, or even an hour?

In their own defense, mass media psychologists point out that listeners and viewers may learn solutions to their problems by hearing others talk. Many also stress that their work is educational, not therapeutic. Nevertheless, the question arises: When does advice become therapy? The American Psychological Association urges media psychologists to discuss problems only of a general nature and not to actually counsel anyone.

Telephone and Internet Therapists

Most distance therapy is conducted one-on-one, via telephone or the Internet. Regardless of how a therapist and client communicate, perhaps the key feature of successful therapy is the establishment of an effective relationship between therapist and client. This could be a problem if, for example, only texting is used. Smiley faces and text message shorthand are poor substitutes for real human interaction, which includes interpersonal cues such as facial expressions and body language. ☺ LOL. Similarly, brief email messages are no way to make a diagnosis. However, the Internet also makes it possible to create two-way audio–video links. Conducting therapy this way lacks the close personal contact of face-to-face interaction, but it also removes many of the objections to doing therapy at a distance (Gros et al., 2013).

It is worth noting that distance therapy does have some distinct advantages and disadvantages. For one thing, clients can more easily remain anonymous. Thus, a person who might hesitate to see a psychologist can seek help privately, by phone or online. (But beware that email counseling may not be completely confidential and could be intercepted and misused.) Of special concern is the fact that distance therapists may or may not be trained professionals. Even if they are, questions exist about whether a psychologist licensed in one state can legally do therapy in another state via the telephone or the Internet.

In closing, under the right circumstances, distance therapy can be successful (Bauer et al., 2011; Brenes, Ingram, & Danhauer, 2011). For example, telephone counseling helps people quit smoking (Rabius, Wiatrek, & McAlister, 2012). Other studies have shown that depressed people, substance abusers, as well as people with social phobia and panic disorder, benefit from Internet therapy (Carlbring et al., 2007; Hermes & Rosenheck, 2016; Klein, Richards, & Austin, 2006; Titov, 2011).

Core Features of Effective Psychotherapy

It's pretty clear there are lots of ways to deliver psychotherapy—are there any similarities between them? Modern therapists typically aim to understand clients' perspectives in order to help them restore hope, courage, and optimism; they also help clients to gain insight, resolve conflicts, improve their sense of self, change unacceptable patterns of behavior, find purpose, mend interpersonal relations, and learn to approach problems rationally (Frank & Frank, 2004; Trull & Prinstein, 2013). To accomplish these goals, the psychotherapies that they use offer the following:

1. Perhaps more than any other single factor, effective therapy provides a **therapeutic alliance**, a caring relationship that unites the client and therapist as they work together to solve the client's problems. The strength of this alliance has a major impact on whether therapy succeeds (Arnow et al., 2013; Bartle-Haring et al., 2016; Constantino et al., 2017). The basis for this relationship is emotional rapport, warmth, friendship, understanding, acceptance, and empathy (Crisp, 2014).
2. Therapy also offers a *protected setting* in which emotional *catharsis* (release) can take place. It is a sanctuary in which the client is free to express fears, anxieties, and personal secrets without fearing rejection or loss of confidentiality.
3. All therapies to some extent offer an *explanation* or *rationale* for the client's suffering. In addition, they propose a line of action that will end this suffering.
4. Therapy provides clients with a *new perspective* about themselves and their situations and a chance to practice *new behaviors* (Prochaska & Norcross, 2014). Insights gained during therapy can bring about lasting changes in clients' lives (Grande et al., 2003).

Human Diversity and Psychotherapy

Understanding another person's perspective is especially important when cultural differences may create a barrier between a client and a therapist (Jun, 2010; La Roche & Lustig, 2013). For example, a published case study describes the story of a young Xhosa man from South Africa. At the age of 23, it was clear to family members that he was suffering from *ifufunyane*, a form of bewitchment common in their culture. However, he was treated by psychiatrists at a hospital in Cape Town who said he had schizophrenia and gave him antipsychotic drugs. The drugs helped, but his family shunned his medical treatment and took him to a traditional healer, who gave him herbs for his ifufunyane. Unfortunately, he got worse and had to be readmitted to the hospital. This time, the psychiatrists included the young man's family in his treatment. Together, they agreed to treat him with a combination of antipsychotic drugs *and* traditional herbs (Niehaus et al., 2005).

As this example illustrates, a **culturally skilled therapist** is trained to work with clients from various cultural backgrounds. To be culturally skilled, a counselor must be able to do all of the following (American Psychological Association, 2008a; Brammer, 2012; Comas-Diaz, 2012):

- Adapt traditional theories and techniques to meet the needs of clients from non-European ethnic or racial groups.
- Be aware of his or her own cultural values and biases.
- Establish rapport with a person from a different cultural background.
- Be open to cultural differences without resorting to stereotypes.
- Treat members of racial or ethnic communities as individuals.
- Be aware of a client's ethnic identity and degree of acculturation to the majority society.
- Use existing helping resources within a cultural group to support efforts to resolve problems.

Cultural awareness has helped broaden our ideas about mental health and optimal development (Brammer, 2012). It also is worth remembering that cultural barriers apply to communication in all areas of life, not just therapy. Although such differences can be challenging, they also are frequently enriching (Fowers & Davidov, 2006).

Effectiveness of Psychotherapy

Does psychotherapy actually work? In 1952, British psychologist Hans Eysenck published the first systematic attempt to empirically answer this question. His answer sent shockwaves through psychology when he found that psychotherapy produces no more improvement in patients than doing nothing (Eysenck, 1952, 1994). Apparently, psychotherapy, and in particular, psychoanalysis, took so long that patients experienced a **spontaneous remission** of symptoms—improvement due to the mere passage of time.

How seriously should the possibility of spontaneous remission be taken? An old joke among doctors is that a cold lasts a week without treatment and seven days with it. In *some* cases, the same may be true of therapy. For example, it's true that problems ranging from hyperactivity to anxiety often improve with the passage of time.

But spontaneous remission is not the only problem we face when evaluating the effectiveness of therapies. Though nine out of ten people who have sought mental health care say their lives improved as a result of the treatment (Howard et al., 2001; Kotkin, Daviet, & Gurin, 1996), you can't always take people's word for it. Perhaps the crisis that triggered the therapy is now nearly forgotten. Or maybe some sort of **therapy placebo effect** has occurred, in which improvement is based on a client's belief that therapy will help. Also, it's possible that the person has received help from other people, such as family, friends, or clergy.

Studying the Science: Empirically Supported Therapies

The real value of Eysenck's critique of the effectiveness of psychoanalysis is that it encouraged psychologists to closely examine whether therapeutic techniques actually work. To establish this, we could carry out an experiment, randomly placing clients in either an experimental group that receives therapy or a control group that does not. We can conclude that the therapy is useful only if people in the experimental group improve more than those in the control group. In some cases, though, the control group may show improvement even without receiving therapy, suggesting that the treatment is not effective (Lambert & Ogles, 2002; Schuck, Keijsers, & Rinck, 2011). Such findings can result from spontaneous remission, but they may also be due to the placebo effect (■ see Section 1.6).

But isn't it unethical to withhold treatment from someone who really needs therapy? Yes—you're absolutely right. One way to deal with this problem is to use a *waiting-list control group.* In this case, people who are waiting to see a therapist are compared with those who receive therapy. Later, those on the waiting list also receive therapy.

In some cases, the American Psychological Association has designated treatments as *empirically supported*, meaning that there is a body of research that consistently supports their effectiveness in dealing with a specific form of psychopathology (American Psychological Association, 2006; Tolin et al., 2015). For example, research clearly demonstrates that behavioral, cognitive, and drug therapies are most helpful in treating obsessive-compulsive disorder.

What factors influence whether a treatment will be effective? Whether treatments are successful or not depends on factors such as *therapist characteristics* (Holdsworth, Brown, Bowen, & Howat, 2014), *client characteristics* (Wiltink et al., 2016), and the *therapist–client relationship* (the therapeutic alliance; Bartle-Haring et al., 2016). In fact, researchers have increasingly noted the importance of tailoring treatments to individuals, leading to new research on the effectiveness of personalized treatments (Schneider, Arch, & Walitzky-Taylor, 2015).

The success of a therapeutic technique also depends on the *nature of the problem.* As you read about the different therapeutic approaches in this chapter, it's important to note that psychotherapy is *not* equally effective for all problems. Chances of improvement are fairly good for phobias, low self-esteem, some sexual problems, and marital conflicts. However, more complex problems can be difficult to solve and some may require medical treatment as well. For example, schizophrenia may not respond to psychotherapy at all, leaving a medical therapy as the only viable treatment option.

Therapeutic alliance A caring relationship that unites a therapist and a client in working to solve the client's problems.

Culturally skilled therapist A therapist who has the awareness, knowledge, and skills necessary to treat clients from diverse cultural backgrounds.

Spontaneous remission Improvement of symptoms due to the mere passage of time.

Therapy placebo effect Improvement caused not by the actual process of therapy but by a client's expectation that therapy will help.

▲ Table 15.1 Elements of Positive Mental Health

- Personal autonomy and independence
- A sense of identity
- Feelings of personal worth
- Skilled interpersonal communication
- Sensitivity, nurturance, and trust
- Genuineness and honesty with self and others
- Self-control and personal responsibility
- Committed and loving personal relationships
- Capacity to forgive others and oneself
- Personal values and a purpose in life
- Self-awareness and motivation for personal growth
- Adaptive coping strategies for managing stresses and crises
- Fulfillment and satisfaction in work
- Good habits of physical health

Source: Adapted from Compton & Hoffman, 2013.

In short, it is often unrealistic to expect psychotherapy to function as a "miracle cure." For many people, the major benefit of psychotherapy is that it provides comfort, support, and a way to make constructive changes (Compton & Hoffman, 2013). But just as it's a mistake to think that psychotherapy can cure all problems, it's also wrong to think that psychotherapy is useful *only* in times of crisis. Even when people are doing well in their lives, therapy can be a way for them to promote personal growth and understand how to use their personal strengths (Trull & Prinstein, 2013). Rather than trying to fix what is "wrong" with a person, then, psychotherapists sometimes seek to nurture positive traits (Compton & Hoffman, 2013). ▲ Table 15.1 lists some of the elements of positive mental health that therapists seek to restore or promote.

Summary

For a summary of major differences among the psychotherapies that will be discussed in this chapter, see ▲ Table 15.2. But before we move on, let's assess your understanding of this chapter so far.

Reflective Practice

The Origins and Effectiveness of Psychotherapy

1. In psychoanalysis, an emotional attachment to the therapist is called
a. free association
b. manifest association
c. resistance
d. transference

2. The approach that is "opposite" to insight therapy is
a. individual therapy
b. action therapy
c. nondirective therapy
d. time-limited psychotherapy

3. To date, the most acceptable type of "distance therapy" is
a. media psychology
b. commercial telephone counseling
c. emoticon-based therapy
d. based on two-way audio and video links

4. Psychological difficulties often improve with the passage of time, a phenomenon known as
a. therapy placebo effect
b. spontaneous remission
c. spontaneous combustion
d. an empirically supported therapy

5. Ethical issues in withholding treatment to patients in experimental studies of the efficacy of therapy can be addressed with
a. spontaneous remission
b. a therapeutic alliance
c. a double-blind study
d. a waiting-list control group

6. Emotional rapport, warmth, understanding, acceptance, and empathy are the core of
a. the therapeutic alliance
b. large-group awareness training
c. role reversals
d. action therapy

7. Culturally skilled therapists do all but one of the following; which does *not* apply?
a. Are aware of the client's degree of acculturation
b. Use helping resources within the client's cultural group
c. Adapt standard techniques to match cultural stereotypes
d. Are aware of their own cultural values

▲ Table 15.2 Comparison of Therapies

	Insight or Action?	Nondirective or Directive?	Individual or Group?	Therapy's Strength
Psychoanalysis	Insight	Directive	Individual	Searching honesty
Brief psychodynamic therapy	Insight	Directive	Individual	Productive use of conflict
Client-centered therapy	Insight	Nondirective	Both	Acceptance, empathy
Existential therapy	Insight	Both	Individual	Personal empowerment
Gestalt therapy	Insight	Directive	Both	Focus on immediate awareness
Behavior therapy	Action	Directive	Both	Observable changes in behavior
Cognitive therapy	Action	Directive	Individual	Constructive guidance
Rational-emotive behavior therapy (REBT)	Action	Directive	Individual	Clarity of thinking and goals
Psychodrama	Insight	Directive	Group	Constructive reenactments
Family therapy	Both	Directive	Group	Shared responsibility for problems

Sources: Adapted from Corsini & Wedding, 2014; Prochaska & Norcross, 2014.

THINK CRITICALLY

8. According to Freud's concept of *transference*, patients "transfer" their feelings onto the psychoanalyst. In light of this idea, to what might the term *countertransference* refer?
9. In your opinion, do psychologists have a duty to protect others who may be harmed by their clients? For example, if a patient has homicidal fantasies about his ex-wife, should she be informed?

SELF-REFLECT

- The use of trepanning, demonology, and exorcism all implied that the mentally ill are "cursed." To what extent are the mentally ill rejected and stigmatized today?
- Would you rather participate in individual therapy or group therapy? What advantages and disadvantages do you think each has?
- What lies at the "heart" of psychotherapy? How would you describe it to a friend?

Answers: 1. d 2. b 3. d 4. b 5. d 6. a 7. c 8. Psychoanalysts (and therapists in general) also are human. They may transfer their own unresolved, unconscious feelings onto *their* patients. This can complicate the therapeutic process (Bunnell, 2016). 9. According to the law, there is a duty to protect others when a therapist could, with little effort, prevent serious harm. However, this duty can conflict with a client's rights to confidentiality and with client–therapist trust. Therapists often must make difficult choices in such situations.

15.2 Behavior Therapies

GATEWAYS LEARNING OUTCOMES:
After reading this section you should be able to:

15.2.1 Describe the main elements of behavior therapies

15.2.2 Describe two therapies that are based on classical conditioning

15.2.3 Describe two therapies that are based on operant conditioning

Imagine that you've got a big problem: You've won a free Caribbean vacation. If you're wondering how this could ever be a problem, we want you now to imagine that the mere thought of traveling on an airplane leaves you paralyzed with fear. What would you do?

Often people do not realize that many phobias, like an overwhelming fear of flying, respond well to a type of *behavior therapy* called systematic desensitization. In just a few weeks, these programs can ease such fears by combining relaxation techniques with lots of exposure to whatever it is that frightens you—heights, spiders, public speaking, and—yes—even airplanes.

Sidney Harris/www.CartoonStock.com

In general, how do behavior therapies like systematic desensitization work? A breakthrough occurred when psychologists realized they could use learning principles to solve human problems (see Chapter 6 for more information about learning principles). **Behavior therapy**, then, is an action therapy that uses learning principles to make constructive changes in behavior. Unlike psychoanalysts, behavior therapists believe that deep insight into one's problems is often unnecessary for improvement. Instead, they try to directly alter troublesome actions and thoughts.

Behavior therapists assume that people have *learned* to be the way they are. If they have learned responses that cause problems, then they can change them by learning more appropriate behaviors. Broadly speaking, **behavior modification** refers to any use of classical or operant (instrumental) conditioning to directly alter human behavior (Miltenberger, 2016; Spiegler, 2016). Behavior therapies include aversion therapy, systematic desensitization, token economies, and the intensive behavioral intervention (IBI) techniques that are used with people diagnosed with autism (Spiegler, 2013a, b). We'll consider therapeutic approaches based on classical conditioning first, and then turn our attention to those that are based on operant conditioning.

Therapies Based on Classical Conditioning

Remind me again: How does classical conditioning work? Classical conditioning is a form of learning based on simple, naturally occurring stimulus–response (called the unconditioned stimulus

Behavior therapy Any therapy designed to actively change behavior.

Behavior modification (applied behavior analysis) The application of learning principles to change human behavior, especially maladaptive behavior.

and unconditioned response) relationships, like reflexes. In classical conditioning, a neutral stimulus (NS) is paired repeatedly with the unconditioned stimulus (US) that produces the unconditioned response (UR). Eventually, the previously neutral stimulus becomes a conditioned stimulus (CS) that is capable of producing a conditioned response (CR) that strongly resembles the UR. For example, imagine that for a child, the sight of a hypodermic needle (NS that becomes a CS) is repeatedly paired with an injection (US) that causes anxiety or fear (UR). Eventually, the sight of a hypodermic needle (the CS) may produce anxiety or fear (a CR) *before* the child gets an injection. (■ For a more thorough review of classical conditioning, return to Section 6.2.)

What does classical conditioning have to do with behavior modification? Classical conditioning has been used in two broad treatment approaches—*aversion therapy* and *exposure therapy*—which we'll examine now.

Aversion Therapy

In **aversion therapy**, clients learn to associate aversive, or negative, experiences (either physical or emotional) with a bad habit that they want to eliminate. In Section 6.1, we discussed how this approach can be used to treat alcoholism, but it has been used for a wide range of other behaviors too, including hiccups, sneezing, stuttering, vomiting, gambling, nail-biting, bed-wetting, compulsive hair-pulling, and drug use.

One of the most common behaviors that is treated with aversion therapy is smoking. In one form of the treatment, smoking (NS that becomes the CS) is paired with electric shock (US) that causes discomfort (UR). Eventually, the sight of cigarettes or even the thought of smoking is enough to bring on feelings of discomfort (CR).

Pairing smoking with the aversive experience of pain caused by the shocks is helpful in getting clients to give up smoking; however, behavior therapists have found that electric shocks and similar aversive stimuli are not required to make smokers uncomfortable. All that is needed is for the smoker to smoke—rapidly, for a long time, at a forced pace. During *rapid smoking,* clients are told to smoke continuously, taking a puff every 6 to 8 seconds. Rapid smoking continues until the smoker is miserable and can stand it no more. By then, most people are thinking, "I never want to see another cigarette for the rest of my life." Rapid smoking has long been known as an effective behavior therapy for smoking (Gifford & Shoenberger, 2009). Nevertheless, anyone tempted to try rapid smoking should realize that it is very unpleasant. In addition, rapid smoking can be dangerous. It should be done only with professional supervision.

Is it really acceptable to treat clients this way? People are often disturbed (shocked?) by the methods associated with aversion therapy. However, clients usually volunteer for aversion therapy because it helps them overcome a destructive habit. Indeed, commercial aversion programs for overeating, smoking, and alcohol abuse have attracted many willing customers. More important, aversion therapy can be justified by its benefits. Many people prefer the short-term discomfort of aversion therapy to the long-term pain caused by a lifetime of struggling with a maladaptive habit.

Studying the Science: The Effectiveness of Aversion Therapy

Various types of aversion therapy have been studied by psychological scientists for decades, so it is a well-studied method for managing negative behaviors. However, research suggests that it is much more effective when combined with other treatment approaches than it is when used on its own (Belendiuk & Riggs, 2014). It's not too hard to understand why this is the case: Aversion therapy requires that clients commit to a treatment plan during which they are subjected to ongoing unpleasant experiences. Unless they have a tremendous amount of motivation to rid themselves of the unwanted behavior, people will often give up on this type of therapy and revert to their old habits.

Exposure Therapy

Another behavioral technique, *exposure therapy*, can be used to help people "unlearn" undesirable behaviors such as phobias (intense, unrealistic fears), strong anxieties, obsessions, and compulsions (Abramowitz, Deacon, Whiteside, 2012; Abramowitz & Jacoby, 2015). The basic premise of **exposure therapy** is that clients are exposed to situations or objects that cause them to feel intense fear, and this type of contact allows the client to learn that their anxiety is unwarranted. Put another way, exposure therapy is a way of trying to eliminate, or extinguish, maladaptive conditioned emotional responses that have been learned through classical conditioning (■ see Section 6.2 for more information about conditioned emotional responses). For example, each of these people might be a candidate for exposure therapy: a teacher with stage fright; a student with test anxiety; a newlywed with an aversion to sexual intimacy; a person with hoarding disorder; or a person who is afraid of flying.

One common form of exposure therapy is called **flooding**, which involves repeatedly exposing people to the object or circumstances that concern them, either in real life (*in vivo flooding*) or in their imagination (*covert flooding*). Often, the therapist will subject their client to very extreme examples of the feared object or situation, bringing about an intense emotional response (Comer & Comer, 2018).

A second type of exposure therapy is referred to as **systematic desensitization**—a much slower and guided reduction in fear that is attained by gradually approaching a feared stimulus while maintaining relaxation (Head & Gross, 2009). For example, suppose that a behavior therapist wanted to help a client named Shanika to overcome her fear of heights (acrophobia). How might he proceed?

While flooding might involve simply forcing Shanika to go out onto a balcony on the 35th floor of her apartment building, this can often prove too traumatic. The key to desensitization—and the primary difference from flooding—is the emphasis that systematic desensitization places on **reciprocal inhibition**—using one emotional state to block another (Heriot & Pritchard, 2004; Trull & Prinstein, 2013). Specifically, clinicians who use this technique believe that if you want to inhibit fear, you must *learn* to relax because it is impossible to be anxious and relaxed at the same time. Put another way, the two states inhibit one another.

One way to voluntarily relax is by using the **tension-release method**. To achieve deep-muscle relaxation, try the following exercise:

> Tense the muscles in your right arm until they tremble. Hold them tight as you slowly count to 10 and then let go. Allow your

hand and arm to go limp and to relax completely. Repeat the procedure. Releasing tension two or three times will allow you to feel whether your arm muscles have relaxed. Repeat the tension-release procedure with your left arm. Compare it with your right arm. Repeat until the left arm is equally relaxed. Apply the tension-release technique to your right leg, to your left leg, to your abdomen, and then to your chest and shoulders. Clench and release your chin, neck, and throat. Wrinkle and release your forehead and scalp. Tighten and release your mouth and face muscles. As a last step, curl your toes and tense your feet and then release.

If you followed these instructions, you should be noticeably more relaxed than you were before you began. Practice the tension-release method until you can achieve complete relaxation quickly (5 to 10 minutes). After you have practiced relaxation once a day for a week or two, you will begin to be able to tell when your body (or a group of muscles) is tense. Also, you will begin to be able to relax on command. This is a valuable skill that you can apply in any situation that makes you feel tense or anxious.

While Shanika learns to voluntarily relax, she and the therapist can also construct her **fear hierarchy**—a list of at least 10 fear-provoking situations related to her fear of heights, arranged from least disturbing to most frightening.

During the process of desensitization, then, Shanika would begin by consciously relaxing while trying to perform the least disturbing item on her fear of heights hierarchy, which might be (1) Stand on a chair. Shanika would continue to practice standing on the chair until she could do so while remaining completely relaxed. Any change from complete relaxation is a signal that Shanika must relax again before continuing. Slowly, Shanika moves up the hierarchy: (2) Climb to the top of a small stepladder, (3) look down one flight of stairs, and so on, until the last item, (20) Stand on the balcony on the top floor of her apartment building, is performed in a relaxed state, without fear.

Working through her fear hierarchy in a safe, relaxed setting allows Shanika to gradually undergo *extinction* of her conditioned fear response. Repeated visits to the staircase should cause fear to disappear in this situation. When Shanika has conquered her fear, we can say that *desensitization* has occurred.

Like flooding, systematic desensitization can be *in vivo* or *covert*. For many phobias, desensitization works best when carried out in vivo, with clients directly exposed to the stimuli and situations they fear (Bourne, 2010; Miltenberger, 2016). For something like a simple spider phobia, this exposure can even be done in groups and may be completed in a single session (Müller et al., 2011).

Fortunately, desensitization works almost as well when it's covert, with the client vividly imagining each step in the hierarchy (Lang, 2016; Yahnke, Sheikh, & Beckman, 2003). If the steps can be visualized without anxiety, fear in the actual situation is reduced. Because imagining feared stimuli can be done at a therapist's office, it is the most common way of doing desensitization.

In an important recent development to covert methods, psychologists are now using virtual reality to treat phobias. As we discussed in ■ Section 4.6, virtual reality is a computer-generated, three-dimensional "world" that viewers enter by wearing a head-mounted video display. **Virtual reality exposure** presents computerized fear stimuli to clients in a realistic yet carefully controlled fashion (Anderson, Edwards, & Goodnight, 2017; Motraghi et al., 2014). It has already been used to treat fears of flying, driving, and public speaking, as well as acrophobia, claustrophobia, and spider phobias (Meyerbröker & Emmelkamp, 2010; Müller et al., 2011; ● Figure 15.1). Virtual reality exposure has also been used to create immersive distracting environments for helping patients reduce the experience of pain (Keefe et al., 2012).

Programs for treating fears of flying combine relaxation, systematic desensitization, group support, and lots of direct and indirect exposure to airliners. Many such programs conclude with a brief flight, so that participants can "test their wings."

A third and final type of exposure therapy is **modeling**. In this method, the problem is handled by having clients observe *models*, including the therapist, who are performing the feared behavior (Bourne, 2010; Eifert & Lejuez, 2000; ● Figure 15.2). A model is a person (either live or filmed) who serves as an example for observational learning (■ for more information about observational learning, see Section 6.4).

Aversion therapy Treatment to reduce unwanted behavior by pairing it with an unpleasant stimulus.

Exposure therapy Alleviating fears and phobias (conditioned emotional responses) by using classical conditioning extinction.

Flooding A form of exposure therapy in which clients are exposed to the object of their fears beginning with examples that provoke the most extreme responses.

Systematic desensitization A reduction in fear, anxiety, or aversion brought about by planned exposure to aversive stimuli.

Reciprocal inhibition The presence of one emotional state can inhibit the occurrence of another, such as joy preventing fear or anxiety inhibiting pleasure.

Tension-release method A procedure for systematically achieving deep relaxation of the body.

Fear hierarchy A list of fears, arranged from least fearful to most fearful, for use in systematic desensitization.

Virtual reality exposure Use of computer-generated images to present fear stimuli while responding to a viewer's head movements and other input.

Modeling A form of exposure therapy in which clients observe models displaying adaptive behavior toward their feared object.

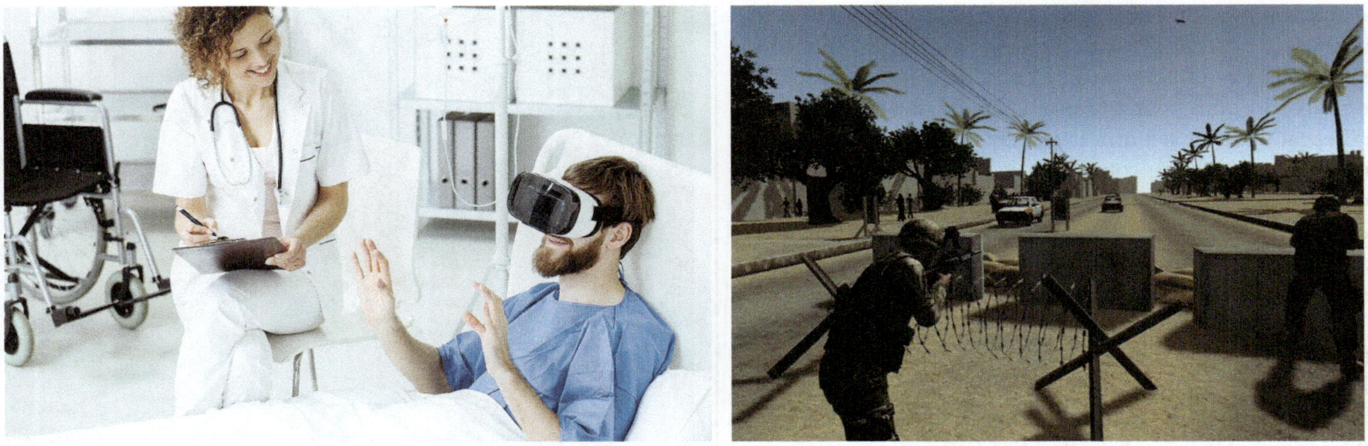

Photographee.eu/Shutterstock.com; Photographs used with permission from University of Southern California Institute for Creative Technologies

Figure 15.1 Treatment of PTSD with virtual reality. (*Left*) A person in the head-mounted display explores a virtual reality system used to expose people to feared stimuli. (*Right*) A computer image from a virtual Iraq or Afghanistan. Veterans suffering from post-traumatic stress disorder (PTSD) can reexperience their traumas. For example, someone whose checkpoint was suddenly attacked by a carload of terrorists can relive that moment, complete with sights, sounds, vibrations, and even smells. Successive exposures result in a reduction of PTSD symptoms (Reger et al., 2016; Rizzo et al., 2015).

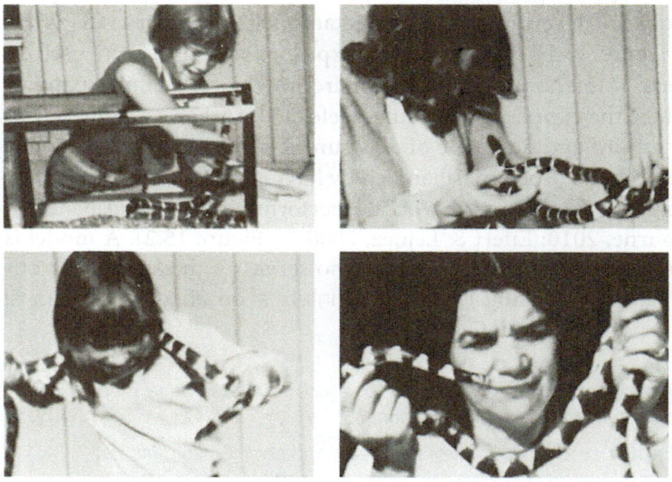

Albert Bandura/Stanford University

Figure 15.2 Treatment of a snake phobia using models in exposure therapy. These classic photographs show models interacting with snakes. To overcome their own fears, phobic subjects observed the models (Bandura, Blanchard, & Ritter, 1969).

Therapies Based on Operant Conditioning

Aversion and exposure therapies are based on classical conditioning, but what about operant conditioning? As you may recall, *operant conditioning* (sometimes called instrumental conditioning) refers to learning based on the consequences of emitting a voluntary behavior. Though there are a number of concepts that are relevant to operant conditioning (■ see Section 6.3 for more details), behavior therapists most often use the following to manage their clients' concerns:

1. **Positive reinforcement.** Responses that are followed by reinforcement tend to occur more frequently. If children whine and are reinforced by getting attention, they will whine more frequently. If you are reinforced for studying by getting straight *A*'s in your psychology class, you will learn that studying is worthwhile and you will be more likely to do it in the future.
2. **Nonreinforcement and extinction.** A behavior that is not followed by reinforcement will occur less frequently. Moreover, if a response is not followed by reward after it has been repeated many times, it will extinguish entirely. For example, imagine that after winning three times, you pull the handle on a slot machine 30 times more without a payoff. What do you do? You stop because you've learned that the behavior—handle pulling—is not worthwhile (for that particular machine, at any rate).
3. **Punishment.** If a behavior is followed by a negative consequence, such as discomfort or another undesirable effect, it will be suppressed (but not necessarily extinguished).
4. **Shaping.** Shaping means reinforcing actions that are closer and closer approximations to a desired response. For example, imagine that you are working with a child who has a developmental delay, and you want to reward him for saying "ball." You might begin by reinforcing the child for saying anything that starts with a *b* sound, and gradually change your reinforcement pattern as he moves closer to saying the whole word.
5. **Time-out.** A time-out procedure usually involves removing the individual from a situation in which reinforcement occurs. Time-out is a variation of punishment: It prevents reward from following an undesirable response. For example, children who fight with each other can be sent to separate rooms and allowed out only when they are able to behave more calmly.

As simple as these principles may seem, they have been used very effectively to overcome difficulties in work, home, school, and industrial settings. For example, here's a good example of using the principles of nonreinforcement and extinction: Imagine that 14-year-old Terrel periodically appeared in the nude in the activity room of a training center for troubled adolescents. This behavior always generated a great deal of attention from staff and other patients. As an experiment, the staff decided to implement operant conditioning principles to manage the behavior. The next time he appeared nude, counselors and other staff members greeted Terrel normally and then ignored him. Attention from other patients rapidly subsided. Sheepishly, he returned to his room and dressed. Over time his inappropriate nudity was completely extinguished.

In the next two sections, we describe two specific types of therapy that make effective use of operant conditioning: *intensive behavioral intervention (IBI)*, which is often used for children on the autism spectrum, and *token economies*.

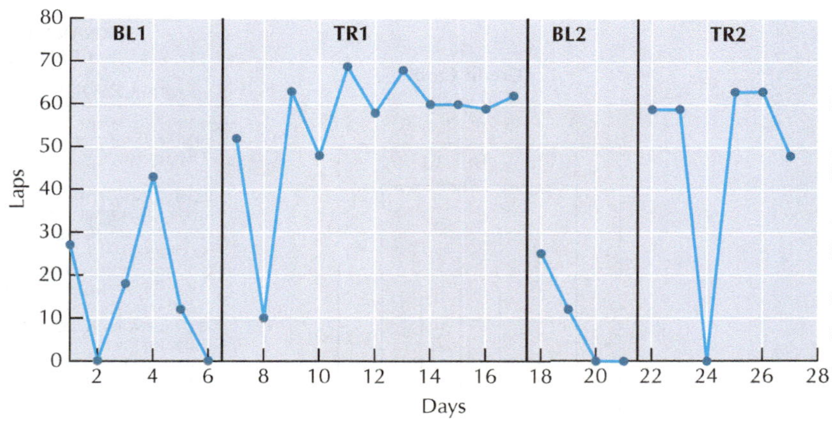

Figure 15.3 Token reinforcers and behavioral change. Adults with intellectual disabilities often struggle with their weight. Paul is overweight and diabetic yet does not get enough exercise. The graph shows the number of laps Paul walks around a short track during an exercise period each day. During baseline periods (BL1 and BL2) he walks fewer laps than during token reinforcer (TR1 and TR2) periods, when he is awarded one token for each lap. After walking, Paul is allowed to exchange his tokens for treats such as Gatorade and Gatorade chews.

Adapted from Krentz, Miltenberger, & Valbuena, 2016.

Intensive Behavioral Intervention

Operant principles—specifically positive reinforcement and shaping—are used by therapists who use intensive behavioral intervention (IBI) to treat children with autism. For example, if the child has limited language then imagine that the goal of treatment is to teach him to make others aware when he wants some juice. The therapist would begin by determining, usually with the parents' help, what kinds of things would serve as positive reinforcement. For some children, this might be a special kind of food or candy, but for others it might be stickers or the use of a toy or tablet. Once the reinforcer is established, the task is broken down into smaller steps; for example, making the "j" sound, saying "jooo," and finally saying the whole word "juice." Initially the child would consistently be given the reinforcer for simply completing the first step ("j"). Once that step has been mastered, reinforcement will only be provided when the child meets the second step ("jooo"), and so on. In this way, the child's behavior is shaped using positive reinforcement until he has met the goal set by the therapist.

Token Economies

Positive reinforcement can also be used in other ways to change behavior. For example, imagine that Paul is a young adult with Down syndrome who is overweight and diabetic. Though it would be beneficial for his health, he does not get enough exercise. One treatment approach that is often used with older children and adults is based on *tokens* (symbolic rewards that can be exchanged for real rewards). Positive responses, such as Paul going out for a walk, can be immediately rewarded with tokens, which may be printed slips of paper, check marks, points, or gold stars. Whatever form they take, tokens serve as rewards because they may be exchanged for candy, food, cigarettes, recreation, or privileges, such as private time with a therapist, outings, or watching TV (Figure 15.3).

Tokens are used in psychiatric hospitals, halfway houses, schools for the intellectually disabled, programs for delinquents, and ordinary classrooms. They usually produce improvements in behavior (Krentz, Miltenberger, & Valbuena, 2016; Maggin et al., 2011). (■ Tokens provide an effective way to change behavior because they are delivered immediately and function as secondary reinforcers. See Section 6.2.)

The full-scale use of tokens in an institutional setting produces a *token economy.* In a **token economy**, patients are rewarded with tokens for a wide range of socially desirable or productive activities (Spiegler, 2016), and they must *pay* tokens to receive privileges and when they engage in problem behaviors (Figure 15.4). For example, tokens are given to patients who dress themselves, take required medication, arrive for meals on time, and so on. Constructive activities, such as gardening, cooking, or cleaning, also may earn tokens. Patients must exchange tokens for meals and private rooms, movies, passes, off-ward activities, and other privileges. They are charged tokens for disrobing in public, talking to themselves, fighting, crying, and similar target behaviors (Morisse et al., 1996; Spiegler, 2016).

Token economies can radically change a patient's overall adjustment and morale. Patients are given an incentive to change and they are held responsible for their actions. The use of tokens may seem manipulative, but it empowers patients. Many "hopelessly" intellectually disabled, mentally ill, and delinquent people have been returned to productive lives by means of token economies (Boerke & Reitman, 2011).

By the time they are ready to leave, patients may be earning tokens on a weekly basis for maintaining responsible and productive behavior (Miltenberger, 2016). Typically, the most effective token economies are those that gradually switch from tokens to *social rewards* such as praise, recognition, and approval. Such rewards are what patients will receive when they return to their family, friends, and community.

Token economy Behavior modification in which desired behaviors earn objects that can be exchanged for positive reinforcers.

OXNARD DAY TREATMENT CENTER
CREDIT INCENTIVE SYSTEM

EARN CREDITS BY		SPEND CREDITS FOR	
MONITOR DAILY	15	COFFEE	5
MENU PLANNING CHAIRMAN	50	LUNCH	10
PARTICIPATE	5	EXCEPT THURSDAY	15
BUY FOOD AT STORE	10	BUS TRIP	5
COOK FOR/PREPARE LUNCH	5	BOWLING	8
WIPE OFF KITCHEN TABLE	3	GROUP THERAPY	5
WASH DISHES	5–10	PRIVATE STAFF TIME	5
DRY AND PUT AWAY DISHES	5	DAY OFF	5–20
MAKE COFFEE AND CLEAN URN	15	WINDOW SHOPPING	5
CLEAN REFRIGERATOR	20	REVIEW WITH DR.	10
ATTEND PLANNING CONFERENCE	1	DOING OWN THING	1
OT PREPARATION	1–5	LATE 1 PER EVERY 10 MIN	
COMPLETE OT PROJECT	5	PRESCRIPTION FROM DR.	10
RETURN OT PROJECT	2		
DUST AND POLISH TABLES	5		
PUT AWAY GROCERIES	3		
CLEAN TABLE	5		
CLEAN 6 ASH TRAYS	2		
CLEAN SINK	5		
CARRY OUT CUPS & BOTTLES	5		
CLEAN CHAIRS	5		
CLEAN KITCHEN CUPBOARDS	5		
ASSIST STAFF	5		
ARRANGE MAGAZINES NEATLY	3		
BEING ON TIME	5		
MONITOR-ANN			

After photographs by Robert P. Liberman.

Figure 15.4 Token economy. Shown here is a token used in one token economy system. In this instance, the token is a card that records the number of credits earned by a patient. Also pictured is a list of credit values for various activities. Tokens may be exchanged for items or for privileges listed on the board.

Reflective Practice

Behavior Therapies

1. Shock plays what role in conditioning an aversion?
   a. conditioned stimulus
   b. unconditioned response
   c. unconditioned stimulus
   d. conditioned response
2. Therapy for phobias that is carried out through the use of live or filmed models is a type of
   a. cognitive therapy
   b. systematic desensitization
   c. Gestalt therapy
   d. exposure therapy
3. Systematic desensitization has three basic steps: constructing a hierarchy, flooding the person with anxiety, and imagining relaxation. T or F?
4. Behavior modification programs aimed at extinction of an undesirable behavior typically use what operant principles?
   a. punishment and stimulus control
   b. punishment and shaping
   c. nonreinforcement and time-out (a variation of punishment)
   d. stimulus control and time-out (a variation of punishment)
5. Attention can be a powerful ________________ for humans.

THINK CRITICALLY

6. A natural form of exposure therapy often takes place in hospitals. Can you guess what it is?

SELF-REFLECT

- Have you ever become naturally desensitized to a stimulus or situation that at first made you anxious (for instance, heights, public speaking, or driving on freeways)? How would you explain your reduced fear?
- See if you can give a personal example of how the following principles have affected your behavior: positive reinforcement, extinction, punishment, shaping, stimulus control, and time-out.

Answers: 1. c 2. d 3. F 4. c 5. reinforcer 6. Doctors and nurses learn to relax and remain calm at the sight of blood and other bodily fluids because of their frequent exposure to them.

15.3 Cognitive and Humanistic Therapies

GATEWAYS LEARNING OUTCOMES:
After reading this section you should be able to:

15.3.1 Describe the main elements of cognitive therapies

15.3.2 Describe the main elements of humanistic therapies

15.3.3 Describe three humanistic therapies

Behavior therapies were prominent in the 1950s, but just a decade later clinicians began to think that a strict focus on behaviors was too simplistic. Two different forms of therapy became very popular during the 1960s: cognitive therapies and humanistic therapies. Let's take a closer look at each one.

Cognitive Therapies

It was influential American psychiatrist Aaron Beck (1967) who launched a revolution in psychotherapy when he proposed that people could alleviate a number of mental health challenges, including depression and anxiety, by actively modifying their conscious *thoughts* and *feelings*. Thus, whereas behavior therapies use the principles of conditioning to change behavior directly, **cognitive therapies** help clients change behavior by altering conscious maladaptive thoughts, beliefs, and feeling patterns (Power, 2010; Rosner, 2012). In particular, these therapeutic techniques focus on trying to change attributions, assumptions, or attitudes that are inaccurate, illogical, or faulty.

As an example, let's consider someone who has been diagnosed with depression. According to Aaron Beck (1967, 1991), depressed persons see themselves, the world, and the future in negative terms because of at least three major distortions in thinking. The first is **selective perception**, which refers to perceiving only certain stimuli in a larger array. If five good things and two bad things happen during the day, depressed people focus only on the bad. A second thinking error in depression is **overgeneralization**, the tendency to think that an upsetting event applies to other, unrelated situations. An example would be Casimir considering himself a total failure or completely worthless if he were to lose a part-time job or fail a test. To complete the picture, depressed persons tend to magnify the importance of undesirable events by engaging in **all-or-nothing thinking**. They see events as completely good or bad, right or wrong, and themselves as either successful or failing miserably (Lam & Mok, 2008).

How do cognitive therapists alter these thinking patterns? Cognitive therapists make a step-by-step effort to correct negative thoughts that lead to depression or similar problems. At first, clients are taught to recognize and keep track of their own thoughts. The client and therapist then look for ideas and beliefs that cause depression, anger, and avoidance (Segal, Williams, & Teasdale, 2013). For example, here's how Casimir's therapist began to challenge his all-or-nothing thinking:

Casimir: I'm feeling really depressed today. No one wants to hire me, and I can't even get a date. I feel completely incompetent!

Therapist: I see. The fact that you are currently unemployed and don't have a girlfriend proves that you are completely and utterly incompetent?

Casimir: Well . . . I can see that seems a bit extreme.

Next, clients are asked to gather information to test their beliefs against reality. For instance, a depressed person like Casimir might list his activities for a week. The list is then used to challenge all-or-nothing thoughts, such as "I had a terrible week" or "I'm a complete failure." With more coaching, clients learn to try out new ways of thinking about their everyday lives that can improve their moods, actions, and relationships.

In an alternative approach, cognitive therapists look for an *absence* of effective coping skills and thinking patterns, rather than the *presence* of self-defeating thoughts (Dobson, Backs-Dermott, & Dozois, 2000). The aim is to teach clients how to cope with anger, depression, shyness, stress, and similar problems. Stress inoculation (■ which was described in Section 13.5) is a good example of this approach.

Cognitive therapy is at least as effective as drugs for treating many cases of depression (Lopez & Basco, 2014). Also, people who have adopted new thinking patterns are less likely to become depressed again—a benefit that drugs can't impart (Eisendrath et al., 2014; Eisendrath, Chartier, & McLane, 2011).

Cognitive Behavior Therapy

In practice, most cognitive therapists, as well as many behavior therapists, have realized that changing maladaptive thoughts and behaviors can be undertaken simultaneously. **Cognitive behavior therapy (CBT)** combines both cognitive and behavioral therapies to optimize treatment outcomes and is currently the most popular approach to nonmedical therapy (Farmer & Chapman, 2016; Pilgrim, 2011). Various forms of CBT have been successfully used as a remedy for many problems, ranging from generalized anxiety disorder and post-traumatic stress disorder (PTSD) to marital distress, anger, and depression (Butler et al., 2006; Eisendrath et al., 2014). For example, hypochondria (now known as somatic

Cognitive therapy Treatment of emotional and behavioral problems by changing maladaptive thoughts, beliefs, and feeling.

Selective perception Perceiving only certain stimuli among a larger array of possibilities.

Overgeneralization Blowing a single event out of proportion by extending it to a large number of unrelated situations.

All-or-nothing thinking Classifying objects or events as absolutely right or wrong, good or bad, acceptable or unacceptable, and so forth.

Cognitive behavior therapy (CBT) Any therapy that combines elements of cognitive therapy and behavior therapy.

symptom disorder) can be greatly reduced by changing a client's thoughts and beliefs about intrusive imagery (McManus et al., 2015).

CBT can assume many forms. For example, Albert Ellis (1913–2007) founded **rational-emotive behavior therapy** (REBT), which is considered to be one of the first established cognitive behavioral therapies. REBT attempts to change self-defeating thoughts and behaviors that cause emotional problems. According to Ellis, the basic idea of REBT is as easy as A-B-C (Ellis, 1995; Ellis & Ellis, 2011).

ABC? Ellis analyzed problems in this way: The letter A stands for an *activating experience,* which the person assumes to be the cause of C, an emotional *consequence.* For instance, a person who is rejected (the activating experience) feels depressed, threatened, or hurt (the consequence). REBT shows the client that the real problem is what comes between A and C: B, which is the client's irrational and unrealistic *beliefs.* In this example, an unrealistic belief leading to unnecessary suffering is "I must be loved and approved by everyone at all times." REBT holds that external conditions or events do not *cause* us to have feelings. We feel as we do because of our beliefs (Dryden, 2011; Kottler & Shepard, 2015). (For some examples, see "Ten Irrational Beliefs—Which Ones Do You Hold?") (■ The REBT explanation of emotional distress is related to the effects of emotional appraisals. See Section 10.4.)

Ten Irrational Beliefs—Which Ones Do You Hold?

REBT therapists have identified numerous beliefs that commonly lead to emotional upsets and conflicts. See if you recognize any of the following irrational beliefs (Dryden, 2011; Ellis & Ellis, 2011; Teyber & McClure, 2011):

1. I must be loved and approved by almost every significant person in my life or it's awful and I'm worthless.
   Example: "One of my classmates doesn't seem to like me. I must be a big loser."
2. I should be completely competent and achieving in all ways to be a worthwhile person.
   Example: "I don't understand my physics class. I guess I really am just stupid."
3. It's terribly upsetting when things don't go my way.
   Example: "I should have gotten a B in that class. The teacher is a total creep."
4. It's not my fault I'm unhappy; I can't control my emotional reactions.
   Example: "You make me feel awful. I would be happy if it weren't for you."
5. I should never forget it if something unpleasant happens.
   Example: "I'll never forget the time my boss insulted me. I think about it every day at work."
6. It is easier to avoid difficulties and responsibilities than to face them.
   Example: "I don't know why my girlfriend is angry. Maybe it will just pass if I ignore it."
7. A lot of people I have to deal with are bad. I should severely punish them for it.
   Example: "The students renting next door are such a pain. I'm going to play my stereo even louder the next time they complain."
8. I should depend on others who are stronger than me.
   Example: "I couldn't survive if she left me."
9. Because something once strongly affected me, it will do so forever.
   Example: "My girlfriend dumped me during my junior year in college. I can never trust a woman again."
10. There is always a perfectly obvious solution to human problems, and it is immoral if this solution is not put into practice.
    Example: "I'm so depressed about politics in this country. It all seems hopeless."

If any of the listed beliefs sound familiar, you may be creating unnecessary emotional distress for yourself by holding on to unrealistic expectations.

Ellis (1979; Ellis & Ellis, 2011) has said that most irrational beliefs come from three core ideas, each of which is unrealistic:

1. I *must* perform well and be approved of by significant others. If I don't, then it is awful, I cannot stand it, and I am a rotten person.
2. You *must* treat me fairly. When you don't, it is horrible, and I cannot bear it.
3. Conditions *must* be the way I want them to be. It is terrible when they are not, and I cannot stand living in such an awful world.

It's easy to see that such beliefs can lead to much grief and needless suffering in a less-than-perfect world. Rational-emotive behavior therapists are very directive in their attempts to change a client's irrational beliefs and "self-talk." The therapist may directly attack clients' logic, challenge their thinking, confront them with evidence contrary to their beliefs, and even assign "homework." Here, for instance, are some examples of statements that dispute irrational beliefs (adapted from Dryden, 2011; Ellis & Ellis, 2011; Kottler & Shepard, 2015):

- "Where is the evidence that you are a loser just because you didn't do well this one time?"
- "Who said the world should be fair? That's your rule."
- "What are you telling yourself to make yourself feel so upset?"
- "Is it really terrible that things aren't working out as you would like? Or is it just inconvenient?"

Many of us would probably do well to give up our irrational beliefs. Improved self-acceptance and a better tolerance of daily annoyances are the benefits of doing so.

Besides REBT, what are some other forms of CBT? Think of times when you have repeatedly "put yourself down" mentally or when you have been preoccupied by needless worries, fears, or other negative and upsetting thoughts. If you want to gain control over such thoughts, a simple form of CBT called **thought stopping** may be helpful. Thought stopping involves interrupting or preventing the upsetting thoughts (Bakker, 2009) that can lead to maladaptive behaviors. You can break your line of thinking by telling yourself "Stop" when the thought occurs (or, as we saw at the beginning of the chapter, you can adopt Chris Evans' method of simply saying "shhhhh"). Another simple thought-stopping technique uses mild physical punishment to suppress upsetting mental images and internal "talk." Simply place a large, flat rubber

Comstock/Stockbyte/Getty Images

Gambling addiction is a growing problem among young people (LaBrie & Shaffer, 2007).

band around your wrist. As you go through the day, apply this rule: Each time you catch yourself thinking the upsetting image or thought, pull the rubber band away from your wrist and snap it. You need not make this terribly painful. Its value lies in drawing your attention to how often you form negative thoughts and in interrupting the flow of thoughts.

CBT in Everyday Life: Gambling Disorder

To see how CBT can be applied, let's consider *gambling disorder*. Imagine that 17-year-old Jonathan has just lost a bundle playing online blackjack. Jonathan started out making $5 bets and then doubled his bet over and over. Surely, he thought, his luck would eventually change. However, he ran out of money after just eight straight losing hands, having lost more than $1,000. Last week, he lost a lot of money playing Texas Hold 'Em. Now Jonathan is in dire straits—he has lost most of his summer earnings, and he's worried about having to drop out of school and tell his parents about his losses. Jonathan has had to admit that he is part of the growing ranks of underage gambling addicts (Dixon et al., 2016; Volberg, 2012).

Like many problem gamblers, Jonathan suffers from several cognitive distortions related to gambling. Here are some mistaken beliefs about gambling (adapted from Toneatto, 2002; Wickwire, Whelan, & Meyers, 2010):

Magnified gambling skill: Your self-confidence is exaggerated, despite the fact that you lose persistently.

Attribution errors: You ascribe your wins to skill but blame your losses on bad luck.

Gambler's fallacy: You believe that a string of losses soon must be followed by wins.

Selective memory: You remember your wins but forget your losses.

Overinterpretation of cues: You put too much faith in irrelevant cues such as bodily sensations or a feeling that your next bet will be a winner.

Luck as a trait: You believe that you are a lucky person in general.

Probability biases: You have incorrect beliefs about randomness and chance events.

Fortunately, a cognitive behavioral therapist helped Jonathan *cognitively restructure* his maladaptive beliefs. He now no longer believes that he can control chance events. Jonathan still gambles a bit, but he does so only recreationally, keeping his losses within his budget and enjoying himself in the process.

Humanistic Therapies

Better self-knowledge was the goal of traditional psychoanalysis. However, Freud claimed that his patients could expect only to change their "hysterical misery into common unhappiness"! Unlike psychoanalysts, humanistic therapists are more optimistic and believe that humans have a natural urge to seek health and self-growth. Also, unlike behavior therapists, humanistic therapists believe humans have a capacity to freely choose to use their potentials fully and live rich, rewarding lives. **Humanistic therapies**, then, tend to be insight therapies intended to help clients gain deeper understanding of their thoughts, emotions, and behavior. Here we discuss three of the most popular humanistic therapies: *client-centered therapy*, *existential therapy*, and *Gestalt therapy*.

Client-Centered Therapy

What is client-centered therapy? How is it different from psychoanalysis? Whereas psychoanalysis is directive and based on insights from the *un*conscious, **client-centered therapy** (or person-centered therapy) is *non*directive and based on insights

Rational-emotive behavior therapy (REBT) Type of treatment designed to identify and change self-defeating thoughts.

Thought stopping The use of aversive stimuli to interrupt or prevent upsetting thoughts.

Humanistic therapies Insight-oriented therapies that help clients better understand themselves with the goal of maximizing their potential.

Client-centered (person-centered) therapy Individual being treated talks without direction, judgment, or interpretation from the therapist.

Psychotherapist Carl Rogers (1902–1987) originated client-centered therapy.

from *conscious* thoughts and feelings (Brodley, 2006; Cain, 2014; Murphy & Joseph, 2016). (Rogers preferred the term client because the word patient implies that a person is sick and needs to be cured.) The client being treated speaks without direction, judgment, or interpretation from the therapist.

A Freudian psychoanalyst tends to take a position of authority, stating what dreams, thoughts, or memories "mean." In contrast, Carl Rogers (1902–1987), who originated client-centered therapy, believed that what is right or valuable for the therapist may be wrong for the client (Rogers, 1959). Consequently, in client-centered therapy, therapists do not try to "fix" clients. Instead, clients must actively seek to solve their problems because they determine what will be discussed during each session (Cooper & McLeod, 2011). The therapist's job is to create a safe "atmosphere of growth" by providing opportunities for change.

How do therapists create such an atmosphere? Rogers believed that effective therapists maintain four basic conditions. First, the therapist offers the client **unconditional positive regard**, or complete, unqualified acceptance of another person as he or she is. The therapist refuses to react with shock, dismay, or disapproval to anything the client says or feels. Total acceptance by the therapist is the first step to self-acceptance by the client.

Second, the therapist attempts to achieve genuine **empathy** by trying to see the world through the client's eyes and feeling some part of what the client is feeling (Grant, 2010).

As a third essential condition, the therapist strives for **authenticity** (to be genuine and honest). The therapist must not hide behind a professional role. Rogers believed that phony fronts destroy the growth atmosphere sought in client-centered therapy.

Fourth, the therapist does not make interpretations, propose solutions, or offer advice. Instead, the therapist relies on **reflection**; that is, rephrasing, summarizing, or repeating the client's thoughts and feelings. This enables the therapist to act as a psychological "mirror" so clients can see themselves more clearly. Rogers theorized that a person armed with a realistic self-image and greater self-acceptance will gradually discover solutions to life's problems.

Existential Therapy

According to the existentialists, "being in the world" (existence) creates deep existential anxiety. Each of us must deal with universal human challenges such as the realities of *death*, the fact that we are *free* to create our private world by making choices, *isolation* on a vast and indifferent planet, and most of all, we must confront feelings of *meaninglessness* (Craig, 2012).

What do these concerns have to do with psychotherapy? **Existential therapy** focuses on the "ultimate concerns" of existence, such as meaning, choice, and responsibility (Vontress, 2013). Like client-centered therapy, it promotes self-knowledge (Adams, 2016). However, there are important differences between the two. Client-centered therapy seeks to uncover a "true self" hidden behind a screen of defenses. In contrast, existential therapy emphasizes free will, the human ability to make choices. Accordingly, existential therapists believe you can choose to become the person you want to be. Existential therapists try to give clients the courage to make rewarding and socially constructive choices.

One example of existential therapy is Victor Frankl's *logotherapy,* which emphasizes the need to find and maintain meaning in life. Frankl (1904–1997) based his approach on experiences that he had as a prisoner in a Nazi concentration camp. In the camp, Frankl saw countless prisoners break down as they were stripped of all hope and human dignity (Frankl, 1955). Those who survived with their sanity did so because they managed to hang on to a sense of meaning (*logos*). Even in less dire circumstances, a sense of purpose in life adds greatly to psychological well-being (Prochaska & Norcross, 2014).

What does the existential therapist do? The therapist helps clients discover self-imposed limitations in personal identity. To be successful, the client must fully accept the challenge of changing his or her life (Bretherton & Orner, 2004). It is interesting that Buddhists seek a similar state that they call "radical acceptance" (Brach, 2003). A key aspect of existential therapy is *confrontation,* in which clients are challenged to be mindful of their values and choices and to take responsibility for the quality of their existence (Claessens, 2009).

An important part of confrontation is the unique, intense, here-and-now encounter between two human beings. When existential therapy is successful, it brings about a renewed sense of purpose and a reappraisal of what's important in life. Some clients even experience an emotional rebirth, as if they had survived a close brush with death.

Gestalt Therapy

Gestalt therapy is based on the idea that perception, or awareness, is disjointed and incomplete in maladjusted persons. The German word *Gestalt* means "whole," or "complete." **Gestalt therapy** helps people rebuild thinking, feeling, and acting into connected wholes. This is achieved by expanding personal awareness; by accepting responsibility for one's thoughts, feelings, and actions; and by filling in gaps in experience (Brownell, 2016).

What are "gaps in experience"? Gestalt therapists believe that we often shy away from expressing or "owning" upsetting feelings. This creates a gap in self-awareness that may become a barrier to personal growth. For example, a person who feels anger after the death of a parent might go for years without fully expressing it. Threatening gaps like this may impair emotional health.

The Gestalt approach is more directive than client-centered or existential therapy, and it is less insight-oriented, instead emphasizing immediate experience. Working either one-on-one or in a group setting, the Gestalt therapist encourages clients to become more aware of their moment-to-moment thoughts, perceptions, and emotions (Frew, 2013). Rather than discussing *why* clients feel guilt, anger, fear, or boredom, the therapist encourages them to have these feelings in the "here and now" and become fully aware of them. The therapist promotes awareness by drawing attention to a client's posture, voice, eye movements, and hand gestures. Clients also may be asked to exaggerate vague feelings until they become clear. Gestalt therapists believe that expressing such feelings allows people to "take care of unfinished business" and break through emotional impasses (Truscott, 2014).

Gestalt therapy is often associated with the work of Fritz Perls (1969). According to Perls, emotional health comes from knowing what you *want* to do, not dwelling on what you *should* do, *ought* to do, or *should want* to do (Wheeler & Axelsson, 2015). In other words, emotional health comes from taking full responsibility for one's feelings and actions. For example, it means changing "I can't" to "I won't," or "I must" to "I choose to."

How does Gestalt therapy help people discover what they really want? Above all else, Gestalt therapy emphasizes present experience (Levin, 2010; Yontef, 2007). Clients are urged to stop intellectualizing and talking about feelings. Instead, they learn to live now; live here; stop imagining; experience the real; stop unnecessary thinking; taste and see; express rather than explain, justify, or judge; give in to unpleasantness and pain just as to pleasure; and surrender to being as you are. Gestalt therapists believe that, paradoxically, the best way to change is to become who you really are (Wheeler & Axelsson, 2015).

Reflective Practice

Cognitive and Humanistic Therapies

Match:

1. ____ Client-centered therapy	A. Changing thought patterns
2. ____ Gestalt therapy	B. Unconditional positive regard
3. ____ Existential therapy	C. Gaps in awareness
4. ____ REBT	D. Choice and becoming

5. The Gestalt therapist tries to *reflect* a client's thoughts and feelings. T or F?

6. Confrontation and encounter are concepts of existential therapy. T or F?

7. According to Beck, selective perception, overgeneralization, and ____________ thinking are cognitive habits that underlie depression.

8. The B in the A-B-C of REBT stands for
a. behavior   c. being
b. belief   d. Beck

THINK CRITICALLY

9. How might using the term *patient* affect the relationship between an individual and a therapist?

SELF-REFLECT

- You are going to play the role of a therapist for a classroom demonstration. How would you act if you were a client-centered therapist? An existential therapist? A Gestalt therapist?
- We all occasionally engage in negative thinking. Can you remember a time recently when you engaged in selective perception? Overgeneralization? All-or-nothing thinking?

Answers: 1. B 2. C 3. D 4. A 5. F 6. T 7. all-or-nothing 8. b 9. The terms *doctor* and *patient* imply a large gap in status and authority between the individual and his or her therapist. Client-centered or person-centered therapy attempts to narrow this gap by making the person the final authority concerning solutions to his or her problems. Also, the word *patient* implies that a person is "sick," and needs to be "cured." Many regard this as an inappropriate way to think about psychological problems.

15.4 Medical Therapies

GATEWAYS LEARNING OUTCOMES:
After reading this section you should be able to:

15.4.1 Name three medical therapies

15.4.2 Explain how hospitalization and community mental health programs can be used to support medical therapies

Psychotherapy can be used to treat many mental disorders, but it may not always be successful. How can you talk someone through their illness if they are suffering a complete psychotic break from reality? And if the primary problem is due to, say, a biochemical imbalance in the brain, it's often better to treat the imbalance itself with medication. For reasons like these, severe mental disorders, such as schizophrenia or major depressive disorders, are more often treated medically—although combinations of medication and psychotherapy can often be helpful (Beck et al., 2009; Trull & Prinstein, 2013).

Three common medical therapies are *drug therapies* (sometimes called *pharmacotherapy*), *brain stimulation therapy*, and *psychosurgery*. They are often done in the context of psychiatric hospitalization, and are typically administered by psychiatrists, who are trained as medical doctors. Let's dig a bit more deeply into each of these three medical therapies before examining the role of hospitalization and community mental health programs in supporting them.

Drug Therapies

The atmosphere in hospital psychiatric wards changed radically in the mid-1950s with the widespread adoption of **pharmacotherapy** (FAR-meh-koe-THER-eh-pea), a term that refers to the use of drugs to treat psychopathology (Prus, 2014). Today, a variety of drugs are used to combat a wide range of problems from the discomforts of milder psychological disorders to the disabling effects of the anxiety disorders, major mood disorders, and even schizophrenia (Maisto, Galizio, & Connors, 2015).

What sort of drugs are used in pharmacotherapy? Five major types of drugs are used (see ▲ Table 15.3 for examples of each

Unconditional positive regard Complete, unqualified acceptance of another person as he or she is.

Empathy A capacity for taking another's point of view; the ability to feel what another is feeling.

Authenticity In Carl Rogers's terms, the ability of a therapist to be genuine and honest about his or her own feelings.

Reflection In client-centered therapy, the process of rephrasing or repeating thoughts and feelings expressed by clients so that they can become aware of what they are saying.

Existential therapy An insight therapy that focuses on the elemental problems of existence, such as death, meaning, choice, and responsibility; emphasizes making courageous life choices.

Gestalt therapy An approach that focuses on immediate experience and awareness to help clients rebuild thinking, feeling, and acting into connected wholes; emphasizes the integration of fragmented experiences.

Pharmacotherapy The use of drugs to treat psychopathology.

▲ Table 15.3 Some Commonly Prescribed Psychiatric Drugs

Class	Examples (trade names)	Effects	Main Mode(s) of Action
Antipsychotics (major tranquilizers)	Clozaril, Haldol, Mellaril, Fanapt, Risperdal, Thorazine, Zyprexa	Reduce agitation, delusions, hallucinations, thought disorders	Reduce effects of dopamine; lesser effects on norepinephrine, serotonin, and acetylcholine
Antianxiety medications (anxiolytics or minor tranquilizers)	Ativan, Klonopin, Librium, Valium, Xanax	Reduce anxiety, tension, fear	Enhance effects of gamma-amino-butyric acid (GABA)
Antidepressants	Brintellix, Effexor, Elavil, Emsam, Nardil, Prozac, Zoloft, Tofranil, Wellbutrin	Counteract depression, some antidepressants also counteract anxiety	Enhance effects of serotonin, dopamine, norepinephrine, or any combination
Mood stabilizers	Lithobid (Lithium)	Counteract bipolar disorder, reduce suicidal tendencies	Currently unclear
Stimulants	Adderall, Concerta, Dexedrine, Ritalin	Counteract attention deficit hyperactivity disorder, narcolepsy	Enhance effects of norepinephrine; lesser effects on dopamine

Sources: Adapted from Abadinsky, 2018; Advokat, Comaty, & Julien, 2014; Prus, 2014.

class of drugs). All achieve their effects by influencing the activity of different brain neurotransmitters (Kalat, 2016; ■ for more information about neurotransmitters, see Section 2.1):

- **Antipsychotic drugs** (major tranquilizers), such as Risperdal, have tranquilizing effects and reduce hallucinations and delusions.

Courtesy of Roger Casier

The work of artist Rodger Casier (1955–2013) illustrates the value of psychiatric care. Despite having a form of schizophrenia, Casier produced artwork that has received public acclaim and has been featured in professional journals. With appropriate treatment, many seriously mentally ill individuals have gone on to lead happy and productive lives.

- **Antianxiety drugs** (anxiolytics [ANG-zee-eh LIT-iks] or minor tranquilizers), such as Valium, produce relaxation or reduce anxiety.
- **Antidepressant drugs**, such as Prozac, are mood-elevating drugs that combat depression.
- **Mood stabilizers** (sometimes called antibipolar drugs), such as Lithobid (lithium), are mood-leveling drugs that level out the extreme mood swings of bipolar disorder.
- **Stimulants**, such as Ritalin, are arousing drugs that paradoxically calm attention deficit hyperactivity disorder.

Studying the Science: Drug Therapy

Evidence consistently suggests that drugs shorten hospital stays, and they have greatly improved the chances that people will recover from major psychological disorders. Drug therapy also has made it possible for many people to return to the community, where they can be treated on an outpatient basis.

Regardless of their benefits, though, drugs are also associated with a number of problems. For example, some antipsychotics, when taken for long periods, can cause *side effects* such as erectile dysfunction and loss of sexual desire (Prus, 2014). Similarly, although the drug clozapine (Clozaril) can relieve the symptoms of schizophrenia, 2 out of 100 patients taking the drug suffer from a potentially fatal blood disease (Mustafa, 2013). Hopefully, newer drugs will improve the risk–benefit ratio in the treatment of severe problems like schizophrenia. One positive development, for example, is that the antipsychotics risperidone (Risperdal) and olanzapine (Zyprexa) appear to be as effective as clozapine without the same degree of risk.

A second problem is that each of the specific drugs that make up each major category of pharmacotherapy has *different effects* and there is no easy way to determine beforehand which is the best specific drug, dosage, or combination of drugs for any given patient. For example, the antidepressant Prozac is an SSRI (selective serotonin reuptake inhibitor) that improves the availability of the neurotransmitter serotonin, while Effexor is an SNRI (serotonin-norepinephrine reuptake inhibitor) that has comparable effects on both serotonin and norepinephrine. Not knowing in advance which one will work better (or at which dosage), however, means that prescription often becomes a frustrating trial-and-error process.

Third, even the best new drugs are *not cure-alls*. They help some people and relieve some problems, but not all. As noted earlier, for many, if not most, mental disorders, a combination of medication and psychotherapy is often very helpful (Kamenov et al., 2016; Oestergaard & Møldrup, 2011). Nevertheless, where schizophrenia and major mood disorders are concerned, drugs will undoubtedly remain the primary mode of treatment (Leucht et al., 2011; Vasa, Carlino, & Pine, 2006).

Brain Stimulation Therapies

In contrast to drug therapies, brain stimulation therapies achieve their effects by altering the electrical activity of the brain. Here we examine three in detail: *electroconvulsive therapy, deep brain stimulation,* and *transcranial magnetic stimulation.*

Electroconvulsive therapy

Electroconvulsive therapy (ECT) is the first, and most dramatic, of the brain stimulation therapies. Widely used since the 1940s, it remains controversial to this day (Case et al., 2013; Choy, Farber, & Kellner, 2017). Although ECT is mainly used to treat depression, it is still occasionally used to treat some other disorders (Cusin et al., 2013; Weiss, Allan, & Greenaway, 2012). In ECT, a 150-volt electrical current is applied to the brain for slightly less than a second. This rather drastic medical treatment for depression triggers a seizure and causes the patient to lose consciousness for a short time. Muscle relaxants and sedative drugs are given before ECT to soften its impact. Treatments are given in a series of sessions spread over several weeks or months.

How does shock help? It is the seizure activity—not the shock—that is believed to be helpful. Proponents of ECT claim that shock-induced seizures alter or "reset" the biochemical and hormonal balance in the brain and body, bringing an end to severe depression and suicidal behavior as well as improving long-term quality of life (Fochtmann, 2016; McCall et al., 2006). Critics have charged that ECT works only by confusing patients so that they can't remember why they were depressed.

Not all professionals support the use of ECT. However, most experts seem to agree on the following four points: (1) At best, ECT produces only temporary improvement—it gets the patient out of a bad spot, but it must be combined with other treatments; (2) ECT can cause memory loss in some patients (Sienaert et al., 2010); (3) ECT should be used only after other treatments have failed; and (4) to lower the chance of a relapse, ECT should be followed by antidepressant drugs (McCall et al., 2011). All told, ECT is considered by many to be a valid treatment for selected cases of depression—especially when it rapidly ends wildly self-destructive or suicidal behavior (Medda et al., 2009). It's interesting to note that most ECT patients feel that the treatment helped them. Most, in fact, would have it done again (Bernstein et al., 1998; Smith et al., 2009).

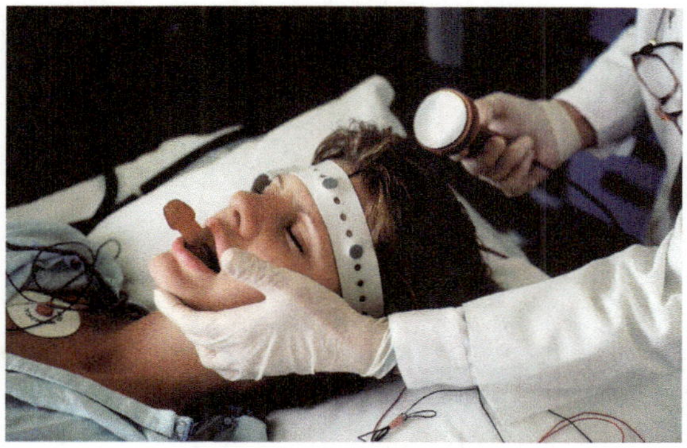
Will McIntyre/Science Source

In ECT, electrodes are attached to the head and a brief electrical current is passed through the brain. ECT is used in the treatment of severe depression.

Deep Brain Stimulation

Unlike ECT, **deep brain stimulation (DBS)** requires surgery to implant electrodes that allow for electrical stimulation of precisely targeted brain regions. In some studies, depressed patients who hadn't benefited from drug therapy and ECT improved when a specific brain region was stimulated (Johansson et al., 2013; Kennedy et al., 2011; Schlaepfer et al., 2008). Also, unlike ECT, DBS can be used to treat disorders other than depression, such as obsessive-compulsive disorder (Haq et al., 2010). (■ Electrical stimulation of the brain is one of several methods used to investigate the brain's inner workings. For more information, see Section 2.2.)

Transcranial Magnetic Stimulation

A promising new technique called **transcranial magnetic stimulation (TMS)** uses magnetic pulses to temporarily block activity in specific parts of the brain (● Figure 15.5). By applying TMS to parts of the frontal lobe, Paulo Boggio and his colleagues (2010) were able to change the way that people made decisions while gambling. It is not a long stretch to imagine that this technique might become a powerful adjunct therapy to cognitive

Antipsychotic drugs (major tranquilizers) Medications that may alleviate hallucinations and delusional thinking associated with mental disorders.

Antianxiety drugs (anxiolytics or minor tranquilizers) Medications that produce relaxation or reduce anxiety.

Antidepressant drugs Medications that combat depression by affecting the levels or activity of neurotransmitters.

Mood stabilizers Medications that combat bipolar disorder by leveling mood swings.

Stimulants (as drugs to treat ADHD) Medications used to calm attention deficit hyperactivity disorder even though they arouse the nervous system.

Electroconvulsive therapy (ECT) Treatment for severe depression in which electrical current is applied to the brain, causing a seizure.

Deep brain stimulation (DBS) Electrical stimulation of precisely targeted brain regions; a surgical procedure is necessary to implant electrodes in the brain that allow for the stimulation.

Transcranial magnetic stimulation (TMS) A device that uses magnetic pulses to temporarily block activity in specific parts of the brain.

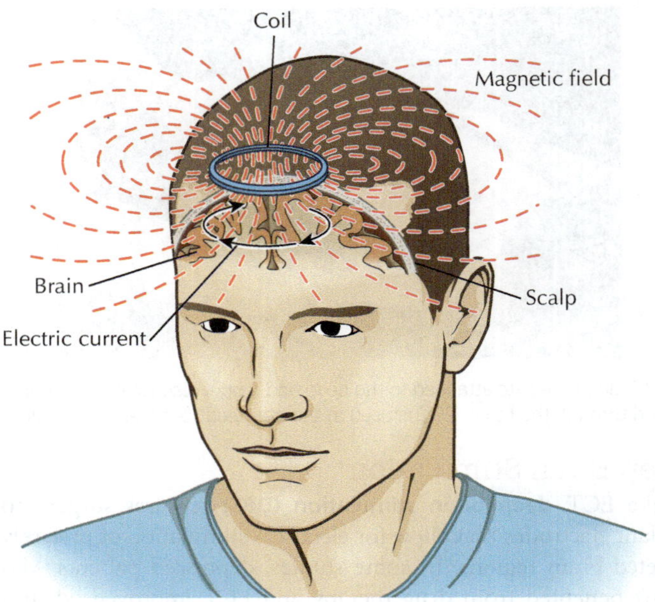

Figure 15.5 Transcranial magnetic stimulation (TMS). TMS uses a small coil held near the surface of the scalp to create magnetic pulses that induce electrical activity in the underlying brain tissue. The result is a temporary blockage of normal brain activity. TMS can be used to study brain function and has already been applied as a medical therapy (Mantovani et al., 2010).

therapy when treating compulsive gambling (Ladouceur, Lachance, & Fournier, 2009). Similarly, patients with obsessive-compulsive disorder have shown marked improvement when TMS disrupted brain areas involved in compulsive behavior (Mantovani et al., 2010).

Psychosurgery

Psychosurgery—any surgical alteration of the brain intended to treat a psychological disorder—is the most extreme medical treatment. The oldest and most radical psychosurgery is the lobotomy. In one specific type—*prefrontal lobotomy*—the frontal lobes are surgically disconnected from other brain areas. This procedure was supposed to calm persons who didn't respond to any other type of treatment.

When the lobotomy was first introduced in the 1940s, there were enthusiastic claims about its success. But later studies suggested that some patients were calmed, some showed no change, and some became mental "vegetables." Lobotomies also produced a high rate of other undesirable side effects, such as seizures, blunted emotions, major personality changes, and stupor. About the same time that such problems became apparent, the first antipsychotic drugs became available. Soon after, the lobotomy was abandoned (Raz, 2013).

To what extent is psychosurgery used now? Psychosurgery is still considered valid by many neurosurgeons. However, most now use *deep lesioning,* in which small target areas are destroyed in the brain's interior. The appeal of deep lesioning is that it targets smaller and more precise regions of the brain, and that it can have value as a remedy for some very specific disorders. For instance, patients suffering from a severe type of obsessive-compulsive disorder may be helped by psychosurgery (Anderson & Booker, 2006; Greenspan & Coghill et al., 2008). (■ Deep lesioning is also a method used to study the brain. See Section 2.2.)

It is worth remembering that psychosurgery cannot be reversed. Whereas a drug can be given or taken away and electrical stimulation can be turned off, you can't take back psychosurgery. Critics argue that psychosurgery should be banned altogether; however, others continue to report success with brain surgery, especially for some very specific and severe disorders (Lévêque, 2014; Sachdev & Chen, 2009).

Hospitalization

Psychiatric hospitalization can be used in conjunction with any of the medical therapies we have discussed and involves placing a person in a protected setting where medical therapy is provided. In fact, hospitalization by itself can also be a form of treatment because staying in a hospital takes patients out of situations that may be sustaining their problems. For example, people with drug addictions may find it nearly impossible to resist the temptations for drug abuse in their daily lives. Hospitalization can help them make a clean break from their self-destructive behavior patterns (André et al., 2003).

At their best, hospitals are sanctuaries that provide diagnosis, support, refuge, and therapy. This is frequently true of psychiatric units in general hospitals and private psychiatric hospitals. At its worst, confinement to an institution can be a brutal experience that leaves people less prepared to face the world than when they arrived. This is more often the case in large state psychiatric hospitals. In most instances, hospitals are best used as a last resort, after other forms of treatment within the community have been exhausted (Trull & Prinstein, 2013).

Another trend in treatment is *partial hospitalization* (Bales & Bateman, 2012). In this approach, some patients spend their days in the hospital but go home at night. Others attend therapy sessions at the hospital during the evening. A major advantage of partial hospitalization is that patients can go home and practice what they've been learning. Overall, partial hospitalization can be

Eric Audras/ONOKY/Getty Images

Depending on the quality of the institution, hospitalization may be a refuge or a brutalizing experience. Many state "asylums" or psychiatric hospitals are antiquated and in need of drastic improvement.

just as effective as full hospitalization (Drymalski & Washburn, 2011; Kiser, Heston, & Paavola, 2006).

Deinstitutionalization

In the last 70 years in the United States, the population in large psychiatric hospitals has dropped by two-thirds. This is largely a result of **deinstitutionalization**, or reduced use of full-time commitment to psychiatric institutions (Hudson, 2016). Long-term institutionalization can lead to dependency, isolation, and continued emotional disturbance (Novella, 2010). Deinstitutionalization was meant to remedy these problems.

How successful has deinstitutionalization been? In truth, its success has been limited (Paulson, 2012). Many states reduced psychiatric hospital populations primarily to save money. The upsetting result is that many chronic patients have been discharged to communities without adequate care. Many former patients have joined the ranks of the homeless. Others are repeatedly jailed for minor crimes. Sadly, patients who trade hospitalization for unemployment, homelessness, and social isolation all too often end up rehospitalized, in jail, or victims of suicide (Hudson, 2016; Markowitz, 2011).

Large psychiatric hospitals may no longer be warehouses for society's unwanted, but many former patients are no better off in bleak nursing homes, single-room hotels, board-and-care homes, shelters, or jails. For example, almost 170,000 mentally ill Americans are currently homeless and almost 385,000 are currently in prison or jail (Treatment Advocacy Center, 2017). These figures suggest that the streets and jails are replacing hospitals as our society's "solution" for mental illness (Markowitz, 2011). Yet, ironically, high-quality care is available in almost every community. As much as anything, a simple lack of money prevents large numbers of people from getting the help they need.

Halfway houses may be a better way to ease a patient's return to the community (Soyez & Broekaert, 2003). A **halfway house** is a short-term group living facility for people making the transition from an institution (mental hospital, prison, and so forth) to independent living. Typically, halfway houses offer supervision and support, without being as restricted and medically oriented as hospitals. They also keep people near their families. Most important, halfway houses can ease a person's return to "normal" life and reduce the chances of being readmitted to a hospital (Davidson et al., 2010).

AP Images/David Goldman

A well-run halfway house can be a humane and cost-effective way to ease people back into the community.

Community Mental Health Programs

Community mental health centers, which offer a wide range of mental health services and psychiatric care, are a bright spot in the area of mental health care (Kloos et al., 2012). Such centers try to help people avoid hospitalization, find answers to mental health problems, and improve mental health literacy (Jorm, 2012; Mark et al., 2013). Typically, they do this by providing short-term treatment, counseling, outpatient care, emergency services, and suicide prevention.

Mental health centers also are concerned with *prevention*. Consultation, education, and **crisis intervention** (skilled management of a psychological emergency) are used to prevent problems before they become serious. Also, some centers attempt to raise the general level of mental health in a community by combating unemployment, delinquency, and drug abuse (Mancini & Wyrick-Waugh, 2013).

Have community mental health centers succeeded in meeting their goals? In practice, they have concentrated much more on providing clinical services than they have on preventing problems. This appears to be primarily the result of wavering government support (translation: money). Overall, community mental health centers have succeeded in making psychological services more accessible than ever. Many of their programs rely on **paraprofessionals**, individuals who work in a near-professional capacity under the supervision of more highly trained staff. Some paraprofessionals are ex-addicts, ex-alcoholics, or ex-patients who have "been there." Many more are persons (paid or volunteer) who have skills in tutoring, crafts, or counseling or who are simply warm, understanding, and skilled at communication. Often, paraprofessionals are more approachable than doctors. This encourages people to seek mental health services that they might otherwise be reluctant to use (Farrand et al., 2009).

Psychosurgery Any surgical alteration of the brain designed to bring about desirable behavioral or emotional changes.

Psychiatric hospitalization Placing a person in a protected, therapeutic environment staffed by mental health professionals.

Deinstitutionalization The reduced use of full-time commitment to mental institutions to treat mental disorders.

Halfway house A community-based facility for individuals making the transition from an institution (mental hospital, prison, and so forth) to independent living.

Community mental health center A facility offering a wide range of mental health services, such as prevention, counseling, consultation, and crisis intervention.

Crisis intervention The skilled management of a psychological emergency.

Paraprofessional An individual who works in a near-professional capacity under the supervision of a more highly trained person.

Reflective Practice

Medical Therapies

1. Major tranquilizers also are known as
   a. anxiolytics
   b. antipsychotics
   c. antidepressants
   d. prefrontal sedatives
2. ECT is a modern form of pharmacotherapy. T or F?
3. Currently, the frontal lobotomy is the most widely used form of psychosurgery. T or F?
4. Deinstitutionalization is an advanced form of partial hospitalization. T or F?

THINK CRITICALLY

5. Residents of Berkeley, California, once voted on a referendum to ban the use of ECT within city limits. Do you think that the use of certain psychiatric treatments should be controlled by law?

SELF-REFLECT

- Keeping in mind that all therapies, and especially medical therapies, have side effects (see, e.g., Casselle, 2009), when is it appropriate to use a medical therapy to treat someone with a mental illness? Why not use psychotherapy instead?
- Why might you choose to combine medical therapy and psychotherapy methods? Can you frame your reasons in terms of the stress-vulnerability model (■ introduced in Section 14.4)?

Answers: 1. b 2. F 3. F 4. F 5. The question of who can prescribe drugs, perform surgery, and administer ECT *is* controlled by law. However, psychiatrists strongly object to residents, city councils, or government agencies making *medical* decisions.

15.5 Psychology and Your Skill Set: Managing Mental Health Issues

GATEWAYS LEARNING OUTCOMES:
After reading this section you should be able to:

15.5.1 Create a plan that will allow you to provide effective help to someone who is experiencing mental health issues

15.5.2 Create a plan that will allow you to find help if you are experiencing mental health issues

We all want to be healthy, strong, and self-reliant. And we often have other people in our lives—children, family, friends, or colleagues—who depend on us. Not wanting to let anyone down, if we are asked, "How are you?" we are prone to respond, "Good, thanks." Admitting you have a problem can be incredibly difficult, but some of the most important skills that we can possess are a self-awareness of our own mental health and, additionally, a willingness to ask for help when we need it. Sometimes all we need is a caring individual to help us work through a problem. Other times we may need more professional help. Mental health issues are common in the United States. Chances are good that at some point you, a friend, or a family member will benefit from mental health services of one kind or another. About 13 percent of all Americans receive treatment for a mental health problem each year (National Institute of Mental Health, 2017).

By the way, we are not counseling you to run for help at the least sign of trouble. By all means, be strong and deal with the issue yourself if you feel that you can (Martin & Pear, 2011; Watson & Tharp, 2014). (■ In Section 6.6, we shared some behavioral self-management skills that can be helpful with a variety of mental health issues.) But if you, or someone you care about, does need help, you should be prepared to act. In the next two sections, we talk about what you can do.

Basic Counseling Skills

While you may not currently be experiencing any mental health problems, perhaps you have a friend who is. If someone close to you asks to talk about his or her troubles, it helps to be prepared. Several general helping skills can be distilled from the various approaches to therapy. Keep these points in mind if you are ever called on to comfort a person in distress, such as a troubled friend or relative (Kottler & Shepard, 2015; Neukrug, 2014; Sharf, 2016) (▲ Table 15.4).

Be an Active Listener

People frequently talk "at" each other without really listening. A person with problems needs to be heard. Make a sincere effort to listen to and understand the person. Try to accept the person's message without judging it or leaping to conclusions. Let the person know you are listening, through eye contact, posture, your tone of voice, and your replies (Kottler & Shepard, 2015).

Reflect Thoughts and Feelings

One of the best things that you can do when offering support to another person is to give feedback by simply restating what is said. This also is a good way to encourage a person to talk. If your

▲ Table 15.4 Helping Behaviors

To help another person gain insight into a personal problem, it is valuable to keep the following comparisons in mind:

Behaviors That Help	Behaviors That Hinder
Active listening	Probing painful topics
Acceptance	Judging/moralizing
Reflecting feelings	Criticism
Open-ended questioning	Threats
Supportive statements	Rejection
Respect	Ridicule/sarcasm
Patience	Impatience
Genuineness	Placing blame
Paraphrasing	Opinionated statements

Source: Adapted from Kottler & Shepard, 2015.

friend seems to be at a loss for words, *restate* or *paraphrase* his or her last sentence. Here's an example:

> *Friend:* I'm really down about school. I can't get interested in any of my classes. I flunked my Spanish test, and somebody stole my notebook for psychology.
> *You:* So you're really upset about school?
> *Friend:* Yeah, and my parents are hassling me about my grades again.
> *You:* You're feeling pressured by your parents?
> *Friend:* Yeah.

As simple as this sounds, it is very helpful to someone trying to sort out feelings. Try it. If nothing else, you'll develop a reputation as a fantastic conversationalist!

Don't Be Afraid of Silence

Counselors tend to wait longer before responding than do people in everyday conversations. Pauses of five seconds or more are not unusual, and interrupting is rare. Listening patiently lets the person feel unhurried and encourages her or him to speak freely.

Ask Open-Ended Questions

Because your goal is to encourage free expression, *open-ended questions* tend to be the most helpful. A *closed question* is one that can be answered yes or no. Open-ended questions call for an open-ended reply. Say, for example, that a friend tells you, "I feel like my boss has it in for me at work." A closed question would be, "Oh, yeah? So, are you going to quit?" Open-ended questions such as, "Do you want to talk about it?" or "How do you feel about it?" are more likely to be helpful.

Clarify Problems

People who have a clear idea of what is wrong in their lives are more likely to discover solutions. Try to understand the problem from the person's point of view. As you do, check your understanding often. For example, you might ask, "Are you saying that you feel depressed just at school? Or in general?" Remember, a problem well defined is often half solved.

Focus on Feelings

Feelings are neither right nor wrong. By focusing on feelings, you can encourage the outpouring of emotion that is the basis for catharsis. Passing judgment on what is said just makes people defensive. For example, a friend confides that he has failed a test. Perhaps you know that he studies very little. If you say, "Just study more and you will do better," he will probably become defensive or hostile. Much more can be accomplished by saying, "You must feel very frustrated" or simply, "How do you feel about it?"

Avoid Giving Advice

Many people mistakenly think that they must solve problems for others. Remember that your goal is to provide understanding and support, not solutions. Of course, it is reasonable to give advice when you are asked for it, but beware of the trap of the "Why don't you . . . ? Yes, but . . ." game. According to psychotherapist Eric Berne (1964), this "game" follows a pattern: Someone says, "I have this problem." You say, "Why don't you do this?" The person replies, "Yes, but . . ." and then tells you why your suggestion won't work. If you make a new suggestion, the reply once again will be, "Yes, but . . . ." Obviously, the person either knows more about his or her personal situation than you do, or he or she has reasons for avoiding your advice. The student described earlier knows that he needs to study. His problem is to understand why he doesn't *want* to study.

Accept the Person's Frame of Reference

Because we all live in different psychological worlds, there is no "correct" view of a life situation. Try to resist imposing your views on the problems of others. A person who feels that his or her viewpoint has been understood feels freer to examine it objectively and to question it.

Maintain Confidentiality

Your efforts to help will be wasted if you fail to respect the privacy of someone who has confided in you. Put yourself in the person's place. Don't gossip.

The points just made help define the qualities of a helping relationship. They also emphasize that each of us can supply two of the greatest mental health resources available at any cost: friendship and honest communication. However, in closing, it is important to remember that only a licensed professional possesses the full set of skills necessary to counsel more serious mental health issues. The *instant* you realize that your problem is beyond your friend's ability to properly address, or that your friend's problem is beyond your ability to address, help your friend find a more qualified counselor. Seeking more professional counseling is not a sign of failure for either you or your friend; it is a testimony to your own wisdom. Although your textbook authors are psychologists, we are not licensed counselors and quite frequently refer students to our college counseling centers.

Getting Counseling

In some cases, mental health challenges are best managed with the support of a professional. In this section, we review some basic information about things to consider should you decide to seek counseling for yourself.

How would I know if I should seek professional help at some point in my life? Although this question has no simple answer, the following guidelines may be helpful:

1. If your level of psychological discomfort (unhappiness, anxiety, or depression, for example) is comparable to a level of physical discomfort that would cause you to see a doctor or dentist, you should consider seeing a psychologist or a psychiatrist.
2. Another signal to watch for is significant changes in behavior, such as the quality of your work (or schoolwork), your rate of absenteeism, your use of drugs (including alcohol), or your relationships with others.
3. Perhaps you have urged a friend or relative to seek professional help and were dismayed because he or she refused to do so. If *you* find friends or relatives making a similar

suggestion, recognize that they may be seeing things more clearly than you are.
4. If you have persistent or disturbing suicidal thoughts or impulses, seek help immediately.

Locating a Therapist

If I wanted to talk to a therapist, how would I find one? Here are some suggestions that can help you get started:

1. **Your family physician.** Your family physician, if you have one, often will be able to help you find the help you are seeking.
2. **Colleges and universities.** If you are a student, don't overlook counseling services offered by a student health center or special student counseling facilities.
3. **Workplaces.** If you have a job, check with your employer. Some employers have employee assistance programs that offer confidential free or low-cost therapy for employees.
4. **Community or county mental health centers.** Most counties and many cities offer public mental health services. (These are listed in the phone book or can be found by searching the Internet.) Public mental health centers usually provide counseling and therapy services directly, and they can refer you to private therapists.
5. **Mental health associations.** Many cities have mental health associations organized by concerned citizens. Groups such as these usually keep listings of qualified therapists and other services and programs in the community.
6. **The Yellow Pages.** Psychologists are listed in the telephone book or on the Internet under "Psychologists," or in some cases under "Counseling Services." Psychiatrists are generally listed as a subheading under "Physicians." Counselors are usually found under the heading "Marriage and Family Counselors." These listings will usually put you in touch with individuals in private practice.
7. **Crisis hotlines.** A typical crisis hotline is a phone service staffed by volunteers. These people are trained to provide information concerning a wide range of mental health problems. They also have lists of organizations, services, and other resources in the community where you can go for help.

▲ Table 15.5 summarizes the sources for psychotherapy, counseling, and referrals we have discussed as well as some additional possibilities.

Therapeutic Options

How would I know what kind of a therapist to see? How would I pick one? The choice between a psychiatrist and a psychologist is somewhat arbitrary. Both are trained to do psychotherapy and can be equally effective as therapists. Although a psychiatrist can administer **somatic therapy** and prescribe drugs, so can psychologists in New Mexico, Louisiana, and Illinois along with psychologists in the US military (Munsey, 2006). A psychologist also can work in conjunction with a physician if such services are needed.

Be aware that most health insurance plans will pay for psychological services. If fees are a problem, keep in mind that many therapists charge on a sliding scale, or ability-to-pay basis, and that community mental health centers almost always charge on that basis as well. In one way or another, help is almost always available for anyone who needs it.

▲ Table 15.5 Mental Health Resources

- Family doctors (for referrals to mental health professionals)
- Mental health specialists, such as psychiatrists, psychologists, social workers, and mental health counselors
- Religious leaders/counselors
- Health maintenance organizations (HMOs)
- Community mental health centers
- Hospital psychiatry departments and outpatient clinics
- University- or medical school-affiliated programs
- State hospital outpatient clinics
- Family service/social agencies
- Private clinics and facilities
- Employee assistance programs
- Local medical, psychiatric, or psychological societies

Some communities and college campuses have counseling services staffed by sympathetic paraprofessionals or peer counselors. These services are free or very low cost. As mentioned previously, paraprofessionals are people who work in a near-professional capacity under professional supervision. **Peer counselors** are nonprofessional persons who have learned basic counseling skills. There is a natural tendency, perhaps, to doubt the abilities of paraprofessionals. However, paraprofessional counselors are often as effective as professionals (Farrand et al., 2009).

Also, don't overlook **self-help groups**, which can add valuable support to professional treatment. Members of a self-help group typically share a particular type of problem, such as eating disorders, alcoholism, or coping with an alcoholic parent. Self-help groups offer members mutual support and a chance to discuss problems. In many instances, helping others also serves as therapy for those who give help. For some problems, self-help groups may be the best choice of all (Dadich, 2010; Galanter et al., 2005).

Look at Qualifications

You can usually find out about a therapist's qualifications simply by asking. A reputable therapist will be glad to reveal his or her background. If you have any doubts, credentials may be checked and other helpful information can be obtained from local branches of any of the following organizations. You also can browse the websites listed here:

American Association for Marriage and Family Therapy (www.aamft.org)
American Family Therapy Academy (www.afta.org)
American Psychiatric Association (www.psych.org)
American Psychological Association (www.apa.org)
Association of Humanistic Psychology (www.ahpweb.org)
Canadian Psychiatric Association (www.cpa-apc.org)
Canadian Psychological Association (www.cpa.ca)
Mental Health America (www.mhanational.org)

The question of how to pick a particular therapist remains. The best way is to start with a short consultation with a respected psychiatrist, psychologist, or counselor. This allows the person that you consult to evaluate your difficulty and recommend a type of therapy, or a therapist who is likely to be helpful. As an alternative, you might ask the person teaching this course for a referral.

Evaluating a Therapist

How would I know a therapist is being effective? A balanced look at psychotherapies suggests that all techniques can be equally successful. However, all therapists are not equally successful (Elliott & Williams, 2003). Former clients consistently rate the person doing the therapy as more important than the type of therapy used (Elliott & Williams, 2003).

Ask yourself if you feel you are establishing a therapeutic alliance with your therapist. A therapist who is working *with* you is usually willing to use whatever method seems most helpful for a client. He or she also can be evaluated on personal characteristics of warmth, integrity, sincerity, and empathy (Okiishi et al., 2003; Prochaska & Norcross, 2014). The relationship between a client and a therapist is the therapist's most basic tool (Hubble, Duncan, & Miller, 1999; Prochaska & Norcross, 2014). This is why you must trust and easily relate to a therapist for therapy to be effective. Here are some danger signals to watch for in psychotherapy:

- Sexual advances by a therapist
- A therapist who makes repeated verbal threats or is physically aggressive
- A therapist who is excessively blaming, belittling, hostile, or controlling
- A therapist who makes excessive small talk; talks repeatedly about his or her own problems
- A therapist who encourages prolonged dependence on him or her
- A therapist who demands absolute trust or tells the client not to discuss therapy with anyone else

An especially important part of the therapeutic alliance is agreement about the goals of therapy (Bartle-Haring et al., 2016). It is therefore a good idea to think about what you want to accomplish by entering therapy. Write down your goals and discuss them with your therapist during the first session. Your first meeting with a therapist should also answer all the following questions:

- Will the information I reveal in therapy remain completely confidential?
- What risks do I face if I begin therapy?
- How long do you expect treatment to last?
- What form of treatment do you expect to use?
- Are there alternatives to therapy that might help me as much or more?

It's always tempting to avoid facing personal problems. With this in mind, you should give a therapist a fair chance and not give up too easily. But don't hesitate to change therapists or to terminate therapy if you lose confidence in the therapist or if you don't relate well to the therapist as a person. After all, you are the person in the best position to judge whether therapy is doing its job—helping you to feel better!

Reflective Practice

Psychology and Your Skill Set: Managing Mental Health Issues

1. Listening to people talk about their problems is usually more helpful than offering them your advice. T or F?
2. Instead of judging people who ask you for help, it is better to
   a. accept their frame of reference
   b. tell them what to do
   c. tell them about your problems
   d. avoid focusing on feelings
3. Persistent emotional discomfort is a clear sign that professional psychological counseling should be sought. T or F?
4. Community mental health centers rarely offer counseling or therapy themselves; they only do referrals. T or F?
5. In many instances, a therapist's personal qualities have more of an effect on the outcome of therapy than the type of therapy used. T or F?

THINK CRITICALLY

6. Would it be acceptable for a therapist to urge a client to break all ties with a troublesome family member?

SELF-REFLECT

- Review the sections of this chapter on behavioral and cognitive therapies. How could you use thought stopping, covert sensitization, and covert reinforcement to change your behavior?
- Just for practice, make a fear hierarchy for a situation that you find frightening. Does vividly picturing items in the hierarchy make you tense or anxious? If so, can you intentionally relax using the tension-release method?
- Which of the basic counseling skills would improve your ability to help a person in distress (or even just have an engaging conversation)?
- Take some time to find out what mental health services are available to you.

Answers: 1. T 2. a 3. T 4. F 5. T 6. Such decisions must be made by clients themselves. Therapists can help clients evaluate important decisions and feelings about significant persons in their lives. However, actively urging a client to sever a relationship borders on unethical behavior.

Somatic therapy Any bodily therapy, such as drug therapy, electroconvulsive therapy, or psychosurgery.

Peer counselor A nonprofessional person who has learned basic counseling skills.

Self-help group A group of people who share a particular type of problem and provide mutual support to one another.

Gateways to Therapy

Summary: Gateways Learning Outcomes

15.1 The Origins and Effectiveness of Psychotherapy

15.1.1 Briefly describe how mental health problems were treated before the 1900s

All psychotherapy aims to facilitate positive changes in personality, behavior, or adjustment. Early approaches to mental illness were dominated by superstition and moral condemnation. Demonology attributed mental disturbance to demonic possession and prescribed exorcism as the cure. More humane treatment began in 1793 with the work of Philippe Pinel in Paris.

15.1.2 Describe the main elements of psychoanalysis

Sigmund Freud developed psychoanalysis, the first psychotherapy, little more than a hundred years ago. As the first true psychotherapy, Freud's psychoanalysis gave rise to modern psychodynamic therapies, although traditional psychoanalysts are now hard to find. The main elements of psychoanalysis include *free association*, *dream analysis*, and *analysis of resistance and transference*, each of which is believed to reveal health-producing insights.

15.1.3 Outline five characteristics that distinguish different psychotherapies

First, therapies may be *insight or action oriented*. Insight therapies rely on gaining a conscious understanding of one's challenges; action therapies focus on changing problematic thoughts and behaviors. Second, therapy can be *directive or non-directive*. The former refers to techniques in which the therapist leads a client through the therapeutic process while the latter involves therapists working to create conditions that allow clients to resolve their own issues. Third, therapy can be *open-ended or time-limited*. Fourth, psychotherapies may be conducted with *individuals or groups*. Fifth, therapies may be effectively conducted either *face-to-face or at a distance*, via telephone and the Internet.

15.1.4 Name four features of effective psychotherapy

The success of any particular therapy depends on the *characteristics of the client*, *characteristics of the therapist*, the relationship between the therapist and client (i.e., the *therapeutic alliance*), and the *nature of the problem* for which therapy is being provided.

15.2 Behavior Therapies

15.2.1 Describe the main elements of behavior therapies

Behavior therapists use the learning principles of classical or operant conditioning to directly change human behavior. This type of psychotherapy does not rely on clients achieving deep insight into their problems but instead focuses on altering maladaptive thoughts and behaviors.

15.2.2 Describe two therapies that are based on classical conditioning

Two therapies based on classical conditioning include *aversion therapy* and *exposure therapy*. In aversion therapy, classical conditioning is used to associate maladaptive behavior (such as smoking or drinking) with pain or other aversive events to inhibit undesirable responses. In exposure therapy, clients are exposed to situations or objects that cause them to feel intense fear. This type of contact allows the client to eliminate conditioned emotional responses originally acquired through classical conditioning by learning that their anxiety is unwarranted. Three types of exposure therapy are flooding, systematic desensitization, and modeling.

15.2.3 Describe two therapies that are based on operant conditioning

Operant principles, such as positive reinforcement, non-reinforcement, extinction, punishment, shaping, stimulus control, and time-out, are used to extinguish undesirable responses and to promote constructive behavior. Nonreward can also help extinguish troublesome behaviors. Often, this is done by simply identifying and eliminating reinforcers, particularly attention and social approval.

Two types of therapy that employ operant principles are *intensive behavioral intervention (IBI)* and *token economies*. IBI uses positive reinforcement and shaping to bring about new behaviors, and is often used with children diagnosed with autism. Tokens are often used to reinforce selected target behaviors; the tokens can be exchanged for other benefits (material goods or privileges) when a sufficient number are accumulated. Full-scale use of tokens in an institutional setting produces a token economy.

15.3 Cognitive and Humanistic Therapies

15.3.1 Describe the main elements of cognitive therapies

Cognitive therapies emphasize changing thought patterns that underlie emotional or behavioral problems. Its goals are to correct distorted thinking, teach improved coping skills, or both. For example, Aaron

Beck's cognitive therapy focuses on changing several major distortions in thinking: selective perception, overgeneralization, and all-or-nothing thinking. Cognitive and behavior therapies can also be combined, resulting in cognitive behavior therapy (CBT). Albert Ellis's early version of cognitive behavior therapy, called rational-emotive behavior therapy (REBT), requires that clients learn to recognize and challenge the irrational beliefs that are at the core of their maladaptive thinking patterns.

15.3.2 Describe the main elements of humanistic therapies

Humanistic therapies are insight-oriented therapies that are focused on helping clients to gain a deeper understanding of their thoughts, emotions, and behaviors.

15.3.3 Describe three humanistic therapies

Client-centered (or person-centered) therapy is non-directive, based on insights gained from conscious thoughts and feelings, and dedicated to creating an atmosphere of growth. Unconditional positive regard, empathy, authenticity, and reflection are combined to give the client a chance to solve his or her own problems. *Existential therapies* focus on the end result of the choices one makes in life. Clients are encouraged through confrontation and encounter to exercise free will and to take responsibility for their choices. *Gestalt therapy* emphasizes immediate awareness of thoughts and feelings. Its goal is to rebuild thinking, feeling, and acting into connected wholes and to help clients break through emotional blockages.

15.4 Medical Therapies

15.4.1 Name three medical therapies

Three medical, or somatic, approaches to treatment are *pharmacotherapy* (that is, the use of drugs), *brain stimulation therapy* (including electroconvulsive therapy [ECT]), and *psychosurgery*.

15.4.2 Explain how hospitalization and community mental health programs can be used to support medical therapies

Hospitalization, including partial hospitalization, involves placing a person in a protected setting where medical therapy is provided. Community mental health centers seek to avoid or minimize hospitalization. They also seek to prevent mental health problems through education, consultation, and crisis intervention.

15.5 Psychology and Your Skill Set: Managing Mental Health Issues

15.5.1 Create a plan that will allow you to provide effective help to someone who is experiencing mental health issues

There are many things that you can do to help when listening to someone else describe their mental health issues. These include: being an active listener, reflecting the person's thoughts and feelings, welcoming silence, asking open-ended questions, clarifying problems, focusing on feelings, avoiding advice, accepting their frame of reference, and maintaining their confidence.

15.5.2 Create a plan that will allow you to find help if you are experiencing mental health issues

There are many places to find counselors, including university and community health centers, family doctors, crisis hotlines, and the Yellow Pages. There are various types of counseling options, including psychologists, psychiatrists, peer counselors, and self-help groups. Practical considerations such as cost and qualifications enter into choosing a therapist. However, the therapist's personal characteristics are of equal importance.

16 Social Thinking and Social Influence

Gateway Theme Humans are social animals. The social world we live in profoundly shapes our thoughts, feelings, perceptions, and behavior.

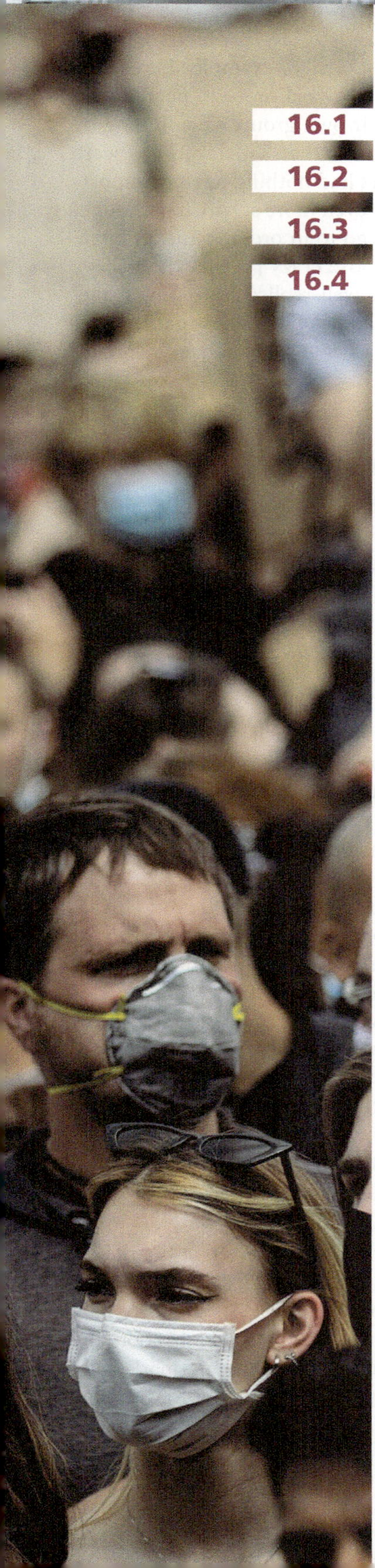

Chapter Outline

I Can't Breathe…

These three words were among the last ones spoken by George Floyd after a Minneapolis police officer attempted to arrest him for passing a suspected counterfeit 20 dollar bill. In front of three fellow policemen and several witnesses, the officer used his knee to pin Mr Floyd's neck to the pavement for more than eight minutes. At the end of that time there was no longer any need for such a dramatic show of force, because by then George Floyd was dead.

In the weeks that followed this incident, George Floyd's words became the rallying cry of the Black Lives Matter movement and protests quickly spread from Minneapolis to other parts of the United States Initially, large public gatherings focused on established norms that seemed to govern law enforcement agencies, including an acceptance of brutality that is disproportionately directed toward Black Americans and other people of color. As the movement gathered strength, though, its focus expanded well beyond policing. America began a difficult reckoning with racist attitudes that continue to pervade the power structures of businesses, government, and social institutions such as health care and education.

In this chapter, we turn our attention to the influence of social groups, examining many of the key concepts that have been underscored by the Black Lives Matter movement. These include group norms, power and status, attitudes, conformity, and obedience to authority. But while group norms and behavior can sometimes lead us to engage in harmful activities, this is not always the case: In the final section of this chapter we explore teamwork, and the many ways that people can come together as a force for positive change.

16.1 The Fundamentals of Social Groups

GATEWAYS LEARNING OUTCOMES:
After reading this section, you will be able to:

16.1.1 Distinguish between ingroups and outgroups, and define ingroup favoritism

16.1.2 Define what is meant by the terms group structure, group cohesiveness, norms, social roles, social status, and social power

16.1.3 Explain how social comparisons are typically carried out

16.1.4 Discriminate between internal and external attributions, and the three factors that determine which type is made

16.1.5 Contrast the fundamental attribution error and the actor–observer bias

Social psychology is the study of how individuals think and behave in social situations; that is, in the actual or imagined presence of others (Baumeister & Bushman, 2017). The impact of others on our behavior begins early and lasts a lifetime: We are born into organized societies, and the **culture**—a set of evolving values, expectations, and behavior patterns—is present when we arrive and is passed from one generation to the next.

Social Groups

Each of us belongs to several social groups, based on our characteristics and the categories with which we identify. Our membership in some of these groups, such as biological sex, can be fixed over time while others, like the football team you support, have the potential to change. We are members of some groups by default (say, the one comprised of citizens from the country where we were born), while membership in other groups (like the one made up of students at your college) is freely chosen. For social psychologists, an **ingroup** is any group to which you feel a sense of belonging; conversely, an **outgroup** is one to which you do not belong.

Very likely, your own ingroups are defined by a combination of prominent social dimensions, such as nationality, ethnicity, age, education, religion, income, political values, gender, sexual orientation, and so forth. Ingroup membership helps define who we are socially. Predictably, we are more likely to attribute positive characteristics to our ingroup and negative qualities to outgroups. We also tend to exaggerate differences between ingroup and outgroup members. This sort of "us and them" can sometimes set the stage for racial and ethnic prejudice and for conflict between groups more generally—topics we will explore in the next chapter.

The tendency to categorize ourselves as a group member is a very powerful one. Indeed, in early experiments, Henri Tajfel found that people needed no prompting to think in terms of ingroups and outgroups, even when those groups had been created based on chance (for example, whether you received heads or tails in a coin toss) or factors that seemed trivial (such as whether you think a hot dog is a sandwich or not) (Tajfel, 1978; Turner, 1975).

In these studies, evidence of allegiance to one's group was seen in clear evidence of *ingroup favoritism* (or ingroup bias), a situation in which we behave in ways that will improve the circumstances of our ingroup. When asked to award points or small amounts of money to anonymous others, for example, there was a reliable tendency for participants to award more to people who were identified as belonging to their own group. This finding by itself was somewhat surprising, given that Tajfel's groups were formed in such a way that members had nothing terribly important in common. What was perhaps even more surprising, though, was the lengths that people would go to in order to discriminate against the outgroup (you know, those crazy people who believe that hot dogs are sandwiches). In a well-replicated finding, Tajfel observed that people would actually make decisions that resulted in a *loss* for the ingroup, *as long as it meant that the outgroup would lose even more.*

Characteristics of Groups

Tajfel's findings provide powerful evidence for a preference to align ourselves with others, and to behave in ways that will benefit other members of our group. In this section, we'll take a closer look at what psychological scientists have learned about groups. In particular, we'll look at three specific characteristics of groups, including their *structure*, *cohesion*, and *norms*.

Structure and Cohesion

Two important dimensions of any group are its structure and its cohesiveness (Forsyth, 2014). **Group structure** consists of the network of roles, communication pathways, and power in a group. Organized groups such as an army or an athletic team have a high degree of structure. In contrast, informal friendship groups may or may not be very structured.

Group cohesiveness refers to the extent to which group members want to remain in the group. Members of cohesive groups often stick together: They tend to stand or sit close together, they pay more attention to one another, and they show more signs of mutual affection. Also, their behavior tends to be closely coordinated (Lin & Peng, 2010). Cohesiveness is the basis for much of the power that groups exert over us. Therapy groups, businesses, sports teams, and the like seek to increase cohesion because it helps people work together more effectively (Boyd et al., 2014; Casey-Campbell & Martens, 2009).

Norms

A third characteristic of groups is the set of norms that they adopt (Matsumoto & Juang, 2017; Miller & Prentice, 2016). A **norm** is a widely accepted (but often unspoken) standard for appropriate behavior within the group. If you have the slightest doubt about the power of norms, try this test: Walk into a crowded supermarket, get in a checkout line, and begin singing loudly at the top of your

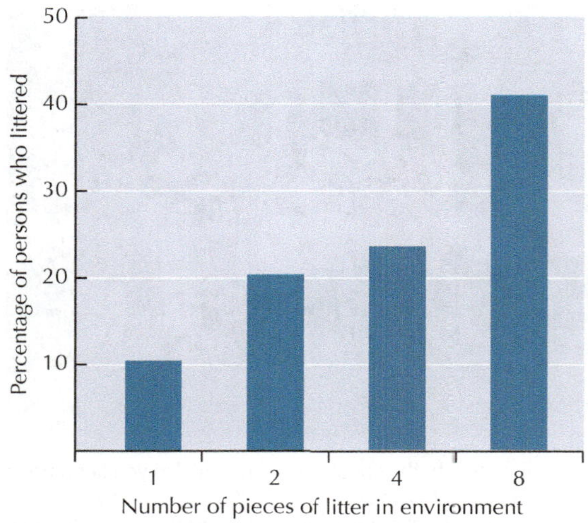

Figure 16.1 Results of an experiment on norms concerning littering. The existence of litter in a public setting implies that littering is acceptable. This encourages others to "trash" the area. (From Cialdini, Reno, & Kallgren, 1990.)

lungs. Are you one of the very rare people who could do this without feeling any discomfort? For most people, this type of behavior violates our society's basic unspoken norms about "appropriate check-out line behavior," and would feel very uncomfortable.

The impact of norms can be seen in a classic study of littering. The question was, "Does the amount of trash in an area affect littering?" To find out, people were given flyers as they walked into a public parking garage. As you can see in Figure 16.1, the more litter there was on the floor, the more likely people were to add to it by dropping their flyer. Apparently, seeing that others had already littered implied a lax social norm about whether littering is acceptable. The moral? The cleaner a public area is kept, the less likely people are to "trash" it (Cialdini, Reno, & Kallgren, 1990; Göckeritz et al., 2010).

Characteristics of Individuals Within Groups

Now that we've had an opportunity to examine some of the features that define social groups, let's turn our attention to the characteristics of individuals that make up the groups, including their *roles*, *status*, and *power* within the group.

Social Roles

We all belong to many overlapping social groups and in each one we occupy a *position* in the *structure* of the group. A **social role** is a pattern of behavior expected of a person in a particular social position within the group (Baumeister & Bushman, 2017). For instance, Amka may simultaneously hold the roles of mother, boss, and daughter, each of which involves different sets of behaviors and expectations. Some roles are *ascribed* (they are assigned to a person or are not under personal control); for example, male or female, son or daughter, infant or adolescent, and so on.

digis/Shutterstock.com

Wrapped in ever-expanding social networks, we are never far from other people. They are always right beside us, just around the next corner, or only a phone call or text message away. Nevertheless, a little solitude can be healthy.

dotshock/Shutterstock.com

Ascribed roles have a powerful impact on social behavior. What kinds of behavior do you expect from your teachers or your coaches? What behaviors do they expect from you? What happens if either of you fails to match the other's expectations?

Social psychology Study of how individuals think and behave in social situations.

Culture An ongoing pattern of life, characterizing a society at a given point in history.

Ingroup A group with which a person identifies.

Outgroup A group with which a person does not identify.

Group structure The network of roles, communication pathways, and power in a group.

Group cohesiveness The degree of attraction among group members or their commitment to remaining in the group.

Norm A widely accepted (but often unspoken) standard of conduct for appropriate behavior.

Social role Expected behavior patterns associated with particular social positions (such as daughter, worker, or student).

Achieved roles are voluntarily attained by special effort; examples include spouse, teacher, scientist, bandleader, and criminal.

Roles streamline daily interactions by allowing us to anticipate what others will do: For example, when a person has the role of doctor, mother, clerk, or police officer, we expect certain behaviors from them. However, roles can have a negative side, too. For example, many people experience **role conflicts**, in which two or more roles make conflicting demands on them (Gordon et al., 2012; Memili et al., 2015). Consider, a teacher who must fail a close friend's son, a mother who has a demanding full-time job, or a soccer coach whose daughter is on the team but isn't a very good athlete. Likewise, the clashing demands of work, family, and school create role conflicts for many students (Senécal, Julien, & Guay, 2003). Role conflicts at work can lead to job burnout and negative health outcomes (Pomaki, Supeli, & Verhoeven, 2007; Schmidt et al., 2014).

Social Status and Social Power

Two additional characteristics of individual group members relate to the extent to which they hold prestige and dominance relative to others within the group. **Social status** refers to the degree to which other group members respect and admire a person, while **social power** refers to the degree to which a person possesses the capacity to control the behavior of other group members (Hays, 2013). A person can be high in both social status and social power (such as a popular chief of police), high in one but not the other (such as a famous actor who has high social status while having little social power), or be low in both (like most homeless people). Incidentally, men generally prefer social power over status while women generally prefer status over power (Hays, 2013).

While higher social power obviously bestows special privileges, so too can higher social status (Albrecht & Albrecht, 2011). For example, in one experiment, a man walked into several bakeries and asked for a pastry while claiming that he did not have enough money to pay for it. Half the time he was well dressed, and the rest of the time he was poorly dressed. If the man was polite when he asked, he was equally likely to be given a free pastry no matter how he was dressed (95 percent vs. 90 percent). However, if he was impolite when he asked, he was much less likely to get a pastry if he was poorly dressed than if he was well dressed (75 percent vs. 20 percent) (Guéguen & Pascual, 2003).

You don't have to be in a bakery for this to work. In most situations, we are more likely to comply with a request made by a high-status (well-dressed) person (Guéguen & Lamy, 2012). Perhaps the better treatment given to people with higher social power or status, even when they are impolite, explains some of our society's preoccupation with expensive clothes, cars, and other social power and status symbols.

Social Cognition: Thinking About Group Members

Social cognition is the process of thinking about ourselves and others in a social context (Happé, Cook, & Bird, 2017; Shook, 2013). In the next few sections, we'll consider two examples of

Visions of America, LLC/Alamy Stock Photo

Have you ever gone to a high school class reunion? Do you keep track of your high school classmates on social media (Cramer, Song, & Drent, 2016)? Apparently, it's hard to resist comparing yourself with former classmates to see how you are doing in life.

social cognition. We begin with *social comparison*, and then move on to consider the process of making *attributions*.

Social Comparison

If you want to know how heavy you are, you simply get on a scale to obtain an objective measure. But how do you know if you are a good athlete, worker, parent, or friend? How do you know if your views on politics, religion, or music are unusual or widely shared? When there are no objective standards, the only available yardstick is provided by comparing yourself with others (Baumeister & Bushman, 2017; Dvash et al., 2010).

Social psychologist Leon Festinger (1919–1989) theorized that group membership fills a need for **social comparison**, which refers to the process of comparing your own actions, feelings, opinions, or abilities to those of others. If you have ever "compared notes" with other students after taking an exam ("How did you do?" "Wasn't that last question hard?"), that's exactly what you were doing (Festinger, 1957; Johnson & Lammers, 2012).

Typically, we don't make social comparisons randomly or on some absolute scale. Meaningful evaluations are usually based on comparing yourself with people of similar backgrounds, abilities, and circumstances (Stapel & Marx, 2007). To illustrate, imagine asking a student named Alex if he is a good basketball player. If Alex compares himself with Michael Jordan, the answer will clearly be no. But a comparison with someone whose level of achievement is exceptionally high isn't typically very helpful, because it tells us little about Alex's relative ability among people with relatively similar experiences or training. On the school basketball team, for example, Alex is regarded as an excellent player. Using this more appropriate scale of comparison, then, Alex is more likely to conclude that he's a good player. In the same way, thinking of yourself as successful, talented, responsible, or fairly paid depends entirely on whom you choose for comparison (Johnson & Stapel, 2010; Strickhouser & Zell, 2015).

There are at least three motives for engaging in social comparison. As Alex's case demonstrates, the first is to *provide information*. However, a second motive is to meet a need for *self-protection or self-enhancement*; in other words, to make yourself feel better

▲ Table 16.1 Making Internal and External Attributions

Why did Ellie yell at Jake?	Consensus?	Distinctiveness?	Consistency?
Internal Attributions—it's something about Ellie—will be made when the behavior is…	**low** in consensus: Ellie is the only one who yells at Jake	**low** in distinctiveness: Ellie yells at lots of people in the class	**high** in consistency: Ellie yells at Jake during every class
External Attributions—it's something about Jake—will be made when the behavior is…	**high** in consensus: Lots of people in the class yell at Jake	**high** in distinctiveness: Ellie doesn't yell at anyone else except Jake	**high** in consistency: Ellie yells at Jake during every class
Situational External Attributions—it's something about the circumstances—will be made when the behavior is…	**low or high** in consensus	**low or high** in distinctiveness	**low** in consistency: This is the first time that Ellie has ever yelled at Jake

(Dvash et al., 2010). If you feel threatened, you may make a **downward comparison** by contrasting yourself with a person who ranks lower on some dimension (Stewart et al., 2013). For example, if you have a part-time job and your employer cuts your hours, you may comfort yourself by thinking about a friend who just lost his job.

The third motive for social comparison is to prompt *self-improvement.* **Upward comparisons**—those that involve comparing ourselves to a person who ranks just a little better on some dimension—can provide strong motivation to improve ourselves (Huguet et al., 2001). If self-improvement is the goal, though, then it's important to choose your point of comparison carefully. As the example with Alex's basketball skills suggests, comparing yourself with people of much greater ability will probably just make you feel bad (Normand & Croizet, 2013; Tyler & Feldman, 2006). For example, when women compare their bodies with those of famous women in the media, their dissatisfaction with their own bodies actually increases (Tiggemann & Polivy, 2010).

Attributions

Aside from social comparisons, attributions are a second important type of social cognition. Imagine yourself in the following situation: You're a college instructor teaching a course in introductory psychology. Today, you have students working in small groups on a discussion question when you notice that one of the students—Ellie—has become angry and is now yelling at another member of the group named Jake. The other students in the class are looking on in shock. What do you make of her behavior?

Every day we try to understand, often from small shreds of evidence, what *causes* other people like Ellie act as they do. We do this through a specific type of social cognition called an **attribution**. In the case of Ellie, you might attribute her behavior to the fact that she's a hostile person. If so, you see the cause of her behavior as being internal. *Internal causes* of behavior, such as ongoing needs or personality traits, lie within the person and are stable over time. But you might also imagine Ellie's behavior as stemming from the fact that Jake was provoking her, or that she's simply tired and stressed because final exams are approaching. If so, you have attributed her actions to an *external cause*—one that lies outside a person and reflects something about the situation or environment.

Making Internal vs. External Attributions

When deciding on whether an internal or external attribution is appropriate, we typically take into account the behavior of the *actor* (the person of interest; Ellie in this case), the *object* or target that the person's action is directed toward (Jake), and the *setting* (social or physical environment) in which the action occurs (Kelley, 1967).

According to Harold Kelley (1921–2003), when we make attributions for behavior like Ellie's, we are sensitive to three factors: *consistency*, *distinctiveness*, and *consensus* (Kelley, 1967). An actor's behavior is *consistent* if it changes very little when we observe it in relation to the same object or target on many different occasions. Here, we'd be asking whether Ellie often gets frustrated with Jake. *Distinctiveness* refers to an assessment of whether the actor's behavior occurs with other objects or targets. In this case, we'd want to know whether Ellie gets angry with other members of the class besides Jake. Finally, *consensus* information relates to how other people respond toward the same object, or target. Here, the question would be whether other students also tend to get angry with Jake.

According to Kelley, when making attributions we look for patterns in those three types of information (see ▲ Table 16.1). Internal attributions (this event reflects something about Ellie) are

Role conflict Trying to occupy two or more roles that make conflicting demands on behavior.

Social status The degree of prestige, admiration, and respect accorded to a member of a group.

Social power The degree to which a group member can control, alter, or influence the behavior of another group member.

Social cognition The process of thinking about ourselves and others in a social context.

Social comparison Making judgments about ourselves through comparison with others.

Downward comparison Comparing yourself with a person who ranks lower than you on some dimension.

Upward comparison Comparing yourself with a person who ranks higher than you on some dimension.

Attribution The act of assigning cause to behavior.

most likely when consistency is high, but distinctiveness and consensus are low. In contrast, we make external attributions about Ellie's behavior (this event reflects something about Jake) when consistency, distinctiveness, and consensus are all high.

In cases where consistency is low, people will be more likely to make a specific type of external attribution—a *situational attribution*—and assume that Ellie's behavior is a product of something unusual about her circumstances, like stress over her upcoming exams. **Situational demands** are pressures or norms that influence behavior in particular settings and social situations. When situational demands are strong, we tend to discount (downgrade) internal causes as a way of explaining a person's behavior. For example, you have probably discounted the motives of professional athletes who praise shaving creams, hair care products, deodorants, and the like. Obviously, the situation—that is, the large sums of money that they receive through their contract—are likely to fully explain their endorsements.

Differences in Attributions About Ourselves and Others

The attributions we make are also influenced by our subjective point of view. Let's say that at the last five parties you've attended, you've seen a woman named Macy talking enthusiastically to lots of people. Based on this consistency in her behavior, you make an internal attribution and assume that Macy is a bit of an extrovert and likes to socialize. When you see Macy at yet another gathering, you mention that she seems to like parties. Somewhat surprisingly, she replies, "Actually, I hate big get-togethers, but I've just started a new business and I'm trying to network so that I can build up my client base."

The truth is, we seldom know the real reasons for others' actions, and consequently we often make attribution errors like the one regarding Macy's sociability. The most common mistake we make is to over-attribute the actions of others to internal causes, a phenomenon called the **fundamental attribution error** (Hooper et al., 2015; Moran, Jolly, & Mitchell, 2014). Specifically, we tend to think that the actions of others have internal causes such as their personality, and we often underestimate the likelihood that their actions are caused by external forces or circumstances. One amusing example of this error is the tendency of people to attribute the actions of actors playing a role to their personalities rather than considering the obvious external cause of their onscreen behavior—that they are under contract and being paid to play a character (Tal-Or & Papirman, 2007).

Tom Hanks was once voted the most trusted person in the United States, according to a *Reader's Digest* poll, ranking above many politicians, judges, religious leaders, and sports figures. Is Tom Hanks actually *that* trustworthy? Or is it that he has played many trustworthy characters in popular films? We are more prone than you might think to attribute to actors the personality traits of the characters they play (Tal-Or & Papirman, 2007).

In an interesting twist, we are more likely to think that external causes explain our own actions. As *observers*, then, we attribute the behavior of others to their internal wants, motives, and personality traits (the fundamental attribution error). As *actors*, however, we tend to find external explanations for our own behavior (Aronson, Wilson, & Akert, 2013; Gordon & Kaplar, 2002). This **actor–observer bias** refers to the fact that when we make attributions *for the same action*, we are far more likely to ascribe others' behavior to internal causes and our own to external causes. For example, other people who don't leave tips in restaurants are cheap and don't care about those who work in low-paying jobs. If you don't leave a tip, it's because the service was bad. And, of course, other people are always late because they are rude and don't value your time. You are late because you were held up by events beyond your control.

Attributions in Everyday Life: Self-Handicapping

Have you ever known someone who partied late into the night before taking an exam or making a speech? Why would a person risk failure in this way? Often, the reason lies in **self-handicapping**; that is, arranging to perform under conditions that impair performance, thus allowing for a plausible external attribution for their own poor performance. In this way, self-handicapping makes people feel better in situations where they might fail (Ferradás et al., 2016).

Any time you set up plausible excuses for a poor performance, you might be self-handicapping. Some other examples include making a half-hearted effort and procrastinating (McCrea & Hirt, 2011). For instance, athletes often protect their self-esteem by practicing *less* before important games or events (Kuczka & Treasure, 2005; Ntoumanis, Taylor, & Standage, 2010). That way, if they don't do well, they have a ready-made external attribution for their poor showing.

What if a person succeeds while "handicapped"? Well, then, so much the better. The person's self-image then gets a boost because she or he succeeded under conditions that normally lower performance.

Drinking alcohol is one of the most popular—and dangerous—self-handicapping strategies. A person who is drunk can attribute failure to being inebriated, while still accepting success if it occurs. Examples of using alcohol for self-handicapping include being drunk for school exams, job interviews, or an important first date. A person who gets drunk at such times should be aware that coping with anxiety in this way can lead to serious alcohol abuse (Zuckerman & Tsai, 2005).

Most of us have used self-handicapping at one time or another. Indeed, life would be harsh if we didn't occasionally give ourselves a break from accepting full responsibility for success or failure. Self-handicapping is mainly a problem when it becomes habitual, because this typically leads to poorer performance, lower self-esteem, poor adjustment, and poor health (Schwinger et al., 2014; Zuckerman & Tsai, 2005).

Reflective Practice

The Fundamentals of Social Groups

1. Social psychology is the study of how people behave in ________________________.
2. Male, female, and adolescent are examples of ________________________ roles.
3. Social status refers to a set of expected behaviors associated with a social position. T or F?
4. Social comparisons are made pretty much at random. T or F?
5. When situational demands are weak, we tend to attribute a person's actions to internal causes. T or F?
6. The fundamental attribution error is to attribute the actions of others to internal causes. T or F?

THINK CRITICALLY

7. People often talk about the fact that American society is becoming more polarized. The ingroup–outgroup distinction that is typically seen as contributing to polarization is political affiliation (Democrats vs. Republicans). Can you think of some other ingroup–outgroup distinctions that may be relevant in polarizing our society?

SELF-REFLECT

- What are the most prominent roles you play? Do they give you any social status or social power? Which are achieved and which are ascribed? What conflicts do they create?
- How has social comparison affected your behavior? Has it influenced who you associate with?
- Have you ever engaged in self-handicapping? Try to relate the concept to a specific example.
- How often do you commit the fundamental attribution error? Again, try to think of a specific personal example that illustrates the concept.

Answers: 1. social situations or the presence of others 2. ascribed 3. F 4. F 5. T 6. T 7. Other ingroup–outgroup distinctions that may contribute to polarization include people who live in rural vs. urban areas, people who identify as being from the south vs. the north (or the east vs. the west coast), or people who identify as wealthy vs. not.

16.2 Attitudes

GATEWAYS LEARNING OUTCOMES:
After reading this section, you will be able to:

16.2.1 Define the term attitude, and outline four ways in which attitudes are formed

16.2.2 Describe three ways to measure attitudes

16.2.3 Outline two factors that may prompt people to change their attitudes

16.2.4 Define cognitive dissonance and outline six ways to minimize dissonance between our beliefs and behaviors

What is your position on affirmative action? What about euthanasia? The situation in the Middle East? How about legalized abortion? Our *attitudes* on these issues and many others are intimately woven into many of our everyday actions, and they reflect our tastes, friendships, preferences, goals, and personalities (Baumeister & Bushman, 2017).

What, specifically, is an attitude? An **attitude** is a positive or negative perception of people, objects, or issues. They summarize your evaluation of these things and, as a result, they can predict or direct future actions. Social psychologists have suggested that attitudes have three components: *cognitions* (or beliefs), *emotions* (or affect), and *behaviors*. The cognitive component of an attitude is what you believe about a particular object or issue. The emotional component consists of your feelings toward the attitudinal object, and the behavioral component refers to your actions toward it.

Consider, for example, your attitude toward gun control. You will have beliefs (or cognitions) about whether gun control would affect rates of crime or violence, and whether there should be mandatory background checks for people who want to buy guns. You will also have particular emotions that are associated with guns, and these might include comfort, fear, pleasure, or threat. In terms of behavior, you will have a tendency to seek out or avoid gun ownership, and you may support organizations that urge or oppose gun control. As you can see, attitudes orient us to the social world. In doing so, they prepare us to act in certain ways (Forgas, Cooper, & Crano, 2010; Jackson, 2011). (For another example, see Figure 16.2.)

Forming Attitudes

Where do our attitudes come from? Attitudes are acquired in at least four ways. Sometimes attitudes come from *direct contact* (personal experience) with the object of the attitude. For example, your attitudes about pollution might stem from witnessing the degradation of a local river as a result of waste being dumped by an upstream factory (Ajzen, 2005).

Second, attitudes can be formed through *chance conditioning* (learning that takes place by luck or coincidence) (Albarracín, Johnson, & Zanna, 2005). Let's say, for instance, that you have had three encounters in your lifetime with psychologists. If all three were negative, you might take an unduly dim view of psychology.

Situational demands Unstated expectations that define desirable or appropriate behavior in various settings and social situations.

Fundamental attribution error Tendency to attribute behavior to internal causes without regard to situational influences.

Actor–observer bias The tendency to attribute the behavior of others to internal causes while attributing one's own behavior to external causes (situations and circumstances).

Self-handicapping Arranging to perform under conditions that usually impair performance, so as to have an excuse for a poor showing.

Attitude Positive or negative perception of people, objects, or issues.

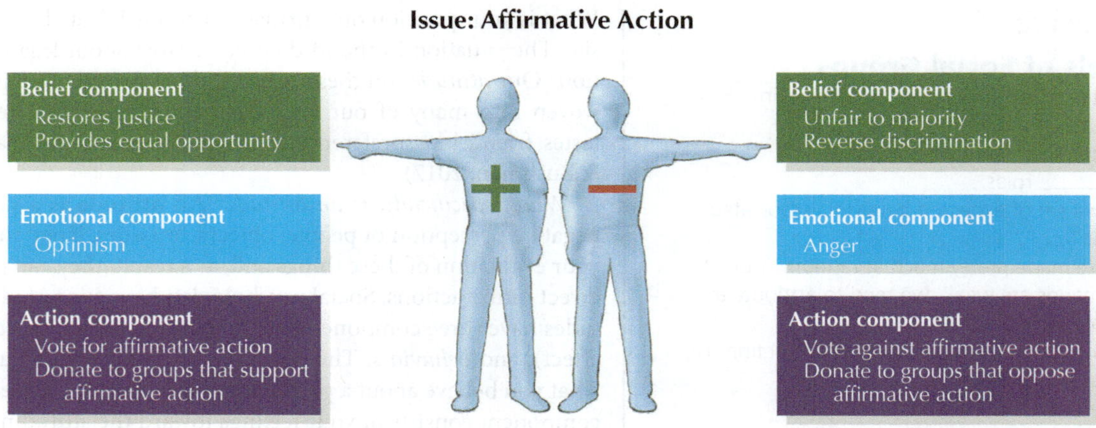

Figure 16.2 Elements of positive and negative attitudes toward affirmative action.

In the same way, people often develop strong attitudes toward cities, foods, or parts of the country on the basis of one or two unusually good or bad experiences (Ledgerwood & Trope, 2010).

Third, attitudes are acquired through *interactions with others*; that is, learning through discussion with other people who hold a particular attitude. For instance, if three of your good friends are volunteers at a local recycling center and you talk with them about their beliefs, you may well come to favor recycling, too. Parental values, beliefs, and practices can also affect the attitudes of their children (Bartram, 2006; Guidetti et al., 2012). For example, if both parents belong to the same political party, chances are good that their children will belong to that same party when they become adults.

Fourth, there is no doubt that attitudes are influenced by the *media*, such as newspapers, television, and the Internet (Mahler, Beckerley, & Vogel, 2010). Teenagers today spend at least 70 hours a week immersed in media, including social media sites, television, video games, the Internet, and movies. Eight-to-twelve-year-olds spend at least 40 hours in similar ways (Rideout, 2015). The information channeled into homes this way can have a powerful impact on attitudes. For instance, frequent television viewers are more likely to mistrust others and overestimate their own chances of being harmed. This suggests that a steady diet of media violence leads some people to develop the attitude that the world is a dangerous and threatening place (Nellis & Savage, 2012). (■ For more on media and observational learning, see Section 6.4.)

Measuring Attitudes

How do researchers measure our attitudes when they study them? Attitudes can be measured in several ways. In an **open-ended interview**, people are asked to freely express their attitudes toward a particular issue. For example, a person might be asked, "What do you think about freedom of speech on college campuses?" Attitudes toward social groups can also be measured with a **social distance scale**. On such scales, people say how willing they are to admit members of a group to various levels of social closeness (Brown, 2011). These levels might include "would exclude from my country," "would rent a room to," or "would admit to marriage in my family." If a person has negative attitudes toward a group, she or he will prefer to remain socially distant from members of the group (Boyle, Blood, & Blood, 2009).

Chip Somodevilla/Getty Images

Attitudes are an important dimension of social behavior. People's attitudes are often greatly influenced by the attitudes of their parents and the groups to which they belong.

Attitude scales are another widely used measure. Attitude scales consist of statements expressing various possible views on an issue (for example, "Socialized medicine would destroy health care in this country" or "This country needs a national health care program"). People might be asked to respond on a five-point scale, indicating their views about the statement from "strongly agree" to "strongly disagree." By combining scores on all items, we can learn whether a person accepts or rejects a particular issue. When used in public opinion polls, attitude scales provide useful information about the feelings of large segments of the population.

Attitude Change

Although attitudes are fairly stable, they do change (Forgas, Cooper, & Crano, 2010; Izuma, 2013). One factor that can drive attitude change is related to the presence of a **reference group**—any group that an individual uses as a standard for social comparison. For example, in the 1930s, Theodore Newcomb studied real-life attitude change among students at Bennington College (Alwin, Cohen, & Newcomb, 1991). Most students came to the college from conservative homes, but Bennington was a very liberal school. Newcomb found that most students shifted toward significantly more liberal attitudes during their four years at Bennington. Those who didn't change kept their parents and hometown friends as primary reference groups. Those who did change identified primarily with the campus community.

Notice that in this study all students could count both the college and their families as membership groups. However, one group or the other tended to become their point of reference. Moreover, it's worth noting that research suggests that it's not necessary to have face-to-face contact with other people for them to be a reference group. Instead, it seems to depend on whether they are people with whom you identify, or whose attitudes and values you care about (Ajzen, 2005; Larimer et al., 2011).

Cognitive Dissonance

In addition to the impact of reference groups, a second route through which attitudes might change is referred to as *cognitive dissonance* (the term "dissonance" means clashing). Developed by Leon Festinger (1957), the theory of **cognitive dissonance** states that when our attitudes contradict one another, or when the cognitive and behavioral aspects of an attitude are inconsistent, we experience a psychological state of discomfort. Put another way, we have a need for *consistency* in our thoughts and behavior, and inconsistency can motivate people to change their attitudes (Cooper, 2007; Festinger, 1957; Gawronski, 2012).

One common everyday situation that may cause dissonance is being *forced to choose between two options*. Have you ever noticed how, once you've made a choice, it can be irksome to notice something positive about a rejected alternative (I should have bought the blue shirt; it had nicer buttons)? Welcome to buyer's regret (Godoy et al., 2010). To minimize such dissonance, we tend to alter our beliefs to emphasize positive aspects of what we choose, while downgrading other alternatives. Thus, you are more likely to

wavebreakmedia/Shutterstock.com

Do you exercise regularly? Like students in the Bennington study, your intentions to exercise are probably influenced by the exercise habits of your reference groups (Ajzen, 2005; Terry & Hogg, 1996).

think that your college courses will be great *after* you have registered for them than before making that commitment. And those courses that you didn't sign up for? They were probably going to be really boring anyway.

A second common dissonance-promoting situation arises when there is a *disconnect between the cognitive and behavioral aspects of attitudes*; that is, what we believe vs. what we do (Johnson & Boynton, 2010). Here's a common example: Imagine that a woman named Amaia knows that automobiles are expensive to operate and add to air pollution. Why would Amaia continue to drive to work every day? What causes this kind of disconnect between beliefs and behavior?

Researchers have suggested at least three explanations for this type of belief–behavior mismatch. First, the *immediate consequences* of our actions weigh heavily on the choices we make. Regardless of Amaia's beliefs about the downside of cars, it may be difficult for her to resist the immediate convenience of driving. Second, expectations about how *others will evaluate* our actions also are important. For example, Amaia may resist taking public transit to work for fear that her coworkers at the auto plant where she works will be critical of her stand on the environment. Third, we must not overlook the effects of longstanding *habits* (Oskamp & Schultz, 2005). Let's say that after years of driving to work Amaia finally vows to shift to public transit. Two months later, it would not be unusual if she found herself driving again because of habit, despite her good intentions (#FailedNewYearsResolution. Enough said.).

Reducing Cognitive Dissonance

How can cognitive dissonance be reduced? That's a great question. To answer it, let's consider another common example of a belief–behavior mismatch that might cause cognitive dissonance: Smokers like Jessica regularly see stories in the media confirming that cigarettes endanger lives, so she obviously has some pretty clear cognitions about the dangers of smoking. In spite of knowing this, though, Jessica lights up and smokes about half a pack each day. How can Jessica resolve the tension (or dissonance) between her beliefs and her actions? ▲ Table 16.2 summarizes the following six ways:

The first possibility is that she could quit smoking; that is, she could *change her behavior* to bring it in line with her beliefs. But Jessica—who has tried and failed to give up smoking a number of times—may not feel that she's able to change her behavior.

A second possibility, then, is that she could *change her belief* about the harm associated with smoking. To do so, it might help for Jessica to prioritize thoughts that smoking is not really that dangerous and may even be helpful. For instance, she might seek

Open-ended interview An interview in which persons are allowed to freely state their views.

Social distance scale A rating of the degree to which a person would be willing to have contact with a member of another group.

Attitude scale A collection of attitudinal statements with which respondents indicate agreement or disagreement.

Reference group Any group that an individual uses as a standard for social comparison.

Cognitive dissonance Psychological state of having related ideas or perceptions that are inconsistent.

▲ Table 16.2 Strategies for Reducing Cognitive Dissonance

LeShawn, who is a college student, has always thought of himself as an environmental activist. Recently, LeShawn "inherited" a car from his parents, who were replacing the family "barge." In the past, LeShawn biked or used public transportation to get around. His parents' old car is an antiquated gas-guzzler, but he has begun to drive it every day. How might LeShawn reduce the cognitive dissonance created by the clash between his environmentalism and his use of an inefficient automobile?

Strategy	Example
Change your behavior.	"I'm only going to use the car when it's impossible to bike or take the bus."
Change your belief.	"Cars are not really a major environmental problem."
De-emphasize dissonant thoughts.	"It's more important for me to support the environmental movement politically than it is to worry about how I get to school and work."
Focus on consonant thoughts.	"This is an old car, so keeping it on the road makes good use of the resources that were consumed when it was manufactured."
Reduce the amount of perceived choice.	"My schedule has become too hectic. I really can't afford to bike or take the bus anymore."
Attribute the belief–behavior mismatch to an external cause.	"My parents told me that I need to use the car because they think my neighborhood is unsafe and if I don't drive then they're going to worry about me when I walk or take the subway to work."

Sources: Franzoi, 2002.

examples of heavy smokers like her Uncle George who lived until he was 93. She could also convince herself that the benefits of smoking, such as reduced anxiety, actually benefit her health (Kneer, Glock, & Rieger, 2012).

If it's too difficult to change a belief completely, then a third way to reduce dissonance is by *diminishing the importance of dissonant thoughts*. Jessica might decide, for example, that research on the risks of smoking are inconclusive. Similarly, a fourth option would be for Jessica to *focus on consonant thoughts*, or those that are in keeping with her behavior and help to justify it ("Just imagine how many people would lose their jobs if everyone stopped smoking.").

A fifth alternative that might help Jessica to reduce feelings of dissonance is to *reduce the amount of perceived choice*. For example, she might persuade herself that she simply can't give up smoking right now because her job is incredibly stressful and she's under so much pressure. Quitting would remove one way that she's able to keep her anxiety and stress under control and would probably compromise her ability to meet her obligations at work.

A sixth and final way that people can reduce dissonance is to *attribute the belief–behavior mismatch to an external cause*. In a classic study, college students did an extremely boring task (turning wooden pegs on a board) for a long time. Afterward, they were asked to help lure others into the experiment by pretending that the task was interesting and enjoyable. Students paid $20 for lying to others did not change their own negative opinion of the task: "That was really boring!" But those who were paid only $1 later rated the task as "pleasant" and "interesting."

How can we explain these results? In both cases, participants were faced with the fact that their behavior (talking up the study to the next participant) conflicted with their belief that the study was actually boring. However, the students paid $20 experienced no dissonance. These students could reassure themselves that anybody would tell a little white lie for $20—in other words, the money provided them with an external justification (or reason) for the fact that their behavior did not align with their beliefs. Consequently, they had no concerns rating the task as boring even though they hadn't communicated that to others.

But it was a different story for those paid just $1. There was no credible external reason for behaving in a way that conflicted with their beliefs—in fact, many of them must have said to themselves, "I lied and I had no good reason to do it." To manage this discrepancy, these students did exactly what cognitive dissonance theory would predict: They changed their belief about the task so that it was more favorable, and more in keeping with what they had said to the next participant (Festinger & Carlsmith, 1959; see Figure 16.3).

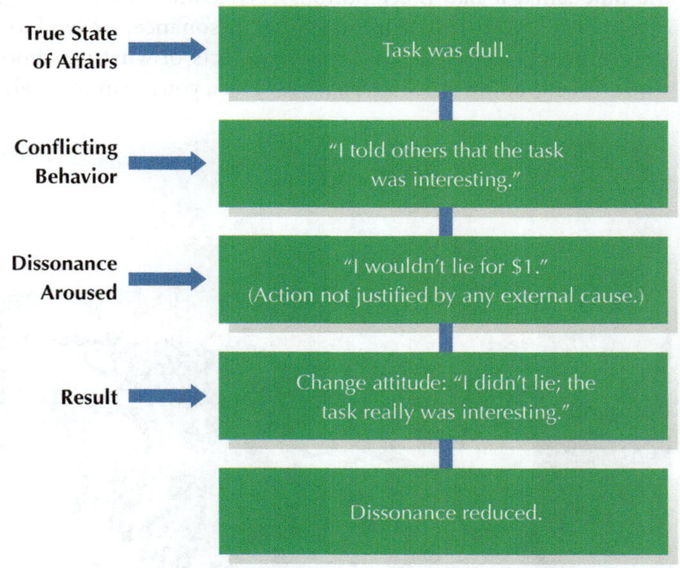

Figure 16.3 Cognitive dissonance. Summary of the Festinger and Carlsmith (1959) study from the viewpoint of a person experiencing cognitive dissonance. (Adapted from Franzoi, 2002.)

Cognitive Dissonance in Everyday Life: The Seekers

A famous example of cognitive dissonance was described by Festinger and his colleagues in the book *When Prophecy Fails*, which provides an account of how these researchers infiltrated a small group of "true believers" led by a woman named Dorothy Martin. Martin claimed that she was in communication with beings on a planet called Clarion whose messages foretold a massive flood that would destroy the Earth. Martin and her followers, the Seekers, were to be rescued from the waters by a flying saucer.

The Seekers' behavior tells us something about their commitment to the belief that they would be whisked away on the UFO: Some of them left their jobs or their spouses, and many of them gave away their money and possessions. When nothing happened at the appointed time (surprise!), the Seekers suffered a bitter and embarrassing disappointment.

You might think that at this point, the Seekers would have gone home with every intention of telling their spouses and bosses that they'd suffered from a temporary lapse in judgment and wanted to come back. Amazingly, though, Dorothy Martin announced that she had received a new message explaining that the Seekers had spread so much light that God had decided to spare the world from devastation. The Seekers actually became *more* convinced than ever before that they were right, calling newspapers and radio stations to let others know of their accomplishment.

To explain what happened here, we need look no further than cognitive dissonance theory. Remember that at the outset, the Seekers' behavior was in alignment with their beliefs: They thought the end was coming, and so they gave up their relationships and possessions. They spent hours out in the cold Michigan winter waiting for a spaceship. When aliens didn't show up, suddenly there was dissonance: their actions no longer seemed to be supported by their beliefs, which had clearly been called into question. How could they bring beliefs and behaviors back into line with one another? They convinced themselves that their beliefs about the flood had been right all along, and further explained away the fact that events did not unfold as expected because of their heroism in saving the world.

Reflective Practice

Attitudes

1. Attitudes have three components, ____________________, ____________________, and ____________________.
2. Which of the following is associated with attitude formation?
   a. direct contact
   b. mass media
   c. chance conditioning
   d. interactions with others
   e. all of the preceding
3. Items such as "would exclude from my country" or "would admit to marriage in my family" are found in which attitude measure?
   a. a reference group scale
   b. a social distance scale
   c. an attitude scale
   d. an open-ended interview
4. Much attitude change is related to a desire to avoid clashing or contradictory thoughts, an idea summarized by ____________________ theory.

THINK CRITICALLY

5. Students entering a college gym are asked to sign a banner promoting water conservation. Later, the students shower at the gym. What effect would you expect signing the banner to have on how long students stay in the shower?
6. Cognitive dissonance theory predicts that false confessions obtained during brainwashing are not likely to bring about lasting changes in attitudes. Why?

SELF-REFLECT

- Describe an attitude that is important to you. What are its three components?
- Which of the various sources of attitudes best explain your own attitudes?
- Imagine that you would like to persuade voters to support an initiative to preserve a small wilderness area by converting it to a park. Using research on persuasion as a guide, what could you do to be more effective?
- How would you explain cognitive dissonance theory to a person who knows nothing about it?

Answers: 1. cognitive (belief), emotional, and behavioral (action) 2. e 3. b 4. cognitive dissonance 5. Cognitive dissonance theory predicts that students who sign the banner will take shorter showers to be consistent with their publicly expressed support of water conservation. This is exactly the result observed in a study done by social psychologist Elliot Aronson. 6. Because there is considerable external pressure that can explain the fact that one offered a false confession. As a result, little cognitive dissonance is created when a prisoner makes statements that contradict his or her beliefs.

16.3 Social Influence

GATEWAYS LEARNING OUTCOMES:
After reading this section, you will be able to:

16.3.1 Distinguish between mere presence, conformity, compliance, obedience, and coercion as methods of social influence

16.3.2 Explain how the mere presence of others can influence behavior

16.3.3 Describe the reasons why people conform, and the conditions under which conformity is most likely

16.3.4 Outline the three factors that impact the persuasiveness of messages intended to elicit compliance

16.3.5 Compare the foot-in-the-door, door-in-the-face, lowball, and nudge techniques as methods of gaining compliance

16.3.6 Explain what we can learn about obedience from Stanley Milgram's studies

16.3.7 Describe how captivity facilitates the brainwashing techniques that are used in coercion

16.3.8 Describe three strategies that facilitate self-assertion

No topic lies nearer to the heart of social psychology than **social influence**—changes in behavior induced by the actions of others. When people interact, they almost always affect one another's behavior (Baer, Cialdini, & Lueth, 2012; Kassin, Fein, & Markus, 2017). For example, in a classic experiment, researchers had actors form groups of various sizes and then asked them to stand on a busy New York City street at different times. Regardless of the group size, everyone in the group would stop and simultaneously look up at a sixth-floor window across the street. A camera recorded how many passersby also stopped to stare in each case. The larger the group size, the more people were swayed to join in staring at the window (Milgram, Bickman, & Berkowitz, 1969).

Though looking up at a building is not a behavior that has any significant consequences, there are many times when the presence of others has the ability to either improve (**social facilitation**) or impair (**social interference**) the performance of others who are working nearby (Cole, Barrett, & Griffiths, 2011). These forms of social influence range from those that are quite mild to those in which a much stronger effect is exerted on behavior.

In this section, we'll talk about five different types of social influence. The gentlest form—*mere presence*—refers to changes in behavior that result from other people being nearby (even when we are not interacting with them). A little further along the scale is *conformity*—we conform when we spontaneously change our behavior to bring it in line with others. *Compliance* is a more directed form of social influence. We comply when we change our behavior in response to another person who has little or no social power or authority. *Obedience* is an even stronger form of social influence. We obey when we change our behavior in direct response to the demands of an authority. The strongest form of social influence is *coercion*, or changing behavior under great pressure from others. Let's take a look at each one of these.

Mere Presence

Imagine that you are pedaling your bike when another rider pulls up beside you without saying anything. Will you pick up your pace? Slow down? Completely ignore the other rider? In 1898, psychologist Norman Triplett's investigation of just such a social situation was the first published social psychology experiment (Strubbe, 2005). According to Triplett, in this situation you are more likely to speed up, owing to the *mere presence* of another person. **Mere presence** refers to the tendency for people to change their behavior just because other people are nearby.

oneinchpunch/Shutterstock.com

Conformity is a subtle dimension of daily life. Notice the similarities in the clothing worn by this group of friends.

Though the mere presence of others can sometimes lead to improvements in performance, that isn't always the case. Whether we see social facilitation or social interference can sometimes be related to *self-confidence*. Specifically, if you're confident in your abilities, your behavior will most likely be facilitated in the presence of others. If you are not, your performance is more likely to be impaired (Uziel, 2007). Another classic study demonstrated this effect with college students shooting pool at a student union. Good players who were confident (sharks?) normally made 71 percent of their shots. Their accuracy improved to 80 percent when others were watching them. Less confident, average players (marks?) who normally made 36 percent of their shots dropped to 25 percent accuracy when someone was watching them (Michaels et al., 1982).

Another example of social impairment that is connected to the presence of others is **social loafing**, or the tendency for people to exert less effort (loaf) when they are part of a group than they do when they are solely responsible for their work (Ferrari & Pychyl, 2012; Hall & Buzwell, 2013). In one study, people playing tug-of-war while blindfolded pulled harder if they thought they were competing alone. When they thought others were on their team, they made less of an effort (Ingham et al., 1974). Research has suggested that social loafing is more likely to occur in groups that are larger and less cohesive, and when individuals feel that their contributions aren't important or won't be recognized (Liden et al., 2004).

Conformity

We show **conformity** when we bring our behavior into agreement with perceived social norms (Carlson & Settle, 2016; Suhay, 2014). Typically, we conform for one of two reasons. The first is that *others can serve as a useful source of information*, and so in situations that are ambiguous, or in which we feel uncertain, it often makes sense to "follow the crowd." The second reason is that humans have *a strong need to be accepted* by our ingroups, and the price of acceptance is often that we conform to group norms (even if we don't always agree with them).

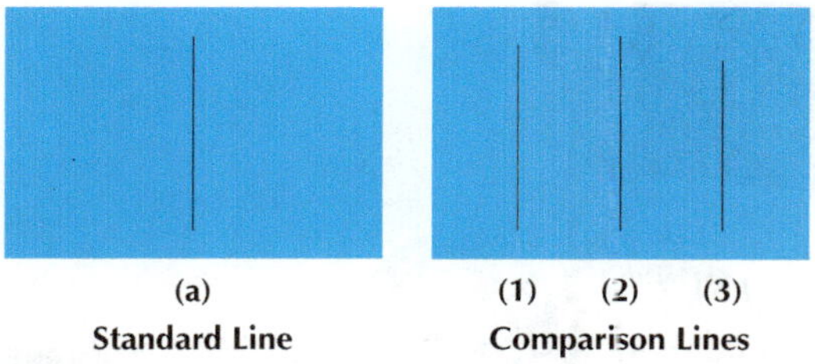

Figure 16.4 Stimuli used in Asch's conformity experiments.

How strong are group pressures for conformity? They're very strong! As mentioned earlier, all groups have unspoken norms. The broadest norms, defined by society as a whole, establish "normal" or acceptable behavior in most situations. Comparing hairstyles, habits of speech, dress, eating habits, and social customs in two or more cultures makes it clear that we all conform to social norms. In fact, a degree of uniformity is necessary if we are to interact comfortably and predict the behavior of those around us: Imagine being totally unable to anticipate the actions of others. In stores, schools, and homes, this would be frustrating and disturbing. On the highways, it would be lethal (LeGros & Cislaghi, 2020).

Sherif's Autokinetic Study

Research concerning humans' tendency to conform with other members of a group has a long history. In one of the first studies in this area, researcher Muzafer Sherif (1935) investigated conformity in a perceptual task that centered on the *autokinetic effect* (the reliable finding that people in a darkened room who stare at a spot of light projected on a wall will perceive that it moves, even though the movement is a visual illusion).

Sherif had groups of three participants come together to experience the autokinetic effect. Unaware that the light's movement was an illusion, group members were asked to publicly estimate how much the point of light moved. Sherif found that over multiple trials, the groups converged on their estimates regarding the extent to which the light moved. Moreover, when participants were tested individually a week later, they tended to provide estimates that were very similar to those that had emerged from their group's session. This finding is noteworthy because it suggested that participants had not felt any pressure to conform during the group session; that is, they had not provided estimates to the other group members that they felt were faulty, just to "go along with the crowd." Instead, it seemed more likely that the participants agreed with the group's assessment about the degree of movement and had internalized that norm.

Asch's Line Judgment Studies

Solomon Asch's research replicated Sherif's findings, but demonstrated that it's also possible to get people to conform even when they *don't* agree with the group. To fully appreciate his studies, imagine yourself as a participant. Assume that you are seated at a table with six other student participants. Your task is quite simple: You are shown three lines on a card, and you must select the line whose length matches a "standard" line (Figure 16.4).

As the testing begins, each person announces an answer for the first card. When your turn comes, you agree with the others about the line that matches the standard. "This isn't hard at all," you say to yourself. For several more trials, your answers agree with those of the group. But then comes a shock: All six people announce that line 1 matches the standard, when you would have said that line 2 matches. You nervously look at the lines again. The room falls silent, and everyone seems to be staring at you. The experimenter awaits your answer. Do you say what you think, or do you conform to the answer provided by the other group members?

In this study, the other six student participants were all actors who purposefully agreed about the same wrong answer about a third of the time, thus creating group pressure (Asch, 1956). "Real" student participants conformed to the group on about one-third of those critical trials. Of those tested, 75 percent yielded and provided the wrong answer at least once. In contrast, people who were tested alone erred in less than 1 percent of their judgments. The pressure to conform to the will of the group is powerful indeed.

Who Conforms? And Why?

How do groups get people to conform to norms? In most groups, we have been rewarded with acceptance and approval for conformity and threatened with rejection or ridicule for nonconformity. These reactions are called **group sanctions**. Negative sanctions range from laughter, staring, or social disapproval to complete rejection or formal exclusion. If you've ever felt the sudden chill of disapproval by others, you understand the power of group sanctions.

Are some people more susceptible to group pressures than others? Yes. First, some *personal traits* are associated with greater conformity, including high needs for structure or certainty, high levels of anxiety and concern about the approval of others, and low levels of self-confidence. Second, people who live in *cultures that emphasize group cooperation* (such as many Asian cultures) also are more likely to conform (Bond & Smith, 1996; Fu et al., 2007). Third, people are more likely to conform *when group membership is important* to them (Stein, 2017). The risk of being rejected can be a threat to our sense of personal identity (Baer, Cialdini, & Lueth, 2012). That's why the Sherif and Asch experiments are impressive:

Social influence Changes in a person's behavior induced by the presence or actions of others.

Social facilitation Tendency to perform better when in the presence of others.

Social interference Tendency to perform more poorly when in the presence of others.

Mere presence The tendency for people to change their behavior just because of the presence of other people.

Social loafing Exerting less effort when performing a specific task with a group than when alone.

Conformity Matching behavior and appearance to perceived social norms.

Group sanctions Rewards and punishments (such as approval or disapproval) administered by groups to enforce conformity among members.

Because these were only temporary groups, sanctions were informal and rejection had no lasting importance. Just the same, the power of the group was evident. Fourth, the *size of the group* also has an influence on conformity. In the sidewalk experiment described previously (in which people stopped to look up), we noted that large groups had more influence. Fifth, in Asch's face-to-face groups, the *size of the majority* also made a difference, but a surprisingly small one. Even more important than the size of the majority is the *unanimity of the group* (total agreement). Having at least one person in your corner can greatly reduce pressures to conform. If you can find at least one other person who sees things as you do, you can be relatively secure in your opposition to other viewpoints. Incidentally, the Internet—and especially social media—now makes it much easier to find that other like-minded person.

Conformity in Everyday Life: Groupthink

Yale psychologist Irving Janis (1918–1990) first proposed the concept of groupthink in an attempt to understand a series of disastrous decisions made by government officials (Janis, 1989, 2007). The core of **groupthink** is a misguided need to conform and maintain other group members' approval, even at the cost of critical thinking (Singer, 2005). Group members are hesitant to "rock the boat," question sloppy thinking, or tolerate alternative views. This self-censorship leads people to believe that there is greater agreement among group members than there actually is (Matusitz & Breen, 2012; Tsintsadze-Maass & Maass, 2014).

Groupthink has been blamed for contributing to many crises, such as the invasion and occupation of Iraq and the *Columbia* space shuttle disaster in 2003 (Houghton, 2008; Post, 2011; Schafer & Crichlow, 2010). Groupthink was also implicated in the failure of Penn State University administrators to deal appropriately with a longstanding pattern of child sexual abuse by then-football coach Jerry Sandusky (Wagner, 2013).

To prevent groupthink, group leaders should take the following steps (Janis, 2007; Schafer & Crichlow, 2010):

- Define each group member's role as a "critical evaluator" and avoid undue pressure.
- Avoid revealing any personal preferences in the beginning. State the problem factually, without bias.
- Invite a group member or and outside expert to specifically play the role of devil's advocate.
- Make it clear that group members will be held accountable for decisions.
- Encourage open inquiry and norms that encourage and reward dissent.

In addition, Janis suggested that a "second-chance" meeting should be held to reevaluate important decisions—that is, each decision should be reached twice.

In fairness to our decision makers, it is worth noting that the presence of too many alternatives can lead to *deadlock*, which can delay taking necessary action (Kowert, 2002). Regardless, in an age clouded by the threat of war, global warming, and terrorism, even stronger solutions to the problem of groupthink would be welcome. Perhaps we should form a group to think about it!

Are you likely to be swayed by this group's message? Successful persuasion is related to the characteristics of the communicator, the message, and the audience.

Compliance and Persuasion

Pressures to "fit in" and conform are usually indirect. In contrast, the term **compliance** refers to situations in which one person bends to the requests of another person who has little or no authority (Cialdini, 2009). Because they have relatively little power, the person seeking your compliance must often resort to persuasion. **Persuasion** is any deliberate attempt to change beliefs or behavior through information and arguments (Gass & Seiter, 2014; Perloff, 2010). The power of persuasive techniques to bring about compliance is clearly evident all around us: Businesses, politicians, and others spend billions of dollars on advertising every year in an effort to get us to comply with their wishes and plans.

Factors That Influence Persuasiveness

Persuasion can range from the daily blitz of media commercials to a personal discussion among friends to a highly structured debate. In most cases, the success or failure of persuasion can be understood if we consider three things: the communicator, the message, and the audience.

In terms of *communicators*, efforts at persuasion will be more successful when the communicator is likable, expressive, trustworthy, an expert on the topic, and is similar or known to the audience in some respect. Moreover, persuasion is more likely when the communicator appears to have nothing to gain if the audience accepts the message.

With respect to the *message*, attempts to persuade people meet with greater success when the message appeals to emotions (particularly fear or anxiety) and provides a clear course of action that will, if followed, reduce fear or produce personally desirable results. Moreover, more persuasive messages state clear-cut conclusions, are backed up by facts and statistics, and are frequently repeated.

Finally, regarding members of the *audience*, researchers have noted that persuasion depends heavily on their motivation and ability to think about the message. Those whose motivation and ability are high will think reflectively about the information being presented. In contrast, people whose motivation and ability are

kagemusha/Shutterstock.com

Would you be willing to help this young woman carry her books to a nearby desk? What if she subsequently asked you to carry them across campus to her car? If you agreed to both, you might have fallen victim to the foot-in-the-door effect. (That is, unless you were attracted to her and were trying to get your own foot in the door!)

low are much more likely to process information automatically and to rely on heuristics or mental shortcuts. (■ see Section 8.1 and 8.3 for more information about reflective vs. automatic processing and heuristics.)

Techniques for Gaining Compliance

There are a number of ways in which people may attempt to gain your compliance. Here, we'll examine four of them: the foot-in-the-door technique, the door-in-the-face technique, the lowball technique, and nudges.

Foot-in-the-Door Technique

People who sell door to door have long recognized that once they get a foot in the door, a sale is almost a sure thing. To state the **foot-in-the-door effect** more formally, a person who first agrees to a small request is more likely to comply with a larger demand later, in an effort to be consistent (Guéguen et al., 2016; Pascual et al., 2013). For instance, if someone asked you to put a large, ugly sign in your front yard to promote safe driving, you would probably refuse. If, however, you had first agreed to put a small sign in your window, you would later be much more likely to allow the big sign in your yard.

Door-in-the-Face Technique

Let's say that a neighbor comes to your door and asks you to feed his dogs, water his plants, and mow his yard while he is out of town for a month. This is quite a major request—one that most people would probably turn down. Feeling only slightly guilty, you tell your neighbor that you're sorry, but you can't help him. Now, what if the same neighbor returns the next day and asks if you would at least pick up his mail while he is gone. Chances are very good that you would honor this request, even if you might have originally turned it down, too.

Psychologist Robert Cialdini coined the term **door-in-the-face effect** to describe the tendency for a person who has refused a major request to agree to a smaller request. In other words, after a person has turned down a major request ("slammed the door in your face"), he or she may be more willing to comply with a lesser demand. This strategy works because a person who abandons a large request appears to have given up something. In response, many people feel that they must reciprocate by giving in to the smaller request (Cialdini, 2009; Meineri et al., 2016). In fact, a good way to get another person to comply with a request is to first do a small favor for the person.

Lowball Technique

Anyone who has purchased an automobile will recognize a third way of inducing compliance. Automobile dealers are notorious for convincing customers to buy cars by offering "lowball" prices that undercut the competition. The dealer first gets the customer to agree to buy at an attractively low price. Then, once the customer is committed, various techniques are used to bump the price up before the sale is concluded.

The **lowball technique**, then, consists of getting a person committed to act and then making the terms of acting less desirable (Pascual et al., 2016). In this case, because you have already complied with a large request, it would be inconsistent to deny the follow-on, smaller additional request. Here's another example: A fellow student asks to borrow $25 for a day. This seems reasonable, and you agree. However, once you have given your classmate the money, he explains that it would be easier to repay you after payday, in two weeks. If you agree, you've succumbed to the lowball technique. Here's another example: Let's say that you ask someone to give you a ride to school in the morning. Only after the person has agreed do you tell her that you have to be there at 6 a.m.

Nudges

Nobel prize-winning economist Richard Thaler and Harvard Law professor Cass Sunstein were the architects of a fourth technique for gaining compliance—nudges (Thaler & Sunstein, 2009). Like a physical nudge, this method of gaining compliance involves creating gentle pressure that pushes people to act in accordance with your wishes. Now used regularly by companies and governments, nudges were developed to address the fact that people often make irrational decisions that are not in their best interests (■ see Section 8.3 for a discussion of biases that interfere with rational decision-making).

It's important to note that when using this method of gaining compliance, an individual's freedom to choose is never restricted.

Groupthink Flawed decision-making in which a collection of individuals favors conformity over critical analysis.

Compliance Bending to the requests of a person who has little or no authority or other form of social power.

Persuasion A deliberate attempt to change beliefs or behavior with information and arguments.

Foot-in-the-door effect The tendency for a person who has first complied with a small request to be more likely later to fulfill a larger request.

Door-in-the-face effect The tendency for a person who has refused a major request to subsequently be more likely to comply with a minor request.

Lowball technique A strategy in which commitment is gained first to reasonable or desirable terms, which are then made less reasonable or desirable.

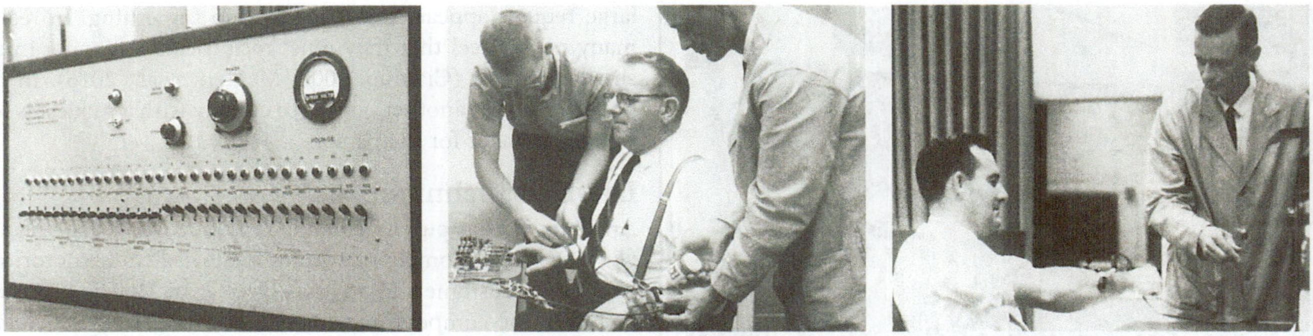

Figure 16.5 Milgram's obedience study. Scenes from Stanley Milgram's most famous study of obedience: the "shock generator," strapping a "learner" into his chair, and a "teacher" being told to administer a severe shock to the learner.

Instead, a nudge simply involves altering the environment in ways that make compliance with a desired behavior the most likely option, given the cognitive biases that generally guide our actions (Benartzi et al., 2017). One example of a nudge might be a company that automatically enrolls all of its employees in a good 401k retirement savings plan (the nudge) but nonetheless allows people to opt out of the plan if they want to do so. Because opting out of the plan requires the kind of effortful decision-making that we are predisposed to avoid, most people will be inclined to stay enrolled in the 401k, an action that is likely to benefit them in the long run.

Obedience: Compliance with Authority Figures

If ordered to do so, would you shock a man with a heart condition who is screaming and asking to be released? Surely most people would refuse to obey a directive like this one. Or would they? In Nazi Germany, obedient soldiers (who were once average citizens) helped slaughter more than 6 million people in concentration camps. Do such inhumane acts reflect deep character flaws? Are they the acts of heartless psychopaths or crazed killers? These are some of the questions that puzzled social psychologist Stanley Milgram (1965) when he began a provocative series of studies on **obedience**, a special type of compliance in which one responds to the demands of an authority.

In this section, we consider the conditions that promote both obedience and disobedience in the face of an authority figure. To get us started, we'll take a look at a series of famous studies that Milgram carried out in the 1960s. As was true of the Asch experiments, Milgram's research is best appreciated by visualizing yourself as a participant:

Imagine answering a newspaper ad to take part in a "learning" experiment at Yale University. When you arrive, a coin is flipped and a second participant, a pleasant-looking man in his fifties, is designated the "learner." By chance, you have become the "teacher."

Your task is to read aloud a list of word pairs. The learner's task is to memorize them. When the learner makes a mistake, you are to punish him by using electric shocks. The learner is taken to an adjacent room, and you watch as he is seated in an "electric chair" apparatus. Electrodes are attached to his wrists. You are then escorted to your position in front of a "shock generator" in the other room. On this device is a row of 30 switches marked from 15 to 450 volts. Corresponding labels range from "Slight Shock" to "Extreme Intensity Shock" and, finally, "Danger: Severe Shock." In the event that the learner makes a mistake and punishment is required, you are told by the experimenter that you must begin with 15 volts and then move one switch (15 volts) higher for each additional mistake (Figure 16.5).

The experiment begins, and the learner soon makes his first error. You flip a switch to deliver 15 volts. More mistakes. Rapidly, you reach the 75-volt level. The learner begins to moan after each shock. At 150 volts, he complains that he has a heart condition and demands to be released. At 315 volts he screams, saying he can no longer give answers and that he's no longer part of the experiment.

At some point, you can imagine that you might begin to protest to the experimenter. "That man has a heart condition," you say. "I'm not going to kill that man." The experimenter says, "Please continue." Another shock and another scream from the learner, and you say, "You mean I've got to keep going up the scale? No, sir." The experimenter replies, "The experiment requires that you continue." The next time, the learner provides no answer at all. You pause and look at the experimenter, who says "It is absolutely essential that you continue." For a time, the learner refuses to answer any questions and screams with each successive shock that you give. You're feeling very, very uncomfortable now and you say, "I'm not going to give him 450 volts!" The experimenter calmly replies, "You have no other choice; you must go on" (Milgram, 1965; Perry, 2013).

It's hard to believe many people would do this. What actually happened? Milgram also doubted that many people would obey his orders. When he polled a group of psychiatrists before the experiment, they predicted that less than 1 percent of those tested would obey. The astounding fact is that in this particular version of the experiment, 65 percent obeyed completely, going all the way to the 450-volt level. Virtually no one stopped short of 300 volts ("Severe Shock") (Figure 16.6).

Was the learner injured? The "learner" was actually an actor who simply turned a tape recorder on and off in the shock room whenever the "teacher" administered a shock. No real shocks were ever administered, but the dilemma for the teacher was quite real.

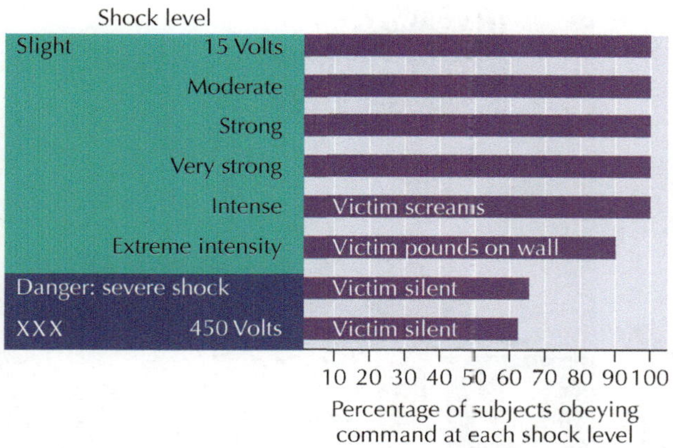

Figure 16.6 Results of Milgram's most famous obedience experiment. In the most widely reported version of Milgram's study, only a minority of participants refused to provide shocks, even at the most extreme intensities (Milgram, 1963). However, when the conditions of the study were varied, obedience sometimes dropped dramatically.

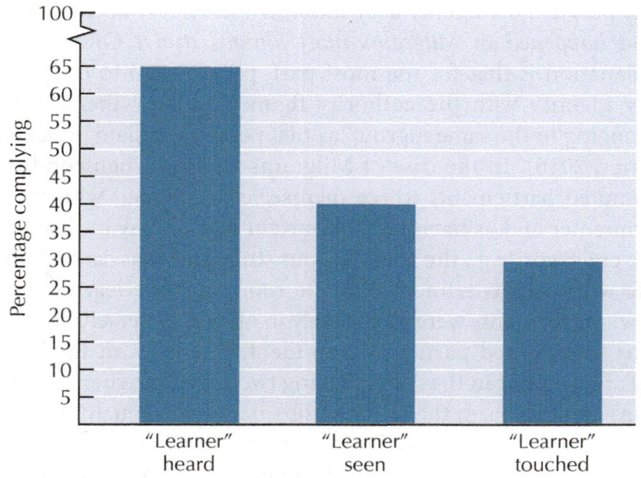

Figure 16.7 Obedience as a function of physical distance. Physical distance from the "learner" had a significant effect on the percentage of participants obeying orders.

Participants playing the teacher protested, sweated, trembled, stuttered, bit their lips, and laughed nervously. Clearly, they were disturbed by what they were doing. Nevertheless, in this version of Milgram's research, most obeyed the experimenter's orders. What should we make of this troubling finding?

Studying the Science: Obedience (and Disobedience) in Milgram's Studies

The study described above is the most famous version of Milgram's experiments, and the one that is most widely reported. For many years, people who read about that research drew the troubling conclusion that humans are capable of very inhumane behavior and that we show a troubling tendency toward "blind obedience" to authority. This idea gained further support when Burger (2009) reported on a slightly modified version of Milgram's famous study, in which he obtained similar results. More recently, though, psychological scientists have examined Milgram's work more closely and suggested that conclusions emphasizing blind obedience may be overly simplistic.

To begin, it's important to note that this single study was one of about 30 that Milgram carried out, and that there were at least 17 variations in the experience provided to participants. For example, one version had two actors play additional teachers (alongside the participant teacher), and these two teachers refused to shock the learner against his will. Another version had two experimenters whose instructions to the participant teacher did not agree with one another. In a third version, the experimenter was not in the room, but instead delivered instructions by telephone. A fourth involved the learner in the same room as the participant teacher, and a fifth was carried out away from Yale, at a run-down office in nearby Bridgeport.

These different conditions of the experiment were aimed at establishing the conditions under which people were more (or less) likely to obey the experimenter, and their results demonstrate the complexity of obedience. For example, Milgram found that the *distance between the teacher and the learner* was important. When participants were in the same room as the learner, only 40 percent obeyed fully. When they were face to face with the learner and were required to force his hand down on a simulated "shock plate," only 30 percent obeyed (Figure 16.7). *Distance from authority* also had an effect. If you consider that Yale University may convey some type of authority, then it's worth noting that when the study was rerun in a shabby office building in Bridgeport, fewer people obeyed (48 percent). Similarly, when the experimenter gave his orders over the phone instead of in person, only 22 percent obeyed. Finally, the *presence of other dissenters* mattered a great deal. Obedience dropped to 10 percent when two actors playing other teachers refused to shock the learner, and to just 5 percent when the two experimenters did not agree with one another (Burger, 2014).

Conclusions from Milgram's Research

Criticisms of Milgram's experiments include the condemnation that his experiments were deeply unethical, and that he actively biased the "teachers" to behave the way they did (Perry, 2013). However, criticisms have also been leveled at the conclusions drawn from this work. For example, when the results of all of the different conditions are considered (instead of the one that was most widely reported), they suggest that humans are not necessarily prone to automatic and blind obedience in the presence of an authority figure (a fact that Milgram himself acknowledged) (Reicher, Haslam, & Smith, 2012). Another interesting finding is that for participants whose resistance meant that the experimenter had to issue the fourth and final prompt ("You have no other choice; you must go on")—the only one that was really a direct order—the rate of compliance was zero. Put another way, if the participant was actually faced with a direct order to continue, they never complied (Burger, 2009).

Obedience Compliance with a request from an authority figure.

If people don't blindly obey authority, then how do you explain what happened in Milgram's most famous study? One alternate explanation is that for the most part, people tend to obey when they identify with the authority figure and view themselves as belonging to the same ingroup as that person (Haslam, Reicher, & Birney, 2016). In the case of Milgram's studies, when conditions prompted participants to see themselves as aligned with the experimenter and as having an important role to play in this scientific endeavor (e.g., the most famous study that was carried out at Yale with the experimenter in the room and the learner out of view), participants were more likely to obey. Conversely, in conditions that pushed participants to identify more with the learner (e.g., the learner in the room; having two other "teachers" say they didn't want to harm the learner), obedience was much lower.

Of course, even if obedience isn't blind, the reality is that in locales as diverse as Cambodia, Rwanda, Bosnia, Vietnam, Darfur, Sri Lanka, Iraq, and Syria, obedience to authority likely played a role in "sanctioned massacres" of chilling proportions (Mastroianni, 2015). Even in everyday life, many people obey orders to do things that they know are dishonest, unethical, or harmful just so that they can keep their jobs (Hinrichs, 2007). As C. P. Snow (1961) observed, "When you think of the long and gloomy history of man, you will find more hideous crimes have been committed in the name of obedience than in the name of rebellion." Nevertheless, the Milgram studies make it clear that there are some conditions—a personal act of courage or moral fortitude by one or two members of a group, for example—that may free others to disobey misguided or unjust authority.

Coercion

We close this section on social influence by examining some forms of *coercion*, the most extreme type of social influence. You are being subjected to **coercion** if you are forced to change your beliefs or your behavior against your will (Baumeister & Bushman, 2017; Moghaddam, 2013). For example, if you're a history enthusiast, you may associate *brainwashing* with techniques used by the Communist Chinese on prisoners during the Korean War (Jowett, 2006). Through various types of "thought reform," the Chinese were able to coerce some prisoners to sign false confessions.

How does brainwashing differ from other persuasive techniques? As we have noted, advertisers, politicians, educators, religious organizations, and others may actively seek to alter our attitudes and opinions. To an extent, their persuasive efforts may seem to resemble brainwashing, but there is an important difference: **Brainwashing**, or forced attitude change, requires a *captive audience*. If you are offended by a television commercial, you can tune it out. In contrast, prisoners are completely at the mercy of their captors. Complete control over the environment allows a degree of psychological manipulation that would be impossible in a normal setting.

How does a captive audience facilitate coercion? Brainwashing typically begins by making the target person feel completely helpless. Physical and psychological abuse, lack of sleep, humiliation, and isolation serve to loosen former values and beliefs. When exhaustion, pressure, and fear become unbearable, change occurs as the person begins to abandon former beliefs. For example, prisoners who reach the breaking point may sign a false confession or cooperate to gain relief. When they do, they are suddenly rewarded with praise, privileges, food, or rest. From that point on, a mixture of hope and fear plus pressures to conform serve to solidify new attitudes (Taylor, 2004).

Aftermath of the mass suicide at Jonestown. Brainwashing is an important part of how cult-like groups recruit new devotees.

How permanent are changes coerced by brainwashing? In most cases, the dramatic shift in attitudes brought about by brainwashing is temporary. Most "converted" prisoners who returned to the United States after the Korean War eventually reverted to their original beliefs. Nevertheless, brainwashing can be powerful, as shown by the success of cults in recruiting new members.

Coercion and Cults

Exhorted by their leader, some 900 members of the Reverend Jim Jones's People's Temple picked up paper cups and drank purple Flavor Aid laced with the deadly poison cyanide. Some even forced their own children to join in. The People's Temple was a classic example of a **cult**, a social group that is defined by its unquestioning devotion to the unusual ideas being put forward by a charismatic leader.

Psychologically, the mass suicide at Jonestown in 1978 is not so incredible as it might seem, given what we have learned about brainwashing (Dein & Littlewood, 2005; Moore, 2009). The inhabitants of Jonestown were isolated in the jungles of Guyana, intimidated by guards, and lulled with sedatives. They were also cut off from friends and relatives and totally accustomed to obeying rigid rules of conduct, which primed them for Jones's final "loyalty test."

Most psychologists regard NXIVM, founded by Keith Raniere, to be a current example of a cult. Cult members, including many celebrities, gave their allegiance to Raniere, who was regarded as infallible,

▲ **Table 16.3 Comparison of Assertive, Aggressive, and Nonassertive Behavior**

	Actor	Receiver of Behavior
Nonassertive behavior	Self-denying, inhibited, hurt, and anxious; lets others make choices; goals not achieved	Feels sympathy, guilt, or contempt for actor; achieves goals at actor's expense
Aggressive behavior	Achieves goals at others' expense; expresses feelings, but hurts others; chooses for others or puts them down	Feels hurt, defensive, humiliated, or taken advantage of; does not meet own needs
Assertive behavior	Self-enhancing; acts in own best interests; expresses feelings; respects rights of others; goals usually achieved; self-respect maintained	Needs respected and feelings expressed; may achieve goal; self-worth maintained

and they followed his dictates without question. Almost always, cult members are victimized by their leaders in one way or another. For example, in October, 2020, Raniere was sentenced to 120 years in prison for sex trafficking and other crimes.

If there is a lesson to be learned from such destructive cults, it is this: All true spiritual leaders have taught love and compassion. They also encourage followers to question their beliefs and to reach their own conclusions about how to live. In contrast, destructive cults show how dangerous it is to trade personal independence and critical thinking for security (Cowan & Bromley, 2008; Goldberg, 2001).

Resisting Social Influence: Assertiveness

Have you ever asserted yourself in any of the following ways: Questioned an error on a restaurant bill? Asked for a raise or a change in working conditions? Said no to something you just didn't feel like doing? Questioned a grade that seemed unfair?

Many people would find performing some—if not all—of these actions to be at least somewhat uncomfortable. In some cases, this discomfort may stem from the fact that we are often rewarded for compliant, obedient, or "good" behavior (Hauck, 2011). In others, not asserting yourself may be related to concerns about making a scene or feeling disliked by others. Whatever the causes, some people suffer significant anxiety in any situation requiring self-assertion that might "make waves" or increase others' workload.

If you have ever had difficulty asserting yourself in similar situations, it might be worth practicing how to be self-assertive (Tavakoli et al., 2009; Wolpe, 1974). The first step is to convince yourself of three basic rights: You have the right to refuse, to request, and to right a wrong. **Self-assertion** involves standing up for these rights by speaking out on your own behalf. It is a direct, honest expression of feelings and desires, and is not exclusively self-serving. In contrast, *aggression*—which we discuss in the next chapter—involves hurting another person or achieving one's goals at the expense of another. Aggression does not take into account the feelings or rights of others. It is an attempt to get one's own way no matter what. While assertion emphasizes firmness, it does not involve aggressive attacks (▲ Table 16.3).

Ideally, assertive actions are practiced until they can be repeated even under stress. For example, let's say it really angers you when a store clerk waits on several people who arrived after you did. To improve your assertiveness in this situation, three strategies can be helpful. First, begin by *rehearsing* the dialogue, posture, and gestures you would use to confront the clerk or the other customer. Working in front of a mirror can be very helpful. Second, you should *role-play* the scene with a friend. Be sure to have your friend take the part of a really aggressive or irresponsible clerk as well as a cooperative one. Rehearsal and role-playing can also be used when you expect a possible confrontation with someone—for example, if you are going to ask for a raise, challenge a grade, or confront a landlord. A third strategy is *overlearning* (practice that continues after initial mastery of a skill). When you rehearse or role-play assertive behavior, it is essential to continue practicing until your responses become almost automatic. This helps prevent you from getting flustered in the actual situation.

AP Images/Jeff Widener

Associated Press photographer Jeff Widener snapped this timeless photo of a lone protester literally standing up on his own behalf while he halted a column of tanks during the pro-democracy rallies in Tiananmen Square in Beijing, China. How many of us would find the courage to assert ourselves against such direct expressions of authority?

Coercion Being forced to change your beliefs or your behavior against your will.

Brainwashing Engineered or forced attitude change involving a captive audience.

Cult A group that professes great devotion to some person and follows that person almost without question; cult members are typically victimized by their leaders in various ways.

Self-assertion A direct, honest expression of feelings and desires.

To summarize, self-assertion does not supply instant poise, confidence, or self-assurance. However, using these three strategies can provide a way of combating anxieties associated with life in an impersonal and sometimes intimidating society (Sarkova et al., 2013). If you are interested in more information, you can consult a book titled *Your Perfect Right* by Alberti and Emmons (2008).

Reflective Practice

Social Influence

1. The effect that one person's behavior has on another is called ____________.
2. The mere presence of others always improves performance. T or F?
3. Nonconformity is punished by negative group ____________.
4. Janis used the term ____________ to describe a compulsion among decision-making groups to maintain an illusion of unanimity.
5. Obedience in Milgram's experiments was related to
   a. distance between learner and teacher
   b. distance between experimenter and teacher
   c. obedience of other teachers
   d. all of the above
6. Brainwashing differs from other persuasive attempts in that brainwashing requires a(n) ____________.
7. Attitude changes brought about by brainwashing are usually permanent. T or F?
8. Overlearning should be avoided when rehearsing assertive behaviors. T or F?

THINK CRITICALLY

9. Modern warfare allows killing to take place impersonally and at a distance. How does this relate to Milgram's experiments?
10. When practicing self-assertion, do you think it would be better to improvise your own responses or imitate those of a person skilled in self-assertion?

SELF-REFLECT

- Have you ever been part of a group that seemed to make a bad decision because of groupthink? How could the group have avoided its mistake?
- You would like to persuade people to donate to a deserving charity. How, specifically, could you use compliance techniques to get people to donate?
- To what extent are governments entitled to use coercion to modify the attitudes or behavior of individuals?
- Pick a specific instance when you could have been more assertive. How would you handle the situation if it occurs again?

Answers: 1. social influence 2. F 3. sanctions 4. groupthink 5. d 6. captive audience 7. F 8. F 9. There is a big difference between killing someone in hand-to-hand combat and killing someone by lining up images on a video screen. Milgram's research suggests that it is easier for a person to follow orders to kill another human when the victim is at a distance and removed from personal contact. 10. One study found that imitating an assertive model is more effective than improvising your own responses (Kipper, 1992). If you know an assertive and self-assured person, you can learn a lot by watching how they handle difficult situations.

16.4 Psychology and Your Skill Set: Teamwork

GATEWAYS LEARNING OUTCOME:
After reading this section, you will be able to:

16.4.1 Create a plan that will allow you to improve your teamwork skills

After a massive earthquake left Haiti devastated in 2010, two former US Marines—Jake Wood and William McNulty—decided that they wanted to help. Along with six other veterans and first responders, they provided assistance to Haitians in remote regions that were getting little aid. Realizing that many former members of the US Armed Forces possess important skills that are desperately needed during such situations, they set about organizing a team that could provide help under these difficult circumstances. This was the beginning of Team Rubicon, an organization that brings veterans together with first responders to assist the victims of natural disasters.

It may surprise you to know that as much as they help others, members of Team Rubicon also help each other: After their years spent in uniform come to an end, the challenges of returning to civilian life are often difficult, and the support they receive from other members of the military can be invaluable. The "team" has now grown to include thousands of past members of the US and Canadian Armed Forces. They volunteer their time to work on community-based projects with organizations such as Habitat for Humanity, as well as disaster relief efforts that take place both at home and in remote corners of the world. Together, these men and women accomplish a great deal of important work. But they're not just a group of individuals working on the same project. Instead, they function as a team. What's the difference, you ask? Let's find out.

Polaris Images/Nepal/Newscom

In this chapter, we examined topics that broadly relate to social psychology—the area of psychology that is most closely aligned to our relationships with other people. In this section, we focus on the importance of those relationships when people have to work together in teams to accomplish a goal.

Isn't "team" just another word for "group"? According to psychologists, a *team* is a special kind of group. Group work involves multiple people working toward a common goal, but group members can often work on their own and then bring their individual contributions together at the end to construct the final product. In contrast, teams are characterized by their *interdependence*: Members of teams have to actively work together at all stages of the project. Progress toward the goal depends on each member of the team providing their expertise that, in turn, enables the others to complete their own tasks more effectively (West, 2012).

Considerable research has been carried out in the area of teamwork by psychologists, including social and personality psychologists, industrial/organizational psychologists (■ psychologists who study people at work and in organizations; see Section 18.1), and cognitive psychologists. Collectively, they have addressed a number of questions including, for example, the costs and benefits of working in teams (rather than individually), cross-cultural differences in perceptions of teamwork, and developmental changes in teams that work together over long periods of time (Caligiuri & Lundby, 2015; Hackman, 2002; Salas et al., 2015). More recently, the global COVID-19 pandemic has led to increased interest among psychologists about virtual collaboration, and how to ensure success among teams that cannot meet face-to-face (Gilson et al., 2015).

In addition to these questions, there's also a large body of literature that addresses the characteristics of both effective and dysfunctional teams, and much of that research examines the role of team members' characteristics and abilities in contributing to positive outcomes. Psychological research has suggested that effective teamwork draws on several skills, including communication, leadership, problem solving, working with diverse others, creativity, emotional intelligence, and integrity (all of which have been discussed in the *Psychology and Your Skill Set* sections in this book!) (Levi, 2017). If a potential employer asks you to talk about your ability to work as part of a team during an interview, then it's useful to have considered your answer in terms of all of these skills. Even better, try to have ready some concrete examples of experiences that you can use to clearly demonstrate that you have these abilities!

When most people think about teamwork, their minds immediately jump to the workplace. They think about teams working together to plan an event, launch a product, or solve a difficult problem. And the literature supports the idea that effective teams are a valuable resource for any organization: A group of people who work well together often creates a synergistic effect, accomplishing more than could be done by each of the team members on their own.

But being a good "team player" isn't just relevant to our working life; these skills are also important in personal relationships as well. Consider, for example, how teamwork is relevant when romantic partners are raising a child, or when siblings are providing care for an elderly parent (Tolkacheva, van Groenou, & van Tilburg, 2014). Consider, too, that teamwork may be necessary for volunteer work and community service projects that you choose to undertake when you are committed to a particular cause.

Becoming a Team Player

If teamwork skills are important across so many aspects of your life, how can you work to improve them? We've already mentioned that good teamwork draws on a number of other skills (e.g., communication, problem solving, and an openness to working with diverse others), so it's important to work on your abilities in these areas. But according to Amy Edmundson at Harvard Business School, there are at least four other things that you can consider if you want to make valuable contributions to a team (Edmondson, 2012).

First, it's important to *help create ground rules*. Setting up norms that team members understand and agree with is important in ensuring that all members of the team understand what's expected of them (and others!).

Second, you should work to *ensure that everyone participates* in group discussions and activities. It's easy sometimes to assume that the right way to proceed is coming from the person who's speaking the loudest. However, making this type of assumption means that you may often miss out on the valuable opinions of those who are more introverted, or people who just need a bit more time to think things through before responding. There are a number of ways to avoid this problem, but one of the simplest is to just make sure that you go around the table and ask for each person's opinion before making a decision. Of course, for this strategy to work, it's also important to create a climate in which everyone feels that their contributions to the team will be valued and considered.

Third, you should *never assume that everyone knows what you do*: Explicitly sharing what you know means that everyone "begins on the same page," and that the project is much more likely to proceed smoothly.

Finally, you should always *model the behavior you want to see in others*. It's an age-old truism that you should treat other people the way that you want to be treated. When you work closely with others, this is particularly important. If characteristics such as openness, acceptance, conscientiousness, and reliability are important to you, then make sure you demonstrate those same characteristics when you interact with other members of the team.

Reflective Practice

Psychology and Your Skill Set: Teamwork

1. Teamwork and group work are essentially the same thing. T or F?
2. One of the most important things that characterizes teams is that its members are interdependent. T or F?
3. Which of the following skills are important to teamwork?
   a. communication
   b. problem solving
   c. emotional intelligence
   d. a, b, and c are all important
4. Teamwork is important in the workplace but is unlikely to be relevant in your personal or family life. T or F?

THINK CRITICALLY

5. What are some of the strategies that you could use to make sure that all members of a team have an opportunity to offer their opinion in a meeting?

SELF-REFLECT

- Do you consider yourself to be a good "team player," or are you someone who prefers to work alone? Given that so many workplaces require teamwork these days, what skills might you need to work on to improve your ability to work well as part of a team?

Answers: 1. F 2. T 3. d 4. F 5. In addition to being supportive and systematically giving all team members the opportunity to speak (by going around the table and asking for each person's opinion, for example), the team may also want to consider circulating a list of questions or issues before the meeting so that people can consider what they'd like to say in advance. This may be particularly helpful for people who aren't always good at "thinking on their feet."

CHAPTER IN REVIEW

Gateways to Social Thinking and Social Influence

Summary: Gateways Learning Outcomes

16.1 The Fundamentals of Social Groups

16.1.1 Distinguish between ingroups and outgroups, and define ingroup favoritism

For social psychologists, an *ingroup* is any group to which you feel a sense of belonging; conversely, an *outgroup* is one to which you do not belong. *Ingroup favoritism* (or ingroup bias) refers to the fact that we behave in ways that will improve the circumstances of our ingroup, sometimes at the expense of the outgroup.

6.1.2 Define what is meant by the terms group structure, group cohesiveness, norms, social roles, social status, and social power

Group structure refers to the organization of roles, communication pathways, and power within a group. *Group cohesiveness* is the degree of attraction among group members. *Norms* are standards of conduct enforced (formally or informally) by groups. *Social roles* define one's position in groups and the behavior patterns associated with those social roles. *Social status* refers to the extent to which other group members respect or admire a person, while *social power* is the degree to which a person can control the behavior of group members.

16.1.3 Explain how social comparisons are typically carried out

Social comparison refers to the fact that we evaluate our own characteristics and abilities by comparing ourselves with others. Typically, it is most useful to compare ourselves with similar others. In some cases, we make *downward comparisons* (comparing ourselves to people who are worse off) in order to serve the goal of self-enhancement or self-protection. In others, we may engage in *upward comparisons* (comparing ourselves to people who are better than we are) to prompt self-improvement.

16.1.4 Discriminate between internal and external attributions, and the three factors that define which type is made

Attribution theory is concerned with how we make inferences about behavior. Internal attributions are those that ascribe behavior to stable needs or characteristics of a person. External attributions ascribe behavior to something about the environment or circumstances (other people, being tired, feeling ill, having too much to do). A variety of factors affect attribution, including *consistency* (the extent to which the behavior is seen regularly under similar conditions), *distinctiveness* (the extent to which the behavior happens in other circumstances), and *consensus* (the extent to which others respond the same way under similar conditions).

16.1.5 Contrast the fundamental attribution error and the actor–observer bias

The *fundamental attribution error* (FAE) refers to a human tendency to ascribe the actions of others to internal causes. The *actor–observer difference* refers to the fact that when making an attribution for the same behavior, we tend to attribute others' behavior to internal causes (the FAE) but our own behavior to external causes.

16.2 Attitudes

16.2.1 Define the term attitude, and outline four ways in which attitudes are formed

Attitudes are learned dispositions made up of a belief component, an emotional component, and an action component. Attitudes may be formed by *direct contact, chance conditioning, interaction with others*, and *interactions with the media*.

16.2.2 Describe three ways to measure attitudes

Attitudes are typically measured with techniques such as *open-ended interviews, social distance scales*, and *attitude scales*. Attitudes expressed in these ways do not always correspond to actual behavior.

16.2.3 Outline two factors that may prompt people to change their attitudes

Attitudes may change as a result of *exposure to a reference group with whom you identify*. Attitudes can also change as a result of *cognitive dissonance*.

16.2.4 Define cognitive dissonance and outline six ways to minimize dissonance between our beliefs and behaviors

Cognitive dissonance refers to a state in which attitudes conflict with one another, or when our cognitions about an issue are inconsistent with our behavior on that issue. Social psychologists have identified at least six ways to reduce dissonance, including: *changing behavior to match the cognition, changing the belief to match the cognition, diminishing the importance of dissonant cognitions, focusing on consonant thoughts, reducing the amount of perceived choice*, and *attributing the belief–behavior mismatch to an external cause*.

16.3 Social Influence

16.3.1 Distinguish between mere presence, conformity, compliance, obedience, and coercion as methods of social influence

Social influence refers to alterations in behavior brought about by the behavior of others. Social influence ranges from milder (mere presence, conformity, and compliance) to stronger (obedience and coercion). The *mere presence* (that is, other people simply being perceived as close) of others can cause changes in behavior. *Conformity* refers to situations in which we bring our behavior into line with perceived social norms. *Compliance* refers to situations in which we go along with direct requests from another person. In some cases, the person has little or no authority. *Obedience* is a special type of compliance that takes place when we go along with the demands of an authority figure. *Coercion* involves forcing people to change their beliefs or behavior against their will.

16.3.2 Explain how the mere presence of others can influence behavior

The presence of others may facilitate or inhibit performance. The extent to which behavior is improved or impaired depends to some extent on self-confidence. The presence of others may also result in social loafing (the tendency to do less work when working with others on a task).

16.3.3 Describe the reasons why people conform, and the conditions under which conformity is most likely

People conform when they feel uncertain about a situation because *others are perceived to be a valuable source of information* about the correct way to behave. In addition, people conform to address the *need to be accepted* by the group. Conformity is most likely when people possess certain *personal traits* (high needs for structure or certainty, high levels of anxiety and concern about the approval of others, and low levels of self-confidence), live in *cultures that emphasize group cooperation* (such as many Asian cultures), *when group membership is important*, when the *size of the group* is large, when the *size of the majority* is large, and when there is *unanimity of the group*.

16.3.4 Outline the three factors that impact the persuasiveness of messages intended to elicit compliance

Effective persuasion occurs when characteristics of the *communicator*, the *message*, and the *audience* are well-matched. In general, a likable and believable communicator who repeats a credible message that arouses emotion (particularly fear) in the audience and states clear-cut conclusions will be persuasive, though persuasiveness also depends on the extent to which the audience is motivated and able to think carefully about the message.

16.3.5 Compare the foot-in-the-door, door-in-the-face, lowball, and nudge techniques as methods of gaining compliance

The *foot-in-the-door effect* refers to situations in which a person who first agrees to a small request is, to be consistent, later more likely to comply with a larger demand. The *door-in-the-face effect* describes the tendency for a person who has refused a major request to agree to a smaller request. The *lowball technique* consists of getting a person committed to act and then making the terms of acting less desirable. *Nudges* involve creating gentle pressure that push people to act in accordance with your wishes.

16.3.6 Explain what we can learn about obedience from Stanley Milgram's studies

Milgram's studies help us to understand the conditions under which obedience to authority is most likely. In general, his studies did not reveal that obedience was always "blind," but rather that it was more likely under conditions when we identify with authority figures and see ourselves as associated with their ingroup.

16.3.7 Describe how captivity facilitates the brainwashing techniques that are used in coercion

Captivity places people at the mercy of their captors, who have control of the environment and can therefore engage in psychological manipulation that would not be possible in a normal setting.

16.3.8 Describe three strategies that facilitate self-assertion

Three strategies that facilitate self-assertion are *rehearsing* the actions you'll want to engage in, *role-playing* (or practicing those actions) with someone else, and *overlearning* (continuing to practice even after you've mastered those actions).

16.4 Psychology and Your Skill Set: Teamwork

16.4.1 Create a plan that will allow you to improve your teamwork skills

Working as an effective member of a team requires that we think carefully about several things, including creating ground rules, ensuring that everyone participates, providing important information to all members of the team, and modeling the behavior that you want to see from others. We hope that after reading this section, you'll be better able to think about how you can use these components to help when you are working with diverse others in your everyday life!

17 Prosocial and Antisocial Behavior

The Washington Post/Getty Images

Gateway Theme Social life is complex, but consistent patterns can be found in our positive and negative interactions with other people.

Chapter Outline

What Does a Reformed Racist Look Like?

Derek Black spends a lot of time trying to help others by talking about the most effective ways to combat racism and anti-Semitism. It's a bit of an odd pastime for him, given that he's the son of a former KKK Grand Wizard. Growing up, he spent years absorbing his family's teachings about White supremacy, and he was widely regarded as being on the path to a leadership position within the White nationalist movement.

That path took a sharp detour when Black decided to attend a very small liberal arts college in Florida. After people on campus learned of his views about race and religion, he was faced with outrage and disgust from fellow students. But then, in a completely unexpected turn of events, an Orthodox Jewish student named Matthew Stevenson invited Derek to a Shabbat dinner with a few other friends from their dorm. The unspoken rule that evening was that there would be no discussion of politics or religion; instead, the dinner was all about connecting with one another as individuals. This effort to improve their understanding of one another was not without consequences: In an interesting twist of intolerance, many of the students then turned on Stevenson and others who attended the dinner, saying that simply associating with Black was like "an act of treason."

That one dinner turned into a weekly Friday gathering that lasted more than two years, and during that time Derek connected—and made friends—with many of the diverse students on that small campus. One conversation at a time, his views and prejudices evolved and changed. In his final year at college he wrote a letter to the Southern Poverty Law Center, disavowing White nationalism and apologizing for his past actions.

Derek Black's story is described in Eli Saslow's Pulitzer-prize winning book *Rising Out of Hatred*. In this chapter, we'll explore several of the ideas that appear in that biography, including the social psychology of both love and hate. We'll look at the human need to affiliate with others, and how those feelings are associated with prosocial behavior, or behavior that supports others. We'll also explore the other side of the coin, examining causes of antisocial behavior including aggression and prejudice. We conclude this chapter with a look at how efforts to promote diversity and inclusion can benefit both our personal and professional lives.

17.1 Affiliation and Attraction

GATEWAYS LEARNING OUTCOMES:
After reading this section, you will be able to:

17.1.1 Provide three reasons that explain why humans seek to affiliate with others

17.1.2 Describe four factors that influence our attraction to others

17.1.3 Describe how relationships deepen, making reference to self-disclosure and social exchange theory

17.1.4 Explain the fundamental ideas behind Sternberg's triangular theory of love

17.1.5 Name and describe the three types of adult attachment

17.1.6 Describe how evolutionary forces shape men's and women's preferences for mates

One common misunderstanding about human nature is that we are engaged in a perennial struggle for survival against one another. In fact, we cooperate with the people around us at least as much as we are in conflict with them. Although at times you may want to be left alone, the fact is that we humans are social animals with a **need to affiliate**—a need to associate with other people—that is rooted in at least three basic human motives.

The first relates to the fact that spending time with others allows us to *engage in comparison*, which in turn allows us to better evaluate ourselves (■ see Section 16.2). Second, we seek the company of others to *alleviate fear or anxiety*. This point is illustrated by a classic experiment in which college women participating in a study were greeted by Dr. Gregor Zilstein, who ominously said to some of them, "We would like to give each of you a series of electric shocks . . . these shocks will hurt, they will be painful." In the room was a frightening electrical device that seemed to verify Zilstein's plans. While waiting to be shocked, each woman was given a choice of waiting alone or with other participants. Women frightened in this way more often chose to wait with others; those for whom Dr. Zilstein had indicated the shock would be "a mild tickle or tingle" were more willing to wait alone (Schachter, 1959).

Martin Barraud/Getty Images

Humans show a natural tendency to affiliate with one another.

Apparently the frightened women found it comforting to be with others. Should we conclude that "misery loves company"? Actually, it may be even more specific than that: In a later experiment, women who expected to be shocked were given the choice of waiting with other future shock recipients, with women waiting to see their college advisers, or alone. Most women chose to wait with other future "victims"—misery seems to love miserable company! In general, we seem to prefer to be with people in circumstances similar to our own (Li et al., 2008).

Is there a reason for that? Seeing that other people are reacting calmly can help reassure and soothe us when a situation is stressful (Kulik, Mahler, & Moore, 2003). Likewise, simply being around other people in times of stress increases levels of the hormone oxytocin, which is sometimes called the "snuggle drug." This, in turn, reduces the stress response (Doom, Doyle, & Gunnar, 2017; Kumsta & Heinrichs, 2013).

Aside from social comparison and alleviating anxiety, a third reason that we tend to affiliate with others stems from the desire to *get and give approval, support, friendship, and love* to close friends and loved ones (Baumeister & Bushman, 2017). But how do we decide who those people will be? Who do we choose for our friends and romantic partners? **Interpersonal attraction**—that is, an affinity for another person—is the basis for most voluntary social relationships (Berscheid, 2010; Finkel & Eastwick, 2015). To form these relationships, we must first identify potential friends and lovers and then get to know them. Deciding whether you would like to get to know another person can happen very quickly, sometimes within just minutes of meeting (Grant-Jacob, 2016). What factors influence this type of attraction? Let's take a closer look.

Factors That Influence Attraction

"Birds of a feather flock together." "Familiarity breeds contempt." "Opposites attract." Are these statements true? At best, the folklore is a mixture of fact and fiction. As you might expect, we look for friends and lovers who will be kind and understanding, and who appear to have *personalities compatible with our own* (Bradbury & Karney, 2010; Park & Lennon, 2008). But there are other factors aside from personality that play a role in our initial attraction to people—let's take a closer look at them.

Familiarity and Proximity

In general, we are attracted to people with whom we are *familiar* (Reis et al., 2011). In fact, our choice of friends (and even lovers) is based more on *physical proximity* (nearness) than we might care to believe. Proximity promotes attraction by increasing the *frequency of contact* between people. The closer people live to each other, the more likely they are to become friends. Likewise, lovers like to think they have found the "one and only" person in the universe for them. In reality, they have probably found the best match in a 5-mile radius (Reis et al., 2011). Marriages are not made in heaven—they are made in local schools, businesses, churches, bars, clubs, and neighborhoods.

In short, there does seem to be a "boy-next-door" or "girl-next-door" effect in romantic attraction, and a "folks-next-door" effect in friendship. It's worth noting, however, that the Internet is making it increasingly easier to stay in constant "virtual contact," which is leading to more and more long-distance friendships and romances (Aron, 2012; Whyte & Torgler, 2017).

Similarity

In everything from casual acquaintance to marriage, similar people are attracted to each other (Montoya & Horton, 2013). *Similarity* refers to how alike you are to another person in background, age, sex, interests, attitudes, ethnicity, beliefs, and so forth.

So similarity also influences mate selection? Yes. In choosing a mate, we often select someone who is like us, a pattern called *homogamy* (huh-MOG-ah-me) (Kalmijn, 2010; Schramm et al., 2012). Studies show that married couples are highly similar in age, education, ethnicity, and religion. To a lesser degree, they also are similar in attitudes and opinions, mental abilities, status, height, and weight. In case you're wondering, homogamy also applies to unmarried couples who are living together (Blackwell & Lichter, 2004).

Physical Attractiveness

People who are *physically attractive* are regarded as good-looking by others. Beautiful people are generally rated as more appealing than average. This is due, in part, to the *halo effect*, a tendency to generalize a favorable impression to unrelated personal characteristics. Because of it, we assume that attractive people also are likable, intelligent, warm, witty, mentally healthy, and socially skilled. Basically, we often act as if "what is beautiful is good" (Lorenzo, Biesanz, & Human, 2010).

In reality, physical attractiveness has little or no connection to intelligence, talents, or abilities. Perhaps that's why beauty affects mainly our initial interest in getting to know others. Later, more meaningful qualities gain in importance. As you discover that someone has a good personality, he or she will start looking even more attractive to you. As you are no doubt aware, it takes more than appearance to make a lasting relationship (Berscheid, 2010; Lewandowski, Aron, & Gee, 2007; Reis et al., 2011).

Reciprocity

Okay, so he or she is someone with whom you are familiar, appears to share a lot in common with you, and is even hot. What else do you need to know before taking it to the next level? Well, it would be nice to know if he or she also is the least bit into you (Greitemeyer, 2010; Montoya & Horton, 2012). In fact, **reciprocity**, which occurs when people respond to each other in similar ways, may be the most important factor influencing the development of relationships. Most people find it easier to reciprocate someone else's overtures than to be the initiator (Montoya & Insko, 2008). That way, at least the embarrassment of an outright rejection can be avoided.

How Relationships Deepen

Once initial contact has been made, it's time to get to know each other. But to get acquainted, you must be willing to talk about more than just the weather, sports, or nuclear physics. Here, we'll look at how relationships deepen through both *self-disclosure* and *social exchange*.

Self-Disclosure

Self-disclosure is the process by which you begin to share private thoughts and feelings and reveal yourself to others. In general, as friends talk, they gradually deepen their level of liking (Sprecher, Treger, & Wondra, 2013; Sprecher & Treger, 2015).

Disclosure requires a degree of trust, though, and many people play it safe, or "close to the vest," with people they do not know well. Indeed, self-disclosure is governed by unspoken rules about what's acceptable, given the closeness of the relationship (Phillips, Rothbard, & Dumas, 2009). When self-disclosure proceeds at a moderate pace it builds trust, intimacy, reciprocity, and positive feelings. This is exactly what happened at the Friday night dinners attended by Derek Black, Matthew Stevenson, and their friends. Over many months, their discussions allowed them to better understand one another as individuals and promoted friendships that probably seemed very unlikely at the outset.

In contrast, overdisclosure exceeds what is appropriate for a relationship or social situation, giving rise to suspicion and

EXImages/Alamy Stock Photo

Overdisclosure is a staple of many reality television shows such as *Catfish* and *90 Day Fiancé*. Guests frequently reveal intimate details about their personal lives, including private family matters, sex and dating, physical or sexual abuse, major embarrassments, and criminal activities. Viewers probably find such intimate disclosures entertaining, rather than threatening, because they don't have to reciprocate.

Need to affiliate The desire to associate with other people.

Interpersonal attraction Social attraction to another person.

Reciprocity A mutual exchange of feelings, thoughts, or things between people.

Self-disclosure The process of revealing private thoughts, feelings, and one's personal history to others.

reducing attraction. For example, imagine standing in line at a store and having the stranger in front of you say, "Lately I've been thinking about how I really feel about myself. I think I'm pretty well adjusted, but I occasionally have some questions about my sexual adequacy." It's interesting to note that on the Internet (and especially on social networking sites), people often feel freer to express their true feelings, which can lead to personal growth and genuine, face-to-face friendships. However, it also can lead to some very dramatic overdisclosures (Jiang, Bazarova, & Hancock, 2013; Special & LiBarber, 2012).

Social Exchange Theory

Self-disclosure involves an exchange of personal information, but other types of exchanges can also help relationships to deepen. In fact, many relationships can be understood as an ongoing series of **social exchanges**—transfers of attention, information, affection, and favors, in addition to personal information. According to **social exchange theory**, we unconsciously weigh social *rewards*, such as positive feelings and intimacy, and *costs*, such as negative feelings and lowered self-esteem. For a relationship to last, it must be *profitable*—its rewards must exceed its costs—for both parties (Kalmijn, 2010). For instance, imagine that Helen and Troy have been dating for two years. Although they still have fun at times, they also frequently argue and bicker. If the friction in their relationship gets much stronger, it will exceed the rewards of staying together. When that happens, they will probably split up.

Generally, the balance between rewards and costs is different for all people and is judged in comparison with what we have come to expect from our past experience. The personal standard that a person uses to evaluate rewards and costs is called the **comparison level**. The comparison level is high for people with histories of satisfying and rewarding relationships, and lower for someone whose relationships have been unsatisfying. Thus, the decision to continue a relationship is affected by your personal comparison level. A lonely person, or one whose friendships have been marginal, might stay longer in a relationship that others would consider unacceptable.

Loving: Dating and Mating

Interpersonal attraction comes in degrees. Casual friendships tend to be based on liking, while deeper friendships and romantic relationships are usually based on various forms of love. Let's do a deeper dive on three theories that help to explain our thoughts and behaviors related to dating and mating: the *triangular theory* of love, *attachment theory*, and *evolutionary theory*.

Triangular Theory of Love

According to psychologist Robert Sternberg's (1988) *triangular theory of love*, different forms of love arise from different combinations of three basic components (● Figure 17.1):

Intimacy refers to feelings of connectedness and affection.
Passion refers to deep emotional and/or sexual feelings.
Commitment involves the determination to stay in a long-term relationship with another person.

How does this triangle work? Try it for yourself. Think of a person to whom you are attracted. Refer to ▲ Table 17.1 as you ask yourself three yes/no questions: Do I feel intimate with this person? Do I feel passion for this person? Am I committed to this person? Find the kind of love that fits your answers.

For example, if you answered *yes* to intimacy but *no* to passion and commitment, you like that person; you are friends. **Romantic love**, in contrast, is based on intimacy as well as high levels of passion (emotional arousal, sexual desire, or both; Marazziti & Baroni, 2012). You are experiencing romantic love as you are "falling in love" (Grant-Jacob, 2016). Romantic love differs from friendship in another interesting way: In contrast to simple liking, romantic love usually involves deep mutual absorption. In other words, lovers (unlike friends) attend

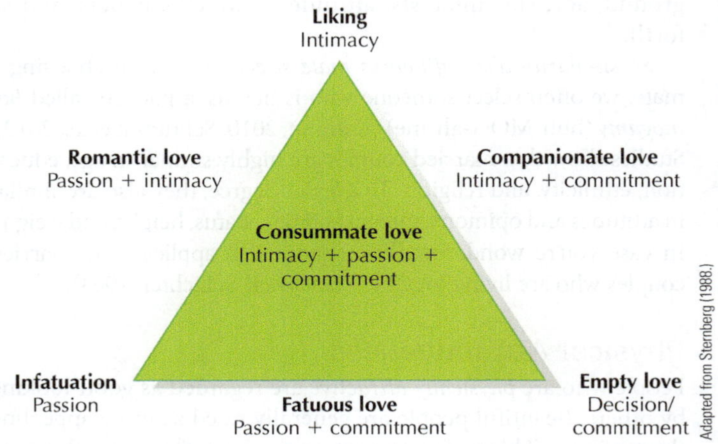

● **Figure 17.1 The triangle of love.** Each of the three basic components of love (intimacy, passion, and commitment) appears at one corner of the triangle and is associated with a form of love. Pairs of components and their associated form of love appear on lines of the triangle. Consummate love, which involves all three components, is pictured at the center of the triangle.

▲ Table 17.1 Sternberg's Triangular Theory of Love

Combinations of intimacy, passion, and commitment

Type of Love	Intimacy	Passion	Commitment
Nonlove			
Liking	Yes		
Infatuated love		Yes	
Empty love			Yes
Romantic love	Yes	Yes	
Companionate love	Yes		Yes
Fatuous love		Yes	Yes
Consummate love	Yes	Yes	Yes

Source: Sternberg (1988).

almost exclusively to one another (Riela et al., 2010). A final interesting characteristic of romantic love is lovers' ability to see their partners in idealized ways (Barelds & Dijkstra, 2009). Nobody's perfect, of course. That's why it's no surprise that relationships are most likely to persist when lovers idealize one another. Doing so doesn't just blind them to their partner's faults; it actually helps them create the relationship they want (Murray, Holmes, & Griffin, 2003).

Alternatively, if you answered *yes* to intimacy and commitment but *no* to passion, then you are feeling **companionate love**. This form of love is more common among couples who have been together for a long time. Such couples often describe themselves as "being in love" rather than "falling in love" (Riela et al., 2010). In contrast, **fatuous love** results when there is passion and commitment, but no intimacy.

Does that mean that the most complete form of love is consummate love? You've got it! We experience **consummate love** when we feel intimacy and passion for another person, *and* we are strongly committed to him or her.

Love and Attachment

Imagine that Sheela has been dating Paul for over a year. Although they have had some rough spots, Sheela is comfortable, secure, and trusting in her love for Paul. Charlene, in contrast, has had a long series of unhappy romances with men. She is basically a loner who has difficulty trusting others. Like Sheela, Eduardo has been dating the same person for a year. However, his relationship with Lizzy has been stormy and troubled. Eduardo is strongly attracted to Lizzy, but he is also in a constant state of anxiety over whether she really loves him.

Sheela, Charlene, and Eduardo might be surprised to learn that the roots of their romantic relationships may lie in childhood. There is growing evidence that early attachments to caregivers can have a lasting impact on how we relate to others (Millings et al., 2013; Vrtička & Vuilleumier, 2012). For example, studies of dating couples have identified secure, avoidant, and ambivalent attachment patterns similar to those seen in early child development (Brumbaugh & Fraley, 2010; Lavy, Mikulincer, & Shaver, 2010). Nationally, about 60 percent of all adults have a secure attachment style, 25 percent are avoidant, and 10 percent have ambivalent attachment styles (Mickelson, Kessler, & Shaver, 1997). (■ Forming a secure attachment to a caregiver is a major event in early child development. See Section 3.3.)

Interesting. How can I figure out my attachment style? Read the following statements and see which best describes your adult relationships:

Secure Attachment Style

In general, I think most other people are well-intentioned and trustworthy.
I find it relatively easy to get close to others.
I am comfortable relying on others and having others depend on me.
I don't worry much about being abandoned by others.
I am comfortable when other people want to get close to me emotionally.

Avoidant Attachment Style

I tend to pull back when things don't go well in a relationship.
I am somewhat skeptical about the idea of true love.
I have difficulty trusting my partner in a romantic relationship.
Other people tend to be too eager to seek commitment from me.
I get a little nervous if anyone gets too close emotionally.

Ambivalent Attachment Style

I have often felt misunderstood and unappreciated in my romantic relationships.
My friends and lovers have been somewhat unreliable.
I love my romantic partner but I worry that she or he doesn't really love me.
I would like to be closer to my romantic partner, but I'm not sure I trust her or him.

Most adults, like Sheela, have a *secure attachment style* that is marked by caring, intimacy, supportiveness, and understanding in love relationships. Secure people regard themselves as friendly, good-natured, and likable. They think of others as generally well-intentioned, reliable, and trustworthy. People with a secure attachment style find it relatively easy to get close to others. They are comfortable depending on others and having others depend on them. In general, they don't worry too much about being abandoned or about having someone become too emotionally close to them. Most people prefer to have a secure partner, whatever their own style might be (Keren & Mayseless, 2013).

While many adults demonstrate a secure attachment pattern, it's not unusual to have an *avoidant attachment style* that reflects a fear of intimacy and a tendency to resist commitment to others. Avoidant people like Charlene tend to pull back

Social exchange Any exchange between two people of attention, information, affection, favors, or the like.

Social exchange theory A theory stating that rewards must exceed costs for relationships to endure.

Comparison level A personal standard used to evaluate rewards and costs in a social exchange.

Intimacy Feelings of connectedness and affection for another person.

Passion Deep emotional and/or sexual feelings for another person.

Commitment The determination to stay in a long-term relationship with another person.

Romantic love Love that is associated with high levels of interpersonal attraction, heightened arousal, mutual absorption, and sexual desire.

Companionate love A form of love characterized by intimacy *and* commitment, but not passion.

Fatuous Love Love characterized by passion and commitment, but not intimacy.

Consummate love A form of love characterized by intimacy, passion, *and* commitment.

when things don't go well in a relationship. The avoidant person is suspicious, aloof, and skeptical about love. She or he tends to see others as either unreliable or overly eager to commit to a relationship. As a result, avoidant people find it hard to completely trust and depend on others, and they get nervous when anyone gets too close emotionally. Basically, as the name suggests, they avoid intimacy (Juhl, Sand, & Routledge, 2012; Lavy, Mikulincer, & Shaver, 2010).

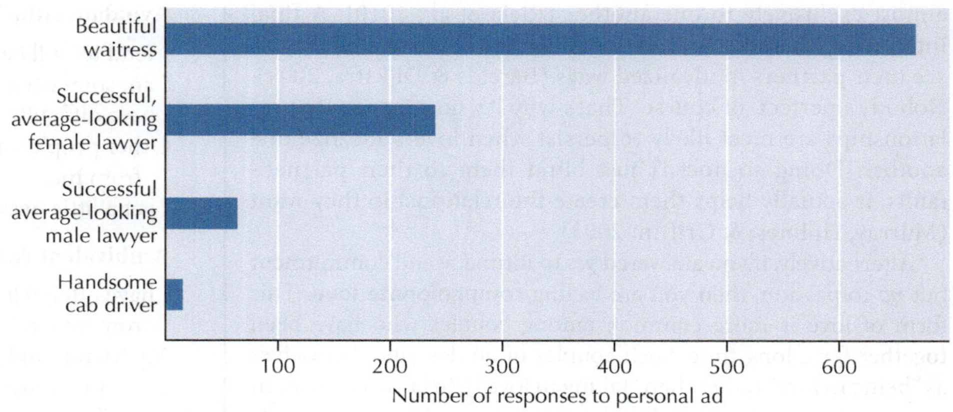

Figure 17.2 Potential dating partners. What do people look for when considering potential dating partners? Here are the results of a study in which four fake personal ads were placed in newspapers, describing (a) a beautiful waitress, (b) a successful, average-looking female lawyer, (c) a successful, average-looking male lawyer, and (d) a handsome male cab driver. All were described as looking for a (heterosexual) romantic relationship. As you can see, men were far more likely to respond to the ads overall (see top two bars as compared to bottom two bars). More interesting was the fact that men were clearly more influenced by looks (compare the top two bars) and women by success (compare the bottom two bars) (Goode, 1996).

People like Eduardo have an *ambivalent attachment style,* marked by mixed feelings about love and friendship. Conflicting feelings of affection, anger, emotional turmoil, physical attraction, and doubt result in an unsettled, ambivalent state. Often, ambivalent people regard themselves as misunderstood and unappreciated. Ambivalent people worry that their romantic partners don't really love them or may leave them. Although they want to be extremely close to their partners, they are also preoccupied with doubts about the partner's dependability and trustworthiness (DeWall et al., 2011).

How could emotional attachments early in life affect adult relationships? It appears that we use early attachment experiences to build mental models about adult relationships. Later, we use these models as a sort of blueprint for forming, maintaining, and breaking bonds of love and affection (Sroufe et al., 2005).

Evolution and Mate Selection

Evolutionary psychology is the study of the evolutionary origins of human behavior patterns (Brown & Cross, 2017; Geher, 2014). Many psychologists believe that evolution left an imprint on men and women that influences everything from sexual attraction and infidelity to jealousy and divorce. According to David Buss, the key to understanding human mating patterns is to understand how evolved behavior patterns guide our choices (Buss, 2015).

In a study of 37 cultures on six continents, Buss found the following patterns: Compared with women, men are more interested in casual sex; they prefer younger, more physically attractive partners; and they get more jealous over real or imagined sexual infidelities than they do over a loss of emotional commitment. Compared with men, women prefer slightly older partners who appear to be industrious, higher in status, or economically successful; women are more upset by a partner who becomes emotionally involved with someone else, rather than one who is sexually unfaithful (Buss, 2015; Regan et al., 2000; Figure 17.2).

Why do such differences exist? Buss and others believe that mating preferences evolved in response to the differing reproductive challenges faced by men and women (Buss, 2015; Frederick & Fales, 2016). As a rule, women must invest more time and energy in reproduction and nurturing their young than men. Consequently, women's interests evolved to focus on whether their partners will stay with them and whether their mates have the resources to provide for their children.

In contrast, the reproductive success of men depends on their mates' fertility. Men, therefore, tend to look for health, youth, and beauty in a prospective mate as signs of suitability for reproduction. This preference, perhaps, is why some older men abandon their first wives in favor of young, beautiful "trophy wives." Evolutionary theory further proposes that the male emphasis on mates' sexual fidelity is based on concerns about the paternity of offspring. From a biological perspective, men do not benefit from investing resources in children they did not sire (Geher, 2014).

Although some evidence supports the evolutionary view of mating, it is important to remember that evolved mating tendencies are subtle at best and are easily overruled by other factors. Some mating patterns may simply reflect the fact that men still tend to control the power and resources in most societies (Fine, 2010). Also, early research may be misleading because women tend to give "polite" answers to questions about jealousy. Privately, they may be just as furious about a mate's sexual infidelity as any man (Harris, 2004).

Whatever the outcome of the debate about evolution and mate selection, it is important to remember this: Potential mates are rated as most attractive if they are kind, secure, intelligent, and supportive (Klohnen & Luo, 2003; Regan et al., 2000). These qualities are love's greatest allies.

Rob Marmion/Shutterstock.com

According to evolutionary psychologists, women tend to be concerned with whether mates will devote time and resources to a relationship. Men place more emphasis on physical attractiveness and sexual fidelity.

Reflective Practice

Affiliation and Attraction

1. The need to affiliate is prompted by a human desire to engage in social comparison, reduce anxiety, and to get and give support, friendship, and love. T or F?
2. Interpersonal attraction is increased by all but one of the following. (Which does ***not*** fit?)
   a. familiarity
   b. reciprocity
   c. similarity
   d. social costs
3. High levels of self-disclosure are reciprocated in even the most casual social encounters. T or F?
4. In Sternberg's triangular theory, infatuated love involves commitment but not passion or intimacy. T or F?
5. The most striking finding about marriage patterns is that most people choose mates whose personalities are quite unlike their own. T or F?
6. Both ambivalent and avoidant attachment patterns are associated with difficulties in trusting a romantic partner. T or F?

THINK CRITICALLY

7. How has the Internet altered the effects of proximity on interpersonal attraction?

SELF-REFLECT

- To what extent does Sternberg's triangular theory of love apply to your own loving relationships with others?
- Can you think of people you know whose adult relationships seem to illustrate each of the attachment styles described in the preceding section?

Answers: 1. T 2. d 3. F 4. F 5. F 6. T 7. The Internet has made actual physical proximity less crucial in interpersonal attraction because frequent contact is possible even at great distances. It has also made self-disclosure (and overdisclosure) easier (be careful, it's just a click away).

17.2 Prosocial Behavior: Helping Others

GATEWAYS LEARNING OUTCOMES:
After reading this section you should be able to:

17.2.1 Define prosocial behavior, and outline three motives that can promote it

17.2.2 Distinguish between prosocial behavior and altruism

17.2.3 Describe three factors that influence helping

17.2.4 Describe the three components of empathy and distinguish empathy from sympathy (or compassion) and personal distress

17.2.5 Explain what is meant by the term bystander apathy, and the three decision points that are relevant in determining whether bystanders will assist others in need

It makes sense that we act kindly toward people to whom we're attracted, or with whom we are friends or lovers. But what about people we don't know? Every year, we hear about people—both trained first responders and private citizens—who risk their lives to save strangers from fires, drowning, animal attacks, electrocution, and suffocation. Volunteers such as organ donors, members of the Peace Corps, and Doctors Without Borders may also assume some level of risk in order to provide help to people that they do not know well. But it's important to remember that highly visible acts of heroism are only one way that people work selflessly to benefit others they may not know very well. In reality, most of the help that's provided comes from people who serve their communities every day in small ways, including volunteering as a tutor or coach, caring for those who are ill, donating blood, or working at fundraisers for local charities.

Prosocial behavior is defined as any action that benefits another person, and may include things like helping, sharing, cooperating, and comforting, as well as more dramatic forms of assistance such as rescuing others (Eagly, 2009). Regardless of its form, though, there's one thing that all prosocial acts have in common: There are costs to the person providing the help, which may include their time, money, effort, or risks to their personal safety. Why, then, do we act prosocially? What motivates us to provide help?

Evolutionary psychology The study of the evolutionary origins of human behavior patterns.

Prosocial behavior Any behavior that has a positive impact on other people.

Three Motives for Prosocial Behavior

One reason that humans assume the costs of prosocial behavior can be explained through *evolutionary forces*. Historically, the chances of survival increased when individuals lived in groups. In particular, cooperative groups (ones in which help was routinely provided and accepted by all members) were particularly effective at ensuring the health and well-being of their members over the longer term.

But while evolution may be valuable for explaining a general tendency for humans to help one another over millions of years, it is less useful for understanding the motives that guide everyday prosocial actions in modern times. Here, we need to consider two other motives: those that are *self-oriented* and those that are *other-oriented*. To appreciate the difference between them, consider these two imaginary scenarios.

> Beatta is a celebrity who has recently had a lot of bad press because she was caught driving while drunk. Her agent suggested that she could improve her image if she volunteered with a well-known organization that was doing good work in the community, such as Habitat for Humanity. Beatta couldn't have cared less about the volunteering, but she agreed that it would help to salvage her reputation. The next month, several media outlets published articles showing photos of Beatta working to build a Habitat for Humanity home for a refugee family in Los Angeles.

> Elsa is a university student who recently did a psychology project on the effects of homelessness. While working on her project, she spent some time at a homeless shelter and did a great deal of reading on the subject. The books and articles she got from the library really emphasized to her how important a secure home was to children's development, including their mental health and achievement at school. Wanting to make a difference for children without secure housing, Elsa volunteered with Habitat for Humanity to build a home for a new immigrant family in her community.

In both scenarios we have a person who has demonstrated prosocial behavior by committing time to a charity that is helping to build a home for a vulnerable family. Do you evaluate their actions in the same way? For most people the answer is no, because Beatta's and Elsa's motives for engaging in prosocial behavior are very different. Beatta is motivated by self-oriented interests: She is volunteering because she wants to improve her own circumstances (in this case, her image). But Elsa's interests are other-oriented: She wants to improve the living conditions of the immigrant family and has nothing to gain herself. (Of course, some people might argue that Elsa does gain from this prosocial behavior if it also makes her feel good about herself; however, if the primary motive for helping is to serve others then it is reasonable to say that it is predominantly an other-oriented action.)

Self- and other-oriented motives lie at the heart of the distinction between prosocial behavior and altruism. Though some people use these terms interchangeably, psychologists see differences between them that are based on motivation (Batson & Powell, 2003). Thus, although both Beatta's and Elsa's actions meet the definition of prosocial behavior (behavior that helps others), psychologists would argue that Beatta's work stems from *egoism* (self-oriented motives) while Elsa's work stems from *altruism* (other-oriented motives). **Altruism**, then, is a specific type of prosocial behavior that is motivated by improving the circumstances of others, with little regard for oneself (Batson & Powell, 2003).

Factors That Influence Helping

Helping behavior is complex and influenced by many variables (Baumeister & Bushman, 2017). Here, we examine three of them: characteristics of the person in need of help, characteristics of the helper, and characteristics of the situation.

Characteristics of Person Needing Help

One of the most well-established findings related to prosocial behavior is that we are more likely to help *people that we perceive to be "like us"*; that is, those who are part of our ingroup (Guéguen, Martin, & Meineri, 2011; Batson, 2010) (■ see Section 16.1 for more about ingroups and outgroups). Moreover, it will not surprise you to know that help is much more often provided to *people we are close to*, such as family and friends, rather than people we do not know well (Clark et al., 2015).

In addition, people are much more likely to give assistance when there is evidence that *the person in need of help is not responsible for their difficulties*. One naturalistic experiment staged in a New York City subway provides support for this idea. When a "victim" (who was an actor) "passed out" in a subway car, he received more help when carrying a cane than when carrying a liquor bottle (Piliavin, Rodin, & Piliavin, 1969).

Characteristics of the Helper

In addition to characteristics of the person in need, psychological scientists have also investigated whether characteristics of the helper predict prosocial behavior. One important characteristic that has received considerable attention is *gender*. Here, the story is in keeping with the gender roles described in ■ Section 11.2: While men are more likely to provide help that requires physical strength, assertiveness, or dominance (such as physically overcoming someone in the middle of committing a crime), women are more likely to engage in prosocial behavior that is focused on developing or maintaining relationships (Eagly, 2009). In this way, gender is likely linked to another factor that seems to influence prosocial behavior; namely, helpers' *beliefs about their competence* to provide the kind of assistance that is needed (Midlarsky, 1984). Not surprisingly, we are more likely to provide the kinds of help that draw on our perceived strengths.

Researchers have also attempted to link *personality characteristics* to prosocial behavior. In particular, agreeableness is a trait that has consistently been linked with helping (Graziano & Habashi, 2015). People who are high on agreeableness tend to be forgiving, cooperative, and sympathetic, all of which are associated with an increased likelihood of providing assistance. A second personality trait that appears to be associated with prosocial responding is honesty/humility. People who score high on this trait are sincere and value fairness, and researchers have found that such individuals are likely to engage in active cooperation with others (Hilbig et al., 2013). (■ For more information about personality traits, including agreeableness and honesty/humility, see Section 12.2.)

Another important helper characteristic is *empathy*. Research has consistently demonstrated that people who are more empathic, or who have been induced to experience empathy, are more likely to behave prosocially (Batson, 2010). Empathy is a complex concept, though, so let's do a deeper dive to see what psychologists have learned about it.

Studying the Science: Empathy

For psychologists, **empathy** is usually narrowly defined as a state in which people, when confronted with someone who is suffering, have an experience that is very similar to the person in distress (Bloom, 2017).

Empathy is assumed to have a *cognitive component* (perspective taking) that allows you to take the perspective of the other person, an *emotional component* (empathic concern) that is associated with the "feelings" you experience, and a *physiological component* (empathic arousal) that is linked to physical arousal (Eisenberg et al., 2010). So, for example, if you are with your friend Assam who is feeling anxious before delivering an important talk to a very large audience, an empathic response would involve you "stepping into Assam's shoes" to understand his experience (the cognitive component), feeling—maybe in a somewhat milder way—that very same sense of anxiety that he is having (the emotional component), and experiencing heightened arousal that might be characterized by increased heart rate, for example (the physiological component).

Of course, sometimes we can understand that another person is having a hard time without necessarily feeling exactly the same emotion in response. Consider a colleague at work who tells you that his mother has passed away. It's pretty clear to you that he is feeling grief as he talks about her time in hospital and the funeral afterward. However, it's entirely possible that you will not experience the same emotion—grief—as you listen to him, especially if you did not know his mother. Instead, you may simply feel a sense of concern and caring for him. Such a reaction is usually referred to as *sympathy* or *compassion*, and it is distinct from empathy because your emotional response is not the same as that of your colleague (Bloom, 2017).

Empathy, sympathy, and compassion can all lead to increased prosocial behavior by motivating us to minimize the distress being experienced by others (Batson, 2011). However, there are at least three situations in which this is not the case: First, in some cases the emotional and physiological responses to someone who is suffering may be so great that they create a state called *personal distress* (Eisenberg, 2010). Personal distress can be so overwhelming that it prompts a need to distance ourselves from the person who is suffering, rather than trying to provide help.

Second, the cognitive component of empathy can be used to promote harmful antisocial behavior. Psychopaths, for example, are very good at understanding the thoughts and feelings of their victims; that is, they are highly skilled at the cognitive component of empathy (perspective taking). However, compared to other people, they show very different emotional and physiological responses to those in distress (Patrick, 2018).

Finally, people will sometimes manipulate empathic responses in the service of promoting hatred and revenge, especially toward outgroups. For example, Paul Bloom at Yale University has pointed out that lynchings in the southern states were often the result of stories that were told about White women who were raped by Black men. More recently, stories about crimes committed by immigrants have been used to turn people against these groups (Bloom, 2017). In both cases, the goal is to have people empathize with the ingroup and direct their hostility toward the outgroup. Social media sites, including Twitter and Facebook, have become a valuable tool for people attempting to create such divisions, as they allow for the manipulation of empathic responding on a much greater scale than was possible in the past.

Characteristics of the Situation

Psychological scientists have established that in addition to characteristics of the helper and person in need, features of the situation may also influence prosocial behavior. For example, sometimes *higher costs to the helper* (such as possible embarrassment, great effort) decrease helping (Zoccola et al., 2011). While this makes some sense, it would seem to imply that in a dangerous situation no one would be inclined to provide help, and we know that this isn't the case. As it turns out, the decision to provide help in emergencies involves some complex decision-making. Let's take a closer look.

Studying the Science: Bystander Intervention in Emergencies

Over the years, the popular media have circulated a number of dispiriting accounts of people failing to help when lives were at stake, even when the cost of doing so was small. For example, some years ago a homeless man helped a young woman fend off an attacker in New York. For his trouble, he was stabbed and fell to the sidewalk where he lay in a pool of his own blood. When emergency aid arrived more than an hour later, Hugo Tale-Yax was already dead. Compounding the horror, surveillance video revealed that no fewer than 25 people walked past him as he lay dying on the street (Livingston, Doyle, & Mangan, 2010). One person actually did stop—but only long enough to take a picture with his cell phone.

It would be easy to just blame this whole incident on the alienation of city life, but the uncharitable view of large cities as breeding grounds for urban apathy has been largely discredited (Gallo, 2015). Having said that, psychological research clearly indicates that *bystander apathy* or the **bystander effect** (the

Altruism A specific type of prosocial behavior motivated primarily by improving the circumstances of others.

Empathy State in which people, when faced with someone who is suffering, experience a feeling state that parallels that of the person in distress.

Bystander effect (bystander apathy) The unwillingness of bystanders to offer help during emergencies or to become involved in others' problems.

Does this person lying on the ground need help? What factors determine whether a person in trouble will receive help in an emergency? Surprisingly, the presence of more potential helpers tends to lower the chances that help will be given.

unwillingness of bystanders to offer help during emergencies) does exist, and not only in large urban centers. According to landmark work by psychologists John Darley and Bibb Latané (1968), failure to help is often related to the number of people present. And though it may seem counterintuitive, over the years many studies have shown that when *more* potential helpers are present, people are *less* likely to help (Fischer et al., 2011; Hortensius & de Gelder, 2014).

Why would people be less willing to help when others are present? Basically, we are likely to assume that someone else will help. The dynamics of this effect are easily illustrated: Suppose that two motorists have stalled at the roadside, one on a sparsely traveled country road and the other on a busy freeway. Who gets help first?

On the freeway, where hundreds of cars pass every minute, each driver can assume that someone else will help. Personal responsibility for helping is spread so thin that no one takes action. On the country road, one of the first few people to drive by will probably stop because the responsibility is clearly theirs. In general, Darley and Latané assume that bystanders are not uncaring; they are inhibited by the presence of others.

Early work on bystander intervention showed that people must pass through three decision points before giving help. First, they must notice that something is happening; that is, they must be paying attention. Next, they must define the event as an emergency. Finally, they must take responsibility and select a course of action (● Figure 17.3). Let's take a closer look at each of these steps.

1. Noticing

What would happen if you fainted or collapsed on the sidewalk, as Hugo Tale-Yax did? Would people stop to help? Would they think you were drunk? Would they even notice you? Darley and Latané suggest that if the sidewalk is crowded, few people will even see you. This has nothing to do with people blocking each other's vision. Instead, it is related to widely accepted norms dictating that people in crowds "keep their eyes to themselves."

Is there any way to show that this is a factor in bystander apathy? To test this idea, students were asked to fill out a questionnaire either alone or in a room full of people. As the students worked, a thick cloud of smoke was blown into the room through a vent. Most students left alone in the room noticed the smoke immediately. Few of the people in groups noticed the smoke until it became difficult to see through it. Participants working in groups politely kept their eyes on their papers and avoided looking at others (or the smoke). In contrast, those who were alone scanned the room from time to time (Latané & Darley, 1970).

2. Defining an Emergency

The study with the smoke-filled room also demonstrates the influence others have on defining a situation as an emergency. When participants in groups finally noticed the smoke, they cast

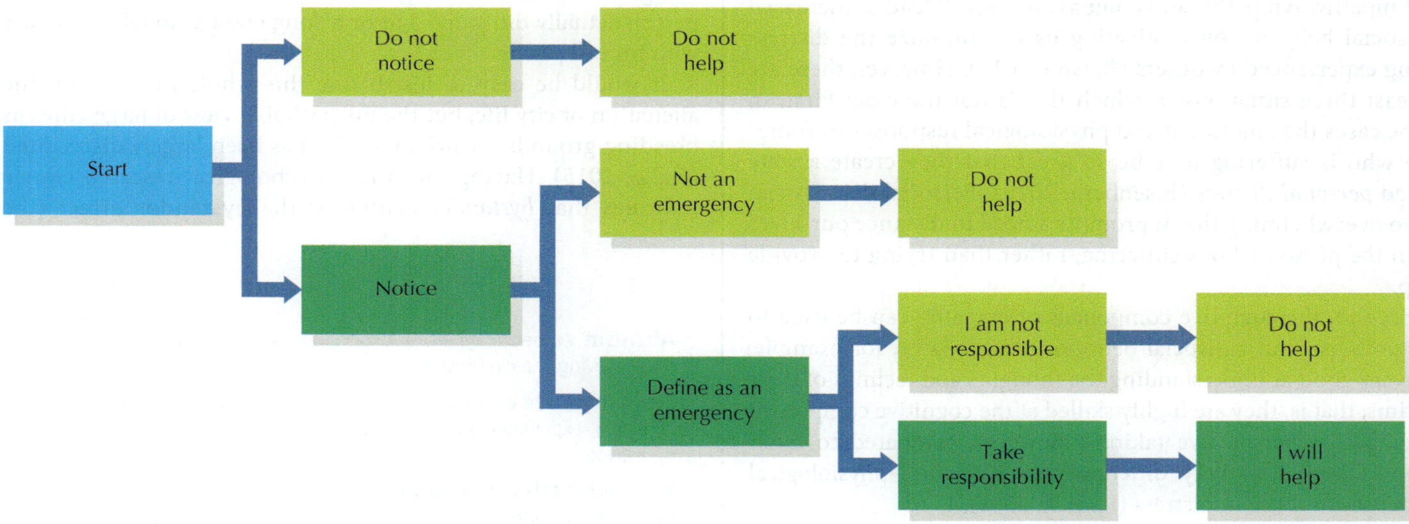

● **Figure 17.3 Steps involved in offering help.** This decision tree summarizes the steps a person must take before making a commitment to offer help, according to Latané and Darley's model.

sidelong glances at others in the room. Apparently, they were searching for clues to help interpret what was happening. No one wanted to overreact or act like a fool if there was no emergency. (Remember social comparison?) However, as participants coolly surveyed the reactions of others, they were themselves being watched. In real emergencies, people sometimes "fake each other out" and underestimate the need for action because each person attempts to appear calm. In short, until someone acts, no one does.

3. Taking Responsibility and Acting

Perhaps the most crucial step in helping is assuming responsibility. In this case, groups limit helping by causing a **diffusion of responsibility**—spreading responsibility among several people (Plötner et al., 2015).

Is that like the unwillingness of drivers to offer help on a crowded freeway? Exactly. It's the feeling that no one is personally responsible for helping. This problem was demonstrated in an experiment in which students participated in a group discussion over an intercom system. However, each group had only one real participant; the others were tape-recorded actors. Each participant was placed in a separate room (supposedly to maintain confidentiality), and discussions of college life were begun. During the discussion, one of the actors simulated an epileptic-like seizure and called out for help. In some cases, the true participants thought they were alone with the seizure victim. Others believed they were members of three- or six-person groups.

People who thought they were alone with the "victim" of this staged emergency reported it immediately or tried to help. Some participants in the three-person groups failed to respond, and those who did were slower. In the six-person groups, over a third of the participants took no action at all. People in this experiment were obviously faced with a conflict like that in many real emergencies: Should they be helpful and responsible, or should they mind their own business? Many were influenced toward inaction by the presence of others.

Research on the bystander effect might very well lead you to worry about what would happen if you ever needed help in a crowd. As it happens, more recent research suggests a somewhat more positive picture of prosocial behavior in emergencies. First, the bystander effect appears to have declined over time (Fischer et al., 2011). Some researchers have attributed this finding to the possibility that people are now more aware of it, and consequently realize the importance of taking action even when others are present. Second, a meta-analysis of many studies indicates that emergency situations actually decrease the bystander effect, making it more likely that people will receive the help they need when they're in danger. This is likely the case because in such circumstances there is no ambiguity about the fact that an emergency is unfolding and that action is required. In addition, the presence of bystanders in dangerous situations may serve to reduce fear because of their ability to provide support.

So how can I make sure I get help from others if I need it? The work we have reviewed here suggests that you should make sure that you are noticed, that people realize there's an emergency, and that they need to take action. At the very least, remember not to just scream. Instead, you should call out "Help!" or "I need help right now!" Whenever possible, define your situation for bystanders. Say, for instance, "I'm being attacked—call the police!" Or, "Stop that man, he has my purse!" You also can directly assign responsibility to a bystander by pointing to someone and saying, "You, call the police" or "I'm injured, I need you to call an ambulance."

Despite the many instances of prosocial behavior that occur every day, people in need are sometimes exploited rather than aided. In the next few sections, we will turn our attention to the dark side of social behavior, often called *antisocial behavior*. Aggression, prejudice, and intergroup conflict are all good examples of antisocial behavior.

Reflective Practice

Prosocial Behavior: Helping Others

1. Altruism is a specific sub-type of prosocial behavior in which the motives for helping primarily center on improving the circumstances of the victim. T or F?
2. Empathy has two components: emotional and cognitive. T or F?
3. Empathy always motivates prosocial responding. T or F?
4. A(n) ______________ of responsibility occurs when individual bystanders in a group do not step forward to help someone in need.
5. Defining an event as an emergency is the first step toward bystander intervention. T or F?
6. Seeing that a person in need is similar to ourselves tends to increase the likelihood that help will be given. T or F?

THINK CRITICALLY

7. If media violence contributes to aggressive behavior in our society, do you think it is possible that media could also promote prosocial behavior?

SELF-REFLECT

- An elderly woman is at the side of the road, trying to change a flat tire. She obviously needs help. You are approaching her in your car. What must happen before you are likely to stop and help her?
- Charitable organizations will sometimes create fundraising videos that show graphic footage of people who are starving or ill, or animals that have been mistreated. How do you respond to such images—do they make you want to respond prosocially by giving money, or do they make you want to turn the video off because they prompt you to feel personal distress?

Answers: 1. T 2. T 3. F 4. diffusion 5. F 6. T 7. Yes. Media could be used to promote helping, cooperation, charity, and brotherhood in the same way that it has encouraged aggression. Numerous studies show, for example, that prosocial behavior in the media increases prosocial behavior by viewers (Greitemeyer, 2009, 2011).

Diffusion of responsibility Spreading the responsibility to act among several people; reduces the likelihood that help will be given to a person in need.

17.3 Antisocial Behavior: Aggression, Conflict, and Prejudice

GATEWAYS LEARNING OUTCOMES:
After reading this section you should be able to:

17.3.1 Distinguish between antisocial behavior and aggression, including the difference between direct aggression and indirect aggression

17.3.2 Outline three potential causes of aggression

17.3.3 Describe some of the ways that aggression can be minimized, at both the societal and individual levels

17.3.4 Name the three components of prejudiced attitudes

17.3.5 Discriminate between explicit and implicit prejudice

17.3.6 Name four factors that are associated with greater levels of prejudice

17.3.7 Outline some of the consequences experienced by victims of prejudice

17.3.8 Describe three ways that prejudice can be reduced

For a time, the Los Angeles Zoo had on display two examples of the world's most dangerous animal—the only animal capable of destroying the Earth and all other animal species. Perhaps you have already guessed which animal it was. In the cage were two college students, representing the species *Homo sapiens*!

Our understanding of social behavior would be incomplete without examining **antisocial behavior**, which is defined as behavior that violates social norms and the rights of others. Antisocial acts may be *non-aggressive* (such as destruction of property, skipping school, lying, and theft) or *aggressive* (Séguin & Tremblay, 2013). The term **aggression** refers to antisocial acts that directly harm another person, and psychological scientists have established that we humans are capable of a wide range of actions that fit into this category. Let's dig a bit deeper to learn more.

Aggression

The human capacity for aggression is staggering. More than 180 million humans were killed by other people (an average of nearly one person every 18 seconds) during the 20th century (Pinker, 2011). War, homicide, riots, family violence, assassination, rape, assault, forcible robbery, and other violent acts offer sad testimony to the realities of human aggression (Shaver & Mikulincer, 2011).

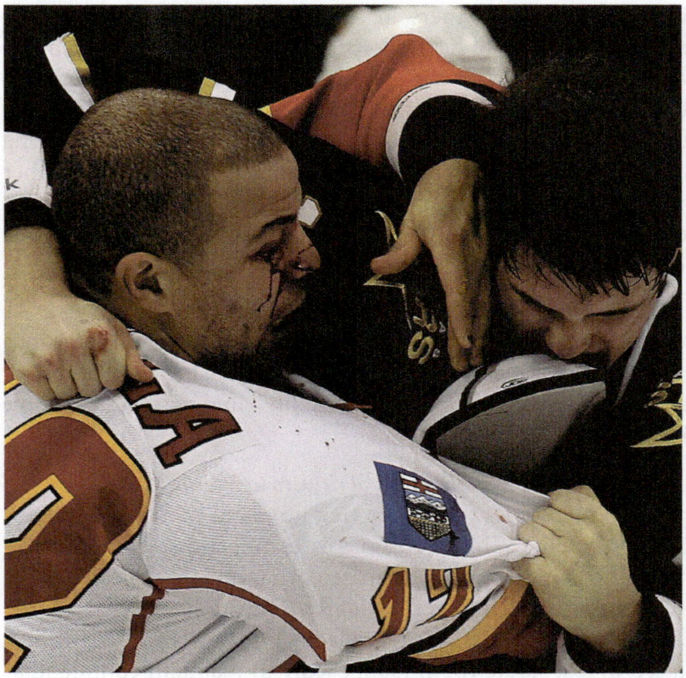
Ronald Martinez/Getty Images Sport Classic/Getty Images

Violent and aggressive behavior is so commonplace that it may be viewed as entertainment. How "natural" is aggressive behavior?

It is worth noting that aggressive behavior can fall in one of two categories. The first is referred to as *direct aggression*, which includes verbal and physical attacks. This may include everything from the truly horrific, such as ethnic cleansing and gangland executions, to the more common, including harassment and the one-finger salute. The second form, *indirect aggression*, refers to aggressive acts that are directed at harming others' reputations, social standing, friendships, or self-esteem.

A good example of aggression is **bullying**, defined as any behavior that deliberately and repeatedly exposes a person to negative experiences (Powell & Ladd, 2010). Bullying is a worldwide phenomenon and occurs among all age groups and in all settings. It can even be found online, in the form of *cyberbullying* (Bonanno & Hymel, 2013).

Bullying can be a direct form of aggression when the bully engages in verbal (name-calling, insults, teasing) or physical (hitting, pushing, confining) actions that harm another person. However, bullying can also be indirectly aggressive when it takes the form of spreading rumors, gossiping or telling lies about others, and purposefully excluding people from groups. While male bullies are more likely than females to engage in direct physical aggression, female bullies tend to specialize in indirect verbal aggression (Field et al., 2009).

Causes of Aggression

What causes aggression? Aggression has many potential causes (DeWall & Anderson, 2011). Let's review three of them: biology, frustration, and social learning.

Biology

Some theorists argue that humans are naturally aggressive, having inherited a "killer instinct" from our animal ancestors (Buss, 2015). While this idea has intuitive appeal, many psychologists question it (Rhee & Waldman, 2011). Just labeling a behavior as due to an **instinct**—an innate impulse that directs or motivates behavior—does little to explain it. More important, we are left with the question of why some individuals or human groups (the Arapesh, the Senoi, the Navajo, the Inuit, and others) show little hostility or aggression. And, thankfully, the vast majority of humans do *not* kill or harm others.

Nevertheless, at least four lines of research suggest that aggression does appear to have biological roots (Rhee & Waldman, 2011). First, researchers have found a relationship between aggression and such *physical factors* as hypoglycemia (low blood sugar) and allergies. Second, physiological studies have shown that some *brain areas* are capable of triggering or ending aggressive behavior, which is why aggression is associated with specific brain injuries and diseases. Third, for both men and women, higher levels of the hormone *testosterone* may be associated with more aggressive behavior (Mehta & Beer, 2010; Montoya et al., 2012). Perhaps because of their higher testosterone levels, men are more likely to engage in physical aggression than women (Anderson & Bushman, 2002). Finally, the effects of *alcohol and other drugs* provide another indication of the role of the brain and biology in violence and aggression. A variety of studies show that alcohol is involved in large percentages of murders and violent crimes. Intoxicating drugs also seem to lower inhibitions to act aggressively—often with tragic results (Banks et al., 2017; Lundholm et al., 2013).

It's important to note that none of these biological factors can be considered a direct cause of aggression. Instead, they probably lower the threshold for aggression, making hostile behavior more likely to occur (Tackett & Krueger, 2011). The fact that we are biologically capable of aggression does not mean that aggression is inevitable or "part of human nature." Humans are fully capable of learning to inhibit aggression. For example, the Quakers and the Amish, who live in this country's increasingly violent culture, adopt nonviolence as a way of life.

Frustration

As we noted in ■ Section 13.3, frustration tends to lead to aggression, a relationship known as the **frustration–aggression hypothesis**.

Does frustration always produce aggression? Although the connection is strong, a moment's thought will show that frustration does not always lead to aggression. For example, frustration may lead to stereotyped responses or a state of "learned helplessness," rather than aggression (■ see Section 13.6). Also, aggression can occur in the absence of frustration. This possibility is illustrated by sports spectators who start fights, throw bottles, tear down goalposts, and so forth after their team has *won*.

Frustration probably encourages aggression because it is uncomfortable. Various *aversive stimuli*, which produce discomfort or displeasure, can heighten hostility and aggression (Morgan, 2005; Simister & Cooper, 2005; ● Figure 17.4). Examples include insults, high air temperatures, pain, and even disgusting scenes or

Road rage and some freeway shootings may be a reaction to the stress and frustration of traffic congestion. The fact that automobiles provide anonymity or a loss of personal identity also may encourage aggressive actions that would not otherwise occur.

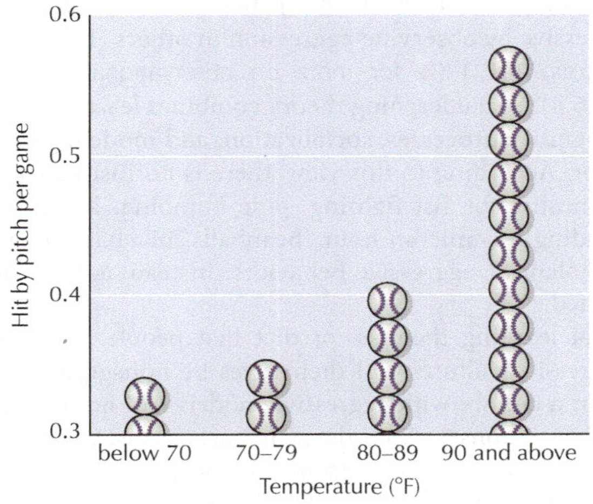

● **Figure 17.4 Hit batters as a function of temperature.** Personal discomfort caused by aversive (unpleasant) stimuli can make aggressive behavior more likely. For example, studies of crime rates show that the incidence of highly aggressive behavior, such as murder, rape, and assault, rises as the air temperature goes from warm to hot to sweltering (Anderson, 1989). The results you see here further support the heat–aggression link. The graph shows that there is a strong association between the temperatures at major league baseball games and the number of batters hit by a pitch during those games. When the temperature goes over 90°, watch out for that fastball (Reifman, Larrick, & Fein, 1991)!

Antisocial behavior Any behavior that has a negative impact on other people.

Aggression Any action carried out with the intention of harming another person.

Bullying The deliberate and repeated use of aggression (whether verbal or physical, direct or indirect) as a tactic for dealing with everyday situations.

Instinct Innate impulse that directs or motivates behavior.

Frustration–aggression hypothesis States that frustration tends to lead to aggression.

odors. Such stimuli probably raise overall arousal levels so that we become more sensitive to *aggression cues*—signals that are associated with aggression (Schwenzer, 2008). Aversive stimuli also tend to activate ideas, memories, and expressions associated with anger and aggression (Morgan, 2005).

While some cues for aggression are internal (angry thoughts, for instance), many are external. For instance, some of the words, actions, and gestures put forward by others are strongly associated with aggressive responses. A raised middle finger, for instance, is an almost universal invitation to aggression in North America. Weapons can also serve as particularly strong cues for aggressive behavior in many situations. The implication of this *weapons effect* seems to be that the symbols and trappings of aggression encourage aggression. A prime example is the fact that murders are more likely to occur in homes in which guns are kept (Siegel, Ross, & King III, 2013).

Social Learning

One of the most widely accepted explanations of aggression is also the simplest. **Social learning theory** holds that we learn to be aggressive by observing aggression in others (Bandura, 2001; Lefrançois, 2012) (■ for more on observational learning, see Section 6.4). Social learning theory combines learning principles with cognitive processes, socialization, and modeling to explain behavior. According to this view, there is no instinctive human programming for fist-fighting, pipe bombing, knife wielding, gun loading, 95-mile-an-hour "beanballs" in a baseball game, or other violent or aggressive behaviors. Instead, aggression must be learned.

Social learning theorists predict that people growing up in nonaggressive cultures will themselves be nonaggressive. Those raised in a culture with aggressive models and heroes will learn aggressive responses. Considered in such terms, it is no wonder that the United States has become one of the more violent countries. As many as 49 percent of US households own at least one firearm (Agresti & Smith, 2016). Children and adults are treated to an almost nonstop parade of aggressive models, in the media as well as through the actual behavior of those around them. (■ See Section 6.4 for a review of the evidence regarding aggression and media exposure to violence.)

Preventing Aggression

What can be done about aggression? Social learning theory implies that "aggression begets aggression" and "kindness begets kindness." For example, children who are physically abused at home, those who suffer severe physical punishment, and those who merely witness violence in the community or in the media are more likely to be involved in fighting, aggressive play, and antisocial behavior at school (Bartholow, Sestir, & Davis, 2005). Similarly, experiences of prosocial behaviors (consisting of actions toward others that are helpful, constructive, or altruistic) reduce aggression by increasing helping, cooperation, charity, and brotherhood (Velez et al., 2016; Greitemeyer et al., 2012). Accordingly, at the societal level, two ways to lower aggression may be to *reduce our society's exposure to violence*, as well as *increasing exposure to prosocial behaviors* (Meier & Wilkowski, 2013).

On an individual level, there are at least three ways that appear to help minimize aggressive actions. First, psychologists have succeeded in teaching some people to control their anger and aggressive impulses (Meier & Wilkowski, 2013; Nay, 2014). Like strengthening a muscle, self-control improves with practice (Denson et al., 2011), and many of the *self-regulation strategies* identified by psychologists may be helpful in this respect. (■ See Section 2.5 for more details about effective self-regulation strategies.)

Second, in ■ Section 13.4 we encountered the distinction between emotion-focused and problem-focused coping. Responding to an upsetting situation by giving into anger is often an ineffective emotion-focused coping strategy. It is usually better to learn to remain calm by *using problem-focused coping strategies*, such as defining upsetting situations as problems to be solved. Therefore, to limit anger, people are taught to do the following:

1. Define the problem as precisely as possible.
2. Make a list of possible solutions.
3. Rank the likely success of each solution.
4. Choose a solution and try it.
5. Assess how successful the solution was, and make adjustments if necessary.

Finally, researchers have suggested that *changing the attributions made for frustrating events* also helps people to manage aggressive impulses, especially when the circumstances are ambiguous (Dodge et al., 2013). If you're not sure whether the person causing your frustration is acting intentionally, then, you should begin by assuming that they are not, and then take steps to assess the situation objectively (■ see Section 16.1 for more information about attributions).

Taking steps such as these has helped many people to lessen tendencies toward child abuse, family violence, and other destructive outbursts (Hall, 2009; Miltenberger, 2012). And let's close with some possible good news: Harvard University psychologist Steven Pinker has suggested that if you compare the amount of violence in the modern world with the more distant past, it appears that we humans are losing our taste for aggression (Pinker, 2011). Improving human rights around the globe, along with reductions in slavery, executions, and torture, are all signs that "the better angels of our nature" are in ascendancy.

Prejudice

In the previous section, we discussed antisocial behaviors that are directed toward specific individuals. Though such acts can have many underlying causes, in some cases they are the product of feelings and beliefs about the group to which a target individual belongs. **Prejudice**, an all-too-common part of daily life, is a particular attitude toward an entire group of people (Biernat & Danaher, 2013). Though we often think about it in negative terms, prejudiced attitudes can actually be either negative or positive.

The Fundamentals of Prejudice

Like other attitudes, prejudice has affective (or emotional), cognitive, and behavioral components. The affective component includes our emotions toward the group in question. These

Sam Forencich/National Basketball Association/Getty Images

Racial stereotypes are common in sports. For example, a study confirmed that many people actually believe that "white men can't jump." This stereotype implies that black basketball players are naturally superior in athletic ability. White players, in contrast, are falsely perceived as smarter and harder-working than black players. Such stereotypes set up expectations that distort the perceptions of fans, coaches, and sportswriters. The resulting misperceptions, in turn, help perpetuate the stereotypes (Stone, Perry, & Darley, 1997).

emotions may be positive (e.g., affection, positive regard) or negative (anger, hatred, mistrust, and fear), depending on whether the prejudiced attitude is positive or negative.

The cognitive component of positive and negative prejudice consists of **social stereotypes**, or oversimplified perceptions of group members that do not take into account their diversity. There is a good chance that you have stereotyped images of at least some of the following groups: African Americans, European Americans, Hispanics, Jews, women, Christians, old people, men, Asian Americans, blue-collar workers, Southerners, politicians, business executives, teenagers, or billionaires. In general, though, the top three categories on which most stereotypes are based are sex, age, and race (Fiske et al., 2002).

Finally, the behavioral component of prejudice is referred to as **discrimination**, or biased actions directed toward a particular group (Kassin, Fein, & Markus, 2017). Again, discrimination can include both actions that benefit the ingroup as well as those that are damaging to the outgroup. Somewhat surprisingly, many instances of discrimination appear to be actions that stem from favoring the ingroup rather than harming the outgroup (Balliet et al., 2014; Brewer, 1979). Of course, ingroup favoritism still raises many concerns. For example, if managers always hired individuals who look and behave "just like them," that's still a problem even though it's motivated by a positive bias toward the ingroup rather than a negative bias toward the outgroup.

At its worst, discrimination may include overt and extreme antisocial behavior toward outgroups we dislike, including destruction of their property or physical and verbal abuse. Sometimes, however, acts of discrimination are more subtle and are not necessarily intended to be hurtful. Researchers refer to these smaller slights as **microaggressions** and have suggested that they often come from well-meaning individuals who do not see themselves as racist and who do not seek to harm others (Sue, 2010). For example, a professor intending to provide a compliment might say to an Asian student that her English is excellent, without considering the possibility that the student was born in the United States and speaks English as a first language.

Studying the Science: Microaggressions

Some psychological scientists have indicated that, over many years, exposure to microaggressions may compromise the self-esteem, health, and well-being of minority groups (Nadal et al., 2014; Williams, 2020). Others have pushed back on this idea, suggesting that responses to microaggressions reflect hypersensitivity and an obsession with political correctness leading people to feel that they are walking on eggshells when speaking to a member of a marginalized group. What do researchers have to say?

One point of agreement among researchers is that microaggressions *are* associated with poorer mental health. Because most of the existing research is correlational rather than experimental, though, it is difficult to make firm statements about whether repeated exposure to microaggressions *causes* these mental health concerns (Lilienfeld, 2020). Nevertheless, the finding that these two variables are consistently associated suggests that microaggressions should be taken very seriously (Williams, 2020).

Of course, there are some points on which researchers disagree as well. Specifically, debates about microaggressions are typically centered on how to best investigate microaggressions rigorously so that we can feel confident about the results of scientific research (Lilienfeld, 2020). For example, questions have been raised about how best to define a microaggression for the purposes of studying them. Should a comment be considered a microaggression if one person from a marginalized group finds it offensive, but another member of that same group does not? A second point of disagreement seems to focus on whether microaggressions should be seen as *intentional* slights intended to hurt and provoke, or whether they are better viewed as unintentional, and the result of a poor understanding or choice of words. The first interpretation would imply that microaggressions really are acts of aggression while the second would not, and this distinction may have important implications for the appropriate way to respond.

Social learning theory A theory that combines learning principles with cognitive processes, socialization, and modeling, to explain behavior.

Prejudice Positive or negative attitude toward an entire group of people.

Social stereotypes Oversimplified images of the traits of individuals who belong to a particular social group.

Discrimination (in social behavior) Unfair actions based on stereotyping and prejudice.

Microaggressions Subtle acts of discrimination that may not be intended to hurt the victim but rather reflect a lack of awareness or sensitivity.

To be clear, though, even researchers who have pushed for more clarity on the subject of microaggressions have not disputed that mild forms of prejudice occur, or that they are important and deserve study. The focus, then, is to ensure that the research being carried out is rigorous, as this will put psychologists in the best position to provide treatment to individuals affected by microaggressions and develop effective training programs to educate the broader public.

Classifying Prejudice

Perhaps the most common way to classify types of prejudice relates to the groups on which these attitudes are based. For example, prejudice directed against people based solely on their race is **racism**. If the sole basis is gender, that is **sexism**, and if the sole basis is age, that is **ageism**. **Heterosexism** is based on the belief that heterosexuality is better or more natural than homosexuality, while **ethnocentrism** refers to placing one's own group "at the center," and believing that the norms associated with one's own culture are superior to those of other cultural groups.

Aside from classifying prejudice based on groups, researchers also distinguish the extent to which such attitudes are *implicit* vs. *explicit*. It is easy to notice **explicit prejudice**; that is, prejudice that is clearly expressed and out in the open (Payne et al., 2010). This is the type of prejudice that Derek Black (described at the beginning of this chapter) expressed before he attended college.

However, because many people realize that crude and obvious explicit prejudice is no longer socially acceptable, the public expression of such attitudes has become much less common. Unfortunately, **implicit prejudice**—unconscious prejudiced thoughts and feelings about members of other groups—is still a significant problem in many societies (Anderson, 2010; Nosek, Greenwald, & Banaji, 2005; Waller, Lampman, & Lupfer-Johnson, 2012).

How can you tell if someone holds implicit prejudiced attitudes? Psychological scientists have long recognized the importance of being able to measure implicit prejudice. Let's try an example of one well-established test that attempts to assess it. To begin, ask yourself whether you are prejudiced against women working outside the family home. Keep in mind your conscious answer to this question as you complete the categorization task in ▲ Table 17.2.

Many people completing this task notice that it takes longer to do the second list and that they make more mistakes. Even people who claim—and genuinely believe—that they are not prejudiced against women working outside the home tend to be slower and less accurate in classifying words into the categories *Male or Family* as opposed to *Female or Career*. Why is there a difference? For many people, *Female* and *Family* seem to go together more naturally than *Female* and *Career* do.

You just completed a version of an *implicit association test*, or IAT for short (adapted from Nosek, Greenwald, & Banaji, 2005). If you Google the term IAT, you will find that such tests have been constructed for race, age, religion, ethnicity, disability, sexual orientation, weight, and many other stereotyped categories (Hofmann et al., 2005; Kite et al., 2005; Waller, Lampman, & Lupfer-Johnson, 2012). Many people find that when they take these tests, their

▲ Table 17.2 The Implicit Association Test

Below you will find two list of 12 words. Your job is to categorize them. Let's begin with List 1. Suppose, for example, that one of the words is *factory.* If you feel that *factory* belongs in the category "Male or Career," then you would touch (or mark) the O to the left of the word. Otherwise, you would mark the O to the right of *factory.* Now, take 20 seconds to classify each of the words in List 1. Place them into the correct categories as quickly and accurately as you can. Got the idea? Ready, set, go! Now try it again with the 12 new words in List 2. The only difference is that the categories have changed. Ready, set, go!

Male or Career		Female or Family	Male or Family		Female or Career
	List 1			**List 2**	
O	Daniel	O	O	Home	O
O	Sally	O	O	Manager	O
O	House	O	O	Domestic	O
O	Kitchen	O	O	Andrew	O
O	Merchant	O	O	In-laws	O
O	Company	O	O	Jane	O
O	Emily	O	O	Workplace	O
O	Relatives	O	O	Sarah	O
O	Employment	O	O	Office	O
O	Baby	O	O	Corporation	O
O	Steven	O	O	Siblings	O
O	Executive	O	O	John	O

Source: Project Implicit, https://implicit.harvard.edu/implicit/

scores suggest that they do harbor implicit prejudices even when they do not explicitly own up to them, or indeed have any conscious sense of holding such attitudes (Anderson, 2010). What should we make of these troubling findings?

Studying the Science: Implicit Bias and the IAT

While the IAT has been around for many decades and is still frequently used, it is not without critics. One significant concern about the IAT is the fact that the results are not always stable across time. Put another way, the test has not always demonstrated good *reliability* (■ recall from Section 9.2 that good measures need to be reliable, providing consistent scores over time). It has been found, for example, that a person may score high on the racial IAT test one week but significantly lower the next week. A second issue is that individuals' IAT scores are not always a good predictor of their behavior in everyday life. People who show high levels of implicit prejudice on the IAT related to age, for example, do not appear to be particularly likely to discriminate against older adults, or show hostility toward them (Vuletich & Payne, 2019).

Does all of this mean that there's no such thing as implicit bias? Keith Payne and his colleagues have argued that nothing could be further from the truth. First of all, these researchers argue that the real value of the IAT doesn't come from an ability to predict the behavior of individuals, but rather its ability to predict the *average behavior of larger groups of people*. For example, a large-scale study of more than 2 million Americans indicated that in areas where the IAT suggests a greater *average* level of implicit racial bias in the population, police use a disproportionate amount of lethal force against Black citizens (Hehman et al., 2018).

Second, there is evidence from many other studies, using multiple other measures, that we do hold biases about other groups and that these biases have consequences for marginalized groups. In one such study, job applications for a lab manager position were shown to researchers working at high-profile American universities (Moss-Racusin et al., 2012). The applications were identical except for the name of the applicant: Half of them had a female name and the other half had a male name. Each researcher was randomly assigned to see one application from either the male or female applicant. The result? On average both male and female researchers viewed the male candidate as being more competent and "hirable" than the (identical!) female candidate—a clear demonstration of implicit bias against females in the sciences.

Factors Associated with Prejudice

Psychologists have established that there are a number of other characteristics that are associated with prejudiced attitudes. Here, we'll take a closer look at four of them: *frustration, social learning, authoritarian beliefs*, and *dehumanization*.

Frustration

One major theory suggests that prejudice is a form of **scapegoating** or blaming a person or a group either for the actions of others or for conditions not of their making. Scapegoating is a type of **displaced aggression** in which hostilities triggered by frustration are redirected at "safer" targets (Glick, 2008; Reijntjes et al., 2013a). This effect is easy to observe in the United States, as people who look "foreign" have become targets for displaced anger and hostility about job losses, crime, and a host of other concerns (Ahluwalia & Pellettiere, 2010).

A classic test of this phenomenon was conducted at a summer camp for young men. The men were given a difficult test that they were sure to fail. In addition, completing the test caused them to miss a trip to the movies, which was normally the high point of their weekly entertainment. Attitudes toward Mexicans and Japanese were measured before the test and after the men had failed the test and missed the movie. Participants in this study, all European Americans, consistently rated members of the two ethnic groups lower after being frustrated (Miller & Bugelski, 1948).

Social Learning

At times, the development of prejudice (like other attitudes) can be traced to direct experiences with members of the rejected group. A child who is repeatedly bullied by members of a particular ethnic group, for example, might develop a lifelong dislike for all members of that group. Yet even subtle influences, such as parents' and teachers' attitudes, the depiction of people in books and on television, and exposure to children of other races can have an impact. Derek Black's experience growing up in a family of White nationalists was clearly a factor in his early views about race and religion. Indeed, evidence suggests that by the time they are three years old, many children already show signs of race bias (Katz, 2003).

The effects of social learning can be seen in a classic experiment carried out by elementary school teacher Jane Elliott. On the first day of the experiment, Elliott announced that brown-eyed children were to sit in the back of the room, and that they could not use the drinking fountain. Blue-eyed children were given extra recess time and got to use the fountain and leave first for lunch. At lunch, brown-eyed children were prevented from taking second helpings because the teacher said that they would "just waste it."

Racism Stereotyping, prejudice, and discrimination directed against someone based solely on their race.

Sexism Stereotyping, prejudice, and discrimination directed against someone based solely on their gender.

Ageism Stereotyping, prejudice, and discrimination directed against someone based solely on their age.

Heterosexism Stereotyping, prejudice, and discrimination directed against someone based solely on the belief that heterosexuality is better or more natural than homosexuality.

Ethnocentrism Placing one's own group or race at the center—that is, tending to reject all other groups but one's own.

Explicit prejudice Prejudice that is conscious and clearly and publicly expressed.

Implicit prejudice Unconscious prejudiced thoughts and feelings about members of other groups.

Scapegoating Blaming a person or a group for the actions of others or for conditions not of their making.

Displaced aggression Redirecting aggression to a target other than the actual source of one's frustration.

Brown-eyed and blue-eyed children were kept from mingling, and the blue-eyed children were told by the teacher that they were "cleaner" and "smarter" (Peters, 1971).

At first, Elliott herself made an effort to criticize and belittle the brown-eyed children. To her surprise, the blue-eyed children learned quickly and rapidly joined her in criticizing their peers. Indeed, these children were soon outdoing her in the viciousness of their attacks. The blue-eyed children began to feel superior, and the brown-eyed children felt just plain awful. Fights broke out. Test scores of the brown-eyed children fell.

How lasting were the effects of this experiment? The effects were short-lived because two days later, the children's roles were reversed. Before long, the same destructive effects occurred again, but this time in reverse. The implications of this experiment are unmistakable. In less than one day, it was possible to *teach* children to behave in very different ways—ways that clearly reflected bias and prejudice—based on eye color and **status inequalities**—differences in power, prestige, or privileges.

You may be thinking that eye color is a trivial basis for creating prejudices. However, people use primarily skin color to make decisions about the race of another person (Glenn, 2009). Surely this is just as superficial a way of judging people as using eye color, especially given recent biological evidence suggesting that it doesn't even make genetic sense to talk about "races" (Bonham, Warshauer-Baker, & Collins, 2005; also ■ see Section 9.4 for more on genes and race).

Authoritarian Beliefs

Other research suggests that prejudice can stem from individual differences in certain personality traits. For example, while studying anti-Semitism, Theodor Adorno and his associates (1950) found that people who are prejudiced against one group tend to be prejudiced against *all* outgroups (Hodson, MacInnis, & Busseri, 2017; Kteily, Sidanius, & Levin, 2011). These researchers referred to this as an **authoritarian personality**, which is marked by ethnocentrism, rigidity, inhibition, and oversimplification (black-and-white thinking, so to speak).

Chris Grieve/Mirrorpix/England United Kingdom/NEWSCOM

Are these children of different "races"? Yes, this *is* a trick question. Only skin color differentiates these nonidentical twins. The odds, by the way, of mixed race parents having a pair of twins like these two are one in a million. How fair will it be when these two children experience differential treatment based solely on their skin color?

Altemeyer (1981) extended this early work on authoritarianism and developed the concept of *right-wing authoritarianism* (RWA). People who score high on RWA defer to strong leaders, appreciate traditional social norms (e.g., heterosexual marriage; traditional gender roles), and demonstrate prejudice toward members of outgroups. RWA is also strongly associated with *social dominance orientation* (SDO). People who score high on SDO seek power and prefer a clear social hierarchy in which higher status groups dominate those with lower status (Bilewicz, 2017; Sidanius, 1993).

Although it may appear that RWA is slanted toward politically conservative authoritarians, rigid and authoritarian personalities can be found at both ends of the political scale (Pettigrew, 2016). (Among those who are more liberal, the term is *left-wing authoritarianism.*) It may be better, therefore, to describe this type of rigid and intolerant thinking as **dogmatism**, an unwarranted certainty in matters of belief or opinion. Dogmatic people find it difficult to change their beliefs, even when the evidence contradicts them (Peterson et al., 2016; White-Ajmani & Bursik, 2011).

Dehumanization

Another factor associated with prejudiced attitudes is a tendency to dehumanize outgroups. **Dehumanization** is associated with the belief that members of outgroups are less than human and *deserve* hatred, discrimination, aggression, and even death. Dehumanization is common when people feel threatened, particularly in the context of war (Leidner et al., 2010; Waytz, Epley, & Cacioppo, 2010). Undoubtedly, this provides a degree of emotional insulation that makes it easier for people to harm others, or support those who do. However, it also makes terrorism, torture, rape, murder, and genocide possible.

Consequences of Prejudice

When prejudiced attitudes pervade a society, there can be a number of consequences for those who are victims. For example, discrimination often *prevents people from doing things they should be able to* do in a free society, such as buying or renting a home, getting a job, or attending a high-quality school (Whitley & Kite, 2010). These, in turn, can impact the ability to earn a good living and provide for a family.

The consequences of prejudice can also be seen in the realm of law enforcement: In many cities, African Americans and Muslims in particular have been the targets of *racial profiling*, with police officers stopping members of these groups (particularly young men) without just cause. Sometimes, they are merely questioned, but many are cited for minor infractions, such as a cracked taillight or an illegal lane change. For many law-abiding citizens, being detained in this manner is a rude awakening (Plous, 2003).

Perhaps just as important is that the effects of prejudice appear to have downstream implications for victims' *physical and mental health*, including the damaging effects of *stereotype threat*. Let's do a deeper dive on these two problems.

Health Consequences of Prejudice

An understanding of the health consequences associated with discrimination goes back hundreds of years. Dr. James McCune Smith, the first Black physician to practice in the United States, noted in the 1800s that the ongoing experience of racism and prejudice had negative implications for the health and well-being of African Americans. He backed up his claims with data from the US census, refuting the idea put forward by the government that slaves enjoyed better mental and physical health than African Americans living in freedom.

Today, there is ample evidence that Dr. McCune Smith was correct, but we now know that it is not only racial discrimination that impacts health: Chronic discrimination based on many characteristics—including sex, gender identity and sexual orientation, religion, and disability, for example—has now been associated with a variety of health conditions such as cancer, high blood pressure, depression, and substance abuse (Khullar, 2017).

Perhaps more important is the fact that newer research has attempted to go beyond mere correlations to establish cause-and-effect relationships between discrimination and health outcomes. These studies have demonstrated, for example, that prior to the civil rights movement the infant mortality rate for African Americans was almost 20 percent higher in states where segregation laws were in place; when those laws were eliminated, that difference declined substantially (Krieger et al., 2013). Moreover, African Americans living in states characterized by more societal racism (that is, racism within institutions such as schools, law enforcement, and government) are more likely to experience heart attacks than those living in states with less racism (Lukachko et al., 2014). These findings are troubling indeed, and suggest that the consequences of discrimination are not confined to the period of time in which it is experienced. Instead, chronic exposure to prejudice can have a lasting impact on victims' future health.

Stereotype Threat

It is especially troubling when people begin to **self-stereotype**, halfway believing the stereotypes applied to them, or at least worrying about how they appear in the presence of stereotypers (Schmader, Croft, & Whitehead, 2014; Tine & Gotlieb, 2013).

Consider Bill, a retired aircraft mechanic, who has agreed to talk to a group of high school students about the early days of commercial aviation. During his talk, Bill is concerned that any slip in his memory will confirm stereotypes about older people being forgetful. Because he is anxious and preoccupied about possible memory lapses, Bill actually "chokes" two or three times during the talk, forgetting what he had planned to say (Jordano & Touron, 2017; Mazerolle et al., 2012).

As Bill's example suggests, negative stereotypes can have a self-fulfilling quality. This is especially true of situations in which a person's abilities are evaluated. For example, African American and other minority group students must often cope with negative stereotypes about their academic abilities (Steele & Aronson, 1995; Owens & Massey, 2011). Could such stereotypes actually impair school performance?

Psychologist Claude Steele has amassed evidence that victims of stereotyping tend to feel **stereotype threat**. They can feel threatened when they think they are being judged in terms of a stereotype. The anxiety that this causes can then lower performance, seemingly confirming the stereotype (Spencer, Logel, & Davies, 2016). An experiment that Steele did demonstrates this effect. In the study, African-American and European-American college students took a very difficult verbal test. Some students were told that the test measured *academic ability*. Others were told that the test was a laboratory *problem-solving task* unrelated to ability. In the ability condition, African-American students performed worse than European Americans. In the problem-solving condition, they performed the same as European Americans (Steele, 1997; Steele & Aronson, 1995). A similar effect has been seen with women, who score lower on math, engineering, and finance tests after being reminded of the stereotype that "women aren't good at math" (Cadaret et al., 2017; Carr & Steele, 2010).

Early research examining stereotype threat had the positive effect of demonstrating a clear effort on the part of researchers to understand the victims of prejudice as well as its perpetrators. However, more recent research in this area has revealed that the phenomenon is not a simple one. For example, some researchers attempting to replicate stereotype threat have been unable to do so, suggesting that the problem may not be a universal one (Flore, Mulder, & Wicherts, 2019).

In trying to understand failures to replicate, researchers have suggested that we need to go beyond simply looking at the effects of stereotype threat on test scores and, in addition, that we need to consider whether perhaps stereotype threat has declined over time (Lewis & Sekaquaptewa, 2016; Lewis & Michalak, 2020). Other research has suggested that it will be important for future studies to go beyond controlled laboratory experiments to study stereotype threat in the "real world," since some of the conditions that characterize experiments are unlikely to be present in everyday settings (Shewach et al., 2019).

Combating Prejudice

Changing the belief component of an attitude—the stereotype, in the case of prejudice—is one of the most direct means of changing the entire attitude. Thus, when we can make people aware that members of various racial and ethnic groups are very diverse and often share the same variety of goals, ambitions, feelings, and frustrations as we do, intergroup relations may be improved (Moskowitz & Li, 2011). Unfortunately, stereotypes are often resistant to change. When a prejudiced person meets a pleasant or likable member of a marginalized group, for example, that outgroup member tends to be perceived as "an exception to the rule," not as evidence against the stereotype. This allows prejudiced people to avoid changing their stereotyped beliefs (Asgari, Dasgupta, & Stout, 2012).

Status inequalities Differences in the power, prestige, or privileges of two or more people or groups.

Authoritarian personality A personality pattern characterized by rigidity, inhibition, prejudice, and an excessive concern with power, authority, and obedience.

Dogmatism An unwarranted positiveness or certainty in matters of belief or opinion.

Dehumanization Beliefs that outgroups are less human and deserve the discrimination that they are subject to.

Self-stereotyping The tendency to apply social stereotypes to one's self.

Stereotype threat The anxiety caused by the fear of being judged in terms of a stereotype.

Coral Sand and Assoc/Shutterstock.com

Ethnic festivals help to introduce the general public to different cultures. Such educational opportunities are helping to slowly replace stereotypes and discrimination. However, despite affirmations of ethnic heritage, the problem of prejudice is far from solved.

wavebreakmedia/Shutterstock.com

Many school districts in the United States require students to wear uniforms. Appearance (including gang colors) is one of the major reasons that kids treat each other differently. Uniforms help minimize status inequalities and ingroup/outgroup distinctions (Sanchez, Yoxsimer, & Hill, 2012).

How, then, can we work to reduce prejudice? Some research suggests that more frequent *equal-status contact* between groups in conflict has the potential to diminish prejudice and stereotyping (Koschate & van Dick, 2011; Pettigrew, 2016). The presence of *superordinate goals* appears to reduce prejudice as well (Sherif et al., 1961). Finally, more recent efforts to reduce prejudice have included *direct instruction* and programs that aim to raise people's awareness of discrimination. Let's take a closer look at each of these.

Equal-Status Contact

Back in the 1950s, psychologist Gordon Allport put forth the *contact hypothesis*, suggesting that prejudice would decline if members of different groups had the opportunity to work closely with one another in situations where all people held equal power. **Equal-status contact** refers to interacting on an equal footing, without obvious differences in power or status. A great deal of evidence suggests that equal-status contact does, in fact, lessen prejudice and it appears to do so by *decreasing anxiety and increasing empathy toward the outgroup* (Pettigrew & Tropp, 2006, 2008). Moreover, interventions that involve increased contact appear to work best among people who express higher levels of prejudice (Hodson, 2011).

The benefits of contact across groups can be seen in one early study, in which European-American women who lived in either integrated or segregated housing projects were compared for changes in attitude toward their African-American neighbors. Women in the integrated project showed a favorable shift in attitudes toward members of the other racial group. Those in the segregated project showed no change or actually became more prejudiced than before (Deutsch & Collins, 1951).

In other studies, mixed-race groups have been formed at work, in the laboratory, and at schools. The conclusion from such research is that personal contact with a disliked group tends to induce friendly behavior, respect, and liking (Abrams et al., 2017). However, these benefits are the most pervasive when personal contact is cooperative and on an equal footing (Moskowitz & Li, 2011).

Superordinate Goals

Prejudice is also reduced in situations that require people of diverse groups to work together to achieve a common, **superordinate goal** that is beneficial to everyone. Cooperation and shared goals seem to help reduce conflict by encouraging people in opposing groups to see themselves as members of a single, larger group—a process that is referred to as *recategorization* (Gaertner et al., 2000; Pettigrew, 2016).

A classic psychology study demonstrated the power of superordinate goals in changing the behavior of 11-year-old boys. When the boys arrived at a summer camp, they were split into two groups and housed in separate cabins. At first, the groups were kept apart to build up separate identities and friendships. Soon each group had a flag and a name (the "Rattlers" and the "Eagles"), and each had staked out its territory. At this point, the two groups were placed in competition with each other. After several clashes, dislike between the groups bordered on hatred: The boys baited each other, started fights, and raided each other's cabins (Sherif et al., 1961).

Were they allowed to go home hating each other? As an experiment in reducing intergroup conflict, and to prevent the boys from remaining enemies, various strategies to reduce tensions were tried. Holding meetings between group leaders did nothing. When the groups were invited to eat together, the event turned into a free-for-all. Finally, emergencies that required cooperation among members of both groups were staged at the camp. For example, the water supply was damaged so that all the boys had to work together to repair it. These emergencies created superordinate goals that exceeded or overrode the lesser competitive goals. Creating superordinate goals helped restore peace between the two groups.

Overall, then, superordinate goals seem to create a "we're all in the same boat" effect on perceptions of group membership. The power of superordinate goals can be seen in the greater unity that prevailed in the United States for months after the 9/11 terrorist attacks.

Can such goals exist on a global scale? Possibly. Examples might include a desire to deal with climate change or manage the continuing threat posed by terrorism and religious extremism. Superordinate goals also are an important ongoing factor in helping peacekeepers constructively engage with people from other nationalities (Boniecki & Britt, 2003; Whitley & Kite, 2010). Finally, we certainly saw evidence of this type of multinational cooperation during the worldwide COVID-19 pandemic, suggesting that when faced with a common problem, even countries with a history of conflict can come together to work on solutions that will benefit everyone.

Direct Instruction

In the spring of 2018, two young African-American men went into a Starbucks coffee shop in Philadelphia and sat down at a table. When a staff member told them that they needed to order something, they indicated that they were waiting for a friend. Unsatisfied, the staff member contacted the police and had the two men arrested. What followed was a media firestorm, and Starbucks responded by closing its 8000 outlets in North America for one day to provide all employees with diversity training.

Starbucks is not unique in this regard: Many companies now have some form of training whose purpose is to directly educate individuals about implicit prejudice. Such programs are aimed at creating greater awareness of the participants' own biases, and then working to reduce them through exercises that focus on, for example, perspective taking, replacing stereotypes and, in some cases, contact with outgroups (Devine et al., 2012).

Given the resources that have been invested in such training, an important question is whether or not they actually work. In some respects, this area of research is still in its infancy and so it is difficult to draw firm conclusions. Some work certainly suggests that there is reason to be optimistic, with clear indications that such programs can be effective (Kang, 2014). Other research, however, has demonstrated that programs are not always successful, and sometimes have the unhappy effect of *increasing* bias toward marginalized groups (Kulik et al., 2000). Overall, it seems that diversity training programs are more likely to be successful when they are longer term, supplemented by other diversity initiatives, and focused on both raising awareness and building skills to work with diverse others (Bezrukova et al., 2016). To learn more about these important skills, take a look at the *Psychology and Your Skill Set* section that follows.

Reflective Practice

Antisocial Behavior: Aggression, Conflict, and Prejudice

1. The position of psychologists is that there is no biological basis for aggression. T or F?
2. Which of the following is ***not*** considered a good strategy for reducing aggression?
   a. drinking alcohol or taking drugs to promote relaxation
   b. enhancing self-regulation strategies
   c. increased use of problem-focused coping
   d. changing attributions for frustrating events
3. Stereotypes may be both positive and negative. T or F?
4. The stereotypes underlying racial and ethnic prejudice can evolve through social learning processes. T or F?
5. Research suggests that prejudice and intergroup conflict may be reduced by ______________ interaction and ______________ goals.

THINK CRITICALLY

6. In court trials, defense lawyers sometimes try to identify and eliminate prospective jurors who have authoritarian personality traits. Can you guess why?

SELF-REFLECT

- Stereotypes exist for many social categories, even ordinary ones such as "college student" or "unmarried young adult." What stereotypes do you think you face in daily life? How do they affect others' responses to you?
- The director of a youth recreation center is concerned about the amount of conflict she is seeing between boys and girls from different racial and ethnic groups. What advice can you give the director?

Answers: 1. F 2. a 3. T 4. T 5. equal-status, superordinate 6. Because authoritarians tend to believe that punishment is effective and tend to take the word of authority figures at face value, they are more likely to vote for conviction.

17.4 Psychology and Your Skill Set: Diversity and Inclusion

GATEWAYS LEARNING OUTCOME:
After reading this section you should be able to:

17.4.1 Create a plan that will allow you to foster improved relationships with diverse others

On his first day of grade 9, Charles McNeill wore a pink polo shirt to school. Outside, bullies said he was gay and were threatening to beat him up until two grade 12 boys intervened. The older boys weren't satisfied with putting an end to the harassment, though. They also bought 50 pink shirts from a discount store and went online to encourage their friends to buy one and wear it to school the following day. But the next morning, there weren't 50 kids who showed up in pink—there were hundreds, some of them dressed in pink from head to toe. What began as a one-day event at a single school eventually became Anti-Bullying Day, marked annually in several countries around the world and supported by the United Nations. It's a day set aside each year to celebrate our differences, and to consider the importance of tolerance.

Most people publicly support policies of equality and fairness. Yet many still have lingering biases and negative images of people seen as being "different." Is it possible to work toward greater acceptance and harmony among people who appear to be so different? Let's find out.

Equal-status contact Social interaction that occurs on an equal footing, without obvious differences in power or status.

Superordinate goal A goal that exceeds or overrides all others; a goal that renders other goals relatively less important.

Carlos Osorio/ZUMA Press/Toronto/ON/Canada/Newscom

Tolerance and Acceptance

It's no secret that the United States is becoming more diverse every year. For example, according to the US Census Bureau, by 2060 the number of senior citizens will have doubled, and this country will become a nation of minorities with no single racial or ethnic group making up 50% of the population (Colby & Ortman, 2016). Add to this the growing acceptance of women into traditionally male roles and people of different sexual orientations into society at large. These are just some examples of the changing face of America, but they raise a point worth thinking about: Going forward it will become increasingly important to have skills that allow you to get along with a variety of people, some of whom may appear—at least at first glance—to be quite different than you.

These population trends mean that your classroom and workplace will become more diverse, but psychologists have found that this type of diversity has many benefits. For example, research from the world of work has suggested that groups with diverse membership are much better at solving complex problems. This is likely because bringing together people with a range of experiences helps to promote the creative and divergent thinking that was discussed in ■ Sections 8.4 and 8.5 (Homan et al., 2015). How, though, can we start to build skills that encourage tolerance and inclusion? It all begins with an attitude of openness.

Being Open to Openness

What do you mean by openness? At the core of successfully navigating relationships with diverse others is accepting the value of *openness to the other*, or the ability to genuinely appreciate those who differ from us. It is important to remember that being open to someone else does not mean that you have to agree with that person all the time, or turn your back on your own values. How can you work toward improving your skill at building positive open relationships with a variety of different people? Here are a few suggestions:

alvarez/E+/Getty Images

Openness to the other is associated with values of tolerance and equality.

Seek Individuating Information

A good way to develop a sense of openness is to get to know individuals from different groups (Inzlicht, Gutsell, & Legault, 2012; Roets & Van Hiel, 2011). We often apply stereotypes when we have only minimal information about a person, but one way to avoid this is to seek **individuating information**—information that helps us see a person as an individual rather than as a member of a group (Jussim, Crawford, & Rubinstein, 2015; Lan Yeung & Kashima, 2010). When you meet individuals from various backgrounds, focus on the *person*, not the *label*.

A good example of the effects of individuating information comes from a Canadian study of English-speaking students in a French-language program. Students who were "immersed" (spent most of their waking hours with French Canadians) became more positive toward them. Immersed students were more likely to say they had come to appreciate and like French Canadians; they were more willing to meet and interact with them and they saw themselves as less different from French Canadians (Lambert, 1987).

Don't Fall Prey to Just-World Beliefs

Do you believe that the world is basically fair, and that people generally get what they deserve? It may not be obvious, but such beliefs can *reduce* the tolerance we feel for other groups (Bizer, Hart, & Jekogian, 2012; Hafer & Sutton, 2016). As an example, suppose you happen to notice Adnan, a member of a visible minority, cleaning the toilets at the airport. **Just-world beliefs**—beliefs that people generally get what they deserve—might lead you to assume that Adnan wouldn't be in this job if he weren't less intelligent than people working in higher-paid positions.

The reality is often very different. As a result of discrimination, social conditions, and circumstances (such as recent immigration policies), many members of minorities are forced to occupy lower socioeconomic positions (Whitley & Kite, 2010). Assuming that Adnan is too lazy or not intelligent enough overlooks the possibility that, say, discrimination in hiring has made it very difficult for him to find a better job. This bit of faulty thinking can reduce feelings of acceptance toward minorities and amounts to blaming people who are victims for their problems. Quite often, people like Adnan are highly educated and highly motivated to take whatever work is available. (Just ask Adnan!)

Be Aware of Self-Fulfilling Prophecies

As noted elsewhere (■ see, for example, Section 1.6), people tend to act in accordance with the behavior expected by others. If you hold strong opinions about members of various groups, a vicious cycle can occur: When you meet people who are different from yourself, you may treat them in a way that is consistent with your initial opinions about their group. If they are influenced by your behavior, they may act in ways that seem to match your stereotype. For example, a person who believes that members of a particular minority group are hostile and unfriendly may treat people in that group in ways that provoke a hostile and unfriendly response. This creates a **self-fulfilling prophecy**—an expectation that prompts people to act in ways that make the expectation come true—which in turn reinforces a belief in the initial expectation.

Look for Commonalities

We live in a society that puts a premium on competition and individual effort. One problem with this is that competing with others fosters desires to minimize and overcome them. When we cooperate with others, we tend to share their joys and suffer when they are in distress (Aronson, 2012). If we don't find ways to cooperate and live in greater harmony, everyone will suffer. That, if nothing else, is one thing that we all have in common. Everyone knows what it feels like to be different. Greater tolerance comes from remembering those times.

Set an Example for Others

People who act in a tolerant fashion can serve as models of tolerance for others, as illustrated by the story about AntiBullying Day at the beginning of this section. Another example is the use of newsletters to promote understanding at an ethnically diverse high school in Houston, Texas. Students wrote stories for the newsletter about situations in which cooperation led to better understanding. For instance, a story about a Hispanic-Anglo friendship in a sports team had this headline: "Don't judge somebody until you know them. The color of the skin doesn't matter." Other stories emphasized the willingness of students to get acquainted with people from other ethnic groups and the new perceptions they had of their abilities. After just five months of modeling tolerance, hostility between ethnic groups was significantly reduced (McAlister et al., 2000).

Remember, Different Does Not Mean Inferior

Some conflicts between groups cannot be avoided. What *can* be avoided is unnecessary **social competition**—rivalry among groups, each of which regards itself as superior to others. The concept of social competition refers to the fact that some individuals seek to enhance their self-esteem by identifying with a group. However, this works only if the group can be seen as superior to others. Because of social competition, groups tend to view themselves as better than their rivals (Branscombe & Baron, 2017).

In one survey, every major ethnic group in the United States rated itself as better than any other group (Njeri, 1991)! A person who has high self-esteem does not need to treat others as inferior in order to feel good about himself or herself. Similarly, it is not necessary to degrade other groups in order to feel positive about one's own group identity (Fowers & Davidov, 2006).

Living comfortably in a diverse society means being open to other groups. Getting acquainted with a person who is different from you can be a wonderful learning experience (Matsumoto & Juang, 2017). No one group has all the answers or the best ways of doing things, but being inclusive and celebrating human differences can enrich our communities and workplaces, as well as being personally rewarding (Fowers & Davidov, 2006).

Reflective Practice

A Psychologist's Skill Set: Diversity and Inclusion

1. Individuating information helps us see a person as an individual rather than as a member of a group. T or F?
2. A self-fulfilling prophecy occurs when one expects something to happen and the opposite occurs, reinforcing their initial belief. T or F?
3. Just-world beliefs are based on the assumption that people generally get what they deserve. T or F?
4. Social competition refers to the idea that certain groups view themselves as inferior to others. T or F?

THINK CRITICALLY

5. You are in the workplace and your coworker is hesitant about collaborating with an international company. Your coworker asks for your opinion. What advice can you give her, based on what you now know from this chapter?

SELF-REFLECT

- Which strategies do you already use to avoid intolerant behaviors? How could you apply the other strategies mentioned in this section to become more inclusive?

Answers: 1. T 2. F 3. T 4. F 5. You might tell your coworker that diversity promotes creativity and effective problem solving which would benefit your company. As well, remind her of biases we sometimes hold that prevent positive relationships from developing between people (e.g., belief in a just world; self-fulfilling prophecies). Finally, you can set an example for your colleague by looking for commonalities between the two companies (e.g., related to their workers, company values).

Individuating information Information that helps define a person as an individual, rather than as a member of a group or social category.

Just-world beliefs Beliefs that people generally get what they deserve.

Self-fulfilling prophecy An expectation that prompts people to act in ways that make the expectation come true.

Social competition Rivalry among groups, each of which regards itself as superior to others.

CHAPTER IN REVIEW

Gateways to Prosocial and Antisocial Behavior

Summary: Gateways Learning Outcomes

17.1 Affiliation and Attraction

17.1.1 Provide three reasons that explain why humans seek to affiliate with others

Affiliation is tied to needs for social comparison, anxiety reduction, and the desire to get and give approval, support, friendship, and love.

17.1.2 Describe four factors that influence our attraction to others

Four factors include *familiarity* (stemming from physical proximity and frequency of contact), *similarity* (in terms of characteristics such as background, age, sex, and attitudes), *physical attractiveness*, and *reciprocity* (responding to one another in similar way).

17.1.3 Describe how relationships deepen, making reference to self-disclosure and social exchange theory

Relationships deepen through self-disclosure, which follows a reciprocity norm: Low levels of self-disclosure are met with low levels in return; moderate self-disclosure elicits more personal replies. However, overdisclosure tends to inhibit self-disclosure by others. According to social exchange theory, we tend to maintain relationships that are profitable; that is, those for which perceived rewards exceed perceived costs.

17.1.4 Explain the fundamental ideas behind Sternberg's triangular theory of love

According to Sternberg's triangular theory of love, romantic love is based on feelings of both intimacy and passion, and fatuous love is based on passion and commitment. Companionate love involves feelings of both intimacy and commitment. Consummate love, involving intimacy, passion, and commitment, is the most complete form of love.

17.1.5 Name and describe the three types of adult attachment

Adult relationships tend to mirror patterns of emotional attachment observed in infancy and early childhood. Secure, avoidant, and ambivalent patterns can be defined on the basis of how a person approaches romantic and affectionate relationships with others. *Secure* adults generally trust others and find it relatively easy to get close to others. *Avoidant* adults tend to be more suspicious of others in close relationships, often worrying that partners will not be reliable. *Ambivalent* adults have conflicted feelings about their close relationships, wanting those close relationships but simultaneously worrying that partners may leave them.

17.1.6 Describe how evolutionary forces shape men's and women's preferences for mates

Evolutionary psychology attributes human mating patterns to the differing reproductive challenges faced by men and women during the course of evolution.

17.2 Prosocial Behavior: Helping Others

17.2.1 Define prosocial behavior, and outline three motives that can promote it

Prosocial behaviors are those that benefit others. Three motives that promote prosocial behaviors are *evolutionary forces, self-oriented motives*, and *other-oriented motives*.

17.2.2 Distinguish between prosocial behavior and altruism

Altruistic acts are a smaller subset of prosocial behaviors that are motivated primarily by other-oriented motives.

17.2.3 Describe three factors that influence helping

Three factors that influence helping include the characteristics of the *person requiring help*, characteristics of the *helper*, and characteristics of the *situation*.

17.2.4 Describe the three components of empathy and distinguish empathy from sympathy (or compassion) and personal distress

Empathy has affective (emotional), cognitive, and behavioral components. It differs from sympathy/compassion on the affective component: An empathic response involves feeling an emotion that is the same as the victim; a sympathetic/compassionate response instead involves an affective response that would be more similar to concern or caring for the victim.

17.2.5 Explain what is meant by the term bystander apathy, and the three decision points that are relevant in determining whether bystanders will assist others in need

Bystander apathy (the bystander effect) refers to the finding that bystanders are often unlikely to provide help when others are present. Three decision points must be passed before a person gives help: noticing, defining an emergency, and taking responsibility/selecting a course of action.

17.3 Antisocial Behavior: Aggression, Conflict, and Prejudice

17.3.1 Distinguish between antisocial behavior and aggression, including the difference between direct aggression and indirect aggression

Antisocial behavior is defined as behavior that violates social norms and the rights of others, and it may be non-aggressive or aggressive. Aggressive acts are a subset of antisocial behaviors and they are specifically defined as actions that harm other people. Direct aggression refers to verbal and physical attacks, while indirect aggression refers to acts that harm others' reputations, social standing, friendships, or self-esteem.

17.3.2 Outline three potential causes of aggression

Three potential causes include *biology* (emphasizing brain mechanisms and physical factors that lower the threshold for aggression), *frustration* (which may increase arousal and make people more sensitive to aggression cues), and *social learning* (which suggests that we learn from aggressive models).

17.3.3 Describe some of the ways that aggression can be minimized, at both the societal and individual levels

At the societal level, aggression could be minimized by *reducing exposure to violence* and *increasing exposure to prosocial behaviors*. At the individual level, strategies may include enhanced *self-regulation*, *problem-focused coping*, and making more charitable *attributions* for events that frustrate us.

17.3.4 Name the three components of prejudiced attitudes

Prejudiced attitudes are comprised of affective (emotional), cognitive (stereotype), and behavioral (discrimination) components.

17.3.5 Discriminate between explicit and implicit prejudice

Explicit prejudice is that which is conscious and publicly displayed. In contrast, implicit prejudice includes attitudes toward groups that reside outside of awareness.

17.3.6 Name four factors that are associated with greater levels of prejudice

Four factors include higher levels of *frustration*, *social learning*, a greater endorsement of *authoritarian beliefs* and *dehumanization*.

17.3.7 Outline some of the consequences experienced by victims of prejudice

Research suggests that victims of prejudice are sometimes unable to do what they wish (e.g., rent an apartment or secure a desired job) and may be victims of racial profiling. They may also experience negative consequences related to their mental and physical health, or fall prey to stereotype threat.

17.3.8 Describe three ways that prejudice can be reduced

Aggression can be reduced through *equal-status contact*, the pursuit of *superordinate goals*, and through *direct instruction* (in diversity training sessions, for example).

17.4 Psychology and Your Skill Set: Diversity and Inclusion

17.4.1 Create a plan that will allow you to foster improved relationships with diverse others

Skillfully managing relationships with diverse others requires that we think carefully about several things, including seeking individuating information, avoiding just-world beliefs, awareness of self-fulfilling prophecies, looking for commonalities, setting a good example for others, and always remembering that different doesn't mean inferior. We hope that after reading this section, you'll be better able to think about how you can use these components to help when you are working with diverse others in your everyday life!

18 Applied Psychology

Paul Morigi/Getty Images Entertainment/Getty Images

Gateway Theme Psychological principles can be used to solve practical problems in a variety of settings.

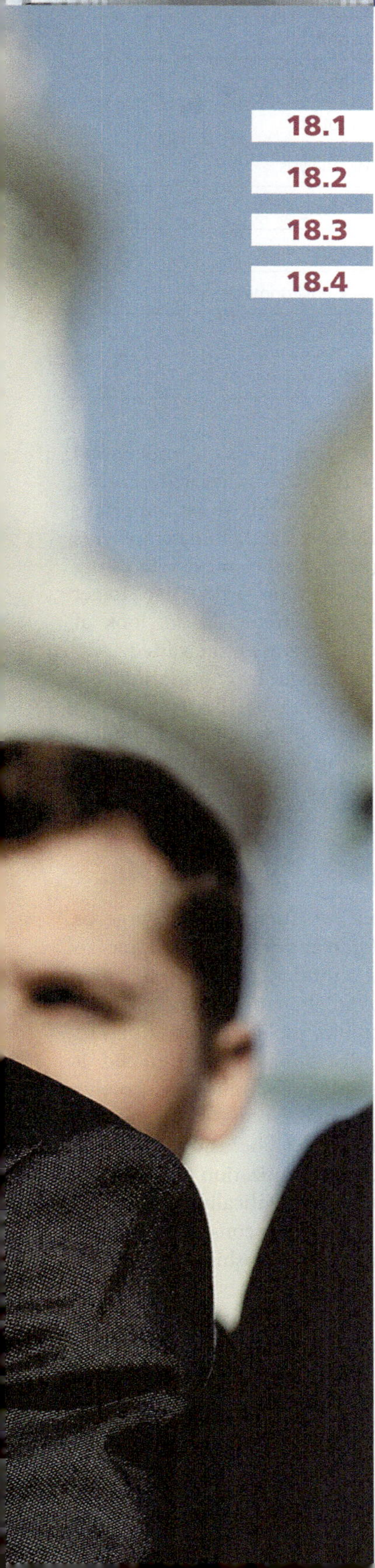

Chapter Outline

Psychology All Around Us

When Wilber Tennant came to see lawyer Robert Bilott, he wanted justice. The factory upriver of his West Virginia farm had been dumping harmful chemicals in the water for years, he said. Moreover, Tennant had a strong suspicion that the toxic waste was the cause of several unexplained deaths in his town, as well as the cancer diagnoses that he and his wife had received. Bilott took the case and discovered that the chemical at the heart of the contamination—perfluorooctanoic acid—did indeed appear to cause cancer and birth defects. Now faced with a class action lawsuit, the company initially agreed to settle the case for $70 million but later reneged on the deal. Undeterred, Bilott decided to take each of the cases to court individually. The jury took less than one day to reach a verdict in the first case. Deciding that the company had acted with malice, jurors awarded the plaintiff $5.1 million dollars in compensation. With thousands of other cases lined up, the company eventually settled for more than $700 million.

This story revolves around a lawyer, but it might surprise you to know that a number of psychologists would also find it interesting. **Applied psychology** refers to the use of psychological principles and research methods to solve practical problems across a wide range of careers. In this particular case, industrial-organizational psychologists who study businesses might notice how the decisions made by the company's senior leadership team led to the disastrous outcome they faced in this case. Environmental psychologists would focus on the impact of human decision-making on the land and water surrounding the town. Community psychologists would take note of how the town came together to work toward a solution. Legal psychologists would, of course, have an interest in how the characteristics of the jury impacted their verdict and decision about compensation for the victims.

In this chapter, we focus on how psychology can be applied to a variety of areas in everyday life. We begin with its connection to businesses and the environment, and then move on to examine how psychology can be applied in legal, community, and sports settings. We conclude with a discussion of career preparation, and how you can get a jump start on using psychology in a field that interests you!

18.1 Industrial/Organizational Psychology

GATEWAYS LEARNING OUTCOMES:
After reading this section, you will be able to:

18.1.1 Explain the role of industrial/organizational psychologists

18.1.2 Define organizational culture, and how it is impacted by hostility in the workplace

18.1.3 Describe how personnel psychologists work to ensure a good fit between people and jobs

18.1.4 Outline two ways in which job satisfaction can be promoted

18.1.5 Distinguish between Theory X, Theory Y, and transformational leadership

Whatever your attitude, the simple fact is that most adults work for a living. Whether you are already employed or plan to begin a career after college, it helps to know something about the psychology of work and organizations.

Industrial/organizational (I/O) psychology, the study of people at work and in organizations, is one of the most important applied areas in psychology (Aamodt, 2016; Bryan & Vinchur, 2013). The efforts of I/O psychologists will likely affect how you are selected for a job, as well as how you would be tested, trained, or evaluated for promotion. Most I/O psychologists are employed by businesses and the government. Typically, they work in two major areas: (1) studying jobs to identify the necessary skills needed for success, which can then guide efforts to select people and train them for jobs that they will find rewarding (the *industrial* part), and (2) studying organizations to understand how to create structures and company cultures that will improve performance (the *organizational* part). Overall, three important goals that are pursued by I/O psychologists are: helping employers deal with employees fairly, helping to make jobs more interesting and satisfying, and helping workers to be more productive. To get a more in-depth idea of what I/O psychologists do, look at ▲ Table 18.1. As you can see, their interests are quite varied.

Pictorial Press Ltd/Alamy Stock Photo

Charlie Chaplin captured the worker as machine perfectly in his 1936 film *Modern Times*. Have you ever worked at a job that made you feel like this?

▲ Table 18.1 Topics of Special Interest to Industrial/Organizational Psychologists

Absenteeism	Minority workers
Decision-making	Pay schedules
Design of organizations	Personnel selection
Employee stress	Personnel training
Employee turnover	Productivity
Interviewing	Promotion
Job enrichment	Task analysis
Job satisfaction	Task design
Labor relations	Work behavior
Leadership	Work environment
Machine design	Work motivation
Management styles	Worker evaluation

In our tour of I/O psychology, we'll begin by considering "the big picture"; that is, organizational culture. We'll then move on to discuss how psychological science has contributed to our understanding of personnel issues (including employee selection and evaluation), job satisfaction, and effective leadership.

Organizational Culture

Businesses and other organizations, whether they are large or small, develop distinct cultures. **Organizational culture** refers to the blend of customs, beliefs, values, attitudes, and rituals that give each organization its unique "flavor" (Chamorro-Premuzic & Furnham, 2010). Organizational culture includes such things as how people are hired and trained, disciplined, and dismissed. It also encompasses how employees dress, communicate, resolve conflicts, share power, identify with organizational goals and values, negotiate contracts, and celebrate special occasions.

People who fit well into a particular organization tend to contribute to its success in ways that are not specifically part of their job description. For example, they are helpful, conscientious, and courteous. They also display good sportsmanship by avoiding pettiness, gossiping, complaining, and making small problems into big ones. Like good citizens, the best workers keep themselves informed about organizational issues by attending meetings and taking part in discussions. Workers with these characteristics display what could be called good **organizational citizenship**.

Understandably, managers and employers highly value workers who are good organizational citizens (Woods & West, 2010).

Of course, sometimes people behave badly at work and this can compromise the organizational culture. Like road rage on the highways, "desk rage," or workplace anger, is a regular occurrence and, at times, erupts into workplace violence or harassment (Niven, Sprigg, & Armitage, 2013). Psychological scientists have helped to identify the common triggers for workplace anger, including particular *personality traits* (such as hostility and paranoia), *job-related stresses* (such as feeling that one has been treated unfairly), *perceived threats* to one's self-esteem, and *work-related conflicts* with others (Einarsen & Hoel, 2008; Spector, 2012). The *economic pressures* that organizations face can also lead to hostile and competitive work environments. However, even in economically difficult times, productivity and a positive organizational culture are closely intertwined. Effective organizations seek to optimize both. For example, companies who pay more attention to the quality of life at work generally suffer fewer productivity losses if they are forced to downsize (i.e., reduce the size of their workforce; Iverson & Zatzick, 2011).

What can be done about harassment and aggression at work? Companies whose organizational culture demonstrates that employees are a valued resource will offer mental health services to troubled employees and trauma counseling in response to workplace violence and harassment. More important, healthy organizations actively promote the well-being of people and try to avoid problems arising in the first place. They do this by openly confronting problems and empowering employees, as well as encouraging participation, cooperation, and the full use of human potential. They also demonstrate compassion and respect for workers' diversity and tolerate the fact that mistakes will sometimes happen (Hodson & Sullivan, 2012; Martinko, Douglas, & Harvey, 2006).

Personnel Psychology

Companies can enhance their chances of developing a positive organizational culture by hiring and promoting the right employees. **Personnel psychology** is concerned with the testing, selection, placement, and promotion of employees (Campbell, 2013; Woods & West, 2010). At present, nine out of ten people are, or will be, employed in business or industry. Thus, nearly everyone who holds a job is placed under the "psychological microscope" of personnel selection sooner or later. Clearly, it is valuable to know how selection for hiring and promotion is done, so let's take a closer look at three key factors in those decisions: job analysis, selection procedures, and performance appraisals.

Job Analysis

Personnel selection begins with **job analysis**, a detailed description of the skills, knowledge, and activities required by a particular job (Paquette & Heitzman, 2014; Sackett, Walmsley, & Laczo, 2013). A job analysis may be done by interviewing expert workers or supervisors, giving them questionnaires, directly observing work, or identifying critical incidents. **Critical incidents** are situations with which competent employees must be able to cope. The ability to deal calmly with a mechanical emergency, for example, is a critical incident for airline pilots. Once job requirements are known, psychologists can state what skills, aptitudes, and interests are needed. In addition, some psychologists are now doing a broader *work analysis*. In this case, they try to identify general characteristics that a person must have to succeed in a variety of work roles, rather than in just one specific job (DuVernet, Dierdorff, & Wilson, 2015).

MixPix/Alamy Stock Photo

Analyzing complex skills during a job analysis has been valuable to the US Navy. When million-dollar aircraft and the lives of pilots are at stake, it makes good sense to do as much training and research as possible on the ground. Navy psychologists use flight simulators such as the one pictured here to analyze the complex skills needed to fly jet fighters. Skills can then be taught without risk on the ground. The CAE P-8 Poseidon simulator shown here uses a computer to generate full-color images that respond realistically to a pilot's use of the controls.

Selection Procedures

After desirable skills and traits are identified, the next step is to learn who has them. Today, the methods most often used for evaluating job candidates include collecting *biodata*, conducting *interviews*, giving *standardized psychological tests*, and employing the *assessment center* approach. Let's see what each one entails.

Applied psychology The use of psychological principles and research methods to solve practical problems.

Industrial/organizational (I/O) psychology A field that focuses on the psychology of work and on behavior within organizations.

Organizational culture The blend of customs, beliefs, values, attitudes, and rituals within an organization.

Organizational citizenship Making positive contributions to the success of an organization in ways that go beyond one's job description.

Personnel psychology A branch of industrial/organizational psychology concerned with testing, selection, placement, and promotion of employees.

Job analysis A detailed description of the skills, knowledge, and activities required by a particular job.

Critical incidents Situations that arise in a job with which a competent worker must be able to cope.

Biodata

As simple as it may seem, one good way to predict job success is to collect detailed biographical information (**biodata**) from applicants (Schultz & Schultz, 2010). The idea behind biodata is that looking at past behavior is a good way to predict future behavior. By learning in detail about a person's life, it is often possible to determine whether the person is suited for a particular type of work (Schmitt & Golubovich, 2013).

Some of the most useful items of biodata include past athletic interests, academic achievements, scientific interests, extracurricular activities, religious activities, social popularity, conflict with brothers and sisters, attitudes toward school, and parents' socioeconomic status (Woods & West, 2010). (It is worth pointing out that there are civil liberty and privacy concerns relating to the collection of sensitive biodata.) Such facts can tell us quite a lot about personality, interests, and abilities. In addition to past experiences, a person's recent life activities also help predict job success. For instance, you might think that college grades are unimportant, but college grade point average (GPA) predicts success in many types of work (Sackett & Lievens, 2008).

Interviews

The traditional personal interview is still one of the most popular ways to select people for jobs or promotions. In a **personal interview**, job applicants are questioned about their qualifications. At the same time, interviewers gain an impression of the applicant's personality (Chamorro-Premuzic & Furnham, 2010).

Unfortunately, interviews are subject to the *halo effect*. (■ Recall that the halo effect is the tendency of interviewers to form favorable or unfavorable impressions about people based on factors that are unrelated to their personalities, including their appearance. See Section 12.3.) In addition, interviewees actively engage in *impression management*, seeking to portray a positive image to interviewers (Kleinmann & Klehe, 2011).

It is for reasons such as these that psychologists continue to look for ways to improve the accuracy of interviews. For instance, some studies suggest that interviews can be improved by giving them *more structure*, with each job candidate being asked the same questions (Levashina et al., 2014; Sackett & Lievens, 2008). Others have noted the value of *behavioral interviews*, which require candidates to describe relevant past experiences (for example, "Tell me about a time when you worked with a team that just wasn't functioning well. What did you do?"). However, even with their limitations, interviews can be a valid and effective way of predicting how people will perform on the job (Hodson & Sullivan, 2012).

Psychological Testing

What kinds of tests do personnel psychologists use? A wide variety of tests are available; we will mention only five of them here. The first type of test that may be used is one that assesses *general mental ability* (that is, intelligence tests). ■ In Section 9.1, we discussed the fact that although these tests have limitations, they can be useful for predicting success in some areas, including those related to work (Aamodt, 2016; Hough & Connelly, 2013; Schmidt & Hunter, 1998).

Second, personnel psychologists make use of *personality tests*, which assess traits such as agreeableness, conscientiousness, extraversion, and neuroticism. (■ These personality traits, which are included in the Big Five and HEXACO models of personality, are discussed in Section 12.2.) Personality traits are important in determining a person's ability to work successfully in particular jobs, but they are also useful for predicting the extent to which that person will get along with other team members and organizational leaders. *Leader-member exchange theory* suggests that the two-way relationship that develops between leaders and workers is associated with mutual trust and respect, and consequently has important implications for productivity and job satisfaction (Day & Miscenko, 2016).

The third type of test often used by personnel psychologists are **vocational interest tests**. These tests assess people's interests and match them to interests found among successful workers in various occupations (Van Iddekinge, Putka, & Campbell, 2011). Tests such as the *Kuder Occupational Interest Survey* and the *Strong-Campbell Interest Inventory* probe interests with items like the following:

I would prefer to
 a. visit a museum
 b. read a good book
 c. take a walk outdoors

Interest inventories typically measure six major themes identified by John Holland (▲ Table 18.2). If you take an interest test and your choices match those of people in a given occupation, it is assumed that you, too, would be comfortable doing the work they do (Meireles & Primi, 2015).

Aptitude tests are a fourth type of test used by personnel psychologists. Such tests rate a person's potential to learn tasks or skills used in various occupations. Tests exist for clerical, verbal, mechanical, artistic, legal, and medical aptitudes, plus many others. (■ Aptitude tests are related to intelligence tests. See Section 9.1 to learn how they differ.) For example, tests of clerical aptitude emphasize the capacity to do rapid, precise, and accurate office work. One section of a clerical aptitude test, therefore, might ask a person to mark all the identical numbers and names in a long list of pairs like those shown here:

49837266	49832766
Global Widgets, Inc.	Global Wigets, Inc.
874583725	874583725
Sevanden Corp.	Sevanden Corp.
Cengage Publishing	Cengage Puhlishing

▲ Table 18.2 Vocational Interest Themes

Themes	Sample College Majors	Sample Occupations
Realistic	Agriculture	Mechanic
Investigative	Physics	Chemist
Artistic	Music	Writer
Social	Education	Counselor
Enterprising	Business	Sales
Conventional	Economics	Clerk

Source: Holland (1997).

After college, there is a chance that you will encounter the fifth means of testing potential employees: an *assessment center*. Many large organizations use **assessment centers** to do in-depth evaluations of job candidates. This approach has become so popular that the list of businesses using it—Ford, IBM, Exxon, Deloitte, and thousands of others—reads like a corporate *Who's Who*.

How do assessment centers differ from the selection methods already described? Assessment centers are primarily used to fill management and executive positions. First, applicants are tested and interviewed. Then, they are observed and evaluated in simulated work situations. Specifically, **situational judgment tests** are used to present difficult but realistic work situations to applicants (Christian, Edwards, & Bradley, 2010; Pollard & Cooper-Thomas, 2015). For example, in one exercise, applicants are given an **in-basket test** that simulates the decision-making challenges executives face. The test consists of a basket full of memos, requests, and typical business problems. Each applicant is asked to quickly read all the materials and to take appropriate action.

In another situational test, applicants take part in a **leaderless group discussion**. This is a test of leadership that simulates group decision-making and problem solving. While the group grapples with a realistic business problem, "clerks" bring in price changes, notices about delayed supplies, and so forth. By observing applicants, it is possible to evaluate leadership skills and to see how job candidates cope with stress (Chamorro-Premuzic & Furnham, 2010). (■ Situational tests are also used to investigate personality traits. See Section 12.2.)

Performance Appraisal

Many of the procedures used to hire employees can also be used by personnel psychologists to periodically evaluate their performance after they have been hired (DeNisi & Murphy, 2017). The results can be used in a variety of ways designed to improve employee job performance. This might include providing employees with feedback, setting goals, and determining appropriate rewards or punishments.

One popular approach is **360° feedback**, the evaluation of employee performance from a variety of perspectives. Although implementations of 360° feedback can vary considerably from company to company, it is fair to say that the key feature of most implementations is a set of anonymous numerical ratings collected from different company stakeholders. Some examples include the employee's managers, coworkers, subordinates, customers—even the employees themselves may be asked to provide a self-assessment. Appraising an employee's performance in this way is more likely to reveal strengths or weaknesses not readily apparent from single-perspective evaluations, such as more traditional manager-only appraisals (Bracken, Rose, & Church, 2016).

Job Satisfaction

When the techniques used by personnel psychologists work well, organizations will have the right people working in the right positions. How, then, do organizations keep people engaged in their work over time? Put another way, how do they keep their workers satisfied?

Job satisfaction refers to the degree to which a person is pleased with his or her work. One factor that contributes to higher satisfaction is the *extent to which we get along with coworkers*. Anyone who has ever been employed has probably encountered at least one perpetually grumpy coworker or difficult boss. Such people often make the work environment difficult to endure, and can significantly impact job satisfaction (Aamodt, 2016).

A second factor that can impact job satisfaction is *a good fit between the work required and employees' characteristics*, including their interests, values, and abilities. Fit is also important with regard to employee expectations (including beliefs about appropriate compensation) and needs (such as the desire for personal growth and challenge) (Aamodt, 2016; Landy & Conte, 2009). Two common means of improving the fit between work and employee characteristics—and therefore enhancing job satisfaction—are *job enrichment* strategies and the use of *flexible working conditions*.

Job Enrichment

With regard to salary expectations and the need for challenge, the trend in business has historically focused on simply tying better pay to more challenging work. However, far too many jobs are routine, repetitive, boring, and do not meet the need for challenge and personal growth. To combat the discontent this can breed, many psychologists recommend a strategy called job enrichment.

Job enrichment involves making a job more personally rewarding or interesting, and has been used successfully by large corporations such as IBM, Maytag, Toyota, and AT&T to lower production costs, increase job satisfaction, reduce boredom, and

Biodata Detailed biographical information about a job applicant.

Personal interview Formal or informal questioning of job applicants to learn their qualifications and to gain an impression of their personalities.

Vocational interest test A paper-and-pencil test that assesses a person's interests and matches them to interests found among successful workers in various occupations.

Aptitude test An evaluation that rates a person's potential to learn skills required by various occupations.

Assessment center A program set up within an organization to conduct in-depth evaluations of job candidates.

Situational judgment test Presenting realistic work situations to applicants in order to observe their skills and reactions.

In-basket test A testing procedure that simulates the individual decision-making challenges that executives face.

Leaderless group discussion A test of leadership that simulates group decision-making and problem solving.

360° feedback Evaluation of employee performance, mainly anonymous numerical ratings, collected from different perspectives.

Job satisfaction The degree to which a person is comfortable with or satisfied with his or her work.

Job enrichment Making a job more personally rewarding, interesting, or intrinsically motivating; typically involves increasing worker knowledge.

decrease absenteeism (Gregory, Albritton, & Osmonbekov, 2010). Merely assigning a person more tasks is usually not enriching. Overloaded workers just feel stressed, and they tend to make more errors. Instead, enrichment strategies involve *removing some of the controls and restrictions* on employees, thus giving them greater freedom, choice, and authority. In some cases, employees also switch to *doing a complete cycle of work*—that is, they complete an entire item or project instead of doing an isolated part of a larger process. Whenever possible, workers are given direct feedback about their work or progress.

True job enrichment helps with the need for challenge and personal development because it increases workers' feelings of empowerment and knowledge—that is, workers are encouraged to continuously learn and exercise a broad range of options, skills, and information related to their occupations (Gregory, Albritton, & Osmonbekov, 2010; Sessa & London, 2006). (■ In this way, job enrichment can be thought of as a way of increasing intrinsic motivation. See Section 10.1.)

Flexible Working Conditions

Besides job enrichment, flexible working conditions can also help to create alignment between work and employee needs and characteristics. If you've ever worked "9 to 5" in an office, you know that traditional time schedules can be confining. They also doom many workers to a daily battle with rush-hour traffic. To improve worker morale, I/O psychologists recommend the use of a variety of flexible work arrangements, one of which is **flextime**, or flexible working hours (Kossek & Michel, 2011). The basic idea of flextime is that starting and quitting times are flexible, so long as employees are present during a core work period. For example, employees might be allowed to arrive between 7:30 a.m. and 10:30 a.m. and depart between 3:30 p.m. and 6:30 p.m. In a common variation called a *compressed workweek*, employees might work fewer days, but put in more hours per day so that the number of hours per week stay the same. A second type of flexibility that employers can provide is **flexplace** (also called *telework* or *telecommuting*), a situation in which work is done outside the workplace, usually at home (Lautsch, Kossek, & Eaton, 2009; Nätti & Häikiö, 2012).

Do flexible working conditions really improve job satisfaction? Generally speaking, yes (Yang & Zheng, 2011). Psychologists theorize that flexible work lowers stress and increases feelings of independence, both of which increase productivity and job satisfaction (Beckmann, Cornelissen, & Kräkel, 2017). For example, flextime typically has a positive effect on workers' productivity, job satisfaction, absenteeism, and comfort with their work schedules (Thompson, Payne, & Taylor, 2015). Similarly, flexplace is especially effective when it allows valued employees to maintain homes in other cities rather than being forced to move to the company's location (Atkin & Lau, 2007). A survey of 3000 employees working at home during the COVID-19 pandemic indicated that 77 percent wanted to continue working from home part-time after restrictions had been lifted, and 16 percent indicated they would prefer not to return to working at the office at all (Global Workplace Analytics, 2020).

Of course, not everyone wants a compressed workweek or to work from home. Ideally, flexible working arrangements should

Daxiao Productions/Shutterstock.com

Connecting with work through the Internet makes it possible to telecommute, or work from home while still interacting with colleagues (Golden, Veiga, & Simsek, 2006).

fit the needs of employees (Rudolph & Baltes, 2016; Troup & Rose, 2012). Perhaps we can conclude that it is better, when possible, to bend working arrangements instead of the workers themselves.

Whether it is enhanced by job enrichment, flexible working conditions or by some other means, job satisfaction is well worth cultivating because positive attitudes toward work are associated with more cooperation, better performance, a greater willingness to help others, more creative problem solving, and less absenteeism (Bowling, 2010; Judge et al., 2017).

Leadership in Organizations

While all employees have some responsibility for an organization's success, leaders have a particularly important role to play (■ Can leadership be learned? See Section 12.5.) How do great business leaders inspire their followers? To some extent, the answer to this question depends on the workers themselves.

Back in the 1950s, Massachusetts Institute of Technology professor Douglas McGregor (1960) outlined two main types of motivation for working. A student of Abraham Maslow, McGregor's ideas about worker motivation were strongly influenced by his mentor's hierarchy of needs (■ see Section 10.3 for a refresher on Maslow's hierarchy). The first type of worker is described by *Theory X*, which describes people whose motivation to work is driven by extrinsic factors (that is, a paycheck). They are likely to avoid taking responsibility, have little ambition, and generally work only because they need their wages to meet Maslow's basic needs for survival. In contrast, *Theory Y* applies to workers who are intrinsically motivated to work, and whose jobs allow them to meet higher-level needs, including the need for personal growth.

McGregor's ideas about Theory X and Y have been used for decades to answer the question about optimal leadership practices. Let's take a look at how his ideas have been applied.

Theory X Leadership

One of the earliest attempts to improve worker efficiency was made in 1923 by Frederick Taylor, an engineer. To speed up production, Taylor standardized work routines and stressed careful planning, control, and orderliness. Today, versions of Taylor's approach are classified as **scientific management**, and they are closely linked to McGregor's ideas about Theory X. Using time-and-motion studies, task analysis, job specialization, assembly lines, pay schedules, and the like, scientific management seeks to increase productivity (Crowley et al., 2010; Paton, 2013).

It sounds like scientific management and Theory X leadership treat people as if they were machines. Is that true? To some extent, it is. In Taylor's day, many large companies were manufacturers with giant assembly lines. They were concerned with improving **work efficiency**, defined as maximum output at lowest cost. As a result, they altered conditions that they believed would affect workers (such as time schedules, work quotas, bonuses, and so on) to meet this goal. Some might even have wished that people *would* act like well-oiled machines.

Leaders who adopt this approach today are those who emphasize a *task orientation*, focusing on the work to be done, rather than a *person orientation*, which focuses on the people doing the work. In keeping with McGregor's Theory X, these leaders tend to assume that workers must be goaded or guided into being productive because they have little motivation—other than their salary—to complete the work they do.

Theory Y Leadership

Most psychologists working in business recognize that psychological efficiency is just as important as work efficiency. **Psychological efficiency** refers to maintaining good morale, labor relations, employee satisfaction, and similar aspects of work behavior. Leadership styles that ignore or mishandle the human element can be devastatingly costly. Studies have consistently found that happy workers are productive workers (Dik, Byrne, & Steger, 2013; Lavy & Littman-Ovadia, 2017).

In keeping with this idea, **Theory Y leadership** refers to managers who adopt a person orientation rather than a task orientation and tend to make different assumptions about their workers' motivation. Specifically, they believe that workers enjoy autonomy and are willing to accept responsibility. They also assume that a worker's needs and goals can be meshed with the company's goals and that people are not naturally passive or lazy.

In short, Theory Y assumes that people are industrious, creative, and motivated by challenging work that meets higher-level needs. It appears that given the proper conditions of freedom and responsibility, many people *will* work hard to gain competence and use their talents. Consider Armando, who is a software engineer. He has been working long hours trying to develop a new way to more quickly predict hurricane activity for a satellite weather system. The work efficiency of Armando's job cannot easily be measured or improved. Instead, his success depends on his own initiative, creativity, and commitment to his work—in short, his intrinsic motivation to do the best job possible. Armando quit his last job because the leaders of that company made him feel like he was "punching the clock," which is something that he does not want to do.

dpa picture alliance/Alamy Stock Photo

As an executive at both Google and Facebook, Sheryl Sandberg constantly faced the incongruity between leadership stereotypes and stereotypes of women.

Human Diversity and Leadership

Aren't women more person-oriented than men? And doesn't that imply that women would make better Theory Y leaders? Good question. As person-oriented Theory Y leadership styles have become more popular, cracks have begun to appear in the *glass ceiling*, the invisible barrier that has historically prevented women from moving into leadership positions (Diehl & Dzubinski, 2016). Today, women are slowly gaining acceptance as leaders and the proportion of American organizations with female CEOs is also slowly increasing (Eagly, 2013; Martin, 2007; Şahin, Gürbüz, & Şeşen, 2017). Moreover, some studies have shown that companies with more women in leadership roles perform better financially and when managing their employees (Krishnan & Park, 2005; Melero, 2011).

Flextime A work schedule that allows flexible starting and quitting times.

Flexplace (telecommuting) An approach to flexible work that involves working at a location away from the office, but using a computer to stay connected throughout the workday.

Theory X leadership (scientific management) An approach to leadership that emphasizes work efficiency.

Work efficiency Maximum output (productivity) at lowest cost.

Psychological efficiency Maintenance of good morale, labor relations, employee satisfaction, and similar aspects of work behavior.

Theory Y leadership A leadership style that emphasizes human relations at work and that views people as industrious, responsible, and interested in challenging work.

Unfortunately, psychologist Alice Eagly has noted that women continue to face unique challenges, including those created by a clash between leadership stereotypes and stereotypes of women (Brescoll, Dawson, & Uhlmann, 2010; Eagly & Carli, 2007). On the one hand, most people expect good leaders to be *agentic*: independent, confident, ambitious, objective, dominant, and forceful. On the other hand, they expect women to be more *communal*: dependent, caring, nurturing, tender, sensitive, and sympathetic. According to traditional gender role stereotypes (■ see Section 11.3), it is men who are agentic (and therefore better) leaders, despite evidence to the contrary (Eagly, 2013).

What does this mean for a woman who moves into a leadership role? If she practices communal, Theory Y leadership, she is seen as weak. She is "not tough enough" or does not "have the right stuff" to be a leader. Yet, if she acts more assertively and confidently, she is scorned for "trying to be a man" (Kark & Eagly, 2010). This conflict was perfectly expressed in a conversation between Oprah Winfrey and Sheryl Sandberg, who has held senior executive positions at both Google and Facebook. According to Sandberg, "We expect people to adhere to stereotypes . . . . The stereotype of men is: leadership qualities. Leader, decisive, going to make things happen. The stereotype of women are communal qualities. Caregiving, sensitive. Because we expect those qualities to be in opposition to each other, it means when a woman does anything other than be nice first, she's judged badly."

Hopefully as traditional gender stereotypes fade, and as Theory Y leadership styles gain wider acceptance, women will add shattering the glass ceiling to their many other successes (Kaiser & Wallace, 2016).

Transformational Leadership

Transformational leadership seeks to transform employees to exceed expectations and look beyond self-interest to help the organization better compete (Guay, 2013; Şahin, Gürbüz, & Şeşen, 2017). The transformational leader achieves these goals in four ways:

1. Idealized influence: Employees are encouraged to work ethically, emphasizing values such as trust.
2. Inspirational motivation: Employees are inspired to see their work as meaningful and challenging.
3. Intellectual stimulation: Employees are empowered to "think outside the box" to find new solutions to problems.
4. Individualized consideration: Employees' individual needs, goals, and abilities are valued; appropriate professional development is available as required.

Two techniques that make transformational leadership (and Theory Y) methods effective are *shared leadership* and *management by objectives*. In **shared leadership (participative management)**, employees at all levels are directly involved in decision-making and problem solving (Neubert et al., 2015; Pearce, Manz, & Sims, 2009). By taking part in decisions that affect them, employees come to see work as a cooperative effort—not as something imposed on them by an egotistical leader. The benefits include greater productivity, more involvement in work, greater job satisfaction, and less job-related stress (Pearce, Conger, & Locke, 2007; Raes et al., 2013).

Monkey Business Images/Shutterstock.com

Shared leadership techniques encourage employees at all levels to become involved in decision-making. Quite often, this arrangement leads to greater job satisfaction.

Management by objectives refers to a situation in which workers are given specific goals to meet so they can tell whether they are doing a good job (Antoni, 2005). Typical objectives include reaching a certain sales total, making a certain number of items, or reducing waste by a specific percentage. In any case, workers are free to choose (within limits) how they will achieve their goals. As a result, they feel more independent and take personal responsibility for their work. Workers are especially productive when they receive feedback about their progress toward goals. Clearly, people like to know what the target is and whether they are succeeding.

Many companies give groups of workers even greater freedom and responsibility than individuals. This is typically done by creating self-managed teams. A **self-managed team** is a group of employees who work together toward shared goals. Self-managed teams can typically choose their own methods of achieving results, so long as they are effective. Self-managed teams tend to make good use of the strengths and talents of individual employees. As a consequence, workers in self-managed teams are much more likely to feel that they are being treated fairly at work and to develop a positive team atmosphere (Chansler, Swamidass, & Cammann, 2003; Gilboa & Tal-Shmotkin, 2012). Self-managed teams also promote new ideas and improve motivation. Most of all, they encourage cooperation and teamwork within organizations (Markova & Perry, 2014).

How can workers below the management level be involved more in their work? One answer is the use of **quality circles**, voluntary discussion groups that seek ways to solve business problems and improve efficiency (Aamodt, 2016). In contrast to self-managed teams, quality circles usually do not have the power to put their suggestions into practice directly. But good ideas speak for themselves and many are adopted by company leaders. Quality circles do have limitations, but nevertheless, studies verify that greater personal involvement can lead to better performance and job satisfaction (Pereira & Osburn, 2007).

Although we have only scratched the surface of industrial/organizational psychology, it is time to move on to look at environmental psychology. Before we begin, though, here's a chance to do some reflective practice on what you've learned.

Reflective Practice

Industrial/Organizational Psychology

1. Theory X leadership, or scientific management, is concerned primarily with improving ______________.
2. Shared leadership management is often a feature of businesses with leaders who adhere to Theory Y or transformational management. T or F?
3. For the majority of workers, job satisfaction is almost exclusively related to the amount of pay received. T or F?
4. Job enrichment is a direct expression of scientific management principles. T or F?
5. Identifying critical work incidents is sometimes included in a thorough ______________.
6. A leaderless group discussion is most closely associated with which approach to employee selection?
   a. aptitude testing
   b. personal interviews
   c. job analysis
   d. assessment center

THINK CRITICALLY

7. In what area of human behavior other than work would a careful task analysis be helpful?

SELF-REFLECT

- If you were leading people in a business setting, which of the leadership concepts do you think you would be most likely to use?
- Do you think women can make effective leaders? In business? In politics?
- Which of the various ways of evaluating job applicants do you regard as most valid? Which would you prefer to have applied to yourself?

Answers: 1. work (or task) efficiency 2. T 3. F 4. F 5. job analysis 6. d 7. One such area is sports psychology. As described later in this chapter, sports skills can also be broken into subparts so that key elements can be identified and taught. Such methods are an extension of techniques first used for job analyses. To a large extent, attempts to identify the characteristics of effective teaching also rely on task analysis.

18.2 Environmental Psychology

GATEWAYS LEARNING OUTCOMES: After reading this section, you will be able to:

18.2.1 Explain the role of environmental psychologists

18.2.2 Explain how crowding, overstimulation, and noise affect human behavior, and how these environmental stressors can be managed

18.2.3 Describe some of the sources of environmental damage, including social dilemmas

18.2.4 Outline four solutions that have been put forward to minimize environmental damage

Environmental psychology is the area of psychology that is concerned with the relationship between environments and human behavior (Winter & Koger, 2010). Environmental psychologists are interested in both **social environments**, defined by groups of people, such as a dance, business meeting, or party, and **physical environments**, whether constructed or natural. They also give special attention to **behavioral settings**, smaller areas within an environment whose use is well defined, such as an office, locker room, church, casino, or classroom. As you have no doubt noticed, various environments and behavioral settings tend to have their own norms, and "demand" certain actions from the people who use them. Consider, for example, the different norms that govern a library and a campus center lounge—if you've ever tried to have an animated discussion with 12 of your friends at the library, you'll know exactly what we mean. ▲ Table 18.3 outlines a number of the topics that are of interest to environmental psychologists.

Throughout this book, we've noted that the social environment—including the people we associate with and the culture in which we grow up—can have an important impact on our thoughts, feelings, and behavior. But the physical environment can also have an important impact on us, though we may not always be aware of its effects. The reverse is also true: People can have a significant impact on the environments in which they live. Nowhere is this more obvious than in the dramatic impact that humans have had on the natural environment. Every time we eat a meal, discard some junk, travel somewhere, or even just sit and breathe, we enlarge our **ecological footprint** (defined as the

Transformational leadership Leadership aimed at transforming employees to exceed expectations and look beyond self-interest to help the organization better compete.

Shared leadership (participative management) A leadership approach that allows employees at all levels to participate in decision-making.

Management by objectives A management technique in which employees are given specific goals to meet in their work.

Self-managed team A work group that has a high degree of freedom with respect to how it achieves its goals.

Quality circle An employee discussion group that makes suggestions for improving quality and solving business problems.

Environmental psychology The formal study of how environments affect behavior.

Social environment An environment defined by a group of people and their activities or interrelationships (such as a parade, revival meeting, or sports event).

Physical environments Natural settings, such as forests and beaches, as well as environments built by humans, such as buildings, ships, and cities.

Behavioral setting A smaller area within an environment whose use is well defined, such as a bus depot, waiting room, or lounge.

Ecological footprint The amount of land and water area required to replenish the resources that a human population consumes.

▲ Table 18.3 Topics of Special Interest to Environmental Psychologists

Architectural design	Noise
Behavioral settings	Personal space
Cognitive maps	Personality and environment
Constructed environments	Pollution
Crowding	Privacy
Energy conservation	Proxemics
Environmental stressors	Resource management
Heat	Territoriality
Human ecology	Urban planning
Littering	Vandalism
Natural environment	

amount of land and water required to replenish the resources that a human population consumes; ● see Figure 18.1). In this section, we examine both of these effects. We begin by considering how the physical environment can impact people, and then we turn our attention to how people impact the environment.

George Sheldon/Shutterstock.com

How big is *your* ecological footprint?

Environmental Influences on Behavior

Much of our behavior is influenced by specific types of environments. For example, a variety of environmental factors influence the amount of vandalism and other crime that occurs in public places (Brown & Devlin, 2003; Hipp et al., 2013; Welsh, Mudge, & Farrington, 2010). In every city, more assaults and burglaries take place near the few restaurants or bars where likely offenders tend to hang out (Buchanan, 2008).

Knowing that the environment can shape our behavior, researchers often concern themselves with questions about how local environments should be designed to encourage desired behavior. For example, many shopping malls and department stores are designed like mazes. Their twisting pathways encourage shoppers to linger and wander while looking at merchandise, increasing the chances that they may buy something. Moreover, because people typically resist trampling flowers and plants, raised flowerbeds are often placed around signs to help protect them from vandals. Or consider the public restroom. Many architects now "harden" and "de-opportunize" public restrooms by adding elements such as doorless toilet stalls and tiled walls to discourage vandalism and graffiti.

So what are some aspects of the environment that impact our thoughts, emotions, and behavior?

Courtesy of John Mitterer

● **Figure 18.1 The cost of bringing up baby.** What will it cost the world to provide for a baby born since the year 2000? Without a major conservation effort, a person born in North America will consume, on average, the resources shown here over a lifetime ("Bringing up Baby," 1999).

John Mitterer

Graffiti, one of the blights of urban life, is more likely to occur in some environments.

John Mitterer

This fly is not real; it is painted onto this urinal at Amsterdam's Schiphol Airport. It's a great example of modifying an environment to change behavior, because men tend to aim at the "fly" and hence are more accurate when they urinate. The result is much cleaner men's washrooms.

Traffic congestion, pollution, crime, and impersonality are urban problems that immediately come to mind. To this list, psychologists have added *crowding, overstimulation*, and *noise* as factors that can affect behavior. Psychological research has begun to clarify the impact of each of these last three elements on human functioning, so let's take a closer look at them (Malan et al., 2008; Thomas, 2013).

Crowding

Nowhere are the effects of urbanization more evident than in teeming cities, including their jammed buses, public spaces, and living quarters, all of which provide ample testimony to the stresses of **crowding**.

Is there any way to assess the effect that crowding has on people? One early approach was to study the effects of overcrowding among animals. Although the results of animal experiments cannot be considered conclusive for humans, they point to some disturbing effects. For example, in an influential classic experiment, John Calhoun (1962) let a group of laboratory rats breed without limit in a confined space. Calhoun provided plenty of food, water, and nesting material for the rats. All that the rats lacked was space. At its peak, the colony numbered 80 rats; yet it was housed in a cage designed to comfortably hold about 50. Overcrowding in the cage was heightened by the actions of the two most dominant males. These animals staked out private territory at opposite ends of the cage, gathered harems of eight to ten females, and prospered. Their actions forced the remaining rats into a small, severely crowded middle area.

What effect did crowding have on the animals? A high rate of pathological behavior developed in both males and females. Females gave up nest building and caring for their young. Pregnancies decreased, and infant mortality ran extremely high. Many of the animals became indiscriminately aggressive and attacked others. Abnormal sexual behavior was rampant, with some animals displaying hypersexuality and others total sexual passivity. Many of the animals died, apparently from stress-caused diseases. The link between these problems and overcrowding is unmistakable.

But does that apply to humans? Many of the same pathological behaviors can be observed in crowded inner-city ghettos. It is, therefore, tempting to assume that the violence, social disorganization, and declining birthrates sometimes seen in these areas are directly related to crowding. However, the connection between crowding and behavior may not be so clear-cut in humans (Evans et al., 2010). For example, in addition to crowding, people living in the inner city also suffer disadvantages in nutrition, education, income, and health care. These conditions, more than crowding, may deserve the blame for pathological behaviors. In fact, most laboratory studies using human subjects have failed to signal any serious ill effects caused by crowding people into small places.

Crowding A subjective feeling of being overstimulated by a loss of privacy or by the nearness of others (especially when social contact with them is unavoidable).

Angela Weiss/AFP/Getty Images

Times Square in New York, New Year's Eve. High densities do not automatically produce feelings of crowding. The nature of the situation and the relationships among crowd members are also important.

This somewhat unexpected finding may result from the fact that crowding is a psychological condition that is separate from **density**. While density is an objective measure of the number of people in a given space, crowding refers to subjective feelings of being overstimulated by social inputs or a loss of privacy. Whether high density is experienced as crowding may depend on the relationships among those involved. In an elevator, subway, or prison, high densities may be uncomfortable or stressful. In contrast, a musical concert, party, or reunion may be most pleasant at high density levels.

Thus, physical crowding may interact with situations to intensify existing stresses or pleasures (Evans, Lercher, & Kofler, 2002). However, when crowding causes a loss of control over one's immediate social environment, stress and health problems are likely to result (Solari & Mare, 2012; Steiner & Wooldredge, 2009). This finding probably explains why death rates increase among prison inmates and psychiatric hospital patients who live in crowded conditions. However, even milder instances of crowding can have a negative impact, as people who live in crowded conditions often become more aggressive or guarded and withdrawn from others (Regoeczi, 2008).

Overstimulation and Noise

One unmistakable consequence of high densities and crowding is overstimulation, or a state that psychologist Stanley Milgram called **attentional overload**. This is a stressful condition that occurs when sensory stimulation, information, and social contacts make excessive demands on our attention. Large cities, in particular, tend to bombard residents with continuous input resulting in sensory and cognitive overload.

One of the most important contributors to this type of sensory overload is noise. A classic study of children attending schools near Los Angeles International Airport suggests that constant noise can be quite damaging. Children from the noisy schools were compared with similar students attending schools farther from the airport (Cohen et al., 1981). The comparison students were from families of similar social and economic makeup. Testing showed that children attending the noisy schools had higher blood pressure than those from the quieter schools. They were more likely to give up attempts to solve a difficult puzzle. And they were poorer at proofreading a printed paragraph—a task that requires close attention and concentration. Other studies of children living near other airports or in noisy neighborhoods have found similar signs of stress, poor reading skills, and other damaging effects (Evans, 2006; Linting et al., 2013; Sörqvist, 2010).

The tendency of the noise-battered children to give up or become distracted is a serious handicap. It may even reveal a state of *learned helplessness* caused by daily, uncontrollable blasts of sound. Even if such damage proves to be temporary, it is clear that **noise pollution**—annoying and intrusive sound—is a major source of environmental stress. (■ Learned helplessness is described in Section 13.2.)

Milgram (1970) believed that city dwellers learn to prevent overstimulation by engaging only in brief, superficial social contacts, by ignoring nonessential events, and by fending off others with cold and unfriendly expressions. In short, many city dwellers find that a degree of callousness is essential for survival (Wilson & Kennedy, 2006). Thus, a blunting of sensitivity to the needs of others may be one of the more serious costs of urban stresses and crowding.

Managing Environmental Stressors

How do psychologists find solutions to problems such as overcrowding, overstimulation, and noise? Solutions often begin with an **environmental assessment** to see how an environment influences the behavior and perceptions of the people using it. For example, anyone who has ever lived in a college dorm knows that, at times, it can feel as though you're living in a zoo. In one well-known environmental assessment, Baum and Valins (1977) found that students housed in long, narrow, corridor-design dormitories often feel crowded and stressed. The crowded students tended to withdraw from others and even made more trips to the campus health center than students living in less-crowded buildings.

Through **architectural psychology**, the study of the effects that buildings have on behavior, psychologists are often able to suggest design changes that solve or avoid these types of problems (Zeisel, 2006). For example, Baum and Valins (1979) studied two basic dorm arrangements. One dorm had a long corridor with one central bathroom. As a result, residents were constantly forced into contact with one another. The other dorm had rooms clustered in threes. Each of these suites shared a small bathroom. Even though the amount of space available to each student was the same in both dorms, students in the long-corridor dorm reported feeling more crowded. They also made fewer friends in their dorm and showed greater signs of withdrawing from social contact.

What sort of solution does this suggest? A later study showed that small architectural changes can greatly reduce stress in high-density living conditions. Baum and Davis (1980) compared students living in a long-corridor dorm housing 40 students with those living in an altered dorm where the hallway was divided in half, with unlocked doors, and the three center bedrooms were turned into a lounge area (● Figure 18.2). At the end of the term, students living in the divided dorm reported less stress from crowding. They also formed more friendships and were more open to social contacts. In comparison, students in the long-corridor dorm felt more crowded, stressed, and unfriendly, and they kept their doors shut much more frequently—presumably because they "wanted to be alone."

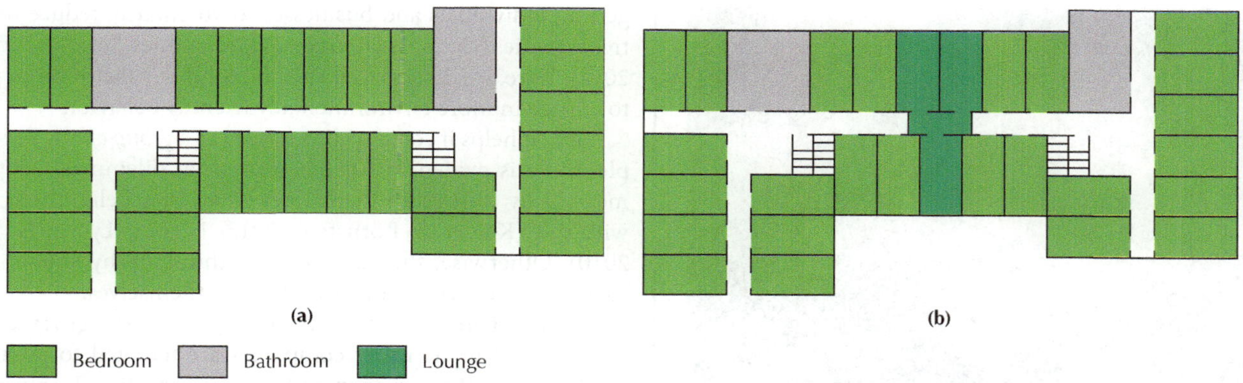

Figure 18.2 **An architectural solution for crowding.** (Psychologists divided a dorm hall like that shown in the left diagram (a) into two shorter halls separated by unlocked doors and a lounge area (b). This simple change minimized unwanted social contacts and greatly reduced feelings of crowding among dorm residents. (Adapted from Baum & Davis, 1980.)

Similar improvements have been made by altering the interior design of businesses, schools, apartment buildings, psychiatric hospitals, and prisons. In general, the more spaces that one must pass through to get from one part of a building to another, the less stressed and crowded people feel (Evans, Lepore, & Schroeder, 1996; Zeisel, 2006).

Human Influences on the Natural Environment

Just as the environment can impact human behavior, so too can human activity impact the environment. Indeed, overpopulation and its environmental impact are surely among the most serious problems facing the world today. The world population has exploded in the last 150 years to more than 7 billion people today, and it may approach 10 billion by 2050 (United Nations, 2016). (See Figure 18.3.)

The human activity associated with our increasing numbers has resulted in drastic changes to the natural environment (Miller & Spoolman, 2016). We burn fossil fuels, destroy forests, use chemical products, and strip, clear, and farm the land. In doing so, we alter natural cycles, animal populations, and the very face of the Earth. The long-range impact of such activities is already becoming evident through global warming, an increase in natural disasters such as flooding and massive forest fires, the extinction of plants and animals, and polluted land, air, and water (Winter & Koger, 2010). Moreover, exposure to toxic hazards, such as radiation, pesticides, and industrial chemicals leads to an elevated risk of physical and mental illness (Evans, 2006).

Sources of Environmental Damage

Given that corporations and governments do significant environmental damage, many of the solutions require changes in politics and policies. Ultimately, though, many of the environmental problems that we face can be traced back to our tendency to overuse natural resources (Global Footprint Network, 2017a; Huang & Rust, 2011). Such overuse by individuals is sometimes related to a thorny problem that psychologists refer to as a *social dilemma*.

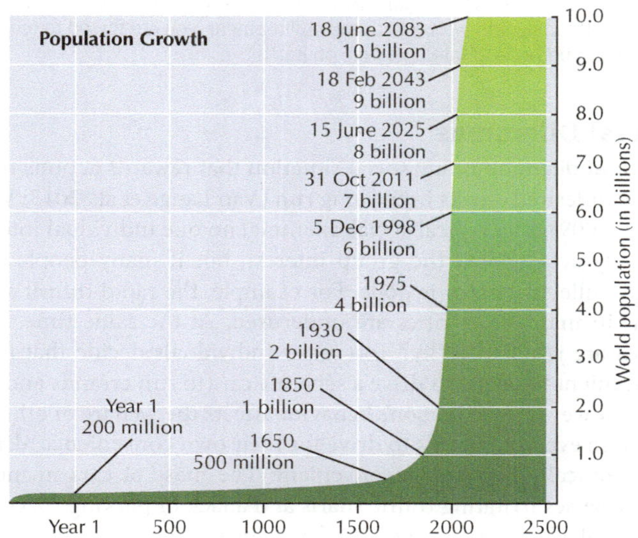

Figure 18.3 **World population growth.** (Population growth has exploded since 1850 and already exceeds 7 billion. Overpopulation and rapid population growth are closely connected with environmental damage, international tensions, and rapid depletion of nonrenewable resources. Some demographers predict that if population growth is not limited voluntarily before it reaches 10 billion, it will be limited by widespread food shortages, disease, infant mortality, and early death (Global Footprint Network, 2017b; United Nations, 2016).

Density The number of people in a given space or, inversely, the amount of space available to each person.

Attentional overload A stressful condition caused when sensory stimulation, information, and social contacts make excessive demands on attention.

Noise pollution Stressful and intrusive noise; usually artificially generated by machinery, but also includes sounds made by animals and humans.

Environmental assessment The measurement and analysis of the effects that an environment has on the behavior and perceptions of people within that environment.

Architectural psychology The study of the effects that buildings have on behavior and the design of buildings using behavioral principles.

AP Images/Itsuo Inouye

After a giant earthquake and tsunami, a Japanese nuclear reactor suffered a catastrophic failure and leaked radiation into the surrounding environment. Major environmental catastrophes like this one have become depressingly common. As the late Carl Sagan once said, "When you look closely, you find so many things going wrong with the environment, you are forced to reassess the hypothesis of intelligent life on Earth."

Social Dilemmas

A **social dilemma** is any social situation that rewards actions that have undesired effects in the long run (Van Lange et al., 2013; Van Vugt, 2009). In a typical social dilemma, no one individual intentionally acts against the group interest, but if many people act alike, collective harm is done. For example, the rapid transit systems in many large cities are underused. At the same time, the roads are jammed. Why? Too many individuals decide that it is convenient to own and drive a separate car (to run errands and so on). However, each person's behavior affects the welfare of others. Because everyone wants to drive for their own convenience, driving ironically becomes inconvenient: The mass of cars in most cities causes irritating traffic snarls and a lack of parking spaces.

Social dilemmas are especially damaging when we are enticed into overuse of scarce resources that must be shared by many people. Again, each person acts in his or her self-interest without necessarily intending to harm others. Collectively, though, everyone ends up suffering in the long run. Ecologist Garrett Hardin (1968) calls these specific social dilemmas the **tragedy of the commons**. A good example is the farmer who applies pesticides to a crop to save it from insect damage. The farmer benefits immediately. However, if other farmers follow suit, the local water system may be permanently contaminated by chemicals in the pesticides, creating problems for *all* the farmers.

In most cases of environmental pollution, immediate individual benefits are gained for polluting, but the major, long-term collective costs are delayed. Overall what the tragedy of the commons demonstrates is that whenever personal comfort, convenience, or profit is involved, it is highly tempting to just let others worry about the consequences of our actions. Yet in the long run, everyone stands to lose (Ansari, Wijen, & Gray, 2013; Van Vugt, 2009).

Solutions for Environmental Damage

Learning about environmental problems and pro-environmental values at home, school, and work has been one of the most effective ways to encourage positive behavioral changes, including getting individuals and businesses to voluntarily reduce destructive activities (Carrico & Riemer, 2011; Matthies, Selge, & Klöckner, 2012). Here, we discuss four specific solutions that prompt people to engage in more environmentally friendly behavior.

First, it helps if conservation is seen as a *group effort*. For example, there is evidence that in most social dilemmas, people are more likely to restrain themselves when they believe that others will, too (Kugler & Bornstein, 2013; Nigbur, Lyons, & Uzzell, 2010). Otherwise, they are likely to think, "Why should I be a sucker? No one else is inconveniencing themselves."

Second, there is evidence that it helps to *rearrange rewards and costs*. For example, many companies are tempted to pollute because it saves them money and increases profits. To reverse the situation, a pollution tax could be levied so that it would cost more, not less, for a business to pollute. Likewise, incentives could be offered for responsible behavior. An example is the rebates offered by governments for installing insulation or buying energy-efficient appliances or electric cars (Schmuck & Vlek, 2003). Similarly, electricity utilities have begun to offer electricity at lower prices during periods of low demand. Savvy consumers can save money by, say, running their dishwasher in the evening rather than during the day. Finally, it's important to remove barriers (another type of cost) and make it easy for people to engage in environmentally responsible behavior. A good example is cities that offer curbside pickup of household recyclables free of charge, or businesses that help customers recycle old computers, printers, and the like. On campus, simply putting marked containers in classrooms is also helpful (Duffy & Verges, 2009).

Third, *persuasive advertising campaigns and initiatives* can be helpful in motivating people to conserve resources or recycle. Effective appeals may be based on self-interest (cost savings), the collective good (protecting one's own children and future generations), or simply an intrinsic motivation to take better care of the planet (Pelletier, Baxter, & Huta, 2011; Winter & Koger, 2010). Unfortunately, even people who believe that recycling is worthwhile are likely to regard it as a boring task. Thus, people are most likely to begin and continue recycling if messages also emphasize the sense of satisfaction that will come from contributing to the environment (Nigbur, Lyons, & Uzzell, 2010).

sunsetman/Shutterstock.com

People are much more likely to recycle if proper attention is given to psychological factors that promote recycling behavior. For example, these recycling bins are designed to make efficient recycling easier.

To date, there have been many different types of media campaigns designed to get people engaged. The widespread use of social media, in particular, is beginning to allow more customized approaches. For example, **social norms marketing** seeks to change attitudes by making social norms more explicit in order to encourage compliance. What would you do if you received a tweet or Facebook post that read, "Seventy-seven percent of your neighbors report taking shorter showers to conserve energy" (Miller & Prentice, 2016, p. 340)? A more precisely targeted approach, **personalized normative feedback**, seeks to change attitudes by comparing feedback about individual performance with the relevant social norms. A sample tweet or post might be "Did you know that you use more water every week than eighty percent of your neighbors?" Both of these social norms-based approaches are proving to be powerful new tools in the battle to encourage greater environmental responsibility (Ferraro, Miranda, & Price, 2011; Ferraro & Price, 2013; Miller & Prentice, 2016).

Fourth and finally, environmental psychologists have found that effective solutions to environmental problems must include *feedback* about our efforts (McCalley, de Vries, & Midden, 2011; Winter & Koger, 2010). Fortunately, many of the same technologies that provide feedback also allow individuals greater control over their conservation efforts. For example, programmable home thermostats and energy-saving settings on appliances and electronics make it possible for conservation-conscious consumers to control their energy consumption more precisely. Psychologists have also demonstrated that giving families and work groups daily feedback about their use of gas or electricity (using smart meters, for instance) can result in lower energy bills (Carrico & Riemer, 2011). Other research suggests that recycling typically increases when families, work groups, dorms, and the like are given feedback on a periodic basis about how much they recycled (Kim, Oah, & Dickinson, 2005). In one study, signs were placed on recycling containers on a college campus. The signs showed how many aluminum cans had been deposited in the previous week. This simple procedure increased recycling by an astonishing 65 percent (Larson, Houlihan, & Goernert, 1995).

Effective feedback about overall resource use is becoming widely available as several organizations provide ecological footprint calculators—websites that allow individuals to calculate (and therefore track) their individual overall resource consumption (Global Footprint Network, 2017a). Similarly, with growing public concern over global warming, many people can now calculate their individual **carbon footprint**, or the volume of greenhouse gases their individual consumption adds to the atmosphere (The Nature Conservancy, 2016).

Conclusion

We have room here only to hint at the creative and highly useful work being done in environmental psychology. Although many environmental problems remain, it is encouraging to see that behavioral solutions exist for at least some of them. Surely, creating and maintaining healthy environments is one of the major challenges facing coming generations (Des Jardins, 2013; Lertzman, 2015).

Reflective Practice

Environmental Psychology

1. Although male rats in Calhoun's crowded animal colony became quite pathological, female rats continued to behave in a relatively normal fashion. T or F?
2. Milgram believed that many city dwellers prevent attentional overload by limiting themselves to superficial social contacts. T or F?
3. Performing an environmental ________________ might be a good prelude to redesigning college classrooms to make them more comfortable and conducive to learning.
4. Using smart meters and ecological footprint calculators to provide feedback is one effective approach for bringing about energy conservation. T or F?
5. So far, the most successful approach for bringing about energy conservation is to add monetary penalties to monthly bills for excessive consumption. T or F?

THINK CRITICALLY

6. Many of the most damaging changes to the environment being caused by humans will not be felt until sometime in the future. How does this complicate the problem of preserving environmental quality?

SELF-REFLECT

- What forms of territorial behavior are you aware of in your own actions?
- Have you ever experienced a stressful level of crowding? Was density or control the key factor?
- Have you ever calculated your carbon footprint? Why not try it? You might be surprised by what you find.
- Would it get you more involved in conservation to be given regular feedback about your conservation activities? About those of your social reference groups?

Answers: 1. F 2. T 3. assessment 4. T 5. F 6. Learning theory tells us that delay of consequences (rewards, benefits, costs, and punishments) tends to reduce their impact on immediate behavior.

Social dilemma A social situation that tends to provide immediate rewards for actions that will have undesired effects in the long run.

Tragedy of the commons A social dilemma in which individuals, each acting in his or her immediate self-interest, overuse a scarce group resource.

Social norms marketing A persuasion technique that seeks to change attitudes by making explicit relevant social norms in order to foster compliance.

Personalized normative feedback A persuasion technique that seeks to change attitudes by comparing feedback about individual performance with relevant social norms in order to foster compliance.

Carbon footprint The volume of greenhouse gases individual consumption adds to the atmosphere.

18.3 Legal, Community, and Sports Psychology

GATEWAYS LEARNING OUTCOMES:
After reading this section, you will be able to:

18.3.1 Explain the role of legal, community, and sports psychologists

18.3.2 Outline four techniques that may be used in scientific jury selection

18.3.3 Describe four factors that impair jurors' ability to reach an impartial verdict

18.3.4 Explain the central ideas that underlie community psychology

18.3.5 Explain what sports psychologists have learned about the development of motor skills and achieving peak performance

In this section, we take a very brief tour of three other areas in which psychological scientists make important contributions: legal psychology, community psychology, and sports psychology.

Legal Psychology

Legal psychology refers to the application of psychological science to the legal system and covers the ways in which the law impacts people, as well as how people influence the law (Cronin, 2019; see ▲ Table 18.4 for a list of topics of interest to legal psychologists). For example, legal psychologists might apply what has been learned about human development, memory, and cognition to questions about eyewitness testimony or children's ability to serve as reliable witnesses. A related area of study—**forensic psychology**—is focused more specifically on the clinical aspects of the law, including competence evaluations for criminals and older adults, counseling both victims of crime and people in prisons, profiling criminals, and helping to select and train police cadets (Greene & Heilbrun, 2014; Wrightsman & Fulero, 2009). In this section, we focus narrowly on what legal psychologists have learned about juries, including how jury selection and behavior can impact the outcome of a trial.

▲ Table 18.4 Topics of Special Interest to Legal Psychologists

Arbitration	Juror attitudes
Attitudes toward law	Jury decisions
Bail setting	Jury selection
Capital punishment	Mediation
Conflict resolution	Memory
Criminal personality	Parole board decisions
Diversion programs	Police selection
Effects of parole	Police stress
Expert testimony	Police training
Eyewitness testimony	Polygraph accuracy
Forensic hypnosis	Sentencing decisions
Insanity plea	White-collar crime

Jury Selection

In many cases, the composition of a jury has a major effect on the verdict of a trial (Kovera & Cutler, 2013). Before a trial begins, opposing attorneys are allowed to disqualify potential jurors who may be biased. For example, a person who knows anyone connected with the trial can be excluded. Beyond this, attorneys try to use jury selection to remove people who may cause trouble for them and keep people who are more likely to return the verdict they are seeking (Morrison, DeVaul-Fetters, & Gawronski, 2016). For instance, juries composed of women are more likely to vote for conviction in child sexual assault trials (Eigenberg et al., 2012; Golding et al., 2007).

Only a limited number of potential jurors can be excused, however. As a result, many attorneys ask psychologists for help in identifying people who will favor or harm their efforts. In **scientific jury selection**, social science principles are applied to the process of choosing a jury (Lieberman, 2011). At least four techniques may be used. As a first step, *demographic information* may be collected for each juror. Much can be guessed by knowing a juror's age, sex, race, occupation, education, political affiliation, religion, and socioeconomic status. Most of this information is available from public records, including social media (Nance, 2015). In the well-publicized case of O. J. Simpson (who was accused of brutally killing his wife and her friend), for example, a majority of African Americans thought that Simpson was innocent during the early stages of the trial. In contrast, the majority of European Americans thought that he was guilty. The opinions of both groups changed little over the course of the year-long trial. (Simpson was eventually acquitted, but he later lost a civil lawsuit brought by the victims' families.) The fact that emerging evidence and arguments had little effect on what people believed shows how the demographic characteristics of the jury may be influential in deciding the outcome of a trial (Cohn et al., 2009).

To supplement demographic information, a second technique is to carry out a *community survey* to find out how local citizens feel about the case. The assumption is that jurors probably have attitudes similar to people with backgrounds like their own. Although talking with potential jurors outside the courtroom is not permitted, other information networks are available. For instance, a psychologist may interview relatives, acquaintances, neighbors, and coworkers of potential jurors.

Third, psychologists also often watch for *authoritarian personality* traits in potential jurors. Authoritarians tend to believe that punishment is effective, and they are more likely to vote for conviction (Devine et al., 2001). (■ Authoritarian personality traits are also related to ethnocentrism and racial prejudice. See Section 17.3.) A fourth strategy that may be employed during scientific jury selection is to have the psychologist observe potential jurors' *nonverbal behavior.* The idea here is to try to learn from body language which side the person favors.

The use of scientific jury selection raises some troubling ethical questions, because while wealthy clients can afford it, most people cannot. Attorneys, of course, can't be blamed for trying to improve their odds of winning a case. And because both sides help select jurors, the net effect in most instances is probably a more balanced jury. At its worst, jury analysis leads to unjust verdicts. At its best, it helps to identify and remove only people who would be highly biased (Kovera & Cutler, 2013).

Death-Qualified Juries

In the United States, murder trials may require a special jury—one made up of people who are not opposed to the death penalty. That way, jurors are capable of voting for the death penalty if they think that it is justified.

Death-qualified juries may be a necessity for the death penalty to have meaning. However, psychologists have discovered that the makeup of such juries tends to be biased. Specifically, death-qualified juries are likely to contain a disproportionate number of people who are male, white, high income, conservative, and authoritarian. Given the same facts, jurors who favor the death penalty are more likely to read criminal intent into a defendant's actions and are much more likely than average to convict a defendant (Butler, 2007; Summers, Hayward, & Miller, 2010).

Could death-qualified juries be too willing to convict? It is nearly impossible to say how often the bias inherent in death-qualified juries results in bad verdicts. However, the possibility that some innocent persons have been executed may be one of the inevitable costs of using death as the ultimate punishment.

Jury Behavior

When a case goes to trial, jurors must listen to days or weeks of testimony and then decide guilt or innocence. How do they reach their decision? Psychological scientists use **mock juries**, or simulated juries, to probe such questions (Bornstein, 2017). In some mock juries, volunteers are simply given written evidence and arguments to read before making a decision. Others watch videotaped trials staged by actors. Either way, studying the behavior of mock juries helps us understand what determines how real jurors vote (Pezdek, Avila-Mora, & Sperry, 2010).

The findings of jury research are unsettling, suggesting at least four challenges to reaching a fair verdict (Peoples et al., 2012). First, studies show that *jurors are rarely able to put aside their biases, attitudes, and values* while making a decision (Buck & Warren, 2010; Stawiski, Dykema-Engblade, & Tindale, 2012). For example, appearance can be unduly influential. Jurors are less likely to find attractive defendants guilty (on the basis of the same evidence) than unattractive defendants. In one mock jury study, defendants were less likely to be convicted if they were wearing eyeglasses than if they were not. Presumably, eyeglasses imply intelligence, and hence, that the defendant wouldn't do anything as foolish as commit the crime for which she was on trial (Brown, Henriquez, & Groscup, 2008).

Jane Flavell Collins/Newscom/European Pressphoto Agency/BOSTON/MASSACHUSETTS/UNITED STATES

A jury of his peers recommended the death sentence after convicting Dzhokhar Tsarnaev on all 30 counts related to the Boston Marathon bombings. Demonstrating the high emotional stakes involved in death penalty cases, some jurors wept when the sentence was read.

A second problem is that jurors are not very good at *separating the evidence from their perceptions of the people involved in the trial,* including the defendant, attorneys, witnesses, and judge. For example, if complex scientific evidence is presented, jurors tend to be swayed more by the expertise of the witness than by the evidence itself (Cooper, Bennett, & Sukel, 1996; Hans et al., 2011). Similarly, today's jurors place too much confidence in DNA evidence because crime-solving programs such as *CSI* make it seem completely objective and simple to obtain (Meyers, 2007).

Third, jurors tend to *inappropriately incorporate information from pretrial publicity into their deliberations,* often without being aware that it has happened (Ruva, McEvoy, & Bryant, 2007). Similarly, the jurors' final verdict is influenced by inadmissible evidence, such as mention of a defendant's prior conviction. When jurors are told to ignore information that slips out in court (even if it is "stricken from the record"), they find it very hard to do so. A related problem occurs when jurors take into account the severity of the punishment that a defendant faces (Sales & Hafemeister, 1985). Jurors are not supposed to let this affect their verdict, but many do.

Legal Psychology The study of the psychological and behavioral dimensions of the legal system.

Forensic Psychology The study of clinical aspects of the law.

Scientific jury selection Using social science principles to choose members of a jury.

Mock jury A group that realistically simulates a courtroom jury.

A fourth and final area of difficulty arises because *jurors usually cannot suspend judgment* until all the evidence is presented. Typically, they form an opinion early in the trial. It then becomes difficult for them to fairly judge evidence that contradicts that opinion. (■ Remember the power of confirmation bias from Section 1.1?)

Problems like these are troubling in a legal system that prides itself on fairness. However, all is not lost. The more severe the crime and the more clear-cut the evidence, the less a jury's quirks affect the verdict. Although it is far from perfect, the jury system works reasonably well in most cases (Greene & Heilbrun, 2014).

Community Psychology

When Nikolas Cruz walked into Marjory Stoneman Douglas school in Parkland, Florida with a semi-automatic rifle, it took him only six minutes to kill three members of staff and fourteen students. In the days that followed, there was a great deal of discussion about this tragedy, and what to do about the problem of gun-related violence in schools. Two clear approaches emerged as people discussed and debated the events that had transpired in Florida. The first assumes an *individual* focus. In the case of Parkland, this approach would involve looking back in time and examining Nikolas Cruz's behavior (for example, his disturbing posts on social media) and state of mental health, and then questioning whether he should have been referred for therapy, and what type of therapy might have been helpful (■ see Chapter 15). Often, the strategies and therapies that define this approach are *reactive*; that is, they are adopted *after* a problem has been identified. In addition, this model often views our ability to change as dependent on the expertise of professionals, including clinicians and medical doctors.

The second approach to the issue of gun violence in schools is very different and is best characterized by the surviving students. Many of these young people did not respond with quiet grief and fear, as one might expect after witnessing such a tragedy. Instead, they stood up and loudly demanded political change. With the support of many Americans, students marched and held rallies, they took to social media using the tag #NeverAgain, and they met with politicians and journalists. Each time, they spoke powerfully about the need to change state and federal laws in ways that would prevent gun-related violence in the future. This second approach, with its focus on *communities* rather than individuals, is in keeping with a branch of psychology referred to as community psychology.

Community psychologists are focused on proactive efforts that improve communities, rather than reacting to problems after the fact. They also press the idea that community members do not always need "experts" to tell them how to bring about change.

From Individuals to Societies

Community psychology is a relatively new area of study whose beginnings in the United States can be traced back to the 1960s. At that time, a group of clinical psychologists gathered together and discussed their shared interest in developing an activist approach to health-related challenges—one that would move beyond traditional psychotherapy (Bond, Serrano-García, Keys, & Shinn, 2017). Given the roots of community psychology, it won't surprise you to learn that psychologists who work in this area tackle health-related challenges quite differently than clinicians. First, their efforts are aimed at moving beyond individuals to *influence health at the level of groups*, including organizations, neighborhoods, and societies. Second, they *emphasize cultural, economic, environmental, and political forces* that shape our health, instead of focusing simply on social factors. Third, community psychology is squarely *focused on empowering people to bring about changes* that they wish to see, rather than waiting for experts to step in on their behalf. And finally, the field is defined by the need to be *proactive* rather than reactive, emphasizing the benefits that come from preventing health-related problems rather than trying to manage them afterward.

Over the past 50 years, community psychologists have participated in a number of successful initiatives that have had a positive impact on the health and well-being of people around the world. In the United States, for example, community psychologists played an important role in large-scale national changes related to smoking and the use of tobacco (Pokorny, Jason, & Schoeny, 2003). But there are many smaller-scale initiatives that have also benefitted from the input of community psychologists. For example, community psychologists have worked on initiatives that promote environmental awareness and sustainability (Browne & Bishop, 2011; Sun & Han, 2018) and rural development (Landini, 2015), as well as positive experiences in schools (McMahon, 2018), healthcare facilities (Franz, Skinner, & Murphy, 2017), and the military (O'Neal, Mallette, & Mancini, 2018). And these are just a small number of the areas where community psychologists are making a difference—each day, they make important contributions to efforts that are aimed at improving the health of communities across the country and around the globe. ▲ Table 18.5 provides some insight into the topics of interest to community psychologists.

How do community psychologists contribute to these efforts? That's a great question! In some cases, they get involved in designing, implementing, and evaluating community-based programs. This might involve working with non-profit agencies, governments, and other organizations, helping them to establish what approaches are most likely to be successful in achieving their goals, putting those plans into action, and measuring success in

▲ Table 18.5 Topics of Special Interest to Community Psychologists

Arbitration	Juror attitudes
Attitudes toward law	Jury decisions
Bail setting	Jury selection
Capital punishment	Mediation
Conflict resolution	Memory
Criminal personality	Parole board decisions
Diversion programs	Police selection
Effects of parole	Police stress
Expert testimony	Police training
Eyewitness testimony	Polygraph accuracy
Forensic hypnosis	Sentencing decisions
Insanity plea	White-collar crime

ways that make sense in that situation. They can also work as consultants, assisting groups in their efforts to promote positive community-based change. And finally, many community psychologists work in colleges and universities helping to educate the next generation of community activists—people just like you!

Sports Psychology

Sports psychology is the study of the behavioral dimensions of sports performance (Cox, 2012; Davis, 2016). On a broad scale, psychological research has provided valuable information about how sports can impact human functioning in the general population. For example, one study of adolescents found a link between sports participation and physical self-esteem that, in turn, was linked with overall self-esteem (Bowker, 2006). In other research, psychologists have learned that the benefits of sport are most likely to occur when competition, rejection, criticism, and the "one-winner mentality" are minimized. When working with children in sports, it is also important to emphasize fair play, intrinsic rewards, self-control of emotions, independence, and self-reliance. Adults, of course, also may benefit from sports through reduced stress, better self-image, and improved general health (Khan et al., 2012; Williams, 2010). Runners, for instance, experience lower levels of tension, anxiety, fatigue, and depression than are found in the nonrunning population.

Psychological Science and Elite Athletes

As almost all serious athletes soon learn, peak performance requires more than physical training. Mental and emotional "conditioning" also are important. Recognizing this fact, many teams, both professional and amateur, now include psychologists on their staff. On any given day, a sports psychologist might teach an athlete how to relax, how to ignore distractions, or how to cope with emotions. The sports psychologist also might provide personal counseling for handling performance-lowering stresses and conflicts (LeUnes, 2008). Other psychologists are interested in studying factors that affect athletic achievement, such as skill learning, the personality profiles of champion athletes, the effects of spectators, and related topics (▲ Table 18.6). In short, sports psychologists seek to understand and improve sports performance and to enhance the benefits of participating in sports (Cox, 2012; Davis, 2016). In this section, we focus on three areas studied by sports psychologists: task analysis, development of motor skills, and achieving peak performance.

▲ Table 18.6 Topics of Special Interest to Sports Psychologists

Achievement motivation	Hypnosis
Athletic personality	Mental practice
Athletic task analysis	Motor learning
Coaching styles	Peak performance
Competition	Positive visualization
Control of attention	Self-regulation
Coping strategies	Skill acquisition
Emotions and performance	Social facilitation
Exercise and mental health	Stress reduction
Goal setting	Team cooperation
Group (team) dynamics	Training procedures

Task Analysis

An ability to do detailed studies of complex skills has been one of the major contributions of sports psychologists. In a **task analysis**, sports skills are broken into subparts so that key elements can be identified and taught (Hewit, Cronin, & Hume, 2012). Such methods are an extension of techniques first used for job analyses, as described previously in this chapter.

For example, it doesn't take much to be off target in the Olympic sport of marksmanship. The object here is to hit a bulls-eye the size of a dime at the end of a 165-foot-long shooting range. Nevertheless, an average of 50 bulls-eyes out of 60 shots is not unusual in international competition (prone position). What does it take—beyond keen eyes and steady hands—to achieve such

Community psychology A branch of psychology that goes beyond an individual focus and integrates social, cultural, economic, political, environmental, and international influences to promote positive change, health, and empowerment at individual and systemic levels.

Sports psychology The study of the psychological and behavioral dimensions of sports performance.

Task analysis Breaking complex skills into their subparts.

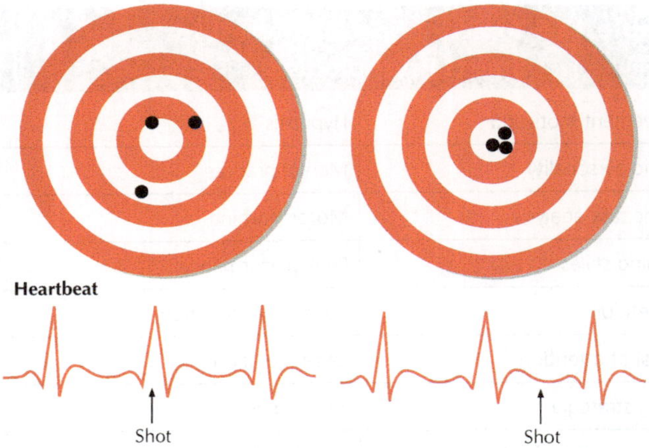

Figure 18.4 Accuracy of target shooting as a function of heartbeats. The target on the left shows what happens when a shooter fires during the heart's contraction. Higher scores, as shown by the three shots on the right, are more likely when shots are taken between heartbeats. (Adapted from Pelton, 1983.)

accuracy? The answer is surprising. Sports psychologists have found that top shooters consistently squeeze the trigger *between* heartbeats (Figure 18.4). Apparently, the tiny tremor induced by a heartbeat is enough to send the shot astray (Pelton, 1983). Without careful psychological study, it is doubtful that this element of marksmanship would have been identified. Now that its importance is known, competitors have begun to use various techniques—from relaxation training to biofeedback—to steady and control their heartbeats. In the future, the best shooters may be those who set their sights on mastering their hearts.

Development of Motor Skills

Successful task analysis often helps with the development of motor skills (Hodges & Williams, 2012). A **motor skill** is a series of actions molded into a smooth and efficient performance. Typing, walking, pole-vaulting, shooting baskets, playing golf, driving a car, writing, and skiing are all motor skills.

Boston Globe/Getty Images

A task analysis by psychologists has shown that umpires can call balls and strikes more accurately if they stand behind the outside corner of home plate. This position supplies better height and distance information because umpires can see pitches pass in front of the batter (Ford et al., 1999).

A basketball player may never make exactly the same shot twice in a game. This makes it almost impossible to practice every shot that might occur. How, then, do athletes become skillful? Typically, athletic performances involve learning *motor programs*. A **motor program** is a mental plan or model of what a skilled movement should be like. Motor programs allow an athlete—or a person simply walking across a room—to perform complex movements that fit changing conditions. If, for example, you have learned a "bike-riding" motor program, you can easily ride bicycles of different sizes and types on a large variety of surfaces.

Throughout life, you will face the challenge of learning new motor skills. How can psychology make your learning more effective? Studies of sports skills suggest that you should keep the following six points in mind for optimal skill learning (Karageorgis & Terry, 2011; Williams, 2010):

1. Begin by observing and imitating a *skilled model*. Modeling provides a good mental picture of the skill. At this point, try simply to grasp a visual image of the skilled movement.
2. Learn *verbal rules* to back up motor learning. Such rules are usually most helpful in the early phases of skill learning. When first learning cross-country skiing, for example, it is helpful to say, "left arm, right foot, right arm, left foot." Later, as a skill becomes more automated, internal speech may actually get in the way.
3. Practice should be as *lifelike* as possible, so artificial cues and responses do not become a part of the skill. A competitive diver should practice on the board, not on a trampoline. If you want to learn to ski, try to practice on snow, not straw.
4. Get *feedback* from a mirror, videotape, coach, or observer. Whenever possible, get someone experienced in the skill to direct attention to *correct responses* when they occur.
5. When possible, it is better to practice *natural units* rather than breaking the task into artificial parts. When learning to type, it is better to start with real words rather than nonsense syllables.
6. Research has shown that **mental practice**, or merely imagining a skilled performance, can aid learning. This technique seems to help by refining motor programs. Although mental practice is not superior to actual practice, it can be a powerful adjunct to actual practice (Caliari, 2008; Frank, Land, & Schack, 2016; Smith & Wakefield, 2016).

Achieving Peak Performance

One of the most interesting topics in sports psychology is the phenomenon of peak performance. During **peak performance**, physical, mental, and emotional states are harmonious and optimal (Bourne & Healy, 2014). Many athletes report episodes during which they felt almost as if they were in a trance. The experience also has been called *flow* because the athlete becomes one with his or her performance and flows with it. At such times, athletes experience intense concentration, detachment, a lack of fatigue and pain, a subjective slowing of time, and feelings of unusual power and control (Dietrich & Stoll, 2010; Hartley, 2012). It is at just such times that "personal bests" tend to occur.

A curious aspect of flow is that it cannot be forced to happen. In fact, if a person stops to think about it, the flow state goes away. Psychologists are now seeking to identify conditions that facilitate peak performance and the unusual mental state that usually accompanies it (Harmison, 2011).

Even though flow may be an elusive state, there is much that athletes and coaches can do mentally to improve performance (Rijken et al., 2016; Williams, 2010). A starting point is to *make sure that their arousal level is appropriate for the task* at hand (■ recall that the Yerkes-Dodson law indicates that the relationship between arousal and performance is an inverted-U shape; Section 10.3).

One way of controlling arousal is to go through a *fixed routine* before each game or event. A second method is to use *imagery and relaxation techniques* to adjust their degree of arousal (LeUnes, 2008). (■ Many of the mental strategies developed by sports psychologists are an extension of stress inoculation techniques. See Section 13.5.) Imaging techniques can be used to focus attention on the athlete's task and to mentally rehearse it beforehand (Gould et al., 2014). For example, golf great Jack Nicklaus "watched a movie" in his head before each shot. Third, during events athletes learn to *use cognitive-behavioral strategies to guide their efforts* in a supportive, positive way (Johnson et al., 2004; ■ see Section 15.3 for more about cognitive-behavioral strategies). For instance, instead of berating herself for being behind in a match, a soccer player could use the time between points to savor a good shot or put an error out of her mind. In general, athletes benefit from avoiding negative, self-critical thoughts that distract them and undermine their confidence (Cox, 2012). Fourth and finally, top athletes tend to use more *self-regulation strategies*, in which they evaluate their performance and make adjustments to keep it at optimum levels (Edwards & Polman, 2012; Puente & Anshel, 2010).

A Look Ahead

Although we have sampled several major areas of applied psychology, by no means are they the only applied specialties. Others that immediately come to mind are human factors psychology, military psychology, and political psychology. The upcoming *Psychology and Your Skill Set* section focuses on *your* transition to work and addresses the steps that you can take to prepare for postgraduate training or a job search.

Reflective Practice

Legal, Community, and Sports Psychology

1. Despite their many limitations, one thing that jurors are good at is setting aside inadmissible evidence. T or F?
2. Which of the following is *not* commonly used by psychologists to aid jury selection?
   a. mock testimony
   b. assessments of authoritarian characteristics
   c. community surveys
   d. demographic data
3. Community psychology emphasizes the importance of economic, environmental, and political forces in relation to our health. T or F?
4. Rather than relying on experts, community psychologists emphasize the importance of empowering ________ to bring about change.
5. Community psychologists stress the importance of being reactive rather than proactive. T or F?
6. The flow experience is closely linked with instances of ________ performance.

THINK CRITICALLY

7. When an athlete follows a set routine before an event, what source of stress has she or he eliminated?

SELF-REFLECT

- What advice would you give a person who is about to serve on a jury if she or he wants to render an impartial decision?
- Consider a social or health-related issue that interests you. If you wanted to address this issue in your community, how might you use what you know about community psychology to approach this problem?
- How could you apply the concepts of task analysis, mental practice, and peak performance to a sport in which you are interested?

Answers: 1. F 2. a 3. T 4. people 5. F 6. peak 7. Stress is reduced when a person feels in control of a situation (see Section 13.2). Following a routine helps athletes maintain a sense of order and control so that they are not excessively aroused when the time comes to perform.

18.4 Psychology and Your Skill Set: Career Preparation

GATEWAYS LEARNING OUTCOME:
After reading this section, you will be able to:

18.4.1 Create a plan that will allow you to begin the process of preparing for a rewarding career

If you've been reading this textbook as a first-year student, chances are that the end of your degree still seems a long way off and worrying about securing a job is probably the last thing on your mind. The reality, though, is that it's never too early to start preparing for the steps that will follow graduation.

Motor skill A series of actions molded into a smooth and efficient performance.

Motor program A mental plan or model that guides skilled movement.

Mental practice Imagining a skilled performance to aid learning.

Peak performance A performance during which physical, mental, and emotional states are harmonious and optimal.

Rawpixel.com/Shutterstock.com

Whether you think you will pursue additional education or look for work, it's often the case that your degree is only one of the things that will be of interest to the people evaluating your application. Many employers are interested in hiring people with relevant experience, even for entry-level jobs: They want to know that you have the *skills* that are needed to be successful, as well as a good understanding of the facts and theories that have been presented in your textbooks. The same is often true for postgraduate programs, where skills such as communication, critical thinking, and the ability to work with others are essential. As a result, it's important to start thinking in advance about building your skill set so that you will be in a strong position to be competitive with your applications, and to distinguish yourself from others.

What's the best way to do this? There are a number of things that you can do while you're at college that will assist you in making an informed decision about a career path that you'll find rewarding. Below we provide a number of suggestions for getting you started. Because the process of building the skills that you'll need can be time consuming, we can't emphasize enough the importance of starting early.

Investigate Potential Career Paths Now

At this stage of your search, you should definitely make use of *on-campus resources* such as a career services office, but the *Internet* can also be a rich source of information about potential jobs. Some of the following sites are useful, though not all of them are exclusively for psychology majors:

- careersinpsychology.org
- apa.org/action/careers
- onetonline.org
- insidecareerinfo.com

As you review information about potential careers, some questions that you should be asking yourself include:

- What does a typical day look like? What are the main tasks that would occupy your time? Ask yourself whether the job looks like it will be a good fit for you in terms of your interests, values, and personality.
- What qualifications are needed for this job? Where can these be obtained, how long will it take, and how much is it likely to cost? Are internships available?
- What is the demand like for this particular career—will there be many jobs available when you finish your education? And is the demand greater in some areas of the country than others?
- What kind of compensation can you expect? Are there working conditions (e.g., weekend work, extensive travel) that you should be aware of? It's important to get a clear sense of whether this job will provide you with the kind of lifestyle that you'd like to have.

You can learn a great deal about particular jobs by searching career-relevant websites, but another way to gather information is to engage in *informational interviews.* Informational interviews are very different from a typical employment interview, because their sole purpose is not to land you a job but rather to allow you to gather job-related information from someone who is currently employed in a field that's of interest to you (Fiske, 2015). Typically, you would make contact with this person via email and set up a time to speak to them for a maximum of 20 to 30 minutes (either in person, on the phone, or by videoconference).

While it's not a formal interview for a job, you should nevertheless carry yourself in a very professional way during an informational interview: Email correspondence should have a formal, businesslike tone and be free of errors. Do some research on the job prior to the interview. Write out and rehearse your questions ahead of time, and dress professionally. Use your time efficiently, and do not go over the agreed-upon amount of time. And don't forget that afterward, it's always a good idea to follow up with a note of thanks (Hettich & Landrum, 2014).

Find Out About Necessary Skills

We've discussed several career-related skills in the *Psychology and Your Skill Set* sections at the end of every chapter of this book. One helpful way of organizing these skills in your mind is to think about them in terms of Five Cs:

- *Communication* obviously includes your oral and written skills (■ see Section 4.7). But don't forget that nonverbal communication is also important. People who are skilled at nonverbal communication are very aware of their own body language and tone of voice, and how those things may be interpreted by the people around them. They are also sensitive to the nonverbal cues of others, "reading" signals that might indicate someone is upset, bored, confused, or enthusiastic. In this respect, nonverbal communication is closely linked to emotional intelligence (■ see Section 9.6).

- *Critical thinking* skills are wide ranging, and include recognizing problems, evaluating the value and reliability of information (information literacy; ■ see Section 1.3), and developing or assessing potential solutions. Critical thinking also includes the ability to think about issues from multiple points of view, as well as your metacognitive skills. You may recall that metacognition refers to your ability to monitor your own knowledge and performance, and to recognize when you might need additional information, or when you might need to change your strategy to accomplish a goal (■ see Section 5.5).
- *Collaboration* skills are those that relate to your ability to work with others. They include broad skills such as teamwork (■ see Section 16.4) and leadership skills (■ see Section 12.5), but as we mentioned in those sections, strong teamwork and leadership abilities depend on a host of other skills, such as integrity (■ see Section 3.5) and the ability to work with diverse others (■ see Section 17.4).
- *Creativity* is an important skill set in many jobs, even those that are not closely connected to the arts. Because creativity is so closely linked to innovation and problem solving (■ see Section 8.5), it is highly valued by employers in many different fields.
- *Character* is a broad category of skills that include a number of personal characteristics that are important for both your personal and professional life. We have discussed a number of them in the *Psychology and Your Skill Set* sections, including self-regulation (■ see Section 2.5), working with diverse others (■ see Section 17.4), and integrity (■ see Section 3.5).

Assess Your Current Skill Set and Your Characteristics

Once you have established what skills you are likely to need for your chosen career path, it's a good idea to do an assessment of your own skills and consider where the gaps are in relation to what's needed. Many tools are available online and through most campus career services centers. Remember that if you rate yourself as being high on a particular skill, you should be able to back up your evaluation with experiences you've had that have allowed you to develop them (Cook, 2013). Students are often inclined to think about their work-related experiences when they think about skill development, but don't forget that course-based assignments and activities can also be valuable. For example, giving presentations or writing papers that have been favorably evaluated by your instructors could be used as evidence of your communication abilities.

Aside from your skills, you should also consider evaluating aspects of your character that are likely to have an influence on your satisfaction with a particular career path (Bolles, 2019). Your values and personality traits are important here, as are the kinds of people whose company you enjoy. The surroundings in which you feel happiest are also important to consider. For example, are you most comfortable working in an organized, structured environment? How do you feel about a high degree of supervision? What about noise level? Flexible hours?

Many students underestimate the importance of these elements of the working environment, focusing instead on issues such as salary and vacation time. However, working with people that you do not like or under conditions that you find challenging will almost certainly make you very unhappy over the long term. When considering potential career paths, then, always think carefully about how well the job will fit with what you know about yourself, and the lifestyle that you hope to have.

Work to Develop and Document Necessary Skills

If there are skills that you feel you will eventually need, but on which you consider yourself to be weak, ask yourself what experiences you could engage in that would help you to build these skills. Consider the possibilities presented by relevant community work and volunteer experiences, as well as opportunities that may be connected to course credit (e.g., service learning courses and study abroad programs). Getting involved in extracurricular activities such as sports teams, campus clubs, and student government may also provide a solid foundation for the development of a variety of skills.

Documenting Key Learning Experiences

Because you'll do many interesting things during the course of your degree, it's important that you begin to record your key learning experiences, and how each one has developed your skills and contributed to your personal growth. You can keep track of them in a career-related journal, or you can document your experiences and skills more formally in a **portfolio**.

While portfolios used to resemble a large scrapbook with printed examples of people's accomplishments and work, they are now increasingly created in a digital format. These newer **e-portfolios** can showcase examples of your work as well as relevant photos, videos, and links to websites (Light, Chen, & Ittelson, 2011). One of the most common e-portfolio platforms is LinkedIn, a professional networking website that is increasingly used by employers to recruit new talent. Users create profiles and build professional connections by following the online activities of other users and companies.

Examine Your Digital Footprint

Aside from providing you with an additional tool to market yourself to prospective employers, e-portfolios also have another benefit: They can help you to begin the process of creating a professional *digital footprint*. The term digital footprint refers to all of the information that is available about you on the Internet. Do you know what you would find if you typed your name and

Portfolio A collection of printed examples of a person's accomplishments and work.

e-Portfolio A digital, rather than hardcopy, collection of printed examples of a person's accomplishments and work.

some basic information about yourself (e.g., your college and the city where you live) into a search engine? For many students, such a search would primarily reveal their participation in social media sites such as Facebook, Twitter, Snapchat, and Instagram. Now ask yourself whether you'd be happy for potential employers to find that information when they carried out this type of online search.

One firm reported that in a study of 275 human resources professionals, more than 75 percent indicated that they actively research potential candidates online. Perhaps more relevant is the fact that of those who carried out Internet-based searches, approximately 70 percent decided *not* to hire someone based on what they found on the web (Cross-Tab, 2010). The moral of the story? Take care to manage your digital footprint, and if you are concerned about any of the hits that are revealed in a Google search about you, then remove those pages and work toward replacing them with web-based content that's more in keeping with what you'd like an employer to see.

We realize that the prospect of moving into the world of work is likely to be a bit intimidating for many students. However, if you start early and take a bit of time during your degree to do some job-based research and planning, you'll put yourself in a strong position to secure an interesting and satisfying career after you graduate. Good Luck!

Reflective Practice

Psychology and Your Skill Set: Career Preparation

1. It's helpful to begin thinking about a potential career early, since developing the necessary skills may take time. T or F?
2. Informational interviews are often used to secure a job in a field of interest to you. T or F?
3. Which of the following is ***not*** one of the skills included in the Five Cs?
   a. communication
   b. creativity
   c. cheerfulness
   d. critical thinking
   e. character
4. It is important to manage your digital footprint carefully because employers are increasingly likely to search for you online to gather information about you. T or F?

THINK CRITICALLY

5. Leadership is a skill that employers often value, but that is difficult to develop in a college classroom or through coursework. What are some activities that you can engage in during your college years that might help you to develop your leadership abilities?

SELF-REFLECT

- What skills do you think you are most likely to need in the career you're planning to pursue?
- What kinds of personality characteristics are likely to be relevant if you want to work in that field?

Answers: 1. T 2. F 3. c 4. T 5. Leadership skills (see also Section 12.5) can often be developed through volunteer or service-learning experiences (e.g., helping to organize a fundraiser for a community-based organization). On-campus activities can also be helpful in developing these skills (e.g., taking on a leadership role in a club or student government). Finally, if the type of leadership that is relevant to your career goals involves mentoring, then consider how you might get involved in an organization that promotes activities of this kind (e.g., working at a summer camp for kids or coaching a team; working for an organization such as Big Brothers/Big Sisters).

CHAPTER IN REVIEW

[ ] Gateways to Applied Psychology

Summary: Gateways Learning Outcomes

18.1 Industrial/Organizational Psychology

18.1.1 Explain the role of industrial/organizational psychologists

Industrial/organizational psychologists enhance quality of work and job satisfaction by studying such topics as organizational structures and culture, personnel issues (e.g., hiring and performance evaluation), and effective leadership.

18.1.2 Define organizational culture, and how it is impacted by hostility in the workplace

Organizational culture refers to the beliefs and values that characterize an organization. It is compromised by hostile actions such as "desk rage" and harassment, which can stem from *personality traits* (such as hostility and paranoia), *job-related stresses* (such as feeling that one has been treated unfairly), *perceived threats* to one's self-esteem, *work-related conflicts* with others, and *economic pressures* that organizations face.

18.1.3 Describe how personnel psychologists work to ensure a good fit between people and jobs

To match people with jobs, personnel psychologists combine job analysis with selection procedures, such as gathering biodata, interviewing, giving standardized psychological tests (including intelligence tests and personality tests), and using assessment centers.

18.1.4 Outline two ways in which job satisfaction can be promoted

Job satisfaction influences productivity, absenteeism, morale, employee turnover, and other factors that affect business efficiency. Two factors that promote job satisfaction are *good relationships with coworkers* and *a good fit between work and a person's interests, abilities, needs, and expectations*. Job enrichment and flexible working conditions often improve the fit between work and people's needs and expectations, and consequently enhance job satisfaction.

18.1.5 Distinguish between Theory X, Theory Y, and transformational leadership

Theory X leadership (scientific management) is mostly concerned with work efficiency, and assumes that workers have little motivation, other than wages to meet basic needs, to complete their work. *Theory Y* leadership (human relations approach) emphasizes psychological efficiency and assumes that people have some intrinsic motivation to work because the job meets their higher-level needs for personal growth. *Transformational leadership* seeks to "transform" workers to exceed expectations and look beyond their own self-interests to help the organization compete. Theory Y and transformational methods include shared leadership (participative management), management by objectives, self-managed teams, and quality circles.

18.2 Environmental Psychology

18.2.1 Explain the role of environmental psychologists

Environmental psychologists are interested in the relationship between people and the environment (both physical and social environments), including environmental influences on human behavior and vice versa.

18.2.2 Explain how crowding, overstimulation, and noise affect human behavior, and how these environmental stressors can be managed

Environmental problems such as crowding, overstimulation, and noise are major sources of urban stress. Animal experiments indicate that excessive crowding can be unhealthy. However, human research shows that psychological feelings of crowding do not always correspond to density. Overstimulation (attentional overload) and noise make excessive demands on attention, and can have effects on health (e.g., blood pressure), and psychological variables (e.g., persistence, learned helplessness) as well as skills (reading). In terms of managing these environmental stressors, environmental and architectural psychologists often begin with a careful environmental assessment that allows them to make alterations to interior and exterior spaces that minimize negative effects.

18.2.3 Describe some of the sources of environmental damage, including social dilemmas

Damage to the environment is often caused by governments and corporations, but a great deal of damage is also caused by individuals. In particular, social dilemmas, such as the tragedy of the commons, arise when individuals are enticed into overuse of scarce, shared resources, leading to a reduction in the availability of that resource, or its degradation. In this way, individual consumption has an important influence on the group as a whole.

18.2.4 Outline four solutions that have been put forward to minimize environmental damage

First, it helps if conservation is seen as a *group effort*. Second, it may be useful to *rearrange rewards and costs*, such as levying taxes, offering incentives, and removing barriers to environmentally friendly behavior. Third, people can consider *persuasive advertising campaigns and initiatives* that are based on self-interest (cost savings), the collective good (protecting one's own children and future generations), or intrinsic motivation to take better care of the planet. Fourth, *feedback* about people's efforts should be included in any environmental initiative.

18.3 Legal, Community, and Sports Psychology

18.3.1 Explain the role of legal, community, and sports psychologists

Legal psychologists apply psychological science to the legal system and investigate the relationship between people and the law. Community psychologists focus on communities rather than individuals, particularly the health of groups such as organizations, neighborhoods, and societies. Sports psychologists seek to enhance sports performance and the benefits of sports participation.

18.3.2 Outline four techniques that may be used in scientific jury selection

In scientific jury selection, jurors' *demographic information* (e.g., age, sex, race, occupation, education, political affiliation, religion) can be helpful in predicting their behavior during a court trial. A second technique is to carry out a *community survey* to find out how local citizens feel about the case. Third, psychologists watch for *authoritarian personality* traits in potential jurors. A fourth strategy is to observe potential jurors' *nonverbal behavior.*

18.3.3 Describe four factors that impair jurors' ability to reach an impartial verdict

Research from mock juries shows that jury decisions are far from impartial. Four challenges to reaching a fair verdict include the fact that jurors are *rarely able to put aside their biases, attitudes, and values* while making a decision, they are not very good at *separating evidence from their perceptions of the people involved in the trial*, they tend to *inappropriately incorporate information from pretrial publicity into their deliberations*, and they *usually cannot suspend judgment* until all the evidence is presented.

18.3.4 Explain the central ideas that underlie community psychology

Community psychologists emphasize the cultural, economic, environmental, and political forces that shape our health. A community psychology approach to health empowers people to bring about the changes that they want to see, rather than waiting for experts to step in and help. Community psychology emphasizes the need to be proactive in preventing health problems rather than trying to manage them after-the-fact.

18.3.5 Explain what sports psychologists have learned about the development of motor skills and achieving peak performance

A motor skill is a nonverbal response chain assembled into a smooth performance. Motor skills are guided by internal mental models called motor programs. Motor skills are refined by observing and imitating a *skilled* model, learning *verbal rules* to back up motor learning, practicing under *lifelike conditions*, getting *feedback* (from a mirror, videotape, coach, or observer), practicing *natural units* rather than breaking the task into artificial parts, and engaging in *mental practice* (imagining a skilled performance).

Peak performance is more likely when athletes go through a *fixed routine* before each event, use *imagery and relaxation techniques* to optimize arousal, use *cognitive-behavioral strategies to guide their efforts* in a supportive, positive way, and use *self-regulation strategies* to evaluate performance and make adjustments to keep it at optimum levels.

18.4 Psychology and Your Skill Set: Career Preparation

18.4.1 Create a plan that will allow you to begin the process of preparing for a rewarding career

Begin the process of *researching careers* early in your degree, making use of resources such as your campus career services office, career-related sites on the Internet, and informational interviewing. *Determine the skills that are necessary* for jobs that interest you and assess yourself on these skills. If you believe that you need to develop any of them further to make yourself competitive, consider what types of experiences would help you to do so. Begin to *document your skills* by building a portfolio or e-portfolio. *Manage your digital footprint* carefully. Remove any web-based material about you that you would not want a potential employer to find, and work to create digital content that is professional (e.g., LinkedIn profile, e-portfolio).

Appendix
A Psychologist's Skill Set: Statistical Literacy

Gateway Theme Statistics allow us to summarize the results of psychological studies and draw valid conclusions about behavior.

Chapter Outline

A Stretch for Samantha and Grandma

Samantha almost decided to avoid majoring in psychology when she found out she needed to take a statistics course to graduate. "I want to work with people, not numbers," she insisted to anyone who would listen. But her attitude started to change as she began to get more involved in a research project exploring the effect of stretching exercises on the quality of sleep among older people. After all, her beloved grandma was often troubled by insomnia, and Samantha hoped to use what she learned from her research to advise older adults about how to get a better night's sleep.

Thankfully, Samantha's curiosity about this research question in particular, and human behavior in general, was stronger than her fear of statistics. By the time she got to her third year and began to design research projects and collect data, she understood that the results of psychological studies are often expressed as numbers, which psychologists must summarize and interpret before they have any meaning.

Psychologists use three major types of statistics. **Descriptive statistics** summarize or "boil down" the data collected from research participants so that the results become more meaningful and easier to communicate to others. **Correlational statistics** provide information about the relationship between variables, and can help us in making predictions. Finally, **inferential statistics** are used to extend experimental conclusions from the people in researchers' samples to larger populations. Let's follow Samantha to get an overview of how statistics are used in psychology.

Descriptive statistics Mathematical techniques used to describe and summarize numeric data.

Correlational statistics Mathematical techniques used to indicate the extent to which variables are related to one another.

Inferential statistics Mathematical techniques for extending experimental conclusions from samples to larger populations.

A.1 Descriptive Statistics: Psychology by the Numbers

GATEWAYS LEARNING OUTCOME:
After reading this section you should be able to:

A.1.1 Explain what descriptive statistics are used for, and provide some examples

Statistics bring greater clarity and precision to psychological thought and research (Gravetter & Wallnau, 2017). In fact, it is difficult to make scientific arguments about human behavior without depending on statistics. Let's say that you have completed a study on human behavior. The results seem interesting, but can you really tell what your data reveal just by looking at a jumble of numbers? To get a clear picture of how people behaved, you will probably turn first to descriptive statistics. By summarizing the results of your study, descriptive statistics will help you make sense of what you observed. To see how statistics help, let's begin by considering three basic types of descriptive statistics: *graphical statistics*, measures of *central tendency*, and measures of *variability.*

Graphical Statistics

Graphical statistics present numbers pictorially, so they are easier to visualize. At one point, Samantha got a chance to administer a short questionnaire to measure sleep quality in a group of elderly retirees. She planned to eventually use the scores from this questionnaire to select participants with poor sleep quality for further study. ▲ Table A.1 shows the sleep quality scores she obtained from 100 retirees.

With so much data, it is hard to form an overall picture of the differences in sleep quality. But by using a *frequency distribution*, large amounts of information can be neatly organized and summarized. A **frequency distribution** is made by breaking down the entire range of possible scores into classes (or groups) of equal size (in this case, 20 points). Next, the number of scores falling into each class is recorded. In ▲ Table A.2, Samantha's raw data from ▲ Table A.1 have been condensed into a frequency distribution. Notice how much clearer the pattern of sleep quality scores for the entire group becomes.

▲ **Table A.1 Raw Sleep Quality Scores**

55	86	52	17	61	57	84	51	16	64
22	56	25	38	35	24	54	26	37	38
52	42	59	26	21	55	40	59	25	57
91	27	38	53	19	93	25	39	52	56
66	14	18	63	59	68	12	19	62	45
47	98	88	72	50	49	96	89	71	66
50	44	71	57	90	53	41	72	56	93
57	38	55	49	87	59	36	56	48	70
33	69	50	50	60	35	67	51	50	52
11	73	46	16	67	13	71	47	25	77

▲ **Table A.2 Frequency Distribution of Sleep Quality Scores Class Interval**

Class Interval	Number of Elders
0–19	10
20–39	20
40–59	40
60–79	20
80–99	10

Let's take Samantha's frequency distribution a bit further now. Frequency distributions can also be shown graphically to make them more "visual." A **frequency histogram**, or graph of a frequency distribution, is made by labeling class intervals on the *abscissa* (*x*-axis, or horizontal line) and frequencies (the number of scores in each class) on the *ordinate* (*y*-axis, or vertical line). Next, bars are drawn for each class interval; the height of each bar is determined by the number of scores in each class (● Figure A.1). An alternative way of graphing scores is the more familiar **frequency polygon** (● Figure A.2). Here, points are placed at the center of each class interval to indicate the number of scores. Then the dots are connected by straight lines.

Measures of Central Tendency

Notice in ▲ Table A.2 that more of Samantha's sleep quality scores fall in the range 40–59 than elsewhere. We can show this quite clearly by using measures of **central tendency**; that is, numbers that describe a "typical score" around which other scores fall. You may be familiar

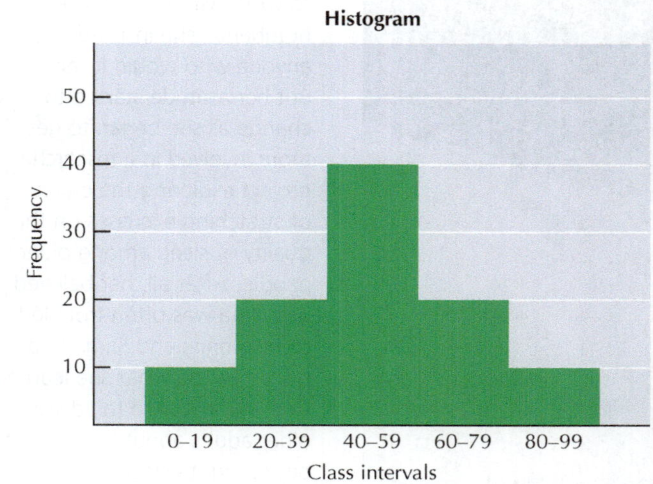

● **Figure A.1 Frequency histogram.** A frequency histogram of the sleep quality scores contained in Table A.2.

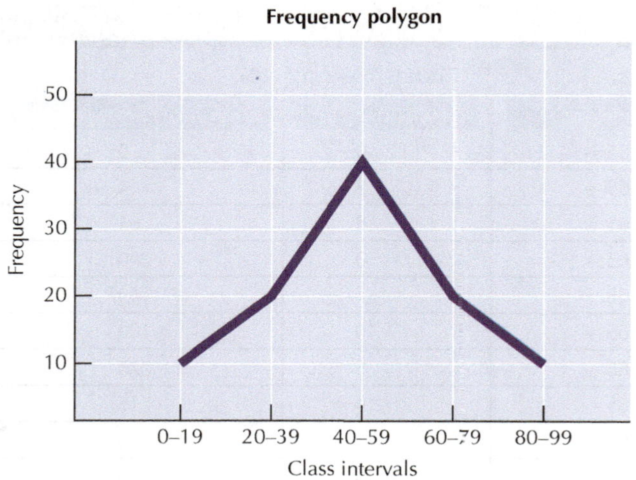

Figure A.2 Frequency polygon. A frequency polygon of the sleep quality scores contained in Table A.2.

with a measure of central tendency called the *mean*, or "average." But as we shall see in a moment, other measures of central tendency can also be used to demonstrate that pattern in Samantha's data.

To illustrate each measure of central tendency, let's work with ▲ Table A.3, which shows the raw data for one of Samantha's preliminary studies. Two small groups of older adults were given the sleep quality questionnaire right after waking up in the morning. The evening before, one group was given an hour of the stretching exercises that Samantha predicted should improve sleep quality. The second group watched television for an hour. Is there a difference in the resulting sleep quality scores between the two groups? It's difficult to tell without looking at measures of central tendency. Here, we'll introduce you to three measures of central tendency: the *mean* (or average), the *median*, and the *mode*.

The Mean

As we noted earlier, one measure of central tendency is the **mean** (or "average score"), which is calculated by adding all the scores for each group and then dividing by the total number of scores. Notice in ▲ Table A.3 that the means reveal a difference between the two groups.

The mean is sensitive to extremely high or low scores in a distribution. For this reason, it is not always the best measure of central tendency. (Imagine how distorted it would be to calculate the mean, or average, yearly incomes from a small sample of people that happened to include a billionaire such as Oprah Winfrey.) In such cases, the middle score in a group of scores—called the *median*—is used instead.

The Median

The **median** is a measure of central tendency that is found by arranging scores from highest to lowest and then selecting the score that falls in the middle. In other words, half the values in a group of scores fall below the median and half fall above it. Consider, for example, the following weights obtained from a small

▲ Table A.3 Raw Sleep Quality Scores After Sleep Preceded by Engaged in Stretching Exercises or Watching Television

Participant 1	Group 1 Stretches	Group 2 Television
1	65	54
2	67	60
3	73	63
4	65	33
5	58	56
6	55	60
7	70	60
8	69	31
9	60	62
10	68	61
Sum	650	540
Mean	65	54
Median	66	60

$$\text{Mean} = \frac{\Sigma X}{N} \text{ or } \frac{\text{sum of all scores, } X}{\text{number of scores}}$$

$$\text{Mean Group 1} = \frac{65 + 67 + 73 + 65 + 58 + 55 + 70 + 69 + 60 + 68}{10} = \frac{650}{10} = 65$$

$$\text{Mean Group 2} = \frac{54 + 60 + 63 + 33 + 56 + 60 + 60 + 31 + 62 + 61}{10} = \frac{540}{10} = 54$$

Median = the middle score or the mean of the two middle scores

Median Group 1 = 55 58 60 65 65 67 68 69 70 73

$$= \frac{65 + 67}{2} = 66$$

Median Group 2 = 31 33 54 56 60 60 60 61 62 63

$$= \frac{60 + 60}{2} = 60$$

Graphical statistics Techniques for presenting numbers pictorially, often by plotting them on a graph.

Frequency distribution A table that divides an entire range of scores into a series of classes and then records the number of scores that fall into each class.

Frequency histogram A graph of a frequency distribution in which the number of scores falling in each class is represented by vertical bars.

Frequency polygon A graph of a frequency distribution in which the number of scores falling in each class is represented by points on a line.

Central tendency The tendency for a majority of scores to fall in the midrange of possible values.

Mean A measure of central tendency calculated by adding a group of scores and then dividing by the total number of scores.

Median A measure of central tendency found by arranging scores from the highest to the lowest and selecting the score that falls in the middle—that is, half the values in a group of scores fall above the median and half fall below it.

class of college students: 105, 111, 123, 126, 148, 151, 154, 162, 182. The median for the group is 148, the middle score. Of course, if there is an even number of scores, there will be no middle score. This problem is handled by averaging the two scores that "share" the middle spot. This procedure yields a single number to serve as the median. (See the bottom panel of ▲ Table A.3.)

The Mode

A final measure of central tendency is the **mode**, which is simply the most frequently occurring score in a group of scores. If you were to take the time to count the scores in ▲ Table A.3, you would find that the mode of Group 1 is 65 and the mode of Group 2 is 60. Although the mode is usually easy to obtain, it can be an unreliable measure, especially in a small group of scores. The mode's advantage is that it gives the score actually obtained by the greatest number of people.

Measures of Variability

Let's say that a researcher discovers two drugs that both lower anxiety in agitated patients. However, let's also assume that one drug consistently lowers anxiety by moderate amounts, whereas the second sometimes lowers it by large amounts, sometimes has no effect, and sometimes may even increase anxiety in patients.

If we look at the average reduction in anxiety that is brought about by each of the drugs, we may find that, overall, there is no difference in the two mean "anxiety reduction" scores. But even if there's no difference between those two average scores, an important difference still exists between the two drugs. As this example shows, it is not enough to simply know the average score in a distribution. Usually, we would also want to know if scores are grouped closely together or scattered widely.

Measures of **variability** provide a single number that tells how "spread out" scores are. When the scores are widely spread (as they would be with the second drug), this number gets larger. When they are close together (as they would be with the first drug), it gets smaller. If you look again at the example in ▲ Table A.3, you will notice that the scores within each group vary widely. How can we show this fact? Two measures of variability can be used to show the "spread" of scores in a data set: the *range* and the *standard deviation.*

The Range

The simplest way to indicate the spread of scores in a data set would be to use the **range**, which is the difference between the highest and lowest scores. In Group 1 of our study, the highest score is 73, and the lowest is 55; thus, the range is 18 (73 − 55 = 18). In Group 2, the highest score is 63, and the lowest is 31; this makes the range 32. Scores in Group 2 are more spread out (that is, they are more variable) than those in Group 1. Unfortunately, one weakness of the range as a measure of variability is that (like the mean) it is very sensitive to very extreme scores.

The Standard Deviation

A better measure of variability is the **standard deviation (SD)**, an index of how much a typical score differs from the mean of a group of scores. To obtain the SD, we find the deviation (or difference) of each score from the mean and then square it (multiply it by itself). These squared deviations are then added and averaged (the total is divided by the number of deviations). Taking the square root of this average yields the SD (▲ Table A.4). Notice again that when we calculate the SD, the variability for Group 1 (5.4) is less than that for Group 2 (where the SD is 11.3).

▲ Table A.4 Computation of the SD

Group 1 Mean = 65

Score Mean	Deviation (d)	Deviation Squared (d^2)
65 − 65 =	0	0
67 − 65 =	2	4
73 − 65 =	8	64
65 − 65 =	0	0
58 − 65 =	−7	49
55 − 65 =	−10	100
70 − 65 =	5	25
69 − 65 =	4	16
60 − 65 =	−5	25
68 − 65 =	3	9
		292

$$SD = \sqrt{\frac{\text{sum of } d^2}{n}} = \sqrt{\frac{292}{10}} = \sqrt{29.2} = 5.4$$

Group 2 Mean = 54

Score Mean	Deviation (d)	Deviation Squared (d^2)
54 − 54 =	0	0
60 − 54 =	6	36
63 − 54 =	9	81
33 − 54 =	−21	441
56 − 54 =	2	4
60 − 54 =	6	36
60 − 54 =	6	36
31 − 54 =	−23	529
62 − 54 =	8	64
61 − 54 =	7	49
		1276

$$SD = \sqrt{\frac{\text{sum of } d^2}{n}} = \sqrt{\frac{1276}{10}} = \sqrt{127.6} = 11.3$$

Standard Scores

A particular advantage of the SD is that it can be used to "standardize" scores in a way that gives them greater meaning. For example, Samantha and her classmate, Rahul, both took psychology midterms, but in different classes. Samantha earned a score of 118, and Rahul scored 110. Who did better? It is impossible to tell for sure without knowing what the average score was on each test and whether Samantha and Rahul scored at the top, middle, or bottom of their classes. We would like to have one number that gives all this information. A number that does this is the *z-score.*

To convert an original score to a **z-score**, we subtract the mean from the score. The resulting number is then divided by the SD for that group of scores. To illustrate, Rahul had a score of 110 in a class with a mean of 100 and an SD of 10. Therefore, his z-score is +1.0 (▲ Table A.5). Samantha's score of 118 came from a class having a mean of 100 and an SD of 18; thus, her z-score is also +1.0 (see ▲ Table A.5). Originally, it looked as if Samantha did better on her midterm than Rahul. But we now see that, relatively speaking, their scores were equivalent. Compared with other students, each was an equal distance above average.

The Normal Curve

When chance events are recorded, we find that some outcomes have a high probability and occur very often, others have a lower probability and occur infrequently, and still others have little probability and occur rarely. As a result, the distribution (or tally) of chance events typically resembles a *normal curve* (● Figure A.3). A **normal curve** is bell-shaped, with a large number of scores in the middle, tapering to very few extremely high and low scores.

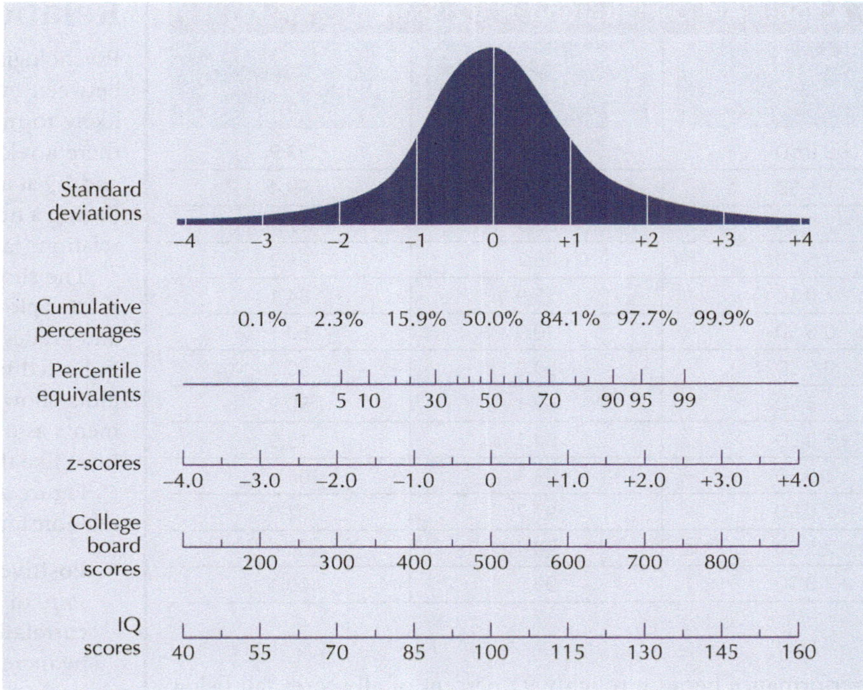

● **Figure A.3 The normal curve.** The normal curve is an idealized mathematical model. However, many measurements in psychology closely approximate a normal curve. The scales shown here show the relationship of SDs, z-scores, and other measures to the curve.

Most psychological traits or events are determined by the action of a large number of factors. Therefore, like chance events, measures of psychological variables tend to roughly match a normal curve. For example, direct measurement has shown such characteristics as height, memory span, and IQ to be distributed approximately along a normal curve. In other words, many people have average height, memory ability, and intelligence. However, as we move above or below average, fewer and fewer people are found.

It is fortunate that so many psychological variables tend to form a normal curve because much is known about the curve. One valuable property concerns the relationship between the SD and the normal curve. Specifically, the SD measures offset proportions of the curve above and below the mean. For example, in Figure A.3, notice that roughly 68 percent of all cases (84.1 − 15.9 = 68.2) fall between one SD above and below the mean (±1 SD); 95 percent of all cases fall between ±2 SD; and 99 percent of the cases can be found within ±3 SD from the mean. This is generally true whether we're talking about IQ scores, memory scores, heights, and many other psychological characteristics.

▲ Table A.6 gives a more complete account of the relationship between z-scores and the percentage of cases found in a particular area of the normal curve. Notice, for example, that 93.3 percent of all cases fall below a z-score of +1.5. A z-score of 1.5 on a test (no matter what the original, or "raw," score was) would be a good

▲ Table A.5 Computation of a z-Score

$z = \frac{X - \bar{X}}{SD}$ = or $\frac{\text{score} - \text{mean}}{\text{standard deviation}}$
Rahul: $z = \frac{110 - 100}{10} = \frac{+10}{10} = +1.0$
Samantha: $z = \frac{118 - 100}{18} = \frac{+18}{18} = +1.0$

Mode A measure of central tendency found by identifying the most frequently occurring score in a group of scores.

Variability The tendency for a group of scores to differ in value. Measures of variability indicate the degree to which a group of scores differs from one another.

Range The difference between the highest and lowest scores in a group of scores.

Standard deviation (SD) A statistical index of how much a typical score differs from the mean of a group of scores.

z-score A number that tells how many standard deviations above or below the mean a score is.

Normal curve A bell-shaped distribution, with a large number of scores in the middle, tapering to very few extremely high and low scores.

▲ Table A.6 Computation of a z-Score

z-Score	Percentage of Area to the Left of This Value	Percentage of Area to the Right of This Value
−3.0 SD	00.1	99.9
−2.5 SD	00.6	99.4
−2.0 SD	02.3	97.7
−1.5 SD	06.7	93.3
−1.0 SD	15.9	84.1
−0.5 SD	30.9	69.1
0.0 SD	50.0	50.0
+0.5 SD	69.1	30.9
+1.0 SD	84.1	15.9
+1.5 SD	93.3	06.7
+2.0 SD	97.7	02.3
+2.5 SD	99.4	00.6
+3.0 SD	99.9	00.1

performance because roughly 93 percent of all scores fall below this mark. Relationships between the SD (or z-scores) and the normal curve do not change. This makes it possible to compare various tests or groups of scores if they come from distributions that are approximately normal, even if they were measured on different scales.

A.2 Correlational Statistics: Seeing Relationships

GATEWAYS LEARNING OUTCOME:
After reading this section you should be able to:

A.2.1 Explain what correlational statistics are used for, and provide an example

As we noted in Chapter 1, many of the statements that psychologists make about behavior do not result from using experimental methods in which variables are controlled by the researcher. Rather, they come from observations about the relationships between measures of existing phenomena. A psychologist might note, for example, that there's a relationship between a couple's socioeconomic status (SES) and the number of children they have: the higher a couple's SES, the fewer children they are likely to have. Another psychologist might observe that grades in high school are related to how well a person is likely to do in college. Or even, as Samantha found, that elders who engage in stretching exercises are better able to sleep. In instances like these where we observe a relationship between measures, we are dealing with a **correlation**—that is, two variables are varying together in some orderly fashion.

Relationships Between Variables

Psychologists are very interested in detecting relationships between events: Are children from single-parent families more likely to misbehave at school? Is wealth related to happiness? Is there a relationship between childhood exposure to the Internet and IQ at age 20? Is the chance of having a heart attack related to having a hostile personality? All of these questions are about correlation (Jackson, 2017).

The simplest way of visualizing a correlation is to construct a **scatter plot**. In a scatter plot, two measures (grades in high school and grades in college, for instance) are obtained. One measure is indicated by the *x*-axis and the second by the *y*-axis. The scatter plots show the intersection (crossing) of each pair of measurements as a single point. Many such measurement pairs give pictures like those shown in ● Figure A.4.

Figure A.4 also shows scatter plots for three basic kinds of relationships between variables (or measures):

- **Positive correlation:** Graphs a, b, and c show *positive relationships* of varying strength. As you can see, in a **positive correlation**, increases in the *X* measure (or score) are matched by increases on the *Y* measure (or score). An example would be finding that higher IQ scores (*X*) are associated with higher college grades (*Y*).

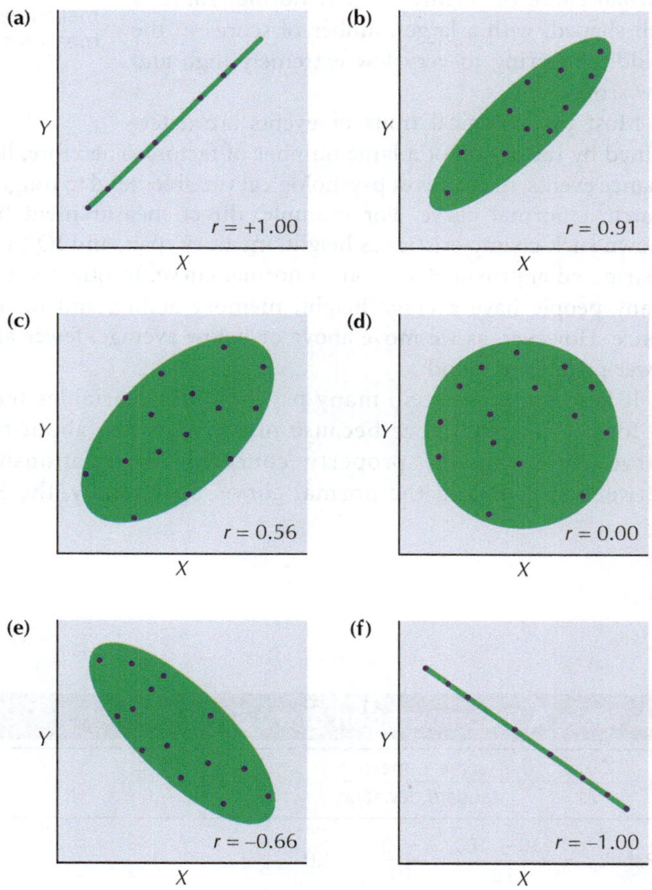

● **Figure A.4 Scatter plots.** Scatter plots showing various degrees of relationship for a positive, zero, and negative correlation.

▲ Table A.7 IQ and Grade Point Average for Computing Pearson *r*

Student No.	IQ (X)	Grade Point Average (Y)	X Score Squared (X^2)	Y Score Squared (Y^2)	X Times Y (XY)
1	110	1.0	12,100	1.00	110.0
2	112	1.6	12,544	2.56	179.2
3	118	1.2	13,924	1.44	141.6
4	119	2.1	14,161	4.41	249.9
5	122	2.6	14,884	6.76	317.2
6	125	1.8	15,625	3.24	225.0
7	127	2.6	16,124	6.76	330.2
8	130	2.0	16,900	4.00	260.0
9	132	3.2	17,424	10.24	422.4
10	134	2.6	17,956	6.76	348.4
11	136	3.0	18,496	9.00	408.0
12	138	3.6	19,044	12.96	496.8
Total	1503	27.3	189,187	69.13	3488.7

$$r = \frac{\Sigma XY - \frac{(\Sigma X)(\Sigma Y)}{N}}{\sqrt{\left[\Sigma X^2 - \frac{(\Sigma X)^2}{N}\right]\left[\Sigma Y^2 - \frac{(\Sigma Y)^2}{N}\right]}}$$

$$= \frac{3488.7 - \frac{1503(27.3)}{12}}{\sqrt{\left[189{,}187 - \frac{(1503)^2}{2}\right]\left[69.132\frac{(27.3)^2}{12}\right]}}$$

$$= \frac{69.375}{81.088} = 0.856 = 0.86$$

- **Zero correlation:** A **zero correlation** suggests that no relationship exists between two measures (see graph d). This might be the result of comparing participants' ha: sizes (X) to their college grades (Y).
- **Negative correlation:** Graphs e and f both show a **negative correlation.** Notice that as values of one measure increase, those of the second become smaller. An example might be the relationship between amount of alcohol consumed and scores on a test of coordination: Higher alcohol levels are correlated with lower coordination scores.

The Correlation Coefficient

The strength of a correlation can also be expressed as a **coefficient of correlation.** This coefficient is simply a number falling somewhere between +1.00 and −1.00. If the correlation is +1.00, a **perfect positive correlation** exists; if the correlation is −1.00, a **perfect negative correlation** has been discovered. The most commonly used correlation coefficient is called the Pearson *r*. Calculation of the Pearson *r* is relatively simple, as shown in ▲ Table A.7. (The numbers shown are hypothetical.)

As stated in Chapter 1, correlations in psychology are rarely perfect. Most fall somewhere between 0 and ±1. If the number is zero or close to zero, it indicates a weak or nonexistent relationship. The closer the correlation coefficient is to +1.00 or −1.00, the stronger the relationship. An interesting example of some typical correlations is provided by a study that compared the IQs of adopted children with the IQs of their biological mothers. At age 4, the children's IQs correlated at .28 with their biological mothers' IQs. By age 7, the correlation was .35. And by age 13, it had grown to .38. Over time, the IQs of adopted children become more similar to the IQs of their biological mothers.

Correlation The existence of a consistent, systematic relationship between two events, measures, or variables.

Scatter plot A graph that shows the intersection of paired measures; that is, the points at which paired *X* and *Y* measures cross.

Positive correlation A mathematical relationship in which increases in one measure are matched by increases in the other (or decreases correspond with decreases).

Zero correlation The absence of a (linear) mathematical relationship between two measures.

Negative correlation A mathematical relationship in which increases in one measure are matched by decreases in the other.

Coefficient of correlation A statistical index ranging from −1.00 to +1.00 that indicates the direction and degree of correlation.

Perfect positive correlation A mathematical relationship in which the correlation between two measures is +1.00.

Perfect negative correlation A mathematical relationship in which the correlation between two measures is −1.00.

Correlations often provide highly useful information. For instance, it is valuable to know that there is a correlation between cigarette smoking and lung cancer rates. Another example is the fact that higher consumption of alcohol during pregnancy is correlated with lower birth weight and a higher rate of birth defects. There is a correlation between the number of recent life stresses experienced and the likelihood of emotional disturbance. Many more examples could be cited, but the point is, correlations help us identify relationships that are worth knowing.

Correlation Coefficients and Prediction

In addition to telling us something about the relationship between two variables, correlations are valuable for making *predictions*. If we know that two measures are correlated and we know a person's score on one measure, we can predict his or her score on the other. For example, most colleges have formulas that use multiple correlations to decide which applicants have the best chances for success. Usually, the formula includes such predictors as high school grade point average (GPA), teacher ratings, extracurricular activities, and scores on the *SAT Reasoning Test* (or some similar test). Although no single predictor is perfectly correlated with success in college, the various predictors together correlate highly and provide a useful technique for screening applicants.

There is an interesting "trick" that you can do with correlations that you may find useful. It works like this: If you *square* the correlation coefficient (multiply r by itself), you will get the **percent of variance**, or amount of variation in scores, accounted for by the correlation. For example, the correlation between IQ scores and college grade point average is .5. Multiplying .5 times .5 gives .25, or 25 percent. This means that 25 percent of the variation in college grades is accounted for by knowing IQ scores. In other words, with a correlation of .5, college grades are "squeezed" into an oval, like the one shown in scatter plot c (● Figure A.4). IQ scores take away some of the possible variation in corresponding grade point averages. If no correlation existed between IQ and grades, grades would be completely free to vary, as shown in scatter plot d (Figure A.4).

Along the same line, a correlation of +1.00 or −1.00 means that 100 percent of the variation in the Y measure is accounted for by knowing the X measure: If you know a person's X score, you can predict exactly what the Y score is. An example that comes close to this state of affairs is the high correlation (.86) between the IQs of identical twins. In any group of identical twins, 74 percent ($.86 \times .86 = .74$) of the variation in the Y twins' IQs is accounted for by knowing the IQs of their siblings (the X twins).

Squaring correlations to obtain the percent of variance accounted for is a useful tool for interpreting the correlations encountered in the media and the psychological literature. For example, sweeping pronouncements about relationships are occasionally made on the basis of correlations in the .25 to .30 range, even though the values mean that only 6 to 9 percent of the variance is accounted for by the observed correlation. Such correlations may document relationships worth noting, but they are rarely something to get excited about.

Correlation and Causation

It is important to reiterate that finding a correlation between two measures does not automatically demonstrate **causation**—that one variable is causing the other. When a correlation exists, the best we can say is that two variables are related. Of course, this does not mean that it is impossible for two correlated variables to have a cause-and-effect relationship. Rather, it means that we cannot conclude, solely on the basis of correlation, that a causal link exists. To gain greater confidence that a cause-and-effect relationship exists, an experiment must be performed (as explained in Section 1.6).

Often, two correlated measures are related as a result of the influence of a third variable. For example, we might observe a correlation demonstrating that the more hours students devote to studying, the better their grades. Although it is tempting to conclude that more studying produces (causes) better grades, it is possible (indeed, it is probable) that this relationship between grades and the amount of study time exists only because both are related to a third variable: the student's amount of motivation or interest.

The difference between cause-and-effect data and data that reveal a relationship of unknown origin is one that should not be forgotten. Because we rarely run experiments in daily life, the information on which we act is largely correlational. This should make us more humble and more tentative in the confidence with which we make pronouncements about human behavior.

A.3 Inferential Statistics: Significant Numbers

GATEWAYS LEARNING OUTCOME:
After reading this section you should be able to:

A.3.1 Explain what inferential statistics are used for

You would like to know whether boys are more aggressive than girls. You observe a group of 5-year-old boys and girls on a playground. After collecting data for a week, you find that the boys committed more aggressive acts than the girls. Could this difference just be a meaningless fluctuation in aggression? Or does it show conclusively that boys are more aggressive than girls? Inferential statistics were created to answer such questions about the differences between groups (Gravetter, Wallnau, & Forzano, 2018).

It's important to note that when researchers carry out studies that compare groups in this way, they're not only interested in these particular individuals. Instead, psychologists usually seek to discover general laws of behavior that apply widely to humans and animals beyond their sample (Babbie, 2016). For example, let's say that a researcher studies the effects of a new therapy on a small group of depressed individuals. Undoubtedly, the researcher would like to know whether the therapy holds any promise for all depressed people. As stated earlier, inferential statistics are techniques that allow us to make such inferences—that is, they allow us to generalize from the behavior of small groups of participants to that of the larger groups they represent.

Samples and Populations

In any scientific study, we would prefer to observe the entire set, or **population**, of participants, objects, or events of interest. However, this is usually impossible or impractical. Observing all terrorists, all cancer patients, or all mothers-in-law could be both impractical (because all are large populations) and impossible (because people change political views, may be unaware of having cancer, and change their status as relatives). In such cases, a **sample** (a smaller cross section of a population) is selected, and observations of the sample are used to draw conclusions about the entire population.

For any sample to be meaningful, it must be **representative**—that is, the sample group must truly reflect the membership and characteristics of the larger population. In Samantha's preliminary study of sleep quality, it would be essential for the sample of 20 people to be representative of the general population of older adults. A very important aspect of representative samples is that their members are chosen by **random selection**. In other words, each member of the population must have an equal chance of being included in the sample.

Significant Differences Between Groups

In Samantha's sleep quality experiment, she found that the average sleep quality score was higher for the group given the stretching exercises than it was for the one that watched TV. Certainly this result is interesting, but could it have occurred by chance? If two groups were repeatedly tested (with neither receiving any exercise or TV), their average sleep quality scores would sometimes differ. How much must two means differ before we can consider the difference "real" (that is, not due to chance)?

Inferential tests of **statistical significance** provide an estimate of how often experimental results could have occurred by chance alone. The results of a significance test are stated as a probability. This probability gives the odds that the observed difference was due to chance. In psychology, any experimental result that could have occurred by chance 5 times (or less) out of 100 (in other words, a probability of .05 or less) is considered *significant*. In Samantha's sleep quality and exercise experiment, the probability turned out to be .025 ($p = .025$, or 2.5 percent) that the group means would differ as much as they did by chance alone. This allows Samantha to conclude with reasonable certainty that the exercise actually did improve sleep quality scores.

Reflective Practice

Psychology and Your Skill Set: Statistical Literacy

1. Three measures of central tendency are the mean, the median, and the ______.
2. As a measure of variability, the standard deviation is defined as the difference between the highest and lowest scores. T or F?
3. A z-score of –1 tells us that a score fell one standard deviation below the mean in a group of scores. T or F?
4. A scatter diagram can be used to plot and visualize a(n) ______ between two groups of scores.
5. It is important to remember that correlation does not demonstrate ______.
6. In inferential statistics, observations of a ______ are used to make inferences and draw conclusions about an entire ______.
7. A representative sample can be obtained by selecting members of the sample at ______.
8. If the results of an experiment could have occurred by chance alone fewer than 25 times out of 100, the result is considered statistically significant. T or F?

THINK CRITICALLY

9. Suppose that it was found that sleeping with your clothes on correlates with waking up with a headache. Could you conclude that sleeping with your clothes on causes headaches?

SELF-REFLECT

- How would you feel about receiving your scores on classroom tests in the form of z-scores?
- Do you think the distribution of scores in Samantha's study of sleep quality in elderly people would form a normal curve? Why or why not?
- See if you can identify at least one positive relationship and one negative relationship involving human behavior that you have observed. How strong do you think the correlation would be in each case? What correlation coefficient would you expect to see?
- If you were trying to test whether a drug causes birth defects, what level of statistical significance would you use? If you were doing a psychology experiment, with what level would you be comfortable?

Answers: 1. mode 2. F 3. T 4. correlation 5. causation 6. sample, population 7. random 8. F 9. No. To reiterate, correlation does not prove causality. It is more likely that a third factor is causing *both* the sleeping with the clothes on at night *and* the headaches (too much alcohol, anyone?).

Percent of variance A portion of the total amount of variation in a group of scores.

Causation The act of causing some effect.

Population An entire group of animals, people, or objects belonging to a particular category (for example, all college students or all married women).

Sample A smaller subpart of a population.

Representative sample A small, randomly selected part of a larger population that accurately reflects characteristics of the whole population.

Random selection Choosing a sample so that each member of the population has an equal chance of being included in the sample.

Statistical significance (statistically significant) The degree to which an event (such as the results of an experiment) is unlikely to have occurred by chance alone.

Gateways to Statistical Literacy

Summary: Gateways Learning Outcomes

A.1 Descriptive Statistics: Psychology by the Numbers

A.1.1 Explain what descriptive statistics are used for, and provide some examples

Descriptive statistics are used to organize and summarize numbers. Summarizing numbers visually, by using various types of graphs such as frequency histograms and frequency polygons, makes it easier to see trends and patterns in the results of psychological investigations.

One example of descriptive statistics is *measures of central tendency*. Measures of central tendency define the "typical score" in a group of scores; examples of central tendency measures include the mean, median, and mode. The mean is found by adding all the scores in a group and then dividing by the total number of scores. The median is found by arranging a group of scores from the highest to the lowest and selecting the middle score. The mode is the score that occurs most frequently in a group of scores.

A second example of descriptive statistics is *measures of variability*. Measures of variability provide a number that shows how much scores vary from the mean, and examples include the range and standard deviation. The range is the difference between the highest score and the lowest score in a group of scores. The standard deviation (SD) shows how much, on average, all the scores in a group differ from the mean.

We can use measures of central tendency to compare scores from different groups, or that have been measured on different scales, by computing a *standard score*. To express an original score as a standard score (or z-score), you must subtract the mean from the score and then divide the result by the SD. Standard scores (z-scores) tell, in SD units, how far above or below the mean a score is. This allows meaningful comparisons between scores from different groups, or measures from different scales.

A.2 Correlational Statistics: Seeing Relationships

A.2.1 Explain what correlational statistics are used for, and provide an example

Pairs of scores that vary together in an orderly fashion (that is, the scores, or variables, show a relationship to one another) are said to be correlated. The degree to which the variables are correlated can be assessed using a *correlation coefficient*.

Correlation coefficients are used to tell us how two groups of scores are related (the relationship can be positive, zero, or negative positively or negatively), and the strength of that relationship. If a correlation is high enough, the correlational statistics can also be used for prediction, because knowing a person's score on one measure allows us to predict his or her score on the second measure. However, correlational statistics cannot be used to demonstrate cause-and-effect links between variables or measures.

A.3 Inferential Statistics: Significant Numbers

A.3.1 Explain what inferential statistics are used for

Inferential statistics are used to make decisions and draw conclusions about observed differences between groups, as well as to generalize from samples. We use inferential statistics because most studies in psychology are based on samples, and researchers often want to know whether their results will generalize to other people. Findings from representative samples are assumed to apply to entire populations. However, observed differences in the average performance of groups could occur purely by chance. Tests of statistical significance tell us if the observed differences between groups are common or rare. If a difference is large enough to be improbable, it suggests that the results did not occur by chance alone.

References

Aamodt, M. G. (2016). *Industrial/ organizational psychology: An applied approach* (8th ed.). Boston, MA: Cengage Learning.

Abadinsky, H. (2018). *Drug use and abuse: A comprehensive introduction* (9th ed.). Boston, MA: Cengage Learning.

Abbott, K. R., & Sherratt, T. N. (2011). The evolution of superstition through optimal use of incomplete information. *Animal Behaviour, 82*(1), 85–92. doi:10.1016/j.anbehav. 2011.04.002

Abbott, S. M., Reid, K. J., et al. (2015). Circadian rhythm sleep-wake disorders. *Psychiatric Clinics of North America, 38*(4), 805–823. doi:10.1016/j.psc.2015.07.012

Abdollahi, A., & Talib, M. A. (2015). Emotional intelligence as a mediator between rumination and suicidal ideation among depressed inpatients: The moderating role of suicidal history. *Psychiatry Research, 228*(3), 591–597. doi:10.1016/j. psychres.2015.05.046

Abel, G. G., Wiegel, M., & Osborn, C. A. (2007). Pedophilia and other paraphilias. In L. VandeCreek, F. L. Peterson, Jr., et al. (Eds.), *Innovations in clinical practice: Focus on sexual health* (pp. 157–175). Sarasota, FL: Professional Resource Press.

Abrahamse, E., Braem, S., et al. (2016). Grounding cognitive control in associative learning. *Psychological Bulletin, 142*(7), 693–728. doi:10.1037/bul0000047

Abramowitz, J. S., & Jacoby, R. J. (2015). Obsessive-compulsive and related disorders: A critical review of the new diagnostic class. *Annual Review of Clinical Psychology, 11,* 165–186. doi:10.1146/annurev-clinpsy-032813-153713

Abramowitz, J. S., Deacon, B. J., et al. (2012). *Exposure therapy for anxiety: Principles and practice.* New York: Guilford.

Abrams, D., Van de Vyver, J., et al. (2017, February 16). Does terror defeat contact? Intergroup contact and prejudice toward Muslims before and after the London bombings. *Peace & Conflict: Journal of Peace Psychology,* n.p. doi:10.1037/pac0000167

Achenbaum, W. A., & Bengtson, V. L. (1994). Re-engaging the disengagement theory of aging: On the history and assessment of theory development in gerontology. *The Gerontologist, 34,* 756–763. doi:10.1093/geront/34.6.756

Ackerman, S. J., Lewis, K. C., et al. (2014). The Thematic Apperception Test: A performance-based assessment technique. In R. P. Archer & S. R. Smith (Eds.), *Personality assessment* (2nd ed., pp. 371–400). New York: Routledge/Taylor & Francis.

Adachi, P. J., & Willoughby, T. (2011a). The effect of violent video games on aggression: Is it more than just the violence? *Aggression & Violent Behavior, 16*(1), 55–62. doi:10.1016/j. avb.2010.12.002

Adachi, P. J., & Willoughby, T. (2011b). The effect of video game competition and violence on aggressive behavior: Which characteristic has the greatest influence? *Psychology of Violence, 1*(4), 259–274. doi:10.1037/a0024908

Adamaszek, M., D'Agata, F., et al. (2016, August 2). Consensus paper: Cerebellum and emotion. *Cerebellum,* n.p. doi:proxy.library.brocku. ca/10.1007/s12311-016-0815-8

Adams, J. (2001). *Conceptual blockbusting* (4th ed.). New York: Basic Books.

Adams, M. (2016). Existential therapy as a skills-learning process. *Existential Analysis, 27*(1), 58–69.

Adamson, K. (2004). *Kate's journey: Triumph over adversity.* Redondo Beach, CA: Nosmada Press.

Adan, A., & Serra-Grabulosa, J. P. (2010). Effects of caffeine and glucose, alone and combined, on cognitive performance. *Human Psychopharmacology: Clinical & Experimental, 25*(4), 310–317. doi:10.1002/hup.1115

Adler, S. A., & Orprecio, J. (2006). The eyes have it: Visual pop-out in infants and adults. *Developmental Science, 9,* 189–206. doi:10.1111/j.1467-7687. 2006.00479.x

Adolph, K. E., & Berger, S. E. (2011). Physical and motor development. In M. H. Bornstein & M. E. Lamb (Eds.), *Cognitive development: An advanced textbook* (pp. 257–318). New York: Psychology Press.

Adolphs, R. (2008). Fear, faces, and the human amygdala. *Current Opinion in Neurobiology, 18*(2), 166–172. doi:10.1016/j.conb.2008.06.006

Adorno, T. W., Frenkel-Brunswik, E., et al. (1950). *The authoritarian personality.* New York: Harper.

Advokat, C. D., Comaty, J. E., & Julien, R. M. (2014). *Julien's primer of drug action.* (13th ed.). New York: Worth.

Afifi, T. O., Brownridge, D. A., et al. (2006). Physical punishment, childhood abuse, and psychiatric disorders. *Child Abuse & Neglect, 30*(10), 1093–1103. doi:10.1016/j. chiabu.2006.04.006

Agbayani, K. A., & Hiscock, M. (2013). Age-related change in Wechsler IQ norms after adjustment for the Flynn effect: Estimates from three computational models. *Journal of Clinical & Experimental Neuropsychology, 35*(6), 642–654. doi: 10.1080/13803395.2013.806650

Agresti, J. D., & Smith, R. K. (2016, August 22). Gun control. *Just Facts.* Retrieved April 6, 2017, from www .justfacts.com/guncontrol.asp

Agrigoroaei, S., & Lachman, M. E. (2011). Cognitive functioning in midlife and old age: Combined effects of psychosocial and behavioral factors. *Journals of Gerontology, 66B,* 130–140. doi:10.1093/geronb/gbr017

Ahima, R. S., & Osei, S. Y. (2004). Leptin signaling. *Physiology & Behavior, 81,* 223–241. doi:10.1016/j.physbeh.2004. 02.014s

Ahluwalia, M. K., & Pellettiere, L. (2010). Sikh men post-9/11: Misidentification, discrimination, and coping. *Asian American Journal of Psychology, 1*(4), 303–314. doi:10.1037/a0022156

Ahrens, K. A., Hutcheon, J. A., et al. (2017, January 19). Reducing unintended pregnancies as a strategy to avert zika-related microcephaly births in the United States: A simulation study. *Maternal & Child Health Journal,* n.p. doi:10.1007/s10995-017-2275-2

Ai, A. L., Huang, B., et al. (2013). Religious attendance and major depression among Asian Americans from a national database: The mediation of social support. *Psychology of Religion & Spirituality, 5*(2), 78–89. doi:10.1037/a0030625

Ainsworth, M. D. (1989). Attachments beyond infancy. *American Psychologist, 44*(4), 709–716.

Aitken, S. J., Lyons, M., & Jonason, P. K. (2013). Dads or cads? Women's strategic decisions in the mating game. *Personality & Individual Differences, 55*(2), 118–122. doi:10.1016/j.paid.2013.02. 017

Ajzen, I. (2005). *Attitudes, personality and behaviour* (2nd ed.). New York: McGraw-Hill.

Åkerstedt, T. (2007). Altered sleep/wake patterns and mental performance. *Physiology & Behavior, 90*(2–3), 209–218. doi:10.1016/j.physbeh.2006. 09.007

Aktas, M., Gelfand, M., & Hanges, P. (2016). Cultural tightness–looseness and perceptions of effective leadership. *Journal of Cross-Cultural Psychology, 47,* 294–309. doi:10.1177/0022022115 606802

Al Yacoub, A. A. (1997, December). How Muslim Arab parents in Western Pennsylvania view the influence of American TV on their children's morality. *Dissertation Abstracts International Section A, 58.*

Alanko, K., Santtila, P., et al. (2010). Common genetic effects of gender atypical behavior in childhood and sexual orientation in adulthood: A study of Finnish twins. *Archives of Sexual Behavior, 39*(1), 81–92. doi:10.1007/s10508-008-9457-3

Albarracín, D., Johnson, B. T., & Zanna, M. P. (Eds.). (2005). *The handbook of attitudes.* Mahwah, NJ: Erlbaum.

Albersen, M., Orabi, H., & Lue, T. F. (2012). Evaluation and treatment of erectile dysfunction in the aging male: A mini-review. *Gerontology, 58*(1), 3–14. doi:10.1159/000329598

Alberti, R., & Emmons, M. (2008). *Your perfect right* (9th ed.). San Luis Obispo, CA: Impact.

Alberto, P. A., & Troutman, A. C. (2013). *Applied behavior analysis for teachers* (9th ed.). Englewood Cliffs, NJ: Prentice Hall.

Alberts, H. M., Thewissen, R. R., & Raes, L. L. (2012). Dealing with problematic eating behaviour. The effects of a mindfulness-based intervention on eating behaviour, food cravings, dichotomous thinking and body image concern. *Appetite, 58*(3), 847–851. doi:10.1016/j.appet.2012.01.009

Albrecht, C. M., & Albrecht, D. E. (2011). Social status, adolescent behavior, and educational attainment. *Sociological Spectrum, 31*(1), 114–137. doi:10.1080/02732173.2011.525698

Albright, D. L., & Thyer, B. (2010). Does EMDR reduce post-traumatic stress disorder symptomatology in combat veterans? *Behavioral Interventions, 25*(1), 1–19. doi:10.1002/bin.295

Alcock, J. E. (2010). The parapsychologist's lament. In S. Krippner & H. L. Friedman (Eds.), *Mysterious minds: The neurobiology of psychics, mediums, and other extraordinary people* (pp. 35–43). Santa Barbara, CA: Praeger.

Alcock, J. E., Burns, J., & Freeman, A. (2003). *Psi wars: Getting to grips with the paranormal.* Exeter, UK: Imprint Academic Press.

Aldwin, C. M., & Gilmer, D. F. (2013). *Health, illness, and optimal aging: Biological and psychosocial perspectives* (2nd ed.). New York: Springer.

Alegre, A. (2011). Parenting styles and children's emotional intelligence: What do we know? *The Family Journal, 19*(1), 56–62. doi:10.1177/1066480710387486

Alegria, A. A., Blanco, C., et al. (2013). Sex differences in antisocial personality disorder: Results from the National Epidemiological Survey on Alcohol and Related Conditions. *Personality Disorders: Theory, Research, & Treatment, 4*(3), 214–222. doi:10.1037/a0031681

Aleman, A. (2013). Use of repetitive transcranial magnetic stimulation for treatment in psychiatry. *Clinical Psychopharmacology & Neuroscience, 11*(2), 53–59. doi:10.9758/cpn.2013.11.2.53

Alessandria, M., Vetrugno, R., et al. (2011). Normal body scheme and absent phantom limb experience in amputees while dreaming. *Consciousness & Cognition, 20*(4), 1831–1834. doi:10.1016/j.concog.2011.06.013

Algoe, S. B., Gable, S. L., et al. (2010). It's the little things: Gratitude as a booster shot for romantic relationships. *Personal Relationships, 17*(2), 217–233.

Ali, M. M., & Dwyer, D. S. (2010). Social network effects in alcohol consumption among adolescents. *Addictive Behaviors, 35*(4), 337–342. doi:10.1016/j.addbeh.2009.12.002

Allemand, M., Steiger, A. E., et al. (2013). Stability of personality traits in adulthood: Mechanisms and implications. *Geropsych: The Journal of Gerontopsychology & Geriatric Psychiatry, 26*(1), 5–13. doi:10.1024/1662-9647/a000080

Allen, A. K., Wilkins, K., et al. (2013). Conscious thoughts from reflex-like processes: A new experimental paradigm for consciousness research. *Consciousness & Cognition, 22*(4), 1318–1331.

Allen, D., Carlson, D., & Ham, C. (2007). Well-being: New paradigms of wellness-inspiring positive health outcomes and renewing hope. *American Journal of Health Promotion, 21*(3), 1–9.

Allen, H. L., Estrada, K., et al. (2010): Hundreds of variants clustered in genomic loci and biological pathways affect human height. *Nature, 467,* 832–838.

Allen, J. L., Lavallee, K. L., et al. (2010). DSM-IV criteria for childhood separation anxiety disorder: Informant, age, and sex differences. *Journal of Anxiety Disorders, 24*(8), 946–952. doi:10.1016/j. janxdis.2010.06.022

Allen, J., & Holder, M. D. (2013, February). Marijuana use and well-being in university students. *Journal of Happiness Studies,* n.p. doi:10.1007/s10902-013-9423-1

Allen, K., Blascovich, J., & Mendes, W. B. (2002). Cardiovascular reactivity in the presence of pets, friends, and spouses: The truth about cats and dogs. *Psychosomatic Medicine, 64*(5), 727–739.

Allen, T. T., & Williams, L. D. (2012). An approach to life skills group work with youth in transition to independent living: Theoretical, practice, and operational considerations. *Residential Treatment for Children & Youth, 29*(4), 324–342. doi:10.1080/0886571X.2012.725375

Allport, G. W. (1958). *The nature of prejudice*. Garden City, NY: Anchor Books, Doubleday.

Allport, G. W. (1961). *Pattern and growth in personality*. New York: Holt, Rinehart, & Winston.

Alstermark, B., & Ekerot, C. (2013). The lateral reticular nucleus: A precerebellar centre providing the cerebellum with overview and integration of motor functions at systems level. A new hypothesis. *Journal of Physiology, 591*(22), 5453–5458. doi:10.1113/jphysiol.2013.256669

Alter, A. L., Aronson, J., et al. (2010). Rising to the threat: Reducing stereotype threat by reframing the threat as a challenge. *Journal of Experimental Social Psychology, 46,* 166–171. doi:10.1016/j.jesp.2009.09.014

Altschul, I., Lee, S. J., & Gershoff, E. T. (2016). Hugs, not hits: Warmth and spanking as predictors of child social competence. *Journal of Marriage & Family, 78*(3), 695–714. doi:10.1111/jomf.12306

Altschuler, G. C. (2001). Battling the cheats. *The New York Times*: Education, January 7, 15.

Alwin, D. F., Cohen, R. L., & Newcomb, T. M. (1991). *Political attitudes over the life span: The Bennington women after fifty years.* Madison, WI: University of Wisconsin Press.

Aly, A., Macdonald, S., et al. (2017). Introduction to the special issue: Terrorist online propaganda and radicalization. *Studies in Conflict & Terrorism, 40*(1), 1–9. doi:10.1080/1057610X.2016.1157402

Alzahabi, R., Becker, M. W., & Hambrick, D. Z. (2017). Investigating the relationship between media multitasking and processes involved in task-switching. *Journal of Experimental Psychology: Human Perception and Performance, 43*(11), 1872–1894. doi:10.1037/xhp0000412

Ambady, N., & Rosenthal, R. (1993). Half a minute: Predicting teacher evaluations from thin slices of nonverbal behavior and physical attractiveness. *Journal of Personality & Social Psychology, 64,* 431–441. doi:10.1037/0022-3514.64.3.431

Ameli, R. (2014). *25 lessons in mindfulness: Now time for healthy living.* Washington, DC: American Psychological Association. doi:10.1037/14257-000

American Academy of Child and Adolescent Psychiatry. (2014). *Child sexual abuse*. Retrieved March 10, 2017, from www.aacap.org/AACAP/Families_and_Youth/Facts_for_Families/FFF-Guide/Child-Sexual-Abuse-009.aspx

American Lung Association. (2017). *Secondhand smoke.* Retrieved May 6, 2017, from www.lungusa.org/stop-smoking/about-smoking/health-effects/secondhand-smoke.html

American Psychiatric Association. (2013). *Diagnostic and statistical manual of mental disorders* (5th ed.). Washington, DC: American Psychiatric Association.

American Psychological Association. (2006). Evidence-based practice in psychology. *American Psychologist, 61,* 271–285. doi:10.1037/0003-066X.61.4.271

American Psychological Association. (2008a). *Report of the Task Force on the Implementation of the Multicultural Guidelines.* Retrieved May 8, 2014, from www.apa.org/about/policy/multicultural-report.pdf

American Psychological Association. (2008b). *Sexual orientation and homosexuality*. Retrieved March 10, 2017, from www.apa.org/topics/lgbt/orientation.pdf

American Psychological Association. (2010). *Report of the APA Task Force on the sexualization of girls.* Retrieved March 10, 2017, from www.apa.org/pi/women/programs/girls/report-full.pdf

American Psychological Association. (2012). *Workplace survey*. Retrieved March 18, 2017, from www.apa.org/news/press/releases/phwa/workplace-survey.pdf

American Psychological Association. (2013). *APA guidelines for the undergraduate major, version 2.0.* Retrieved April 26, 2017, from http://www.apa.org/ed/precollege/about/psymajor-guidelines.pdf

American Psychological Association. (2015a). *2015: APA member profiles*. Retrieved April 26, 2017, from www.apa.org/workforce/publications/15-member/index.aspx

American Psychological Association. (2015b). *2005–13: Demographics of the U.S. psychology workforce.* Retrieved April 26, 2017, from www.apa.org/workforce/publications/3-dem-acs/index.aspx

American Psychological Association. (2017a). *Ethical principles of psychologists and code of conduct: Including 2010 and 2016 amendments.* Retrieved April 26, 2017, from www.apa.org/ethics/code/index.aspx

American Psychological Association. (2017b). *Civic engagement*. Retrieved February 22, 2017, from http://www.apa.org/education/undergrad/civic-engagement.aspx

American Psychological Association. (2017c). *Psychologist locator.* Retrieved June 11, 2017 from http://locator.apa.org

Andersen, M. L., Poyares, D., et al. (2007). Sexsomnia: Abnormal sexual behavior during sleep. *Brain Research Reviews, 56*(2), 271–282. doi:10.1016/j.brainresrev.2007.06.005

Anderson, C. A. (1989). Temperature and aggression. *Psychological Bulletin, 106,* 74–96. doi:10.1037/0033-2909.106.1.74

Anderson, C. A., & Bushman, B. J. (2002). Human aggression. *Annual Review of Psychology, 53,* 27–51. doi:10.1146/annurev.psych.53.100901.135231

Anderson, C. A., Berkowitz, L., et al. (2003). The influence of media violence on youth. *Psychological Science in the Public Interest, 4,* 81–100. doi:10.1111/j.1529-1006.2003.pspi_1433.x

Anderson, C. A., Gentile, D. A., & Buckley, K. E. (2007). *Violent video game effects on children and adolescents: Theory, research, and public policy*. New York: Oxford University Press.

Anderson, J. R. (2014). *Cognitive psychology and its implications* (8th ed.). New York: Worth.

Anderson, K. J. (2010). *Benign bigotry: The psychology of subtle prejudice*. New York: Cambridge University Press.

Anderson, L. W. (2003). *Benjamin S. Bloom: His life, his works, and his legacy*. In B. J. Zimmerman & D. H. Schunk (Eds.), *Educational psychology: A century of contributions* (p. 367–389). Lawrence Erlbaum Associates Publishers.

Anderson, M., & Jiang, J. (2018). *Teens, Social Media & Technology 2018*. Retrieved from https://www.pewinternet.org/2018/05/31/teens-social-media-technology-2018/

Anderson, M. C., & Huddleston, E. (2012). Towards a cognitive neurobiological model of motivated forgetting. In R. F. Belli (Ed.), *True and false recovered memories: Toward a reconciliation of the debate* (pp. 53–120). New York: Springer. doi:10.1007/978-1-4614-1195-6_3

Anderson, M. C., Reinholz, J., et al. (2011). Intentional suppression of unwanted memories grows more difficult as we age. *Psychology & Aging, 26*(2), 397–405. doi:10.1037/a0022505

Anderson, P. L., Edwards, S. M., & Goodnight, J. R. (2017). Virtual reality and exposure group therapy for social anxiety disorder: Results from a 4–6 year follow-up. *Cognitive Therapy & Research, 41*(2), 230–236. doi:10.1007/s10608-016-9820-y

Anderson, P. L., Zimand, E., Hodges, L. F., & Rothbaum, B. O. (2005). Cognitive behavioral therapy for public-speaking anxiety using virtual reality for exposure. *Depression and Anxiety, 22*(3), 156-158. doi:10.1002/da.20090

Anderson, S. W., & Booker, M. B. (2006). Cognitive behavioral therapy versus psychosurgery for refractory obsessive-compulsive disorder. *Journal of Neuropsychiatry & Clinical Neurosciences, 18*(1), 129. doi:10.1176/appi.neuropsych.18.1.129

Anderson, S., & Hunter, S. C. (2012). Cognitive appraisals, emotional reactions, and their associations with three forms of peer-victimization. *Psicothema, 24*(4), 621–627.

André, C., Jaber-Filho, J. A., et al. (2003). Predictors of recovery following involuntary hospitalization of violent substance abuse patients. *American Journal on Addictions,12*(1), 84–89. doi:10.1080/10550490390143394

Andreasen, N. C., Nopoulos, P., et al. (2011). Progressive brain change in schizophrenia: A prospective longitudinal study of first-episode schizophrenia. *Biological Psychiatry, 70*(7), 672–679. doi:10.1016/j.biopsych.2011.05.017

Anekonda, T. S. (2006). Resveratrol: A boon for treating Alzheimer's disease? *Brain Research Reviews, 52*(2), 316–326. doi:10.1016/j.brainresrev.2006.04.004

Anema, H. A., & Dijkerman, H. (2013). Motor and kinesthetic imagery. In S. Lacey & R. Lawson (Eds.). *Multisensory imagery* (pp. 93–113). New York: Springer. doi:10.1007/978-1-4614-5879-1_6

Annesi, J. J., & Marti, C. N. (2011). Path analysis of exercise treatment-induced changes in psychological factors leading to weight loss. *Psychology & Health, 26*(8), 1081–1098. doi:10.1080/08870446.2010.534167

Ansari, S., Wijen, F., et al. (2013). Constructing a climate change logic: An institutional perspective on the "tragedy of the commons." *Organization Science, 24*(4), 1014–1040. doi:10.1287/orsc.1120.0799

Anthony, J. S., Clayton, K. E., & Zusho, A. (2013). An investigation of students' self-regulated learning strategies: Students' qualitative and quantitative accounts of their learning strategies. *Journal of Cognitive Education & Psychology, 12*(3), 359–373. doi:10.1891/1945-8959.12.3.359

Antoni, C. (2005). Management by objectives: An effective tool for teamwork? *International Journal of Human Resource Management, 16*(2), 174–184.

Apperly, I. A. (2012). What is "theory of mind"? Concepts, cognitive processes, and individual differences. *Quarterly Journal of Experimental Psychology, 65*(5), 825–839. doi:10.1080/17470218.2012.676055

Arch, J. J., Ayers, C. R., et al. (2013). Randomized clinical trial of adapted mindfulness-based stress reduction versus group cognitive behavioral therapy for heterogeneous anxiety disorders. *Behaviour Research & Therapy, 51*(4–5), 185–196. doi:10.1016/j.brat.2013.01.003

Ardila, A., Bernal, B., et al. (2016). The role of Wernicke's area in language comprehension. *Psychology & Neuroscience, 9*(3), 340–343. doi:10.1037/pne0000060

Ariely, D., & Loewenstein, G. (2006). The heat of the moment: The effect of sexual arousal on sexual decision making. *Journal of Behavioral Decision Making, 19*(2), 87–98.

Ariely, D., & Wertenbroch, K. (2002). Procrastination, deadlines, and performance: Self-control by precommitment. *Psychological Science, 13*(3), 219–224. doi:10.1111/1467-9280.00441

Arnett, J. J. (2010, February 9). The empathic civilization: The young pioneers of the empathic generation. Retrieved February 23, 2017, from http://www.huffingtonpost.com/jeffrey-jensen-arnett/theempathic-civilization_b_454211.html

Arnett, J. J. (2011). The cultural psychology of a new life stage. In L. A. Jensen (Ed.), *Emerging adulthood(s): The cultural psychology of a new life stage* (pp. 255–275). New York: Oxford University Press.

Arnett, J. J. (2016). Does emerging adulthood theory apply across social classes? National data on a persistent question. *Emerging Adulthood, 4*(4), 227–235. doi:10.1177/2167696815613000

Arnow, B. A., Steidtmann, D., et al. (2013). The relationship between the therapeutic alliance and treatment outcome in two distinct psychotherapies for chronic depression. *Journal of Consulting & Clinical Psychology, 81*(4), 627–638. doi:10.1037/a0031530

Arnsten, A., Mazure, C. M., & Sinha, R. (2012, April). This is your brain on meltdown. *Scientific American, 306*, 48–53. doi:10.1038/scientificamerican0412-48

Aron, A. (2012). Online dating: The current status—and beyond. *Psychological Science in the Public Interest, 13*(1), 1–2. doi:10.1177/1529100612438173

Aron, L., & Starr, K. (2013). *A psychotherapy for the people: Toward a progressive psychoanalysis*. New York: Routledge.

Aronson, E. (2012). *The social animal* (11th ed.). New York: Worth.

Aronson, E., Wilson, T. D., & Akert, R. M. (2013). *Social psychology* (8th ed.). Englewood Cliffs, NJ: Prentice Hall.

Aronson, K. (2003). Alcohol: A recently identified risk factor for breast cancer. *Canadian Medical Association Journal, 168*(9), 1147–1148.

Arshamian, A., Iannilli, E., et al. (2013). The functional neuroanatomy of odor evoked autobiographical memories cued by odors and words. *Neuropsychologia, 51*(1), 123–131. doi:10.1016/j.neuropsychologia.2012.10.023

Artz, S. (2005). To die for: Violent adolescent girls' search for male attention. In D. J. Pepler, K. C. Madsen, et al. (Eds.), *The development and treatment of girlhood aggression* (pp. 137–160). Mahwah, NJ: Erlbaum.

Asch, S. E. (1956). Studies of independence and conformity: A minority of one against a unanimous majority. *Psychological Monographs, 70*(9, Whole No. 416). doi:10.1037/h0093718

Aselton, P. (2012). Sources of stress and coping in American college students who have been diagnosed with depression. *Journal of Child & Adolescent Psychiatric Nursing, 25*(3), 119–123. doi:10.1111/j.1744-6171.2012.00341.x

Asendorpf, J. (2009). Personality: Traits and situations. In P. J. Corr & G. Matthews (Eds.), *The Cambridge handbook of personality psychology* (pp. 43–53). Cambridge: Cambridge University Press.

Asgari, S., Dasgupta, N., & Stout, J. G. (2012). When do counterstereotypic ingroup members inspire versus deflate? The effect of successful professional women on young women's leadership self-concept. *Personality & Social Psychology Bulletin, 38*(3), 370–383. doi:10.1177/0146167211431968

Ash, D. W., & Holding, D. H. (1990). Backward versus forward chaining in the acquisition of a keyboard skill. *Human Factors, 32*(2), 139–146. doi:10.1177/001872089003200202

Ashby, F. G., & Maddox, W. T. (2005). Human category learning. *Annual Review of Psychology, 56*, 149–178. doi:10.1146/annurev.psych.56.091103.070217

Ashcraft, D. (2015). *Personality theories workbook* (6th ed.). Boston, MA: Cengage Learning.

Ashton, M. C. (2018). *Individual differences and personality* (3rd ed.). San Diego, CA: Elsevier.

Ashton, M. C., & Lee, K. (2001). A theoretical basis for the major dimensions of personality. *European Journal of Personality, 15*, 327–353. doi:10.1002/per.417

Askenasy, J., & Lehmann, J. (2013). Consciousness, brain, neuroplasticity. *Frontiers in Psychology, 4*, 412. doi:10.3389/fpsyg.2013.00142

Asthana, H. S. (2015). Wilhelm Wundt. *Psychological Studies, 60*(2), 244–248. doi:10.1007/s12646-014-0295-1

Athenasiou, R., Shaver, P., & Tavris, C. (1970). Sex. *Psychology Today, 4*(2), 37–52.

Atkin, D. J., & Lau, T. Y. (2007). Information technology and organizational telework. In C. A. Lin & D. J. Atkin (Eds.), *Communication technology and social change: Theory and implications* (pp. 79–100). Mahwah, NJ: Erlbaum.

Atkinson, C., & Mayer, R. E. (2004). *Five ways to reduce PowerPoint overload*. Retrieved January 31, 2017 from http://slideplayer.com/slide/7096121

Atkinson, R. C., & Shiffrin, R. M. (1968). Human memory: A proposed system and its control processes. In K. W. Spence & J. T. Spence (Eds.), *The psychology of learning and motivation* (Vol. 2, pp. 742–775). London: Academic Press. doi:10.1016/S0079-7421(08)60422-3

Atwood, J. D. (2006). Mommy's little angel, daddy's little girl: Do you know what your pre-teens are doing? *American Journal of Family Therapy, 34*(5), 447–467.

Au, S., & Stavinoha, P. L. (2008). *Stress-free potty training: A commonsense guide to finding the right approach for your child.* New York: AMACOM.

Ausubel, D. P. (1978). In defense of advance organizers: A reply to the critics. *Review of Educational Research, 48,* 251–257.

Avery, D. H., Eder, D. N., et al. (2001). Dawn simulation and bright light in the treatment of SAD. *Biological Psychiatry, 50*(3), 205–216. doi:10.1016/S0006-3223(01)01200-8

Awadallah, N., Vaughan, A., et al. (2005). Munchausen by proxy: A case, chart series, and literature review of older victims. *Child Abuse & Neglect, 29*(8), 931–941. doi:10.1016/j.chiabu.2004.11.007

Axmacher, N., Do Lam, A. T., et al. (2010). Natural memory beyond the storage model: Repression, trauma, and the construction of a personal past. *Frontiers in Human Neuroscience, 4,* 211. doi:10.3389/fnhum.2010.00211

Ayal, S., Gino, F., et al. (2015). Three principles to REVISE people's unethical behavior. *Perspectives on Psychological Science, 10*(6), 738–741. doi:10.1177/1745691615598512

Azadyecta, M. (2011). Relationship between hardiness and parenting styles among high school girls of Tehran. *Psychological Research, 14*(1), 65–78.

Baad-Hansen, L., Abrahamsen, R., et al. (2013). Somatosensory sensitivity in patients with persistent idiopathic orofacial pain is associated with pain relief from hypnosis and relaxation. *Clinical Journal of Pain, 29*(6), 518–526.

Baas, M., Nijstad, B. A., et al. (2015). The cognitive, emotional and neural correlates of creativity. *Frontiers in Human Neuroscience, 9,* 275. doi:10.3389/fnhum.2015.00275

Baas, M., Nijstad, B. A., et al. (2016). Mad genius revisited: Vulnerability to psychopathology, biobehavioral approach-avoidance, and creativity. *Psychological Bulletin, 142*(6), 668–692. doi:10.1037/bul0000049

Babbie, E. R. (2016). *The practice of social research* (14th ed.). Boston, MA: Cengage Learning.

Baddeley, A. (2012). Working memory: Theories, models, and controversies. *Annual Review of Psychology, 63,* 1–29. doi:10.1146/annurev-psych-120710-100422

Baddeley, A., Eysenck, M. W., & Anderson, M. C. (2009). *Memory.* Hove, UK: Psychology Press.

Bader, S. M., Schoeneman-Morris, K. A., et al. (2008). Exhibitionism: Findings from a Midwestern police contact sample. *International Journal of Offender Therapy & Comparative Criminology, 52*(3), 270–279. doi:10.1177/0306624X07307122

Baer, N., Cialdini, R. B., & Lueth, N. (2012). *Influence: Science and practice: The Comic.* Highland Park, IL: Roundtable.

Bailey, C. H., & Kandel, E. R. (2004). Synaptic growth and the persistence of long-term memory: A molecular perspective. In M. S. Gazzaniga (Ed.), *The cognitive neurosciences* (3rd ed., pp. 647–663). Cambridge, MA: MIT Press.

Bailey, M. J., Sun, S., & Timpe, B. (2018, November). *Prep school for poor kids: The long-run impacts of Head Start on human capital and economic self-sufficiency.* Retrieved from https://news.umich.edu/head-start-slashes-likelihood-of-adult-poverty/

Baillargeon, R. (1991). Reasoning about the height and location of a hidden object in 4.5- and 6.5-month-old infants. *Cognition, 38*(1), 13–42. doi:10.1016/0010-0277(91)90021-U

Baillargeon, R. (2004). Infants' reasoning about hidden objects: Evidence for event-general and event-specific expectations. *Developmental Science, 7*(4), 391–424. doi:10.1111/j.1467-7687.2004.00357.x

Baillargeon, R., & DeVos, J. (1991). Object permanence in young infants: Further evidence. *Child Development, 62,* 1227–1246. doi:10.1111/j.1467-8624.1991.tb01602.x

Baillargeon, R., De Vos, J., & Graber, M. (1989). Location memory in 8-month-old infants in a nonsearch AB task. *Cognitive Development, 4,* 345–367. doi:10.1016/S0885-2014(89)90040-3

Baillargeon, R., Scott, R. M., et al. (2016). Psychological reasoning in infancy. *Annual Review of Psychology, 67,* 159–186. doi:10.1146/annurev-psych-010213-115033

Baker, S. C., & Serdikoff, S. L. (2013). Addressing the role of animal research in psychology. In D. S. Dunn, R. A. R. Gurung, et al. (Eds.), *Controversy in the psychology classroom: Using hot topics to foster critical thinking* (pp. 105–112). Washington, DC: American Psychological Association. doi:10.1037/14038-007

Bakker, G. M. (2009). In defence of thought stopping. *Clinical Psychologist, 13*(2), 59–68. doi:10.1080/13284200902810452

Bales, D., & Bateman, A. W. (2012). Partial hospitalization settings. In A. W. Bateman & P. Fonagy (Eds.), *Handbook of mentalizing in mental health practice* (pp. 197–226). Arlington, VA: American Psychiatric Publishing.

Balk, D. E., Lampe, S., et al. (1998). TAT results in a longitudinal study of bereaved college students. *Death Studies, 22*(1), 3–21. doi:10.1080/074811898201704

Ball, H. L., & Volpe, L. E. (2013). Sudden Infant Death Syndrome (SIDS) risk reduction and infant sleep location: Moving the discussion forward. *Social Science & Medicine, 79,* 84–91. doi:10.1016/j.socscimed.2012.03.025

Balliet, D., Wu, J., & De Dreu, C. K. W. (2014). Ingroup favoritism in cooperation: A meta-analysis. *Psychological Bulletin, 140*(6), 1556–1581. doi:10.1037/a0037737

Ballonoff Suleiman, A., & Brindis, C. D. (2014). Adolescent school-based sex education: Using developmental neuroscience to guide new directions for policy and practice. *Sexuality Research & Social Policy: A Journal of the NSRC,* doi:10.1007/s13178-014-0147-8

Balmas, M. (2014). When fake news becomes real: Combined exposure to multiple news sources and political attitudes of inefficacy, alienation, and cynicism. *Communication Research, 41*(3), 430–454. doi:10.1177/0093650212453600

Balon, R. (2016a). Exhibitionistic disorder. In R. Balon (Ed.), *Practical guide to paraphilia and paraphilic disorders* (pp. 77–91). Cham, Switzerland: Springer. doi:10.1007/978-3-319-42650-1_6

Balon, R. (Ed.). (2016b). *Practical guide to paraphilia and paraphilic disorders.* Cham, Switzerland: Springer International Publishing. doi:10.1007/978-3-319-42650-1

Balthazart, J. (2012). *Biology of homosexuality.* New York: Oxford University Press.

Bandura, A. (1971). *Social learning theory.* New York: General Learning Press.

Bandura, A. (2001). Social cognitive theory: An agentic perspective. *Annual Review of Psychology, 52,* 1–26. doi:10.1146/annurev.psych.52.1.1

Bandura, A., Blanchard, E. B., & Ritter, B. (1969). Relative efficacy of desensitization and modeling approaches for inducing behavioral, affective, and attitudinal changes. *Journal of Personality & Social Psychology, 13*(3), 173–199. doi:10.1037/h0028276

Bandura, A., Ross, D., & Ross, S. A. (1963). Vicarious reinforcement and imitative learning. *Journal of Abnormal & Social Psychology, 67,* 601–607. doi:10.1037/h0045550

Banerjee, D., & Nisbet, A. (2011). Sleepwalking. *Sleep Medicine Clinics, 6*(4), 401–416. doi:10.1016/j.jsmc.2011.07.001

Banich, M. T., & Compton, R. J. (2011). *Cognitive neuroscience* (3rd ed.). Boston, MA: Cengage Learning.

Banks, A., & Gartrell, N. K. (1995). Hormones and sexual orientation: A questionable link. *Journal of Homosexuality, 28*(3–4), 247–268.

Banks, G., Hadenfeldt, K., et al. (2017, February 16). Gun violence and substance abuse. *Aggression & Violent Behavior,* n.p. doi:10.1016/j.avb.2017.02.002

Bar-Anan, Y., Wilson, T. D., & Hassin, R. R. (2010). Inaccurate self-knowledge formation as a result of automatic behavior. *Journal of Experimental Social Psychology, 46*(6), 884–894. doi:10.1016/j.jesp.2010.07.007

Barabasz, A., & Watkins, J. G. (2005). *Hypnotherapeutic techniques* (2nd ed.). Washington, DC: Taylor & Francis.

Barber, J. P., Abrams, M. J., et al. (2005). Explanatory style change in supportive-expressive dynamic therapy. *Journal of Clinical Psychology, 61*(3), 257–268. doi:10.1002/jclp.20114

Barber, N. (2010). Applying the concept of adaptation to societal differences in intelligence. *Cross-Cultural Research, 44*(2), 116–150. doi:10.1177/1069397109358041

Bardone-Cone, A. M., Joiner, Jr., T. E., et al. (2008). Examining a psychosocial interactive model of binge eating and vomiting in women with bulimia nervosa and subthreshold bulimia nervosa. *Behaviour Research & Therapy, 46*(7), 887–894. doi:10.1016/j.brat.2008.04.003

Barelds, D. P., & Dijkstra, P. (2009). Positive illusions about a partner's physical attractiveness and relationship quality. *Personal Relationships, 16*(2), 263–283. doi:10.1111/j.1475-6811.2009.01222.x

Barkan, R., Ayal, S., et al. (2012). The pot calling the kettle black: Distancing response to ethical dissonance. *Journal of Experimental Psychology: General, 141,* 757–773. doi:10.1037/a0027588

Barkataki, I., Kumari, V., et al. (2006). Volumetric structural brain abnormalities in men with schizophrenia or antisocial personality disorder. *Behavioural Brain Research, 169*(2), 239–247. doi:10.1016/j.bbr.2006.01.009

Barlow, D. H. (2000). Unraveling the mysteries of anxiety and its disorders from the perspective of emotion theory. *American Psychologist, 55,* 1247–1263. doi:10.1037/0003-066X.55.11.1247

Barlow, D. H., Durand, V. M., et al. (2018). *Abnormal psychology: An integrative approach* (8th ed.). Boston, MA: Cengage Learning.

Barnett, J., Behnke, S. H., et al. (2007). In case of ethical dilemma, break glass: Commentary on ethical decision making in practice. *Professional Psychology: Research & Practice, 38*(1), 7–12. doi:10.1037/0735-7028.38.1.7

Barnett, N. P., Ott, M. Q., et al. (2013, December). Peer associations for substance use and exercise in a college student social network. *Health Psychology,* n.p. doi:10.1037/a0034687

Barnier, A. J., McConkey, K. M., & Wright, J. (2004). Posthypnotic amnesia for autobiographical episodes: Influencing memory accessibility and quality. *International Journal of Clinical & Experimental Hypnosis, 52*(3), 260–279. doi:10.1080/0020714049052351

Baron-Cohen, S., Burt, L., Smith-Laittan, F., Harrison, J., & Bolton, P. (1996). Synaesthesia: Prevalence and familiality. *Perception, 25*(9), 1073–1079. doi:10.1068/p251073

Barr, M. S., Farzan, F., et al. (2013). Can repetitive magnetic stimulation improve cognition in schizophrenia? Pilot data from a randomized controlled trial. *Biological Psychiatry, 73*(6), 510–517. doi:10.1016/j.biopsych.2012.08.020

Barratt, B. B. (2013). *What is psychoanalysis? 100 years after Freud's "secret committee."* New York: Taylor & Francis.

Barreto, M. L., & Frazier, L. D. (2012). Coping with life events through possible selves. *Journal of Applied Social Psychology, 42*(7), 1785–1810. doi:10.1111/j.1559-1816.2012.00918.x

Barrett, F. S., Grimm, K. J., et al. (2010). Music-evoked nostalgia: Affect, memory, and personality. *Emotion, 10*(3), 390–403. doi:10.1037/a0019006

Barrett, L. F. (2017). *How emotions are made: The secret life of the brain.* Boston: Houghton Mifflin Harcourt.

Barron, F. (1958). The psychology of imagination. *Scientific American, 199*(3), 150–170. doi:10.1038.scientificamerican0958-150

Barrouillet, P. (2015). Theories of cognitive development: From Piaget to today. *Developmental Review, 38,* 1–12. doi:10.1016/j.dr.2015.07.004

Barry, J. G., Sabisch, B., et al. (2011). Encoding: The keystone to efficient functioning of verbal short-term memory. *Neuropsychologia, 49*(13), 3636–3647. doi:10.1016/j.neuropsychologia.2011.09.018

Barry, S. R., & Sacks, O. (2009). *Fixing my gaze.* New York: Basic Books.

Bartels, J. M. (2015). The Stanford prison experiment in introductory psychology textbooks: A content analysis. *Psychology Learning & Teaching, 14*(1), 36–50. doi:10.1177/1475725714568007

Bartholow, B. D., & Anderson, C. A. (2002). Effects of violent video games on aggressive behavior. *Journal of Experimental Social Psychology, 38*(3), 283–290. doi:10.1006/jesp.2001.1502

Bartholow, B. D., Sestir, M. A., & Davis, E. B. (2005). Correlates and consequences of exposure to video game violence: Hostile personality, empathy, and aggressive behavior. *Personality & Social Psychology Bulletin, 31*(11), 1573–1586. doi:10.1177/0146167205277205

Bartle-Haring, S., Shannon, S., et al. (2016, February 29). Therapist differentiation and couple clients' perceptions of therapeutic alliance. *Journal of Marital & Family Therapy.* doi:10.1111/jmft.12157

Bartram, B. (2006). An examination of perceptions of parental influence on attitudes to language learning. *Educational Research, 48*(2), 211–222. doi:10.1080/00131880600732298

Basner, M., & Dinges, D. (2009). Dubious bargain: Trading sleep for Leno and Letterman. *Sleep, 32*(6), 747–752.

Bass, J., & Takahashi, J. S. (2010). Circadian integration of metabolism and energetics. *Science, 330*(6009), 1349–1354. doi:10.1126/science.1195027

Basson, R., & Brotto, L. A. (2009). Disorders of sexual desire and subjective arousal in women. In R. Balon & R. T. Segraves (Eds.), *Clinical manual of sexual disorders* (pp. 119–159). Arlington, VA: American Psychiatric Publishing.

Batelaan, N. M., de Graaf, R., et al. (2010). The course of panic attacks in individuals with panic disorder and subthreshold panic disorder: A population-based study. *Journal of Affective Disorders, 121*(1–2), 30–38. doi:10.1016/j.jad.2009.05.003

Bateman, A. W., & Fonagy, P. (2012). Antisocial personality disorder. In A. W. Bateman & P. Fonagy (Eds.), *Handbook of mentalizing in mental health practice* (pp. 289–308). Arlington, VA: American Psychiatric Publishing.

Batson, C. D. (2006). "Not all self-interest after all": Economics of empathy-induced altruism. In D. De Cremer, M. Zeelenberg, et al. (Eds.), *Social psychology and economics* (pp. 281– 299). Mahwah, NJ: Erlbaum.

Batson, C. D. (2010). Empathy-induced altruistic motivation. In M. Mikulincer & P. R. Shaver (Eds.), *Prosocial motives, emotions, and behavior: The better angels of our nature* (pp. 15–34). Washington, DC: American Psychological Association. doi:10.1037/12061-001

Batson, C. D. (2011). *Altruism in humans.* New York: Oxford.

Batson, C. D., & Powell, A. A. (2003). Altruism and prosocial behavior. In T. Millon & M. J. Lerner (Eds.), *Handbook of psychology: Personality and social psychology* (Vol. 5, pp. 463– 484). New York: Wiley.

Bauer, A., Schneider, S., et al. (2017). Selective visual attention towards oneself and associated state body satisfaction: An eye-tracking study in adolescents with different types of eating disorders. *Journal of Abnormal Child Psychology,* n.p. doi:10.1007/s10802-017-0263-z

Bauer, J. J., McAdams, D. P., & Pals, J. L. (2008). Narrative identity and eudaimonic well-being. *Journal of Happiness Studies, 9*(1), 81–104. doi:10.1007/s10902-006-9021-6

Bauer, S., Wolf, M., et al. (2011). The effectiveness of Internet chat groups in relapse prevention after inpatient psychotherapy. *Psychotherapy Research, 21*(2), 219–226. doi:10.1080/10503307.2010.547530

Baugh, C. M., Stamm, J. M., et al. (2012). Chronic traumatic encephalopathy: Neurodegeneration following repetitive concussive and subconcussive brain trauma. *Brain Imaging & Behavior, 6*(2), 244–254. doi:10.1007/s11682-012-9164-5

Baughman, H. M., Dearing, S., Giammarco, E., & Vernon, P. A. (2012). Relationships between bullying behaviours and the Dark Triad: A study with adults. *Personality and Individual Differences, 52*(5), 571–575.

Baum, A., & Davis, G. E. (1980). Reducing the stress of high-density living: An architectural intervention. *Journal of Personality & Social Psychology, 38,* 471–481.

Baum, A., & Valins, S. (1979). Architectural mediation of residential density and control: Crowding and the regulation of social contact. *Advances in Experimental & Social Psychology, 12,* 131–175.

Baum, A., & Valins, S. (Eds.). (1977). *Human response to crowding: Studies of the effects of residential group size.* Mahwah, NJ: Erlbaum.

Bauman, L. J., Karasz, A., & Hamilton, A. (2007). Understanding failure of condom use intention among adolescents: Completing an intensive preventive intervention. *Journal of Adolescent Research, 22*(3), 248–274.

Baumeister, R. F. (2015, April). Conquer yourself, conquer the world. *Scientific American, 312*(4), 60–65.

Baumeister, R. F., & Bushman, B. (2017). *Social psychology and human nature* (4th ed.). Boston, MA: Cengage Learning.

Baumeister, R. F., Campbell, J. D., et al. (2003). Does high self-esteem cause better performance, interpersonal success, happiness, or healthier lifestyles? *Psychological Science in the Public Interest, 4*(1), 1–44. doi:10.1111/1529-1006.01431

Baumrind, D. (1991). The influence of parenting style on adolescent competence and substance use. *Journal of Early Adolescence, 11*(1), 56–95. doi:10.1177/0272431691111004

Baumrind, D. (2005). Patterns of parental authority and adolescent autonomy. In J. Smetana (Ed.), *New directions for child development: Changes in parental authority during adolescence* (pp. 61–69). San Francisco, CA: Jossey-Bass.

Bayne, R., & Jinks, G. (2013). *Applied psychology: Research, practice and new directions* (2nd ed.). Thousand Oaks: Sage.

Beans, D. R. (2009). *Integrative endocrinology*: New York: Routledge.

Bearman, P. S., Moody, J., & Stovel, K. (2004). Chains of affection: The structure of adolescent romantic and sexual networks. *American Journal of Sociology, 110*(1), 44–91.

Beaulieu, C. M. J. (2004). Intercultural study of personal space: A case study. *Journal of Applied Social Psychology, 34*(4), 794–805.

Beck, A. T. (1967). *Depression.* New York: Harper & Row.

Beck, A. T. (1991). Cognitive therapy. *American Psychologist, 46*(4), 368–375. doi:10.1037/0003-066X.46.4.368

Beck, A. T., Rector, N. A., et al. (2009). *Schizophrenia: Cognitive theory, research, and therapy.* New York: Guilford.

Beck, H. P., Levinson, S., & Irons, G. (2009). Finding little Albert: A journey to John B. Watson's infant laboratory. *American Psychologist, 64*(7), 605–614. doi:10.1037/a0017234

Becker, A. E., Fay, K., et al. (2010). Development of a measure of "acculturation" for ethnic Fijians: Methodologic and conceptual considerations for application to eating disorders research.

Transcultural Psychiatry, 47(5), 754–788. doi:10.1177/1363461510382153
Becker, S. W., & Eagly, A. H. (2004). The heroism of women and men. *American Psychologist, 59*(3),163–178.
Beckmann, M., Cornelissen, T., et al. (2017). Self-managed working time and employee effort: Theory and evidence. *Journal of Economic Behavior & Organization, 133,* 285-302. doi:10.1016/j.jebo.2016.11.013
Bedny, M., Pascual-Leone, A., et al. (2012). A sensitive period for language in the visual cortex: Distinct patterns of plasticity in congenitally versus late blind adults. *Brain & Language, 122*(3), 162–170. doi:10.1016/j.bandl.2011.10.005
Beeber, L. S., Chazan-Cohen, R., et al. (2007). The Early Promotion and Intervention Research Consortium (EPIRC): Five approaches to improving infant/toddler mental health in Early Head Start. *Infant Mental Health Journal, 28*(2), 130–150. doi:10.1002/imhj.20126
Begg, D. P., Sinclair, A. J., & Weisinger, R. S. (2012). Thirst deficits in aged rats are reversed by dietary omega-3 fatty acid supplementation. *Neurobiology of Aging, 33*(10), 2422–2430. doi:10.1016/j.neurobiolaging.2011.12.001
Behne, T., Liszkowski, U., et al. (2012). Twelve-month-olds' comprehension and production of pointing. *British Journal of Developmental Psychology, 30*(3), 359–375. doi:10.1111/j.2044-835X.2011.02043.x
Beidel, D. C., Frueh, B. C., et al. (2019). Trauma management therapy with virtual-reality augmented exposure therapy for combat-related PTSD: A randomized controlled trial. *Journal of Anxiety Disorders, 61,* 64–74. doi:10.1016/j.janxdis.2017.08.005
Bekinschtein, T. A., Shalom, D. E., et al. (2009). Classical conditioning in the vegetative and minimally conscious state. *Nature Neuroscience, 12,* 1343–1349. doi:10.1038/nn.2391
Belicki, K., Chambers, E., et al. (1997). Sleep quality and nightmares. *Sleep Research, 26,* 637.
Belsky, J., Ruttle, P. L., et al. (2015). Early adversity, elevated stress physiology, accelerated sexual maturation, and poor health in females. *Developmental Psychology, 51*(6), 816–822. doi:10.1037/dev0000017
Bem, S. L. (1974). The measurement of psychological androgyny. *Journal of Consulting & Clinical Psychology, 42*(2), 155–162. doi:10.1037/h0036215
Bem, S. L. (1975). Androgyny vs. the tight little lives of fluffy women and chesty men. *Psychology Today, 31,*58–62.
Bem, S. L. (1981). Gender schema theory. A cognitive account of sex typing. *Psychological Review, 88,* 354–364.
Ben Abdallah, N. M.-B., Slomianka, L., et al. (2010). Early age-related changes in adult hippocampal neurogenesis in C57 mice. *Neurobiology of Aging, 31*(1), 151–161. doi:10.1016/j.neurobiolaging.2008.03.002
Ben-Itzhak, S., Bluvstein, I., et al. (2012). The effectiveness of brief versus intermediate duration psychodynamic psychotherapy in the treatment of adjustment disorder. *Journal of Contemporary Psychotherapy, 42*(4), 249–256. doi:10.1007/s10879-012-9208-6
Ben-Shakhar, G., & Dolev, K. (1996). Psychophysiological detection through the guilty knowledge technique: Effect of mental countermeasures. *Journal of Applied Psychology, 81*(3), 273–281. doi:10.1037/0021-9010.81.3.273
Benartzi, S., Beshears, J., et al. (2017). Should governments invest more in nudging? *Psychological Science, 28*(8), 1041–1055. doi:10.1177/0956797617702501
Benedetti, F. (2009). *Placebo effects: Understanding the mechanisms in health and disease.* New York: Oxford University Press.
Benitz, L. (2009). Becoming biliterate: A study of two-way bilingual immersion education. *Journal of Language, Identity, & Education, 8*(1), 54–57. doi:10.1080/15348450802620001
Benjafield, J. G. (2015). *A history of psychology* (4th ed.). New York: Oxford University Press.
Benjafield, J. G., Smilek, D., & Kingstone, A. (2010). *Cognition* (4th ed.). New York: Oxford University Press.
Benjamin, O., & Tlusten, D. (2010). Intimacy and/or degradation: Heterosexual images of togetherness and women's embracement of pornography. *Sexualities, 13*(5), 599–623.
Benloucif, S., Bennett, E. L., & Rosenzweig, M. R. (1995). Norepinephrine and neural plasticity: The effects of xylamine on experience-induced changes in brain weight, memory, and behavior. *Neurobiology of Learning & Memory, 63*(1), 33–42. doi:10.1006/nlme.1995.1003
Bensafi, M., Zelano, C., et al. (2004). Olfaction: From sniff to percept. In M. S. Gazzaniga (Ed.), *The cognitive neurosciences* (3rd ed., pp. 259–280). Cambridge, MA: MIT Press.
Bensley, L., & Van Eenwyk, J. (2001). Video games and real-life aggression. *Journal of Adolescent Health, 29*(4), 244–257. doi:10.1016/S1054-139X(01)00239-7
Bentley-Condit, V. K., & Smith, E. O. (2010). Animal tool use: Current definitions and an updated comprehensive catalog. *Behaviour, 147*(2), 185–221. doi:10.1163/000579509X12512865686555
Bento, A. I., Nguyen, T., Wing, C., Lozano-Rojas, F., Ahn, Y., & Simon, K. (2020). Evidence from internet search data shows information-seeking responses to news of local COVID-19 cases. *Proceedings of the National Academy of Sciences, 117*(21), 11220–11222. doi:10.1073/pnas.2005335117
Berenbaum, S. A., Blakemore, J., & Beltz, A. M. (2011). A role for biology in gender-related behavior. *Sex Roles, 64*(11–12), 804–825. doi:10.1007/s11199-011-9990-8
Berg, J. (2013). Opposition to pro-immigrant public policy: Symbolic racism and group threat. *Sociological Inquiry, 83*(1), 1–31. doi:10.1111/j.1475-682x.2012.00437.x
Bergeron, S., & Lord, M. J. (2003). The integration of pelvi-perineal reeducation and cognitive-behavioral therapy in the multidisciplinary treatment of the sexual pain disorders. *Sexual & Relationship Therapy, 18,* 135–141.
Bergstrom, H. C., McDonald, C. G., et al. (2013). Neurons activated during fear memory consolidation and reconsolidation are mapped to a common and new topography in the lateral amygdala. *Brain Topography, 26*(3), 468–478. doi:10.1007/s10548-012-0266-6
Berlin, H. A. (2011). The neural basis of the dynamic unconscious. *Neuropsychoanalysis, 13*(1), 5–31.
Berman, M. G., Yourganov, G., et al. (2013). Dimensionality of brain networks linked to life-long individual differences in self-control. *Nature Communications, 4,* 1373. doi:10.1038/ncomms2374
Berman, S. L., Weems, C. F., & Stickle, T. R. (2006). Existential anxiety in adolescents: Prevalence, structure, association with psychological symptoms, and identity development. *Journal of Youth & Adolescence, 35*(3), 303–310. doi:10.1007/s10964-006-9032-y
Bermudez-Silva, F. J., Viveros, M. P., et al. (2010). The endocannabinoid system, eating behavior and energy homeostasis: The end or a new beginning? *Pharmacology, Biochemistry & Behavior, 95*(4), 375–382. doi:10.1016/j.pbb.2010.03.012
Bernard, R. S., Cohen, L. L., & Moffett, K. (2009). A token economy for exercise adherence in pediatric cystic fibrosis: A single-subject analysis. *Journal of Pediatric Psychology, 34*(4), 354–365. doi:10.1093/jpepsy/jsn101
Berne, E. (1964). *Games people play*. New York: Grove.
Bernstein, D. A. (2018). Does active learning work? A good question, but not the right one. *Scholarship of Teaching and Learning in Psychology, 4,* 290–307. doi:10.1037/stl0000124
Bernstein, D. A., & Lucas, S. G. (2008). Functional fixedness in problem solving. In Benjamin L. T. (Ed.), *Favorite activities for the teaching of psychology* (pp. 143–144). Washington, DC: American Psychological Association.
Bernstein, D. M., & Loftus, E. F. (2009). How to tell if a particular memory is true or false. *Perspectives on Psychological Science, 4*(4), 370–374. doi:10.1111/j.1745-6924.2009.01140.x
Bernstein, H. J., Beale, M. D., et al. (1998). Patient attitudes about ECT after treatment. *Psychiatric Annals, 28*(9), 524–527.
Bernstein, I. H., Rush, A. J., et al. (2008). Symptom features of postpartum depression: Are they distinct? *Depression & Anxiety, 25*(1), 20–26.
Bernthal, M. J. (2008). How viewing professional wrestling may affect children. *The Sport Journal, 6*(3). Retrieved January 27, 2017, from http://www.thesportjournal.org/article/effect professional wrestling-viewership-children
Bersamin, M. M., Zamboanga, B. L., et al. (2014). Risky business: Is there an association between casual sex and mental health among emerging adults? *Journal of Sex Research, 51*(1), 43–51. doi:10.1080/00224499.2013.772088
Berscheid, E. (2010). Love in the fourth dimension. *Annual Review of Psychology, 61,* 1–25. doi:10.1146/annurev.psych.093008.100318
Bersoff, D. M. (1999). Why good people sometimes do bad things: Motivated reasoning and unethical behavior. *Personality & Social Psychology Bulletin, 25*(1), 28–39. doi:10.1177/0146167299025001003
Bertakis, K. D., Azari, R., Helms, L. J., Callahan, E. J., & Robbins, J. A. (2000). Gender differences in the utilization of health care services. *Journal of Family Practice, 49*(2), 147.
Beseler, C. L., Taylor, L. A., & Leeman, R. F. (2010). An item-response theory analysis of DSM-IV alcohol-use

disorder criteria and "binge" drinking in undergraduates. *Journal of Studies on Alcohol & Drugs, 71*(3), 418–423.

Besnard, D., & Cacitti, L. (2005). Interface changes causing accidents: An empirical study of negative transfer. *International Journal of Human-Computer Studies, 62*(1), 105–125.

Best, D. (2002). Cross-cultural gender roles. In J. Worell (Ed.), *Encyclopedia of women and gender* (pp. 279–290). New York: Oxford.

Beyers, W., & Seiffge-Krenke, I. (2010). Does identity precede intimacy? Testing Erikson's theory on romantic development in emerging adults of the 21st century. *Journal of Adolescent Research, 25*(3), 387–415. doi:10.1177/0743558410361370

Bezrukova, K., Spell, C. S., Perry, J. L., & Jehn, K. A. (2016). A meta-analytical integration of over 40 years of research on diversity training evaluation. *Psychological Bulletin, 142*(11), 1227–1274. doi:10.1037/bul0000067

Bialystok, E., & Barac, R. R. (2012). Emerging bilingualism: Dissociating advantages for metalinguistic awareness and executive control. *Cognition, 122*(1), 67–73. doi:10.1016/j.cognition.2011.08.003

Bick, A. S., Leker, R. R., et al. (2013). Implementing novel imaging methods for improved diagnosis of disorder of consciousness patients. *Journal of the Neurological Sciences, 334*(1), 130–138. doi:10.1016/j.jns.2013.08.009

Biernat, M., & Danaher, K. (2013). Prejudice. In H. Tennen, J. Suls, et al. (Eds.), *Handbook of psychology* (Vol. 5): *Personality and social psychology* (2nd ed., pp. 341–367). New York: Wiley.

Bilewicz, M., Soral, W., et al. (2017). When authoritarians confront prejudice. Differential effects of SDO and RWA on support for hate-speech prohibition. *Political Psychology, 38*(1), 87–99. doi:10.1111/pops.12313

Binder, J. L., & Betan, E. J. (2013). Essential activities in a session of brief dynamic/interpersonal psychotherapy. *Psychotherapy, 50*(3), 428–432. doi:10.1037/a0032521

Binder, J., Zagefka, H., et al. (2009). Does contact reduce prejudice or does prejudice reduce contact? A longitudinal test of the contact hypothesis among majority and minority groups in three European countries. *Journal of Personality & Social Psychology, 96*(4), 843–856. doi:10.1037/a0013470

Binik, Y. M. (2010). The DSM diagnostic criteria for dyspareunia. *Archives of Sexual Behavior, 39*(2), 292–303. doi:10.1007/s10508-009-9563-x

Binning, K. R., Sherman, D. K., et al. (2010). Seeing the other side: Reducing political partisanship via self-affirmation in the 2008 presidential election. *Analyses of Social Issues & Public Policy,* (1), 276–292. doi:10.1111/j.1530-2415.2010.01210.x

Birchwood, M., Michail, M., et al. (2014). Cognitive behaviour therapy to prevent harmful compliance with command hallucinations (COMMAND): A randomised controlled trial. *The Lancet Psychiatry, 1*(1), 23–33. doi:10.1016/S2215-0366(14)70247-0

Birgegård, A., Norring, C., & Clinton, D. (2012). DSM-IV versus DSM-5: Implementation of proposed DSM-5 criteria in a large naturalistic database. *International Journal of Eating Disorders, 45*(3), 353–361. doi:10.1002/eat.20968

Biro, F. M., Galvez, M. P., et al. (2010). Pubertal assessment method and baseline characteristics in a mixed longitudinal study of girls. *Pediatrics, 126*(3), e583–e590. doi:10.1542/peds.2009-3079

Bisson, J. I., Ehlers, A., et al. (2007). Psychological treatments for chronic post-traumatic stress disorder: Systematic review and meta-analysis. *British Journal of Psychiatry, 190*(2), 97–104. doi:10.1192/bjp.bp.106.021402

Bitzer, J., Giraldi, A., & Pfaus, J. (2013). Sexual desire and hypoactive sexual desire disorder in women. Introduction and overview. Standard operating procedure (SOP Part 1). *Journal of Sexual Medicine, 10*(1), 36–49. doi:10.1111/j.1743-6109.2012.02818.x

Bizer, G. Y., Hart, J., & Jekogian, A. M. (2012). Belief in a just world and social dominance orientation: Evidence for a mediational pathway predicting negative attitudes and discrimination against individuals with mental illness. *Personality & Individual Differences, 52*(3), 428–432. doi:10.1016/j.paid.2011.11.002

Bjork, R. A., & Bjork, E. L. (2013). Optimizing treatment and instruction: Implications of a new theory of disuse. In L. Nilsson & N. Ohta (Eds.), *Memory and society: Psychological perspectives* (pp. 119–143). London: Psychology Press.

Bjorklund, D. F. (2012). *Children's thinking* (5th ed.). Boston, MA: Cengage Learning.

Bjorklund, D. F., & Hernández Blasi, C. (2012). *Child and adolescent development*. Boston, MA: Cengage Learning.

Bjornstrom, E. E. (2011). An examination of the relationship between neighborhood income inequality, social resources, and obesity in Los Angeles County. *American Journal of Health Promotion, 26*(2), 109–115. doi:10.4278/ajhp.100326-QUAN-93

Black, D. W. (2015). The natural history of antisocial personality disorder. *Canadian Journal of Psychiatry, 60*(7), 309–314.

Blackmore, S. (2000, November 4). First person: Into the unknown. *New Scientist,* 55.

Blackwell, B. (2012). Obituary: Jose Manuel Rodriguez Delgado. *Neuropsychopharmacology, 37*(13), 2883–2884.

Blackwell, D. L., & Lichter, D. T. (2004). Homogamy among dating, cohabiting, and married couples. *Sociological Quarterly, 45*(4), 719–737. doi:10.1111/j.1533-8525.2004.tb02311.x

Blair, K. S., Richell, R. A., et al. (2006). They know the words, but not the music: Affective and semantic priming in individuals with psychopathy. *Biological Psychology, 73*(2), 114–123. doi:10.1016/j.biopsycho.2005.12.006

Blake, A. B., Nazarian, M., et al. (2015). The Apple of the mind's eye: Everyday attention, metamemory, and reconstructive memory for the Apple logo. *Quarterly Journal of Experimental Psychology, 68*(5), 858–865. doi:10.1080/17470218

Blakemore, C., & Cooper, G. (1970). Development of the brain depends on the visual environment. *Nature, 228,* 477–478. doi:10.1038/228477a0

Blanchard, E. B., Kuhn, E., et al. (2004). Studies of the vicarious traumatization of college students by the September 11th attacks: Effects of proximity, exposure, and connectedness. *Behaviour Research & Therapy, 42*(2), 191–205.

Blandón-Gitlin, I., Pezdek, K., et al. (2014). Oxytocin eliminates the own-race bias in face recognition memory. *Brain Research, 1580,* 180–187. doi10.1016/j.brainres.2013.07.015

Bliese, P. D., Edwards, J. R., et al. (2017). Stress and well-being at work: A century of empirical trends reflecting theoretical and societal influences. *Journal of Applied Psychology, 102*(3), 389–402. doi:10.1037/apl0000109

Bloom, B. S. (1956). *Taxonomy of educational objectives: The classification of educational goals* (1st ed.). Harlow, Essex, England: Longman Group.

Bloom, C. M., & Lamkin, D. M. (2006). The Olympian struggle to remember the cranial nerves: Mnemonics and student success. *Teaching of Psychology, 33*(2), 128–129. doi:1207/s15328023top3302_8

Bloom, L., & Bloom, C. (2012). What's so special about *Fifty Shades of Gray?* Retrieved March 10, 2017, from www.psychologytoday.com/blog/stronger-the-broken-places/201212/whats-so-special-about-fifty-shades-gray

Bloom, P. (2017). Empathy and its discontents. *Trends in Cognitive Sciences, 21*(1), 24–31. doi:10.1016/j.tics.2016.11.004

Blundon, J. A., & Zakharenko, S. S. (2008). Dissecting the components of long-term potentiation. *The Neuroscientist, 14*(6), 598–608.

Bodner, E. (2009). On the origins of ageism among older and younger adults. *International Psychogeriatrics, 21*(6), 1003–1014. doi:10.1017/S104161020999055X

Boduroglu, A., Shah, P., & Nisbett, R. E. (2009). Cultural differences in allocation of attention in visual information processing. *Journal of Cross-Cultural Psychology, 40*(3), 349–360. doi:10.1177/0022022108331005

Boerke, K. W., & Reitman, D. (2011). Token economies. In W. W. Fisher, C. C. Piazza, et al. (Eds.), *Handbook of applied behavior analysis* (pp. 370–382). New York: Guilford.

Bogaert, A. F. (2006). Toward a conceptual understanding of asexuality. *Review of General Psychology, 10,* 241–250.

Bogaert, A. F. (2012). *Understanding asexuality*. Lanham, MD: Rowman & Littlefield.

Bogaert, A. F. (2015). Asexuality: What it is and why it matters. *Journal of Sex Research, 52*(4), 362–379. doi:10.1080/00224499.2015.1015713

Bogaert, A. F., & Skorska, M. (2011). Sexual orientation, fraternal birth order, and the maternal immune hypothesis: A review. *Frontiers in Neuroendocrinology, 32*(2), 247–254. doi:10.1016/j.yfrne.2011.02.004

Boggio, P. S., Campanhã, C., et al. (2010). Modulation of decision-making in a gambling task in older adults with transcranial direct current stimulation. *European Journal of Neuroscience, 31*(3), 593–597. doi:10.1111/j.1460-9568.2010.07080.x

Bohbot, V., & Corkin, S. (2007). Posterior parahippocampal place learning in H. M. *Hippocampus, 17*(9), 863–872. doi:10.1002/hipo.20313.

Bohner, G., & Dickel, N. (2010). Attitudes and attitude change. *Annual Review of Psychology, 62,* 391–417.

doi:10.1146/annurev.psych.121208.131609

Bohns, V. K. (2016). (Mis)understanding our influence over others: A review of the underestimation-of-compliance effect. *Current Directions in Psychological Science, 25*(2), 119–123. doi:10.1177/0963721415628011

Boiger, M., & Mesquita, B. (2012). The construction of emotion in interactions, relationships, and cultures. *Emotion Review, 4*(3), 221–229. doi:10.1177/1754073912439765

Boivin, D. B., Czeisler, C. A., et al. (1997). Complex interaction of the sleep-wake cycle and circadian phase modulates mood in healthy subjects. *Archives of General Psychiatry, 54*(2), 145–152. doi:10.1001/archpsyc.1997.01830140055010

Boldero, J. M., Moretti, M. M., et al. (2005). Self-discrepancies and negative affect: A primer on when to look for specificity and how to find it. *Australian Journal of Psychology, 57*(3), 139–147. doi:10.1080/00049530500048730

Bolles, R. N. (2016). *What color is your parachute?* New York: Ten Speed Press.

Bolt, D. M., Piper, M. E., et al. (2012). Why two smoking cessation agents work better than one: Role of craving suppression. *Journal of Consulting & Clinical Psychology, 80*(1), 54–65. doi:10.1037/a0026366

Bonanno, R. A., & Hymel, S. (2013). Cyber bullying and internalizing difficulties: Above and beyond the impact of traditional forms of bullying. *Journal of Youth & Adolescence, 42*, 685–697. doi:10.1007/s10964-013-9937-1

Bond, M. A., Serrano-García, I., Keys, C. B., & Shinn, M. (2017). *APA handbook of community psychology: Theoretical foundations, core concepts, and emerging challenges, Vol. 1.* Washington DC: American Psychological Association.

Bond, R., & Smith, P. B. (1996). Culture and conformity: A meta-analysis of studies using Asch's (1952, 1956) line judgment task. *Psychological Bulletin, 119*(1), 111–137. doi:10.1037/0033-2909.119.1.111

Bongard, S., al'Absi, M., & Lovallo, W. R. (1998). Interactive effects of trait hostility and anger expression on cardiovascular reactivity in young men. *International Journal of Psychophysiology, 28*(2), 181–191. doi:10.1016/S0167-8760(97)00095-0

Bonham, V., Warshauer-Baker, E., & Collins, F. S. (2005). Race and ethnicity in the genome era: The complexity of the constructs. *American Psychologist, 60*(1), 9–15. doi:10.1037/0003-066X.60.1.9

Boniecki, K. A., & Britt, T. W. (2003). Prejudice and the peacekeeper. In T. W. Britt & A. B Adler (Eds.), *The psychology of the peacekeeper: Lessons from the field* (pp. 53–70). Westport, CT: Praeger.

Bonk, W. J., & Healy, A. F. (2010). Learning and memory for sequences of pictures, words, and spatial locations: An exploration of serial position effects. *American Journal of Psychology, 123*(2), 137–168.

Bonnardel, N., & Didier, J. (2016). Enhancing creativity in the educational design context: An exploration of the effects of design project-oriented methods on students' evocation processes and creative output. *Journal of Cognitive Education & Psychology, 15*(1), 80–101. doi:10.1891/1945-8959.15.1.80

Bood, S., Sundequist, U., et al. (2006). Eliciting the relaxation response with the help of flotation-REST (Restricted Environmental Stimulation Technique) in patients with stress-related ailments. *International Journal of Stress Management, 13*(2), 154–175. doi:10.1037/1072-5245.13.2.154

Bora, E., Fornito, A., et al. (2011). Neuroanatomical abnormalities in schizophrenia: A multimodal voxelwise meta-analysis and meta-regression analysis. *Schizophrenia Research, 127*(1), 46–57. doi:10.1016/j.schres.2010.12.020

Borch-Jacobsen, M., & Shamdasani, S. (2011). *The Freud files: An inquiry into the history of psychoanalysis.* London: Cambridge University Press.

Borg, C., Peters, M. L., et al. (2012). Vaginismus: Heightened harm avoidance and pain catastrophizing cognitions. *Journal of Sexual Medicine, 9*(2), 558–567. doi:10.1111/j.1743-6109.2011.02535.x

Bornstein, B. H. (2017). Jury simulation research: Pros, cons, trends, and alternatives. In M. B. Kovera (Ed.). *The psychology of juries* (pp. 207–226). Washington, DC: American Psychological Association. doi:10.1037/0000026-010

Bornstein, R. F. (2012). Rorschach score validation as a model for 21st-century personality assessment. *Journal of Personality Assessment, 94*(1), 26–38. doi:10.1080/00223891.2011.627961

Boroditsky, L. (2011, February). How language shapes thought. *Scientific American*, 62–65. doi:10.1038/scientificamerican0211-62

Boroditsky, L., & Gaby, A. (2010). Remembrances of times east: Absolute spatial representations of time in an Australian Aboriginal community. *Psychological Science, 21*(11), 1635–1639. doi:10.1177/0956797610386621

Borst, G., & Kosslyn, S. M. (2010). Fear selectively modulates visual mental imagery and visual perception. *Quarterly Journal of Experimental Psychology, 63*(5), 833–839. doi:10.1080/17470211003602420

Borzekowski, D. L. G., Schenk, S., et al. (2010). e-Ana and e-Mia: A content analysis of pro–eating disorder web sites. *American Journal of Public Health, 100*(8), 1526–1534.

Boskey, E. (2016). *Is oral sex safe sex?* Retrieved March 10, 2017, from http://std.about.com/od/riskfactors forstds/a/oralsexsafesex.htm

Bosley, H. G., & Eagleman, D. M. (2015). Synesthesia in twins: Incomplete concordance in monozygotes suggests extragenic factors. *Behavioural Brain Research, 286*, 93–96. doi:10.1016/j.bbr.2015.02.024

Bostwick, W. B., Boyd, C. J., et al. (2014). Discrimination and mental health among lesbian, gay, and bisexual adults in the United States. *American Journal of Orthopsychiatry, 84*(1), 35–45. doi:10.1037/h0098851

Botti, S., Orfali, K., & Iyengar, S. S. (2009). Tragic choices: Autonomy and emotional responses to medical decisions. *Journal of Consumer Research, 36*(3), 337–352. doi:10.1086/598969

Bouchard, T. J. Jr. (2004). Genetic influence on human psychological traits: A survey. *Current Directions in Psychological Science, 13*(4), 148–151. doi:10.1111/j.0963-7214.2004.00295.x

Boudry, M., Blancke, S., et al. (2015). What makes weird beliefs thrive? The epidemiology of pseudoscience. *Philosophical Psychology, 28*(8), 1177–1198. doi:10.1080/09515089.2014.971946

Bourgeois, J. A., Kahn, D., et al. (2009). *Casebook of psychosomatic medicine.* Washington, DC: American Psychiatric Publishing.

Bourne, E. J. (2010). *The anxiety & phobia workbook* (5th ed.). Oakland, CA: New Harbinger.

Bourne, L. R., & Healy, A. F. (2014). *Train your mind for peak performance: A science-based approach for achieving your goals.* Washington, DC: American Psychological Association. doi:10.1037/14319-000

Bowden, S. C., Petrauskas, V. M., et al. (2013). Exploring the dimensionality of Digit Span. *Assessment, 20*(2), 188–198. doi:10.1177/1073191112457016

Bowe, A. G., Desjardins, C. D., et al. (2017). Urban elementary single-sex math classrooms: Mitigating stereotype threat for African American girls. *Urban Education, 52*(3), 370–398. doi:10.1177/0042085915574521

Bowe, F. (2000). *Universal Design in education: Teaching nontraditional students.* Westport, CT: Bergin & Garvey.

Bowen, N. K., Wegmann, K. M., & Webber, K. C. (2013). Enhancing a brief writing intervention to combat stereotype threat among middle-school students. *Journal of Educational Psychology, 105*(2), 427–435. doi:10.1037/a0031177

Bower, G. H. (1981). Mood and memory. *American Psychologist, 36*, 129–148. doi:10.1037/0003-066X.36.2.129

Bower, G. H., & Springston, F. (1970). Pauses as recoding points in letter series. *Journal of Experimental Psychology, 83*, 421–430. doi:10.1037/h0028863

Bowker, A. (2006). The relationship between sports participation and self-esteem during early adolescence. *Canadian Journal of Behavioural Science, 38*(3), 214–229.

Bowlby, J. (1978). Attachment theory and its therapeutic implications. *Adolescent Psychiatry, 6*, 5–33.

Bowling, N. A. (2010). Effects of job satisfaction and conscientiousness on extra-role behaviors. *Journal of Business & Psychology, 25*(1), 119–130.

Bowyer, K. W. (2004). Face recognition technology: Security versus privacy. *IEEE Technology and Society Magazine, 23*(1), 9–19.

Boyd, J., & Munroe, K. J. (2003). The use of imagery in climbing. *Athletic Insight: The Online Journal of Sport Psychology, 5*(2). Retrieved March 4, 2017, from www.athleticinsight.com/Vol5Iss2/ClimbingImagery.htm

Boyd, J., Harris, S., & Knight, J. R. (2012). Screening and brief interventions for the addiction syndrome: Considering the vulnerability of adolescence. In H. Shaffer, D. A. LaPlante, et al. (Eds.), *APA addiction syndrome handbook* (Vol. 2): *Recovery, prevention, and other issues* (pp. 169–194). Washington, DC: American Psychological Association. doi:10.1037/13750-008

Boyd, M., Kim, M., et al. (2014). Perceived motivational team climate in relation to task and social cohesion among male college athletes. *Journal of Applied Social Psychology, 44*(2), 115–123. doi:10.1111/jasp.12210

Boyle, M. P., Blood, G. W., & Blood, I. M. (2009). Effects of perceived causality on perceptions of persons who stutter. *Journal of Fluency Disorders, 34*(3), 201–218.

Boysen, G. A. (2011). The scientific status of childhood dissociative identity disorder: A review of published research. *Psychotherapy & Psychosomatics, 80*(6), 329–334. doi:10.1159/000323403

Boysen, G. A., & VanBergen, A. (2013). A review of published research on adult dissociative identity disorder: 2000–2010. *Journal of Nervous & Mental Disease, 201*(1), 5–11. doi:10.1097/NMD.0b013e31827aaf81

Brach, T. (2003). *Radical acceptance.* New York: Bantam Books.

Bracken, D. W., Rose, D. S., et al. (2016). The evolution and devolution of 360° feedback. *Industrial & Organizational Psychology: Perspectives on Science & Practice, 9*(4), 761–794. doi:10.1017/iop.2016.93

Bradbury, J. W., & Vehrencamp, S. L. (2011). *Principles of animal communication* (2nd ed.). Sunderland, MA: Sinauer.

Bradbury, T. N., & Karney, B. R. (2010). *Intimate relationships.* New York: Norton.

Bradley, R. T., McCraty, R., et al. (2010). Emotion self-regulation psychophysiological coherence, and test anxiety: Results from an experiment using electrophysiological measures. *Applied Psychophysiology & Biofeedback, 35*(4), 261–283. doi:10.1007/s10484-010-9134-x

Bradshaw, C., Kahn, A. S., & Saville, B. K. (2010). To hook up or date: Which gender benefits? *Sex Roles, 62*(9–10), 661–669.

Braga, J. N., Ferreira, M. B., Sherman, S. J., Mata, A., Jacinto, S., & Ferreira, M. (2018). What's next? Disentangling availability from representativeness using binary decision tasks. *Journal of Experimental Social Psychology, 76,* 307–319. doi:10.1016/j.jesp.2018.03.006

Brainerd, C. J. (2003). Jean Piaget, learning research, and American education. In B. J. Zimmerman & D. H. Schunk (Eds.), *Educational psychology: A century of contributions* (pp. 251–287). Mahwah, NJ: Erlbaum.

Brakel, T. M., Dijkstra, A., et al. (2011). Impact of social comparison on cancer survivors' quality of life: An experimental field study. *Health Psychology, 31,* 660–670. doi:10.1037/a0026572

Bramerson, A., Johansson, L., et al. (2004). Prevalence of olfactory dysfunction: The Skovde population-based study. *Laryngoscope, 114*(4), 733–737. doi:10.1097/00005537-200404000-00026

Brammer, R. (2012). *Diversity in counseling* (2nd ed.). Boston, MA: Cengage Learning.

Brand, S., Gerber, M., et al. (2010). High exercise levels are related to favorable sleep patterns and psychological functioning in adolescents: A comparison of athletes and controls. *Journal of Adolescent Health, 46*(2), 133–141. doi:10.1016/j.jadohealth.2009.06.018

Brang, D., & Ramachandran, V. S. (2010). Visual field heterogeneity, laterality, and eidetic imagery in synesthesia. *Neurocase, 16*(2), 169–174. doi:10.1080/13554790903339645

Brannon, L. (2011). *Gender: Psychological perspectives.* Boston, MA: Pearson/Allyn & Bacon.

Brannon, L., Feist, J., & Updegraff, J. (2014). *Health psychology: An introduction to behavior and health* (8th ed.). Boston, MA: Cengage Learning.

Branscombe, N. R., & Baron, R. A. (2017). *Social psychology.* New York: Pearson.

Brauer, J. R., & Tittle, C. R. (2012). Social learning theory and human reinforcement. *Sociological Spectrum, 32*(2), 157–177. doi:10.1080/02732173.2012.646160

Braun, K. A., Ellis, R., & Loftus, E. F. (2002). Make my memory: How advertising can change memories of the past. *Psychology & Marketing, 19,* 1–23. doi 10.1002/mar.1000

Braun, T., Fung, B. C., Iqbal, F., & Shah, B. (2018). Security and privacy challenges in smart cities. *Sustainable Cities and Society, 39,* 499–507. doi:10.1016/j.scs.2018.02.039

Breedlove, S. M., Watson, N. V., et al. (2013). *Biological psychology: An introduction to behavioral and cognitive neuroscience* (7th ed.). Sunderland, MA: Sinauer Associates.

Breiding, M. G., Smith, S. G., et al. (2014). *Prevalence and characteristics of sexual violence, stalking, and intimate partner violence victimization—National Intimate Partner and Sexual Violence Survey, United States, 2011.* Retrieved March 10, 2017, from www.cdc.gov/mmwr/preview/mmwrhtml/ss6308a1.htm

Brenes, G. A., Ingram, C. W., & Danhauer, S. C. (2011) Benefits and challenges of conducting psychotherapy by telephone. *Professional Psychology: Research & Practice, 42*(6), 543–549. doi:10.1037/a0026135

Brescoll, V. L., Dawson, E., & Uhlmann, E. L. (2010). Hard won and easily lost: The fragile status of leaders in gender-stereotype-incongruent occupations. *Psychological Science, 21*(11), 1640–1642.

Bressan, P., & Pizzighello, S. (2008). The attentional cost of inattentional blindness. *Cognition, 106*(1), 370–383. doi:10.1016/j.cognition.2007.03.001

Bressi, C., Albonetti, S., & Razzoli, E. (1998). "Communication deviance" and schizophrenia. *New Trends in Experimental & Clinical Psychiatry, 14*(1), 33–39.

Bretherton, R., & Orner, R. J. (2004). Positive psychology and psychotherapy: An existential approach. In P. A. Linley & S. Joseph (Eds.), *Positive psychology in practice* (pp. 420–430). New York: Wiley.

Brevers, D., Dan, B., et al. (2011). Sport superstition: Mediation of psychological tension on nonprofessional sportsmen's superstitious rituals. *Journal of Sport Behavior, 34*(1), 3–24.

Brewer, J. A., Mallik, S., et al. (2011). Mindfulness training for smoking cessation: Results from a randomized controlled trial. *Drug & Alcohol Dependence, 119*(1–2), 72–80. doi:10.1016/j.drugalcdep.2011.05.027

Brewer, M. B. (1979). In-group bias in the minimal intergroup situation: A cognitive-motivational analysis. *Psychological Bulletin, 86*(2), 307–324. doi:10.1037/0033-2909.86.2.307

Bridge, J. A., Greenhouse, et al. (2020). Association between the release of Netflix's 13 Reasons Why and suicide rates in the United States: An interrupted times series analysis. *Journal of the American Academy of Child and Adolescent Psychiatry, 59,* 236–243. doi:10.1016/j.jaac.2019.04.020

Bridges, K. M. B. (1932). Emotional development in early infancy. *Child Development, 3,* 324–341. doi:10.2307/1125359

Bridgett, D. J., Gartstein, M. A., et al. (2009). Maternal and contextual influences and the effect of temperament development during infancy on parenting in toddlerhood. *Infant Behavior & Development, 32*(1), 103–116. doi:10.1016/j.infbeh.2008.10.007

Bridgman, T., Cummings, S., & Ballard, J. (2019). Who built Maslow's pyramid? A history of the creation of management studies' most famous symbol and its implications for management education. *Academy of Management Learning & Education, 18*(1), 81–98. doi:10.5465/amle.2017.0351

Briley, D. A., & Tucker-Drob, E. M. (2017). Comparing the developmental genetics of cognition and personality over the life span. *Journal of Personality, 85*(1), 51–64. doi:10.1111/jopy.12186

Brinch, C. N., & Galloway, T. (2012). Schooling in adolescence raises IQ scores. *Proceedings of the National Academy of Sciences, 109*(2), 425–430. doi:10.1073/pnas.1106077109

Bringing Up Baby. (1999, January–February). *Sierra,* 17.

Britton, P. C., Duberstein, P. R., et al. (2008). Reasons for living, hopelessness, and suicide ideation among depressed adults 50 years or older. *American Journal of Geriatric Psychiatry, 16*(9), 736–741. doi:10.1097/JGP.0b013e31817b609a

Brodley, B. T. (2006). Nondirectivity in client-centered therapy. *Person-Centered & Experiential Psychotherapies, 5*(1), 36–52.

Brody, S., & Weiss, P. (2011). Simultaneous penile–vaginal intercourse orgasm is associated with satisfaction (sexual, life, partnership, and mental health). *Journal of Sexual Medicine, 8*(3), 734–741. doi:10.1111/j.1743-6109.2010.02149.x

Brondolo, E., ver Halen, N. B., et al. (2011). Racism as a psychosocial stressor. In R. J. Contrada & A. Baum (Eds.), *The handbook of stress science: Biology, psychology, and health* (pp. 167–184). New York: Springer.

Brooks, M. (2009). Rise of the robogeeks. *New Scientist, 2697,* 34–36.

Brotto, L.A., Knudson, G., et al. (2010). Asexuality: A mixed-methods approach. *Archives of Sexual Behavior, 39*(3), 599–618.

Brough, P., Drummond, S., et al. (2017, February 13). Job support, coping, and control: Assessment of simultaneous impacts within the occupational stress process. *Journal of Occupational Health Psychology,* n.p. doi:10.1037/ocp0000074

Browne, A. L., & Bishop, B. J. (2011). Chasing our tails: Psychological, institutional and societal paradoxes in natural resource management, sustainability, and climate change in Australia. *American Journal of Community Psychology, 47,* 354–361. doi:10.1007/s10464-010-9390-1

Brower, A. M. (2002). Are college students alcoholics? *Journal of American College Health, 50*(5), 253–255. doi:10.1080/07448480209595716

Brown, A. S. (2012). *The tip of the tongue state.* New York: Psychology Press.

Brown, A. S., & Marsh, E. J. (2010). Digging into déjà vu: Recent research on possible mechanisms. In B. H. Ross (Ed.), *The psychology of learning and motivation: Advances in research and theory* (Vol. 53, pp. 33–62). San Diego, CA: Elsevier. doi:10.1016/S0079-7421(10)53002-0

Brown, A., Charlwood, A., & Spencer, D. A. (2012). Not all that it might seem: Why job satisfaction is worth studying despite it being a poor summary measure of job quality. *Work, Employment & Society, 26*(6), 1007–1018. doi:10.1177/0950017012461837

Brown, G., & Devlin, A. S. (2003). Vandalism: Environmental and social factors. *Journal of College Student Development, 44*(4), 502–516.

Brown, G. R., & Cross, C. P. (2017). Evolutionary approaches to human psychology. In J. Call, G. M. Burghardt, et al. (Eds.). *APA handbook of comparative psychology: Basic concepts, methods, neural substrate, and behavior* (Vol. 1, pp. 299–313). Washington, DC: American Psychological Association. doi:10.1037/0000011-015

Brown, J. D., Cai, H., et al. (2009). Cultural similarities in self-esteem functioning: East is east and west is west, but sometimes the twain do meet. *Journal of Cross-Cultural Psychology, 40*(1), 140–157. doi:10.1177/0022022108326280

Brown, L. M. (2005). *Girlfighting: Betrayal and rejection among girls.* New York: New York University Press.

Brown, M. J., Henriquez, E., & Groscup, J. (2008). The effects of eyeglasses and race on juror decisions involving a violent crime. *American Journal of Forensic Psychology, 26*(2), 25–43.

Brown, P. (1990). The name game. *Journal of Mind & Behavior, 11,* 385–406.

Brown, R., & Kulik, J. (1977). Flashbulb memories. *Cognition, 5,* 73–99. doi:10.1016/0010-0277(77)90018-X.

Brown, R., & McNeill, D. (1966). The "tip of the tongue" phenomenon. *Journal of Verbal Learning & Verbal Behavior, 5,* 325–337. doi:10.1016/S0022-5371(66)80040-3

Brown, S. A. (2011). Standardized measures for substance use stigma. *Drug & Alcohol Dependence, 116*(1–3), 137–141.

Brown, S. A., Tapert, S. F., et al. (2000). Neurocognitive functioning of adolescents: Effects of protracted alcohol use. *Alcoholism: Clinical & Experimental Research, 24*(2), 164– 171. doi:10.1111/j.1530-0277.2000.tb04586.x

Brown, S. D., Lent, R. W., et al. (2011). Social cognitive career theory, conscientiousness, and work performance: A meta-analytic path analysis. *Journal of Vocational Behavior, 79*(1), 81–90. doi:10.1016/j.jvb.2010.11.009

Brown, T. A., & Barlow, D. H. (2017). *Casebook in abnormal psychology* (5th. ed.). Boston, MA: Cengage Learning.

Brown, V., Tumeo, M., et al. (1998). Modeling cognitive interactions during group brainstorming. *Small Group Research, 29*(4), 495–526.

Brownell, P. (2016). Contemporary Gestalt therapy. In Cain, D. J., Keenan, K., & Rubin, S. (Eds.), *Humanistic psychotherapies: Handbook of research and practice* (2nd ed., pp. 219–250). Washington, DC: American Psychological Association. doi:10.1037/14775-008

Bruchmüller, K., Margraf, J., et al. (2012). Is ADHD diagnosed in accord with diagnostic criteria? Overdiagnosis and influence of client gender on diagnosis. *Journal of Consulting & Clinical Psychology, 80*(1), 128–138. doi:10.1037/a0026582

Bruehl, S. S., Burns, J. W., et al. (2012). What do plasma beta-endorphin levels reveal about endogenous opioid analgesic function? *European Journal of Pain, 16*(3), 370–380. doi:10.1002/j.1532-2149.2011.00021.x

Brumbaugh, C. C., & Fraley, R. C. (2010). Adult attachment and dating strategies: How do insecure people attract mates? *Personal Relationships, 17*(4), 599–614.

Bruner, J. (1973). *Going beyond the information given.* New York: Norton.

Bruner, J. (1983). *Child's talk.* New York: Norton.

Brunet, A., & Berger, S. L. (2014). Epigenetics of aging and aging-related disease. *The Journals of Gerontology: Series A 69*(Suppl 1), S17–S20. doi:10.1093/gerona/glu042

Bryan, L., & Vinchur, A. J. (2013). Industrial-organizational psychology. In D. K. Freedheim & I. B. Weiner (Eds.), *Handbook of psychology* (Vol. 1): *History of psychology* (2nd ed., pp. 407–428). New York: Wiley.

Brydon, L., Strike, P. C., et al. (2010). Hostility and physiological responses to laboratory stress in acute coronary syndrome patients. *Journal of Psychosomatic Research, 68*(2), 109–116. doi:10.1016/j.jpsychores.2009.06.007

Buchanan, M. (2008, April 30). Sin cities: The geometry of crime. *New Scientist,* 36–39.

Bucher, S. G. (2011). *344 questions: The creative person's do-it-yourself guide to insight, survival, and artistic fulfillment.* Berkeley, CA: New Riders Publishing.

Buck, J. A., & Warren, A. R. (2010). Expert testimony in recovered memory trials: Effects on mock jurors' opinions, deliberations and verdicts. *Applied Cognitive Psychology, 24*(4), 495–512.

Buckels, E. E., Jones, D. N., & Paulhus, D. L. (2013). Behavioral confirmation of everyday sadism. *Psychological Science, 24*(11), 2201–2209. doi:10.1177/0956797613490749

Buckels, E. E., Trapnell, P. D., & Paulhus, D. L. (2014). Trolls just want to have fun. *Personality and Individual Differences, 67,* 97–102. doi:10.1016/j.paid.2014.01.016

Buckner, J. D., Ecker, A. H., & Cohen, A. S. (2010). Mental health problems and interest in marijuana treatment among marijuana-using college students. *Addictive Behaviors, 35*(9), 826–833. doi:10.1016/j.addbeh.2010.04.001

Buckworth, J., Lee, R. E., et al. (2007). Decomposing intrinsic and extrinsic motivation for exercise: Application to stages of motivational readiness. *Psychology of Sport & Exercise, 8*(4), 441–461. doi:10.1016/j.psychsport.2006.06.007

Buehner, M. J., & May, J. (2003). Rethinking temporal contiguity and the judgement of causality: Effects of prior knowledge, experience, and reinforcement procedure. *Quarterly Journal of Experimental Psychology, 56*(5), 865–890. doi:10.1080/02724980244000675

Bukach, C. M., Cottle, J., et al. (2012). Individuation experience predicts other-race effects in holistic processing for both Caucasian and Black participants. *Cognition, 123,* 319–324. doi:10.1016/j.cognition.2012.02.007

Bunde, J., & Suls, J. (2006). A quantitative analysis of the relationship between the Cook-Medley hostility scale and traditional coronary artery disease risk factors. *Health Psychology, 25*(4), 493–500. doi:10.1037/0278-6133.25.4.493

Bundy, H., Stahl, D., & MacCabe, J. H. (2011). A systematic review and meta-analysis of the fertility of patients with schizophrenia and their unaffected relatives. *Acta Psychiatrica Scandinavica, 123*(2), 98–106. doi:10.1111/j.1600-0447.2010.01623.x

Bunk, J. A., & Magley, V. J. (2013). The role of appraisals and emotions in understanding experiences of workplace incivility. *Journal of Occupational Health Psychology, 18*(1), 87–105. doi:10.1037/a0030987

Bunn, G. C. (2012). *The truth machine: A social history of the lie detector.* Baltimore, MD: Johns Hopkins University Press.

Bunnell, D. W. (2016). Gender socialization, countertransference and the treatment of men with eating disorders. *Clinical Social Work Journal, 44*(1), 99–104. doi:10.1007/s10615-015-0564-z

Burbach, M. E., Matkin, G. S., et al. (2004). Teaching critical thinking in an introductory leadership course utilizing active learning strategies: A confirmatory study. *College Student Journal, 38*(3), 482–493.

Burchinal, M., Skinner, D., et al. (2010). European American and African American mothers' beliefs about parenting and disciplining infants: A mixed method analysis. *Parenting: Science & Practice, 10,* 79–96. doi:10.1080/15295190903212604

Burger, J. M. (2009). Replicating Milgram: Would people still obey today? *American Psychologist, 64*(1), 1–11. doi:10.1037/a0010932

Burger, J. M. (2015). *Personality* (9th ed.). Boston, MA: Cengage Learning.

Burgess, C. A., & Kirsch, I. (1999). Expectancy information as a moderator of the effects of hypnosis on memory. *Contemporary Hypnosis, 16*(1), 22–31. doi:10.1002/ch.146

Burlingame, G. M., Fuhriman, A., & Mosier, J. (2003). The differential effectiveness of group psychotherapy: A meta-analytic perspective. *Group Dynamics: Theory, Research, & Practice, 7*(1), 3–12. doi:10.1037/1089-2699.7.1.3

Burn, S. M. (2019). The psychology of sexual harassment. *Teaching of Psychology, 46*(1), 96–103. doi:10.1177/0098628318816183

Burns, J. M., & Swerdlow, R. H. (2003). Right orbitofrontal tumor with pedophilia symptom and constructional apraxia sign. *Archives of Neurology, 60*(3), 437–440. doi:10.1001/archneur.60.3.437

Burón, P., Jimenez-Trevino, L., et al. (2016). Reasons for attempted suicide in Europe: Prevalence, associated factors, and risk of repetition. *Archives of Suicide Research, 20*(1), 45–58. doi: 10.1080/13811118.2015.1004481

Burt, S. A., McGue, M., et al. (2007). The different origins of stability and change in antisocial personality disorder symptoms. *Psychological Medicine, 37*(1), 27–38. doi:10.1017/S0033291706009020

Burton, C. M., & King, L. A. (2004). The health benefits of writing about intensely positive experiences. *Journal of Research in Personality, 38*(2), 150–163. doi:10.1016/S0092-6566(03)00058-8

Burtt, H. E. (1941). An experimental study of early childhood memory: Final report. *Journal of General Psychology, 58,* 435–439.

Buss, A. H. (2012). *Pathways to individuality: Evolution and development of personality traits.* Washington, DC: American Psychological Association.

Buss, D. M. (2015). *Evolutionary psychology: The new science of the mind* (5th ed.). Boston, MA: Psychology Press.

Bussell, H., & Forbes, D. (2002). Understanding the volunteer market: The what, where, who and why of volunteering. *International Journal of Nonprofit & Voluntary Sector*

Marketing, 7(3), 244–257. doi:10.1002/nvsm.183
Butcher, J. N. (2011). *A beginner's guide to the MMPI-2* (3rd ed.). Washington, DC: American Psychological Association.
Butcher, J. N., Mineka, S., & Hooley, J. (2010). *Abnormal psychology* (14th ed.). Boston, MA: Allyn & Bacon.
Butler, A. C., Chapman, J. E., et al. (2006). The empirical status of cognitive-behavioral therapy: A review of meta-analyses. *Clinical Psychology Review, 26*(1), 17–31. doi:10.1016/j.cpr.2005.07.003
Butler, B. (2007). The role of death qualification in capital trials involving juvenile defendants. *Journal of Applied Social Psychology, 37*(3), 549–560.
Butler, J. C. (2000). Personality and emotional correlates of right-wing authoritarianism. *Social Behavior & Personality, 28*(1), 1–14. doi:10.2224/sbp.2000.28.1.1
Butler, R. (1954). Curiosity in monkeys. *Scientific American, 190*(18), 70–75. doi:10.1038/scientificamerican0254-70
Byrne, J. S., & O'Brien, E. J. (2014). Interpersonal views of narcissism and authentic high self-esteem: It is not all about you. *Psychological Reports, 115*(1), 243–260. doi:10.2466/21.09.PR0.115c15z9
Byrne, S., Barry, D., & Petry, N. M. (2012). Predictors of weight loss success: Exercise vs. dietary self-efficacy and treatment attendance. *Appetite, 58*(2), 695–698. doi:10.1016/j.appet.2012.01.005
Byrnes, J. P., Miller, D. C., & Schafer, W. D. (1999). Gender differences in risk taking: A meta-analysis. *Psychological Bulletin, 125*(3), 367–383.
Cabrera, A. (2016). Pound puppy turned police "porn dog." *CNN*. Retrieved January 9, 2017, from www.cnn.com/2016/09/05/us/police-dog-sniffs-out-flash-drives-in-porn-cases
Cadaret, M. C., Hartung, P. J., et al. (2017). Stereotype threat as a barrier to women entering engineering careers. *Journal of Vocational Behavior, 99*, 40–51. doi:10.1016/j.jvb.2016.12.002
Cadet, P. (2011). Androgen insensitivity syndrome with male sex-of-living. *Archives of Sexual Behavior, 40*(6), 1101–1102. doi:10.1007/s10508-011-9823-4
Caharel, S., Fiori, N., et al. (2006). The effects of inversion and eye displacements of familiar and unknown faces on early and late-stage ERPs. *International Journal of Psychophysiology, 62*(1), 141–151. doi:10 1016/j.ijpsycho.2006.03.002
Cain, D. J. (2014). Person-centered therapy. In G. R. VandenBos, E. Meidenbauer, et al. (Eds.), *Psychotherapy theories & techniques: A reader* (pp. 251–259). Washington, DC: American Psychological Association. doi:10.1037/14295-027
Cain, S. (2012). *Quiet: The power of introverts in a world that can't stop talking*. New York: Crown Publishers/Random House.
Calabrese, F., Molteni, R., et al. (2009). Neuronal plasticity: A link between stress and mood disorders. *Psychoneuroendocrinology, 34*(Suppl. 1), S208–S216. doi:10.1016/j.psyneuen.2009.05.014
Calabria, B., Degenhardt, L., et al. (2010). Systematic review of prospective studies investigating "remission" from amphetamine, cannabis, cocaine, or opioid dependence. *Addictive Behaviors, 35*(8), 741–749. doi:10.1016/j.addbeh.2010.03.019
Calhoun, J. B. (1962). A "behavioral sink." In E. L. Bliss (Ed.), *Roots of behavior* (pp. 295–315). New York: Harper & Row.
Caliari, P. (2008). Enhancing forehand acquisition in table tennis: The role of mental practice. *Journal of Applied Sport Psychology, 20*(1), 88–96.
Caligiuri, P., & Lundby, K. (2015). Developing cross-cultural competencies through global teams. In J. L. Wildman & R. L. Griffith (Eds.), *Leading global teams* (pp. 123– 139). New York: Springer.
Calvin, C. M., Fernandes, C., et al. (2010). Sex, intelligence, and educational achievement in a national cohort of over 175,000 11-year-old schoolchildren in England. *Intelligence, 38*(4), 424–432.
Calzada, E. J., Fernandez, Y., & Cortes, D. E. (2010). Incorporating the cultural value of *respeto* into a framework of Latino parenting. *Cultural Diversity & Ethnic Minority Psychology, 16*(1), 77–86. doi:10.1037/a0016071
Cambron, M. J., Acitelli, L. K., & Pettit, J. W. (2009). Explaining gender differences in depression: An interpersonal contingent self-esteem perspective. *Sex Roles, 61*(11–12), 751–761. doi:10.1007/s11199-009-9616-6
Cameron, H. A., & Glover, L. R. (2015). Adult neurogenesis: Beyond learning and memory. *Annual Review of Psychology, 66*, 53–81. doi:10.1146/annurev-psych-010814-015006
Cameron, J., & Pierce, W. D. (2002). *Rewards and intrinsic motivation: Resolving the controversy*. Westport, CO: Bergin & Garvey.
Cameron, M., Crane, N., et al. (2013). Promoting well-being through creativity: How arts and public health can learn from each other. *Perspectives in Public Health, 133*(1), 52–59. doi:10.1177/1757913912466951
Campbell, B. (2008). *Handbook of differentiated instruction using the multiple intelligences*. Boston, MA: Pearson/Allyn & Bacon.
Campbell, J. P. (2013). Assessment in industrial and organizational psychology: An overview. In K. F. Geisinger, B. A. Bracken, et al. (Eds.), *APA handbook of testing and assessment in psychology* (Vol. 1): *Test theory and testing and assessment in industrial and organizational psychology* (pp. 355–395). Washington, DC: American Psychological Association. doi:10.1037/14047-022
Camperio Ciani, A. S., Fontanesi, L., et al. (2012). Factors associated with higher fecundity in female maternal relatives of homosexual men. *Journal of Sexual Medicine, 9*(11), 2878–2887. doi:10.1111/j.1743-6109.2012.02785.x
Campo, M., Laborde, S., et al. (2015). Emotional intelligence training: Implications for performance and health. In A. M. Columbus (Ed.), *Advances in psychology research* (Vol. 101, pp. 75–92). Hauppage, NY: Nova Science Publishers.
Campos, A., Camino, E., & Pérez-Fabello, M. (2011). Using the keyword mnemonics method among adult learners. *Educational Gerontology, 37*(4), 327–335. doi:10.1080/03601271003608886
Campos, A., Rodríguez-Pinal, M. D., & Pérez-Fabello, M. (2013). Receptive and productive recall with the keyword mnemonics in bilingual students. *Current Psychology*. doi:10.1007/s12144-013-9197-y
Canadian Psychological Association. (2017). Careers in and related to psychology. Retrieved April 26, 2017, from http://www.cpa.ca/students/career/careersinpsychology/
Cannon, D. M., Klaver, J. M., et al. (2013). Gender-specific abnormalities in the serotonin transporter system in panic disorder. *International Journal of Neuropsychopharmacology, 16*(4), 733–743. doi:10.1017/S1461145712000776
Cannon, W. B. (1932). *The wisdom of the body*. New York: Norton.
Cannon, W. B. (1934). Hunger and thirst. In C. Murchinson (Ed.), *Handbook of general experimental psychology* (pp. 247–263). Worcester, MA: Clark University Press. doi:10.1037/11374-005
Cannon, W. B., & Washburn, A. L. (1912). An explanation of hunger. *American Journal of Physiology, 29*, 441–454.
Caplan, P. J. (1995). *They say you're crazy*. Reading, MA: Addison-Wesley.
Caporro, M., Haneef, Z., et al. (2012). Functional MRI of sleep spindles and K-complexes. *Clinical Neurophysiology, 123*(2), 303–309. doi:10.1016/j.clinph.2011.06.018
Caputi, A. A., Aguilera, P. A., et al. (2013). On the haptic nature of the active electric sense of fish. *Brain Research, 1536*, 27–43. doi:10.1016/j.brainres.2013.05.028
Carcaillon, L., Brailly-Tabard, S., et al. (2013, September 10). Low testosterone and the risk of dementia in elderly men: Impact of age and education. *Alzheimer's & Dementia*, n.p. doi:10.1016/j.jalz.2013.06.006
Cardeña, E., Winkelman, M., et al. (Eds.). (2011). *Altering consciousness: Multidisciplinary perspectives* (Vol. 1): *History, culture, and the humanities*. Westport, CT: Praeger.
Carey, B. (2015). *How we learn: The surprising truth about when, where, and why it happens*. New York: Random House.
Carlbring, P., Gunnarsdóttir, M., et al. (2007). Treatment of social phobia: Randomized trial of Internet-delivered cognitive-behavioural therapy with telephone support. *British Journal of Psychiatry, 190*(2), 123–128. doi:10.1192/bjp.bp.105.020107
Carlson, J., & Maniacci, M. P. (Eds.). (2012). *Alfred Adler revisited*. New York: Routledge.
Carlson, N. R. (2013). *Physiology of behavior* (11th ed.). Boston, MA: Allyn & Bacon.
Carlson, T. N., & Settle, J. E. (2016). Political chameleons: An exploration of conformity in political discussions. *Political Behavior, 38*(4), 817–859. doi:10.1007/s11109-016-9335-y
Carman, C. A. (2013). Comparing apples and oranges: Fifteen years of definitions of giftedness in research. *Journal of Advanced Academics, 24*(1), 52–70. doi:10.1177/1932202X12472602
Carnagey, N. L., & Anderson, C. A. (2004). Violent video game exposure and aggression: A literature review. *Minerva Psichiatrica, 45*(1), 1–18.
Carnagey, N. L., Anderson, C. A., & Bushman, B. J. (2007). The effect of video game violence on physiological desensitization to real-life violence. *Journal of Experimental Social Psychology, 43*(3), 489–496. doi:10.1016/j.jesp.2006.05.003

Carney, R. N., & Levin, J. R. (2003). Promoting higher-order learning benefits by building lower-order mnemonic connections. *Applied Cognitive Psychology, 17*(5), 563–575. doi:10.1002/acp.889

Carney, R. N., & Levin, J. R. (2014). Learning more about and with the face–name mnemonic strategy. *Applied Cognitive Psychology, 28*(4), 569–578. doi:10.1002/acp.3036

Carr, P. B., & Steele, C. M. (2010). Stereotype threat affects financial decision making. *Psychological Science, 21*(10), 1411–1416. doi:10.1177/0956797610384146

Carrico, A. R., & Riemer, M. (2011). Motivating energy conservation in the workplace: An evaluation of the use of group-level feedback and peer education. *Journal of Environmental Psychology, 31*(1), 1–13. doi:10.1016/j.jenvp.2010.11.004

Carroll, D. W. (2008). *Psychology of language* (5th ed.). Boston, MA: Cengage Learning.

Carroll, J. L. (2016). *Sexuality now: Embracing diversity* (5th ed.). Boston, MA: Cengage Learning.

Carroll, J. M., & Russell, J. A. (1996). Do facial expressions signal specific emotions? Judging emotion from the face in context. *Journal of Personality & Social Psychology, 70*(2), 205–218. doi:10.1037/0022-3514.70.2.205

Carroll, J. S., Padilla-Walker, L. M., et al. (2008). Generation XXX: Pornography acceptance and use among emerging adults. *Journal of Adolescent Research, 23*(1), 6–30. doi:10.1177/0743558407306348

Carskadon, M. A., Acebo, C., & Jenni, O. C. (2004). Regulation of adolescent sleep: Implications for behavior. *Annals of the New York Academy of Science, 1021,* 276–291. doi:10.1196/annals.1308.032

Carstensen, L. L., & DeLiema, M. (2018). The positivity effect: A negativity bias in youth fades with age. *Current Opinion in Behavioral Sciences, 19,* 7–12. doi:10.1016/j.cobeha.2017.07.009

Carstensen, L. L., Isaacowitz, D. M., & Charles, S. T. (1999). Taking time seriously: A theory of socioemotional selectivity. *American Psychologist, 54,* 165–181. doi:10.1037/0003-066X.54.3.165

Carter, D. A., Simkins, B. J., & Simpson, W. G. (2003). Corporate governance, board diversity, and firm value. *Financial Review, 38,* 33–53.

Carter, G., Campbell, A. C., & Muncer, S. (2014). The dark triad personality: Attractiveness to women. *Personality & Individual Differences, 56,* 57–61. doi:10.1016/j.paid.2013.08.021

Carter, M. J. (2013). Advancing identity theory: Examining the relationship between activated identities and behavior in different social contexts. *Social Psychology Quarterly, 76*(3), 203–223.

Caruso, D. R., Salovey, P., et al. (2015). The ability model of emotional intelligence. In S. Joseph (Ed.), *Positive psychology in practice: Promoting human flourishing in work, health, education, and everyday life* (2nd ed., pp. 545–558). New York: Wiley.

Carver, C. S., & Scheier, M. F. (2014). Dispositional optimism. *Trends in Cognitive Sciences, 18,* 293–299. doi:10.1016/j.tics.2014.02.003

Case, B. G., Bertollo, D. N., et al. (2013). Declining use of electroconvulsive therapy in United States general hospitals. *Biological Psychiatry, 73*(2), 119–126. doi:10.1016/j.biopsych.2012.09.005

Casey, A. A., Elliott, M., et al. (2008). Impact of the food environment and physical activity environment on behaviors and weight status in rural U.S. communities. *Preventive Medicine, 47*(6), 600–604. doi:10.1016/j.ypmed.2008.10.001

Casey-Campbell, M., & Martens, M. L. (2009). Sticking it all together: A critical assessment of the group cohesion–performance literature. *International Journal of Management Reviews, 11*(2), 223–246. doi:10.1111/j.1468-2370.2008.00239.x

Cassady, J. C. (2004). The influence of cognitive test anxiety across the learning-testing cycle. *Learning & Instruction, 14*(6), 569–592.

Casselle, G. (2009). What is it really like to have electroconvulsive therapy? *Journal of ECT, 25*(4), 289. doi:10.1097/YCT.0b013e3181a59f97

Castañeda, H., Holmes, S. M., et al. (2015). Immigration as a social determinant of health. *Annual Review of Public Health, 36,* 375–392. doi:10.1146/annurev-publhealth-032013-182419

Castañeda, T. R., Tong, J., et al. (2010). Ghrelin in the regulation of body weight and metabolism. *Frontiers in Neuroendocrinology, 31*(1), 44–60. doi:10.1016/j.yfrne.2009.10.008

Castellano, J. A., & Frazier, A. D. (Eds.). (2011). *Special populations in gifted education: Understanding our most able students from diverse backgrounds.* Waco, TX: Prufrock Press.

Castle, D., Murray, R., et al. (Eds.). (2012). *Marijuana and madness* (2nd ed.). London: Cambridge University Press.

Castles, E. E. (2012). *Inventing intelligence: How America came to worship IQ.* Santa Barbara, CA: Praeger.

Castro-Schilo, L., & Kee, D. W. (2010). Gender differences in the relationship between emotional intelligence and right hemisphere lateralization for facial processing. *Brain & Cognition, 73*(1), 62–67. doi:10.1016/j.bandc.2010.03.003

Cattell, R. B. (1965). *The scientific analysis of personality.* Baltimore, MD: Penguin.

Cattell, R. B. (1973, July). Personality pinned down. *Psychology Today,* 40–46.

Caulfield, M. (2017). *Web literacy for student fact-checkers.* This is a self-published e-book, retrieved from https://webliteracy.pressbooks.com/front-matter/web-strategies-for-student-fact-checkers/

Cavaco, S., Anderson, S. W., et al. (2004). The scope of preserved procedural memory in amnesia. *Brain: A Journal of Neurology, 127*(8), 1853–1867. doi:10.1093/brain/awh208

Cavanaugh, J. C., & Blanchard-Fields, F. (2015). *Adult development and aging* (7th ed.). Boston, MA: Cengage Learning.

Cavazotte, F., Moreno, V., et al. (2012). Effects of leader intelligence, personality and emotional intelligence on transformational leadership and managerial performance. *The Leadership Quarterly, 23*(3), 443–455. doi:10.1016/j.leaqua.2011.10.003

Ceci, S. J., & Williams, W. M. (2010). *The mathematics of sex: How biology and society conspire to limit talented women and girls.* New York: Oxford University Press.

Cellard, C., Lefèbvre, A.-A., et al. (2010). An examination of the relative contribution of saturation and selective attention to memory deficits in patients with recent-onset schizophrenia and their unaffected parents. *Journal of Abnormal Psychology, 119*(1), 60–70. doi:10.1037/a0018397

Center for Behavioral Health Statistics and Quality. (2016). *Key substance use and mental health indicators in the United States: Results from the 2015 National Survey on Drug Use and Health* (HHS Publication No. SMA 16-4984, NSDUH Series H-51). Retrieved May 6, 2017, from www.samhsa.gov/data/sites/default/files/NSDUH-FFR1-2015/NSDUH-FFR1-2015/NSDUH-FFR1-2015.pdf

Center on the Developing Child at Harvard University. (2011). Building the brain's "air traffic control" system: How early experiences shape the development of executive function: Working paper no. 11. Retrieved May 1, 2017, from developingchild.harvard.edu/resources/building-the-brains-air-traffic-control-system-how-early-experiences-shape-thedevelopment-of-executive-function/

Centers for Disease Control. (2012). *Short sleep duration among workers—United States, 2010.* Retrieved January 15, 2014, from www.cdc.gov/mmwr/preview/mmwrhtml/mm6116a2.htm?s_cid=mm6116a2_w

Centers for Disease Control. (2015a). *Understanding suicide.* Retrieved March 27, 2017, from www.cdc.gov/violenceprevention/pdf/suicide_factsheet-a.pdf

Centers for Disease Control. (2015b). *Drowsy driving: Asleep at the wheel.* Retrieved February 18, 2016, from http://www.cdc.gov/Features/dsDrowsyDriving/index.html

Centers for Disease Control. (2015c). *Health, United States, 2014.* DHHS Publication No. 2015-1232. Retrieved March 10, 2017, from www.cdc.gov/nchs/data/hus/hus14.pdf

Centers for Disease Control. (2015d). *Drowsy driving: Asleep at the wheel.* Retrieved January 2, 2017, from www.cdc.gov/Features/dsDrowsyDriving/index.html

Centers for Disease Control. (2016a). *Adult cigarette smoking in the United States: Current estimate.* Retrieved March 18, 2017, from www.cdc.gov/tobacco/data_statistics/fact_sheets/adult_data/cig_smoking/index.htm

Centers for Disease Control. (2016b). *Electronic aggression.* Retrieved June 4, 2017, from www.cdc.gov/ViolencePrevention/youthviolence/electronicaggression/index.html

Centers for Disease Control. (2016c). *Injury prevention & control: Opioid overdose.* Retrieved January 3, 2017, from https://www.cdc.gov/drugoverdose/

Centers for Disease Control. (2016d). *Youth Risk Behavior Surveillance—United States, 2015.* Retrieved March 10, 2017, from www.cdc.gov/mmwr/volumes/65/ss/ss6506a1.htm

Centers for Disease Control. (2016e). *Fragile X Syndrome (FXS).* Retrieved May 19, 2017, from www.cdc.gov/ncbddd/fxs/data.html

Centers for Disease Control. (2016f). *Reported STDs in the United States: 2015 national data for chlamydia, gonorrhea, and syphilis.* Retrieved March 10, 2017, from http://www.cdc.gov/std/stats14/std-trends-508.pdf

Centers for Disease Control. (2016g). *Facts about microcephaly (FXS).* Retrieved February 16, 2017, from www.cdc.gov/ncbddd/birthdefects/microcephaly.html

Centers for Disease Control. (2016h). *HIV in the United States: At a glance.* Retrieved March 10, 2017, from http://www.cdc.gov/hiv/statistics/overview/ataglance.html

Centers for Disease Control. (2017a). *Injury prevention & control: Opioid overdose.* Retrieved May 6, 2017, from www.cdc.gov/drugoverdose

Centers for Disease Control. (2017b). *Quitting smoking.* Retrieved May 6, 2017, from www.cdc.gov/tobacco/data_statistics/fact_sheets/cessation/quitting/index.htm

Centers for Disease Control. (2017c). *Reproductive health: Teen pregnancy.* Retrieved March 10, 2017, from http://www.cdc.gov/teenpregnancy/index.htm

Centers for Disease Control and Prevention. (2015). *Percentage of U.S. adults who looked up health information on the Internet in the past year, by type of locality—National Health Interview Survey, 2012–2014.* Downloaded from https://www.cdc.gov/mmwr/preview/mmwrhtml/mm6449a5.htm?s_cid=mm6449a5_w

Centers for Disease Control and Prevention. (2020). *Data and publications.* Retrieved from https://www.cdc.gov/mentalhealth/data_publications/index.htm

Centofanti, A. T., & Reece, J. (2006). The cognitive interview and its effect on misleading postevent information. *Psychology, Crime & Law, 12*(6), 669–683. doi:10.1080/10683160600558394

Centre for Addiction and Mental Health. (2012). *CAMH and harm reduction: A background paper on its meaning and application for substance use issues.* Retrieved January 2, 2017, from www.camh.ca/en/hospital/about_camh/influencing_public_policy/public_policy_submissions/harm_reduction/Pages/harmreductionbackground.aspx

Cervone, D., & Pervin, L. A. (2013). *Personality: Theory & research* (12th ed.). New York: Wiley.

Ceylan, M., & Sayin, A. (2012). Neurobiology of repression: A hypothetical interpretation. *Integrative Psychological & Behavioral Science, 46*(3), 395–409. doi:10.1007/s12124-012-9197-8

Chabas, D., Taheri, S., et al. (2003). The genetics of narcolepsy. *Annual Review of Genomics & Human Genetics, 4,* 459–483. doi:10.1146/annurev.genom.4.070802.110432

Chabris, C. F., Hebert, B. M., et al. (2012). Most reported genetic associations with general intelligence are probably false positives. *Psychological Science, 23*(11), 1314–1323. doi:10.1177/0956797611435528

Chabris, C. F., Lee, J. J., Cesarini, D., Benjamin, D. J., & Laibson, D. I. (2015). The fourth law of behavior genetics. *Current Directions in Psychological Science, 24*(4), 304–312. doi:10.1177/0963721415580430

Chaffee, J. (2015). *Thinking critically* (11th ed.). Boston, MA: Cengage Learning.

Challacombe, F., Oldfield, V. B., & Salkovskis, P. M. (2011). *Break free from OCD: Overcoming obsessive compulsive disorder using CBT.* London: Vermillion.

Chalmers. D. J. (2010). *The character of consciousness.* New York: Oxford University Press.

Chambers, R. (2012, December 29). Adult hippocampal neurogenesis in the pathogenesis of addiction and dual diagnosis disorders. *Drug & Alcohol Dependence,* n.p. doi:10.1016/j.drugalcdep.2012.12.005

Chamorro-Premuzic, T., & Furnham, A. (2003). Personality predicts academic performance. *Journal of Research in Personality, 37*(4), 319–338. doi:10.1016/S0092-6566(02)00578-0

Chamorro-Premuzic, T., & Furnham, A. (2010). *The psychology of personnel selection.* New York: Cambridge University Press.

Chance, P. (2014). *Learning and behavior* (7th ed.). Boston, MA: Cengage Learning.

Chang, B., Dusek, J. A., & Benson, H. (2011). Psychobiological changes from relaxation response elicitation: Long-term practitioners vs. novices. *Psychosomatics: Journal of Consultation Liaison Psychiatry, 52*(6), 550–559.

Chang, C., Pan, W., et al. (2012). Postural activity and motion sickness during video game play in children and adults. *Experimental Brain Research, 217*(2), 299–309. doi:10.1007/s00221-011-2993-4

Chang, J.-H. (2009). Chronic pain: Cultural sensitivity to pain. In S. Eshun, & R. A. R. Gurung (Eds.), *Culture and mental health: Sociocultural influences, theory, and practice* (pp. 71–89). New York: Wiley-Blackwell. doi:10.1002/9781444305807.ch5

Chansler, P. A., Swamidass, P. M., & Cammann, C. (2003). Self-managing work teams: An empirical study of group cohesiveness in "natural work groups" at a Harley-Davidson Motor Company plant. *Small Group Research, 34*(1), 101–120.

Chapleau, K. M., & Oswald, D. L. (2010). Power, sex, and rape myth acceptance: Testing two models of rape proclivity. *Journal of Sex Research, 47*(1), 66–78.

Charmaraman, L., & Grossman, J. M. (2010). Importance of race and ethnicity: An exploration of Asian, Black, Latino, and multiracial adolescent identity. *Cultural Diversity & Ethnic Minority Psychology, 16*(2), 144–151. doi:10.1037/a0018668

Chartrand, T. L., & Lakin, J. L. (2013). The antecedents and consequences of human behavioral mimicry. *Annual Review of Psychology, 64,* 285–308. doi:10.1146/annurev-psych-113011-143754

Chase, W. G., & Simon, H. A. (1973). Perception in chess. *Cognitive Psychology, 4*(1), 55–81. doi:10.1016/0010-0285(73)90004-2

Chaudry, A., Pedroza, J., et al. (2011, November). *Child care choices of low-income working families.* Retrieved from https://www.urban.org/research/publication/child-care-choices-low-income-working-families

Chaves, J. F. (2000). Hypnosis. In A. Kazdin (Ed.), *Encyclopedia of psychology* (Vol. 4, pp. 211–216). Washington, DC: American Psychological Association.

Cheah, C. L., Leung, C. Y., & Zhou, N. (2013). Understanding "tiger parenting" through the perceptions of Chinese immigrant mothers: Can Chinese and U.S. parenting coexist? *Asian American Journal of Psychology, 4*(1), 30–40. doi:10.1037/a0031217

Check, J. V., & Malamuth, N. M. (1983). Sex role stereotyping and reactions to depictions of stranger versus acquaintance rape. *Journal of Personality & Social Psychology, 45,* 344–356.

Chein, J. M., & Fiez, J. A. (2010). Evaluating models of working memory through the effects of concurrent irrelevant information. *Journal of Experimental Psychology: General, 139*(1), 117–137. doi:10.1037/a0018200

Chen, C., Lin, Y., & Hsiao, C. (2012). Celebrity endorsement for sporting events using classical conditioning. *International Journal of Sports Marketing & Sponsorship, 13*(3), 209–219.

Chen, Z., Mo, L., & Honomichl, R. (2004). Having the memory of an elephant. *Journal of Experimental Psychology: General, 133*(3), 415–433.

Cheng, C., & Lin, Y. (2012). The effects of aging on lifetime of auditory sensory memory in humans. *Biological Psychology, 89*(2), 306–312. doi:10.1016/j.biopsycho.2011.11.003

Cherner, R. A., & Reissing, E. D. (2013). A comparative study of sexual function, behavior, and cognitions of women with lifelong vaginismus. *Archives of Sexual Behavior, 42*(8), 1605–1614. doi:10.1007/s10508-013-0111-3

Chernev, A., Böckenholt, U., et al. (2015). Choice overload: A conceptual review and meta-analysis. *Journal of Consumer Psychology, 25*(2), 333–358. doi:10.1016/j.jcps.2014.08.002

Chess, S., & Thomas, A. (1986). *Know your child.* New York: Basic.

Chew, S. L., & Cerbin, W. J. (2017, December). Teaching and learning: Lost in a buzzword wasteland. *Inside Higher Education.* Retrieved from https://www.insidehighered.com/views/2017/12/05/need-theory-learning-opinion

Cheyne, J. A., & Girard, T. A. (2009). The body unbound: Vestibular-motor hallucinations and out-of-body experiences. *Cortex, 45*(2), 201–215. doi:10.1016/j.cortex.2007.05.002

Chi, M. T., Feltovich, P. J., & Glaser, R. (1981). Categorization and representation of physics problems by experts and novices. *Cognitive Science, 5*(2), 121–152. doi:10.1207/s15516709cog0502_2

Chipman, M., & Jin, Y. L. (2009). Drowsy drivers: The effect of light and circadian rhythm on crash occurrence. *Safety Science, 47*(10), 1364–1370. doi:10.1016/j.ssci.2009.03.005

Choi, O. (2015). Using fMRI for lie detection: Ready for court? In K. J. Weiss & Watson, C. (Eds.), *Psychiatric expert testimony: Emerging applications* (pp. 84–101). New York: Oxford University Press. doi:10.1093/med/9780199346592.003.0006

Chomsky, N. (1986). *Knowledge of language.* New York: Praeger.

Choy, M. M., Farber, K. G., et al. (2017). Electroconvulsive therapy (ECT) in the news: "Balance" leads to bias. *Journal of ECT, 33*(1), 1–2. doi:10.1097/YCT.0000000000000376

Christakis, N. A., & Fowler, J. H. (2007). The spread of obesity in a large social network over 32 years. *New England Journal of Medicine, 357*(4), 370–379.

Christakis, N. A., & Fowler, J. H. (2008). The collective dynamics of smoking in a large social network. *New England Journal of Medicine, 358*(21), 2249–2258. doi:10.1056/NEJMsa0706154

Christakis, N. A., & Fowler, J. H. (2009). *Connected: The surprising power of our social networks and how they shape our lives.* New York: Little, Brown.

Christensen, K., Nørskov, S., et al. (2016). In search of new product ideas: Identifying ideas in online communities by machine learning and text mining. *Creativity and Innovation Management*. Retrieved December 17, 2020 from http://www.ccrs.uzh.ch/dam/jcr:94c30066-bdec-4286-baf6-55d611f774ea/2016.12.Search %20of%20new%20product%20ideas %20JS-et-al.pdf

Christian, M. S., Edwards, B. D., et al. (2010). Situational judgment tests: Constructs assessed and a meta-analysis of their criterion-related validities. *Personnel Psychology, 63*(1), 83–117.

Chua, A. (2011). *Battle hymn of the tiger mother*. New York: Penguin.

Chua, H. F., Boland, J. E., et al. (2005). Cultural variation in eye movements during scene perception. *Proceedings of the National Academy of Sciences, 102*(35), 12629–12633. doi:10.1073/pnas.0506162102

Cialdini, R. B. (2009). *Influence: Science and practice* (5th ed.). Boston, MA: Allyn & Bacon.

Cialdini, R. B., & Griskevicius, V. (2010). Social influence. In R. F. Baumeister & E. J. Finkel (Eds.), *Advanced social psychology: The state of the science* (pp. 385–417). New York: Oxford University Press.

Cialdini, R. B., Reno, R. R., & Kallgren, C. A. (1990). A focus theory of normative conduct: Recycling the concept of norms to reduce littering in public places. *Journal of Personality & Social Psychology, 58*(6), 1015–1026. doi:10.1037/0022-3514.58.6.1015

Cicchetti, D. (2016). Socioemotional, personality, and biological development: Illustrations from a multilevel developmental psychopathology perspective on child maltreatment. *Annual Review of Psychology, 67,* 187–211. doi:10.1146/annurev-psych-122414-033259

Cicciola, E., Foschi, R., et al. (2014). Making up intelligence scales: De Sanctis's and Binet's tests, 1905 and after. *History of Psychology, 17*(3), 223–236. doi:10.1037/a0033740

Ciobanu, L. G., Sachdev, P. S., et al. (2016). Differential gene expression in brain and peripheral tissues in depression across the life span: A review of replicated findings. *Neuroscience & Biobehavioral Reviews, 71,* 281–293. doi:10.1016/j.neubiorev.2016.08.018

Cipani, E., & Schock, K. (2010). *Functional behavioral assessment, diagnosis, and treatment: A complete system for education and mental health settings* (2nd ed.). New York: Springer.

Cipolli, C., Mazzetti, M., & Plazzi, G. (2013). Sleep-dependent memory consolidation in patients with sleep disorders. *Sleep Medicine Reviews, 17*(2), 91–103. doi:10.1016/j.smrv.2012.01.004

Cisler, J. M., Olatunji, B. O., et al. (2010). Emotion regulation and the anxiety disorders: An integrative review. *Journal of Psychopathology & Behavioral Assessment, 32*(1), 68–82. doi:10.1007/s10862-009-9161-1

Citrome, L. (2011). Neurochemical models of schizophrenia: Transcending dopamine. *Annals of Clinical Psychiatry, 23*(4), S10–S14.

Claessens, M. (2009). Mindfulness and existential therapy. *Existential Analysis, 20*(1), 109–119.

Clark, J. A., & Fessler, D. M. T. (2014). Recontextualizing the behavioral immune system within psychoneuroimmunology. *Evolutionary Behavioral Sciences, 8*(4), 235–243. doi:10.1037/ebs0000024

Clark, M. S., Boothby, E. J., Clark-Polner, E., & Reis, H. T. (2015). Understanding prosocial behavior requires understanding relational context. In D. A. Schroeder & W. G. Graziano (Eds.), *The Oxford handbook of prosocial behavior* (pp. 329–345). New York, NY: Oxford University Press. doi:10.1093/oxfordhb/9780195399813.001.0001

Clark, S. E., Rush, R. A., & Moreland, M. B. (2013). Constructing the lineup: Law, reform, theory, and data. In B. L. Cutler (Ed.), *Reform of eyewitness identification procedures* (pp. 87–112). Washington, DC: American Psychological Association. doi:10.1037/14094-005

Clarke, J., & Mack, A. (2015). Iconic memory for natural scenes: Evidence using a modified change-detection procedure. *Visual Cognition, 23*(7), 917–938. doi:10.1080/13506285.2015.1103826

Claudat, K., White, E. K., & Warren, C. S. (2016). Acculturative stress, self-esteem, and eating pathology in Latina and Asian American female college students. *Journal of Clinical Psychology, 72*(1), 88–100. doi:10.1002/jclp.22234

Clayton, N. S. (2017). Episodic-like memory and mental time travel in animals. In J. Call, G. M. Burghardt, et al. (Eds.). *APA handbook of comparative psychology: Basic concepts, methods, neural substrate, and behavior: Perception, learning, and cognition* (Vol. 2, pp. 227–243). Washington, DC: American Psychological Association.

Clayton, N. S., Russell, J., & Dickinson, A. (2009). Are animals stuck in time or are they chronesthetic creatures? *Topics in Cognitive Science, 1*(1), 59–71. doi:10.1111/j.1756-8765.2008.01004.x

Clayton, N. S., Yu, K. S., & Dickinson, A. (2001). Scrub jays (Aphelocoma coerulescens) form integrated memories of the multiple features of caching episodes. *Journal of Experimental Psychology: Animal Behavior Processes, 27,* 17–29. doi:10.1037/0097-7403.27.1.17

Clearfield, M. W., & Nelson, N. M. (2006). Sex differences in mothers' speech and play behavior with 6-, 9-, and 14-month-old infants. *Sex Roles, 54*(1–2), 127–137.

Clements, A. M., Rimrodt, S. L., et al. (2006). Sex differences in cerebral laterality of language and visuospatial processing. *Brain & Language, 98*(2), 150–158.

Clifford, A., Lang, L., & Chen, R. (2012). Effects of maternal cigarette smoking during pregnancy on cognitive parameters of children and young adults: A literature review. *Neurotoxicology & Teratology, 34*(6), 560–570. doi:10.1016/j.ntt.2012.09.004

Cnattingius, S., Signorello, L. B., et al. (2000). Caffeine intake and the risk of first-trimester spontaneous abortion. *New England Journal of Medicine, 343*(25), 1839–1845.

Cobb, N. K., & Abrams, D. B. (2011). E-cigarette or drug-delivery device? Regulating novel nicotine products. *New England Journal of Medicine, 365*(3), 193–195. doi:10.1056/NEJMp1105249

Cochran, G. M., & Harpending, H. (2009). *The 10,000 year explosion.* New York: Basic Books.

Coe-Odess, S. J., Narr, R. K., & Allen, J. P. (2019). Emergent Emotions in Adolescence. In V. LoBue, K. Pérez-Edgar, & K. A. Buss (Eds.), *Handbook of Emotional Development* (pp. 595–625). Cham, Switzerland: Springer.

Coelho, V. A., Marchante, M., et al. (2017). Promoting a positive middle school transition: A randomizedcon-trolled treatment study examining self-concept and self-esteem. *Journal of Youth & Adolescence, 46*(3), 558–569. doi:10.1007/s10964-016-0510-6

Coffield, F., Moseley, D., et al. (2004). *Learning styles and pedagogy in post-16 learning. A systematic and critical review.* London: Learning and Skills Research Centre.

Cohen, H. (2006). Two stories of PTSD. *Psych Central.* Retrieved on January 31, 2017, from psychcentral.com/lib/two-stories-of-ptsd

Cohen, K., & Collens, P. (2012). The impact of trauma work on trauma workers: A metasynthesis on vicarious trauma and vicarious posttraumatic growth. *Psychological Trauma,* n.p. doi:10.1037/a0030388

Cohen, L. J., Forman, H., et al. (2010). Comparison of childhood sexual histories in subjects with pedophilia or opiate addiction and healthy controls: Is childhood sexual abuse a risk factor for addictions? *Journal of Psychiatric Practice, 16*(6), 394–404. doi:10.1097/01.pra.0000390758.27451.79

Cohen, S., Evans, G. W., et al. (1981). Cardiovascular and behavioral effects of community noise. *American Scientist, 69,* 528–535.

Cohen, S., Tyrrell, D. A., & Smith, A. P. (1993). Negative life events, perceived stress, negative affect, and susceptibility to the common cold. *Journal of Personality & Social Psychology, 64*(1), 131–140. doi:10.1037/0022-3514.64.1.131

Cohen, S., & Wills, T. A. (1985). Stress, social support, and the buffering hypothesis. *Psychological Bulletin, 98*(2), 310–357. doi:10.1037/0033-2909.98.2.310

Cohn, E., Bucolo, D., et al. (2009). Reducing white juror bias: The role of race salience and racial attitudes. *Journal of Applied Social Psychology, 39*(8), 1953–1973. doi:10.1111/j.1559-1816.2009.00511.x

Colangelo, J. J. (2007). Recovered memory debate revisited: Practice implications for mental health counselors. *Journal of Mental Health Counseling, 29*(2), 93–120.

Colby, S. L., & Ortman, J. M. (2016). *Projections of the size and composition of the U.S. Population: 2014 to 2060.* Retrieved April 26, 2017, from www.census.gov/content/dam/Census/library/publications/2015/demo/p25-1143.pdf

Cole, M. W., Yarkoni, T., et al. (2012). Global connectivity of prefrontal cortex predicts cognitive control and intelligence. *Journal of Neuroscience, 32*(26), 8988–8999. doi:10.1523/JNEUROSCI.0536-12.2012

Cole, T., Barrett, D. J. K., & Griffiths, M. D. (2011). Social facilitation in online and offline gambling: A pilot study. *International Journal of Mental Health & Addiction, 9*(3), 240–247. doi:10.1007/s11469-010-9281-6

Colin, A. K., & Moore, K., & West, A. N. (1996). Creativity, oversensitivity, and rate of habituation. *EDRA: Environmental Design Research Association, 20*(4), 423–427. doi:10.1016/0191-8869(95)00193-X

Collins, A. M., & Quillian, M. R. (1969). Retrieval time from semantic memory. *Journal of Verbal Learning & Verbal Behavior, 8,* 240–247. doi:10.1016/S0022-5371(69)80069-1

Colom, R., Burgaleta, M., et al. (2013). Neuroanatomic overlap between intelligence and cognitive factors: Morphometry methods provide support for the key role of the frontal lobes. *Neuroimage, 72,* 143–152. doi:10.1016/j.neuroimage.2013.01.032

Comas-Diaz, L. (2012). *Multicultural care: A clinician's guide to cultural competence.* Washington, DC: American Psychological Association.

Comer, R. J. (2013). *Abnormal psychology* (8th ed.). New York: Worth.

Compton, W. C., & Hoffman, E. (2013). *Positive psychology: The science of happiness and flourishing* (2nd ed.). Boston, MA: Cengage Learning.

Concha, A., Mills, D. S., et al. (2014). Using sniffing behavior to differentiate true negative from false negative responses in trained scent-detection dogs. *Chemical Senses, 39*(9), 749–754. doi:10.1093/chemse/bju045

Conley, T. D., Moors, A. C., et al. (2011). Women, men, and the bedroom: Methodological and conceptual insights that narrow, reframe, and eliminate gender differences in sexuality. *Current Directions in Psychological Science, 20*(5), 296–300. doi:10.1177/0963721411418467

Conlon, K. E., Ehrlinger, J., et al. (2011). Eyes on the prize: The longitudinal benefits of goal focus on progress toward a weight-loss goal. *Journal of Experimental Social Psychology, 47,* 853–855. doi:10.1016/j.jesp.2011.02.005

Connolly, T. M., Boyle, E. A., et al. (2012). A systematic literature review of empirical evidence on computer games and serious games. *Computers & Education, 59*(2), 661–686. doi:10.1016/j.compedu.2012.03.004

Conron, K. J., Mimiaga, M. J., & Landers, S. J. (2010). A population-based study of sexual orientation identity and gender differences in adult health. *American Journal of Public Health, 100*(10), 1953–1960. doi:10.2105/AJPH.2009.174169

Constantino, M. J., Coyne, A. E., et al. (2017, February 9). Therapeutic alliance, subsequent change, and moderators of the alliance–outcome association in Interpersonal Psychotherapy for depression. *Psychotherapy,* n.p. doi:10.1037/pst0000101

Conway, M. A., Cohen, G., & Stanhope, N. (1992). Very long-term memory for knowledge acquired at school and university. *Applied Cognitive Psychology, 6*(6), 467–482. doi:10.1002/acp.2350060603

Cook, R., Bird, G., et al. (2014). Mirror neurons: From origin to function. *Behavioral & Brain Sciences, 37*(2), 177–192. doi:10.1017/S0140525X13000903

Cook, S. G. (2013). Behavioral interviews: Hire for the competencies needed. *Women in Higher Education, 22*(3), 23–24. doi:10.1002/whe.10437

Coolidge, F. L., & Wynn, T. (2009). *The rise of Homo Sapiens: The evolution of modern thinking.* New York: Wiley-Blackwell.

Cooper, H. (2010). *Research synthesis and meta-analysis.* Thousand Oaks, CA: Sage.

Cooper, J. (2007). *Cognitive dissonance: Fifty years of a classic theory.* Thousand Oaks, CA: Sage.

Cooper, J., Bennett, E. A., & Sukel, H. L. (1996). Complex scientific testimony: How do jurors make decisions? *Law & Human Behavior, 20*(4), 379–394.

Cooper, M., & McLeod, J. (2011). Person-centered therapy: A pluralistic perspective. *Person-Centered & Experiential Psychotherapies, 10*(3), 210–223. doi:10.1080/14779757.2011.599517

Cooper, P. J., & Murray, L. (2001). The treatment and prevention of postpartum depression and associated disturbances in child development. *Archives of Women's Mental Health, 3*(Suppl. 2), 5.

Cooper, R. P., Abraham, J., et al. (1997). The development of infants' preference for motherese. *Infant Behavior & Development, 20*(4), 477–488. doi:10.1016/S0163-6383(97)90037-0

Cooper, S. J. (2008). From Claude Bernard to Walter Cannon: Emergence of the concept of homeostasis. *Appetite, 51*(3), 419–427. doi:10.1016/j.appet.2008.06.005

Corbin, W. R., & Fromme, K. (2002). Alcohol use and serial monogamy as risks for sexually transmitted diseases in young adults. *Health Psychology, 21*(3), 229–236.

Corcoran, R. (2010). The allusive cognitive deficit in paranoia: The case for mental time travel or cognitive self-projection. *Psychological Medicine, 40*(8), 1233–1237. doi:10.1017/S003329170999211X

Cordaro, D. T., Sun, R., Keltner, D., Kamble, S., Huddar, N., & McNeil, G. (2018). Universals and cultural variations in 22 emotional expressions across five cultures. *Emotion, 18,* 75–93. doi:10.1037/emo0000302

Coren, S. (1996). *Sleep thieves.* New York: Free Press.

Corenblum, B. (2013). Development of racial–ethnic identity among First Nation children. *Journal of Youth & Adolescence.* doi:10.1007/s10964-013-0007-5

Corey, G. (2016). *Theory and practice of group counseling* (9th ed.). Boston, MA: Cengage Learning.

Corey, G., & Corey, M. S. (2014). *I never knew I had a choice: Explorations in personal growth* (10th ed.). Boston, MA: Cengage Learning.

Cornelius, J. R., Kirisci, L., et al. (2010). PTSD contributes to teen and young adult cannabis use disorders. *Addictive Behaviors, 35*(2), 91–94. doi:10.1016/j.addbeh.2009.09.007

Corr, C. A., Nabe, C. M., & Corr, D. M. (2013). *Death and dying, life and living* (7th ed.). Boston, MA: Cengage Learning.

Corradini, A., & Antonietti, A. (2013). Mirror neurons and their function in cognitively understood empathy. *Consciousness & Cognition, 22*(3), 1152–1161. doi:10.1016/j.concog.2013.03.003

Correa-Chávez, M., Rogoff, B., & Arauz, R. M. (2005). Cultural patterns in attending to two events at once. *Child Development, 76*(3), 664–678. doi:10.1111/j.1467-8624.2005.00870.x

Corrigan, P. W., & Watson, A. C. (2005). Findings from the National Comorbidity Survey on the frequency of violent behavior in individuals with psychiatric disorders. *Psychiatry Research, 136*(2–3), 153–162. doi:10.1016/j.psychres.2005.06.005

Corsini, R. J., & Wedding, D. (2014). *Current psychotherapies* (10th ed.). Boston, MA: Cengage Learning.

Cortina, M. (2016). Quo vadis? The future of psychoanalysis. *Psychoanalytic Review, 103*(6), 793–817. doi:10.1521/prev.2016.103.6.793

Costa, M. (2012). Territorial behavior in public settings. *Environment & Behavior, 44*(5), 713–721. doi:10.1177/0013916511403803

Counotte, D. S., Smit, A. B., et al. (2011). Development of the motivational system during adolescence, and its sensitivity to disruption by nicotine. *Developmental Cognitive Neuroscience, 1*(4), 430–443. doi:10.1016/j.dcn.2011.05.010

Cowen, A., Sauter, D., Tracy, J. L., & Keltner, D. (2019). Mapping the passions: Toward a high-dimensional taxonomy of emotional experience and expression. *Psychological Science in the Public Interest, 20*(1), 69–90. doi:10.1177/1529100619850176

Cowan, D. E., & Bromley, D. G. (2008). *Cults and new religions: A brief history.* Malden, MA: Blackwell.

Cowles, J. T. (1937). Food tokens as incentives for learning by chimpanzees. *Comparative Psychology,* Monograph, *14*(5, Whole No. 71).

Cox, R. H. (2012). *Sport psychology: Concepts and applications* (7th ed.). New York: McGraw-Hill.

Coxell, A. W., & King, M. B. (2010). Male victims of rape and sexual abuse. *Sexual & Relationship Therapy, 25*(4), 380–391.

Coyle, T. R., Pillow, D. R., et al. (2011). Processing speed mediates the development of general intelligence (g) in adolescence. *Psychological Science, 22*(10), 1265–1269. doi:10.1177/0956797611418243

Craig, E. (2012). Human existence (cún zài): What is it? What's in it for us as existential psychotherapists? *The Humanistic Psychologist, 40*(1), 1–22. doi:10.1080/08873267.2012.643680

Craig, L. (2006). Does father care mean fathers share? A comparison of how mothers and fathers in intact families spend time with children. *Gender & Society, 20*(2), 259–281. doi:10.1177/0891243205285212

Craig, R. J. (2013). Assessing personality and psychopathology with interviews. In J. R. Graham, J. A. Naglieri, et al. (Eds.), *Handbook of psychology* (Vol. 10): *Assessment psychology* (2nd ed., pp. 558–582). Hoboken, NJ: John Wiley & Sons Inc.

Craik, F. I. M. (1970). The fate of primary items in free recall. *Journal of Verbal Learning & Verbal Behavior, 9,* 143–148. doi:10.1016/S0022-5371(70)80042-1

Cramer, E. M., Song, H., et al. (2016). Social comparison on Facebook: Motivation, affective consequences, self-esteem, and Facebook fatigue. *Computers in Human Behavior, 64,* 739–746. doi:10.1016/j.chb.2016.07.049

Crandall, C. S., Bahns, A. J., et al. (2011). Stereotypes as justifications of prejudice. *Personality & Social Psychology Bulletin, 37*(11), 1488–1498. doi:10.1177/0146167211411723

Crane, L., Pring, L., et al. (2010). Executive functions in savant artists with autism. *Research in Autism Spectrum Disorders, 5*(2), 790–797.

Craver-Lemley, C., & Reeves, A. (2013). Is synesthesia a form of mental imagery? In S. Lacey & R. Lawson (Eds.), *Multisensory imagery* (pp. 185–206). New York: Springer. doi:10.1007/978-1-4614-5879-1_10

Crawford, S. A., & Caltabiano, N. J. (2011). Promoting emotional well-being through the use of humour. *Journal of Positive Psychology, 6*(3), 237–252. doi:10.1080/17439760.2011.577087

Crews, F. T., & Boettiger, C. A. (2009). Impulsivity, frontal lobes, and risk for addiction. *Pharmacology, Biochemistry, & Behavior, 93*(3), 237–247. doi:10.1016/j.pbb.2009.04.018

Crisp, R. (2014). Characteristics of master therapists and the influence of Carl Rogers: A discussion. *Counselling Psychology Review, 29*(3), 55–64.

Crist, M., & Requarth, T. (2012, October 25). Why IQs rise. *New Republic.* Retrieved March 5, 2014, from www.newrepublic.com/book/review

/are-we-getting-smarter-rising -IQs-james-flynn
Crivelli, C., Russell, J. A., et al. (2017). Recognizing spontaneous facial expressions of emotion in a small-scale society of Papua New Guinea. *Emotion, 17*(2), 337–347. doi:10.1037/emo0000236
Crone, T. S., & Portillo, M. C. (2013). Jigsaw variations and attitudes about learning and the self in cognitive psychology. *Teaching of Psychology, 40*(3), 246–251. doi:10.1177/0098628313487451
Cronin, C. (2019). *Forensic psychology: An applied approach* (3rd ed.). Dubuque: Kendall-Hunt.
Crooks, R., & Baur, K. (2017). *Our sexuality* (13th ed.). Boston, MA: Cengage Learning.
Cross-Tab. (2010, January). *Online reputation in a connected world* (Public report prepared for Microsoft). Retrieved April 12, 2017, from www.job-hunt.org/guides /DPD_Online-Reputation-Research _overview.pdf
Crowley, M., Tope, D., et al. (2010). Neo-Taylorism at work: Occupational change in the post-Fordist Era. *Social Problems, 57*(3), 421–447.
Crown, C. L., Feldstein, S., et al. (2002). The cross-modal coordination of interpersonal timing. *Journal of Psycholinguistic Research, 31*(1), 1–23. doi:10.1023/A:1014301303616
Crowther, J. H., Sanftner, J., et al. (2001). The role of daily hassles in binge eating. *International Journal of Eating Disorders, 29,* 449–454. doi:10.1002/eat.1041
Cruse, D., Chennu, S., et al. (2011). Bedside detection of awareness in the vegetative state: A cohort study. *Lancet, 378*(9809), 2088–2094. doi:10.1016/S0140-6736(11)61224-5
Cservenka, A., Herting, M. M., et al. (2013). High and low sensation seeking adolescents show distinct patterns of brain activity during reward processing. *Neuroimage, 66,* 184–193. doi:10.1016/j.neuroimage.2012.11.003
Csikszentmihalyi, M., Abuhamdeh, S., Nakamura, J. (2005). Flow. In A. J. Elliot, & C. S. Dweck (Eds.), *Handbook of competence and motivation* (pp. 598–608). New York: Guilford.
Cuevas, J. (2015). Is learning styles-based instruction effective? A comprehensive analysis of recent research on learning styles. *Theory and Research in Education, 13*(3), 308–333. doi:10.1177/1477878515606621
Cuijpers, P., Cristea, I. A., et al. (2016). Psychological treatment of depression in college students: A metaanalysis. *Depression & Anxiety, 33*(5), 400–414. doi:10.1002/da.22461
Cuijpers, P., Geraedts, A. S., et al. (2011). Interpersonal psychotherapy for depression: A meta-analysis. *The American Journal of Psychiatry, 168*(6), 581–592. doi:10.1176/appi.ajp.2010.10101411
Culver, R., & Ianna, P. (1988). *Astrology: True or false?* Buffalo, NY: Prometheus Books.
Cummings, M. R. (2016). *Human heredity: Principles and issues* (11th ed.). Boston, MA: Cengage Learning.
Cunningham, R. L., Lumia, A. R., & McGinnis, M. Y. (2013). Androgenic anabolic steroid exposure during adolescence: Ramifications for brain development and behavior. *Hormones & Behavior, 64*(2), 350–356. doi:10.1016/j.yhbeh.2012.12.009
Curci, A., & Luminet, O. (2006). Follow-up of a crossnational comparison on flashbulb and event memory for the September 11th attacks. *Memory, 14*(3), 329–344. doi:10.1080/09658210903081827
Curtis, D., Vine, A. E., et al. (2011). Case–case genome-wide association analysis shows markers differentially associated with schizophrenia and bipolar disorder and implicates calcium channel genes. *Psychiatric Genetics, 21*(1), 1–4. doi:10.1097/YPG.0b013e3283413382
Cushen, P. J., & Wiley, J. (2012). Cues to solution, restructuring patterns, and reports of insight in creative problem solving. *Consciousness & Cognition, 21*(3), 1166–1175. doi:10.1016/j.concog.2012.03.013
Cushing, L., Morello-Frosch, R., et al. (2015). The haves, the have-nots, and the health of everyone: The relationship between social inequality and environmental quality. *Annual Review of Public Health, 36,* 193–209. deoi:10.1146/annurev-publhealth -031914-122646
Cusin, C., Franco, F., et al. (2013). Rapid improvement of depression and psychotic symptoms in Huntington's disease: A retrospective chart review of seven patients treated with electroconvulsive therapy. *General Hospital Psychiatry, 35,* 678.e3-5. doi:10.1016/j.genhosppsych.2013.01.015
Czeisler, C. A., Duffy, J. F., et al. (1999). Stability, precision, and near-24-hour period of the human circadian pacemaker. *Science, 284*(5423), 2177–2181. doi:10.1126/science.284.5423.2177
Czerniak, E., & Davidson, M. (2012). Placebo: A historical perspective. *European Neuropsychopharmacology, 22*(11), 770–774. doi:10.1016/j.euroneuro.2012.04.003
D'Agostino, A., & Limosani, I. (2010). Hypnagogic hallucinations and sleep paralysis. In M. Goswami, S. R. Pandi-Perumal, et al. (Eds.), *Narcolepsy: A clinical guide* (pp. 87–97). Totowa, NJ: Humana Press. doi:10.1007/978 -1-4419-0854-4_8
Dadich, A. (2010). Expanding our understanding of self-help support groups for substance use issues. *Journal of Drug Education, 40*(2), 189–202.
Dai, D. Y. (2010). *The nature and nurture of giftedness: A new framework for understanding gifted education.* New York: Teachers College Press.
Dailey, M. N., Joyce, C., et al. (2010). Evidence and a computational explanation of cultural differences in facial expression recognition. *Emotion, 10*(6), 874–893. doi:10.1037/a0020019
Dalton, A. N., Chartrand, T. L., & Finkel, E. J. (2010). The schema-driven chameleon: How mimicry affects executive and self-regulatory resources. *Journal of Personality & Social Psychology, 98*(4), 605–617.
Dalton, R. P., & Lomvardas, S. (2015). Chemosensory receptor specificity and regulation. *Annual Review of Neuroscience, 38,* 331–349. doi:10.1146/annurev-neuro-071714-034145
Damisch, L., Stoberock, B., & Mussweiler, T. (2010). Keep your fingers crossed! How superstition improves performance. *Psychological Science, 21*(7), 1014–1020. doi:10.1177/0956797610372631
Damman, M., Henkens, K., & Kalmijn, M. (2011). The impact of midlife educational, work, health, and family experiences on men's early retirement. *Journals of Gerontology, 66B*(5), 617–627. doi:10.1093/geronb/gbr092
Danaei, G., Ding, E. L., et al. (2009). The preventable causes of death in the United States: Comparative risk assessment of dietary, lifestyle, and metabolic risk factors. *PLoS Med, 6*(4), e1000058. doi:10.1371/journal.pmed.1000058
Dang-Vu, T. T., McKinney, S. M., et al. (2010). Spontaneous brain rhythms predict sleep stability in the face of noise. *Current Biology, 20*(15), R626–R627. doi:0.06/j.cub.200.06.032
Dani, J. A., & Balfour, D. J. K. (2011). Historical and current perspective on tobacco use and nicotine addiction. *Trends in Neurosciences, 34*(7), 383–392. doi:10.1016/j.tins.2011.05.001
Daniels, H. (2005). Vygotsky and educational psychology: Some preliminary remarks. *Educational & Child Psychology, 22*(1), 6–17.
Danielsson, H., Henry, L., et al. (2010). Executive functions in individuals with intellectual disability. *Research in Developmental Disabilities, 31,* 1299–1304.
Danziger, N., Prkachin, K. M., & Willer, J.-C. (2006). Is pain the price of empathy? The perception of others' pain in patients with congenital insensitivity to pain. *Brain: A Journal of Neurology, 129*(9), 2494–2507. doi:10.1093/brain/awl155
Darley, J. M., & Latané, B. (1968). Bystander intervention in emergencies: Diffusion of responsibility. *Journal of Personality & Social Psychology, 8,* 377–383. doi:10.1037/h0025589
Darou, W. S. (1992). Native Canadians and intelligence testing. *Canadian Journal of Counselling, 26*(2), 96–99.
Daruna, J. H. (2012). *Introduction to psychoneuroimmunology* (2nd ed.). San Diego, CA: Academic Press.
Darwin, C. (1872). *The expression of emotion in man and animals.* Chicago, IL: University of Chicago Press.
Das, J. P. (2000). Mental retardation. In A. Kazdin (Ed.), *Encyclopedia of psychology* (Vol. 5, pp. 193–197). Washington, DC: American Psychological Association.
Davey, G. (Ed.). (2011). *Applied psychology.* New York: Wiley-Blackwell.
Davidson, J. E. (2003). Insights about insightful problem solving. In J. E. Davidson & R. J. Sternberg (Eds.), *The psychology of problem solving* (pp. 149–175). New York: Cambridge University Press. doi:10.1017/CBO9780511615771.006
Davidson, L., Shaw, J., et al. (2010). "I don't know how to find my way in the world": Contributions of user-led research to transforming mental health practice. *Psychiatry: Interpersonal and Biological Processes, 73*(2), 101–113. doi:10.1521/psyc.2010.73.2.101
Davidson, R. J., Kabat-Zinn, J., et al. (2003). Alternations in brain and immune function produced by mindfulness meditation. *Psychosomatic Medicine, 65*(4), 564–570. doi:10.1097/01.PSY.0000077505.67574.E3
Davis, D., & Follette, W. C. (2002). Rethinking the probative value of evidence. *Law & Human Behavior, 26*(2), 133–158. doi:10.1023/A:1014693024962
Davis, M. A. (2009). Understanding the relationship between mood and creativity: A meta-analysis. *Organizational Behavior & Human Decision Processes, 108*(1), 25–38. doi:10.1016/j.obhdp.2008.04.001
Davis, P. A. (Ed.). (2016). *The psychology of effective coaching and management.* Hauppauge, NY: Nova Science Publishers.
Davis, R., Campbell, R., et al. (2015). Theories of behaviour and behaviour

change across the social and behavioural sciences: A scoping review. *Health Psychology Review, 9*(3), 323–344. doi:10.1080/17437199.2014.941722

Davison, G. C., & Neale, J. M. (2006). *Abnormal psychology* (10th ed.). San Francisco, CA: Jossey-Bass.

Day, D. O., & Moseley, R. L. (2010). Munchausen by proxy syndrome. *Journal of Forensic Psychology Practice, 10*(1), 13–36. doi:10.1080/15228930903172981

Day, D. V., Fleenor, J. W., et al. (2014). Advances in leader and leadership development: A review of 25 years of research and theory. *The Leadership Quarterly, 25*(1), 63–82. doi:10.1016/j.leaqua.2013.11.004

Day, D. V., & Miscenko, D. (2016). *Leader-member exchange (LMX): Construct evolution, contributions, and future prospects for advancing leadership theory.* In T. N. Bauer & B. Erdogan (Eds.), *Oxford library of psychology. The Oxford handbook of leader-member exchange* (pp. 9–28). Oxford: Oxford University Press.

Dazzi, C., & Pedrabissi, L. (2009). Graphology and personality: An empirical study on validity of handwriting analysis. *Psychological Reports, 105,* 1255–1268. doi:10.2466/pr0.105.F.1255-1268

de Bono, E. (1992). *Serious creativity.* New York: HarperCollins.

De Cuypere, G., Knudson, G., & Bockting, W. (2011). Second response of the world professional association for transgender health to the proposed revision of the diagnosis of gender dysphoria for DSM 5. *International Journal of Transgenderism, 13*(2), 51–53. doi:10.1080/15532739.2011.624047

de Gelder, B. (2013). From body perception to action preparation: A distributed neural system for viewing bodily expressions of emotion. In K. L. Johnson, & M. Shiffrar (Eds.), *People watching: Social, perceptual, and neurophysiological studies of body perception* (pp. 350–368). New York: Oxford University Press.

De Groot, A. D. (1946/1978). *Thought and choice in chess* (2nd ed.). The Hague: Mouton Publishers.

de Jong, P. J., & Muris, P. (2002). Spider phobia. *Journal of Anxiety Disorders, 16*(1), 51–65. doi:10.1016/S0887-6185(01)00089-5

De Leng, W. E., Stegers-Jager, K. M., et al. (2016, October 18). Scoring method of a situational judgment test: Influence on internal consistency reliability, adverse impact and correlation with personality? *Advances in Health Sciences Education*, n.p. doi:10.1007/s10459-016-9720-7

de Rios, M. D., & Grob, C. S. (2005). Editors' introduction: Ayahuasca use in cross-cultural perspective. *Journal of Psychoactive Drugs, 37*(2), 119–121.

De Schuymer, L., De Groote, I., et al. (2011). Preverbal skills as mediators for language outcome in preterm and full-term children. *Early Human Development, 87*(4), 265–272. doi:10.1016/j.earlhumdev.2011.01.029

De Tanti, A., Saviola, D., et al. (2016). Recovery of consciousness after 7 years in vegetative state of non-traumatic origin: A single case study. *Brain Injury, 30*(8), 1029–1034. doi:10.3109/02699052.2016.1147078

de Vries, S.-K., & Meule, A. (2016). Food addiction and bulimia nervosa: New data based on the Yale Food Addiction Scale 2.0. *European Eating Disorders Review, 24*(6), 518–522. doi:10.1002/erv.2470

Dean, D. Jr., & Kuhn, D. (2007). Direct instruction vs. discovery: The long view. *Science Education, 91*(3), 384–397.

Dean, M. L., & Tate, C. C. (2016, December 12). Extending the legacy of Sandra Bem: Psychological androgyny as a touchstone conceptual advance for the study of gender in psychological science. *Sex Roles,* n.p. doi:10.1007/s11199-016-0713-z

Deardorff, J., Hayward, C., et al. (2007). Puberty and gender interact to predict social anxiety symptoms in early adolescence. *Journal of Adolescent Health, 41*(1), 102–104. doi:10.1016/j.jadohealth.2007.02.013

Deary, I. J., Harris, S. E., & Hill, W. D. (2019). What genome-wide association studies reveal about the association between intelligence and physical health, illness, and mortality. *Current Opinion in Psychology, 27,* 6–12. doi:10.1016/j.copsyc.2018.07.005

DeBord, K. A., Fischer, A. R., et al. (Eds.). (2017). *Handbook of sexual orientation and gender diversity in counseling and psychotherapy.* Washington, DC: American Psychological Association. doi:10.1037/15959-000

DeCarolis, N. A., & Eisch, A. J. (2010). Hippocampal neurogenesis as a target for the treatment of mental illness: A critical evaluation. *Neuropharmacology, 58*(6), 884–893. doi:10.1016/j.neuropharm.2009.12.013

Deckers, L. (2014). *Motivation: Biological, psychological, and environmental* (4th ed.). Boston, MA: Pearson/Allyn and Bacon.

Deckro, G. R., Ballinger, K. M., et al. (2002). The evaluation of a mind/body intervention to reduce psychological distress and perceived stress in college students. *Journal of American College Health, 50*(6), 281–287. doi:10.1080/07448480209603446

Dein, S., & Littlewood, R. (2005). Apocalyptic suicide: From a pathological to an eschatological interpretation. *International Journal of Social Psychiatry, 51*(3), 198–210. doi:10.1177/0020764005056762

Dekker, S., Lee, N. C., et al. (2012). Neuromyths in education: Prevalence and predictors of misconceptions among teachers. *Frontiers in Psychology: Educational Psychology, 429,* 1–8. doi:10.3389/fpsyg.2012.00429

del Casale, A., Ferracuti, S., et al. (2012). Neurocognition under hypnosis: Findings from recent functional neuroimaging studies. *International Journal of Clinical and Experimental Hypnosis, 60*(3), 286–317. doi:10.1080/00207144.2012.675295

Delavest, M. M., Even, C. C., et al. (2012). Association of the intronic rs2072621 polymorphism of the X-linked GPR50 gene with affective disorder with seasonal pattern. *European Psychiatry, 27*(5), 369–371. doi:10.1016/j.eurpsy.2011.02.011

Delgado, B. M., & Ford, L. (1998). Parental perceptions of child development among low-income Mexican American families. *Journal of Child & Family Studies, 7*(4), 469–481. doi:10.1023/A:1022958026951

Dell, P. F. (2009). The long struggle to diagnose multiple personality disorder (MPD): MPD. In P. F. Dell & J. A. O'Neil (Eds.), *Dissociation and the dissociative disorders: DSM-V and beyond* (pp. 667–692). New York: Routledge.

Della Sala, S. (Ed.). (2010). *Forgetting.* Hove, UK: Psychology Press.

Demos, J. N. (2005). *Getting started with neurofeedback.* New York: Norton.

DeNisi, A. S., & Murphy, K. R. (2017). Performance appraisal and performance management: 100 years of progress? *Journal of Applied Psychology, 102*(3), 421–433. doi:10.1037/apl0000085

Denmark, F. L., Rabinowitz, V. C., & Sechzer, J. A. (2005). *Engendering psychology: Women and gender revisited* (2nd ed.). Boston, MA: Allyn & Bacon.

Denney, J. T., Rogers, R. G., et al. (2009). Adult suicide mortality in the United States: Marital status, family size, socioeconomic status, and differences by sex. *Social Science Quarterly, 90*(5), 1167–1185. doi:10.1111/j.1540-6237.2009.00652.x

Denson, T. F., Capper, M. M., et al. (2011). Self-control training decreases aggression in response to provocation in aggressive individuals. *Journal of Research in Personality, 42,* 252–256.

Deręgowski, J. B. (2013). Short and sweet: On the Müller-Lyer illusion in the Carpentered World. *Perception, 42*(7), 790–792. doi:10.1068/p7424

Des Jardins, J. R. (2013). *Environmental ethics* (5th ed.). Boston, MA: Cengage Learning.

DeSantis, A. D., & Hane, A. C. (2010). "Adderall is definitely not a drug": Justifications for the illegal use of ADHD stimulants. *Substance Use & Misuse, 45*(1–2), 31–46. doi:10.3109/10826080902858334

Desmarais, S., Evers, F., et al. (2013). *The peer helper program at the University of Guelph: Analysis of skills objectives.* Toronto, Canada: Higher Education Quality Council of Ontario.

Deutsch, M., & Collins, M. E. (1951). *Interracial housing.* Minneapolis, MA: University of Minnesota.

Deutschendorf, H. (2009). *The other kind of smart: Simple ways to boost your emotional intelligence for greater personal effectiveness and success.* New York: AMACOM.

Devine, D. J., Clayton, L. D., et al. (2001). Jury decision making: 45 years of empirical research on deliberating groups. *Psychology, Public Policy, & Law, 7*(3), 622–727.

Devine, P. G., Forscher, P. S., Austin, A. J., & Cox, W. T. (2012). Long-term reduction in implicit race bias: A prejudice habit-breaking intervention. *Journal of Experimental Social Psychology, 48*(6), 1267–1278. doi:10.1016/j.jesp.2012.06.003

DeWall, C. N., & Anderson, C. A. (2011). The general aggression model. In P. R. Shaver & M. Mikulincer (Eds.), *Human aggression and violence: Causes, manifestations, and consequences* (pp. 15–33). Washington, DC: American Psychological Association. doi:10.1037/12346-001

DeWall, C. N., Lambert, N. M., et al. (2011). So far away from one's partner, yet so close to romantic alternatives: Avoidant attachment, interest in alternatives, and infidelity. *Journal of Personality & Social Psychology, 101*(6), 1302–1316. doi:10.1037/a0025497

Dewar, M., Della Sala, S., et al. (2010). Profound retroactive interference in anterograde amnesia: What interferes? *Neuropsychology, 24*(3), 357–367. doi:10.1037/a0018207

Dewey, J. (1910). *How we think.* Lexington, MA: D.C. Health.

Dexter, C. A., Wong, K., et al. (2013). Parenting and attachment among low-income African American and Caucasian preschoolers. *Journal of

Family Psychology, 27(4), 629–638. doi:10.1037/a0033341

DeYoung, C. G., Hirsh, J. B., et al. (2010). Testing predictions from personality neuroscience: Brain structure and the Big Five. *Psychological Science, 21*(6), 820–828. doi:10.1177/0956797610370159

Di Lorenzo, P. M., & Youngentob, S. L. (2013). Taste and olfaction. In R. J. Nelson, S. Y. Mizumori, & I. B. Weiner (Eds.), *Handbook of psychology* (Vol. 3): *Behavioral neuroscience* (2nd ed., pp. 272–305). New York: Wiley.

Diamond, M. (2009). Human intersexuality: Difference or disorder? *Archives of Sexual Behavior, 38*(2), 172.

Diano, S., Farr, S. A., et al. (2006). Ghrelin controls hippocampal spine synapse density and memory performance. *Nature Neuroscience, 9,* 381–388. doi:10.1038/nn1656

Dick-Niederhauser, A., & Silverman, W. K. (2006). Separation anxiety disorder. In J. E. Fisher & W. T. O'Donohue (Eds.), *Practitioner's guide to evidence-based psychotherapy* (pp. 627–633). New York: Springer. doi:10.1007/978-0-387-28370-8_62

Dicke-Bohmann, A. K., & Cox, C. B. (2015, December 23). Predicting successful responses to emergencies: The emergency responsiveness scale. *Current Psychology,* n.p. doi:10.1007/s12144-015-9402-2

Diehl, A. B., & Dzubinski, L. M. (2016). Making the invisible visible: A cross-sector analysis of gender-based leadership barriers. *Human Resource Development Quarterly, 27*(2), 181–206. doi:10.1002/hrdq.21248

Diehl, M., Chui, H., et al. (2014). Change in coping and defense mechanisms across adulthood: Longitudinal findings in a European American sample. *Developmental Psychology, 50*(2), 634–648.

Diekelmann, S., & Born, J. (2010). The memory function of sleep. *Nature Reviews Neuroscience, 11*(2), 114–126.

Diener, E. (2013). The remarkable changes in the science of subjective well-being. *Perspectives on Psychological Science, 8*(6), 663–666. doi:10.1177/1745691613507583

Diener, E., & Chan, M. Y. (2011). Happy people live longer: Subjective well-being contributes to health and longevity. *Applied Psychology: Health & Well-Being, 3*(1), 1–43. doi:10.1111/j.1758-0854.2010.01045.x

Diener, E., Scollon, C. N., & Lucas, R. E. (2009). The evolving concept of subjective well-being: The multifaceted nature of happiness. *Social Indicators Research* Series, *39,* 67–100. doi:10.1007/978-90-481-2354-4_4

Dieterich, S. E., Assel, M. A., et al. (2006). The impact of early maternal verbal scaffolding and child language abilities on later decoding and reading comprehension skills. *Journal of School Psychology, 43*(6), 481–494. doi:10.1016/j.jsp.2005.10.003

Dietrich, A., & Stoll, O. (2010). Effortless attention, hypofrontality, and perfectionism. In B. Bruya (Ed.), *Effortless attention: A new perspective in the cognitive science of attention and action* (pp. 159–178). Cambridge, MA: MIT Press.

Dietz, W. H. (2015). The response of the US Centers for Disease Control and Prevention to the obesity epidemic. *Annual Review of Public Health, 36,* 575–596. doi:10.1146/annurev-publhealth-031914-122415

Dik, B. J., Byrne, Z. S., & Steger, M. F. (2013). *Purpose and meaning in the workplace.* Washington, DC: American Psychological Association. doi:10.1037/14183-000

Dikotter, F., Laamann, L., & Xun, Z. (2008). *Narcotic culture: A history of drugs in China.* Chicago, IL: University of Chicago Press.

Dillard, A. J., Midboe, A. M., et al. (2009). The dark side of optimism: Unrealistic optimism about problems with alcohol predicts subsequent negative event experiences. *Personality & Social Psychology Bulletin, 35,* 1540–1550. doi:10.1177/0146167209343124

DiMatteo, M. R., Giordani, P. J., Lepper, H. S., & Croghan, T. W. (2002). Patient adherence and medical treatment outcomes: A meta-analysis. *Medical Care, 40,* 794–811. doi:10.1097/01.MLR.0000024612.61915.2D

DiMatteo, M. R., Lepper, H. S., & Croghan, T. W. (2000). Depression is a risk factor for noncompliance with medical treatment: Meta-analysis of the effects of anxiety and depression on patient adherence. *Archives of Internal Medicine, 160*(14), 2101–2107. doi:10.1001/archinte.160.14.2101

Dimberg, U., & Söderkvist, S. (2011). The voluntary facial action technique: A method to test the facial feedback hypothesis. *Journal of Nonverbal Behavior, 35*(1), 17–33. doi:10.1007/s10919-010-0098-6

Dimsdale, J. E. (2011). Medically unexplained symptoms: A treacherous foundation for somatoform disorders? *Psychiatric Clinics of North America, 34*(3), 511– 513. doi:10.1016/j.psc.2011.05.003

Dingus, T. A., Klauer, S. G., et al. (2006). The 100-car naturalistic driving study: Phase II. Results of the 100-car field experiment. *National Highway Traffic Safety Administration Report No. DOT HS 810 593.* Retrieved April 26, 2017, from ntl.bts.gov/lib/jpodocs/repts_te/14302.htm

Distin, K. (2006). *Gifted children: A guide for parents and professionals.* London: Jessica Kingsley Publishers.

Dixon, M. J., Smilek, D., & Merikle, P. M. (2004). Not all synaesthetes are created equal: Projector versus associator synaesthetes. *Cognitive, Affective, & Behavioral Neuroscience, 4*(3), 335–343. doi:10.3758/CABN.4.3.335

Dixon, R. W., Youssef, G. J., et al. (2016). The relationship between gambling attitudes, involvement, and problems in adolescence: Examining the moderating role of coping strategies and parenting styles. *Addictive Behaviors, 58,* 42–46. doi:10.1016/j.addbeh.2016.02.011

Dixon, S. V., Graber, J. A., & Brooks-Gunn, J. (2008). The roles of respect for parental authority and parenting practices in parent-child conflict among African American, Latino, and European American families. *Journal of Family Psychology, 22*(1), 1–10. doi:10.1037/0893-3200.22.1.1

Dobelle, W. H. (2000). Artificial vision for the blind by connecting a television camera to the visual cortex. *American Society of Artificial Internal Organs, 46,* 3–9.

Dobson, K. S., Backs-Dermott, G. J., & Dozois, D. J. A. (2000). Cognitive and cognitive-behavioral therapies. In C. R. Snyder & R. E. Ingram (Eds.), *Hand—book of psychological change: Psychotherapy processes and practices for the 21st century* (pp. 409–428). New York: Wiley.

Dobson, P. W., & Gerstner, E. (2010). For a few cents more: Why supersize unhealthy food?. *Marketing Science, 29*(4), 770–778. doi:10.1287/mksc.1100.0558

Dodge, K. A., Godwin, J., & Conduct Problems Prevention Research Group. (2013). Social-information-processing patterns mediate the impact of preventive intervention on adolescent antisocial behavior. *Psychological Science, 24*(4), 456–465. doi:10.1177/0956797612457394

Dodge, T., Williams, K. J., et al. (2012). Judging cheaters: Is substance misuse viewed similarly in the athletic and academic domains? *Psychology of Addictive Behaviors, 26*(3), 678–682. doi:10.1037/a0027872

Dodson, E. R., & Zee, P. C. (2010). Therapeutics for circadian rhythm sleep disorders. *Sleep Medicine Clinics, 5*(4), 701–715. doi:10.1016/j.jsmc.2010.08.001

Doebler, P., & Scheffler, B. (2016). The relationship of choice reaction time variability and intelligence: A meta-analysis. *Learning & Individual Differences, 52,* 157–166. doi:10.1016/j.lindif.2015.02.009

Doherty, M. J. (2009). *Theory of mind: How children understand others' thoughts and feelings.* New York: Psychology Press.

Dollard, J., & Miller, N. E. (1950). *Personality and psychotherapy: An analysis in terms of learning, thinking and culture.* New York: McGraw-Hill.

Domhoff, G. W. (2003). *The scientific study of dreams: Neural networks, cognitive development, and content analysis.* Washington, DC: American Psychological Association.

Domhoff, G. W. (2011). Dreams are embodied simulations that dramatize conceptions and concerns: The continuity hypothesis in empirical, theoretical, and historical context. *International Journal of Dream Research, 4*(2), 50–62.

Domhoff, G. W., & Schneider, A. (2008). Similarities and differences in dream content at the crosscultural, gender, and individual levels. *Consciousness & Cognition, 17*(4), 1257–1265. doi:10.1016/j.concog.2008.08.005

Domingo, R. A., & Goldstein-Alpern, N. (1999). "What dis?" and other toddler-initiated expressive language-learning strategies. *Infant-Toddler Intervention, 9*(1), 39–60.

Domingos, A. I., Vaynshteyn, J., et al. (2011). Leptin regulates the reward value of nutrient. *Nature Neuroscience, 14*(12), 1562–1568. doi:10.1038/nn.2977

Domjan, M. (2015). *The principles of learning and behavior* (7th ed.). Boston, MA: Cengage Learning.

Dömötör, Z., Ruíz-Barquín, R., & Szabo, A. (2016). Superstitious behavior in sport: A literature review. *Scandinavian Journal of Psychology, 57*(4), 368–382. doi:10.1111/sjop.12301

Donaldson, J. M., Vollmer, T. R., et al. (2013). Effects of a reduced time-out interval on compliance with the timeout instruction. *Journal of Applied Behavior Analysis, 46*(2), 369–378.

Donate-Bartfield, E., & Passman, R. H. (2004). Relations between children's attachments to their mothers and to security blankets. *Journal of Family Psychology, 18*(3), 453–458.

Dong, L., Lee, J. Y., & Harvey, A. G. (2017). Do improved patient recall and the provision of memory support enhance treatment adherence? *Journal of Behavior Therapy and Experimental Psychiatry, 54,* 219–228. doi:10.1016/j.jbtep.2016.08.017

Donnellan, M., Kenny, D. A., et al. (2012). Using trait-state models to evaluate the longitudinal

consistency of global self-esteem from adolescence to adulthood. *Journal of Research in Personality, 46*(6), 634–645. doi:10.1016/j.jrp.2012.07.005
Dooling, D. J., & Lachman, R. (1971). Effects of comprehension on retention of prose. *Journal of Experimental Psychology, 88,* 216–222. doi:10.1037/h0030904
Doom, J. R., Doyle, C. M., et al. (2017). Social stress buffering by friends in childhood and adolescence: Effects on HPA and oxytocin activity. *Social Neuroscience, 12*(1), 8–21. doi:10.1080/17470919.2016.1149095
Doran, S. M., Van Dongen, H. P., & Dinges, D. F. (2001). Sustained attention performance during sleep deprivation. *Archives of Italian Biology, 139,* 253–267.
Doty, R. L. (2012). Has human olfaction evolved primarily to provide flavor to foods? *Trends in Neurosciences, 35*(2), 79–80. doi:10.1016/j.tins.2011.10.001
Douglas, K. S., Guy, L. S., & Hart, S. D. (2009). Psychosis as a risk factor for violence to others: A meta-analysis. *Psychological Bulletin, 135*(5), 679–706. doi:10.1037/a0016311
Doumas, D. M., Miller, R., & Esp, S. (2017). Impulsive sensation seeking, binge drinking, and alcohol-related consequences: Do protective behavioral strategies help high risk adolescents? *Addictive Behaviors, 64,* 6–12. doi:10.1016/j.addbeh.2016.08.003
Dovidio, J. F., & Penner, L. A. (2001). Helping and altruism. In M. Hewstone & M. Brewer (Eds.), *Handbook of social psychology* (pp. 162–195). London: Blackwell.
Dovidio, J. F., Gaertner, S. L., et al. (2002). Why can't we just get along? *Cultural Diversity & Ethnic Minority Psychology, 8*(2), 88–102. doi:10.1037/1099-9809.8.2.88
Dovidio, J. F., Piliavin, J. A., et al. (2006). *The social psychology of prosocial behavior*. Mahwah, NJ: Erlbaum.
Dowling, K. W. (2005). The effect of lunar phases on domestic violence incident rates. *Forensic Examiner, 14*(4), 13–18.
Doyle, D. M., & Molix, L. (2016). Disparities in social health by sexual orientation and the etiologic role of self-reported discrimination. *Archives of Sexual Behavior, 45*(6), 1317–1327. doi:10.1007/s10508-015-0639-5
Drane, C. F., Modecki, K. L., & Barber, B. L. (2017). Disentangling development of sensation seeking, risky peer affiliation, and binge drinking in adolescent sport. *Addictive Behaviors, 66,* 60–65. doi:10.1016/j.addbeh.2016.11.001
Dresler, M., Wehrle, R., et al. (2012). Neural correlates of dream lucidity obtained from contrasting lucid versus non-lucid REM sleep: A combined EEG/fMRI case study. *Sleep, 35*(7), 1017–1020.
Drew, T., Võ, M. L.-H., & Wolfe, J. M. (2013). The invisible gorilla strikes again: Sustained inattentional blindness in expert observers. *Psychological Science, 24*(9), 1848–1853. doi:10.1177/0956797613479386
Drews, F. A., Yazdani, H., et al. (2009). Text messaging during simulated driving. *Human Factors, 51*(5), 762–770. doi:10.1177/0018720809353319
Drigotas, S. M. (2002). The Michelangelo phenomenon and personal well-being. *Journal of Personality, 70*(1), 59–77. doi:10.1111/1467-6494.00178
Driver, J. L., & Gottman, J. M. (2004). Daily marital interactions and positive affect during marital conflict among newlywed couples. *Family Process, 43*(3), 301–314.
Drummond, M., Douglas, J., & Olver, J. (2007). Anosmia after traumatic brain injury: A clinical update. *Brain Impairment, 8*(1), 31–40. doi:10.1375/brim.8.1.31
Drury, S., Hutchens, S. A., et al. (2012). Philip G. Zimbardo on his career and the Stanford Prison Experiment's 40th anniversary. *History of Psychology, 15*(2), 161–170. doi:10.1037/a0025884
Dryden, W. (2011). *Understanding psychological health: The REBT perspective.* New York: Routledge/Taylor & Francis.
Dryer, R., Tyson, G. A., & Kiernan, M. J. (2013). Bulimia nervosa: Professional and lay people's beliefs about the causes. *Australian Psychologist, 48*(5), 338–344.
Drymalski, W. M., & Washburn, J. J. (2011). Sudden gains in the treatment of depression in a partial hospitalization program. *Journal of Consulting & Clinical Psychology, 79*(3), 364–368. doi:10.1037/a0022973
D'Souza, J., & Gurin, M. (2016). The universal significance of Maslow's concept of self-actualization. *The Humanistic Psychologist, 44*(2), 210–214. doi:10.1037/hum0000027
Duckitt, J., & Sibley, C. G. (2010). Personality, ideology, prejudice, and politics: A dual-process motivational model. *Journal of Personality, 78*(6), 1861–1893. doi:10.1111/j.1467-6494.2010.00672.x
Duckworth, A. L., Gendler, T. S., et al. (2014). Self-control in school-age children. *Educational Psychologist, 49*(3), 199–217. doi:10.1080/00461520.2014.926225
Duckworth, A. L., Peterson, C., et al. (2007). Grit: Perseverance and passion for long-term goals. *Journal of Personality & Social Psychology, 92*(6), 1087–1101. doi:10.1037/0022-3514.92.6.1087
Duffy, S., & Verges, M. (2009). It matters a hole lot: Perceptual affordances of waste containers influence recycling compliance. *Environment & Behavior, 41*(5), 741–749.
Duggan, M. (2017, July 11). *Online harassment 2017.* Retrieved from http://www.pewinternet.org/2017/07/11/online-harassment-2017
Duncan, C. C. (2013). The Genain Quadruplets: A 55-year follow-up of two of four monozygous sisters with schizophrenia. *Schizophrenia Research, 48,* 186–187. doi:10.1016/j.schres.2013.06.011
Duncker, K. (1945). On problem solving. *Psychological Monographs, 58*(270).
Dunlop, S. M., & Romer, D. (2010). Adolescent and young adult crash risk: Sensation seeking, substance use propensity and substance use behaviors. *Journal of Adolescent Health, 46*(1), 90–92. doi:10.1016/j.jadohealth.2009.06.005
Dunlosky, J., & Rawson, K. A. (2015). Practice tests, spaced practice, and successive relearning: Tips for classroom use and for guiding students' learning. *Scholarship of Teaching & Learning in Psychology, 1*(1), 72–78. doi:10.1037/stl0000024
Dunlosky, J., Rawson, K. A., et al. (2013). Improving students' learning with effective learning techniques: Promising directions from cognitive and educational psychology. *Psychological Science in the Public Interest, 14,* 4–58. doi:10.1177/1529100612453266
Dunning, D., Heath, C., & Suls, J. M. (2004). Flawed self-assessment: Implications for health, education, and the workplace. *Psychological Science in the Public Interest, 5*(3), 69–106. doi:10.1111/j.1529-1006.2004.00018.x
Durán, L. K., Roseth, C. J., Hoffman, P. (2010). An experimental study comparing English-only and Transitional Bilingual Education on Spanish-speaking preschoolers' early literacy development. *Early Childhood Research Quarterly, 25*(2), 207–217. doi:10.1016/j.ecresq.2009.10.002
Durand, V. M., & Barlow, D. H. (2016). *Essentials of abnormal psychology* (7th ed.). Boston, MA: Cengage Learning.
Durham, M. G. (2009). *The Lolita effect.* New York: Overlook Press.
Dutton, D. G., & Aron, A. P. (1974). Some evidence for heightened sexual attraction under conditions of high anxiety. *Journal of Personality & Social Psychology, 30,* 510–517. doi:10.1037/h0037031
DuVernet, A. M., Dierdorff, E. C., et al. (2015). Exploring factors that influence work analysis data: A meta-analysis of design choices, purposes, and organizational context. *Journal of Applied Psychology, 100*(5), 1603–1631. doi:10.1037/a0039084
Dvash, J., Gilam, G., et al. (2010). The envious brain: The neural basis of social comparison. *Human Brain Mapping, 31*(11), 1741–1750. doi:10.1002/hbm.20972
Dweck, C. S. (2008). *Mindset: The new psychology of success.* New York: Random House.
Dweck, C. S. (2012). Mindsets and human nature: Promoting change in the Middle East, the schoolyard, the racial divide, and willpower. *American Psychologist, 67,* 614–622. doi:10.1037/a0029783
Dweck, C. (2016). What having a "growth mindset" actually means. *Harvard Business Review*, 13–16.
Dweck, C. S. (2017). The journey to children's mindsets—and beyond. *Child Development Perspectives, 11,* 139–144. doi:10.1111/cdep.12225
Dyer, J., Gregersen, H., et al. (2013). *The innovator's DNA: Mastering the five skills of disruptive innovators*. Boston, MA: Harvard Business Press.
Dyer, K. A. (2001). *Dealing with death and dying in medical education and practice.* Retrieved May 1, 2017, from www.journeyofhearts.org/kirstimd/AMSA/outline.htm
Dyukova, G. M., Glozman, Z. M., et al. (2010). Speech disorders in right-hemisphere stroke. *Neuroscience & Behavioral Physiology, 40*(6), 593–602. doi:10.1007/s11055-010-9301-9
Dywan, J., & Bowers, K. S. (1983). The use of hypnosis to enhance recall. *Science, 222,* 184–185. doi:10.1126/science.6623071
Eagly, A. H. (2009). The his and hers of prosocial behavior: An examination of the social psychology of gender. *American Psychologist, 64*(8), 644–658. doi:10.1037/0003-066X.64.8.644
Eagly, A. H. (2013). Women as leaders: Paths through the labyrinth. In M. C. Bligh & R. E. Riggio (Eds.), *Exploring distance in leader-follower relationships: When near is far and far is near* (pp. 191–214). New York: Routledge/Taylor & Francis.
Eagly, A. H., & Carli, L. L. (2007). *Through the labyrinth: The truth about how women become leaders.* Watertown, MA: HBS Press Book.
Eagly, A. H., Eaton, A., et al. (2012). Feminism and psychology: Analysis of a half-century of research on women and gender. *American Psychologist, 67*(3), 211–230. doi:10.1037/a0027260

Eardley, A. F., & Pring, L. (2007). Spatial processing, mental imagery, and creativity in individuals with and without sight. *European Journal of Cognitive Psychology, 19*(1), 37–58. doi:10.1080/09541440600591965

Earleywine, M. (2011). *Humor 101*. New York: Springer.

Easterbrooks, M., Bartlett, J., et al. (2013). Social and emotional development in infancy. In R. M. Lerner, M. Easterbrooks, et al. (Eds.), *Handbook of psychology* (Vol. 6): *Developmental psychology* (2nd ed., pp. 91–120). New York: Wiley.

Eastman, C. I., Molina, T. A., et al. (2012). Blacks (African Americans) have shorter free-running circadian periods than Whites (Caucasian Americans). *Chronobiology International, 29*(8), 1072–1077. doi:10.3109/07420528.2012.700670

Ebben, M. R., & Spielman, A. J. (2009). Non-pharmacological treatments for insomnia. *Journal of Behavioral Medicine, 32*(3), 244–254. doi:10.1007/s10865-008-9198-8

Ebbinghaus, H. (1885). *Memory: A contribution to experimental psychology* (H. A. Ruger, & C. E. Bussenius, Trans.). New York: New York Teacher's College, Columbia University.

Eckardt, M. H. (2005). Karen Horney: A portrait: The 120th anniversary, Karen Horney, September 16, 1885. *American Journal of Psychoanalysis, 65*(2), 95–101.

Eckert, M. J., & Racine, R. J. (2006). Long-term depression and associativity in rat primary motor cortex following thalamic stimulation. *European Journal of Neuroscience, 24*(12), 3553–3560. doi:10.1111/j.1460-9568.2006.05220.x

Edenfield, T. M., & Blumenthal, J. A. (2011). Exercise and stress reduction. In R. J. Contrada & A. Baum (Eds.), *The handbook of stress science: Biology, psychology, and health* (pp. 301–319). New York: Springer.

Edgerly, S. (2015). Red media, blue media, and purple media: News repertoires in the colorful media landscape. *Journal of Broadcasting & Electronic Media, 59*(1), 1–21. doi:10.1080/08838151.2014.998220

Edmondson, A. (2012). *Teaming: How organizations learn, innovate, and compete in the knowledge economy.* New York: Wiley.

Education Endowment Fund. (2019, July). *Changing mindsets*. Retrieved July 21, 2019, from https://educationendowmentfoundation.org.uk/

Edwards, A., & Polman, R. (2012). *Pacing in sport and exercise: A psychophysiological perspective.* Hauppauge, NY: Nova Science Publishers.

Ehret, A. M., Joormann, J., & Berking, M. (2015). Examining risk and resilience factors for depression: The role of self-criticism and self-compassion. *Cognition & Emotion, 29*(8), 1496–1504. doi:10.1080/02699931.2014.992394

Eidelson, R. J., & Eidelson, J. I. (2003). Dangerous ideas. *American Psychologist, 58*(3), 182–192. doi:10.1037/0003-066X.58.3.182

Eifert, G. H., Hodson, S. E., Tracey, D. R., Seville, L., & Gunawardane, K. (1996). Heart-focused anxiety, illness beliefs, and behavioral impairment: Comparing healthy heart-anxious patients with cardiac and surgical inpatients. *Journal of Behavioral Medicine, 19*(4), 385–399. doi:10.1007/BF01904764

Eifert, G. H., & Lejuez, C. W. (2000). Aversion therapy. In A. E. Kazdin (Ed.), *Encyclopedia of psychology* (Vol. 1, pp. 348–350). Washington, DC: American Psychological Association.

Eigenberg, H., McGuffee, K., et al. (2012). Doing justice: Perceptions of gender neutrality in the jury selection process. *American Journal of Criminal Justice, 37*(2), 258–275. doi:10.1007/s12103-011-9139-x

Einarsen, S., & Hoel, H. (2008). Bullying and mistreatment at work: How managers may prevent and manage such problems. In A. Kinder, R. Hughes, & C. L. Cooper (Eds.), *Employee well-being support: A workplace resource* (pp. 161–173). New York: Wiley.

Eisenberg, N., Eggum, N. D., & Di Giunta, L. (2010). Empathy-related responding: Associations with prosocial behavior, aggression, and intergroup relations. *Social Issues and Policy Review, 4*(1), 143–180. doi:10.1111/j.1751-2409.2010.01020.x

Eisendrath, S. J., Chartier, M., et al. (2011). Adapting mindfulness-based cognitive therapy for treatment-resistant depression. *Cognitive & Behavioral Practice, 18*(3), 362–370. doi:10.1016/j.cbpra.2010.05.004

Eisendrath, S. J., Gillung, E., et al. (2014, January 28). A preliminary study: Efficacy of mindfulness-based cognitive therapy versus sertraline as first-line treatments for major depressive disorder. *Mindfulness*, n.p. doi:10.1007/s12671-014-0280-8

Eisler, I., Simic, M., et al. (2007). A randomized controlled treatment trial of two forms of family therapy in adolescent anorexia nervosa: A five-year follow-up. *Journal of Child Psychology & Psychiatry, 48*(6), 552–560. doi:10.1111/j.1469-7610.2007.01726.x

Ekman, P. (1993). Facial expression and emotion. *American Psychologist, 48*(4), 384–392. doi:10.1037/0003-066X.48.4.384

Ekman, P., & Cordaro, D. (2011). What is meant by calling emotions basic. *Emotion Review, 3*(4), 364–370. doi:10.1177/1754073911410740

Ekman, P., Levenson, R. W., & Friesen, W. V. (1983). Autonomic nervous system activity distinguishes among emotions. *Science, 221,* 1208–1210. doi:10.1126/science.6612338

Eldridge, M., Saltzman, E., & Lahav, A. (2010). Seeing what you hear: Visual feedback improves pitch recognition. *European Journal of Cognitive Psychology, 22*(7), 1078–1091. doi:10.1080/09541440903316136

Elfenbein, H. A. (2013). Nonverbal dialects and accents in facial expressions of emotion. *Emotion Review, 5,* 90–96. doi:10.1177/1754073912451332

Eliot, L. (2009). *Pink brain, blue brain.* New York: Houghton Mifflin Harcourt.

Elkington, K. S., Hackler, D., et al. (2012). Perceived mental illness stigma among youth in psychiatric outpatient treatment. *Journal of Adolescent Research, 27*(2), 290–317. doi:10.1177/0743558411409931

Elkins, G. R., Barabasz, A. F., et al. (2015). Advancing research and practice: The revised APA Division 30 definition of hypnosis. *American Journal of Clinical Hypnosis, 57*(4), 378–385. doi:10.1080/00029157.2015.1011465

Elli, K. A., & Nathan, P. J. (2001). The pharmacology of human working memory. *International Journal of Neuropsychopharmacology, 4*(3), 299–313. doi:10.1017/S1461145701002541

Ellickson, P. L., Martino, S. C., & Collins, R. L. (2004). Marijuana use from adolescence to young adulthood. *Health Psychology, 23*(3), 299–307. doi:10.1037/0278-6133.23.3.299

Elliott, M., & Williams, D. (2003). The client experience of counselling and psychotherapy. *Counselling Psychology Review, 18*(1), 34–38.

Elliott, M., Browne, K., & Kilcoyne, J. (1995). Child sexual abuse prevention: What offenders tell us. *Child Abuse & Neglect, 19*(5), 579–594.

Elliott, R., & Farber, B. A. (2010). Carl Rogers: Idealistic pragmatist and psychotherapy research pioneer. In L. G. Castonguay, J. C. Muran, et al. (Eds.), *Bringing psychotherapy research to life: Understanding change through the work of leading clinical researchers* (pp. 17–27). Washington, DC: American Psychological Association.

Ellis, A. (1979). The practice of rational-emotive therapy. In A. Ellis & J. Whiteley (Eds.), *Theoretical and empirical foundations of rational-emotive therapy* (pp. 1–6). Monterey, CA: Brooks/Cole.

Ellis, A. (1995). Changing rational-emotive therapy (RET) to rational emotive behavior therapy (REBT). *Journal of Rational-Emotive & Cognitive Behavior Therapy, 13*(2), 85–89. doi:10.1007/BF02354453

Ellis, A., & Ellis, D. J. (2011). *Rational emotive behavior therapy*. Washington, DC: American Psychological Association.

Ellis, D. (2016). *The essential guide to becoming a master student* (4th ed.). Boston, MA: Cengage Learning.

Ellison-Wright, I., & Bullmore, E. (2010). Anatomy of bipolar disorder and schizophrenia: A meta-analysis. *Schizophrenia Research, 117*(1), 1–12. doi:10.1016/j.schres.2009.12.022

Emerson, E. (2009). Relative child poverty, income inequality, wealth, and health. *Journal of the American Medical Association, 301*(4), 425–426. doi:10.1001/jama.2009.8

Engel, G. L. (2012). The need for a new medical model: A challenge for biomedicine. *Psychodynamic Psychiatry, 40*(3), 377–396. doi:10.1521/pdps.2012.40.3.377

Engelen, E., & Röttger-Rössler, B. (2012). Current disciplinary and interdisciplinary debates on empathy. *Emotion Review, 4*(1), 3–8. doi:10.1177/1754073911422287

Engelhard, I. M., van Uijen, S. L., et al. (2015). The effects of safety behavior directed towards a safety cue on perceptions of threat. *Behavior Therapy, 46*(5), 604–610. doi:10.1016/j.beth.2014.12.006

Engler, B. (2014). *Personality theories* (9th ed.). Boston, MA: Cengage Learning.

English, T., John, O. P., et al. (2012). Emotion regulation and peer-rated social functioning: A 4-year longitudinal study. *Journal of Research in Personality, 46*(6), 780–784. doi:10.1016/j.jrp.2012.09.006

Enns, M. W., Cox, B. J., & Clara, I. P. (2005). Perfectionism and neuroticism: A longitudinal study of specific vulnerability and diathesis-stress models. *Cognitive Therapy & Research, 29*(4), 463–478. doi:10.1007/s10608-005-2843-04

Enrici, I., Adenzato, M., et al. (2011). Intention processing in communication: A common brain network for language and gestures. *Journal of Cognitive Neuroscience, 23*(9), 2415–2431. doi:10.1162/jocn.2010.21594

Epstein, S. (2003). Cognitive-experiential self-theory of personality. In T. Millon & M. J. Lerner (Eds.), *Comprehensive handbook of*

psychology: Personality and social psychology (Vol. 5, pp. 159–184). New York: Wiley.

Erez, D. L., Levy, J., et al. (2010). Assessment of cognitive and adaptive behaviour among individuals with congenital insensitivity to pain and anhidrosis. *Developmental Medicine & Child Neurology, 52*(6), 559–562. doi:10.1111/j.1469-8749.2009.03567.x

Erickson, C. D., & Al-Timimi, N. R. (2001). Providing mental health services to Arab Americans. *Cultural Diversity & Ethnic Minority Psychology, 7*(4), 308–327. doi:10.1037/1099-9809.7.4.308

Erikson, E. H. (1963). *Childhood and society*. New York: Norton.

Ericsson, K. A., & Charness, N. (1994). Expert performance. *American Psychologist, 49*(8), 725–747. doi:10.1037/0003-066X.49.8.725

Ericsson, K. A., & Chase, W. G. (1982). Exceptional memory. *American Scientist, 70,* 607–615.

Ericsson, K. A., & Pool, R. (2016). *Peak: Secrets from the new science of expertise*. New York: Houghton Mifflin Harcourt.

Erikson, E. H. (1963). *Childhood and society*. New York: Norton.

Erlacher, D., & Schredl, M. (2004). Dreams reflecting waking sport activities: A comparison of sport and psychology students. *International Journal of Sport Psychology, 35*(4), 301–308.

Ertmer, D. J., & Jung, J. (2012). Prelinguistic vocal development in young cochlear implant recipients and typically developing infants: Year 1 of robust hearing experience. *Journal of Deaf Studies & Deaf Education, 17*(1), 116–132. doi:10.1093/deafed/enr021

España, R. A., Oleson, E. B., et al. (2010). The hypocretin orexin system regulates cocaine self-administration via actions on the mesolimbic dopamine system. *European Journal of Neuroscience, 31*(2), 336–348. doi:10.1111/j.1460-9568.2009.07065.x

Essien, E. J., Monjok, E., et al. (2010). Correlates of HIV knowledge and sexual risk behaviors among female military personnel. *AIDS & Behavior, 14*(6), 1401–1414.

Estefan, L. F., Coulter, M. L., & VandeWeerd, C. (2016). Depression in women who have left violent relationships: The unique impact of frequent emotional abuse. *Violence Against Women, 22*(11), 1397–1413. doi:10.1177/1077801215624792

Ethier, K. A., Kershaw, T., et al. (2003). Adolescent women underestimate their susceptibility to sexually transmitted infections. *Sexually Transmitted Infections, 79,* 408–411.

Evans, A. D., O'Connor, A. M., Bruer, K. C., & Price, H. L. (2019). Children who disclose a minor transgression often neglect disclosing secrecy and coaching. *Journal of Applied Developmental Psychology, 62,* 199–204. doi:10.1016/j.appdev.2019.03.002

Evans, G. W. (2006). Child development and the physical environment. *Annual Review of Psychology, 57,* 423–451.

Evans, G. W., & Fuller-Rowell, T. E. (2013). Childhood poverty, chronic stress, and young adult working memory: The protective role of self-regulatory capacity. *Developmental Science, 16*(5), 688–696. doi:10.1111/desc.12082

Evans, G. W., Lepore, S. J., & Schroeder, A. (1996). The role of interior design elements in human responses to crowding. *Journal of Personality & Social Psychology, 70*(1), 41–46.

Evans, G. W., Lercher, P., & Kofler, W. W. (2002). Crowding and children's mental health: The role of house type. *Journal of Environmental Psychology, 22,* 221–231.

Evans, G. W., Ricciuti, H. N., et al. (2010). Crowding and cognitive development: The mediating role of maternal responsiveness among 36-month-old children. *Environment & Behavior, 42*(1), 135–148.

Evans, G. W., Lepore, S. J., & Schroeder, A. (1996). The role of interior design elements in human responses to crowding. *Journal of Personality & Social Psychology, 70*(1), 41–46.

Evardone, M., Alexander, G. M., & Morey, L. C. (2007). Hormones and borderline personality features. *Personality & Individual Differences, 44*(1), 278–287. doi:10.1016/j.paid.2007.08.007

Everitt, B. J., & Robbins, T. W. (2016). Drug addiction: Updating actions to habits to compulsions ten years on. *Annual Review of Psychology, 67,* 23–50. doi:10.1146/annurev-psych-122414-033457

Ewart, C. K., Elder, G. J., Laird, K. T., Shelby, G. D., & Walker, L. S. (2014). Can agonistic striving lead to unexplained illness? Implicit goals, pain tolerance, and somatic symptoms in adolescents and adults. *Health Psychology, 33*(9), 977–985. doi:10.1037/a0033496

Eysenck, H. J. (1952). The effects of psychotherapy: An evaluation. *Journal of Consulting Psychology, 16,* 319–324.

Eysenck, H. J. (1994). The outcome problem in psychotherapy: What have we learned? *Behaviour Research & Therapy, 32*(5), 477–495. doi:10.1016/0005-7967(94)90135-X

Eysenck, H. J. (Ed.). (1981). *A model for personality*. New York: Springer-Verlag.

Fabian, J. (2011). Neuropsychology, neuroscience, volitional impairment and sexually violent predators: A review of the literature and the law and their application to civil commitment proceedings. *Aggression & Violent Behavior,* doi:10.1016/j.avb.2011.07.002

Fain, G. L. (2003). *Sensory transduction*. Sunderland, MA: Sinauer.

Fandakova, Y., Shing, Y., & Lindenberger, U. (2012). Differences in binding and monitoring mechanisms contribute to lifespan age differences in false memory. *Developmental Psychology,* doi:10.1037/a0031361

Fang, A., & Wilhelm, S. (2015). Clinical features, cognitive biases, and treatment of body dysmorphic disorder. *Annual Review of Clinical Psychology, 11,* 187–212. doi:10.1146/annurev-clinpsy-032814-112849

Farah, M. J. (2004). *Visual agnosia* (2nd ed.). Cambridge, MA: MIT Press.

Farah, M. J., Haimm, C., et al. (2009). When we enhance cognition with Adderall, do we sacrifice creativity? A preliminary study. *Psychopharmacology, 202*(1–3), 541–547. doi:10.1007/s00213-008-1369-3

Farah, M. J., Illes, J., et al. (2004). Neurocognitive enhancement: What can we do and what should we do? *Nature Reviews Neuroscience, 5,* 421–425. doi:10.1038/nrn1390

Faraut, B., Boudjeltia, K. Z., et al. (2011). Benefits of napping and an extended duration of recovery sleep on alertness and immune cells after acute sleep restriction. *Brain, Behavior, & Immunity, 25*(1), 16–24. doi:10.1016/j.bbi.2010.08.001

Farmer, R. F., & Chapman, A. L. (2016). *Behavioral interventions in cognitive behavior therapy: Practical guidance for putting theory into action* (2nd ed.). Washington, DC: American Psychological Association. doi:10.1037/14691-000

Farr, R. H. (2017). Does parental sexual orientation matter? A longitudinal follow-up of adoptive families with school-age children. *Developmental Psychology, 53*(2), 252–264. doi:10.1037/dev0000228

Farrand, P., Confue, P., et al. (2009). Guided self-help supported by paraprofessional mental health workers: An uncontrolled before-after cohort study. *Health & Social Care in the Community, 17*(1), 9–17. doi:10.1111/j.1365-2524.2008.00792.x

Farroni, T., Massaccesi, S., et al. (2004). Gaze following in newborns. *Infancy, 5*(1), 39–60. doi:10.1207/s15327078in0501_2

Fava, G. A. (2016). Psychosomatic medicine. In G. Fink (Ed.). (2016). *Stress: Concepts, cognition, emotion, and behavior* (pp. 457–463). San Diego, CA: Elsevier.

Fawcett, J. M., Russell, E. J., et al. (2013). Of guns and geese: A meta-analytic review of the 'weapon focus' literature. *Psychology, Crime, & Law, 19*(1), 35–66. doi:10.1080/1068316X.2011.599325

Federal Bureau of Investigation. (2016). *FBI Releases 2015 Crime Statistics*. Retrieved June 26, 2017, from www.fbi.gov/news/pressrel/press-releases/fbi-releases-2015-crime-statistics

Feinberg, T. E., & Mallatt, J. (2016). The nature of primary consciousness. A new synthesis. *Consciousness & Cognition, 43,* 113–127. doi:10.1016/j.concog.2016.05.009

Feldman, R., Gordon, I., et al. (2013). Parental oxytocin and early caregiving jointly shape children's oxytocin response and social reciprocity. *Neuropsychopharmacology, 38*(7), 1154–1162. doi:10.1038/npp.2013.22

Fenesi, B., Heisz, J. J., et al. (2014). Combining best-practice and experimental approaches: Redundancy, images, and misperceptions in multimedia learning. *Journal of Experimental Education, 82*(2), 253–263. doi:10.1080/00220973.2012.745472

Fenton, M. C., Keyes, K., et al. (2012). Psychiatric comorbidity and the persistence of drug use disorders in the United States. *Addiction, 107*(3), 599–609. doi:10.1111/j.1360-0443.2011.03638.x

Ferguson, C. J. (2015). Does media violence predict societal violence? It depends on what you look at and when. *Journal of Communication, 65,* E1–E22. doi:10.1111/jcom.12129

Ferguson, C. J., & Dyck, D. (2012). Paradigm change in aggression research: The time has come to retire the General Aggression Model. *Aggression & Violent Behavior, 17*(3), 220–228. doi:10.1016/j.avb.2012.02.007

Ferguson, C. J., Miguel, C. N., & Hartley, R. D. (2009). A multivariate analysis of youth violence and aggression: The influence of family, peers, depression, and media violence. *Journal of Pediatrics, 155*(6), 904–908. doi:10.1016/j.jpeds.2009.06.021

Ferini-Strambi, L. L., Marelli, S. S., et al. (2013). Effects of continuous positive airway pressure on cognition and neuroimaging data in sleep apnea. *International Journal of Psychophysiology, 89*(2), 203–212. doi:10.1016/j.ijpsycho.2013.03.022

Fernald, A. (1989). Intonation and communicative intent in mothers' speech to infants: Is the melody the message? *Child Development, 60*(6), 1497–1510. doi:10.2307/1130938

Fernald, A., Perfors, A., & Marchman, V. A. (2006). Picking up speed in understanding: Speech processing efficiency and vocabulary growth across the 2nd year. *Developmental Psychology, 42*(1), 98–116. doi:10.1037/0012-1649.42.1.98

Fernandez, J., Grizzell, J., & Wecker, L. (2013). The role of estrogen receptor β and nicotinic cholinergic receptors in postpartum depression. *Progress in Neuro-Psychopharmacology & Biological Psychiatry, 40,* 199–206. doi:10.1016/j.pnpbp.2012.10.002

Ferradás, M., Freire, C., et al. (2016, November 10). Motivational profiles in university students. Its relationship with self-handicapping and defensive pessimism strategies. *Learning & Individual Differences,* n.p. doi:10.1016/j.lindif.2016.10.018

Ferrara, P., Vitelli, O., et al. (2013). Factitious disorders and Münchausen syndrome: The tip of the iceberg. *Journal of Child Health Care, 17*(4), 366–374. doi:10.1177/1367493512 462262

Ferrari, J. R., & Pychyl, T. A. (2012). "If I wait, my partner will do it": The role of conscientiousness as a mediator in the relation of academic procrastination and perceived social loafing. *North American Journal of Psychology, 14*(1), 13–24.

Ferraro, P. J., & Price, M. K. (2013). Using non-pecuniary strategies to influence behavior: Evidence from a large-scale field experiment. *Review of Economics & Statistics, 95*(1), 64–73. doi:10.3386/w17189

Ferraro, P. J., Miranda, J. J., et al. (2011). Persistence of treatment effects with norm-based policy instruments: Evidence from a randomized environmental policy experiment. *American Economic Review, 101*(3), 318–322. doi:10.1257/aer.101.3.318

Festinger, L. (1957). *A theory of cognitive dissonance.* Stanford, CA: Stanford University Press.

Festinger, L., & Carlsmith, J. M. (1959). Cognitive consequences of forced compliance. *Journal of Abnormal & Social Psychology, 58,* 203–210. doi:10.1037/h0041593

Ficca, G., Axelsson, J., et al. (2010). Naps, cognition and performance. *Sleep Medicine Reviews, 14*(4), 249–258. doi:10.1016/j.smrv.2009.09.005

Field, J. E., Kolbert, J. B., et al. (2009). *Understanding girl bullying and what to do about it: Strategies to help heal the divide.* Thousand Oaks, CA: Corwin Press.

Fields, R. D. (2013). Neuroscience: Map the other brain. *Nature, 501*(7465), 25–27.

Fields, R. M., & Margolin, J. (2001). *Coping with trauma.* Washington, DC: American Psychological Association.

Filbey, F. M., Schacht, J. P., et al. (2009). Marijuana craving in the brain. *Proceedings of the National Academy of Sciences, 106*(31), 13016–13021. doi:10.1073/pnas.0903863106

Fine, C. (2010). *Delusions of gender.* New York: Norton.

Fine, L. E. (2011). Minimizing heterosexism and homophobia: Constructing meaning of out campus LGB life. *Journal of Homosexuality, 58*(4), 521–546. doi:10.1080/00918369 .2011.555673

Fink, M. (2013). Rediscovering catatonia: The biography of a treatable syndrome. *Acta Psychiatrica Scandinavica, 127*(Suppl. 441), 1–47. doi:10.1111/acps.12038

Finkel, E. J., & Eastwick, P. W. (2015). Interpersonal attraction: In search of a theoretical Rosetta Stone. In M. Mikulincer, P. R. Shaver, et al. (Eds.). *In APA handbook of personality and social psychology, Volume 3: Interpersonal relations* (pp. 179–210). Washington, DC: American Psychological Association. doi:10.1037/14344-007

Fiore, D., Dimaggio, G., et al. (2008). Metacognitive interpersonal therapy in a case of obsessive-compulsive and avoidant personality disorders. *Journal of Clinical Psychology, 64*(2), 168–180. doi:10.1002/jclp.20450

Fiorina, C. (2006). *Tough choices: A memoir.* New York: Penguin.

Fireman, G., Kose, G., & Solomon, M. J. (2003). Self-observation and learning: The effect of watching oneself on problem solving performance. *Cognitive Development, 18*(3), 339–354. doi:10.1016/S0885-2014(03)00038-8

Firestone, P., Kingston, D. A., et al. (2006). Long-term follow-up of exhibitionists: Psychological, phallometric, and offense characteristics. *Journal of the American Academy of Psychiatry & the Law, 34*(3), 349–359.

Fischbach, A., Baudson, T. G., et al. (2013). Do teacher judgments of student intelligence predict life outcomes? *Learning & Individual Differences, 27,* 109–119. doi:10.1016/j.lindif.2013.07.004

Fischer, A. H., Manstead, A. S. R., et al. (2004). Gender and culture differences in emotion. *Emotion, 4*(1), 87–94. doi:10.1037/1528-3542.4.1.87

Fischer, C., & Kächele, H. (2009). Comparative analysis of patients' dreams in Freudian and Jungian treatment. *International Journal of Psychotherapy, 13*(3), 34–40.

Fischer, P., & Greitemeyer, T. (2013). The positive bystander effect: Passive bystanders increase helping in situations with high expected negative consequences for the helper. *Journal of Social Psychology, 153*(1), 1–5. doi:1 0.1080/00224545.2012.697931

Fischer, P., Kastenmüller, A., & Greitemeyer, T. (2010). Media violence and the self: The impact of personalized gaming characters in aggressive video games on aggressive behavior. *Journal of Experimental Social Psychology, 46*(1), 192–195. doi:10.1016/j.jesp.2009.06.010

Fischer, P., Krueger, J. I., et al. (2011). The bystander-effect: A meta-analytic review on bystander intervention in dangerous and non-dangerous emergencies. *Psychological Bulletin, 137*(4), 517–537. doi:10.1037/a0023304

Fisher, B. S., Cullen, F. T., & Daigle, L. E. (2005). The discovery of acquaintance rape: The salience of methodological innovation and rigor. *Journal of Interpersonal Violence, 20*(4), 493–500.

Fisher, R. P., & Geiselman, R. E. (1987). Enhancing eyewitness memory with the cognitive interview. In M. M. Gruneberg, P. E. Morris, et al. (Eds.), *Practical aspects of memory: Current research and issues* (pp. 34–39). New York: Wiley.

Fiske, P. (2015). Know your network. *Nature, 524*(7566), 507–508. doi:10.1038/nj7566-507a

Fiske, S. T., Cuddy, A. J., et al. (2002). A model of (often mixed) stereotype content: Competence and warmth respectively follow from perceived status and competition. *Journal of Personality & Social Psychology, 82*(6), 878–902. doi:10.1037/0022 -3514.82.6.878

Fite, R. E., Lindeman, M. I. H., et al. (2017). Knowing oneself and long-term goal pursuit: Relations among self-concept clarity, conscientiousness, and grit. *Personality & Individual Differences, 108,* 191–194. doi:10.1016/j.paid.2016.12.008

Fitzgerald, L. F., Swan, S., & Magley, V. J. (1997). But was it really sexual harassment? Legal, behavioral, and psychological definitions of the workplace victimization of women. In W. O'Donohue (Ed.), *Sexual harassment: Theory, research, and treatment* (pp. 5–28). Needham Heights, MA: Allyn & Bacon.

Flaskerud, J. H. (2009). What do we need to know about the culture-bound syndromes? *Issues in Mental Health Nursing, 30*(6), 406–407. doi:10.1080/01612840902812947

Flegal, K. M., Carroll, M. D., et al. (2010). Prevalence and trends in obesity among U.S. adults, 1999–2008. *Journal of the American Medical Association, 303*(3), 235–241. doi:10.1001/jama.2009.2014

Fleming, J. (2012). The effectiveness of eye movement desensitization and reprocessing in the treatment of traumatized children and youth. *Journal of EMDR Practice and Research, 6*(1), 16–26. doi:10.1891/1933-3196.6.1.16

Fletcher, R., St. George, J., & Freeman, E. (2013). Rough and tumble play quality: Theoretical foundations for a new measure of father–child interaction. *Early Child Development & Care, 183*(6), 746–759. doi:10.1080/ 03004430.2012.723439

Flinker, A., Korzeniewska, A., et al. (2015). Redefining the role of Broca's area in speech. *Proceedings of the National Academy of Sciences, 112*(9), 2871–2875. doi:10.1073/ pnas.1414491112

Flora, J., & Segrin, C. (2015). Family conflict and communication. In L. H. Turner & R. West (Eds.), *The SAGE handbook of family communication* (pp. 91–106). Thousand Oaks, CA: Sage.

Flore, P. C., Mulder, J., & Wicherts, J. M. (2019). The influence of gender stereotype threat on mathematics test scores of Dutch high school students: A registered report. *Comprehensive Results in Social Psychology,* 1–35. doi:10.1080/23743603.2018.1559647

Floresco, S. B. (2015). Noradrenaline and dopamine: Sharing the workload. *Trends in Neurosciences, 38*(8), 465–467. doi:10.1016/j.tins.2015.07.001

Florida Medical Examiners Commission. (2016). *Drugs identified in deceased persons by Florida Medical Examiners: 2015 annual report.* Retrieved January 2, 2017, from www.fdle.state.fl.us/cms /MEC/Publications-and-Forms /Documents/Drugs-in-Deceased -Persons/2015-Annual-Drug-Report.aspx

Flowe, H. D., & Ebbese, E. B. (2007). The effect of lineup member similarity on recognition accuracy in simultaneous and sequential lineups. *Law & Human Behavior, 31*(1), 33–52. doi:10.1007/s10979-006-9045-9

Flowers, S. (2011). Mindfully shy. In B. Boyce (Ed.), *The mindfulness revolution: Leading psychologists, scientists, artists, and meditation teachers on the power of mindfulness in daily life* (pp. 166–176). Boston, MA: Shambhala Publications.

Flynn, B. S., Worden, J. K., et al. (2011). Evaluation of smoking prevention television messages based on the elaboration likelihood model. *Health Education Research, 26*(6), 976–987. doi:10.1093/her/cyr082

Flynn, J. R. (2012). *Are we getting smarter? Rising IQ in the twenty-first century.* New York: Cambridge University Press. doi:10.1017/CBO 9781139235679

Flynn, K. J., & Fitzgibbon, M. (1998). Body images and obesity risk among Black females: A review of the literature. *Annals of Behavioral Medicine, 20*(1), 13–24.

Fochtmann, L. J. (2016). Evidence for the continuing benefits of electroconvulsive therapy. *American Journal of Psychiatry, 173*(11), 1071–1072. doi:10.1176/appi.ajp.2016.16080880

Foley, S., & Gambescia, N. (2015). The complex etiology of delayed ejaculation: Assessment and treatment implications. In K. M. Hertlein, G. R. Weeks, et al. (Eds.). *Systemic sex therapy* (2nd ed., pp. 107–124). New York: Routledge/Taylor & Francis.

Folkman, S., & Moskowitz, J. T. (2004). Coping: Pitfalls and promise. *Annual Review of Psychology, 55,* 745–774. doi:10.1146/annurev.psych.55.090902.141456

Fonken, L. K., Aubrecht, T. G., et al. (2013). Dim light at night disrupts molecular circadian rhythms and increases body weight. *Journal of Biological Rhythms, 28*(4), 262–271. doi:10.1177/0748730413493862

Fontaine, K. R., Redden, D. T., et al. (2003). Years of life lost due to obesity. *Journal of the American Medical Association, 289,* 187–193. doi:10.1001/jama.289.2.187

Forbes, G. B., Adams-Curtis, L. E., & White, K. B. (2004). First- and second-generation measures of sexism, rape myths and related beliefs, and hostility toward women: Their interrelationships and association with college students' experiences with dating aggression and sexual coercion. *Violence Against Women, 10*(3), 236–261.

Ford, D., Easton, D. F., Bishop, D. T., Narod, S. A., & Goldgar, D. E. (1994). Risks of cancer in BRCA1-mutation carriers. *The Lancet, 343*(8899), 692–695. doi:10.1016/S0140-6736(94)91578-4

Ford, G. G., Gallagher, S. H., et al. (1999). Repositioning the home plate umpire to provide enhanced perceptual cues and more accurate ball-strike judgments. *Journal of Sport Behavior, 22*(1), 28–44.

Ford, J. D. (2012). Ethnoracial and educational differences in victimization history, trauma-related symptoms, and coping style. *Psychological Trauma: Theory, Research, Practice, & Policy, 4*(2), 177–185. doi:10.1037/a0023670

Forgeard, M. J. C., & Seligman, M. E. P. (2012). Seeing the glass half full: A review of the causes and consequences of optimism. *Pratiques Psychologiques, 18*(2), 107–120. doi:10.1016/j.prps.2012.02.002

Forgas, J. P. (2011). She just doesn't look like a philosopher…? Affective influences on the halo effect in impression formation. *European Journal of Social Psychology, 41*(7), 812–817. doi:10.1002/ejsp.842

Forgas, J. P., Cooper, J., & Crano, W. D. (Eds.) (2010). *The psychology of attitudes and attitude change.* New York: Psychology Press.

Forney, W. S., Forney, J. C., & Crutsinger, C. (2005). Developmental stages of age and moral reasoning as predictors of juvenile delinquents' behavioral intention to steal clothing. *Family & Consumer Sciences Research Journal, 34*(2), 110–126. doi:10.1177/1077727X05280666

Forsyth, D. R. (2014). *Group dynamics* (6th ed.). Boston, MA: Cengage Learning.

Fortunato, L., Young, A. M., et al. (2010). Hook-up sexual experiences and problem behaviors among adolescents. *Journal of Child & Adolescent Substance Abuse, 19*(3), 261–278.

Foster, C. A., Witcher, B. S., et al. (1998). Arousal and attraction: Evidence for automatic and controlled processes. *Journal of Personality & Social Psychology, 74*(1), 86–101. doi:10.1037/0022-3514.74.1.86

Foster, G., & Ysseldyke, J. (1976). Expectancy and halo effects as a result of artificially induced teacher bias. *Contemporary Educational Psychology, 1,* 37–45. doi:10.1016/0361-476X(76)90005-9

Fournier, N. M., & Duman, R. S. (2012). Role of vascular endothelial growth factor in adult hippocampal neurogenesis: Implications for the pathophysiology and treatment of depression. *Behavioural Brain Research, 227*(2), 440–449. doi:10.1016/j.bbr.2011.04.022

Fowers, B. J., & Davidov, B. J. (2006). The virtue of multiculturalism: Personal transformation, character, and openness to the other. *American Psychologist, 61*(6), 581–594. doi:10.1037/0003-066X.61.6.581

Fowler, J. H., & Christakis, N. A. (2010). Cooperative behavior cascades in human social networks. *Proceedings of the National Academy of Sciences, 107*(12), 5334–5338. doi:10.1073/pnas.0913149107

Fox, J. B., & Shaw, F. E. (2014). Relationship of income and health care coverage to receipt of recommended clinical preventive services by adults—United States, 2011–2012. *Morbidity and Mortality Weekly Report, 63*(31), 666.

Fox, K. C. R., Dixon, M. L., et al. (2016). Functional neuroanatomy of meditation: A review and meta-analysis of 78 functional neuroimaging investigations. *Neuroscience & Biobehavioral Reviews, 65,* 208–228. doi:10.1016/j.neubiorev.2016.03.021

Fox, M., Thayer, Z., & et al. (2017). Assessment of acculturation in minority health research. *Social Science & Medicine, 176,* 123–132. doi:10.1016/j.socscimed.2017.01.029

Frajo-Apor, B., Pardeller, S., et al. (2016). Emotional intelligence deficits in schizophrenia: The impact of nonsocial cognition. *Schizophrenia Research, 172,* 131–136. doi:10.1016/j.schres.2016.02.027

Frances, A. (2012). DSM 5 is guide not bible—Ignore its ten worst changes. *Psychology Today.* Retrieved May 8, 2014, from March 27, 2017, from www.psychologytoday.com/blog/dsm5-in-distress/201212/dsm-5-is-guide-not-bible-ignore-its-ten-worst-changes

Frank, C., Land, W. M., et al. (2016, January 8). Perceptual-cognitive changes during motor learning: The influence of mental and physical practice on mental representation, gaze behavior, and performance of a complex action. *Frontiers in Psychology, 6,* Article 1981.

Frank, J. D., & Frank, J. (2004). Therapeutic components shared by all psychotherapies. In A. Freeman, M. J. Mahoney, et al. (Eds.), *Cognition and psychotherapy* (2nd ed., pp. 45–78). New York: Springer.

Frankl, V. (1955). *The doctor and the soul.* New York: Knopf.

Franz, B. A., Skinner, D., & Murphy, J. W. (2017). Defining "community" in community health evaluation: Perspectives from a sample of nonprofit Appalachian hospitals. American Journal of Evaluation, 39, 237–256 doi:10.1177/1098214017722857

Franzoi, S. L. (2002). *Social psychology.* New York: McGraw-Hill.

Frass, M., Strassl, R. P., Friehs, H., Müllner, M., Kundi, M., & Kaye, A. D. (2012). Use and acceptance of complementary and alternative medicine among the general population and medical personnel: A systematic review. *The Ochsner Journal, 12*(1), 45–56.

Frazier, A. (2012). The possible selves of high-ability African males attending a residential high school for highly able youth. *Journal for the Education of the Gifted, 35*(4), 366–390. doi:10.1177/0162353212461565

Freberg, L. A. (2016). *Discovering behavioral neuroscience: An introduction to biological psychology* (3rd ed.). Boston, MA: Cengage Learning.

Fréchette, S., Zoratti, M., et al. (2015). What is the link between corporal punishment and child physical abuse? *Journal of Family Violence, 30*(2), 135–148. doi:10.1007/s10896-014-9663-9

Frederick, D. A., & Fales, M. R. (2016). Upset over sexual versus emotional infidelity among gay, lesbian, bisexual, and heterosexual adults. *Archives of Sexual Behavior, 45*(1), 175–191. doi:10.1007/s10508-014-0409-9

Frederickson, N., Petrides, K. V., & Simmonds, E. (2012). Trait emotional intelligence as a predictor of socioemotional outcomes in early adolescence. *Personality & Individual Differences, 52*(3), 323–328. doi:10.1016/j.paid.2011.10.034

Fredrickson, B. L. (2003). The value of positive emotions. *American Scientist, 91,* 330–335. doi:10.1511/2003.4.330

Fredrickson, B. L., & Branigan, C. (2005). Positive emotions broaden the scope of attention and thought-action repertoires. *Cognition & Emotion, 19*(3), 313–332. doi:10.1080/02699930441000238

Fredrickson, B. L., Roberts, T., et al. (1998). That swimsuit becomes you. *Journal of Personality & Social Psychology, 75*(1), 269–284.

Freedman, D. H. (2011, February). How to fix the obesity crisis. *Scientific American,* pp. 40–47. doi:10.1038/scientificamerican0211-40

Freeman, D., & Garety, P. A. (2004). *Paranoia: The psychology of persecutory delusions.* New York: Routledge.

Freeman, N. K. (2007). Preschoolers' perceptions of gender appropriate toys and their parents' beliefs about genderized behaviors: Miscommunication, mixed messages, or hidden truths?. *Early Childhood Education Journal, 34*(5), 357–366. doi:10.1007/s10643-006-0123-x

Freidson, E. (1960). Client control and medical practice. *American Journal of Sociology, 65*(4), 374–382. doi:10.1086/222726

French, S. E., Kim, T. E., & Pillado, O. (2006). Ethnic identity, social group membership, and youth violence. In N. G. Guerra & E. P. Smith (Eds.), *Preventing youth violence in a multicultural society* (pp. 47–73). Washington, DC: American Psychological Association.

Freud, S. (1900). *The interpretation of dreams.* London: Hogarth.

Freud, S. (1949). *An outline of psychoanalysis.* New York: Norton.

Freund, A. M., & Ritter, J. O. (2009). Midlife crisis: A debate. *Gerontology, 55*(5), 582–591. doi:10.1159/000227322

Frew, J. (2013). Gestalt therapy. In J. Frew & M. D. Spiegler (Eds.), *Contemporary psychotherapies for a diverse world* (pp. 215–257). New York: Routledge/Taylor & Francis.

Fridriksson, J., Hubbard, H., et al. (2012). Speech entrainment enables patients with Broca's aphasia to produce fluent speech. *Brain: A Journal of Neurology, 135*(12), 3815–3829. doi:10.1093/brain/aws301

Friedman, H. S. (2002). *Health psychology* (2nd ed.). Englewood Cliffs, NJ: Prentice Hall.

Friedman, M., & Rosenman, R. H. (1983). *Type A behavior and your heart.* New York: Knopf.

Friese, M., Messner, C., & Schaffner, Y. (2012). Mindfulness meditation counteracts self-control depletion. *Consciousness & Cognition, 21*(2), 1016–1022. doi:10.1016/j.concog.2012.01.008

Friesen, P. (2019). Mesmer, the placebo effect, and the efficacy paradox: Lessons for evidence-based medicine and complementary and alternative medicine. *Critical Public Health, 29*(4), 435–447. doi:10.1080/09581596.2019.1597967

Fritz, C. O., Morris, P. E., et al. (2007). Comparing and combining retrieval practice and the keyword mnemonic for foreign vocabulary learning. *Applied Cognitive Psychology, 21*(4), 499–526. doi:10.1002/acp.1287

Fritzell, J., Rehnberg, J., et al. (2015). Absolute or relative? A comparative analysis of the relationship between poverty and mortality. *International Journal of Public Health, 60*(1), 101–110. doi:10.1007/s00038-014-0614-2

Fry, R. (2012). *Improve your memory* (6th ed.). Boston, MA: Cengage Learning.

Fryar, C. D., Carroll, M. D., et al. (2014). Prevalence of overweight, obesity and extreme obesity among adults: United States, 1960–62 through 2011–2012. *National Center for Health Statistics Health E-Stats, September.* Retrieved March 10, 2017, from www.cdc.gov/nchs/data/hestat/obesity_adult_11_12/obesity_adult_11_12.htm

Fryar, C. D., Hirsch, R., et al. (2007). Drug use and sexual behaviors reported by adults: United States, 1999–2002. *Advance data from vital and health statistics; no. 384.* Retrieved May 8, 2014, from www.cdc.gov/nchs/data/ad/ad384.pdf

Fu, J. H., Morris, M. W., et al. (2007). Epistemic motives and cultural conformity: Need for closure, culture, and context as determinants of conflict judgments. *Journal of Personality & Social Psychology, 92*(2), 191–207. doi:10.1037/0022-3514.92.2.191

Fuchs, G. (2013). Low versus high sensation-seeking tourists: A study of backpackers' experience risk perception. *International Journal of Tourism Research, 15*(1), 81–92. doi:10.1002/jtr.878

Fukai, S., Akishita, M., et al. (2010). Effects of testosterone in older men with mild-to-moderate cognitive impairment. *Journal of the American Geriatrics Society, 58*(7), 1419–1421.

Fuller-Rowell, T. E., Evans, G. W., & Ong, A. D. (2012). Poverty and health: The mediating role of perceived discrimination. *Psychological Science, 23*(7), 734–739. doi:10.1177/0956797612439720

Fuller, T. E. (2012). *The insanity offense: How America's failure to treat the seriously mentally ill endangers its citizens.* New York: Norton.

Funder, D. C. (2010). *The personality puzzle* (5th ed.). New York: Norton.

Furman, D., Campisi, J., et al. (2019). Chronic inflammation in the etiology of disease across the life span. *Nature Medicine, 25*(12), 1822–1832. doi:10.1038/s41591-019-0675-0

Furnham, A., Chamorro-Premuzic, T., & Callahan, I. (2003). Does graphology predict personality and intelligence? *Individual Differences Research, 1*(2), 78–94.

Furnham, A., Richards, S. C., & Paulhus, D. L. (2013). The dark triad of personality: A 10-year review. *Social & Personality Psychology Compass, 7*(3), 199–216. doi:10.1111/spc3.12018

Gable, S. L., Reis, H. T., et al. (2004). What do you do when things go right? *Journal of Personality & Social Psychology, 87*(2), 228–245. doi:10.1037/0022-3514.87.2.228

Gaertner, S. L., Dovidio, J. F., et al. (2000). Reducing intergroup conflict: From superordinate goals to decategorization, recategorization, and mutual differentiation. *Group Dynamics, 4*(1), 98–114. doi:10.1037/1089-2699.4.1.98

Gainforth, H. L., West, R., et al. (2015). Assessing connections between behavior change theories using network analysis. *Annals of Behavioral Medicine, 49*(5), 754–761. doi:10.1007/s12160-015-9710-7

Galanter, M., Hayden, F., et al. (2005). Group therapy, self-help groups, and network therapy. In R. J. Frances, S. I. Miller, et al. (Eds.), *Clinical textbook of addictive disorders* (3rd ed., pp. 502–527). New York: Guilford.

Galati, D., Scherer, K. R., & Ricci-Bitti, P. E. (1997). Voluntary facial expression of emotion: Comparing congenitally blind with normally sighted encoders. *Journal of Personality & Social Psychology, 73*(6), 1363–1379. doi:10.1037/0022-3514.73.6.1363

Galatzer-Levy, R. M. (2012). Obscuring desire: A special pattern of male adolescent masturbation, Internet pornography, and the flight from meaning. *Psychoanalytic Inquiry, 32*(5), 480–495. doi:10.1080/07351690.2012.703582

Galea, S., & Resnick, H. (2005). Post-traumatic stress disorder in the general population after mass terrorist incidents: Considerations about the nature of exposure. *CNS Spectrums, 10*(2), 107–115.

Galea, S., Ahern, J., et al. (2002). Psychological sequelae of the September 11 terrorist attacks in New York City. *New England Journal of Medicine, 346*(13), 982–987. doi:10.1056/NEJMsa013404

Gallagher, S. (2004). Nailing the lie: An interview with Jonathan Cole. *Journal of Consciousness Studies, 11*(2), 3–21.

Gallese, V., Rochat, M. J., & Berchio, C. (2013). The mirror mechanism and its potential role in autism spectrum disorder. *Developmental Medicine & Child Neurology, 55*(1), 15–22. doi:10.1111/j.1469-8749.2012.04398.x

Galliher, R. V., Jones, M. D., & Dahl, A. (2011). Concurrent and longitudinal effects of ethnic identity and experiences of discrimination on psychosocial adjustment of Navajo adolescents. *Developmental Psychology, 47*(2), 509–526. doi:10.1037/a0021061

Gallo, M. M. (2015). *"No one helped": Kitty Genovese, New York City, and the myth of urban apathy.* Ithaca, NY: Cornell University Press.

Galsworthy-Francis, L., & Allan, S. (2014). Cognitive behavioural therapy for anorexia nervosa: A systematic review. *Clinical Psychology Review, 34*(1), 54–72. doi:10.1016/j.cpr.2013.11.001

Gambescia, N., & Weeks, G. R. (2015). Systemic treatment of erectile disorder. In K. M. Hertlein, G. R. Weeks, et al. (Eds.), *Systemic sex therapy* (2nd ed., pp. 72–89). New York: Routledge/Taylor & Francis.

Ganis, G. (2013). Visual mental imagery. In S. Lacey & R. Lawson (Eds.), *Multisensory imagery* (pp. 9–28). New York: Springer. doi:10.1007/978-1-4614-5879-1_2

Ganna, A., Verweij, K. J., et al. (2019). Large-scale GWAS reveals insights into the genetic architecture of same-sex sexual behavior. *Science, 365*(6456), eaat7693. doi:10.1126/science.aat7693

Ganster, D. C., Fox, M. L., & Dwyer, D. J. (2001). Explaining employees' health care costs: A prospective examination of stressful job demands, personal control, and physiological reactivity. *Journal of Applied Psychology, 86,* 954–964. doi:10.1037/0021-9010.86.5.954

Garcia, E. E. (2008). Bilingual education in the United States. In J. Altarriba & R. R. Heredia (Eds.), *An introduction to bilingualism: Principles and processes* (pp. 321–343). Mahwah, NJ: Erlbaum.

Garcia-Barrera, M. A., Direnfeld, E., et al. (2013). Psychological assessment: From interviewing to objective and projective measurement. In C. A. Noggle & R. S. Dean (Eds.), *The neuropsychology of psychopathology* (pp. 473–493). New York: Springer.

García-Rodríguez, O., Secades-Villa, R., et al. (2013). Probability and predictors of relapse to smoking: Results of the National Epidemiologic Survey on Alcohol and Related Conditions (NESARC). *Drug & Alcohol Dependence, 132*(3), 479–485. doi:10.1016/j.drugalcdep.2013.03.008

Garcia-Sierra, A., Rivera-Gaxiola, M., et al. (2011). Bilingual language learning: An ERP study relating early brain responses to speech, language input, and later word production. *Journal of Phonetics, 39*(4), 546–557. doi:10.1016/j.wocn.2011.07.002

Gardner, H. (2008). Birth and the spreading of a "meme." In J. Q. Chen, S. Moran, et al. (Eds.), *Multiple intelligences around the world* (pp. 3–16). San Francisco, CA: Jossey-Bass.

Gardner, H. (2011). The theory of multiple intelligences. In M. A. Gernsbacher, R. W. Pew, et al. (Eds.), *Psychology and the real world: Essays illustrating fundamental contributions to society* (pp. 122–130). New York: Worth.

Gardner, S. E., Betts, L. R., et al. (2017). The role of emotion regulation for coping with school-based peer-victimisation in late childhood. *Personality & Individual Differences, 107,* 108–113. doi:10.1016/j.paid.2016.11.035

Garety, P. A., & Freeman, D. (2013). The past and future of delusions research: From the inexplicable to the treatable. *British Journal of Psychiatry, 203,* 327–333.

Garlow, S. J., Purselle, D. C., & Heninger, M. (2007). Cocaine and alcohol use preceding suicide in African American and white adolescents. *Journal of Psychiatric Research, 41*(6), 530–536. doi:10.1016/j.jpsychires.2005.08.008

Garrosa, E., Moreno-Jiménez, B., et al. (2008). The relationship between socio-demographic variables, job stressors, burnout, and hardy personality in nurses: An exploratory study. *International Journal of Nursing Studies, 45*(3), 418–427. doi:10.1016/j.ijnurstu.2006.09.003

Garza-Villarreal, E. A. (2016). Music-induced analgesia: The neurobiology of the analgesic effects of music in acute and chronic pain. M. Hashefi (Ed.), *Music therapy in the management of medical conditions* (pp. 9–23). Hauppauge, NY: Nova Science Publishers, viii, 157 pp.

Gass, R. H., & Seiter, J. S. (2014). *Persuasion: Social influence and compliance gaining* (5th ed.). Boston, MA: Allyn & Bacon.

Gastner, M. T., Shalizi, C. R., & Newman, M. E. J. (2005). Maps and cartograms of the 2004 US presidential election results. *Advances in Complex Systems, 8*(1), 117–123. doi:10.1142/S0219525905000397

Gates, A. I. (1917). Recitation as a factor in memorizing. *Archives of Psychology, 40,* 104.

Gaumon, S., Paquette, D., et al. (2016). Anxiety and attachment to the mother in preschoolers receiving psychiatric care: The father–child activation relationship as a protective factor. *Infant Mental Health Journal, 37*(4), 372–387. doi:10.1002/imhj.21571

Gavett, B. E., & Horwitz, J. E. (2012). Immediate list recall as a measure of short-term episodic memory: Insights from the serial position effect and item response theory. *Archives of Clinical Neuropsychology, 27*(2), 125–135. doi:10.1093/arclin/acr104

Gawronski, B. (2012). Back to the future of dissonance theory: Cognitive consistency as a core motive. *Social Cognition, 30*(6), 652–668. doi:10.1521/soco.2012.30.6.652

Gazzaniga, M. S. (2015). *Tales from both sides of the brain: A life in neuroscience.* New York: Ecco/HarperCollins.

Geddes, L. (2008, October 3). Could brain scans ever be safe evidence? *New Scientist,* pp. 8–9.

Gegenfurtner, K. R., & Kiper, D. C. (2003). Color vision. *Annual Review of Neuroscience, 26,* 181–206. doi:10.1146/annurev.neuro.26.041002.131116

Geher, G. (2014). *Evolutionary psychology 101.* New York: Springer.

Geiselman, R. E., Fisher, R. P., et al. (1986). Enhancement of eyewitness memory with the cognitive interview. *American Journal of Psychology, 99,* 385–401.

Gejman, P. V., Sanders, A. R., & Duan, J. (2010). The role of genetics in the etiology of schizophrenia. *Psychiatric Clinics of North America, 33*(1), 35–66. doi:10.1016/j.psc.2009.12.003

Gentile, M. (2010). *Giving voice to values: How to speak your mind when you know what's right.* New Haven, CT: Yale University Press.

Genty, E., Breuer, T., et al. (2009). Gestural communication of the gorilla (Gorilla gorilla): Repertoire, intentionality, and possible origins. *Animal Cognition, 12*(3), 527–546. doi:10.1007/s10071-009-0213-4

German, T. P., & Defeyter, M. A. (2000). Immunity to functional fixedness in young children. *Psychonomic Bulletin & Review, 7*(4), 707–712. doi:10.3758/BF03213010

Gershoff, E. T., & Bitensky, S. H. (2007). The case against corporal punishment of children: Converging evidence from social science research and international human rights law and implications for U.S. public policy. *Psychology, Public Policy, & Law, 13*(4), 231–272. doi:10.1037/1076-8971.13.4.231

Gershoff, E. T., & Grogan-Kaylor, A. (2016). Spanking and child outcomes: Old controversies and new meta-analyses. *Journal of Family Psychology, 30*(4), 453-469. doi:10.1037/fam0000191

Gerstein, E. R. (2002, March–April). Manatees, bioacoustics, and boats. *American Scientist, 90,* 154–163. doi:10.1511/2002.2.154

Gewin, V. (2019, April 22). Why some anti-bias training misses the mark. *Nature.* https://www.nature.com/articles/d41586-019-01301-8

Gheitury, A., Sahraee, A., & Hoseini, M. (2012). Language acquisition in late critical period: A case report. *Deafness & Education International, 14*(3), 122–135. doi:10.1179/1557069X12Y.0000000008

Giancola, P. R., Josephs, R. A., et al. (2010). Alcohol myopia revisited: Clarifying aggression and other acts of disinhibition through a distorted lens. *Perspectives on Psychological Science, 5*(3), 265–278. doi:10.1177/1745691610369467

Giarratano, J. C., & Riley, G. (2004). *Expert systems, principles and programming* (4th ed.). Boston, MA: Cengage Learning.

Gibson, E. J., & Walk, R. D. (1960). The "visual cliff." *Scientific American, 202*(4), 67–71. doi:10.1038/scientificamerican0460-64

Gick, M. L., & Holyoak, K. J. (1980). Analogical problem solving. *Cognitive Psychology, 12*(3), 306–355. doi:10.1016/0010-0285(80)90013-4

Gifford, E. V., & Shoenberger, D. (2009). Rapid smoking. In W. T. O'Donohue, & J. E. Fisher (Eds.), *General principles and empirically supported techniques of cognitive behavior therapy* (pp. 513–519). New York: Wiley.

Gilboa, A., & Tal-Shmotkin, M. (2012). String quartets as self-managed teams: An interdisciplinary perspective. *Psychology of Music, 40*(1), 19–41. doi:10.1177/0305735610377593

Gilchrist, A. L., Cowan, N., & Naveh-Benjamin, M. (2009). Investigating the childhood development of working memory using sentences: New evidence for the growth of chunk capacity. *Journal of Experimental Child Psychology, 104*(2), 252–265. doi:10.1016/j.jecp.2009.05.006

Giletta, M., Calhoun, C. D., et al. (2015). Multi-level risk factors for suicidal ideation among at-risk adolescent females: The role of hypothalamicp-ituitary-adrenal axis responses to stress. *Journal of Abnormal Child Psychology, 43*(5), 807–820. doi:10.10007/s10802-014-9897-2

Gillan, C. M., & Robbins, T. W. (2014). Goal-directed learning and obsessive-compulsive disorder. *Philosophical Transactions of Royal Society B.* Retrieved March 27, 2017, from http://rstb.royalsocietypublishing.org/content/369/1655/20130475

Gillan, C. M., & Sahakian, B. J. (2015). Which is the driver, the obsessions or the compulsions, in OCD? *Neuropsychopharmacology, 40*(1), 247–248. doi:10.1038/npp.2014.201

Gillespie-Lynch, K., Greenfield, P. M., et al. (2011). The role of dialogue in the ontogeny and phylogeny of early symbol combinations: A cross-species comparison of bonobo, chimpanzee, and human learners. *First Language, 31*(4), 442–460. doi:10.1177/0142723711406882

Gillespie-Lynch, K., Greenfield, P. M., et al. (2014). Gestural and symbolic development among apes and humans: Support for a multimodal theory of language evolution. *Frontiers in Psychology, 5,* Article 1228. doi:10.3389/fpsyg.2014.01228

Gillespie, C. F., & Nemeroff, C. B. (2007). Corticotropin-releasing factor and the psychobiology of early-life stress. *Current Directions in Psychological Science, 16*(2), 85–89. doi:10.1111/j.1467-8721.2007.00481.x

Gilligan, C. (1982). *In a different voice.* Cambridge, MA: Harvard University Press.

Gilroy, K. E., & Pearce, J. M. (2014). The role of local, distal, and global information in latent spatial learning. *Journal of Experimental Psychology: Animal Learning & Cognition, 40*(2), 212–224. doi:10.1037/xan0000017

Gilson, L. L., Maynard, M. T., et al. (2015). Virtual teams research 10 Years, 10 themes, and 10 opportunities. *Journal of Management, 41*(5), 1313–1337. doi:10.1177/0149206314559946

Ginet, M., Py, J., & Colomb, C. (2014). The differential effectiveness of the cognitive interview instructions for enhancing witnesses' memory of a familiar event. *Swiss Journal of Psychology, 73*(1), 25–34. doi:10.1024/1421-0185/a000118

Gino, F., & Flynn, F. J. (2011). Give them what they want: The benefits of explicitness in gift exchange. *Journal of Experimental Social Psychology, 47,* 915–922. doi:10.1016/j. jesp. 2011.03.015

Giordano, P. C. (2003). Relationships in adolescence. *Annual Review of Sociology, 29*(1), 257–281. doi:10.1146/annurev.soc.29.010202.100047

Giummarra, M. J., Gibson, S. J., et al. (2007). Central mechanisms in phantom limb perception: The past, present, and future. *Brain Research Reviews, 54*(1), 219–232. doi:10.1016/j.brainresrev.2007.01.009

Gladwell, M. (2005). *Blink: The power of thinking without thinking.* New York: Little, Brown.

Glass, D., Meyer, A., & Rose, D. H. (2013). Universal design for learning and the arts. *Harvard Educational Review, 83*(1), 98–119.

Glassgold, J. M., Beckstead, L., et al. (2009). *Report of the American Psychological Association Task Force on appropriate therapeutic responses to sexual orientation.* Retrieved May 8, 2014, from http://www.apa.org/pi/lgbt/resources/therapeutic-response.pdf

Gleason, J. B., & Ratner, N. B. (2013). *The development of language* (8th ed.). Boston, MA: Allyn & Bacon.

Gleason, O. C., Pierce, A. M., et al. (2013). The two-way relationship between medical illness and late-life depression. *Psychiatric Clinics of North America, 36*(4), 533–544. doi:10.1016/j.psc.2013.08.003

Glenn, E. N. (Ed.). (2009). *Shades of difference: Why skin color matters.* Palo Alto, CA: Stanford University Press.

Glick, P. (2008). When neighbors blame neighbors: Scapegoating and the breakdown of ethnic relations. In V. M. Esses & R. A. Vernon (Eds.), *Explaining the breakdown of ethnic relations: Why neighbors kill: Social issues and interventions* (pp. 123–146). Malden, MA: Blackwell. doi:10.1002/9781444303056.ch6

Global Footprint Network. (2017a). *Personal footprint.* Retrieved April 12, 2017, from www.footprintnetwork.org/en/index.php/GFN/page/personal_footprint

Global Footprint Network. (2017b). *Ecological footprint.* Retrieved April 12, 2017, from www.footprintnetwork.org/our-work/ecological-footprint/#worldfootprint

Global Workplace Analytics. (2020). *Work from home experience survey results.* https://globalworkplaceanalytics.com/global-work-from-home-experience-survey#AboutSurvey

Gloria-Bottini, F., Magrini, A., & Bottini, E. (2009). The effect of genetic and seasonal factors on birth weight. *Early Human Development, 85*(7), 439–441. doi:10.1016/j.earlhumdev.2009.02.004

Glover, R. J. (2001). Discriminators of moral orientation: Gender role or personality? *Journal of Adult Development, 8*(1), 1–7.

Gobet, F. (2005). Chunking models of expertise: Implications for education. *Applied Cognitive Psychology, 19*(2), 183–204. doi:10.1002/acp.1110

Gobet, F., & Simon, H. A. (1996). Recall of random and distorted chess positions: Implications for the theory of expertise. *Memory & Cognition, 24*(4), 493–503. doi:10.3758/BF03200937

Göckeritz, S., Schultz, P. W., et al. (2010). Descriptive normative beliefs and conservation behavior: The moderating roles of personal involvement and injunctive normative beliefs. *European Journal of Social Psychology, 40*(3), 514–523. doi:10.1002/ejsp.643

Godnig, E. C. (2003). Tunnel vision: Its causes & treatment strategies. *Journal of Behavioral Optometry, 14*(4), 95–99.

Godoy, R., Zeinalova, E., et al. (2010). Does civilization cause discontentment among indigenous Amazonians? Test of empirical data from the Tsimane' of Bolivia. *Journal of Economic Psychology, 31,* 587–598.

Goel, N. (2012). Genetics of sleep timing, duration, and homeostasis in humans. *Sleep Medicine Clinics, 7*(3), 443–454. doi:10.1016/j.jsmc.2012.06.013

Goforth, A., Pham, A., & Oka, E. (2015). Parent–child conflict, acculturation gap, acculturative stress, and behavior problems in Arab American adolescents. *Journal of Cross-Cultural Psychology, 46*(6), 821–836. doi:10.1177/0022022115585140

Gogate, L. J., Bahrick, L. E., & Watson, J. D. (2000). A study of multimodal motherese: The role of temporal synchrony between verbal labels and gestures. *Child Development, 71*(4), 878–894. doi:10.1111/1467-8624.00197

Goldberg, C. (2001). Of prophets, true believers, and terrorists. *The Dana Forum on Brain Science, 3*(3), 21–24.

Goldberg, R. (2014). *Drugs across the spectrum* (7th ed.). Boston, MA: Cengage Learning.

Golden, T. D., Veiga, J. F., & Simsek, Z. (2006). Telecommuting's differential impact on work-family conflict: Is there no place like home? *Journal of Applied Psychology, 91*(6), 1340–1350.

Goldenberg, A., & Gross, J. J. (2020). Digital emotion contagion. *Trends in Cognitive Sciences, 24,* 316–328. doi:10.1016/j.tics.2020.01.009

Goldenberg, H., & Goldenberg, I. (2013). *Family therapy: An overview* (8th ed.). Pacific Grove, CA: Brooks/Cole.

Goldfried, M. R. (2001). Integrating gay, lesbian, and bisexual issues into mainstream psychology. *American Psychologist, 56*(11), 977–987.

Golding, J. M., Bradshaw, G. S., et al. (2007). The impact of mock jury gender composition on deliberations and conviction rates in a child sexual assault trial. *Child Maltreatment, 12*(2), 182–190.

Goldstein, A., Déry, N., et al. (2016). Stress and binge drinking: A toxic combination for the teenage brain. *Neuropsychologia, 90,* 251–260. doi:10.1016/j.neuropsychologia.2016.07.035

Goldstein, E. B. (2019). *Cognitive psychology: Connecting mind, research, and everyday experience* (5th ed.). Boston, MA: Cengage Learning.

Goldstein, E. B., & Brockmole, J. R. (2017). *Sensation and perception* (10th ed.). Boston, MA: Cengage Learning.

Goldstein, M. H., Schwade, J., et al. (2010). Learning while babbling: Prelinguistic object-directed vocalizations indicate a readiness to learn. *Infancy, 15*(4), 362–391. doi:10.1111/j.1532-7078.2009.00020.x

Goldston, D. B., Molock, S. D., et al. (2008). Cultural considerations in adolescent suicide prevention and psychosocial treatment. *American Psychologist, 63*(1), 14–31. doi:10.1037/0003-066X.63.1.14

Goman, C. K. (2008). *The nonverbal advantage: Secrets and science of body language at work.* San Francisco, CA: Berrett-Koehler.

Gomes, A. R., Faria, S., & Lopes, H. (2016). Stress and psychological health: Testing the mediating role of cognitive appraisal. *Western Journal of Nursing Research, 38*(11), 1448–1468. doi:10.1177/0193945916654666

González-Vallejo, C., Lassiter, G. D., et al. (2008). "Save angels perhaps": A critical examination of unconscious thought theory and the deliberation-without-attention effect. *Review of General Psychology, 12*(3), 282–296. doi:10.1037/a0013134

Gonzalez, M., Durrant, J. E., et al. (2008). What predicts injury from physical punishment? A test of the typologies of violence hypothesis. *Child Abuse & Neglect, 32*(8), 752–765. doi:10.1016/j.chiabu.2007.12.005

Gonzalez, V. M., Reynolds, B., & Skewes, M. C. (2011). Role of impulsivity in the relationship between depression and alcohol problems among emerging adult college drinkers. *Experimental & Clinical Psychopharmacology, 19*(4), 303–313. doi:10.1037/a0022720

Goode, E. (1996). Gender and courtship entitlement: Responses to personal ads. *Sex Roles, 34*(3–4), 141–169. doi:10.1007/BF01544293

Goodman, G. S., Quas, J. A., Ogle, C. M. (2010). Child maltreatment and memory. *Annual Review of Psychology, 61,* 325–351. doi:10.1146/annurev.psych.093008.100403

Gopie, N., Craik, F. I. M., & Hasher, L. (2011). A double dissociation of implicit and explicit memory in younger and older adults. *Psychological Science, 22*(5), 634–640. doi:10.1177/0956797611403321

Gopnik, A. (2016). *The gardener and the carpenter: What the new science of child development tells us about the relationship between parents and children.* New York: Farrar, Straus & Giroux.

Gordon, A. K., & Kaplar, M. E. (2002). A new technique for demonstrating the actor-observer bias. *Teaching of Psychology, 29*(4), 301–303. doi:10.1207/S15328023TOP2904_10

Gordon, I., Zagoory-Sharon, O., et al. (2010). Oxytocin and the development of parenting in humans. *Biological Psychiatry, 68*(4), 377–382. doi:10.1016/j.biopsych.2010.02.005

Gordon, J. R., Pruchno, R. A., et al. (2012). Balancing caregiving and work: Role conflict and role strain dynamics. *Journal of Family Issues, 33*(5), 662–689. doi:10.1177/0192513X11425322

Gordon, K. A., Wong, D. D. E., et al. (2011). Use it or lose it? Lessons learned from the developing brains of children who are deaf and use cochlear implants to hear. *Brain Topography, 24*(3–4), 204–219. doi:10.1007/s10548-011-0181-2

Gordon, R. M. (2001). MMPI/MMPI-2 changes in long-term psychoanalytic psychotherapy. *Issues in Psychoanalytic Psychology, 23*(1–2), 59–79.

Gorman, A. D., Abernethy, B., & Farrow, D. (2011). Investigating the anticipatory nature of pattern perception in sport. *Memory & Cognition, 39*(5), 894–901. doi:10.3758/s13421-010-0067-7

Gorman, A. D., Abernethy, B., & Farrow, D. (2013). The expert advantage in dynamic pattern recall persists across both attended and unattended display elements. *Attention, Perception, & Psychophysics, 75*(5), 835–844. doi:10.3758/s13414-013-0423-3

Gosling, S. D., & Mason, W. (2015). Internet research in psychology. *Annual Review of Psychology, 66,* 877–902. doi:10.1146/annurev-psych-010814-015321

Gottman, J. M. (1994). *Why marriages succeed or fail.* New York: Simon & Schuster.

Gottman, J. M., & Krokoff, L. J. (1989). Marital interaction and satisfaction: A longitudinal view. *Journal of Consulting & Clinical Psychology, 57*(1), 47–52.

Gould, D., Voelker, D. K., et al. (2014). Imagery training for peak performance. In J. L. Van Raalte & B. W. Brewer (Eds.), *Exploring sport and exercise psychology* (3rd ed., pp. 55–82). Washington, DC: American Psychological Association. doi:10.1037/14251-004

Gould, E., Schieder, J., & Geier, K. (2016). What is the gender pay gap and is it real? The complete guide to how women are paid less than men and why it can't be explained away. Retrieved March 10, 2017, from www.epi.org/publication/what-is-the-gender-pay-gap-and-isit-real/#epi-toc-13

Gourville, J. T., & Soman, D. (2005). Overchoice and assortment type: When and why variety backfires. *Marketing Science, 24*(3), 382–395. doi:10.1287/mksc.1040.0109

Gow, A. J., Johnson, W., et al. (2010). Stability and change in intelligence from age 11 to ages 70, 79, and 87: The Lothian birth cohorts of 1921 and 1936. *Psychology & Aging, 26*(1), 232–240. doi:10.1037/a0021072

Gowensmith, W., Murrie, D. C., & Boccaccini, M. T. (2013). How reliable are forensic evaluations of legal sanity? *Law & Human Behavior, 37*(2), 98–106. doi:10.1037/lhb0000001

Graham, J., Haidt, J., et al. (2009). Liberals and conservatives rely on different sets of moral foundations. *Journal of Personality and Social Psychology, 96*(5), 1029–1046. doi:10.1037/a0015141

Graham, J., Nosek, B. A., et al. (2011). Mapping the moral domain. *Journal of Personality and Social Psychology, 101*(2), 366–385. doi:10.1037/a0021847

Grande, T., Rudolf, G., et al. (2003). Progressive changes in patients' lives after psychotherapy. *Psychotherapy Research, 13*(1), 43–58. doi:10.1093/ptr/kpg006

Grandner, M. A., & Kripke, D. F. (2004). Self-reported sleep complaints with long and short sleep: A nationally representative sample. *Psychosomatic Medicine, 66,* 239–241. doi:10.1097/01.PSY.0000107881.53228.4D

Grangeon, M., Guillot, A., & Collet, C. (2011). Postural control during visual and kinesthetic motor imagery. *Applied Psychophysiology & Biofeedback, 36*(1), 47–56. doi:10.1007/s10484-011-9145-2

Granrud, C. E. (2006). Size constancy in infants: 4-month-olds' responses to physical versus retinal image size. *Journal of Experimental Psychology: Human Perception & Performance, 32*(6), 1398–1404. doi:10.1037/0096-1523.32.6.1398

Granrud, C. E. (2009). Development of size constancy in children: A test of the metacognitive theory. *Attention, Perception, & Psychophysics, 71*(3), 644–654. doi:10.3758/APP.71.3.644

Grant, B. (2010). Getting the point: Empathic understanding in nondirective client-centered therapy. *Person-Centered & Experiential Psychotherapies, 9*(3), 220–235. doi:10.1080/14779757.2010.9689068

Grant, B. F., Hasin, D. S., et al. (2006). The epidemiology of DSM-IV panic disorder and agoraphobia in the United States: Results from the National Epidemiologic Survey on Alcohol and Related Conditions. *Journal of Clinical Psychiatry, 67*(3), 363–374. doi:10.4088/JCP.v67n0305

Grant, I., Gonzalez, R., et al. (2001, August 13). Long-term neurocognitive consequences of marijuana. In *National Institute on Drug Abuse Workshop on Clinical Consequences of Marijuana*, Rockville, MD.

Grant, T. M., Jack, D. C., et al. (2011). Carrying the burdens of poverty, parenting, and addiction: Depression symptoms and self-silencing among ethnically diverse women. *Community Mental Health Journal, 47*(1), 90–98. doi:10.1007/s10597-009-9255-y

Grant-Jacob, J. A. (2016). Love at first sight. *Frontiers in Psychology, 7,* Article 1113. doi:10.3389/fpsyg.2016.01113

Gravetter, F. J., & Forzano, L.-A. B. (2016). *Research methods for the behavioral sciences* (5th ed.). Boston, MA: Cengage Learning.

Gravetter, F. J., & Wallnau, L. B. (2017). *Statistics for the behavioral sciences* (10th ed.). Boston, MA: Cengage Learning.

Gravetter, F. J., Wallnau, L. B., & Forzano, L.-A. B. (2018). *Essentials of statistics for the behavioral sciences* (8th ed.).

Gravitz, L. (2019). The importance of forgetting. *Nature, 574,* S12–S14.

Gray, S. A. O., & Sweeney, K. K., et al. (2016). "Am I doing the right thing?": Pathways to parenting a gender variant child. *Family Process, 55*(1), 123–138. doi:10.1111/famp.12128

Gray, S. J., & Gallo, D. A. (2016). Paranormal psychic believers and skeptics: A large-scale test of the cognitive differences hypothesis. *Memory & Cognition, 44*(2), 242–261. doi:10.3758/s13421-015-0563-x

Graziano, W. G., & Habashi, M. M. (2015). Searching for the prosocial personality. In D. A. Schroeder & W. G. Graziano (Eds.), *The Oxford handbook of prosocial behavior* (pp. 231–255). New York, NY: Oxford University Press. doi:10.1093/oxfordhb/9780195399813.001.0001

Gredler, M. E. (2012). Understanding Vygotsky for the classroom: Is it too late? *Educational Psychology Review, 24*(1), 113–131. doi:10.1007/s10648-011-9183-6

Greene, D. C., & Britton, P. J. (2012). Stage of sexual minority identity formation: The impact of shame, internalized homophobia, ambivalence over emotional expression, and personal mastery. *Journal of Gay & Lesbian Mental Health, 16*(3), 188–214. doi:10.1080/19359705.2012.671126

Greene, D., & Lepper, M. R. (1974). How to turn play into work. *Psychology Today, 8*(4), 49.

Greene, E., & Heilbrun, K. (2014). *Wrightsman's psychology and the legal system* (8th ed.). Boston, MA: Cengage Learning.

Greenfield, P. M. (1997). You can't take it with you: Why abilities assessments don't cross cultures. *American Psychologist, 52,* 1115–1124. doi:10.1037/0003-066X.52.10.1115

Greenspan, J. D., Coghill, R. C., et al. (2008). Quantitative somatic sensory testing and functional imaging of the response to painful stimuli before and after cingulotomy for obsessive-compulsive disorder (OCD). *European Journal of Pain, 12*(8), 990–999. doi:10.1016/j.ejpain.2008.01.007

Greenwood, J. G., Greenwood, J. J., et al. (2006). A survey of sidedness in Northern Irish schoolchildren: The interaction of sex, age, and task. *Laterality. Asymmetries of Body, Brain, & Cognition, 12*(1), 1–18. doi:10.1080/13576500600886630

Gregoire, C. (2016). *Why psychology should be a part of the fight against climate change.* Retrieved April 14, 2017, from www.huffingtonpost.com/entry/climate-change-psychology_us_5674272ee4b014efe0d52186

Gregory, B. T., Albritton, M. D., & Osmonbekov, T. (2010). The mediating role of psychological empowerment on the relationships between P–O fit, job satisfaction, and in-role performance. *Journal of Business & Psychology, 25*(4), 639–647.

Gregory, D. (2016). Inner speech, imagined speech, and auditory verbal hallucinations. *Review of Philosophy & Psychology, 7*(3), 653–673. doi:10.1007/s13164-015-0274-z

Gregory, R. L. (1990). *Eye and brain: The psychology of seeing.* Princeton, NJ: Princeton University Press.

Gregory, R. L. (2000). Visual illusions. In A. Kazdin (Ed.), *Encyclopedia of psychology* (Vol. 8, pp. 193–200). Washington, DC: American Psychological Association.

Gregory, R. L. (2003). Seeing after blindness. *Nature Neuroscience, 6*(9), 909–910.

Greifeneder, R., Scheibehenne, B., & Kleber, N. (2010). Less may be more when choosing is difficult: Choice complexity and too much choice. *Acta Psychologica, 133*(1), 45–50. doi:10.1016/j.actpsy.2009.08.005

Greitemeyer, T. (2009). Effects of songs with prosocial lyrics on prosocial thoughts, affect, and behavior. *Journal of Experimental Social Psychology, 45*(1), 186–190.

Greitemeyer, T. (2010). Effects of reciprocity on attraction: The role of a partner's physical attractiveness. *Personal Relationships, 17*(2), 317–330. doi:10.1111/j.1475-6811.2010.01278.x

Greitemeyer, T. (2011). Effects of prosocial media on social behavior: When and why does media exposure affect helping and aggression? *Current Direction in Psychological Science, 20,* 251–255.

Greitemeyer, T., et al. (2012). Acting prosocially reduces retaliation: Effects of prosocial video games on aggressive behavior. *European Journal of Social Psychology, 42,* 235–242.

Grello, C. M., Welsh, D. P., & Harper, M. S. (2006). No strings attached: The nature of casual sex in college students. *Journal of Sex Research, 43*(3), 255–267.

Grenèche, J., Krieger, J., et al. (2011). Short-term memory performances during sustained wakefulness in patients with obstructive sleep apnea–hypopnea syndrome. *Brain & Cognition, 75*(1), 39–50. doi:10.1016/j.bandc.2010.10.003

Grenier, G., & Byers, E. S. (1995). Rapid ejaculation: A review of conceptual, etiological, and treatment issues. *Archives of Sexual Behavior, 24*(4), 447–472.

Griffin, W. A. (2002). Family therapy. In M. Hersen & W. H. Sledge (Eds.), *Encyclopedia of psychotherapy* (pp. 787– 791). San Diego, CA: Academic Press.

Griffiths, M. D. (2012). Internet sex addiction: A review of empirical research. *Addiction Research & Theory, 20*(2), 111–124. doi:10.3109/16066359.2011.588351

Griggs, R. A. (2015). The Kitty Genovese story in introductory psychology textbooks: Fifty years later. *Teaching of Psychology, 42*(2), 149–152. doi:10.1177/0098628315573138

Griggs, R. A. (2017). Milgram's obedience study: A contentious classic reinterpreted. *Teaching of Psychology, 44*(1), 32–37. doi:10.1177/0098628316677644

Grigorenko, E. L. (2005). The inherent complexities of gene-environment interactions. *Journals of Gerontology, 60B*(1), 53–64. doi:10.1093/geronb/60.Special_Issue_1.53

Grilly, D. M., & Salamone, J. (2012). *Drugs, brain, and behavior* (6th ed.). Englewood Cliffs, NJ: Prentice Hall.

Grobstein, P., & Chow, K. L. (1975). Perceptive field development and individual experience. *Science, 190,* 352–358.

Grönbladh, A., Nylander, E., & Hallberg, M. (2016). The neurobiology and addiction potential of anabolic androgenic steroids and the effects of growth hormone. *Brain Research Bulletin, 126,* 127–137. doi:10.1016/j.brainresbull.2016.05.003

Gros, D. F., Morland, L. A., et al. (2013). Delivery of evidence-based psychotherapy via video telehealth. *Journal of Psychopathology & Behavioral Assessment, 35*(4), 506–521. doi:10.1007/s10862-013-9363-4

Gross, J. J. (2013). Emotion regulation: Taking stock and moving forward. *Emotion, 13,* 359–365. doi:10.1037/a0032135

Gruberger, M., Levkovitz, Y., et al. (2015). I think therefore I am: Rest-related prefrontal cortex neural activity is involved in generating the sense of self. *Consciousness & Cognition, 33,* 414–421. doi:10.1016/j.concog.2015.02.008

Grubin, D., & Madsen, L. (2005). Lie detection and the polygraph: A historical review. *Journal of Forensic Psychiatry & Psychology, 16*(2), 357–369. doi:10.1080/1478994041 2331337353

Grusec, J. E., & Hastings, P. D. (Eds.). (2007). *Handbook of socialization: Theory and research.* The Guilford Press.

Grusec, J. E., Rudy, D. D., & Martini, T. S. (1997). The study of parenting cognitions: Some implications for understanding parenting behavior and children's internalization of values. In J. E. Grusec and L. Kuczynski (Eds.), *Parenting strategies and children's internalization of values: A handbook of theoretical and research perspectives.* Toronto: Wiley.

Guadagno, R. E., Rempala, D. M., Murphy, S., & Okdie, B. M. (2013). What makes a video go viral? An analysis of emotional contagion and Internet memes. *Computers in Human Behavior, 29*(6), 2312–2319. doi:10.1016/j.chb.2013.04.016

Guay, R. P. (2013). The relationship between leader fit and transformational leadership. *Journal of Managerial Psychology, 28*(1), 55–73. doi:10.1108/0268394131 1298869

Güçlütürk, Y., Jacobs, R., & van Lier, R. (2016). Liking versus complexity: Decomposing the inverted U-curve. *Frontiers in Human Neuroscience, 10,* Article 112.

Guéguen, N., & Lamy, L. (2012). Men's social status and attractiveness: Women's receptivity to men's date requests. *Swiss Journal of Psychology, 71*(3), 157–160. doi:10.1024/1421-0185/a000083

Guéguen, N., & Pascual, A. (2003). Status and people's tolerance towards an ill-mannered person: A field study. *Journal of Mundane Behavior, 4*(1), 29–36.

Guéguen, N., Jacob, C., & Meineri, S. (2011). Effects of the door-in-the-face technique on restaurant customers' behavior. *International Journal of Hospitality Management, 30*(3), 759–761. doi:10.1016/j.ijhm.2010.12.010

Guéguen, N., Martin, A., & Meineri, S. (2011). Similarity and social interaction: When similarity fosters implicit behavior toward a stranger. *Journal of Social Psychology, 151*(6), 671–673. doi:10.1080/00224545.2010.522627

Guéguen, N., Martin, A., et al. (2016). The foot-in-the-door technique, crime, and the responsive bystander: A field experiment. *Crime Prevention & Community Safety, 18*(1), 60–68. doi:10.1057/cpcs.2015.20

Guerin, S. A., Robbins, C. A., et al. (2012). Retrieval failure contributes to gist-based false recognition. *Journal of Memory & Language, 66*(1), 68–78. doi:10.1016/j. jml.2011.07.002

Gugliandolo, M. C., Costa, S., et al. (2015). Trait emotional intelligence and behavioral problems among adolescents: A cross-informant design. *Personality and Individual Differences, 74,* 16–21. doi:10.1016/j.paid.2014.09.032

Guidetti, M., Conner, M., et al. (2012). The transmission of attitudes towards food: Twofold specificity of similarities with parents and friends. *British Journal of Health Psychology, 17*(2), 346–361. doi:10.1111/j.2044-8287.2011.02041.x

Gujar, N., McDonald, S., et al. (2011). A role for REM sleep in recalibrating the sensitivity of the human brain to specific emotions. *Cerebral Cortex, 21*(1), 115–123. doi:10.1093/cercor/bhq064

Gündogan, N. Ü., Durmazlar, N., et al. (2005). Projected color slides as a method for mass screening test for color vision deficiency (a preliminary study). *International Journal of Neuroscience, 115*(8), 1105–1117. doi:10.1080/00207450590914365

Gupta, M. A. (2013). Review of somatic symptoms in post-traumatic stress disorder. *International Review of Psychiatry, 25*(1), 86–99. doi:10.3109/09540261.2012.736367

Gurlitt, J., Dummel, S., et al. (2012). Differently structured advance organizers lead to different initial schemata and learning outcomes. *Instructional Science, 40*(2), 351–369. doi:10.1007/s11251-011-9180-7

Gurung, R. (2014). *Health psychology: A cultural approach* (3rd ed.). Boston, MA: Cengage Learning.

Gurung, R. (2019). *Health psychology: Well-being in a diverse world* (4th ed.). Thousand Oaks: Sage.

Gustavson, C. R., & Garcia, J. (1974, May). Pulling a gag on the wily coyote. *Psychology Today,* pp. 68–72.

Güth, W., Levati, M. V., & von Wangenheim, G. (2010). Mutual interdependence versus repeated interaction: An experiment studying voluntary social exchange. *Rationality & Society, 22*(2), 131–158. doi:10.1177/1043463110366230

Guthrie, R. V. (2004). *Even the rat was white: A historical view of psychology* (2nd ed.). Boston, MA: Allyn & Bacon.

Haaken, J., & Reavey, P. (Eds.). (2010). *Memory matters: Contexts for understanding sexual abuse recollections.* New York: Routledge/Taylor & Francis.

Haas, B. W., Omura, K., et al. (2007). Is automatic emotion regulation associated with agreeableness? A perspective using a social neuroscience approach. *Psychological Science, 18*(2), 130–132.

Haber, R. N. (1970). How we remember what we see. *Scientific American, 222*(5), 104–112. doi:10.1038/scientificamerican0570-104

Haber, R. N., & Haber, L. (2000). Eidetic imagery. In A. E. Kazdin (Ed.), *Encyclopedia of psychology* (Vol. 3, pp. 147–149). Washington, DC: American Psychological Association.

Hackman, R. (2002). *Leading teams: Setting the stage for great performances.* Boston, MA: Harvard Business School Press.

Hafer, C. L., & Sutton, R. (2016). Belief in a just world. In C. Sabbagh & M. Schmitt (Eds.), *Handbook of social justice theory and research* (pp. 145–160). New York: Springer.

Haga, S. M., Kraft, P., & Corby, E.-K. (2010). Emotion regulation: Antecedents and well-being outcomes of cognitive reappraisal and expressive suppression in crosscultural samples. *Journal of Happiness Studies, 10*(3), 271–291. doi:10.1007/s10902-007-9080-3

Haghbin, M., McCaffrey, A., & Pychyl, T. A. (2012). The complexity of the relation between fear of failure and procrastination. *Journal of Rational-Emotive & Cognitive-Behavior Therapy, 30*(4), 249–263. doi:10.1007/s10942-012-0153-9

Haidt, J. (2007). The new synthesis in moral psychology. *Science, 316*(5827), 998–1002. doi:10.1126/science.1137651

Haidt, J. (2012). *The righteous mind: Why good people are divided by politics and religion.* New York: Pantheon.

Haidt, J. (2013). Moral psychology for the twenty-first century. *Journal of Moral Education, 42*(3), 281–297. doi:10.1080/03057240.2013.817327

Haier, R. J. (2017). *The neuroscience of intelligence.* New York: Cambridge.

Haier, R. J., Jung, R. E., et al. (2004). Structural brain variation and general intelligence. *NeuroImage, 23,* 425–433.

Hakun, J. G., Ruparel, K., et al. (2009). Towards clinical trials of lie detection with fMRI. *Social Neuroscience, 4*(6), 518–527. doi:10.1080/17470910802188370

Hald, G. M., Seaman, C., & Linz, D. (2014). Sexuality and pornography. In D. L. Tolman, L. M. Diamond, et al. (Eds.), *APA handbook of sexuality and psychology* (Vol. 2): *Contextual approaches* (pp. 3–35). Washington, DC: American Psychological Association. doi:10.1037/14194-001

Hales, D. (2015). *An invitation to health: Choosing to change* (16th ed.). Boston, MA: Cengage Learning.

Halim, M., Ruble, D. N., & Amodio, D. M. (2011). From pink frilly dresses to "one of the boys": A social-cognitive analysis of gender identity development and gender bias. *Social & Personality Psychology Compass, 5*(11), 933–949. doi:10.1111/j.1751-9004.2011.00399.x

Hall, D., & Buzwell, S. (2013). The problem of free-riding in group projects: Looking beyond social loafing as reason for non-contribution. *Active Learning in Higher Education, 14*(1), 37–49. doi:10.1177/1469787412467123

Hall, E. T. (1966). *The hidden dimension.* Garden City, NY: Doubleday.

Hall, N. C., Perry, R. P., et al. (2007). Attributional retraining and elaborative learning: Improving academic development through writing-based interventions. *Learning & Individual Differences, 17*(3), 280–290. doi:10.1016/j.lindif.2007.04.002

Hall, S. P. (2009). *Anger, rage, and relationships. An empathic approach to anger management.* New York: Routledge/Taylor & Francis.

Hallahan, D. P., Kauffman, J. M., & Pullen, P. C. (2015). *Exceptional learners* (13th ed.). Boston, MA: Pearson/Allyn & Bacon.

Halliday, G. (2010). Reflections on the meanings of dreams prompted by reading Stekel. *Dreaming, 20*(4), 219–226. doi:10.1037/a0020880

Halmai, Z., Dome, P., et al. (2013). Associations between depression severity and purinergic receptor p2rx7 gene polymorphisms. *Journal of Affective Disorders, 150*(1), 104–109. doi:10.1016/j.jad.2013.02.033

Halonen, J. S., & Santrock, J. W. (2013). *Your guide to college success: Strategies for achieving your goals* (7th ed.). Boston, MA: Cengage Learning.

Halpern-Felsher, B. L., Cornell, J., et al. (2005). Oral versus vaginal sex among adolescents: Perceptions, attitudes, and behavior. *Pediatrics, 115,* 845–851.

Halpern, D. F. (2003). *Thought and knowledge: An introduction to critical thinking* (4th ed.). Mahwah, NJ: Erlbaum.

Hamlin, J. (2013). Moral judgment and action in preverbal infants and toddlers: Evidence for an innate moral core. *Current Directions in Psychological Science, 22*(3), 186–193. doi:10.1177/0963721412470687

Hammond, D. C. (2008). Hypnosis as sole anesthesia for major surgeries: Historical & contemporary perspectives. *American Journal of Clinical Hypnosis, 51*(2), 101–121. doi:10.1080/00029157.2008.10401653

Hammond, D. C. (2013). A review of the history of hypnosis through the late 19th century. *American Journal of Clinical Hypnosis, 56*(2), 174–191.

Hampshire, A., Highfield, R. R., et al. (2012). Fractionating human intelligence. *Neuron, 76*(6), 1225–1237.

Hampson, S. E., Edmonds, G. W., et al. (2013). Childhood conscientiousness relates to objectively measured adult physical health four decades later. *Health Psychology, 32*(8), 925–928. doi:10.1037/a0031655

Hancock, J. (2011). *Brilliant memory training: Stop worrying about your memory and start using it—to the full!* Upper Saddle River, NJ: FT Press.

Haney, C., Banks, C., & Zimbardo, P. (1973). Interpersonal dynamics in a simulated prison. *International Journal of Criminology & Penology, 1,* 69–97. Downloaded April 3, 2017, from http://pdf.prisonexp.org/ijcp1973.pdf

Hans, V. P., Kaye, D. H., et al. (2011). Science in the jury box: Jurors' comprehension of mitochondrial DNA evidence. *Law & Human Behavior, 35*(1), 60–71.

Hansen, C. J., Stevens, L. C., & Coast, J. R. (2001). Exercise duration and mood state: How much is enough to feel better? *Health Psychology, 20*(4), 267–275. doi:10.1037/0278-6133.20.4.267

Hansen, K., Höfling, V., et al. (2013). Efficacy of psychological interventions aiming to reduce chronic nightmares: A meta-analysis. *Clinical Psychology Review, 33*(1), 146–155. doi:10.1016/j.cpr.2012.10.012

Hanton, S., Mellalieu, S. D., & Hall, R. (2004). Self-confidence and anxiety interpretation: A qualitative investigation. *Psychology of Sport & Exercise, 5*(4), 477–495. doi:10.1016/S1469-0292(03)00040-2

Hanyu, H., Sato, T., et al. (2010). The progression of cognitive deterioration and regional cerebral blood flow patterns in Alzheimer's disease: A longitudinal SPECT study. *Journal of the Neurological Sciences, 290*(1–2), 96–101. doi:10.1016/j.jns.2009.10.022

Happé, F., Cook, J. L., et al. (2017). The structure of social cognition: In(ter)dependence of sociocognitive processes. *Annual Review of Psychology, 68,* 243–267. doi:10.1146/annurev-psych-010416-044046

Haq, I. U., Foote, K. D., et al. (2010, March 10). Smile and laughter induction and intraoperative predictors of response to deep brain stimulation for obsessive-compulsive disorder. *NeuroImage,* [np].

Harb, G. C., Brownlow, J. A., et al. (2016). Posttraumatic nightmares and imagery rehearsal: The possible role of lucid dreaming. *Dreaming, 26*(3), 238–249. doi:10.1037/drm0000030

Harb, G. C., Thompson, R., et al. (2012). Combat-related PTSD nightmares and imagery rehearsal: Nightmare characteristics and relation to treatment outcome. *Journal of Traumatic Stress, 25*(5), 511–518. doi:10.1002/jts.21748

Hard, B. M. (2017, January) *Creating lectures that tell a story.* Paper presented at the National Institute on the Teaching of Psychology, St. Pete Beach, FL.

Hardaway, C. A., & Gregory, K. B. (2005). Fatigue and sleep debt in an operational navy squadron. *International Journal of Aviation Psychology, 15*(2), 157–171. doi:10.1207/s15327108ijap1502_3

Harden, K. P., Quinn, P. D., & Tucker-Drob, E. M. (2012). Genetically influenced change in sensation seeking drives the rise of delinquent behavior during adolescence. *Developmental Science, 15*(1), 150–163. doi:10.1111/j.1467-7687.2011.01115.x

Hardin, G. (1968). The tragedy of the commons. *Science, 162,* 1243–1248.

Hardin, M., & Greer, J. D. (2009). The influence of gender-role socialization, media use and sports participation on perceptions of gender-appropriate sports. *Journal of Sport Behavior, 32*(2), 207–226.

Harding, D. J., Fox, C., et al. (2002). Studying rare events through qualitative case studies: Lessons from a study of rampage school shootings. *Sociological Methods & Research, 31*(2), 174–217. doi:10.1177/0049124102031002003

Hare, R. D. (2006). Psychopathy: A clinical and forensic overview. *Psychiatric Clinics of North America, 29*(3), 709–724. doi:10.1016/j.psc.2006.04.007

Harel, A., Gilaie-Dotan, S., et al. (2010). Top-down engagement modulates the neural expressions of visual expertise. *Cerebral Cortex, 20*(10), 2304–2318. doi:10.1093/cercor/bhp316

Harley, T. A. (2014). *The psychology of language: From data to theory* (4th ed.). Hove, UK: Psychology Press.

Harlow, H. F., & Harlow, M. K. (1962). Social deprivation in monkeys. *Scientific American, 207,* 136–146.

Harlow, J. M. (1868). Recovery from the passage of an iron bar through the head. *Publications of the Massachusetts Medical Society, 2,* 327–347.

Harmison, R. J. (2011). Peak performance in sport: Identifying ideal performance states and developing athletes' psychological skills. *Sport, Exercise, & Performance Psychology, 1*(S), 3–18. doi:10.1037/2157-3905.1.S.3

Harms, P. L., & Roebuck, D. B. (2010). Teaching the art and craft of giving and receiving feedback. *Business Communication Quarterly, 73,* 413–431. doi:10.1177/1080569910385565

Harper, J., Lima, G., et al. (2018). The fluidity of gender and implications for the biology of inclusion for transgender and intersex athletes. *Current Sports Medicine Reports, 17*(12), 467–472. doi:10.1249/JSR.0000000000000543

Harrell, J. P., & Medford, E. (2012). History, prejudice, and the study of social inequities. *Behavioral & Brain Sciences, 35*(6), 433–434. doi:10.1017/S0140525X12001203

Harrington, R. (2013). *Stress, health and well-being: Thriving in the 21st century.* Boston, MA: Cengage Learning.

Harris, C. (2004). The evolution of jealousy. *American Scientist, 92,* 62–71.

Harris, J. C. (2010). *Intellectual disability: A guide for families and professionals.* New York: Oxford University Press.

Harris, J., Hirsh-Pasek, K., & Newcombe, N. S. (2013). Understanding spatial transformations: Similarities and differences between mental rotation and mental folding. *Cognitive Processing, 14*(2), 105–115. doi:10.1007/s10339-013-0544-6

Harris, L. R., & Jenkin, M. R. M. (Eds.). (2011). *Vision in 3D environments.* New York: Cambridge University Press.

Hart, D., & Carlo, G. (2005). Moral development in adolescence. *Journal of Research on Adolescence, 15*(3), 223–233. doi:10.1111/j.1532-7795.2005.00094.x

Hart, J. E., Mourot, J. E., & Aros, M. (2012). Children of same-sex parents: In and out of the closet. *Educational Studies, 38*(3), 277–281. doi:10.1080/03055698.2011 598677

Hartgens, F., & Kuipers, H. (2004). Effects of androgenic-anabolic steroids in athletes. *Sports Medicine, 34*(8), 513–554.

Hartley, S. (2012). *Peak performance every time.* New York: Routledge/Taylor & Francis.

Hartmann, A. S., Greenberg, J. L., & Wilhelm, S. (2013). The relationship between anorexia nervosa and body dysmorphic disorder. *Clinical Psychology Review, 33,* 675–685. doi:10.1016/j.cpr.2013.04.002

Hartmann, E. (2011). *The nature and functions of dreaming.* New York: Oxford University Press.

Hartmann, P., Reuter, M., & Nyborg, H. (2006). The relationship between date of birth and individual differences in personality and general intelligence: A large-scale study. *Personality & Individual Differences, 40*(7), 1349–1362. doi:10.1016/j.paid.2005.11.017

Hartung, C. M., Lefler, E. K., et al. (2010). Halo effects in ratings of ADHD and ODD: Identification of susceptible symptoms. *Journal of Psychopathology & Behavioral Assessment, 32*(1), 128–137. doi:10.1007/s10862-009-9135-3

Hashimoto, I., Suzuki, A., et al. (2004). Is there training-dependent reorganization of digit representations in area 3b of string players? *Clinical Neurophysiology, 115*(2), 435–447. doi:10.1016/S1388-2457(03)00340-7

Hasin, D. S., Kerridge, B. T., et al. (2016). Prevalence and correlates of DSM-5 cannabis use disorder, 2012–2013: Findings from the National Epidemiologic Survey on Alcohol and Related Conditions–III. *American Journal of Psychiatry, 173*(6), 588–599. doi:10.1176/appi.ajp.2015.15070907

Haskard-Zolnierek, K. B., Miller, T. A., & DiMatteo, M. R. (2017). Promoting treatment adherence. In D. W. Kissane et al. (Eds.), *Oxford textbook of communication in oncology and palliative care* (pp. 239–248). Oxford, UK: Oxford University Press.

Haslam, S. A., & Reicher, S. (2006). Debating the psychology of tyranny: Fundamental issues of theory, perspective and science. *British Journal of Social Psychology, 45,* 55–63.

Haslam, S. A., Reicher, S. D., et al. (2016). Questioning authority: New perspectives on Milgram's 'obedience' research and its implications for intergroup relations. *Current Opinion in Psychology, 11,* 6–9. doi:10.1016/j.copsyc.2016.03.007

Hatch, L. (2011). The American Psychological Association Task Force on the Sexualization of Girls: A review, update and commentary. *Sexual Addiction & Compulsivity, 18*(4), 195–211. doi:10.1080/10720162.2011.613326

Hattie, J. (2017). *250+ influences on student achievement.* Downloaded from https://www.visiblelearningplus.com/content/research-john-hattie

Hattie, J., & Donoghue, G. M. (2016). Learning strategies: A synthesis and conceptual model. *NPJ Science of Learning, 1,* 16013. doi:10.1038/npjscilearn.2016.13

Hauck, P. A. (2011). Assertion strategies. In H. G. Rosenthal (Ed.), *Favorite counseling and therapy techniques* (2nd ed., pp. 155–157). New York: Routledge.

Hausenblas, H. A., Campbell, A., et al. (2013). Media effects of experimental presentation of the ideal physique on eating disorder symptoms: A meta-analysis of laboratory studies. *Clinical Psychology Review, 33*(1), 168–181. doi:10.1016/j.cpr.2012.10.011

Hawe, P. (2015). Lessons from complex interventions to improve health. *Annual Review of Public Health, 36,* 307–323. doi:10.1146/annurevpublhealth-031912-114421

Hawks, J., Wang, E. T., et al. (2007). Recent acceleration of human adaptive evolution. *Proceedings of the National Academy of Sciences, 104*(52), 20753–20758.

Haycraft, E., & Blissett, J. (2010). Eating disorder symptoms and parenting styles. *Appetite, 54*(1), 221–224. doi:10.1016/j.appet.2009.11.009

Hayes, M. R. (2012). Neuronal and intracellular signaling pathways mediating GLP-1 energy balance and glycemic effects. *Physiology & Behavior, 106*(3), 413–416. doi:10.1016/j.physbeh.2012.02.017

Hayes, M. R., De Jonghe, B. C., & Kanoski, S. (2010). Role of the glucagon-like-peptide-1 receptor in the control of energy balance. *Physiology & Behavior, 100*(5), 503–510. doi:10.1016/j.physbeh.2010.02.029

Hayes, R. M., Abbott, R. L., et al. (2016). It's her fault: Student acceptance of rape myths on two college campuses. *Violence Against Women, 22*(13), 1540–1555. doi:10.1177/1077801216 630147

Hayes, S. C., Strosahl, K. D., & Wilson, K. G. (2012). *Acceptance and commitment therapy: The process and practice of mindful change* (2nd ed.). New York: Guilford.

Hayne, H., & Rovee-Collier, C. (1995). The organization of reactivated memory in infancy. *Child Development, 66*(3), 893–906. doi:10.2307/1131957

Hays, N. A. (2013). Fear and loving in social hierarchy: Sex differences in preferences for power versus status. *Journal of Experimental Social*

Psychology, 49(6), 1130–1136. doi:10.1016/j.jesp.2013.08.007

Hayward, L. C., & Coles, M. E. (2009). Elucidating the relation of hoarding to obsessive compulsive disorder and impulse control disorders. *Journal of Psychopathology & Behavioral Assessment, 31*(3), 220–227. doi:10.1007/s10862-008-9106-0

Head, L. S., & Gross, A. M. (2009). Systematic desensitization. In W. T. O'Donohue & J. E. Fisher (Eds.), *General principles and empirically supported techniques of cognitive behavior therapy* (pp. 640–647). New York: Wiley.

Healey, C., Morriss, R., et al. (2013). Self-harm in postpartum depression and referrals to a perinatal mental health team: An audit study. *Archives of Women's Mental Health, 16*(3), 237–245. doi:10.1007/s00737-013-0335-1

Hearn, S., Saulnier, G., et al. (2012). Between integrity and despair: Toward construct validation of Erikson's eighth stage. *Journal of Adult Development, 19*(1), 1–20.

Heath, R. G. (1963). Electrical self-stimulation of the brain in man. *American Journal of Psychiatry, 120,* 571–577.

Hebb, D. O. (1949). *The organization of behavior*. New York: Wiley & Sons.

Hebblethwaite, S., & Norris, J. (2011). Expressions of generativity through family leisure: Experiences of grandparents and adult grandchildren. *Family Relations, 60*(1), 121–133. doi:10.1111/j.1741-3729.2010.00637.x

Hebl, M. R., King, E. G., & Lin, J. (2004). The swimsuit becomes us all: Ethnicity, gender, and vulnerability to self-objectification. *Personality & Social Psychology Bulletin, 30,* 1322–1331.

Hecht, J. (2007). *The happiness myth: Why what we think is right is wrong*. New York: HarperCollins.

Hedden, T., Ketay, S., et al. (2008). Cultural influences on neural substrates of attentional control. *Psychological Science, 19*(1), 12–17. doi:10.1111/j.1467-9280.2008.02038.x

Hehman, E., Flake, J. K., & Calanchini, J. (2018). Disproportionate use of lethal force in policing is associated with regional racial biases of residents. *Social Psychological and Personality Science, 9*(4), 393–401. doi:10.1177/1948550617711229

Heidemeier, H., & Göritz, A. S. (2016). The instrumental role of personality traits: Using mixture structural equation modeling to investigate individual differences in the relationships between the Big Five traits and life satisfaction. *Journal of Happiness Studies, 17*(6), 2595–2612. doi:10.1007/s10902-015-9708-7

Heimann, M., & Meltzoff, A. N. (1996, March). Deferred imitation in 9- and 14-month-old infants: A longitudinal study of a Swedish sample. *British Journal of Developmental Psychology, 14,* 55–64. doi:10.1111/j.2044-835X.1996.tb00693.x

Hein, L. C., & Berger, K. C. (2012). Gender dysphoria in children: Let's think this through. *Journal of Child & Adolescent Psychiatric Nursing, 25*(4), 237–240. doi:10.1111/jcap.12014

Heinrichs, R. W. (2001). *In search of madness: Schizophrenia and neuroscience*. New York: Oxford University Press.

Heisel, M. J., Flett, G. L., & Hewitt, P. L. (2003). Social hopelessness and college student suicide ideation. *Archives of Suicide Research, 7*(3), 221–235. doi:10.1080/13811110301557

Helenius, D., Munk-Jørgensen, P., & Steinhausen, H. (2012). Family load estimates of schizophrenia and associated risk factors in a nationwide population study of former child and adolescent patients up to forty years of age. *Schizophrenia Research, 139*(1–3), 183–188. doi:10.1016/j.schres.2012.05.014

Helgeson, V. S. (2012). *The psychology of gender* (4th ed.). Englewood Cliffs, NJ: Prentice Hall.

Hélie, S., & Sun, R. (2010). Incubation, insight, and creative problem solving: A unified theory and a connectionist model. *Psychological Review, 117*(3), 994–1024. doi:10.1037/a0019532

Helle, L., & Säljö, R. (2012). Collaborating with digital tools and peers in medical education: Cases and simulations as interventions in learning. *Instructional Science, 40*(5), 737–744. doi:10.1007/s11251-012-9216-7

Helton, W. S. (2007). Skill in expert dogs. *Journal of Experimental Psychology: Applied, 13*(3), 171–178. doi:10.1037/1076-898X.13.3.171

Helton, W. S. (2009). Exceptional running skill in dogs requires extensive experience. *Journal of General Psychology, 136*(3), 323–332. doi:10.3200/GENP.136.3.323-336

Henderson, T. L., Roberto, K. A., & Kamo, Y. (2010). Older adults' responses to Hurricane Katrina: Daily hassles and coping strategies. *Journal of Applied Gerontology, 29*(1), 48–69. doi:10.1177/0733464809334287

Hennenlotter, A., Dresel, C., et al. (2009). The link between facial feedback and neural activity within central circuitries of emotion: New insights from botulinum toxin-induced denervation of frown muscles. *Cerebral Cortex, 19*(3), 537–542. doi:10.1093/cercor/bhn104

Hennessey, B. A., & Amabile, T. M. (2010). Creativity. *Annual Review of Psychology, 61,* 569–598. doi:10.1146/annurev.psych.093008.100416

Henningsen, D., & Henningsen, M. (2013). Generating ideas about the uses of brainstorming: Reconsidering the losses and gains of brainstorming groups relative to nominal groups. *Southern Communication Journal, 78*(1), 42–55. doi:10.1080/1041794X.2012.717684

Hennink-Kaminski, H., & Reichert, T. (2011). Using sexual appeals in advertising to sell cosmetic surgery: A content analysis from 1986 to 2007. *Sexuality & Culture, 15*(1), 41–55. doi:10.1007/s12119-010-9081-y

Henrich, J., Heine, S. J., & Norenzayan, A. (2010). The weirdest people in the world? *Behavioral & Brain Sciences, 33,* 61–135. doi:10.1017/S0140525X0999152X

Henry, J. F., & Sherwin, B. B. (2012). Hormones and cognitive functioning during late pregnancy and postpartum: A longitudinal study. *Behavioral Neuroscience, 126*(1), 73–85. doi:10.1037/a0025540

Henry, P. K., Murnane, K. S., et al. (2010). Acute brain metabolic effects of cocaine in rhesus monkeys with a history of cocaine use. *Brain Imaging & Behavior, 4*(3–4), 212–219. doi:10.1007/s11682-010-9100-5

Henry, S. G., Penner, L. A., et al. (2016, December 19). Associations between thin slice ratings of affect and rapport and perceived patient-centeredness in primary care: Comparison of audio and video recordings. *Patient Education & Counseling,* n.p. doi:10.1016/j.pec.2016.12.020

Hensley, B. J. (2016). *An EMDR therapy primer: From practicum to practice* (2nd ed.). New York: Springer.

Hensley, L. C. (2016). The draws and drawbacks of college students' active procrastination. *Journal of College Student Development, 57*(4), 465–471. doi:10.1353/csd.2016.0045

Hepper, P. G., Dornan, J. C., & Lynch, C. (2012). Fetal brain function in response to maternal alcohol consumption: Early evidence of damage. *Alcoholism: Clinical & Experimental Research, 36*(12), 2168–2175. doi:10.1111/j.1530-0277.2012.01832.x

Herbenick, D., Reece, M., et al. (2010a). Sexual behavior in the United States: Results from a national probability sample of men and women ages 14–94. *Journal of Sexual Medicine, 7*(Suppl. 5), 255–265. doi:10.1111/j.1743-6109.2010.02012.x.

Herbenick, D., Reece, M., et al. (2010b). An event-level analysis of the sexual characteristics and composition among adults ages 18–59: Results from a national probability sample in the United States. *Journal of Sexual Medicine, 7*(Suppl. 5), 346–361. doi:10.1111/j.1743-6109.2010.02020.x

Herculano-Houzel, S. (2012). The remarkable, yet not extraordinary, human brain as a scaled-up primate brain and its associated cost. *Proceedings of the National Academy of Sciences, 109*(Suppl. 1), 10661–10668. doi:10.1073/pnas.1201895109

Hergenhahn, B. R., & Henley, T. (2014). *An introduction to the history of psychology* (7th ed.). Boston, MA: Cengage Learning.

Heriot, S. A., & Pritchard, M. (2004). "Reciprocal inhibition as the main basis of psychotherapeutic effects" by Joseph Wolpe (1954). *Clinical Child Psychology & Psychiatry, 9*(2), 297–307. doi:10.1177/1359104504041928

Hermanto, N., Moreno, S., & Bialystok, E. (2012). Linguistic and metalinguistic outcomes of intense immersion education: How bilingual? *International Journal of Bilingual Education & Bilingualism, 15*(2), 131–145. doi:10.1080/13670050.2011.652591

Hermes, E. D. A., & Rosenheck, R. A. (2016). Implementing computer-based psychotherapy among veterans in outpatient treatment for substance use disorders. *Psychiatric Services, 67*(2), 176–183. doi:10.1176/appi.ps.201400532

Herodotou, C. (2018). Mobile games and science learning: A comparative study of 4 and 5 years olds playing the game Angry Birds. *British Journal of Educational Technology, 49*(1), 6–16. doi:10.1111/bjet.12546

Herren, C., In-Albon, T., & Schneider, S. (2013). Beliefs regarding child anxiety and parenting competence in parents of children with separation anxiety disorder. *Journal of Behavior Therapy & Experimental Psychiatry, 44*(1), 53–60. doi:10.1016/j.jbtep.2012.07.005

Hertenstein, M. J., Holmes, R., McCullough, M., & Keltner, D. (2009). The communication of emotion via touch. *Emotion, 9,* 566–573. doi:10.1037/a0016108

Hettich, P. I., & Landrum, R. E. (2014). *Your undergraduate degree in psychology: From college to career*. Thousand Oaks: Sage.

Hewit, J. K., Cronin, J. B., & Hume, P. A. (2012). Understanding change of direction performance: A technical analysis of a 180° ground-based turn and sprint task. *International Journal of Sports Science & Coaching, 7*(3), 493–501.

Heyns, M. M., & Kerr, M. D. (2018). Generational differences in workplace motivation. *SA Journal of Human Resource Management, 16*(1), 1–10. doi:10.4102/sajhrm.v16i0.967

Hickok, G. (2014). *The myth of mirror neurons: The real science of*

communication and cognition. New York: Norton.

Hyde, T. S., & Jenkins, J. J. (1973). Recall for words as a function of semantic, graphic, and syntactic orienting tasks. *Journal of Verbal Learning and Verbal Behavior, 12*(5), 471–480. doi:10.1016/S0022-5371(73)80027-1

Higbee, K. L., Clawson, C., et al. (1990). Using the link mnemonic to remember errands. *Psychological Record, 40*(3), 429–436.

Higham, P. A., & Gerrard, C. (2005). Not all errors are created equal: Metacognition and changing answers on multiple-choice tests. Canadian *Journal of Experimental Psychology, 59*(1), 28–34. doi:10.1037/h0087457

Hilbig, B. E., Zettler, I., Leist, F., & Heydasch, T. (2013). It takes two: Honesty–Humility and agreeableness differentially predict active versus reactive cooperation. *Personality and Individual Differences, 54*(5), 598–603. doi:10.1016/j.paid.2012.11.008

Hilgard, E. R. (1977). *Divided consciousness* (pp. 32–51). New York: Wiley.

Hilgard, E. R. (1994). Neodissociation theory. In S. J. Lynn & J. W. Rhue (Eds.), *Dissociation: Clinical, theoretical and research perspectives* (pp. 32–51). New York: Guilford.

Hilgard, J., Engelhardt, C. R., Rouder, J. N., Segert, I. L., & Bartholow, B. D. (2019). Null effects of game violence, game difficulty, and 2D:4D digit ratio on aggressive behavior. *Psychological Science, 30,* 606–616. doi:10.1177/0956797619829688

Hill, C., & Kearl, H. (2011). *Crossing the line: Sexual harassment at school.* Washington, DC: AAUW.

Hinrichs, K. T. (2007). Follower propensity to commit crimes of obedience: The role of leadership beliefs. *Journal of Leadership & Organizational Studies, 14*(1), 69–76. doi:10.1177/1071791907304225

Hintzman, D. L. (2005). Memory strength and recency judgments. *Psychonomic Bulletin & Review, 12*(5), 858–864. doi:10.3758/BF03196777

Hinzman, L., & Kelly, S. D. (2013). Effects of emotional body language on rapid out-group judgments. *Journal of Experimental Social Psychology, 49*(1), 152–155. doi:10.1016/j.jesp.2012.07.010

Hipp, J. R., Butts, C. T., et al. (2013). Extrapolative simulation of neighborhood networks based on population spatial distribution: Do they predict crime? *Social Networks, 35*(4), 614–625. doi:10.1016/j.socnet.2013.07.002

Hirsch, E. D. (2016). *Why knowledge matters: Rescuing our children from failed educational theories.* Cambridge, MA: Harvard Education Press.

Hirst, A. (2001). *Links between volunteering and employability.* London, England: Department for Education and Skills.

Hirstein, W. (2005). *Brain fiction: Self-deception and the riddle of confabulation.* Cambridge, MA: MIT Press.

Hobson, J. A. (2000). Dreams: Physiology. In A. Kazdin (Ed.), *Encyclopedia of psychology* (Vol. 3, pp. 78–81). Washington, DC: American Psychological Association.

Hobson, J. A. (2005). Sleep is of the brain, by the brain and for the brain. *Nature, 437*(7063), 1254–1256. doi:10.1038/nature04283

Hobson, J. A. (2009). The neurobiology of consciousness: Lucid dreaming wakes up. *International Journal of Dream Research, 2*(2), 41–44.

Hobson, J. A., & Schredl, M. (2011). The continuity and discontinuity between waking and dreaming: A dialogue between Michael Schredl and Allan Hobson concerning the adequacy and completeness of these notions. *International Journal of Dream Research, 4*(1), 3–7.

Hodges, N., & Williams, M. (Eds.). (2012). *Skill acquisition in sport: Research, theory and practice.* New York: Psychology Press.

Hodgins, H. S., & Adair, K. C. (2010). Attentional processes and meditation. *Consciousness & Cognition, 19*(4), 872–878. doi:10.1016/j.concog.2010.04.002

Hodson, G. (2011). Do ideologically intolerant people benefit from intergroup contact? *Current Directions in Psychological Science, 20*(3), 154–159. doi:10.1177/0963721411409025

Hodson, G., & Hewstone, M. (Eds.). (2013). *Advances in intergroup contact.* New York: Psychology Press.

Hodson, G., Hogg, S. M., & MacInnis, C. C. (2009). The role of "dark personalities" (narcissism, Machiavellianism, psychopathy), Big Five personality factors, and ideology in explaining prejudice. *Journal of Research in Personality, 43*(4), 686–690. doi:10.1016/j.jrp.2009.02.005

Hodson, G., MacInnis, C. C., & et al. (2017). Bowing and kicking: Rediscovering the fundamental link between generalized authoritarianism and generalized prejudice. *Personality & Individual Differences, 104,* 243–251. doi:10.1016/j.paid.2016.08.018

Hodson, R., & Sullivan, T. A. (2012). *The social organization of work* (5th ed.). Boston, MA: Cengage Learning.

Hoeft, F., Gabrieli, J. E., et al. (2012). Functional brain basis of hypnotizability. *JAMA Psychiatry, 69*(10), 1064–1072. doi:10.1001/archgenpsychiatry.2011.2190

Hoenig, K., Müller, C., et al. (2011). Neuroplasticity of semantic representations for musical instruments in professional musicians. *Neuroimage, 56*(3), 1714– 1725. doi:10.1016/j.neuroimage.2011.02.065

Hoerger, M., Chapman, B. P., et al. (2012). Emotional intelligence: A theoretical framework for individual differences in affective forecasting. *Emotion, 12*(4), 716–725. doi:10.1037/a0026724.

Hoff, E. (2014). *Language development* (5th ed.). Boston, MA: Cengage Learning.

Hoff, E., & Tian, C. (2005). Socioeconomic status and cultural influences on language. *Journal of Communication Disorders, 38*(4), 271–278. doi:10.1016/j.jcomdis.2005.02.003

Hoffart, A. (2005). Interpersonal therapy for social phobia: Theoretical model and review of the evidence. In M. E. Abelian (Ed.), *Focus on psychotherapy research* (pp. 121–137). Hauppauge, NY: Nova Science Publishers.

Hoffman, E. (2008). Abraham Maslow: A biographer's reflections. *Journal of Humanistic Psychology, 48*(4), 439–443. doi:10.1177/0022167808320534

Hofmann, W., Gawronski, B., et al. (2005). A meta-analysis on the correlation between the implicit association test and explicit self-report measures. *Personality & Social Psychology Bulletin, 31*(10), 1369–1385.

Hogan, E. H., Hornick, B. A., & Bouchoux, A. (2002). Focus on communications: Communicating the message: Clarifying the controversies about caffeine. *Nutrition Today, 37,* 28–35.

Hohwy, J., & Fox, E. (2012). Preserved aspects of consciousness in disorders of consciousness: A review and conceptual analysis. *Journal of Consciousness Studies, 19*(3–4), 87–120.

Holbrook, T., Moore, C., & Zoss, M. (2010). Equitable intent: Reflections on universal design in education as an ethic of care. *Reflective Practice, 11*(5), 681–692.

Holden, C. (1980, November). Twins reunited. *Science 80,* 55–59.

Holdsworth, E., Bowen, E., et al. (2014). Client engagement in psychotherapeutic treatment and associations with client characteristics, therapist characteristics, and treatment factors. *Clinical Psychology Review, 34*(5), 428–450. doi:10.1016/j.cpr.2014.06.004

Holland, J. L. (1997). *Making vocational choices.* Odessa, FL: Psychological Assessment Resources.

Holliday, R. E., Humphries, J. E., et al. (2012). Reducing misinformation effects in older adults with cognitive interview mnemonics. *Psychology and Aging, 27*(4), 1191–1203. doi:10.1037/a002203

Hollins, M. (2010). Somesthetic senses. *Annual Review of Psychology, 61,* 243–271. doi:10.1146/annurev.psych.093008.100419

Holloway, T., Moreno, J. L., et al. (2013). Prenatal stress induces schizophrenia-like alterations of serotonin 2A and metabotropic glutamate 2 receptors in the adult offspring: Role of maternal immune system. *Journal of Neuroscience, 33*(3), 1088–1098. doi:10.1523/JNEUROSCI.2331-12.2013

Holly, J. E., & Harmon, S. M. (2012). Sensory conflict compared in microgravity, artificial gravity, motion sickness, and vestibular disorders. *Journal of Vestibular Research: Equilibrium & Orientation, 22*(2–3), 81–94.

Holman, A., & Sillars, A. (2012). Talk about "hooking up": The influence of college student social networks on nonrelationship sex. *Health Communication, 27*(2), 205–216. doi:10.1080/10410236.2011.575540

Holman, E. A., Silver, R. C., et al. (2008). Terrorism, acute stress, and cardiovascular health: A 3-year national study following the September 11th attacks. *Archives of General Psychiatry, 65*(1), 73–80. doi:10.1001/archgenpsychiatry.2007.6

Holmes, E. K., & Huston, A. C. (2010). Understanding positive father–child interaction: Children's, father's, and mother's contributions. *Fathering, 8*(2), 203–225. doi:10.3149/fth.1802.203

Holmes, M. (2002). Rethinking the meaning and management of intersexuality. *Sexualities, 5*(2), 159–180. doi:10.1177/1363460702005002002

Holmes, T. H., & Rahe, R. H. (1967). The social readjustment rating scale. *Journal of Psychosomatic Research, 11*(2), 213–218. doi:10.1016/0022-3999(67)90010-4

Holz, J., Piosczyk, H., et al. (2012). EEG sigma and slow-wave activity during NREM sleep correlate with overnight declarative and procedural memory consolidation. *Journal of Sleep Research, 21*(6), 612–619. doi:10.1111/j.1365-2869.2012.01017.x

Hölzel, B. K., Lazar, S. W., et al. (2011). How does mindfulness meditation work? Proposing mechanisms of action from a conceptual and neural perspective. *Perspectives on Psychological Science, 6*(6), 537–559. doi:10.1177/1745691611419671

Homan, A. C., Buengeler, C., et al. (2015). The interplay of diversity training and diversity beliefs on team creativity in nationality diverse teams. *Journal of Applied Psychology, 100*(5), 1456–1467. doi:10.1037/apl000001

Hooper, N., Erdogan, A., et al. (2015). Perspective taking reduces the fundamental attribution error. *Journal of Contextual Behavioral Science, 4*(2), 69–72. doi:10.1016/j.jcbs.2015.02.002

Hooyman, N., & Kiyak, H. A. (2011). *Social gerontology: A multidisciplinary perspective* (9th ed.). Boston, MA: Pearson/Allyn & Bacon.

Hopton, A., Thomas, K., & MacPherson, H. (2013). The acceptability of acupuncture for low back pain: A qualitative study of patient's experiences nested within a randomised controlled trial. *PLoS ONE, 8*(2). doi:10.1371/journal.pone.0056806

Hopwood, C. J., Donnellan, M. B., et al. (2011). Genetic and environmental influences on personality trait stability and growth during the transition to adulthood: A three-wave longitudinal study. *Journal of Personality & Social Psychology, 100*(3), 545–556. doi:10.1037/a0022409

Horne, M. R., Gilroy, K. E., et al. (2012). Latent spatial learning in an environment with a distinctive shape. *Journal of Experimental Psychology: Animal Behavior Processes, 38*(2), 139–147. doi:10.1037/a0027288

Horsley, R. R., Osborne, M., et al. (2012). High-frequency gamblers show increased resistance to extinction following partial reinforcement. *Behavioural Brain Research, 229*(2), 438–442. doi:10.1016/j. bbr.2012 .01.024

Hortensius, R., & de Gelder, B. (2014). The neural basis of the bystander effect: The influence of group size on neural activity when witnessing an emergency. *NeuroImage, 93*, 53–58. doi:10.1016/j.neuroimage.2014.02.025

Hosch, H. M., & Cooper, D. S. (1982). Victimization as a determinant of eyewitness accuracy. *Journal of Applied Psychology, 67*, 649–652. doi:10.1037/0021-9010.67.5.649

Hosemans, D. (2014, January 4). Meditation: A process of cultivating enhanced well-being. *Mindfulness*, n.p. doi:10.1007/s12671-013-0266-y

Hough, L. M., & Connelly, B. S. (2013). Personality measurement and use in industrial and organizational psychology. In K. F. Geisinger, B. A. Bracken, et al. (Eds.), *APA handbook of testing and assessment in psychology* (Vol. 1): *Test theory and testing and assessment in industrial and organizational psychology* (pp. 501–531). Washington, DC: American Psychological Association. doi:10.1037/14047-028

Houghton, D. P. (2008). Invading and occupying Iraq: Some insights from political psychology. *Peace & Conflict: Journal of Peace Psychology, 14*(2), 169–192. doi:10.1080/10781910802017297

Howard, I. P. (2012). *Perceiving in depth* (Vol. 3): *Other mechanisms of depth perception*. New York: Oxford University Press. doi:10.1093/acprof:oso/9780199764167.001.0001

Howard, K. I., Krause, M. S., et al. (2001). Syzygy, science, and psychotherapy: The Consumer Reports study. *Journal of Clinical Psychology, 57*(7), 865–874. doi:10.1002/jclp.1055

Howe, L. C., & Krosnick, J. A. (2017). Attitude strength. *Annual Review of Psychology, 68*, 327–351. doi:10.1146/annurev-psych-122414-033600

Howes, O., McCutcheon, R., et al. (2015). Glutamate and dopamine in schizophrenia: An update for the 21st century. *Journal of Psychopharmacology, 29*(2), 97–115.doi:10.1177/0269881114563634

Howren, M. B., Suls, J., & Martin, R. (2009). Depressive symptomatology, rather than neuroticism, predicts inflated physical symptom reports. *Psychosomatic Medicine, 71*(9), 951–957. doi: 10.1097/PSY.0b013e3181b9b2d7

Hsieh, P., Colas, J. T., & Kanwisher, N. (2011). Pop-out without awareness: Unseen feature singletons capture attention only when top-down attention is available. *Psychological Science, 22*(9), 1220–1226. doi:10.1177/0956797611419302

Hu, Y., & Ericsson, K. A. (2012). Memorization and recall of very long lists accounted for within the Long-Term Working Memory framework. *Cognitive Psychology, 64*(4), 235–266. doi:10.1016/j.cogpsych.2012.01.001

Hu, Y., Ericsson, K. A., et al. (2009). Superior self-paced memorization of digits in spite of a normal digit span: The structure of a memorist's skill. *Journal of Experimental Psychology: Learning, Memory, & Cognition, 35*(6), 1426–1442. doi:10.1037/a0017395

Huang, M.-H., & Rust, R. T. (2011). Sustainability and consumption. *Journal of the Academy of Marketing Science, 39*(1), 40–54.

Hubble, M.A., Duncan, B. L., & Miller, S. D. (Eds.). (1999). *The heart and soul of change: What works in therapy*. Washington, DC: American Psychological Association.

Hubel, D. H., & Wiesel, W. N. (2005). *Brain & visual perception: The story of a 25-year collaboration*. New York: Oxford University Press.

Hübner, R., & Volberg, G. (2005). The integration of object levels and their content: A theory of global/local processing and related hemispheric differences. *Journal of Experimental Psychology: Human Perception & Performance, 31*(3), 520–541. doi:10.1037/0096-1523.31.3.520

Hudson, C. G. (2016). A model of deinstitutionalization of psychiatric care across 161 nations: 2001–2014. *International Journal of Mental Health, 45*(2), 135–153. doi:10.1080/00207411.2016.1167489

Hudson, N. W., & Fraley, R. C. (2015). Volitional personality trait change: Can people choose to change their personality traits? *Journal of Personality & Social Psychology, 109*(3), 490–507. doi:10.1037/pspp0000021

Huebner, R. B., & Kantor, L. (2011). Advances in alcoholism treatment. *Alcohol Research & Health, 33*(4), 295–299.

Hughes, A. (2008). The use of urban legends to improve critical thinking. In L. T. Benjamin, Jr. (Ed.), *Favorite activities for the teaching of psychology*. Washington, DC: American Psychological Association.

Hughes, D. F. (2013). Charles Bonnet syndrome: A literature review into diagnostic criteria, treatment, and implications for nursing practice. *Journal of Psychiatric & Mental Health Nursing, 20*(2), 169–175. doi:10.1111/j.1365-2850.2012.01904.x

Hughes, J. R., & Callas, P. W. (2011). Is delaying a quit attempt associated with less success? *Nicotine & Tobacco Research, 13*(12), 1228–1232. doi:10.1093/ntr/ntr207

Hughes, M., Brymer, M., et al. (2011). Posttraumatic stress among students after the shootings at Virginia Tech. *Psychological Trauma, 3*(4), 403–411. doi:10.1037/a0024565

Huguet, P., Dumas, F., et al. (2001). Social comparison choices in the classroom: Further evidence for students' upward comparison tendency and its beneficial impact on performance. *European Journal of Social Psychology, 31*(5), 557–578.

Human Connectome Project. (2013). Retrieved May 1, 2017, from www .humanconnectomeproject.org

Human, L. J., Biesanz, J. C., et al. (2014). To thine own self be true: Psychological adjustment promotes judgeability via personality–behavior congruence. *Journal of Personality & Social Psychology, 106*(2), 286–303. doi:10.1037/a0034860

Humphrey, R. H. (2014). *Effective leadership: Theory, cases and applications*. Thousand Oaks, CA: Sage.

Hunter, J. P., Katz, J., & Davis, K. D. (2003). The effect of tactile and visual sensory inputs on phantom limb awareness. *Brain, 126*(3), 579–589. doi:10.1093/brain/awg054

Hunter, S., Hurley, R. A., & Taber, K. H. (2013). A look inside the mirror neuron system. *Journal of Neuropsychiatry & Clinical Neurosciences, 25*(3), 170–175.

Huntsinger, J. R. (2013). Does emotion directly tune the scope of attention?. *Current Directions in Psychological Science, 22*(4), 265–270. doi:10.1177/0963721413480364

Huston, H. C., & Bentley, A. C. (2010). Human development in societal context. *Annual Review of Psychology, 61*, 411–437. doi:10.1146/annurev.psych.093008.100442

Hutchinson, S. R. (2004). Survey research. In K. deMarrais & S. D. Lapan (Eds.), Foundations for research: *Methods of inquiry in education and the social sciences: Inquiry and pedagogy across diverse contexts* (pp. 283–301). Mahwah, NJ: Erlbaum.

Hutchinson, S., Lee, L. H., et al. (2003). Cerebellar volume of musicians. *Cerebral Cortex, 13*(9), 943–949. doi:10.1093/cercor/13.9.943

Hutchison, K. E., McGeary, J., et al. (2002). The DRD4 VNTR polymorphism moderates craving after alcohol consumption. *Health Psychology, 21*(2), 139–146. doi:10.1037/0278-6133.21.2.139

Hyde, J. S., & DeLamater, J. D. (2014). *Understanding human sexuality* (12th ed.). New York: McGraw-Hill.

Hyde, J. S., & Else-Quest, N. (2013). *Half the human experience* (8th ed.). Boston, MA: Cengage Learning.

Hyman, R. (2007). Talking with the dead, communicating with the future and other myths created by cold reading. In S. Della Sala (Ed.), *Tall tales about the mind & brain: Separating fact from fiction* (pp. 218–232). New York: Oxford University Press.

Hysenbegasi, A., Hass, S. L., & Rowland, C. R. (2005). The impact of depression on the academic productivity of university students. *Journal of Mental Health Policy & Economics, 8*(3), 145–151.

Iacono, W. G. (2008). Effective policing: Understanding how polygraph tests work and are used. *Criminal Justice & Behavior, 35*(10), 1295–1308. doi:10.1177/0093854808321529

Iacono, W. G. (2011). Encouraging the use of the Guilty Knowledge Test (GKT): What the GKT has to offer law enforcement. In B. Verschuere, G. Ben-Shakhar, et al. (Eds.), *Memory detection: Theory and application of the Concealed Information Test* (pp. 12–23). New York: Cambridge University Press.

Iannone, M., Bulotta, S., et al. (2006, February 16). Electrocortical effects of MDMA are potentiated by acoustic stimulation in rats. *BMC Neuroscience*, 7–13. doi:10.1186/1471-2202-7-13

Imbimbo, C., Verze, P., et al. (2009). A report from a single institute's 14-year experience in treatment of male-to-female transsexuals. *Journal of Sexual Medicine, 6*(10), 2736–2745.

Immordino-Yang, M. H. (2008). How we can learn from children with half a brain? *New Scientist, 2664,* 44–45.

Impett, E. A., Strachman, A., et al. (2008). Maintaining sexual desire in intimate relationships: The importance of approach goals. *Journal of Personality & Social Psychology, 94*(5), 808–823.

Impett, E. A., Gordon, A. M., et al. (2010). Moving toward more perfect unions: Daily and long-term consequences of approach and avoidance goals in romantic relationships. *Journal of Personality & Social Psychology, 99*(6), 948–963.

IMS Institute for Healthcare Informatics. (2013). *Avoidable costs in US health care: 2013.* Downloaded from: http://www.imshealth.com/deployedfiles/imshealth/Global/Content/Corporate/IMS%20Institute/RUOM-2013/IHII_Responsible_Use_Medicines_2013.pdf

Imuta, K., Henry, J. D., et al. (2016). Theory of mind and prosocial behavior in childhood: A meta-analytic review. *Developmental Psychology, 52*(8), 1192–1205. doi:10.1037/dev0000140

Ingalhalikar, M., Smith, A., et al. (2013, December 2). Sex differences in the structural connectome of the human brain. *Proceedings of the National Academy of Sciences.* doi:10.1073/pnas.1316909110

Ingham, A. G., Levinger, G., et al. (1974). The Ringelmann effect: Studies of group size and group performance. *Journal of Personality & Social Psychology, 10,* 371–384. doi:10.1016/0022-1031(74)90033-X

Ingiosi, A. M., Opp, M. R., & Krueger, J. M. (2013). Sleep and immune function: Glial contributions and consequences of aging. *Current Opinion in Neurobiology, 23*(5), 806–811. doi:10.1016/j.conb.2013.02.003

Ingravallo, F., Gnucci, V., et al. (2012). The burden of narcolepsy with cataplexy: How disease history and clinical features influence socioeconomic outcomes. *Sleep Medicine, 13*(10), 1293–1300. doi:10.1016/j.sleep.2012.08.002

Innocence Project. (2016). *Exonerated by DNA.* Retrieved May 5, 2017, from www.innocenceproject.org/all-cases/#exonerated-by-dnap;lo

Insel, T. R. (2010). Rethinking schizophrenia. *Nature, 468*(7321), 187–193. doi:10.1038/nature09552

Inta, D., Meyer-Lindenberg, A., & Gass, P. (2011). Alterations in postnatal neurogenesis and dopamine dysregulation in schizophrenia: A hypothesis. *Schizophrenia Bulletin, 37*(4), 674–680. doi:10.1093/schbul/sbq134

Intaitė, M., Noreika, V., et al. (2013). Interaction of bottom-up and top-down processes in the perception of ambiguous figures. *Vision Research, 89,* 24–31. doi:10.1016/j.visres.2013.06.011

Inzlicht, M., & Schmeichel, B. J. (2012). What is ego depletion? Toward a mechanistic revision of the resource model of self-control. *Perspectives on Psychological Science, 7*(5), 450–463. doi:10.1177/1745691612454134

Inzlicht, M., Gutsell, J. N., & Legault, L. (2012). Mimicry reduces racial prejudice. *Journal of Experimental Social Psychology, 48*(1), 361–365. doi:10.1016/j.jesp.2011.06.007

Iosif, A., & Ballon, B. (2005). Bad moon rising: The persistent belief in lunar connections to madness. *Canadian Medical Association Journal, 173*(12), 1498–1500. doi:10.1503/cmaj.051119

Ipser, J. C., Singh, L., & Stein, D. J. (2013). Meta-analysis of functional brain imaging in specific phobia. *Psychiatry & Clinical Neurosciences, 67*(5), 311–322. doi:10.1111/pcn.12055

Irish, M., Landin-Romero, R., et al. (2017, March 10). Evolution of autobiographical memory impairments in Alzheimer's disease and frontotemporal dementia: A longitudinal neuroimaging study. *Neuropsychologia,* n.p. doi:10.1016/j.neuropsychologia.2017.03.014

Irish, M., & Piguet, O. (2013). The pivotal role of semantic memory in remembering the past and imagining the future. *Frontiers in Behavioral Neuroscience, 7,* 27. doi:10.3389/fnbeh.2013.00027

Irwin, M. R. (2015). Why sleep is important for health: A psychoneuroimmunology perspective. *Annual Review of Psychology, 66,* 143–172. doi:10.1146/annurev-psych-010213-115205

Isaacs, D. (2011). Corporal punishment of children: Changing the culture. *Journal of Paediatrics and Child Health, 47*(8), 491–492. doi:10.1111/j.1440-1754.2011.02143.x

Isbell, E., Stevens, C., et al. (2016). 5-HTTLPR polymorphism is linked to neural mechanisms of selective attention in preschoolers from lower socioeconomic status backgrounds. *Developmental Cognitive Neuroscience, 22,* 36–47. doi:10.1016/j.dcn.2016.10.002

Iskra-Golec, I. (2016). Individual differences in circadian rhythm parameters and work-family spillover in shift workers. In I. Iskra-Golec, J. Barnes-Farrell, & P. Bohle (Eds.), *Social and family issues in shift work and non standard working hours* (pp. 181–202). Cham, Switzerland: Springer International Publishing. doi:10.1007/978-3-319-42286-2_9

Iuga, A. O., & McGuire, M. J. (2014). Adherence and health care costs. *Risk Management and Healthcare Policy, 7,* 35–44. doi:10.2147/RMHP.S19801

Ivanco, T. L., & Racine, R. J. (2000). Long-term potentiation in the pathways between the hippocampus and neocortex in the chronically implanted, freely moving rat. *Hippocampus, 10,* 143–152.

Iverson, R. D., & Zatzick, C. D. (2011). The effects of downsizing on labor productivity: The value of showing consideration for employees' morale and welfare in high-performance work systems. *Human Resource Management, 50*(1), 29–44.

Ivtzan, I., Gardner, H. E., et al. (2013). Wellbeing through self-fulfilment: Examining developmental aspects of self-actualization. *The Humanistic Psychologist, 41*(2), 119–132. doi:10.1080/08873267.2012.712076

Iyengar, S. S., & Lepper, M. R. (2000). When choice is demotivating: Can one desire too much of a good thing? *Journal of Personality & Social Psychology, 79*(6), 995–1006. doi:10.1037/0022-3514.79.6.995

Izard, C. E. (1990). Facial expressions and the regulation of emotions. *Journal of Personality & Social Psychology, 58*(3), 487–498. doi:10.1177/1754073911410737

Izard, C. E. (2007). Basic emotions, natural kinds, emotion schemas, and a new paradigm. *Perspectives on Psychological Science, 2,* 260–280.

Izard, C. E. (2011). Forms and functions of emotions: Matters of emotion–cognition interactions. *Emotion Review, 3*(4), 371–378. doi:10.1177/1754073911410737

Izard, C. E., Woodburn, E. M., & Finlon, K. J. (2010). Extending emotion science to the study of discrete emotions in infants. *Emotion Review, 2*(2), 134–136. doi:10.1177/1754073909355003

Izuma, K. (2013). The neural basis of social influence and attitude change. *Current Opinion in Neurobiology, 23,* 456–462. doi:10.1016/j.conb.2013.03.009

Jack, D. C., & Ali, A. (2010). *Silencing the self across cultures: Depression and gender in the social world.* New York: Oxford University Press.

Jackson, D., & Newberry, P. (2016). *Critical thinking: A user's manual* (2nd ed.). Boston, MA: Cengage Learning.

Jackson, L. M. (2011). *The psychology of prejudice: From attitudes to social action.* Washington, DC: American Psychological Association.

Jackson, S. L. (2016). *Research methods and statistics: A critical thinking approach* (5th ed.). Boston, MA: Cengage Learning.

Jackson, S. L. (2017). *Statistics plain and simple* (4th ed.). Boston, MA: Cengage Learning.

Jacobs-Stewart, T. (2010). *Mindfulness and the 12 steps: Living recovery in the present moment.* Center City, MN: Hazelden Foundation.

Jacobs, J., Lega, B., & Anderson, C. (2012). Explaining how brain stimulation can evoke memories. *Journal of Cognitive Neuroscience, 24*(3), 553–563. doi:10.1162/jocn_a_00170

Jacobs, N., van Os, J., et al. (2008). Heritability of intelligence. *Twin Research & Human Genetics, 10*(Suppl), 11–14. doi:10.1375/twin.10.supp.11

Jacobs, S. R., & Dodd, D. K. (2003). Student burnout as a function of personality, social support, and workload. *Journal of College Student Development, 44*(3), 291–303. doi:10.1353/csd.2003.0028

Jaeggi, S. M., Buschkuehl, M., et al. (2008). Improving fluid intelligence with training on working memory. *Proceedings of the National Academy of Sciences, 105*(19), 6829–6833. doi:10.1073/pnas.0801268105

Jaehnig, W., & Miller, M. L. (2007). Feedback types in programmed instruction: A systematic review. *Psychological Record, 57*(2), 219–232.

Jaffe, J., Beatrice, B., et al. (2001). Rhythms of dialogue in infancy. *Monographs of the Society for Research in Child Development, 66*(2), i–vi, 1–132.

James, W. (1890). *The principles of psychology.* Retrieved May 8, 2014, from psychclassics.yorku.ca/James/Principles/

Jamieson, J. P., & Mendes, W. B. (2016). Social stress facilitates risk in youths. *Journal of Experimental Psychology: General, 145*(4), 467–485. doi:10.1037/xge0000147

Jamison, K. R. (1996). *Touched with fire: Manic-depressive illness and the artistic temperament.* New York: Free Press.

Janis, I. L. (1989). *Crucial decisions.* New York: Free Press.

Janis, I. L. (2007). Groupthink. In R. P. Vecchio (Ed.), *Leadership: Understanding the dynamics of power and influence in organizations* (2nd ed., pp. 163–176). Notre Dame, IN: University of Notre Dame Press.

Janssen, S. A., & Arntz, A. (2001). Real-life stress and opioid-mediated analgesia in novice parachute jumpers. *Journal of Psychophysiology, 15*(2), 106–113. doi:10.1027//0269-8803.15.2.106

Janusek, L., Cooper, D., & Mathews, H. L. (2012). Stress, immunity, and health outcomes. In V. Rice (Ed.), *Handbook of stress, coping, and health: Implications for nursing research, theory, and practice* (2nd ed., pp. 43–70). Thousand Oaks, CA: Sage.

Jarrold, C., & Hall, D. (2013). The development of rehearsal in verbal short-term memory. *Child Development Perspectives, 7*(3), 182–186. doi:10.1111/cdep.12034

Jaschik, S. (2011). The enduring gender gap in pay. Inside Higher Ed, April 5. Retrieved March 10, 2017, from www.insidehighered.com/news/2011/04/052/the_enduring_gender_gap_in_faculty_pay

Javitt, D. C., Zukin, S. R., et al. (2012). Has an angel shown the way? Etiological and therapeutic implications of the PCP/NMDA model of schizophrenia. *Schizophrenia Bulletin, 38*(5), 958–966. doi:10.1093/schbul/sbs069

Jeffries, F. W., & Davis, P. (2013). What is the role of eye movements in eye movement desensitization and reprocessing (EMDR) for post-traumatic stress disorder (PTSD)? A review. *Behavioural & Cognitive Psychotherapy, 41*(3), 290–300. doi:10.1017/S1352465812000793

Jegindø, E., Vase, L., et al. (2013). Pain and sacrifice: Experience and modulation of pain in a religious piercing ritual. *International Journal for the Psychology of Religion, 23*(3), 171–187. doi:10.1080/10508619.2012.759065

Jenkins, A. C., & Mitchell, J. P. (2011). Medial prefrontal cortex subserves diverse forms of self-reflection. *Social Neuroscience, 6*(3), 211–218. doi:10.1080/17470919.2010.507948

Jenkins, J. G., & Dallenbach, K. M. (1924). Oblivescence during sleep and waking. *American Journal of Psychology, 35,* 605–612.

Jenkins, S. R., Dobbs, L., & Leeper, M. (2015). Using the Thematic Apperception Test to assess interpersonal decentering in violent relationships. *Rorschachiana, 36*(2), 156–179. doi:10.1027/1192-5604/a000064

Jerabek, I., & Standing, L. (1992). Imagined test situations produce contextual memory enhancement. *Perceptual & Motor Skills, 75*(2), 400.

Jervis, L. L., Boland, M. E., et al. (2010). American Indian family caregivers' experiences with helping elders. *Journal of Cross-Cultural Gerontology, 25*(4), 355–369. doi:10.1007/s10823-010-9131-9

Jiang, L., Bazarova, N. N., & Hancock, J. T. (2013). From perception to behavior: Disclosure reciprocity and the intensification of intimacy in computer-mediated communication. *Communication Research, 40*(1), 125–143. doi:10.1177/0093650211405313

Jirout, J. J., & Newcombe, N. S. (2015). Building blocks for developing spatial skills: Evidence from a large, representative US sample. *Psychological Science, 26*(3), 302–310. doi:10.1177/0956797614563338

Joel, S., Gordon, A. M., et al. (2013). The things you do for me: Perceptions of a romantic partner's investments promote gratitude and commitment. *Personality & Social Psychology Bulletin, 39*(10), 1333–1345.

Joffe, R. T. (2006). Is the thyroid still important in major depression? *Journal of Psychiatry & Neuroscience, 31*(6), 367–368.

Johansson, V., Garwicz, M., et al. (2013). Beyond blind optimism and unfounded fears: Deep brain stimulation for treatment resistant depression. *Neuroethics, 6*(3), 457–471. doi:10.1007/s12152-011-9112-x

Johnson, B. T., & Boynton, M. H. (2010). Putting attitudes in their place: Behavioral prediction in the face of competing variables. In J. P. Forgas, J. Cooper, et al. (Eds.), *The psychology of attitudes and attitude change* (pp. 19–38). New York: Psychology Press.

Johnson, C. S., & Lammers, J. (2012). The powerful disregard social comparison information. *Journal of Experimental Social Psychology, 48*(1), 329–334. doi:10.1016/j.jesp.2011.10.010

Johnson, C. S., & Stapel, D. A. (2010). It depends on how you look at it: Being versus becoming mindsets determine responses to social comparisons. *British Journal of Social Psychology, 49*(4), 703–723. doi:10.1348/014466609X476827

Johnson, J. J. M., Hrycaiko, D. W., et al. (2004). Self-talk and female youth soccer performance. *Sport Psychologist, 18*(1), 44–59.

Johnson, K. J., & Fredrickson, B. L. (2005). "We all look the same to me": Positive emotions eliminate the own-race bias in face recognition. *Psychological Science, 16*(11), 875–881. doi:10.1111/j.1467-9280.2005.01631.x

Johnson, M. W., & Griffiths, R. R. (2013). Comparative abuse liability of GHB and ethanol in humans. *Experimental & Clinical Psychopharmacology, 21,* 112–123. doi:10.1037/a0031692

Johnson, R., Nessler, D., et al. (2013). Temporally specific divided attention tasks in young adults reveal the temporal dynamics of episodic encoding failures in elderly adults. *Psychology & Aging, 28*(2), 443–456. doi:10.1037/a0030967

Johnson, S. J., Batey, M., & Holdsworth, L. (2009). Personality and health: The mediating role of trait emotional intelligence and work locus of control. *Personality & Individual Differences, 47*(5), 470–475. doi:10.1016/j.paid.2009.04.025

Johnson, T. J. (2002). College students' self-reported reasons for why drinking games end. *Addictive Behaviors, 27*(1), 145–153. doi:10.1016/S0306-4603(00)00168-4

Johnstone, P. M., Nábelek, A. K., & Robertson, V. S. (2010). Sound localization acuity in children with unilateral hearing loss who wear a hearing aid in the impaired ear. *Journal of the American Academy of Audiology, 21*(8), 522–534. doi:10.3766/jaaa.21.8.4

Joiner, T. E., Jr. (2010). *Myths about suicide.* Cambridge, MA: Harvard University Press.

Joinson, C., Heron, J., et al. (2009). A prospective study of age at initiation of toilet training and subsequent daytime bladder control in school-age children. *Journal of Developmental & Behavioral Pediatrics, 30*(5), 385–393. doi:10.1097/DBP.0b013e3181ba0e77

Jolly, J. L., Treffinger, D. J., et al. (Eds.). (2011). *Parenting gifted children: The authoritative guide from the National Association for Gifted Children.* Waco, TX: Prufrock Press.

Jonason, P. K., Koenig, B. L., & Tost, J. (2010). Living a fast life: The Dark Triad and life history theory. *Human Nature, 21*(4), 428–442. doi:10.1007/s12110-010-9102-4

Jonason, P. K., & Lavertu, A. N. (2017). The reproductive costs and benefits associated with the Dark Triad traits in women. *Personality & Individual Differences, 110,* 38–40. doi:10.1016/j.paid.2017.01.024

Jonason, P. K., & Webster, G. D. (2010). The dirty dozen: A concise measure of the dark triad. *Psychological Assessment, 22*(2), 420–432. doi:10.1037/a0019265

Jonason, P. K., Webster, G. D., et al. (2012). The antihero in popular culture: Life history theory and the dark triad personality traits. *Review of General Psychology, 16*(2), 192–199. doi:10.1037/a0027914

Jones, G. (2012). Why chunking should be considered as an explanation for developmental change before short-term memory capacity and processing speed. *Frontiers in Psychology, 3,* 167. doi:10.3389/fpsyg.2012.00167

Jones, K. L., & Streissguth, A. P. (2010). Fetal alcohol syndrome and fetal alcohol spectrum disorders: A brief history. *Journal of Psychiatry & Law, 38*(4), 373–382.

Jones, O. D., Marois, R., et al. (2013). Law and neuroscience. *Journal of Neuroscience, 33*(45), 17624–17630. doi:10.1523/JNEUROSCI.3254-13.2013

Jones, P., Blunda, M., et al. (2013). Can mindfulness-based interventions help adolescents with cancer? *Psycho-Oncology, 22*(9), 2148–2151. doi:10.1002/pon.3251

Jones, S. R., & Fernyhough, C. (2007). A new look at the neural diathesis–stress model of schizophrenia: The primacy of social evaluative and uncontrollable situations. *Schizophrenia Bulletin, 33*(5), 1171–1177. doi:10.1093/schbul/sbl058

Jones, W. R., & Morgan, J. F. (2010). Eating disorders in men: A review of the literature. *Journal of Public Mental Health, 9*(2), 23–31. doi:10.5042/jpmh.2010.0326

Jonides, J., Lewis, R. L., et al. (2008). The mind and brain of short-term memory. *Annual Review of Psychology, 59,* 193–224. doi:10.1146/annurev.psych.59.103006.093615

Joo, E. Y., Tae, W. K., et al. (2010). Reduced brain gray matter concentration in patients with obstructive sleep apnea syndrome. *Sleep: Journal of Sleep & Sleep Disorders Research, 33*(2), 235–241.

Jordan, K. (2010). Vicarious trauma: Proposed factors that impact clinicians. *Journal of Family Psychotherapy, 21*(4), 225–237. doi:10.1080/08975353.2010.529003

Jordan, M. I., & Mitchell, T. M. (2015). Machine learning: Trends, perspectives, and prospects. *Science, 349*(6245), 255–260. doi:10.1126/science.aaa8415

Jordano, M. L., & Touron, D. R. (2017). Stereotype threat as a trigger of mind-wandering in older adults. *Psychology & Aging*, n.p. doi:10.1037/pag0000167

Jorm, A. F. (2012). Mental health literacy: Empowering the community to take action for better mental health. *American Psychologist, 67*(3), 231–243. doi:10.1037/a0025957

Joseph, D. L., Jin, J., et al. (2015). Why does self-reported emotional intelligence predict job performance? A meta-analytic investigation of mixed EI. *Journal of Applied Psychology, 100*(2), 298–342. doi:10.1037/a0037681

Jou, J., & Flores, S. (2013). How are false memories distinguishable from true memories in the Deese-Roediger-McDermott paradigm? A review of the findings. *Psychological Research, 77*(6), 671–686. doi:10.1007/s00426-012-0472-6

Jowett, G. S. (2006). Brainwashing: The Korean POW controversy and the origins of a myth. In G. S. Jowett & V. O'Donnell (Eds.), *Readings in propaganda and persuasion: New and classic essays* (pp. 201–211). Thousand Oaks, CA: Sage.

Juarez, L., Soto, E., et al. (2012). Drive for muscularity and drive for thinness: The impact of pro-anorexia websites. *Eating Disorders: The Journal of Treatment & Prevention, 20*(2), 99–112. doi:10.1080/10640266.2012.653944

Judge, T. A., Weiss, H. M., et al. (2017). Job attitudes, job satisfaction, and job affect: A century of continuity and of change. *Journal of Applied Psychology, 102*(3), 356–374. doi:10.1037/apl0000181

Judson, S. S., Johnson, D. M., & Perez, A. U. (2013). Perceptions of adult sexual coercion as a function of victim gender. *Psychology of Men & Masculinity*, doi:10.1037/a0030448

Juhl, J., Sand, E. C., & Routledge, C. (2012). The effects of nostalgia and avoidant attachment on relationship satisfaction and romantic motives. *Journal of Social & Personal Relationships, 29*(5), 661–670. doi:10.1177/0265407512443433

Juliano, L. M., & Griffiths, R. R. (2004). A critical review of caffeine withdrawal: Empirical validation of symptoms and signs, incidence, severity, and associated features. *Psychopharmacology, 176*(1), 1–29. doi:10.1007/s00213-004-2000-x

Julien, R. M. (2011). *A primer of drug action* (12th ed.). New York: Worth.

Jun, H. (2010). *Social justice, multicultural counseling, and practice: Beyond a conventional approach.* Thousand Oaks, CA: Sage.

Jung, C. G. (1961). *Memories, dreams, reflections.* New York: Pantheon.

Jurd, R. R. (2011). TiNS special issue: Hippocampus and memory. *Trends in Neurosciences, 34*(10), 499–500. doi:10.1016/j.tins.2011.08.008

Jussim, L., Crawford, J. T., & Rubinstein, R. S. (2015). Stereotype (in)accuracy in perceptions of groups and individuals. *Current Directions in Psychological Science, 24*(6), 490–497. doi:10.1177/0963721415605257

Jussim, L., & Harber, K. D. (2005). Teacher expectations and self-fulfilling prophecies: Knowns and unknowns, resolved and unresolved controversies. *Personality & Social Psychology Review, 9*(2), 131–155. doi:10.1207/s15327957pspr0902_3

Justman, S. (2011). From medicine to psychotherapy: The placebo effect. *History of the Human Sciences, 24*(1), 95–107. doi:10.1177/0952695110386655

Kafka, M. P. (2010). Hypersexual disorder: A proposed diagnosis for DSM-V. *Archives of Sexual Behavior, 39*(2), 377–400.

Kahlenberg, S. G., & Hein, M. M. (2010). Progression on Nickelodeon? Gender-role stereotypes in toy commercials. *Sex Roles, 62*(11–12), 830–847. doi:10.1007/s11199-009-9653-1

Kahn, R. E., Ermer, E., et al. (2016). Emotional intelligence and callous–unemotional traits in incarcerated adolescents. *Child Psychiatry & Human Development, 47*, 903–917. Advance online publication. doi:10.1007/s10578-015-0621-4

Kahneman, D. (2011). *Thinking, fast and slow.* New York: Macmillan.

Kahneman, D., & Tversky, A. (1972). Subjective probability: A judgment of representativeness. *Cognitive Psychology, 3*, 430–454. doi:10.1016/0010-0285(72)90016-3

Kahneman, D., Slovic, P., & Tversky, A. (1982). *Judgment under uncertainty: Heuristics and biases.* Cambridge, MA: Cambridge University Press.

Kail, R. V., & Cavanaugh, J. C. (2016). *Human development: A life-span view* (7th ed.). Boston, MA: Cengage Learning.

Kaiser, R. B., & Wallace, W. T. (2016). Gender bias and substantive differences in ratings of leadership behavior: Toward a new narrative. *Consulting Psychology Journal: Practice & Research, 68*(1), 72–98. doi:10.1037/cpb0000059

Kalat, J. W. (2016). *Biological psychology* (12th ed.). Boston, MA: Cengage Learning.

Kalat, J. W., & Shiota, M. N. (2012). *Emotion* (2nd ed.). Belmont, CA: Wadsworth.

Kalmijn, M. (2010). Educational inequality, homogamy, and status exchange in Black-White intermarriage: A comment on Rosenfield. *American Journal of Sociology, 115*(4), 1252–1263.

Kalyuga, S., & Hanham, J. (2011). Instructing in generalized knowledge structures to develop flexible problem solving skills. *Computers in Human Behavior, 27*(1), 63–68. doi:10.1016/j.chb.2010 05.024

Kalyuga, S., Renkl, A., & Paas, F. (2010). Facilitating flexible problem solving: A cognitive load perspective. *Educational Psychology Review, 22*(2), 175–186. doi:10.1007/s10648-010-9132-9

Kamenov, K., Twomey, C., et al. (2016, October 26). *The efficacy of psychotherapy, pharmacotherapy and their combination on functioning and quality of life in depression: A meta-analysis*, n.p. doi:10.1017/S0033291716002774

Kamimori, G. H., Johnson, D., et al. (2005). Multiple caffeine doses maintain vigilance during early morning operations. *Aviation, Space, & Environmental Medicine, 76*(11), 1046–1050.

Kamin, L. J. (1981). *The intelligence controversy.* New York: Wiley.

Kammrath, L. K., Mendoza-Denton, R., & Mischel, W. (2005). Incorporating If . . . Then . . . personality signatures in person perception: Beyond the person-situation dichotomy. *Journal of Personality & Social Psychology, 88*(4), 605–618.

Kan, K., Wicherts, J. M., et al. (2013). On the nature and nurture of intelligence and specific cognitive abilities: The more heritable, the more culture dependent. *Psychological Science, 24*(12), 2420–2428. doi:10.1177/0956797613493292

Kanas, N., & Manzey, D. (2008). *Space psychology and psychiatry* (2nd ed.). New York: Springer.

Kanayama, G., Kean, J., et al. (2012, December 14). Cognitive deficits in long-term anabolic-androgenic steroid users. *Drug & Alcohol Dependence*, n.p. doi:10.1016/j.drugalcdep.2012.11.008

Kandler, C. (2012). Knowing your personality is knowing its nature: The role of information accuracy of peer assessments for heritability estimates of temperamental and personality traits. *Personality & Individual Differences, 53*(4), 387–392. doi:10.1016/j.paid.2012.01.004

Kang, Y., Gray, J. R., Dovido, J. F. (2014). The nondiscriminating heart: Lovingkindness meditation training decreases implicit intergroup bias. *Journal of Experimental Psychology: General, 143(3)*, 1306–1313. doi:10.1037/a0034150

Kann, L., McManus, M. S., et al. (2015). *Youth risk behavior surveillance: United States, 2015.* Atlanta, GA: Centers for Disease Control. Retrieved March 18, 2017, from www.cdc.gov/mmwr/volumes/65/ss/ss6506a1.htm

Kansky, J., Allen, J. P., & Deiner, E. (2016). Early adolescent affect predicts later life outcomes. *Health and Well-being, 8*, 192–212. doi:10.1111/aphw.12068

Kapinos, K. A., & Yakusheva, O. (2011). Environmental influences on young adult weight gain: Evidence from a natural experiment. *Journal of Adolescent Health, 48*(1), 52–58. doi:10.1016/j.jadohealth.2010.05.021

Kaplan, A., & Haenlein, M. *(2019,* January). Siri, Siri, in my hand: Who's the fairest in the land? On the interpretations, illustrations, and implications of artificial intelligence. *Business Horizons, 62*(1), 15–25. doi:10.1016/j.bushor.2018.08.004

Kaplan, J. S. (2012). The effects of shared environment on adult intelligence: A critical review of adoption, twin, and MZA studies. *Developmental Psychology, 48*(5), 1292–1298. doi:10.1037/a0028133

Kaplan, P. S. (1998). *The human odyssey.* Pacific Grove, CA: Brooks/Cole.

Kaplan, R. M., & Saccuzzo, D. P. (2018). *Psychological testing: Principles, applications, and issues* (9th ed.). Boston, MA: Cengage Learning.

Kapleau, P. (1966). *The three pillars of Zen.* New York: Harper & Row.

Kappe, R., & van der Flier, H. (2010). Using multiple and specific criteria to assess the predictive validity of the Big Five personality factors on academic performance. *Journal of Research in Personality, 44*(1), 142–145. doi:10.1016/j.jrp.2009.11.002

Karagheorgis, C. I., & Terry, P. C. (2011). *Inside sport psychology.* Champaign, IL: Human Kinetics.

Kardas, E. P. (2014). *History of psychology: The making of a science.* Boston, MA: Cengage Learning.

Kark, R., & Eagly, A. H. (2010). Gender and leadership: Negotiating the labyrinth. In J. C. Chrisler & D. R. McCreary (Eds.), *Handbook of gender research in psychology* (Vol. 2): *Gender research in social and applied psychology* (pp. 443–470). New York: Springer.

Karpicke, J. D., & Blunt, J. R. (2011). Retrieval practice produces more learning than elaborative studying with concept mapping. *Science, 331*(6018), 772–775. doi:10.1126/science.1199327

Karpicke, J. D., & Smith, M. A. (2012). Separate mnemonic effects of retrieval practice and elaborative encoding. *Journal of Memory and Language, 67*(1), 17–29.

Kasser, T. (2016). Materialistic values and goals. *Annual Review of Psychology, 67*, 489–514. doi:10.1146/annurev-psych-122414-033344

Kassin, S. M. (2005). On the psychology of confessions: Does innocence put innocents at risk? *American Psychologist, 60*(3), 215–228. doi:10.1037/0003-066X.60.3.215

Kassin, S. M., Fein, S., & et al. (2017). *Social psychology* (10th ed.). Boston, MA: Houghton Mifflin.

Kastytis, S., Nida, Z., et al. (2015). Type A behavior pattern is not a predictor of premature mortality. *International Journal of Behavioral Medicine, 22*(2), 161–169. doi:10.1007/s12529-014-9435-1

Kataria, S. (2004). A clinical guide to pediatric sleep: Diagnosis and management of sleep problems. *Journal of Developmental & Behavioral Pediatrics, 25*(2), 132–133. doi:10.1097/00004703-200404000-00012

Katwala, A. (2019, May 1). *The controversial science behind the Caster Semenya verdict*. Wired.

Katz, D. L., & Meller, S. (2014). Can we say what diet is best for health? *Annual Review of Public Health, 35,* 83–103. doi:10.1146/annurev-publhealth-032013-182351

Katz, J. (2013). The three-block model of universal design for learning (UDL): Engaging students in inclusive education. *Canadian Journal of Education, 36*(1), 153–194.

Katz, P. A. (2003). Racists or tolerant multiculturalists? *American Psychologist, 58*(11), 897–909.

Kaufman, J. C. (2009). *Creativity 101.* New York: Springer.

Kaufman, J. C., & Sternberg, R. J. (Eds.). (2010). *The Cambridge handbook of creativity*. New York: Cambridge University Press.

Kaulich, T., Fohre, W., Kutz, D. F., Gerwig, M., Timmann, D., & Kolb, F. P. (2010). Differences in unconditioned and conditioned responses of the human withdrawal reflex during stance: Muscle responses and biomechanical data. *Brain Research, 1326,* 81–95. doi:10.1016/j.brainres.2010.02.051

Kawada, R., Yoshizumi, M., et al. (2009). Brain volume and dysexecutive behavior in schizophrenia. *Progress in Neuro-Psychopharmacology & Biological Psychiatry, 33*(7), 1255–1260. doi:10.1016/j.pnpbp.2009.07.014

Kaye, W. H., Wierenga, C. E., et al. (2013). Nothing tastes as good as skinny feels: The neurobiology of anorexia nervosa. *Trends in Neurosciences, 36*(2), 110–120. doi:10.1016/j.tins.2013.01.003

Kearney, A. J. (2006). A primer of covert sensitization. *Cognitive & Behavioral Practice, 13*(2), 167–175. doi:10.1016/j.cbpra.2006.02.002

Kearney, C., & Trull, T. (2018). *Abnormal psychology and life: A dimensional approach* (3rd ed.). Boston, MA: Cengage Learning.

Kearney, M. S., & Levine, P. B. (2012). Why is the teen birth rate in the United States so high and why does it matter? *Journal of Economic Perspectives, 26*(2), 141–163.

Keating, C. (2010). Theoretical perspective on anorexia nervosa: The conflict of reward. *Neuroscience & Biobehavioral Reviews, 34*(1), 73–79. doi:10.1016/j.neubiorev.2009.07.004

Keefe, F. J., Huling, D. A., et al. (2012). Virtual reality for persistent pain: A new direction for behavioral pain management. *Pain, 153*(11), 2163–2166.

Keegan, J., Parva, M., et al. (2010). Addiction in pregnancy. *Journal of Addictive Diseases, 29*(2), 175–191. doi:10.1080/10550881003684723

Keel, P. K., & Klump, K. L. (2003). Are eating disorders culture-bound syndromes? Implications for conceptualizing their etiology. *Psychological Bulletin, 129*(5), 747–769. doi:10.1037/0033-2909.129.5.747

Keith, T. Z., & Reynolds, M. R. (2010). Cattell-Horn-Carroll abilities and cognitive tests: What we've learned from 20 years of research. *Psychology in the Schools, 47*(7), 635–650. doi:10.1002/pits.20496

Kell, C. A., Morillon, B., et al. (2011). Lateralization of speech production starts in sensory cortices: A possible sensory origin of cerebral left dominance for speech. *Cerebral Cortex, 21*(4), 932–937. doi:10.1093/cercor/bhq167

Kelley, H. H. (1967). Attribution in social psychology. *Nebraska Symposium on Motivation, 15,* 192–238.

Kelly, E. (2010). I always knew I was a girl. Retrieved May 8, 2014, from www.salon.com/life/feature/2010/11/20/how_i_became_a_woman

Kelly, M. P., Strassberg, D. S., & Turner, C. M. (2006). Behavioral assessment of couples' communication in female orgasmic disorder. *Journal of Sex & Marital Therapy, 32*(2), 81–95. doi:10.1080/00926230500442243

Keltner, D. (2019). Toward a consensual taxonomy of emotions. *Cognition and Emotion, 33*(1), 14–19. doi:10.1080/02699931.2019.1574397

Keltner, D., Sauter, D., Tracy, J., & Cowen, A. (2019). Emotional expression: Advances in basic emotion theory. *Journal of Nonverbal Behavior*, 1–28. doi:10.1007/s10919-019-00293-3.

Kendon, A. (2016, July 20). Reflections on the "gesture-first" hypothesis of language origins. *Psychonomic Bulletin & Review,* n.p. doi:10.3758/s13423-016-1117-3

Kennedy, M., Kreppner, J., et al. (2016). Early severe institutional deprivation is associated with a persistent variant of adult attention-deficit/hyperactivity disorder: Clinical presentation, developmental continuities and life circumstances in the English and Romanian adoptees study. *Journal of Child Psychology & Psychiatry, 57*(10), 1113–1125. doi:10.1111/jcpp.12576

Kennedy, S. H., Giacobbe, P., et al. (2011). Deep brain stimulation for treatment-resistant depression: Follow-up after 3 to 6 years. *The American Journal of Psychiatry, 168*(5), 502–510. doi:10.1176/appi.ajp.2010.10081187

Kenny, P. J., & Markou, A. (2006). Nicotine self-administration acutely activates brain reward systems and induces a long-lasting increase in reward sensitivity. *Neuropsychopharmacology, 31*(6), 1203–1211. doi:10.1038/sj.npp.1300905

Kenrick, D. T., Griskevicius, V., et al. (2010). Renovating the pyramid of needs: Contemporary extensions built upon ancient foundations. *Perspectives on Psychological Science, 5,* 292–314. doi:10.1177/1745691610369469

Keren, E., & Mayseless, O. (2013). The freedom to choose secure attachment relationships in adulthood. *Journal of Genetic Psychology: Research & Theory on Human Development, 174*(3), 271–290. doi:10.1080/00221325.2012.681326

Kern, J. K., Geier, D. A., et al. (2012). Evidence of parallels between mercury intoxication and the brain pathology in autism. *Acta Neurobiologiae Experimentalis, 72*(2), 113–153.

Kernis, M. H., & Goldman, B. M. (2005). Authenticity, social motivation, and psychological adjustment. In J. P. Forgas, K. D. Williams, & S. M. Laham (Eds.), *Social motivation: Conscious and unconscious processes* (pp. 210–227). New York: Cambridge University Press.

Kernis, M. H., & Lakey, C. E. (2010). Fragile versus secure high self-esteem: Implications for defensiveness and insecurity. In R. M. Arkin, K. C. Oleson, & P. J. Carroll (Eds.), *Handbook of the uncertain self* (pp. 360–378). New York: Psychology Press.

Kerns, R. D., Sellinger, J., & Goodin, B. R. (2011). Psychological treatment of chronic pain. *Annual Review of Clinical Psychology, 7,* 411–434. doi:10.1146/annurev-clinpsy-090310-120430

Kessen, W., & Cahan, E. D. (1986). A century of psychology: From subject to object to agent. *American Scientist, 74,* 640–649.

Kessler, D. A. (2009). *The end of overeating: Taking control of the insatiable American appetite*. Emmaus, PA: Rodale Press.

Kessler, R. C. (2010). The prevalence of mental illness. In T. L. Scheid & T. N. Brown (Eds.), *A handbook for the study of mental health: Social contexts, theories, and systems* (2nd ed., pp. 46–63). New York: Cambridge University Press.

Kety, S. S. (1979, September). Disorders of the human brain. *Scientific American, 241,* 202–214. doi:10.1038/scientificamerican0979-202

Khan, K. M., Thompson, A. M., et al. (2012). Sport and exercise as contributors to the health of nations. *The Lancet, 380*(9836), 59–64. doi:10.1016/S0140-6736(12)60865-4

Khullar, D. (2017, June 8). How prejudice can harm your health. *New York Times.* https://www.nytimes.com/2017/06/08/upshot/how-prejudice-can-harm-your-health.html

Kida, T. E. (2006). *Don't believe everything you think.* Buffalo, NY: Prometheus.

Kiddoo, D. A. (2012). Toilet training children: When to start and how to train. *Canadian Medical Association Journal, 184*(5), 511–512. doi:10.1503/cmaj.110830

Kiecolt-Glaser, J. (2010). Stress, food, and inflammation: Psychoneuroimmunology and nutrition at the cutting edge. *Psychosomatic Medicine, 72*(4), 365–369. doi:10.1097/PSY.0b013e3181dbf489

Kiernan, M., Brown, S. D., et al. (2013). Promoting healthy weight with "stability skills first": A randomized trial. *Journal of Consulting & Clinical Psychology, 81*(2), 336–346. doi:10.1037/a0030544

Kievit, R. A., van Rooijen, H., et al. (2012). Intelligence and the brain: A model-based approach. *Cognitive Neuroscience, 3,* 89–97. doi:10.1080/17588928.2011.628383

Kiff, C. J., Lengua, L. J., & Bush, N. R. (2011). Temperament variation in sensitivity to parenting: Predicting changes in depression and anxiety. *Journal of Abnormal Child Psychology, 39*(8), 1199–1212. doi:10.1007/s10802-011-9539-x

Kihlstrom, J. F. (2013). Neurohypnotism: Prospects for hypnosis and neuroscience. *Cortex, 49*(2), 365–374. doi:10.1016/j.cortex.2012.05.016

Kim, K. H., Cramond, B., & VanTassel-Baska, J. (2010). The relationship between creativity and intelligence. In J. C. Kaufman & R. J. Sternberg (Eds.), *The Cambridge handbook of creativity* (pp. 395–412). New York: Cambridge University Press.

Kim, S., Oah, S., & Dickinson, A. M. (2005). The impact of public feedback on three recycling-related behaviors in South Korea. *Environment & Behavior, 37*(2), 258–274. doi:10.1177/0013916504267639

Kim, S.-K., Lee, Y. M., et al. (2013). The defensible space theory for creating safe urban neighborhoods: Perceptions and design implications in the United States and South Korea. *Journal of Architectural & Planning Research, 30*(3), 181–196.

Kimhi, Y. (2014). Theory of mind abilities and deficits in autism spectrum disorders. *Topics in Language Disorders, 34*(4), 329–343. doi:10.1097/TLD.0000000000000033

Kimmerer, R. W. (2013). *Braiding sweetgrass: Indigenous wisdom, scientific knowledge, and the teachings of plants.* Minneapolis: Milkweed.

Kimura, R., MacTavish, D., et al. (2012). Beta amyloid-induced depression of hippocampal long-term potentiation is mediated through the amylin receptor. *Journal of Neuroscience, 32*(48), 17401–17406. doi:10.1523/JNEUROSCI.3028-12.2012

King, B. E. (2012). *Human sexuality today* (7th ed.). Englewood Cliffs, NJ: Prentice Hall.

King, N. J., Muris, P., & Ollendick, T. H. (2005). Childhood fears and phobias: Assessment and treatment. *Child & Adolescent Mental Health, 10*(2), 50–56. doi:10.1111/j.1475-3588.2005.00118.x

King, P. M. (2009). Principles of development and developmental change underlying theories of cognitive and moral development. *Journal of College Student Development, 50*(6), 597–620. doi:10.1353/csd.0.0104

Kinnunen, L. H., Moltz, H., et al. (2004). Differential brain activation in exclusively homosexual and heterosexual men produced by the selective serotonin reuptake inhibitor, fluoxetine. *Brain Research, 1024*(1–2), 251–254. doi:10.1016/j.brainres.2004.07.070

Kinsey, A., Pomeroy, W., & Martin, C. (1948). *Sexual behavior in the human male.* Philadelphia: Saunders.

Kinsey, A., Pomeroy, W., (1953). *Sexual behavior in the human female.* Philadelphia: Saunders.

Kipp, M. (2016). Remyelination strategies in multiple sclerosis: A critical reflection. *Expert Review of Neurotherapeutics, 16*(1), 1–3. doi:10.1586/14737175.2016.1116387

Kipper, D. A. (1992). The effect of two kinds of role playing on self-evaluation of improved assertiveness. *Journal of Clinical Psychology, 48*(2), 246–250.

Kirby, D. B. (2008). The impact of abstinence and comprehensive sex and STD/HIV education programs on adolescent sexual behavior. *Sexuality Research & Social Policy, 5*(3), 18–27.

Kirk, S. A., Gallagher, J. J., & Coleman, M. R. (2015). *Educating exceptional children* (14th ed.). Boston, MA: Cengage Learning.

Kirlin, M. (2002). Civic skill building: The missing component in service programs? *Political Science & Politics, 35,* 571–575. doi:10.1017/S1049096502000872

Kirmayer, L. J., & Ryder, A. G. (2016). Culture and psychopathology. *Current Opinion in Psychology, 8,* 143–148. doi:10.1016/j.copsyc.2015.10.020

Kirsch, I., & Lynn, S. J. (1995). The altered state of hypnosis. *American Psychologist, 50*(10), 846–858. doi:10.1037/0003-066X.50.10.846

Kirsch, I., & Sapirstein, G. (1998). Listening to Prozac but hearing placebo: A meta-analysis of antidepressant medication. *Prevention & Treatment, 1,* art. 0002a. doi:10.1037/1522-3736.1.1.12a

Kirschner, P. A., Sweller, J., & Clark, R. E. (2006). Why minimal guidance during instruction does not work: An analysis of the failure of constructivist, discovery, problem-based, experiential, and inquiry-based teaching. *Educational Psychologist, 41*(2), 75–86. doi:10.1207/s15326985ep4102_1

Kirsh, S. J. (2010). *Children, adolescents, and media violence: A critical look at the research* (2nd ed.). Thousand Oaks, CA Sage.

Kiser, L. J., Heston, J. D., & Paavola, M. (2006). Day treatment centers/Partial hospitalization settings. In T. A. Petti & C. Salguero (Eds.), *Community child & adolescent psychiatry: A manual of clinical practice and consultation* (pp. 189–203). Washington, DC: American Psychiatric Publishing.

Kish, A. M., & Newcombe, P. A. (2015). "Smacking never hurt me!": Identifying myths surrounding the use of corporal punishment. *Personality & Individual Differences, 87,* 121–129. doi:10.1016/j.paid.2015.07.035

Kishimoto, N., Yamamuro, K., et al. (2016). Distinctive Rorschach profiles of young adults with schizophrenia and autism spectrum disorder. *Neuropsychiatric Disease & Treatment, 12,* 2403–2410.

Kisilevsky, B. S., & Hains, S. J. (2011). Onset and maturation of fetal heart rate response to the mother's voice over late gestation. *Developmental Science, 14*(2), 214–223.

Kitayama, S., Markus, H. R., & Kurokawa, M. (2000). Culture, emotion, and well-being: Good feelings in Japan and the United States. *Cognition & Emotion, 14,* 93–124. doi:10.1080/026999300379003

Kitchin, R. (2016). The ethics of smart cities and urban science. *Philosophical Transactions of the Royal Society A: Mathematical, Physical and Engineering Sciences, 374*(2083), 20160115.

Kite, M. E., Stockdale, G. D., et al. (2005). Attitudes toward younger and older adults: An updated meta-analytic review. *Journal of Social Issues, 61*(2), 241–266.

Kjellgren, A., Buhrkall, H., & Norlander, T. (2011). Preventing sick-leave for sufferers of high stress-load and burnout syndrome: A pilot study combining psychotherapy and the flotation tank. *International Journal of Psychology & Psychological Therapy, 11*(2), 297–306.

Klahr, D., & Nigam, M. (2004). The equivalence of learning paths in early science instruction: Effects of direct instruction and discovery learning. *Psychological Science, 15,* 661–667.

Kleiman, E. M., Miller, A. B., & Riskind, J. H. (2012). Enhancing attributional style as a protective factor in suicide. *Journal of Affective Disorders, 143*(1–3), 236–240. doi:10.1016/j.jad.2012.05.014

Klein, B., Richards, J. C., & Austin, D. W. (2006). Efficacy of Internet therapy for panic disorder. *Journal of Behavior Therapy & Experimental Psychiatry, 37*(3), 213–238. doi:10.1016/j.jbtep.2005.07.001

Klein, D. W., & Kihlstrom, J. F. (1986). Elaboration, organization, and the self-reference effect in memory. *Journal of Experimental Psychology: General, 115,* 26–38.

Klein, G. (2013). *Seeing what others don't: The remarkable ways we gain insights.* New York: Public Affairs Books.

Klein, K., & Boals, A. (2001). Expressive writing can increase working memory capacity. *Journal of Experimental Psychology: General, 130*(3), 520–533. doi:10.1037/0096-3445.130.3.520

Klein, L. A., & Houlihan, D. (2010). Relationship satisfaction, sexual satisfaction, and sexual problems in sexsomnia. *International Journal of Sexual Health, 22*(2), 84–90. doi:10.1080/19317610903510489

Kleinfield, N. R., & Buckley, C. (2011, September 30). Wall Street Occupiers, protesting till whenever. *New York Times.* Retrieved February 23, 2017, from www.nytimes.com/2011/10/01/nyregion/wall-street-occupiers-protesting-till-whenever.html

Kleinmann, M., & Klehe, U. (2011). Selling oneself: Construct and criterion-related validity of impression management in structured interviews. *Human Performance, 24*(1), 29–46. doi:10.1080/08959285.2010.530634

Klinger, E. (2013). Goal commitments and the content of thoughts and dreams: Basic principles. *Frontiers in Psychology, 4,* 415.

Klohnen, E. C., & Luo, S. (2003). Interpersonal attraction and personality: What is attractive—self similarity, ideal similarity, complementarity or attachment security? *Journal of Personality & Social Psychology, 85*(4), 709–722. doi:10.1037/0022-3514.85.4.709

Kloos, B., Hill, J., et al. (2012). *Community psychology: Linking individuals and communities* (3rd ed.) Boston, MA: Cengage Learning.

Klösch, G., & Holzinger, B. (2014). Dream content analysis: Methodological and theoretical approaches. *Psychotherapie Forum, 19*(3–4), 121–129. doi:10.1007/s00729-014-0023-2

Knafo, D. (2012). Alone together: Solitude and the creative encounter in art and psychoanalysis. *Psychoanalytic Dialogues, 22*(1), 54–71.

Kneer, J., Glock, S., & Rieger, D. (2012). Fast and not furious? Reduction of cognitive dissonance in smokers. *Social Psychology, 43*(2), 81–91. doi:10.1027/1864-9335/a000086

Knickmeyer, R. C., & Baron-Cohen, S. (2006). Fetal testosterone and sex differences. *Early Human Development, 82*(12), 755–760.

Knoops, K. T., de Groot, L. C., et al. (2004). Mediterranean diet, lifestyle factors, and 10-year mortality in elderly European men and women. *Journal of the American Medical Association, 292*(12), 1433–1439. doi:10.1001/jama.292.12.1433

Koch, A. R., & Binnewies, C. (2015). Setting a good example: Supervisors as work-life-friendly role models within the context of boundary management. *Journal of Occupational Health Psychology, 20,* 82–92. doi:10.1037/a0037890

Koch, I., Lawo, V., et al. (2011). Switching in the cocktail party: Exploring intentional control of auditory selective attention. *Journal of Experimental Psychology: Human Perception & Performance, 37*(4), 1140–1147. doi:10.1037/a0022189

Koch, I., Poljac, E., Müller, H., & Kiesel, A. (2018). Cognitive structure, flexibility, and plasticity in human multitasking—An integrative review of dual-task and task-switching research. *Psychological Bulletin, 144*(6), 557–583. doi:10.1037/bul0000144

Koch, M., Varela, L., Kim, J. G., Kim, J. D., Hernández-Nuño, F., Simonds, S. E., et al. (2015). Hypothalamic POMC neurons promote cannabinoid-induced feeding. *Nature, 519*(7541), 45–50. doi:10.1038/nature14260

Koçkaya, G., & Wertheimer, A. (2011). Can we reduce the cost of illness with more compliant patients? An estimation of the effect of 100% compliance with hypertension treatment. *Journal of Pharmacy Practice, 24*(3), 345–350. doi:10.1177/0897190010389336

Koek, W. (2011). Drug-induced, state-dependent learning: Review of an operant procedure in rats. *Behavioural Pharmacology, 22*(5–6), 430–440. doi:10.1097/FBP.0b013e328348ed3b

Kohen, D. P. (2011). Chronic daily headache: Helping adolescents help themselves with self-hypnosis. *American Journal of Clinical Hypnosis, 54*(1), 32–46. doi:10.1080/00029157.2011.566767

Kohlberg, L. (1969). The cognitive-developmental approach to socialization. In A. Goslin (Ed.), *Handbook of socialization theory and research* (pp. 1–134). Chicago, IL: Rand McNally.

Kohlberg, L. (1981). *Essays on moral development* (Vol. I): *The philosophy of moral development*. San Francisco, CA: Harper.

Kohler, P. K., Manhart, L. E., & Lafferty, W. E. (2008). Abstinence-only and comprehensive sex education and the initiation of sexual activity and teen pregnancy. *Journal of Adolescent Health, 42*(4), 344–351.

Kok, B. E., Coffey, K. A., et al. (2013). How positive emotions build physical health: Perceived positive social connections account for the upward spiral between positive emotions and vagal tone. *Psychological Science, 24*(7), 1123–1132. doi:10.1177/0956797612470827

Köke, A., Schouten, J. S., et al. (2004). Pain-reducing effect of three types of transcutaneous electrical nerve stimulation in patients with chronic pain: A randomized crossover trial. *Pain, 108*(1–2), 36–42. doi:10.1016/j.pain.2003.11.013

Kolb, B., & Whishaw, I.Q. (2013). *Introduction to brain and behaviour* (4th ed.). New York: Freeman-Worth.

Kolb, B., Gibb, R., & Gorny, G. (2003). Experience-dependent changes in dendritic arbor and spine density in neocortex vary with age and sex. *Neurobiology of Learning & Memory, 79*(1), 1–10. doi:10.1016/S1074-7427(02)00021-7

Kolb, B., Mychasiuk, R., et al. (2011). Brain plasticity and recovery from early cortical injury. *Developmental Medicine & Child Neurology, 53*, 4–8. doi:10.1111/j.1469-8749.2011.04054.x

Kolodny, A., Courtwright, D. T., et al. (2015). The prescription opioid and heroin crisis: A public health approach to an epidemic of addiction. *Annual Review of Public Health, 36*, 559–574. doi:10.1146/annurev-publhealth-031914-122957

Komisaruk, B. R., Beyer-Flores, C., & Whipple, B. (2006). *The science of orgasm*. Baltimore, MD: Johns Hopkins University Press.

Kornhaber, M. L., & Gardner, H. (2006). Multiple intelligences: Developments in implementation and theory. In M. A. Constas & R. J. Sternberg (Eds.), *Translating theory and research into educational practice: Developments in content domains, large-scale reform, and intellectual capacity* (pp. 255–276). Mahwah, NJ: Erlbaum.

Kornilov, S. A., Tan, M., et al. (2012). Gifted identification with aurora: Widening the spotlight. *Journal of Psychoeducational Assessment, 30*(1), 117–133. doi:10.1177/0734282911428199

Koschate, M., & van Dick, R. (2011). A multilevel test of Allport's contact conditions. *Group Processes & Intergroup Relations, 14*(6), 769–787. doi:10.1177/1368430211399602

Kossek, E. E., & Michel, J. S. (2011). Flexible work schedules. In S. Zedeck (Ed.). (2011). *APA handbook of industrial and organizational psychology* (Vol. 1): *Building and developing the organization* (pp. 535–572). Washington, DC: American Psychological Association.

Kosslyn, S. M. (1983). *Ghosts in the mind's machine*. New York: Norton.

Kosslyn, S. M. (1985). Stalking the mental image. *Psychology Today, 19*(5), 22–28.

Kosslyn, S. M., Ball, T. M., & Reiser, B. J. (1978). Visual images preserve metric spatial information: Evidence from studies of image scanning. *Journal of Experimental Psychology: Human Perception & Performance, 4*, 47–60. doi:10.1037/0096-1523.4.1.47

Kosson, D. S., Suchy, Y., et al. (2002). Facial affect recognition in criminal psychopaths. *Emotion, 2*(4), 398–411. doi:10.1037/1528-3542.2.4.398

Kost, K., & Maddow-Zimet, I. (2016). *U.S. teenage pregnancies, births and abortions, 2011: State trends by age, race and ethnicity*. New York: Guttmacher Institute. Retrieved March 10, 2017, from www.guttmacher.org/pubs/USTPtrends10.pdf

Kosten, T. R., Wu, G., et al. (2012, August 18). Pharmacogenetic randomized trial for cocaine abuse: Disulfiram and dopamine β-hydroxylase. *Biological Psychiatry*, n.p. doi:10.1016/j.biopsych.2012.07.011

Kotagal, S. (2012). Hypersomnia in children. *Sleep Medicine Clinics, 7*(2), 379–389. doi:10.1016/j.jsmc.2012.03.010

Kotkin, M., Daviet, C., & Gurin, J. (1996). The *Consumer Reports* mental health survey. *American Psychologist, 51*(10), 1080–1082. doi:10.1037/0003-066X.51.10.1080

Kott, A. A. (2011). Masturbation is associated with partnered sex among adolescent males and females. *Perspectives on Sexual and Reproductive Health, 43*(4), 264. doi:10.1363/4326411_1

Kottler, J. A., & Chen, D. D. (2011). *Stress management and prevention: Applications to daily life* (2nd ed.). New York: Routledge.

Kottler, J. A., & Shepard, D. S. (2015). *Introduction to counseling* (8th ed.). Boston, MA: Cengage Learning.

Kouzes, J., & Posner, B. (2014). *The student leadership challenge*. San Francisco, CA: Wiley.

Kovera, M., & Cutler, B. L. (2013). *Jury selection*. New York: Oxford University Press.

Kovrov, G. V., Rusakova, I. M., et al. (2012). Specificity of sleep-wakefulness cycle during a 105-day isolation. *Human Physiology, 38*(7), 695–698. doi:10.1134/S0362119712070109

Kowert, P. A. (2002). *Groupthink or deadlock: When do leaders learn from their advisors? SUNY series on the presidency*. Albany, NY: State University of New York Press.

Kozica, S. L., Deeks, A. A., et al. (2012). Health-related behaviors in women with lifestyle-related diseases. *Behavioral Medicine, 38*(3), 65–73. doi:10.1080/08964289.2012.685498

Krahé, B., & Möller, I. (2010). Longitudinal effects of media violence on aggression and empathy among German adolescents. *Journal of Applied Developmental Psychology, 31*(5). 401–409. doi:10.1016/j.appdev.2010.07.003

Krahé, B., Möller, I., et al. (2011). Desensitization to media violence: Links with habitual media violence exposure, aggressive cognitions, and aggressive behavior. *Journal of Personality & Social Psychology, 100*(4), 630–646. doi:10.1037/a0021711

Krakow, B., & Zadra, A. (2006). Clinical management of chronic nightmares: Imagery rehearsal therapy. *Behavioral Sleep Medicine, 4*(1), 45–70. doi:10.1207/s15402010bsm0401_4

Krall, E. A., Garvey, A. J., & Garcia, R. I. (2002). Smoking relapse after 2 years of abstinence: Findings from the VA Normative Aging Study. *Nicotine & Tobacco Research, 4*(1), 95–100. doi:10.1080/14622200110098428

Kramer, A. D., Guillory, J. E., & Hancock, J. T. (2014). Experimental evidence of massive-scale emotional contagion through social networks. *Proceedings of the National Academy of Sciences, 111*(24), 8788–8790. doi:10.1073/pnas.1320040111

Kramer, U., Despland, J.-N., et al. (2010). Change in defense mechanisms and coping over the course of short-term dynamic psychotherapy for adjustment disorder. *Journal of Clinical Psychology, 66*(12), 1232–1241. doi:10.1002/jclp.20719

Krantz, M. J., Sabel, A. L., et al. (2012). Factors influencing QT prolongation in patients hospitalized with severe anorexia nervosa. *General Hospital Psychiatry, 34*(2), 173–177. doi:10.1016/j.genhosppsych.2011.08.003

Krathwohl, D. R. (2002). A revision of Bloom's taxonomy: An overview. *Theory into practice, 41*(4), 212–218. doi:10.1207/s15430421tip4104_2

Kraus, N., & Slater, J. (2016). Beyond words: How humans communicate through sound. *Annual Review of Psychology, 67*, 83–103. doi:10.1146/annurev-psych-122414-033318

Kreager, D. A., & Staff, J. (2009). The sexual double standard and adolescent peer acceptance. *Social Psychology Quarterly, 72*(2), 143–164.

Kreger Silverman, L. (2013). *Giftedness 101*. New York: Springer.

Krentz, H., Miltenberger, R., & Valbuena, D. (2016). Using token reinforcement to increase walking for adults with intellectual disabilities. *Journal of Applied Behavior Analysis, 49*(4), 745–750. doi:10.1002/jaba.326

Krettenauer, T., Colasante, T., et al. (2014). The development of moral emotions and decision-making from adolescence to early adulthood: A 6-year longitudinal study. *Journal of Youth & Adolescence, 43*(4), 583–596. doi:10.1007/s10964-013-9994-5

Krieger, N., Chen, J. T., Coull, B., Waterman, P. D., & Beckfield, J. (2013). The unique impact of abolition of Jim Crow laws on reducing inequities in infant death rates and implications for choice of comparison groups in analyzing societal determinants of health. *American Journal of Public Health, 103*(12), 2234–2244. doi:10.2105/AJPH.2013.301350

Krishnan, H. A., & Park, D. (2005). A few good women—on top management teams. *Journal of Business Research, 58,* 1712–1720.

Ksir, C. J., Hart, C. L., et al. (2015). *Drugs, behavior, and society* (2nd ed.). New York: McGraw-Hill.

Kteily, N., Hodson, G., et al. (2016). They see us as less than human: Meta-dehumanization predicts intergroup conflict via reciprocal dehumanization. *Journal of Personality & Social Psychology, 110,* 343–370. doi:10.1037/pspa0000044

Kteily, N., Sidanius, J., & Levin, S. (2011). Social dominance orientation: Cause or 'mere effect'? Evidence for SDO as a causal predictor of prejudice and discrimination against ethnic and racial outgroups. *Journal of Experimental Social Psychology, 47*(1), 208–214. doi:10.1016/j.jesp.2010.09.009

Ku, K. Y. L., & Ho, I. T. (2010). Metacognitive strategies that enhance critical thinking. *Metacognition & Learning, 5*(3), 251–267.

Kübler-Ross, E. (1975). *Death: The final stage of growth.* Englewood Cliffs, NJ: Prentice Hall.

Kuczka, K. K., & Treasure, D. C. (2005). Self-handicapping in competitive sport: Influence of the motivational climate, self-efficacy and perceived importance. *Psychology of Sport & Exercise, 6*(5), 539–550.

Kudo, F. T., Longhofer, J. L., & Floersch, J. E. (2012). On the origins of early leadership: The role of authoritative parenting practices and mastery orientation. *Leadership, 8*(4), 345–375.

Kuehn, B. M. (2012). Marijuana use starting in youth linked to IQ loss. *Journal of the American Medical Association, 308*(12). doi:10.1001/2012.jama.12205

Kuehner, C. (2017). Why is depression more common among women than among men? *The Lancet Psychiatry, 4*(2), 146–158. doi:10.1016/S2215-0366(16)30263-2

Kugler, T., & Bornstein, G. (2013). Social dilemmas between individuals and groups. *Organizational Behavior & Human Decision Processes, 120*(2), 191–205. doi:10.1016/j.obhdp.2012.07.007

Kuiper, N. A., & McHale, N. (2009). Humor styles as mediators between self-evaluative standards and psychological well-being. *Journal of Psychology: Interdisciplinary & Applied, 143*(4), 359–376. doi:10.3200/JRLP.143.4.359-376

Kulik, C. T., Perry, E. L., & Bourhis, A. C. (2000) Ironic evaluation processes: Effects of thought suppression on evaluations of older job applicants. *Journal of Organizational Behavior, 21*(6), 689–711. doi:10.1002/1099-1379(200009)21:6<689::AID-JOB52>3.0.CO;2-W

Kulik, J., Mahler, H. I. M., & Moore, P. J. (2003). Social comparison affiliation under threat: Effects on recovery from major surgery. In P. Salovey & A. J. Rothman (Eds.), *Social psychology of health: Key readings in social psychology* (pp. 199–226). New York: Psychology Press.

Kumsta, R., & Heinrichs, M. (2013). Oxytocin, stress and social behavior: Neurogenetics of the human oxytocin system. *Current Opinion in Neurobiology, 23*(1), 11–16. doi:10.1016/j.conb.2012.09.004

Kupfersmid, J. (2012). The Oedipus complex: It made no sense then, it makes no sense now. In M. Holowchak (Ed.), *Radical claims in Freudian psychoanalysis: Point/Counterpoint* (pp. 27–40). Lanham, MD: Jason Aronson.

Kyaga, S., Landén, M., et al. (2013). Mental illness, suicide and creativity: 40-year prospective total population study. *Journal of Psychiatric Research, 47*(1), 83–90. doi:10.1016/j.jpsychires.2012.09.010

Laasonen, M., Kauppinen, J., et al. (2012). Project DyAdd: Classical eyeblink conditioning in adults with dyslexia and ADHD. *Experimental Brain Research, 223*(1), 19–32. doi:10.1007/s00221-012-3237-y

LaBar, K. S. (2007). Beyond fear: Emotional memory mechanisms in the human brain. *Current Directions in Psychological Science, 16*(4), 173–177. doi:10.1111/j.1467-8721.2007.00498.x

LaBerge, S. (2014). Lucid dreaming: Paradoxes of dreaming consciousness. In E. Cardeña, S. Lynn, et al. (Eds.), *Varieties of anomalous experience: Examining the scientific evidence* (2nd ed., pp. 145–173). Washington, DC: American Psychological Association. doi:10.1037/14258-006

Labov, W. (1973). The boundaries of words and their meanings. In C. J. N. Bailey & R. W. Shuy (Eds.), *New ways of analyzing variation in English* (pp. 340–373). Washington, DC: Georgetown University Press.

LaBrie, R. A., & Shaffer, H. J. (2007). Gambling with adolescent health. *Journal of Adolescent Health, 40*(5), 387–389. doi:10.1016/j.jadohealth.2007.02.009

Lackner, J. R., & DiZio, P. (2005). Vestibular, proprioceptive, and haptic contributions to spatial orientation. *Annual Review of Psychology, 56,* 115–147. doi:10.1146/annurev.psych.55.090902.142023

Ladouceur, R., Lachance, S., & Fournier, P.-M. (2009). Is control a viable goal in the treatment of pathological gambling? *Behaviour Research & Therapy, 47*(3), 189–197. doi:10.1016/j.brat.2008.11.004

Laible, D. J., & Thompson, R. A. (2002). Mother-child conflict in the toddler years: Lessons in emotion, morality, and relationships. *Child Development, 73*(4), 1187–1203. doi:10.1111/1467-8624.00466

Lam, R., & Mok, H. (2008). *Depression.* New York: Oxford.

Lamb, R. J., Kirby, K. C., et al. (2010). Shaping smoking cessation in hard-to-treat smokers. *Journal of Consulting & Clinical Psychology, 78*(1), 62–71. doi:10.1037/a0018323

Lambert, E. G., Clarke, A., et al. (2009). Multivariate analysis of reasons for death penalty support between male and female college students: Empirical support for Gilligan's "ethic of care." *Criminal Justice Studies: A Critical Journal of Crime, Law, & Society, 22*(3), 239–260. doi:10.1080/14786010903166957

Lambert, M. J., & Ogles, B. M. (2002). The efficacy and effectiveness of psychotherapy. In M. J. Lambert (Ed.), *Handbook of psychotherapy and behavior change* (5th ed., pp. 130–193). New York: Wiley.

Lambert, W. E. (1987). The effects of bilingual and bicultural experiences on children's attitudes and social perspectives. In P. Homel, M. Palij, et al. (Eds.), *Childhood bilingualism* (pp. 197–221). Hillsdale, NJ: Erlbaum.

Lammers, G. J., Bassetti, C., et al. (2010). Sodium oxybate is an effective and safe treatment for narcolepsy. *Sleep Medicine, 11*(1), 105–106. doi:10.1016/j.sleep.2009.08.003

Lammers, J., Stoker, J. I., et al. (2016). To have control over or to be free from others? The desire for power reflects a need for autonomy. *Personality & Social Psychology Bulletin, 42*(4), 498–512. doi:10.1177/0146167216634064

Lamont, K. T., Somers, S., et al. (2011). Is red wine a SAFE sip away from cardioprotection? Mechanisms involved in resveratrol- and melatonin-induced cardioprotection. *Journal of Pineal Research, 50,* 374–380. doi:10.1111/j.1600-079X.2010.00853.x

Lampinen, J. M., Neuschatz, J. S., & Cling, A. D. (2012). *The psychology of eyewitness identification.* Hove, UK: Psychology Press.

Lamprecht, R., Dracheva, S., et al. (2009). Fear conditioning induces distinct patterns of gene expression in lateral amygdala. *Genes, Brain, & Behavior, 8*(8), 735–743. doi:10.1111/j.1601-183X.2009.00515.x

Lamy, L., Fischer-Lokou, J., & Guéguen, N. (2012). Priming emotion concepts and helping behavior: How unlived emotions can influence action. *Social Behavior and Personality, 40*(1), 55–62. doi:10.2224/sbp.2012.40.1.55

Lan Yeung, V. W., & Kashima, Y. (2010). Communicating stereotype-relevant information: How readily can people individuate? *Asian Journal of Social Psychology, 13*(4), 209–220. doi:10.1111/j.1467-839X.2010.01313.x

Lanciano, T., Curci, A., & Semin, G. (2010). The emotional and reconstructive determinants of emotional memories: An experimental approach to flashbulb memory investigation. *Memory, 18*(5), 473–485. doi:10.1080/09658211003762076

Landa, Y., Silverstein, S. M., et al. (2006). Group cognitive behavioral therapy for delusions: Helping patients improve reality testing. *Journal of Contemporary Psychotherapy, 36*(1), 9–17. doi:10.1007/s10879-005-9001-x.

Landini, F. (2015). Contributions of community psychology to rural advisory services: An analysis of Latin American rural extensionists' point of view. *American Journal of Community Psychology, 55,* 359–368. doi:10.1007/s10464-015-9712-4

Landy, F. J., & Conte, J. M. (2009). *Work in the 21st century: An introduction to industrial and organizational psychology* (3rd ed.). Malden, MA: Blackwell.

Lane, C. (2009, June 3). The slippery slope of bitterness disorder and other psychiatric diagnoses. *Psychology Today,* Retrieved May 8, 2014, from www.psychologytoday.com/blog/side-effects/200906/the-slippery-slope-bitterness-disorder-and-other-psychiatric-diagnoses

Lane, R. D. (2014). Is it possible to bridge the biopsychosocial and biomedical models? *Biopsychosocial Medicine, 8,* 3.

Lane, R. D., Ryan, L., et al. (2015). Memory reconsolidation, emotional arousal, and the process of change in psychotherapy: New insights from brain science. *Behavioral & Brain Sciences, 38,* e1. doi:10.1017/S0140525X14000041

Lang, P. J. (2016). Imagery in therapy: An information processing analysis of fear. *Therapy, 47*(5), 688–701. doi:10.1016/j.beth.2016.08.011

Langens, T. A., & Schmalt, H.-D. (2002). Emotional consequences of positive daydreaming: The moderating role of fear of failure. *Personality & Social Psychology Bulletin, 28*(12), 1725–1735.

Langeslag, S. E., Schmidt, M., et al. (2013). Functional connectivity between parietal and frontal brain regions and intelligence in young children: The Generation R study. *Human Brain Mapping, 34*(12), 3299–3307. doi:10.1002/hbm.22143

Langleben, D. D. (2008). Detection of deception with fMRI: Are we there yet? *Legal & Criminological Psychology, 13*(1), 1–9. doi:10.1348/135532507X251641

Langleben, D. D., & Moriarty, J. (2013). Using brain imaging for lie detection: Where science, law, and policy collide. *Psychology, Public Policy, & Law, 19*(2), 222–234. doi:10.1037/a0028841

Langleben, D. D., Loughead, J. W., et al. (2005). Telling truth from a lie in individual subjects with fast event-related fMRI. *Human Brain Mapping, 26*(4), 262–272. doi:10.1002/hbm.20191

Lankford, A., & Madfis, E. (2018). Don't name them, don't show them, but report everything else: A pragmatic proposal for denying mass killers the attention they seek and deterring future offenders. *American Behavioral Scientist, 62*, 260–279. doi:10.1177/0002764218763476

Långsjö, J. W., Alkire, M. T., et al. (2012). Returning from oblivion: Imaging the neural core of consciousness. *Journal of Neuroscience, 32*(14), 4935–4943. doi:10.1523/JNEUROSCI.4962-11.2012

Lanphear, B. P. (2015). The impact of toxins on the developing brain. *Annual Review of Public Health, 36*, 211–230 doi:10.1146/annurev-publhealth-031912-114413

Larimer, M. E., Neighbors, C., et al. (2011). Descriptive drinking norms: For whom does reference group matter? *Journal of Studies on Alcohol & Drugs, 72*(5), 833–843.

La Roche, M., & Lustig, K. (2013). Being mindful about the assessment of culture: A cultural analysis of culturally adapted acceptance-based behavior therapy approaches. *Cognitive & Behavioral Practice, 20*(1), 60–63. doi:10.1016/j.cbpra.2012.04.002

Larsen, L., Hartmann, P., & Nyborg, H. (2008). The stability of general intelligence from early adulthood to middle-age. *Intelligence, 36*(1), 29–34.

Larsen, R. J., & Buss, D. M. (2014). *Personality psychology* (5th ed.). New York: McGraw-Hill.

Larsen, R. J., & Kasimatis, M. (1990). Individual differences in entrainment of mood to the weekly calendar. *Journal of Personality & Social Psychology, 58*(1), 164–171. doi:10.1037/0022-3514.58.1.164

Larson, M. E., Houlihan, D., & Goernert, P. N. (1995). Effects of informational feedback on aluminum can recycling. *Behavioral Interventions, 10*(2), 111–117.

Larsson, B., Carlsson, J., et al. (2005). Relaxation treatment of adolescent headache sufferers: Results from a school-based replication series. *Headache: The Journal of Head & Face Pain, 45*(6), 692–704. doi:10.1111/j.1526-4610.2005.05138.x

Larsson, J.-O., Larsson, H., & Lichtenstein, P. (2004). Genetic and environmental contributions to stability and change of ADHD symptoms between 8 and 13 years of age: A longitudinal twin study. *Journal of the American Academy of Child & Adolescent Psychiatry, 43*(10), 1267–1275. doi:10.1097/01.chi.0000135622.05219.bf

Latané, B., & Darley, J. M. (1970). *The unresponsive bystander: Why doesn't he help?* Upper Saddle River: Prentice Hall.

Lattal, K. A., Reilly, M. P., & Kohn, J. P. (1998). Response persistence under ratio and interval reinforcement schedules. *Journal of the Experimental Analysis of Behavior, 70*(2), 165–183. doi:10.1901/jeab.1998.70-165

Lau, C. Q. (2012). The stability of same-sex cohabitation, different-sex cohabitation, and marriage. *Journal of Marriage & Family, 74*(5), 973–988.

Laughlin, P. R. (2011). *Group problem solving*. Princeton, NJ: Princeton University Press.

Laukka, P., Elfenbein, H. A., et al. (2016). The expression and recognition of emotions in the voice across five nations: A lens model analysis based on acoustic features. *Journal of Personality and Social Psychology, 111*(5), 686–705. doi:10.1037/pspi0000066

Laureys, S., & Boly. M. (2007). What is it like to be vegetative or minimally conscious? *Current Opinion in Neurology, 20*, 609–613.

Laureys, S., Antoine, S., et al. (2002). Brain function in the vegetative state. *Acta Neurologica Belgica, 102*(4), 177–185.

Lautsch, B. A., Kossek, E. E., & Eaton, S. C. (2009). Supervisory approaches and paradoxes in managing telecommuting implementation. *Human Relations, 62*(6), 795–827.

Lavigne, F., Dumercy, L., et al. (2012). Dynamics of the semantic priming shift: Behavioral experiments and cortical network model. *Cognitive Neurodynamics, 6*(6), 467–483. doi:10.1007/s11571-012-9206-0

Lavin, M. (2012). On behalf of free association. In M. Holowchak (Ed.), *Radical claims in Freudian psychoanalysis: Point/Counterpoint* (pp. 153–166). Lanham, MD: Jason Aronson.

Lavy, S., & Littman-Ovadia, H. (2017). My better self: Using strengths at work and work productivity, organizational citizenship behavior, and satisfaction. *Journal of Career Development, 44*(2), 95–109. doi:10.1177/0894845316634056

Lavy, S., Mikulincer, M., & Shaver, P. R. (2010). Autonomy–proximity imbalance: An attachment theory perspective on intrusiveness in romantic relationships. *Personality & Individual Differences, 48*(5), 552–556.

Lawson, T. J., Jordan-Fleming, M. K., et al. (2015). Measuring psychological critical thinking: An update. *Teaching of Psychology, 42*, 248–253. doi:10.1177/0098628315587624

Lawson, T. T. (2008). *Carl Jung, Darwin of the mind*. London, UK: Karnac Books.

Lazar, A. S., Santhi, N., et al. (2013). Circadian period and the timing of melatonin onset in men and women: Predictors of sleep during the weekend and in the laboratory. *Journal of Sleep Research, 22*(2), 155–159. doi:10.1111/jsr.12001

Lazarevich, I., Irigoyen, C., et al. (2016). Relationship among obesity, depression, and emotional eating in young adults. *Appetite, 107*, 639–644. doi:10.1016/j.appet.2016.09.011

Lazarus, R. S. (1991a). Cognition and motivation in emotion. *American Psychologist, 46*(4), 352–367. doi:10.1037/0003-066X.46.4.352

Lazarus, R. S. (1991b). Progress on a cognitive–motivational–relational theory of emotion. *American Psychologist, 46*(8), 819–834. doi:10.1037/0003-066X.46.8.819

Lazarus, R. S., & Folkman, S. (1984). *Stress, appraisal, and coping*. New York: Springer.

Lazenka, M. F., Legakis, L. P., et al. (2016). Opposing effects of dopamine D1- and D2-like agonists on intracranial self-stimulation in male rats. *Experimental & Clinical Psychopharmacology, 24*(3), 193–205. doi:10.1037/pha0000067

Le Berre, A. P., Rauchs, G. G., et al. (2012, November 24). Impaired decision-making and brain shrinkage in alcoholism. *European Psychiatry*, n.p. doi:10.1016/j.eurpsy.2012.10.002

Le Pelley, M. E., Reimers, S. J., et al. (2010). Stereotype formation: Biased by association. *Journal of Experimental Psychology: General, 139*(1), 138–161. doi:10.1037/a0018210

Le, T. N. (2011). Life satisfaction, openness value, self-transcendence, and wisdom. *Journal of Happiness Studies, 12*(2), 171–182. doi:10.1007/s10902-010-9182-1

Leal, M. C., Shin, Y. J., et al. (2003). Music perception in adult cochlear implant recipients. *Acta Oto-Laryngologica, 123*(7), 826–835. doi:10.1177/8755123312437050

Leander, N., Chartrand, T. L., & Bargh, J. A. (2012). You give me the chills: Embodied reactions to inappropriate amounts of behavioral mimicry. *Psychological Science, 23*(7), 772–779. doi:10.1177/0956797611434535

Ledgerwood, A., & Trope, Y. (2010). Attitudes as global and local action guides. In J. P. Forgas, J. Cooper, et al. (Eds.), *The psychology of attitudes and attitude change* (pp. 39–58). New York: Psychology Press.

LeDoux, J. E. (2000). Emotion circuits in the brain. *Annual Review of Neuroscience, 23*, 155–184. doi:10.1146/annurev.neuro.23.1.155

LeDoux, J. E. (2012). A neuroscientist's perspective on debates about the nature of emotion. *Emotion Review, 4*(4), 375–379. doi:10.1177/1754073912445822

Lee, H., Peng, W., Steel, A., Reid, R., Sibbritt, D., & Adams, J. (2019). Complementary and alternative medicine research in practice-based research networks: A critical review. *Complementary Therapies in Medicine, 43*, 7–19. doi:10.1016/j.ctim.2018.12.023

Lee, J., Husman, J., et al. (2016). Development and validation of the persistent academic possible selves scale for adolescents (PAPSS). *Learning & Individual Differences, 52*, 19–28. doi:10.1016/j.lindif.2016.09.005

Lee, K., & Ashton, M. C. (2012). Getting mad and getting even: Agreeableness and Honesty-Humility as predictors of revenge intentions. *Personality and Individual Differences, 52*(5), 596–600. doi:10.1016/j.paid.2011.12.004

Lee, S. W., Clemenson, G. D., & Gage, F. H. (2011, October 18). New neurons in an aged brain. *Behavioural Brain Research*, n.p. doi:10.1016/j.bbr.2011.10.009

Lee, Y.-H., Dunbar, N., et al. (2016). Digital game based learning for undergraduate calculus education: Immersion, calculation, and conceptual understanding. *International Journal of Gaming & Computer-Mediated Simulations, 8*(1), 13–27. doi:10.4018/IJGCMS.2016010102

Leenaars, A. A., Lester, D., & Wenckstern, S. (2005). Coping with suicide: The art and the research. In R. I. Yufit & D. Lester (Eds.), *Assessment, treatment, and prevention of suicidal behavior* (pp. 347–377). New York: Wiley.

Leeper, R. W. (1935). A study of a neglected portion of the field of learning: The development of sensory organization. *Pedagogical Seminary & Journal of Genetic Psychology, 46*, 41–75.

Lefebvre, C. D., Marchand,Y., et al. (2007). Determining eyewitness identification accuracy using event-related brain potentials (ERPs). *Psychophysiology, 44*(6), 894–904.

Lefkowitz, E. S., & Zeldow, P. B. (2006). Masculinity and femininity predict optimal mental health: A belated test of the androgyny hypothesis. *Journal of Personality Assessment, 87*(1), 95–101.

Lefmann, T., & Combs-Orme, T. (2013). Early brain development for social work practice: Integrating neuroscience with Piaget's theory of cognitive development. *Journal of Human Behavior in the Social Environment, 23*(5), 640–647. doi:10 .1080/10911359.2013.775936

Lefrançois, G. R. (2012). *Theories of human learning: What the professors said* (6th ed.). Boston, MA: Cengage Learning.

Legros, S., & Cislaghi, B. (2020). Mapping the social-norms literature: An overview of reviews. *Perspectives on Psychological Science, 15*(1), 62–80. doi:10.1177/1745691619866455

Leidner, B., Castano, E., et al. (2010). Ingroup glorification, moral disengagement, and justice in the context of collective violence. *Personality & Social Psychology Bulletin, 36*(8), 1115–1129.

Leiter, M. P., & Maslach, C. (2005). *Banishing burnout: Six strategies for improving your relationship with work.* San Francisco, CA: Jossey-Bass.

Leiter, M. P., Gascón, S., & Martínez-Jarreta, B. (2010). Making sense of work life: A structural model of burnout. *Journal of Applied Social Psychology, 40*(1), 57–75. doi:10.1111/ j.1559-1816.2009.00563.x

Lejuez, C. W., Eifert, G. H., et al. (2000). Preference between onset predictable and unpredictable administrations of 20 carbon-dioxide-enriched air: Implications for better understanding the etiology and treatment of panic disorder. *Journal of Experimental Psychology: Applied, 6*(4), 349–358. doi:10.1037/1076-898X.6.4.349

Leming, M. R., & Dickinson, G. E. (2016). *Understanding dying, death, and bereavement* (8th ed.). Boston, MA: Cengage Learning.

Lemma, A., Target, M., & Fonagy, P. (2011). The development of a brief psychodynamic intervention (dynamic interpersonal therapy) and its application to depression: A pilot study. *Psychiatry: Interpersonal & Biological Processes, 74*(1), 41–48. doi:10.1521/psyc.2011.74.1.41

Lemogne, C., Nabi, H., et al. (2010). Hostility may explain the association between depressive mood and mortality: Evidence from the French GAZEL cohort study. *Psychotherapy & Psychosomatics, 79*(3), 164–171. doi:10.1159/000286961

Lenze, S. N., & Potts, M. A. (2017). Brief Interpersonal Psychotherapy for depression during pregnancy in a low-income population: A randomized controlled trial. *Journal of Affective Disorders, 210*, 151–157. doi:10.1016/j.jad.2016.12.029

Lenzenweger, M. F., & Gottesman, I. I. (1994). Schizophrenia. In V. S. Ramachandran (Ed.), *Encyclopedia of human behavior* (Vol. 4, pp. 41–59). San Diego, CA: Academic.

León, I., & Hernández, J. A. (1998). Testing the role of attribution and appraisal in predicting own and other's emotions. *Cognition & Emotion, 12*(1), 27–43. doi:10.1080/ 026999398379763

Leotti, L. A., Iyengar, S. S., & Ochsner, K. N. (2010). Born to choose: The origins and value of the need for control. *Trends in Cognitive Sciences, 14*(10), 457–463. doi:10.1016/j. tics.2010.08.001

Lepage, M. M., Sergerie, K. K., et al. (2011). Emotional face processing and flat affect in schizophrenia: Functional and structural neural correlates. *Psychological Medicine, 41*(9), 1833–1844. doi:10.1017/S0033291711000031

LePort, A. K. R., Mattfeld, A. T., et al. (2012). Behavioral and neuroanatomical investigation of Highly Superior Autobiographical Memory (HSAM). *Neurobiology of Learning & Memory, 98*(1), 78–92. doi:10.1016/j.nlm.2012.05.002

Leppänen, J. M. (2011). Neural and developmental bases of the ability to recognize social signals of emotions. *Emotion Review, 3*(2), 179–188. doi:10.1177/1754073910387942

Lerner, J. S., Li, Y., et al. (2015). Emotion and decision making. *Annual Review of Psychology, 66*, 799–823. doi:10.1146/annurev-psych-010213-115043

Lertzman, R. (2015). *Environmental melancholia.* London, UK: Routledge.

Lerum, K., & Dworkin, S. L. (2009). "Bad girls rule": An interdisciplinary feminist commentary on the report of the APA task force on the sexualization of girls. *Journal of Sex Research, 46*(4), 250–263.

Lessow-Hurley, J. (2013). *Foundations of dual language instruction* (6th ed.). Boston, MA: Allyn & Bacon.

Lester, D. (2006). Sexual orientation and suicidal behavior. *Psychological Reports, 99*(3), 923–924.

Le Texier, T. (2019). Debunking the Stanford prison experiment. *American Psychologist, 74*(7), 823–839. doi:10.1037/amp0000401

Lettvin, J. Y. (1961). Two remarks on the visual system of the frog. In W. Rosenblith (Ed.), *Sensory communication* (pp. 757–776). Cambridge, MA: MIT Press.

Leucht, S., Heres, S., et al. (2011). Evidence-based pharmacotherapy of schizophrenia. *International Journal of Neuropsychopharmacology, 14*(2), 269–284. doi:10.1017/ S1461145710001380

LeUnes, A. (2008). *Sport psychology* (4th ed.). New York: Psychology Press.

Leung, K., & Wang, J. (2015). Social processes and team creativity in multicultural teams: A sociotechnical framework. *Journal of Organizational Behavior, 36*(7), 1008–1025. doi:10.1002/job.2021

Levant, R. F. (2003). Treating male alexithymia. In L. B. Silverstein & T. J. Goodrich (Eds.), *Feminist family therapy: Empowerment in social context* (pp. 177–188). Washington, DC: American Psychological Association.

Levant, R. F. (2011). Research in the psychology of men and masculinity using the gender role strain paradigm as a framework. *American Psychologist, 66*(8), 765–776. doi:10.1037/a0025034

Levant, R. F., Allen, P. A., & Lien, M. (2014). Alexithymia in men: How and when do emotional processing deficiencies occur? *Psychology of Men & Masculinity, 15, 324–344,* doi:10.1037/a0033860

Levant, R. F., Good, G. E., et al. (2006). The Normative Male Alexithymia Scale: Measurement of a gender-linked syndrome. *Psychology of Men & Masculinity, 7*(4), 212–224. doi:10.1037/1524-9220.7.4.212

Levant, R. F., Hall, R. J., et al. (2009). Gender differences in alexithymia. *Psychology of Men & Masculinity, 10*(3), 190–203.

Levant, R. F., & Powell, W. A. (2017). The gender role strain paradigm. In R. F. Levant, & Y. J. Wong, Y. (Eds.), *The psychology of men and masculinities* (pp. 15–43). Washington, DC: American Psychological Association. doi:10.1037/0000023-002

Levashina, J., Hartwell, C. J., et al. (2014). The structured employment interview: Narrative and quantitative review of the research literature. *Personnel Psychology, 67*(1), 241–293. doi:10.1111/peps.12052

LeVay, S. (2011). *Gay, straight, and the reason why.* New York: Oxford University Press.

LeVay, S., Baldwin, J., et al. (2015). *Discovering human sexuality* (3rd ed.). Sunderland, MA: Sinauer Associates.

Levenson, E. A. (2012). Psychoanalysis and the rite of refusal. *Psychoanalytic Dialogues, 22*(1), 2–6. doi:10.1080/104 81885.2012.646593

Levenston, G. K., Patrick, C. J., et al. (2000). The psychopathic observer. *Journal of Abnormal Psychology, 109*, 373–385. doi:10.1037/0021-843X.109.3.373

Leventhal, E. A., Hansell, S., Diefenbach, M., Leventhal, H., & Glass, D. C. (1996). Negative affect and self-report of physical symptoms: Two longitudinal studies of older adults. *Health Psychology, 15*(3), 193–199. doi:10.1037/0278-6133.15.3.193

Lévêque, M. (2014). *Psychosurgery: New techniques for brain disorders.* Cham, Switzerland: Springer International Publishing. doi:10.1007/978-3-319-01144-8

Levi, A. M. (1998). Are defendants guilty if they were chosen in a lineup? *Law & Human Behavior, 22*(4), 389–407. doi:10.1023/A:1025718909499

Levi, D. (2017). *Group dynamics for teams.* Thousand Oaks: Sage.

Levin, J. (2010). Gestalt therapy: Now and for tomorrow. *Gestalt Review, 14*(2), 147–170.

Levin, R., & Fireman, G. (2002). Nightmare prevalence, nightmare distress, and self-reported psychological disturbance. *Sleep: Journal of Sleep & Sleep Disorders Research, 25*(2), 205–212.

Levin, R., & Nielsen, T. (2009). Nightmares, bad dreams, and emotion dysregulation: A review and new neurocognitive model of dreaming. *Current Directions in Psychological Science, 18*(2), 84–88. doi:10.1111/j.1467-8721.2009.01614.x

Levy, D. L., Coleman, M. J., et al. (2010). The genetic basis of thought disorder and language and communication disturbances in schizophrenia. *Journal of Neurolinguistics, 23*(3), 176–192. doi:10.1016/j. jneuroling.2009.08.003

Lewandowski, G. W. Jr., Aron, A., & Gee, J. (2007). Personality goes a long way: The malleability of opposite-sex physical attractiveness. *Personal Relationships, 14*(4), 571–585. doi:10.1111/j.1475-6811.2007.00172.x

Lewis, C., & Lovatt, P. J. (2013). Breaking away from set patterns of thinking: Improvisation and divergent thinking. *Thinking Skills & Creativity, 9*, 46–58. doi:10.1016/j.tsc.2013.03.001

Lewis, M. B. (1995, January–February). Self-conscious emotions. *American Scientist, 83*, 68–78.

Lewis, M. B. (2012). Exploring the positive and negative implications of facial feedback. *Emotion, 12*(4), 852–859. doi:10.1037/a0029275

Lewis Jr, N., & Michalak, N. M. (2021). Has stereotype threat dissipated over time? A cross-temporal meta-analysis. *Comprehensive Results in Social Psychology.* This is in press, not yet published. It is available via PsyArXiv (open science repository) via https://psyarxiv.com/w4ta2/

Lewis Jr, N. A., & Sekaquaptewa, D. (2016). Beyond test performance: A broader view of stereotype threat. *Current Opinion in Psychology, 11,* 40–43. doi:10.1016/j.copsyc.2016.05.002

Li, C., Ford, E. S., et al. (2009). Associations of health risk factors and chronic illnesses with life dissatisfaction among U.S. adults: The Behavioral Risk Factor Surveillance System, 2006. *Preventive Medicine, 49*(2–3), 253–259. doi:10.1016/j.ypmed.2009.05.012

Li, N. P., Halterman, R. A., et al. (2008). The stress-affiliation paradigm revisited: Do people prefer the kindness of strangers or their attractiveness? *Personality & Individual Differences, 44*(2), 382–391. doi:10.1016/j.paid.2007. 08.017

Li, W., Farkas, G., et al. (2012, November 5). Timing of high-quality child care and cognitive, language, and preacademic development. *Developmental Psychology,* n.p. doi:10.1037/a0030613

Liddell, S. K. (2003). *Grammar, gesture and meaning in American Sign Language.* Cambridge, MA: Cambridge University Press.

Liden, R. C., Wayne, S. J., Jaworski, R. A., & Bennett, N. (2004). Social loafing: A field investigation. *Journal of Management, 30*(2), 285–304. doi:10.1016/j.jm.2003.02.002

Lieberman, J. D. (2011). The utility of scientific jury selection: Still murky after 30 years. *Current Directions in Psychological Science, 20*(1), 48–52. doi:10.1177/0963721410396628

Liechti, M. E., Dolder, P. C., et al. (2016, October 7). Alterations of consciousness and mystical-type experiences after acute LSD in humans. *Psychopharmacology,* n.p. doi:10.1007/s00213-016-4453-0

Light, T. P., Chen, H. L., et al. (2011). *Documenting learning with e-portfolios.* New York: Jossey-Bass.

Liles, E. E., & Packman, J. (2009). Play therapy for children with fetal alcohol syndrome. *International Journal of Play Therapy, 18*(4), 192–206. doi:10.1037/a0015664

Lilgendahl, J., Helson, R., & John, O. P. (2013). Does ego development increase during midlife? The effects of openness and accommodative processing of difficult events. *Journal of Personality, 81*(4), 403–416. doi:10.1111/jopy.12009

Lilienfeld, S. O., Ammirati, R., & Landfield, K. (2009). Giving debiasing away: Can psychological research on correcting cognitive errors promote human welfare? *Perspectives on Psychological Science, 4*(4), 390–398. doi:10.1111/j.1745-6924.2009.01144.x

Lilienfeld, S. O., Lynn, S. J., et al. (2010). *50 great myths of popular psychology: Shattering widespread misconceptions about human behavior.* London: Wiley-Blackwell.

Lilienfeld, S. O., Ruscio, J., & Lynn, S. J. (Eds.). (2008). *Navigating the mindfield: A user's guide to distinguishing science from pseudoscience in mental health.* Buffalo, NY: Prometheus Books.

Lin, F. R., Thorpe, R., et al. (2011). Hearing loss prevalence and risk factors among older adults in the United States. *Journals of Gerontology: Series A: Biological Sciences & Medical Sciences, 66A*(5), 582–590. doi:10.1093/gerona/glr002

Lin, T., & Peng, T. K. (2010). From organizational citizenship behaviour to team performance: The mediation of group cohesion and collective efficacy. *Management & Organization Review, 6*(1), 55–75. doi:10.1111/j.1740-8784.2009.00172.x

Lindemann, B. (2001). Receptors and transduction in taste. *Nature, 413,* 219–225. doi:10.1038/35093032

Linderoth, B., & Foreman, R. D. (2006). Mechanisms of spinal cord stimulation in painful syndromes: Role of animal models. *Pain Medicine, 7*(Suppl. 1), S14–S26. doi:10.1111/j.1526-4637.2006.00119.x

Lindsay, R. L., Kalmet, N., et al. (2013). Confidence and accuracy of lineup selections and rejections: Postdicting rejection accuracy with confidence. *Journal of Applied Research in Memory & Cognition, 2*(3), 179–184. doi:10.1016/j.jarmac.2013.06.002

Lindsey, B. J., Fabiano, P., & Stark, C. (2009). The prevalence and correlates of depression among college students. *College Student Journal, 43*(4, PtA), 999–1014.

Lindson-Hawley, N., Banting, M., et al. (2016, March 15). Gradual versus abrupt smoking cessation: A randomized, controlled noninferiority trial. *Annals of Internal Medicine,* doi:10.7326/M14-2805

Linsley, P., Digan, J., et al. (2016). Emotional intelligence as part of clinical engagement. *British Journal of Mental Health Nursing, 5*(1), 32–37. doi:10.12968/bjmh.2016.5.1.32

Linting, M., Groeneveld, M. G., et al. (2013). Threshold for noise in daycare: Noise level and noise variability are associated with child wellbeing in home-based childcare. *Early Childhood Research Quarterly, 28,* 960–971. doi:10.1016/j.ecresq.2013.03.005

Lipka, J., Miltner, W. H. R., & Straube, T. (2011). Vigilance for threat interacts with amygdala responses to subliminal threat cues in specific phobia. *Biological Psychiatry, 70*(5), 472–478. doi:10.1016/j.biopsych.2011.04.005

Lippke, S., Nigg, C. R., & Maddock, J. E. (2012). Health-promoting and health-risk behaviors: Theory-driven analyses of multiple health behavior change in three international samples. *International Journal of Behavioral Medicine, 19*(1), 1–13. doi:10.1007/s12529-010-9135-4

Littleton, H., & Breitkopf, C. R. (2006). Coping with the experience of rape. *Psychology of Women Quarterly, 30*(1), 106–116. doi:10.1111/j.1471-6402.2006.00267.x

Liu, Y., Gao, J., et al. (2000). The temporal response of the brain after eating revealed by functional MRI. *Nature, 405,* 1058–1062. doi:10.1038/35016590

Livingston, I., Doyle, J., & Mangan, D. (2010, April 25). Stabbed hero dies as more than 20 people stroll past him. *New York Post.* Retrieved May 8, 2014, from http://nypost.com/2010/04/24/stabbed-hero-dies-as-more-than-20-people-stroll-past-him/

Livingston-Thomas, J., Nelson, P., et al. (2016). Exercise and environmental enrichment as enablers of task-specific neuroplasticity and stroke recovery. *Neurotherapeutics, 13*(2), 395–402. doi:10.1007/s13311-016-0423-9

Llorens, R., & Noé, E. (2016). Through the eyes of neglect patients: A preliminary eye-tracking study of unilateral spatial neglect. *Journal of Neuropsychiatry & Clinical Neurosciences, 28*(1), e8–e9. doi:10.1176/appi.neuropsych.15060156

Lobbestael, J., Cima, M., & Arntz, A. (2013). The relationship between adult reactive and proactive aggression, hostile interpretation bias, and antisocial personality disorder. *Journal of Personality Disorders, 27*(1), 53–66. doi:10.1521/pedi.2013.27.1.53

Loeber, R., & Hay, D. (1997). Key issues in the development of aggression and violence from childhood to early adulthood. *Annual Review of Psychology, 48,* 371–410. doi:10.1146/annurev.psych.48.1.371

Loehlin, J. C., McCrae, R. R., Costa Jr, P. T., & John, O. P. (1998). Heritabilities of common and measure-specific components of the Big Five personality factors. *Journal of Research in Personality, 32*(4), 431–453. doi:10.1006/jrpe.1998.2225

Loftus, E. F. (2003). Make-believe memories. *American Psychologist, 58*(11), 867–873. doi:10.1037/0003-066X.58.11.867

Loftus, E. F., & Palmer, J. C. (1974). Reconstruction of automobile destruction: An example of interaction between language and memory. *Journal of Verbal Learning & Verbal Behavior, 13,* 585–589. doi:10.1016/S0022-5371(74)80011-3

Lokuge, S., Frey, B. N., et al. (2011). Depression in women: Windows of vulnerability and new insights into the link between estrogen and serotonin. *Journal of Clinical Psychiatry, 72*(11), 1563–1569. doi:10.4088/JCP.11com07089

LoLordo, V. M. (2001). Learned helplessness and depression. In M. E. Carroll & J. B. Overmier (Eds.), *Animal research and human health: Advancing human welfare through behavioral science* (pp. 63–77). Washington, DC: American Psychological Association.

Long, C. R., Seburn, M., et al. (2003). Solitude experiences: Varieties, settings, and individual differences. *Personality & Social Psychology Bulletin, 29*(5), 578–583.

Longo, M. R., Long, C., & Haggard, P. (2012). Mapping the invisible hand: A body model of a phantom limb. *Psychological Science, 23*(7), 740–742. doi:10.1177/0956797612441219

Lopez, M. A., & Basco, M. A. (2014, April 2). Effectiveness of cognitive behavioral therapy in public mental health: Comparison to treatment as usual for treatment-resistant depression. *Administration & Policy in Mental & Mental Health Services Research,* n.p. doi:10.1007/s10488-014-0546-4

López, S. R., & Guarnaccia, P. J. J. (2000). Cultural psychopathology. *Annual Review of Psychology, 51,* 571–598. doi:10.1146/annurev.psych.51.1.571

Lord, C., & Bishop, S. L. (2015). Recent advances in autism research as reflected in DSM-5 criteria for autism spectrum disorder. *Annual Review of Clinical Psychology, 11,* 53–70. doi:10.1146/annurev-clinpsy-032814-112745

Lorenzo, G. L., Biesanz, J. C., & Human, L. J. (2010). What is beautiful is good and more accurately understood: Physical attractiveness and accuracy in first impressions of personality. *Psychological Science, 21*(12), 1777–1782. doi:10.1177/0956797610388048

Lounsbury, D. W., & Mitchell, S. G. (2009). Introduction to special issue on social ecological approaches to community health research and action. *American Journal of Community Psychology, 44*(3–4), 213–220. doi:10.1007/s10464-009-9266-4

Lovibond, S. H., Mithiran, X., et al. (1979). The effects of three experimental prison environments on the behavior of non-convict volunteer subjects. *Australian Psychologist, 14,* 273–287.

Lowman, R. L. (Ed.). (2013). *Internationalizing multiculturalism: Expanding professional competencies in a globalized world.* Washington, DC: American Psychological Association.

Lu, Z.-L., & Dosher, B. (2014). *Visual psychophysics: From laboratory to theory*. Cambridge, MA: MIT Press.

Lucas, C., & Bayley, R. (2011). Variation in sign languages: Recent research on ASL and beyond. *Language & Linguistics Compass, 5*(9), 677–690. doi:10.1111/j.1749-818X.2011.00304.x

Lucy, J. A. (2016). Recent advances in the study of linguistic relativity in historical context: A critical assessment. *Language Learning, 66*(3), 487–515. doi:10.1111/lang.12195

Lum, D. (2011). *Culturally competent practice: A framework for understanding* (4th ed.). Boston, MA: Cengage Learning.

Lum, J. A., & Bleses, D. (2012). Declarative and procedural memory in Danish-speaking children with specific language impairment. *Journal of Communication Disorders, 45*(1), 46–58. doi:10.1016/j.jcomdis.2011.09.001

Lumley, M. A. (2004). Alexithymia, emotional disclosure, and health: A program of research. *Journal of Personality, 72*(6), 1271–1300. doi:10.1111/j.1467-6494.2004.00297.x

Lundholm, L., Haggård, U., et al. (2013). The triggering effect of alcohol and illicit drugs on violent crime in a remand prison population: A case crossover study. *Drug & Alcohol Dependence, 129*(1–2), 110–115. doi:10.1016/j.drugalcdep.2012.09.019

Luppa, M., Heinrich, S., et al. (2007). Cost-of-illness studies of depression: A systematic review. *Journal of Affective Disorders, 98*(1–2), 29–43. doi:10.1016/j.jad.2006.07.017

Luria, A. R. (1968). *The mind of a mnemonist*. New York: Basic.

Lusardi, A., Schneider, D., & Tufano, P. (2015). The economic crisis and medical care use: Comparative evidence from five high-income countries. *Social Science Quarterly, 96*(1), 202–213. doi:10.1111/ssqu.12076

Lussier, R., & Achua, C. (2015). *Leadership: Theory, application, & skill development.* Boston, MA: Cengage Learning.

Lutz, J., Brühl, A. B., et al. (2016). Neural correlates of mindful self-awareness in mindfulness meditators and meditation-naïve subjects revisited. *Biological Psychology, 119,* 21–30. doi:10.1016/j.biopsycho.2016.06.010

Luyster, F. S., Strollo, P. R., et al. (2012). Sleep: A health imperative. *Sleep: Journal of Sleep & Sleep Disorders Research, 35*(6), 727–734.

Luyten, P., & Blatt, S. J. (2011). Integrating theory-driven and empirically-derived models of personality development and psychopathology: A proposal for DSM V. *Clinical Psychology Review, 31*(1), 52–68. doi:10.1016/j.cpr.2010.09.003

Lykken, D. T. (1998). *A tremor in the blood: Uses and abuses of the lie detector*. New York: Plenum.

Lykken, D. T. (2001). Lie detection. In W. E. Craighead & C. B. Nemeroff (Eds.), *The Corsini Encyclopedia of psychology and behavioral science* (3rd ed., pp. 878–880). New York: Wiley.

Lyn, H., Franks, B., & Savage-Rumbaugh, E. S. (2008). Precursors of morality in the use of the symbols "good" and "bad" in two bonobos (Pan paniscus) and a chimpanzee (Pan troglodytes). *Language & Communication, 28*(3), 213–224. doi:10.1016/j.langcom.2008.01.006

Lynn, S. J., Green, J. P., et al. (2015). Grounding hypnosis in science: The "new" APA Division 30 definition of hypnosis as a step backward. *American Journal of Clinical Hypnosis, 57*(4), 390–401. doi:10.1080/00029157.2015.1011472

Lynn, S. J., & Kirsch, I. (2006). Introduction: Definitions and early history. In S. J. Lynn & I. Kirsch (Eds.), *Essentials of clinical hypnosis: An evidence-based approach* (pp. 3–15). Washington, DC: American Psychological Association.

Lynn, S. J., Kirsch, I., et al. (2010). An introduction to clinical hypnosis. In S. Lynn, J. W. Rhue, & I. Kirsch (Eds.), *Handbook of clinical hypnosis* (2nd ed., pp. 3–18). Washington, DC: American Psychological Association.

Lynn, S. J., & O'Hagen, S. (2009). The sociocognitive and conditioning and inhibition theories of hypnosis. *Contemporary Hypnosis, 26*(2), 121–125. doi:10.1002/ch.378

Lynne-Landsman, S. D., Graber, J. A., et al. (2011). Is sensation seeking a stable trait or does it change over time? *Journal of Youth & Adolescence, 40*(1), 48–58. doi:10.1007/s10964-010-9529-2

Lyons, H., Manning, W., et al. (2013). Predictors of heterosexual casual sex among young adults. *Archives of Sexual Behavior, 42*(4), 585–593. doi:10.1007/s10508-012-0051-3

Lyons, R. (2011). The spread of evidence-poor medicine via flawed social -network analysis. *Statistics, Politics, & Policy, 2*(1). doi:10.2202/2151-7509.1024

Lyubomirsky, S., & Tucker, K. L. (1998). Implications of individual differences in subjective happiness for perceiving, interpreting, and thinking about life events. *Motivation & Emotion, 22*(2), 155–186. doi:10.1023/A:1021396422190

MacDuffie, K., & Mashour, G. A. (2010). Dreams and the temporality of consciousness. *American Journal of Psychology, 123*(2), 189–197. doi:10.5406/amerjpsyc.123.2.0189

Macht, M., & Simons, G. (2011). Emotional eating. In I. NykliČek, A. Vingerhoets, & M. Zeelenberg (Eds.), *Emotion regulation and well-being* (pp. 281–295). New York: Springer.

MacIver, K., Lloyd, D. M., et al. (2008). Phantom limb pain, cortical reorganization, and the therapeutic effect of mental imagery. *Brain: A Journal of Neurology, 131*(8), 2181–2191. doi:10.1093/brain/awn124

MacKay, D. G., & Hadley, C. (2009). Supra-normal age-linked retrograde amnesia: Lessons from an older amnesic (H. M.). *Hippocampus, 19*(5), 424–445. doi:10.1002/hipo.20531

MacKenzie, M. J., Nicklas, E., et al. (2015). Spanking and children's externalizing behavior across the first decade of life: Evidence for transactional processes. *Journal of Youth & Adolescence, 44*(3), 658–669. doi:10.1007/s10964-014-0114-y

Maddi, S. R. (2013). *Hardiness: Turning stressful circumstances into resilient growth*. New York: Springer.

Maddi, S. R., Harvey, R. H., et al. (2009). The personality construct of hardiness, IV: Expressed in positive cognitions and emotions concerning oneself and developmentally relevant activities. *Journal of Humanistic Psychology, 49*(3), 292–305. doi:10.1177/0022167809331860

Maddock, J. E., & Glanz, K. (2005). The relationship of proximal normative beliefs and global subjective norms to college students' alcohol consumption. *Addictive Behaviors, 30*(2), 315–323. doi:10.1016/j.addbeh.2004.05.021

Maddock, J. E., Laforge, R. G., et al. (2001). The College Alcohol Problems Scale. *Addictive Behaviors, 26,* 385–398. doi:10.1016/S0306-4603(00)00116-7

Maddox, K. B. (2004). Perspectives on racial phenotypicality bias. *Personality & Social Psychology Review, 8*(4), 383–401. doi:10.1207/s15327957pspr0804_4

Madison, G., Mosing, M. A., et al. (2016). Common genetic influences on intelligence and auditory simple reaction time in a large Swedish sample. *Intelligence, 59,* 157–162. doi:10.1016/j.intell.2016.10.001

Madon, S., Willard, J., et al. (2011). Self-fulfilling prophecies: Mechanisms, power, and links to social problems. *Social & Personality Psychology Compass, 5*(8), 578–590. doi:10.1111/j.1751-9004.2011.00375.x

Madras, B. K. (2013). History of the discovery of the antipsychotic dopamine D2 receptor: A basis for the dopamine hypothesis of schizophrenia. *Journal of the History of the Neurosciences, 22*(1), 62–78. doi:10.1080/0964704X.2012.678199

Maggin, D. M., Chafouleas, S. M., et al. (2011). A systematic evaluation of token economies as a classroom management tool for students with challenging behavior. *Journal of School Psychology, 49*(5), 529–554. doi:10.1016/j.jsp.2011.05.001

Maguire, E. A., Intraub, H., & Mullally, S. L. (2016). Scenes, spaces, and memory traces: What does the hippocampus do? *Neuroscientist, 22*(5), 432–439. doi:10.1177/1073858415600389

Maguire-Jack, K., Gromoske, A. N., et al. (2012). Spanking and child development during the first 5 years of life. *Child Development, 83*(6), 1960–1977. doi:10.1111/j.1467-8624.2012.01820.x

Mah, K., & Binik, Y. M. (2001). The nature of human orgasm: A critical review of major trends. *Clinical Psychology Review, 21*(6), 823–856.

Mahler, H. I. M., Beckerley, S. E., & Vogel, M. T. (2010). Effects of media images on attitudes toward tanning. *Basic & Applied Social Psychology, 32*(2), 118–127. doi:10.1080/01973531003738296

Mahmoodabadi, S. Z., Ahmadian, A., et al. (2010). A fast expert system for electrocardiogram arrhythmia detection. *Expert Systems, 27*(3), 180–200.

Maier, N. R. F. (1949). *Frustration*. New York: McGraw-Hill.

Maier, S. F., & Seligman, M. E. P. (2016). Learned helplessness at fifty: Insights from neuroscience. *Psychological Review, 123*(4), 349–367. doi:10.1037/rev0000033

Maisto, S. A., Galizio, M., & Connors, G. J. (2015). *Drug use and abuse* (7th ed.). Boston, MA: Cengage Learning.

Malan, L., Hamer, M., et al. (2012). Defensive coping, urbanization, and neuroendocrine function in Black Africans: The THUSA study. *Psychophysiology, 49*(6), 807–814. doi:10.1111/j.1469-8986.2012.01362.x

Malan, L., Malan, N. T., et al. (2008). Coping with urbanization: A cardiometabolic risk? The THUSA study. *Biological Psychology, 79*(3), 323–328.

Malhi, G. S., & Outhred, T. (2016). Therapeutic mechanisms of lithium in bipolar disorder: Recent advances and current understanding. *CNS Drugs, 30*(10), 931–949. doi:10.1007/s40263-016-0380-1

Malhotra, A., Redberg R.F., & Meier P. (2017). Saturated fat does not clog the arteries: Coronary heart disease is a chronic inflammatory condition, the risk of which can be effectively reduced from healthy lifestyle interventions. *British Journal of Sports Medicine, 51,* 1111–1112. doi:10.1136/bjsports-2016-097285

Malmberg, L., & Flouri, E. (2011). The comparison and interdependence of maternal and paternal influences on young children's behavior and resilience. *Journal of Clinical Child & Adolescent Psychology, 40*(3), 434–444. doi:10.1080/15374416.2011.563469

Mamen, M. (2004). *Pampered child syndrome: How to recognize it, how to manage it and how to avoid it.* Carp, ON: Creative Bound.

Mancini, M. A., & Wyrick-Waugh, W. (2013). Consumer and practitioner perceptions of the harm reduction approach in a community mental health setting. *Community Mental Health Journal, 49*(1), 14–24. doi:10.1007/s10597-011-9451-4

Mangos, P. M., & Hulse, N. A. (2017). Advances in machine learning applications for scenario intelligence: Deep learning. *Theoretical Issues in Ergonomics Science, 18*(2), 184–198. doi:10.1080/1463922X.2016.1166406

Manning, R., Levine, M., & Collins, A. (2007). The Kitty Genovese murder and the social psychology of helping: The parable of the 38 witnesses. *American Psychologist, 62*(6), 555–562. doi:10.1037/0003-066X.62.6.555

Manning, R. P. C., Dickson, J. M., et al. (2017). A systematic review of adult attachment and social anxiety. *Journal of Affective Disorders, 211,* 44–59. doi:10.1016/j.jad.2016.12.020

Mantovani, A., Simpson, H. B., et al. (2010). Randomized sham-controlled trial of repetitive transcranial magnetic stimulation in treatment-resistant obsessive-compulsive disorder. *International Journal of Neuropsychopharmacology, 13*(2), 217–227. doi:10.1017/S1461145709990435

Mantyla, T. (1986). Optimizing cue effectiveness: Recall of 600 incidentally learned words. *Journal of Experimental Psychology: Learning, Memory, & Cognition, 12*(1), 66–71. doi:10.1037/0278-7393.12.1.66

Maples-Keller, J. L., Bunnell, B. E., Kim, S. J., & Rothbaum, B. O. (2017). The use of virtual reality technology in the treatment of anxiety and other psychiatric disorders. *Harvard Review of Psychiatry, 25*(3), 103–113. doi:10.1097/HRP.0000000000000138

Maran, M. (2010). *My lie: A true story of false memory.* San Francisco, CA: Jossey-Bass/Wiley.

Marazziti, D., & Baroni, S. (2012). Romantic love: The mystery of its biological roots. *Clinical Neuropsychiatry, 9*(1), 14–19.

Marcel, M. (2005). *Freud's traumatic memory: Reclaiming seduction theory and revisiting Oedipus.* Pittsburgh, PA: Duquesne University Press.

Marco, E. M., Romero-Zerbo, S. Y., et al. (2012). The role of the endocannabinoid system in eating disorders: Pharmacological implications. *Behavioural Pharmacology, 23*(5–6), 526–538. doi:10.1097/FBP.0b013e328356c3c9

Marecek, J., & Gavey, N. (2013). DSM-5 and beyond: A critical feminist engagement with psychodiagnosis. *Feminism & Psychology, 23*(1), 3–9. doi:10.1177/0959353512467962

Marian, D. E., & Shimamura, A. P. (2012). Emotions in context: Pictorial influences on affective attributions. *Emotion, 12*(2), 371–375. doi:10.1037/a0025517

Mariani, R., Mello, C., et al. (2011). Effect of naloxone and morphine on arcaine-induced state-dependent memory in rats. *Psychopharmacology, 215*(3), 483–491. doi:10.1007/s00213-011-2215-6

Mark, G. P., Shabani, S., et al. (2011). Cholinergic modulation of mesolimbic dopamine function and reward. *Physiology & Behavior, 104*(1), 76–81. doi:10.1016/j.physbeh.2011.04.052

Mark, K., Janssen, E., & Milhausen, R. (2011). Infidelity in heterosexual couples: Demographic, interpersonal, and personality-related predictors of extradyadic sex. *Archives of Sexual Behavior, 40*(5), 971–982. doi:10.1007/s10508-011-9771-z

Mark, T., Tomic, K., et al. (2013). Hospital readmission among Medicaid patients with an index hospitalization for mental and/or substance use disorder. *Journal of Behavioral Health Services & Research, 40*(2), 207–221. doi:10.1007/s11414-013-9323-5

Markoff, J. (2011). *Computer wins on Jeopardy!: Trivial, it's not.* Retrieved February 10, 2017, from www.nytimes.com/2011/02/17/science/17jeopardy-watson.html

Markova, G., & Perry, J. T. (2014). Cohesion and individual well-being of members in self-managed teams. *Leadership & Organization Development Journal, 35*(5), 429–441. doi:10.1108/LODJ-04-12-0058

Markowitz, F. E. (2011). Mental illness, crime, and violence: Risk, context, and social control. *Aggression & Violent Behavior, 16,* 36–44. doi:10.1016/j.avb.2010.10.003

Markowitz, J. C. (2017). *Interpersonal psychotherapy for posttraumatic stress disorder.* New York: Oxford University Press.

Marks, L. E. (2014). Synesthesia: A teeming multiplicity. In E. Cardeña, S. Lynn, et al. (Eds.), *Varieties of anomalous experience: Examining the scientific evidence* (2nd ed., pp. 79–108). Washington, DC: American Psychological Association. doi:10.1037/14258-004

Markus, H. R., Uchida, Y., et al. (2006). Going for the gold: Models of agency in Japanese and American contexts. *Psychological Science, 17*(2), 103–112. doi:10.1111/j.1467-9280.2006.01672.x

Markus, H., & Nurius, P. (1986). Possible selves. *American Psychologist, 41,* 954–969. doi:10.1037/0003-066X.41.9.954

Marshall, R. D., Bryant, R. A., et al. (2007). The psychology of ongoing threat: Relative risk appraisal, the September 11 attacks, and terrorism-related fears. *American Psychologist, 62*(4), 304–316. doi:10.1037/0003-066X.62.4.304

Martens, R., & Trachet, T. (1998). *Making sense of astrology.* Amherst, MA: Prometheus.

Martin, B. (2011). *Children at play: Learning gender in the early years.* Sterling, VA: Trentham Books.

Martin, C. L., & Ruble, D. N. (2009). Patterns of gender development. *Annual Review of Psychology, 61,* 353–381.

Martin, D., & Yurkovich, E. (2014). "Close-knit" defines a healthy Native American, Indian family. *Journal of Family Nursingi, 20*(1), 51–72. doi:10.1177/1074840713508604

Martin, E. K., Taft, C. T., & Resick, P. A. (2007). A review of marital rape. *Aggression & Violent Behavior, 12*(3), 329–347.

Martin, E., & Weiss, K. J. (2010). Knowing moral and legal wrong in an insanity defense. *Journal of the American Academy of Psychiatry & the Law, 38*(2), 286–288.

Martin, G., & Pear, J. (2011). *Behavior modification: What it is and how to do it* (9th ed.). Upper Saddle River, NJ: Prentice Hall.

Martin, L. R., Friedman, H. S., & Schwartz, J. E. (2007). Personality and mortality risk across the life span: The importance of conscientiousness as a biopsychosocial attribute. *Health Psychology, 26*(4), 428–436. doi:10.1037/0278-6133.26.4.428

Martin, L. R., Williams, S. L., Haskard, K. B., & DiMatteo, M. R. (2005). The challenge of patient adherence. *Therapeutics and Clinical Risk Management, 1*(3), 189–199.

Martin, S. (2007, July–August). The labyrinth of leadership. *Monitor on Psychology,* 90–91.

Martin-Raugh, M. P., Kell, H. J., et al. (2016). Prosocial knowledge mediates effects of agreeableness and emotional intelligence on prosocial behavior. *Personality & Individual Differences, 90,* 41–49. doi:10.1016/j.paid.2015.10.024

Martínez-Alvarez, R., Mah, Y. H., et al. (2016). A fast pathway for fear in human amygdala. *Nature Neuroscience, 19*(8), 1041–1049. doi:10.1038/nn.4324

Martinez-Gonzalez, M. A., Gual, P., et al. (2003). Parental factors, mass media influences, and the onset of eating disorders in a prospective population-based cohort. *Pediatrics, 111,* 315–320. doi:10.1542/peds.111.2.315

Martinko, M. J., Douglas, S. C., & Harvey, P. (2006). Understanding and managing workplace aggression. *Organizational Dynamics, 35*(2),117–130

Martynhak, B. J., Louzada, F. M., et al. (2010). Does the chronotype classification need to be updated? Preliminary findings. *Chronobiology International, 27*(6), 1329–1334. doi:10.3109/07420528.2010.490314

Maslow, A. H. (1954). *Motivation and personality.* New York: Harper.

Maslow, A. H. (1967). Self-actualization and beyond. In J. F. T. Bugental (Ed.), *Challenges of humanistic psychology* (pp. 279–286). New York: McGraw-Hill.

Maslow, A. H. (1969). *The psychology of science.* Chicago, IL: Henry Regnery.

Maslow, A. H. (1970). *Motivation and personality.* New York: Harper & Row.

Maslow, A. H. (1971). *The farther reaches of human nature.* New York: Viking.

Masse, L. C., & Tremblay, R. E. (1997). Behavior of boys in kindergarten and the onset of substance use during adolescence. *Archives of General Psychiatry, 54*(1), 62–68. doi:10.1001/archpsyc.1997.01830130068014

Masten, A. S. (2014). *Ordinary magic: Resilience in development.* New York: Guilford.

Masters, J. L., & Holley, L. M. (2006). A glimpse of life at 67: The modified future-self worksheet. *Educational Gerontology, 32*(4), 261–269. doi:10.1080/03601270500494022

Masters, W. H., & Johnson, V. E. (1966). *Human sexual response.* Boston, MA: Little, Brown.

Masters, W. H., & Johnson, V. E. (1970). *The pleasure bond: A new look at sexuality and commitment*. Boston, MA: Little, Brown.

Mastroianni, G. R. (2015). Obedience in perspective: Psychology and the Holocaust. *Theory & Psychology, 25*(5), 657–669. doi:10.1177/0959354315608963

Masuda, T., Gonzalez, R., et al. (2008). Culture and aesthetic preference: Comparing the attention to context of East Asians and Americans. *Personality & Social Psychology Bulletin, 34*(9), 1260–1275. doi:10.1177/0146167208320555

Mather, M. (2016). The affective neuroscience of aging. *Annual Review of Psychology, 67,* 213–238. doi:10.1146/annurev-psych-122414-033540

Mathy, F., & Feldman, J. (2012). What's magic about magic numbers? Chunking and data compression in short-term memory. *Cognition, 122*(3), 346–362. doi:10.1016/j.cognition.2011.11.003

Matsumoto, D., & Hwang, H. S. C. (2019). Culture, emotion, and expression. In K. D. Keith (Ed.), *Cross-cultural psychology: Contemporary themes and perspectives* (2nd ed., pp. 501–515) doi:10.1002/9781119519348.ch24.

Matsumoto, D., Hwang, H. C., et al. (2016). *The body: Postures, gait, proxemics, and haptics*. In D. Matsumoto, D., H. C. Hwang, & M. G. Frank (Eds.), *APA handbook of nonverbal communication* (pp. 387–400). Washington, DC: American Psychological Association. doi:10.1037/14669-015

Matsumoto, D., & Juang, L. (2017). *Culture and psychology* (6th ed.). Boston, MA: Cengage Learning.

Mattanah, J. F., Lopez, F. G., & Govern, J. M. (2011). The contributions of parental attachment bonds to college student development and adjustment: A meta-analytic review. *Journal of Counseling Psychology, 58,* 565–596. doi:10.1037/a0024635

Matthews, K. A., & Gallo, L. C. (2011). Psychological perspectives on pathways linking socioeconomic status and physical health. *Annual Review of Psychology, 62,* 501–530. doi:10.1146/annurev.psych.031809. 130711

Matthews, P. H., & Matthews, M. S. (2004). Heritage language instruction and giftedness in language minority students: Pathways toward success. *Journal of Secondary Gifted Education, 15*(2), 50–55. doi:10.4219/jsge-2004-448

Matthies, E., Selge, S., & Klöckner, C. A. (2012). The role of parental behaviour for the development of behaviour specific environmental norms The example of recycling and re-use behaviour. *Journal of Environmental Psychology, 32*(3), 277–284. doi:10.1016/j.jenvp.2012.04.003

Matusitz, J., & Breen, G. (2012). An examination of pack journalism as a form of groupthink: A theoretical and qualitative analysis. *Journal of Human Behavior in the Social Environment, 22*(7), 896–915. doi:10.1080/10911359.2012.707933

Mayer, J. D. (2005). A tale of two visions: Can a new view of personality help integrate psychology? *American Psychologist, 60*(4), 294–307. doi:10.1037/0003-066X.60.4.294

Mayer, R. E. (2011). *Applying the science of learning*. Boston, MA: Allyn & Bacon.

Mayer, R. E. (2014). Research-based principles for designing multimedia instruction. In V. A. Benassi, C. E. Overson, et al. (Eds.), *Applying science of learning in education: Infusing psychological science into the curriculum*. Retrieved January 31, 2017, from teachpsych.org/ebooks/asle2014/index.php

Mayes, S. D., Calhoun, S. L., et al. (2009). IQ and neuropsychological predictors of academic achievement. *Learning & Individual Differences, 19*(2), 238–241.

Mazar, N., Amir, O., & Ariely, D. (2008). The dishonesty of honest people: A theory of self-concept maintenance. *Journal of Marketing Research, 45*(6), 633–644.

Mazerolle, M., Régner, I., et al. (2012). Stereotype threat strengthens automatic recall and undermines controlled processes in older adults. *Psychological Science, 23*(7), 723–727. doi:10.1177/0956797612437607

Mazzoni, G., Heap, M., & Scoboria, A. (2010). Hypnosis and memory: Theory, laboratory research, and applications. In S. J. Lynn, J. W. Rhue, et al. (Eds.) *Handbook of clinical hypnosis* (2nd ed., pp. 709–741). Washington, DC: American Psychological Association.

McAdams, D. P., & McLean, K. C. (2013). Narrative identity. *Current Directions in Psychological Science, 22*(3), 233–238.

McAdams, D. P., & Pals, J. L. (2006). A new Big Five: Fundamental principles for an integrative science of personality. *American Psychologist, 61*(3), 204–217. doi:10.1037/0003-066X.61.3.204

McAlister, A. L., Ama, E., et al. (2000). Promoting tolerance and moral engagement through peer modeling. *Cultural Diversity & Ethnic Minority Psychology, 6*(4), 363–373.

McCabe, M. P. (2015). Female orgasmic disorder. In K. M. Hertlein, G. R. Weeks, et al. (Eds.), *Systemic sex therapy* (2nd ed., pp. 171–190). New York: Routledge/Taylor & Francis.

McCabe, D. L., Butterfield, K. D., & Trevino, L. K. (2012). *Cheating in college: Why students do it and what educators can do about it*. Baltimore, MD: Johns Hopkins University Press.

McCabe, M. P. (2015). Female orgasmic disorder. In K. M. Hertlein, G. R. Weeks, et al. (Eds.), *Systemic sex therapy* (2nd ed., pp. 171–190). New York: Routledge/Taylor & Francis.

McCaffrey, T. (2012). Innovation relies on the obscure: A key to overcoming the classic problem of functional fixedness. *Psychological Science, 23*(3), 215–218. doi:10.1177/0956797611429580

McCall, W. V., Prudic, J., et al. (2006). Health-related quality of life following ECT in a large community sample. *Journal of Affective Disorders, 90*(2–3), 269–274. doi:10.1016/j.jad.2005.12.002

McCall, W. V., Rosenquist, P. B., et al. (2011). Health-related quality of life in a clinical trial of ECT followed by continuation pharmacotherapy: Effects immediately after ECT and at 24 weeks. *The Journal of ECT, 27*(2), 97–102. doi:10.1097/YCT.0b013e318 205c7d7

McCalley, L. T., de Vries, P. W., & Midden, C. J. (2011). Consumer response to product-integrated energy feedback: Behavior, goal level shifts, and energy conservation. *Environment and Behavior, 43*(4), 525–545. doi:10.1177/0013916510371053

McCarthy, B. W. (1995). Bridges to sexual desire. *Journal of Sex Education & Therapy, 21*(2), 132–141.

McCarthy, B. W., & Fucito, L. M. (2005). Integrating medication, realistic expectations, and therapeutic interventions in the treatment of male sexual dysfunction. *Journal of Sex & Marital Therapy, 31*(4), 319–328.

McCarthy, M. M., Arnold, A. P., et al. (2012). Sex differences in the brain: The not-so-inconvenient truth. *Journal of Neuroscience, 32*(7), 2241–2247. doi:10.1523/JNEUROSCI.5372-11.2012

McCaulley, M. H. (2000). Myers-Briggs Type Indicator: A bridge between counseling and consulting. *Consulting Psychology Journal: Practice and Research, 52*(2), 117–132. doi:10.1037/1061-4087.52.2.117

McClelland, D. C. (1961). *The achieving society*. New York: Van Nostrand.

McClelland, D. C. (1975). *Power: The inner experience*. New York: Irvington.

McClelland, D. C. (1994). The knowledge-testing-educational complex strikes back. *American Psychologist, 49*(1), 66–69. doi:10.1037/0003-066X.49.1.66

McClung, C. A. (2011). Circadian rhythms and mood regulation: Insights from pre-clinical models. *European Neuropsychopharmacology, 21,* S683–S693. doi:10.1016/j.euroneuro.2011.07.008

McCluskey, U. (2002). The dynamics of attachment and systems-centered group psychotherapy. *Group Dynamics, 6*(2), 131–142. doi:10.1037/1089-2699.6.2.131

McCormick, N. B. (2010). Sexual scripts: Social and therapeutic implications. *Sexual & Relationship Therapy, 25*(1), 96–120.

McCoy, D. C., Yoshikawa, H., Ziol-Guest, K. M., Duncan, G. J., Schindler, H. S., Magnuson, K., et al. (2017). Impacts of early childhood education on medium- and long-term educational outcomes. *Educational Researcher, 46*(8), 474–487. doi:10.3102/0013189X17737739

McCrae, R. R., & Costa, P. T. (2001). A five-factor theory of personality. In L. A. Pervin & O. P. John (Eds.), *Handbook of personality* (pp. 139–153). New York: Guilford.

McCrae, R. R., & Costa, P. Jr. (2013). Introduction to the empirical and theoretical status of the five-factor model of personality traits. In T. A. Widiger & P. Jr. Costa (Eds.), *Personality disorders and the five-factor model of personality* (3rd ed., pp. 15–27). Washington, DC: American Psychological Association. doi:10.1037/13939-002

McCrea, S. M., & Hirt, E. R. (2011). Limitations on the substitutability of self-protective processes: Self-handicapping is not reduced by related-domain self-affirmations. *Social Psychology, 42*(1), 9–18.

McCrory, C., & Cooper, C. (2005). The relationship between three auditory inspection time tasks and general intelligence. *Personality & Individual Differences, 38*(8), 1835–1845.

McDaniel, M. A., Maier, S. F., & Einstein, G. O. (2002). "Brain-specific" nutrients: A memory cure? *Psychological Science in the Public Interest, 3*(1), 12–38. doi:10.1111/1529-1006.00007

McDermott, P. A., Watkins, M. W., & Rhoad, A. M. (2014). Whose IQ is it?—Assessor bias variance in high-stakes psychological assessment. *Psychological Assessment, 26*(1), 207–214. doi:10.1037/a0034832

McFadden, J. R., & Rawson Swan, K. T. (2012). Women during midlife: Is it transition or crisis? *Family and Consumer Sciences Research Journal,*

40(3), 313–325. doi:10.1111/j.1552-3934.2011.02113.x

McGaugh, J. L. (2018). Emotional arousal regulation of memory consolidation. *Current Opinion in Behavioral Sciences, 19*, 55–60. doi:10.1016/j.cobeha.2017.10.003

McGaugh, J. L., & Roozendaal, B. (2009). Drug enhancement of memory consolidation: Historical perspective and neurobiological implications. *Psychopharmacology, 202*(1–3), 3–14. doi:10.1007/s00213-008-1285-6

McGowan, S., & Behar, E. (2013). A preliminary investigation of stimulus control training for worry: Effects on anxiety and insomnia. *Behavior Modification, 37*(1), 90–112. doi:10.1177/0145445512455661

McGrath, R. E., & Carroll, E. J. (2012). The current status of "projective" "tests." In H. Cooper (Ed.), *APA handbook of research methods in psychology: Foundations, planning, measures, and psychometrics* (Vol. 1, pp. 329–348). Washington, DC: American Psychological Association.

McGrath, R. E., & Moore, B. A. (Eds.). (2010). *Pharmacotherapy for psychologists: Prescribing and collaborative roles*. Washington, DC: American Psychological Association.

McGregor, D. (1960). *The human side of enterprise*. New York: McGraw-Hill.

McGregor, I., McAdams, D. P., & Little, B. R. (2006). Personal projects, life stories, and happiness: On being true to traits. *Journal of Research in Personality, 40*(5), 551–572. doi:10.1016/j.jrp.2005.05.002

McGrew, S., Ortega, T., Breakstone, J., & Wineburg, S. (2017). The challenge that's bigger than fake news: Civic reasoning in a social media environment. *American Educator, 41*(3), 4–9.

McGue, M., Bouchard, T. R., et al. (1993). Behavioral genetics of cognitive ability: A life-span perspective. In R. Plomin & G. E. McClearn (Eds.), *Nature, nurture & psychology* (pp. 59–76). Washington, DC: American Psychological Association. doi:10.1037/10131-003

McGuinness, T. M., Dyer, J. G., & Wade, E. H. (2012). Gender differences in adolescent depression. *Journal of Psychosocial Nursing & Mental Health Services, 50*(12), 17–20. doi:10.3928/02793695-20121107-04

McIntosh, W. D., Harlow, T. F., & Martin, L. L. (1995). Linkers and nonlinkers: Goal beliefs as a moderator of the effects of everyday hassles on rumination, depression, and physical complaints. *Journal of Applied Social Psychology, 25*(14), 1231–1244. doi:10.1111/j.1559-1816.1995.tb02616.x

McKay, A. (2005). Sexuality and substance use: The impact of tobacco, alcohol, and selected recreational drugs on sexual function. *Canadian Journal of Human Sexuality, 14*(1–2), 47–56.

McKeever, L. (2006). Online plagiarism detection services: Saviour or scourge? *Assessment & Evaluation in Higher Education, 31*(2), 155–165. doi:10.1080/02602930500262460

McKeganey, N. (2012). Harm reduction at the crossroads and the rediscovery of drug user abstinence. *Drugs: Education, Prevention & Policy, 19*(4), 276–283. doi:10.3109/09687637.2012.671867

McKenna, M. W., & Ossoff, E. P. (1998). Age differences in children's comprehension of a popular television program. *Child Study Journal, 28*(1), 52–68.

McKim, W. A. (2013). *Drugs & behavior: Introduction to behaviorial pharmacology* (7th ed.). Englewood Cliffs, NJ: Prentice Hall.

McLay, R. N., & Spira, J. L. (2009). Use of a portable biofeedback device to improve insomnia in a combat zone, a case report. *Applied Psychophysiology & Biofeedback, 34*(4), 319–321. doi:10.1007/s10484-009-9104-3

McLean, K. C., & Pasupathi, M. (2012). Processes of identity development: Where I am and how I got there. *Identity: An International Journal of Theory and Research, 12*(1), 8–28. doi:10.1080/15283488.2011.632363.

McLewin, L. A., & Muller, R. T. (2006). Childhood trauma, imaginary companions, and the development of pathological dissociation. *Aggression & Violent Behavior, 11*(5), 531–545. doi:10.1016/j.avb.2006.02.001

McMahon, C. G., Jannini, E., et al. (2013). Standard operating procedures in the disorders of orgasm and ejaculation. *Journal of Sexual Medicine, 10*(1), 204–229. doi:10.1111/j.1743-6109.2012.02824.x

McMahon, S., & Koltzenburg, M. (2013). *Wall & Melzack's textbook of pain* (6th ed.). San Diego, CA: Elsevier.

McMahon, S. D. (2018). Schools as vehicles to assess experiences, improve outcomes, and effect social change. *American Journal of Community Psychology, 61*, 267–275. doi:10.1002/ajcp.12253

McMahon, T. (2014, January 20). Will quitting porn improve your life? *Macleans Magazine*. Retrieved March 10, 2017, from www.macleans.ca/society/life/can-swearing-off-porn-improve-your-life/

McMahon, T. R., Kenyon, D. B., et al. (2013). "My culture, my family, my school, me": Identifying strengths and challenges in the lives and communities of American Indian youth. *Journal of Child & Family Studies, 22*(5), 694–706. doi:10.1007/s10826-012-9623-z

McManus, F., Muse, K., et al. (2015). Relating differently to intrusive images: The impact of mindfulness-based cognitive therapy (MBCT) on intrusive images in patients with severe health anxiety (hypochondriasis). *Mindfulness, 6*(4), 788–796. doi:10.1007/s12671-014-0318-y

McManus, I. C., Moore, J., et al. (2010). Science in the making: Right hand, left hand. III: Estimating historical rates of left-handedness. *Laterality: Asymmetries of Body, Brain, & Cognition, 15*(1–2), 186–208. doi:10.1080/13576500802565313

McNally, R. J., & Clancy, S. A. (2005). Sleep paralysis, sexual abuse, and space alien abduction. *Transcultural Psychiatry, 42*(1), 113–122. doi:10.1177/1363461505050715

McNamara, D. S., & Scott, J. L. (2001). Working memory capacity and strategy use. *Memory & Cognition, 29*(1), 10–17. doi:10.3758/BF03195736

McNamara, P. (2011). *Spirit possession and exorcism: History, psychology, and neurobiology* (Vols. 1 & 2). Westport, CT: Praeger.

Mcquaid, N. E., Bibok, M. B., & Carpendale, J. I. M. (2009). Relation between maternal contingent responsiveness and infant social expectations. *Infancy, 14*(3), 390–401. doi:10.1080/15250000902839955

McVea, C. S., Gow, K., & Lowe, R. (2011). Corrective interpersonal experience in psychodrama group therapy: A comprehensive process analysis of significant therapeutic events. *Psychotherapy Research, 21*(4), 416–429. doi:10.1080/10503307.2011.577823

Meadow, T. (2011). "Deep down where the music plays": How parents account for childhood gender variance. *Sexualities, 14*(6), 725–747. doi:10.1177/1363460711420463

Meara, E., White, C., & Cutler, D. M. (2004). Trends in medical spending by age, 1963–2000. *Health Affairs, 23*(4), 176–183. doi:10.1377/hlthaff.23.4.176

Mecklinger, A. (2010). The control of long-term memory: Brain systems and cognitive processes. *Neuroscience & Biobehavioral Reviews, 34*(7), 1055–1065. doi:10.1016/j.neubiorev.2009.11.020

Medda, P., Perugi, G., et al. (2009). Response to ECT in bipolar I, bipolar II and unipolar depression. *Journal of Affective Disorders, 118*(1–3), 55–59. doi:10.1016/j.jad.2009.01.014

Meeks, T. W., & Jeste, D. V. (2009). Neurobiology of wisdom: A literature overview. *Archives of General Psychiatry, 66*(4), 355–365. doi:10.1001/archgenpsychiatry.2009.8

Meevissen, Y. M., Peters, M. L., et al. (2011). Become more optimistic by imagining a best possible self: Effects of a two week intervention. *Journal of Behavior Therapy & Experimental Psychiatry, 42*(3), 371–378. doi:10.1016/j.jbtep.2011.02.012

Mega, C., Ronconi, L., & De Beni, R. (2014). What makes a good student? How emotions, self-regulated learning, and motivation contribute to academic achievement. *Journal of Educational Psychology, 106*(1), 121–131. doi:10.1037/a0033546

Megreya, A. M., White, D., & Burton, A. M. (2011). The other-race effect does not rely on memory: Evidence from a matching task. *Quarterly Journal of Experimental Psychology, 64*(8), 1473–1483. doi:10.1080/17470218.2011.575228

Meguerditchian, A., Vauclair, J., & Hopkins, W. D. (2013). On the origins of human handedness and language: A comparative review of hand preferences for bimanual coordinated actions and gestural communication in nonhuman primates. *Developmental Psychobiology, 55*(6), 637–650. doi:10.1002/dev.21150

Mehta, P. J., & Beer, J. (2010). Neural mechanisms of the testosterone-aggression relation: The role of orbitofrontal cortex. *Journal of Cognitive Neuroscience, 22*(10), 2357–2368.

Meichenbaum, D. (2009). Stress inoculation training. In W. T. O'Donohue & J. E. Fisher (Eds.), *General principles and empirically supported techniques of cognitive behavior therapy* (pp. 627–630). Hoboken, NJ: Wiley.

Meier, B. P., & Wilkowski, B. M. (2013). Reducing the tendency to aggress: Insights from social and personality psychology. *Social & Personality Psychology Compass, 7*(6), 343–354. doi:10.1111/spc3.12029

Meijer, E. H., & Verschuere, B. (2010). The polygraph and the detection of deception. *Journal of Forensic Psychology Practice, 10*(4), 325–338. doi:10.1080/15228932.2010.481237

Meineri, S., Dupré, M., et al. (2016). Door-in-the-face and but-you-are-free: Testing the effect of combining two no-pressure compliance paradigms. *Psychological Reports, 119*(1), 276–289. doi:10.1177/0033294116657064

Meini, C., & Paternoster, A. (2012). Mirror neurons as a conceptual mechanism? *Mind & Society, 11*(2), 183–201. doi:10.1007/s11299-012-0106-0

Meireles, E., & Primi, R. (2015). Validity and reliability evidence for assessing Holland's career types. *Paidéia, 25*(62), 307–315. doi:10.1590/1982-43272562201504

Melero, E. (2011). Are workplaces with many women in management run differently? *Journal of Business Research, 64*(4), 385–393. doi:10.1016/j.jbusres.2010.01.009

Melrose, S. (2015). Seasonal affective disorder: An overview of assessment and treatment approaches. *Depression Research & Treatment,* Article ID 178564. doi:10.1155/2015/1785

Meltzoff, A. N. (2005). Imitation and other minds: The "Like Me" Hypothesis. In S. Hurley & N. Chater (Eds.), *Perspectives on imitation: From neuroscience to social science* (Vol. 2): *Imitation, human development, and culture* (pp. 55–77). Cambridge, MA: MIT Press.

Melzack, R. (1999, August). From the gate to the neuromatrix. *Pain, 6* (Suppl.), S121–S126. doi:10.1016/S0304-3959(99)00145-1

Melzack, R., & Katz, J. (2006). Pain in the 21st century: The neuromatrix and beyond. In G. Young, A. W. Kane, et al. (Eds.), *Psychological knowledge in court: PTSD, pain, and TBI* (pp. 129–148). New York: Springer.

Memili, E., Chang, E. P. C., et al. (2015). Role conflicts of family members in family firms. *European Journal of Work & Organizational Psychology, 24*(1), 143–151. doi:10.1080/13594 32X.2013.839549

Memon, A., Meissner, C. A., & Fraser, J. (2010). The Cognitive Interview: A meta-analytic review and study space analysis of the past 25 years. *Psychology, Public Policy, & Law, 16*(4), 340–372. doi:10.1037/a0020518

Mendelson, D., & Goes, F. S. (2011). A 34-year-old mother with religious delusions, filicidal thoughts. *Psychiatric Annals, 41*(7), 359–362.

Méndez-Bértolo, C., Moratti, S., et al. (2016). A fast pathway for fear in human amygdala. *Nature Neuroscience, 19*(8), 1041–1049. doi:10.1038/nn.4324

Mercer, T., & McKeown, D. (2010). Interference in short-term auditory memory. *Quarterly Journal of Experimental Psychology, 63*(7), 1256–1265. doi:10.1080/17470211003802467

Meyer, G. J., Finn, S. E., et al. (2001). Psychological testing and psychological assessment: A review of evidence and issues. *American Psychologist, 56*(2), 128–165. doi:10.1037/0003-066X.56.2.128

Meyer, I. H., Ouellette, S. C., et al. (2011). "We'd be free": Narratives of life without homophobia, racism, or sexism. *Sexuality Research & Social Policy, 8*(3), 204–214. doi:10.1007/s13178-011-0063-0

Meyer, T. (2014). Type D personality is unrelated to major adverse cardiovascular events in patients with coronary artery disease treated by intracoronary stenting. *Annals of Behavioral Medicine, 48*(2), 156–162. doi:10.1007/s12160-014-9590-2

Meyerbröker, K., & Emmelkamp, P. M. (2010). Virtual reality exposure therapy in anxiety disorders: A systematic review of process-and-outcome studies. *Depression & Anxiety, 27*(10), 933–944. doi:10.1002/da.20734

Meyers, L. (2006). Behind the scenes of the *Dr. Phil* show. *Monitor on Psychology, 37*(9), 63.

Meyers, L. (2007). The problem with DNA. *Monitor on Psychology, 38*(6), 52–53.

Michaels, J. W., Blommel, J. M., et al. (1982). Social facilitation and inhibition in a natural setting. *Replications in Social Psychology, 2,* 21–24.

Michaliszyn, D., Marchand, A., et al. (2010). A randomized, controlled clinical trial of in virtuo and in vivo exposure for spider phobia. *Cyberpsychology, Behavior, & Social Networking, 13*(6), 689–695. doi:10.1089/cyber.2009.0277

Michalko, M. (2001). *Cracking creativity.* Berkeley, CA: Ten Speed Press.

Michalko, M. (2006). *Thinkertoys: A handbook of creative-thinking techniques* (2nd ed.). Berkeley, CA: Ten Speed Press.

Mickelson, K. D., Kessler, R. C., & Shaver, P. R. (1997). Adult attachment in a nationally representative sample. *Journal of Personality & Social Psychology, 73*(5), 1092–1106.

Mickes, L., Flowe, H. D., & Wixted, J. T. (2012). Receiver operating characteristic analysis of eyewitness memory: Comparing the diagnostic accuracy of simultaneous versus sequential lineups. *Journal of Experimental Psychology: Applied, 18*(4), 361–376. doi:10.1037/a0030609

Middlehurst, R. (2015). Investing in leadership development: The UK experience. *International Higher Education.* Retrieved March 19, 2017, from https://ejournals.bc.edu/ojs/index.php/ihe/article/view/8613

Middleton, H. (2015). The medical model: What is it, where did it come from and how long has it got? In D. Loewenthal (Ed.), *Critical psychotherapy, psychoanalysis and counselling: Implications for practice* (pp. 29–40). New York: Palgrave Macmillan, xxxviii, 309. doi:10.1057/9781137460585.0008

Midlarsky, E. (1984). Competence and helping. In E. Staub, D. Bar-Tal, J. Karylowski, & J. Reykowski (Eds.), *Development and maintenance of prosocial behavior. Critical issues in social justice* Vol. 31, pp. 291–308). New York, NY: Springer. doi:10.1007/978-1-4613-2645-8_17

Miehls, D. (2017). Hegemonic views of masculinity and bullying: Clinical work with men who were bullied as children. *Clinical Social Work Journal, 45*(1), 56–64. doi:10.1007/s10615-016-0581-6

Mikulincer, M., & Shaver, P. R. (Eds.). (2010). *Prosocial motives, emotions, and behavior: The better angels of our nature.* Washington, DC: American Psychological Association.

Miles, L. K., Karpinska, K., et al. (2010). The meandering mind: Vection and mental time travel. *PLoS ONE, 5*(5): e10825. doi:10.1371/journal.pone.0010825.

Milgram, S. (1963). Behavioral study of obedience. *Journal of Abnormal & Social Psychology, 67,* 371–378. doi:10.1037/h0040525

Milgram, S. (1965). Some conditions of obedience and disobedience to authority. *Human Relations, 18,* 57–76. doi:10.1177/001872676501800105

Milgram, S. (1970). The experience of living in the cities: A psychological analysis. *Science, 167,* 1461–1468.

Milgram, S., Bickman, L., & Berkowitz, L. (1969). Note on the drawing power of crowds of different size. *Journal of Personality & Social Psychology, 13,* 79–82. doi:10.1037/h0028070

Miller, A. L., Lambert, A. D., & Neumeister, K. (2012). Parenting style, perfectionism, and creativity in high-ability and high-achieving young adults. *Journal for the Education of the Gifted, 35*(4), 344–365.

Miller, D. T., & Prentice, D. A. (2016). Changing norms to change behavior. *Annual Review of Psychology, 67,* 339–361. doi:10.1146/annurev-psych-010814-015013

Miller, G. A. (1956). The magical number seven, plus or minus two: Some limits on our capacity for processing information. *Psychological Review, 63,* 81–97. doi:10.1037/0033-295X.101.2.343

Miller, G. T., Jr., & Spoolman, S. (2016). *Environmental science* (15th ed.). Boston, MA: Cengage Learning.

Miller, J., & Garran, A. M. (2008). *Racism in the United States: Implications for the helping professions.* Boston, MA: Cengage Learning.

Miller, L. E., Grabell, A., et al. (2012). The associations between community violence, television violence, intimate partner violence, parent–child aggression, and aggression in sibling relationships of a sample of preschoolers. *Psychology of Violence, 2,* 165–178. doi:10.1037/a0027254

Miller, M. A., & Rahe, R. H. (1997). Life changes scaling for the 1990s. *Journal of Psychosomatic Research, 43*(3), 279–292. doi:10.1016/S0022-3999(97)00118-9

Miller, M., Hemenway, D., & Azraela, D. (2007). State-level homicide victimization rates in the US in relation to survey measures of household firearm ownership, 2001–2003. *Social Science & Medicine, 64*(3), 656–664. doi:10.1016/j.socscimed.2006.09.024

Miller, N. E. (1944). Experimental studies of conflict. In J. McV. Hunt (Ed.), *Personality and the behavior disorders* (Vol. 1, pp. 431–465). New York: Ronald Press.

Miller, N. E., & Bugelski. R. (1948). Minor studies of aggression: II. The influence of frustration imposed by the in-group on attitudes expressed toward out-groups. *Journal of Psychology, 25,* 437–442. doi:10.1080/00223980.1948.9917387

Miller, N., Pedersen, W. C., et al. (2003). A theoretical model of triggered displaced aggression. *Personality & Social Psychology Review, 7*(1), 75–97. doi:10.1207/S15327957PSPR0701_5

Miller, P. H. (2011). Piaget's theory: Past, present, and future. In U. Goswami (Ed.), *Piaget's theory: Past, present, and future* (pp. 649–672). West Sussex, UK: Wiley-Blackwell.

Miller, W. R., & Munoz, R. F. (2005). *Controlling your drinking: Tools to make moderation work for you.* New York: Guilford.

Millings, A., Walsh, J., et al. (2013). Good partner, good parent: Responsiveness mediates the link between romantic attachment and parenting style. *Personality & Social Psychology Bulletin, 39*(2), 170–180. doi:10.1177/0146167212468333

Millman, R. B., & Ross, E. J. (2003). Steroid and nutritional supplement use in professional athletes. *American Journal on Addictions, 12*(Suppl. 2), S48–S54. doi:10.1080/713830544

Mills, S., White, M., et al. (2017). Health and social determinants and outcomes of home cooking: A systematic review of observational studies. *Appetite, 111,* 116–134. doi:10.1016/j.appet.2016.12.022

Milne, R., & Bull, R. (2002). Back to basics: A componential analysis of the original cognitive interview mnemonics with three age groups. *Applied Cognitive Psychology, 16*(7), 743–753. doi:10.1002/acp.825

Milner, B. (1965). Memory disturbance after bilateral hippocampal lesions. In P.

Milner & S. Glickman (Eds.), *Cognitive processes and the brain* (pp. 97–111). Princeton, NJ: Van Nostrand.

Miltenberger, R. G. (2012). *Behavior modification: Principles and procedures* (5th ed.). Boston, MA: Cengage Learning.

Miltenberger, R. G. (2016). *Behavior modification: Principles and procedures* (6th ed.). Boston, MA: Cengage Learning.

Milton, F., Bealing, P., at al. (2017). The neural correlates of similarity- and rule-based generalization. *Journal of Cognitive Neuroscience, 29*(1), 150–166. doi:10.1162/jocn_a_01024.

Minda, J. P., & Smith, J. D. (2011). Prototype models of categorization: Basic formulation, predictions, and limitations. In E. M. Pothos & A. J. Wills (Eds.), *Formal approaches in categorization* (pp. 40–64). New York: Cambridge University Press.

Minnes, S., Min, M. O., et al. (2016). Executive function in children with prenatal cocaine exposure (12–15 years). *Neurotoxicology & Teratology, 57,* 79–86. doi:10.1016/j.ntt.2016.07.002

Minton, H. L. (2000). Psychology and gender at the turn of the century. *American Psychologist, 55*(6), 613–615. doi:10.1037/0003-066X.55.6.613

Miotto, K., Darakjian, J., et al. (2001). Gamma-hydroxybutyric acid: Patterns of use, effects, and withdrawal. *American Journal on Addictions, 10*(3), 232–241. doi:10.1080/105504901750532111

Mirsky, A. F., & Duncan, C. C. (2005). Pathophysiology of mental illness: A view from the fourth ventricle. *International Journal of Psychophysiology, 58*(2–3), 162–178. doi:10.1016/j.ijpsycho.2005.06.004

Mirsky, A. F., Bieliauskas, L. M., et al. (2000). A 39-year follow-up of the Genain quadruplets. *Schizophrenia Bulletin, 3,* 5–18.

Mischel, W. (1974). Processes in the delay of gratification. *Advances in Experimental Social Psychology, 7,* 249–292. doi:10.1016/S0065-2601(08)60039-8

Mischel, W. (2004). Toward an integrative science of the person. *Annual Review of Psychology, 55,* 1–22. doi:10.1146/annurev.psych.55.042902.130709

Mischel, W. (2014). *The marshmallow test: Mastering self-control.* New York: Little, Brown, & Co.

Mischel, W., & Shoda, Y. (2010). The situated person. In B. Mesquita, L. F. Barrett, et al. (Eds.), *The mind in context* (pp. 149–173). New York: Guilford.

Mischel, W., Shoda, Y., & Smith, R. E. (2008). *Introduction to personality: Toward an integration* (8th ed.). Hoboken, NJ: Wiley.

Mitchell, D. (1987, February). Firewalking cults: Nothing but hot air. *Laser,* 7–8.

Mitchell, J. (2015). *Individualism and moral character: Karen Horney's depth psychology.* Piscataway, NJ: Transaction Publishers.

Mitchell, M. E., Lebow, J. R., et al. (2011). Internet use, happiness, social support, and introversion: A more fine-grained analysis of person variables and Internet activity. *Computers in Human Behavior, 27*(5), 1857–1861. doi:10.1016/j.chb.2011.04.008

Mitchell, N. S., Dickinson, L. M., et al. (2010). Determining the effectiveness of Take Off Pounds Sensibly (TOPS), a nationally available nonprofit weight loss program. *Obesity, 19,* 568–573. doi:10.1038/oby.2010.202

Mitka, M. (2009). College binge drinking still on the rise. *Journal of the American Medical Association, 302*(8), 836–837. doi:10.1001/jama.2009.1154

Mizock, L., & Harkins, D. (2011). Diagnostic bias and conduct disorder: Improving culturally sensitive diagnosis. *Child & Youth Services, 32*(3), 243–253. doi:10.1080/01459 35X.2011.605315

Moayedi, M., & Davis, K. D. (2013). Theories of pain: From specificity to gate control. *Journal of Neurophysiology, 109*(1), 5–12. doi:10.1152/jn.00457.2012

Mock, S. E., & Eibach, R. P. (2012). Stability and change in sexual orientation identity over a 10-year period in adulthood. *Archives of Sexual Behavior, 41*(3), 641–648. doi:10.1007/s10508011-9761-1

Moerman, D. E. (2002). The meaning response and the ethics of avoiding placebos. *Evaluation & the Health Professions, 25*(4), 399–409. doi:10.1177/0163278702238053

Moffitt, T. E., Arseneault, L., et al. (2011). A gradient of childhood self-control predicts health, wealth, and public safety. *Proceedings of the National Academy of Sciences, 108*(7), 2693–2698. doi:10.1073/pnas.1010076108

Moghaddam, B. (2002). Stress activation of glutamate neurotransmission in the prefrontal cortex. *Biological Psychiatry, 51*(10), 775–787. doi:10.1016/S0006-3223(01)01362-2

Moghaddam, F. M. (2013). *The psychology of dictatorship.* Washington, DC: American Psychological Association. doi:10.1037/14138-008

Mojtabai, R., Olfson, M., et al. (2011). Barriers to mental health treatment: Results from the national comorbidity survey replication. *Psychological Medicine, 41*(8), 1751–1761. doi:10.1017/S0033291710002291

Mokdad, A. H., Marks, J. S., et al. (2004). Actual causes of death in the United States, 2000. *Journal of the American Medical Association, 291,* 1238–1245. doi:10.1001/jama.291.10.1238

Moksnes, U. K., & Espnes, G. A. (2012). Self-esteem and emotional health in adolescents: Gender and age as potential moderators. *Scandinavian Journal of Psychology, 53*(6), 483–489. doi:10.1111/sjop.12021

Molenberghs, P., Cunnington, R., & Mattingley, J. B. (2012). Brain regions with mirror properties: A meta-analysis of 125 human fMRI studies. *Neuroscience & Biobehavioral Reviews, 36*(1), 341–349. doi:10.1016/j.neubiorev.2011.07.004

Molenberghs, P., Halász, V., et al. (2013). Seeing is believing: Neural mechanisms of action–perception are biased by team membership. *Human Brain Mapping, 34*(9), 2055–2068. doi:10.1002/hbm.22044

Moller, A. C., Merchant, G., et al. (2017). Applying and advancing behavior change theories and techniques in the context of a digital health revolution: Proposals for more effectively realizing untapped potential. *Journal of Behavioral Medicine, 40*(1), 85–98. doi:10.1007/s10865-016-9818-7

Monahan, C. I., Beeber, L. S., et al. (2012). Finding family strengths in the midst of adversity: Using risk and resilience models to promote mental health. In S. Summers & R. Chazan-Cohen (Eds.), *Understanding early childhood mental health: A practical guide for professionals* (pp. 59–78). Baltimore, MD: Paul H. Brookes.

Monahan, J., Steadman, H. J., et al. (2001). *Rethinking risk assessment: The MacArthur study of mental disorder and violence.* New York: Oxford University Press.

Monde, K., Ketay, S., et al. (2013). Preliminary physiological evidence for impaired emotion regulation in depersonalization disorder. *Psychiatry Research, 209,* 235–238. doi:10.1016/j.psychres.2013.02.020

Moneta, G. B. (2012). Opportunity for creativity in the job as a moderator of the relation between trait intrinsic motivation and flow in work. *Motivation & Emotion, 36*(4), 491–503. doi:10.1007/s11031-012-9278-5

Mongeau, P. A., Knight, K., et al. (2013). Identifying and explicating variation among friends with benefits relationships. *Journal of Sex Research, 50*(1), 37–47. doi:10.1080/00224499.2011.623797

Montgomery, P., & Dennis, J. (2004). A systematic review of non-pharmacological therapies for sleep problems in later life. *Sleep Medicine Reviews, 8*(1), 47–62. doi:10.1016/S1087-0792(03)00026-1

Monti, M. M. (2012). Cognition in the vegetative state. *Annual Review of Clinical Psychology, 8,* 431–454. doi:10.1146/annurev-clinpsy-032511-143050

Monti, M. M., Vanhaudenhuyse, A., et al. (2010). Willful modulation of brain activity in disorders of consciousness. *New England Journal of Medicine, 362*(7), 579–589. doi:10.1056/NEJMoa0905370

Montoya, E. R., Terburg, D., et al. (2012). Testosterone, cortisol, and serotonin as key regulators of social aggression: A review and theoretical perspective. *Motivation & Emotion, 36*(1), 65–73. doi:10.1007/s11031-011-9264-3

Montoya, R. M., & Horton, R. S. (2012). The reciprocity of liking effect. In M. A. Paludi (Ed.), *The psychology of love* (Vols. 1–4, pp. 39–57). Santa Barbara, CA: Praeger.

Montoya, R. M., & Horton, R. S. (2013). A meta-analytic investigation of the processes underlying the similarity-attraction effect. *Journal of Social & Personal Relationships, 30*(1), 64–94. doi:10.1177/0265407512452989

Montoya, R. M., & Insko, C. A. (2008). Toward a more complete understanding of the reciprocity of liking effect. *European Journal of Social Psychology, 38,* 477–498.

Montreal Declaration on Intellectual Disabilities. (2004). Retrieved February 10, 2017, from http://www.bioethicsanddisability.org/montreal.html

Moon, T. R. (2016). Commentary regarding Bui, Craig, and Imberman (2011): Is gifted education a bright idea? Assessing the impacts of gifted and talented programs on achievement. *Journal of Advanced Academics, 27*(2), 90–98. doi:10.1177/1932202X166 31110

Mooneyham, B. W., & Schooler, J. W. (2013). The costs and benefits of mind-wandering: A review. *Canadian Journal of Experimental Psychology, 67*(1), 11–18. doi:10.1037/a0031569

Moore, R. (2009). *Understanding Jonestown and Peoples Temple.* Westport, CT: Praeger.

Moore, R. C., Viglione, D. J., et al. (2013). Rorschach measures of cognition relate to everyday and social functioning in schizophrenia. *Psychological Assessment, 25*(1), 253–263. doi:10.1037/a0030546

Moore, S. A., & Zoellner, L. A. (2007). Overgeneral autobiographical memory and traumatic events: An evaluative review. *Psychological Bulletin, 133*(3), 419–437. doi:10.1037/0033-2909.133.3.419

Moors, A. (2016). Automaticity: Componential, causal, and mechanistic explanations. *Annual Review of Psychology, 67,* 263–287. doi:10.1146/annurev-psych-122414-033550

Moran, E. F. (2010). *Environmental social science: Human–environment interactions and sustainability.* Malden, MA: Wiley-Blackwell.

Moran, F. (2010). *The paradoxical legacy of Sigmund Freud.* London: Karnac Books.

Moran, J. M., Jolly, E., et al. (2014). Spontaneous mentalizing predicts the fundamental attribution error. *Journal of Cognitive Neuroscience, 26*(3), 569–576. doi:10.1162/jocn_a_0051

Morehead, K., Dunlosky, J., & Rawson, K. A. (2019). How much mightier is the pen than the keyboard for note-taking? A replication and extension of Mueller and Oppenheimer (2014). *Educational Psychology Review*, 1–28. doi:10.1007/s10648-019-09468-2

Moreno-Cabrera, J. (2011). Speech and gesture: An integrational approach. *Language Sciences, 33*(4), 615–622. doi:10.1016/j.langsci.2011.04.021

Moreno, J. L. (1953). *Who shall survive?* New York: Beacon.

Moreno, M. M., Linster, C., et al. (2009). Olfactory perceptual learning requires adult neurogenesis. *Proceedings of the National Academy of Sciences, 106*(42), 17980–17985. doi:10.1073/pnas.0907063106

Morgan, J. P. (Ed.). (2005). *Psychology of aggression.* Hauppauge, NY: Nova Science Publishers.

Morin, A. (2006). Levels of consciousness and self-awareness: A comparison and integration of various neurocognitive views. *Consciousness & Cognition, 15*(2), 358–371. doi:10.1016/j.concog.2005.09.006

Morina, N., Ijntema, H., et al. (2015). Can virtual reality exposure therapy gains be generalized to real-life? A meta-analysis of studies applying behavioral assessments. *Behaviour Research & Therapy, 74,* 18–24. doi:10.1016/j.brat.2015.08.010

Morisse, D., Batra, L., et al. (1996). A demonstration of a token economy for the real world. *Applied & Preventive Psychology, 5*(1), 41–46. doi:10.1016/S0962-1849(96)80025-4

Morley, T. E., & Moran, G. (2011). The origins of cognitive vulnerability in early childhood: Mechanisms linking early attachment to later depression. *Clinical Psychology Review, 31*(7), 1071–1082. doi:10.1016/j.cpr.2011. 06.006

Morrison, M. (2012). *Using humor to maximize living: Connecting with humor* (2nd ed.). Lanham, MD: Rowman & Littlefield Education.

Morrison, M., DeVaul-Fetters, A., et al. (2016). Stacking the jury: Legal professionals' peremptory challenges reflect jurors' levels of implicit race bias. *Personality & Social Psychology Bulletin, 42*(8), 1129–1141. doi:10.1177/0146167216651853

Morrison, R. G., & Wallace, B. (2001). Imagery vividness, creativity and the visual arts. *Journal of Mental Imagery, 25*(3–4). 135–152.

Moscovitch, M., Cabeza, R., et al. (2016). Episodic memory and beyond: The hippocampus and neocortex in transformation. *Annual Review of Psychology, 67,* 105–134. doi:10.1146/annurev-psych-113011-143733

Moseley, P., Fernyhough, C., et al. (2013). Auditory verbal hallucinations as atypical inner speech monitoring, and the potential of neurostimulation as a treatment option. *Neuroscience & Biobehavioral Reviews, 37,* 2794–2805, doi:10.1016/j.neubiorev.2013.10.001

Mosher, W. D., Chandra, C., & Jones, J. (2005). Sexual behavior and selected health measures: Men and women 15–44 years of age, United States, 2002. U.S Department of Health and Human Services, Centers for Disease Control and Prevention. Retrieved March 10, 2020, from www.cdc.gov/nchs/data/ad/ad362.pdf

Moskowitz, G. B., & Li, P. (2011). Egalitarian goals trigger stereotype inhibition: A proactive form of stereotype control. *Journal of Experimental Social Psychology, 47*(1), 103–116.

Mosley, M. (2011). *Alien Hand Syndrome sees woman attacked by her own hand.* Retrieved May 1, 2017, from www.bbc.co.uk/news/uk-12225163

Moss-Racusin, C. A., Dovidio, J. F., Brescoll, V. L., Graham, M. J., & Handelsman, J. (2012). Science faculty's subtle gender biases favor male students. *Proceedings of the National Academy of Sciences, 109*(41), 16474–16479. doi:10.1073/pnas.1211286109

Motivala, S. J., & Irwin, M. R. (2007). Sleep and immunity: Cytokine pathways linking sleep and health outcomes. *Current Directions in Psychological Science, 16*(1), 21–25. doi:10.1111/j.1467-8721.2007.00468.x

Motraghi, T. E., Seim, R. W., et al. (2014). Virtual reality exposure therapy for the treatment of posttraumatic stress disorder: A methodological review using CONSORT guidelines. *Journal of Clinical Psychology, 70*(3), 197–208. doi:10.1002/jclp.22051

Mõttus, R., Johnson, W., & Deary, I. J. (2012). Personality traits in old age: Measurement and rank-order stability and some mean-level change. *Psychology & Aging, 27*(1), 243–249. doi:10.1037/a0023690

Moutsiana, C., Fearon, P., et al. (2014). Making an effort to feel positive: Insecure attachment in infancy predicts the neural underpinnings of emotion regulation in adulthood. *Journal of Child Psychology & Psychiatry, 55,* 999–1008.

Mowbray, T. (2012). Working memory, test anxiety and effective interventions: A review. *Australian Educational & Developmental Psychologist, 29*(2), 141–156. doi:10.1017/edp.2012.16

Mukherjee, A. (2015). Effective use of discovery learning to improve understanding of factors that affect quality. *Journal of Education for Business, 90*(8), 413–419. doi:10.1080/08832323.2015.1081866

Mulavara, A. P., Feiveson, A. H., et al. (2010). Locomotor function after long-duration space flight: Effects and motor learning during recovery. *Experimental Brain Research, 202*(3), 649–659.

Müller, B. C. N., Gerasimova, A., et al. (2016). Concentrative meditation influences creativity by increasing cognitive flexibility. *Psychology of Aesthetics, Creativity, & the Arts, 10*(3), 278–286. doi:10.1037/a0040335

Müller, B. H., Kull, S., et al. (2011). One-session computer-based exposure treatment for spider-fearful individuals: Efficacy of a minimal self-help intervention in a randomised controlled trial. *Journal of Behavior Therapy & Experimental Psychiatry, 42*(2), 179–184. doi:10.1016/j.jbtep.2010.12.001

Müller, V. C. (2012). Introduction: Philosophy and theory of artificial intelligence. *Minds & Machines, 22*(2), 67–69. doi:10.1007/s11023-012-9278-y

Munroe-Chandler, K., Hall, C., & Fishburne, G. (2008). Playing with confidence: The relationship between imagery use and self-confidence and self-efficacy in youth soccer players. *Journal of Sports Sciences, 26*(14), 1539–1546. doi:10.1080/02640410802315419

Munsey, C. (2006, June). RxP legislation made historic progress in Hawaii. *APA Monitor, 37*(7), 42.

Murayama, K., Kitagami, S., et al. (2017, January 16). People's naiveté about how extrinsic rewards influence intrinsic motivation. *Motivation Science*, n.p. doi:10.1037/mot0000040

Murayama, K., Matsumoto, M., et al. (2015). How self-determined choice facilitates performance: A key role of the ventromedial prefrontal cortex. *Cerebral Cortex, 25*(5), 1241–1251. doi:10.1093/cercor/bht317

Murimi, M.W., & Harpel, T. (2010). Practicing preventive health: The underlying culture among low-income rural populations. *The Journal of Rural Health, 26,* 273–282. doi:10.1111/j.1748-0361.2010.00289.x

Murphy, B. C., & Dillon, C. (2015). *Interviewing in action in a multicultural world* (5th ed.). Boston, MA: Cengage Learning.

Murphy, D., & Joseph, S. (2016). Person-centered therapy: Past, present, and future orientations. In Cain, D. J., Keenan, K., & Rubin, S. (Eds.). *Humanistic psychotherapies: Handbook of research and practice* (2nd ed., pp. 185–218). Washington, DC: American Psychological Association. doi:10.1037/14775-007

Murphy, D., & Page, I. (2008). Exhibitionism: Psychopathology and theory. In D. Laws & W. O'Donohue (Eds.), *Sexual deviance: Theory, assessment, and treatment* (2nd ed.). New York: Guilford.

Murphy, G., & Greene, C. M. (2016). Perceptual load induces inattentional blindness in drivers. *Applied Cognitive Psychology, 30*(3), 479–483. doi:10.1002/acp.3216

Murray, A., McKenzie, K., et al. (2013). Estimating the level of functional ability of children identified as likely to have an intellectual disability. *Research in Developmental Disabilities, 34*(11), 4009–4016. doi:10.1016/j.ridd.2013.08.008

Murray, C. D., Pettifer, S., et al. (2007). The treatment of phantom limb pain using immersive virtual reality: Three case studies. *Disability & Rehabilitation, 29*(18), 1465–1469. doi:10.1080/09638280601107385

Murray, D. A. B. (Ed.). (2009). *Homophobias: Lust and loathing across time and space.* Durham, NC: Duke University Press.

Murray, S. L., & Holmes, J. G. (1993). Seeing virtues in faults. *Journal of Personality & Social Psychology, 65*(4), 707–722.

Murray, S., Holmes, J. G., & Griffin, D. W. (2003). Reflections on the self-fulfilling effects of positive illusions. *Psychological Inquiry, 14*(3–4), 289–295. doi:10.1080/1047840X.2003.9682895

Murrell, A. R., Christoff, K. A., & Henning, K. R. (2007). Characteristics of domestic violence offenders: Associations with childhood exposure to violence. *Journal of Family Violence, 22*(7). 523–532. doi:10.1007/s10896-007-9100-4

Music, G. (2011). *Nurturing natures: Attachment and children's emotional, sociocultural, and brain development*. Hove, UK: Psychology Press.

Mussen, P. H., Conger, J. J., et al. (1979). *Psychological development: A life span approach*. New York: Harper & Row.

Mustafa, F. (2013). Schizophrenia past clozapine: What works? *Journal of Clinical Psychopharmacology, 33*(1), 63–68. doi:10.1097/JCP.0b013e31827a813b

Mustanski, B. S., Chivers, M. L., & Bailey, J. M. (2002). A critical review of recent biological research on human sexual orientation. *Annual Review of Sex Research, 13*, 89–140.

Myers, L., & Midence, K. (1998). *Adherance to treatment in medical conditions*. Boca Raton: CRC Press.

Myers, M. W., & Hodges, S. D. (2013). Empathy: Perspective taking and prosocial behavior: Caring for others like we care for the self. In J. J. Froh & A. C. Parks (Eds.), *Activities for teaching positive psychology: A guide for instructors* (pp. 77–83). Washington, DC: American Psychological Association. doi:10.1037/14042-013

Myers, S. G., & Wells, A. (2015). Early trauma, negative affect, and anxious attachment: The role of metacognition. *Anxiety, Stress, & Coping: An International Journal, 28*, 634–649. doi: 10.1080/10615806.2015.1009832

Nadal, K. L., Griffin, K. E., Wong, Y., Hamit, S., & Rasmus, M. (2014). The impact of racial microaggressions on mental health: Counseling implications for clients of color. *Journal of Counseling & Development, 92*(1), 57–66. doi:10.1002/j.1556-6676.2014.00130.x

Nadel, L. L., Hupbach, A. A., et al. (2012). Memory formation, consolidation, and transformation. *Neuroscience & Biobehavioral Reviews, 36*(7), 1640–1645. doi:10.1016/j.neubiorev.2012.03.001

Nahari, G. (2012). Elaborations on credibility judgments by professional lie detectors and laypersons: Strategies of judgment and justification. *Psychology, Crime & Law, 18*(6), 567–577. doi:10.1080/1068316X.2010.511222

Nakajima, S., & Nagaishi, T. (2005). Summation of latent inhibition and overshadowing in a generalized bait shyness paradigm of rats. *Behavioural Processes, 69*(3), 369–377.

Nakamura, Y., Goto, T. K., et al. (2011). Localization of brain activation by umami taste in humans. *Brain Research, 1406*, 18–29. doi:10.1016/j.brainres.2011.06.029

Nakayama, H. (2010). Development of infant crying behavior: A longitudinal case study. *Infant Behavior & Development, 33*(4), 463–471. doi:10.1016/j.infbeh.2010.05.002

Nance, A. R. (2015). Social media selection: How jury consultants can use social media to build a more favorable jury. *Law & Psychology Review, 39*, 267–286.

Nandagopal, K., & Ericsson, K. (2011). An expert performance approach to the study of individual differences in self-regulated learning activities in upper-level college students. *Learning & Individual Differences*, doi:10.1016/j.lindif.2011.11.018

National Academies of Sciences, Engineering, and Medicine. (2017). *The health effects of cannabis and cannabinoids: The current state of evidence and recommendations for research*. Washington, DC: The National Academies Press. doi:10.17226/24625.

National Academy of Sciences. (2003). *The polygraph and lie detection*. Washington, DC: The National Academies Press.

National Alliance on Mental Illness. (2016). *Risk of suicide*. Retrieved March 27, 2017, from www.nami.org/Learn-More/Mental-Health-Conditions/Related-Conditions/Suicide

National Center for PTSD. (2017). *Epidemiology of PTSD*. Retrieved May 6, 2017, from www.ptsd.va.gov/professional/PTSD-overview/epidemiological-facts-ptsd.asp

National Down Syndrome Society. (2017). *What is Down syndrome?* Retrieved February 10, 2017, from www.ndss.org/Down-Syndrome/What-Is-Down-Syndrome

National Institute of Child Health and Human Development. (2010). *Link between child care and academic achievement and behavior persists into adolescence*. Retrieved May 1, 2017, from www.nichd.nih.gov/news/releases/051410-early-child-care.cfm

National Institute of Child Health and Human Development. (2014). *Sudden infant death syndrome (SIDS) overview*. Retrieved May 6, 2017, from www.nichd.nih.gov/health/topics/sids/Pages/default.aspx

National Institutes of Health. (2016). *Color vision deficiency*. Retrieved May 5, 2017, from http://ghr.nlm.nih.gov/condition/color-vision-deficiency

National Institute of Mental Health. (2013). *Postpartum depression facts*. Retrieved March 27, 2017, from https://www.nimh.nih.gov/health/publications/postpartum-depression-facts/index.shtml

National Institute of Mental Health. (2015). *Depression: What you need to know*. Retrieved March 18, 2017, from www.nimh.nih.gov/health/publications/depression-what-you-need-to-know-12-2015/index.shtml#pub12

National Institute of Mental Health. (2016). *Attention deficit hyperactivity disorder*. Retrieved January 2, 2017, from www.nimh.nih.gov/health/topics/attention-deficit-hyperactivity-disorder-adhd/index.shtml

National Institute of Mental Health. (2017). *Statistics*. Retrieved March 27, 2017, from www.nimh.nih.gov/health/statistics/index.shtml

National Institute of Neurological Disorders and Stroke. (2014). *Brain basics: Understanding sleep*. Retrieved January 2, 2017, from www.ninds.nih.gov/disorders/brain_basics/understanding_sleep.htm

National Institute on Aging. (2019). *Hearing loss: A common problem for older adults*. Retrieved from https://www.nia.nih.gov/health/hearing-loss-common-problem-older-adults

National Institute on Alcohol Abuse and Alcoholism. (2015). College drinking. Retrieved May 6, 2017, from pubs.niaaa.nih.gov/publications/CollegeFactSheet/CollegeFactSheet.pdf

National Institute on Alcohol Abuse and Alcoholism. (2016). *Tips to try*. Retrieved January 2, 2017, from rethinkingdrinking.niaaa.nih.gov/Strategies/TipsToTry.asp

National Institute on Deafness and Other Communication Disorders. (2016). *Quick statistics about hearing*. Retrieved May 5, 2017, from www.nidcd.nih.gov/health/statistics/quick-statistics-hearing

National Institute on Deafness and Other Communication Disorders. (2017). *Noise-induced hearing loss*. Retrieved May 5, 2017, from www.nidcd.nih.gov/health/noise-induced-hearing-loss

National Institute on Drug Abuse. (2012). *Tobacco addiction*. Retrieved January 2, 2017, from www.drugabuse.gov/sites/default/files/tobaccorrs_v16_0.pdf

National Institute on Drug Abuse. (2014). *Drugs, brains, and behavior: The science of addiction*. Retrieved January 2, 2017, from www.drugabuse.gov/publications/drugs-brains-behavior-science-addiction/preface

National Institute on Drug Abuse. (2016a). *DrugFacts: Fentanyl*. Retrieved January 3, 2017, from www.drugabuse.gov/publications/drugfacts/fentanyl

National Institute on Drug Abuse. (2016b). *DrugFacts: MDMA (Ecstasy or Molly)*. Retrieved January 2, 2017, from www.drugabuse.gov/publications/drugfacts/mdma-ecstasymolly

National Institute on Drug Abuse. (2017). *Marijuana*. Retrieved May 6, 2017, from www.drugabuse.gov/publications/research-reports/marijuana/letter-director

National Institutes of Health. (2016). *Color vision deficiency*. Retrieved December 17, 2016, from http://ghr.nlm.nih.gov/condition/color-vision-deficiency

Nätti, J., & Häikiö, L. (2012). Flexible work and work–family interaction. *Community, Work & Family, 15*(4), 381–382. doi:10.1080/13668803.2012.725548

Nau, S. D., & Lichstein, K. L. (2005). Insomnia: Causes and treatments. In P. R. Carney, J. D. Geyer, et al. (Eds.), *Clinical sleep disorders* (pp. 157–190). Philadelphia, PA: Lippincott Williams & Wilkins.

Nawrot, E., Mayo, S. L., & Nawrot, M. (2009). The development of depth perception from motion parallax in infancy. *Attention, Perception, & Psychophysics, 71*(1), 194–199.

Nay, W. R. (2014). *The anger management workbook: Use the STOP method to replace destructive responses with constructive behavior*. New York: Guilford.

Neff, L. A., & Geers, A. L. (2013). Optimistic expectations in early marriage: A resource or vulnerability for adaptive relationship functioning? *Journal of Personality & Social Psychology, 105*(1), 38–60. doi:10.1037/a0032600

Negriff, S., & Trickett, P. K. (2010). The relationship between pubertal timing and delinquent behavior in maltreated male and female adolescents. *Journal of Early Adolescence, 30*(4), 518–542. doi:10.1177/0272431609338180

Nehlig, A. (Ed.). (2004). *Coffee, tea, chocolate, and the brain*. Boca Raton, FL: CRC Press.

Neikrug, A. B., & Ancoli-Israel, S. (2012). Diagnostic tools for REM sleep behavior disorder. *Sleep Medicine Reviews, 16*(5), 415–429. doi:10.1016/j.smrv.2011.08.004

Neisser, U. (1967) *Cognitive psychology*. New York: Appleton-Century-Crofts.

Neitz, J., & Neitz, M. (2011). The genetics of normal and defective color vision. *Vision Research, 51*(7), 633–651. doi:10.1016/j.visres.2010.12.002.

Nellis, A., & Savage, J. (2012). Does watching the news affect fear of terrorism? The importance of media exposure on terrorism fear. *Crime & Delinquency, 58*(5), 748–768. doi:10.1177/0011128712452961

Nelson, C. A. (1999). How important are the first 3 years of life? *Applied Developmental Science, 3*(4), 235–238. doi:10.1207/s1532480xads0304_8

Nelson, G., Van Andel, A. K., et al. (2012). Exploring outcomes through narrative: The long-term impacts of better beginnings, better futures on the turning point stories of youth at ages 18–19. *American Journal of Community Psychology, 49*(1–2), 294–306. doi:10.1007/s10464-011-9466-6

Nelson, J. L., Lewis, D. A., & Lei, R. (2016). Digital democracy in America: A look at civic engagement in an Internet age. *Journalism & Mass Communication Quarterly, 94,* 318–334. doi:1077699016681969

Nelson, T. D. (2005). Ageism: Prejudice against our feared future self. *Journal of Social Issues, 61*(2), 207–221. doi:10.1111/j.1540-4560.2005.00402.x

Nestor, P. G., Nakamura, M., et al. (2015). Attentional control and intelligence: MRI orbital frontal gray matter and neuropsychological correlates. *Behavioural Neurology,* Article 354186.

Nettle, D. (2005). An evolutionary perspective on the extraversion continuum. *Evolution & Human Behavior, 26,* 363–373. doi:10.1016/j.evolhumbehav.2004.12.004

Nettle, D. (2008, February 9). The personality factor: What makes you unique? *New Scientist,* 36–39.

Neubert, J. C., Mainert, J., et al. (2015, June). The assessment of 21st century skills in industrial and organizational psychology: Complex and collaborative problem solving. *Industrial & Organizational Psychology, 8*(2), 238–268. doi:10.1017/iop.2015.14

Neufeind, J., Dritschel, B., et al. (2009). The effects of thought suppression on autobiographical memory recall. *Behaviour Research & Therapy, 47*(4), 275–284. doi:10.1016/j.brat.2008.12.010

Neufeld, R. W. J., Carter, J. R., et al. (2003). Schizophrenia. In P. Firestone & W. L. Marshall (Eds.), *Abnormal psychology: Perspectives* (2nd ed., pp. 343–370). Toronto: Prentice Hall.

Neukrug, E. S. (2014). *A brief orientation to counseling.* Boston, MA: Cengage Learning.

Neukrug, E. S., & Fawcett, R. C. (2015). *Essentials of testing and assessment: A practical guide for counselors, social workers, and psychologists* (3rd ed.). Boston, MA: Cengage Learning.

Neville, H. A., Awad, G. H., et al. (2013). Color-blind racial ideology: Theory, training, and measurement implications in psychology. *American Psychologist, 68*(6), 455–466. doi:10.1037/a0033282

Nevo, E., & Breznitz, Z. (2013). The development of working memory from kindergarten to first grade in children with different decoding skills. *Journal of Experimental Child Psychology, 114*(2), 217–228. doi:10.1016/j.jecp.2012.09.004

Newell, B. R. (2012). Levels of explanation in category learning. *Australian Journal of Psychology, 64*(1), 46–51.

Newman, B. R., & Newman, P. R. (2015). *Development through life: A psychosocial approach* (12th ed.). Boston, MA: Cengage Learning.

Newman, R. S., Rowe, M. L., et al. (2016). Input and uptake at 7 months predicts toddler vocabulary: The role of child-directed speech and infant processing skills in language development. *Journal of Child Language, 43*(5), 1158–1173. doi:10.1017/S0305000915000446.

Ng, T. H., & Feldman, D. C. (2010). Human capital and objective indicators of career success: The mediating effects of cognitive ability and conscientiousness. *Journal of Occupational & Organizational Psychology, 83*(1), 207–235. doi:10.1348/096317909X414584

Nguyen, T. Q., Gwynn, R. C., et al. (2008). Population prevalence of reported and unreported HIV and related behaviors among the household adult population in New York City 2004. *AIDS, 22*(2), 281–287. doi:10.1097/QAD.0b013e3282f2ef58

Nichols, E. S., Wild, C. J., Stojanoski, B., Battista, M. E., & Owen, A. M. (2020). Bilingualism affords no general cognitive advantages: A population study of executive function in 11,000 people. *Psychological Science.* doi:10.1177/0956797620903113

Nickerson, C., Diener, E., & Schwarz, N. (2011). Positive affect and college success. *Journal of Happiness Studies, 12*(4), 717–746. doi:10.1007/s10902-010-9224-8

Nickerson, R. S., & Adams, M. J. (1979). Long-term memory for a common object. *Cognitive Psychology, 11,* 287–307. doi:10.1016/0010-0285(79)90013-6

Nicoletti, A. (2009). Teens and drug facilitated sexual assault. *Journal of Pediatric & Adolescent Gynecology, 22*(3), 187.

Niedzwienska, A. (2004). Metamemory knowledge and the accuracy of flashbulb memories. *Memory, 12*(5), 603–613. doi:10.1080/09658210344000134

Niehaus, D. J. H., Stein, D. J., et al. (2005). A case of "Lufunyane": A Xhosa culture-bound syndrome. *Journal of Psychiatric Practice, 11*(6), 411–413. doi:10.1097/00131746-200511000-00009

Niehaus, J. L., Cruz-Bermúdez, N. D., & Kauer, J. A. (2009). Plasticity of addiction: A mesolimbic dopamine short-circuit? *American Journal on Addictions, 18*(4), 259–271. doi:10.1080/10550490902925946

Nielsen, J. A., Zielinski, B. A., et al. (2013). An evaluation of the left-brain vs. right-brain hypothesis with resting state functional connectivity magnetic resonance imaging. *PLoS ONE, 8*(8), e71275. doi:10.1371/journal.pone.0071275

Nielsen, M., & Dissanayake, C. (2004). Pretend play, mirror self-recognition, and imitation: A longitudinal investigation through the second year. *Infant Behavior & Development, 27*(3), 342–365. doi:10.1016/j.infbeh.2003.12.006

Nieuwoudt, J. E., Zhou, S., et al. (2012). Muscle dysmorphia: Current research and potential classification as a disorder. *Psychology of Sport & Exercise, 13*(5), 569–577. doi:10.1016/j.psychsport.2012.03.006

Nigbur, D., Lyons, E., & Uzzell, D. (2010). Attitudes, norms, identity, and environmental behaviour: Using an expanded theory of planned behaviour to predict participation in a kerbside recycling programme. *British Journal of Social Psychology, 49*(2), 259–284.

Nijboer, T. W., & Jellema, T. (2012). Unequal impairment in the recognition of positive and negative emotions after right hemisphere lesions: A left hemisphere bias for happy faces. *Journal of Neuropsychology, 6*(1), 79–93. doi:10.1111/j.1748-6653.2011.02007.x

Nijstad, B. A., De Dreu, C. W., et al. (2010). The dual pathway to creativity model: Creative ideation as a function of flexibility and persistence. *European Review of Social Psychology, 21*(1), 34–77.doi:10.1080/10463281003765323

Nirenberg, S., & Pandarinath, C. (2012). Retinal prosthetic strategy with the capacity to restore normal vision. *Proceedings of the National Academy of Sciences, 109*(37), 15012–15017. doi:10.1073/pnas.1207035109

Nisbett, R. E. (2005). Heredity, environment, and race differences in IQ: A commentary on Rushton and Jensen. *Psychology, Public Policy, & Law, 11*(2), 302–310. doi:10.1037/1076-8971.11.2.302

Nisbett, R. E. (2009). *Intelligence and how to get it: Why schools and cultures count.* New York: Norton.

Nisbett, R. E., Aronson, J., et al. (2012). Intelligence: New findings and theoretical developments. *American Psychologist, 67*(2), 130–159. doi:10.1037/a0026699

Nisbett, R. E., & Miyamoto, Y. (2005). The influence of culture: Holistic versus analytic perception. *Trends in Cognitive Sciences, 9*(10), 467–473. doi:10.1016/j.tics.2005.08.004

Nisbett, R. E., & Wilson, T. D. (1977). Telling more than we can know: Verbal reports on mental processes. *Psychological Review, 84*(3), 231–259. doi:10.1037/0033-295X.84.3.231

Niven, K., Sprigg, C. A., & Armitage, C. J. (2013). Does emotion regulation protect employees from the negative effects of workplace aggression? *European Journal of Work & Organizational Psychology, 22*(1), 88–106. doi:10.1080/1359432X.2011.626200

Njeri, I. (1991, January 13). Beyond the melting pot. *Los Angeles Times,* E-1–E-8.

Noftle, E. E., & Fleeson, W. (2010). Age differences in Big Five behavior averages and variabilities across the adult life span: Moving beyond retrospective, global summary accounts of personality. *Psychology & Aging, 25*(1), 95–107. doi:10.1037/a0018199

Noland, J. S., Singer, L. T., et al. (2005). Prenatal drug exposure and selective attention in preschoolers. *Neurotoxicology & Teratology, 27*(3), 429–438. doi:10.1016/j.ntt.2005.02.001

Nolen-Hoeksema, S. (2011). *Abnormal psychology* (5th ed.). New York: McGraw-Hill.

Nolet, K., Rouleau, J.-L., et al. (2016). How ego depletion affects sexual self-regulation: Is it more than resource depletion? *Journal of Sex Research, 53*(8), 994–1007. doi:10.1080/00224499.2015.1096887

Noltemeyer, A., Bush, K., et al. (2012). The relationship among deficiency needs and growth needs: An empirical investigation of Maslow's theory. *Children & Youth Services Review, 34*(9), 1862–1867. doi:10.1016/j.childyouth.2012.05.021

Norenzayan, A., & Nisbett, R. E. (2000). Culture and causal cognition. *Current Directions in Psychological Science, 9,* 132–135. doi:10.1111/1467-8721.00077

Norlander, T., Bergman, H., & Archer, T. (1998). Effects of flotation rest on creative problem solving and originality. *Journal of Environmental Psychology, 18*(4), 399–408. doi:10.1006/jevp.1998.0112

Norlander, T., Bergman, H., & Archer, T. (1999). Primary process in competitive archery performance: Effects of flotation REST. *Journal of Applied Sport Psychology, 11*(2), 194–209. doi:10.1080/10413209908404200

Norman, D. A. (1994) *Things that make us smart.* Menlo Park, CA: Addison-Wesley.

Norman, P., Conner, M. T., & Stride, C. B. (2012). Reasons for binge drinking among undergraduate students: An application of behavioural reasoning theory. *British Journal of Health Psychology, 17*(4), 682–698. doi:10.1111/j.2044-8287.2012.02065.x

Norman, T. R. (2009). Melatonin: Hormone of the night. *Acta Neuropsychiatrica, 21*(5), 263–265. doi:10.1111/acn.2009.21.issue-510.1111/j.1601-5215.2009.00411.x

Normand, A., & Croizet, J. (2013). Upward social comparison generates attentional focusing when the dimension of comparison is self-threatening. *Social Cognition, 31*(3), 336–348.

Northouse, P. G. (2016). *Leadership: Theory and practice* (7th ed.). Thousand Oaks, CA: Sage.

Nosek, B. A., Greenwald, A. G., & Banaji, M. R. (2005). Understanding and using the implicit association test: II. Method variables and construct validity. *Personality & Social Psychology Bulletin, 31*(2), 166–180. doi:10.1177/0146167204271418

Novak, J. R., Peak, T., Gast, J., & Arnell, M. (2019). Associations between masculine norms and health-care utilization in highly religious, heterosexual men. *American Journal of Men's Health, 13*(3), 1557988319856739. doi:10.1177/1557988319856739

Novella, E. J. (2010). Mental health care in the aftermath of deinstitutionalization: A retrospective and prospective view. *Health Care Analysis, 18*(3), 222–238. doi:10.1007/s10728-009-0138-8

Novelli, D., Drury, J., & Reicher, S. (2010). Come together: Two studies concerning the impact of group relations on 'personal space'. *British Journal of Social Psychology, 49*(2), 223–236.

November Learning. (2017). *How to read a web address.* Retrieved April 26, 2017, from novemberlearning.com/educational-resources-for-educators/information-literacy-resources/4-how-to-read-a-web-address

Ntoumanis, N., Taylor, I. M., & Standage, M. (2010). Testing a model of antecedents and consequences of defensive pessimism and self-handicapping in school physical education. *Journal of Sports Sciences, 28*(14), 1515–1525.

Nucci, L. P., & Gingo, M. (2011). The development of moral reasoning. In U. Goswami (Ed.), *The development of moral reasoning* (pp. 420–444). London: Wiley-Blackwell.

Nunes, K. L., Hermann, C. A., et al. (2013). Childhood sexual victimization, pedophilic interest, and sexual recidivism. *Child Abuse & Neglect, 37*(9), 703–711. doi:10.1016/j.chiabu.2013.01.008

O'Conner, T. G., Marvin, R. S., et al. (2003). Child–parent attachment following early institutional deprivation. *Development & Psychopathology, 15*(1), 19–38. doi:10.1017/S0954579403000026

O'Neal, C. W., Mallette, J. K. and Mancini, J. A. (2018). The importance of parents' community connections for adolescent well-being: An examination of military families. *American Journal of Community Psychology, 61*, 204–217. doi:10.1002/ajcp.12222

O'Neill, P. (2005). The ethics of problem definition. *Canadian Psychology, 46*, 13–20. doi:10.1037/h0085819

Oakley, D. A., Whitman, L. G., & Halligan, P. W. (2002). Hypnotic imagery as a treatment for phantom limb pain: Two case reports and a review. *Clinical Rehabilitation, 16*(4), 368–377. doi:10.1191/0269215502cr507oa

Oakley, R. (2004). How the mind hurts and heals the body. *American Psychologist, 59*(1), 29–40. doi:10.1037/0003-066X.59.1.29

Oates, J. M., & Reder, L. M. (2011). Memory for pictures: Sometimes a picture is not worth a single word. In A. S. Benjamin (Ed.), *Successful remembering and successful forgetting: A festschrift in honor of Robert A. Bjork* (pp. 447–461). New York: Psychology Press.

Oberle, E. (2009). The development of Theory of Mind reasoning in Micronesian children. *Journal of Cognition & Culture, 9*(1–2), 39–56. doi:10.1163/156853709X414629

Oberman, L. M., & Ramachandran, V. S. (2015). The role of the mirror neuron system in the pathophysiology of autism spectrum disorder. In P. F. Ferrari & G. Rizzolatti (Eds.), *New frontiers in mirror neurons research* (pp. 380–396). New York: Oxford University Press. doi:10.1093/acprof:oso/9780199686155.003.0021

Odinot, G., Wolters, G., & van Giezen, A. (2013). Accuracy, confidence, and consistency in repeated recall of events. *Psychology, Crime, & Law, 19*(7), 629–642. doi:10.1080/1068316X.2012.660152

Oestergaard, S., & Møldrup, C. (2011). Optimal duration of combined psychotherapy and pharmacotherapy for patients with moderate and severe depression: A meta-analysis. *Journal of Affective Disorders, 131*(1–3), 24–36. doi:10.1016/j.jad.2010.08.014

Oexle, N., Ajdacic-Gross, V., et al. (2017). Mental illness stigma, secrecy and suicidal ideation. *Epidemiology & Psychiatric Sciences, 26*(1), 53–60. doi:10.1017/S2045796015001018

Ogden, C. L., Carroll, M. D., et al. (2010). Prevalence of high body mass index in U.S. children and adolescents, 2007–2008. *Journal of the American Medical Association, 303*(3), 242–249. doi:10.1001/jama.2009.2012

Ogrodniczuk, J. S., Piper, W. E., & Joyce, A. S. (2011). Effect of alexithymia on the process and outcome of psychotherapy: A programmatic review. *Psychiatry Research, 190*(1), 43–48. doi:10.1016/j.psychres.2010.04.026

Oishi, S., Kesebir, S., & Diener, E. (2011). Income inequality and happiness. *Psychological Science, 22*(9), 1095–1100. doi:10.1177/0956797611417262

Okiishi, J., Lambert, M. J., et al. (2003). Waiting for supershrink: An empirical analysis of therapist effects. *Clinical Psychology & Psychotherapy, 10*(6), 361–373. doi:10.1002/cpp.383

Olafsen, A. H., Halvari, H., et al. (2015). Show them the money? The role of pay, managerial need support, and justice in a self-determination theory model of intrinsic work motivation. *Scandinavian Journal of Psychology, 56*(4), 447–457. doi:10.1111/sjop.12211

Ollendick, T. H., & Muris, P. (2015). The scientific legacy of Little Hans and Little Albert: Future directions for research on specific phobias in youth. *Journal of Clinical Child & Adolescent Psychology, 44*(4), 689–706. doi:10.1080/15374416.2015.1020543

Olpin, M., & Hesson, M. (2016). *Stress management for life: A research-based experiential approach* (4th ed.). Boston, MA: Cengage Learning.

Olshansky, M. P., Bar, R. J., et al. (2015). Supplementary motor area and primary auditory cortex activation in an expert break-dancer during the kinesthetic motor imagery of dance to music. *Neurocase, 21*(5), 607–617. doi:10.1080/13554794.2014.960428

Olson, M., & Hergenhahn, B. (2013). *Introduction to the theories of learning* (9th ed.). Englewood Cliffs, NJ: Prentice Hall.

Olsson, A., Nearing, K., & Phelps, E. A. (2007). Learning fears by observing others: The neural systems of social fear transmission. *Social Cognitive & Affective Neuroscience, 2*(1), 3–11. doi:10.1093/scan/nsm005

Olsson, E. M., El Alaoui, S., et al. (2010). Internet-based biofeedback-assisted relaxation training in the treatment of hypertension: A pilot study. *Applied Psychophysiology & Biofeedback, 35*(2), 163–170. doi:10.1007/s10484-009-9126-x

Ong, A. D., Zautra, A. J., & Reid, M. C. (2010). Psychological resilience predicts decreases in pain catastrophizing through positive emotions. *Psychology & Aging, 25*(3), 516–523. doi:10.1037/a0019384

Oppliger, P. A. (2007). Effects of gender stereotyping on socialization. In R. W. Preiss, B. M. Gayle, et al. (Eds.), *Mass media effects research: Advances through meta-analysis* (pp. 199–214). Mahwah, NJ: Erlbaum.

Oral Cancer Foundation. (2017). *Oral cancer facts.* Retrieved May 6, 2017, from oralcancerfoundation.org/facts/index.htm

Oren, E. E., & Solomon, R. R. (2012). EMDR therapy: An overview of its development and mechanisms of action. *European Review of Applied Psychology, 62*(4), 197–203. doi:10.1016/j.erap.2012.08.005

Orenstein, P. (2011). *Cinderella ate my daughter.* New York: HarperCollins.

Orleans, C. T., Gruman, J., & Hollendonner, J. K. (1999). Rating our progress in population health promotion: Report card on six behaviors. *American Journal of Health Promotion, 14*(2), 75–82. doi:10.4278/0890-1171-14.2.75

Ormrod, J. E. (2014). *Educational psychology: Developing learners* (8th ed.). Boston, MA: Allyn & Bacon.

Orr, A. C., & Hammig, S. B. (2009). Inclusive postsecondary strategies for teaching students with learning disabilities: A review of the literature. *Learning Disability Quarterly, 32*(3), 181–196.

Osgood, C. E. (1952). The nature and measurement of meaning. *Psychological Bulletin, 49*, 197–237. doi:10.1037/h0055737

Oskamp, S., & Schultz, P. W. (2005). *Attitudes and opinions* (3rd ed.). Mahwah, NJ: Erlbaum.

Ossorio, P. N. (2011). Myth and mystification: The science of race and IQ. In S. Krimsky & K. Sloan (Eds.), *Race and the genetic revolution: Science, myth, and culture* (pp. 173–194). New York: Columbia University Press.

Otgaar, H., & Smeets, T. (2010). Adaptive memory: Survival processing increases both true and false memory in adults and children. *Journal of Experimental Psychology: Learning, Memory, & Cognition, 36*(4), 1010–1016. doi:10.1037/a0019402

Overholser, J. C. (2010). Psychotherapy that strives to encourage social interest: A simulated interview with Alfred Adler. *Journal of Psychotherapy Integration, 20*(4), 347–363.

Overmier, J. B., & LoLordo, V. M. (1998). Learned helplessness. In W. T. O'Donohue (Ed.), *Learning and behavior therapy* (pp. 352–373). Boston, MA: Allyn & Bacon.

Overson, C. E. (2014). Applying multimedia principles to slide shows for academic presentation. In V. A. Benassi, C. E. Overson, et al. (Eds.), *Applying science of learning in education: Infusing psychological science into the curriculum*. Retrieved January 31, 2017, from teachpsych.org/ebooks/asle2014/index.php

Owens, J., & Massey, D. S. (2011). Stereotype threat and college academic performance: A latent variables approach. *Social Science Research, 40*(1), 150–166. doi:10.1016/j.ssresearch.2010.09.010

Oyserman, D., Bybee, D., et al. (2004). Possible selves as roadmaps. *Journal of Research in Personality, 38*(2), 130–149. doi:10.1016/S0092-6566(03)00057-6

Page, M., Taylor, J., et al. (2012). Context effects and observer bias—implications for forensic odontology. *Journal of Forensic Sciences, 57*(1), 108–112. doi:10.1111/j.1556-4029.2011.01903.x

Pagel, J. F. (2012). The synchronous electrophysiology of conscious states. *Dreaming, 22*(3), 173–191.

Palermo, L., Geberhiwot, T., et al. (2017, January 12). Cognitive outcomes in early-treated adults with phenylketonuria (PKU): A comprehensive picture across domains. *Neuropsychology*, n.p. doi:proxy.library.brocku.ca/10.1037/neu0000337

Palmer, S. E., & Beck, D. M. (2007). The repetition discrimination task: An objective method for studying perceptual grouping. *Perception & Psychophysics, 69*(1), 68–78. doi:10.3758/BF03194454

Pan, Y., Storm, D. R., & Xia, Z. (2013). Role of adult neurogenesis in hippocampus-dependent memory, contextual fear extinction, and remote contextual memory: New insights from ERK5 MAP kinase. *Neurobiology of Learning & Memory, 105*, 81–92. doi:10.1016/j.nlm.2013.07.011

Pancer, S. M. (2015). *The psychology of citizenship and civic engagement*. New York: Oxford University Press.

Panksepp, J., & Pasqualini, M. S. (2005). The search for the fundamental brain/mind sources of affective experience. In J. Nadel & D. Muir (Eds.), *Emotional development: Recent research advances* (pp. 5–30). New York: Oxford University Press.

Panksepp, J., & Watt, D. (2011). What is basic about basic emotions? Lasting lessons from affective neuroscience. *Emotion Review, 3*(4), 387–396. doi:10.1177/1754073911410741

Papanicolaou, A. C. (Ed.). (2006). *The amnesias: A clinical textbook of memory disorders*. New York: Oxford University Press.

Paquette, S., & Heitzman, A. M. (2014). Job analysis. In R. H. Robinson (Ed.), *Foundations of forensic vocational rehabilitation* (pp. 145– 166). New York: Springer.

Paradis, C. M., Solomon, L. Z., et al. (2004). Flashbulb memories of personal events of 9/11 and the day after for a sample of New York City residents. *Psychological Reports, 95*(1), 304–310. doi:10.2466/PR0.95.5.304-310

Park, E., Shipp, D. B., et al. (2011). Postlingually deaf adults of all ages derive equal benefits from unilateral multichannel cochlear implant. *Journal of the American Academy of Audiology, 22*(10), 637–643. doi:10.3766/jaaa.22.10.2

Park, H. J., Li, R. X., et al. (2009). Neural correlates of winning and losing while watching soccer matches. *International Journal of Neuroscience, 119*(1), 76–87. doi:10.1080/00207450802480069

Park, H., & Lennon, S. J. (2008). Beyond physical attractiveness: Interpersonal attraction as a function of similarities in personal characteristics. *Clothing & Textiles Research Journal, 26*(4), 275–289. doi:10.1177/0887302X07309714

Park, I., Lee, N., et al. (2012). Volumetric analysis of cerebellum in short-track speed skating players. *Cerebellum, 11*(4), 925–930. doi:10.1007/s12311-012-0366-6

Park, Y. S., Kim, B. K., et al. (2010). Acculturation, enculturation, parental adherence to Asian cultural values, parenting styles, and family conflict among Asian American college students. *Asian American Journal of Psychology, 1*(1), 67–79. doi:10.1037/a0018961

Parke, R. D. (2004). Development in the family. *Annual Review of Psychology, 55*, 365–399. doi:10.1146/annurev.psych.55.090902.141528

Parker, A., Ngu, H., & Cassaday, H. J. (2001). Odour and Proustian memory. *Applied Cognitive Psychology, 15*(2), 159–171.

Parker, E. S., Cahill, L., & McGaugh, J. L. (2006). A case of unusual autobiographical remembering. *Neurocase, 12*(1), 35–49. doi:10.1080/13554790500473680

Parker, K., & Funk, C. (2017, December 14). Gender discrimination comes in many forms for today's working women. Retrieved from http://www.pewresearch.org/fact-tank/2017/12/14/gender-discrimination-comes-in-many-forms-for-todays-working-women/

Parker, P. D., & Salmela-Aro, K. (2011). Developmental processes in school burnout: A comparison of major developmental models. *Learning & Individual Differences, 21*, 244–248. doi:10.1016/j.lindif.2011.01.005

Parlade, M., Messinger, D. S., et al. (2009). Anticipatory smiling: Linking early affective communication and social outcome. *Infant Behavior & Development, 32*(1), 33–43. doi:10.1016/j.infbeh.2008.09.007

Pascual, A., Carpenter, C. J., et al. (2016). A meta-analysis of the effectiveness of the low-ball compliance-gaining procedure. *European Review of Applied Psychology, 66*(5), 261–267. doi:10.1016/j.erap.2016.06.004

Pascual, A., Guéguen, N., et al. (2013). Foot-in-the-door and problematic requests: A field experiment. *Social Influence, 8*(1), 46–53. doi:10.1080/15534510.2012.696038

Pashler, H., McDaniel, M., et al. (2008). Learning styles: Concepts and evidence. *Psychological Science in the Public Interest, 9*(3), 105–119. doi:10.1111/j.1539-6053.2009.01038.x. Epub 2008 Dec 1

Patall, E. A., Cooper, H., & Robinson, J. C. (2008). The effects of choice on intrinsic motivation and related outcomes: A meta-analysis of research findings. *Psychological Bulletin, 134*(2), 270–300. doi:10.1037/0033-2909.134.2.270

Paternoster, R., & Pogarsky, G. (2009). Rational choice, agency and thoughtfully reflective decision making: The short and long-term consequences of making good choices. *Journal of Quantitative Criminology, 25*(2), 103–127.

Paton, S. (2013). Introducing Taylor to the knowledge economy. *Employee Relations, 35*(1), 20–38. doi:10.1108/01425451311279393

Patrick, C. J. (Ed.). (2018). *Handbook of psychopathy*. New York: Guilford.

Paulhus, D. L., & Williams, K. M. (2002). The dark triad of personality: Narcissism, Machiavellianism, and psychopathy. *Journal of Research in Personality, 36*(6), 556–563. doi:10.1016/S0092-6566(02)00505-6

Paulson, G. W. (2012). *Closing the asylums: Causes and consequences of the deinstitutionalization movement*. Jefferson, NC: McFarland.

Pavlov, I. P. (1927). *Conditioned reflexes*. Translated by G. V. Anrep. New York: Dover.

Payne, B. K., Krosnick, J. A., et al. (2010). Implicit and explicit prejudice in the 2008 American presidential election. *Journal of Experimental Social Psychology, 46*(2), 367–374.

Payne, K. (2009). Winning the battle of ideas: Propaganda, ideology, and terror. *Studies in Conflict & Terrorism, 32*(2), 109–128. doi:10.1080/10576100802627738

Payne, K., & Sheeran, P. (2018, July 3). Try to resist misinterpreting the Marshmallow Test. *Behavioral Scientist*. Retrieved from https://behavioralscientist.org/try-to-resist-misinterpreting-the-marshmallow-test/

Pearce, C. L., Conger, J. A., & Locke, E. A. (2007). Shared leadership theory. *Leadership Quarterly, 18*(3), 281–288.

Pearce, C. L., Manz, C. C., & Sims, H. P., Jr. (2009). Where do we go from here? Is shared leadership the key to team success? *Organizational Dynamics, 38*(3), 234–238.

Pedersen, A. F., Bovbjerg, D. H., & Zachariae, R. (2011). Stress and susceptibility to infectious disease. In R. J. Contrada & A. Baum (Eds.), *The handbook of stress science: Biology, psychology, and health* (pp. 425–445). New York: Springer.

Pedraza, C., García, F. B., & Navarro, J. F. (2009). Neurotoxic effects induced by gammahydroxybutyric acid (GHB) in male rats. *International Journal of Neuropsychopharmacology, 12*(9), 1165–1177. doi:10.1017/S1461145709000157

Peira, N., Fredrikson, M., & Pourtois, G. (2013, December 27). Controlling the emotional heart: Heart rate biofeedback improves cardiac control during emotional reactions. *International Journal of Psychophysiology*, n.p. doi:10.1016/j.ijpsycho.2013.12.008

Pelletier, L. G., Baxter, D., & Huta, V. (2011). Personal autonomy and environmental sustainability. In V. I. Chirkov, R. N. Ryan, et al. (Eds.), *Human autonomy in cross-cultural context: Perspectives on the psychology of agency, freedom, and well-being* (pp. 257–278). New York: Springer.

Pelton, T. (1983). The shootists. *Science, 83, 4*(4), 84–86.

Pemment, J. (2013). The neurobiology of antisocial personality disorder: The quest for rehabilitation and treatment. *Aggression & Violent Behavior, 18*(1), 79–82. doi:10.1016/j.avb.2012.10.004

Penfield, W. (1957, April 27). Brain's record of past a continuous movie film. *Science News Letter*, 265.

Penfield, W. (1958). *The excitable cortex in conscious man*. Springfield, IL: Charles C. Thomas.

Penke, L. L., Maniega, S. M., et al. (2012). Brain-wide white matter tract integrity is associated with information processing speed and general intelligence. *Molecular Psychiatry, 17*(10), doi:10.1038/mp.2012.127

Pennebaker, J. W. (2004). *Writing to heal: A guided journal for recovering from trauma and emotional upheaval*. Oakland, CA: New Harbinger Press.

Pennebaker, J. W., & Chung, C. K. (2007). Expressive writing, emotional upheavals, and health. In H. S. Friedman & R. C. Silver (Eds.),

Foundations of health psychology (pp. 263–284). New York: Oxford University Press.

Peoples, C. D., Sigillo, A. E., et al. (2012). Friendship and conformity in group opinions: Juror verdict change in mock juries. *Sociological Spectrum, 32*(2), 178–193. doi:10.1080/02732173 2012.646163

Peplau, L. A. (2003). Human sexuality: How do men and women differ? *Current Directions in Psychological Science, 12*(2), 37–40.

Pepperberg, I. M. (2016, July 1). Animal language studies: What happened? *Psychonomic Bulletin & Review,* n.p. doi:10.3758/s13423-016-1101-y

Pereira, G. M., & Osburn, H. G. (2007). Effects of participation in decision making on performance and employee attitudes: A quality circles meta-analysis. *Journal of Business & Psychology, 22*(2), 145–153. doi:10.1007/s10869-007-9055-8

Pereira, M., Estramiana, J., & Gallo, I. (2010). Essentialism and the expression of social stereotypes: A comparative study of Spain, Brazil and England. *Spanish Journal of Psychology, 13*(2), 808–817.

Perkins, D. N. (1995). *Outsmarting IQ: The emerging science of learnable intelligence.* New York: Free Press.

Perkins, D. N., & Grotzer, T. A. (1997). Teaching intelligence. *American Psychologist, 52*(10), 1125–1133.

Perloff, R. M. (2010). *The dynamics of persuasion: Communication and attitudes in the 21st century.* New York: Psychology Press.

Perls, F. (1969). *Gestalt therapy verbatim.* Lafayette, CA: Real People Press.

Perry, G. (2013). *Behind the shock machine: The untold story of the notorious Milgram psychology experiments.* New York: New Press.

Perry, J. L., Joseph, J. E., et al. (2011). Prefrontal cortex and drug abuse vulnerability: Translation to prevention and treatment interventions. *Brain Research Reviews, 65,* 124–149. doi:10.1016/j. brainresrev.2010.09.001

Perry, R. P. (2003). Perceived (academic) control and causal thinking in achievement settings. *Canadian Psychology, 44*(4), 312–331. doi:10.1037/h0086956

Pérusse, F., Boucher, S., & Fernet, M. (2012). Observation of couple interactions: Alexithymia and communication behaviors. *Personality & Individual Differences, 53*(8), 1017–1022. doi:10.1016/j.paid.2012.07.022

Pesant, N., & Zadra, A. (2006). Dream content and psychological well-being: A longitudinal study of the continuity hypothesis. *Journal of Clinical Psychology, 62*(1), 111–121. doi:10.1002/jclp.20212

Pescatello, L. S. (2001). Exercising for health. *Western Journal of Medicine, 174*(2), 114–118.

Peters, M. L., Meevissen, Y. M., et al. (2013). Specificity of the best possible self intervention for increasing optimism: Comparison with a gratitude intervention. *Terapia Psicologica, 31,* 93–100.

Peters, W. A. (1971). *A class divided.* Garden City, NY: Doubleday.

Peterson, B. E., Pratt, M. W., et al. (2016). The authoritarian personality in emerging adulthood: Longitudinal analysis using standardized scales, observer ratings, and content coding of the life story. *Journal of Personality, 84*(2), 225–236. doi:10.1111/jopy.12154

Peterson, C., & Chang, E. C. (2003). Optimism and flourishing. In C. Keyes & J. Haidt (Eds.), *Flourishing: Positive psychology and the life well-lived* (pp. 55–79). Washington, DC: American Psychological Association.

Peterson, C., & Park, N. (2010). What happened to self-actualization? Commentary on Kenrick et al. (2010). *Perspectives on Psychological Science, 5*(3), 320–322. doi:10.1177/ 1745691610369471

Peterson, C., & Seligman, M. E. P. (2004). *Character strengths and virtues.* Washington, DC: American Psychological Association.

Peterson, C., Semmel, A., et al. (1982). The attributional style questionnaire. *Cognitive Therapy & Research, 6,* 287–299. doi:10.1007/BF01173577

Peterson, C., & Vaidya, R. S. (2001). Explanatory style, expectations, and depressive symptoms. *Personality & Individual Differences, 31*(7), 1217– 1223. doi:10.1016/S0191-8869(00) 00221-X

Peterson, L. R., & Peterson, M. J. (1959). Short-term retention of individual verbal items. *Journal of Experimental Psychology, 58,* 193–198. doi:10.1037/ h0049234

Petri, H. L., & Govern, J. M. (2013). *Motivation: Theory, research, and application* (6th ed.). Boston, MA: Cengage Learning.

Petrovsky, N., Ettinger, U., et al. (2014). Sleep deprivation disrupts prepulse inhibition and induces psychosis-like symptoms in healthy humans. *Journal of Neuroscience, 34*(27), 9134–9140. doi:10.1523/JNEUROSCI.0904-14.2014

Pett, M. A., & Johnson, M. J. M. (2005). Development and psychometric evaluation of the Revised University Student Hassles Scale. *Educational & Psychological Measurement, 65*(6), 984–1010. doi:10.1177/0013164405275661

Petticrew, M. P., Lee, K., et al. (2012). Type A behavior pattern and coronary heart disease: Philip Morris's "crown jewel." *American Journal of Public Health, 102*(11), 2018–2025. doi:10.2105/AJPH.2012.300816

Pettigrew, T. F. (2016). In pursuit of three theories: Authoritarianism, relative deprivation, and intergroup contact. *Annual Review of Psychology, 67,* 1–21. doi:10.1146/annurev-psych -122414-033327

Pettigrew, T. F., & Tropp, L. R. (2006). A meta-analytic test of intergroup contact theory. *Journal of Personality and Social Psychology, 90*(5), 751–783. doi:10.1037/0022-3514.90.5.751

Pettigrew, T. F., & Tropp, L. R. (2008). How does intergroup contact reduce prejudice? Meta-analytic tests of three mediators. *European Journal of Social Psychology, 38*(6), 922–934. doi:10.1002/ejsp.504

Peverly, S. T., Brobst, K. E., et al. (2003). College adults are not good at self-regulation. *Journal of Educational Psychology, 95*(2), 335–346.

Pezdek, K., Avila-Mora, E., & Sperry, K. (2010). Does trial presentation medium matter in jury simulation research? Evaluating the effectiveness of eyewitness expert testimony. *Applied Cognitive Psychology, 24*(5), 673–690.

Philippe, F. L., Koestner, R., & Lekes, N. (2013). On the directive function of episodic memories in people's lives: A look at romantic relationships. *Journal of Personality & Social Psychology, 104*(1), 164–179. doi:10.1037/a0030384

Phillips, D. A., & Lowenstein, A. E. (2011). Early care, education, and child development. *Annual Review of Psychology, 62,* 483–500. doi:10.1146/ annurev.psych.031809.130707

Phillips, J., Sharpe, L., et al. (2010). Subtypes of postnatal depression? A comparison of women with recurrent and de novo postnatal depression. *Journal of Affective Disorders, 120*(1–3), 67–75.

Phillips, K. M., Jim, H. L., et al. (2012). Effects of self-directed stress management training and home-based exercise on stress management skills in cancer patients receiving chemotherapy. *Stress & Health, 28*(5), 368–375. doi:10.1002/smi.2450

Phillips, K. W., Rothbard, N. P., & Dumas, T. L. (2009). To disclose or not to disclose? Status distance and self-disclosure in diverse environments. *Academy of Management Review, 34*(4), 710–732.

Piaget, J. (1951, original French, 1945). *The psychology of intelligence.* New York: Norton.

Piaget, J. (1952). *The origins of intelligence in children.* New York: International University Press.

Piaget, J., & Inhelder, B. (1956). *The child's conception of space.* London: Routledge & Kegan Paul.

Pilgrim, D. (2011). The hegemony of cognitive-behaviour therapy in modern mental health care. *Health Sociology Review, 20*(2), 120–132.

Piliavin, I. M., Rodin, J., & Piliavin, J. A. (1969). Good Samaritanism: An underground phenomenon? *Journal of Personality & Social Psychology, 13,* 289–299. doi:10.1037/h0028433

Piliavin, J. A., & Siegl, E. (2015). Health and well-being consequences of formal volunteering. In D. A. Schroeder & W. G. Graziano (Eds.), *The Oxford handbook of prosocial behavior* (pp. 494–523). New York: Oxford University Press.

Pinel, J. P. J., Assanand, S., & Lehman, D. R. (2000). Hunger, eating, and ill health. *American Psychologist, 55*(10), 1105–1116. doi:10.1037//0003-066X.55.10.1105

Pinel, P., & Dehaene, S. (2010). Beyond hemispheric dominance: Brain regions underlying the joint lateralization of language and arithmetic to the left hemisphere. *Journal of Cognitive Neuroscience, 22*(1), 48–66. doi:10.1162/jocn.2009.21184

Pinker, S. (2011). *The better angels of our nature: Why violence has declined.* New York: Viking.

Pinker, S., & Jackendoff, R. (2005). The faculty of language: What's special about it? *Cognition, 95*(2), 201–236. doi:10.1016/j.cognition.2004.08.004

Piomelli, D. (2014). More surprises lying ahead: The endocannabinoids keep us guessing. *Neuropharmacology, 76*(Part B), 228–234.

Piper, A., Jr. (2008). Multiple personality disorder: Witchcraft survives in the twentieth century. In S. O. Lilienfeld, J. Ruscio, & S. J. Lynn (Eds.), *Navigating the mindfield: A user's guide to distinguishing science from pseudoscience in mental health* (pp. 249–268). Amherst, NY: Prometheus Books.

Pirson, M., I, A., & Langer, E. (2012). Seeing what we know, knowing what we see: Challenging the limits of visual acuity. *Journal of Adult Development, 19*(2), 59–65.

Plakun, E. (2012). Treatment resistance and psychodynamic psychiatry: Concepts psychiatry needs from psychoanalysis. *Psychodynamic Psychiatry, 40*(2), 183–209. doi:10.1521/pdps.2012.40.2.183

Plassmann, H., O'Doherty, J., et al. (2008). Marketing actions can modulate neural representations of experienced pleasantness. *Proceedings of the National Academy of Sciences, 105*(3), 1050–1054. doi:10.1073/ pnas.0706929105

Plaze, M., Paillère-Martinot, M., et al. (2011). Where do auditory hallucinations come from? A brain morphometry study of schizophrenia patients with inner- or outer-space hallucinations. *Schizophrenia Bulletin, 37*(1), 212–221. doi:10.1093/schbul/sbp081

Plazzi, G., Vetrugno, R., et al. (2005). Sleepwalking and other ambulatory behaviours during sleep. *Neurological Sciences, 26*(Suppl. 3), s193–s198. doi:10.1007/s10072-005-0486-6

Pliner, P., & Mann, N. (2004). Influence of social norms and palatability on amount consumed and food choice. *Appetite, 42*(2), 227–237. doi:10.1016/j.appet.2003.12.001

Plomin, R., & Deary, I. J. (2015). Genetics and intelligence differences: Five special findings. *Molecular Psychiatry, 20*(1), 98–108. doi:10.1038/mp.2014.105

Plötner, M., Over, H., et al. (2015). Young children show the bystander effect in helping situations. *Psychological Science, 26*(4), 499–506. doi:10.1177/0956797615569579

Plous, S. (2003). *Understanding prejudice and discrimination*. New York: McGraw-Hill.

Pokorny, S. B., Jason, L. A., & Schoeny, M. E. (2003). The relation of retail tobacco availability to initiation and continued smoking. *Journal of Clinical Child & Adolescent Psychology, 32,* 193–204. doi:10.1207/S15374424JCCP3202_4

Poland, J., & Caplan, P. J. (2004). The deep structure of bias in psychiatric diagnosis. In P. J. Caplan & L. Cosgrove (Eds.), *Bias in psychiatric diagnosis. A project of the association for women in psychology* (pp. 9–23). Lanham, MD: Jason Aronson.

Polit, D. F., & Beck, C. (2013). Is there still gender bias in nursing research? An update. *Research in Nursing & Health, 36*(1), 75–83. doi:10.1002/nur.21514

Polivy, J., & Herman, C. P. (2002). Causes of eating disorders. *Annual Review of Psychology, 53,* 187–213. doi:10.1146/annurev.psych.53.100901.135103

Pollard, S., & Cooper-Thomas, H. D. (2015). Best practice recommendations for situational judgment tests. *Australasian Journal of Organisational Psychology, 8,* Article e7. doi:10.1017/orp.2015.6

Polusny, M. A., Ries, B. J., et al. (2011). Effects of parents' experiential avoidance and PTSD on adolescent disaster-related posttraumatic stress symptomatology. *Journal of Family Psychology, 25*(2), 220–229. doi:10.1037/a0022945

Pomaki, G., Supeli, A., & Verhoeven, C. (2007). Role conflict and health behaviors: Moderating effects on psychological distress and somatic complaints. *Psychology & Health, 22*(3), 317–335. doi:10.1080/14768320600774561

Portugal, E., Cevada, T., et al. (2013). Neuroscience of exercise: From neurobiology mechanisms to mental health. *Neuropsychobiology, 68*(1), 1–14.

Post, J. M. (2011). Crimes of obedience: "Groupthink" at Abu Ghraib. *International Journal of Group Psychotherapy, 61*(1), 49–66. doi:10.1521/ijgp.2011.61.1.48

Post, L. M., Feeny, N. C., et al. (2015). Post-traumatic stress disorder and depression co-occurrence: Structural relations among disorder constructs and trait and symptom dimensions. *Psychology & Psychotherapy: Theory, Research & Practice*. Advance online publication. doi:10.1111/papt.12087

Powell, M. D., & Ladd, L. D. (2010). Bullying A review of the literature and implications for family therapists. *American Journal of Family Therapy, 38*(3), 189–206. doi:10.1080/01926180902961662

Powell, R. A , Honey, P. L., et al. (2017). *Introduction to learning and behavior* (5th ed.). Boston, MA: Cengage Learning

Power, M. (2010). *Emotion-focused cognitive therapy*. New York: Wiley/Blackwell.

Prat-Sala, M., & Redford, P. (2012). Writing essays: Does self-efficacy matter? The relationship between self-efficacy in reading and in writing and undergraduate students' performance in essay writing. *Educational Psychology, 32*(1), 9–20. doi:10.1080/01443410.2011.621411

Prause, N. (2012). Theoretical, statistical, and construct problems perpetuated in the study of female orgasm. *Sexual & Relationship Therapy, 27*(3), 260–271. doi:10.1080/14681994.2012.732262

Pressnitzer, D., Graves, J., Chambers, C., De Gardelle, V., & Egré, P. (2018). Auditory perception: Laurel and Yanny together at last. *Current Biology, 28*(13), R739–R741. doi:10.1016/j.cub.2018.06.002

Price, D. D., Finniss, D. G., & Benedetti, F. (2008). A comprehensive review of the placebo effect: Recent advances and current thought. *Annual Review of Psychology, 59,* 565–590. doi:10.1146/annurev.psych.59.113006.095941

Price, J., & Davis, B. (2009). *The woman who can't forget: The extraordinary story of living with the most remarkable memory known to science—A memoir.* New York: Simon & Schuster.

Prichard, E., Propper, R. E., & Christman, S. D. (2013). Degree of handedness, but not direction, is a systematic predictor of cognitive performance. *Frontiers in Psychology, 4,* 9.

Prime, D. J., & Jolicoeur, P. (2010). Mental rotation requires visual short-term memory: Evidence from human electric cortical activity. *Journal of Cognitive Neuroscience, 22*(11), 2437–2446. doi:10.1162/jocn.2009.21337

Prochaska, J. O., & Norcross, J. C. (2014). *Systems of psychotherapy: A transtheoretical analysis* (8th ed.). Boston, MA: Cengage Learning.

Prochnow, D. D., Höing, B. B., et al. (2013). The neural correlates of affect reading: An fMRI study on faces and gestures. *Behavioural Brain Research, 237,* 270–277. doi:10.1016/j.bbr.2012.08.050

Prodan, C. I., Orbelo, D. M., & Ross, E. D. (2007). Processing of facial blends of emotion: Support for right hemisphere cognitive aging. *Cortex, 43*(2), 196–206. doi:10.1016/S0010-9452(08)70475-1

Prokhorov, A. V., Kelder, S. H., et al. (2010). Project aspire: An interactive, multimedia smoking prevention and cessation curriculum for culturally diverse high school students. *Substance Use & Misuse, 45*(6), 983–1006.doi:10.3109/10826080903038050

Protopapas, A., Archonti, A., & Skaloumbakas, C. (2007). Reading ability is negatively related to Stroop interference. *Cognitive Psychology, 54*(3), 251–282. doi:10.1016/j.cogpsych.2006.07.003

Proyer, R. T., Gander, F., et al. (2013). What good are character strengths beyond subjective well-being? The contribution of the good character on self-reported health-oriented behavior, physical fitness, and the subjective health status. *Journal of Positive Psychology, 8*(3), 222–232. doi:10.1080/17439760.2013.777767

Pruessner, M., Cullen, A. E., et al. (2017). The neural diathesis-stress model of schizophrenia revisited: An update on recent findings considering illness stage and neurobiological and methodological complexities. *Neuroscience & Biobehavioral Reviews, 73,* 191–218. doi:10.1016/j.neubiorev.2016.12.013

Prus, A. (2014). *An introduction to drugs and the neuroscience of behavior*. Boston, MA: Cengage Learning.

Przepiorka, A., Błachnio, A., & Díaz-Morales, J. F. (2016). Problematic Facebook use and procrastination. *Computers in Human Behavior, 65,* 59–64. doi:10.1016/j.chb.2016.08.022

Przybylski, A. K., Weinstein, N., et al. (2012). The ideal self at play: The appeal of video games that let you be all you can be. *Psychological Science, 23*(1), 69–76. doi:10.1177/0956797611418676

Puente, R., & Anshel, M. H. (2010). Exercisers' perceptions of their fitness instructor's interacting style, perceived competence, and autonomy as a function of self-determined regulation to exercise, enjoyment, affect, and exercise frequency. *Scandinavian Journal of Psychology, 51*(1), 38–45.

Purnell, L. (2003). The Purnell Model for Cultural Competence: A Model for all Healthcare Providers. *The Medical Network, 1 (1),* 8–17. (no doi available)

Putnam, R. (2000). *Bowling alone: The collapse and revival of American community*. New York: Touchstone.

Putwain, D. W., & Aveyard, B. (2016, November 10). Is perceived control a critical factor in understanding the negative relationship between cognitive test anxiety and examination performance? *School Psychology Quarterly,* n.p. doi:10.1037/spq0000183

Pychyl, T. A. (2013). *Solving the procrastination puzzle: A concise guide to strategies for change.* New York: Tarcher/Penguin.

Quednow, B. B., Jessen, F., et al. (2006). Memory deficits in abstinent MDMA (ecstasy) users: Neuropsychological evidence of frontal dysfunction. *Journal of Psychopharmacology, 20*(3), 373–384. doi:10.1177/0269881106061200

Quick, J. C., & McFadyen, M. A. (2017). Sexual harassment: Have we made any progress? *Journal of Occupational Health Psychology, 22*(3), 286–298. doi:10.1037/ocp0000054

Quinn, P. C., Bhatt, R. S., & Hayden, A. (2008). Young infants readily use proximity to organize visual pattern information. *Acta Psychologica, 127*(2), 289–298. doi:10.1016/j.actpsy.2007.06.002

Rabinak, C. A., Angstadt, M., et al. (2013). Cannabinoid facilitation of fear extinction memory recall in humans. *Neuropharmacology, 64,* 396–402. doi:10.1016/j.neuropharm.2012.06.063

Rabius, V., Wiatrek, D., & McAlister, A. L. (2012). African American participation and success in telephone counseling for smoking cessation. *Nicotine & Tobacco Research, 14*(2), 240–242. doi:10.1093/ntr/ntr129

Rachman, S. (2013). *Anxiety* (3rd ed.). New York: Routledge.

Radermacher, A., & Walia, G. (2013, March). Gaps between industry expectations and the abilities of graduates. In *Proceedings of the 44th ACM technical symposium on computer science education*

(pp. 525–530). Retrieved March 19, 2017, from http://dl.acm.org/citation.cfm?id=2445351

Radke, A. K., Rothwell, P. E., & Gewirtz, J. C. (2011). An anatomical basis for opponent process mechanisms of opiate withdrawal. *The Journal of Neuroscience, 31*(20), 7533–7539. doi:10.1523/JNEUROSCI.0172-11.2011

Radvansky, G. A. (2017). *Human memory* (3rd ed.). Boston, MA: Pearson/Allyn & Bacon.

Raes, E., Decuyper, S., et al. (2013). Facilitating team learning through transformational leadership. *Instructional Science, 41*(2), 287–305. doi:10.1007/s11251-012-9228-3

Raffin, E., Richard, N., et al. (2016). Primary motor cortex changes after amputation correlate with phantom limb pain and the ability to move the phantom limb. *NeuroImage, 130,* 134–144. doi:10.1016/j.neuroimage.2016.01.063

Ralston, A. (2004). *Between a rock and a hard place.* New York: Atria Books.

Ramachandran, V. S. (1995). 2-D or not 2-D—That is the question. In R. Gregory, J. Harris, P. Heard, & D. Rose (Eds.), *The artful eye* (pp. 249–267). Oxford: Oxford University Press.

Raman, R., & Sarkar, S. (2016). Predictive coding: A possible explanation of filling-in at the blind spot. *PLoS ONE, 11*(3), Article e0151194.

Range, F., Möslinger, H., & Virányi, Z. (2012). Domestication has not affected the understanding of means-end connections in dogs. *Animal Cognition, 15*(4), 597–607. doi:10.1007/s10071-012-0488-8

Rantanen, J., Metsäpelto, R. L., et al. (2007). Long-term stability in the Big Five personality traits in adulthood. *Scandinavian Journal of Psychology, 48*(6), 511–518. doi:10.1111/j.1467-9450.2007.00609.x

Raphael-Leff, J. (2012). "Terrible twos" and "terrible teens": The importance of play. *Journal of Infant, Child, & Adolescent Psychotherapy, 11*(4), 299–315. doi:10.1080/15289168.2012.732841

Raposo, A., Han, S., & Dobbins, I. G. (2009). Ventrolateral prefrontal cortex and self-initiated semantic elaboration during memory retrieval. *Neuropsychologia, 47*(11), 2261–2271. doi:10.1016/j.neuropsychologia.2008.10.024

Rasmussen, S. A., Eisen, J. L., & Greenberg, B. D. (2013). Toward a neuroanatomy of obsessive-compulsive disorder revisited. *Biological Psychiatry, 73*(4), 298–299. doi:10.1016/j.biopsych.2012.12.010

Rathus, R., Nevid, J., & Fichner-Rathus, L. (2013). *Human sexuality in a world of diversity* (9th ed.). Boston, MA: Allyn & Bacon.

Rathus, S. A. (2014). *Childhood and adolescence: Voyages in development* (5th ed.). Boston, MA: Cengage Learning.

Raval, V. V., & Walker, B. L. (2019). Unpacking "culture": Caregiver socialization of emotion and child functioning in diverse families. *Developmental Review, 51,* 146–174. doi:10.1016/j.dr.2018.11.001

Ray, S. L., Wong, C., et al. (2013). Compassion satisfaction, compassion fatigue, work life conditions, and burnout among frontline mental health care professionals. *Traumatology, 19*(4), 255–267. doi:10.1177/1534765612471144

Raymo, J. M., Warren, J. R., et al. (2010). Later-life employment preferences and outcomes: The role of midlife work experiences. *Research on Aging, 32*(4), 419–466.

Raymond, D., & Noggle, C. (2013). *Clinical neuropsychology: Biological and cognitive foundations for evaluation and rehabilitation.* New York: Springer.

Raz, M. (2013). *The lobotomy letters: The making of American psychosurgery.* Rochester: University of Rochester Press.

Reason, J. (2000). The Freudian slip revisited. *The Psychologist, 13*(12), 610–611.

Recht, D. R., & Leslie, L. (1988). Effect of prior knowledge on good and poor readers' memory of text. *Journal of Educational Psychology, 80*(1), 16–20. doi:10.1037/0022-0663.80.1.16

Reed, J. D., & Bruce, D. (1982). Longitudinal tracking of difficult memory retrievals. *Cognitive Psychology, 14,* 280–300. doi:10.1016/0010-0285(82)90011-1

Reed, S. K. (2013). *Cognition: Theory and applications* (9th ed.). Boston, MA: Cengage Learning.

Regan, P. C., Levin, L., et al. (2000). Partner preferences: What characteristics do men and women desire in their short-term sexual and long-term romantic partners? *Journal of Psychology & Human Sexuality, 12*(3), 1–21. doi:10.1300/J056v12n03_01

Reger, G. M., Koenen-Woods, P., et al. (2016). Randomized controlled trial of prolonged exposure using imaginal exposure vs. virtual reality exposure in active duty soldiers with deployment-related posttraumatic stress disorder (PTSD). *Journal of Consulting & Clinical Psychology, 84*(11), 946–959. doi:10.1037/ccp0000134

Regev, L. G., Zeiss, A., & Zeiss, R. (2006). Orgasmic disorders. In J. E. Fisher & W. T. O'Donohue (Eds.), *Practitioner's guide to evidence-based psychotherapy* (pp. 469–477). New York: Springer Science.

Regnerus, M., & Uecker, J. (2011). *Premarital sex in America: How young Americans meet, mate, and think about marrying.* New York: Oxford University Press.

Regoeczi, W. C. (2008). Crowding in context: An examination of the differential responses of men and women to high-density living environments. *Journal of Health & Social Behavior, 49*(3), 254–268. doi:10.1177/002214650804900302

Reid, M. R., Mackinnon, L. T., & Drummond, P. D. (2001). The effects of stress management on symptoms of upper respiratory tract infection, secretory immunoglobulin A, and mood in young adults. *Journal of Psychosomatic Research, 51*(6), 721–728. doi:10.1016/S0022-3999(01)00234-3

Reid, R. C., Carpenter, B. N., et al. (2012). Report of findings in a DSM-5 field trial for hypersexual disorder. *Journal of Sexual Medicine, 9*(11), 2868–2877. doi:10.1111/j.1743-6109.2012.02936.x

Reiff, S., Katkin, E. S., & Friedman, R. (1999). Classical conditioning of the human blood pressure response. *International Journal of Psychophysiology, 34*(2), 135–145. doi:10.1016/S0167-8760(99)00071-9

Reifman, A. S., Larrick, R. P., & Fein, S. (1991). Temper and temperature on the diamond: The heat-aggression relationship in major league baseball. *Personality & Social Psychology Bulletin, 17*(5), 580–585. doi:10.1177/0146167291175013

Reijntjes, A., Kamphuis, J. H., et al. (2013a). Too calloused to care: An experimental examination of factors influencing youths' displaced aggression against their peers. *Journal of Experimental Psychology: General, 142*(1), 28–33. doi:10.1037/a0028619

Reijntjes, A., Thomaes, S., et al. (2013b). Youths' displaced aggression against in- and out-group peers: An experimental examination. *Journal of Experimental Child Psychology, 115*(1), 180–187. doi:10.1016/j.jecp.2012.11.010

Reilly, D., Neumann, D. L., & Andrews, G. (2016). Sex and sex-role differences in specific cognitive abilities. *Intelligence, 54,* 147–158. doi:10.1016/j.intell.2015.12.004

Reinberg, A., & Ashkenazi, I. (2008). Internal desynchronization of circadian rhythms and tolerance to shift work. *Chronobiology International, 25*(4), 625–643. doi:10.1080/07420520802256101

Reis, H. T., Maniaci, M. R., et al. (2011). Familiarity does indeed promote attraction in live interaction. *Journal of Personality & Social Psychology, 101*(3), 557–570. doi:10.1037/a0022885

Reis, S. M. (Ed.). (2016). *Reflections on gifted education: Critical works by Joseph S. Renzulli and colleagues.* Waco, TX: Prufrock Press.

Reis, S. M., & Renzulli, J. S. (2010). Is there still a need for gifted education? An examination of current research. *Learning & Individual Differences, 20*(4), 308–317. doi:10.1016/j.lindif.2009.10.012

Reisner, A. D. (2006). A case of Munchausen syndrome by proxy with subsequent stalking behavior. *International Journal of Offender Therapy & Comparative Criminology, 50*(3), 245–254. doi:10.1177/0306624X05281880

Reivich, K., Gillham, J. E., et al. (2013). From helplessness to optimism: The role of resilience in treating and preventing depression in youth. In S. Goldstein & R. B. Brooks (Eds.), *Handbook of resilience in children* (2nd ed., pp. 201–214). New York: Springer. doi:10.1007/978-1-4614-3661-4_12

Reker, M., Ohrmann, P., et al. (2010). Individual differences in alexithymia and brain response to masked emotion faces. *Cortex, 46*(5), 658–667. doi:10.1016/j.cortex.2009.05.008

Remland, M. S., Jones, T. S., et al. (1991). Proxemic and haptic behavior in three European countries. *Journal of Nonverbal Behavior, 15*(4), 215–232.

Rescorla, R. A. (1987). A Pavlovian analysis of goal-directed behavior. *American Psychologist, 42*i, 119–129. doi:10.1037/0003-066X.42.2.119

Resnick, B. (2017). Brain activity is too complicated for humans to decipher: Machines can decode it for us. Retrieved February 10, 2017, from www.vox.com/science-and-health/2016/12/29/13967966/machine-learning-neuroscience

Restak, R. M. (2001). *The secret life of the brain.* New York: Dana Press.

Revillo, D. A., Paglini, M. G., et al. (2014). Spontaneous recovery from extinction in the infant rat. *Behavioural Brain Research, 274,* 149–157. doi:10.1016/j.bbr.2014.08.009

Revonsuo, A., Kallio, S., & Sikka, P. (2009). What is an altered state of consciousness? *Philosophical Psychology, 22*(2), 187–204. doi:10.1080/09515080902802850

Reynolds, B. W., Basso, M. R., Miller, A. K., Whiteside, D. M., & Combs, D. (2019). Executive function, impulsivity, and risky behaviors in young adults. *Neuropsychology, 33*(2), 212–221. doi:10.1037/neu0000510

Rhee, S. H., & Waldman, I. D. (2011). Genetic and environmental influences on aggression. In P. R. Shaver & M. Mikulincer (Eds.), *Human aggression and violence: Causes, manifestations, and consequences* (pp. 143–163). Washington, DC: American Psychological Association.

Ribeiro, A. C., LeSauter, J., et al. (2009). Relationship of arousal to circadian anticipatory behavior: Ventromedial hypothalamus: One node in a hunger arousal network. *European Journal of Neuroscience, 30*(9), 1730–1738. doi:10.1111/j.1460-9568.2009.06969.x

Rice, K. G., Richardson, C. E., & Clark, D. (2012). Perfectionism, procrastination, and psychological distress. *Journal of Counseling Psychology, 59*(2), 288–302. doi:10.1037/a0026643

Rice, L., & Markey, P. M. (2009). The role of extraversion and neuroticism in influencing anxiety following computer-mediated interactions. *Personality & Individual Differences, 46*(1), 35–39. doi:10.1016/j.paid.2008.08.022

Richardson, K. (2013). The eclipse of heritability and the foundations of intelligence. *New Ideas in Psychology, 31*(2), 122–129. doi:10.1016/j.newideapsych.2012.08.002

Ridenour, T. A., Maldonado-Molina, M., et al. (2005). Factors associated with the transition from abuse to dependence among substance abusers: Implications for a measure of addictive liability. *Drug & Alcohol Dependence, 80*(1), 1–14.

Rideout, V. (2015). *The common sense census: Media use by tweens and teens.* Retrieved April 2, 2017, from www.commonsensemedia.org/sites/default/files/uploads/research/census_researchreport.pdf

Rideout, V., Foehr, U. G., & Roberts, D. F. (2010). *Generation M2: Media in the lives of 8–18-year-olds.* Retrieved January 27, 2017, from www.kff.org/entmedia/upload/8010.pdf

Riela, S., Rodriguez, G., et al. (2010). Experiences of falling in love: Investigating culture, ethnicity, gender, and speed. *Journal of Social & Personal Relationships, 27*(4), 473–493. doi:10.1177/0265407510363508

Rigakos, G. S., Davis, R. C., et al. (2009). Soft targets? A national survey of the preparedness of large retail malls to prevent and respond to terrorist attack after 9/11. *Security Journal, 22*(4), 286–301. doi:10.1057/palgrave.sj.8350084

Righetti, F., Rusbult, C., & Finkenauer, C. (2010). Regulatory focus and the Michelangelo phenomenon: How close partners promote one another's ideal selves. *Journal of Experimental Social Psychology, 46*(6), 972–985. doi:10.1016/j.jesp.2010.06.001

Rihmer, Z., Dome, P., et al. (2012). Psychiatry should not become hostage to placebo: An alternative interpretation of antidepressant–placebo differences in the treatment response in depression. *European Neuropsychopharmacology, 22*(11), 782–786. doi:10.1016/j.euroneuro.2012.03.002

Rijken, N. H., Soer, R., et al. (2016). Increasing performance of professional soccer players and elite track and field athletes with peak performance training and biofeedback: A pilot study. *Applied Psychophysiology & Biofeedback, 41*(4), 421–430. doi:10.1007/s10484-016-9344-y

Riley, W., Jerome, A., et al. (2002). Feasibility of computerized scheduled gradual reduction for adolescent smoking cessation. *Substance Use & Misuse, 37*(2), 255–263.

Rind, B., Tromovitch, P., & Bauserman, R. (1998). A meta-analytic examination of assumed properties of child sexual abuse using college samples. *Psychological Bulletin, 124*(1), 22–53.

Rindermann, H., Becker, D., et al. (2017). Survey of expert opinion on intelligence: The Flynn effect and the future of intelligence. *Personality & Individual Differences, 106,* 242–247. doi:10.1016/j.paid.2016.10.061

Rindermann, H., Flores-Mendoza, C., & Mansur-Alves, M. (2010). Reciprocal effects between fluid and crystallized intelligence and their dependence on parents' socioeconomic status and education. *Learning & Individual Differences, 20*(5), 544–548.

Riquelme, H. (2002). Can people creative in imagery interpret ambiguous figures faster than people less creative in imagery? *Journal of Creative Behavior, 36*(2), 105–116. doi:10.1002/j.2162-6057.2002.tb01059.x

Riser, R. E., & Kosson, D. S. (2013). Criminal behavior and cognitive processing in male offenders with antisocial personality disorder with and without comorbid psychopathy. *Personality Disorders: Theory, Research, & Treatment, 4*(4), 332–340. doi:10.1037/a0033303

Ritchey, M., Dolcos, F., et al. (2011). Neural correlates of emotional processing in depression: Changes with cognitive behavioral therapy and predictors of treatment response. *Journal of Psychiatric Research, 45*(5), 577–587. doi:10.1016/j.jpsychires.2010.09.007

Ritchhart, R., & Perkins, D. N. (2005). Learning to think: The challenges of teaching thinking. In K. J. Holyoak & R. G. Morrison (Eds.), *The Cambridge handbook of thinking and reasoning* (pp. 775–802). Cambridge, MA: Cambridge University Press.

Ritchie, S. J., Bates, T. C., et al. (2013). Education is associated with higher later life IQ scores, but not with faster cognitive processing speed. *Psychology & Aging, 28*(2), 515–521. doi:10.1037/a0030820

Ritchie, T. D., Sedikides, C., et al. (2011). Self-concept clarity mediates the relation between stress and subjective well-being. *Self & Identity, 10*(4), 493–508. doi:10.1080/15298868.2010.493066

Ritter, S. M., van Baaren, R. B., & Dijksterhuis, A. (2012). Creativity: The role of unconscious processes in idea generation and idea selection. *Thinking Skills & Creativity, 7*(1), 21–27. doi:10.1016/j.tsc.2011.12.002

Rivers, S. E., Brackett, M. A., et al. (2012). Measuring emotional intelligence in early adolescence with the MSCEIT-YV psychometric properties and relationship with academic performance and psychosocial functioning. *Journal of Psychoeducational Assessment, 30*(4), 344–366. doi:10.1177/0734282912449443

Rizzo, A., Cukor, J., et al. (2015). Virtual reality exposure for PTSD due to military combat and terrorist attacks. *Journal of Contemporary Psychotherapy, 45*(4), 255–264. doi:10.1007/s10879-015-9306-3

Rizzolatti, G., Fogassi, L., & Gallese, V. (2006). Mirrors in the mind. *Scientific American, 295*(5), 54–61.

Roberto, M., & Koob, G. F. (2009). First congress of "Alcoholism and stress: A framework for future treatment strategies": Introduction to the proceeding. *Alcohol, 43*(7), 489–490. doi:10.1016/j.alcohol.2009.10.008

Roberts, B. W., & Mroczek, D. (2008). Personality trait change in adulthood. *Current Directions in Psychological Science, 17*(1), 31–35. doi:10.1111/j.1467-8721.2008.00543.x

Roberts, R. D., & Lipnevich, A. A. (2012). From general intelligence to multiple intelligences: Meanings, models, and measures. In K. R. Harris, S. Graham, et al. (Eds.), *APA educational psychology handbook* (Vol 2): *Individual differences and cultural and contextual factors* (pp. 33–57). Washington, DC: American Psychological Association. doi:10.1037/13274-002

Roberts, T., & Zurbriggen, E. L. (2013). The problem of sexualization: What is it and how does it happen? In E. L. Zurbriggen & T. Roberts (Eds.), *The sexualization of girls and girlhood: Causes, consequences, and resistance* (pp. 3–21). New York: Oxford University Press.

Roberts, W. A. (2002). Are animals stuck in time? *Psychological Bulletin, 128*(3), 473–489. doi:10.1037/0033-2909.128.3.473

Roberts, W. A., & Roberts, S. (2002). Two tests of the stuck-in-time hypothesis. *Journal of General Psychology, 129*(4), 415–429. doi:10.1080/00221300209602105

Robins, R. W., Gosling, S. D., & Craik, K. H. (1998). Psychological science at the crossroads. *American Scientist, 86,* 310–313. doi:10.1511/1998.4.310

Robinson, A. (2010). *Sudden genius? The gradual path to creative breakthroughs.* New York: Oxford University Press.

Robinson, D. N. (2008). *Consciousness and mental life.* New York: Columbia University Press.

Robinson, T. E., & Berridge, K. C. (2003). Addiction. *Annual Review of Psychology, 54,* 25–53. doi:10.1146/annurev.psych.54.101601.145237

Roca, M., Parr, A., et al. (2010). Executive function and fluid intelligence after frontal lobe lesions. *Brain: A Journal of Neurology, 133*(1), 234–247. doi:10.1093/brain/awp269

Rock, A. (2004). *The mind at night: The new science of how and why we dream.* New York: Basic Books.

Rodríguez-Villagra, O., Göthe, K., et al. (2012, December 10). Working memory capacity in a go/no-go task: Age differences in interference, processing speed, and attentional control. *Developmental Psychology,* n.p. doi:10.1037/a0030883

Roebers, C. M., & Feurer, E. (2015, November 25). Linking executive functions and procedural metacognition. *Child Development Perspectives,* n.p. doi:10.1111/cdep.12159

Roediger, H. L. III, & McDermott, K. B. (1995). Creating false memories: Remembering words not presented on lists. *Journal of Experimental Psychology: Learning, Memory, and Cognition, 21*(4), 803–814. doi:10.1037/0278-7393.21.4.803

Roese, N. J., Pennington, G. L., et al. (2006). Sex differences in regret: All for love or some for lust? *Personality & Social Psychology Bulletin, 32*(6), 770–780.

Roets, A., & Van Hiel, A. (2011). Allport's prejudiced personality today: Need for closure as the motivated cognitive basis of prejudice. *Current Directions*

in Psychological Science, 20(6), 349–354. doi:10.1177/0963721411424894

Roffman, J. L., Brohawn, D. G., et al. (2011). MTHFR 677C.T effects on anterior cingulate structure and function during response monitoring in schizophrenia: A preliminary study. *Brain Imaging & Behavior, 5*(1), 65–75. doi:10.1007/s11682-010-9111-2

Rogers, C. R. (1959). A theory of therapy, personality, and interpersonal relationships, as developed in the client-centered framework. In S. Koch (Ed.), *Psychology: A study of a science* (Vol. 3, pp. 184–256). New York: McGraw-Hill.

Rogers, C. R. (1961). *On becoming a person: A therapist's view of psychotherapy*. Boston, MA: Houghton Mifflin.

Rogers, P., & Soule, J. (2009). Cross-cultural differences in the acceptance of Barnum profiles supposedly derived from Western versus Chinese astrology. *Journal of Cross-Cultural Psychology, 40*(3), 381–399. doi:10.1177/0022022109332843

Rogowsky, B. A., Calhoun, B. M., et al. (2015). Matching learning style to instructional method: Effects on comprehension. *Journal of Educational Psychology, 107*(1), 64–78. doi:10.1037/a0037478

Roid, G. H., & Pomplun, M. (2012). The Stanford-Binet Intelligence Scales, Fifth Edition. In D. P. Flanagan & P. L. Harrison (Eds.), *Contemporary intellectual assessment: Theories, tests, and issues* (3rd ed., pp. 249–268). New York: Guilford Press.

Roja, I., & Roja, Z. (2010). Use of cognitive hypnotherapy and couples therapy for female patients with psychogenic vaginismus. *Contemporary Hypnosis, 27*(2), 88–94.

Rollero, C., Gattino, S., & De Piccoli, N. (2013). A gender lens on quality of life: The role of sense of community, perceived social support, self-reported health and income. *Social Indicators Research,* doi:10.1007/s11205-013-0316-9

Rollins, A. L., Bond, G. R., et al. (2010). Coping with positive and negative symptoms of schizophrenia. *American Journal of Psychiatric Rehabilitation, 13*(3), 208–223. doi:10.1080/15487768.2010.501297

Rolls, E. T. (2008). Top-down control of visual perception: Attention in natural vision. *Perception, 37*(3), 333–354. doi:10.1068/p5877

Rolls, E. T. (2014). *Emotion and decision-making explained*. New York: Oxford University Press.

Romero, M., Usart, M., & Ott, M. (2015). Can serious games contribute to developing and sustaining 21st century skills? *Games & Culture, 10*(2), 148–177. doi:10.1177/1555412014548919

Roney, J. R. (2003). Effects of visual exposure to the opposite sex: Cognitive aspects of mate attraction in human males. *Personality & Social Psychology Bulletin, 29,* 393–404.

Roos, P. E., & Cohen, L. H. (1987). Sex roles and social support as moderators of life stress adjustment. *Journal of Personality & Social Psychology, 52,* 576–585.

Rosa, N. M., & Gutchess, A. H. (2011). Source memory for action in young and older adults: Self vs. close or unknown others. *Psychology & Aging, 26*(3), 625–630. doi:10.1037/a0022827

Rosch, E. (1977). Classification of real-world objects: Origins and representations in cognition. In P. N. Johnson-Laird & P. C. Wason (Eds.), *Thinking: Reading in cognitive science* (pp. 212–222). Cambridge, UK: Cambridge University Press.

Rosen, R. C., Marx, B. P., et al. (2012). Project VALOR: Design and methods of a longitudinal registry of post-traumatic stress disorder (PTSD) in combat-exposed veterans in the Afghanistan and Iraqi military theaters of operations. *International Journal of Methods in Psychiatric Research, 21*(1), 5–16. doi:10.1002/mpr.355

Rosenhan, D. L. (1973). On being sane in insane places. *Science, 179*(4070), 250–258. doi:10.1126/science.179.4070.250

Rosenkranz, M. A., Jackson, D. C., et al. (2003). Affective style and in vivo immune response: Neurobehavioral mechanisms. *Proceedings of the National Academy of Sciences, 100,* 11148–11152. doi:10.1073/pnas.1534743100

Rosenthal, M. (2013). *Human sexuality: From cells to society*. Boston, MA: Cengage Learning.

Rosenthal, N. E. (2013). *Winter blues: Everything you need to know to beat seasonal affective disorder* (4th ed.). New York: Guilford.

Rosenthal, R. (1973, September). The Pygmalion effect lives. *Psychology Today*, 56–63.

Rosenthal, R. (1994). Science and ethics in conducting, analyzing, and reporting psychological research. *Psychological Science, 5,* 127–134. doi:10.1111/j.1467-9280.1994.tb00644.x

Rosmalen, J. G., Neeleman, J., Gans, R. O., & de Jonge, P. (2007). The association between neuroticism and self-reported common somatic symptoms in a population cohort. *Journal of Psychosomatic Research, 62*(3), 305–311. doi:10.1016/j.jpsychores.2006.10.014

Rosner, R. I. (2012). Aaron T. Beck's drawings and the psychoanalytic origin story of cognitive therapy. *History of Psychology, 15*(1), 1–18. doi:10.1037/a0023892

Ross, C. A., Schroeder, E., & Ness, L. (2013). Dissociation and symptoms of culture-bound syndromes in North America: A preliminary study. *Journal of Trauma & Dissociation, 14*(2), 224–235. doi:10.1080/15299732.2013.724338

Ross, M., & Wang, Q. (2010). Why we remember and what we remember: Culture and autobiographical memory. *Perspectives on Psychological Science, 5*(4), 401–409.

Ross, M., Heine, S. J., et al. (2005). Cross-cultural discrepancies in self-appraisals. *Personality & Social Psychology Bulletin, 31*(9), 1175–1188. doi:10.1177/0146167204274080

Ross, M., & Sicoly, F. (1979). Egocentric biases in availability and attribution. *Journal of Personality and Social Psychology, 37*(3), 322–336. doi:10.1037/0022-3514.37.3.322

Ross, P. E. (2006). The expert mind. *Scientific American, 294*(7), 64–71.

Rossignol, S., & Frigon, A. (2011). Recovery of locomotion after spinal cord injury: Some facts and mechanisms. *Annual Review of Neuroscience, 34,* 413–440. doi:10.1146/annurev-neuro-061010-113746

Rotter, J. B., & Hochreich, D. J. (1975). *Personality*. Glenview, IL: Scott, Foresman.

Rowland, D. L. (2007). Sexual health and problems: Erectile dysfunction, premature ejaculation, and male orgasmic disorder. In J. E. Grant & M. N. Potenza (Eds.), *Textbook of men's mental health* (pp. 171–203). Washington, DC: American Psychiatric Publishing.

Rowley, S. J., Varner, F., et al. (2012). Toward a model of racial identity and parenting in African Americans. In J. M. Sullivan & A. M. Esmail (Eds.), *African American identity: Racial and cultural dimensions of the Black experience* (pp. 273–288). Lanham, MD: Lexington Books.

Royle, N. A., Booth, T., et al. (2013). Estimated maximal and current brain volume predict cognitive ability in old age. *Neurobiology of Aging, 34*(12), 2726–2733. doi:10.1016/j.neurobiolaging.2013.05.015

Rozin, P., Kabnick, K., et al. (2003). The ecology of eating: Smaller portion sizes in France than in the United States help explain the French paradox. *Psychological Science, 14*(5), 450–454. doi:10.1111/1467-9280.02452

Rubenstein, C., & Tavris, C. (1987). Special survey results: 2600 women reveal the secrets of intimacy. *Redbook, 159,* 147–149.

Rucker, D. D., Tormala, Z. L., et al. (2014). Consumer conviction and commitment: An appraisal-based framework for attitude certainty. *Journal of Consumer Psychology, 24*(1), 119–136. doi:10.1016/j.jcps.2013.07.001

Rudolph, C. W., & Baltes, B. B. (2016, February 25). Age and health jointly moderate the influence of flexible work arrangements on work engagement: Evidence from two empirical studies. *Journal of Occupational Health Psychology,* n.p. doi:10.1037/a0040147

Ruggiero, V. R. (2015). *Becoming a critical thinker* (8th ed.). Boston, MA: Cengage Learning.

Runco, M. A. (2012). *Creativity: An interdisciplinary perspective*. New York: Routledge.

Runco, M. A. (2015). Meta-creativity: Being creative about creativity. *Creativity Research Journal, 27*(3), 295–298. doi:10.1080/10400419.2015.1065134

Runco, M. A., & Acar, S. (2012). Divergent thinking as an indicator of creative potential. *Creativity Research Journal, 24*(1), 66–75. doi:10.1080/10400419.2012.652929

Rusconi, E., & Mitchener-Nissen, T. (2013). Prospects of functional magnetic resonance imaging as lie detector. *Frontiers in Human Neuroscience, 7,* 594.

Rushton, J. P., & Jensen, A. R. (2005). Thirty years of research on race differences in cognitive ability. *Psychology, Public Policy, & Law, 11,* 235–294. doi:10.1037/1076-8971.11.2.235

Russell, A., Stevenson, R. J., et al. (2015). Chocolate smells pink and stripy: Exploring olfactory-visual synesthesia. *Cognitive Neuroscience, 6*(2–3), 77–88. doi:10.1080/17588928.2015.1035245

Russell, S., & Norvig, P. (2014). *Artificial intelligence: A modern approach* (3rd ed., paperback). Englewood Cliffs, NJ: Prentice Hall.

Russo, M. B., Brooks, F. R., et al. (1998). Conversion disorder presenting as multiple sclerosis. *Military Medicine, 163*(10), 709–710.

Rutter, M., Beckett, C., et al. (2009). Effects of profound early institutional deprivation: An overview of findings from a UK longitudinal study of Romanian adoptees. In G. Wrobel & E. Neil (Eds.), *International advances in adoption research for practice* (pp. 147–167). London, UK: Wiley-Blackwell.

Rutter, V. B., & Singer, T. (Eds.). (2015). *Ancient Greece, modern psyche: Archetypes evolving.* New York: Routledge.

Rutz, C., & St. Clair, J. H. (2012). The evolutionary origins and ecological context of tool use in New Caledonian crows. *Behavioural Processes, 89*(2), 153–165. doi:10.1016/j.beproc.2011.11.005

Ruva, C., McEvoy, C., & Bryant, J. B. (2007). Effects of pre-trial publicity and jury deliberation on juror bias and source memory errors. *Applied Cognitive Psychology, 21*(1), 45–67. doi:10.1002/acp.1254

Ryan, K. M. (2011). The relationship between rape myths and sexual scripts: The social construction of rape. *Sex Roles, 65*(11–12), 774–782. doi:10.1007/s11199-011-0033-2

Ryan, M. P. (2001). Conceptual models of lecture learning: Guiding metaphors and model-appropriate notetaking practices. *Reading Psychology, 22*(4), 289–312. doi:10.1080/02702710127638

Ryan, R. M., Curren, R. R., & Deci, E. L. (2013). What humans need: Flourishing in Aristotelian philosophy and self-determination theory. In A. S. Waterman (Ed.), *The best within us: Positive psychology perspectives on eudaimonia* (pp. 57–75). Washington, DC: American Psychological Association. doi:10.1037/14092-004

Ryan, R. M., & Deci, E. L. (2017). *Self-determination theory: Basic psychological needs in motivation, development, and wellness.* New York: Guilford.

Ryckman, R. M. (2013). *Theories of personality* (10th ed.). Boston, MA: Cengage Learning.

Ryff, C. D., & Singer, B. (2009). Understanding healthy aging: Key components and their integration. In V. L. Bengston, D. Gans, D., et al. (Eds.), *Handbook of theories of aging* (2nd ed., pp. 117–144). New York: Springer.

Saarimäki, H., Gotsopoulos, A., et al. (2016). Discrete neural signatures of basic emotions. *Cerebral Cortex, 26*(6), 2563–2573. doi:10.1093/cercor/bhv086

Sachdev, P. S., & Chen, X. (2009). Neurosurgical treatment of mood disorders: Traditional psychosurgery and the advent of deep brain stimulation. *Current Opinion in Psychiatry, 22*(1), 25–31. doi:10.1097/YCO.0b013e32831c8475

Sackett, P. R., & Lievens, F. (2008). Personnel selection. *Annual Review of Psychology, 59,* 419–450.

Sackett, P. R., Walmsley, P. T., & Laczo, R. M. (2013). Job and work analysis. In N. W. Schmitt, S. Highhouse, et al. (Eds.), *Handbook of psychology* (Vol. 12): *Industrial and organizational psychology* (2nd ed., pp. 61–81). New York: Wiley.

Sacks, O. (2010). *The mind's eye.* New York: Knopf.

Şahin, F., Gürbüz, S., et al. (2017). Leaders' managerial assumptions and transformational leadership: The moderating role of gender. *Leadership & Organization Development Journal, 38*(1), 105–125. doi:10.1108/LODJ-11-2015-0239

Sailor, W. (2015). Advances in schoolwide inclusive school reform. *Remedial & Special Education, 36*(2), 94–99. doi:10.1177/0741932514555021

Sakaluk, J. K., & Milhausen, R. R. (2012). Factors influencing university students' explicit and implicit sexual double standards. *Journal of Sex Research, 49*(5), 464–476. doi:10.1080/00224499.2011.569976

Saksida, L. M., & Wilkie, D. M. (1994). Time-of-day discrimination by pigeons. *Animal Learning & Behavior, 22,* 143–154. doi:10.3758/BF03199914

Salas, E., Shuffler, M. L., et al. (2015). Understanding and improving teamwork in organizations: A scientifically-based practical guide. *Human Resources Management, 54,* 599–622. doi:10.1002/hrm.21628

Sales, B. D., & Hafemeister, T. L. (1985). Law and psychology. In E. M. Altmeir & M. E. Meyer (Eds.), *Applied specialties in psychology* (pp. 331–373). New York: Random House.

Salimpoor, V. N., Benovoy, M. M., et al. (2011). Anatomically distinct dopamine release during anticipation and experience of peak emotion to music. *Nature Neuroscience, 14*(2), 257–262. doi:10.1038/nn.2726

Salisbury, A. G., & Burker, E. J. (2011). Assessment, treatment, and vocational implications of combat-related PTSD in veterans. *Journal of Applied Rehabilitation Counseling, 42*(2), 42–49.

Sallinen, M., Holm, A., et al. (2008). Recovery of cognitive performance from sleep debt: Do a short rest pause and a single recovery night help? *Chronobiology International, 25*(2–3), 279–296. doi:10.1080/07420520802107 10

Sallinen, M., Sihvola, M., et al. (2017). Sleep, alertness and alertness management among commercial airline pilots on short-haul and long-haul flights. *Accident Analysis & Prevention. 98,* 320–329. doi:10.1016/j.aap.2016.10.029

Salloum, A., & Overstreet, S. (2012). Grief and trauma intervention for children after disaster: Exploring coping skills versus trauma narration. *Behaviour Research & Therapy, 50*(3), 169–179. doi:10.1016/j.brat.2012.01.001

Salomons, T. V., Nusslock, R., et al. (2015). Neural emotion regulation circuitry underlying anxiolytic effects of perceived control over pain. *Journal of Cognitive Neuroscience, 27*(2), 222–233. doi:10.1162/jocn_a_00702

Sam, D. L., & Berry, J. W. (2010). Acculturation: When individuals and groups of different cultural backgrounds meet. *Perspectives on Psychological Science, 5*(4), 472–481. doi:10.1177/1745691610373075

Sample, I. (2014, February 14). Male sexual orientation influenced by genes, study shows. *The Guardian.* Retrieved May 20, 2014, from www.theguardian.com/science/2014/feb/14/genes-influence-male-sexual-orientation-study

Samson, D., & Apperly, I. A. (2010). There is more to mind reading than having theory of mind concepts: New directions in theory of mind research. *Infant & Child Development, 19*(5), 443–454.

Sana, F., Weston, T., & Cepeda, N. J. (2013). Laptop multitasking hinders classroom learning for both users and nearby peers. *Computers & Education, 62,* 24–31. doi:10.1016/j.compedu.2012.10.003

Sanchez, J. E., Yoxsimer, A., et al. (2012). Uniforms in the middle school: Student opinions, discipline data, and school police data. *Journal of School Violence, 11*(4), 345–356. doi:10.1080/15388220.2012.706873

Sandvik, A. M., Bartone, P. T., et al. (2013). Psychological hardiness predicts neuroimmunological responses to stress. *Psychology, Health & Medicine, 18*(6), 705–713. doi:10.1080/13548506.2013.772304

Sanes, J. R., & Masland, R. H. (2015). The types of retinal ganglion cells: Current status and implications for neuronal classification. *Annual Review of Neuroscience, 38,* 221–246. doi:10.1146/annurev-neuro-071714-034120

Sansone, R. A., & Sansone, L. A. (2010). Road rage: What's driving it? *Psychiatry, 7*(7), 14–18.

Sansone, R. A., Leung, J. S., & Wiederman, M. W. (2013). Self-reported bullying in childhood: Relationships with employment in adulthood. *International Journal of Psychiatry in Clinical Practice, 17*(1), 64–68. doi:10.3109/13651501.2012.709867

Santarcangelo, E. L., & Scattina, E. (2016). Complementing the latest APA definition of hypnosis: Sensory-motor and vascular peculiarities involved in hypnotizability. *International Journal of Clinical & Experimental Hypnosis, 64*(3), 318–330. doi:10.1080/00207144.2016.1171093

Santelices, M. P., Guzmán, G. M., et al. (2011). Promoting secure attachment: Evaluation of the effectiveness of an early intervention pilot programme with mother–infant dyads in Santiago, Chile. *Child: Care, Health, & Development, 37*(2), 203–210. doi:10.1111/j.1365-2214.2010.01161.x

Santrock, J. W., & Halonen, J. S. (2013). *Your guide to college success: Strategies for achieving your goals* (7th ed.). Boston, MA: Cengage Learning.

Sapolsky, R. (2005). Sick of poverty. *Scientific American, 293*(6), 92–99.

Sarason, I. G., & Sarason, B. R. (2005). *Abnormal psychology* (11th ed.). Mahwah, NJ: Prentice Hall.

Sarkova, M., Bacikova-Sleskova, M., et al. (2013). Associations between assertiveness, psychological well-being, and self-esteem in adolescents. *Journal of Applied Social Psychology, 43*(1), 147–154. doi:10.1111/j.1559-1816.2012.00988.x

Sauce, B., & Matzel, L. D. (2018). The paradox of intelligence: Heritability and malleability coexist in hidden gene-environment interplay. *Psychological Bulletin, 144*(1), 26–47. doi:10.1037/bul0000131

Savin-Williams, R., Joyner, K., et al. (2012). Prevalence and stability of self-reported sexual orientation identity during young adulthood. *Archives of Sexual Behavior, 41*(1), 103–110.

Saxbe, D. E. (2017). Birth of a new perspective? A call for biopsychosocial research on childbirth. *Current Directions in Psychological Science, 26*(1), 81–86. doi:10.1177/0963721416677096

Saxton, M. (2010). *Child language: Acquisition and development.* Thousand Oaks, CA: Sage.

Saxvig, I. W., Lundervold, A. J., et al. (2008). The effect of a REM sleep deprivation procedure on different aspects of memory function in humans. *Psychophysiology, 45*(2), 309–317. doi:10.1111/j.1469-8986.2007.00623.x

Scannell, S., & Mulvilhill, M. (2012). *Big book of brainstorming games.* New York: McGraw-Hill.

Schachter, S. (1959). *Psychology of affiliation.* Stanford, CA: Stanford University Press.

Schachter, S., & Wheeler, L. (1962). Epinephrine, chlorpromazine and amusement. *Journal of Abnormal and Social Psychology, 65,* 121–128. doi:10.1037/h0040391

Schacter, D. L. (1996). *Searching for memory: The brain, the mind, and the past.* New York: Basic Books.

Schacter, D. L. (2012). Adaptive constructive processes and the future of memory. *American Psychologist, 67*(8), 603–613. doi:10.1037/a0029869

Schafer, M., & Crichlow, S. (2010). *Groupthink versus high-quality decision making in international relations.* New York: Columbia University Press.

Schaie, K. W. (2005). *Developmental influences on adult intelligence: The Seattle longitudinal study.* New York: Oxford University Press.

Schalke, D., Brunner, M., et al. (2013). Stability and change in intelligence from age 12 to age 52: Results from the Luxembourg MAGRIP study. *Developmental Psychology, 49*(8), 1529–1543. doi:10.1037/a0030623

Schechter, E. (2012). Intentions and unified agency: Insights from the split-brain phenomenon. *Mind & Language, 27*(5), 570–594. doi:10.1111/mila.12003

Scheibe, S., Sheppes, G., & Staudinger, U. M. (2015). Distract or reappraise? Age-related differences in emotion-regulation choice. *Emotion, 15,* 677–681. doi:10.1037/a0039246

Scheinkman, M. (2008). The multi-level approach: A road map for couples therapy. *Family Process, 47*(2), 197–213.

Schenck, C. H., & Mahowald, M. W. (2005). Rapid eye movement and non-REM sleep parasomnias. *Primary Psychiatry, 12*(8), 67–74.

Scherbaum, C. A., Sabet, J., et al. (2013). Examining faking on personality inventories using unfolding item response theory models. *Journal of Personality Assessment, 95*(2), 207–216. doi:10.1080/00223891.2012.725439

Schermer, V. L. (2015). Psychodrama in perspective: An interview with Jonathan Moreno on his father, Jacob Moreno, and the lasting impact of his ideas. *Group Analysis, 48*(2), 187–201. doi:10.1177/0533316415580539

Schetter, C. D. (2011). Psychological science on pregnancy: Stress processes, biopsychosocial models, and emerging research issues. *Annual Review of Psychology, 62,* 531–558. doi:10.1146/annurev.psych.031809.130727

Schick, T., & Vaughn, L. (2014). *How to think about weird things: Critical thinking for a new age* (7th ed.). New York: McGraw-Hill.

Schifrin, N. (2013, October 7). How Malala Yousafzai's courage inspired a nation: "We are no longer afraid." *ABC News.* Retrieved March 18, 2017, from http://abcnews.go.com/International/malala-yousafzais-courage-inspired-nation-longer-afraid/story?id=20452967

Schiller, D., Eichenbaum, H., et al. (2015). Memory and space: Towards an understanding of the cognitive map. *Journal of Neuroscience, 35*(41), 13904–13911. doi:10.1523/JNEUROSCI.2618-15.2015

Schiller, P. H., Slocum, W. M., et al. (2011). The integration of disparity, shading, and motion parallax cues for depth perception in humans and monkeys. *Brain Research, 1377,* 67–77. doi:10.1016/j.brainres.2011.01.003

Schinazi, V. R., Nardi, D., et al. (2013). Hippocampal size predicts rapid learning of a cognitive map in humans. *Hippocampus, 23*(6), 515–528. doi:10.1002/hipo.22111

Schiraldi, G. R., & Brown, S. L. (2001). Primary prevention for mental health: Results of an exploratory cognitive-behavioral college course. *Journal of Primary Prevention, 22*(1), 55–67. doi:10.1023/A:1011040231249

Schizophrenia Working Group of the Psychiatric Genomics Consortium. (2014). Biological insights from 108 schizophrenia-associated genetic loci. *Nature, 511*(7510), 421–425. doi:10.1038/nature13595

Schlaepfer, T. E., Cohen, M. X., et al. (2008). Deep brain stimulation to reward circuitry alleviates anhedonia in refractory major depression. *Neuropsychopharmacology, 33*(2), 368–377. doi:10.1038/sj.npp.1301408

Schleicher, S. S., & Gilbert, L. A. (2005). Heterosexual dating discourses among college students: Is there still a double standard? *Journal of College Student Psychotherapy, 19*(3), 7–23.

Schlund, M. W., & Cataldo, M. F. (2010). Amygdala involvement in human avoidance, escape and approach behavior. *NeuroImage, 53*(2), 769–776. doi:10.1016/j.neuroimage.2010.06.058

Schmader, T., Croft, A., & Whitehead, J. (2014). Why can't I just be myself? A social cognitive analysis of the working self-concept under stereotype threat. *Social Psychological & Personality Science, 5*(1), 4–11. doi:10.1177/1948550613482988

Schmahmann, J. D. (2010). The role of the cerebellum in cognition and emotion: Personal reflections since 1982 on the dysmetria of thought hypothesis, and its historical evolution from theory to therapy. *Neuropsychology Review, 20*(3), 236–260. doi:10.1007/s11065-010-9142-x.

Schmalzl, L., Thomke, E., et al. (2011). "Pulling telescoped phantoms out of the stump": Manipulating the perceived position of phantom limbs using a full-body illusion. *Frontiers in Human Neuroscience, 5,* 121. doi:10.3389/fnhum.2011.00121

Schmelz, M. (2010). Itch and pain. *Neuroscience & Biobehavioral Reviews, 34*(2), 171–176. doi:10.1016/j.neubiorev.2008.12.004

Schmidt, F. L., & Hunter, J. E. (1998). The validity and utility of selection methods in personnel psychology. *Psychological Bulletin, 124*(2), 262–274.

Schmidt, S., Roesler, U., et al. (2014). Uncertainty in the workplace: Examining role ambiguity and role conflict, and their link to depression—A meta-analysis. *European Journal of Work & Organizational Psychology, 23*(1), 91–106. doi:10.1080/1359432X.2012.711523

Schmitt, D. P., & Allik, J. (2005). Simultaneous administration of the Rosenberg Self-Esteem Scale in 53 nations: Exploring the universal and culture-specific features of global self-esteem. *Journal of Personality & Social Psychology, 89*(4), 623–642.doi:10.1037/0022-3514.89.4.623

Schmitt, N., & Golubovich, J. (2013). Biographical information. In K. F. Geisinger, B. A. Bracken, et al. (Eds.), *APA handbook of testing and assessment in psychology* (Vol. 1): *Test theory and testing and assessment in industrial and organizational psychology* (pp. 437–455). Washington, DC: American Psychological Association. doi:10.1037/14047-025

Schmuck, P., & Vlek, C. (2003). Psychologists can do much to support sustainable development. *European Psychologist, 8*(2), 66–76.

Schnakers, C. C., Perrin, F. F., et al. (2009). Detecting consciousness in a total locked-in syndrome: An active event-related paradigm. *Neurocase, 15*(4), 271–277. doi:10.1080/13554790902724904

Schnakers, C., & Laureys, S. (2012). *Coma and disorders of consciousness.* New York: Springer. doi:10.1007/978-1-4471-2440-5

Schneider, A., Ligsay, A., & Hagerman, R. J. (2013). Fragile X syndrome: An aging perspective. *Developmental Disabilities Research Reviews, 18*(1), 68–74. doi:10.1002/ddrr.1129

Schneider, K. J., Bugental, J. F. T., & Pierson, J. F. (2001). *The handbook of humanistic psychology.* Thousand Oaks, CA: Sage.

Schneider, R. L., Arch, J. J., & Wolitzky-Taylor, K. B. (2015). The state of personalized treatment for anxiety disorders: A systematic review of treatment moderators. *Clinical Psychology Review, 38,* 39–54. doi:10.1016/j.cpr.2015.02.004

Schneider, W., Niklas, F., et al. (2014). Intellectual development from early childhood to early adulthood: The impact of early IQ differences on stability and change over time. *Learning & Individual Differences, 32,* 156–162. doi:10.1016/j.lindif.2014.02.001

Schneiderman, N., Antoni, M. H., et al. (2001). Health psychology: Psychological and biobehavioral aspects of chronic disease management. *Annual Review of Psychology, 52,* 555–580. doi:10.1146/annurev.psych.52.1.555

Schramm, D. G., Marshall, J. P., et al. (2012). Religiosity, homogamy, and marital adjustment: An examination of newlyweds in first marriages and remarriages. *Journal of Family Issues, 33*(2), 246–268. doi:10.1177/0192513X11420370

Schreiber, F. R. (1973). *Sybil.* Chicago, IL: Regency.

Schuck, K., Keijsers, G. P. J., & Rinck, M. (2011). The effects of brief cognitive-behaviour therapy for pathological skin picking: A randomized comparison to wait-list control. *Behaviour Research & Therapy, 49*(1), 11–17. doi:10.1016/j.brat.2010.09.005

Schultz, D. H., & Helmstetter, F. J. (2010). Classical conditioning of autonomic fear responses is independent of contingency awareness. *Journal of Experimental Psychology: Animal Behavior Processes, 36*(4), 495–500. doi:10.1037/a0020263

Schultz, D. P., & Schultz, S. E. (2010). *Psychology and work today* (10th ed.). Englewood Cliffs, NJ: Prentice Hall.

Schultz, D. P., & Schultz, S. E. (2016). *A history of modern psychology* (11th ed.). Boston, MA: Cengage Learning.

Schultz, D. P., & Schultz, S. E. (2017). *Theories of personality* (11th ed.). Boston, MA: Cengage Learning.

Schuster, J., Hoertel, N., & Limosin, F. (2011). The man behind Philippe Pinel: Jean-Baptiste Pussin (1746–1811): Psychiatry in pictures. *British Journal of Psychiatry, 198*(3), 198–241. doi:10.1192/bjp.198.3.241a

Schuster, M. A., Stein, B. D., et al. (2001). A national survey of stress reactions after the September 11, 2001, terrorist attacks. *New England Journal of Medicine, 345*(20), 1507–1512. doi:10.1056/NEJM200111153452024

Schwab, S. G., & Wildenauer, D. B. (2013). Genetics of psychiatric disorders in the GWAS era: An update on schizophrenia. *European Archives of Psychiatry & Clinical Neuroscience, 263*(Suppl. 2), 147–154. doi:10.1007/s00406-013-0450-z

Schwartz, B. (2004). *The paradox of choice: Why less is more.* New York: Ecco.

Schwarz, N., Bless, H., Strack, F., Klumpp, G., Rittenauer-Schatka, H., & Simons, A. (1991). Ease of retrieval as information: Another look at the availability heuristic. *Journal of Personality and Social Psychology, 61*(2), 195–202. doi:10.1037/0022-3514.61.2.195

Schweckendiek, J., Klucken, T., et al. (2011). Weaving the (neuronal) web: Fear learning in spider phobia. *NeuroImage, 54*(1), 681–688. doi:10.1016/j.neuroimage.2010.07.049

Schwenzer, M. (2008). Prosocial orientation may sensitize to aggression-related cues. *Social Behavior & Personality, 36*(8), 1009–1010. doi:10.2224/sbp.2008.36.8.1009

Schwinger, M., Wirthwein, L., et al. (2014). Academic self-handicapping and achievement: A meta-analysis. *Journal of Educational Psychology,* doi:10.1037/a0035832

Sclafani, A., & Springer, D. (1976). Dietary obesity in adult rats: Similarities to hypothalamic and human obesity syndromes. *Psychology & Behavior, 17,* 461–471. doi:10.1016/0031-9384(76)90109-8

Scoboria, A., Mazzoni, G., et al. (2002). Immediate and persisting effects of misleading questions and hypnosis on memory reports. *Journal of Experimental Psychology: Applied, 8*(1), 26–32. doi:10.1037/1076-898X.8.1.26

Scoboria, A., Mazzoni, G., et al. (2012). Personalized and not general suggestion produces false autobiographical memories and suggestion-consistent behavior. *Acta Psychologica, 139*(1), 225–232. doi:10.1016/j.actpsy.2011.10.008

Scollon, C. N., Koh, S., & Au, E. W. M. (2011). Cultural differences in the subjective experience of emotion: When and why they occur. *Social & Personality Psychology Compass, 5*(11), 853–864. doi:10.1111/j.1751-9004.2011.00391.x

Scott, R. (2012). Amphetamine-induced psychosis and defences to murder. *Psychiatry, Psychology & Law, 19*(5), 615–645. doi:10.1080/13218719.2012.738022

Scruggs, T. E., & Mastropieri, M. A. (2007). Science learning in special education: The case for constructed versus instructed learning. *Exceptionality, 15*(2), 57–74.

Sears, S., & Kraus, S. (2009). I think therefore I om: Cognitive distortions and coping style as mediators for the effects of mindfulness meditation on anxiety, positive and negative affect, and hope. *Journal of Clinical Psychology, 65*(6), 561–573. doi:10.1002/jclp.20543

Segal, N. L. (2012). *Born together—reared apart: The landmark Minnesota Twin Study.* Cambridge, MA: Harvard University Press. doi:10.4159/harvard.9780674065154

Segal, Z. V., Williams, J. G., & Teasdale, J. D. (2013). *Mindfulness-based cognitive therapy for depression* (2nd ed.). New York: Guilford.

Segerdahl, P., Fields, W., & Savage-Rumbaugh, S. (2005). *Kanzi's primal language: The cultural initiation of primates into language.* New York: Palgrave MacMillan.

Segerstrom, S., & Miller, G. E. (2004). Psychological stress and the human immune system: A meta-analytic study of 30 years of inquiry. *Psychological Bulletin, 130*(4), 601–630. doi:10.1037/0033-2909.130.4.601

Segraves, R., & Woodard, T. (2006). Female hypoactive sexual desire disorder: History and current status. *Journal of Sexual Medicine, 3*(3), 408–418.

Segraves, T., & Althof, S. (2002). Psychotherapy and pharmacotherapy for sexual dysfunctions. In P. E. Nathan & J. M. Gorman (Eds.), *A guide to treatments that work* (2nd ed., pp. 497–524). London: Oxford.

Seidman, B. F. (2001, January–February). Medicine wars. *Skeptical Inquirer,* 28–35.

Seitz, A., & Watanabe, T. (2005). A unified model for perceptual learning. *Trends in Cognitive Sciences, 9*(7), 329–334. doi:10.1016/j.tics.2005.05.010

Sela, L., & Sobel, N. (2010). Human olfaction: A constant state of change-blindness. *Experimental Brain Research, 205,* 13–29. doi:10.1007/s00221-010-2348-6

Seli, P., Carriere, J. S. A., Wammes, J. D., Risko, E. F., Schacter, D. L., & Smilek, D. (2018). On the clock: Evidence for the rapid and strategic modulation of mind wandering. *Psychological Science, 29*(8), 1247–1256. doi:10.1177/0956797618761039

Seligman, M. E. P. (1972). For helplessness: Can we immunize the weak? In *Readings in Psychology Today* (2nd ed.). Del Mar, CA: CRM.

Seligman, M. E. P. (1989). *Helplessness.* New York: Freeman.

Seligman, M. E. P. (1998). *Learned optimism.* New York: Pocket Books.

Selye, H. (1976). *The stress of life.* New York: Knopf.

Senécal, C., Julien, E., & Guay, F. (2003). Role conflict and academic procrastination: A self-determination perspective. *European Journal of Social Psychology, 33*(1), 135–145. doi:10.1002/ejsp.144

Serfass, D. G., & Sherman, R. A. (2013). Personality and perceptions of situations from the Thematic Apperception Test. *Journal of Research in Personality, 47*(6), 708–718. doi:10.1016/j.jrp.2013. 06.007

Serra, M. J., & Metcalfe, J. (2009). Effective implementation of metacognition. In D. J. Hacker, J. Dunlosky, et al. (Eds.), *Handbook of metacognition in education* (pp. 278–298). New York: Routledge.

Sessa, V. I., & London, M. (2006). *Continuous learning in organizations: Individual, group, and organizational perspectives.* Mahwah, NJ: Erlbaum.

Sethi-Iyengar, S., Huberman, G., & Jiang, W. (2004). How much choice is too much? Contributions to 401(k) retirement plans. In O. S. Mitchell & S. P. Utkus (Eds.), *Pension design and structure: New lessons from behavioral finance* (pp. 84–96). New York: Oxford University Press.

Seto, M. C. (2008). *Pedophilia and sexual offending against children: Theory, assessment, and intervention.* Washington, DC: American Psychological Association.

Seto, M. C. (2009). Pedophilia. *Annual Review of Clinical Psychology, 5,* 391–407.

Seto, M. C., Cantor, J. M., & Blanchard, R. (2006). Child pornography offenses are a valid diagnostic indicator of pedophilia. *Journal of Abnormal Psychology, 115*(3), 610–615.

Seybolt, D. C., & Wagner, M. K. (1997). Self-reinforcement, gender-role, and sex of participant in prediction of life satisfaction. *Psychological Reports, 81*(2), 519–522. doi:10.2466/PR0.81.6.519-522

Seyle, D. C., & Newman, M. L. (2006). A house divided? The psychology of red and blue America. *American Psychologist, 61*(6), 571–580. doi:10.1037/0003-066X.61.6.571

Shaffer, D. R. (2009). *Social and personality development* (6th ed.). Boston, MA: Cengage Learning.

Shaffer, D. R., & Kipp, K. (2014). *Developmental psychology: Childhood and adolescence* (9th ed.). Boston, MA: Cengage Learning.

Shafton, A. (1995). *Dream reader.* Albany, NY: SUNY Press.

Shager, H. M., Schindler, H. S., et al. (2013). Can research design explain variation in Head Start research results? A meta-analysis of cognitive and achievement outcomes. *Educational Evaluation & Policy Analysis, 35*(1), 76–95.

Shamloul, R. (2010). Natural aphrodisiacs. *Journal of Sexual Medicine, 7*(1, Pt 1), 39–49. doi:10.1111/j.1743-6109.2009.01521.x

Shapiro-Mendoza, C. K., Kimball, M., et al. (2009). US infant mortality trends attributable to accidental suffocation and strangulation in bed from 1984 through 2004: Are rates increasing? *Pediatrics, 123*(2), 533–539. doi:10.1542/peds.2007-3746

Shapiro, F. (2012). EMDR therapy: An overview of current and future research. *European Review of Applied Psychology, 62*(4), 193–195. doi:10.1016/j.erap.2012.09.005

Shapiro, J. M. (2006). A "memory-jamming" theory of advertising. *Social Science Research Network.* Retrieved January 31, 2017, from papers.ssrn.com/sol3/papers.cfm?abstract_id=903474

Shapiro, S. L., & Walsh, R. (2006). The meeting of meditative disciplines and Western psychology: A mutually enriching dialogue. *American Psychologist, 61*(3), 227–239. doi:10.1037/0003-066X.61.3.227

Sharf, R. S. (2016). *Theories of psychotherapy & counseling: Concepts and cases* (6th ed.). Boston, MA: Cengage Learning.

Sharma, S., Powers, A., et al. (2016). Gene × environment determinants of stress- and anxiety-related disorders. *Annual Review of Psychology, 67,* 239–261. doi:10.1146/annurev-psych-122414-033408

Shaver, P. R., & Mikulincer, M. (Eds.). (2011). *Human aggression and violence: Causes, manifestations, and consequences.* Washington, DC: American Psychological Association.

Shaw, E., & Delaporte, Y. (2011). New perspectives on the history of American Sign Language. *Sign Language Studies, 11*(2), 158–204. doi:10.1353/sls.2010.0006

Shaywitz, B. A., Shaywitz, S. E., et al. (1995). Sex differences in the functional organization of the brain for language. *Nature, 373,* 607–609. doi:10.1038/373607a0

Shepard, R. N. (1975). Form, formation, and transformation of internal representations. In R. L. Solso (Ed.), *Information processing and cognition: The Loyola Symposium* (pp. 87–122). Hillsdale, NJ: Erlbaum.

Sheppes, G., Suri, G., et al. (2015). Emotion regulation and

psychopathology. *Annual Review of Clinical Psychology, 11,* 379–405. doi:10.1146/annurev-clinpsy-032814-112739
Sherif, M. (1935). A study of some social factors in perception. *Archives of Psychology (Columbia University), 187,* 60.
Sherif, M., Harvey, O. J., et al. (1961). *Intergroup conflict and cooperation: The Robbers Cave experiment.* University of Oklahoma, Institute of Group Relations. Retrieved April 6, 2017, from http://psychclassics.yorku.ca/Sherif/
Shermer, L. O., Rose, K. C., & Hoffman, A. (2011). Perceptions and credibility: Understanding the nuances of eyewitness testimony. *Journal of Contemporary Criminal Justice, 27*(2), 183–203. doi:10.1177/1043986211405886
Shermer, M. (2011). *The believing brain.* New York: Holt.
Shewach, O. R., Sackett, P. R., & Quint, S. (2019). Stereotype threat effects in settings with features likely versus unlikely in operational test settings: A meta-analysis. *Journal of Applied Psychology, 104*(12), 1514–1534. doi:10.1037/apl0000420
Shih, J. J., & Krusienski, D. J. (2012). Signals from intraventricular depth electrodes can control a brain–computer interface. *Journal of Neuroscience Methods, 203*(2), 311–314. doi:10.1016/j.jneumeth.2011.10.012
Shillingsburg, M. A., Kelley, M. E., et al. (2009). Evaluation and training of yes-no responding across verbal operants. *Journal of Applied Behavior Analysis, 42*(2), 209–223. doi:10.1901/jaba.2009.42-209
Shimotake, A., Matsumoto, R., et al. (2015). Direct exploration of the role of the ventral anterior temporal lobe in semantic memory: Cortical stimulation and local field potential evidence from subdural grid electrodes. *Cerebral Cortex, 25*(10), 3802–3817. doi:10.1093/cercor/bhu262
Shiner, R. L., Buss, K. A., et al. (2012). What is temperament now? Assessing progress in temperament research on the twenty-fifth anniversary of Goldsmith et al. (1987). *Child Development Perspectives, 6*(4), 436–444. doi:10.1111/j.1750-8606.2012.00254.x
Shins, S. H., Miller, D. P., & Teicher, M. H. (2012). Exposure to childhood neglect and physical abuse and developmental trajectories of heavy episodic drinking from early adolescence into young adulthood. *Drug & Alcohol Dependence, 127*(1–3), 31–38. doi:10.1016/j.drugalcdep.2012.06.005
Shmerling, R. H. (2019, December 10). Can vaping damage your lungs? What we do (and don't) know. *Harvard Health Blog.* https://www.health.harvard.edu/blog/can-vaping-damage-your-lungs-what-we-do-and-dont-know-2019090417734
Shook, J. R. (2013). Social cognition and the problem of other minds. In D. D. Franks & J. H. Turner (Eds.), *Handbook of neurosociology* (pp. 33–46). New York: Springer. doi:10.1007/978-94-007-4473-8_4
Shorrock, S. T., & Isaac, A. (2010). Mental imagery in air traffic control. *International Journal of Aviation Psychology, 20*(4), 309–324. doi:10.1080/10508414.2010.487008
Shrout, P. E., & Rodgers, J. L. (2018). Psychology, science, and knowledge construction: Broadening perspectives from the replication crisis. *Annual Review of Psychology, 69,* 487–510. doi:10.1146/annurev-psych-122216-011845
Shutter, J. M., & Camras, L. A. (2010). Emotional facial expressions in infancy. *Emotion Review, 2*(2), 120–129. doi:10.1177/1754073909352529
Sidanius, J. (1993). The psychology of group conflict and the dynamics of oppression: A social dominance perspective. In Iyengar, Shanto, McGuire, William James (Eds.), *Explorations in political psychology. Duke studies in political psychology* (pp. 183–219). Durham, NC: Duke University Press.
Siefert, C. J. (2010). Screening for personality disorders in psychiatric settings: Four recently developed screening measures. In L. Baer & M. A. Blais (Eds.), *Handbook of clinical rating scales and assessment in psychiatry and mental health* (pp. 125–144). Totowa, NJ: Humana Press.
Siegel, M., Ross, C. S., & et al. (2013). The relationship between gun ownership and firearm homicide rates in the United States, 1981–2010. *American Journal of Public Health, 103*(11), 2098–2105. doi:10.2105/AJPH.2013.301409
Siegel, R. D. (2010). *The mindfulness solution: Everyday practices for everyday problems.* New York: Guilford.
Siegel, R. K. (2005). *Intoxication: The universal drive for mind-altering substances.* Rochester, VT: Park Street Press.
Siegler, R. S. (2005). *Children's thinking* (4th ed.). Mahwah, NJ: Erlbaum.
Siegler, R. S., DeLoache, J. S., & Eisenberg, N. (2014). *How children develop* (4th ed.). New York: Worth.
Siegman, A. W., & Feldstein, S. (2014). *Nonverbal behavior and communication.* Hove, UK: Psychology Press.
Sielski, R., Rief, W., & Glombiewski, J. A. (2017). Efficacy of biofeedback in chronic back pain: A meta-analysis. *International Journal of Behavioral Medicine, 24*(1), 25–41. doi:10.1007/s12529-016-9572-9
Sienaert, P., Vansteelandt, K., et al. (2010). Randomized comparison of ultra-brief bifrontal and unilateral electroconvulsive therapy for major depression: Cognitive side-effects. *Journal of Affective Disorders, 122*(1–2), 60–67. doi:10.1016/j.jad.2009.06.011
Sigelman, C. K., & Rider, E. A. (2015). *Life-span human development* (8th ed.). Boston, MA: Cengage Learning.
Silber, B. Y., & Schmitt, J. A. J. (2010). Effects of tryptophan loading on human cognition, mood, and sleep. *Neuroscience & Biobehavioral Reviews, 34*(3), 387–407. doi:10.1016/j.neubiorev.2009.08.005
Silla, I., & Gamero, N. (2014). Shared time pressure at work and its health-related outcomes: Job satisfaction as a mediator. *European Journal of Work & Organizational Psychology, 23*(3), 405–418. doi:10.1080/1359432X.2012.752898
Silveri, M. C., Ciccarelli, N., & Cappa, A. (2011). Unilateral spatial neglect in degenerative brain pathology. *Neuropsychology, 25*(5), 554–566. doi:10.1037/a0023957
Silverman, W. H. (2013). The future of psychotherapy: One editor's perspective. *Psychotherapy, 50*(4), 484–489. doi:10.1037/a0030573
Silverstein, C. (2009). The implications of removing homosexuality from the DSM as a mental disorder. *Archives of Sexual Behavior, 38*(2), 161–163.
Silvia, P. J. (2015). Intelligence and creativity are pretty similar after all. *Educational Psychology Review, 27*(4), 599–606. doi:10.1007/s10648-015-9299-1
Simeonova, D., Chang, K. D., et al. (2005). Creativity in familial bipolar disorder. *Journal of Psychiatric Research, 39*(6), 623–631.
Simister, J., & Cooper, C. (2005). Thermal stress in the U.S.A.: Effects on violence and on employee behaviour. *Stress & Health, 21,* 3–15. doi:10.1002/smi.1029
Simner, M. L., & Goffin, R. D. (2003). A position statement by the International Graphonomics Society on the use of graphology in personnel selection testing. *International Journal of Testing, 3*(4), 353–364. doi:10.1207/S15327574IJT0304_4
Simon-Thomas, E. R., Role, K. O., & Knight, R. T. (2005). Behavioral and electrophysiological evidence of a right hemisphere bias for the influence of negative emotion on higher cognition. *Journal of Cognitive Neuroscience, 17*(3), 518–529. doi:10.1162/0898929053279504
Simons, D. A., & Wurtele, S. K. (2010). Relationships between parents' use of corporal punishment and their children's endorsement of spanking and hitting other children. *Child Abuse & Neglect, 34*(9), 639–646. doi:10.1016/j.chiabu.2010.01.012
Simons, D. J., & Chabris, C. F. (1999). Gorillas in our midst: Sustained inattentional blindness for dynamic events. *Perception, 28,* 1059–1074. doi:10.1068/p2952
Simons, D. J., & Levin, D. T. (1998). Failure to detect changes to people during a real-world interaction. *Psychonomic Bulletin & Review, 5*(4), 644–649. doi:10.3758/BF03208840
Simonton, D. K. (2009). Varieties of (scientific) creativity: A hierarchical model of domain-specific disposition, development, and achievement. *Perspectives on Psychological Science, 4*(5), 441–452. doi:10.1111/j.1745-6924.2009.01152.x
Simonton, D. K. (2016, January 25). Defining creativity: Don't we also need to define what is not creative? *Journal of Creative Behavior,* n.p. doi:10.1002/jocb.137
Simpson, J. A., & Rholes, W. S. (2017). Adult attachment, stress, and romantic relationships. *Current Opinion in Psychology, 13,* 19–24. doi:10.1016/j.copsyc.2016.04.006
Simpson, K. J. (2002). Anorexia nervosa and culture. *Journal of Psychiatric & Mental Health Nursing, 9,* 65–71.
Sims, T., Hogan, C. L., & Carstensen, L. L. (2015). Selectivity as an emotion regulation strategy: Lessons from older adults. *Current Opinion in Psychology, 3,* 80–84. doi:10.1016/j.copsyc.2015.02.012
Singer, J. D. (2005). Explaining foreign policy: U.S. decision-making and the Persian Gulf War. *Political Psychology, 26*(5), 831–834.
Singh, B., Murad, M., et al. (2013). Meta-analysis of Glasgow Coma Scale and Simplified Motor Score in predicting traumatic brain injury outcomes. *Brain Injury, 27*(3), 293–300. doi:10.3109/02699052.2012.743182
Singh, K., Dawson, M. E., et al. (2013). Can human autonomic classical conditioning occur without contingency awareness? The critical importance of the trial sequence. *Biological Psychology, 93*(1), 197–205. doi:10.1016/j.biopsycho.2013.02.007
Sinha, R., Garcia, M., et al. (2006). Stress-induced cocaine craving and

hypothalamic-pituitary-adrenal responses are predictive of cocaine relapse outcomes. *Archives of General Psychiatry, 63*(3), 324–331. doi:10.1001/archpsyc.63.3.324

Sipos, A., Rasmussen, F., et al. (2004). Paternal age and schizophrenia: A population based cohort study. *British Medical Journal, 329*(7474), 1070. doi:10.1136/bmj.38243.672396.55

Sirin, S. R., Ryce, P., et al. (2013). The role of acculturative stress on mental health symptoms for immigrant adolescents: A longitudinal investigation. *Developmental Psychology, 49*(4), 736–748. doi:10.1037/a0028398

Sirois, F. M., & Tosti, N. (2012). Lost in the moment? An investigation of procrastination, mindfulness, and well-being. *Journal of Rational-Emotive & Cognitive Behavior Therapy, 30*(4), 237–248.

Sisk, V. F., Burgoyne, A. P., Sun, J., Butler, J. L., & Macnamara, B. N. (2018). To what extent and under which circumstances are growth mind-sets important to academic achievement? Two meta-analyses. *Psychological Science, 29*, 549–571. 10.1177/0956797617739704

Skeels, H. M. (1966). Adult status of children with contrasting early life experiences. *Monograph of the Society for Research in Child Development, 31*(3), 1–56.

Skinner, B. F. (1938). *The behavior of organisms*. Englewood Cliffs, NJ: Prentice Hall.

Slagt, M., Dubas, J. S., et al. (2016). Differences in sensitivity to parenting depending on child temperament: A meta-analysis. *Psychological Bulletin, 142*(10), 1068–1110. doi:10.1037/bul0000061

Slof-Op't Landt, M. C. T., Claes, L., et al. (2016). Classifying eating disorders based on "healthy" and "unhealthy" perfectionism and impulsivity. *International Journal of Eating Disorders, 49*(7), 673–680. doi:10.1002/eat.22557

Sloman, A. (2008). The well-designed young mathematician. *Artificial Intelligence, 172*(18), 2015–2034. doi:10.1016/j.artint.2008.09.004

Smallwood, J., & Schooler, J. W. (2006). The restless mind. *Psychological Bulletin, 132*(6), 946–958. doi:10.1037/0033-2909.132.6.946

Smith, A. P., Christopher, G., & Sutherland, D. (2013). Acute effects of caffeine on attention: A comparison of non-consumers and withdrawn consumers. *Journal of Psychopharmacology, 27*(1), 77–83.

Smith, A. P., Clark, R., & Gallagher, J. (1999). Breakfast cereal and caffeinated coffee: Effects on working memory, attention, mood, and cardiovascular function. *Physiology & Behavior, 67*(1), 9–17. doi:10.1016/S0031-9384(99)00025-6

Smith, C. A., & Kirby, L. D. (2011). The role of appraisal and emotion in coping and adaptation. In R. J. Contrada & A. Baum (Eds.), *The handbook of stress science: Biology, psychology, and health* (pp. 195–208). New York: Springer.

Smith, D., & Wakefield, C. (2016). Imagery in sport. In A. M. Lane (Ed.), *Sport and exercise psychology* (2nd ed., pp. 232–249). New York: Routledge/Taylor & Francis.

Smith, J. (2013, April 1). Prototypes, exemplars, and the natural history of categorization. *Psychonomic Bulletin & Review*, n.p. doi:10.3758/s13423-013-0506-0

Smith, M., Vogler, J., et al. (2009). Electroconvulsive therapy: The struggles in the decision-making process and the aftermath of treatment. *Issues in Mental Health Nursing, 30*(9), 554–559. doi:10.1080/01612840902807947

Smith, S. J., Zanotti, D. C., et al. (2011). Individuals' beliefs about the etiology of same-sex sexual orientation. *Journal of Homosexuality, 58*(8), 1110–1131. doi:10.1080/00918369.2011.598417

Smith, T. W. (2006). *American sexual behavior: Trends, socio-demographic differences, and risk behavior.* University of Chicago National Opinion Research Center GSS Topical Report No. 25. Retrieved March 10, 2017, from www.norc.org/NR/rdonlyres/2663F09F-2E74-436E-AC81-6FFBF288E183/0/AmericanSexualBehavior2006.pdf

Smith, T. W., & Traupman, E. K. (2011). Anger, hostility, and aggressiveness in coronary heart disease: Clinical applications of an interpersonal perspective. In R. Allan & J. Fisher (Eds.), *Heart and mind: The practice of cardiac psychology* (2nd ed., pp. 187–198). Washington, DC: American Psychological Association

Smith, T. W., Ruiz, J. M., & Uchino, B. N. (2004). Mental activation of supportive ties, hostility, and cardiovascular reactivity to laboratory stress in young men and women. *Health Psychology, 23*(5), 476–485. doi:10.1037/0278-6133.23.5.476

Smyth, J. M., & Pennebaker, J. W. (2008). Exploring the boundary conditions of expressive writing: In search of the right recipe. *British Journal of Health Psychology, 13*(1), 1–7. doi:10.1348/135910707X260117

Smyth, J. M., Pennebaker, J. W., & Arigo, D. (2012). What are the health effects of disclosure? In A. Baum, T. A. Revenson, et al. (Eds.), *Handbook of health psychology* (2nd ed., pp. 175–191). New York: Psychology Press.

Snitz, B. E., O'Meara, E. S., et al. (2009). Ginkgo biloba for preventing cognitive decline in older adults: A randomized trial. *Journal of the American Medical Association, 302*(24), 2663–2670. doi:10.1001/jama.2009.1913

Snow, C. P. (1961, February). Either-or. *Progressive*, 24.

Snowman, J., & McCown, R. (2015). *Psychology applied to teaching* (14th ed.). Boston, MA: Cengage Learning.

Snyder, A., Bahramali, H., et al. (2006). Savant-like numerosity skills revealed in normal people by magnetic pulses. *Perception, 35*(6), 837–845. doi:10.1068/p5539

Snyder, C. R., Lopez, S. J., & Pedrotti, J. T. (2011). *Positive psychology: The scientific and practical explorations of human strengths* (2nd ed.). Thousand Oaks, CA: Sage.

Sobczak, J. A. (2009). Alcohol use and sexual function in women: A literature review. *Journal of Addictions Nursing, 20*(2), 71–85. doi:10.1080/10884600902850095

Sobel, E., Shine, D., et al. (1996). Condom use among HIV/infected patients in South Bronx, New York. *AIDS, 10*(2), 235–236.

Sobolewski, J. M., & Amato, P. R. (2005). Economic hardship in the family of origin and children's psychological well-being in adulthood. *Journal of Marriage & Family, 67*(1), 141–156. doi:10.1111/j.0022-2445.2005.00011.x

Soderstrom, M. (2007). Beyond babytalk: Re-evaluating the nature and content of speech input to preverbal infants. *Developmental Review, 27*(4), 501–532. doi:10.1016/j.dr.2007.06.002

Soemer, A., & Schwan, S. (2012). Visual mnemonics for language learning: Static pictures versus animated morphs. *Journal of Educational Psychology, 104*(3), 565–579. doi:10.1037/a0029272

Solari, C. D., & Mare, R. D. (2012). Housing crowding effects on children's well-being. *Social Science Research, 41*(2), 464–476. doi:10.1016/j.ssresearch.2011.09.012

Solomon, J. L., Marshall, P., & Gardner, H. (2005). Crossing boundaries to generative wisdom: An analysis of professional work. In R. J. Sternberg & J. Jordan (Eds.), *A handbook of wisdom: Psychological perspectives* (pp. 272–296). New York: Cambridge University Press.

Solomon, R. L. (1980). The opponent-process theory of acquired motivation. *American Psychologist, 35*, 691–721.

Solowij, N., Stephens, R. S., et al. (2002). Cognitive functioning of long-term heavy cannabis users seeking treatment. *Journal of the American Medical Association, 287*, 1123–1131. doi:10-1001/pubs.JAMA-ISSN-0098-7484-287-9-joc11416

Soman, D. (2010, Fall). Option overload: How to deal with choice complexity. *Rotman Magazine*, pp. 42–47.

Sommer, I. E. (2010). Sex differences in handedness, brain asymmetry, and language lateralization. In K. Hugdahl & R. Westerhausen (Eds.), *The two halves of the brain: Information processing in the cerebral hemispheres*. Cambridge, MA: MIT Press.

Sommerville, J. A., Schmidt, M. H., et al. (2013). The development of fairness expectations and prosocial behavior in the second year of life. *Infancy, 18*(1), 40–66. doi:10.1111/j.1532-7078.2012.00129.x

Sorge, G. B., Toplak, M. E., et al. (2016, February 14). Interactions between levels of attention ability and levels of bilingualism in children's executive functioning. *Developmental Science*, n.p. doi:10.1111/desc.12408

Sorkhabi, N. (2012). Parent socialization effects in difference cultures: Significance of directive parenting. *Psychological Reports, 110*(3), 854–878. doi:10.2466/10.02.17.21.PR0.110.3.854-878

Sörqvist, P. (2010). Effects of aircraft noise and speech on prose memory: What role for working memory capacity? *Journal of Environmental Psychology, 30*(1), 112–118.

Sousa, K., Orfale, A. G., et al. (2009). Assessment of a biofeedback program to treat chronic low back pain. *Journal of Musculoskeletal Pain, 17*(4), 369–377. doi:10.3109/10582450903284828

Soussignan, R. (2002). Duchenne smile, emotional experience, and autonomic reactivity. *Emotion, 2*(1), 52–74. doi:10.1037/1528-3542.2.1.52

Soyez, V., & Broekaert, E. (2003). How do substance abusers and their significant others experience the re-entry phase of therapeutic community treatment: A qualitative study. *International Journal of Social Welfare, 12*(3), 211–220. doi:10.1111/1468-2397.00454

Spalding, K. L., Arner, E., et al. (2008). Dynamics of f.at cell turnover in humans. *Nature, 453*, 783–787. doi:10.1038/nature06902

Sparfeldt, J. R., Rost, D. H., et al. (2013). Test anxiety in written and oral examinations. *Learning & Individual*

Differences, 24, 198–203. doi:10.1016/j.lindif.2012.12.010

Special, W. P., & Li-Barber, K. (2012). Self-disclosure and student satisfaction with Facebook. *Computers in Human Behavior, 28*(2), 624–630. doi:10.1016/j.chb.2011.11.008

Spector, P. E. (2012). *Industrial and organizational psychology: Research and practice* (6th ed.). New York: Wiley.

Spence, S. A., Kaylor-Hughes, C., et al. (2009). Toward a cognitive neurobiological account of free association. *Neuropsychoanalysis, 11*(2), 151–163.

Spencer, S. J., Logel, C., et al. (2016). Stereotype threat. *Annual Review of Psychology, 67i,* 415–437. doi:10.1146/annurev-psych-073115-103235

Spencer-Thomas, S., & Jahn, D. R. (2012). Tracking a movement: U.S. milestones in suicide prevention. *Suicide & Life-Threatening Behavior, 42*(1), 78–85. doi:10.1111/j.1943-278X.2011.00072.x

Spengler, M., Brunner, M., et al. (2015). Student characteristics and behaviors at age 12 predict occupational success 40 years later over and above childhood IQ and parental socioeconomic status. *Developmental Psychology, 51*(9), 1329–1340. doi:10.1037/dev0000025

Spenhoff, M., Kruger, T. C., et al. (2013). Hypersexual behavior in an online sample of males: Associations with personal distress and functional impairment. *Journal of Sexual Medicine, 10*(12), 2996–3005. doi:10.1111/jsm.12160

Sperry, R. W. (1968). Hemisphere deconnection and unity in conscious awareness. *American Psychologist, 23,* 723–733. doi:10.1037/h0026839

Spiegler, M. D. (2013a). Behavior therapy I: Traditional behavior therapy. In J. Frew & M. D. Spiegler (Eds.), *Contemporary psychotherapies for a diverse world* (pp. 259–300). New York: Routledge/Taylor & Francis.

Spiegler, M. D. (2013b). Behavior therapy II: Cognitive-behavioral therapy. In J. Frew & M. D. Spiegler (Eds.), *Contemporary psychotherapies for a diverse world* (pp. 301–337). New York: Routledge/Taylor & Francis.

Spiegler, M. D. (2016). *Contemporary behavior therapy* (6th ed.). Boston, MA: Cengage Learning.

Spiro Wagner, P., & Spiro, C. S. (2005). *Divided minds: Twin sisters and their journey through schizophrenia.* New York: St. Martin's Press.

Sporer, S. L. (2001). Recognizing faces of other ethnic groups. *Psychology, Public Policy, & Law, 7*(1), 36–97. doi:10.1037/1076-8971.7.1.36

Sporns, O. (2011). *Networks of the brain.* Cambridge, MA: MIT Press.

Sporns, O. (2013). The human connectome: Origins and challenges. *Neuroimage, 80,* 53–61. doi:10.1016/j.neuroimage.2013.03.023

Sporns, O., & Betzel, R. F. (2016). Modular brain networks. *Annual Review of Psychology, 67,* 613–640. doi:10.1146/annurev-psych-122414-033634

Sprecher, S., & Treger, S. (2015). The benefits of turn-taking reciprocal self-disclosure in get-acquainted interactions. *Personal Relationships, 22*(3), 460–475. doi:10.1111/pere.12090

Sprecher, S., Treger, S., & Wondra, J. D. (2013). Effects of self-disclosure role on liking, closeness, and other impressions in get-acquainted interactions. *Journal of Social & Personal Relationships, 30*(4), 497–514.

Squire, L. R. (2004). Memory systems of the brain: A brief history and current perspective. *Neurobiology of Learning & Memory, 82,* 171–177. doi:10.1016/j.nlm.2004.06.005

Squire, L. R., & Wixted, J. T. (2011). The cognitive neuroscience of human memory since H. M. *Annual Review of Neuroscience, 34,* 259–288. doi:10.1146/annurev-neuro-061010-113720

Sroufe, L. A., Egeland, B., et al. (2005). Placing early attachment experiences in developmental context: The Minnesota Longitudinal Study. In K. E. Grossmann, K. Grossmann, et al. (Eds.), *Attachment from infancy to adulthood: The major longitudinal studies* (pp. 48–70). New York: Guilford.

Stacks, A. M., Oshio, T., et al. (2009). The moderating effect of parental warmth on the association between spanking and child aggression: A longitudinal approach. *Infant & Child Development, 18*(2), 178–194. doi:10.1002/icd.596

Stall-Meadows, C., & Hebert, P. R. (2011). The sustainable consumer: An in situ study of residential lighting alternatives as influenced by infield education. *International Journal of Consumer Studies, 35*(2), 164–170.

Stallen, M., De Dreu, C. W., et al. (2012). The herding hormone: Oxytocin stimulates in-group conformity. *Psychological Science, 23*(11), 1288–1292. doi:10.1177/0956797612446026

Stangor, C. (2015). *Research methods for the behavioral sciences* (5th ed.). Boston, MA: Cengage Learning.

Stanovich, K. E. (2013). *How to think straight about psychology* (10th ed.). Boston, MA: Allyn & Bacon.

Stapel, D. A., & Marx, D. M. (2007). Distinctiveness is key: How different types of self-other similarity moderate social comparison effects. *Personality & Social Psychology Bulletin, 33*(3), 439–448. doi:10.1177/0146167206296105

Starkman, B. G., Sakharkar, A. J., & Pandey, S. C. (2012). Epigenetics: Beyond the genome in alcoholism. *Alcohol Research: Current Reviews, 34*(3), 293–305.

Stawiski, S., Dykema-Engblade, A., & Tindale, R. (2012). The roles of shared stereotypes and shared processing goals on mock jury decision making. *Basic & Applied Social Psychology, 34*(1), 88–97. doi:10.1080/01973533.2011.637467

Steblay, N. K. (2013). Lineup instructions. In B. L. Cutler (Ed.), *Reform of eyewitness identification procedures* (pp. 65–86). Washington, DC: American Psychological Association. doi:10.1037/14094-004

Steele, C. M. (1997). A threat in the air: How stereotypes shape intellectual identity and performance. *American Psychologist, 52*(6), 613–629. doi:10.1037/0003-066X.52.6.613

Steele, C. M., & Aronson, J. (1995). Stereotype threat and the intellectual test performance of African Americans. *Journal of Personality & Social Psychology, 69*(5), 797–811. doi:10.1037/0022-3514.69.5.797

Steele, V. R., Rao, V., et al. (2017). Machine learning of structural magnetic resonance imaging predicts psychopathic traits in adolescent offenders. *NeuroImage, 145*(Part B), 265–273. doi:10.1016/j.neuroimage.2015.12.013

Stefurak, T., Taylor, C., & Mehta, S. (2010). Gender-specific models of homosexual prejudice: Religiosity, authoritarianism, and gender roles. *Psychology of Religion & Spirituality, 2*(4), 247–261.

Steiger, A. (2007). Neurochemical regulation of sleep. *Journal of Psychiatric Research, 41,* 537–552. doi:10.1016/j.jpsychires.2006.04.007

Stein, G. L., Cupito, A. M., et al. (2014). Familism through a developmental lens. *Journal of Latina/o Psychology, 2*(4), 224–250. doi:10.1037/lat0000025

Stein, L. M., & Memon, A. (2006). Testing the efficacy of the cognitive interview in a developing country. *Applied Cognitive Psychology, 20*(5), 597–605. doi:10.1002/acp.1211

Stein, M. D., & Friedmann, P. D. (2005). Disturbed sleep and its relationship to alcohol use. *Substance Abuse, 26*(1), 1–13. doi:10.1300/J465v26n01_01

Stein, M. I. (1974). *Stimulating creativity* (Vol. 1). New York: Academic.

Stein, M. T., & Ferber, R. (2001). Recent onset of sleepwalking in early adolescence. *Journal of Development, Behavior, & Pediatrics, 22,* S33–S35.

Stein, R. (2017). "Trumping" conformity: Urges towards conformity to ingroups and nonconformity to morally opposed outgroups. *Journal of Experimental Social Psychology, 70,* 34–40. doi:10.1016/j.jesp.2016.12.007

Steinberg, L. (2001). Adolescent development. *Annual Review of Psychology, 52,* 83–110. doi:10.1146/annurev.psych.52.1.83

Steiner, B., & Wooldredge, J. (2009). Rethinking the link between institutional crowding and inmate misconduct. *The Prison Journal, 89*(2), 205–233.

Steinman, S. A., Smyth, F. L., et al. (2013). Anxiety-linked expectancy bias across the adult lifespan. *Cognition & Emotion, 27*(2), 345–355. doi:10.1080/02699931.2012.711743

Steinmayr, R., & Spinath, B. (2009). The importance of motivation as a predictor of school achievement. *Learning & Individual Differences, 19*(1), 80–90. doi:10.1016/j.lindif.2008.05.004

Steketee, G., Frost, R. O., et al. (2010). Waitlist-controlled trial of cognitive behavior therapy for hoarding disorder. *Depression & Anxiety, 27*(5), 476–484. doi:10.1002/da.20673

Stemler, S. E., & Sternberg, R. J. (2006). Using situational judgment tests to measure practical intelligence. In J. A. Weekley & R. E. Ployhart (Eds.), *Situational judgment tests: Theory, measurement, and application* (pp. 107–131). Mahwah, NJ: Erlbaum.

Stephens, D. P. (2012). The influence of mainstream hip hop's female sexual scripts on African American women's dating relationship experiences. In M. A. Paludi (Ed.), *The psychology of love* (Vols. 1–4, pp. 169–183). Santa Barbara, CA: Praeger.

Stephens, K., Kiger, L., et al. (1999). Use of nonverbal measures of intelligence in identification of culturally diverse gifted students in rural areas. *Perceptual & Motor Skills, 88*(3, Pt 1), 793–796. doi:10.2466/PMS.88.3.793-796

Stephenson, E., King, D. B., & DeLongis, A. (2016). Coping process. In G. Fink (Ed.), *Stress: Concepts, cognition, emotion, and behavior* (pp. 359–364). Cambridge: Academic Press.

Stern, S. L., Dhanda, R., & Hazuda, H. P. (2001). Hopelessness predicts mortality in older Mexican and

European Americans. *Psychosomatic Medicine, 63*(3), 344–351.
Sternberg, R. J. (1988). *The triangle of love.* New York: Basic.
Sternberg, R. J. (2004). Culture and intelligence. *American Psychologist, 59*(5), 325–338. doi:10.1037/0003-066X.59.5.325
Sternberg, R. J. (2007, October 27). Race and intelligence: Not a case of black and white. *New Scientist,* 16.
Sternberg, R. J. (2017). *Cognitive psychology* (7th ed.). Boston, MA: Cengage Learning.
Sternberg, R. J., & Grigorenko, E. L. (2005). Cultural explorations of the nature of intelligence. In A. F. Healy (Ed.), *Experimental cognitive psychology and its applications* (pp. 225–235). Washington, DC: American Psychological Association.
Sternberg, R. J., Grigorenko, E. L., & Bundy, D. A. (2001). The predictive value of IQ. *Merrill-Palmer Quarterly, 47*(1), 1–41. doi:10.1353/mpq.2001.0005
Sternberg, R. J., Grigorenko, E. L., et al. (2011). Intelligence, race, and genetics. In S. Krimsky & K. Sloan (Eds.), *Race and the genetic revolution: Science, myth, and culture* (pp. 195–237). New York: Columbia University Press.
Stevens, F. L. (2016). The anterior cingulate cortex in psychopathology and psychotherapy: Effects on awareness and repression of affect. *Neuropsychoanalysis, 18*(1), 53–68. doi:10.1080/15294145.2016.1149777
Stevens, R., Bernadini, S., & Jemmott, J. B. (2013). Social environment and sexual risk-taking among gay and transgender African American youth. *Culture, Health, & Sexuality, 15*(10), 1148–1161. doi:10.1080/13691058.2013.809608
Stewart, T. L., Chipperfield, J. G., et al. (2013). Downward social comparison and subjective well-being in late life: The moderating role of perceived control. *Aging & Mental Health, 17*(3), 375–385. doi:10.1080/13607863.2012.743963
Stickgold, R. (2013). Parsing the role of sleep in memory processing. *Current Opinion in Neurobiology, 23*(5), 847– 853. doi:10.1016/j.conb.2013.04.002
Stickgold, R., & Walker, M. (2004). To sleep, perchance to gain creative insight? *Trends in Cognitive Sciences, 8*(5), 191–192. doi:10.1016/j.tics.2004.03.003
Stinson, F. S., Dawson, D. A., et al. (2007). The epidemiology of DSM-IV specific phobia in the USA: Result from the National Epidemiologic Survey on Alcohol and Related Conditions. *Psychological Medicine, 37*(7), 1047–1059. doi:10.1017/S0033291707000086
Stix, G. (2011). The neuroscience of true grit. *Scientific American, 304,* 28–33. doi:10.1038/scientificamerican0111-29a
Stöber, J. (2004). Dimensions of test anxiety: Relations to ways of coping with pre-exam anxiety and uncertainty. *Anxiety, Stress & Coping, 17*(3), 213–226. doi:10.1080/10615800412331292615
Stokes, D., & Lappin, M. (2010, February 2). Neurofeedback and biofeedback with 37 migraineurs: A clinical outcome study. *Behavioral & Brain Functions, 6,* ArtID 9. Retrieved March 18, 2017, from www.ncbi.nlm.nih.gov/pubmed/20205867
Stone, J., Perry, Z. W., & Darley, J. M. (1997). "White men can't jump." *Basic & Applied Social Psychology, 19*(3), 291–306. doi:10.1207/15324839751036977
Stoop, R., Hegoburu, C., & van den Burg, E. (2015). New opportunities in vasopressin and oxytocin research: A perspective from the amygdala. *Annual Review of Neuroscience, 38,* 369–388. doi:10.1146/annurev-neuro-071714-033904
Stoppard, J. M., & McMullen, L. M. (Eds.). (2003). *Situating sadness: Women and depression in social context.* New York: New York University Press.
Storr, A. (1988). *Solitude: A return to the self.* New York: Free Press.
Strack, F., Martin, L. L., & Stepper, S. (1988). Inhibiting and facilitating conditions of facial expressions: A non-obtrusive test of the facial feedback hypothesis. *Journal of Personality & Social Psychology, 54,* 768–777. doi:10.1037/0022-3514.54.5.768
Straub, R. (2012). *Health psychology* (3rd ed.). New York: Worth.
Strayer, D. L., Drews, F. A., & Crouch, D. J. (2006). A comparison of the cell phone driver and the drunk driver. *Human Factors, 48*(2), 381–391. doi:10.1518/001872006777724471
Strenger, C. (2016). *Freud's legacy in the global era.* New York: Routledge/Taylor & Francis.
Strenze, T. (2007). Intelligence and socioeconomic success: A meta-analytic review of longitudinal research. *Intelligence, 35*(5), 401–426.
Stricker, G. (2011). PsyD programs. In J. C. Norcross, G. R. VandenBos, et al. (Eds.), *History of psychotherapy: Continuity and change* (2nd ed., pp. 630–639). Washington, DC: American Psychological Association. doi:10.1037/12353-040
Strickhouser, J. E., & Zell, E. (2015). Self-evaluative effects of dimensional and social comparison. *Journal of Experimental Social Psychology, 59,* 60–66. doi:10.1016/j.jesp.2015.03.001
Strickhouser, J. E., Zell, E., et al. (2017). Does personality predict health and well-being? A metasynthesis. *Health Psychology,* n.p. doi:10.1037/hea0000475
Strickland, S. A. (2015). Pedophilia. In D. L. Dobbert, & T. X. Mackey (Eds.), *Deviance: Theories on behaviors that defy social norms* (pp. 171–180). Santa Barbara, CA: Praeger/ABC-CLIO.
Striedter, G. F., Srinivasan, S., & Monuki, E. S. (2015). Cortical folding: When, where, how, and why? *Annual Review of Neuroscience, 38,* 291–307. doi:10.1146/annurev-neuro-071714-034128
Stroebe, W., Papies, E. K., & Aarts, H. (2008). From homeostatic to hedonic theories of eating: Self-regulatory failure in food-rich environments. *Applied Psychology, 57,* 172–193. doi:10.1111/j.1464-0597.2008.00360.x
Strong, B., DeVault, C., & Cohen, T. C. (2011). *The marriage and family experience: Intimate relationships in a changing society* (11th ed.). Boston, MA: Cengage Learning.
Strote, J., Lee, J. E., & Wechsler, H. (2002). Increasing MDMA use among college students: Results of a national survey. *Journal of Adolescent Health, 30*(1), 64–72. doi:10.1016/S1054-139X(01)00315-9
Strubbe, M. J. (2005). What did Triplett really find? A contemporary analysis of the first experiment in social psychology. *American Journal of Psychology, 118,* 271–286.
Stumbrys, T., Erlacher, D., et al. (2012). Induction of lucid dreams: A systematic review of evidence. *Consciousness & Cognition, 21*(3), 1456–1475. doi:10.1016/j.concog.2012.07.003
Stuss, D. T., & Knight, R. T. (2002). *Principles of frontal lobe function.* New York: Oxford University Press.
Suarez, E., & Gadalla, T. M. (2010). Stop blaming the victim: A meta-analysis on rape myths. *Journal of Interpersonal Violence, 25*(11), 2010–2035.
Sue, D. W. (2010). *Microaggressions in everyday life: Race, gender, and sexual orientation.* New York: John Wiley & Sons.
Sue, D., Sue, D. W., et al. (2016). *Understanding abnormal behavior* (11th ed.). Boston, MA: Cengage Learning.
Sue, D., Sue, D. W., et al. (2017). *Essentials of understanding abnormal behavior* (3rd ed.). Boston, MA: Cengage Learning.
Suedfeld, P., & Borrie, R. A. (1999). Health and therapeutic applications of chamber and flotation restricted environmental stimulation therapy (REST). *Psychology & Health, 14*(3), 545–566. doi:10.1080/08870449908407346
Suedfeld, P., & Steel, G. D. (2000). The environmental psychology of capsule habitats. *Annual Review of Psychology, 51,* 227–253.
Suh, H., Rice, K. G., et al. (2016). Measuring acculturative stress with the SAFE: Evidence for longitudinal measurement invariance and associations with life satisfaction. *Personality & Individual Differences, 89,* 217–222. doi:10.1016/j.paid.2015.10.002
Suhay, E. (2014, November 30). Explaining group influence: The role of identity and emotion in political conformity and polarization. *Political Behavior,* n.p. doi:10.1007/s11109-014-9269-1
Suinn, R. M. (1975). *Fundamentals of behavior pathology* (2nd ed.). New York: Wiley.
Suinn, R. M. (1999, March). Scaling the summit: Valuing ethnicity. *APA Monitor,* 2.
Suls, J. M., Luger, T., & Martin, R. (2010). The biopsychosocial model and the use of theory in health psychology. In J. M. Suls, K. W. Davidson, et al. (Eds.), *Handbook of health psychology and behavioral medicine* (pp. 15–27). New York: Guilford.
Summers, A., Hayward, R. D., & Miller, M. K. (2010). Death qualification as systematic exclusion of jurors with certain religious and other characteristics. *Journal of Applied Social Psychology, 40*(12), 3218–3234.
Sun, Y., & Han, Z. (2018). Climate change risk perception in Taiwan: Correlation with individual and societal factors. *International Journal of Environmental Research & Public Health, 15,* 91–100. doi:10.3390/ijerph15010091
Sunnafrank, M., Ramirez, A., & Metts, S. (2004). At first sight: Persistent relational effects of get-acquainted conversations. *Journal of Social & Personal Relationships, 21*(3), 361–379. doi:10.1177/0265407504042837
Sunnhed, R., & Jansson-Fröjmark, M. (2014). Are changes in worry associated with treatment response in cognitive behavioral therapy for insomnia? *Cognitive Behaviour Therapy, 43*(1), 1–11. doi:10.1080/16506073.2013.846399
Susilo, T., Wright, V., et al. (2015). Acquired prosopagnosia without word recognition deficits. *Cognitive Neuropsychology, 32*(6), 321–339. doi:10.1080/02643294.2015.1081882
Sussman, G. (Ed.). (2011). *The propaganda society: Promotional*

culture and politics in global context. New York: Peter Lang.

Sutin, A. R., & Costa, P. T. Jr. (2010). Reciprocal influences of personality and job characteristics across middle adulthood. *Journal of Personality, 78*(1), 257–288. doi:10.1111/j.1467-6494.2009.00615.x

Sutterer, D. W., & Awh, E. (2016). Retrieval practice enhances the accessibility but not the quality of memory. *Psychonomic Bulletin & Review, 23*(3), 831–841. doi:10.3758/s13423-015-0937-x

Suzuki, L., & Aronson, J. (2005). The cultural malleability of intelligence and its impact on the racial/ethnic hierarchy. *Psychology, Public Policy, & Law, 11,* 320–327. doi:10.1037/1076-8971.11.2.320

Swanson, S. A., Crow, S. J., et al. (2011). Prevalence and correlates of eating disorders in adolescents: Results from the national comorbidity survey replication adolescent supplement. *Archives of General Psychiatry, 68*(7), 714–723. doi:10.1001/archgenpsychiatry.2011.22

Swartz, T. B., & Arce, A. (2014). New insights involving the home team advantage. *International Journal of Sports Science & Coaching, 9*(4), 681–692. doi:10.1260/1747-9541.9.4.681

Syed, E. C. J., Grima, L. L., et al. (2016). Action initiation shapes mesolimbic dopamine encoding of future rewards. *Nature Neuroscience, 19*(1), 34–36. doi:10.1038/nn.4187

Synhorst, L. L., Buckley, J. A., et al. (2005). Cross informant agreement of the Behavioral and Emotional Rating Scale: 2nd Edition (BERS-2) parent and youth rating scales. *Child & Family Behavior Therapy, 27*(3), 1–11. doi:10.1300/J019v27n03_01

Szaflarski, J. P., Rajagopal, A., et al. (2011). Left-handedness and language lateralization in children. *Brain Research, 1433,* 85–97. doi:10.1016/j.brainres.2011.11.026

Szollos, A. (2009). Toward a psychology of chronic time pressure: Conceptual and methodological review. *Time & Society, 18*(2–3), 332–350. doi:10.1177/0961463X09337847

Szpak, A., & Allen, D. (2012). A case of acute suicidality following excessive caffeine intake. *Journal of Psychopharmacology, 26*(11), 1502–1510. doi:10.1177/0269881112442788

Tabak, N. T., Green, M. F., et al. (2015). Perceived emotional intelligence is impaired and associated with poor community functioning in schizophrenia and bipolar disorder. *Schizophrenia Research, 162*(1), 189–195. doi:10.1016/j.schres.2014.12.005

Taber, K. H., Black, D. N., et al. (2012). Neuroanatomy of dopamine: Reward and addiction. *Journal of Neuropsychiatry & Clinical Neurosciences, 24*(1), 1–4. doi:10.1176/appi.neuropsych.24.1.1

Tackett, J. L., & Krueger, R. F. (2011). Dispositional influences on human aggression. In P. R. Shaver & M. Mikulincer (Eds.), *Human aggression and violence: Causes, manifestations, and consequences* (pp. 89–104). Washington, DC: American Psychological Association.

Tafarodi, R. W., Shaughnessy, S. C., et al. (2011). The reporting of self-esteem in Japan and Canada. *Journal of Cross-Cultural Psychology, 42*(1), 155–164. doi:10.1177/0022022110386373

Tafrate, R. C., & Kassinove, H. (2009). *Anger management for everyone: Seven proven ways to control anger and live a happier life.* Atascadero, CA: Impact Publishers.

Taitz, I. (2011). Learning lucid dreaming and its effect on depression in undergraduates. *International Journal of Dream Research, 4*(2), 117–126.

Tajfel, H. (Ed.). (1978). *Differentiation between social groups: Studies in the social psychology of intergroup relations.* Cambridge, MA: Academic Press.

Tal-Or, N., & Papirman, Y. (2007). The fundamental attribution error in attributing fictional figures' characteristics to the actors. *Media Psychology, 9*(2), 331–345. doi:10.1080/15213260701286049

Talbot, N. L., & Gamble, S. A. (2008). IPT for women with trauma histories in community mental health care. *Journal of Contemporary Psychotherapy, 38*(1), 35–44. doi:10.1007/s10879-007-9066-9

Tamis-LeMonda, C. S., Shannon, J. D., et al. (2004). Fathers and mothers at play with their 2- and 3-year-olds: Contributions to language and cognitive development. *Child Development, 75*(6), 1806–1820. doi:10.1111/j.1467-8624.2004.00818.x

Tandon, R., Heckers, S., et al. (2013). Catatonia in DSM-5. *Schizophrenia Research, 150,* 26–30. doi:10.1016/j.schres.2013.04.034

Tang, C. Y., Eaves, E. L., et al. (2010). Brain networks for working memory and factors of intelligence assessed in males and females with fMRI and DTI. *Intelligence, 38*(3), 293–303. doi:10.1016/j.intell.2010.03.003

Tannen, D. (1995, September–October). The power of talk: Who gets heard and why. *Harvard Business Review.* Retrieved May 5, 2017, from hbr.org/1995/09/the-power-of-talk-who-gets-heardand-why#

Taraban, R., Rynearson, K., & Kerr, M. (2000). College students' academic performance and self-reports of comprehension strategy use. *Reading Psychology, 21*(4), 283–308. doi:10.1080/027027100750061930

Tarquinio, C. C., Brennstuhl, M. J., et al. (2012). Eye movement desensitization and reprocessing (EMDR) therapy in the treatment of victims of domestic violence: A pilot study. *European Review of Applied Psychology, 62*(4), 205–212. doi:10.1016/j.erap.2012.08.006

Tatum, J. L., & Foubert, J. D. (2009). Rape myth acceptance, hypermasculinity, and SAT scores as correlates of moral development: Understanding sexually aggressive attitudes in first-year college men. *Journal of College Student Development, 50*(2), 195–209. doi:10.1353/csd.0.0062

Tauber, A. I. (2010). *Freud, the reluctant philosopher.* Princeton, NJ: Princeton University Press.

Tavakoli, S., Lumley, M. A., et al. (2009). Effects of assertiveness training and expressive writing on acculturative stress in international students: A randomized trial. *Journal of Counseling Psychology, 56*(4), 590–596. doi:10.1037/a0016634

Tavris, C., & Aronson, E. (2007). *Mistakes were made (but not by me): Why we justify foolish beliefs, bad decisions, and hurtful acts.* New York: Harcourt.

Tay, L., & Diener, E. (2011). Needs and subjective well-being around the world. *Journal of Personality and Social Psychology, 101*(2), 354–365. doi:10.1037/a0023779

Taylor, D. J., & Roane, B. M. (2010). Treatment of insomnia in adults and children: A practice-friendly review of research. *Journal of Clinical Psychology, 66*(11), 1137–1147. doi:10.1002/jclp.20733

Taylor, G. J., & Taylor-Allan, H. L. (2007). Applying emotional intelligence in understanding and treating physical and psychological disorders: What we have learned from alexithymia. In R. Bar-On, M. J. G. Reuven, et al. (Eds.), *Educating people to be emotionally intelligent* (pp. 211–223). Westport, CT: Praeger.

Taylor, K. (2004). *Brainwashing: The science of thought control.* New York: Oxford University Press.

Taylor, L. D., & Ruiz, J. (2013). Empowerment and aggression: Understanding violence in America's girls. *Analyses of Social Issues & Public Policy, 13*(1), 401–403. doi:10.1111/asap.12010

Taylor, R., Thomson, H., et al. (2017). Does working memory have a single capacity limit? *Journal of Memory & Language, 93,* 67–81. doi:10.1016/j.jml.2016.09.004

Taylor, S. E. (2011). The future of social-health psychology: Prospects and predictions. *Social & Personality Psychology Compass, 5,* 275–284. doi:10.1111/j.1751-9004.2011.00360.x

Taylor, S. E. (2021). *Health psychology* (11th ed.). New York: McGrawHill.

Taylor, S. E., & Master, S. L. (2011). Social responses to stress: The tend-and-befriend model. In R. J. Contrada & A. Baum (Eds.), *The handbook of stress science: Biology, psychology, and health* (pp. 101–109). New York: Springer.

Teff, K. L., & Silva, C. M. (2015). Waking up to the importance of sleep and circadian rhythms for metabolic health: The need for in-depth phenotyping. *Sleep: Journal of Sleep & Sleep Disorders Research, 38*(12), 1847–1848. doi:10.5665/sleep.5224

Teglasi, H. (2010). *Essentials of TAT and other storytelling assessments* (2nd ed.). Hoboken, NJ: Wiley.

Tennie, C., Greve, K., et al. (2010). Two-year-old children copy more reliably and more often than nonhuman great apes in multiple observational learning tasks. *Primates, 51*(4), 337–351. doi:10.1007/s10329-010-0208-4

Teo, A. R., & Gaw, A. C. (2010). Hikikomori, a Japanese culture-bound syndrome of social withdrawal? A proposal for DSM-5. *Journal of Nervous & Mental Disease, 198*(6), 444–449. doi:10.1097/NMD.0b013e3181e086b1

Teresi, L., & Haroutunian, H. (2011). *Hijacking the brain: How drug and alcohol addiction hijacks our brains. The science behind Twelve-Step recovery.* Bloomington, IN: AuthorHouse.

Terman, L. M., & Merrill, M. A. (1937/1960). *Stanford-Binet Intelligence Scale.* Boston, MA: Houghton Mifflin.

Terman, L. M., & Oden, M. (1959). *The gifted group in mid-life* (Vol. 5): *Genetic studies of genius.* Stanford, CA: Stanford University Press.

Terry, C. (2006). History of treatment of people with mental illness. In J. R. Matthews, C. E. Walker, et al. (Eds.), *Your practicum in psychology: A guide for maximizing knowledge and competence* (pp. 81–103). Washington, DC: American Psychological Association.

Terry, D. J., & Hogg, M. A. (1996). Group norms and the attitude-behavior relationship. *Personality & Social Psychology Bulletin, 22*(8), 776–793.doi:10.1177/0146167296228002

Teufel-Shone, N. I., Staten, L. K., et al. (2005). Cohesion and conflict in an American Indian community. *American Journal of Health Behavior, 29*(5), 413–422. doi:10.5993/AJHB.29.5.4

Teutsch, S. M., McCoy, M. A., Woodbury, R. B., & Welp, A. (2016). *Making eye health a population health imperative: Vision for tomorrow.* Washington (DC): National Academies Press. https://www.ncbi.nlm.nih.gov/books/NBK402366/

Teyber, E., & McClure, F. H. (2011). *Interpersonal process in therapy: An integrative model* (6th ed.). Boston, MA: Cengage Learning.

Thakral, P. P. (2011). The neural substrates associated with inattentional blindness. *Consciousness & Cognition, 20*(4), 1768–1775. doi:10.1016/j.concog.2011.03.013

Thaler, R. H. (2016). Behavioral economics: Past, present, and future. *American Economic Review, 106*(7), 1577–1600. doi:10.1257/aer.106.7.1577

Thaler, R. H., & Ganser, L. J. (2015). *Misbehaving: The making of behavioral economics.* New York: WW Norton.

Thaler, R., & Sunstein, C. (2008). *Nudge: Improving decisions on health, wealth, and happiness.* New Haven: Yale University Press.

Thanellou, A., & Green, J. T. (2011). Spontaneous recovery but not reinstatement of the extinguished conditioned eyeblink response in the rat. *Behavioral Neuroscience, 125*(4), 613–625. doi:10.1037/a0023582

Thase, M. E. (2006). Major depressive disorder. In F. Andrasik (Ed.), *Comprehensive handbook of personality and psychopathology* (Vol. 2): *Adult psychopathology* (pp. 207–230). New York: Wiley.

The Nature Conservancy. (2016). *Carbon footprint calculator.* Retrieved February 23, 2016, from www.nature.org/greenliving/carboncalculator

Thoma, C. A., Bartholomew, C. C., & Scott, L. A. (2009). *Universal design for transition: A roadmap for planning and instruction.* Baltimore, MD: Brookes Publishing.

Thomas, A. K., Bulevich, J. B., & Dubois, S. J. (2011). Context affects feeling-of-knowing accuracy in younger and older adults. *Journal of Experimental Psychology: Learning, Memory, & Cognition, 37*(1), 96–108. doi:10.1037/a0021612.

Thomas, E. M. (2004). *Aggressive behaviour outcomes for young children: Change in parenting environment predicts change in behaviour.* Ottawa, ON: Statistics Canada. Retrieved January 27, 2017, from http://publications.gc.ca/Collection/Statcan/89-599-MIE/89-599-MIE2004001.pdf

Thomas, S. P. (2013). The global phenomenon of urbanization and its effects on mental health. *Issues in Mental Health Nursing, 34*(3), 139–140. doi:10.3109/01612840.2013.762857

Thompson, E. R., & Barnes, K. (2012). Meaning of sexual performance among men with and without erectile dysfunction. *Psychology of Men & Masculinity,* doi:10.1037/a0029104

Thompson, R. J., Payne, S. C., et al. (2015). Applicant attraction to flexible work arrangements: Separating the influence of flextime and flexplace. *Journal of Occupational & Organizational Psychology, 88*(4), 726–749. doi/10.1111/joop.12095/pdf

Thornton, S. N. (2010). Thirst and hydration: Physiology and consequences of dysfunction. *Physiology & Behavior, 100*(1), 15–21. doi:10.1016/j.physbeh.2010.02.026

Thrift, A. G. (2010). Design and methods of population surveys. *Neuroepidemiology, 34*(4), 267–269. doi:10.1159/000297758

Thurson, T. (2008). *Think better: An innovator's guide to productive thinking.* New York: McGraw-Hill.

Thyen, U., Richter-Appelt, H., et al. (2005). Deciding on gender in children with intersex conditions: Considerations and controversies. *Treatments in Endocrinology, 4*(1), 1–8.

Tiggemann, M., & Polivy, J. (2010). Upward and downward: Social comparison processing of thin idealized media images. *Psychology of Women Quarterly, 34*(3), 356–364.

Tikotzky, L., Chambers, A. S., et al. (2012). Postpartum maternal sleep and mothers' perceptions of their attachment relationship with the infant among women with a history of depression during pregnancy. *International Journal of Behavioral Development, 36*(6), 440–448.

Till, B. D., & Priluck, R. L. (2000). Stimulus generalization in classical conditioning: An initial investigation and extension. *Psychology & Marketing, 17*(1), 55–72. doi:10.1002/(SICI)1520-6793(200001)17:1<55::AID-MAR4>3.0.CO;2-C

Till, B. D., Stanley, S. M., & Priluck, R. (2008). Classical conditioning and celebrity endorsers: An examination of belongingness and resistance to extinction. *Psychology & Marketing, 25*(2), 179–196. doi:10.1002/mar.20205

Tine, M., & Gotlieb, R. (2013). Gender-, race-, and income-based stereotype threat: The effects of multiple stigmatized aspects of identity on math performance and working memory function. *Social Psychology of Education, 16*, 353–376. doi:10.1007/s11218-013-9224-8

Tinti, C., Schmidt, S., et al. (2013, November 12). Distinct processes shape flashbulb and event memories. *Memory & Cognition,* n.p. doi:10.3758/s13421-013-0383-9

Tipples, J., Atkinson, A. P., & Young, A. W. (2002). The eyebrow frown: A salient social signal. *Emotion, 2*(3), 288–296. doi:10.1037/1528-3542.2.3.288

Titov, N. (2011). Internet-delivered psychotherapy for depression in adults. *Current Opinion in Psychiatry, 24*(1), 18–23. doi:10.1097/YCO.0b013e32833ed18f

Tolin, D. F., McKay, D., et al. (2015). Empirically supported treatment: Recommendations for a new model. *Clinical Psychology: Science & Practice, 22*(4), 317–338. doi:10.1111/cpsp.12122

Tolkacheva, N., van Groenou, M. B., et al. (2014). Sibling similarities and sharing the care of older parents. *Journal of Family Issues, 35*(3), 312–330. doi:10.1177/0192513X12470619

Tolman, E. C., & Honzik, C. H. (1930). Degrees of hunger, reward and non-reward and maze performance in rats. *University of California Publications in Psychology, 4*, 241–256.

Tolman, E. C., Ritchie, B. F., & Kalish, D. (1946). Studies in spatial learning: II. Place learning versus response learning. *Journal of Experimental Psychology, 36*, 221–229. doi:10.1037/h0060262

Tom, G., Tong, S., & Hesse, C. (2010). Thick slice and thin slice teaching evaluations. *Social Psychology of Education, 13*(1), 129–136. doi:10.1007/s11218-009-9101-7

Tomasi, D., & Volkow, N. D. (2012). Laterality patterns of brain functional connectivity: Gender effects. *Cerebral Cortex, 22*(6), 1455–1462. doi:10.1093/cercor/bhr230

Toneatto, T. (2002). Cognitive therapy for problem gambling. *Cognitive & Behavioral Practice, 9*(3), 191–199. doi:10.1016/S1077-7229(02)80049-9

Torrente, M. P., Gelenberg, A. J., & Vrana, K. E. (2012). Boosting serotonin in the brain: Is it time to revamp the treatment of depression? *Journal of Psychopharmacology, 26*(5), 629–635. doi:10.1177/0269881111430744

Toyota, H., & Kikuchi, Y. (2005). Encoding richness of self-generated elaboration and spacing effects on incidental memory. *Perceptual & Motor Skills, 101*(2), 621–627.

Trainor, L. J., & Desjardins, R. N. (2002). Pitch characteristics of infant-directed speech affect infants' ability to discriminate vowels. *Psychonomic Bulletin & Review, 9*(2), 335–340. doi:10.3758/BF03196290

Tramontana, J. (2011). *Sports hypnosis in practice: Scripts, strategies, and case examples.* Bethel, CT: Crown House Publishing.

Tran, L., & Rimes, K. A. (2017). Unhealthy perfectionism, negative beliefs about emotions, emotional suppression, and depression in students: A mediational analysis. *Personality & Individual Differences, 110*, 144–147. doi:10.1016/j.paid.2017.01.042

Treatment Advocacy Center. (2017). *Fast facts.* Retrieved April 1, 2017, from www.treatmentadvocacycenter.org/evidence-and-research/fast-facts

Treffert, D. A. (2010). *Islands of genius: The bountiful mind of the autistic, acquired, and sudden savant.* London, UK: Jessica Kingsley Publishers.

Treffert, D. A. (2014). Savant syndrome: Realities, myths and misconceptions. *Journal of Autism & Developmental Disorders, 44*(3), 564–571.

Treffert, D. A., & Christensen, C. D. (2005). Inside the mind of a savant. *Scientific American, 293*(6), 108–113. doi:10.1038/scientificamerican1205-108

Tregear, S., Resto, J., et al. (2010). Continuous positive airway pressure reduces risk of motor vehicle crash among drivers with obstructive sleep apnea: Systematic review and meta-analysis. *Sleep: Journal of Sleep & Sleep Disorders Research, 33*(10), 1373–1380.

Trehub, S. E., Unyk, A. M., & Trainor, L. J. (1993). Adults identify infant-directed music across cultures. *Infant Behavior & Development, 16*(2), 193–211.

Trémolière, B., & De Neys, W. (2014). When intuitions are helpful: Prior beliefs can support reasoning in the bat-and-ball problem. *Journal of Cognitive Psychology, 26*, 486–490. doi:10.1080/20445911.2014.899238

Trentowska, M., Bender, C., & Tuschen-Caffier, B. (2013). Mirror exposure in women with bulimic symptoms: How do thoughts and emotions change in body image treatment? *Behaviour Research & Therapy, 51*(1), 1–6. doi:10.1016/j.brat.2012.03.012

Treves, T. A., & Korczyn, A. D. (2012). Modeling the dementia epidemic. *CNS Neuroscience & Therapeutics, 18*(2), 175–181. doi:10.1111/j.1755-5949.2011.00242.x

Triandis, H. C., & Suh, E. M. (2002). Cultural influences on personality. *Annual Review of Psychology, 53*, 133–160. doi:10.1146/annurev.psych.53.100901.135200

Tripp, D. A., Stanish, W., et al. (2011). Fear of reinjury, negative affect, and catastrophizing predicting return to sport in recreational athletes with anterior cruciate ligament injuries at 1 year postsurgery. *Sport, Exercise, & Performance Psychology, 1*(S), 38–48. doi:10.1037/2157-3905.1.S.38

Trocmé, N., MacLaurin, B., et al. (2001). *Canadian Incidence Study of Reported Child Abuse and Neglect*. Retrieved May 8, 2014, from www.phac-aspc.gc.ca/publicat/cissr-ecirc

Troll, L. E., & Skaff, M. M. (1997). Perceived continuity of self in very old age. *Psychology & Aging, 12*(1), 162–169. doi:10.1037/0882-7974.12.1.162

Troup, C., & Rose, J. (2012). Working from home: Do formal or informal telework arrangements provide better work–family outcomes? *Community, Work & Family, 15*(4), 471–486. doi:1 0.1080/13668803.2012.724220

Trujillo, L. T., Kornguth, S., & Schnyer, D. M. (2009). An ERP examination of the different effects of sleep deprivation on exogenously cued and endogenously cued attention. *Sleep, 32*(10), 1285–1297.

Trull, T., & Prinstein, M. (2013). *Clinical psychology* (8th ed.). Boston, MA: Cengage Learning.

Truscott, D. (2014). Gestalt therapy. In G. R. VandenBos, E. Meidenbauer, et al. (Eds.), *Psychotherapy theories & techniques: A read* (pp. 187–194). Washington, DC: American Psychological Association. doi:10.1037/14295-021

Tryon, R. C. (1929). The genetics of learning ability in rats. *University of California Publications in Psychology, 4*, 71–89.

Tsai, C., Hoerr, S. L., & Song, W. O. (1998). Dieting behavior of Asian college women attending a US university. *Journal of American College Health, 46*(4), 163–168.

Tsai, J., El-Gabalawy, R., Sledge, W. H., Southwick, S. M., & Pietrzak, R. H. (2015). Post-traumatic growth among veterans in the USA: Results from the National Health and Resilience in Veterans Study. *Psychological Medicine, 45*(1), 165–179. doi:10.1017/S0033291714001202

Tsintsadze-Maass, E., & Maass, R. W. (2014). Groupthink and terrorist radicalization. *Terrorism & Political Violence, 26*(5), 735–758. doi:10.1080/09546553.2013.805094

Tully, H. M. Ishak, G. E., et al. (2016). Two hundred thirty-six children with developmental hydrocephalus: Causes and clinical consequences. *Journal of Child Neurology, 31*(3), 309–320. doi:10.1177/0883073815592222

Tulving, E. (1989). Remembering and knowing the past. *American Scientist, 77*(4), 361–367.

Tulving, E. (2002). Episodic memory. *Annual Review of Psychology, 53*, 1–25. doi:10.1146/annurev.psych.53.100901.135114

Tunney, R. J., & Fernie, G. (2012). Episodic and prototype models of category learning. *Cognitive Processing, 13*(1), 41–54.

Turenius, C. I., Htut, M. M., et al. (2009). GABA(A) receptors in the lateral hypothalamus as mediators of satiety and body weight regulation. *Brain Research, 1262*, 16–24. doi:10.1016/j.brainres.2009.01.016

Turgoose, D., Glover, N., et al. (2017, March 2). Empathy, compassion fatigue, and burnout in police officers working with rape victims. *Traumatology*, n.p. doi:10.1037/trm0000118

Turiano, N. A., Mroczek, D. K., et al. (2013). Big 5 personality traits and interleukin-6: Evidence for "healthy neuroticism" in a U.S. population sample. *Brain, Behavior, & Immunity, 28*, 83–89. doi:10.1016/j.bbi.2012.10.020

Turkheimer, E., Haley, A., et al. (2003). Socioeconomic status modifies heritability of IQ in young children. *Psychological Science, 14*, 623–628. doi:10.1046/j.0956-7976.2003.psci_1475.x

Turkheimer, E., Harden, K. P., & Nisbett, R. E. (2017, June). *There's still no good reason to believe black-white IQ differences are due to genes*. Retrieved from https://www.vox.com/the-big-idea/2017/6/15/15797120/race-black-white-iq-response-critics

Turner, J. C. (1975). Social comparison and social identity: Some prospects for intergroup behaviour. *European Journal of Social Psychology, 5*(1), 1–34. doi:10.1002/ejsp.2420050102

Tversky, A., & Kahneman, D. (1981). The framing of decisions and the psychology of choice. *Science, 211*, 453–458. doi:10.1126/science.7455683

Tversky, A., & Kahneman, D. (1982). Judgments of and by representativeness. In D. Kahneman, P. Slovic, & A. Tversky (Eds.), *Judgment under uncertainty: Heuristics and biases* (pp. 84–98). Cambridge, UK: Cambridge University Press.

Tversky, A., & Kahneman, D. (1983). Extensional versus intuitive reasoning: The conjunction fallacy in probability judgment. *Psychological Review, 90*(4), 293–315. doi:10.1037/0033-295X.90.4.293

Twenge, J. M. (2014). *Generation me—revised and updated: Why today's young Americans are more confident, assertive, entitled—and more miserable than ever before*. New York: Simon & Schuster.

Twenge, J. (2019, March 14). *The mental health crisis among America's youth is real–and staggering*. Retrieved from https://theconversation.com/the-mental-health-crisis-among-americas-youth-is-real-and-staggering-113239

Twenge, J. M., Campbell, W. K., & Freeman, E. C. (2012). Generational differences in young adults' life goals, concern for others, and civic orientation, 1966–2009. *Journal of Personality and Social Psychology, 102*, 1045–1062. doi:10.1037/a0027408

Tyler, J. M., & Feldman, R. S. (2006). Deflecting threat to one's image: Dissembling personal information as a self-presentation strategy. *Basic & Applied Social Psychology, 27*(4), 371–378.

United Nations. (2016). *World population prospects 2015*. Retrieved April 12, 2017, from esa.un.org/unpd/wpp

United Nations Programme on HIV/AIDS. (2016). *Global AIDS update*. Retrieved March 10, 2017, from www.unaids.org/sites/default/files/media_asset/global-AIDS-update-2016en.pdf

Underwood, B. J. (1957). Interference and forgetting. *Psychological Review, 64*, 49–60. doi:10.1037/h0044616

United Nations. (2016). *World population prospects 2015*. Retrieved April 12, 2017, from http://esa.un.org/unpd/wpp/

United Nations Programme on HIV/AIDS. (2016). *Global AIDS update*. Retrieved March 10, 2017, from www.unaids.org/sites/default/files/media_asset/global-AIDS-update-2016_en.pdf

Unsworth, G., & Ward, T. (2001). Video games and aggressive behaviour. *Australian Psychologist, 36*(3), 184–192. doi:10.1080/00050060108259654

Unsworth, N. (2017). Examining the dynamics of strategic search from long-term memory. *Journal of Memory & Language, 93*, 135–153. doi:1016/j.jml.2016.09.005

Unsworth, N., Brewer, G. A., & Spillers, G. J. (2012). Variation in cognitive failures: An individual differences investigation of everyday attention and memory failures. *Journal of Memory and Language, 67*(1), 1–16. doi:10.1016/j.jml.2011.12.005

U.S. Census Bureau. (2016). *Poverty: 2014 and 2015*. Retrieved May 1, 2017, from www.census.gov/content/dam/Census/library/publications/2016/demo/acsbr15-01.pdf

U.S. Department of Energy Office of Science. (2015). *All About the Human Genome Project (HGP)*. Retrieved May 1, 2017, from www.genome.gov/10001772/#al-2

U.S. Department of Energy. (2017). *What is the smart grid?* Retrieved April 14, 2017, from www.smartgrid.gov

Uziel, L. (2007). Individual differences in the social facilitation effect: A review and meta-analysis. *Journal of Research in Personality, 41*(3), 579–601. doi:10.1016/j.jrp.2006.06.008

Vadillo, M. A., & Luque, D. (2013). Dissociations among judgments do not reflect cognitive priority: An associative explanation of memory for frequency information in contingency learning. *Canadian Journal of Experimental Psychology, 67*(1), 60–71. doi:10.1037/a0027617

Vago, D. R., & Nakamura, Y. (2011). Selective attentional bias towards pain-related threat in fibromyalgia: Preliminary evidence for effects of mindfulness meditation training. *Cognitive Therapy & Research, 35*(6), 581–594. doi:10.1007/s10608-011-9391-x

Valadez, J. J., & Ferguson, C. J. (2012). Just a game after all: Violent video game exposure and time spent playing effects on hostile feelings, depression, and visuospatial cognition. *Computers in Human Behavior, 28*, 608–616. doi:10.1016/j.chb.2011.11.006

Valeggia, C. R., & Snodgrass, J. J. (2015). Health of indigenous peoples. *Annual Review of Anthropology, 44*, 117–135. doi:10.1146/annurev-anthro-102214-013831

Valins, S. (1967). Emotionality and information concerning internal reactions. *Journal of Personality & Social Psychology, 6*, 458–463. doi:10.1037/h0024842

Valkenburg, P. M., Peter, J., & Walther, J. B. (2016). Media effects: Theory and research. *Annual Review of Psychology, 67*, 315–338. doi:10.1146/annurev-psych-122414-033608

Vallerand, R. J., Paquet, Y., et al. (2010). On the role of passion for work in burnout: A process model. *Journal of Personality, 78*(1), 289–312. doi:10.1111/j.1467-6494.2009.00616.x

Van Blerkom, D. L. (2012). *College study skills: Becoming a strategic learner* (7th ed.). Boston, MA: Cengage Learning.

van Dam, C. (2006). *The socially skilled child molester: Differentiating the guilty from the falsely accused*. Binghamton, NY: Haworth Maltreatment & Trauma Press.

van de Pol, P. C., & Kavussanu, M. (2012). Achievement motivation across training and competition in individual and team sports. *Sport,*

Exercise, & Performance Psychology, 1(2), 91–105. doi:10.1037/a0025967

van der Hart, O., Lierens, R., & Goodwin, J. (1996). Jeanne Fery: A sixteenth-century case of dissociative identity disorder. *Journal of Psychohistory, 24*(1), 18–35.

van der Kamp, J., & Cañal-Bruland, R. (2011). Kissing right? On the consistency of the head-turning bias in kissing. *Laterality: Asymmetries of Body, Brain, & Cognition, 16*(3), 257–267. doi:10.1080/13576500903530778

van Dierendonck, D., & Te Nijenhuis, J. (2005). Flotation restricted environmental stimulation therapy (REST) as a stress-management tool: A meta-analysis. *Psychology & Health, 20*(3), 405–412. doi:10.1080/0887044 0412331337093

van Dierendonck, D., Díaz, D., et al. (2008). Ryff's six-factor model of psychological well-being, a Spanish exploration. *Social Indicators Research, 87*(3), 473–479. doi:10.1007/s11205-007-9174-7

van Dijk, E., Parks, C. D., & van Lange, P. M. (2013). Social dilemmas: The challenge of human cooperation. *Organizational Behavior & Human Decision Processes, 120*(2), 123–124. doi:10.1016/j.obhdp.2012.12.005

van Duijvenbode, N., Didden, R., et al. (2013). Executive control in long-term abstinent alcoholics with mild to borderline intellectual disability: The relationship with IQ and severity of alcohol use-related problems. *Research in Developmental Disabilities, 34*(10), 3583–3595. doi:10.1016/j.ridd.2013.07.003

Van Iddekinge, C. H., Putka, D. J., & Campbell, J. P. (2011). Reconsidering vocational interests for personnel selection: The validity of an interest-based selection test in relation to job knowledge, job performance, and continuance intentions. *Journal of Applied Psychology, 96*(1), 13–33.

Van Lange, P. M., Joireman, J., et al. (2013). The psychology of social dilemmas: A review. *Organizational Behavior & Human Decision Processes, 120*(2), 125–141. doi:10.1016/j.obhdp.2012.11.003

Van Lawick-Goodall, J. (1971). *In the shadow of man.* New York: Houghton Mifflin.

Van Volkom, M. (2009). The effects of childhood tomboyism and family experiences on the self-esteem of college females. *College Student Journal, 43*(3), 736–743.

Van Vugt, M. (2009). Averting the tragedy of the commons: Using social psychological science to protect the environment. *Current Directions in Psychological Science, 18*(3), 169–173.

Vandenbeuch, A., Tizzano, M., et al. (2010). Evidence for a role of glutamate as an efferent transmitter in taste buds. *BMC Neuroscience, 11,* 77. doi:10.1186/1471-2202-11-77

Vance, A. (2015). *Elon Musk: Tesla, SpaceX and the quest for a fantastic future.* New York: HarperCollins.

Vance, E. (2016). *Suggestible you: The curious science of your brain's ability to deceive, transform, and heal.* Washington, DC: National Geographic Books.

Vandewalle, G., Hébert, M., et al. (2011). Abnormal hypothalamic response to light in seasonal affective disorder. *Biological Psychiatry, 70*(10), 954–961. doi:10.1016/j.biopsych.2011.06.022

Vandewater, E. A., Ostrove, J. M., & Stewart, A. J. (1997). Predicting women's well-being in midlife: The importance of personality development and social role involvements. *Journal of Personality and Social Psychology, 72*(5), 1147–1160. doi:10.1037/0022-3514.72.5.1147

Vanheule, S., Vandenbergen, J., et al. (2010). Interpersonal problems in alexithymia: A study in three primary care groups. *Psychology & Psychotherapy: Theory, Research & Practice, 83*(4), 351–362. doi:10.1348/147608309X481829

Vargas-Perez, H., Ting-A-Kee, R., & van der Kooy, D. (2009). Different neural systems mediate morphine reward and its spontaneous withdrawal aversion *European Journal of Neuroscience, 29*(10), 2029–2034.

Vartanian, O., & Suedfeld, P. (2011). The effect of the flotation version of restricted environmental stimulation technique (REST) on jazz improvisation. *Music & Medicine, 3*(4), 234–238. doi:10.1177 /1943862111407640

Vasa, R. A., Carlino, A. R., & Pine, D. S. (2006). Pharmacotherapy of depressed children and adolescents: Current issues and potential directions. *Biological Psychiatry, 59*(11), 1021–1028. doi:10.1016/j.biopsych.2005.10.010

Vasquez, E. A., Lickel, B., & Hennigan, K. (2010). Gangs, displaced, and group-based aggression. *Aggression & Violent Behavior, 15*(2), 130–140. doi:10.1016/j.avb.2009.08.001

Vaughn, L. (2016). *The power of critical thinking: Effective reasoning about ordinary and extraordinary claims* (5th ed.). New York: Oxford University Press.

Veale, J. F., Clarke, D. E., & Lomax, T. C. (2010). Biological and psychosocial correlates of adult gender-variant identities: A review. *Personality & Individual Differences, 48*(4), 357–366.

Velakoulis, D., & Pantelis, C. (1996). What have we learned from functional imaging studies in schizophrenia? The role of frontal, striatal and temporal areas. *Australian & New Zealand Journal of Psychiatry, 30*(2), 195–209. doi:10.3109 /00048679609076095

Velez, J. A., Greitemeyer, T., et al. (2016). Violent video games and reciprocity: The attenuating effects of cooperative game play on subsequent aggression. *Communication Research, 43*(4), 447–467. doi:10.1177/0093650214552519

Verma, M. M., & Howard, R. J. (2012). Semantic memory and language dysfunction in early Alzheimer's disease: A review. *International Journal of Geriatric Psychiatry, 27*(12), 1209–1217. doi:10.1002/gps.3766

Vernon-Feagans, L., Garrett-Peters, P., et al. (2011, July 1). Chaos, poverty, and parenting: Predictors of early language development. *Early Childhood Research Quarterly,* n.p., doi:10.1016/j.ecresq.2011.11.001

Vesoulas, A. (2020, March 11) Coronavirus may disproportionately affect the poor. And that's bad for everyone. *Time Magazine*. Retrieved from https://time.com/5800930 /how-coronavirus-will-hurt-the-poor/

Vieira, V. J., & Valentine, R. J. (2009). Mitochondrial biogenesis in adipose tissue: Can exercise make fat cells "fit"? *Journal of Physiology, 587*(14), 3427–3428. doi:10.1113/ jphysiol.2009.175307

Vincent, N., Lewycky, S., & Finnegan, H. (2008). Barriers to engagement in sleep restriction and stimulus control in chronic insomnia. *Journal of Consulting & Clinical Psychology, 76*(5), 820–828. doi:10.1037/0022-006X.76.5.820

Visser, B. A., Bay, D., et al. (2010). Psychopathic and antisocial, but not emotionally intelligent. *Personality & Individual Differences, 48*(5), 644–648. doi:10.1016/j.paid.2010.01.003

Vlachou, S., & Markou, A. (2011). Intracranial self-stimulation. In M. C. Olmstead (Ed.), *Animal models of drug addiction* (pp. 3–56). Totowa, NJ: Humana Press.

Vogler, R. E., Weissbach, T. A., et al. (1977). Integrated behavior change techniques for problem drinkers in the community. *Journal of Consulting & Clinical Psychology, 45,* 267–279.

Vojdanoska, M., Cranney, J., & Newell, B. R. (2010). The testing effect: The role of feedback and collaboration in a tertiary classroom setting. *Applied Cognitive Psychology, 24*(8), 1183–1195. doi:10.1002/acp.1630

Volberg, R. A. (2012). Still not on the radar: Adolescent risk and gambling, revisited. *Journal of Adolescent Health, 50*(6), 539–540. doi:10.1016/j. jadohealth.2012.03.009

Volk, L., Chiu, S.-L., et al. (2015). Glutamate synapses in human cognitive disorders. *Annual Review of Neuroscience, 38,* 127–149. doi:10.1146/annurev-neuro -071714-033821

Volpicelli, J. R., Ulm, R. R., et al. (1983). Learned mastery in the rat. *Learning & Motivation, 14,* 204–222. doi:10.1016/0023-9690(83)90006-1

Vontress, C. E. (2013). Existential therapy. In J. Frew & M. D. Spiegler (Eds.), *Contemporary psychotherapies for a diverse world* (pp. 131–164). New York: Routledge/Taylor & Francis.

Voss, J. L., Lucas, H. D., & Paller, K. A. (2012). More than a feeling: Pervasive influences of memory processing without awareness of remembering. *Cognitive Neuroscience, 3,* 193–207. doi:org/10.1080/17588928.2012.674935

Vriends, N., Michael, T., et al. (2012). Associative learning in flying phobia. *Journal of Behavior Therapy & Experimental Psychiatry, 43*(2), 838–843. doi:10.1016/j.jbtep.2011.11.003

Vrtička, P., & Vuilleumier, P. (2012). Neuroscience of human social interactions and adult attachment style. *Frontiers in Human Neuroscience, 6.* doi:10.3389/ fnhum.2012.00212

Vuillermot, S., Weber, L., et al. (2010). A longitudinal examination of the neurodevelopmental impact of prenatal immune activation in mice reveals primary defects in dopaminergic development relevant to schizophrenia. *Journal of Neuroscience, 30*(4), 1270–1287. doi:10.1523/ JNEUROSCI.5408-09.2010

Vuletich, H. A., & Payne, B. K. (2019). Stability and change in implicit bias. *Psychological Science, 30*(6), 854–862. doi:10.1177/0956797619844270

Vygotsky, L. S. (1962). *Thought and language.* Cambridge, MA: MIT Press.

Vygotsky, L. S. (1978). *Mind in society.* Cambridge, MA: Harvard University Press.

Wade, K. A., Green, S. L., & Nash, R. A. (2010). Can fabricated evidence induce false eyewitness testimony? *Applied Cognitive Psychology, 24*(7), 899–908. doi:10.1002/acp.1607

Wagenmakers, E.-J., Beek, T., et al. (2016). Registered replication report: Strack, Martin, & Stepper (1988). *Perspectives on Psychological Science, 11*(6), 917–928. doi:10.1177/ 1745691616674458

Wager, T. D., Rilling, J. K., et al. (2004, February 20). Placebo-induced changes in MRI in the anticipation and experience of pain. *Science, 303,* 1162–1166. doi:10.1126/science.1093065

Wagner, M. (2012). Sensory and cognitive explanations for a century of size constancy research. In G. Hatfield & S. Allred (Eds.), *Visual experience: Sensation, cognition, and constancy* (pp. 63–86). New York: Oxford University Press. doi:10.1093/acprof:oso/9780199597277.003.0004

Wagner, S. H. (2013). Leadership and responses to organizational crisis. *Industrial & Organizational Psychology: Perspectives on Science & Practice, 6*(2), 140–144. doi:10.1111/iops.12024

Wagner, S. L. (2020). *The United States healthcare system: Overview, driving forces, and outlook for the future.* Chicago, IL: Health Administration Press.

Waiter, G. D., Deary, I. J., et al. (2009). Exploring possible neural mechanisms of intelligence differences using processing speed and working memory tasks: An fMRI study. *Intelligence, 37*(2), 199–206.

Wakefield, J. C. (1992). The concept of mental disorder. *American Psychologist, 47*(3), 373–388. doi:10.1037/0003-066X.47.3.373

Waldinger, M. D. (2009). Delayed and premature ejaculation. In R. Balon & R. T. Segraves (Eds.), *Clinical manual of sexual disorders* (pp. 267–292). Arlington, VA: American Psychiatric Publishing.

Walen, H. R., & Lachman, M. E. (2000). Social support and strain from partner, family, and friends: Costs and benefits for men and women in adulthood. *Journal of Social and Personal Relationships, 17,* 5–30. doi:10.1177/0265407500171001

Walker, E., Kestler, L., et al. (2004). Schizophrenia: Etiology and course. *Annual Review of Psychology, 55,* 401–430. doi:10.1146/annurev.psych.55.090902.141950

Walker, I., & Crogan, M. (1998). Academic performance, prejudice, and the Jigsaw classroom. *Journal of Community & Applied Social Psychology, 8*(6), 381–393. doi:10.1002/(SICI)1099-1298(199811/12)8:6<381::AID-CASP457>3.0.CO;2-6

Walker, M. P., & Stickgold, R. (2006). Sleep, memory, and plasticity. *Annual Review of Psychology, 57,* 139–166. doi:10.1146/annurev.psych.56.091103. 070307

Walker, S. P., Wachs, T. D., et al. (2011). Inequality in early childhood Risk and protective factors for early child development. *Lancet, 378*(9799), 1325–1338. doi:10.1016/S0140-6736(11)60555-2

Wallach, M. A., & Kogan, N. (1965). *Modes of thinking in young children.* New York: Holt.

Waller, G., Gray, E., et al. (2014). Cognitive-behavioral therapy for bulimia nervosa and atypical bulimic nervosa: Effectiveness in clinical settings. *International Journal of Eating Disorders, 47*(1), 13–17. doi:10.1002/eat.22181

Waller, T., Lampman, C., & Lupfer-Johnson, G. (2012). Assessing bias against overweight individuals among nursing and psychology students: An implicit association test. *Journal of Clinical Nursing, 21*(23–24), 3504–3512. doi:10.1111/j.1365-2702.2012.04226.x

Wallis, J., Lipp, O. V., & Vanman, E. J. (2012). Face age and sex modulate the other-race effect in face recognition. *Attention, Perception, & Psychophysics, 74*(8), 1712–1721. doi:10.3758/s13414-012-0359-z

Wallisch, P. (2017). Illumination assumptions account for individual differences in the perceptual interpretation of a profoundly ambiguous stimulus in the color domain: "The dress." *Journal of Vision, 17*(4), 5. doi:10.1167/17.4.5

Walters, G. D. (2011). Criminal thinking as a mediator of the mental illness–prison violence relationship: A path analytic study and causal mediation analysis. *Psychological Services, 8*(3), 189–199. doi:10.1037/a0024684

Wampold, B. E., Minami, T., et al. (2005). The placebo is powerful: Estimating placebo effects in medicine and psychotherapy from randomized clinical trials. *Journal of Clinical Psychology, 61*(7), 835–854. doi:10.1002/jclp.20129

Wandersman, A., & Florin, P. (2003). Community interventions and effective prevention. *American Psychologist, 58*(6/7), 441–448. doi:10.1037/0003-066X

Wang, Q. (2013). *The autobiographical self in time and culture.* New York: Oxford University Press.

Wang, Q., & Conway, M. A. (2004). The stories we keep: Autobiographical memory in American and Chinese middle-aged adults. *Journal of Personality, 72*(5), 911–938.

Wang, S. S., & Brownell, K. D. (2005). Public policy and obesity: The need to marry science with advocacy. *Psychiatric Clinics of North America, 28*(1), 235–252. doi:10.1016/j.psc.2004.09.001

Wang, S.-H., & Morris, R. G. M. (2010). Hippocampal-neocortical interactions in memory formation, consolidation, and reconsolidation. *Annual Review of Psychology, 61,* 49–79. doi:10.1146/annurev.psych.093008.100523

Wang, Z., Han, W., et al. (2014). The neuroprotection of Rattin against amyloid β peptide in spatial memory and synaptic plasticity of rats. *Hippocampus, 24*(1), 44–53. doi:10.1002/hipo.22202

Ward, A. F. (2013). Supernormal: How the Internet is changing our memories and our minds. *Psychological Inquiry, 24*(4), 341–348. doi:10.1080/1047840X.2013.850148

Ward, L. M. (2004). Wading through the stereotypes: Positive and negative associations between media use and Black adolescents' conceptions of self. *Developmental Psychology, 40,* 284–294.

Wark, G. R., & Krebs, D. L. (1996). Gender and dilemma differences in real-life moral judgment. *Developmental Psychology, 32*(2), 220–230.

Warren, D. J., & Normann, R. A. (2005). Functional reorganization of primary visual cortex induced by electrical stimulation in the cat. *Vision Research, 45,* 551–565. doi:10.1016/j.visres.2004.09.021

Washton, A. M., & Zweben, J. E. (2009). *Cocaine and methamphetamine addiction: Treatment, recovery, and relapse prevention.* New York: Norton.

Waters, F., Blom, J. D., et al. (2016). What is the link between hallucinations, dreams, and hypnagogic–hypnopompic experiences? *Schizophrenia Bulletin, 42*(5), 1098–1109. doi:10.1093/schbul/sbw076

Watson, D. L., & Tharp, R. G. (2014). *Self-directed behavior: Self-modification for personal adjustment* (10th ed.). Boston, MA: Cengage Learning.

Watson, J. B. (1913/1994). Psychology as the behaviorist views it. *Psychological Review, 101*(2), 248–253. doi:10.1037/0033-295X.101.2.248

Watson, J. M., & Strayer, D. L. (2010). Supertaskers: Profiles in extraordinary multitasking ability. *Psychonomic Bulletin & Review, 17*(4), 479–485. doi:10.3758/PBR.17.4.479

Watts, T. W., Duncan, G. J., & Quan, H. (2018). Revisiting the Marshmallow Test: A conceptual replication investigating links between early delay of gratification and later outcomes. *Psychological Science, 29*(7), 1159–1177. doi:10.1177/0956797618761661

Waytz, A., Epley, N., & Cacioppo, J. T. (2010). Social cognition unbound: Insights into anthropomorphism and dehumanization. *Current Directions in Psychological Science, 19*(1), 58–62. doi:10.1177/0963721409359302

Weaver, Y. (2009). Mid-life: A time of crisis or new possibilities? *Existential Analysis, 20*(1), 69–78.

Weber, K., Giannakopoulos, P., et al. (2012). Personality traits are associated with acute major depression across the age spectrum. *Aging & Mental Health, 16*(4), 472–480. doi:10.1080/13607863.2011.630375

Wechsler, D. (2008). *Wechsler Adult Intelligence Scale, Fourth Edition (WAIS-IV).* San Antonio, TX: Pearson.

Wedding, D., & Corsini, R. J. (2014). *Case studies in psychotherapy* (7th ed.). Boston, MA: Cengage Learning.

Weeks, G. R., & Gambescia, N. (2009). A systemic approach to sensate focus. In K. M. Hertlein, G. R. Weeks, et al. (Eds.), *Systemic sex therapy* (pp. 341–362). New York: Routledge/Taylor & Francis.

Weigold, A., Weigold, I. K., & Russell, E. J. (2013). Examination of the equivalence of self-report survey-based paper-and-pencil and internet data collection methods. *Psychological Methods, 18*(1), 53–70. doi:10.1037/a0031607

Weinberg, R. A. (1989). Intelligence and IQ. *American Psychologist, 44*(2), 98–104. doi:10.1037/0003-066X.44.2.98

Weiner, B. A., & Carton, J. S. (2012). Avoidant coping: A mediator of maladaptive perfectionism and test anxiety. *Personality & Individual Differences, 52*(5), 632–636. doi:10.1016/j.paid.2011.12.009

Weingarten, K. (2010). Reasonable hope: Construct, clinical applications, and supports. *Family Process, 49*(1), 5–25. doi:10.1111/j.1545-5300.2010.01305.x

Weinstein, N. D. (1989, December 8). Optimistic biases about personal risks. *Science, 246,* 1232–1233. doi:10.1126/science.2686031

Weinstein, Y., & Shanks, D. R. (2010). Rapid induction of false memory for pictures. *Memory, 18*(5), 533–542. doi:10.1080/09658211.2010.483232

Weintraub, M. I. (1983). *Hysterical conversion reactions.* New York: SP Medical & Scientific Books.

Weir, K. (2013, July–August). The health-wealth gap. *Monitor on Psychology, 44*(9), 36–41.

Weishaar, M. E. (2006). A cognitive-behavioral approach to suicide risk reduction in crisis intervention. In A. R. Roberts & K. R. Yeager (Eds.), *Foundations of evidence-based social work practice* (pp. 181–193). New York: Oxford University Press.

Weiss, M., Allan, B., & Greenaway, M. (2012). Treatment of catatonia with electroconvulsive therapy in adolescents. *Journal of Child & Adolescent Psychopharmacology,*

22(1), 96–100. doi:10.1089/cap.2010.0052

Weissman, A. M., Jogerst, G. J., & Dawson, J. D. (2003). Community characteristics associated with child abuse in Iowa. *Child Abuse & Neglect, 27*(10), 1145–1159. doi:10.1016/j.chiabu.2003.09.002

Weitzenhoffer, A. M., & Hilgard, E. R. (1959). *Stanford Hypnotic Susceptibility Scale: Forms A and B.* Palo Alto, CA: Consulting Psychologists Press.

Wellings, K., Collumbien, M., et al. (2006). Sexual behaviour in context: A global perspective. *Lancet, 368*(9548), 1706–1738.

Wells, G. L. (2001). Police lineups: Data, theory, and policy. *Psychology, Public Policy, & Law, 7*(4), 791–801.

Wells, G. L., & Olsen, E. A. (2003). Eyewitness testimony. *Annual Review of Psychology, 54,* 277–295. doi:10.1146/annurev.psych.54.101601.145028

Welsh, B. C., Mudge, M. E., & Farrington, D. P. (2010). Reconceptualizing public area surveillance and crime prevention: Security guards, place managers and defensible space. *Security Journal, 23*(4), 299–319. doi:10.1057/sj.2008.22

Weltzin, T. E., Weisensel, N., et al. (2005). Eating disorders in men: Update. *Journal of Men's Health & Gender, 2*(2), 186–193. doi:10.1016/j.jmhg.2005.04.008

Wentland, J. J., & Reissing, E. D. (2011). Taking casual sex not too casually: Exploring definitions of casual sexual relationships. *Canadian Journal of Human Sexuality, 20*(3), 75–91.

Wenzel, A. J., & Lucas-Thompson, R. G. (2012). Authenticity in college-aged males and females, how close others are perceived, and mental health outcomes. *Sex Roles, 67*(5–6), 334–350. doi:10.1007/s11199-012-0182-y

Wertheimer, M. (1959). *Productive thinking*. New York: Harper & Row.

Werthmann, J., Roefs, A., et al. (2011). Can(not) take my eyes off it: Attention bias for food in overweight participants. *Health Psychology, 30*(5), 561–569. doi:10.1037/a0024291

Wessel, I., & Wright, D. B. (Eds.). (2004). *Emotional memory failures*. Hove, UK: Psychology Press.

Weltzin, T. E., Weisensel, N., et al. (2005). Eating disorders in men: Update. *Journal of Men's Health & Gender, 2*(2), 186–193. doi:10.1016/j.jmhg.2005.04.008

West, D., & Sutton-Spence, R. (2012). Shared thinking processes with four deaf poets: A window on "the creative" in "creative sign language." *Sign Language Studies, 12*(2), 188–210. doi:10.1353/sls.2011.0023

West, M. A. (2012). *Effective teamwork: Practical lessons from organizational research*. Oxford, UK: Blackwell.

Wester, W., & Hammond, D. (2011). Solving crimes with hypnosis. *American Journal of Clinical Hypnosis, 53*(4), 249–263. doi:10.1080/00029157.2011.10404355

Wethington, E., Kessler, R. C., & Shiner Pixley, J. E. (2004). Turning points in adulthood. In O. G. Brim, C. D. Ryff, et al. (Eds.), *How healthy are we? A national study of well-being at midlife* (pp. 425–450). Chicago, IL: University of Chicago Press.

Wheeler, G., & Axelsson, L. (2015). *Gestalt therapy*. Washington, DC: American Psychological Association. doi:10.1037/14527-000

Whitbourne, S. K., & Halgin, R. P. (2013). *Abnormal psychology: Clinical perspectives on psychological disorders* (7th ed.). New York: McGraw-Hill.

White-Ajmani, M., & Bursik, K. (2011). What lies beneath: Dogmatism, intolerance, and political self-identification. *Individual Differences Research, 9*(3), 153–164.

White, T. L., & McBurney, D. H. (2013). *Research methods* (9th ed.). Boston, MA: Cengage Learning.

Whitebread, D. (2012). *Developmental psychology and early childhood education*. London: Sage.

Whitley, B. E., & Kite, M. E. (2010). *The psychology of prejudice and discrimination* (2nd ed.). Boston, MA: Cengage Learning.

Whyte, S., & Torgler, B. (2017). Preference versus choice in online dating. *Cyberpsychology, Behavior, & Social Networking, 20*(3), 150–156. doi:10.1089/cyber.2016.0528

Wicherts, J. M. (2019). Publication bias examined in meta-analyses from psychology and medicine: A meta-meta-analysis. *PLoS ONE, 14*(4), doi:10.1371/journal.pone.0215052

Wickwire, E. M., Whelan, J. P., & Meyers, A. W. (2010). Outcome expectancies and gambling behavior among urban adolescents. *Psychology of Addictive Behaviors, 24*(1), 75–88. doi:10.1037/a0017505

Widen, S. C., & Russell, J. A. (2008). Children acquire emotion categories gradually. *Cognitive Development, 23,* 291–312. doi:10.1016/j.cogdev.2008.01.002

Widner, R. L., Otani, H., & Winkelman, S. E. (2005). Tip-of-the-tongue experiences are not merely strong feeling-of-knowing experiences. *Journal of General Psychology, 132*(4), 392–407. doi:10.3200/GENP.132.4.392-407

Wiebe, S. A., & Johnson, S. M. (2016). A review of the research in emotionally focused therapy for couples. *Family Process, 55*(3), 390–407. doi:10.1111/famp.12229

Wiederman, M. W. (1999). Volunteer bias in sexuality research using college student participants. *Journal of Sex Research, 36*(1), 59–66.

Wiederman, M. W. (2001). Gender differences in sexuality: Perceptions, myths, and realities. *Family Journal-Counseling & Therapy for Couples & Families, 9*(4), 468–471.

Wiggins, G. (2012). Seven keys to effective feedback. *Educational Leadership, 70,* 10–16.

Wild, B., Rodden, F. A., et al. (2003). Neural correlates of laughter and humour. *Brain: A Journal of Neurology, 126*(10), 2121–2138. doi:10.1093/brain/awg226

Wilhelm, K., Wedgwood, L., et al. (2010). Predicting mental health and well-being in adulthood. *Journal of Nervous and Mental Disease, 198*(2), 85–90.

Williams, M. T. (2020). Microaggressions: Clarification, evidence, and impact. *Perspectives on Psychological Science, 15,* 3–26. doi:10.1177/1745691619827499

Willingham, D. T. (2009). *Why don't students like school? A cognitive scientist answers questions about how the mind works and what it means for the classroom*. New York: Wiley.

Willingham, D. T., & Riener, C. (2019). *Cognition: The thinking animal* (4th ed). New York: Cambridge University Press.

Willoughby, M. T., Wylie, A. C., & Little, M. H. (2019). Testing longitudinal associations between executive function and academic achievement. *Developmental Psychology, 55*(4), 767–779. doi:10.1037/dev0000664

Wilke, J., & Saad, L. (2013). Older Americans' moral attitudes changing. Retrieved March 10, 2017 from www.gallup.com/poll/162881/older-americans-moral-attitudes-changing.aspx

Wilkinson, D., & Abraham, C. (2004). Constructing an integrated model of the antecedents of adolescent smoking. *British Journal of Health Psychology, 9*(3), 315–333. doi:10.1348/1359107041557075

Wilkinson, M. (2006). The dreaming mindbrain: A Jungian perspective. *Journal of Analytical Psychology, 51*(1), 43–59. doi:10.1111/j.0021-8774.2006.00571.x

Wilkinson, R. G., & Pickett, K. E. (2006). Income inequality and population health: A review and explanation of the evidence. *Social Science & Medicine, 62*(7), 1768–1784. doi:10.1016/j.socscimed.2005. 08.036

Wilkinson, R. G., & Pickett, K. E. (2009). Income inequality and social dysfunction. *Annual Review of Sociology, 35,* 493–511. doi:10.1146/annurev-soc-070308-115926

Willander, J., & Larsson, M. (2006). Smell your way back to childhood: Autobiographical odor memory. *Psychonomic Bulletin & Review, 13*(2), 240–244. doi:10.3758/BF03193837

Williams, D. G., & Morris, G. (1996). Crying, weeping or tearfulness in British and Israeli adults. *British Journal of Psychology, 87*(3), 479–505. doi:10.1111/j.2044-8295.1996.tb02603.x

Williams, J. L., Aiyer, S. M., et al. (2014). The protective role of ethnic identity for urban adolescent males facing multiple stressors. *Journal of Youth & Adolescence, 43*(10), 1728–1741. doi:10.1007/s10964-013-0071-x

Williams, J. M. (2010). *Applied sport psychology: Personal growth to peak performance* (6th ed.). New York: McGraw-Hill.

Williams, R. (1989). *The trusting heart: Great news about Type A behavior*. New York: Random House.

Williams, R. L. (2013). Overview of the Flynn effect. *Intelligence, 41*(6), 753–764. doi:10.1016/j.intell.2013.04.010

Williams, R. L., & Eggert, A. (2002). Note-taking predictors of test performance. *Teaching of Psychology, 29*(3), 234–237.

Wilson, S. B., & Kennedy, J. H. (2006). Helping behavior in a rural and an urban setting: Professional and casual attire. *Psychological Reports, 98*(1), 229–233.

Wilson, S. L. (2003). Postinstitutionalization: The effects of early deprivation on development of Romanian adoptees. *Child & Adolescent Social Work Journal, 20*(6), 473–483. doi:10.1023/B:CASW.0000003139.14144.06

Wilson, T. D. (2004). *Strangers to ourselves: Discovering the adaptive unconscious*. Cambridge, MA: Harvard University Press.

Wilson, T. D. (2009). Know thyself. *Perspectives on Psychological Science, 4*(4), 384–389.

Wilson, T. D., & Nisbett, R. E. (1978). The accuracy of verbal reports about the effects of stimuli on evaluations and behavior. *Social Psychology, 41*(2), 118–131. doi:10.2307/3033572

Wiltink, J., Hoyer, J., et al. (2016). Do patient characteristics predict outcome of psychodynamic psychotherapy for social anxiety disorder? *PloS ONE, 11*(1). doi:10.1371/journal.pone.0147165

Wimpenny, J. H., Weir, A. A., et al. (2009). Cognitive processes associated with sequential tool use in New Caledonian crows. *PLoS ONE, 4*(8): e6471. doi:10.1371/journal. pone.0006471.

Winfree, L. T. Jr., & Jiang, S. (2010). Youthful suicide and social support: Exploring the social dynamics of suicide-related behavior and attitudes within a national sample of U.S. adolescents. *Youth Violence & Juvenile Justice, 8*(1), 19–37. doi:10.1177/1541204009338252

Wingood, G. M., DiClemente, R. J., et al. (2003). A prospective study of exposure to rap music videos and African American female adolescents' health. *American Journal of Public Health, 93,* 437–439. doi:10.2105/AJPH.93.3.437

Winkleby, M., Ahn, D., & Cubbin, C. (2006). Effect of cross-level interaction between individual and neighborhood socioeconomic status on adult mortality rates. *American Journal of Public Health, 96*(12), 2145–2153. doi:10.2105/AJPH.2004.060970

Winner, E. (2003). Creativity and talent. In M. H. Bornstein, L. Davidson, et al. (Eds.), *Well-being: Positive development across the life course* (pp. 371–380). Mahwah, NJ: Erlbaum.

Winter, D. D. N., & Koger, S. M. (2010). *The psychology of environmental problems* (3rd ed.). New York: Psychology Press.

Wise, R. A., & Safer, M. A. (2010). A comparison of what U.S. judges and students know and believe about eyewitness testimony. *Journal of Applied Social Psychology, 40*(6), 1400–1422. doi:10.1111/j.1559-1816.2010.00623.x

Wise, R. A., Gong, X., et al. (2010). A comparison of Chinese judges' and U.S. judges' knowledge and beliefs about eyewitness testimony. *Psychology, Crime, & Law, 16*(8), 695–713. doi:10.1080/10683160903153893

Wiseman, M., & Davidson, S. (2012). Problems with binary gender discourse: Using context to promote flexibility and connection in gender identity. *Clinical Child Psychology & Psychiatry, 17*(4), 528–537. doi:10.1177/1359104511424991

Witherington, D. C., Campos, J. J., et al. (2005). Avoidance of heights on the visual cliff in newly walking infants. *Infancy, 7*(3), 285–298. doi:10.1207/s15327078in0703_4

Witkiewitz, K., Villarroel, N., et al. (2011). Drinking outcomes following drink refusal skills training: Differential effects for African American and non-Hispanic White clients. *Psychology of Addictive Behaviors, 25*(1), 162–167. doi:10.1037/a0022254

Witt, C. M., Schützler, L., et al. (2011). Patient characteristics and variation in treatment outcomes: Which patients benefit most from acupuncture for chronic pain? *Clinical Journal of Pain, 27*(6), 550–555. doi:10.1097/AJP.0b013e31820dfbf5

Wixted, J. T. (2004). The psychology and neuroscience of forgetting. *Annual Review of Psychology, 55,* 235–269. doi:10.1146/annurev.psych.55.090902.141555

Wohl, M. J. A., Pychyl, T. A., & Bennett, S. H. (2010). I forgive myself, now I can study: How self-forgiveness for procrastinating can reduce future procrastination. *Personality & Individual Differences, 48*(7), 803–808.

Wolff, J. M., Rospenda, K. M., & Colaneri, A. S. (2017). Sexual harassment, psychological distress, and problematic drinking behavior among college students: an examination of reciprocal causal relations. *The Journal of Sex Research, 54*(3), 362–373. doi:10.1080/00224499.2016.1143439

Wolpe, J. (1974). *The practice of behavior therapy* (2nd ed.). New York: Pergamon.

Wong, P. T. (2011). Positive psychology 2.0: Towards a balanced interactive model of the good life. *Canadian Psychology, 52*(2), 69–81. doi:10.1177/0022167811408729

Wong, W. (2015). *Essential study skills* (8th ed.). Boston, MA: Cengage Learning.

Wood, W., & Rünger, D. (2016). Psychology of habit. *Annual Review of Psychology, 67,* 289–314. doi:10.1146/annurev-psych-122414-033417

Woods, A. M., Racine, S. E., & Klump, K. L. (2010). Examining the relationship between dietary restraint and binge eating: Differential effects of major and minor stressors. *Eating Behaviors, 11*(4), 276–280. doi:10.1016/j.eatbeh.2010.08.001

Woods, J. (2013). Group analytic therapy for compulsive users of internet pornography. *Psychoanalytic Psychotherapy, 27*(4), 306–318. doi:10.1080/02668734.2013.853907

Woods, S., & West, M. (2010). *The psychology of work and organizations.* Boston, MA: Cengage Learning.

Woods, S. B. (2019). Biopsychosocial theories. In B. H. Fiese, M. Celano, K. Deater-Deckard, E. N. Jouriles, & M. A. Whisman (Eds.), *APA handbooks in psychology series. APA handbook of contemporary family psychology: Foundations, methods, and contemporary issues across the lifespan* (pp. 75–92). Washington, DC, US: American Psychological Association. doi:10.1037/0000099-005

Woods, S. C., & Ramsay, D. S. (2011). Food intake, metabolism and homeostasis. *Physiology & Behavior, 104*(1), 4–7. doi:10.1016/j.physbeh.2011.04.026

Wooldridge, T., & Lytle, P. (2012). An overview of anorexia nervosa in males. *Eating Disorders: The Journal of Treatment & Prevention, 20*(5), 368–378. doi:10.1080/10640266.2012.715515

Woollett, K., & Maguire, E. A. (2011). Acquiring "the Knowledge" of London's layout drives structural brain changes. *Current Biology, 21*(24), 2109–2114. doi:10.1016/j.cub.2011.11.018

World Bank. (2016). *Poverty and shared prosperity 2016: Taking on inequality.* Washington, DC: World Bank. doi:10.1596/978-1-4648-0958-3. Retrieved March 19, 2017, from www.worldbank.org/en/publication/poverty-and-shared-prosperity

World Bank. (2020). *Poverty.* Retrieved from https://www.worldbank.org/en/topic/poverty/overview

World Health Organization. (2013). *WHO report on the global tobacco epidemic, 2013: Warning about the dangers of tobacco.* Retrieved January 2, 2017, from apps.who.int/iris/bitstream/10665/85381/1/WHO_NMH_PND_13.2_eng.pdf

World Health Organization. (2017). *Deafness and hearing loss.* Retrieved May 5, 2017, from www.who.int/mediacentre/factsheets/fs300/en

Worley, J. (2019). Virtual reality for individuals with substance use disorders. *Journal of Psychosocial Nursing and Mental Health Services, 57*(6), 15–19. doi:10.3928/02793695-20190430-01

Worthen, J. B., & Hunt, R. R. (2010). *Mnemonology: Mnemonics for the 21st century.* Hove, UK: Psychology Press.

Wortman, J., Lucas, R. E., & Donnellan, M. (2012). Stability and change in the Big Five personality domains: Evidence from a longitudinal study of Australians. *Psychology & Aging, 27*(4), 867–874. doi:10.1037/a0029322

Wraga, M. J., Boyle, H. K., & Flynn, C. M. (2010). Role of motor processes in extrinsically encoding mental transformations. *Brain & Cognition, 74*(3), 193–202. doi:10.1016/j.bandc.2010.07.005

Wright, J. P., Dietrich, K. N., et al. (2008). Association of prenatal and childhood blood lead concentrations with criminal arrests in early adulthood. *Proceedings of the National Academy of Sciences, 5*(5), e101. doi:10.1371/journal.pmed.0050101

Wright, K. R., Bogan, R. K., & Wyatt, J. K. (2013). Shift work and the assessment and management of shift work disorder (SWD). *Sleep Medicine Reviews, 17*(1), 41–54. doi:10.1016/j.smrv.2012.02.002

Wright, P. B., & Erdal, K. J. (2008). Sport superstition as a function of skill level and task difficulty. *Journal of Sport Behavior, 31*(2), 187–199.

Wright, T. A., & Bonett, D. G. (2007). Job satisfaction and psychological well-being as nonadditive predictors of workplace turnover. *Journal of Management, 33*(2), 141–160.

Wright, P. J., Tokunaga, R. S., et al. (2017, March 2). Pornography consumption and satisfaction: A meta-analysis. *Human Communication Research,* n.p. doi:10.1111/hcre.12108

Wrightsman, L. S., & Fulero, S. M. (2009). *Forensic psychology* (3rd ed.). Boston, MA: Cengage Learning.

Wroe, A. L., & Wise, C. (2012). Evaluation of an adapted cognitive behavioural therapy (CBT) group programme for people with obsessive compulsive disorder: A case study. *Cognitive Behaviour Therapist, 5*(4), 112–123.

Wrosch, C., Jobin, J., & Scheier, M. F. (2016). Do the emotional benefits of optimism vary across older adulthood? A life-span perspective. *Journal of Personality, 85,* 388–397. doi:10.1111/jopy.12247

Wyatt, J. W., Posey, A., et al. (1984). Natural levels of similarities between identical twins and between unrelated people. *The Skeptical Inquirer, 9,* 62–66.

Xavier, M. J., Roman, S. D., Aitken, R. J., & Nixon, B. (2019). Transgenerational inheritance: How impacts to the epigenetic and genetic information of parents affect offspring health. *Human Reproduction Update, 25*(5), 519–541. doi:10.1093/humupd/dmz017

Xerri, C. (2012). Plasticity of cortical maps: Multiple triggers for adaptive reorganization following brain damage and spinal cord injury. *Neuroscientist, 18*(2), 133–148. doi:10.1177/1073858410397894

Xu, T.-X., & Yao, W.-D. (2010). D1 and D2 dopamine receptors in separate circuits cooperate to drive associative long-term potentiation in the prefrontal cortex. *Proceedings of the National Academy of Sciences, 107*(37), 16366–16371. doi:10.1073/pnas.1004108107

Yahnke, B. H., Sheikh, A. A., & Beckman, H. T. (2003). Imagery and the treatment of phobic disorders. In A. A. Sheikh (Ed.), *Healing images: The role of imagination in health* (pp. 312–342). Amityville, NY: Baywood Publishing.

Yamamoto, N., & Philbeck, J. W. (2013). Peripheral vision benefits spatial learning by guiding eye movements. *Memory & Cognition, 41*(1), 109–121. doi:10.3758/s13421-012-0240-2

Yanchar, S. C., Slife, B. D., & Warne, R. (2008). Critical thinking as disciplinary practice. *Review of General Psychology, 12*(3), 265–281. doi:10.1037/1089-2680.12.3.265

Yang, L., & Ornstein, T. J. (2011). The effect of emotion-focused orientation at retrieval on emotional memory in young and older adults. *Memory, 19*(3), 305–313. doi:10.1080/09658211.2011.561803

Yang, S., & Zheng, L. (2011). The paradox of de-coupling: A study of flexible work program and workers' productivity. *Social Science Research, 40*(1), 299–311.

Yapko, M. D. (2011). *Mindfulness and hypnosis: The power of suggestion to transform experience.* New York: Norton.

Yarbus, A. L. (1967). *Eye movements and vision.* New York: Plenum Press.

Yarmey, D. (2010). *Eyewitness testimony.* In J. M. Brown & E. A. Campbell (Eds.), *The Cambridge handbook of forensic psychology* (pp. 177–186). New York: Cambridge University Press.

Yedidia, M. J., & MacGregor, B. (2001). Confronting the prospect of dying. *Journal of Pain & Symptom Management, 22*(4), 807–819. doi:10.1016/S0885-3924(01)00325-6

Yi, H., & Qian, X. (2009). A review on neurocognitive research in superior memory. *Psychological Science (China), 32*(3), 643–645.

Yiend, J. (2010). The effects of emotion on attention: A review of attentional processing of emotional information. *Cognition & Emotion, 24*(1), 3–47. doi:10.1080/02699930903205698

Yim, I. S., Tanner, S., et al. (2015). Biological and psychosocial predictors of postpartum depression: Systematic review and call for integration. *Annual Review of Clinical Psychology, 11,* 99–137. doi:10.1146/annurev-clinpsy-101414-020426

Yonas, A., Elieff, C. A., & Arterberry, M. E. (2002). Emergence of sensitivity to pictorial depth cues: Charting development in individual infants. *Infant Behavior & Development, 25*(4), 495–514. doi:10.1016/S0163-6383(02)00147-9

Yontef, G. (2007). The power of the immediate moment in gestalt therapy. *Journal of Contemporary Psychotherapy, 37*(1), 17–23. doi:10.1007/s10879-006-9030-0

Yoonessi, A., & Baker, C. L. (2011). Contribution of motion parallax to segmentation and depth perception. *Journal of Vision, 11*(9), 1–21. doi:10.1167/11.9.13

Youn, H., Sutton, L., et al. (2016). On the universal structure of human lexical semantics. *Proceedings of the National Academy of Sciences, 113*(7), 1766–1771. doi:10.1073/pnas.1520752113

Young, J. K. (2012). *Hunger, thirst, sex, and sleep: How the brain controls our passions.* Lanham, MD: Rowman & Littlefield.

Young, R. (2005). Neurobiology of savant syndrome. In C. Stough (Ed.), *Neurobiology of exceptionality* (pp. 199–215). New York: Kluwer Academic Publishers.

Young, S. M., & Pinsky, D. (2006). Narcissism and celebrity. *Journal of Research in Personality, 40*(5), 463–471. doi:10.1016/j.jrp.2006.05.005

Yuille, J. C., & Daylen, J. (1998). The impact of traumatic events on eyewitness memory. In C. Thompson, D. Herrmann, et al. (Eds.), *Eyewitness memory: Theoretical and applied perspectives* (pp. 155–178). Mahwah, NJ: Erlbaum.

Zachariae, R. (2009). Psychoneuroimmunology: A bio-psycho-social approach to health and disease. *Scandinavian Journal of Psychology, 50*(6), 645–651. doi:10.1111/j.1467-9450.2009.00779.x

Zammit, A. R., Ezzati, A., et al. (2017). Roles of hippocampal subfields in verbal and visual episodic memory. *Behavioural Brain Research, 317,* 157–162. doi:10.1016/j.bbr.2016.09.038

Zampetakis, L. A., & Moustakis, V. (2011). Managers' trait emotional intelligence and group outcomes: The case of group job satisfaction. *Small Group Research, 42*(1), 77–102. doi:10.1177/1046496410373627

Zaraska, N. M. (2016, November–December). Hear the violet, Taste the velvet. *Scientific American Mind,* 64–69.

Zarcadoolas, C., Pleasant, A., & Greer, D. S. (2006). *Advancing health literacy: A framework for understanding and action.* San Francisco, CA: Jossey-Bass.

Zeidan, F., Johnson, S. K., et al. (2010). Effects of brief and sham mindfulness meditation on mood and cardiovascular variables. *Journal of Alternative & Complementary Medicine, 16*(8), 867–873. doi:10.1089/acm.2009.0321

Zeidner, M., Matthews, G., et al. (2012). The emotional intelligence, health, and well-being nexus: What have we learned and what have we missed? *Applied Psychology: Health & Well-Being, 4*(1) 1–30. doi:10.1111/j.1758-0854.2011.01062.x

Zeigler-Hill, V., Holden, C. J., et al. (2016). The dark sides of high and low self-esteem. In V. Zeigler-Hill, & Marcus, David K. (Eds.), *The dark side of personality: Science and practice in social, personality, and clinical psychology* (pp. 325–340). Washington, DC: American Psychological Association. doi:10.1037/14854-017

Zeiler, K., & Wickström, A. (2009). Why do "we" perform surgery on newborn intersexed children? The phenomenology of the parental experience of having a child with intersex anatomies. *Feminist Theory, 10*(3), 359–377.

Zeisel, J. (2006). *Inquiry by design: Environment/behavior/neuroscience in architecture, interiors, landscape, and planning.* New York: Norton.

Zell, E., & Krizan, Z. (2014). Do people have insight into their abilities? A metasynthesis. *Perspectives on Psychological Science, 9*(2), 111–125. doi:10.1177/1745691613518075

Zellner, D. A., Harner, D. E., & Adler, R. L. (1989). Effects of eating abnormalities and gender on perceptions of desirable body shape. *Journal of Abnormal Psychology, 98*(1), 93–96. doi:10.1037/0021-843X.98.1.93

Zellner, M. (2011). The cognitive unconscious seems related to the dynamic unconscious: But it's not the whole story. *Neuropsychoanalysis, 13*(1), 59–63.

Zemishlany, Z., Aizenberg, D., & Weizman, A. (2001). Subjective effects of MDMA ("Ecstasy") on human sexual function. *European Psychiatry, 16*(2), 127–130. doi:10.1016/S0924-9338(01)00550-8

Zenasni, F., Mourgues, C., et al. (2016). How does creative giftedness differ from academic giftedness? A multidimensional conception. *Learning & Individual Differences, 52,* 216–223. doi:10.1016/j.lindif.2016.09.003

Zentall, T. R. (2002). A cognitive behaviorist approach to the study of animal behavior. *Journal of General Psychology. Special Issue: Animal Behavior, 129*(4), 328–363.

Zentall, T. R. (2010). Coding of stimuli by animals: Retrospection, prospection, episodic memory and future planning. *Learning & Motivation, 41*(4), 225–240. doi:10.1016/j.lmot.2010.08.001

Zentall, T. R. (2011). Perspectives on observational learning in animals. *Journal of Comparative Psychology, 126*(2), 114–128. doi:10.1037/a0025381

Zhang Zepeda, C. D., Richey, J. E., et al. (2015). Direct instruction of metacognition benefits adolescent science learning, transfer, and motivation: An in vivo study. *Journal of Educational Psychology, 107*(4), 954–970. doi:10.1037/edu0000022

Zhang, B., Hao, Y. L., et al. (2010). Fatal familial insomnia: A middle-age-onset Chinese family kindred. *Sleep Medicine, 11*(5), 498–499. doi:10.1016/j.sleep.2009.11.005

Zhaurova, K. (2008). Genetic causes of adult-onset disorders. *Nature Education, 1,* 49.

Ziegler, M., Dietl, E., et al. (2011). Predicting training success with general mental ability, specific ability tests, and (un)structured interviews: A meta-analysis with unique samples. *International Journal of Selection & Assessment, 19*(2), 170–182. doi:10.1111/j.1468-2389.2011.00544.x

Zietsch, B. P., Miller, G. F., et al. (2011). Female orgasm rates are largely independent of other traits: Implications for "female orgasmic disorder" and evolutionary theories of orgasm. *Journal of Sexual Medicine, 8*(8), 2305–2316. doi:10.1111/j.1743-6109.2011.02300.x

Zimbardo, P. G. (2007). *The Lucifer effect: Understanding how good people turn evil.* New York: Random House.

Zink, N., & Pietrowsky, R. (2013). Relationship between lucid dreaming, creativity and dream characteristics. *International Journal of Dream Research, 6*(2), 98–103.

Zippert, E. L., Daubert, E. N., Scalise, N. R., Noreen, G. D., & Ramani, G. B. (2019). "Tap space number three": Promoting math talk during parent-child tablet play. *Developmental Psychology, 55*(8), 1605–1614. doi:10.1037/dev0000769

Ziv, I., Leiser, D., & Levine, J. (2011). Social cognition in schizophrenia: Cognitive and affective factors. *Cognitive Neuropsychiatry, 16*(1), 71–91. doi:10.1080/13546805.2010.492693

Zoccola, P. M., Green, M. C., et al. (2011). The embarrassed bystander: Embarrassability and the inhibition of helping. *Personality & Individual Differences, 51*(8), 925–929. doi:10.1016/j.paid.2011.07.026

Zuckerman, M., & Tsai, F-R. (2005). Costs of self-handicapping. *Journal of Personality, 73*(2), 411–442.

Zvyagintsev, M., Clemens, B., et al. (2013). Brain networks underlying mental imagery of auditory and visual information. *European Journal of Neuroscience, 37*(9), 1421–1434.

1000 Genomes Project Consortium. (2015). A global reference for human genetic variation. *Nature, 526,* 68–74. doi:10.1038/nature15393

Author Index

D

E

F

Q

R

S

X

Y

Z

Subject Index / Glossary

B

C

E

F

H